D1004299

Business Communication

PROCESS & PRODUCT

10e

Mary Ellen Guffey

Professor Emerita of Business
Los Angeles Pierce College

Dana Loewy

Business Communication Program, Emerita
California State University, Fullerton

CENGAGE

Australia • Brazil • Canada • Mexico • Singapore • United Kingdom • United States

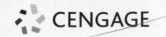
CENGAGE

Business Communication, Process and Product, 10th Edition
Mary Ellen Guffey, Dana Loewy

Senior Vice President, Higher Education & Skills Product: Erin Joyner

Product Director: Joe Sabatino

Product Manager: Heather Thompson

Senior Product Assistant: Juleah Morehouse

Learning Designer: Megan Guiliani

Senior Content Manager: Allie Janneck

Digital Delivery Lead: Drew Gaither

Senior Director, Marketing: Kristen Hurd

Marketing Manager: Andrew Stock

IP Analyst: Diane Garrity

IP Project Manager: Nick Barrows

Production Service: SPi Global

Art Director: Bethany Bourgeois

Text Designer: Joe Devine/Red Hangar Design

Cover Designer: Joe Devine/Red Hangar Design

Cover Image: ©metamorworks/ShutterStock.com

Design Images:

©rangizzz/ShutterStock.com
©IM_photo/ShutterStock.com
©LightField Studios/ShutterStock.com
©ByGurzoglu/ShutterStock.com
©Patthana Nirangkul/ShutterStock.com

For product information and technology assistance, contact us at
**Cengage Customer & Sales Support, 1-800-354-9706
or support.cengage.com.**

For permission to use material from this text or product, submit all requests online at **www.cengage.com/permissions.**

Library of Congress Control Number: 2020922962

Soft-cover Edition:
ISBN: 978-0-357-12923-4

Loose-leaf Edition:
ISBN: 978-0-357-12930-2

Cengage Learning
200 Pier 4 Boulevard, Suite 400
Boston, MA 02210
USA

Cengage is a leading provider of customized learning solutions with employees residing in nearly 40 different countries and sales in more than 125 countries around the world. Find your local representative at **www.cengage.com.**

To learn more about Cengage platforms and services, register or access your online learning solution, or purchase materials for your course, visit **www.cengage.com.**

Printed in the United States of America
Print Number: 01   Print Year: 2021

Business Communication
PROCESS & PRODUCT 10e

Dear Business Communication Instructors and Students:

Welcome to the Tenth Edition of *Business Communication: Process and Product*! We are eager to invite you to examine this substantially revised edition that focuses on developing job-ready and recession-proof skills for students entering today's complex mobile and social workplace. After leading the business communication textbook market for nearly thirty years, this book has become an even more valuable teaching/learning package.

Dr. Mary Ellen Guffey and Dr. Dana Loewy

All the features that made this award-winning book so successful over the decades have been updated with relevant, current research converted to stimulating content and learning activities. Our goal is to help students develop much-needed communication skills while also easing the instructor's workload in delivering superior online and classroom resources. A few key features of the Tenth Edition are listed here:

- **Trusted content.** This new edition reflects the prevalence of communication technologies in today's social and mobile workplace. We have thoroughly revised the book to present best practices for e-mailing, texting, instant messaging, blogging, podcasting, working in face-to-face and remote teams, and using social media.

- **Development of job-ready and recession-proof skills.** Students will find special emphasis on emotional intelligence, professionalism, listening, teaming, critical thinking, and other skills that cannot be replaced by artificial intelligence and other technological advances, thus making them recession-proof and future-ready.

- **MindTap.** A multimedia learning experience, MindTap provides a complete ebook combined with unparalleled resources to achieve success in the course. Those resources include abundant grammar/mechanics review including a pre-course diagnostic, Learn It activities featuring narrated lessons coupled with comprehension-check questions, chapter assignments with rich feedback, model document videos, skills-based activities, and flashcards. This multimedia learning experience seamlessly integrates chapter content with your college's preferred learning management system allowing instructors to customize activities.

- **Latest trends in job searching and interviewing.** True to our goal of making students job ready, Chapters 15 and 16 provide countless tips on today's job search, how to build a personal brand, and how to network. Students benefit from knowing the latest trends in résumé and interview practices, including tips for successful one- and two-way interviewing.

For additional helpful instructor resources such as ready-to-use exercises with solutions, please visit the Guffey Team blog at *https://bizcombuzz.com*, and follow us on Facebook and Twitter (@danaloewy).

Cordially,

Mary Ellen Guffey and Dana Loewy

Dr. Mary Ellen Guffey
Emerita Professor of Business
Los Angeles Pierce College
m.e.guffey@cox.net

Dr. Dana Loewy
Business Communication Program, Emerita
California State University, Fullerton
dloewy@fullerton.edu

Business Communication
PROCESS AND PRODUCT 10e

This book and this course may well be the most important in your entire college curriculum!

This leading text and MindTap guide you in developing the communication competencies most important for professional success in today's hyperconnected digital age. Refine the skills that employers value most, such as superior writing, speaking, presentation, critical thinking, and teamwork skills.

Survey after survey reveals that employers are seeking new-hires with these key skills:

- Written and oral communication skills
- Critical thinking and analytical reasoning
- Ethical decision making
- Teamwork skills
- Professionalism

No other college course gives you training in all of these skills at once! Based on interviews with successful practitioners and extensive research into the latest trends, technologies and practices, this edition offers synthesized advice on building your personal brand, using LinkedIn effectively, and résumé writing. A signature 3-x-3 writing process, meaningful assignments, and digital practice tools further equip you with the communication skills to stand out in business today.

Business Communication
PROCESS & PRODUCT 10e

1 Prewriting

Analyze:
Decide on the message purpose. What do you want the receiver to do or believe?

Anticipate:
What does the audience already know? How will it receive this message?

Adapt:
Think about techniques to present this message most effecively. Consider how to elicit feedback.

2 Drafting

Research:
Gather background data by searching files and the Internet.

Organize:
Arrange direct messages with the big idea first. For persuasive or negative messages, use an indirect, problem-solving strategy.

Draft:
Prepare the first draft, using active-voice sentences, coherent paragraphs, and appropriate transitional expressions.

3 Revising

Edit:
Eliminate wordy fillers, long lead-ins, redundancies, and trite business phrases. Strive for parallelism, clarity, conciseness, and readability.

Proofread:
Check carefully for errors in spelling, grammar, punctuation, and format.

Evaluate:
Will this message achieve your purpose? Is the tone pleasant? Did you encourage feedback?

Business Communication: Process and Product, 10e, covers the following topics you will find indispensable in the digital-age workplace:

- Expert writing techniques geared to developing your writing skills plus interactive Documents for Analysis, authentic model documents, and engaging activities in which you apply your skills

- Presentation skills featuring contemporary examples including coverage of smartphone best practices to prepare you for the realities of workplace communication and technology

- Critical-thinking questions and activities in every chapter to stimulate and develop skills

- Ethics Checks in addition to guidance and tools provided through discussion questions and ethical dilemma scenarios

- Teamwork skills with a heavy emphasis on professionalism and etiquette in the workplace so that you will know how to meet employer expectations

- Coverage of social media and mobile technology showing how their explosive growth has sparked disruptive new business models in the new sharing economy

- Two updated employment chapters providing tips for a labor market that is more competitive, mobile, and technology-driven than ever before

Business Communication
PROCESS & PRODUCT 10e

Premium Online Resources with Mindtap

- **MindTap for *Business Communication: Process & Product*, 10th Edition helps you see the importance of communication skills in practice.** Each unit opens with a "**Why Does This Matter to Me?**" activity, showcasing how each unit you're learning about connects to your future business success.

- **"Learn It" modules** cover the basic concepts for each section of a chapter in digestible video tutorials. These brief videos are coupled with questions that reinforce understanding of each learning objective and provide immediate feedback about your performance.

- **"Apply It" activities** include the comprehensive **Chapter Assignment** that challenges you to apply what you're learning within examples and business communication scenarios—delivering detailed immediate feedback to underscore chapter concepts in context. Flex your growing communication skills muscle with **video activities** challenging you to apply what you're learning in real time.

- A comprehensive **Grammar/Mechanics Diagnostic** provides an opportunity to assess your basic language skills in key areas and receive a custom report about your proficiency in each, with options for further review. Upon reviewing your results, you can continue to hone your language skills with targeted Grammar/Mechanics tutorials and put those skills into practice with additional Grammar/Mechanics Check-Ups.

- **Model Document Videos** included throughout the chapters explain and illustrate many concepts and walk you through how to create model documents including positive, bad-news, persuasive, and sales messages.

- The **Cengage Mobile App** enables you to learn on your terms. Read or listen to your textbook on your mobile device and study with the included tools.

Social Media Networks and Mobile Technology

The authors address workplace social media and communication technology in a chapter solely dedicated to best practices on the job. Because these skills are fundamental in the contemporary world of work, social media and communication technology are integrated in each chapter.

Every chapter reflects the pervasive influence of communication technology on business writing. This state-of-the-art coverage makes it clear that writing and speaking are more important than ever in the rapidly changing world of work. Careers are made or thwarted based on one's online digital persona.

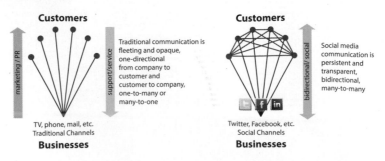

Business Communication
PROCESS & PRODUCT 10e

- New sections discussing current digital workplace tools are complemented by brand-new coverage of social media's dark side to help you hone your critical thinking skills.
- New activities, identified with the Social Media and Communication Technology icon, reflect the preeminence of writing in the digital workplace and prompt you to develop your professional social networking skills.

SOCIAL NETWORKERS VS. OTHER U.S. WORKERS: COMPARING ATTITUDES TOWARDS QUESTIONABLE BEHAVIOR		
Do you feel it is acceptable to...?	**Active Social Networkers**	**Other U.S. Workers**
"Friend" a client/customer on a social network	59%	28%
Blog or tweet negatively about your company or colleagues	42%	6%
Buy personal items with your company credit card as long as you pay it back	42%	8%
Do a little less work to compensate for cuts in benefits or pay	51%	10%
Keep a copy of confidential work documents in case you need them in your next job	50%	15%
Take a copy of work software home and use it on your personal computer	46%	7%
Upload vacation pictures to the company network or server so you can share them with co-workers	50%	17%
Use social networking to find out what my company's competitors are doing	54%	30%

- Opening scenarios in each chapter illustrate social media and technology use, teamwork, meetings, persuasion, and more by companies that you know and interact with, such as Nordstrom, Lyft, Walmart, Taco Bell, Volkswagen, Seventh Generation, Jeep, Netflix, and Juul.

Zooming In

Juul—Suspicions Unlikely to Evaporate

"We created ridiculous enthusiasm for the hashtag 'Vaporized,'" bragged marketing agency Cult Collective about its Juul campaign. On its website, Cult gushed that its strategy promoting the popular e-cigarette vaporizer "aligned perfectly with those we knew would be our best customers."[1] But who exactly were Juul's intended customers?

The Federal Trade Commission wants to know. It's investigating whether e-cigarette startup Juul Labs used social media and influencers to appeal to minors, as vaping among teens surged by 78 percent from 2017 to 2018, and one in five high schoolers admitted to having vaped in the last 30 days, according to the CDC.[2] Regulators, parents, schools, and public health advocates are alarmed by what the Food and Drug Administration has called an "epidemic of e-cigarette use among teenagers."[3] At least three lawsuits are pending against Juul Labs for deceptively marketing its products as safe.[4] Stanford researchers found that Juul's colorful ads showing attractive twentysomethings having fun while "Juuling" appeared to mimic tobacco industry marketing in style and content. Most important, though, was that Juul "exploited social media" to reach young users, the researchers said.[5] Since its inception in 2015, Juul has rocketed past competitors to own 75 percent of the e-cigarette market.[6]

Users love the small, sleek vaporizer that produces little odor. Juul is a fad that's seemingly everywhere: "I saw everyone doing it, so I wanted to try it," said one teenager. Most of all, the "pod" flavors—e.g., fruit, crème, cucumber, or mango—appear to be a factor. A young man explained Juuling is "like having a cookies milkshake, that's what it tastes like in your mouth."[7] All fruit flavors are now banned in the United States leaving only mint and menthol to mask the harshness of the aerosol.[8] Many Juul users believe they are inhaling harmless flavored water vapor, unaware of the nicotine in the pods, each of which equals 20 regular cigarettes. Nicotine is highly addictive and particularly harmful to the developing brain. In addition, toxic metals, potentially leeching from the metal coil that's heating the e-liquid, were discovered in the aerosol users inhale.[9] Recent regulation mandates highly visible health warnings on all vaping products.

Juul strenuously denies having deliberately targeted young people: "We were completely surprised by the youth usage of the product," Ashley Gould, chief administrative officer at Juul Labs, asserted and claimed, "Juul is a switching product, not a cessation product, and it is intended for adult smokers to enable them to switch from combustible cigarettes."[10] Juul's stated mission is "improving the lives of the one billion adult smokers."[11] When e-cigarettes were first introduced, they were touted as smoking cessation devices or less harmful smoking alternatives. You will learn more about Juul and be asked to complete a relevant task at the end of this chapter.

Critical Thinking

- Why might teenagers and young adults be susceptible to Juul, and what type of appeal was the e-cigarette startup using?
- What could explain the huge success of Juul, the startup that burst onto a crowded e-cigarette scene in 2015 and within three years grabbed a 75-percent share of the vaping market?
- The marketing agency Cult Collective has removed the Juul case study from its website, and it's available only in the Internet Archive. Why may Cult have pulled the case from its e-portfolio?

Brief Contents

CHAPTER 3
Intercultural Communication   80

UNIT 2 The Writing Process in the Digital Era

CHAPTER 4
...ning Business Messages   118

Contents

wavebreakmedia/Shutterstock.com

CHAPTER 5
Organizing and Drafting Business Messages   148

CHAPTER 6
Revising Business Messages   176

UNIT 3 Workplace Communication

CHAPTER 7
Short Workplace Messages and Digital Media   202

CHAPTER 8
Positive and Neutral Messages   242

C H A P T E R   9
Negative Messages   282

C H A P T E R   1 0
Persuasive and Sales Messages   324

UNIT 4 Reports, Proposals, and Presentations

CHAPTER 11
Report Writing Basics   368

CHAPTER 12
Informal Business Reports   410

CHAPTER 13
Proposals, Business Plans, and Formal Business Reports   454

CHAPTER 14
Business Presentations   492

UNIT 5 Employment Communication

C H A P T E R   1 5
The Job Search, Résumés, and Cover Letters in the Digital Age   536

C H A P T E R   1 6
Interviewing and Following Up   580

Appreciation for Support

No successful textbook reaches a No. 1 position without a great deal of help. We are exceedingly grateful to the reviewers and other experts who contributed their pedagogic and academic expertise in shaping *Business Communication: Process and Product*.

We extend sincere thanks to many professionals at Cengage Learning including Erin Joyner, Senior Vice President, Higher Education & Skills Product; Michael Schenk, Vice President, Product Management - B&E, 4LTR & Support Programs; Joe Sabatino, Product Director; Heather Thompson, Product Manager; John Rich, Manager, Content Creation; Megan Guiliani, Learning Designer; Allie Janneck, Senior Content Manager; Bethany Bourgeois, Art Director; Juleah Morehouse, Senior Product Assistant; Diane Garrity, Intellectual Property Analyst; and Nick Barrows, Intellectual Property Project Manager.

Our heartfelt appreciation also goes to the following for their expertise in creating exceptional instructor and student support materials: Carolyn M. Seefer, Diablo Valley College and Nicky Adams, University of Dayton.

Mary Ellen Guffey
Dana Loewy

Grateful Thanks to Reviewers

Janet G. Adams, *Minnesota State University, Mankato*

Leslie Adams, *Houston Baptist University*

Kehinde A. Adesina, *Contra Costa College*

Asberine Parnell Alford, *Suffolk Community College*

Virginia Allen, *Joliet Junior College*

Cynthia Anderson, *Youngstown State University*

Linda Landis Andrews, *University of Illinois, Chicago*

Vanessa D. Arnold, *University of Mississippi*

Lois J. Bachman, *Community College of Philadelphia*

Rebecca Barksdale, *University of Central Florida*

Sandra Berill, *Arkansas State University*

Teresa L. Beyer, *Sinclair Community College*

Cathie Bishop, *Parkland College*

Randi Blank, *Indiana University*

Elizabeth Bowers, *Orange Coast College and Golden West College*

Martha E. Bradshaw, *Southeastern Louisiana Univ.*

Bernadine Branchaw, *Western Michigan University*

Maryanne Brandenburg, *Indiana University of Pennsylvania*

Charles P. Bretan, *Northwood University*

Paula E. Brown, *Northern Illinois University*

Vivian R. Brown, *Loredo Community College*

Domenic Bruni, *University of Wisconsin Oshkosh*

Phyllis C. Bunn, *Delta State University*

Mary Ann Burris, *Pueblo Community College*

Roosevelt D. Butler, *College of New Jersey*

Jane Campanizzi-Mook, *Franklin University*

James F. Carey, *Onondaga Community College*

Leila Chambers, *Cuesta College*

Patricia H. Chapman, *University of South Carolina*

Judie C. Cochran, *Grand Canyon University*

Marjorie Coffey, *Oregon State University*

Randy E. Cone, *University of New Orleans*

James Conley, *Eastern Michigan University*

Billie Miller Cooper, *Cosumnes River College*

Linda W. Cooper, *Macon State College*

Jane G. Corbly, *Sinclair Community College*

Martha Cross, *Delta State University*

Linda Cunningham, *Salt Lake Community College*

Lajuan Davis, *University of Wisconsin-Whitewater*

Fred DeCasperis, *Siena College*

Guy Devitt, *Herkimer County Community College*

Linda Di Desidero, *University of Maryland University College*

John Donnellan, *University of Texas at Austin*

J. Yellowless Douglas, *University of Florida*

Bertha Du-Babcock, *City University of Hong Kong*

Dorothy Drayton, *Texas Southern University*

Kay Durden, *University of Tennessee*

Anna Easton, *Indiana University*

Lorena B. Edwards, *Belmont University*

Donald E. English, *Texas A&M University*

Margaret Erthal, *Southern Illinois University*

Donna R. Everett, *Morehead State University*

Gwendolyn Bowie Ewing, *Southwest Tennessee Community College*

Anne Finestone, *Santa Monica Community College*

Peggy B. Fisher, *Ball State University*

Terry M. Frame, *University of South Carolina*

Gen Freese, *Harrisburg Area Community College*

Kerry J. Gambrill, *Florida Community College*

Judith L. Graham, *Holyoke Community College*

Carolyn G. Gray, *The University of Texas, Austin*

Diane Gruber, *Arizona State University West*

Susan Guzmán-Treviño, *Temple College*

David Hamilton, *Bemidji State University*

Bill Hargrave, *University of West Georgia*

Paul Hegele, *Elgin Community College*

Susan A. Heller, *Reading Area Community College*

K. Virginia Hemby, *Middle Tennessee State University*

Rovena L. Hillsman, *California State University, Sacramento*

Kenneth Hoffman, *Emporia State University*

Shirley Houston, *University of Nebraska*

Warren B. Humphrey, *University of Central Florida*

Robert G. Insley, *University of North Texas*

Edna Jellesed, *Lane Community College*

Glen J. Jenewein, *Portland Community College*

Kathy Jesiolowski, *Milwaukee Area Technical College*

Carolyn Spillers Jewell, *Pembroke State University*

Pamela R. Johnson, *California State University, Chico*

Eric Johnstone, *Montana State University*

Cheryl L. Kane, *University of North Carolina Charlotte*

Diana K. Kanoy, *Central Florida Community College*

Tina S. Kazan, *University of Illinois, Chicago*

Carolyn E. Kerr, *University of Pittsburgh*

Sonia Khatchadourian, *University of Wisconsin-Milwaukee*

Margaret S. Kilcoyne, *Northwestern State University*

G. Scott King, *Sinclair Community College*

Suzanne P. Krissler, *Orange County Com. College*

Linda L. Labin, *Husson College*

Gary E. Lacefield, *University of Texas at Arlington*

Richard Lacy, *California State University, Fresno*

Suzanne Lambert, *Broward Community College*

Marilyn L. Lammers, *California State University, Northridge*

Lorita S. Langdon, *Columbus State Community College*

Joyce N. Larsen, *Front Range Community College*

Marianna Larsen, *Utah State University*

Barbara Lea, *West Valley College*

Claire E. Legowski, *North Dakota State University*

Mary E. Leslie, *Grossmont College*

Kathy Lynn Lewis-Adler, *University of North Alabama*

Kristie J. Loescher, *The University of Texas at Austin*

Jennifer Cook Loney, *Portland State University*

Mary Jean Lush, *Delta State University*

Sonia Maasik, *University of California, Los Angeles*

Bruce MacBeth, *Clarion University of Pennsylvania*

Georgia E. Mackh, *Cabrillo College*

Andrew Madson, *Milwaukee Area Technical College*

Anna Maheshwari, *Schoolcraft College*

Maureen L. Margolies, *University of Cincinnati*

Leon Markowicz, *Lebanon Valley College*

Thomas A. Marshall II, *Robert Morris College*

Jeanette Martin, *University of Mississippi*

John F. Mastriani, *El Paso Community College*

Cynthia H. Mayfield, *York Technical College*

Susan Smith McClaren, *Mt. Hood Community College*

Beryl C. McEwen, *North Carolina A&T State University*

Marya McFadden, *California State University Northridge*

Nancy McGee, *Davenport University*

Diana McKowen, *Indiana University*

Mary C. Miller, *Ashland University*

Marci Mitchell, *South Texas Community College*

Nancy B. Moody, *Sinclair Community College*

Danne Moore, *Shawnee State University*

Wayne A. Moore, *Indiana University of Pennsylvania*

Paul W. Murphey, *Southwest Wisconsin Technical College*

Lin Nassar, *Oakland Community College*

Beverly H. Nelson, *University of New Orleans*

Matt Newby, *Heald College*

John P. Nightingale, *Eastern Michigan University*

Ed Nagelhout, *University of Nevada*

Jeanne E. Newhall, *Middlesex Community College*

Alexa B. North, *State University of West Georgia*

Nancy Nygaard, *University of Wisconsin-Milwaukee*

Rosemary Olds, *Des Moines Area Community College*

James S. O'Rourke IV, *University of Notre Dame*

Smita Jain Oxford, *University of Mary Washington*

Ed Peters, *University of Texas at Arlington*

Melinda Phillabaum, *Indiana University*

Richard David Ramsey, *Southeastern Louisiana University, Hammond*

Betty Jane Robbins, *University of Oklahoma*

Janice Rowan, *Rowan University*

Calvin R. Parks, *Northern Illinois University*

Pamela A. Patey, *Riverside Community College*

Shara Toursh Pavlow, *University of Miami*

William Peirce, *Prince George's Community College and University of Maryland University College*

Joan Policano, *Onondaga Community College*

Paula J. Pomerenke, *Illinois State University*

Jean Anna Sellers, *Fort Hays State University*

Appreciation for Support

Deborah Von Spreecken, *Anoka-Ramsey Community College*

Karen Sterkel Powell, *Colorado State University*

Gloria Power, *Delgado Community College*

Richard P. Profozich, *Prince George's Community College*

Carolyn Mae Rainey, *Southeast Missouri State University*

Richard David Ramsey, *Southeastern Louisiana University*

Richard G. Raspen, *Wilkes University*

Virginia L. Reynolds, *Cleveland State University*

Ruth D. Richardson, *University of North Alabama*

Joseph H. Roach, *Middlesex County College*

Terry D. Roach, *Arkansas State University*

Betty Jane Robbins, *University of Oklahoma*

Linda Sarlo, *Rock Valley College*

Christine A. Saxild, *Mt. Senario College*

Joseph Schaffner, *State University of New York at Alfred*

Annette Schley, *North Seattle Community College*

Betty L. Schroeder, *Northern Illinois University*

Carolyn M. Seefer, *Diablo Valley Community College*

Marilyn Simonson, *Lakewood Community College*

Sue C. Smith, *Palm Beach Community Collage*

Kathleen M. Sole, *University of Phoenix*

Charles L. Snowden, *Sinclair Community College*

Gayle A. Sobolik, *California State University, Fresno*

Jeanette Spender, *Arkansas State University*

Jan Starnes, *The University of Texas at Austin*

Judy Steiner-Williams, *Indiana University*

Ted D. Stoddard, *Brigham Young University*

Susan Switzer, *Central Michigan University*

Roni Szeliga, *Gateway Technical College*

Leslie S. Talley, *University of Central Florida*

Barbara P. Thompson, *Columbus State Community College*

Sally J. Tiffany, *Milwaukee Area Technical College*

Lori M. Townsend, *Niagara County Community College*

Mary L. Tucker, *Ohio University*

Richard F. Tyler, *Anne Arundel Community College*

Deborah Valentine, *Emory University*

Doris A. Van Horn Christopher, *California State University, Los Angeles*

David Victor, *Eastern Michigan University*

Lois Ann Wagner, *Southwest Wisconsin Technical College*

John L. Waltman, *Eastern Michigan University*

Marion Webb, *Cleveland State University*

Beverly A. Westbrook, *Delta College*

Carol Smith White, *Georgia State University*

Carol M. Williams, *Pima County Community College*

Debbie J. Williams, *Abilene Christian University*

Jane D. Williams, *J. Sargeant Reynolds Community College*

Rosemary B. Wilson, *Washtenaw Community College*

Beverly C. Wise, *State University of New York, Morrisville*

William E. Worth, *Georgia State University*

Myron D. Yeager, *Chapman University*

Karen Zempel, *Bryant and Stratton College*

About the Authors

Dr. Mary Ellen Guffey

A dedicated professional, Mary Ellen Guffey has taught business communication and business English topics for over thirty-five years. She received a bachelor's degree, summa cum laude, from Bowling Green State University; a master's degree from the University of Illinois, and a doctorate in business and economic education from the University of California, Los Angeles (UCLA). She has taught at the University of Illinois, Santa Monica College, and Los Angeles Pierce College.

Now recognized as the world's leading business communication author, Dr. Guffey corresponds with instructors around the globe who are using her books. She is the founding author of the award-winning *Business Communication: Process and Product,* the leading business communication textbook in this country. She also wrote *Business English*, which serves more students than any other book in its field; *Essentials of College English*; and *Essentials of Business Communication*, the leading text/workbook in its market. Dr. Guffey is active professionally, serving on the review boards of the *Business and Professional Communication Quarterly* and the *Journal of Business Communication,* publications of the Association for Business Communication. She participates in national meetings, sponsors business communication awards, and is committed to promoting excellence in business communication pedagogy and the development of student writing skills.

Dr. Dana Loewy

Dana Loewy has taught business communication at California State University, Fullerton for two decades. She enjoyed introducing undergraduates to business writing and honing the skills of graduate students in managerial communication. Concurrently, she has also taught various German courses and was a regular guest lecturer at Fachhochschule Nürtingen, Germany. In addition to completing numerous brand-name consulting assignments, she is a business etiquette consultant certified by The Protocol School of Washington. Dr. Loewy has played an increasingly significant role in collaborating with Dr. Guffey on recent editions of *Business Communication: Process and Product* as well as on *Essentials of Business Communication.*

Dr. Loewy holds a master's degree from Bonn University, Germany, and earned a PhD in English from the University of Southern California. Fluent in several languages, among them German and Czech, her two native languages, Dr. Loewy has authored critical articles in many areas of interest—literary criticism, translation, business communication, and business ethics. Before teaming up with Dr. Guffey, Dr. Loewy worked as a professional translator for 25 years, during which she provided subtitles for thousands of films and videos. She also published various poetry and prose translations, most notably *The Early Poetry* of Jaroslav Seifert and *On the Waves of TSF*. Active in the Association for Business Communication, Dr. Loewy focuses on creating effective teaching/learning materials for undergraduate and graduate business communication students.

UNIT 1

Communication Foundations

Nebojsa Tatomirov/Shutterstock.com

Business Communication in the Digital Age

LEARNING OUTCOMES

After studying this chapter, you should be able to do the following:

1 Explain how communication skills fuel career success in a technology-driven, social, and mobile workplace.

2 Understand the impact of powerful interpersonal skills and a college education for your professional success in the hyperconnected digital age workplace.

3 Describe significant communication trends in today's dynamic, networked work environment.

4 Identify how information flows internally and externally in organizations through formal and informal channels.

5 Recognize the tools for doing the right thing as an ethical business communicator.

Zooming In

Nordstrom: A Century-Old Retailer Keeps Reinventing Itself

Management giant Peter Drucker's maxim "Innovate or die" may explain the longevity of Nordstrom, a 118-year-old clothing retailer that is keeping its brand fresh and its customers happy. While other clothing retailers are shuttering stores, Nordstrom is defying trends by opening new retail outlets and upgrading existing stores. The company's co-presidents Blake, Erik, and Peter Nordstrom know that to future-proof their business, they must resist conventional wisdom. At the same time, the great-grandsons of the founder uphold a proud tradition of exceptional customer service while adapting to their customers' changing needs.

So far, Nordstrom's winning formula has been to combine extraordinary concierge in-store service with cutting-edge technology. After spending more than $500 million to establish an exclusive men's store in Manhattan, the retailer has most recently opened a unique flagship store for women and children in Manhattan.[1] In addition, the company established several "service hubs" in New York City and Los Angeles called Nordstrom Local. These boutique-style stores provide pampered service and convenience—but no clothes! Shoppers buy online and pick up their items in the store, where stylists and tailors stand by. Customers can enjoy refreshments and visit a nail salon, shoe repair, or other services. "There aren't store customers or online customers," Erik Nordstrom describes the company's concept, "there are just customers who are more empowered than ever to shop on their terms."[2]

Consequently, the retailer has invested heavily in technology, for example, to allow shoppers to integrate its inventory management system with its website and the Nordstrom app. As a result, the company's online and offline worlds are seamlessly linked, and customers can find what they want in one place. Salespeople track customer requests and needs online. A strong social media engagement is key to Nordstrom's strategy to provide superb customer experiences and drive traffic to its e-commerce site. As one of America's most connected companies,[3] it relies on crowdsourcing to learn which items to stock, and it responds rapidly to queries, in Spanish when needed. Nordstrom has also pioneered the use of popular social media influencers to capture younger audiences.[4]

With such public engagement, it's not surprising that Nordstrom has clearly defined social media use guidelines. Approved employees may connect with customers during working hours and even after hours, if allowed. They are asked to use good judgment and abide by all corporate policies. They are told to be respectful, responsible, and ethical. Furthermore, the policy forbids the sharing of confidential corporate information as well as employees' and customers' personal information. Conflicts of interest are to be avoided, and compensated endorsements must be disclosed.

Whether Nordstrom's strategy will succeed remains to be seen, and the retailer's recent lackluster stock performance has irked Wall Street. In response, the family attempted to take Nordstrom private but was unable to raise enough capital. You will learn more about Nordstrom and be asked to complete a relevant task at the end of this chapter.

Critical Thinking

- Wall Street analysts have criticized Nordstrom for its lagging profits in recent months; the company's bold new ventures have been called a "gamble." What explains this clash between the Nordstrom family's vision and the reaction of the stock market?

- Why does Nordstrom allow only *approved and trained* employees to use company-owned social media accounts, logos, and videos on behalf of Nordstrom?

- Why do Nordstrom's social media guidelines emphasize ethical behavior and ethical communication?

1-1 Thriving in a Digital, Mobile, and Social Workplace

LEARNING OUTCOME

1 Explain how communication skills fuel career success in a technology-driven, social, and mobile workplace.

What will the workplace of the future look like, and will you have the skills to succeed in it? Technologies in many disciplines are rapidly evolving and transforming how we work and communicate. In his book *The Fourth Industrial Revolution*, renowned economist Klaus Schwab describes changes that can be expected. Robots, automation, and artificial intelligence (AI) are already radically reshaping and even destroying some occupations. Consider self-driving vehicles, automated supermarket checkout stands, devices reading X-rays, or algorithms flagging fraudulent bank transactions—many tasks formerly performed by humans can be executed by machines. Experts estimate that close to half of all present jobs will disappear in the next decade, although new jobs are likely to emerge.[5]

Automation will gobble up work that machines can do better and faster, for example, food preparation, operating machinery, and data processing. On the other hand, future-proof occupations include those that require communication, managing people, creativity, and specialized knowledge. This radical transformation of the workplace demands a well-trained workforce equipped with so-called soft skills, sometimes also called emotional intelligence. However, these powerful social and interpersonal skills are anything but "soft" or inferior. To reflect their growing importance, we prefer to use the terms interpersonal skills or professional skills, which may be defined as a combination of communication, logical reasoning, critical thinking, teamwork, and time management skills.[6]

The contemporary workplace is a fast-paced, competitive, and highly connected digital environment. Communication technology provides unmatched mobility and connects individuals anytime and anywhere in the world. Technology-savvy businesses such as Nordstrom have recognized the power of social media and created a seamless customer experience that's integrated across all channels. These businesses know that to survive, they must innovate and constantly reinvent themselves. Individuals, too, must remain flexible, ready to remake themselves when needed. The COVID-19 pandemic is a case in point. It has devastated the economy and forced millions to work from home. Confronting such a major crisis requires a robust skill set.

In an increasingly complex, networked, and mobile environment, communication skills matter more than ever.[7] Job candidates with exceptional communication skills immediately stand out. In this chapter, you will learn about communication skills in the digital era and about the contemporary world of work. Later you will study tools to help you negotiate ethical minefields and do the right thing. Each section covers the latest information about communicating in business while also providing tips to help you function effectively in today's fast-moving, technology-driven workplace.

1-1a Communication Skills: Your Ticket to Work

When we discuss communication skills, we generally mean reading, listening, nonverbal, speaking, and writing skills. In addition, workers today must be media savvy and exercise good judgment when posting messages on the Internet and writing e-mails. To be successful, they must guard their online image and protect the reputation of their employers.

In making hiring decisions, employers often rank communication skills among the most desirable competencies.[8] No wonder. According to one survey, the average worker spends almost 12 hours per week answering e-mail at the office and another five hours from home.[9] Many employees also write reports, memos, presentations, social media posts, and more. As one writing coach puts it: "Having excellent writing skills can make you an indispensable member of your team or company. And it's one of the best ways to remain consistently employable—no matter your profession."[10] The ability to communicate well is an always-in-demand, transferable skill.

Writing has been variously called a "career sifter," a "threshold skill," and "the price of admission,"[11] indicating that effective writing skills can be a stepping-stone to great job opportunities. Poorly developed writing skills, however, may derail a career. Writing is a marker of high-skill, high-wage, professional work, according to Bob Kerrey, former university president and chair of the National Commission on Writing. If you can't express yourself clearly, he says, you limit your opportunities for many positions.[12]

If interpersonal skills matter greatly, writing effectively can be even more critical. Ever since the digital revolution swept the workplace, most workers write their own messages. New communication channels appeared, including the Internet and e-mail, followed by instant messaging, blogs, and social media networks. We communicate more than ever. With our smart devices, we communicate on the go. Americans now devote almost 70 percent of their waking hours to screen time. According to market research firm Nielsen, adults in the United States on average spend more than 11 hours daily interacting with all kinds of media, primarily TV, but almost four hours on their smartphones and tablets.[13]

The mobile revolution is stimulating huge economic growth and has profoundly changed how we communicate; it has become the fastest-adopted technology of all time.[14] Figure 1.1 displays the emergence of new technology and the rapid growth of Internet users over the last two decades. So far, the number of Internet users has roughly doubled every five years.

Writing matters more than ever because online media require more of it, not less. An important PayScale study revealed an unexpected finding. The skill most lacking among recent college

Note: Because this is a well-researched textbook, you will find small superscript numbers in the text. These announce information sources. Citations are located in the References section at the end of the book. This edition uses a modified American Psychological Association (APA) reference citation format.

Note: Following major publication guides, in this book direct quotations will be presented verbatim, i.e., exactly as the words and punctuation appeared in the original text. Occasionally, the quotation style may clash with the book style. For example, the authors prefer *e-mail*, but the quotation shows *email*.

FIGURE 1.1 Time Line: Evolving Technology and Social Media

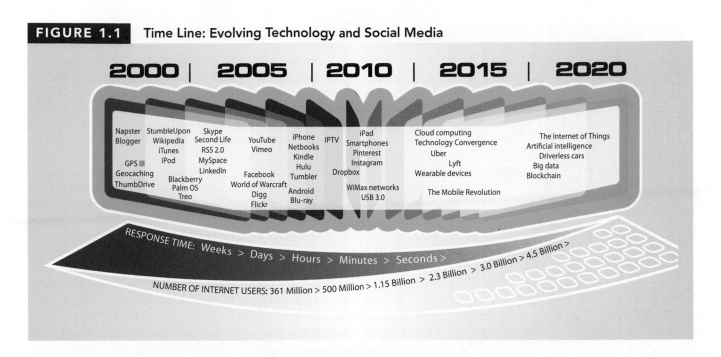

graduates, said 44 percent of the managers polled, was writing proficiency.[15] Dan Schawbel, research director at Future Workplace, agreed: "No working day will be complete without writing an email or tackling a new challenge, so the sooner you develop these skills, the more employable you will become."[16] Breaking with the norm, PayScale considers writing and speaking skills to be "hard" skills, perhaps as a nod to their tremendous importance.

1-1b It's Up to You: Communication Skills Can Be Learned

By enrolling in a business writing class, you have already taken the first step toward improving or polishing your communication skills. The goals of this course and this book include teaching you basic business communication skills, such as how to write an effective e-mail, a short message on a mobile device, or a clear business letter, and how to make a memorable presentation with various digital media.

Thriving in the challenging interconnected work world depends on many factors, some of which you cannot control. However, one factor that you do control is how well you communicate. You are not born with the abilities to read, listen, speak, and write effectively. These skills must be learned. This book and this course may well be the most important in your entire college curriculum because they will equip you with the skills most needed in today's fast-paced information- and data-driven workplace.

Reality Check

Robot-Proof Workplace Survival Skills

"Many jobs require ... very human qualities like communication, empathy, creativity, strategic thinking, questioning, and dreaming. Collectively, we often refer to these qualities as 'soft skills,' but don't let the name fool you; these soft skills are going to be hard currency in the job market as AI and technology take over some of the jobs that can be performed without people."[17]

—Bernard Marr, *author, consultant, futurist*

1-2 Building Future-Proof Skills for the Twenty-First-Century Workplace

Information technology has changed how we work, play, and communicate. It has never been easier to access and share information via various digital media from a vast network of sources and distribute it nearly instantly and to widespread audiences. What hasn't changed is that communication skills need time and effort to develop. To achieve literacy in the digital age means not only using multimedia applications and snazzy late-model gadgets but also thinking critically

LEARNING OUTCOME

2 Understand the impact of powerful interpersonal skills and a college education for your professional success in the hyperconnected digital age workplace.

VLADGRIN/Shutterstock.com

about new media. It means using technology thoughtfully and in a professional manner to achieve success in a hyperconnected world.

The twenty-first-century economy depends mainly on information and knowledge. Previously, in the Industrial Age, raw materials and physical labor were the key ingredients in the creation of wealth. Today, however, individuals in the workforce offer their knowledge, not their muscles. Knowledge workers (a term first coined by management guru Peter Drucker) get paid for their education and their ability to learn.[18]

More recently, we are hearing the term information worker to describe those who produce and consume information in the workplace.[19] Regardless of the terminology, knowledge and information workers engage in mind work. They must make sense of words, figures, and data. At the same time, according to professional services firm Deloitte, roughly 90 percent of all existing data generated on our planet was created just in the last five years. The data that humans create and copy annually in the "digital universe" is doubling every 12 months.[20] This exponential growth of knowledge is expected to continue and accelerate.

In this light, it may not surprise you that jobs in the information technology sector are likely to increase 13 percent by 2026.[21] Mobile technology generated almost $3.3 trillion in revenue globally in one year alone and is responsible for 11 million jobs, according to Boston Consulting.[22] However, even in a strong economy and a very tight U.S. labor market, hundreds of thousands of jobs in science, technology, engineering, and math (STEM) remain unfilled, primarily in sought-after fields such as data analytics, AI, cloud computing, and IT security.[23] Experts also worry about domestic talent shortages in skilled manufacturing.[24] In such a quick-changing environment, continuous, lifelong learning will make you more competitive and valuable to future employers. Only an adaptable, highly skilled workforce is well equipped to weather any economic climate as well as global competition.

1-2a Why Should You Care?

As an information worker in the digital age, you can expect to be generating, processing, and exchanging information. You will need to be able to transmit it effectively across various communication channels and multiple media. You might be called on to use e-mail, multimedia slide presentations, podcasts, or Instagram and Facebook as well as other social media in a professional setting. With added job responsibilities, you will be expected to make sound decisions and solve complex problems. Yet in a PayScale survey, half of the employers said new-hires are not workplace ready, mainly lacking critical-thinking and reasoning skills.[26] As you can see, if you possess or develop your critical thinking ability, you will thrive.

In college, you are learning to think, read, and ask questions to function in a complex networked world. The avalanche of information that engulfs you daily requires you to evaluate all sources critically because not all news outlets were created equal. Some engage in deliberate disinformation as they pursue a hidden political agenda. Others may be purposely manipulated by hostile powers engaging in a cyber war. Bots and fake accounts have been found to spread propaganda via social media—untruths planted to divide Americans and disrupt public discourse.

As a discerning businessperson and voter in a democracy, you will be challenged to stay informed, detect fake news stories, and withstand attempts at manipulation. However, even the very definition of the catch phrase fake news is complex. After

BigNazik/Shutterstock.com

all, many types of misinformation (accidental untruth) and disinformation (intentional untruth) exist. Two U.S. economists have presented research defining fake news as "news stories that have no factual basis but are presented as facts."[27] In partisan politics, the term *fake news* has also been used to describe unwelcome evidence that some people find uncomfortable because it clashes with their convictions. The key ability to accurately evaluate new information—a hallmark of information literacy—will be discussed in Chapter 11. A questioning, critical-thinking mindset is an important interpersonal skill in any profession.

1-2b Thinking Critically in the Digital Age

In an age of automation that will devour millions of jobs, positions that require thinking, brainpower, and decision-making skills are likely to remain plentiful. Whether you work in m-commerce (mobile technology businesses), e-commerce (Internet-based businesses), or brick-and-mortar commerce, nearly three out of four jobs involve some form of mind work. To be successful in these jobs, you will need to be able to think critically, make decisions, and communicate those decisions.

Management and employees work together in such areas as product development, quality control, and customer satisfaction. All workers, from executives to subordinates, need to think creatively and critically. Toyota's corporate culture of continuous improvement (kaizen) by engaged and empowered workers has been the envy of the manufacturing world. Competing with Google and Uber Technologies in the race for connected, autonomous, and electric cars, Toyota created a centralized group of 200 workers to adapt continuous improvement to new business such as car sharing and consumer robots.[29] When your boss or team leader says, "What do you think we ought to do?" you want to be able to supply good ideas and demonstrate that you can think critically. This means having opinions that are backed by reasons and evidence.

Faced with a problem or an issue, most of us do a lot of worrying before separating the issues or deciding. Figure 1.2

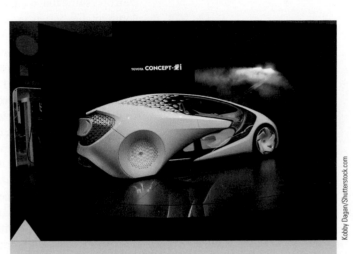

Kobby Dagan/Shutterstock.com

Toyota's futuristic electric vehicle Concept-i is equipped with an AI assistant, dubbed Yui, designed to interpret drivers' emotions and learn to adjust to the passengers' needs, foreshadowing an AI companion capable of a full-fledged natural-language conversation.

FIGURE 1.2 Osborn–Parnes Creative Problem-Solving Process

1 Explore the Challenge	2 Generate Ideas	3 Implement Solutions
Identify the challenge	Come up with many ideas to solve the problem	Select and strengthen solutions
Gather information and clarify the problem	Pick the most promising ideas	Plan how to bring your solution to life and implement it

provides a three-point plan to help you think critically and solve problems competently. As you can see, understanding the problem is essential and must come first. Generating and selecting the most feasible ideas is the intermediate step. Finally, the problem-solving model prompts you to refine, justify, and implement the solution. At the end of each chapter in this text, you will find activities and problems that will help you develop and apply your critical-thinking skills.

1-2c Managing Your Career Well: Guarding Your Credibility

To find an entry-level job and advance, you will need to be proactive and exercise greater control over your career than college graduates before you did. Like most workers today, you will not find nine-to-five jobs, predictable pay increases, lifetime security, and even conventional workplaces. Quite likely, your future employer may first observe your online presence before deciding to invite you for an interview.

Don't presume that companies will provide you with a clearly defined career path or planned developmental experiences. Your opportunities may broaden when the economy is humming, even if your skills are not up to speed. However, only adequate skills will recession-proof your career. In the private sector, you will most likely work for multiple employers, moving back and forth between work and education, and between work and family responsibilities. Increasingly, the workplace and your career will resemble not a vertical corporate ladder but a more intricate, open, fluid, and interconnected framework—a **corporate lattice**.[30]

To keep up with evolving technologies and procedures, you can expect lifelong learning and career training. After all, you might have to pursue four or five different careers (not just jobs) in your lifetime.[31] Primarily because technology is changing lightning fast, traditional colleges and universities cannot keep pace; often their graduates are not workplace ready. Therefore, in a tight job market, some companies have started to offer boot camp-style academies to nontraditional candidates. For example, Capital One Financial and health-care company DaVita are trying to attract and train the skilled workers they need before hiring the best of them.[32] Scrambling to fill its 150,000 vacant IT support jobs, Google is partnering with a Texas community college to develop an IT certification program.[33] Whether you are currently employed or about to enter today's demanding workplace, you must be willing to continually learn new skills that supplement the basic skills you are acquiring in college.

In addition, in a hyperconnected professional environment, you must manage and guard your reputation—at the office and online. How you present yourself in the virtual world, meaning how well you communicate and protect your **brand**, may very well determine how successful your career will be. Your credibility is a precious asset. Well-crafted tweets, astute comments on LinkedIn, Instagram, and Facebook, competent e-mails, and thoughtful blog posts will help you continually make a positive impression. As one career advisor explains: "Every interaction—from how you greet your coworkers in the morning to how you summarize a status update in an email—contributes to how people view you."[35] In short, you will need to nurture and safeguard your professionalism online and off. You will learn more about interpersonal skills and professionalism in Chapter 2.

1-2d Acquiring Crisis-Proof Skills to Weather Any Job Market

The upheaval of the economy following the COVID-19 pandemic turned the job market upside down. Recent college graduates and entry-level workers were especially hard hit. However, as the economy recovers, new grads who are flexible and well-prepared are finding opportunities even in a tough job market.[36] In one of its much-noted Job Outlook studies, the National Association of Colleges and Employers (NACE) recently asked employers what attributes they seek in new college graduates.

FIGURE 1.3 Powerful Job Skills Employers Seek

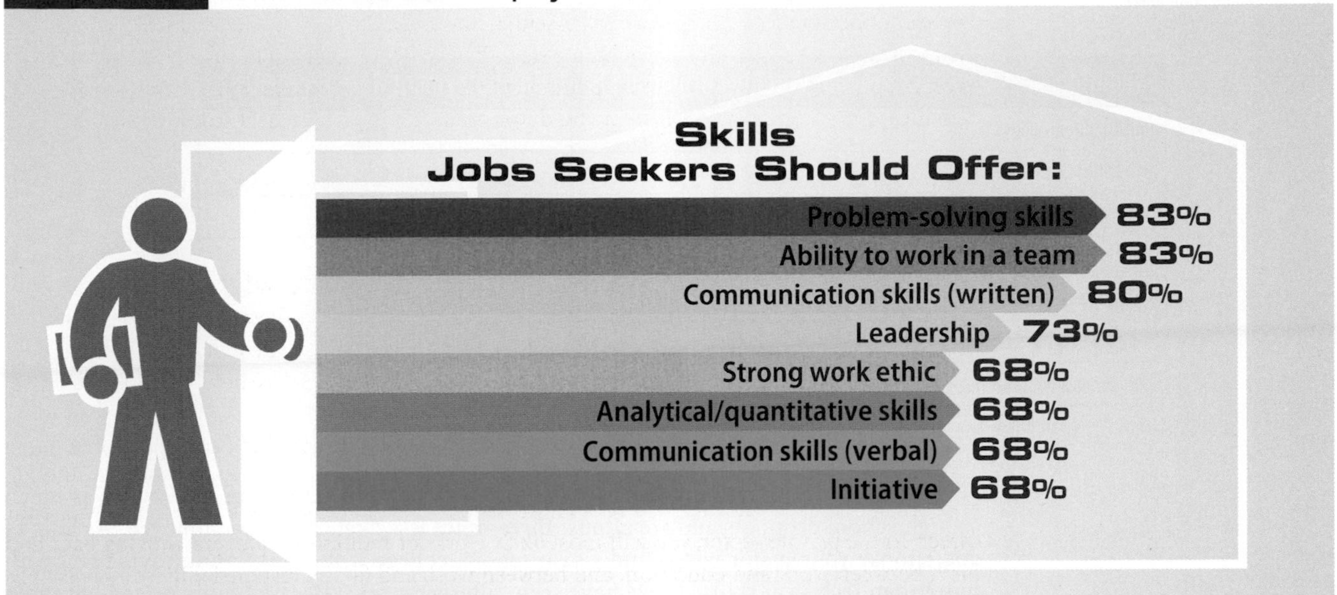

Skills
Jobs Seekers Should Offer:

Skill	Percentage
Problem-solving skills	83%
Ability to work in a team	83%
Communication skills (written)	80%
Leadership	73%
Strong work ethic	68%
Analytical/quantitative skills	68%
Communication skills (verbal)	68%
Initiative	68%

Source: Job Outlook 2018, National Association of Colleges and Employers, p. 30.

First, a prospective employee must meet the employer's fundamental criteria, including having the required major, course work, and GPA. By the way, fewer employers screen candidates by GPA than just five years ago; however, GPA continues to serve as a crucial distinguishing factor in most industries, with 3.0 (a B average) as a cutoff.[37] If a candidate passes these hurdles, then employers look for interpersonal and professional skills such as problem solving, teamworking, and writing ability, as shown in Figure 1.3.[38]

Although employers seek these skills, they are not always pleased with what they find. The Association of American Colleges and Universities (AACU) asked executives and hiring managers about graduates' career readiness. The employers noted that students were adequately trained for entry-level jobs but were not equipped for advancement. In their view, promotable graduates excel at oral communication, critical thinking, ethical judgment, teamwork, independent work, self-motivation, writing, and real-world application of learning. However, only 40 percent are well prepared, said the executives.[39] To make sure you don't disappoint future employers, take advantage now of opportunities to strengthen your writing, presentation, and critical-thinking skills.

1-2e Understanding How Your Education Drives Your Income

As college tuition rises steeply and student debt mounts, you may wonder whether going to college is worthwhile. The American public seems to share this skepticism, as a Gallup poll suggests. Fewer than half of adults in the United States expressed confidence in higher education.[40] Yet the effort and money you invest in earning your college degree will most likely pay off. College graduates earn more, suffer less unemployment, and can choose from a wider variety of career options than workers without a college education. Moreover, college graduates have access to the highest-paying and fastest-growing careers, many of which require a degree. A college education also correlates positively with better health care and longer life expectancy.[41]

Reality Check

"New-Collar Skills" Needed Beyond a College Degree

"[Many jobs at IBM] require a certain set of skills; we call them new-collar skills that maybe require a two-year degree or just different skill sets. We think the capabilities and the skills are even more important than the degree because things change so quickly in a lot of hot new fields: cybersecurity, analytics, cognitive, even things we're doing within marketing or design."[44]

—Jennifer Ryan Crozier, *former president of IBM Foundation and VP, IBM Corporate Citizenship*

FIGURE 1.4 The Education Bonus: Higher Income, Lower Unemployment

Education	Median Weekly Earnings ($)	Unemployment Rate (Percent)
High school dropout	520	6.5
High school diploma	712	4.6
Some college, no degree	774	4.0
Associate's degree	836	3.4
Bachelor's degree	1,173	2.5
Master's degree	1,401	2.2
Professional/doctoral degree	1,790	1.5

Source: U.S. Bureau of Labor Statistics (2017). Employment projections: Unemployment rates and earnings by educational attainment.

As Figure 1.4 shows, graduates with bachelor's degrees earn more than twice as much as high school dropouts and are almost three times less likely to be unemployed. As long as you choose your major wisely and finish school, college will pay off and provide you with more than technical skills. As we have seen, interpersonal skills are highly prized but often in short supply. Workers who lack them are fired. One researcher even claims that half of all terminations are attributable to poor "soft" skills.[42] A survey of employers confirms that interpersonal skills such as communication ability can tip the scales in favor of one job applicant over another.[43] Your ticket to winning in any job market and launching a successful career is good communication skills.

LEARNING OUTCOME

3 Describe significant communication trends in today's dynamic, networked work environment.

1-3 Trends and Challenges Affecting You in the Information Age Workplace

As a businessperson and especially as a business communicator, you will undoubtedly be affected by many trends. Some of those trends include new, disruptive technologies and social media, expectations of around-the-clock availability, and global competition. Other trends include flattened management hierarchies, team projects, a diverse workforce, and the mobile or virtual office. The workplace continues to change rapidly and profoundly. The following overview reveals how communication skills are closely tied to your success in a constantly evolving networked workplace.

1-3a Social Media Use in Business and Disruptive Technologies

Interacting with others on Instagram, Snapchat, YouTube, Facebook, FaceTime, or Twitter may be a daily necessity to you, and once employed, you will be expected to keep up with new technology. In the twenty-first-century workplace, technology savvy is so important that businesses are unlikely to thrive without it. Despite security risks and the precarious handling of user data by organizations such as Google and Facebook, technology will remain central to organizations. Most large enterprises are completely plugged in and have created a positive presence with the help of both traditional and social media.

New platforms that predominantly function via smartphone apps have given rise to the sharing economy. Consider Uber and Lyft. These app-based ride-sharing platforms are disrupting long-established business models to the delight of their core passengers—young, affluent urbanites. However, ride-hailing apps are testing labor laws and local ordinances; they irk cab drivers and city officials around the world, leading to bans and lawsuits. Other new players in urban transportation are bike-sharing, car-sharing, and now e-scooter-sharing apps such as

Bird, Lime, and Spin. Similarly, the home-sharing platform Airbnb has disrupted the hospitality industry worldwide and encouraged a growing host network.

Sparking new radical technologies, social media continue to connect vast numbers of people all over the world. The 336 million monthly active Twitter users clock an average 500 million tweets per day.[45] Ordinary citizens can organize protests and boycotts within hours, even minutes. Bad customer service experiences or overt political leanings can damage an organization's reputation with long-term economic consequences.[46] In short, word of mouth, positive and negative, can travel instantly at the speed of a few taps on a smartphone keyboard. The various social media channels offer undeniable advantages. However, even their most avid users are learning that their go-to technologies also come with significant downsides—for example, data breaches, invasion of privacy, identity theft, manipulation, and disinformation, as Figure 1.5 illustrates.

Tech-savvy companies are embracing digital tools to connect with consumers, invite feedback, and improve their products and services. They may announce promotions and events in blog posts, in tweets, on their company websites, and by social media. Above all, plugged-in businesses realize that to manage public perceptions of their brands, they need to be proactive but also respond quickly and deftly within social media when a crisis hits. They need to go where their customers are and attempt to establish and keep a loyal following. It has never been easier to interact so fast with so many people at once.

Even if they still have not mastered their social media strategies, nearly all business-people today in some way rely on the Internet to collect information, serve customers, and sell products and services. Figure 1.6 illustrates many common office and communication

---

FIGURE 1.5 Communication Technology in a Mobile and Social World—Costs and Benefits

Benefits

- Empowerment of the individual; potentially everyone has a voice
- Unparalleled access to nearly unlimited information
- Transparency: People and organizations face scrutiny and pressure to behave
- Companies can collect productivity and behavioral data
- Unprecedented mobility; the anywhere, anytime office
- Cloud-based data storage and applications independent of device
- Convenience and speed of e-commerce
- Connectedness with friends, family, and larger social groups

Trade-Offs

- Proliferation of conspiracy theorists, radicals, criminals and crackpots in the absence of gatekeepers
- Cyber war, disinformation, bots, propaganda by foreign powers
- Transparency: Privacy violations, spying, cyber stalking, identify theft
- Indiscretions potentially following individuals forever
- Relentless pursuit of productivity; "Big Data"; loss of control over one's information
- 24/7 availability; threat to work–life balance
- Hacking and data breaches
- Fake news stories, doctored videos

Pepsco Studio/Shutterstock.com

FIGURE 1.6 Communication and Collaborative Technologies

Communication Technologies at Work

Becoming familiar with communication technology in business can help you succeed on the job. Today's digital workplace is shaped by mobile devices, mobile apps, social media, superfast broadband and wireless access, and other technologies that allow workers to share information, work from remote locations, and be more productive in or away from the office. With today's tools you can exchange ideas, solve problems, develop products, forecast future performance, and complete team projects any time of the day or night anywhere in the world.

Cloud Computing, Web 2.0, and Beyond: A Social, Mobile, and Smart Future

Increasingly, applications and data are stored in remote locations online, *in the cloud*. This ability to access data on remote servers with a computer or mobile device is called *cloud computing*, and it has helped fuel unparalleled mobility and information sharing. All social media platforms are cloud-based, as are typical workplace applications such as Microsoft's Office 365 or Adobe's Creative Suite. Websites and Internet-based applications have shifted from one-way, read-only communication to multidirectional, social, read-write communication. This profound change, dubbed Web 2.0, has allowed workers to collaborate and network in unprecedented ways.

More changes on the horizon beyond Web 2.0 will transform our lives and communication; they include intelligent devices and appliances—the *Internet of things*—*artificial intelligence* (AI), *augmented reality* (AR) and *virtual reality* (VR), voice-activated digital assistants such as Alexa or Siri, and self-driving vehicles. The emergence of the digital currency Bitcoin has introduced *blockchain technology*, a decentralized network of shared and continuously reconciled information, a vast database hosted by millions of computers at once. Some believe that blockchain will revolutionize the Internet.

VoIP Phone Systems

Savvy businesses are switching from traditional phone service to voice over Internet protocol (VoIP). This technology allows callers to communicate using a fast Internet connection, thus eliminating long-distance and local telephone charges. Higher-end VoIP systems now support unified voice mail, e-mail, click-to-call capabilities, and softphones (Internet-based applications or mobile apps, such as Google Voice, for calling and messaging). Other free or low-cost options include Skype and FaceTime. Most messaging apps—such as WhatsApp and Facebook Messenger—now offer wireless voice calling and recorded voice messages.

Smart Mobile Devices and Digital Convergence

Lightweight, ever-smaller devices provide phone, e-mail, Web browsing, and calendar options anywhere there is a cellular or Wi-Fi network. Tablets and smartphones such as Android devices and the iPhone and iPad allow workers to tap into corporate databases and intranets from distant locations. Users can check customers' files, complete orders, collect payment, and send out receipts remotely. The need for separate electronic gadgets is waning as digital smart devices are becoming multifunctional. With streaming video, connectivity between smart TVs and computers, and networked mobile devices, technology is converging, consolidating into increasingly more powerful devices. Many smart devices today can replace digital point-and-shoot still photography and video cameras. Mobile smart devices are also competing with TVs and computers for primacy. Mobile apps rival the capabilities of full-fledged software applications on laptops, on desktops, and in the cloud.

KANUT PHOTO/Shutterstock.com

Wearable Devices: Smartwatches, AR and VR Headsets

A growing trend in mobile computing is wearable devices. Activity trackers such as Fitbit, Apple Watch, and similar accessories do more than record fitness activities. They are powerful mobile devices that can sync with other smart electronics. Google Glass failed to capture a larger consumer market; however, with Google Lens, the company continues to pursue innovative augmented-reality head-mounted devices. More affordable virtual-reality goggles, for example, Oculus Rift, are popular with gamers, but VR headsets are also used in simulators, in training, and in patient therapy.

Speech Recognition

Computers and mobile devices equipped with speech-recognition software enable users to dictate hands-free with accurate transcription. Speech recognition is particularly helpful to disabled workers and professionals with heavy dictation loads, such as physicians and attorneys. Users can create documents, enter data, compose and send e-mails, search the Web, and control their notebooks, laptops, and desktops—all by voice. Smart devices can also execute tasks with voice command apps—for example, to dial a call, find a route, or transcribe voice mail.

Electronic Presentations and Data Visualization

Business presentations in PowerPoint, Prezi, or Keynote can be projected from a laptop, tablet, or smartphone. They can be posted and accessed online. Sophisticated presentations may include animation, sound effects, digital photos, video clips, or hyperlinks. In some industries, PowerPoint and other electronic slides (decks) are replacing or supplementing traditional hard-copy reports. Data visualization tools such as SAS help businesses make sense of increasing amounts of complex data.

Social Media

The term *social media* describes technology that enables participants to connect and share in social networks online. For example, Facebook, Instagram, and Twitter allow users to post their latest news, photos, other media, and links. Businesses use microblogging services such as Twitter and Tumblr to message the public, drive traffic to their blogs and websites, or announce events and promotions. Twitter and Tumblr also allow businesses to track what is being said about them and their products and to respond immediately.

Similarly, organizations use social networks such as Facebook, Instagram, and others to interact with customers

Tero Vesalainen/Shutterstock.com

and build their brands. Companies may also prospect for talent using social media networks, LinkedIn in particular. Many companies are using corporate social networks for messaging, collaboration, project management, and data storage. Various popular enterprise-grade platforms include Slacker, Yammer, Asana, Atlassian HipChat, and SharePoint.

Blogs, Podcasts, and Wikis

Businesses use *blogs* to keep customers and employees informed and to receive feedback. Company news can be posted, updated, and categorized for easy cross-referencing. *Podcasts* are popular audio files played back from a website or downloaded to a digital audio player, typically a smart device. A *wiki* is an Internet or intranet site that allows multiple users to collaboratively create, edit, and store digital files. Information can get lost in e-mails and chat threads, but wikis provide easy access to important organizational documents and serve as a knowledge management tool. Wikis for business are often integrated within powerful enterprise social networks, for instance, in Slack.

Web Conferencing and Videoconferencing

With services such as Zoom, WebEx, GoToMeeting, and Skype for Business, users need only a computer or smart device and an Internet connection to hold a meeting (*webinar*) with customers or colleagues in real time. Although the functions are constantly evolving, Web conferencing incorporates screen sharing, chats, slide presentations, text messaging, and application sharing. All services also provide voice and video, making them videoconferencing tools as well. Best of all, they can be accessed across all devices.

Some companies have invested in sophisticated videoconferencing rooms equipped with HD video cameras and large video screens. Two to 200 individuals can see each other and interact in real time, although they may be far apart.

Gamification

Gamification is the application of game design techniques to increase motivation and engagement. Much like computer games, gamification platforms in business are designed to be fun and in turn increase productivity as well as revenue. Gamification techniques include using badges or points to tap into workers' natural desires for competition, status, and achievement but also altruism and collaboration. Gamification is used in marketing, sales, customer retention, and training, allowing employers to collect large amounts of productivity data.

technologies you will find in today's workplace. To make the most of these resources, you, as a skilled business communicator, must develop a tool kit of new communication skills. You will want to know how to select the best communication channel, how to use each channel effectively, and how to build and safeguard your credibility. All of these topics are covered in later chapters.

1-3b Anytime, Anywhere: 24/7/365 Availability

The dizzyingly fast connectedness across time zones and vast distances has a downside. In the last two decades, the line between work and leisure has become increasingly blurry. In many industries, information workers are expected to remain tethered to their workplaces with laptops, tablets, and smartphones around the clock and on weekends. As you rise on the career ladder, you may be expected to work long hours without extra compensation and be available practically anytime and anywhere should a crisis strike at work.

The physical office is extending its reach, sometimes overreaching, perhaps. Compared to workers in most European countries, Americans put in the longest hours (about 50 percent more). They also receive the shortest paid vacations. In contrast, workers in the European Union enjoy four to six weeks of paid time off per year. Most are also protected from working more than 48 hours per week. In France, a labor law guarantees workers the right to disconnect from work communication.[48] Similarly, the Japanese government enacted a law at least partially limiting work hours after a young employee of an advertising firm committed suicide. Her death was blamed on karoshi, death by overwork.[49]

In the United States, workers tend to be always plugged in. Employees spend eight hours a week on average answering work e-mails after hours. Almost a third of males and nearly a quarter of females regularly bring work home, to social outings, and even on vacation.[50] Recently, the Global Wellness Summit issued a report cautioning that constant connectedness may lead to depression and anxiety.[51] Sociologist Simon Gottschalk cites research showing that "digital overload" after hours is a major stressor, leading to burnout.[52] Be that as it may, the office today and in the future is mobile, social, and always on.

In a global economy in which corporations own far-flung operations around the world, a networked information-driven workforce never goes off duty or offline. Managers exert power beyond the physical office. Moreover, work in the digital age demands that participants stay on until the project is finished, not when the clock strikes five or six at the end of the day. As your professional responsibilities grow, you can expect not only to be accessible 24/7 but also to feel the significant impact of globalization.

New communication technologies, free-trade agreements, low transportation costs, and saturated domestic markets have given rise to globalization.

1-3c Global Markets and Competition

New communication technologies, free-trade agreements, falling transportation costs, and saturated local markets—all these developments have encouraged companies to enter emerging markets around the world. Small, medium, and large companies in the United States and abroad have expanded and created supply chains overseas. Wealthy countries gained new markets, and formerly poor nations such as China rose and became integrated into the global economy. Consumers everywhere benefited from affordable goods. A global middle class arose.

Globalization also caused negative outcomes, however. Entire industries and regions manufacturing low-tech products were devastated. As a result, opposition against globalization by those who felt left out has grown, leading to calls for protectionism in the United States and elsewhere. Still, even as trade barriers are beginning to rise again, globalization is unlikely to experience a serious reversal, experts believe.[53] Most likely it will just change. Advances in cross-border communication and connectivity will likely lead to global competition for high-end technology jobs and more complex products, such as automobiles or microprocessors. David Autor, a prominent economist, believes that the real challenge in the future will be struggles over intellectual property and innovative industries.[54]

The consequences of this shift should alarm anyone who lacks an advanced education and faces a career that can be automated or outsourced. Even highly educated Americans will be competing with their smart counterparts across the globe, many of whom will be willing to work for less money. Routine, blue-collar jobs will continue to be outsourced, but high-end research, marketing, and design work will gravitate to the United States.[55]

Many traditional U.S. companies are global players now and generate more profit abroad than at home. Coca-Cola, Accenture, Mars, 3M, Intel, Medtronic, and American Express are admired multinational corporations with U.S. headquarters. International carmakers Volkswagen and Toyota produce vehicles in the United States to sell them domestically and export them to China. Global interconnectedness is here to stay.

Doing business in faraway countries means dealing with people who may be very different from you. They may practice different religions, follow different customs, have different lifestyles, and rely on different approaches in business. Now add the complications of multiple time zones, vast distances between offices, and different languages.

Successful communication in new markets requires developing new skills and attitudes. These include cultural awareness, flexibility, and patience. Because these skills and attitudes may be difficult to achieve, you will receive special communication training to help you deal with intercultural business transactions.

1-3d Flattened Management Layers

In traditional companies, information flows through many levels of managers. In response to intense global competition and other pressures, however, innovative businesses have for years been cutting costs and flattening their management hierarchies. This flattening means that fewer layers of managers separate decision makers from line workers. In flat organizations,

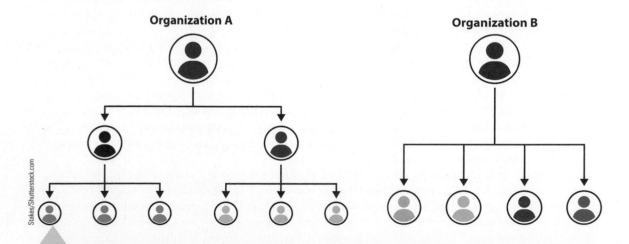

Organization A

Organization B

Stakes/Shutterstock.com

The simple chart is showing Organization A with middle management and Organization B with a flat management structure without middle managers.

in which the lines of communication are shorter, decision makers can react more quickly to market changes. Removing middle management, the belief was, would make companies more agile; it would encourage collaboration and spark creativity by banishing bureaucracy. It would save costs, too.

Not surprisingly, tech firms—start-ups in particular—gravitate toward a **bossless organizational structure**. Chief among them, online shoe retailer Zappos introduced a radical experiment—a system of self-management its CEO Tony Hsieh called **holacracy**. He abolished job titles and managers. Zappos workers digitally tracked decisions and outcomes with an app.[56] Hundreds of businesses adopted the model. Like Zappos, tech firm Bonitasoft created "circles" to tackle work projects autonomously. California tomato processor Morning Star has no formal management and a happy staff.[57] Most recently, electric carmaker Tesla decided to go lean, too.

However, in the absence of midlevel bosses to keep workers on track and motivated, some companies have started to struggle. Zappos suffered substantial staff departures. Bonitasoft learned that its members became too passive and experienced "almost too much democracy."[58] Studies found that workers prefer structure and perceive overly flattened workplaces as disorienting.[59] Hierarchies seem to provide clarity and direction. Critics point to one major disadvantage for executives of thinning management layers: "interaction fatigue." Internal social platforms and companywide Slack channels force top managers to spend ever more time communicating and collaborating. CEOs may become too accessible to the rank-and-file.[60]

Today's flatter organizations pose communication challenges. In the past, authoritarian and hierarchical management structures did not require that every employee be a skilled communicator. Managers simply passed along messages to the next level. Today, however, frontline employees as well as managers participate in critical thinking and decision making. Nearly everyone is a writer and a communicator.

1-3e Collaborative Environments and Teaming

Teamwork has become a reality in business. Many companies have created cross-functional teams to empower employees and boost their involvement in decision making. Such stable teams of people have learned to work well together over time. Traditional teams helped turn around Simmons Bedding Company a decade ago by reducing waste in operations, boosting sales, and improving the relationships with dealers. Customer satisfaction and employee morale also soared.[62] Eager to speed up innovation, global conglomerate Siemens AG bypassed its own research and development arm. Instead, the company launched Next47, an independent product-innovation unit, to invite creative collaboration in its medical equipment and electrical gear business. For its first project, Next47 teamed up with aircraft manufacturer Airbus to build a quiet, fuel-efficient hybrid-powered jet engine.[63]

The complex and unpredictable challenges in today's workplace require rapid changes in course and greater flexibility, says Harvard management professor Amy Edmondson. She argues that the new era of business requires a new strategy she calls **teaming**: "Teaming is teamwork on the fly: a pickup basketball game rather than plays run by a team that has trained as a unit for years."[64] This means that instead of traditional standing teams, organizations are now forming **ad hoc teams** to solve problems. Such project-based teams disband once they have accomplished their objectives. Although the challenges of making such diverse and potentially dispersed teams function well are many, teaming is here to stay.

Not surprisingly, the independent workforce is growing, enabled by digital platforms. Much has been written about the **gig economy**, a sector of the labor market relying on free agents hired on a project basis or doing other short-term, independent work. Some economists estimate that 20 to 30 percent of working-age American adults hold nontraditional jobs.[65] Online platforms facilitate a marketplace in which independent contractors are moonlighting as Lyft and Uber drivers or as odd-jobbers for TaskRabbit. Gloomy predictions describe a contingent workforce of the future without well-defined credentials, benefits, and job security. The upside of nontraditional work is flexibility; most independent workers

Ethics ✔ Check

Too Informal?

Executives typically spend 80 percent of their workday communicating. Thanks to Slack and other internal communication platforms, some top managers come close to 90 percent. One CEO complained that an entry-level hire pinged him on Slack to find out where his kids go to school.[61] Why was the CEO unhappy?

report being highly satisfied with their work arrangements.[66] In certain sectors, such as aerospace and entertainment, employers will continue to rely on a network of contractors for short-term projects.

Whether companies form standing or ad hoc teams, individuals must work together and share information. Working relationships can become strained when individuals don't share the same location, background, knowledge, or training. Some companies even hire communication coaches to help teams get along. Such experts work to develop interpersonal, negotiation, and collaboration techniques. However, companies would prefer to hire new workers who already possess these skills. That is why so many advertisements for new employees say "must possess excellent communication skills"—which you are learning in this book and this course.

1-3f Growing Workforce Diversity

In addition to pervasive communication technology, advanced team management, and distant work environments, today's workplace is changing in yet another area. The U.S. workforce is becoming increasingly diverse. As shown in Figure 1.7, the population of non-Hispanic whites in the United States is expected to drop from 61 percent in 2016 to 53 percent in 2035. Hispanics will climb from 18 percent to 23 percent, while African Americans will hold steady at around 13 percent relative to the growing total U.S. population within that time period. Asians and Pacific Islanders will probably rise from 5 percent to 7 percent by 2035.[67]

Women attain higher education in greater numbers than men do; 39 percent of women ages twenty-five to twenty-nine earned a bachelor's degree, as opposed to 32 percent of men. In other words, women earn 57.34 percent of all bachelor's degrees, resulting in a gender gap of 25.6 percent for men, as they earn 74.4 degrees for every 100 degrees earned by women.[68] However, in many industries and in executive positions, females are still the minority. According to the National Science Foundation, the gender gap is most pronounced in the high-tech industry (26 percent) and science and engineering (28 percent).[69] The U.S. Bureau of Labor Statistics projects that, overall, women will peak at 47 percent of the labor force in 2025 and then level off to 46 percent by 2060.[70]

FIGURE 1.7 **Racial and Ethnic Makeup of U.S. Population, 2016–2055 (Projected)**

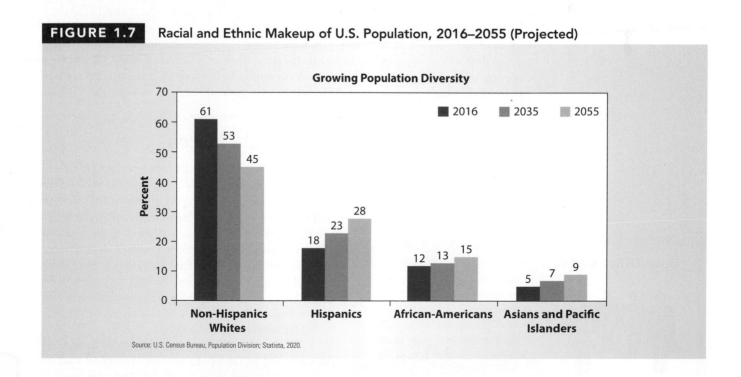

Source: U.S. Census Bureau, Population Division; Statista, 2020.

FOR THE RECORD

Digital Nomads Check in From Paradise

Are you dreaming of becoming a digital nomad working from home, in a café, or on the beach? If so, you may get your wish. Smartphones, tablets, and ever smaller netbooks have given rise to mobile workers who can do their jobs from any place that provides connectivity. Even before the COVID-19 pandemic instantly confined many workers to their home offices, experts believed that within a few years, more than 105 million Americans will work remotely in some form. That's nearly 75 percent of the domestic labor force![75]

Studies show that mobile workers are happier and more productive. However, working without traditional offices creates unique challenges, including the lack of face-to-face communication with colleagues. What are some ways virtual workers can effectively communicate with stakeholders?

In addition to increasing numbers of minorities, the workforce will see a big jump in older workers. By 2024, the number of workers aged fifty-five and older will have grown to a quarter of the labor force, almost double the number in 2000.[71] Aging baby boomers are healthier and enjoy greater longevity than previous generations. Because they are also better educated, mature workers tend to work later in life and bring invaluable know-how and experience to the table.[72] Workers with disabilities are another group benefiting from a tight labor market as they must overcome prejudice.[73] However, businesses such as Ford Motor, Microsoft, JPMorgan Chase, and SAP have formed a task force to boost the hiring of autistic workers because tech workers on the spectrum more than make up for their lack of social skills with analytical skills, tenacity, and focus.[74] As a result of these and other demographic trends, businesses must create work environments that value and support all people.

Communicating in this diverse work environment requires new attitudes and skills. Acquiring these new employment skills is certainly worth the effort because of the benefits diversity brings to consumers, work teams, and business organizations. A diverse staff is better able to read trends and respond to the increasingly diverse customer base in local and world markets.

In the workplace, diversity also makes good business sense. Teams made up of people with various experiences are more likely to create the products consumers demand. Customers also want to deal with companies that respect their values. They are more likely to say, "If you are a company whose ads do not include me, or whose workforce does not include me, I will not buy from you." Learning to cooperate and communicate successfully with diverse coworkers should be a major priority for all businesspeople.

1-3g Virtual and Nonterritorial Offices

Today's physical work environments are changing profoundly. You may have heard people refer to the **virtual office**, a workspace that's mobile and decentralized. Thanks largely to nearly ever-present Internet access, millions of workers telecommute. They no longer report to nine-to-five jobs that confine them to offices. They have flexible working arrangements, so they can work remotely at home, on the road, and at the customer's place of business. The **anytime, anywhere office** a teleworker needs requires only a smartphone, a laptop, and an Internet connection. Perhaps the most untethered type is the **digital nomad**, a worker with a wandering lifestyle enabled by technology, who often travels to exotic locales for extended periods of time.

Reliable data tracking office road warriors are lacking, but according to Gallup, 43 percent of employed adults work remotely at least some of the time and increasingly longer. In finance, health care, client services,

Open Office Rules

Rules for sharing open workspaces:

1. Don't hang around.
2. Limit chitchat.
3. Don't sneak up on anyone.
4. Don't eavesdrop or otherwise spy on others.
5. Speak in a soft voice.
6. Wear headphones.

transportation, and IT, intermittent telework is common among more than half of the workforce.[76] Yahoo under Marissa Mayer's leadership famously pulled the plug on telecommuting, but companies such as Amazon, Dell, Xerox, Toyota, and UnitedHealth Group lure applicants with a better work–life balance. Matt Welsh, vice president of global recruiting at Hilton, believes that "Offering our Team Members flexibility in their work schedule and location is one way that we can help them thrive."[77] The concerns about telework include plummeting productivity, social isolation, and lagging promotions.

To save on office real estate, a number of companies such as American Express and drug maker GlaxoSmithKline provide **nonterritorial workspaces**. Also known as mobile platforms and hot desks, these unassigned workspaces are up for grabs. The first to arrive gets the best desk and the corner window. But some workers rebelled against corporate penny-pinching and generic open office layouts, and now several IT businesses are experimenting with a **palette of places**, to cater to the various work tasks knowledge workers tackle. Such variable spaces include tiny soundproof rooms for intense concentration, team spaces, standing desks, and even technology-free lounges.[78]

Increasingly, telecommuters and home office workers resort to **coworking** as an alternative to holding business meetings at the local coffee shop or in the living room. Coworkers are professionals who share a communal office space on an as-needed basis. Although most coworking spaces provide monthly memberships, some offer day or hourly passes. Not just small businesses, but also major corporations, such as GE, KPMG, PepsiCo, and Merck, are moving workers into trendy shared offices.[79] WeWork and LiquidSpace are doing for office real estate what Uber has started for ride sharing—a platform for users to offer and seek flexible access to workspaces. Digital nomads benefit from new **co-living** platforms such as Roam or PodShare that provide coworking spaces and accommodations in the United States and around the world.[80]

Although Facebook bet on building the largest open-office space in the word, many knowledge workers prefer quiet spaces when they must concentrate.

Even in more traditional offices, employees work in open-plan spaces with flexible workstations, shared conference rooms, and boomerang-shaped desks that save space and discourage territorial behavior while encouraging casual interactions as well as spontaneous collaborations.

1-4 Communication Channels in Organizations and Media Richness

Businesspeople almost always communicate strategically—that is, purposefully, hoping to achieve a desired outcome. Business communication functions can be summarized in three simple categories: (a) to inform, (b) to persuade, and/or (c) to promote goodwill. Most business messages have one of these functions as their purpose. Informing or sharing information is perhaps the most common communication function in all organizations today. On the job, you will have a dizzying array of channels to help you share information and stay connected both internally and externally. You will need to know which media are most suitable to accomplish your goal and be able to distinguish between formal and informal channels.

1-4a The Workplace in a Hyperconnected World

Social media and other information technology coupled with flatter hierarchies have greatly changed the way people communicate internally and externally at work. One major shift is away from one-sided, slow forms of communication such as hard-copy memos and letters to interactive, instant, less paper-based communication. Speeding up the flow of communication in organizations are e-mail, instant messaging (IM) and collaboration platforms, texting, blogging, and interacting with social media such as Facebook, Instagram, Twitter, and LinkedIn. Figure 1.8 shows a side-by-side comparison between the traditional one-directional business communication model and today's hyperconnected, many-to-many social media communication model.

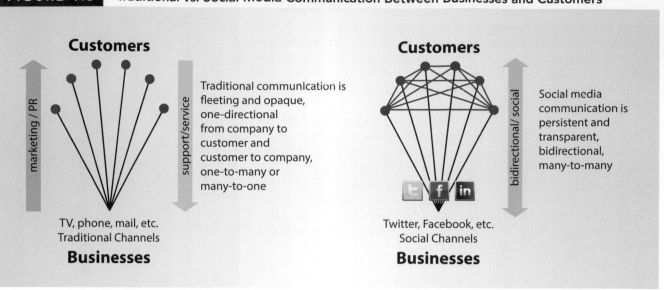

Fearing openly accessible social networks, many large organizations have developed their own internal social media platforms behind corporate firewalls. These enterprise social networks (e.g., Adobe's Unicom) combine e-mail, phone, chat, presence technology, and other communication tools, as you will study in Chapter 7. Collaboration platforms such as Slack, Google Hangouts, Cisco Spark, Hive, Fuze, or Yammer allow messaging, file sharing and editing, and project management. To stay connected on the go, business communicators rely on mobile electronic devices and mobile apps that enhance work productivity.

Mobility and Interactivity.
Mobility has revolutionized the way we communicate on the job. Internet access is nearly ever present, whether provided by cell phone companies or wireless networks. Wireless access is increasingly blanketing entire office buildings, airports, hotels, hospitals, restaurants, school and college campuses, cities, and other public spaces.

Other forms of interactive and mobile communication in the contemporary workplace are intranets (secured local area networks within organizations), corporate websites, audio and video podcasting, videoconferencing, and live chats. The latter is rapidly becoming the preferred communication channel for online customer service. Consumers shopping online or inquiring about billing or technical support use the company website and chat with customer service representatives in real time by typing their questions. Live service agents respond with typed replies. Some companies are experimenting with automated chat bots for routine tasks.

Smart Devices.
The revolution in mobile communication technology that we have come to depend on is fueled by smart mobile electronics. They include smartphones, tablets, notebooks, and, more recently, wearable technology such as the Apple Watch, activity trackers, and Google Glass.

To understand the pervasiveness of mobile technology, consider that the world population now stands at 7.7 billion people; of those, 5.1 billion are mobile device users who own 8.5 billion smart electronic gadgets. Mobile access reached a tipping point in 2014, overtaking traditional stationary Internet access; today the share of Web traffic now stands at almost 53 percent for mobile phones (without tablets) to 45 percent for laptops and desktops.[81] When Apple launched its phenomenally successful iPad, the gadget was hailed as a game changer. Although consumer sales of the most popular tablet have slowed, many businesses choose iPads on the go because they are lighter and cheaper than laptops.

Ahead of the iPhone, Google's Android platform has taken the smartphone market by storm worldwide. Android, primarily represented by Samsung devices, has grabbed a global market share of 88 percent; Apple's iOS market share has fluctuated between 14 and 21 percent.[82] Low-cost Android handsets also dominate the smartphone market in Africa, India, and China. Thus, millions of people access the Internet by mobile phone not only in industrialized nations but also in regions of the world where smartphones provide the only online access.

1-4b Internal and External Communication

Digital age businesspeople communicate with many stakeholders outside their organizations, and internally with coworkers and other employees. They must anticipate public scrutiny and potential leaks of information that may reach unintended audiences. Although most businesses rely on e-mail and digital files for communication, they still produce some paper-based documents, as will be discussed in later chapters.

Internal communication includes exchanging ideas and messages with superiors, coworkers, and subordinates. When those messages must be written, you will probably choose e-mail—the most prevalent communication channel in the workplace today. Some of the functions of internal communication are to issue and clarify procedures and policies, inform management of progress, develop new products and services, persuade employees or management to make changes or improvements, coordinate activities, and evaluate and reward employees. Brief messages and status updates may be conveyed by text message or IM especially when the writer is traveling.

External communication is also handled by e-mail in most routine cases. When you are communicating externally with customers, suppliers, the government, and the public, e-mail correspondence is generally appropriate. Hard-copy letters sent by traditional snail mail are becoming increasingly rare, especially under time constraints. However, some businesses do create signed paper documents to be faxed, or they scan and e-mail them. External functions involve answering inquiries about products or services, persuading customers to buy products or services, clarifying supplier specifications, issuing credit, collecting bills, responding to government agencies, and promoting a positive image of the organization.

When communicating with internal and external audiences, businesspeople must now also consider leaks and the backchannel. **Backchannel communication** is a simultaneous electronic background conversation during a conference presentation, lecture, or entertainment program. For example, when you live tweet or IM your friends while watching the latest episode of *Game of Thrones,* you are having a backchannel conversation.

In business, backchannel describes the synchronous digital interactions that run in the background parallel to a meeting or presentation. When AOL chief Tim Armstrong infamously fired a subordinate during an internal conference call in front of 1,100 colleagues, the audio was instantly leaked and went viral. Business communicators must always anticipate unintended audiences and public criticism.

1-4c Media Richness and Social Presence

Business communicators must be able to choose from a wide range of communication channels the one most suitable to get the job done—that is, most likely to elicit the desired outcome. How to choose the appropriate medium to avoid ambiguity, confusing messages, and misunderstandings has long been studied by researchers. Media richness theory and the concept of social presence are particularly useful for evaluating the effectiveness of old and new media in a given situation.

Media Richness. Daft and Lengel's media richness theory attempts to classify media in organizations according to how much clarifying information they are able to convey from a sender to a recipient.[83] The more helpful cues and immediate feedback the medium provides, the richer it is; face-to-face and on the telephone, managers can best deal with complex organizational issues. For routine, unambiguous problems, however, media of lower richness, such as memos, reports, and other written communication, usually suffice. Figure 1.9 displays contemporary and traditional media based on their richness and, hence, their likely communication effectiveness.

Ideally, senders would choose the richest medium necessary to communicate the message to the recipient with as little ambiguity as possible. Because a rich medium (such as a face-to-face conversation) is not always available, communicators must often use leaner media (for example, e-mail) that may not be as effective in reducing ambiguity and decreasing the risk of miscommunication. Just think how hard it is to know whether a text or an e-mail is sarcastic.

FIGURE 1.9 **Communication Channels from Richest to Leanest**

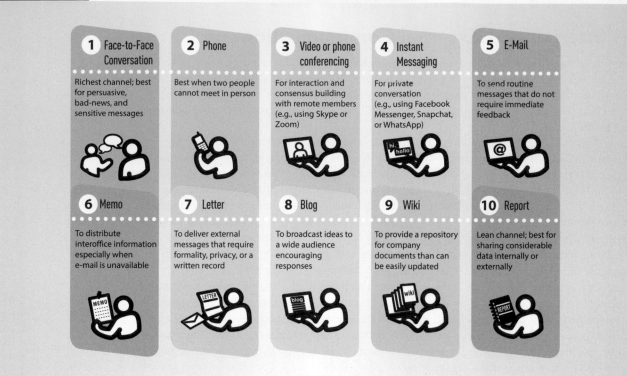

1 Face-to-Face Conversation

Richest channel; best for persuasive, bad-news, and sensitive messages

2 Phone

Best when two people cannot meet in person

3 Video or phone conferencing

For interaction and consensus building with remote members (e.g., using Skype or Zoom)

4 Instant Messaging

For private conversation (e.g., using Facebook Messenger, Snapchat, or WhatsApp)

5 E-Mail

To send routine messages that do not require immediate feedback

6 Memo

To distribute interoffice information especially when e-mail is unavailable

7 Letter

To deliver external messages that require formality, privacy, or a written record

8 Blog

To broadcast ideas to a wide audience encouraging responses

9 Wiki

To provide a repository for company documents than can be easily updated

10 Report

Lean channel; best for sharing considerable data internally or externally

Social Presence. The degree to which people are engaged online and ready to connect with others is called **social presence**. As proposed by Short, Williams, and Christie, however, social presence is the degree of salience (being there) between a sender and receiver using a communication medium.[84] Media with high social presence convey warmth and are personal. Social presence is greatest face-to-face and less so in mediated and written communication, such as phone conversations and text messages. Likewise, social presence is greater in synchronous communication (live chat, IM) than in asynchronous communication (e-mail, forum post), which is rather impersonal.

Face-to-face we receive many more signals than just speech. For example, nonverbal cues, emotional disposition, and voice inflection help us interpret a message. In real time, we can ask the author of a message to clarify—something we cannot do as easily when the message arrives with a delay and is enabled by technology. You could say that social presence means how much awareness of the sender is conveyed along with the message. Communication can succeed as long as the chosen communication medium offers enough social presence to complete the task.[85]

1-4d Formal Communication Channels

Information within organizations flows through formal and informal communication channels. A free exchange of information helps organizations respond rapidly to changing markets, boost efficiency and productivity, build employee morale, serve the public, and take full advantage of the ideas of today's knowledge workers. Official information within an organization typically flows through formal channels in three directions: downward, upward, and horizontally, as shown in Figure 1.10.

Formal channels of communication generally follow an organization's chain of command. That is, a message originates with executives and flows down through managers to supervisors and finally to lower-level employees. Many organizations have formulated communication policies that encourage regular open communication through newsletters, the corporate intranet,

FIGURE 1.10 Information Flow in Organizations

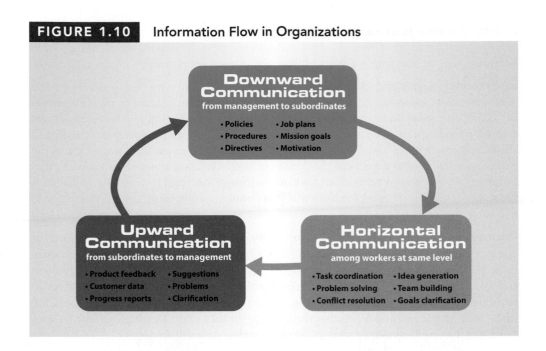

official messages, company-provided social networks, and blogs. Free-flowing, open communication invigorates organizations and makes them successful. Barriers, however, can obstruct the flow of communication, as summarized in Figure 1.11, and must be overcome if the organization is to thrive.

Improving Downward Information Flow. To improve communication and to compete more effectively, many of today's companies have restructured and reengineered themselves into smaller operating units and work teams. Rather than being bogged down with long communication chains, management speaks directly to employees. In addition to shorter chains of communication, management can improve the downward flow of information through

FIGURE 1.11 Barriers Blocking the Flow of Communication in Organizations

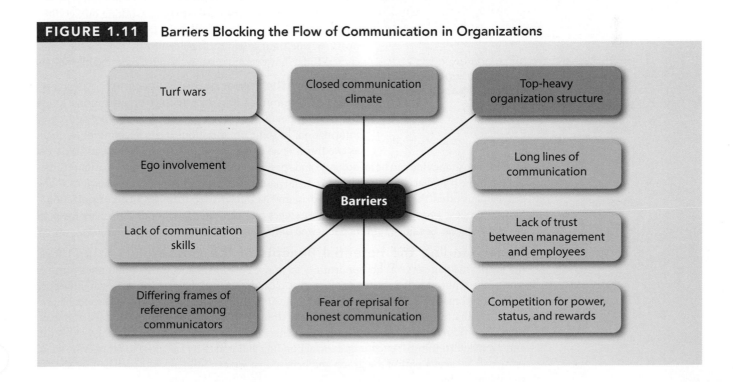

company publications, announcements, meetings, videos, podcasts, and other channels. Instead of hoarding information at the top, today's managers recognize the importance of letting workers know how well the company is doing and what new projects are planned.

Improving Upward Information Flow.　To improve the upward flow of communication, some companies are (a) hiring communication coaches to train employees, (b) asking employees to report customer complaints, (c) encouraging regular meetings with staff, (d) providing a trusting, nonthreatening environment in which employees can comfortably share their observations and ideas with management, and (e) offering incentive programs that encourage employees to collect and share valuable feedback. Companies are also building trust by setting up hotlines for anonymous feedback to management and by installing ombudsman programs. An *ombudsman* is a mediator who hears employee complaints, investigates, and seeks to resolve problems fairly.

Improving Horizontal Information Flow.　To improve horizontal communication, companies are (a) training employees in teamwork and communication techniques, (b) establishing reward systems based on team achievement rather than individual achievement, and (c) encouraging full participation in team functions. However, employees must also realize that they are personally responsible for making themselves heard, for really understanding what other people say, and for getting the information they need. Developing those business communication skills is exactly what this book and this course will do for you.

1-4e Informal Communication Channels

Most organizations today share company news through consistent, formal channels such as e-mail, intranet posts, blogs, and staff meetings. Regardless, even within organizations with consistent formal channels, people still spread rumors about the company and gossip about each other.

The **grapevine** is an informal channel of communication that carries organizationally relevant gossip. This powerful but informal channel functions through social relationships; people talk about work when they are lunching, working out, golfing, and carpooling, as well as in e-mails, texts, and social media posts. At one time gossip took place mostly around the water cooler. Today, however, gossip travels much more rapidly online.

Respecting the Power of the Grapevine.　Researchers studying communication flow within organizations know that the grapevine can be a powerful, pervasive source of information. In some organizations it can account for as much as two thirds of an employee's information. Is this bad? Well, yes and no. The grapevine can be an accurate and speedy source of organization information. Studies have demonstrated accuracy ratings of 75 to 80 percent for many grapevine transmissions.[86] The grapevine is often the fastest channel to disseminate information throughout an organization.[87] However, like a game of telephone, such messages can introduce falsehoods the longer the path the news travels. Sensitive rumors publicized online have cost many workers their jobs.

Understanding the Potential Benefits of the Grapevine.　In deft hands, the grapevine can serve as an opportunity to praise coworkers and subtly build one's positive workplace reputation.[88] Sometimes office gossip can be downright positive. A Dutch university study found that up to 90 percent of office conversation consists of gossip. The authors believe that such chatter may foster group cohesion, strengthen the bonds among workers, and even improve productivity by making poor performers work harder.[89] To many of us, gossip is fun and even entertaining. It encourages social bonding and makes us feel close to others who share our trust. We feel a part of the group and believe that we can influence others when we share a significant tidbit.

PR Image Factory/Shutterstock.com

Feared by management, the office grapevine can be an accurate and speedy source of information in organizations with poor formal communication and lack of transparency.

As opposed to the offline grapevine, consumer-generated information online in social media, forums, Internet discussion boards, blogs, Facebook posts, and tweets provides an unsparing, revealing glimpse of what employees and the public are thinking. Social networking sites such as Glassdoor offer anonymous reviews that expose the inner workings of companies. Glassdoor also enables users to share typical interview questions with other job seekers and provides invaluable insider information. High-profile leaks spread fast online, and their accuracy can be verified more easily than rumors in an offline grapevine.

Using the Grapevine Productively.   Managers can use the grapevine productively by doing the following: (a) respecting employees' desire to know, (b) increasing the amount of information delivered through formal channels, (c) sharing bad as well as good news, (d) monitoring the grapevine, and (e) acting promptly to correct misinformation.[90] In addition, managers should model desirable behavior and not gossip themselves.[91]

As we have seen, office gossip online or off is complex and sometimes harmful. Productivity and morale may suffer as mistrust spreads. As a result, worker engagement plummets and turnover increases. If pervasive gossip qualifies as "malicious harassment," it may expose a company to legal liability.[92] Malicious gossip spread in e-mails, via text messages, or on social media sites can be used in defamation cases. It can become evidence against employers in supporting charges of harassment or maintaining a hostile work environment. In addition, employers look upon gossip as a productivity drain. The time spent gossiping reduces the time spent working.

Responsive organizations are better able to correct inaccuracies and misperceptions regardless of the channel used. Through formal and informal channels of communication, smart companies keep employees and the public informed.

1-5 Ethics in the Workplace Needed More Than Ever

Business ethics continue to grab headlines and dominate public debate. The Great Recession of 2007–2009 was triggered by the collapse of the housing bubble and ensuing banking crisis. Many economists blame greed and ethical lapses for the worst economic tailspin in more than 70 years. Subsequent corporate scandals, allegations of executive misconduct, and fraud investigations have ensured that business ethics remain in the spotlight.

Consider one egregious example—Wells Fargo's systemic consumer abuses at a time when U.S. banks' reputations were still tarnished by the financial crisis. The bank admitted that thousands of its employees had created 3.5 million fake accounts to earn bonuses. Wells Fargo also charged unfair mortgage fees and ripped off service members. Nearly $1.2 billion in fines followed—a huge sum historically, but one that is dwarfed by Wells Fargo's annual revenue of $22 billion.[93] Of similar magnitude, Volkswagen AG's massive diesel emissions fraud led to lawsuits in 55 countries and a fine of $1.2 billion. In all, "Dieselgate" has cost VW $35 billion in buybacks and litigation. The German carmaker had rigged 11 million vehicles to bypass diesel-emissions regulations.[94] Each new tale of impropriety erodes consumer confidence and feeds into the perception that all business is dishonest.

Most individuals understand that lying is "corrosive," undermining trust in the workplace and destroying personal integrity.[95] Warren Buffett's much-quoted maxim applies here: "It takes 20 years to build a reputation and five minutes to ruin it."[96] More tangibly, lying in the form of fraud can cost a typical business about 5 percent of its annual revenue, leading, according to an association of investigators, to a projected global loss of nearly $4 trillion a year.[97] Harvey Weinstein's sexual indiscretions destroyed his production company; the scandal triggered the #MeToo movement and led to the firing of prominent public figures.

Americans want change. An important study reveals that millennials prefer brands with sustainable manufacturing and ethical business practices.[98] A PwC study suggests that corporate boards will not be able to overlook executives' ethical lapses. Activist shareholders and technology make discovering malfeasance easier and amplify public outrage via social media. A Stanford poll found that almost half of Americans want dishonest CEOs to be fired or sent to prison. Only 15 percent oppose punishment.[99] Figure 1.12 reveals the results of a global ethics study. The survey

FIGURE 1.12 Global Business Ethics Survey

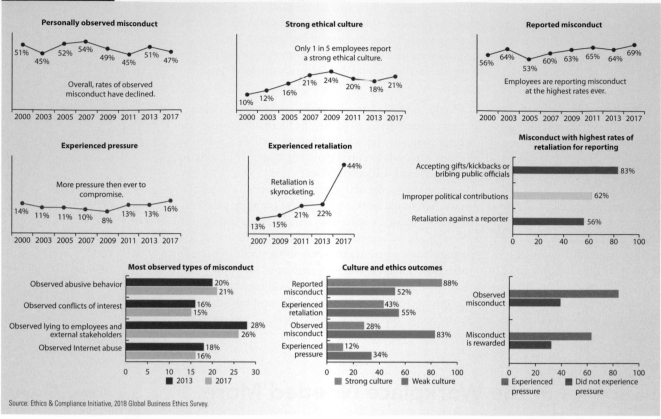

Source: Ethics & Compliance Initiative, 2018 Global Business Ethics Survey.

concludes that strong workplace cultures prioritizing ethics suffer fewer lapses, but the number of such workplaces remains stagnant.

The topic of ethics could fill entire books. However, we will examine aspects that specifically concern you as a business communicator in today's workplace.

1-5a Defining Ethics

Ethics refers to conventional standards of right and wrong that prescribe what people should do. These standards usually consist of rights, obligations, and benefits to society. They also include virtues such as fairness, honesty, loyalty, and concern for others. Ethics is about having values and taking responsibility. Ethical individuals follow the law and refrain from theft, murder, assault, slander, and fraud. Figure 1.13 depicts some of the influences that form our awareness of ethics and help us develop a value system that guides our decisions. In the following discussion, we examine ethics in the workplace, study goals of ethical business communicators, and learn tools for doing the right thing.

As a business communicator, you should understand basic ethical principles so that you can make logical decisions when faced with dilemmas in the workplace. Professionals in any field deal with moral dilemmas on the job. However, just being a moral person and having sound personal or professional ethics may not be sufficient to handle the ethical issues you may face in the workplace. Consider the following ethical dilemmas:

- **E-mail message** You accidentally receive a message outlining your company's restructuring plan. You see that your coworker's job will be eliminated. He and his wife are about to purchase a new home. Should you tell him that his job is in danger?

- **Customer e-mail** You are replying to an e-mail from to a customer who is irate over a mistake you made. Should you blame it on a computer glitch, point the finger at another department, or take the blame and risk losing this customer's trust and possibly your job?

FIGURE 1.13 The Context of Ethical Decision Making

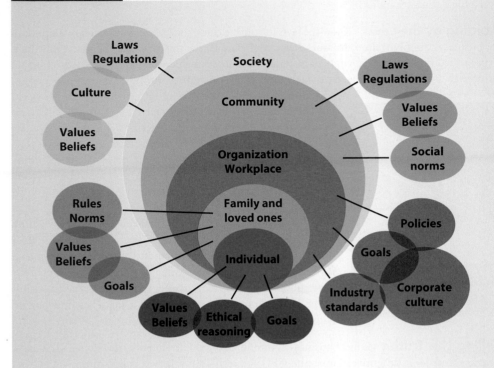

Various influences shape an individual's value system and affect ethical decision making. Most of us exist in a family, workplace, one or several communities, and society at large. Each of these environments may emphasize different norms. Not surprisingly, sometimes the various rules and beliefs clash, causing ethical dilemmas that need to be resolved.

- **Progress report** Should you write a report that ignores problems in a project, as your boss asks? Your boss controls your performance evaluation.

- **Sales report** Should you inflate sales figures so that your team can meet its quarterly goal? Your team leader strongly urges you to do so, and you receive a healthy bonus if your team meets its goal.

- **Presentation** You are rushing to prepare a presentation. On the Internet you find perfect wording and great graphics. Should you lift the graphics and wording but change a few words? You figure that if it is online, it must be in the public domain.

- **Proposal** Your company urgently needs a revenue-producing project. Should you submit a proposal that unrealistically suggests a short completion schedule to ensure that you get the job?

- **Résumé** Should you inflate your grade point average or give yourself more experience or a higher job title than your experience warrants to make your résumé more attractive? The job market in your field is very competitive.

On the job you will face many dilemmas, and you will want to react ethically. Determining the right thing to do, however, is not always an easy task. No solid rules guide us. For some people, following the law seems to be enough. They think that anything legal must also be ethical or moral. Most people, however, believe that ethical standards rise to a higher level. What are those standards? Although many ethical dilemmas have no right answer, one solution is often better than another. In deciding on that solution, keep in mind the goals of ethical business communicators.

1-5b Doing What Ethical Communicators Do

Taking ethics into consideration can be painful in the short term. In the long term, however, ethical behavior makes sense and pays off. Dealing honestly with colleagues and customers develops trust and builds strong relationships. The following guidelines can help you set specific ethical goals. Although these goals hardly constitute a formal code of conduct, they will help you maintain a high ethical standard.

Abiding by the Law.   Know the laws in your field and follow them. Particularly important for business communicators are issues of copyright law. Under the concept of fair use, individuals have limited rights to use copyrighted material without seeking permission. To be safe, you should assume that anything produced privately after 1989—including words, charts, graphs, photos, and music—is copyrighted. More information about copyright law and fair use appears in Chapter 11.

30 generator/Shutterstock.com

By the way, don't assume that Internet items are in the public domain and free to be used or shared. Files and media posted on the Internet are covered by copyright laws. The Recording Industry Association of America (RIAA) and the Motion Picture Association of America (MPAA) have sued individuals, website operators, and Internet service providers for allowing illicit downloading or sharing of music and movies. Tough penalties can include a felony conviction, up to five years in jail, and fines up to $250,000. If you are in accounting, financial management, investing, or corporate management, you should be aware of the restrictions set forth by the Sarbanes–Oxley Act or the provisions of the Dodd–Frank Act. Whatever your field, become familiar with its regulations.

Telling the Truth.   Ethical business communicators do not intentionally make statements that are untrue or deceptive. Samsonite CEO Ramesh Tainwala was called out by an activist investor for claiming a doctoral degree he had not earned and was forced to resign a week later. Hewlett-Packard CEO Mark Hurd was ousted in scandal after a probe into his relationship with a female contractor revealed that he had submitted inaccurate expense reports. Former Volkswagen CEO Martin Winterkorn faces years in prison and stiff fines for allegedly helping to conceal cheating software in the company's massive diesel emissions scandal. According to a Stanford study, lying and cheating CEOs had a lingering effect on their companies' reputations—on average for five years after their departure.[100] The big-time lies made headlines, and you may see no correlation to your life. On a personal level, however, we all may lie and deceive in various ways. We say things that are not so. We may exaggerate to swell the importance of our assertions.

Labeling Opinions.   Sensitive communicators know the difference between facts and opinions. Facts are verifiable and often are quantifiable; opinions are beliefs held with confidence but without substantiation. It is a fact, for example, that women are starting businesses at five times the rate of men.[101] It is an opinion, though, that the so-called glass ceiling has held women back, forcing them to start their own businesses. Such a cause-and-effect claim would be difficult to prove. It is a fact that many corporations are spending billions of dollars to be socially responsible, including using ethically made products and developing eco-friendly technology. It is an opinion that corporate social responsibility is an obligation for all businesses. Assertions that cannot be proved are opinions, and stating opinions as if they were facts is unethical and, well, foolish.

Being Objective.   Ethical business communicators recognize their own biases and strive to keep them from distorting a message. Suppose you are asked to investigate laptop computers and write a report recommending a brand for your office. As you visit stores, you discover that an old high school friend is selling Brand X. Because you always liked this individual and have faith in his judgment, you may be inclined to tilt your recommendation in his direction. However, it is unethical to misrepresent the facts in your report or to put a spin on your arguments based on friendship. To be ethical, you could note in your report that you have known the person for ten years and that you respect his opinion. In this way, you have disclosed your relationship as well as the reasons for your decision. Honest reporting means presenting the whole picture and relating all facts fairly.

Communicating Clearly.   Ethical business communicators feel an obligation to write clearly so that receivers understand easily and quickly. Some states have even passed plain English

Chapter 1 Business Communication in the Digital Age

(also called plain language) laws requiring businesses to write policies, warranties, and contracts in language comprehensible to average readers. Under former chairman Arthur Levitt, the Securities and Exchange Commission issued *A Plain English Handbook* explaining how to create clear SEC disclosure documents. Persistent lobbying efforts by plain-language advocacy groups at the federal level culminated in the Plain Writing Act. The law mandates that government agencies use unadorned prose in documents addressing the public. Plain English means short sentences, simple words, and clear organization. Communicators who intentionally obscure the meaning with long sentences and difficult words are being unethical.

Using Inclusive Language.   Ethical business communicators use language that includes rather than excludes. They avoid expressions that discriminate against individuals or groups on the basis of their sex, ethnicity, disability, race, sexual orientation, or age. Language is discriminatory when it stereotypes, insults, or excludes people. You will learn more about how to use inclusive, bias-free language in Chapter 4.

Giving Credit.   Ethical communicators give credit for ideas by (a) referring to originators' names within the text, (b) using quotation marks, and (c) documenting sources with endnotes, footnotes, or internal references. You will learn how to do this in Chapter 11 and Appendix B. Don't suggest that you did all the work on a project if you had help. In school or on the job, stealing ideas, words, graphics, or any other original material is unethical.

In addition to legal and regulatory restrictions in their fields, many professionals uphold their own rigorous rules of conduct; for example, physicians, psychologists, and accountants follow standards of professional ethics much higher than the restrictions imposed by law. Similarly, members of the International Association of Business Communicators have developed a code of ethics with 12 guidelines that spell out criteria for determining what is right and wrong for members of its organization. Search for *IABC Code of Ethics for Professional Communicators* on the Web.

Reality Check

Corporate Ethics Is Front and Center Again

"While some Fortune 100 executives have gone to jail trying to deliver financial results at all costs, others have pushed their businesses forward with decisions rooted in integrity and a commitment to employees, customers, and shareholders. ... If leaders do not operate from a place of integrity, it sets the tone for everything and everyone else and directly and negatively impacts the bottom line."[102]

—Nicole Alvino, *co-founder and CSO of SocialChorus*

1-5c Choosing Tools for Doing the Right Thing

It's easy to commit ethical lapses because of natural self-interest and the desire to succeed. In composing messages or engaging in other activities on the job, business communicators can't help being torn by conflicting loyalties. Do we tell the truth and risk our jobs? Do we show loyalty to friends even if it means bending the rules? Should we be tactful or totally honest? Is it our duty to make a profit or to be socially responsible?

Acting ethically means doing the right thing given the circumstances. Each set of circumstances requires analyzing issues, evaluating choices, and acting responsibly. Resolving ethical issues is never easy, but the task can be made less difficult if you know how to identify key issues. The five questions in Figure 1.14 may help you resolve most ethical dilemmas. The checklist begins by asking whether an action is legal. You should go forward only if the action complies with the law. If it does, then test the ethical soundness of your plan by asking the remaining questions: Would you proceed if you were on the receiving end of the action, and can you rule out better options? Even if the answer is *yes,* consider then how a trusted mentor or your family, friends, and coworkers would view your decision.

Traditionally, it has been argued that the best advice in ethical matters is contained in the **Golden Rule**: Treat others the way you wish to be treated. The principle of reciprocity has a long tradition and exists in many religions and cultures. However, more recently, author Tony Alessandra proposed the **Platinum Rule**: "Treat others as *they* wish to be treated," acknowledging that people may have standards and wishes different from our own. The ultimate solution to all ethics problems is treating others fairly and doing what is right to achieve what is good. In succeeding chapters, you will find additional discussions of ethical questions as they relate to relevant topics.

FIGURE 1.14 Five Questions to Guide Ethical Decisions

1. Is the action legal?

2. Would you do it if you were on the opposite side?

3. Can you rule out a better alternative?

4. Would a trusted advisor agree?

5. Would family, friends, employer, or coworkers approve?

If yes, GO!

If the action is illegal, STOP!

Even if it is legal, proceed with CAUTION

Ethics hold us to a higher standard than the law. Even when an action is legal, it may violate generally accepted principles of right and wrong.

Zooming In

Your Turn:
Applying Your Skills at Nordstrom

Customers expect speed and convenience, says Jamie Nordstrom, president of stores, regardless of where they shop, online or in a physical store. The great-grandson of the company founder believes that "the retailers that deliver on those customers' expectations are the ones that are going to get their business."[103]

He grew up with the threat of new competitors unseating the family business, Jamie Nordstrom says, but he points to the company's longevity and continued success. Its secret? Engaging customers and listening to their needs: "We have to remind ourselves on a daily basis that if we're not listening to the customer, then we're probably not going to make a good decision—so that's our focus."[104]
And listen Nordstrom does.

Your Task

You are an intern in the User Experience and Optimization division overseen by Jamie Nordstrom, president of stores.

You are learning about the "Nordie" ethos of truly believing in helping others and genuinely loving customer service. As the former chairman Bruce A. Nordstrom put it: "We can hire nice people and teach them to sell, but we can't hire salespeople and teach them to be nice."[105] Naturally, this means being kind online.

The intern supervisor wants you to study Facebook interactions among customers and Nordstrom representatives to learn about the friendly, casual tone employed in such virtual encounters. How are the Nordstrom posters helping their Facebook followers? What are some of their most prominent strategies? Read several days' worth of Facebook posts. Summarize your observations in an e-mail. Refer to Chapter 8 for information about how to draft an e-mail. Be sure to select two or three specific posts representing a pattern or strategy. For example, discuss particularly successful responses, whether they are prompted by an inquiry, complaint, or praise.

SUMMARY OF LEARNING OUTCOMES

1 Explain how communication skills fuel career success in a technology-driven, social, and mobile workplace.

- In the age of automation, augmented reality, and artificial intelligence, also called the Fourth Industrial Revolution, communication and other interpersonal skills can future-proof well-trained workers.

- Superior communication skills—reading, writing, listening, nonverbal, speaking and writing skills—are always in demand; they rank high among the most desirable job competencies.

- Workers communicate more than ever; they must write their own messages and are glued to their screens for hours each day. Employers expect more of workers, not less.

- Writing skills can be learned; they are not innate.

2 Understand the impact of powerful interpersonal skills and a college education for your professional success in the hyperconnected digital age workplace.

- In the information age, which has allowed us to access and share vast amounts of resources via digital media, you will engage in mind work.

- Expect to be a knowledge worker who must think critically and develop opinions backed by evidence, particularly in an era of disinformation, manipulation, and fake news.

- You are learning to think, read, and ask questions in a networked world in which employers demand professionalism.

- Be prepared to take charge of your career as you are less likely to find predictable employment, pay increases, or even conventional workplaces.

- Because technologies are constantly evolving, you must engage in lifelong learning; expect to pursue several careers, not just jobs, but your education will most likely cause your income to grow.

3 Describe significant communication trends in today's dynamic, networked work environment.

- The trends affecting today's workers include new disruptive technologies and social media, expectations of around-the-clock availability, and global competition.

- Flattened management hierarchies, team projects, a diverse workforce, and the mobile or virtual office operating practically 24/7/365 are other significant trends.

- Workers need new skills and attitudes to collaborate successfully as team members in workplaces that are increasingly diverse and as potential telecommuters.

- Today's changing work environments include coworking spaces and flexible office design, requiring adaptability and mobility; some workers become digital nomads traveling the world.

4 Identify how information flows internally and externally in organizations through formal and informal channels.

- Business communicators are strategic; they always seek to achieve a particular objective, aided by rapidly changing communication technologies.

- The mobile digital workplace is unthinkable without smart mobile devices for accessing e-mail, messaging, company intranets, corporate websites, podcasts, videoconferences, and live chats.

- Internal communication involves superiors, coworkers, and subordinates, whereas external communication includes customers, suppliers, government agencies, and the public.

- Media richness and social presence describe the communication media most suitable to avoid ambiguity in any workplace interaction.

- Formal channels of communication follow an organization's rank order; informal channels, such as the grapevine, deliver unofficial news among coworkers. Gossip can be damaging.

5 Recognize the tools for doing the right thing as an ethical business communicator.

- Ethics describes standards of right and wrong prescribing what people should do and includes virtues such as fairness, honesty, and loyalty. Ethical standards are more rigorous than the law.

- The goals of ethical communicators include abiding by the law, telling the truth, labeling opinions, being objective, communicating clearly, using inclusive language, and giving credit.

- To do the right thing, ask these questions: (a) Is the action legal? (b) Would you do it if you were on the opposite side? (c) Can you rule out a better alternative? (d) Would a trusted advisor agree? and (e) Would your family, friends, employer, or coworkers approve?

Key Terms

soft skills *4*

emotional intelligence *4*

interpersonal skills or professional skills *4*

knowledge workers *6*

information worker *6*

fake news *6*

information literacy *7*

m-commerce *7*

e-commerce *7*

brick-and-mortar commerce *7*

kaizen *7*

corporate lattice *8*

brand *8*

smartphone apps *10*

sharing economy *10*

disrupting *10*

credibility *14*

karoshi *14*

bossless organizational structure *16*

holacracy *16*

teaming *16*

ad hoc teams *16*

gig economy *16*

virtual office *18*

anytime, anywhere office *18*

digital nomad *18*

nonterritorial workspaces *19*

palette of places *19*

coworking *19*

co-living *19*

backchannel communication *21*

social presence *22*

grapevine *24*

#MeToo movement *25*

ethics *26*

golden rule *29*

platinum rule *29*

Critical Thinking

1. All this talk about interpersonal skills and future-proofing your career may make you nervous, especially if your communication skills are shaky. Do you think workers today can be successful if they lack communication skills and write poorly? (L.O. 1)

2. Sharing various digital media impulsively can lead to embarrassment and worse. Have you or has someone you know ever regretted posting a comment, photo, or other media online? (L.O. 2)

3. Despite laws dictating a 40-hour workweek, many young Chinese tech workers work the dreaded 9-9-6 schedule: 9 a.m. to 9 p.m., six days a week. How do you feel about work–life balance? What effects on your health and personal life do you anticipate? (L.O. 3)

4. Critics complain that texting and instant messaging lead to *textspeak,* poor writing characterized by acronyms, abbreviations, and emoticons. Others have claimed that emoji help supply important missing cues in lean media channels that are "toneless" otherwise.[106] What do you think? (L.O. 3, 4)

5. **Ethical Issue:** Author and entrepreneur Dave Kerpen believes that doing unto others as we would want done to us is insufficient. He prefers the *Platinum Rule*: Do unto others as *they* would want done to *them*. "The Golden Rule, as great as it is, has limitations, since all people and all situations are different. When you follow the Platinum Rule, however, you can be sure you're actually doing what the other person wants done and assure yourself of a better outcome."[107] Do you agree? Why does Kerpen think the Platinum Rule beats the Golden Rule? (L.O. 4).

Activities

1.1 Fact Checking: Digging Deep to Spot Fake News (L.O. 1, 2, 5)

`E-Mail` `Web`

Fake news is all the rage now. Literally. It is a term applied to misleading, usually deceptive, or wholly invented information. Most serious communicators apply the incendiary phrase to news that indeed is bogus and can be reliably fact-checked. Others use the cry of fake news to discredit opponents. The onslaught of often-conflicting news stories each day may leave you wondering what to believe. How can we find the truth in an age of bots and disinformation campaigns from domestic and hostile foreign sources?

Fortunately, there is help. Librarians are superheroes of information literacy. Many have created free online resources to vet information. Chances are that your college library offers such guides or workshops on spotting hoaxes and false information. But even librarians and journalists rely on independent fact-checking organizations dedicated to keeping politicians, other public figures, and the media honest. Who pays the fact checkers? Like Wikipedia, Snopes is user-funded, so consider donating when you rely on it a lot. Created by the Tampa Bay Times, PolitiFact is operated by the nonprofit Poynter Institute, and FactCheck.org relies on support from the reputable Annenberg Public Policy Center. Following the money is key in establishing who can be trusted. Many more reliable fact checkers exist, e.g., Hoax Slayer or NPR Fact Check.

YOUR TASK For starters, use your favorite Web browser to visit Snopes, FactCheck.org, and PolitiFact. Familiarize yourself with their interfaces. Check out the latest outrageous claims being debunked. If you are concerned about your privacy every time you search (and you should be!), use Duck Duck Go, a search engine that neither tracks the visitor nor sells clicks. For best results from several fact checkers at once, accurately type the following syntax in the browser search window: *your search term* **site:factcheck.org site:snopes.com site:politifact.com site:washingtonpost.com/news/fact-checker**

Search for a businessperson or topic you are curious about. Use the fact checkers to find hoaxes and memes about these subjects. Pick the most interesting business-related story and save your results. Your instructor may ask you to report your findings orally in class or summarize them in an e-mail or a memo. For instance, try the mercurial Tesla and SpaceX CEO, Elon Musk.

1.2 Exploring Remote and Flexible Work: Meet Distributed Companies (L.O. 1, 3)

Communication Technology | **E-Mail** | **Team** | **Web**

Will one of your future careers allow for remote work? Find out. Millennials increasingly want to telecommute, and FlexJobs is a platform helping them find full-time or part-time work and achieve better work–life balance. Currently 170 companies in the United States are fully virtual, that is, they are distributed companies without physical headquarters operating mostly in the cloud. The largest among them are Automattic, AnswerConnect, inVision, and Toptal.[108] The latter is itself a platform for top-notch talent.

YOUR TASK Your instructor may divide the class into teams that investigate a single company or compare two or more remote distributed businesses. Start by browsing their websites and social media pages. Take notes to capture information about how these organizations operate, how many workers they employ or refer to other employers, and how they present themselves online. Answer questions such as the following: What is their core business? Who are their principals and their customers? What is their mission or vision? What benefits or perks do they offer to the lucky few they successfully vet and place? Which jobs are

most sought-after, and what types of qualifications would an applicant have to offer? End by concluding whether you would want to work remotely—part-time, full-time, or even as an all-out digital nomad. Your instructor may assign you to present your search results orally in class—individually or as a member of a team. Or you may be asked to summarize your findings in an e-mail or memo.

1.3 Analyzing the "Holy Grail" of Interpersonal Skills: Iowa Core (L.O. 1, 2)

Employers have long complained that job candidates lack professional skills. The Department of Education in Iowa decided to do something about it and launched a project, dubbed "Iowa Core," to identify key interpersonal skills that could be taught in Iowa schools.[109] The result was a group of six categories of skills considered general or universal, with 24 skills subordinated to those main categories:

CRITICAL THINKING: 1) Access and analyze information; 2) develop solutions to complex problems that have no clear answer; 3) challenge assumptions with thoughtful questions; 4) deploy processes that analyze, select, use and evaluate various approaches to develop solutions.

COMPLEX COMMUNICATION: 5) Successfully share information through multiple means that include visual, digital, verbal and nonverbal interactions; 6) interact effectively with people of different cultures; 7) successfully navigate through nuances of effective communication.

CREATIVITY: 8) Incorporate curiosity and innovation into processes to generate new or original thoughts, interpretations, products, works or techniques; 9) combine seemingly unrelated ideas into something new; 10) think divergently; 11) reconfigure current thought within a new context.

COLLABORATION: 12) Work among and across personal global networks to achieve common goals; 13) understand and apply effective group processes to solve problems; 14) respectfully disagree; 15) respect complex processes that require individuals to contribute and participate in meaningful interactions.

FLEXIBILITY AND ADAPTABILITY: 16) Respond and adjust to situational needs; 17) meet the challenges of new roles, paradigms and environments; 18) intellectually embrace change; 19) balance one's core beliefs and the appropriate reaction to change; 20) respond to dissonance in productive ways.

PRODUCTIVITY AND ACCOUNTABILITY: 21) Prioritize, plan and apply knowledge and skills to make decisions that create quality results. 22) demonstrate accountability through efficient time management and resource allocation. 23) self-learn and 24) be self-confident.

YOUR TASK Your instructor may invite a discussion in the classroom or divide the class into teams, each to analyze one of the six "universal constructs," or general principles identified in Iowa. Individually or as a team, consider one main skill and its subcategories. First ensure that you fully understand the definitions of requisite skills. Look up unfamiliar words as needed. Imagine workplace scenarios when each category of powerful interpersonal skills might be required. Do you believe you possess this skill set? How would you convince a recruiter that you do? Provide detailed examples. If you believe you don't have what it takes, how could you acquire the skills you lack? Do you think you are learning these skills in college? After completing an exhaustive group discussion or your individual analysis, report to the class orally or in writing.

1.4 Facing Screen Time (L.O. 1–4)

Communication Technology **E-Mail** **Social Media** **Team** **Web**

Are you a *digital native*? If you are a millennial (born after 1985), you do not remember a time without computer technology and cell phones in wide use. People born in the 1990s have only known a society that depends on the Internet and mobile technology. Social media are second nature to most of these young people who seem to be inseparably attached to their smart devices.

Very likely, you live, learn, work, play, network, and shop in the digital world. Even if you are not crazy about the latest gadgets and gizmos, your daily life depends on technology. Your smartphone, smart TV, gaming console, and other electronics wouldn't exist without modern technology and are increasingly networked.

To prepare for this assignment, do the following first: Take stock of your Internet, social media, and other technology use. First establish useful criteria—for example, categories such as consumer electronics, social networking sites, preferred modes of communication with friends and family, and so forth. Within each category, list the technology you use most frequently. For instance, for social media networks, indicate your use of Facebook, Instagram, Snapchat, Twitter, YouTube, LinkedIn, and more. How do you use each? Estimate how often you access these sites per day and indicate the tools you use (e.g., smartphone, tablet, laptop). How much do you text every day?

YOUR TASK Your instructor may ask you to create at least three categories of communication technology, list the tools you use within each category, and describe your use in writing. Then compare your three lists within a group of five classmates or in assigned teams. Share your results individually or in groups, either verbally or in writing. Your instructor may ask you to summarize your observations about how plugged in you and your classmates are in a post on a discussion board or in an e-mail.

Attention, shortcut! If you own an Apple device running iOS 12, you have a built-in app called Screen Time. If you use Android and have a Google Pixel phone with Android 9 Pie, you can set up Android Digital Wellbeing. You may be surprised when you see the statistics! Pew Research reports that teens spend nine hours a day on average interacting with their smart devices.[110] How do you measure up?

1.5 Practicing Critical Thinking: Analyzing the Opening Case Scenario (L.O. 1–5)

Team **Web**

Each chapter opens with a two-part case study of a well-known company. To help you develop collaboration and speaking skills, as well as to learn about the target company and apply the chapter concepts, your instructor may ask you to do the following.

YOUR TASK Individually or as part of a three-student team during your course, work on one of the 16 case studies in the textbook. Answer the questions posed in both parts of the case study, look for additional information in articles or on the Internet, complete the application assignment, and then make a five- to ten-minute presentation to the class of your findings and reactions.

1.6 Polishing Those Interpersonal Skills: Introductions (L.O. 1, 2)

Communication Technology **E-Mail** **Social Media**

In a large business communication classroom, as in most professional settings, you want to stand out favorably right from the start. Make a powerful impression. Your instructor wants to know more about you, your motivation for taking this course, your career goals, and your writing skills.

YOUR TASK Send an e-mail or write a memo of introduction to your instructor. See Appendix A for memo formats and Chapters 7 and 8 for tips on preparing an e-mail message. In your message include the following:

a. Your reasons for taking this class

b. Your career goals (both temporary and long-term)

c. A brief description of your employment, if any, and your favorite activities

d. An assessment and discussion of your current communication skills, including your strengths and weaknesses

Alternatively, your instructor may ask you to (a) create a profile for LinkedIn, the social networking site for professionals or (b) develop a profile within a learning-management system (e.g., Blackboard or Moodle) to introduce yourself to your classmates. If your class is small, your instructor may challenge you to compose your introduction in 140 or fewer characters (see

Chapter 6 for tips on writing tweets and other short messages effectively).

1.7 Exercising Those Interpersonal Skills: Introduce Your Team (L.O. 1, 2)

Team

Teamwork is the lifeblood of many business organizations today. To help you develop coveted speaking, listening, and teamwork skills, your instructor may assign team projects. One of the first jobs in any team is selecting members and becoming acquainted.

YOUR TASK Your instructor will divide your class into small groups or teams. At your instructor's direction, either (a) interview another group member and introduce that person to the group or (b) introduce yourself to the group. Think of this as an informal interview for a team assignment or a job. You will want to make notes from which to speak. Your introduction should include information such as the following:

a. Where did you grow up?

b. What work and extracurricular activities have you engaged in?

c. What are your interests and talents? What are you good at doing?

d. What have you achieved?

e. How familiar are you with various computer technologies?

f. What are your professional and personal goals? Where do you expect to be five years from now?

g. Name one thing about you that others might not guess upon your first meeting.

To develop listening skills, team members should practice good listening techniques (see Chapter 2) and take notes. They should be prepared to discuss three important facts as well as remember details about each speaker.

Alternatively, expanding the task under (a), you could be asked to write a short professional biographical blurb after your interview of a group member. After feedback to ensure that it is correct, discuss with your partner or the whole group whether the bio would be attractive to employers looking for communication skills and other employability skills as presented in this chapter.

1.8 Honing Your Communication Skills: What Employers Want (L.O. 1)

Team **Web**

What do employers dream of? Examining listed job openings in your field, you can find out.

YOUR TASK Individually or in teams, check the listings at an online job board such as Monster, Indeed, College Recruiter, CareerBuilder, or CollegeGrad. In fact, you can look up dozens of *employment websites* if you browse using that search term. Follow the instructions to search job categories and locations. Also check college resources and peek at local newspaper listings of job openings (online). Don't forget Craigslist. Find five or more job listings in your field. If possible, print or download the results of your search. If you cannot print, save the information on a thumb drive or a mobile device. You may also be able to use Dropbox or your course-management platform (Blackboard, Moodle). You could also go "old school" and simply make handwritten notes on what you find.

Examine the skills requested. How often do the job listings mention communication, teamwork, and computer skills? What tasks do the job listings mention? Discuss your findings with your team members. Prepare a list of the most frequently requested skills. Your instructor may ask you to submit your findings and/or report to the class.

1.9 Focusing on Writing Skills: So You Think You Won't Have to Write? (L.O. 1–3)

Team

Writing can be scary to some people, yet it's essential. Occasionally, job candidates experience a disconnect between what they expect to be doing in their career fields and what they actually will do.

YOUR TASK In teams or in class, discuss the accuracy of the following statements. Are they myths or facts?

a. No one really writes anymore. They just text and send e-mails.

b. Because I'm in a technical field, I will work with numbers, not words.

c. Secretaries will clean up my writing problems.

d. Technical writers do most of the real writing on the job.

e. Today's sophisticated software programs can fix any of my writing mistakes.

f. I can use forms and templates for most messages.

1.10 Exploring Work–Life Balance and Tweeting About It (L.O. 1–4)

Social Media **Web**

Trying to balance work and life seems ever challenging and elusive. It continues to be a hot-button topic. *The Huffington Post* is devoting an entire section to articles on work–life balance. Some discuss the dangers of work encroaching on Americans' lives and families; others blame social media and mobile communication technology for the demise of work–life balance. Bloomberg Business put it bluntly: "Work–life balance is steadily becoming a unicorn in the working world."[111] Unicorns are mythic creatures of fantasy and as such truly rare! This statement suggests that work–life balance is unattainable.

If you feel adventurous, you could explore work–life balance in Europe and compare. The *Times* of London might be a good start. Most German publications provide complete English-language Web pages that you could search, too.

YOUR TASK Select your publication, for example, *The Huffington Post*. Input your search term *work–life balance*. Among the ten or so pages of articles, select one piece. Read it closely. Unless your instructor uses Twitter (or Tumblr) for this exercise, write a tweet in a messaging app or MS Word of no more than 260 characters out of the 280 allowed. Leave room for a comment in a retweet. Use a hashtag to start a conversation on the topic. Shorten long URLs (Web addresses) by visiting TinyURL. Note that although Twitter doubled the number of characters allowed for tweets, most users still keep their messages under 140 characters because they appreciate conciseness. Your tweets should be teasers that induce the reader to click the link and read the article.

If directed, also write a social media post—think LinkedIn—of no more than 30 words. In addition, you could be asked to write a summary of the article of no more than 10 percent of the total word count. Do not copy from the original. Tweet, post, and summarize from memory. When submitting your work, indicate the character and word count of both the original article and your messages. Word count is easy once you select and copy the entire article and paste it into an empty MS Word page. Your instructor may show you Twitter examples.

1.11 Speaking or Writing: Explore Media Richness (L.O. 4)

`Communication Technology` / `E-Mail` `Social Media`

YOUR TASK Decide whether the following messages need to be communicated orally or in writing. After consulting the media richness diagram in Figure 1.9, consider how rich the medium must be in each communication situation to convey the message most appropriately and reliably. You may want to choose channels such as e-mail, letter, report, texting, instant messaging, telephone call, live chat, teleconferencing, face-to-face conversation, or team meeting. Describe the advantages and disadvantages of each choice.

a. As a junior sales assistant, you are expected to join your division sales manager at company headquarters, where you both must attend an important meeting. It looks as though you will be at least 15 minutes late. What to do?

b. Working at 8 a.m. in your Philadelphia office, you need to get in touch with your counterpart at your company's San Diego office and ask a few clarifying formatting questions about a report on which the two of you are collaborating.

c. Axel, the information technology vice president, must tell employees about a new company social media policy. He has two employees in mind who particularly need this information.

d. As soon as possible, you need to learn from Callie in the Imaging Department whether she can make copies of a set of architectural blueprints. If she cannot, you need her advice on where you can get it done.

e. As a manager in your Human Resources Department, you must terminate three employees in a companywide initiative to reduce costs.

f. It wasn't your fault, but a print order of fine letterhead stationery for a longtime corporate customer was mishandled. The stationery is not ready, and the customer is angry.

g. As chair of the Employee Benefits Committee, you have worked with your committee for two months evaluating several health plan options. You are now ready to convey the recommendations of the committee to management.

1.12 Probing Active Social Media Users' Attitudes Toward Ethics (L.O. 5)

`Communication Technology` / `Ethics` `Social Media`

Test yourself and see how your ethical decision making compares with the attitudes of other active social media users. The National Business Ethics Survey of 4,800 U.S. males ages nineteen to forty-five found that active social networkers showed a much greater acceptance of questionable workplace behavior than did other U.S. workers. Here are the survey questions:

Do you feel it is acceptable to…?		
"Friend" a client/ customer on a social network	YES	NO
Blog or tweet negatively about your company or colleagues	YES	NO
Buy personal items with your company credit card as long as you pay it back	YES	NO
Do a little less work to compensate for cuts in benefits or pay	YES	NO
Keep a copy of confidential work documents in case you need them in your next job	YES	NO
Take a copy of work software home and use it on your personal computer	YES	NO
Upload vacation pictures to the company network or server so that you can share them with coworkers	YES	NO
Use social networking to find out what your company's competitors are doing	YES	NO

FIGURE 1.15

SOCIAL NETWORKERS VS. OTHER U.S. WORKERS: COMPARING ATTITUDES TOWARDS QUESTIONABLE BEHAVIOR		
Do you feel it is acceptable to...?	**Active Social Networkers**	**Other U.S. Workers**
"Friend" a client/customer on a social network	59%	28%
Blog or tweet negatively about your company or colleagues	42%	6%
Buy personal items with your company credit card as long as you pay it back	42%	8%
Do a little less work to compensate for cuts in benefits or pay	51%	10%
Keep a copy of confidential work documents in case you need them in your next job	50%	15%
Take a copy of work software home and use it on your personal computer	46%	7%
Upload vacation pictures to the company network or server so you can share them with co-workers	50%	17%
Use social networking to find out what my company's competitors are doing	54%	30%

Source: National Business Ethics Survey, Social Media Week.

YOUR TASK Answer the survey questions. Then view the survey results in Figure 1.15. How do your responses stack up? In class share your impressions of the survey. What surprised you and why? With your classmates and your instructor, discuss the behaviors addressed in the study. Are some particularly egregious? Do some seem pretty harmless? Why or why not? Apply the tools for doing the right thing introduced in this chapter (see Figure 1.14, Five Questions to Guide Ethical Decisions). Your instructor may ask you to post your views on Blackboard, Moodle, or another discussion forum and to respond to your peers' posts.

1.13 Doing the Right Thing: Resolving Ethical Dilemmas (L.O. 5)

Ethics / Team

In your career, your ethics will frequently be put to the test. As you face various ethical dilemmas, many factors can determine your choice of an action to take.

YOUR TASK Study the seven dilemmas appearing in this chapter. Select four of them and apply the tools for doing the right thing in Figure 1.14, choosing an appropriate action. In a memo to your instructor or in a team discussion, explain the action you would take for each dilemma. Analyze your response to each question (Is the action you are considering legal? How would you see the problem if you were on the opposite side? and so forth).

Test Your Workplace Etiquette IQ

New communication platforms and casual workplace environments have blurred the lines of appropriateness, leaving workers wondering how to navigate uncharted waters. Check your workplace etiquette IQ by deciding whether the following statements are true or false. Then see if you agree with the responses on p. Key-5.

1. The boss is traveling, and fellow worker Cole begs you to sign the boss's name on an application that he insists must be mailed immediately. As the boss's assistant, you should sign the boss's name because you think he wouldn't mind, and it would help Cole immensely.

_____ True _____ False

2. As you begin a leisurely weekend at home, you receive an e-mail from your product manager asking for information. Because it's not urgent, the best plan is to respond early on Monday.

_____ True _____ False

3. McKayla is your go-to colleague with all the answers, but she's on vacation. You need to ask her a quick question that you're sure she could answer—if you could just reach her. Because she has a cell phone connected to work e-mail, it's perfectly acceptable to give her a quick call.

_____ True _____ False

Chat About It

In each chapter, you will find five discussion questions related to the chapter material. Your instructor may assign these topics for you to discuss in class, in an online chat room, or on an online discussion board. Some of the discussion topics may require outside research. You may also be asked to read and respond to postings made by your classmates.

TOPIC 1: Should college education in the United States be free as it is in many parts of Europe? Advocates of tuition-free higher education say it is an investment in the future of our society. Opponents argue that expecting American taxpayers to shoulder the cost is unfair.

TOPIC 2: Do you think that always being plugged in can erode performance, as some executives have claimed in a recent survey? One leader pointed out that major scientific breakthroughs occurred outside the laboratory when the scientist was engaged in a mundane task—or even asleep.

TOPIC 3: Google employees railed against Dragonfly, a search app developed in secret that would restrict content banned by China. They also protested an AI project for the Pentagon. Then, thousands of Google employees staged a global mass walkout against sexual misconduct by executives. In your work, have you faced ethical dilemmas? Would you join a protest?

TOPIC 4: Within the next few decades, automation is expected to wipe out almost half of all currently existing jobs in the United States. What consequences of that development can you foresee and what can you do to future-proof your career?

TOPIC 5: Some experts believe that although computer technology is improving our lives in many ways, it might be impairing our ability to think critically by putting answers at our fingertips. What do you think?

Grammar and Mechanics Review 1

Each chapter includes an exercise based on Appendix D, Grammar and Mechanics. This appendix is a business communicator's condensed guide to language usage, covering 50 of the most used and abused language elements. It also includes a list of frequently misspelled words as well as a list of confusing words. In the first nine chapters, each exercise focuses on a specific set of grammar/mechanics guidelines. In the last seven chapters, exercises review all the guidelines plus spelling and confusing words. In addition to these chapter reviews, you will find checkpoint quizzes in Appendix D and in-depth grammar/mechanics exercises in Aplia.

Sentence Structure

Study sentence structure in Guides 1–3 of Appendix D beginning at the end of the book. Then on a separate sheet, identify the faults in the following sentences. If incorrect, write a correct version. Avoid adding new phrases or rewriting in your own words. When finished, compare your responses with the key at the end of the book.

a. Correctly punctuated

b. Fragment [Guide 1]

c. Run-on [Guide 2]

d. Comma splice [Guide 3]

EXAMPLE: The job market is improving, however competition is fierce.

REVISION: The job market is improving; **however**, competition is fierce. [d, Guide 3, Comma splice]

1. The current graduating class will enter the most challenging job market in years, many graduates do not know where to apply.

2. Researchers predict that a booming U.S. economy may not return quickly it may take years for the job market to regain stability.

3. Because recent graduates are entering a fast-paced, competitive, and highly connected digital environment. Communication and technology skills are critical to career success.

4. Many applicants will apply for openings those with exceptional communication skills will immediately stand out.

5. Surprisingly, many employers say that the ability to think critically, communicate clearly, and solve complex problems is more important than a candidate's undergraduate major.

6. The 9-to-5 job may soon be a relic of the past. If millennials have their way.

7. Knowledge workers must be able to explain their decisions they must be critical thinkers.

8. Informal communication travels through the grapevine. Which is generally word-of-mouth communication.

9. Ethical companies experience less litigation, they also are the target of less government regulation.

10. Even when an action is legal. It may violate generally accepted principles of right and wrong.

CHAPTER 2

Professionalism: Team, Meeting, Listening, Nonverbal, and Etiquette Skills

LEARNING OUTCOMES

After studying this chapter, you should be able to do the following:

1 Explain why teamwork is important in the digital-era workplace and how you can contribute to excellent team performance.

2 Identify effective practices and technologies for planning and participating in face-to-face meetings and virtual meetings.

3 Describe and apply active listening techniques.

4 Discuss how effective nonverbal communication can help you advance your career.

5 Examine how developing professionalism and business etiquette skills can improve your competitive advantage.

Monkey Business Images/Shutterstock.com

Zooming In

Uplifting Others: Collaboration and Team-Orientation at Lyft

Today's sharing economy is disrupting entire industries, especially transportation. While Uber aggressively spread the game-changing idea of ride sharing, its scrappy smaller rival Lyft, known for its glowing pink-mustache branding, is betting on strategic partnerships to compete. In the wake of Uber's long turmoil that ended with the CEO's forced exit, Lyft has leveraged its more favorable image to grow market share, increase its valuation, and cooperate with much larger partners. Lyft's co-founders, John Zimmer and CEO Logan Green, are co-equal leaders who have created a friendly, driver-centered culture—in stark contrast to the hard-driving antics of ousted Uber chief, Travis Kalanick.

Operating solely in North America, Lyft has a strategic local focus. It forged exclusive deals with a city in Colorado to provide subsidized transportation for light rail riders, and with Boston, offering on-demand service for riders with disabilities. The company has become the official ride-sharing partner for the Honda Center, home to the Anaheim Ducks. More important, Lyft contracted with hundreds of health-care organizations to give car-less patients rides using a new Web-based request platform. Lyft has also attracted large corporate clients, such as Apple and Airbnb,[1] and has partnered with security firm ADT.[2] Like its larger rival, Lyft is betting big on autonomous vehicles and urban bike sharing. However, Lyft is collaborating with others to launch self-driving cars instead of building costly expertise in-house.[3] The company's market share of 30 percent has doubled in the last three years.[4]

This success may be owed to Lyft's core values: *Be yourself, create fearlessly, uplift others,* and *make it happen. Uplift others* refers to a seamless ride experience and collaboration among employees, called team members.[5] Lyft so values teamwork that part of the test new-hires must pass is a culture fit to determine whether they share the Lyft ethos of collaboration and mutual respect. CEO Logan Green says, "When we build a team, we look for incredibly smart, compassionate people who are all motivated by the same goal."[6] In fact, Lyft's organizational structure is a series of teams instead of departments found in more traditional businesses. Team members regularly approach colleagues to solve problems. One software engineer praises being surrounded by "friendly people willing to help get things done."[7] A brand designer boasts, "All teams are very supportive and respectful to each other" and that Lyft's collaborative spirit fosters team "camaraderie, energy, and creativity."[8]

Lyft and its ever-growing teams dedicated to a shared vision embody teamwork in the digital workplace. Lyft may have a pink-fur-lined elevator, boast a dog-friendly office, and allow flip-flops and casual clothing, but effective communication skills, respect for fellow workers, and professionalism are key factors that have contributed to its growing success.

You will have a chance to complete a relevant task related to this case study at the end of this chapter.

Critical Thinking

- Why is Lyft partnering with much larger organizations?

- Why does Lyft test new-hires for their *culture fit,* and why is it valuable for employer and employee?

- What attitudes and behaviors contribute to effective teams?

2-1 Excelling in Professional Teams

Most businesses seek employees who can get along and deliver positive results that increase profits and boost their image. As a budding business professional, you have a stake in acquiring skills that will make you recession-proof and future-ready.

LEARNING OUTCOME

1 Explain why teamwork is important in the digital era workplace and how you can contribute to excellent team performance.

2-1a Impressing Digital Age Employers

Employers are typically interested in four key areas: education, experience, hard skills, and soft skills. **Hard skills** traditionally refer to the technical expertise in your field. **Soft skills** are commonly defined as interpersonal or social skills, professional skills, or, more broadly, emotional intelligence. As we have established in Chapter 1, these powerful skills are not "soft" or somehow less. On the contrary! In today's collaborative, hyperconnected workplaces and in the approaching age of automation, they are indispensable. Therefore, we prefer to call them social skills, interpersonal skills, or professional skills.

Desirable competencies include not only oral and written communication skills but also active listening skills, appropriate nonverbal behavior, and proper business etiquette. In addition, employers such as Lyft want efficient and productive team members. They want managers and employees who are comfortable with diverse audiences, listen actively to customers and colleagues, make eye contact, and display good workplace manners. These social skills are immensely important not only to be hired but also to be promoted.

Hiring managers naturally expect you to have technical expertise in your field and know the latest communication technology. Such skills and an impressive résumé may get you in the door. However, your long-term success depends on how well you communicate with your boss, coworkers, and customers, and whether you can be an effective and contributing team member. Even in fields such as information technology, employers are looking for interpersonal skills. A recent global survey of chief information officers found that "the talent gap in soft digital skills is more pronounced than in hard digital skills." The CIOs believe that the much-debated skills gap in some technology occupations is slowing down digital transformation in organizations.[9]

As we discussed in Chapter 1, collaboration is the rule today, and an overwhelming majority of white-collar professionals (85 percent) need to partner with others to complete their work.[11] Research by design company Gensler shows that the 4,000 knowledge workers surveyed nationally spent on average about 28 percent of their time collaborating.[12] In addition, 84 percent of U.S. employees are members of so-called matrixed teams. This means that their job tasks are spread out across multiple teams and they don't always work with the same people or report to the same manager.[13] Workers collaborate not only at their desks but also informally in hallways and flexible unassigned workspaces or remotely with the latest teleconferencing tools. Needless to say, solid interpersonal skills rule in face-to-face and far-flung teams.

This chapter focuses on developing team, meeting, listening, nonverbal, and etiquette skills. These are some of the professional skills that employers seek in the hyperconnected, competitive work environment of the digital age.

2-1b Understanding the Purpose of Teams

The workplace is teeming with teams. You might find yourself a part of a work team, project team, customer support team, supplier team, design team, planning team, functional team, cross-functional team, or some other group. All these teams are formed to accomplish specific goals.

It's no secret that one of the most important objectives of businesses is finding ways to do jobs better at less cost. This objective helps explain the popularity of teams, which are formed for the following reasons:

- **Better decisions.** Decisions are generally more accurate and effective because group and team members contribute different expertise and perspectives.
- **Faster responses.** When action is necessary to respond to competition or to solve a problem, small groups and teams can act rapidly.
- **Increased productivity.** Because they are often closer to the action and the customer, team members can see opportunities for improving efficiency.
- **Greater buy-in.** Decisions arrived at jointly are usually better received because members are committed to the solution and more willing to support it.
- **Less resistance to change.** People who have input into decisions are less hostile, aggressive, and resistant to change.
- **Improved employee morale.** Personal satisfaction and job morale increase when teams are successful.
- **Reduced risks.** Responsibility for a decision is diffused on a team, thus carrying less risk for any individual.

Despite the current popularity of teams, however, they are not a solution for all workplace problems, particularly if such groups are dysfunctional. The late Harvard professor J. Richard Hackman claimed that research "consistently shows that teams underperform despite all their extra resources."[15] This team expert and other studies suggest that organizations must strike a balance between solo effort—in highly creative endeavors—and collective action. "The most spectacularly creative people" are often introverted and prefer to work alone, which is when they do their best and most innovative work.[16] Subsequent research discusses the downsides of multitasking and frequent interruptions common in collaboration.[17]

The demands of the always-on workplace often lead to overwork, even burnout. Because time demands have skyrocketed more than 50 percent in the last ten years, some knowledge and information workers who struggle to set boundaries experience collaborative overload. Constant interaction inflates their workload, they fall behind, and their performance suffers.[18] However, in most models of future organizations, teams—not individuals—function as the primary performance units.

2-1c Collaborating in Virtual Teams

In addition to working side by side with potential teammates, you can expect to collaborate with coworkers remotely—at home, in other cities, and even in other countries. Such collaborations are referred to as virtual teams. This is a group of dispersed people who, aided by communication technology, must accomplish shared tasks without face-to-face contact across geographic boundaries, sometimes on different continents and across time zones.[19]

Although Yahoo and Best Buy have reversed their acclaimed work-at-home policies, remote work and virtual teams are here to stay. Some tech companies have become fully dispersed, having ditched the idea of a physical office. "When I started Toptal, I was working with people in several different countries right from the very beginning," explains Taso DuVal, the founder of the tech talent platform. "It didn't make sense to have an office anywhere."[20]

Many well-known German companies with a global reach maintain headquarters in picturesque small German towns (think Volkswagen, Adidas, Hugo Boss, and software corporation SAP). Virtual technology enables them to connect with their facilities in locations around the globe, wherever needed talent may reside.[21] SAP is headquartered in idyllic Walldorf, Germany, but it has established research and development centers in India, China, Israel, and the United States to save costs and take advantage of global know-how. Depending on the competence needed, employees from different locations form virtual teams that pool their expertise to complete ad hoc assignments.[22] These teams must coordinate their work and complete their tasks across time and geographic zones. As you can see, work is increasingly viewed as what you do rather than a place you go.

In some organizations remote coworkers may be permanent employees from the same office or specialists called together for special projects. Regardless of the assignment, virtual teams can benefit from shared views, skills, and diversity.

Rawpixel.com/Shutterstock.com

Project teams can be pulled together from all corners of the globe as needed to tackle complex problems while benefiting from diverse expertise.

2-1d Outlining the Four Phases of Team Development

Regardless of their specific purpose, teams normally go through predictable phases as they develop. The psychologist B. A. Tuckman identified four phases: *forming, storming, norming,* and *performing*, as Figure 2.1 illustrates.[23] Some groups get lucky and move quickly from forming to

FIGURE 2.1 Four Phases of Team Development in Decision Making

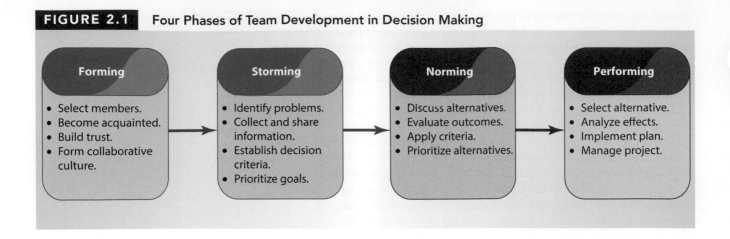

Forming	Storming	Norming	Performing
• Select members. • Become acquainted. • Build trust. • Form collaborative culture.	• Identify problems. • Collect and share information. • Establish decision criteria. • Prioritize goals.	• Discuss alternatives. • Evaluate outcomes. • Apply criteria. • Prioritize alternatives.	• Select alternative. • Analyze effects. • Implement plan. • Manage project.

performing. Other teams may never reach the final stage of performing. However, most struggle through disruptive, although ultimately constructive, team-building stages.

Forming.   During the first stage, individuals get to know each other. They often are overly polite and feel a bit awkward. As they search for similarities and attempt to bond, they begin to develop trust in each other. Members discuss fundamental topics such as why the team is necessary, who "owns" the team, whether membership is mandatory, how large the team should be, and what talents members can contribute. A leader functions primarily as a traffic director. Groups and teams should resist the efforts of some members to dash through the first stages and race to the performing stage. Moving slowly through the stages is necessary to build a cohesive, productive unit.

Storming.   During the second phase, members define their roles and responsibilities, decide how to reach their goals, and iron out the rules governing how they interact. Unfortunately, this stage often produces conflict, resulting in storming. A good leader, however, should step in to set limits, control the chaos, and offer suggestions. Team leaders are most successful if they act like a coach rather than a cop. Teams composed of dissimilar personality types may take longer to progress through the storming phase. Tempers may flare, sleep may be lost, and leaders may be deposed. But most often the storm passes, and a cohesive group emerges.

Norming.   Once the sun returns to the sky, teams and groups enter the norming stage. Tension subsides, roles are clarified, and information begins to flow among members. The group periodically checks its agenda to remind itself of its progress toward its goals. People are careful not to shake the hard-won camaraderie and formation of a single-minded purpose. Formal leadership is unnecessary because everyone takes on leadership functions. Important data are shared with the entire group, and mutual interdependence becomes typical. The group or team begins to move smoothly in one direction. Figure 2.1 shows how a team might proceed through the four phases while solving a problem and reaching a decision.

Performing.   In Tuckman's team growth model, some groups never reach the final stage of performing. For those that survive the first three phases, however, the final stage is gratifying. Group members have established routines and a shared language. They develop loyalty and a willingness to resolve all problems. A can-do mentality pervades as they progress toward their goal. Fights are clean, and members continue working together without grudges. Best of all, information flows freely, deadlines are met, and production exceeds expectations.

2-1e Recognizing Positive and Negative Team Behavior

By displaying positive behavior, team members show their commitment to achieving the group's purpose. How can you be a valuable team member? The most effective groups have members who are willing to establish rules and abide by them. Effective team members are able to analyze tasks and define problems so that they can work toward solutions. They offer information and try out their ideas on the group to stimulate discussion. They show interest in others' ideas by listening actively. Helpful team members also seek to involve silent members. They strive to resolve differences, and they encourage a warm, supportive climate by praising and agreeing with others. When they sense that agreement is near, they review significant points and move the group toward its goal by synthesizing points of understanding.

Not all groups, however, have members who contribute positively. Negative behavior emerges when some constantly put down the ideas and suggestions of others. They insult, criticize, and aggress against others. They waste the group's time with unnecessary recounting of personal achievements or irrelevant topics. The team clown distracts the group with excessive joke-telling, inappropriate comments, and disruptive antics. Also disturbing are team members who withdraw and refuse to be drawn out. They have nothing to say, either for or against ideas being considered. To be a productive and welcome member of a group, be prepared to perform the positive tasks described in Figure 2.2. Avoid the negative behaviors.

2-1f Combating Groupthink

Successful teams can resolve conflict using the methods you just learned. They understand that some friction is normal, even healthy, in team interactions. They "engage in the productive conflict, the listening and debating, that help you get to the right answer," an expert says.[24] However, some teams avoid conflict at their own risk. They smooth things over and in doing so may fall victim to groupthink. This is a term coined by theorist Irving Janis to describe faulty decision-making processes by team members who are overly eager to agree with one another.[25] Apparently, when we deviate from a group, we fear rejection. Scientists variously call this natural reluctance "the pain of independence"[26] or describe it as "the hazards of courage."[27]

Several conditions can lead to groupthink: team members with similar backgrounds, a lack of systematic procedures, a demand for a quick decision, or a strong leader who favors a specific outcome. Symptoms of groupthink include pressure placed on any member who argues against the group's mutual beliefs, self-censorship of thoughts that stray from the group's agreement, collective efforts to rationalize, and an unquestioned belief in the group's moral authority. Teams suffering from groupthink fail to check alternatives, are biased in collecting and evaluating information, and ignore the risks of the preferred choice. They may also neglect to work out a contingency plan in case the preferred choice fails.[28]

Effective teams avoid groupthink by striving for team diversity—in age, gender, background, experience, and training. They encourage open discussion, search for relevant information,

---

FIGURE 2.2 Positive and Negative Group Behaviors

GROUP BEHAVIORS   POSITIVE

+ Setting rules and abiding by them

+ Analyzing tasks and defining problems

+ Contributing information and ideas

+ Showing interest by listening actively

+ Encouraging members to participate

NEGATIVE   **GROUP BEHAVIORS**

− Blocking the ideas of others

− Insulting and criticizing others

− Making improper jokes and comments

− Failing to stay on task

− Withdrawing, failing to participate

evaluate many alternatives, consider how a decision will be implemented, and plan for contingencies in case the decision doesn't work out.

2-1g Reaching Group Decisions

The way teams reach decisions greatly affects their morale and commitment, as well as the implementation of any team decision. In U.S. culture the majority usually rules, but other methods, five of which are discussed here, may be more effective. As you study these methods, think about which would be best for routine decisions and which would be best for dealing with emergencies.

- **Majority.** Group members vote and a majority wins. This method results in a quick decision but may leave an alienated minority uncommitted to implementation.
- **Consensus.** Discussion continues until all team members have aired their opinions and, ultimately, agree. This method is time consuming; however, it produces creative, high-quality discussion and generally elicits commitment by all members to implement the decision.
- **Minority.** Typically, a subcommittee investigates and makes a recommendation for action. This method is useful when the full group cannot get together to make a decision or when time is short.
- **Averaging.** Members haggle, bargain, wheedle, and negotiate to reach a middle position, which often requires compromise. With this method, the opinions of the least knowledgeable members may cancel the opinions of the most knowledgeable.
- **Authority rule with discussion.** The leader, boss, or manager listens to team members' ideas, but the final decision is that person'. This method encourages lively discussion and results in participatory decision making. However, team members must have good communication skills. This method also requires a leader who is willing to make decisions.

2-1h Defining High-Performing Teams

The use of teams has been called the solution to many ills in today's workplace.[29] It's an old saw in business to claim that TEAM means Together, Everyone Achieves More.[30] However, teams that do not work well together can increase frustration, lower productivity, and create employee dissatisfaction. Experts who have studied team dynamics and decisions have discovered that effective teams share some or all of the following characteristics.

Stay Small and Embrace Diversity. Teams may range from two to 25 members, although four to six is an optimal number for most projects. Teams smaller than ten members tend to agree more easily on a common objective and form more cohesive units.[31] For the most creative decisions, teams generally have male and female members who differ in age, ethnicity, social background, training, and experience. The key business advantage of diversity is the ability to view a project from multiple perspectives. Many organizations are finding that diverse teams can produce innovative solutions with broader applications than homogeneous teams can.

microstock3D/Shutterstock.com

Agree on a Purpose. An effective team begins with a purpose. Working from a general purpose to specific goals typically requires a huge investment of time and effort. Meaningful discussions, however, motivate team members to buy in to the project. Responding to an aging workforce and wishing to boost its hiring, construction company TDIndustries teamed up with United Way of Greater Houston to train and recruit female candidates. The partnership resulted in a 12-week tradeswomen program geared to easing skilled female workers into the male-dominated profession. Despite a few initial challenges, the collaboration was so successful that TDIndustries plans to extend the program to its other divisions in Texas and Arizona.[32]

Establish Procedures. The best teams develop procedures to guide them. They set up intermediate goals with deadlines. They assign roles and tasks, requiring all members to

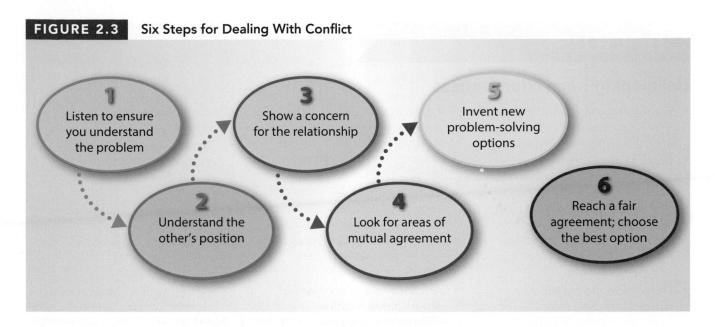

FIGURE 2.3 Six Steps for Dealing With Conflict

1. Listen to ensure you understand the problem
2. Understand the other's position
3. Show a concern for the relationship
4. Look for areas of mutual agreement
5. Invent new problem-solving options
6. Reach a fair agreement; choose the best option

contribute equivalent amounts of real work. They decide how they will make decisions, whether by majority vote, consensus, or other methods discussed earlier. Procedures are continually evaluated to ensure movement toward the attainment of the team's goals.

Confront Conflict. Poorly functioning teams avoid conflict, preferring sulking, gossiping, or backstabbing. A better plan is to acknowledge conflict and address the root of the problem openly using the six-step plan outlined in Figure 2.3. Although it may feel emotionally risky, direct confrontation saves time and enhances team commitment in the long run. To be constructive, however, confrontation must be task oriented, not person oriented. An open airing of differences, in which all team members have a chance to speak their minds, should center on the strengths and weaknesses of the various positions and ideas—not on personalities. After hearing all sides, team members must negotiate a fair settlement, no matter how long it takes.

Communicate Effectively. The best teams exchange information and contribute ideas freely in an informal environment often facilitated by technology. Team members speak and write clearly and concisely, avoiding generalities. They encourage feedback. Listeners become actively involved, read body language, and ask clarifying questions before responding. Tactful, constructive disagreement is encouraged. Although a team's task is taken seriously, successful teams are able to inject humor into their face-to-face interactions.

Collaborate Rather Than Compete. Effective team members are genuinely interested in achieving team goals instead of receiving individual recognition. They contribute ideas and feedback unselfishly. They monitor team progress, including what's going right, what's going wrong, and what to do about it. They celebrate individual and team accomplishments.

Accept Ethical Responsibilities. Teams as a whole have ethical responsibilities to their members, to their larger organizations, and to society. Members have a number of specific responsibilities to each other. As a whole, teams have a responsibility to represent the organization's view and respect its privileged information. They should not discuss any sensitive issues with outsiders without permission. In addition, teams have a broader obligation to avoid advocating actions that would endanger members of society at large.

Share Leadership. Effective teams often have no formal leader. Instead, leadership rotates to those with the appropriate expertise as the team evolves and moves from one phase to another. Many teams operate under a democratic approach. This approach can achieve buy-in to team decisions, boost morale, and create fewer hurt feelings and less resentment. In times of crisis, however, a strong team member may need to step up as a leader.

The following checklist summarizes effective techniques for developing successful teams.

Checklist

Developing Team Effectiveness

- **Establish small teams.** Smaller teams function more efficiently and effectively than larger teams.
- **Encourage diversity.** Innovative teams typically include members who differ in age, gender, ethnicity, and background. Team members should possess the necessary technical expertise, problem-solving skills, and interpersonal skills.
- **Determine the purpose, procedures, and roles.** Members must understand the task at hand and what is expected of them. Teams function best when operating procedures are ironed out early and each member assumes a specific role.
- **Acknowledge and manage conflict.** Conflict is productive when it motivates a team to search for new ideas,

increase participation, delay premature decisions, or discuss disagreements. Keep conflict centered on issues rather than on people.
- **Cultivate effective communication skills.** Productive team members articulate ideas clearly and concisely, recognize nonverbal cues, and listen actively.
- **Advance an environment of open communication.** Teams are most productive when members trust each other and feel free to discuss all viewpoints openly in an informal atmosphere.
- **Encourage collaboration and discourage competition.** Sharing information in a cooperative effort to achieve the team purpose must be more important than competing with

other members for individual achievement.
- **Share leadership.** Members with the most expertise should lead at various times during the project's evolution.
- **Strive to make fair decisions.** Effective teams resolve problems without forcing members into a win–lose situation.
- **Lighten up.** The most successful teams take their task seriously, but they are also able to laugh at themselves and interject humor to enliven team proceedings.
- **Continually assess performance.** Teams should establish checkpoints along the way to determine whether they are meeting their objectives and adjust procedures if progress is unsatisfactory.

LEARNING OUTCOME

2 Identify effective practices and technologies for planning and participating in face-to-face meetings and virtual meetings.

2-2 Preparing and Participating in Face-to-Face and Virtual Meetings

As you prepare to join the workforce, expect to attend meetings—lots of them! One conservative estimate suggests that workers on average spend more than a fifth of their work time in meetings and consider 25 percent of that time as wasted.[33] Top managers spend even more time in meetings. A U.S. study of chief executives reveals that CEOs devote 72 percent of their workweeks to meetings with the average meeting taking an hour or less, but 17 percent exceeded two hours.[34] In one survey, managers considered more than a third of meeting time unproductive and reported that two thirds of meetings fell short of their stated objectives.[35]

Business meetings consist of three or more people who assemble to pool information, solicit feedback, clarify policy, seek consensus, and solve problems. However, as growing numbers of employees work at distant locations, meetings have changed. Workers cannot always meet face-to-face. To be able to exchange information effectively and efficiently, you will need to know how to plan and participate in face-to-face as well as virtual meetings.

2-2a Contributing in Face-to-Face Meetings

Meetings may be inevitable and commonplace, but most workers dread them. Yet another survey, commissioned by the National Statistics Council, concluded that a whopping 37 percent of workers' time is spent in meetings and that nearly half of employees view too many meetings as the biggest time waster, more than social media or e-mail.[37] One business reporter complained that "long-winded colleagues consume all available oxygen, killing good ideas by asphyxiation."[38] Embracing the latest antidote to hated hourlong meetings, some companies are resorting to daily five-minute huddles or scrums. Meeting participants can speak for only 15 to 30 seconds at a time or risk being cut off.[39] Whether such brevity destroys relationship building, an intangible byproduct of meetings, remains to be seen. Be it as it may, your task as a business communicator is to learn how to make your workplace meetings more efficient, satisfying, and productive.

After all, although meetings are disliked, they can be career-critical. Meeting participation, if well played, can bring you favorable status and help build your reputation.[40] Therefore, instead of treating meetings as thieves of your valuable time, try to see them as golden opportunities to demonstrate your leadership, communication, and problem-solving skills. To help you make the most of these opportunities, this section outlines best practices for running and contributing to meetings.

2-2b Determining the Purpose of a Meeting

A face-to-face meeting provides the most nonverbal cues and other signals that help us interpret the intended meaning of words. Thus, an in-person meeting is the richest of available media. No meeting should be called unless it is important, can't wait, and requires an exchange of ideas. If people are merely being informed, send an e-mail, text message, memo, or letter. Leave a phone or voice mail message, but don't call a costly meeting. Remember, the real expense of a meeting is the lost productivity of all the people attending. To decide whether the purpose of the meeting is valid, consult the key people who will be attending. Ask them what outcomes they desire and how to achieve those goals. This consultation also sets a collaborative tone and encourages full participation.

Selecting Meeting Participants.

The purpose of the meeting determines the number of participants, as shown in Figure 2.4. If the meeting purpose is motivational, such as an awards ceremony for sales reps of cosmetics giant Avon or nutrition supplement seller Herbalife, then the number of participants is potentially unlimited. However, to make decisions, the best number is no more than seven to eight participants, as studies suggest.[41] For effective decision making, consultants recommend limiting the session to four to seven participants.[42]

Ideally, decision makers and people with the information necessary to make the decision should attend. Also attending should be people who will be responsible for implementing the decision and representatives of groups who will benefit from the decision. Let's consider Timberland and its signature employee volunteer program. Company leaders might meet with managers, employee representatives, and community leaders to decide how best to improve school grounds, give back to veterans, or maintain community gardens.[43] Inviting key stakeholders who represent various interests, perspectives, and competencies ensures valuable input and, therefore, is more likely to lead to informed decisions.

Business meetings consist of three or more people who assemble to pool information, solicit feedback, clarify policy, seek consensus, and solve problems.

Oberon/Shutterstock.com

FIGURE 2.4 Meeting Purpose and Number of Participants

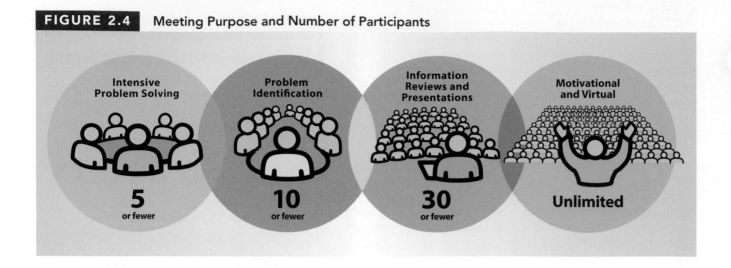

Intensive Problem Solving — **5** or fewer

Problem Identification — **10** or fewer

Information Reviews and Presentations — **30** or fewer

Motivational and Virtual — **Unlimited**

Using Digital Calendars to Schedule Meetings. Finding a time when everyone can meet is often difficult. Fortunately, digital calendars make the task quick and efficient. Popular programs and mobile apps are Google Calendar, Apple Calendar, and the business favorite, Outlook Calendar (shown in Figure 2.5). Online calendars and mobile apps enable users to make appointments, schedule meetings, and keep track of daily activities.

To schedule meetings, you enter a meeting request and add the names of attendees. You select a date, enter a start and end time, and list the meeting subject and location. Then the meeting request goes to each attendee. Later you check the attendee availability tab to see a list of all meeting attendees. As the meeting time approaches, the program automatically sends reminders to attendees. The free Web-based meeting scheduler and mobile app Doodle is growing in popularity because it helps users poll participants to determine the best date and time for a meeting.

Distributing an Agenda and Other Information. At least two days before a meeting, distribute an agenda of topics to be discussed. Also include any reports or materials that participants should read in advance. For continuing groups, you might also include a copy of the minutes of the previous meeting. To keep meetings productive, limit the number of agenda items. Remember, the narrower the focus, the greater the chances for success. A good agenda, as illustrated in Figure 2.6, covers the following information:

- Date and place of meeting
- Start time and end time
- Brief description of each topic, in order of priority, including the names of individuals who are responsible for performing some action
- Proposed allotment of time for each topic
- Any premeeting preparation expected of participants

2-2c Managing the Meeting

Whether you are the meeting leader or a participant, it is important to act professionally during the meeting. Meetings can be more efficient and productive if leaders and participants recognize how to get the meeting started, establish ground rules, move the meeting along, and handle conflict.

FIGURE 2.5 Using Calendar Programs

Calendar programs ease the frustration of scheduling meetings for busy people. The program allows you to check colleagues' calendars (if permission is given), locate a free time, schedule a meeting, send out an initial announcement, and follow up with reminders.

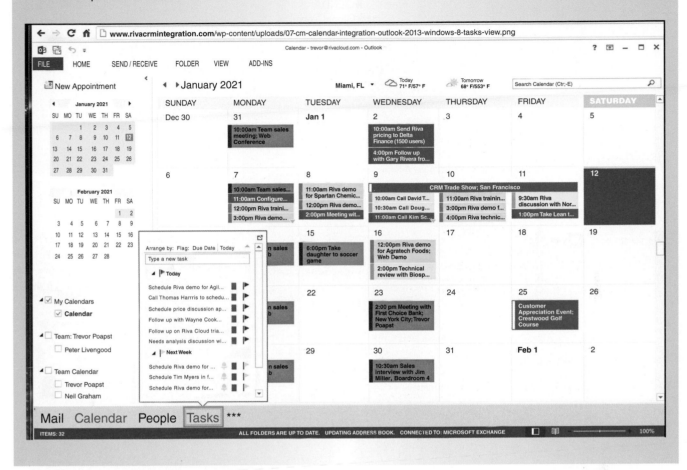

Getting Started and Establishing Ground Rules.

Even if some participants are missing, start meetings promptly to avoid wasting time and irritating attendees. For the same reasons, don't give quick recaps to latecomers. Open the meeting with a three- to five-minute introduction that includes the following:

- Goal and length of the meeting
- Background of topics or problems
- Possible solutions and constraints
- Tentative agenda
- Ground rules to be followed

Typical ground rules are communicating openly, being supportive, listening carefully, participating fully, confronting conflict frankly, silencing cell phones and other digital devices, and following the agenda. More formal groups follow parliamentary procedures based on Robert's Rules. The next step is to assign one attendee to take minutes and one to act as a recorder. The recorder uses a computer and projector or stands at a flipchart or whiteboard to list the main ideas being discussed and agreements reached.

Moving the Meeting Along.

An effective leader lets others talk and tries to involve all participants. If the group has one member who dominates, the leader might say, *Thanks, Tom, for*

FIGURE 2.6 Typical Meeting Agenda

AGENDA
Smart Global Travel
Staff Meeting
September 4, 2021
10 to 11 a.m.
Conference Room

		Person	Proposed Time
I.	Call to order; roll call		
II.	Approval of agenda		
III.	Approval of minutes from previous meeting		
IV.	Committee reports		
	A. Social media news update	Mason	5 minutes
	B. Tour packages	Minerva	10 minutes
V.	Old business		
	A. Equipment maintenance	Scott	5 minutes
	B. Client escrow accounts	Olivia	5 minutes
	C. Internal e-newsletter	Evelyn	5 minutes
VI.	New business		
	A. New accounts	Javier	5 minutes
	B. Pricing policy for Asian tours	Thanh	15 minutes
VII.	Announcements		
VIII.	Chair's summary, adjournment		

that perspective, but please hold your next point while we hear how Alana would respond to that. This technique also encourages quieter participants to speak up.

To avoid allowing digressions to sidetrack the group, try generating a parking lot list (a list of important but divergent issues that should be discussed later). Another way to handle digressions is to say, *Folks, we're drifting astray here. Please forgive me for pressing on, but let's return to the central issue of . . . .* It is important to adhere to the agenda and the schedule. Equally important, when the group seems to have reached a consensus, is to summarize the group's position and check to see whether everyone agrees.

Participating Actively and Productively. Meetings are an opportunity for you to showcase your abilities and boost your career. To get the most out of the meetings you attend, try these techniques: [44]

- **Arrive early.** You show respect and look well organized when you arrive a little early.
- **Come prepared.** Bring the agenda and any distributed materials. Study the topics and be ready with questions, comments, and good ideas.
- **Have a positive attitude.** Use positive body language; speak energetically.
- **Contribute respectfully.** Wait your turn to speak; raise your hand to be recognized.

- **Wait for others to finish.** Show respect and good manners by not interrupting.
- **Keep your voice calm and pleasant, yet energetic.** Avoid showing anger as this focuses attention on your behavior rather than on your ideas.
- **Give credit to others.** Gain allies and enhance your credibility by recognizing others in front of peers and superiors.
- **Use your cell phone, tablet, and laptop only for meeting-related tasks.** Focus your attention on the meeting, not on answering e-mails or working on your computer.
- **Help summarize.** Assist the meeting leader by reviewing points you have noted.
- **Express your views IN the meeting.** Build trust by not holding postmeeting sidebars that involve criticism and judgments.
- **Follow up.** Send the signal that you are efficient and caring by completing the actions assigned to you.

Productive meeting participants use their electronic devices only for meeting-related tasks and focus on the meeting, not on texting and answering e-mail.

Handling Conflict in Meetings. As you learned earlier, conflict is natural and even desirable. However, it can also cause awkwardness and uneasiness. In meetings, conflict typically develops when people feel unheard or misunderstood. If two people clash, the best approach is to encourage each to make a complete case while group members give their full attention. Let each one question the other. Then, the leader should summarize what was said, and the participants should offer comments. The group may modify a recommendation or suggest alternatives before reaching consensus on a direction to follow.

Concluding and Following Up. End the meeting at the agreed time or sooner. The leader should summarize all decisions, assigned tasks, and deadlines. It may be necessary to ask attendees to volunteer for completing action items. All participants should understand what was accomplished. One effective technique that encourages full participation is a round-robin in which people take turns summarizing briefly their interpretations of what was decided and what happens next. Of course, this closure technique works best with smaller groups. The leader should conclude by asking the group to set a time for the next meeting. He or she should assure the group that a report will follow. Finally, the leader should thank participants for attending.

If minutes were taken, they should be distributed within a couple of days of the meeting. Meeting management programs and mobile apps offer a structured template such as that shown in Figure 2.7, which includes brief meeting minutes, key points and decisions, and action items. The leader needs to ensure that decisions are executed. The leader may need to contact participants to remind them of their assignments and solicit help if necessary.

2-2d Preparing for Virtual Meetings

Virtual meetings are real-time gatherings of dispersed participants who connect with communication technology. As travel costs rise and companies slash budgets, many organizations are cutting back on meetings that require travel. Instead, people may meet in audioconferences using telephones or in videoconferences using the Internet. Steady improvements in telecommunications networks, software applications, and bandwidth continue to fuel the shift to virtual meetings. These meetings have many purposes, including training employees, making sales presentations, coordinating team activities, and talking to customers.

FIGURE 2.7 E-Mail Meeting Minutes

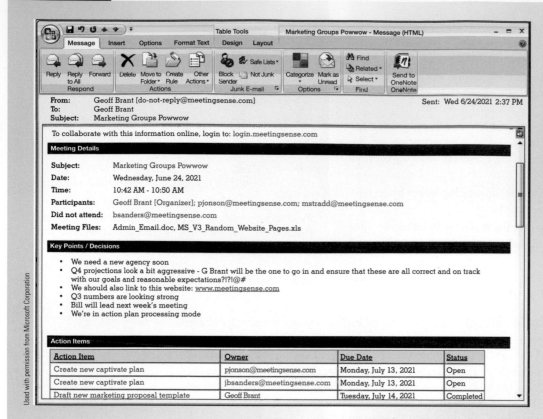

Meeting proceedings are efficiently recorded in a summary distribution template that provides subject, date, time, participant names, absentee names, meeting documents and files, key points, decisions, and action items.

Used with permission from Microsoft Corporation

Although the same good meeting management techniques discussed for face-to-face meetings prevail, additional skills and practices are important in virtual meetings. The following best practices recommended by experienced meeting facilitators will help you address premeeting issues such as technology glitches, scheduling across time zones, and language challenges.[47] Creating ground rules, anticipating limited media richness, managing turn-taking, and humanizing the interaction with remote members all achieve the best results during virtual meetings.

- **Select the most appropriate technology.** Decide whether audio- or videoconferencing is needed. Choose the appropriate program or application.

- **Ensure that all participants are able to use the technology.** Coach attendees who may need help before the session begins.

- **Encourage participants to log in 15 minutes early.** Some programs require downloads and installations that can cause immense frustration if not done early.

- **Be aware of different time zones.** Use Coordinated Universal Time (UTC) to minimize confusion resulting from mismatched local times. Avoid spanning a lunch hour or holding someone overtime.

- **Rotate your meeting time to be fair to all dispersed group members.** Ensure that everyone shares the burden of an inconvenient time.

- **Decide what language to use.** If the meeting language may be difficult for some participants, think about using simple expressions and repeating major ideas. Always follow up in writing.

- **Explain how questions may be asked and answered.** Many meeting programs allow participants to virtually raise their hands using an icon on the computer screen and type in their questions.

FOR THE RECORD

Far Away, So Close—Telepresence Rooms Mimic Face-to-Face Communication

You may be familiar with FaceTime, Skype, or perhaps Zoom—low-cost teleconferencing tools available to anyone and favored by small to midsize businesses. Videoconferencing has changed the way employees communicate. However, in some large organizations with many dispersed team members, workers connect remotely using sophisticated communication technology. These virtual meetings take place in high-tech telepresence rooms—conference spaces with high-end equipment dedicated to videoconferencing—and enable employees at different locations to simulate face-to-face meetings. Such virtual meetings demand specific etiquette and behavior, including making eye contact with people on the screen, paying close attention, and not typing or eating. Experts also advise against interruptions and leaving suddenly.[46] Why does videoconferencing require distinct behavior and etiquette?

- **Ensure it is clear who is speaking in audioconferences.** Ask participants to always say their names before beginning to comment.

- **Remind the group to silence all electronic alerts and alarms.** Ask participants to mute ringers and buzzers and control background noise, or you may also hear dogs barking, telephones ringing, and toilets flushing.

- **Don't multitask.** Giving your full attention is critical. That includes texting and checking e-mail.

- **Anticipate the limitations of virtual technology.** Given the lack of nonverbal cues, be as precise as possible. Use simple language and summarize the discussion often. Confirm your understanding of the discussion. Project an upbeat, enthusiastic, and strong voice.

- **Manage turn-taking.** Ask questions of specific people. Invite each participant to speak for 30 seconds without interruption. Avoid asking vague questions such as *Does everyone agree?*

- **Humanize virtual meetings.** Build camaraderie and trust. Leave time for small talk to establish a warm environment. Build trust and interest by logging in early and greeting others as they join in.

Companies with a global reach or a distributed domestic workforce could not function without teleconferencing. For Mozilla's Chief Innovation Officer Katharina Borchert, 70 percent of her daily meetings are video calls because her company has many remote employees: "I cannot imagine a world without video calls anymore. Video is equally important for my professional communication and for staying in touch with friends and family back in Europe."[48] Figure 2.8 shows how athletic gear company EverSports used video conferencing to meet virtually and design a new activity tracker.

FIGURE 2.8 Understanding Video Conferencing

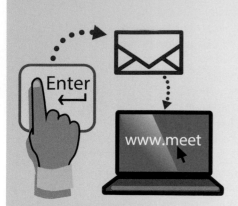

1. E-Mail Contact:
Mark K., president of EverSports, an athletic gear company in Seattle, WA, sends an e-mail to Jen S., chief designer at Digital Interactive Partners in Tucson, AZ, to discuss a new fitness tracker. The e-mail includes meeting date and time and a link to launch the session.

2. Virtual Meeting:
When the Web conference begins, participants see live video of each other's faces on their screens. They look at photos of fitness trackers, share ideas, sketch designs on a shared "virtual whiteboard," and review contract terms.

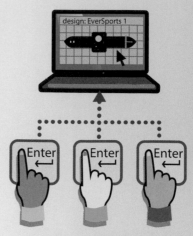

3. Design Collaboration:
Digital Interactive artists and EverSports managers use peer-to-peer software that allows them to share spaces on each other's computers. The software enables them to take turns modifying the designs, and it also tracks all the changes.

Although many acknowledge that virtual meetings may not be as effective as face-to-face meetings, virtual meetings are here to stay.[49] Learning to plan and participate in them professionally will enhance your career as a business communicator. The following checklist summarizes helpful techniques for both face-to-face and virtual meetings.

Checklist

Planning and Participating in Productive Meetings

Before the Meeting

- **Consider alternatives.** Unless a topic is important and pressing, avoid calling a meeting. Perhaps an e-mail message, telephone call, or intranet post would serve the purpose.

- **Invite the right people.** Invite people who have information and authority to make the decision and implement it.

- **Use a calendar program.** If available, use calendaring software to set a meeting date, issue invitations, and send the agenda.

- **Distribute an agenda.** Prepare an agenda that includes the date and place of the meeting, the starting and ending time, a brief description of each topic, the names of the people responsible for any action, and a proposed time allotment for each topic.

- **Train participants on technology.** Especially for virtual meetings, be sure participants are comfortable with the conferencing software.

During the Meeting

- **Start on time and introduce the agenda.** Discuss the goal and length of the meeting, provide backgrounds of topics for discussion, suggest possible solutions and constraints, propose a tentative agenda, and clarify the ground rules for the meeting.

- **Appoint a secretary and a recorder.** Ask one attendee to take notes of the proceedings, and ask another person to record discussion topics on a flipchart or whiteboard.

- **Encourage participation.** Ensure that all participants' views are heard and that no one monopolizes the discussion. Avoid digressions by steering the group back to the topics on the agenda. In virtual meetings be sure participants identify themselves before speaking.

- **Confront conflict frankly.** Encourage people who disagree to explain their positions completely. Then restate each position and ask for group comments. The group may modify a recommendation or suggest alternatives before agreeing on a plan of action.

- **Summarize along the way.** When the group seems to reach a consensus, summarize and see whether all members agree.

Ending the Meeting and Following Up

- **Review meeting decisions.** At the end of the meeting, consider using a round-robin to be sure everyone understands what has been decided. Discuss action items, and establish a schedule for completion.

- **Distribute minutes of the meeting.** A few days after the meeting, distribute the minutes. Use an e-mail template, if available.

- **Remind people of action items**. Follow up by calling people to see whether they are completing the actions recommended at the meeting.

2-3 Practicing Active Listening

The famous American entrepreneur and publisher Malcolm Forbes wrote, "The art of conversation lies in listening." Now, you may be thinking, everyone knows how to listen. Most of us believe that listening is an automatic response to noise. We do it without thinking. Perhaps that explains why so many of us are poor listeners. In this section we explore the importance of listening, the kinds of listening required in the workplace, and improving listening skills. Although many of the tips for improving your listening skills will be effective in your personal life, our discussion centers primarily on workplace and employment needs.

As you learned earlier, workers are communicating more than ever before, largely because of nearly omnipresent Internet access, unprecedented mobility afforded by electronic devices, social media, teamwork, global competition, and an emphasis on customer service. Experts point out that listening is an important leadership skill.[50] Researchers tell us that active, empathic listening—when we sincerely strive to understand others' viewpoints—is the most effective form of listening.[51] Only when we are mindful, meaning fully present, can we truly listen to build trust and gain respect.

Listening skills are important for career success, organization effectiveness, and worker satisfaction. Numerous studies and experts report that good listeners make good managers; in fact, good listeners achieve success at all stages of their careers.[52] Studies of Fortune 500 companies report that professional and interpersonal skills such as listening, writing, and speaking are most likely to determine hiring and career success.[53] Levi Strauss CEO Chip Bergh succeeded in returning Levi Strauss to profitability. As soon as he took the helm of the ailing company, Bergh started with a "listening tour" to assess the extent of cultural change needed. Then, an in-home visit with a family in Bangalore, India, inspired a new Levi's tagline and showed Bergh "how much value can come from listening to consumers."[54]

Reality Check

Listening: An Overlooked Leadership Skill

"360 listening: This is where the magic happens. You're not only listening to what the person is saying, but how they're saying it—and, even better, what they're *not* saying. . . . Even in a world of limitless, instantaneous, global connection, the most powerful mode of communication is that of two people listening."[55]

—Melissa Daimler, *Head of Learning and Organizational Development at Twitter*

2-3a Identifying Poor Listening Habits

Although executives and employees devote the bulk of their communication time to listening, research suggests that they're not very good at it. In fact, most of us are poor listeners. Experts say that most people recall only between 25 and 50 percent of what they hear. Expect your boss, your coworkers, and your customers to retain only half or less of the conversation.[56]

Poor listening habits may result from several factors. Lack of training is one significant factor. Few schools give as much emphasis to listening as they do to the development of reading, speaking, and writing skills. In addition, our listening skills may be less than perfect because of the large number of competing sounds and stimuli in our lives that interfere with concentration. Finally, we are inefficient listeners because we are able to process speech much faster than others can speak. Although most speakers talk at about 125 to 175 words per minute, listeners can listen at 450 words per minute.[57] The resulting lag time fosters daydreaming, which clearly reduces listening efficiency.

2-3b Understanding Workplace Listening

On the job you can expect to be involved in many types of listening. These include listening to supervisors, colleagues, and customers. If you are an entry-level employee, you will probably be most concerned with listening to superiors. But you also must develop skills for listening to colleagues and team members. As you advance in your career and enter the ranks of management, you will need skills for listening to subordinates. Finally, the entire organization must listen to customers, employees, government agencies, all stakeholders, and the public at large to compete in today's social and mobile business environment, in a service-oriented economy.

Listening to Supervisors   One of your most important tasks will be listening to instructions, assignments, and explanations about how to do your work. You will be listening to learn and comprehend. To focus totally on the speaker, be sure you are not distracted by noisy surroundings or other tasks. Don't take phone calls, and don't try to complete another job while listening with one ear. Show your interest by leaning forward and striving for good eye contact.

Above all, take notes. Don't rely on your memory. Details are easy to forget. Taking selective notes also conveys to the speaker your seriousness about hearing accurately and completely. Don't interrupt. When the speaker finishes, paraphrase the instructions in your own words. Ask pertinent questions in a nonthreatening manner. Don't be afraid to ask "dumb" questions, if it means you won't have to do a job twice. Avoid criticizing or arguing when you are listening to a supervisor. Your goals should be to hear accurately and convey an image of competence.

Listening to Colleagues and Teammates   Much of your listening will take place during interactions with coworkers and teammates. In these exchanges two kinds of listening are important. Critical listening enables you to judge and evaluate what you are hearing. You will be listening to decide whether the speaker's message is fact, fiction, or opinion. You will also be listening to decide whether an argument is based on logic or emotion. Critical listening requires an effort on your part. You must remain objective, particularly when you disagree with what you are hearing. Control your tendency to prejudge. Let the speaker complete the message before you evaluate it. Discriminative listening is necessary when you must discern, understand, and remember. It means you must identify main ideas, understand a logical argument, and recognize the purpose of the message.

Listening to Customers   The U.S. economy is heavily service oriented, and the management mantra is *Customers rule*. Many organizations know that listening to customers results in increased sales and profitability as well as improved customer acquisition and retention. Abercrombie & Fitch Company's CEO Fran Horowitz believes that listening helped her reposition her brands and made the company culture more customer-centric and digitally focused. For example, consumer feedback led Hollister to start offering jeans with zippers in addition to the button fly.[58] The simple truth is that consumers feel better about companies that value their opinions—views that are amplified with unprecedented speed and reach by social media.

Andrey_Popov/Shutterstock.com

Smart devices connect us with others potentially across vast distances, but they can also separate us from those closest to us. A person holding a smartphone signals unavailability for a conversation and listening.

FIGURE 2.9 Listening to Customers: Comparing Trained and Untrained Listeners

Untrained Listeners	Trained Listeners
☒ Tune out some of what the customer is saying because they know the answer	☑ Defer judgment; listen for the customer's feelings and assess the situation
☒ Focus on style; mentally dismiss grammar, voice tone, and speech mannerisms	☑ Pay most attention to content, not to appearances, form, or other surface issues
☒ Tend to listen mainly for facts and specific bits of information	☑ Listen completely, trying to really understand every nuance
☒ Attempt to take in everything being said, including exaggerations and errors ("fogging"), only to refute each comment	☑ Listen primarily for the main idea and avoid replying to everything, especially sidetracking issues
☒ Divide their attention among two or more tasks because listening is automatic	☑ Do one thing at a time, realizing that listening is a full-time job
☒ Tend to become distracted by emotional words, have difficulty controlling anger	☑ Control their anger and refuse to fight fire with fire
☒ Interrupt the customer	☑ Are silent for a few seconds after speakers finish to let them complete their thought
☒ Give few, if any, verbal responses	☑ Give affirming statements and invite additional comments

How can organizations improve their customer listening techniques? Because employees are the eyes and ears of the organization, smart companies begin by hiring staff members who genuinely care about customers. Organizations intent on listening also train their employees to listen actively and to ask gentle, probing questions to ensure clear understanding. As you can see in Figure 2.9, employees trained in listening techniques are far more likely to elicit customer feedback and promote goodwill than untrained employees are.

2-3c Improving Workplace Listening

Listening on the job is more difficult than listening in college classes in which experienced professors present well-organized lectures and repeat important points. Workplace listening is more challenging because information is often exchanged casually or under time pressure. It may be disorganized, unclear, and cluttered with extraneous facts. Moreover, your coworkers are often friends. Because they are familiar with you, they may not be as polite and respectful as they are with strangers. Friends tend to interrupt, jump to conclusions, and take each other for granted.

Listening in groups or listening to nonnative speakers further complicates the listening process. In groups, more than one person talks at once, and topics change rapidly. Group members are monitoring both verbal and nonverbal messages to learn what relates to their group roles. Listening to nonnative speakers often creates special challenges. Chapter 3 presents suggestions for communicating across cultures.

2-3d Building Powerful Listening Skills

Despite the complexities and challenges of workplace listening, good listeners on the job must remember that their goal is to listen carefully and to *understand* what is being said so that they can do their work well. The following recommendations can help you improve your workplace listening effectiveness.

1. **Eliminate external and internal distractions.** Move to an area where you can hear without conflicting noises or conversations. Block out surrounding physical distractions. Silence and put away your smartphone, turn off the computer monitor, or shut the laptop. Internally, try to focus totally on the speaker. If other projects are on your mind, put them on the back burner temporarily. When you are emotionally charged, whether angry or extremely happy, it is a good idea to postpone any serious listening.

2. **Become actively involved.** Show that you are listening closely by leaning forward and maintaining eye contact with the speaker. Don't fidget or try to complete another task at the same time you are listening. Listen to more than the spoken words. How are they said? What implied meaning, reasoning, and feelings do you hear behind the spoken words? Does the speaker's body language (eye contact, posture, movements) support or contradict the main message?

3. **Separate facts from opinions.** Facts are truths known to exist; for example, *Apple is located in Cupertino, California*. Opinions are statements of personal judgments or preferences; for example, *Apple stock is always a good investment*. Some opinions are easy to recognize because speakers preface them with statements such as *I think, It seems to me,* and *As far as I'm concerned.* Often, however, listeners must evaluate assertions to decide their validity. Good listeners consider whether speakers are credible and speaking within their areas of competence. They do not automatically accept assertions as facts.

4. **Identify important facts.** Speakers on the job often intersperse important information with casual conversation. Unrelated topics pop up—ball scores, a customer's weird request, a computer glitch, the boss's extravagant new sports car. Your task is to select what's crucial and register it mentally. What step is next in your project? Who does what? What is your role?

5. **Avoid interrupting.** When someone else has the floor, do not interrupt with a quick reply or opinion. Don't signal nonverbal disagreement such as negative head shaking, rolling eyes, sarcastic snorting, or audible sighs. Good listeners let speakers have their say. Interruptions are not only impolite but also prevent you from hearing the speaker's complete thought. Listeners who interrupt with their opinions sidetrack discussions and cause hard feelings.

6. **Ask clarifying questions.** Good listeners wait for the proper moment and then ask questions that do not attack the speaker. Instead of saying, *But I don't understand how you can say that,* a good listener seeks clarification with statements such as *Please help me understand by explaining more about . . . .* Because questions can put you in the driver's seat, think about them in advance. Use **open-ended questions** (those without set answers) to draw out feelings, motivations, ideas, and suggestions. Use **close-ended questions** (those that require a choice among set answers) to identify key factors in a discussion.[59] By the way, don't ask a question unless you are ready to be quiet and listen to the answer.

7. **Paraphrase to increase understanding.** To make sure you understand a speaker, rephrase and summarize a message in your own words. Be objective and nonjudgmental. Remember, your goal is to understand what the speaker has said—not to show how mindless the speaker's words sound when parroted. Remember, too, that other workplace listeners will also benefit from a clear summary of what was said.

8. **Capitalize on lag time.** While you are waiting for a speaker's next idea, use the time to review what the speaker is saying. Separate the central idea, key points, and details. Sometimes you may have to supply the organization. Use lag time to silently rephrase and summarize the speaker's message. Another effective trick for keeping your mind from drifting is to try to guess what a speaker's next point

Humans always communicate, even if they don't speak.

IgorZD/Shutterstock.com

Chapter 2 Professionalism: Team, Meeting, Listening, Nonverbal, and Etiquette Skills will be. Most important, keep your mind focused on the speaker and that person's ideas—not on all the other work waiting for you.

9. **Take notes to ensure retention.** A wise person once said that he would rather have a short pencil than a long memory. If you have a hallway conversation with a colleague and don't have a pen or smart electronic device handy, make a mental note of the important items. Then write them down as soon as possible. Even with seemingly easily remembered facts or instructions, jot them down to ease your mind and to be sure you understand them correctly. Two weeks later you will be glad you did. Be sure you have a good place to store notes about various projects, such as file folders, notebooks, digital files, or handy apps such as Evernote.

10. **Adopt an empathic, humble attitude.** Effective listening requires an empathic mindset. Empathy is being called "the linchpin soft skill" and "the cornerstone of smart leadership"—the arguably most critical quality of the human worker in forming relationships.[61] **Empathy** describes the ability to understand other people's perspectives and emotionally respond to their experiences.[62] Newer research has focused on **humility** as a core quality of leaders that fosters deep listening, respect for diverse views, and an openness to suggestions and feedback.[63] If you are the brash, chatty type who dominates conversations, try to break the habit by letting others talk without interrupting and by asking questions.

Being aware of these tendencies will make you a more sensitive and knowledgeable listener. The checklist that follows sums up useful tips for effective listening.

Checklist

Improving Listening

- **Stop talking.** Accept the role of listener by concentrating on the speaker's words, not on your response.

- **Work hard at listening.** Become actively involved; expect to learn something.

- **Block out competing thoughts.** Concentrate on the message. Don't daydream during lag time.

- **Control the listening environment.** Move to a quiet area where you won't be interrupted by calls, texts, or visitors. Check to be certain that listeners can hear speakers.

- **Maintain an open mind.** Know your biases and try to correct for them. Be tolerant of less abled and different-looking speakers. Provide verbal and nonverbal feedback. Encourage the speaker with comments such as *Yes, I see, OK,* and *Uh huh.* Ask polite questions, and demonstrate alertness by leaning forward.

- **Paraphrase the speaker's ideas.** Silently repeat the message in your own words, sort out the main points, and identify supporting details. In conversation sum up the main points to confirm what was said.

- **Listen between the lines and validate emotion.** Observe nonverbal cues and interpret the feelings of the speaker: What is really being said? Acknowledge the feelings even if you disagree on substance.

- **Distinguish between facts and opinions.** Know the difference between factual statements and opinions stated as assertions.

- **Capitalize on lag time.** Use spare moments to organize, review, anticipate, challenge, and weigh the evidence.

- **Use memory devices.** If the information is important, develop acronyms, links, or rhymes to help you remember it.

- **Take selective notes.** If you are hearing instructions or important data, record the major points; then, revise your notes immediately or verify them with the speaker. Resist the temptation to type your notes or risk becoming distracted. Moreover, research shows that handwritten notes are more memorable.[64]

LEARNING OUTCOME

4 Discuss how effective nonverbal communication can help you advance your career.

2-4 Communicating Nonverbally

Understanding messages often involves more than merely listening to spoken words. Nonverbal cues, in fact, can speak louder than words. These cues include eye contact, facial expression, body movements, time, space, territory, and appearance. All these nonverbal cues affect how a message is interpreted, or decoded, by the receiver.

Defining Nonverbal Communication   Nonverbal communication includes all unwritten and unspoken messages, whether intended or not. These silent signals have a strong effect on receivers. However, understanding them is not simple. Does a downward glance indicate modesty? Fatigue? Does a constant stare reflect coldness? Dullness? Aggression? Do crossed arms mean defensiveness, withdrawal, or just that the person is shivering?

Resolving Clashes Between Words and Nonverbal Cues   Messages are even harder to decipher when the verbal and nonverbal cues do not agree. What will you think if Andrew says he is not angry, but he slams the door when he leaves? What if Rosa assures the hostess that the meal is excellent, but she eats very little? The nonverbal messages in these situations speak louder than the words. In fact, researchers believe that most messages we receive have a strong nonverbal component.

Nonverbal cues contradicting verbal messages speak louder than the words uttered. In one experiment speakers delivered a positive message but averted their eyes as they spoke. Listeners perceived the overall message to be negative. Moreover, listeners thought that gaze aversion suggested deception or lack of respect.[65] The lesson here is that effective communicators must be certain that all their nonverbal messages reinforce their spoken words and their professional goals. To make sure that you're on the right track to nonverbal communication competency, let's look at the silent nonverbal messages our bodies send.

2-4a Your Body Sends Silent Messages

Psychologist and philosopher Paul Watzlawick claimed that we cannot not communicate.

This means that every behavior is sending a message even if we don't use words. The eyes, face, and body convey meaning without a single syllable being spoken. Although this discussion covers many forms of nonverbal communication, we are especially concerned with workplace applications. Think about how you can use the following nonverbal cues positively in your career.

Eye Contact.   The eyes have been called the windows to the soul. Even if they don't reveal the soul, the eyes are often the best predictor of a speaker's true feelings and attitudes. Most of us cannot look another person straight in the eye and lie. As a result, in North American culture we tend to believe people who look directly at us. Sustained eye contact suggests trust and admiration; brief eye contact signals fear or stress. Prolonged eye contact or staring, though, can be intrusive and intimidating.

Good eye contact enables the message sender to see whether a receiver is paying attention, showing respect, responding favorably, or feeling distress. From the receiver's perspective, good eye contact, in North American culture, reveals the speaker's sincerity, confidence, and truthfulness. However, nonverbal cues, including eye contact, have different meanings in different cultures. Chapter 3 presents more information about cultural influences on nonverbal cues.

Facial Expression.   The expression on a communicator's face can be almost as revealing of emotion as the eyes. Experts estimate that the human face can display more than 250,000 expressions.[66] To hide their feelings, some people can control these expressions and maintain so-called poker faces. Most of us, however, display our emotions openly and often unintentionally. Raising or lowering the eyebrows, squinting the eyes, swallowing nervously, clenching the jaw, smiling broadly—these voluntary and involuntary facial expressions can add to or entirely replace verbal messages.

Posture and Gestures.   An individual's posture can convey anything from high status and self-confidence to shyness and submissiveness. Leaning toward a speaker suggests attentiveness and interest; pulling away or shrinking back denotes fear, distrust, anxiety, or disgust. Similarly, gestures can communicate entire thoughts via simple movements. However, the meanings of some of these movements differ in other cultures. In the United States and Canada, for example, forming the thumb and forefinger in a circle means everything is OK. But in parts of South America, the OK sign is obscene.

In the workplace you can make a good impression by controlling your posture and gestures. When speaking, make sure your upper body is aligned with the person to whom you're talking. Erect posture sends a message of confidence, competence, diligence, and strength. Women are advised to avoid tilting their heads to the side when making an important point. This gesture undermines their perceived self-confidence.[67]

Be careful, however, before attaching specific meanings to gestures or actions, because behavior and its interpretations strongly depend on context and on one's cultural background, as you will see in Chapter 3.

2-4b Time, Space, and Territory Send Silent Messages

In addition to nonverbal messages transmitted by your body, three external elements convey information in the communication process: time, space, and territory.

Time. How we structure and use time tells observers about our personality and attitudes. For example, when Warren Buffett, industrialist, investor, and philanthropist, gives a visitor a prolonged interview, he signals his respect for, interest in, and approval of the visitor or the topic being discussed. By sharing his valuable time, he sends a clear nonverbal message. Likewise, when Arron Sota twice arrives late for a meeting, it could mean that the meeting has low priority to Arron, that he is a self-centered, perhaps hostile person, or that he has little self-discipline. These are assumptions that typical Americans might make. In other cultures and regions, though, punctuality is viewed differently. In the workplace you can send positive nonverbal messages by being on time for meetings and appointments, staying on task during meetings, and giving ample time to appropriate projects and individuals.

Space. How we order the space around us tells something about ourselves and our objectives. Whether the space is a bedroom, a dorm room, or an office, people reveal themselves in the design and grouping of their furniture. Generally, the more formal the arrangement, the more formal and closed the communication style. An executive who seats visitors in a row of chairs across from his desk sends a message of aloofness and a desire for separation. A team

FIGURE 2.10   Four Space Zones for Social Interaction

Intimate Zone
(1 to 1.5 feet)

Personal Zone
(1.5 to 4 feet)

Social Zone
(4 to 12 feet)

Public Zone
(12 or more feet)

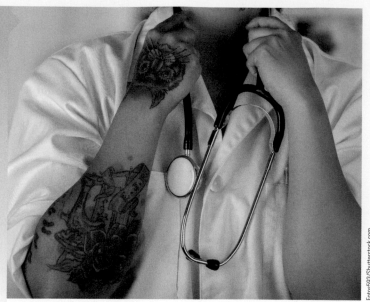

Fotos593/Shutterstock.com

leader who arranges chairs informally in a circle rather than in straight rows or a rectangular pattern conveys her desire for a more open, egalitarian exchange of ideas. A manager who creates an open office space with few partitions separating workers' desks seeks to encourage an unrestricted flow of communication and work among departments.

Territory.   Each of us has a certain area that we feel is our own territory, whether it is a specific spot or just the space around us. Your father may have a favorite chair in which he is most comfortable, a cook might not tolerate intruders in the kitchen, and veteran employees may feel that certain work areas and tools belong to them. We all maintain zones of privacy in which we feel comfortable. Figure 2.10 categorizes the four zones of social interaction among North Americans, as formulated by anthropologist Edward T. Hall.[70] Notice that North Americans are a bit standoffish; only intimate friends and family may stand closer than about 1.5 feet. If someone violates that territory, we may feel uncomfortable and step back to reestablish our space. In the workplace be aware of the territorial needs of others and don't invade their space.

2-4c Appearance Sends Silent Messages

Much like the personal appearance of an individual, the physical appearance of a business document transmits immediate and important nonverbal messages. Ideally, these messages should be pleasing to the eye.

Eye Appeal of Business Documents.   The way an e-mail, letter, memo, or report looks can have either a positive or a negative effect on the receiver. Sloppy e-mails send a nonverbal message that you are in a terrific hurry or that you do not care about the receiver. Envelopes—through their postage, stationery, and printing—can suggest that the messages they carry are routine, important, or junk mail. Letters and reports can look neat, professional, well organized, and attractive—or just the opposite.

In succeeding chapters you will learn how to create documents that send positive nonverbal messages through their appearance, format, organization, readability, and correctness.

Personal Appearance.   The way you look—your clothing, grooming, and posture—transmits an instant nonverbal message about you. Based on what they see, viewers make quick judgments about your status, credibility, personality, and potential. Business communicators who look the part are more likely to be successful in working with supervisors, colleagues, and customers. Because appearance is such a powerful force in business, some aspiring professionals are turning for help to image consultants (who charge up to $500 an hour!).

What do image consultants say? They suggest investing in appropriate, professional-looking clothing and accessories. Remember that quality is more important than quantity. Avoid flashy garments, clunky jewelry, garish makeup, and overpowering colognes. Pay attention to good grooming, including a neat hairstyle, body cleanliness, polished shoes, and clean nails. Project confidence in your posture, both standing and sitting.

In recent years the trend is the movement toward one or more days per week of casual dress at work. Be aware, though, that casual clothes change the image you project and also may affect your work style. It doesn't help that many workers are confused about what constitutes "business casual." See the Career Coach box regarding the pros and cons of casual apparel.

In the preceding discussion of nonverbal communication, you learned that each of us sends and responds to thousands of nonverbal messages daily in our personal and work lives. You can harness the power of silent messages by reviewing Figure 2.11 and studying the tips in the following checklist.

FIGURE 2.11   **Sending Positive Nonverbal Signals in the Workplace**

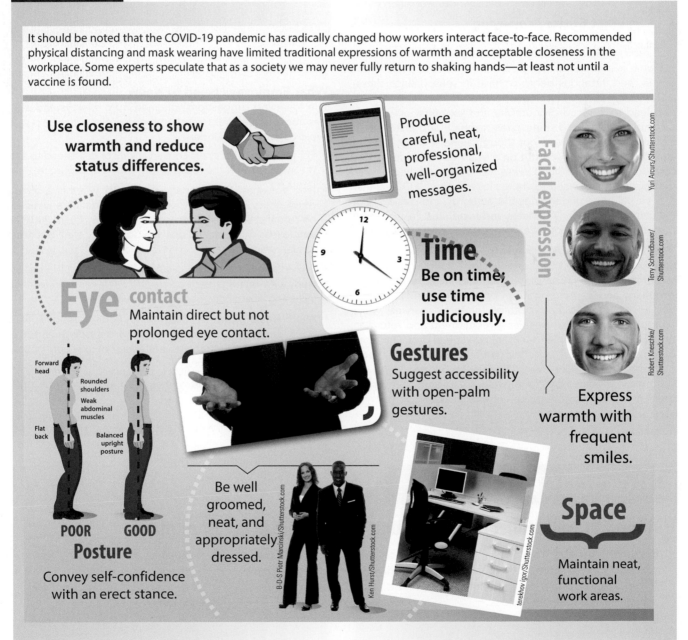

It should be noted that the COVID-19 pandemic has radically changed how workers interact face-to-face. Recommended physical distancing and mask wearing have limited traditional expressions of warmth and acceptable closeness in the workplace. Some experts speculate that as a society we may never fully return to shaking hands—at least not until a vaccine is found.

Use closeness to show warmth and reduce status differences.

Produce careful, neat, professional, well-organized messages.

Facial expression

Eye contact
Maintain direct but not prolonged eye contact.

Time
Be on time; use time judiciously.

Forward head
Rounded shoulders
Weak abdominal muscles
Flat back
Balanced upright posture

Gestures
Suggest accessibility with open-palm gestures.

Express warmth with frequent smiles.

POOR   GOOD
Posture
Convey self-confidence with an erect stance.

Be well groomed, neat, and appropriately dressed.

Space
Maintain neat, functional work areas.

Career Coach

Dressing the Part

Your choice of work clothes sends a strong nonverbal message about you. Unfortunately, wardrobe policies vary greatly in American businesses. Overall, the start-up culture and remote work have prompted even traditional bastions of formal attire, banking and consulting, to relax their once-stringent dress codes. After JPMorgan Chase and PricewaterhouseCoopers embraced business casual wear, Goldman Sachs too is allowing a rather vague "firmwide flexible dress code."[71] Yet poorly written gender-based dress codes can expose companies to litigation and negatively affect transgender workers.[72]

What Critics Are Saying

Some employers oppose casual dress because, in their opinion, too many workers push the boundaries of what is acceptable. They contend that absenteeism, tardiness, and flirtatious behavior have increased since dress-down policies were first implemented. Relaxed dress codes also lead to reduced productivity and lax behavior.[73] British psychologist Karen J. Pine cites research suggesting that clothing not only reflects our thoughts and feelings but can change them, too: "[W]e put on a smart outfit, we feel more confident. We slob around in casual clothes and there's a risk that our thinking becomes more slovenly too."[74] Others fear that casual attire undermines the authority and credibility of executives, particularly females and minorities.[75] Also, some customers might disapprove of casually attired employees.

What Supporters Are Saying

Supporters argue that comfortable clothes and relaxed working environments lift employee morale, increase employee creativity, and improve internal communication.[76] Employees appreciate reduced clothing-related expenses, while employers use casual dress as a recruitment and retention tool. Because employees seem to love casual dress, nine out of ten employers have adopted casual-dress days for at least part of the workweek—even if it is just on Fridays during the summer. Advocates of casual wear also argue that formal dress is exclusive and tends to entrench class divisions.[77]

marvent/Shutterstock.com

What Employees Need to Know

The following suggestions, gleaned from surveys and articles about casual-dress trends in the workplace, can help you avoid casual-attire blunders.

- For job interviews, dress conservatively or call ahead to ask the interviewer or the receptionist what is appropriate.

- Find out what your company allows. Ask whether a dress-down policy is in place. Observe what others are wearing on casual-dress days. JPMorgan Chase provided its 240,000 employees with detailed dos and don'ts to define business casual wear.

- If your company has no casual-attire policy, volunteer to work with management to develop relevant guidelines, including illustrations of suitable casual attire.

- Avoid wearing the following items: T-shirts, sandals, flip-flops, shoes without socks, backless dresses, tank tops, shorts, miniskirts, spandex, athletic shoes, hiking boots, baseball caps, and visors.

- When meeting customers, dress as well as or better than they do.

Checklist

Building Strong Nonverbal Communication Skills in the Workplace

- **Establish and maintain eye contact.** Remember that in North America appropriate eye contact signals interest, attentiveness, confidence, and credibility.

- **Use posture to show interest.** Encourage interaction by leaning forward, sitting or standing erect, and looking alert.

- **Reduce or eliminate physical barriers.** Move out from behind a desk or lectern; arrange meeting chairs in a circle.

- **Improve your decoding skills.** Watch facial expressions and body language to understand the complete verbal and nonverbal message being communicated.

- **Probe for more information.** When you perceive nonverbal cues that contradict verbal meanings, politely seek additional clues (*I'm not sure I understand, Please tell me more about ...* or *Do you mean that ... ?*).

- **Interpret nonverbal meanings in context.** Make nonverbal assessments only when you understand a situation or a culture.

- **Associate with people from diverse cultures.** Learn about other cultures to widen your knowledge and tolerance of intercultural nonverbal messages.

- **Appreciate the power of appearance.** Keep in mind that the appearance of your business documents, your business space,

and yourself sends immediate positive or negative messages to others.

- **Observe yourself on video.** Ensure that your verbal and nonverbal messages are in sync by recording and evaluating yourself making a presentation.

- **Enlist friends and family.** Ask friends and family members to monitor your conscious and unconscious body movements and gestures to help you become a more effective communicator.

2-5 Developing Professionalism and Business Etiquette Skills at the Office and Online

LEARNING OUTCOME

5 Examine how developing professionalism and business etiquette skills can improve your competitive advantage.

As you have seen in Chapter 1, interpersonal skills are the hallmark of a professional. Your future employer will expect you to possess emotional intelligence or interpersonal skills in addition to your technical training. Besides complex communication skills, these twenty-first-century attributes include curiosity, creativity, adaptability, resilience, and critical thinking, as well as the ability to collaborate and thrive in diverse environments.[78] Consulting firm McKinsey identifies "cognitive skills, creativity, social and emotional skills" as safeguards—along with higher educational attainment—against job loss from automation.[79] In the digital age, professionalism also means maintaining a positive online presence, a subject we discuss in Chapters 1 and 7.

Business etiquette is more about attitude than about formal rules of behavior. Attitude is a desire to show others consideration, courtesy, and respect. It includes a desire to make others feel comfortable. Good manners and a businesslike, professional demeanor are among the top interpersonal skills that employers seek in job candidates. But can you really learn how to be courteous, civil, and professional? Of course! This section gives you a few pointers.

2-5a Understanding Professionalism and the Cost of Incivility

Not every job seeker is aware of the employer's expectations, even the most basic ones. In some regions of the United States where the opioid crisis is raging, factories struggle to fill openings with candidates who can pass a drug test. One official puts it bluntly: "Employers just want someone who will get up, dress up, show up, shut up, and never give up."[80] Some new-hires have no idea that absenteeism or tardiness is grounds for termination. Many employees are sabotaging their careers by sprinkling their conversation with *like, you know,* and uptalk (making declarative statements sound like questions).

Projecting and maintaining a professional image can make a real difference in helping you obtain the job of your dreams. Once you get that job, you are more likely to be taken seriously and much more likely to be promoted if you look and sound professional. Do not send the wrong message with unwitting or unprofessional behavior. Figure 2.12 reviews seven areas you will want to check to be sure you are projecting professionalism.

FIGURE 2.12 Projecting Professionalism When You Communicate

Unprofessional | Professional

Unprofessional		Professional
Uptalk, a singsong speech pattern, making sentences sound like questions; *like* used as a filler; *go* for *said*; slang; poor grammar and profanity.	**Speech habits**	Recognizing that your credibility can be seriously damaged by sounding uneducated, crude, or adolescent.
Sloppy messages with incomplete sentences, misspelled words, exclamation points, IM slang, and mindless chatter. E-mail addresses such as *partyanimal@gmail.com, snugglykitty@icloud.com,* or *hotmama@outlook.com.*	**E-mail**	Messages with subjects, verbs, and punctuation free from IM abbreviations; messages that are concise and spelled correctly even when brief. E-mail addresses that include a name, or a positive, businesslike expression.
Suggestive Twitter handles and user names that point to an immature, unhealthy lifestyle. Posts that reveal political, religious, and other personal learnings.	**Internet, social media**	Real name Twitter handles and user names that don't sound cute or like chatroom nicknames. Posts in good taste, fit for public consumption.
An outgoing message with strident background music, weird sounds, or a joke message.	**Voice mail**	An outgoing message that states your name or phone number and provides instructions for leaving a message.
Soap operas, thunderous music, or a TV football game playing noisily in the background when you answer the phone.	**Telephone presence**	A quiet background when you answer the telephone, especially if you are expecting a prospective employer's call.
Using electronics during business meetings for unrelated purposes or during conversations with fellow employees; raising your voice (cell yell); forcing others to overhear your calls.	**Cell phones, tablets**	Turning off phone and message notification, both audible and vibrate, during meetings; using your smart devices only for meeting-related purposes.
Sending and receiving text messages during meetings, allowing texting to interrupt face-to-face conversations, or texting when driving.	**Texting**	Sending appropriate business text messages only when necessary (perhaps when a cell phone call would disturb others).

2-5b Gaining an Etiquette Edge in a Networked World

In the job market today and in the future, employers will reward your awareness of etiquette and courtesy. Business etiquette, civility, and goodwill may seem out of place in today's fast-paced offices. However, when two candidates have equal qualifications, the one who appears to be more polished and professional is more likely to be hired and promoted.

As workloads increase and face-to-face meetings decline, bad behavior is becoming alarmingly common in the American workplace and may exact a high cost. Researchers found that even low-level rude exchanges spread like contagion; they taint a worker's entire day.[81] Employers, of course, suffer from the resulting drop in productivity and exodus of talent. Employees, too, suffer. They are more likely to disengage or quit and experience stress responses such as digestive problems, sleeplessness, and headaches.[82] Workplace rudeness also turns customers away.[83] Businesses are responding to increasing incidents of desk rage and cyberbullying in American workplaces by establishing policies to enforce civility. In short, it is not hard to understand why employers are looking for people who are courteous, polite, respectful, and well mannered.

Figure 2.13 summarizes the many components of professional workplace behavior and identifies six main dimensions that will ease your entry into the world of work.

Good manners, on the other hand, convey a positive image of an organization. People like to do business with those who show respect and treat others politely. Most of us also like to work in a pleasant environment. Considering how much time Americans spend at work, it makes sense

FIGURE 2.13 The Six Dimensions of Professional Behavior

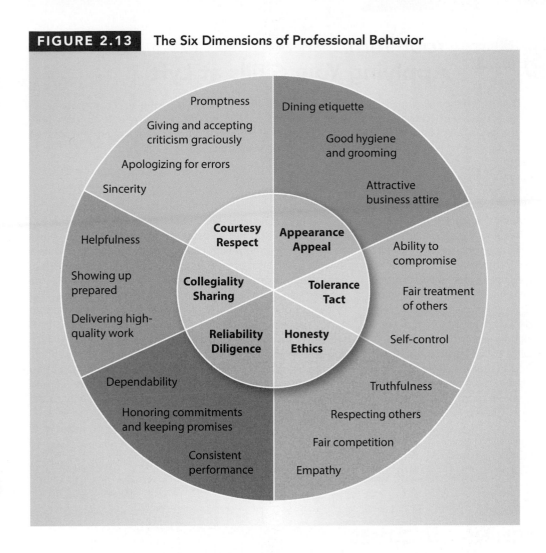

that people prefer an agreeable environment to one that is rude and uncivil. Remember, too, that bad behavior can be recorded and posted for the world to see, practically forever!

You don't have to become an etiquette nut, but you might need to polish your social competencies a little to be an effective businessperson today. Here are a few simple pointers:

- **Use polite words.** Be generous with words and phrases such as *please, thank you*, and *you're welcome.*

- **Express sincere appreciation and praise.** Tell coworkers how much you appreciate their efforts. Remember that written and specific thank-you notes are even better than saying thanks.

- **Be selective in sharing personal information.** Avoid talking about health concerns, personal relationships, or finances in the office.

- **Don't put people down.** If you have a reputation for criticizing people, your coworkers will begin to wonder what you are saying behind their backs.

- **Respect coworkers' space.** Turn down the ringer on your business phone, minimize the use of speakerphones, and turn your personal cell phone down or off during business hours. Avoid wearing heavy perfumes or bringing strong-smelling food.

- **Rise above others' rudeness.** Don't use profanity or participate in questionable joke-telling.

- **Be considerate when sharing space and equipment with others.** Clean up after yourself.

- **Choose the high road in conflict.** Avoid letting discussions degenerate into shouting matches. Keep a calm voice tone and focus on the work rather than on personality differences.

- **Disagree agreeably.** You may not agree with everyone, but you should respect their opinions.

Zooming In

Your Turn:
Applying Your Skills at Lyft

Uber outperforms its smaller rival internationally, but Lyft is pursuing its research and development partnerships with great resolve, even abroad. A team in Lyft's new Level 5 office in Munich, Germany, is now developing specialized mapping software that will help maneuver the company's fully autonomous cars through urban landscapes. The Germans have not yet visited Lyft's unique Mission Bay headquarters in San Francisco. They are not familiar with the sprawling office or with their American counterparts' informal work culture. An on-site visit is scheduled later in the year.

With an open office space and relaxed atmosphere, Lyft is designed to encourage teamwork. Informal collaboration may occur when several employees gather over company-provided lunches. Shorter, planned meetings take place in small meeting rooms named after animals. However, as different as Lyft's culture is from traditional companies, its leaders know the importance of keeping employees informed *and* motivated. Sometimes that means meetings.

Before beginning your task, take a moment to watch the six-minute video *Lyft's Fuzzy Pink Mission Headquarters* on YouTube, which illustrates Lyft's one-of-a-kind corporate headquarters. Check out *Life at Lyft* while you're at it. To learn more about benefits at corporate Lyft and what staffers think of their workplace, visit Glassdoor.

Your Task

You are a new-hire at Lyft, and your boss, Anika, is preparing a virtual meeting that will involve 15 staffers from the Lyft headquarters and ten software engineers in Munich. Anika would like your help with organizing the meeting and asks that you draft a list of tasks needed to ensure that the video-conference is productive. The main purpose is to welcome the German team and introduce the headquarters as well as Lyft's corporate culture. Anika also wants your ideas about adding an element of fun and humor to the meeting, as is typical at the company. Write an e-mail to your boss in which you outline the steps that lead to effective virtual meetings, or discuss the steps with a teammate before presenting them in class. Use your creativity and what you've learned about Lyft to decide whether and how to bring levity to the meeting.

SUMMARY OF LEARNING OUTCOMES

1 **Explain why teamwork is important in the digital-era workplace and how you can contribute to excellent team performance.**

- Teams are popular because they lead to better decisions, faster responses, increased productivity, greater buy-in, less resistance to change, improved morale, and reduced risks.

- Virtual teams are collaborations among remote coworkers connecting with technology.

- The four phases of team development are forming, storming, norming, and performing.

- Positive group behaviors include establishing and following rules, resolving differences, being supportive, praising others, and summarizing points of understanding.

- Negative behaviors include showing contempt for others, wasting the team's time, and withdrawing.

- Successful teams are small and diverse, agree on a purpose and procedures, confront conflict, communicate well, don't compete but collaborate, are ethical, and share leadership.

2 **Identify effective practices and technologies for planning and participating in face-to-face meetings and virtual meetings.**

- Before a meeting businesspeople determine its purpose and location, choose participants, use a digital calendar, and distribute an agenda.

- Experienced meeting leaders establish ground rules, move the meeting along, and confront any conflict; they end the meeting on time, make sure everyone is heard, and distribute meeting minutes promptly.

- Virtual meetings save travel costs but require attention to communication technology and the needs of dispersed participants regarding issues such as different time zones and language barriers.

- Virtual meetings demand specific procedures to handle questions, noise, lack of media richness, and turn-taking. Because they are impersonal, virtual meetings benefit from building camaraderie and trust.

3 Describe and apply active listening techniques.

- Most of us are poor listeners; careers and organizational success depend on active listening.

- A fast processing speed allows us to let our minds wander; as untrained listeners, we are easily distracted.

- Listening to supervisors on the job, workers should take notes, avoid interrupting, ask pertinent questions, and paraphrase what they hear.

- When dealing with coworkers, good listeners identify facts, main ideas, and logical arguments.

- When listening to customers, employees should ask gentle, probing questions to ensure understanding.

- Effective listeners control distractions, show active involvement, separate facts from opinions, identify important facts, refrain from interrupting, ask clarifying questions, paraphrase, take advantage of lag time, take notes to ensure retention, and adopt an empathic, humble attitude.

4 Discuss how effective nonverbal communication can help you advance your career.

- Be aware of nonverbal cues such as eye contact, facial expression, and posture that send silent, highly believable messages.

- Understand that how you use time, space, and territory is interpreted by the receiver, who also reads the eye appeal of your business documents and your personal appearance.

- Build solid nonverbal skills by keeping eye contact, maintaining good posture, reducing physical barriers, improving your decoding skills, and probing for more information.

- Interpret nonverbal meanings in context, learn about other cultures, and understand the impact of appearance—of documents, your office space, and yourself.

5 Examine how developing professionalism and business etiquette skills can improve your competitive advantage.

- Interpersonal skills and emotional intelligence are characteristics of a professional; communication skills, curiosity, creativity, adaptability, resilience, and critical thinking are desirable workplace behaviors that are complemented by a positive online presence.

- Business etiquette is an attitude or desire to show others consideration, courtesy, and respect. Good manners are among the top skills employers seek.

- Practicing business etiquette on the job and online can put you ahead of others who lack polish.

- Good workplace behavior includes using polite words, giving sincere praise, respecting coworkers' space, rising above others' rudeness, taking the high road in conflict, and disagreeing agreeably.

Key Terms

hard skills 41

soft skills 41

matrixed teams 42

collaborative overload 43

virtual teams 43

groupthink 45

social loafing 46

virtual meetings 48

ghosted, ghosting 50

empathic listening 57

mindful 57

critical listening 58

discriminative listening 58

open-ended questions 60

close-ended questions 60

empathy 61

humility 61

desk rage 68

cyberbullying 68

Critical Thinking

1. Cal Newport, computer scientist and author, blames open-office layouts and relentless collaboration for a decline in concentrated deep thinking. He cites research suggesting that even short interruptions significantly increase the total time needed to complete a task. Other studies show that multitasking not only drags out work but reduces its quality. One researcher believes that jumping from one task to another reduces

efficiency because of "attention residue." As the mind turns to a new task, it is still thinking about the old task.[84] Are you easily distracted? What techniques help you concentrate? (L.O. 1)

2. Evaluate the following humorous analogy between the murder of a famous Roman emperor and the deadening effect of meetings: "This month is the 2,053rd anniversary of the death of Julius Caesar, who pronounced himself dictator for life before running the idea past the Roman Senate. On his way to a meeting, he was met by a group of senators who, wishing to express their unhappiness with his vocational aspirations, stabbed him to death. Moral of the story: Beware of meetings."[85] Is the comparison fitting? What might the author of the article have wanted to convey? (L.O. 2)

3. Why do executives and managers spend more time listening than do workers? (L.O. 3)

4. What arguments could you give for or against the idea that body language is a science with principles that specialists can interpret accurately? (L.O. 4)

5. **Ethical Issue:** In his book *The Ideal Team Player*, management consultant Patrick Lencioni describes what he calls the three virtues that effective team members possess: They are *humble*, *hungry*, and *smart*, he believes. Humble means little ego and giving credit to others. Hungry describes the drive to get things done. Smart refers to emotional intelligence, to being interpersonally aware and appropriate. How does the emphasis on humility square with the conspicuous, hard-driving bosses like Elon Musk or Jerry Jones, the brash owner of the Dallas Cowboys? (L.O. 1).

Activities

2.1 Team Decision Making: Majority, Consensus, or What? (L.O. 1)

Team

YOUR TASK In small groups decide which decision strategy is best for the following situations:

a. A large Internet retailer needs to identify a strategic location for a second headquarters.

b. A team of 12 workers at a freight-forwarding company must decide whether to choose the iPad or an Android tablet for their new equipment. Some team members dislike Apple's closed system and prefer the more open Android platform. However, Apple offers more apps.

c. Company employees numbering more than 1,200 must decide whether to adopt new health-care and long-term-care plans proposed by management or stay with the current plans. A yes-or-no vote is required.

d. The owner of your company is meeting with all managers to decide which departments will move into a new facility.

e. Appointed by management, an employee team is charged with proposing new guidelines for casual Fridays. Management feels that too many employees are abusing the privilege.

f. Members of a business club must select new officers.

g. A group of town officials and volunteers must decide how to organize a town website and social media presence. Only a few members have technical expertise.

h. An ad-hoc personnel committee of three members (two supervisors and the manager) must decide on promotions within a department.

2.2 Workplace Conflict Resolution: Put the Six-Step Procedure to Work (L.O. 1)

Team

Although conflict is a normal part of every workplace, if unresolved, it can create hard feelings and reduce productivity.

YOUR TASK Analyze the following scenarios. In teams, discuss each scenario and apply the six-step procedure for dealing with conflict outlined in Figure 2.3. Choose two of the scenarios to role-play with two of your team members taking roles.

a. During an important meeting, several agenda items deal require actions that are crucial to the success of a current project. They require that key decisions be made—fast! As usual, Jill is telling entertaining anecdotes without regard for the meeting's urgency. John is becoming impatient and irritated. He doesn't understand why the other meeting participants, and the boss in particular, don't stop Jill's antics.

b. Kacey, an accountant, cannot complete her report until Rashawn, a salesman, provides her with all the necessary numbers and documentation. Kacey thinks that Rashawn is a procrastinator who forces her to deliver a rush job, thus causing her great stress and increasing the likelihood of error. Rashawn believes that Kacey is exerting pressure on both of them and setting unrealistic deadlines. As the conflict intensifies, productivity decreases.

c. A company policy manual is posted and updated on the company intranet. Employees must sign that they have read and understand the manual. A conflict arises when team member Alvaro insists that employees should sign electronically. Fellow team member Hallie thinks that a paper form should be signed by employees so that better records may be kept.

d. The author of a lengthy report refuses to collaborate with a colleague on future projects because she believes that her colleague's review of her document was superficial, short, and essentially useless. The report author is angry at the lack of attention her 25-page paper received.

e. Two management team members disagree about a new company social media policy. One wants to ban Facebook and Twitter use totally. The other believes that an outright ban is impossible to implement and might raise the ire of employees. He is more concerned with limiting Internet misuse, including visits to online game, pornography, and shopping sites. The management team members agree that they need a social media policy, but they disagree on what to allow and what to prohibit.

f. A manager and his assistant plan to attend a conference together at a resort location. Six weeks before the conference, the company announces a cutback and limits conference attendance to one person. The assistant, who has developed a presentation specifically for the conference, feels that he should be the one to attend. Travel arrangements must be made immediately.

2.3 H Is for Humility: Test Your H Factor
(L.O. 1, 3)

`E-Mail` `Social Media` `Team` `Web`

The outdoor apparel company Patagonia selects job candidates based on humility when they first set foot in the building. After the interview, recruiters ask receptionists how the applicants interacted with the front desk. Disrespectful or self-absorbed behavior gets the boot. Kibeom Lee and Michael Ashton, two Canadian researchers studying personality and leadership behavior, have created what they call the H factor. It is a cluster of personal characteristics the experts observed consistently in people who refuse to manipulate others, who don't bend the rules, and who avoid greed and hypocrisy. Put positively, the H factor is a mix of traits such as sincerity, modesty, fairness, truthfulness, and unpretentiousness.[86] To measure humility and thus assess a person's H factor, Lee and Ashton developed a free online test they dubbed the HEXACO Personal Inventory.

A lead researcher in business ethics at Brigham Young University found that teams with humble chief executives performed better and did higher-quality work than teams led by managers exhibiting less humility. Charismatic, opinionated, and attention-seeking bosses are not always good for the health of their organizations, another expert believes: "[S]uch leaders tend to ruin their companies because they take on more than they can handle, are overconfident and don't listen to feedback from others."[87]

YOUR TASK Individually or as a team, visit the **Hexaco.org** website (search using the name) and take the HEXACO-PI-R inventory. Expect to spend approximately 15 minutes answering multiple-choice questions. Your responses will provide you with scores measuring the six major personality categories: Honesty-Humility, Emotionality, eXtraversion, Agreeableness (versus Anger), Conscientiousness, and Openness to Experience as well as multiple subcategories for each. Select Self-Report if you wish to assess yourself or Observer-Report if you want to fill out the questionnaire about someone else. Once you receive your scores in the six broad factors and 25 narrow facets, download the HEXACO-PI-R as a PDF from the website.

Compare your results with the median scores and the middle 80 percent of all test takers' scores (10th to 90th percentiles). Do you believe the test has measured your personality traits accurately? You may compare scores with teammates or in class, as directed by your instructor. If asked to summarize your results or those of your teammates, write an e-mail or memo (see Chapter 7) discussing the main outcomes of the inventory. Alternatively, your instructor may ask you to describe (orally in class or in writing) which personal characteristics are most suitable for a businessperson in a leadership role and explain why. You may also be asked to tweet about the inventory, inviting others to take the test.

2.4 Scheduling a Meeting With a Doodle Poll (L.O. 2)

`Communication Technology` `Team`

Have you ever planned an event for multiple invitees? If yes, then you know how difficult it is to find a date and time that works for most participants. Businesspeople use Outlook and other calendar apps that allow them to call a meeting, but even then, picking the right day and time can be a challenge and occasionally a hit-and-miss proposition. Enter Doodle. This free Web-based poll generator will help you schedule the best date and time for your group.

YOUR TASK Your instructor may divide the class into teams and ask a representative of each team to call a study group meeting or a social event for your business society. As the designated group leader, you will open a free account with Doodle (go to **doodle.com**). You won't need to input much personal information and can start sending out free basic scheduling polls almost instantly.

Follow these steps: After creating your free account, name your event. Add a location and an optional note. Follow the on-screen options. Suggest several dates and times in the calendar. Invite participants by typing their e-mail addresses. If you synced your address book, the e-mail addresses will appear automatically. Or e-mail the link you generate at the end of the poll to your group members. After your invitees fill in their available slots, confirm the date and time that works best for most if not all participants. If possible, rotate the responsibilities within the team; share the scheduling duties with the other group members and in class.

2.5 Making the Most of Meetings (L.O. 2)

`Team` `Web`

"Meetings are indispensable when you don't want to do anything," observed the late economist John Kenneth Galbraith, and management guru Peter Drucker claimed: "Meetings are a symptom of a bad organization. The fewer meetings, the better."[88] More recently, Tesla and SpaceX founder and CEO Elon Musk grumbled that "Excessive meetings are the blight of big companies and almost always get worse over time."[89] Amazon chief executive Jeff Bezos hates unproductive meetings and keeps them small by employing his two pizza rule. He never invites more people than could be fed by two pizzas.[90]

Much venomous ink has been spilled decrying meetings, but they won't go away because—despite their potential shortcomings—many workplace gatherings are necessary.

YOUR TASK Examine the preceding quotations and perhaps other statements deriding meetings. Are they exaggerations or accurate assessments? If the assertions of wastefulness are true, what does that mean for the health of organizations conducting large numbers of meetings? Individually or as a team, search the Internet for information in defense of meetings. (a) Begin by discussing your own and classmates' experience with workplace meetings. (b) Interview your parents, other relatives, and friends about meetings. (c) Finding gripes is easy, but search the Web for advice on making meetings more effective.

What information beyond the tips in this book can you find? In a class discussion or individually—perhaps in writing or in a slide presentation, such as PowerPoint, if your instructor directs—introduce your findings.

2.6 Five-Minute Meetings: The Answer to Meeting Bloat? (L.O. 2)

`E-Mail` `Team`

Tired of long, boring meetings, some companies have embraced five-minute huddles or desk "drive-bys" for minor decision making. The CEO of a New York digital agency likes to cut people short when they talk too long by resorting to being "politely blunt." Brief daily check-in meetings are common in marketing, e-commerce, advertising, and related fields.[91] These mini meetings are so short that PowerPoint is out. So are long-winded speeches. Participants learn to boil down their contributions or they risk being cut off—brutally.

An account director at a digital agency in Phoenix says that the resulting bluntness "feels like having the wind knocked out of you." An executive creative director tactfully concludes: "You sort of need to check your ego at the door." Some companies limit even video meetings to five minutes. A Boston software developer holds lightning meetings that he praises for their energy and fast action. This breakneck efficiency leaves no time for idle chitchat about the kids or the weather.

YOUR TASK As a team, brainstorm all possible applications of quick meetings. What types of businesses could benefit from such meetings? How would you ensure on-time arrival, participation and order during the meeting, and turn-taking? What type of sanctions would you impose for violations? What are some potential drawback of the five-minute scrum? If your instructor directs, write an e-mail (see Chapter 7) to persuade your current or past boss to adopt five-minute meetings.

2.7 Virtual Meetings: Creating Buy-In (L.O. 2)

`Communication Technology` `Team` `Web`

Jaclyn Hadley works at the headquarters for a large HMO that contracts with physicians across the nation. Her position requires her to impose organizational objectives and systems on smaller groups that often resist such interference. Jaclyn recently needed to inform regional groups that the home office was instituting a system-wide change to hiring practices. To save costs, she set up a teleconference between her office in Baltimore and others in Chicago, Denver, and Sacramento. Jaclyn set the meeting for 10 a.m. Eastern Standard Time. At the designated date and hour, she found that the Sacramento team was not logged in and she had to delay the session. When the Sacramento team finally did log in, Jaclyn launched into her presentation. She explained the reasons behind the change in a PowerPoint presentation that contained complex data she had not distributed prior to the conference. Jaclyn heard cell phone ringtones and typing in the background as she spoke. Still, she pushed through her one-hour presentation without eliciting any feedback.

YOUR TASK In teams, discuss ways Jaclyn might have improved the teleconference. Prepare a list of recommendations from your team.

2.8 Virtual Meetings: Connecting by Skype to Clarify an Order (L.O. 2)

Communication Technology / **Social Media** / **Web**

Paramount Fitness Corporation, a commercial strength equipment manufacturer in California, contracts with several distributors overseas who exclusively sell Paramount weight machines to gyms and fitness studios, not to the general public. The distributor in the UK, Blake Luca, has sent a confusing order by e-mail containing incorrect item numbers and product names as well as inconsistent quantities of items. Mr. Luca doesn't respond to telephone calls or e-mail requests for clarification. You remember that you conversed with Mr. Luca via Skype and notice to your delight that your distributor is online.

YOUR TASK Using Skype, FaceTime, or Zoom, call a classmate designated to play Mr. Luca and request clarification of the rather large order. Improvise the details of the order in a Skype, FaceTime, or Zoom call to your peer (with or without a camera) applying the tips for virtual meetings in this chapter. Alternatively, your instructor may introduce a short background fact sheet or script for each participant, guiding your conversation and defining your roles and the particulars of the order. To use teleconferencing apps with or without a camera, select a laptop, computer lab desktop computer, smartphone, or iPad. This exchange can occur in the classroom or computer lab where the image can be projected onto a screen. The person playing the remote partner should leave the room and connect from a quiet place outside. Fellow students and your instructor will evaluate your virtual meeting with Mr. Luca.

2.9 Assessment Quiz: How Good a Listener Are You? (L.O. 3)

Psychologists say that listening is an act of connection. Even if we can't touch or see others, we feel connected hearing their voices. In a relationship, listening is an act of love, we are told.[92] In business, assertiveness and strong opinions tend to rule and drown out other voices. Leaders wishing to exude decisiveness speak more than they listen and are not even aware of their domineering behavior. Yet researchers tell us that active, empathic listening is key to being successful in teams and in leadership roles. They advise businesspeople to examine their bad habits, validate opinions of others, verify what is being said, watch for speakers' nonverbal cues, and control their own reactions and body language.[93]

How do you measure up? Do you know how good your listening skills are? Try this self-assessment:[94]

Score yourself on each question as 1 (the statement is not true for me at all), 2 (I mildly disagree), 3 (I partly agree

and partly disagree with the statement), 4 (I mildly agree), or 5 (the statement is totally true for me).

___ 1. I prefer talking to listening to what others may say.
___ 2. It mostly doesn't occur to me to ask questions.
___ 3. When others are talking I'm often thinking about what I'll say next.
___ 4. The main point of talking is to impress people, or at least to entertain them.
___ 5. My perspective is usually right, so if others disagree, I convince them to see it my way.
___ 6. It bothers me when people get their facts wrong.
___ 7. It's important to point out when people are wrong about something.
___ 8. Most people are boring, so I usually do most of the talking.
___ 9. When my body tries to talk to me with pain or other discomforts, I tune my body out.
___ Total score

YOUR TASK Record your score. Your instructor will share the interpretation of the results with you. Did you score high or low? Try the following experiment at home with your loved ones: Pick an object, a "listening stick" or a "listening stone," that will indicate turn-taking. Only the person in possession of the listening object will be allowed to speak. Not until the speaker is ready to give up the stick or stone can another person talk. Is it difficult for you to remain silent until you get your hands on the listening object? Are you truly present during the conversation? Do you listen without waiting impatiently to speak? Share your observations in class. The instructor may ask you to submit your findings and/or report in writing. What could you do to further improve your listening skills?

2.10 Listening: An In-Person or Virtual Social Media Interview (L.O. 3)

Communication Technology / **Social Media** / **Team**

How much and to whom do businesspeople listen?

YOUR TASK Interview a businessperson about that person's workplace listening. Connect with a worker in your circle of friends, family, and acquaintances; in your campus network; at a prior or current job; or via LinkedIn or Facebook. Come up with questions to ask about listening—for example: (a) How much active listening do you practice daily? (b) To whom do you listen on the job? (c) How do you know that others are listening or not listening to you? (d) Can you share anecdotes of poor listening that led to negative outcomes? (e) Do you have tips for better listening? Alternatively, interview a businessperson about face-to-face or virtual meetings.

2.11 Nonverbal Communication: Reading Body Language (L.O. 4)

YOUR TASK What attitudes do the following body movements suggest to you? Do these movements always mean the same thing? What part does context play in your interpretations?

a. Whistling, wringing hands

b. Bowed posture, twiddling thumbs

c. Steepled hands, sprawling sitting position

d. Rubbing hand through hair

e. Open hands, unbuttoned coat

f. Wringing hands, tugging ears

2.12 Nonverbal Communication: Casual Attire at Work (L.O. 4)

`Communication Technology` `E-Mail` `Social Media` `Team` `Web`

Although many employers allow casual attire, not all employers and customers are happy with the results. To learn more about the implementation, acceptance, and effects of casual-dress programs, select one of the following activities, all of which involve some form of interviewing.

YOUR TASK

a. In teams, gather information from human resources directors to determine which companies allow casual-dress, or dress-down, days, how often, and under what conditions. The information may be collected by personal interviews, e-mail, telephone, or instant messaging.

b. In teams, conduct inquiring-reporter interviews. Ask individuals in the community how they react to casual dress in the workplace. Develop a set of standard interview questions.

c. In teams, visit local businesses on both casual-dress days and traditional business-dress days.

Compare and contrast the effects of business-dress standards on such factors as the projected image of the company, the nature of the interactions with customers and with fellow employees, the morale of employees, and the productivity of employees. What generalizations can you draw from your findings?

2.13 Express Yourself? Perceptions of Tattoos on the Job (L.O. 4)

`Communication Technology` `E-Mail` `Social Media` `Team`

Tattoos are increasingly mainstream at work today and less likely to be viewed as a sign of immoral behavior. Nearly 40 percent of eighteen- to twenty-nine-year-olds sport tattoos. According to a Statista survey, tattoos are most common among Americans between the ages of thirty and thirty-nine; more than half of this age group has body ink. Overall, almost a third of Americans now have one or more tattoos, but about 80 percent of them prefer to hide their visible tattoos at work.[95] The perception of body art seems to be generational. Fewer than 25 percent of millennials consider tattoos unprofessional, compared with 63 percent among those 60 years and older.[96] Experts recommend that job candidates cover up their tattoos when interviewing for customer-facing positions or in more conservative sectors such as banking or law to avoid being judged and potentially rejected. Caution is indicated when candidates are interviewing for jobs in management.[97] Although negative attitudes toward body art are softening, tattoos on hands, face, and neck are still largely unacceptable in most workplaces.[98]

Many organizations today have policies covering body adornment, some requiring employees with customer contact to conceal such decoration, for example, Sea World Orlando, Walt Disney World, Walmart, Delta, and more. In general, companies have a constitutional right to ban or fire employees with tattoos, especially when the employer has reason to fear that tattooed employees could hurt their professional image. A Harris poll found that nearly a quarter of people with tattoos regretted being inked.[99] The removal of even small pieces of body art can be expensive. The American Academy of Pediatrics reported that the price per square inch of laser treatment ranges from $49 to $300.[100]

YOUR TASK In teams or in class, discuss tattoos as a form of self-expression in the workplace. Gauge the attitudes toward tattoos and piercings in your class. Consider the limits to self-expression on the job. Think about casual clothing or blogging and tweeting about your employer. What is different? What are some of the similarities among these forms of self-expression? What types of nonverbal cues do body adornments send? Summarize your discussion orally or in an e-mail to your instructor. Alternatively, your instructor may ask you to post your responses to an online discussion board or some other forum that allows individual postings.

2.14 Nonverbal Communication Around the World (L.O. 4)

`Intercultural` `Web`

Gestures play an important role when people communicate. Because culture shapes the meaning of gestures, miscommunication and misunderstanding can easily result in international situations.

YOUR TASK Use the Internet to research the meanings of selected gestures. Make a list of ten gestures (other than those discussed in the text) that have different meanings in different countries. Consider the hand pyramid, fingertip kiss, nose thumb, eyelid pull, nose tap, head shake, and other gestures. How are the meanings different in other countries?

2.15 Business Etiquette in Meetings: Kicking the Smartphone Habit (L.O.5)

Communication Technology | **Social Media** | **Team**

Typical smartphone users whip out their devices to check them about 80 times a day, according to Apple.[101] Out of boredom or to catch up, some businesspeople compulsively eyeball their smartphones and tablets to read e-mail, search the Internet, and check Facebook, Instagram, or Twitter even during meetings. However, many professionals are growing tired of disruptions caused by electronic gadgets during meetings. Fortunately, nine in ten people oppose using smart devices during meetings, movies, church services, or other places where attentiveness is expected.[102]

Etiquette consultants concur: "Electronic devices are like the smoking of the '90s," says Pamela Eyring, president of the Protocol School of Washington. "Companies are aggravated and losing productivity." Businesses hire her to enact formal policies and to teach workers "why it's not a good idea to be texting while your boss is speaking at the podium," Eyring says.[103] Nancy Flynn, executive director of the ePolicy Institute and author of *The Handbook of Social Media*, has this suggestion: "Require employees to turn off mobile devices during business-related meetings, seminars, conferences, luncheons and any other situation in which a ringing phone or tapping fingers are likely to disrupt proceedings or interrupt a speaker's or participant's train of thought."

Flynn notes that banning electronic devices in meetings is not just about interruptions: "You don't want employees shooting video via a smartphone during a meeting in which company secrets are discussed, then uploading the video to YouTube or sharing it with a competitor, reporter or other third party."[104]

YOUR TASK Many organizations have established policies on smartphone use in meetings. Assume that your team has been asked to develop such a policy. Your boss can't decide whether to ask your team to develop a short, general policy or a more rigorous one. Unable to make a decision, he asks for two statements: (a) a short statement that treats employees as grown-ups who can exercise intelligent judgment and (b) a more complete set of guidelines that spell out exactly what should and should not be done.

Test Your Workplace Etiquette IQ

New communication platforms and casual workplace environments have blurred the lines of appropriateness, leaving workers wondering how to navigate uncharted waters. Check your workplace etiquette IQ by deciding whether the following statements are true or false. Then see if you agree with the responses on p. Key-5.

1. You are attending a business function designed to help people network and make contacts. To be polite, you should plan to spend 10 to 15 minutes with each individual and then move on.

   _____ True _____ False

2. When a business meeting is long and you are not directly involved, it is acceptable for you to perform minor grooming tasks such as combing your hair, applying lipstick, or clipping your fingernails—as long as you do it discreetly.

   _____ True _____ False

3. Even though you may be working on a team project together, you should not open the closed door of a coworker without knocking first.

   _____True _____ False

Chat About It

In each chapter you will find five discussion questions related to the chapter material. Your instructor may assign these topics for you to discuss in class, in an online chat room, or on an online discussion board. Some of the discussion topics may require outside research. You may also be asked to read and respond to postings made by your classmates.

TOPIC 1: Research by the late communication expert Clifford Nass suggests that young people are spending so much time looking at screens that they are losing the ability to read nonverbal communication and learn other skills necessary for one-on-one interactions. Have you observed social awkwardness in your own life? Would the loss of social skills be worrisome?

TOPIC 2: A clothing manufacturer argues that America's love affair with comfort manifests itself not only in the way we dress, but also in the way we design our homes, furniture, cars, and even how we consume our food. He believes that a well-made suit can fit like a glove and be comfortable, but most people prefer baggy clothes and stretchy fabrics. Do you agree? Do you feel different when you dress formally?

TOPIC 3: Psychologists say that we fear rejection when deviating from group consensus; we try to avoid the "hazards of courage" and may consequently fall victim to groupthink. Recall a past or present team experience. Can you relate to feeling "the pain of independence" when going against the majority opinion?

TOPIC 4: Consider a situation in your family, in your circle of friends, in high school, at college, during an internship, or at work that shows the potential risks of poor listening skills. How could the resulting misunderstandings or other negative consequences have been prevented? Which techniques would have helped avert the undesirable outcome?

TOPIC 5: A realtor who missed out on a $12,000 commission because he was serving on a sequestered jury that prohibited the use of cell phones has no regrets. He considers it rude to answer a phone during a meeting with a client and purposely leaves his phone in the car to avoid temptation.[104] What events would justify remaining permanently tethered to your mobile phone? What types of situations would warrant turning off or at least ignoring your electronic devices?

Grammar and Mechanics Review 2

Verbs

Review Guides 4 through 9 in Appendix D, Grammar and Mechanics, beginning on page D-2. On a separate sheet, revise the following sentences to correct any errors in verb use. For each error that you locate, write the guide number that reflects this usage. If a sentence is correct, write C.

EXAMPLE: If Madison was manager, she would have acted ethically.

REVISION: If Madison **were** manager, she would have acted ethically. [Guide 5]

1. Conflict and disagreement is normal and should be expected in team interactions.

2. Have you wrote to other members of the virtual team?

3. One of the most frequently requested professional skills during job interviews are writing proficiency.

4. I wish the CEO was more supportive of our current team project.

5. Better decisions and faster response time explains why organizations are using teams.

6. Neither the speaker nor members of the team was bothered by the technical mishap.

7. Every piece of information including e-mails and texts were made public during the trial.

8. A committee of students and faculty are examining strategies to improve campus conservation efforts.

9. Each of the newly hired employees must chose a team to join.

10. When two candidates have equal qualifications, the one who appears to be more polished and professional is more likely to be hired and promoted.

Intercultural Communication

LEARNING OUTCOMES

After studying this chapter, you should be able to do the following:

1 Explain the powerful effects of globalization and the major trends fueling it.

2 Identify the primary characteristics and key dimensions of culture.

3 Discuss strategies for enhancing intercultural effectiveness and communication across cultures.

4 Examine the complexities of ethics across cultures, including business practices abroad, bribery, prevailing customs, and methods for coping.

5 Describe the advantages and challenges of workforce diversity as well as approaches for improving communication among diverse workplace audiences.

Zooming In

Walmart:
Global Expansion Marred by Intercultural Blunders and Legal Woes

Walmart's global intercultural missteps and legal lapses continue to serve as rich case studies of how not to expand abroad.[1] After explosive growth worldwide, Walmart was forced to withdraw from its first European market, Germany, at a loss of $1 billion. Walmart has also struggled in Asia. Cultural differences and fierce local competition forced the world's second largest retailer (after Amazon) to exit South Korea. Consumers in this and other Asian countries don't buy in bulk. In Japan Walmart's one-stop low-cost business model didn't appeal to discerning consumers who equate discounts with poor quality and don't trust a broad merchandise selection.[2] Walmart's American everyday-low-price approach also failed to translate in Brazil.[3]

However, despite setbacks in both countries, the big-box retailer is going big in India and China to compete with Amazon for primacy in online sales.[4] Toward this purpose, Walmart has acquired the Indian digital sales giant Flipkart, launched its first online store in Japan with strategic partner Rakuten, and jumpstarted its e-commerce and delivery business in China with JD.com, a leading online mall operator.[5] Why the focus on online sales and speedy delivery? In China e-commerce accounts for 21 percent of all retail (12 percent in the U.S.), as customers demand convenience.[6] JP Suarez, a top corporate officer at Walmart International, confidently declared: "Customers around the world are kind of the same. They want quality, a great assortment, a great price, and they want it whenever they want it."[7]

In addition to addressing costly intercultural stumbles, Walmart was compelled to improve its ethical practices abroad. Investigative reporting by *The New York Times* triggered a massive seven-year probe by federal regulators into Walmart's operations under the Foreign Corrupt Practices Act, which forbids U.S. corporations from bribing overseas officials. The Securities and Exchange Commission and the Department of Justice found that, for more than a decade, Walmart's foreign subsidiaries in Mexico, Brazil, China, and India had paid millions of dollars to middlemen to speed up licenses and store permits. The SEC blamed Walmart's "low-cost philosophy" for a lack of policies and internal controls that would flag corruption risks. One official concluded that the retailer "valued international growth and cost-cutting over compliance."[8] In joint ventures Walmart had failed to vet local partners for signs of corruption. Ignoring whistleblower warnings cost Walmart dearly—$900 million in legal fees and $282 million in fines. The scandal damaged Walmart's reputation, prompted investor lawsuits, and forced out high-level executives.[9]

Will Walmart do better in its future international endeavors?

You will learn more about Walmart and be asked to complete a relevant task at the end of this chapter.

Critical Thinking

- The late marketing guru Theodore Levitt, who coined the term *globalization,* argued that the customer is central to all business endeavors. However, his most provocative assertion, debated to this day, is that the "global corporation" of the future would sell standardized consumer products, not cater to local differences in taste. Walmart's JP Suarez believes that all customers want the same. Should companies stick to a standardized approach or adapt to local markets?

- What domestic and global changes enable the international expansion of companies such as Walmart?

- What other businesses have merged with overseas companies or expanded to become multinational or global? Have you heard of any notable successes or failures?

3-1 Building Intercultural Communication Skills in a Globalized World

LEARNING OUTCOME

1 Explain the powerful effects of globalization and the major trends fueling it.

The global village predicted many years ago is here, making intercultural communication skills ever more important. In North America and around the world, the global economy is now a fact of life, despite recent trade skirmishes over tariffs. To tap into new markets and grow their profits, many organizations are expanding overseas. If you visit a European, South-American, or Asian city, you will see many familiar U.S. chains such as Subway, Abercrombie & Fitch, Guess, Dunkin', American Eagle Outfitters, Apple, and KFC. To be immediately competitive, some companies form strategic alliances with local players. For example, in India Starbucks has partnered with Tata Global Beverages to form a joint venture called Tata Starbucks Private Limited, operating as Starbucks: A Tata Alliance.

Similarly, in the biggest e-commerce deal to date, Walmart allied with Indian online retailer Flipkart. After all, the mega-retailer's past tribulations showcased the risks U.S. corporations take in expanding to countries with different political cultures and legal systems. Confusion and clashes can result from intercultural differences. You may face such intercultural differences in your current or future jobs. Your employers, coworkers, or customers could very well be from other countries, ethnic groups, and cultures. You may travel abroad for your employer or on your own. Learning more about the powerful effect culture has on behavior will help you reduce tensions and misunderstandings in your dealings with people who are not like you. Before examining strategies for helping you overcome intercultural obstacles, let's take a closer look at globalization and the trends fueling it.

3-1a The Emergence of Global Markets

Having an international presence is now commonplace for many businesses. Four U.S.-based multinationals have placed among the top five most trusted brands in India: Dell, Jeep, Amazon, and iPhone.[11] McDonald's, Burger King, KFC, and Starbucks serve hungry customers around the world. An old rivalry is playing out overseas: PepsiCo India aims to double its local snack business by 2022 while Coca-Cola Hong Kong is betting on a new energy drink specifically targeting young consumers who multitask and yearn for freedom.[12]

Not only are familiar businesses expanding their markets beyond their borders, but acquisitions, mergers, alliances, and buyouts are obscuring the nationality of many companies. The iconic U.S. brand GE Appliances, founded in 1905, is now majority-owned by Haier, based in Qingdao, China.[13] Chinese corporations have been acquiring assets around the world at a fast clip. Most notably, the Chinese own and operate more than 10,000 enterprises in Africa, a resource-rich continent shunned by Western businesses fearing political instability and poor infrastructure.[14] In the U.S., the nation's largest movie theater chain, AMC, is now Chinese-owned. So is New York's legendary Waldorf-Astoria hotel and former handset leader Motorola Mobility.[15] A proposed Chinese takeover of the Chicago Stock Exchange drew sharp protests and was blocked by the SEC.[16]

Many home-grown companies with famous brands—such as Ford, Firestone, Coca-Cola, AT&T, Colgate, and JPMorgan Chase—have become global enterprises. When the Japanese beverage empire Suntory bought Beam Inc., distiller of whiskey brands Jim Beam and Maker's Mark, the deal caused a social media storm, including calls for a boycott.[17] Another Japanese company owns the omnipresent convenience store chain 7-Eleven. The British-Dutch multinational Unilever controls Vermont's beloved ice cream purveyor Ben & Jerry's as well as Hellmann's Mayonnaise. The American hotel chain Holiday Inn was acquired by British InterContinental Hotels. Budweiser beer, an American classic, was sold to InBev, a Belgian beer empire.[18] Last, "Your Neighborhood Grocery Store," Trader Joe's, is owned by Germany's discount grocer, Aldi, and now the parent company itself is aggressively expanding across the United States, spending $5.3 billion to compete with Walmart and Kroger.[19]

To succeed in today's interdependent global village, multinational companies try to negotiate two seemingly opposite approaches based on their target demographic.[20] On the one hand, they introduce new products in new territories—for example, tempting wine-loving Italians with American beer or awakening in Chinese consumers a penchant for potato chips and coffee. On the other hand, they localize their offerings to match each market. In China McDonald's and KFC highlight salads in response to the Chinese preference for grains, protein, and vegetables in each meal and have made rice more prominent than fries. In India McDonald's dropped beef and pork from its menu, instead substituting Chicken McGrill and vegetarian options, such as a McAloo Tikki burger, to suit the sizable proportion of Indians who don't eat meat.[21] At McDonald's in Germany, beer is on the menu.

As Figure 3.1 shows, Starbucks has established itself successfully in China and India by focusing on fast growth and targeting well-heeled urban populations. However, market saturation and a premium-pricing strategy could backfire.[22]

Not all overseas expansions succeed. In Shanghai toy company Mattel splurged on the world's largest House of Barbie. The six-story structure—complete with a restaurant, spa, hair

---

FIGURE 3.1   Starbucks—Localization and Premium Pricing in China and India

Starbucks is a global brand that has successfully adapted to a very different market and modified its business model to fit China while remaining faithful to its core values. In India so far Starbucks has 174 outlets and plans to continue to grow in a difficult market for cafés.

Sorbis/Shutterstock.com

Starbucks' Coffee Wars in China

Introduced flavors appealing to local tastes, such as green-tea flavored coffee drinks

A new location opens in China every 15 hours. Currently 4,125 outlets in China: looming threat of cannibalization

China: Starbucks' largest market outside the U.S.

Offers dine-in service and a comfortable environment with air conditioning

$ premium pricing strategy

Superb service equal to 5-star hotels

Even consumers who prefer competing coffee products prefer Starbucks for its service.

Trouble is brewing: Luckin Coffee, a scrappy fast-growing start-up, embracing technology and speedy delivery at 20 percent lower prices; KFC/Yum China, second largest coffee retailer by cups sold, more than 90 million servings

Outlets: meeting places for executives and gatherings of friends

Carrying a cup: a little personal luxury, a status symbol, a way to show sophistication

Coffee conquering tea cultures

Coffee consumption has nearly doubled over last 10 years.

Coffee, a "sexy" beverage to enjoy.

Coffee has become the "in" thing.

Neutral place to go and sit, hang out

Starbucks Growing in India—a $30 billion tea market

Strategic launch of Teavana: premium teas such as masala and mint, hibiscus tea with pomegranate pearls—both hot and cold

Growth of **café culture,** not so much of coffee

Competition

Instead of traditional coffee, young Indians favor Café Coffee Day's cold, sweet milkshakes and teas.

Indians prefer over-the-top, plush outlets.

singh_lens/Shutterstock.com

Lavazza of Italy and Coffee Bean & Tea Leaf have outlets in India.

A small cappuccino costs $1.75 at Café Coffee Day, India's largest café chain, $2.80 at Starbucks

Sources: Rein, S. (2012, February 13). Why Starbucks succeeds in China. CNBC guest blog. Retrieved from http://www.cnbc.com/id/46186635/Rein_Why_Starbucks_Succeeds_in_China; Bailay, R. (2014, April 14). Coffee chain Starbucks expanding aggressively in India. The Economic Times. Retrieved from http://articles.economictimes.indiatimes.com/2014-04-14/news/49126396_1_costa-coffee-cafe-coffee-day-coffee-chain

---

and nail salon, and cocktail bar—featured all things Barbie in its Chinese incarnation (Ling) but ended up confusing Chinese shoppers. Two years later the store closed due to high costs and low sales.[23] Then there are linguistic gaffes: Mercedes-Benz entered the Chinese market as "Bensi," sounding similar to "Benz." However, the word translated as "rush to die." KFC's familiar tagline "finger-lickin' good" in Chinese invited customers to "eat their fingers off."[24] In a U.S. ad campaign, Swedish vacuum maker Electrolux bragged about its vacuums' power with the slogan "Nothing sucks like an Electrolux."[25] Before venturing abroad, enterprises must do their homework, and even then, success is not guaranteed.

3-1b Trends Fueling Globalization

Although some companies fail, many domestic and international businesses are rushing to expand around the world. What is causing this dash toward the globalization of markets and blurring of national identities? Like Walmart, many companies are looking overseas as domestic markets mature. They can no longer expect double-digit sales growth at home. As summarized in Figure 3.2, aside from shrinking domestic markets, several trends fuel global expansion.

International Free-Trade Agreements. A significant factor in the expansion of global markets was the passage of free-trade agreements. The General Agreement on Tariffs and Trade (GATT) and its successor, the World Trade Organization (WTO), promote open trade and the reduction of trade barriers globally. The 1994 North American Free Trade Agreement (NAFTA) expanded free trade among Canada, the United States, and Mexico. NAFTA created one of the largest and richest free-trade regions on earth. Most recently, NAFTA was updated and is awaiting ratification as the U.S.-Mexico-Canada Agreement (USMCA). The new pact would promote peaceful trade relations for at least 16 years, toughen car-industry rules, protect farmers, strengthen labor as well as environmental standards, and set digital trade rules.[26]

Additional trade agreements are causing markets to expand. At this writing the United States has 14 free-trade agreements (FTAs) in force with 20 countries and is negotiating several other regional FTAs.[27] These agreements have significantly opened global markets to imports and exports.

FIGURE 3.2 Trends Fueling Globalization

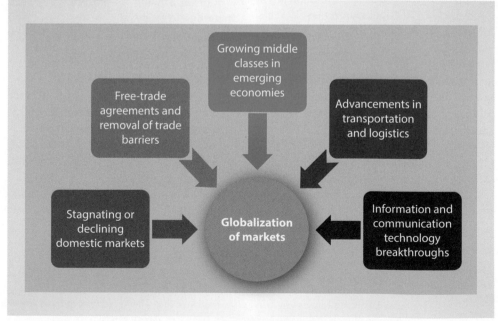

A Growing Global Middle Class.

Economists recently marked "a global income tipping point," as half the world population, 3.8 billion, is now middle class or wealthier. The middle class is the fastest growing segment of the global income distribution; it is the main driver of demand in the global economy.[29] By 2030 the global middle class is projected to reach 5.3 billion people. Consumers in China, India, and South and Southeast Asia will account for almost 90 percent of that new growth.[30] McKinsey predicts that by 2022 China's 550-million middle class alone will surpass today's entire U.S. population one-and-a-half times and the U.S. middle class two-and-a-half times.[31] Consumers in these emerging economies crave everything from cola to smartphones, high-definition TVs, refrigerators, or washing machines. They will have discretionary income to spend on entertainment, eating out, or vacations. Global trade has lifted a billion people out of poverty.

Travel mania/Shutterstock.com

However, experts acknowledge that international trade has not been a boon to everyone. The manufacturing sector in the United States has been decimated; whole communities were devastated when well-paying skilled work was outsourced to countries where labor is cheaper, and environmental laws and labor practices are less restrictive.[32] Deep dissatisfaction in postindustrial regions of the United States and other Western democracies has erupted in a backlash of political polarization, trade tensions, economic nationalism, and protectionism in the form of tariffs.

Innovation in Transportation and Logistics.

Of paramount importance in explaining the explosive growth of global markets are advancements in transportation and logistics. Supersonic planes carry goods and passengers to other continents overnight. Produce shoppers in Japan can choose from the finest artichokes, avocados, and apples only hours after they were picked in California. Americans enjoy bouquets of tulips, roses, and exotic lilies soon after harvesting in Holland and Colombia. Fruits and vegetables such as strawberries and asparagus, once available only in season, are now enjoyed nearly year-round. New ultra-large container ships (ULCS), mostly operating on Far East routes, carry between 10,000 and soon even 23,350 containers (TEU) each.[33] They are symptomatic of the steadily growing maritime industry as demand for more freight capacity and cost pressures keep increasing.

Breakthroughs in transportation technology also enabled globalization. Now, large transportation companies are launching **blockchain technology**. Blockchain was first conceived as a new decentralized network to distribute the virtual currency Bitcoin. In shipping, blockchain allows users to digitize paper-based processes, increase security, improve administrative efficiency, and allow all supply chain partners to trace a package from shipment to smart locker. Barcode scanners and sensors help track goods and generate valuable data. Digitization not only helps optimize delivery routes but also monitor individuals' driving behavior.[34] Warehouse operators are deploying AI-powered robots to speed up e-commerce orders. Mobile collaborative robots or **cobots** are helping workers find merchandise or bring it to them. Some autonomous robots even execute their tasks automatically.[35] Self-driving trucks are on the horizon as are delivery drones.

As a new wrinkle brought on by trade disputes, recent trade barriers and tariffs have also affected the shipping industry. Imports into western U.S. ports have declined by double digits.[36]

Information and Communication Technologies.

The Internet, wireless networks, mobile electronic devices, and other communication media have transformed the world of business. Geographic location has become nearly irrelevant for many activities and services. Using teleconferencing, instant messaging, virtual private networks, and social media, workers have access to company records, software programs, and colleagues. They may be working at home, in the office, or at the beach. Managers in Miami or Milwaukee can use high-speed data systems to edit marketing plans in real time with their counterparts in Milan or Munich. Fashionistas can snap a digital photo of a garment on a runway in Europe and immediately transmit it to manufacturers in Cambodia and Bangladesh.

Enter artificial intelligence (AI) that will inform every part of business within a few years, as experts predict.[37] Some likely applications include natural language generation, used in customer service or report creation to produce text from computer data; speech recognition, as AI helps transcribe human speech into formats readable by computer applications; virtual agents such as chatbots deployed in customer service; and biometrics that enable more natural human-machine interactions, such as image and touch recognition, speech, and body language.[38]

The changing landscape of business clearly demonstrates the need for technology savvy and connectedness around the world. Career success and personal wealth depend on the ability to use technology effectively.

3-1c The Increasing Diversity of the Domestic Workforce

As global commerce becomes more interconnected, another trend makes proficient intercultural communication increasingly important: people are on the move. Lured by the prospects of peace, prosperity, education, or a fresh start, people from many cultures are moving to countries promising to fulfill their dreams. For generations the two most popular destinations have been the United States and Canada.

Because of increases in immigration over time, foreign-born people comprise an ever-growing portion of the total U.S. population, from 45 million in 2017 (14 percent of the U.S. population) to an estimated 78 million by 2065. The population of the United States is expected to grow by approximately 26 percent over the next 40 years. In absolute terms, the growth will extend from about 330 million in 2020 to 417 million persons in 2060. If current trends hold, immigrants and their descendants may account for 88 percent of U.S. population growth through 2065.[40]

This influx of immigrants is reshaping American and Canadian societies. Earlier immigrants were thought to be part of a melting pot of ethnic groups. Today, they are more like a tossed salad or spicy stew, with each group contributing its own unique flavor. Instead of the exception, cultural diversity is increasingly the norm. As we seek to accommodate multiethnic neighborhoods, multinational companies, and an intercultural workforce, we can expect some changes to happen smoothly. Other changes will involve conflict and resentment, especially for people losing their positions of power and privilege. Learning to accommodate and manage intercultural change is an important part of the education of any business communicator.

LEARNING OUTCOME

2 Identify the primary characteristics and key dimensions of culture.

3-2 Understanding Culture and Communication

Even when communicators share the same culture, comprehending the verbal and nonverbal meanings of a message is difficult. When different cultures come together, special sensitivity and skills are necessary. Although global business, new communication technologies, the Internet, and social media span the world and reduce distances, cultural differences still exist and can cause significant misunderstandings—even here at home, in the increasingly multiethnic United States.

For our purposes, **culture** may be defined as the complex system of values, traits, morals, and customs shared by a society. Culture is a powerful operating force that molds the way we think, behave, and communicate. The objective of this chapter is to broaden your view of culture and open your mind to flexible attitudes so that you can avoid frustration when cultural adjustment is necessary.

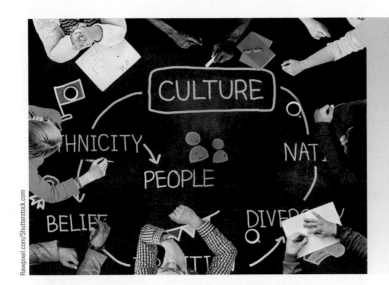

Rawpixel.com/Shutterstock.com

3-2a Characteristics of Culture

Every country or region within a country has a unique common heritage, joint experience, or shared learning. This shared background creates its culture. Despite the homogenizing effects of globalization, interculturalism, and social networking, we do need to adjust and adopt new attitudes when encountering individuals from cultures very different from our own. However, first we must understand some basic characteristics of culture.

Culture Is Learned.   Rules, values, and attitudes of a culture are learned and passed down from generation to generation. For example, in many Middle Eastern and some Asian cultures, same-sex people may walk hand-in-hand in the street, but opposite-sex people may not do so. In Arab cultures conversations are sometimes held nose to nose. However, in Western cultures if a person stands too close, one may react as if violated: *He was all over me like a rash.* Cultural rules of behavior learned from your family and society are conditioned from early childhood.

Cultures Are Inherently Logical.   The rules in any culture reinforce that culture's values and beliefs. They act as normative forces. For example, even Mattel's localized Chinese version of Barbie called Ling was a flop because it didn't match consumers' views of *femininity*. Also, Chinese parents prefer educational toys that focus their children on academics. Mattel responded with a lower-priced, more studious Violin Soloist Barbie sold on e-commerce site Alibaba.[42]

Although current cultural behavior may seem silly and illogical to some people, nearly all serious rules and values originate in deep-seated beliefs. Acknowledging the inherent logic of a culture is extremely important when encountering behavior that differs from one's own cultural norms.

Culture Is the Basis of Self-Identity and Community.   Culture is the basis for how we tell the world who we are and what we believe. People build their identities through cultural overlays to their primary culture. When North Americans make choices in education, career, place of employment, and life partner, they consider certain rules, manners, ceremonies, beliefs, languages, and values. These considerations add to their total cultural outlook and are major expressions of their self-identity.

Culture Combines the Visible and Invisible.   To outsiders, the way we act—those things we do in daily life and work—are the most visible parts of our culture. On the surface, we recognize numerous signs of culture including the words we use, our body language and gestures, the way we dress, and our outward behavior. Under the surface, however, lie unspoken rules governing these outward signs. These unspoken and often unconscious rules are determined by our beliefs and values, attitudes and biases, feelings and fears, and upbringing. The elements of the invisible structure of culture vastly outnumber those of the visible structure, as illustrated by the iceberg concept shown in Figure 3.3.

FIGURE 3.3 **Culture Combines the Visible and Invisible**

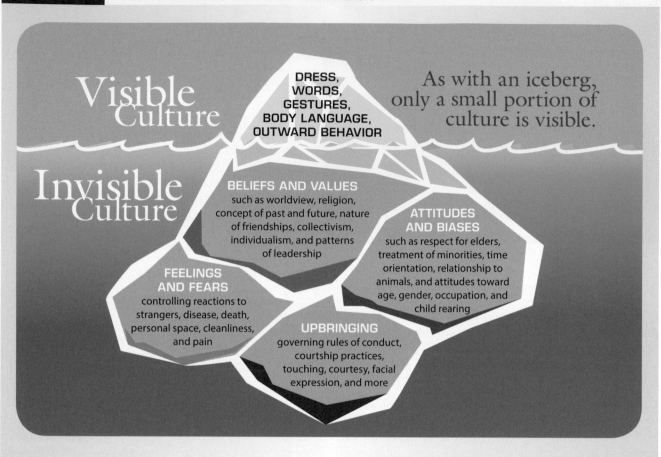

Visible Culture

DRESS, WORDS, GESTURES, BODY LANGUAGE, OUTWARD BEHAVIOR

As with an iceberg, only a small portion of culture is visible.

Invisible Culture

BELIEFS AND VALUES
such as worldview, religion, concept of past and future, nature of friendships, collectivism, individualism, and patterns of leadership

ATTITUDES AND BIASES
such as respect for elders, treatment of minorities, time orientation, relationship to animals, and attitudes toward age, gender, occupation, and child rearing

FEELINGS AND FEARS
controlling reactions to strangers, disease, death, personal space, cleanliness, and pain

UPBRINGING
governing rules of conduct, courtship practices, touching, courtesy, facial expression, and more

Culture is Dynamic.   Over time, cultures change. Changes are caused by advancements in technology and communication, as discussed earlier. Local differences are modified or slowly erased. Change is also caused by events such as migration, natural disasters, and wars. The American Civil War, for instance, produced far-reaching cultural changes for both the North and the South. Another major event in the United States was the exodus of people from farms. When families moved to cities, major changes occurred in the way family members interacted. Attitudes, behaviors, and beliefs change in open societies more quickly than in closed societies.

When social media networks emerged and added to the pull exerted by traditional mass media—for example, influential TV shows—deeply held cultural norms in the United States changed swiftly. In a 2004 poll, Pew Research found that 60 percent of Americans opposed same-sex marriage versus 31 percent who supported it. Fifteen years later, 61 percent of Americans favored same-sex marriage, compared to 31 percent who opposed it. Generational change in part accounted for the shift; younger Americans were more supportive, Pew showed.[43]

3-2b **Basic Dimensions of Culture**

The more you know about culture in general and your own culture, the better able you will be to adopt an intercultural perspective. In this book it is impossible to describe fully the infinite facets of culture, but we can outline some key dimensions identified by social scientists.

To help you better understand your culture and how it contrasts with other cultures, we describe five key dimensions of culture: context, individualism, time orientation, power distance, and communication style.

High and Low Context.   Context is probably the most important cultural dimension and also the most difficult to define. It is a concept developed by cultural anthropologist Edward T. Hall. In his model, context refers to the stimuli, environment, or ambience surrounding an

FIGURE 3.4 Comparing Low- and High-Context Cultures

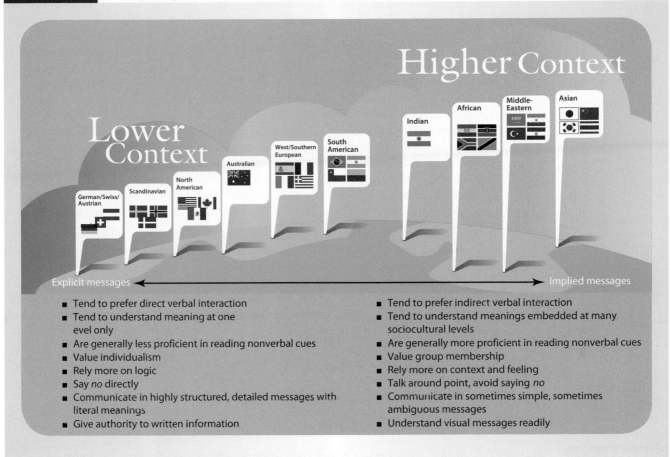

Tend to prefer direct verbal interaction

- Tend to prefer direct verbal interaction
- Tend to understand meaning at one level only
- Are generally less proficient in reading nonverbal cues
- Value individualism
- Rely more on logic
- Say *no* directly
- Communicate in highly structured, detailed messages with literal meanings
- Give authority to written information

- Tend to prefer indirect verbal interaction
- Tend to understand meanings embedded at many sociocultural levels
- Are generally more proficient in reading nonverbal cues
- Value group membership
- Rely more on context and feeling
- Talk around point, avoid saying *no*
- Communicate in sometimes simple, sometimes ambiguous messages
- Understand visual messages readily

event. Communicators in low-context cultures (such as those in North America, Scandinavia, and Germany) depend little on the context of a situation and shared experience to convey their meaning. They assume that messages must be explicit, and listeners rely exclusively on the written or spoken word. In high-context cultures (such as those in Japan, China, and Middle Eastern countries), much is left unsaid because the listener is assumed to be already *contexted* and does not require much background information.[44] To identify low- and high-context countries, Hall arranged them on a continuum, as shown in Figure 3.4.[45]

Low-context cultures tend to be logical, analytical, and action oriented. Business communicators stress clearly articulated messages that they consider to be objective, professional, and efficient. High-context cultures are more likely to be intuitive and contemplative. Communicators in high-context cultures pay attention to more than the spoken or written words. They emphasize interpersonal relationships, nonverbal expression, physical setting, and social setting. For example, a Japanese communicator might say *yes* when he really means *no*. From the context of the situation, the Japanese speaker would indicate whether *yes* really means *yes* or whether it means *no*. The context, tone, time taken to answer, facial expression, and body cues convey the meaning of *yes*.[46] Thus, in high-context cultures, communication cues are transmitted by posture, voice inflection, gestures, and facial expression. Establishing relationships is an important part of communicating and interacting.

In terms of thinking patterns, low-context communicators tend to use **linear logic**. They proceed from Point A to Point B to Point C and finally arrive at a conclusion. High-context communicators, however, may use **spiral logic**, circling around a topic indirectly and looking at it from many tangential or divergent viewpoints. A conclusion may be implied but not argued directly. Figure 3.4 shows a scale ranking low- and high-context cultures.

Individualism and Collectivism.   An attitude of independence and freedom from control characterizes individualism. Members of low-context cultures, particularly Americans, tend to value individualism. They believe that initiative and self-assertion result in personal achievement. They believe in individual action and personal responsibility, and they desire a large degree of freedom in their personal lives.

Members of high-context cultures are more collectivist. They emphasize membership in organizations, groups, and teams; they encourage acceptance of group values, duties, and decisions. They typically resist independence because it fosters competition and confrontation instead of consensus. In group-oriented cultures such as those in many Asian societies, for example, self-assertion and individual decision making are discouraged. "The nail that sticks up gets pounded down" is a common Japanese saying. Business decisions are often made by all who have competence in the matter under discussion. Similarly, in China managers also focus on the group rather than on the individual, preferring a consultative management style over an autocratic style.[47]

Many cultures, of course, are quite complex and cannot be characterized as totally individualistic or group oriented. For example, Americans of European descent are generally quite individualistic, whereas African Americans are less so, and Americans with a Latinx or Hispanic heritage are closer to the group-centered dimension.[48] Figure 3.5 shows selected countries ranked according to their expression of collectivism and individualism as well as power distance.

Time Orientation. North Americans consider time a precious commodity to be conserved. They correlate time with productivity, efficiency, and money. Keeping people waiting for business appointments is considered a waste of time and rude.

In other cultures time may be perceived as an unlimited resource to be enjoyed. A North American businessperson, for example, was kept waiting two hours past a scheduled appointment time in South America. She wasn't offended, though, because she was familiar with South Americans' more relaxed concept of time.

Although Asians are punctual in general, their need for deliberation and contemplation sometimes clashes with Americans' desire for speedy decisions. They do not like to be rushed. A Japanese businessperson considering the purchase of American appliances, for example, asked for five minutes to consider the seller's proposal. The potential buyer crossed his arms, sat back, and closed his eyes in concentration. A scant 18 seconds later, the American resumed his sales pitch to the obvious bewilderment of the Japanese buyer.[49]

FIGURE 3.5 Selected Countries' Ranking in Collectivism, Individualism, and Power Distance

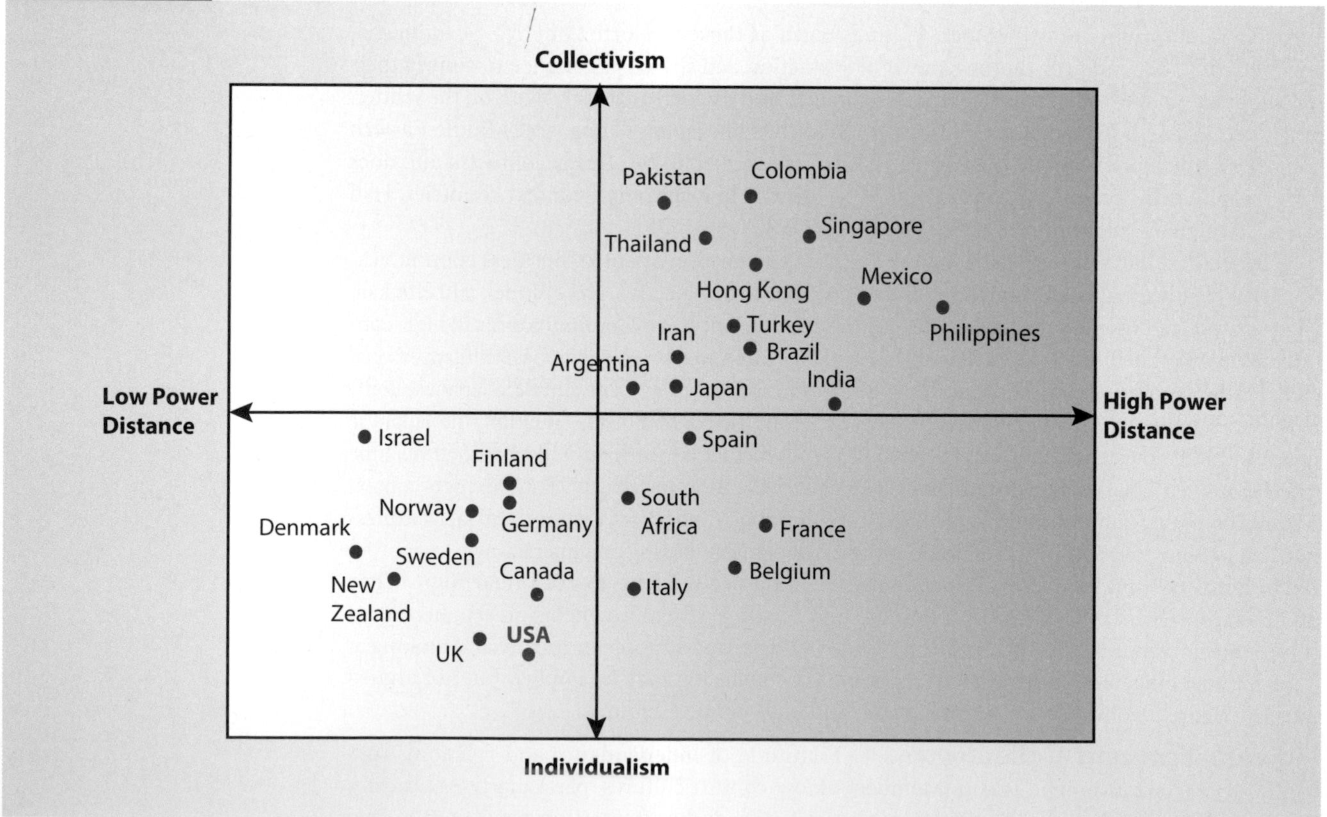

Power Distance. One important element of culture is power distance, first introduced by influential social psychologist Geert Hofstede. The Power Distance Index measures how people in different societies cope with inequality; in other words, how they relate to more powerful individuals. In high-power-distance countries, subordinates expect formal hierarchies and embrace relatively authoritarian, paternalistic power relationships. In low-power-distance cultures, however, subordinates consider themselves as equals of their supervisors. They confidently voice opinions and participate in decision making. Relationships between high-powered individuals and people with little power tend to be more democratic, egalitarian, and informal.

As you have probably guessed, in Western cultures people are more relaxed about social status and the appearance of power.[50] Deference is not generally paid to individuals merely because of their wealth, position, seniority, or age. In many Asian cultures, however, these characteristics are important and must be respected. Walmart, facing many hurdles in breaking into the Japanese market, admits to having had difficulty training local employees to speak up to their bosses. In the Japanese culture, lower-level employees do not question management. Deference and respect are paid to authority and power. Recognizing this cultural pattern, Marriott Hotel managers learned to avoid placing a lower-level Japanese employee on a floor above a higher-level executive from the same company. The degree of power distance in selected countries is illustrated in Figure 3.5.

Communication Style. People in low- and high-context cultures tend to communicate differently with words. To Americans and Germans, words are very important, especially in contracts and negotiations. People in high-context cultures, on the other hand, place more emphasis on the surrounding context than on the words describing a negotiation. Greek businesspeople may see a contract as a formal statement announcing the intention to build a business for the future. The Japanese may treat contracts as statements of intention, and they assume changes will be made as projects develop. Mexicans may treat contracts as artistic exercises of what might be accomplished in an ideal world. They do not necessarily expect contracts to apply consistently in the real world. Some Arab cultures may be insulted by merely mentioning a contract; a person's word is more binding.[51]

North Americans tend to take words literally, whereas Latinos enjoy plays on words; and Arabs and South Americans sometimes speak with extravagant or poetic figures of speech that may be misinterpreted if taken literally. Nigerians prefer a quiet, clear form of expression; and Germans tend to be direct but understated.[52]

In communication style North Americans value straightforwardness, are suspicious of evasiveness, and distrust people whom they perceive as having a hidden agenda or playing their cards too close to the chest.[53] North Americans also tend to be uncomfortable with silence and impatient with delays. Some Asian businesspeople have learned that the longer they drag out negotiations, the more concessions impatient North Americans are likely to make.

As you can see, high-context cultures differ from low-context cultures in many dimensions. These differences can be significant for companies engaging in international business.

3-3 Becoming Interculturally Proficient

LEARNING OUTCOME

3 Discuss strategies for enhancing intercultural effectiveness and communication across cultures.

Being aware of your own culture and how it contrasts with others is an important first step in achieving intercultural proficiency. Another step involves recognizing barriers to intercultural accommodation and striving to overcome them. Some of these barriers occur quite naturally and require conscious effort to surmount. You might be thinking, why bother? Probably the most important reasons for becoming interculturally competent are that your personal life will be more satisfying and your work life will be more productive, gratifying, and effective.

3-3a Improving Intercultural Effectiveness

Remember that culture is learned. Developing cultural competence often involves changing attitudes. Through exposure to other cultures and through training, such as you are receiving in this course, you can learn new attitudes and behaviors that help bridge gaps between cultures. Following are some suggestions to help you boost your intercultural savvy.

Building Cultural Self-Awareness. Begin to think of yourself as a product of your culture, and understand that your culture is just one among many. Take any opportunity to travel or study abroad, if possible. You will learn much, not only about other cultures but also about your own. Try to stand outside and look at yourself. Do you see any reflex reactions and automatic thought patterns that are a result of your upbringing? These may be invisible to you until challenged by difference. Remember, your culture was designed to help you succeed and survive in a certain environment. Be sure to keep what works and yet be ready to adapt as environments change. Flexibility is an important survival skill.

Curbing Ethnocentrism. The belief in the superiority of one's own race is known as **ethnocentrism**, a natural attitude inherent in all cultures. If you were raised in North America, many of the dimensions of culture described previously probably seem right to you. For example, it is only logical to think that time is money and you should not waste it. Everyone knows that, right? That is why an American businessperson in an Arab or Asian country might feel irritated at time spent over coffee or other social rituals before any *real* business is transacted. In these cultures, however, time is viewed differently. Moreover, personal relationships must be established and nurtured before credible negotiations may proceed.

Ethnocentrism causes us to judge others by our own values. We expect others to react as we would, and they expect us to behave as they would. Misunderstandings naturally result. A North American smiling broadly, joking, and presenting excitedly a proposed project to German business partners may be perceived as lacking credibility. In turn, German businesspeople who respond soberly and ask direct, probing questions may appear rude and humorless. These knee-jerk ethnocentric judgments can be reduced through knowledge of other cultures and increased intercultural sensitivity.

Political conflict can reinforce ethnocentric gut-level reactions that are often fueled by ignorance and fear. Since the terrorist attacks on September 11, 2001 to this day, 40 percent of Americans harbor fear that they or a family member might be killed by terrorists, although experts put the yearly risk of dying from any terrorist act since 2001 to the present at 1 in 40 million.[54] Radical Islam, the wars in Iraq and Afghanistan, as well as well-publicized terrorist attacks at home and around the world have fueled irrational anti-Muslim sentiments. Battling such deep-seated prejudice and even hate can be a tall order.

Analyzing Generalizations and Stereotyping. Most experts recognize that it is impossible to talk about cultures without using mental categories, representations, and generalizations. These categories are sometimes considered stereotypes. Because the term **stereotype** has a negative meaning, intercultural authors Varner and Beamer suggested that we distinguish between *stereotype* and **prototype**.

In social psychology *stereotype* is defined as an oversimplified behavioral pattern applied uncritically to groups. Although they may be exaggerated and overgeneralized beliefs when applied to groups of people, stereotypes are not always entirely false.[55] However, when a stereotype develops into a rigid attitude and when it is based on erroneous beliefs or preconceptions, then it is hurtful and should be called a **prejudice**.

Varner and Beamer recommended using the term *prototype* to describe "mental representations based on general characteristics that are not fixed and rigid, but rather are open to new definitions."[56] Prototypes, then, are dynamic and change with fresh experience. Prototypes based on objective observations usually have a considerable amount of truth in them. That is why they can be helpful in studying culture. For example, South American businesspeople often talk about their families before getting down to business. This prototype is generally accurate, but it may not universally apply, and it may change over time.

Some people object to making any generalizations about cultures whatsoever. It is wise to remember, however, that whenever we are confronted with something new and unfamiliar, we naturally strive to categorize the data to make sense of them. In categorizing these new data, we are generalizing. Significant intellectual discourse and science would be impossible without generalizations. Unfounded generalizations about people and cultures, of course, can lead to bias and prejudice. However, for our purposes, when we discuss cultures, it is important to be able to generalize and describe cultural prototypes.

Being Open-Minded.

One desirable attitude in achieving intercultural proficiency is that of tolerance. Closed-minded people cannot look beyond their own ethnocentrism. But as global markets expand and as our own society becomes increasingly multiethnic, tolerance becomes especially significant. Not only that: With greater knowledge and compassion, tolerance may lead to *acceptance* and *understanding*.[57] Some job descriptions now include statements such as *Must be able to interact with diverse personnel*.

To improve tolerance, you will want to practice empathy. This means trying to see the world through another's eyes. It means being less judgmental and more eager to seek common ground. One way to promote greater understanding is to work toward a common goal and, as a result, learn about each other. The Arava Institute, an environmental studies center at Kibbutz Ketura in Israel, brings together Jews, Muslims, and Christians to tackle water scarcity in the Middle East, home to 10 of the 15 most water-starved countries in the world. The diverse student body is Jewish Israeli, Arab, and non–Middle Eastern in almost three equal parts. Aside from learning to solve a common challenge in caring for the environment, the students attend peace-building forums in which they discuss race, religion, culture, and politics. For many, studying at Arava is the first encounter with counterparts of a different nationality or religion. The center develops one of the region's scarcest resources—trust.[58]

Being tolerant also involves patience. If a nonnative speaker is struggling to express an idea in English, Americans must avoid the temptation to finish the sentence and provide the word they presume is wanted. When we put words into their mouths, our foreign friends often smile and agree out of politeness, but our words may not express their thoughts. Remaining silent is another means of exhibiting tolerance. Instead of filling every lapse in conversation, North Americans, for example, should recognize that in Asian cultures people deliberately use periods of silence for reflection and contemplation.

Saving Face.

In business transactions North Americans often assume that economic factors are the primary motivators of people. It is wise to remember, though, that strong cultural influences are also at work. Saving face, for example, is important in many parts of the world. *Face* refers to the image a person holds in that person's social network. Positive comments raise a person's social standing, but negative comments lower it.

People in low-context cultures are less concerned with face. Germans and North Americans, for instance, value honesty and directness; they generally come right to the point and tell it like it is. Mexicans, Asians, and members of other high-context cultures, on the other hand, are more concerned with preserving social harmony and saving face. They are indirect and go to great lengths to avoid offending by saying *no*. The Japanese, in fact, have 16 ways to avoid an outright *no*. The empathic listener recognizes the language of refusal and pushes no further. Accepting cultural differences and adapting to them with tolerance and empathy often results in a harmonious compromise.

Ethics ✔ Check

How Ugly Are Today's U.S. Tourists?

Sixty years ago the blockbuster novel *The Ugly American* exposed arrogant, ethnocentric U.S. diplomats in Southeast Asia. Today's ugliest tourists may be Chinese, British, German, or Russian, depending on whom pollsters ask.[59] Rowdy and drunken behavior is the most frequently mentioned infraction. And Americans? Here are a few behaviors that others find annoying: Referring to oneself as "American" in South America, where Argentines or Chileans are Americans, too; being indignant that the locals don't accept dollars in Ireland, a eurozone country; infuriating Czechs for confusing them with Russians, their problematic neighbor; puzzling Austrians for choosing McDonald's over one of the country's legendary cafes; treating medieval European cities like theme parks; taunting the Queen's Guard in London; and insisting on sightseeing in the slums of Rio de Janeiro. Most common criticisms of U.S. visitors include sloppy attire, ignorance of local customs, and over-the-top patriotism.[60] Are such perceptions fair?

3-3b Communicating Nonverbally Across Cultures

Verbal skills in another culture can generally be mastered by studying hard enough. But nonverbal skills are much more difficult to learn. Nonverbal behavior includes the areas described in Chapter 2, such as eye contact, facial expression, posture, gestures, and the use of time, space, and territory. Fortunately, you can learn techniques to boost your intercultural competence.

Nonverbal Cues Influencing Communication. The messages sent by body language and the way we arrange time and space have always been open to interpretation. Does a raised eyebrow mean that your boss doubts your statement or just that she is seriously considering it? Does that closed door to an office mean that your coworker is angry or just that he is working on a project that requires concentration? Deciphering nonverbal communication is difficult for people who are culturally similar, and it is even more troublesome when cultures differ.

In Western cultures, for example, people perceive silence as negative. It suggests rejection, unhappiness, depression, regret, embarrassment, or ignorance. The English expression "The silence was deafening" conveys its oppressiveness. However, the Japanese admire silence and consider it a key to success. A Japanese proverb says, "Those who know do not speak; those who speak do not know." Silence is equated with respect and wisdom.[61]

Although nonverbal behavior is ambiguous within cultures and even more problematic between cultures, it nevertheless conveys meaning. If you've ever had to talk with someone who does not share your language, you probably learned quickly to use gestures to convey basic messages. Because gestures can create very different reactions in different cultures, one must be careful in using and interpreting them. In some societies it is extremely bad form to point one's finger, as in giving directions. Other hand gestures can also cause trouble. The thumbs-up symbol may be used to indicate approval in North America, but in Iran and Ghana it is a vulgar gesture.

As businesspeople increasingly interact with their counterparts from other cultures, they become more aware of these differences. Numerous lists of cultural dos and don'ts have been compiled. However, learning all the nuances of nonverbal behavior in other cultures is impossible; such lists are merely the tip of the cultural iceberg (see Figure 3.3). Striving to associate with people from different cultures can further broaden your intercultural savvy.

Achieving Intercultural Competence. For improving effectiveness and achieving intercultural competence, one expert, M. R. Hammer, suggested that three processes or attitudes are effective. Descriptiveness refers to the use of concrete and specific feedback. As you will learn in Chapter 4 about the process of communication, descriptive feedback is more effective than judgmental feedback. For example, using objective terms to describe the modest attire of Muslim women is more effective than describing it as unfeminine or motivated by the oppressive and unequal treatment of females.

A second attitude is what Hammer called nonjudgmentalism. This attitude goes a long way in preventing defensive reactions from communicators. Most important in achieving effective communication is supportiveness. This attitude requires us to support others positively with head nods, eye contact, facial expression, and physical proximity.[62]

From a practical standpoint, when interacting with businesspeople in other cultures, you would be wise to follow their lead. If they avoid intense eye contact, don't stare. If no one is putting elbows on a table, don't be the first to do so. Until you are knowledgeable about the meaning of gestures, it is probably a good idea to keep yours to a minimum. Learning the words for *please, yes,* and *thank you,* some of which are shown in Figure 3.6, is even better than relying on gestures.[63] Intercultural competence in nonverbal behavior may never be fully attained, but sensitivity, a nonjudgmental attitude, and respect for others go a long way toward improving interactions.

FIGURE 3.6 Basic Expressions in Other Languages

ENGLISH

hello
please
thank you
yes
no
goodbye
sorry

ARABIC

as-salam alaykum
min fadhlik
shukran
aiwa/na'am
la
ma'a salama
asef(a)

FRENCH

bonjour
s'il vous plaît
merci
oui
non
au revoir
pardon

GERMAN

guten Tag
bitte
danke
ja
nein
auf Wiedersehen
Entschuldigung

ITALIAN

buon giorno
per favore
grazie
sì
no
arrivederci
scusa

JAPANESE

konnichiwa
onegai shimasu
arigato goizamasu
hai
iie [ee-yeh]
sayonara
sumimasen

NORWEGIAN

god dag
vær så snill
takk
ja
nei
ha det
beklager

RUSSIAN

zdravstvujte
požalujsta
spasiba
da
net [nyet]
do svidanija
izvinite

SPANISH

hola
por favor
gracias
sí
no
adiós
perdón

Filip Bjorkman/Shutterstock.com; Viktorija Reuta/Shutterstock.com

3-3c Technology and Social Media Affecting Intercultural Communication

Much has been made of the unprecedented hyperconnectivity facilitated by social media and communication technology today. Certainly, users can interact instantly across time zones and vast distances. With minimal resources, they can also potentially reach out to more individuals and groups all over the world than ever before in history. Not surprisingly, social media may potentially bridge cultural differences as well as reinforce them, depending on their users.

Social Media: Blurring Boundaries? What we make of the potential for connectedness and intercultural communication online is as much up to us as it would be at a dinner party at which we don't know any of the other guests. Some authors believe that social media blur cultural gaps, reduce hierarchies, and empower people to change their circumstances.[64] At the same time, the online environment may deepen feelings of social isolation, leading to the much debated *loneliness epidemic*.[65] One recent study suggests that humans tend to experience negative events online more strongly than positive encounters. Social media can worsen depression, but users who are already depressed may be more likely to depend on social media, or have negative experiences with it, researchers say.[66]

Online, as in real life, we tend to gravitate toward people who seem similar to us, believes social entrepreneur Rajiv Vinnakota. Social media divide us because we inhabit "echo chambers" online instead of "bridging social capital" and interacting with people not like us as we used to do offline, he says.[67]

Twitter and other social media can boost intercultural communication; however, we must be willing to reach out across the boundaries that separate us. Shared causes can mobilize social media users halfway across the globe. The current pro-democracy student protesters in Hong Kong are skilled in documenting, organizing, and assembling large-scale protests with the help of social media. They not only are able to stay anonymous, spread information, and galvanize demonstrators, but they also work to win the hearts and minds of the public.[68] In response, mainland Chinese authorities are using Twitter and Facebook to spread disinformation about Hong Kong.[69]

Social Media: Global and Local?   Despite the equalizing influence of globalization, regional and cultural differences persist, as those who design media for markets in other countries know. Asian users may prefer muted pastel colors and anime-style graphics that North Americans would find strange. Knowledge of color symbolism across cultures is indispensable for designers lest they commit cultural blunders. Consider yellow—a hue with generally positive connotations in Western cultures, but one that also represents cowardice—stands for courage in Japan. Orange, the signature color of the Dutch royal court, epitomizes the harvest and fall in North America and Europe. Likewise, in Asia, orange is an auspicious hue; however, in the Middle East, orange signifies mourning and loss. Green is a color with pleasing associations in Western cultures, Asia, and the Middle East.[70]

More serious differences nationally as well as globally are now caused by geopolitical turmoil, Russian influence operations, and restricted access to the Internet in authoritarian countries around the world—a trend that has been called **digital nationalism**. Some predictions foresee a so-called **Splinternet**, a fragmentation of the Internet, once viewed as a unified global network.[71] It remains to be seen whether the deep divides will dissipate or continue to grow.

3-3d Improving Intercultural Communication

Although speaking a foreign language fluently is best, many Americans lack that skill. Fortunately, global business transactions are increasingly conducted in English. English has become the language of technology, the language of Hollywood, and the language of business even in traditionally non-English-speaking countries. English is so dominant that when Korean, Russian, and Mexican officials recently met in Beijing at the Asia-Pacific Economic Cooperation (APEC) summit, they communicated in English. It's the only official language of APEC, even when that organization meets in China.[72] However, Americans and others who communicate with nonnative speakers are more likely to be understood if they observe a few polite and helpful suggestions.

Refining Oral Communication.   Americans abroad make a big mistake in thinking that nonnative speakers of English can always follow the conversation. Comprehension can be superficial. Even though they speak English, foreign nationals appreciate if you learn greetings and a few phrases in their language. It's also wise to speak slowly, use simple English, opt for short sentences, and avoid long, complex words. Following are additional suggestions to improve oral intercultural communication:

- **Observe eye messages.** Be alert to a glazed expression or wandering eyes. These tell you that the listener is lost.

- **Encourage accurate feedback.** Ask probing questions, and encourage the listener to paraphrase what you say. Do not assume that a *yes*, a nod, or a smile indicates comprehension.

- **Accept blame.** If a misunderstanding results, graciously accept the blame for not making your meaning clear.

- **Listen without interrupting.** Curb your desire to finish sentences or to fill out ideas for the speaker. Keep in mind that North Americans abroad are often accused of listening too little and talking too much.

- **Smile when appropriate.** The smile is often considered the single most understood and most useful form of communication. However, in some cultures excessive smiling may seem insincere.

- **Follow up in writing.** After conversations or oral negotiations, confirm the results and agreements with written messages. For proposals and contracts, hire a professional translator.

Perfecting Written Communication. In sending letters, e-mails, and other documents to businesspeople in other cultures, try to adjust your writing style and tone. For example, in cultures in which formality and tradition are important, be scrupulously polite. Don't even think of sharing the latest joke. Humor translates very poorly and can cause misunderstanding and negative reactions. Familiarize yourself with customary channels of communication. Are letters, e-mails, and faxes common? Would a direct or indirect organizational pattern be more effective? What's more, forget about trying to cut through red tape: In some cultures bureaucracy is widely accepted. The following additional suggestions can help you prepare successful written messages for intercultural audiences.

- **Use short sentences and short paragraphs.** Sentences with fewer than 20 words and paragraphs with fewer than 8 lines are most readable.

- **Observe titles and rank.** Use last names, titles, and other signals of rank and status. Send messages to higher-status people and avoid sending copies to lower-rank people.

- **Avoid ambiguous expressions.** Include relative pronouns (*that, which, who*) for clarity in introducing clauses. Stay away from contractions (especially ones such as *Here's the problem*). Avoid idioms and figurative clichés (*once in a blue moon*), slang (*my presentation really bombed*), acronyms (*ASAP,* for *as soon as possible*), abbreviations (*DBA,* for *doing business as*), jargon (*input, bottom line*), and sports references (*play ball, slam dunk, ballpark figure*). Use action-specific verbs (*purchase a printer* rather than *get a printer*).

- **Strive for clarity.** Avoid words that have many meanings (the word *light* has 18 meanings). If necessary, clarify words that may be confusing. Replace two-word verbs with clear single words (*return* instead of *bring back; delay* instead of *put off; maintain* instead of *keep up*).

- **Use correct grammar.** Be careful about misplaced modifiers, dangling participles, and sentence fragments. Use conventional punctuation.

- **Cite numbers carefully.** In international trade learn and use the metric system. In citing numbers use figures (*12*) instead of spelling them out (*twelve*). Always convert dollar figures into local currency. Avoid using figures to express the month of the year. In North America, for example, May 11, 2017, might be written as 5/11/17, whereas in Europe the same date might appear as 11.5.17. Figure 3.7 shows common international data formats. The International Organization for Standardization (ISO) has created the least ambiguous date and time representations, but the formats have not been universally adopted. Based on guideline ISO 8601, the date of June 12, 2021 would be represented as 2021-06-12.

FIGURE 3.7   Typical Data Formats

	United States	United Kingdom	France	Germany	Argentina
Dates	June 12, 2022 06/12/2022	12 June 2022 12/06/2022	12 juin 2022 12.06.2022	12. Juni 2022 12.06.2022	12 de junio 2022 12/06/2022 or 12-VI-2022
Time	9:45 p.m.	9:45 p.m.	21:45 21 h 45	21:45 Uhr 21.45 Uhr	21:45 21h45
Currency	$123.45 USD 123.45	£123.45 GBP 123.45	123,45 € EUR 123,45	123,45 € EUR 123,45	$123,45 123,45 ARS
Large numbers	1,234,567.89	1,234,567.89	1.234.567,89	1.234.567,89	1.234.567,89
Phone numbers	(302) 567–1234 +1 302 567 1234	020 7734 8624 +44 20 7734 8624	01 43 36 17 00 +33 1 43 36 1700	(030) 2261 1004 +49 30 2261 1004	(11) 1234-5678 +54 11 1234 5678

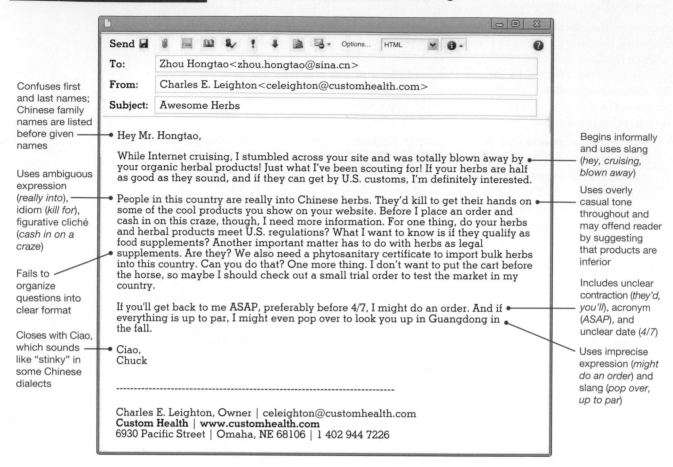

Confuses first and last names; Chinese family names are listed before given names

Uses ambiguous expression (*really into*), idiom (*kill for*), figurative cliché (*cash in on a craze*)

Fails to organize questions into clear format

Closes with Ciao, which sounds like "stinky" in some Chinese dialects

Begins informally and uses slang (*hey, cruising, blown away*)

Uses overly casual tone throughout and may offend reader by suggesting that products are inferior

Includes unclear contraction (*they'd, you'll*), acronym (*ASAP*), and unclear date (4/7)

Uses imprecise expression (*might do an order*) and slang (*pop over, up to par*)

To: Zhou Hongtao<zhou.hongtao@sina.cn>
From: Charles E. Leighton<celeighton@customhealth.com>
Subject: Awesome Herbs

Hey Mr. Hongtao,

While Internet cruising, I stumbled across your site and was totally blown away by your organic herbal products! Just what I've been scouting for! If your herbs are half as good as they sound, and if they can get by U.S. customs, I'm definitely interested.

People in this country are really into Chinese herbs. They'd kill to get their hands on some of the cool products you show on your website. Before I place an order and cash in on this craze, though, I need more information. For one thing, do your herbs and herbal products meet U.S. regulations? What I want to know is if they qualify as food supplements? Another important matter has to do with herbs as legal supplements. Are they? We also need a phytosanitary certificate to import bulk herbs into this country. Can you do that? One more thing. I don't want to put the cart before the horse, so maybe I should check out a small trial order to test the market in my country.

If you'll get back to me ASAP, preferably before 4/7, I might do an order. And if everything is up to par, I might even pop over to look you up in Guangdong in the fall.

Ciao,
Chuck

Charles E. Leighton, Owner | celeighton@customhealth.com
Custom Health | **www.customhealth.com**
6930 Pacific Street | Omaha, NE 68106 | 1 402 944 7226

3-3e Examining an Inadequate Intercultural E-Mail Message

Model Document 3.1 illustrates an ineffective intercultural message. The writer uses a casual, breezy tone in a message to a Chinese company when a formal tone would be more appropriate. In addition, the e-mail includes slang and ambiguous expressions that would almost surely confuse a reader for whom English is not a first language.

In the effective version in Model Document 3.2, the writer adopts a formal but pleasant, polite tone, striving for complete sentences and correct grammar. The effective e-mail message avoids slang (*up to par*), idioms, imprecise words (*put the cart before the horse, I might do an order*), unclear abbreviations (*ASAP*), and confusing dates (4/7). To further aid comprehension, the writer organizes the message into a bulleted list with clear questions.

As the world economies continue to intermingle and globalization spreads, more businesspeople are adopting Western ways. Although Japanese writers may open letters with a seasonable greeting (*Cherry trees will soon be blooming*), many pragmatic U.S. writers prefer streamlined messages. Forced friendliness and cliché openings (*I hope this finds you well*) sound canned and delay the main message. If the situation requires a relaxed opening, find a more creative way to be friendly and courteous while staying professional.[73]

The following checklist summarizes suggestions for improving communication with intercultural audiences.

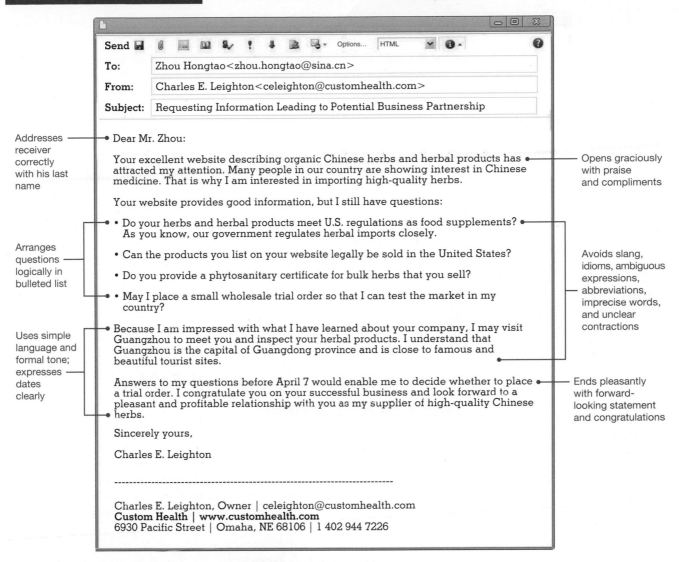

Addresses receiver correctly with his last name

Arranges questions logically in bulleted list

Uses simple language and formal tone; expresses dates clearly

Opens graciously with praise and compliments

Avoids slang, idioms, ambiguous expressions, abbreviations, imprecise words, and unclear contractions

Ends pleasantly with forward-looking statement and congratulations

---

Send | Options... | HTML

To: Zhou Hongtao<zhou.hongtao@sina.cn>

From: Charles E. Leighton<celeighton@customhealth.com>

Subject: Requesting Information Leading to Potential Business Partnership

Dear Mr. Zhou:

Your excellent website describing organic Chinese herbs and herbal products has attracted my attention. Many people in our country are showing interest in Chinese medicine. That is why I am interested in importing high-quality herbs.

Your website provides good information, but I still have questions:

- Do your herbs and herbal products meet U.S. regulations as food supplements? As you know, our government regulates herbal imports closely.

- Can the products you list on your website legally be sold in the United States?

- Do you provide a phytosanitary certificate for bulk herbs that you sell?

- May I place a small wholesale trial order so that I can test the market in my country?

Because I am impressed with what I have learned about your company, I may visit Guangzhou to meet you and inspect your herbal products. I understand that Guangzhou is the capital of Guangdong province and is close to famous and beautiful tourist sites.

Answers to my questions before April 7 would enable me to decide whether to place a trial order. I congratulate you on your successful business and look forward to a pleasant and profitable relationship with you as my supplier of high-quality Chinese herbs.

Sincerely yours,

Charles E. Leighton

Charles E. Leighton, Owner | celeighton@customhealth.com
Custom Health | www.customhealth.com
6930 Pacific Street | Omaha, NE 68106 | 1 402 944 7226

Checklist

Achieving Intercultural Proficiency

- **Examine your own culture.** Culture is learned. Study your customs, biases, and views and how they differ from those in other societies. This may improve your understanding and acceptance of the values and behavior of people in other cultures.

- **Explore other cultures.** Education can help you alter cultural misconceptions, reduce fears, and minimize misunderstandings. Knowledge of other cultures opens your eyes and enriches your life.

- **Curb ethnocentrism.** Avoid judging others by your personal views. Overcome the view that other cultures are incorrect, defective, or primitive. Try to develop an open mind-set.

- **Treat each individual you meet as a *prototype*.** Be open to questioning and adjusting your perceptions of other cultures. Generalizations are natural and unavoidable, but beware of stereotypes and prejudice. Most people like to be treated as unique individuals, not typical representatives of an entire group.

- **Observe nonverbal cues in your culture.** Become more alert to the meanings of eye contact, facial expression, posture, gestures, and the use of time, space, and territory. How do they differ in other cultures?

- **Embrace nonjudgmental attitude.** Strive to accept unfamiliar behavior as different, rather than as right or wrong. However, try not to be defensive in justifying your own culture. Strive for objectivity.

- **Be aware of culture when using communication technology.** Don't expect that individuals from other cultures think and act the same way you do; at the same time, try to reach out to others over common interests.

- **Use plain English.** Speak and write in short sentences using simple words and standard English. Eliminate puns, slang, jargon, acronyms, abbreviations, and any words that cannot be easily translated.

- **Encourage accurate feedback.** In conversations ask probing questions and listen attentively without interrupting. Do not assume that a *yes* or a smile indicates agreement or comprehension.

- **Adapt to local preferences.** Shape your writing to reflect the document styles of the reader's culture, if appropriate. Express currency in local figures. Write out months of the year for clarity.

LEARNING OUTCOME

4 Examine the complexities of ethics across cultures, including business practices abroad, bribery, prevailing customs, and methods for coping.

3-4 Considering Culture and Ethical Business Practices

When you do business around the world, whose values, culture, and, ultimately, laws do you follow? In a global economy, conscientious organizations and individuals face this perplexing problem: Do you heed the customs of your country or those of the host country? Despite a slew of international antigraft laws, corrupt payments are "an unspoken rule" in China, for example. In real estate and construction, 38 to 44 percent of U.S. companies cite "competitive pressure" to justify grease payments and gifts to officials to operate.[74]

3-4a Doing Business Abroad

As companies do more and more business around the globe, their assumptions about ethics are put to the test. Businesspeople may face simple questions regarding the appropriate amount of money to spend on a business gift or the legitimacy of payments to agents and distributors to "expedite" business. They may also encounter out-and-out bribery, child-labor abuse, environment mistreatment, and unscrupulous business practices. Despite recent pressure toward loosening enforcement of bribery abroad, the ethics of U.S. businesses are being scrutinized by lawmakers who want to punish not only the payer of a bribe but the recipient as well.[75] Violators of laws or company policies can land in big trouble, as Walmart did in Brazil and several other countries.

Today most companies that are active in global markets have ethical codes of conduct. These codes are public documents and can usually be found on company websites, whether Lululemon or Northrop Grumman. They are an accepted part of governance. The growing sophistication of these codes results in ethics training programs that often include complicated hypothetical questions. Ethics trainers teach employees to solve problems by reconciling legal requirements, company policies, and conflicting cultural norms.

Businesses in other countries are also adopting ethics codes and helping employees live up to the standards. After entering the market and investing $4 billion in Russia, IKEA decided to halt further expansion. Safety inspectors, expecting bribes, were withholding permission for additional stores outside Moscow. The company cited "zero tolerance on corruption" and refused to pay up.[76] After overcoming such tribulations, the Swedish furniture powerhouse is wildly successful in Russia today.

Transparency International, a Berlin-based watchdog group, compiles an annual ranking of perceived public sector corruption in 180 countries. Based on surveys of businesspeople and analysts, the index shown in Figure 3.9 reflects perceptions of corruption in the public sector.[77] Gauging corruption precisely is impossible. However, this graph reflects the feelings of individuals doing business in the countries shown. Of the countries selected for this graph, the least corrupt were Denmark, New Zealand, Finland, Singapore, Sweden, and Switzerland. The most corrupt were Syria, South Sudan, and Somalia.

FIGURE 3.9 Corruption Perceptions Index: Clean or Corrupt?

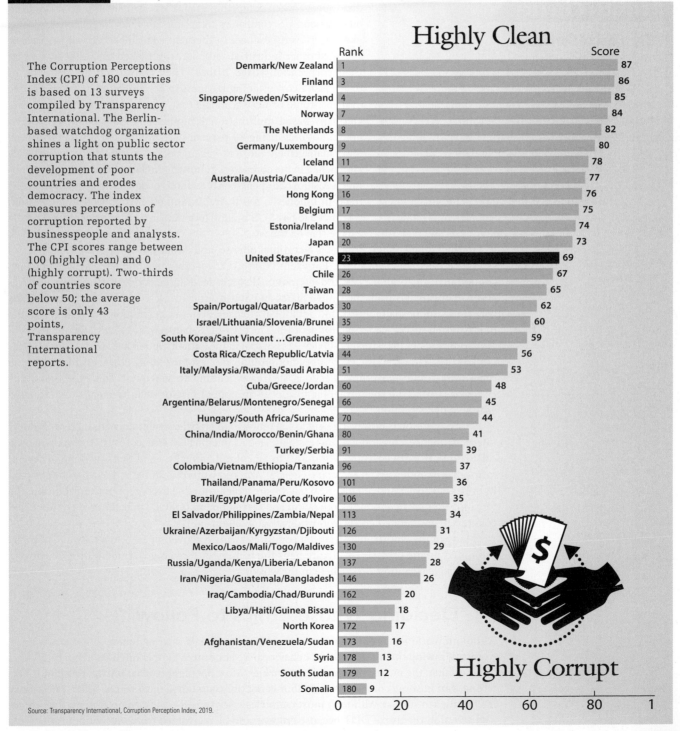

The Corruption Perceptions Index (CPI) of 180 countries is based on 13 surveys compiled by Transparency International. The Berlin-based watchdog organization shines a light on public sector corruption that stunts the development of poor countries and erodes democracy. The index measures perceptions of corruption reported by businesspeople and analysts. The CPI scores range between 100 (highly clean) and 0 (highly corrupt). Two-thirds of countries score below 50; the average score is only 43 points, Transparency International reports.

Highly Clean

	Rank	Score
Denmark/New Zealand	1	87
Finland	3	86
Singapore/Sweden/Switzerland	4	85
Norway	7	84
The Netherlands	8	82
Germany/Luxembourg	9	80
Iceland	11	78
Australia/Austria/Canada/UK	12	77
Hong Kong	16	76
Belgium	17	75
Estonia/Ireland	18	74
Japan	20	73
United States/France	23	69
Chile	26	67
Taiwan	28	65
Spain/Portugal/Quatar/Barbados	30	62
Israel/Lithuania/Slovenia/Brunei	35	60
South Korea/Saint Vincent ...Grenadines	39	59
Costa Rica/Czech Republic/Latvia	44	56
Italy/Malaysia/Rwanda/Saudi Arabia	51	53
Cuba/Greece/Jordan	60	48
Argentina/Belarus/Montenegro/Senegal	66	45
Hungary/South Africa/Suriname	70	44
China/India/Morocco/Benin/Ghana	80	41
Turkey/Serbia	91	39
Colombia/Vietnam/Ethiopia/Tanzania	96	37
Thailand/Panama/Peru/Kosovo	101	36
Brazil/Egypt/Algeria/Cote d'Ivoire	106	35
El Salvador/Philippines/Zambia/Nepal	113	34
Ukraine/Azerbaijan/Kyrgyzstan/Djibouti	126	31
Mexico/Laos/Mali/Togo/Maldives	130	29
Russia/Uganda/Kenya/Liberia/Lebanon	137	28
Iran/Nigeria/Guatemala/Bangladesh	146	26
Iraq/Cambodia/Chad/Burundi	162	20
Libya/Haiti/Guinea Bissau	168	18
North Korea	172	17
Afghanistan/Venezuela/Sudan	173	16
Syria	178	13
South Sudan	179	12
Somalia	180	9

Highly Corrupt

0   20   40   60   80   1

Source: Transparency International, Corruption Perception Index, 2019.

The United States earned its lowest CPI score in eight years; Transparency International calls the United States a country to watch for "threats to its system of checks and balances," "ever-increasing influence of special interests" and "the use of anonymous shell companies . . . to hide illicit activities."[78]

3-4b Understanding Antibribery Laws

The United States is not at the top on the index of least corrupt countries. However, it has taken the global lead in fighting corruption. In 1977 the U.S. government passed the Foreign Corrupt Practices Act (FCPA). It prohibits payments to foreign officials for the purpose of obtaining or retaining business. But the law applies only to U.S. companies. Therefore, they are at a decided disadvantage when competing against less scrupulous enterprises from other nations. U.S. companies complained that they lost billions of dollars in contracts every year because they refused to bribe their way to success.

Most other industrialized countries looked the other way when their corporations used bribes. They considered the greasing of palms just a cost of doing business in certain cultures. After a string of high-profile bribery scandals that led to penalties of $1.6 billion, Germany-based multinational engineering giant Siemens cleaned house, not only firing 80 percent of its top executives, but thinning lower management ranks as well to root out corruption that was deeply entrenched in the company's culture.[80] Similarly, French energy corporation Alstom had spent tens of millions of dollars in bribes to win contracts in Indonesia, Saudi Arabia, and other countries. In all, Alstom was forced to pay $772 million to settle the corruption charges,[81] hardly a mere slap on the wrist.

In the United States, bribery is a criminal offense, and American corporate officials found guilty are fined and sent to jail. For example, the U.S. government conducted a sweeping corruption investigation of FIFA, the international soccer federation. Sports-marketing executives and soccer officials from the United States and South America were convicted of racketeering, wire fraud, money laundering, and additional offenses. Systemic corruption was rampant in the international soccer leadership for decades. The use of U.S. banks was its downfall.[82]

Domestically, the Sarbanes–Oxley Act is a tool in the anticorruption battle. It forbids off-the-book bribes. However, the FCPA does not prohibit modest *facilitating payments* that may ease the way for routine government actions, such as expediting a visa request. This exception in the FCPA has been criticized for failing to specify an upper limit for such payments and created a gray area of corruption.[83]

More attention is now being paid to the problem of global corruption. With increased global interdependence, corruption is increasingly seen as unethical as well as costly. According to one calculation, bribery costs the world $1.5 to $2 trillion annually—and that's just one of several forms of corruption.[84] UN Secretary-General António Guterres estimates that $1 trillion is paid in bribes each year and another $2.6 trillion are stolen—all due to corruption.[85] In addition, the Organization for Economic Cooperation and Development (OECD) puts the value of imported counterfeit and pirated goods worldwide at $509 billion.

Many of the world's industrialized countries formally agreed in 1999 to a new global treaty promoted by the OECD. This treaty bans the bribery of foreign government officials. Today, bribery is illegal almost everywhere in the world.

3-4c Deciding Whose Ethics to Follow

Although world leaders seem to agree that bribing officials is wrong, many other shady areas persist. Drawing the lines of ethical behavior here at home is hard enough. When faced with a cultural filter, the picture becomes even murkier. Most people agree that mistreating children is wrong. But in some countries, child labor is not only condoned but also considered necessary for families to subsist. Although most countries want to respect the environment, they might also sanction the use of DDT because crops would be consumed by insects without it.

The exchanging of gifts is another tricky subject. In many non-Western cultures, the gift exchange tradition has become a business ritual. Gifts not only are a sign of gratitude and hospitality but also generate a future obligation and trust. Americans, of course, become uneasy when gift-giving seems to move beyond normal courtesy and friendliness. If it even remotely suggests influence peddling, they back off. Many companies suggest $50 as a top limit for gifts.

Whose ethics prevail across borders? Doing the right thing can be subject to huge economic pressures. China's global influence is growing. In the interest of commerce, Western democracies have long ago stopped criticizing the increasingly authoritarian regime on its poor human rights record.[86] More often than not, businesspeople in countries where bribes are common know corruption is wrong and may dislike it, but they view the practice as a cost of doing business.[87] Systemic change is slow to come.

Beyond moral values, non-governmental organizations such as the International Monetary Fund convincingly argue that fighting global corruption offers tangible rewards, for example, the retrieval of $1 trillion in lost tax revenues and social gains such as restoring the public's trust in government.[88]

3-4d Making Ethical Decisions Across Borders

Instead of trying to distinguish *good* ethics and *bad* ethics, perhaps the best plan is to look for practical solutions to the cultural challenges of global business interaction. Following are suggestions that acknowledge different values but also emphasize moral initiative.[89]

- **Broaden your view.** Become more sensitive to the values and customs of other cultures. Look especially at what they consider moral, traditional, practical, and effective.

- **Create virtuous incentives for staff.** Compensation should reward proper legal and ethical behavior.

- **Find alternatives.** Instead of caving to government payoffs, perhaps offer nonmonetary public service benefits, technical expertise, or additional customer service.

- **Refuse business if options violate your basic values.** If an action seriously breaches your own code of ethics or that of your firm, give up the transaction.

- **Embrace transparency.** Conduct all relations and negotiations as openly as possible.

- **Don't rationalize shady decisions.** Avoid agreeing to actions that cause you to say, *This isn't really illegal or immoral, This is in the company's best interest,* or *No one will find out.*

- **Resist legalistic strategies.** Don't use tactics that are legally safe but ethically questionable. For example, don't call agents (who are accountable to employers) distributors (who are not).

When faced with an intercultural ethical dilemma, you can apply the same five-question test you learned in Chapter 1, Figure 1.14. Even in another culture, these questions can guide you to the best decision.

1. Is the action legal?
2. Would you do it if you were on the opposite side?
3. Can you rule out a better alternative?
4. Would a trusted advisor agree?
5. Would family, friends, an employer, or coworkers approve?

> **Reality Check**
>
> ### Diversity Boosts Competitiveness
>
> "It makes sense that a diverse and inclusive employee base—with a range of approaches and perspectives—would be more competitive in a globalized economy. [. . .] Companies with the most ethnically/culturally diverse boards worldwide are 43% more likely to experience higher profits."[90]
>
> —McKinsey & Company, *Delivering through Diversity Report*

3-5 Evaluating Benefits and Challenges of Workplace Diversity

LEARNING OUTCOME

5 Describe the advantages and challenges of workforce diversity as well as approaches for improving communication among diverse workplace audiences.

While North American companies are expanding global operations and adapting to a variety of emerging markets, the domestic workforce is also becoming more diverse. This diversity has many dimensions—race, ethnicity, age, religion, gender, national origin, physical ability, sexual orientation, and others. No longer, say the experts, will the workplace be predominantly Anglo-oriented or male.

As discussed in Chapter 1, many groups now considered minorities (African Americans, Hispanics, Asians, Native Americans) already comprise 39 percent of the U.S. population. New projections indicate that 2045 will be the year of the majority–minority crossover, the point at which minorities will represent the majority of the U.S. population at 50.3 percent.[91] The minority-white tipping point has already arrived for youth under 18 years of age and will be reached in 2027 for the age group between 18 and 29.[92] Women comprise nearly 50 percent of the workforce. Moreover, latest U.S. Census data suggest that the share of the population over sixty-five will jump from 15 percent now to almost 22 percent in 2050. By 2030 all baby boomers will be over the age of 65, so that 1 in 5 residents will have reached retirement age, outnumbering children for the first time in U.S. history.[93] Trends suggest that many of these older people will remain in the workforce. Because of technological advances, more physically challenged people are also joining the workforce.

3-5a Advantages of Diversity

As society and the workforce become more diverse, successful interactions and communication among identity groups bring distinct advantages in three areas.

Ethical Insight

Gender Identity: A New Frontier in Workplace Diversity and Inclusion Efforts

Gay and lesbian Americans have won gains culminating in marriage equality. However, transgender and gender nonconforming people have yet to reach accommodation, much less acceptance on the job and in society. Yet ignoring this potential talent pool may prove unwise, not just in a tight job market.

Growing Diversity by the Numbers

According to Pew Research, millennials now comprise more than one-third of workers, the largest generation participating in the U.S. labor force.[94] Of these millennials, about 20 percent identify as LGBTQ+, twice as many as the boomers and two-thirds more than Generation X. Roughly 12 percent of this cohort (ages 21 to 36) identify as transgender or gender nonconforming, a Harris Poll/GLAAD survey has found.[95] One study estimates that 1.4 million adults in the United States identify as transgender and gender nonbinary.[96] Forward-looking organizations realize that they need to address gender beyond the ongoing controversy over restroom facilities.

Companies Are Taking Notice

Large companies are beginning to acknowledge nonbinary employees and customers by introducing gender-neutral language and training their representatives to ask about preferred pronouns.[97] Some 515 major businesses provide gender transition guidelines, suggesting that corporate America is moving toward transgender acceptance.[98] Financial services giant TIAA expects client-facing employees to share their pronouns in introductions and ask clients whether they wish to be referred to as *he*, *she*, *they*, or *ze*. Netflix has adopted this practice in hiring, and United Airlines offers nonbinary gender booking options, including *Mx*.[99] Eleven U.S. states and D.C. issue driver's licenses that include a gender-neutral option. However, employers are struggling with binary gender limitations in current HR software systems, health insurance plans, and on federal forms.

Challenges Persist

Despite the growing awareness, gender nonbinary workers still face many hurdles. In one poll 30 percent of transgender workers reported they were fired, denied promotions, or not hired because of their gender identity or expression.[100] Many of these individuals struggle with mistreatment, harassment, and violence. They are more likely to be poor, homeless, depressed, and suicidal. The biggest challenge, however, is just getting hired. Unemployment among transgender workers runs three times higher than the national jobless rate.[101]

At consulting firm Accenture, Ellyn Shook introduces herself to new-hires by stating her name, education, and her pronouns, *she* and *her*. "When you're in a war for talent, you need to be committed to helping people both professionally and personally," the HR executive believes. "It's incumbent on me and my colleagues to make sure every single person feels like they belong."[102]

Did you know what these terms mean?

Transgender: An umbrella term describing people who don't identify by the male/female gender definitions, although some do identify as he or she; they may or may not have surgery to physically reassign their sex; transgender individuals can express any sexuality just as nontrans people do.

Gender nonbinary: Those who don't identify as male or female and believe neither gender fits them.

Gender nonconforming: Like nonbinary people, nonconforming people don't identify within the binary gender norms of male or female. Gender nonbinary and gender nonconforming are often used as synonyms.

Gender fluid: Individuals whose gender identity is flexible and shifting.

Gender nonbinary, nonconforming, and fluid individuals may ask that the gender nonspecific, singular pronouns *they/their* or *ze/hir*—not *he/his* or *she/her*—be used to refer to them. Some may adopt the honorific *Mx*. (pronounced *mix*), not *Mr.* or *Ms.*

Consumers.   A diverse staff is better able to read trends and respond to the increasingly diverse customer base in local and world markets. Diverse consumers now want goods and services tailored to their needs. Teams made up of people with different experiences are better equipped to create products that these markets require. Consumers also want to deal with companies that respect their values and reflect themselves.

The CEO of PR firm Gravity, Yuriy Boykiv, speaks to this relationship between a diverse staff and customers: "My company's collective work calls for reaching consumers of multiple ethnicities, which is impossible to do without a deep understanding of a wide range of cultures. Our team consists of more than 40 people who collectively speak 20 different languages." Boykiv urges fellow executives to "Tap into the diversity of your workplace to gain a deep understanding of your workforce and your potential customer base."[103]

Work Teams.   As you learned in Chapter 2, employees today often work in teams. Team members with different backgrounds may come up with more innovative and effective solutions than homogeneous teams. Leadership and ethics professor Katherine Phillips said she believes that "Diversity enhances creativity. It encourages the search for novel information and perspectives, leading to better decision making and problem solving. . . . Even simply being exposed to diversity can change the way you think."[104] Aside from creativity, diverse teams are 45 percent more likely to increase market share and 70 percent more likely to capture a new market.[105]

Business Organizations.   Companies that set aside time and resources to cultivate and capitalize on diversity suffer fewer discrimination lawsuits, fewer union clashes, and less government regulatory action. Most important, though, is the growing realization among organizations that diversity is a critical bottom-line business strategy to increase revenue, engage employees, and spur innovation. According to a McKinsey report, gender and ethnically diverse executive teams were 33 percent more likely to lead their industry in profitability.[106] Researchers compiling *Fortune's* annual list of Best Workplaces for Diversity suggest that inclusion not only makes business sense but also benefits all workers. "The best workplaces forge bonds among co-workers of different political views, different backgrounds, different job titles," says Ann Nadeau, chief people officer at Great Place to Work. She adds: "At a time when our national social fabric has frayed, workplaces that are great for all people can play an important role in mending America."[107]

Developing a diverse staff that can work together is one of the biggest challenges facing business organizations today.

3-5b Challenges of Diversity

Diversity can be a positive force within organizations. However, sometimes it may lead to divisiveness, discontent, and clashes. Many of the identity groups, the so-called workforce disenfranchised, have legitimate gripes.

Women complain of the glass ceiling, that invisible barrier of attitudes, prejudices, and old boy networks blocking them from reaching important corporate positions. Some women feel that they are the victims of sexual harassment, unequal wages, sexism, and even their style of communication. See the Career Coach box to learn more about gender talk and gender tension. On the other hand, men, too, have gender issues. A male HR professional complained that he was passed over for promotion because the hiring managers thought he was not warm enough, potentially a code for a female leadership style.[108]

Older employees believe that the deck is stacked in favor of younger employees. Minorities complain that they are discriminated against in hiring, retention, wages, and promotions. People with disabilities feel that their limitations should not hold them back, and they fear that their potential is often prejudged. Religious affiliation too can lead to uneasy workplace relations. In fact, religion-based conflict in the American workplace is rising. "It's the fastest growth area in discrimination," says Robert E. Gregg, an attorney in Madison, Wisconsin. Religion has surpassed even sex and racial discrimination in the volume of litigation.[109]

Despite progress, much remains to be done to get diversity and inclusion right. Instances of unconscious bias leading to the arrest of two African Americans at Starbucks in Philadelphia, the age discrimination lawsuit filed against IBM for firing 20,000 older workers over five years, or the flood of sexual harassment claims around the country[111] speak volumes.

He Said, She Said: Gender Talk and Gender Tension

Fewer Americans appear to make gender-based assumptions any longer. Gender differences are fading: Gallup has found that a 55 percent majority of Americans have no preferences about the gender of their boss; men (68 percent) are even more likely than women (44 percent) to be indifferent. Younger workers under 35 prefer a female boss over a male by 14 points. The pollsters speculate that the sexual misconduct cases that spawned the #MeToo movement may have shifted favor toward female leaders.[110] It is also conceivable that increasingly eroding gender roles and growing gender fluidity are factors.

In its day Deborah Tannen's book *You Just Don't Understand: Women and Men in Conversation*, as well as John Gray's *Men Are From Mars, Women Are From Venus*, caused an avalanche of discussion (and some hostility) by comparing the communication styles of men and women.

Gender theorists argued that one reason women can't break the glass ceiling is that their communication style is less authoritative than that of men. Compare the following observations (greatly simplified) from gender theorists:

	Women	Men
Object of talk	Establish rapport, make connections, negotiate inclusive relationships	Preserve independence, maintain status, exhibit skill and knowledge
Listening behavior	Attentive, steady eye contact; remain stationary; nod head	Less attentive, sporadic eye contact; move around
Pauses	Frequent pauses, giving chance for others to take turns	Infrequent pauses; interrupt each other to take turns
Small talk	Personal disclosure	Impersonal topics
Focus	Details first, pulled together at end	Big picture
Gestures	Small, confined	Expansive
Method	Questions, apologies; "we" statements; hesitant, indirect, soft speech	Assertions; "I" statements; clear, loud, take-charge speech

3-5c Improving Communication Among Diverse Workers

Harmony and acceptance do not happen automatically when people who are dissimilar work together. This means that organizations must commit to diversity. Harnessed effectively, diversity can enhance productivity and propel a company to success. Mismanaged, it can become a tremendous drain on a company's time and resources. How companies deal with diversity will make all the difference in how they compete in a global environment. The following suggestions can help you and your organization find ways to improve communication and interaction.

- **Seek training.** Especially if an organization is experiencing diversity problems, awareness-raising sessions may be helpful. Spend time reading and learning about workforce diversity and how it can benefit organizations. Look upon diversity as an opportunity, not a threat. Intercultural communication, team building, and conflict resolution are skills that can be learned in diversity training programs. Resolve to leave your comfort zone and seek out people who are not like you.

- **Understand the value of differences.** Diversity makes an organization innovative and creative. Sameness fosters an absence of critical thinking called groupthink, discussed in Chapter 2. Former senior executive at Citigroup and other banks, Sallie Krawcheck, cites data suggesting that lack of diversity may have led to overconfidence and blind agreement in the financial industry: "I concluded that if Wall Street had looked more like the country did in the years leading up to 2008—that is, if all big Wall Street banks had had more diversity (and more women)—the financial crisis would have been less severe."[112] Bank of England chief Mark Carney concurs: "Almost all decisions in finance are taken under uncertainty, making it especially important that decision makers are exposed to a range of views and engage in open debates with people whose perspectives challenge the prevailing wisdom."[113]

- **Don't expect conformity.** Long gone are the days when businesses could say, "This is our culture. Conform or leave."[114] Today's workers are prized for their creativity, and for being curious and authentic.[115] U.K. banker Sue Baines views diversity and inclusion in the workplace as recruiting tools: "It's important on many levels to attract and retain talent. We're all fighting for top talent. If you're not a diverse and inclusive firm, you're restricting access to that top talent." Dax Dasilva, a tech entrepreneur, believes that "difference is a teacher." "The solutions for the future come out of diverse perspectives," he says.[116]

- **Make fewer assumptions.** Be careful of seemingly insignificant, innocent workplace assumptions. For example, don't assume that everyone wants to observe the holidays with a Christmas party and a decorated tree. Celebrating only Christian holidays in December and January excludes those who honor Hanukkah, Kwanzaa, and the Lunar New Year. Moreover, in workplace discussions don't assume anything about others' sexual orientation or attitude toward marriage. For invitations, avoid phrases such as *managers and their wives. Spouses* or *partners* is more inclusive. Valuing diversity means making fewer assumptions that everyone is like you or wants to be like you.

- **Build on similarities.** Look for areas in which you and others not like you can agree or at least share opinions. Be prepared to consider issues from many perspectives, all of which may be valid. Accept that there is room for different points of view to coexist peacefully. Although you can always find differences, it is much harder to find similarities. Look for common ground in shared experiences, mutual goals, and similar values.[117] Concentrate on your objective even when you may disagree on how to reach it.

Zooming In

Your Turn:
Applying Your Skills at Walmart

Until 2016 Walmart regularly landed on 24/7 Wall St.'s annual list of America's Most Hated Companies.[118] However, since then the company's significant efforts may have burnished its image and appealed to consumers who value good corporate citizenship. Although the mega-retailer still scores low in "employee engagement & development," it ranked No. 14 on the Drucker Institute's Management Top 250 list for innovation, financial strength, and social responsibility.[119]

Sustainability has perhaps been Walmart's most significant virtue. The company is committed to creating zero waste and to generating 100 percent renewable energy long term, sourcing at least 50 percent of its energy needs from renewables by 2025. The retailer is spearheading 136 projects around the world that will generate two billion kilowatt hours, or two gigawatt hours, of renewable energy—equal to six months of electricity generated by the Hoover Dam. In India, 90 percent of Walmart stores are equipped with rooftop solar panels. The company decided to decrease greenhouse gas in its global supply chain by working with suppliers on optimizing agricultural production and training farmers in emerging markets. Its so-called Project Gigaton aims to avoid one billion tons (a gigaton) of ozone-depleting greenhouse gases.[120] To put this potential savings in perspective, saving one gigaton would equal the annual carbon dioxide emissions of the two highest polluting U.S. states, Texas and California, combined.

Last, in defiance of the federal government that pulled the United States out of the Paris Climate Agreement, Walmart and several thousand American businesses pledged their continued commitment to it.[121] Due to its sheer size, Walmart sets an example in the industry and beyond, and other major retailers frequently follow suit.

Your Task

As a junior member of a task force assembled by EVP for Corporate Affairs at Walmart, Dan Bartlett, you are working to improve the image of the global retailer. Despite many praiseworthy initiatives, Walmart is still viewed by many with suspicion. As a team, discuss the global effect of Walmart's admirable sustainability effort. Create a communication plan that includes answers to questions such as the following: How should Walmart spread the news about its sustainability policies to reach the broader public and young people in particular? Consider the use of social media such as Instagram, Facebook, and Twitter. Your team may be asked to explain its decision to the class or to write a summary of the pros and cons of each option. Be prepared to support your choice.

SUMMARY OF LEARNING OUTCOMES

1 Explain the powerful effects of globalization and the major trends fueling it.

- Intercultural competency is needed to contend with several major trends. Global markets resulting from free-trade agreements are now a reality, recent trade disputes notwithstanding.

- Advancements in transportation and logistics have made the world smaller and more intertwined.

- Communication and information technologies extend the global reach of business.

- In emerging economies the middle class is growing.

- The domestic workforce is becoming increasingly diverse as immigrants settle in North America, and their offspring outnumber the descendants of non-Hispanic whites.

2 Identify the primary characteristics and key dimensions of culture.

- Culture is the complex system of values, traits, morals, and customs shared by a society.

- Significant characteristics of culture include the following: (a) culture is learned, (b) cultures are inherently logical, (c) culture is the basis of self-identity and community, (d) culture combines the visible and invisible, and (e) culture is dynamic.

- Members of low-context cultures (e.g., North America, Scandinavia, and Germany) depend on words to express meaning.

- Members of high-context cultures (e.g., Japan, China, and Arab countries) rely more on context, such as social setting and a person's history, status, and position to convey meaning.

- Other key dimensions of culture include individualism, time orientation, power distance, and communication style.

3 Discuss strategies for enhancing intercultural effectiveness and communication across cultures.

- To function effectively in a global economy, we must learn about other cultures and be willing to change our attitudes once we become aware of our own cultural assumptions and biases.

- Ethnocentrism refers to the belief that one's own culture is superior to all others and holds all truths; to overcome stereotypes and become more tolerant, we need to practice empathy.

- Nonverbal miscommunication can be avoided by recognizing that body language, such as eye contact, posture, gestures, use of time, space, and territory, is largely culture dependent.

- Communicating in social media, people tend to seek out those who are like them; whether users reach out across boundaries depends on whether they are outgoing or introverted.

- To improve intercultural written messages, communicators accommodate the reader in organization, tone, and style; use short sentences and paragraphs; observe titles and rank; avoid ambiguous expressions; use correct grammar; and cite numbers carefully.

4 Examine the complexities of ethics across cultures, including business practices abroad, bribery, prevailing customs, and methods for coping.

- Doing business abroad, businesspeople encounter differing views about ethical practices.

- To uphold sound ethical principles abroad, businesspeople should broaden their understanding of values and customs in other cultures but need to follow U.S. anticorruption laws.

- Seeking alternative solutions, refusing business if the options violate one's basic values, and conducting all relations as openly as possible are additional techniques for ethical dealings.

- Businesspeople who wish to uphold good business practices abroad should resist legalistic strategies, avoid rationalizing shady decisions, and apply a five-question ethics test when faced with a perplexing ethical dilemma.

5 Describe the advantages and challenges of workforce diversity as well as approaches for improving communication among diverse workplace audiences.

- A diverse workforce can benefit consumers, work teams, and business organizations.

- Diversity can also cause discord among identity groups.

- Business communicators should be aware of and sensitive to differences in the communication styles of men and women.

- To foster harmony and communication in diverse workplaces, many organizations develop diversity training programs.

- Workers are tasked with understanding and accepting the value of differences; they should not expect conformity, make fewer assumptions about others, and look for common ground.

Key Terms

blockchain technology *85*

cobots *85*

culture *86*

cultural intelligence *87*

spiral logic *89*

linear logic *89*

ethnocentrism *92*

stereotype *92*

prototype *92*

prejudice *92*

tolerance *93*

empathy *93*

saving face *93*

descriptiveness *94*

nonjudgmentalism *94*

supportiveness *94*

digital nationalism *96*

Splinternet *96*

glass ceiling *105*

Critical Thinking

1. When Procter & Gamble launched its Pampers brand in Japan, the diaper package confused and disturbed customers. As in the United States, the package featured the picture of a stork delivering a baby. Why were Japanese parents perturbed? It turns out that the myth of a stork carrying babies to expectant parents is unknown in Japan. Instead, according to Japanese lore, giant floating peaches deliver offspring.[122] Can you explain what may have caused the intercultural blunder? How could Procter & Gamble have avoided it? (L.O. 2, 3)

2. When we travel or work abroad, we tend to be perceived not so much as individuals but as members of racial, ethnic, or national groups. For example, when visiting Europe, Americans can expect to be questioned on U.S. foreign policy, military actions, and economic influence. How can you ensure that you function as an effective ambassador of your country when working and traveling overseas? (L.O. 1, 3, and 5)

3. A stereotype is an oversimplified perception of a behavioral pattern or characteristic applied to entire groups. For example, the Swiss are hardworking, efficient, and neat; Germans are formal, reserved, and blunt; Americans are loud, friendly, and impatient; Canadians are polite, trusting, and tolerant; Asians are gracious,

humble, and inscrutable. In what way are such stereotypes harmless or harmful? (L.O. 2, 3)

4. You know that it's not acceptable to make ethnic jokes, least of all in the workplace, but a colleague of yours keeps invoking the worst ethnic and racial stereotypes. How do you respond? Do you remain silent and change the subject, or do you speak up? What other options do you have in dealing with such a coworker? Consider whether your answer would change if the offender were your boss. (L.O. 3, 5)

5. **Ethical Issue**: Transparency International, the global antibribery watchdog, severely criticizes *wasta*, a social norm common in many Arab countries. It is the practice of using family and social contacts to speed up government paperwork or improve access to schools, hospitals, or jobs. Whom people know determines the speed and quality of services they receive. Wasta is deeply ingrained in the fabric of society. "Wasta is a way of life. . . . I expect that even on Judgment Day we will need wasta too," said a young Arab man in an interview with *Vice Magazine*.[123] After reading this chapter, can you explain why using one's connections to receive preferential treatment may cause harm? (L.O. 2, 4)

Activities

3.1 Intercultural Missteps and Bias Amplified on Social Media (L.O. 1–3, 5)

`Intercultural` `Social Media`

Once a gaffe blows up on social media, it is difficult to contain. Consider the worst, most embarrassing intercultural mistake or bigotry incident, and then imagine it amplified a thousandfold or millionfold for everyone to see. What follows is a list of diversity and inclusion blunders as well as awkward social media slip-ups with intercultural implications.[124]

YOUR TASK Consider the gravity of each offense; then, individually or in groups, discuss each for its take-away, the lesson to be learned from it.

a. In a case of awful timing, WW, formerly Weight Watchers, released a New Year's campaign #ThisIsMyWW on Twitter just as the United States launched a targeted drone strike that killed Iran's top general, Qasem Soleimani in Iraq, causing international consternation. Thus, WW's promoted trend campaign clashed with the unfortunate trending hashtag WWIII. The company immediately pulled its campaign and Twitter helped by removing the promoted trend within one hour of its launch. Even so, more than 870,000 people would belabor the topic over the course of three days on Twitter alone.[125]

b. Papa John's pizza company forced out its founder and CEO, John Schnatter, after he had used a racial slur and made other racially-tinged comments during a conference call with executives and the company's advertising agency. Predictably, his remarks made it onto social media, and Papa John's sales dropped 10.5 percent in the following weeks.

c. Home improvement chain Lowe's allowed a discussion on its Facebook page to get out of hand after withdrawing its advertising from a TLC reality show about Muslim families. The 23,000 comments on Facebook that followed were mostly critical of the company, but some praised the home improvement giant. Only when the media picked up the story did the company respond to offensive and racist posts by deleting all the messages and explaining its late intervention as "respect for the transparency of social media."[126]

d. Facebook has faced public scrutiny after reports that the company had failed to safeguard users' data and privacy. The outrage grew when the platform admitted that data firm Cambridge Analytica had misused almost 87 million Facebook users' information. Marketing efforts to address privacy concerns failed, however, when the public soon learned that Facebook had shared users' private messages with Netflix, Spotify, and other companies. It also had provided private information to Amazon and Microsoft.

e. Two African American men were arrested at a Philadelphia Starbucks, the victims of apparent racial bias. The two men were waiting for an associate and asked to use the restroom without making a purchase. The situation escalated, and police were called. Social media blew up with negative tweets. Starbucks' brand perception among customers plummeted to its lowest in 10 years. Starbucks closed 8,000 U.S. stores for sensitivity training.

3.2 Learning From Epic Intercultural Fails
(L.O. 1—3)

Intercultural

As business organizations become increasingly global in their structure and marketing, they face communication problems resulting from cultural misunderstandings. They also must deal with culture clashes and radically different values around the world.

YOUR TASK Based on what you have learned in this chapter, describe several broad principles that could be applied in helping the individuals involved understand what went wrong in the following events. What suggestions could you make for remedying the problems?

a. Social media leaders are not immune to intercultural missteps that go viral. Twitter CEO Jack Dorsey landed in hot water in India for posing with a group of female activists and holding a controversial sign. The slogan "Smash Brahminical Patriarchy" caused outrage because it is calling for the dismantling of the oppressive Hindu caste system and male dominance with it. Many Twitter users called it hate speech and were furious. Twitter publicly apologized but then reaped criticism for caving in to the ruling class and silencing marginalized voices.[127]

b. When Susan Kramer served as the British transportation minister, she faced embarrassment after presenting the mayor of Taipei, Taiwan, Ko Wen-je, with a watch—a taboo in Chinese culture. Ko remarked to reporters that he would "sell it to a scrap dealer" because a watch would be useless to him. *Giving a clock* and *attending an old person's funeral* sound very similar in Chinese.[128]

c. During a state dinner for a delegation from Singapore visiting the government of the Czech Republic, the conversation turned to the tasty main course they were eating. One of the Czech hosts explained to the inquiring foreign guests that they were enjoying a Czech specialty, rabbit, known for its light white meat. The Singaporeans' faces mirrored shock, embarrassment, and irritation. As inconspicuously as possible, they put down their silverware. Only later did the Czech hosts learn that rabbit is a pet in Singapore much like the house cat in European or North American households.[129]

d. As China's economic power grows, professionals suffer the same signs of job stress experienced in Western countries. Multinational companies have long offered counseling to their expatriate managers. Locals, however, frowned on any form of psychological therapy. When China's largest bank hired Chestnut Global Partners to offer employee counseling services, Chestnut learned immediately that it could not talk about such issues as conflict management. Instead, Chestnut stressed workplace harmony. Chestnut also found that Chinese workers refused one-on-one counseling. They preferred group sessions or online counseling.[130] What cultural elements were at work here?

e. More than half of Japanese hotels do not allow guests with tattoos in their *onsens* or hot spring bathing facilities. Some operators do, but only if the guests cover up their body art. In Japan tattoos are associated with organized crime. The bans were put in place to keep yakuza gangsters out and to prevent complaints from Japanese guests. A controversy erupted when a Maori woman (a member of the indigenous Polynesian people from New Zealand) was barred from a public bath in Hokkaido for her traditional face tattoos.[131] Critics of the restrictive Japanese policies pointed out the pervasive presence of tattoos in many western countries.

3.3 Connecting Across Time Zones
(L.O. 1–3)

Communication Technology | **Intercultural** | **Web**

Assume you are a virtual assistant working from your home. As part of your job, you schedule webcasts, online chats, and teleconference calls for businesspeople who are conducting business around the world.

YOUR TASK To broaden your knowledge of time zones, respond to the following questions.

a. What does the abbreviation UTC indicate? (Use Google and search for *UTC definition*.)

b. Internationally, time is shown with a 24-hour clock (sometimes called military time). What time does 14.00 indicate? (Use Google and search for *24-hour clock*.) How is a 12-hour clock different from a 24-hour clock? With which are you most familiar?

c. You must schedule an audioconference for a business-person in Omaha, Nebraska, who wants to talk with a person in Seoul, South Korea. What are the best business hours (between 8 a.m. and 5 p.m.) for them to talk? (Many websites provide time zone converters. For example, visit *timeanddate.com*. Several websites display time and date in any time zone on Earth.)

d. What are the best business hours for an online chat between an executive in New Orleans and a vendor in Mombasa, Kenya?

e. When should two businesspeople, one in Nevada and the other in Colorado, start a Zoom conference call with a contact in the Netherlands during office hours? Your instructor may select other cities for you to search.

f. Why did your new business partner in Ankara, Turkey, call you at 2 a.m. in the Eastern Standard Time zone (UTC-5) and was understandably shocked that he woke you up?

3.4 Twitter: A Window to Other Countries and Cultures (L.O. 1, 3)

E-Mail | **Intercultural** | **Social Media** | **Web**

Twitter feeds provide up-to-the-second news from war-torn regions, violent incidents, mass protests, and sites of natural disasters at home and around the world. Twitter has also changed how public opinion of political events is formed and expressed. The so-called back channel, a running commentary on events still unfolding, often decides the winner of a political debate even before the debate concludes.

Breath-taking speed and potential influence may explain why Twitter and other social media have become important news sources to many Americans. Two-thirds of adults in the United States (68 percent) say they at least occasionally go to social media for news, according to Pew Research. Fortunately, most respondents are concerned about truthfulness: As many as 57 percent say that they expect news on social media to be inaccurate. Accuracy is their top concern. However, they appreciate the convenience of receiving their news that way. Facebook and YouTube are the most popular social media news sources, with Twitter in third place at 12 percent. At 42 percent, the most avid Twitter users range in age between thirty to fourty-nine, followed by eighteen- to twenty-nine-year-olds at 33 percent.[132] The social and political impact of Twitter, however, exceeds these percentages by far.

Even if some of the information on social media may be unreliable, tweets provide instant cross-border, globe-spanning communication as a high-speed alternative to mainstream media.

YOUR TASK Start by viewing *trending topics* on Twitter. Some may be business related. A few may be international. Use the search box to type any current international or business event to see what Twitter users are saying about it. For instance, check out the tweets of Christiane Amanpour, Katrina vanden Heuvel, Arianna Huffington, or those of other well-known journalists, for example, Nick Gillespie, Paul Krugman, Bret Stevens, or George Will. In the classroom, discuss the usefulness of Twitter as you see it. Your instructor may ask you to prepare an e-mail or memo identifying and summarizing three trending business topics. In your opinion, how accurately do the tweets convey the trend? Can trends be summarized in 140 to 280 characters? You will learn more about the business use of Twitter and other social media in Chapter 7.

3.5 Value Conflicts Haunt IKEA in Russia and Poland (L.O. 1, 2, 4 and 5)

E-Mail | **Communication Technology** | **Intercultural** | **Team**

In this chapter we have raised questions about whose ethics should prevail when companies do business abroad. Consider the following intercultural scenarios.[133]

IKEA IN RUSSIA When Russia passed a so-called "homosexual propaganda" law, sanctioning the persecution of the LGBTQ+ community, protests erupted in western countries. Although it has cultivated a gay-friendly image, IKEA cut a feature about a lesbian couple and their child from the Russian edition of its magazine. The two women were depicted as bonding over furnishing their small apartment. IKEA responded that it had merely obeyed the law of the land. Yet as early as 1994, the Swedish company had resisted pressure from religious conservatives and featured same-sex couples in U.S. ads. A decade ago IKEA also braved outrage in Italy with an ad featuring a gay couple; one newspaper branded the ad campaign "Swedish Imperialism." Russia is the company's fifth best-selling region, with 6 percent of IKEA's total sales.

IKEA IN POLAND IKEA has introduced explicit LGBTQ+-inclusive nondiscrimination policies across all its operations, including in deeply Catholic Poland. A Polish IKEA worker was fired after denouncing in an incendiary intranet post an event supportive of the LGBTQ+ community. He had quoted scripture and had alleged religious discrimination. His case drew widespread protests in Poland in the man's defense, accompanied by calls for a boycott of the Swedish company. The conservative Law and Justice party railed against "LGBT ideology," allegedly an imported "threat to Polish identity." IKEA owns over a dozen plants in Poland and as many retail stores. About 4,000 products are manufactured in Poland for IKEA stores around the world.

YOUR TASK In small groups or as a class, examine the information summarized earlier. Compare IKEA's various decisions and consider questions such as these: How do you feel about IKEA's pulling the article from the Russian edition of its magazine? How valid is IKEA's defense that it was only following Russian law? Why was the Russian law rejected by western countries and in an EU court? What other reasons may have prompted IKEA's withdrawal of the article? What is meant by "Swedish Imperialism"? In what ways may IKEA's corporate policies be perceived as a "threat to Polish identity"? Was IKEA justified in firing the Polish worker?

Perhaps you have heard about similar culture clashes businesses have faced at home or as they expanded to countries with different value systems. If your instructor directs, summarize your responses in an e-mail or a discussion-board post.

3.6 Navigating a Looming Culture Clash
(L.O. 2, 3)

`Intercultural`

Reaching agreement on the terms of contracts, proposals, and anything that involves bargaining is often tough. The difficulties grow, though, when business partners hail from different cultures.

YOUR TASK Discuss the causes and implications of the following common mistakes made by North Americans in their negotiations with foreigners.

a. Getting upset when a Brazilian or Chilean business partner arrives substantially late.

b. Expecting that a final agreement is set in stone.

c. Lacking patience and rushing matters along more quickly than the pace preferred by the locals.

d. Thinking that an interpreter is always completely accurate.

e. Believing that individuals abroad who speak English understand every nuance of meaning.

f. Ignoring rank when greeting and addressing a Chinese team.

3.7 Learning Languages with Duolingo, Busuu, or Babbel (L.O. 2, 3)

`E-Mail` `Intercultural` `Social Media` `Web`

Social media are playing a huge role in how we communicate and socialize online; therefore, it's not surprising that social media platforms have formed around various interests and pursuits. At least six popular language learning websites and apps have united people eager to learn or practice a foreign language. The three major ones are Duolingo, Busuu, and Babbel. Each offers what is known as the *freemium* model—free basic instruction and premium fee-based content without ads in a number of popular languages.

YOUR TASK Compare the online language learning communities. Consider these and similar questions: How many languages do they support? How do they operate, and how much do they cost? What features do they offer? How many users do they have? Are they engaging? How? Which languages are most popular? In addition, learn a few phrases in a language that interests you and report back to class. Your instructor may ask you to summarize your findings in writing, in either an e-mail or an online post.

3.8 Exploring the International Face of Facebook (L.O. 1, 3)

`Intercultural` `Social Media` `Team` `Web`

With 2.4 billion monthly active users at this writing, Facebook is the largest social networking site; it is available in 101 languages.[134] A whopping 85 percent of daily active users are located outside the United States. Consider India. Facebook has taken the country by storm. India boasts the highest number of active monthly users (270 million), followed by the United States (190 million), and Indonesia (123 million). Africa occupies the opposite side of the spectrum. The continent has an Internet usage rate of approximately 40 percent, the lowest of the seven continents. Facebook has hardly made a dent. With a population of $1.3 billion, a mere 204 million of Africans are on Facebook (a 15.5 percent usage rate).

YOUR TASK As a team or alone, visit any of the Facebook tracking websites—for example, Socialbakers or Internet World Stats. Study the tables listing the top countries in various categories. Which country is currently the fastest-growing country in absolute numbers? Do not rely solely on absolute numbers, but compare population figures and Internet penetration (usage) rates; that is, the ratio between Facebook use and population.

Even if you don't speak another language, visit at last one non-English Facebook region and evaluate surface similarities and differences. Chances are that you will recognize some familiar features. Discuss similarities and differences in class. If you speak a foreign language, can you spot any customization that suggests adaptation to local preferences and customs? Of course, you can always switch the foreign Facebook page to your own preferred language! If you don't know how, your instructor will provide guidance. You may also want to try one of these large companies with a huge global presence: Google, Samsung, or Nokia. Your instructor may assign a different corporation to each team.

As you will learn in Chapter 15, Facebook is also playing an increasing role in recruiting and other business applications.

3.9 Investigating Cultural Stereotypes
(L.O. 2, 3)

Intercultural | **Team** | **Web**

Almost all of us at some point in our lives are subject to stereotyping by others, whether we are immigrants, minorities, women, members of certain professions, or Americans abroad. Negative stereotypes sting. However, even positive stereotypes can offend or embarrass because they fail to acknowledge the differences among individuals. As you have learned in this chapter, generalizations are necessary as we acquire and categorize new knowledge. As long as we remain open to new experiences, we won't be limited by rigid, stereotypical perceptions of other cultures.

YOUR TASK Think about a nation or culture about which you have only a hazy idea. Jot down a few key traits that come to mind. For example, you may not know much about the Netherlands and the Dutch people. You can probably think of gouda cheese, wooden clogs, Heineken beer, tulips, and windmills. Anything else? Then consider a culture with which you are very familiar, whether it is yours or that of a country you have visited or studied. In one column, write down a few stereotypical perceptions that are positive. Then, in another column, record negative stereotypes you associate with that culture. Share your notes with your team or the whole class, as the instructor may direct. How do you respond to others' descriptions of your culture? Which stereotypes irk you and why? For a quick fact check and overview at the end of this exercise, google the *CIA World Factbook* or *BBC News Country Profiles*.

3.10 Fixing a Tricky International E-Mail (L.O. 3)

E-Mail | **Intercultural**

American writers sometimes forget that people in other countries, even if they understand English, are not aware of the meanings of certain words and phrases.

YOUR TASK Study the following e-mail to be sent by a U.S. firm to a potential supplier in another country. Identify specific weaknesses that may cause troubles for intercultural readers. Revise of rewrite the e-mail if your instructor assigns this task.

> Dear Zayan:
>
> Because of the epic horse-trading with one of our shilly-shally subcontractors, we were dragging our feet a bit before finally writing to you. We were royally ticked off by their shoddy merchandise, the excuses they made up, and the way they dissed some of our customers. Since we have our good rep to keep up, we have decided to get down to brass tacks and see if you would be interested in bidding on the contract for spare parts.
>
> By playing ball with us, your products are sure to score big. So please give it your best shot and fire off your price list ASAP. We will need it by 4/6 if you are to be in the running.
>
> Yours,

3.11 Be My Guest: Avoiding Intercultural Confusion (L.O. 3)

Intercultural | **Team**

In conversations, North Americans often issue casual invitations to new acquaintances and even virtual strangers, such as *Give me a call when you come to New York* or *Make Yourself at Home*. However, nonnative speakers and visitors may misinterpret such offhand remarks. They may embarrass their hosts and suffer disappointment by taking the spontaneous invitation literally and acting on it. Those interacting across cultures would be wise to avoid using expressions that have multiple meanings.

YOUR TASK Assume you are a businessperson engaged in exporting and importing. As such, you are in constant communication with suppliers and customers around the world. In messages sent abroad or in situations with nonnative speakers of English at home, what kinds of ambiguous expressions should you avoid? In teams or individually, list three to five original examples of idioms, slang, acronyms, sports references, abbreviations, jargon, and two-word verbs. Which phrases or behavior could be taken literally by a person from a different culture?

3.12 Bribery by Many Names: *Baksheesh, Mordida,* and *Kumshah* (L.O. 4)

Ethics | **Intercultural**

Although it takes place in many parts of the world, bribery is not officially sanctioned by any country. In the Middle East, bribes are called *baksheesh*. In Mexico, they are *mordida*; and in Southeast Asia, *kumshah*. In the United States, the Foreign Corrupt Practices Act prohibits giving anything of value to a foreign official to win or retain business. However, this law does allow *facilitating payments* that may be necessary to expedite or secure "routine governmental action." For instance, a company could make small payments to obtain permits and licenses or to process visas or work orders. Also allowed are payments to secure telephone service and power and water supplies, as well as payments for the loading and unloading of cargo.

YOUR TASK In light of what you have learned in this chapter, how should you act in the following situations? Are the actions legal or illegal?[135]

a. Your company's shares are traded in the U.S.; therefore, your Germany-based auto company must file SEC reports. You sell passenger vehicles and trucks all over the world. In Turkmenistan you provide a birthday gift to a government official—a $300,000 armored Mercedes Benz S-class limousine.

b. Your global pharma company sends doctors on luxurious trips, treats them to lavish meals, and books the costs as necessary expenses. The purpose of these incentives is to prompt health-care workers to increase sales of your company's drugs.

c. Officials in the Dominican Republic seized an aircraft that belongs to your company claiming that the plane was used to smuggle illicit drugs. However, this charge is unfounded, and you realize that the Dominicans would release the plane for a "facilitating payment" of $15,000 to various officials.

d. Your company is in the business of arranging hunting trips to East Africa. You are encouraged to give guns and travel allowances to officials in a wildlife agency that has authority to issue licenses to hunt big game. The officials have agreed to keep the gifts quiet. Should you make the gifts?

e. Your firm has just moved you to Malaysia, and the shipping container with your personal effects is not being released to you. You have a sense that you might be able pay the customs official to do his duty and expedite the inspection of your personal effects. You also have a hunch that paying the official to forego the inspection entirely could be a possibility as well. Which is legal?

f. In Mexico your firm has been working hard to earn lucrative contracts with the national oil company, Pemex. One government official has hinted elaborately that his son would like to do marketing studies for your company. Should you hire the son?

3.13 Gifts and Entertainment Limits: What Is Nominal Value? (L.O. 4)

`E-Mail` / `Ethics` / `Intercultural` / `Team` / `Web`

You are one of a group of new-hires at a large company. As part of your onboarding, your director asks your team to investigate the codes of conduct of other organizations. In particular, the manager asks you to find comparison information on gifts, gratuities, kickbacks, and entertainment limits.

YOUR TASK Search the Internet for sections in codes of conduct that relate to gifts, gratuities, kickbacks, and entertainment. From three companies or organizations (such as a health-care group, a financial company, or a university), investigate specific restrictions. What do these organizations allow and restrict? Prepare a list and summarize your findings in your own words, possibly in an e-mail at your instructor's direction.

3.14 When Cultures Clash, or Do They?
(L.O. 2-5)

`E-Mail` / `Intercultural` / `Team`

INTERCULTURAL SCENARIO 1 What's in a mustache? A lot, if you're the Japan-born U.S. ambassador to South Korea. Harry Binkley Harris, Jr., a former U.S. Navy officer, has caused offense with his chevron-shaped mustache. That's because it reminds many South Koreans of brutal colonial rule during the occupation 1910-1945 of their country when Japanese governor generals typically wore chevron mustaches. During World War II, the Japanese committed atrocities in Korea, subjecting the population to forced labor, sexual slavery, and other grave human rights abuses. Ambassador Harris in turn accused his critics of attacking him for his ethnic origin: "I have been criticized in the media here, especially on social media, because of my ethnic background, because I'm a Japanese American," he told reporters. He defended his look as a lifestyle change after serving in the Navy. At a press conference, America's top diplomat in South Korea handed out little black mustaches.[136]

INTERCULTURAL SCENARIO 2 Fired for being French? Guillaume Rey was dismissed from his Vancouver restaurant job after warnings that he was being "combative and aggressive" toward other staff. When he reduced a fellow server to tears over a disagreement, he was let go for violating workplace policy. The Milestones restaurant admitted that Rey was professional and friendly with guests and often served as shift lead. The waiter filed a complaint with British Columbia's Human Rights Tribunal. He alleged discrimination and claimed that French culture "tends to be more direct and expressive." He insisted he was let go for having acquired high standards in France along with a "direct, honest and professional personality." An employment consultant in B.C. agrees that most French-speaking people from Europe tend to be direct, whereas Canadians are steeped in a non-conflict culture, particularly on the job. A French ex-patriot living in London believes that many French dislike chitchat such as talking about the weather. They get to the point. Talking or even smiling at strangers strikes them as intrusive, she says.[137]

YOUR TASK Critically analyze the scenarios in small teams or as a class. If your instructor directs, write a discussion forum post or an e-mail evaluating one of the intercultural encounters (or both). Consider questions such as the following to get to the bottom of each controversy:

(1) What are the grievances the South Koreans voiced against Ambassador Harris? Why are they so upset about facial hair? How did the ambassador respond? Is his reaction to the criticism adequate and justified? Could he have reacted differently? What does it tell you that Harris distributed little black mustaches at the press conference, considering his role in South Korea?

(2) What is the fundamental conflict here? Was Guillaume Rey a competent waiter? Do you find his claims and his defense credible? Does his official complaint have merit? Did the restaurant act reasonably? In how far is the incident an intercultural one? Is it the result of a cultural misunderstanding?

3.15 Making Corporations More Diverse
(L.O. 5)

E-Mail | **Intercultural** | **Team**

Despite strides by some global companies toward greater diversity, the Alliance for Board Diversity (ABD) reports that women and minorities are still underrepresented in U.S. corporate boardrooms. The alliance, which includes the leadership organization Catalyst, found that white men still occupied 51 percent of new board seats at Fortune 100 companies. White males' share among new directors was even higher in Fortune 500 companies, at 60 percent. The ABD concluded that despite advances for women and minorities, overall progress is still slow.[138]

However, as we have seen, diversity and inclusion seem to be good for business: Catalyst found that diverse organizations attract and retain talent more easily; inclusive workplaces experience less aggression or harassment and are more productive. Diverse teams are innovative and less likely to succumb to groupthink.

Moreover, gender-diverse companies enjoy excellent reputations, as 78 percent of American adults say gender diversity at work is important.[139] A McKinsey survey of more than 1,000 companies in 12 countries produced similar results. Overall, businesses with culturally and ethnically diverse executives were 33 percent more likely to be more profitable than their industry rivals—43 percent if they had diverse boards.[140]

European countries such as Norway, Germany, the UK, France, and the Netherlands are taking radical measures. They are imposing mandatory quotas to increase the percentage of women on the largest companies' corporate boards. California, too, has recently enacted a controversial law requiring that corporate boards include at least one woman, two by late 2021. Critics contend that rigid quotas could jeopardize the very goal of greater diversity, unduly burden smaller companies, and encourage the appointment of token women just to satisfy the requirement. Rather, they suggest that politicians and business leaders pursue voluntary targets and appeal to customers and investors to step up the pressure on companies to change.[141]

Academic research recommends that rather than narrowly pursue numeric increases of women on corporate boards, businesses should cast a wide net, choosing "the very best directors from the largest talent pool possible," including females who bring different insights to all-male boards. Merely adding women won't boost financial performance, the scholars say. Instead, boards should aim to achieve "cognitive diversity" to better solve complex problems and find innovative solutions.[142] Others agree that "Diversity of thought, not more women, brings success."[143]

YOUR TASK Individually or in groups, discuss whether the United States should rely on the marketplace to effect change or whether the government should speed change along. If your instructor directs, summarize your thoughts in a concise e-mail message or a post on Blackboard, Moodle, or another online discussion board or chat room.

Test Your Workplace Etiquette IQ

New communication platforms and casual workplace environments have blurred the lines of appropriateness, leaving workers wondering how to navigate uncharted waters. Check your workplace etiquette IQ by deciding whether the following statements are true or false. Then see if you agree with the responses on p. Key-5.

1. The best way to show confidence and friendliness when greeting people in other countries is by shaking hands and making direct eye contact.

_____ True _____ False

2. When representing your organization abroad on business, you should show your enthusiasm and friendliness with expansive gestures and first-name conversations.

_____ True _____ False

3. If you are traveling abroad, open doors and allow older businesspeople to enter a room and be seated before you.

_____ True _____ False

Chat About It

In each chapter you will find five discussion questions related to the chapter material. Your instructor may assign these topics for you to discuss in class, in an online chat room, or on an online discussion board. Some of the discussion topics may require outside research. You may also be asked to read and respond to postings made by your classmates.

TOPIC 1: In his article "It's Time for 'They,'" *New York Times* columnist Farhad Manjoo muses, while observing his young children, that the traditional male/female binary is restrictive: "Gender is a ubiquitous prison for the mind, reinforced everywhere, by everyone, and only rarely questioned." What does Manjoo mean? Debate his statement from the perspective of a gender-nonconforming person.

TOPIC 2: Discuss the dos and don'ts when traveling abroad, or establish criteria of appropriate behavior you would expect from tourists to your country. Be specific and give reasons.

TOPIC 3: Identify a situation in which you were aware of ethnocentrism in your own actions or those of friends, family members, or colleagues. In general terms, describe what happened. What made you think the experience involved ethnocentrism?

TOPIC 4: Netflix is admired for a lengthy manifesto that describes its culture. Workers are asked to be "curious about how our different backgrounds affect us at work, rather than pretending they don't affect us." "You recognize we all have biases, and work past them. You intervene if someone else is being marginalized." How do you interpret these statements? What do they mean?

TOPIC 5: Transparency International's annual Corruption Perception Index ranks 180 countries based on apparent public sector corruption. How does the ranking from clean to highly corrupt relate to the countries' political systems, wealth, and stability? Discuss a few countries with which you are familiar.

Grammar and Mechanics Review 3

Nouns and Pronouns

Review Guides 10 through 18 about noun and pronoun usage in Appendix D, Grammar and Mechanics, beginning on page D-4. On a separate sheet, revise the following sentences to correct errors in nouns and pronouns. For each error you locate, write the guide number that reflects this usage. Some sentences may have two errors. If the sentence is correct, write *C*. When you finish, check your answers on page D-14.

EXAMPLE: When my friend and me traveled to Japan, we learned that they often avoid saying no.

REVISION: When my friend and I traveled to Japan, we learned that they often avoid saying no. [Guide 12]

1. Just between you and I, do you know how to curb ethnocentrism?

2. During the bribery hearing, both attornies questioned all witnesses thoroughly.

3. Please send texts to my manager and I so that she and I both understand the situation.

4. Its natural for most of us to gravitate toward those who are similar to us.

5. Starbucks has established itself successfully in China and India by adjusting it's brand to local markets.

6. Please send your report to the administrative assistant or myself when it's finished.

7. Every online sales rep must improve their writing skills to handle chat sessions.

8. The contract will be awarded to whomever submits the lowest bid.

9. Most applications were made in time, but your's and her's missed the deadline.

10. It must have been she who sent the e-mail to Mason and myself.

Planning Business Messages

LEARNING OUTCOMES

After studying this chapter, you should be able to do the following:

1 List the steps in the communication process.

2 Describe the goals of business writers and three phases of the writing process.

3 Identify the intended purpose and audience of a message to select the best communication channel.

4 Discuss expert writing techniques that improve business messages.

5 Explain the purpose of collaborative workplace writing and tools that facilitate it.

Dezay/Shutterstock.com

Zooming In

Words Matter!
VisibleThread Strives to Improve Readability in Corporate Writing

Fergal McGovern believes intensely that words matter. Following his conviction, he founded VisibleThread, a company that helps financial organizations and money managers improve the readability of their websites and documents by using plain language.

To ground his vision, McGovern's researchers studied the websites of 69 global financial organizations and money managers.[1] This research revealed that readability of the website content was surprisingly difficult. A total of 98.5 percent of the websites studied did not meet basic readability levels, according to McGovern's measures. The primary faults were overly long sentences, passive instead of active voice, wordiness, and complex language.

He suggested that money managers in the investment field might intentionally strive to keep their content incomprehensible. Why? To perpetuate the idea that only they had the expertise to manage the investor's money.[2] On the other hand, making financial documents difficult to read has many disadvantages. Customers become discouraged when they can't find what they want or can't understand what they read. They waste time, become frustrated, and, most important, begin to lose trust in dealing with their financial organizations.

McGovern argues that the financial industry could improve trust and better meet government compliance requirements by improving the readability of documents and websites. He

developed criteria to evaluate the clarity and readability of documents by counting words in long sentences and totaling the number of syllables in words. He also identified unfamiliar words and jargon. Many of his tools use the same mechanics as the Flesch-Kincaid readability tests, which measure how easy a document is to read. Similarly, the writing principles that McGovern advocates are not new; most are included in The Plain Writing Act of 2010. It requires U.S. government-created content to meet basic readability standards. The Act presents sensible techniques that help writers make their documents easier to read and comprehend.

McGovern is particularly interested in improving readability in the financial services industry. However, his emphasis on plain language holds true for nearly all business writing. In this chapter you will learn more about the communication process, the 3-x-3 writing process, and the use of plain language. As you progress through this three-chapter unit on the writing process, you will meet more of McGovern's guidelines and see many of the superior writing techniques advocated in The Plain Writing Act.

Critical Thinking

- Why do you think Fergal McGovern is motivated to focus so intensely on readability in documents and websites in the financial industry?

- Technology has changed the way people read, McGovern contends. Today's readers have short attention spans and gather information by skim reading. Why is readability particularly important for online readers who are reading quickly to find information?

- McGovern suggests that low readability scores in financial documents may result from a desire to impress clients with a lofty tone. Does inflated language encourage or damage trust? Why is it critical that financial institutions offer readable documents that build trust?

Ken Felepchuk/Shutterstock.com

4-1 Exploring the Communication Process

LEARNING OUTCOME

1 List the steps in the communication process.

The digital revolution and the rise of the Internet have vastly changed nearly everything in our lives—the way we work, play, learn, socialize, conduct business, and connect with each other. As the world becomes increasingly interconnected, people are communicating more than ever. They are sending a staggering number of messages often delivered over social media platforms.

FIGURE 4.1 The Communication Process

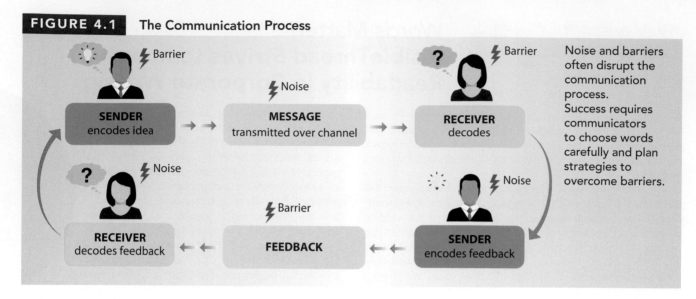

Noise and barriers often disrupt the communication process. Success requires communicators to choose words carefully and plan strategies to overcome barriers.

However, even as we have accepted e-mail, chatbots, texting, Twitter, Slack, Zoom, and a myriad of other interactive media, the nature of communication remains unchanged.

At VisibleThead, Fergal McGovern created a business centered on improving the way financial institutions connect with their customers. He primarily focused on one part of the communication process—the readability of business messages. This is one important aspect of the planning of business messages. However, before we explore the specifics of creating business messages, it is important to understand basic elements of the communication process. Regardless of how the digital era has changed the way we communicate, the communication process remains largely unchanged.

In its simplest form, **communication** may be defined as the *transmission of information and meaning from a sender to a receiver*. The crucial element in this definition is *meaning*. The process is successful only when the receiver understands an idea as the sender intended it. How does an idea travel from one person to another? It involves a sensitive circular process, shown in Figure 4.1. This process can easily be sidetracked resulting in miscommunication. The process of communication is successful only when both the sender and receiver understand the process and how to make it work. In our discussion we are most concerned with professional communication in the workplace so that you can be successful as a business communicator in your career.

4-1a Sender Has Idea

The communication process begins when the sender has an idea. The form of the idea may be influenced by complex factors surrounding the sender. These factors include mood, frame of reference, background, culture, and physical makeup, as well as the context of the situation and many other factors. Senders shape their ideas based on their own experiences and assumptions. A manager sending an e-mail request to employees asking them to conserve energy in the building assumes that they will be receptive. On the other hand, a direct-mail advertiser promoting a new credit card assumes that receivers may give only a quick glance to something perceived as junk mail. To gain attention, the direct-mail piece must offer something special. What exactly does the sender want to achieve? How is the message likely to be received? When senders know their purpose and anticipate the expected response, they are better able to shape successful messages.

4-1b Sender Encodes Idea

The next step in the communication process involves **encoding**. This means converting the idea into words or gestures that will convey meaning. A major problem in communicating any message verbally is that words have different meanings for different people. Recognizing how easy it is to be misunderstood, skilled communicators choose familiar, concrete words. In choosing proper words and symbols, senders must be alert to the receiver's communication skills, attitudes, background, experiences, and culture. Including a smiley face emoji in an e-mail announcement to stockholders may turn them off.

International messages require even more care. In Great Britain, the press called a new recycling program a *scheme*, which seriously offended the New York–based sponsor of the program, RecycleBank. In the United States, *scheme* connotes deceit. In Britain, however, it carries no such negative meaning.[4] The most successful messages use appropriate words, gestures, and symbols selected specifically to match the situation. Good messages also encourage feedback and make it easy for the receiver to respond.

4-1c Sender Selects Channel and Transmits Message

The medium over which the message travels is the channel. Messages may be delivered by computer, wireless network, smartphone, social network, letter, memorandum, report, announcement, picture, spoken word, fax, Web page, or some other channel. Today's messages are increasingly carried over digital networks with much opportunity for distraction and breakdown. Receivers may be overloaded with incoming messages or unable to receive messages clearly on their devices. Only well-crafted messages may be accepted, understood, and acted on. Anything that interrupts the transmission of a message in the communication process is called noise. Channel noise may range from a weak Internet signal to sloppy formatting and typos in e-mail messages. Noise may even include the annoyance a receiver feels when the sender chooses an improper channel for transmission or when the receiver is jammed with too many messages and information.

4-1d Receiver Decodes Message

The individual for whom the message is intended is the receiver. Translating the message from its symbol form into meaning involves decoding. Only when the receiver understands the meaning intended by the sender—that is, successfully decodes the message—does communication take place. Such success is often difficult to achieve because a number of barriers block the process.

No two people share the same life experiences or have the same skills. Decoding can be disrupted internally by the receiver's lack of attention, by bias against the sender, or by competing messages. It can be disrupted externally by loud sounds or illegible words. Decoding can also be sidetracked by semantic obstacles, such as misunderstood words or emotional reactions to certain terms. A memo that refers to women in the office as chicks or babes, for example, may disturb its receivers so much that they fail to focus on the total message. On the receiving end, successful decoding is more likely to be achieved when the receiver creates a receptive environment and ignores distractions. Alert receivers strive to understand both verbal and nonverbal cues, avoid prejudging the message, and expect to learn something.

4-1e Feedback Returns to Sender

The verbal and nonverbal responses of the receiver create feedback, a vital part of the communication process. Feedback helps the sender know that the message was received and understood. Senders can encourage feedback by asking questions such as *Am I making myself clear?* and *Is there anything you don't understand?* Senders can further improve feedback by timing the delivery appropriately and by providing only as much information as the receiver can handle. Receivers improve the communication process by providing clear and complete feedback.

In the business world, one of the best ways to advance understanding is to paraphrase the sender's message with comments such as, *Let me try to explain that in my own words.* The best feedback tends to be descriptive rather than evaluative. Here's a descriptive response: *I understand you want to sell sunglasses for cool dogs, and you would call them Doggles.*[6] Here's an evaluative response: *Your business ideas are always wacky!* An evaluative response is judgmental and

Bypassing or False Advertising?

J. C. Penney produced a T-shirt emblazoned with a ferocious red and blue eagle beneath the words *American Made*. However, a small label inside revealed that the shirt was made in Mexico. In response to complaints that the slogan was deceptive, a Penney spokeswoman said that *American Made* referred to the person wearing the shirt, not to the manufacturer.[5] Was this a simple case of miscommunication?

The idea of sunglasses for cool dogs could receive both judgmental and evaluative feedback.

doesn't tell the sender whether the receiver actually understood the message. When the receiver returns feedback, this person then becomes the sender of a new cycle of communication with all of the same concerns as the original sender.

4-1f Communication Barriers May Ruin the Process

The communication process is successful only when the receiver understands the message as intended by the sender. It sounds quite simple. Yet it's not. How many times have you thought that you delivered a clear message only to learn later that your intentions were misunderstood? Most messages that we send reach their destinations, but many are only partially understood.

You can improve your chances of communicating successfully by learning to recognize barriers that are known to disrupt the process. Some of the most significant barriers for individuals are bypassing, differing frames of reference, lack of language skill, and distractions.

Bypassing. An important barrier to clear communication involves words. Each of us attaches a little bundle of meanings to every word, and these meanings are not always similar. Bypassing happens when people miss each other with their meanings.[7] Let's say your boss asks you to help with a large customer mailing. When you arrive to do your share, you learn that you are expected to do the whole mailing yourself. You and your boss attached different meanings to the word *help*. Bypassing can lead to major miscommunication because people assume that meanings are contained in words. Actually, meanings are in people. For communication to be successful, the receiver and sender must attach the same symbolic meanings to their words. One study revealed a high likelihood of miscommunication when people use common but vague words such as *probably, always, never, usually, often, soon,* and *right away*. What do these words really mean?[8]

Differing Frames of Reference. Another barrier to clear communication is your **frame of reference**. Everything you see and feel in the world is translated through your individual frame of reference. Your unique frame is formed by a combination of your experiences, education, culture, expectations, personality, and other elements. As a result, you bring your own biases and expectations to any communication situation. Because your frame of reference is different from everyone else's, you will never see things exactly as others do. American managers eager to reach an agreement with a Chinese parts supplier, for example, were disappointed with the slow negotiation process. The Chinese managers, on the other hand, were pleased that so much time had been taken to build personal relationships with the American managers. Wise business communicators strive to prevent miscommunication by being alert to both their own frames of reference and those of others.

Weak Language Skills. No matter how extraordinary the idea is, it won't be understood or fully appreciated unless the communicators involved have good language skills. Each individual needs an adequate vocabulary and skill in oral and written expression. Using unfamiliar words, jargon, and unrecognizable abbreviations can seriously impede the transmission of meaning. Consider the following message posted on LinkedIn regarding social media and search engines: *Although SEO is part of SEM, you can't just lump in SMM and PR under the SEO banner!* Translation: *Although search engine optimization (SEO) is part of search engine marketing (SMM),* *you can't just lump social media marketing (SMM) and public relations (PR) under the search engine optimization (SEO) banner!* You will learn more about using plain language and familiar words later in this chapter.

Distractions. Other communication barriers are emotional interference, physical distractions, and digital interruptions. Shaping an intelligent message is difficult when one is feeling joy, fear, resentment, hostility, sadness, or some other strong emotion. It's also difficult to stay focused when physical distractions such as faulty acoustics, noisy surroundings, or a poor mobile connection disrupt oral communication. Similarly, sloppy appearance, poor printing, careless formatting, and typographical or spelling errors can disrupt written messages.

What's more, ever-increasing digital distractions continue to reduce attention span and disrupt communication processes. Nearly 70 percent of respondents in a recent workplace study reported feeling distracted on the job.[10] The focus of workers is constantly diverted by e-mail, text messages, Snapchat notifications, Facebook messages, chatty coworkers, Slack chats, Instagram live, office noise, and attempts to multitask. It's small wonder that the attention span of the average person is said to have declined from 12 seconds to 8. A much-circulated juicy tidbit holds that a goldfish, with a 9-second attention span, is better able to focus. Although largely debunked, the goldfish analogy has raised awareness of ever-increasing distractions.[11] Clear communication requires focusing on what is important and shutting out interruptions.

Common communication obstacles range from loud conversations to nonstop pings of incoming messages. How can employees in today's fast-paced digital workplace avoid distractions?

4-1g Overcoming Communication Obstacles

Careful communicators can conquer barriers in a number of ways. Half the battle in communicating successfully is recognizing that the entire process is sensitive and susceptible to breakdown. Like a defensive driver anticipating problems on the road, a good communicator anticipates problems in encoding, transmitting, and decoding a message. Effective communicators also focus on the receiver's environment and frame of reference. They ask themselves questions such as *How is that individual likely to react to my message?* or *What does the receiver already know about the subject?*

Misunderstandings are less likely if you arrange your ideas logically and use words precisely. Mark Twain was right when he said, "The difference between an almost-right word and the right word is like the difference between lightning and the lightning bug." Communicating, however, is more than expressing yourself well. A large part of successful communication is listening. Management advisor Peter Drucker observed that "too many executives think they are wonderful with people because they talk well. They don't realize that being wonderful with people means listening well."[12]

Effective communicators create an environment that encourages useful feedback. In oral communication, this means asking questions such as *Do you understand?* and *What questions do you have?* as well as encouraging listeners to repeat instructions or paraphrase ideas. As a listener, it means providing feedback that describes rather than evaluates. In written communication, it means asking questions and providing access: *Do you have my cell number in case you have questions? Or Here's my e-mail address so that you can give me your response immediately.*

LEARNING OUTCOME

2 Describe the goals of business writers and three phases of the writing process.

4-2 Applying the 3-x-3 Writing Process to Business Messages

Today's new media and digital technologies enable you to choose from innumerable communication channels to create, transmit, and respond to messages. Regardless of the channel, nearly all communication revolves around writing. Because writing is central to nearly all business communication, this chapter presents a systematic plan for planning messages in the digital era.

4-2a Understanding the Goals of Business Writers

One thing you should immediately recognize about business writing is that it differs from other writing you have done. In preparing high school or college compositions and term papers, you probably focused on discussing your feelings or displaying your knowledge. Your instructors wanted to see your thought processes, and they wanted assurance that you had internalized the subject matter. You may have been required to meet a minimum word count. Business writing is definitely not like that! It also differs from personal texts you may exchange with your friends and family. Those messages enabled you to stay connected and express your feelings. In the workplace, however, writing should be:

- **Purposeful.** Your goal will be to solve problems and convey information. Each message should have a definite strategy.

- **Economical.** You will try to present ideas clearly but concisely. Length is not rewarded.

- **Audience oriented.** You will look at a problem from the perspective of the audience instead of seeing it from your own.

These distinctions actually ease your task. No more searching your imagination for creative topic ideas. No stretching your ideas to make them appear longer. Writing consultants and businesspeople complain that many college graduates entering the workplace have a conscious—or perhaps unconscious—perception that quantity enhances quality. Wrong! Get over the notion that longer is better. Whether you are presenting your ideas in print, online, or in person, conciseness and clarity are what count in business.

The ability to prepare purposeful, concise, and audience-centered messages does not come naturally. Very few people, especially beginners, can sit down and draft an effective e-mail message, letter, or report without training. However, following a systematic process, studying model messages, and practicing the craft can make nearly anyone a successful business writer or speaker.

Reality Check

Why Is Business Writing So Bad?

Author David Silverman blasts "an educational system that rewards length over clarity." Students learn to overwrite, he says, in hopes that at least some of their sentences "hit the mark." Once on the job, they continue to act as if they were paid by the word, a perception that must be unlearned.[13]

—David Silverman, *entrepreneur, author,* Harvard Business Review Blog

4-2b Following the 3-x-3 Writing Process

Regardless of what you are writing or planning, the process will be easier if you follow a systematic plan. The 3-x-3 writing process breaks the entire task into three phases: *prewriting, drafting,* and *revising,* as shown in Figure 4.2.

To illustrate the writing process, let's say that you own a local McDonald's restaurant. Management recently installed digital kiosks to automate ordering. You aren't delighted with the new plan because customers are confused, and many refuse to use the digital kiosk. To assist customers, an employee must stand nearby to help. After placing an order, a customer often must still go to a cashier to pay. You fail to see how kiosk ordering is boosting your profit. Your customers definitely prefer cashiers to kiosk ordering, especially when they are ordering more than one item. You want to convince other franchise owners to join you in protesting this unwanted change. To convince others, you could make a lot of telephone calls or send many text messages. However, you want to present a serious argument with

FIGURE 4.2 The 3-x-3 Writing Process

1 Prewriting	2 Drafting	3 Revising
Analyze • What is your purpose? • What do you want the receiver to do or believe? • What channel should you choose: face-to-face conversation, group meeting, e-mail, memo, letter, report, blog, wiki, tweet? • What are the benefits or barriers of each channel?	**Research** • Gather data to provide facts. • Review previous correspondence. • Search company files for background information. • Talk with the boss and colleagues. • Search the Internet. • What do you need to know to write this message?	**Edit** • Edit your message to be sure it is clear, concise, conversational, and readable. • Revise to eliminate wordy fillers, long lead-ins, redundancies, and trite business phrases. • Consider using headings and numbered and bulleted lists for quick reading.
Anticipate • What is the audience profile? • What does the receiver already know? • Will the receiver's response be neutral, positive, or negative? How will the response affect your organizational stategy?	**Organize** • Organize direct messages with the big idea first, followed by an explanation in the body and an action request in the closing. • For persuasive or negative messages, use an indirect problem-solving strategy.	**Proofread** • Take the time to read the message carefully. • Look for errors in spelling, grammar, punctuation, names, and numbers. • Check to be sure the format is consistent.
Adapt • What techniques can you use to adapt your message to its audience? • How can you promote feedback? • What can you do to ensure positive, conversational, and courteous language?	**Draft** • Prepare a first draft usually writing quickly. • Focus on short, clear sentences using the active voice. • Build paragraph coherence by repeating key ideas, using pronouns, and incorporating appropriate transitional expressions.	**Evaluate** • Will this message achieve its purpose? • Does the tone sound pleasant and friendly rather than curt? • Have you thought enough about the audience to be sure this message is appealing? • Did you encourage feedback?

compelling points that they will remember and be willing to act on when they gather for their next district meeting. Texting doesn't enable you to make a serious argument. You decide to send a persuasive e-mail that you hope will win their support.

Prewriting.   The first phase of the writing process prepares you to write. It involves analyzing the audience and your purpose for writing. The audience for your message will be other franchise owners, some highly educated and others not. Your purpose in writing is to convince them that a change in policy would improve customer service and please customers.

You think that a single-line system, such as that used in banks, would reduce chaos and make customers happier because they would not have to worry about where they are in line.

Prewriting also involves anticipating how your audience will react to your message. You are sure that some of the other owners will agree with you, but others might fear that customers seeing a long single line might go elsewhere. In adapting your message to the audience, you try to think of the right words and the right tone that will win approval.

Drafting.   The second phase involves researching, organizing, and then drafting the message. In researching information for this message, you would probably investigate other kinds of businesses that use single lines for customers. You might check your competitors. What are Wendy's and Burger King doing? You might do some calling to see whether other franchise owners are concerned about chaotic

---

Reality Check   ✓

What Mistake Do Many Writers Make?

"Before you put pen to paper or hands to keyboard, consider what you want to say. The mistake that many people make is they start writing prematurely. They work out the thoughts as they're writing, which makes their writing less structured, meandering, and repetitive. Ask yourself: What should my audience know or think after reading this e-mail, proposal, or report? If the answer isn't immediately clear, you're moving too quickly."[14]

—Bryan A. Garner, *professor, lexicographer, acclaimed author,* Black's Law Dictionary

lines. Before writing to the entire group, you might brainstorm with a few owners to see what ideas they have for solving the problem.

Once you have collected enough information, you would focus on **organizing** your message. Should you start out by offering your solution? Or should you work up to it slowly, describing the problem, presenting your evidence, and then ending with the solution? The final step in the second phase of the writing process is actually **drafting** the letter. At this point, many writers write quickly, knowing that they will polish their ideas when they revise.

Revising.   The third phase of the process involves editing, proofreading, and evaluating your message. After writing the first draft, you will spend considerable time **editing** the message for clarity, conciseness, tone, and readability. Could parts of it be rearranged to make your point more effectively? This is the time when you look for ways to improve the organization and tone of your message. Next, you will spend time **proofreading** carefully to ensure correct spelling, grammar, punctuation, and format. The final phase involves **evaluating** your message to decide whether it accomplishes your goal.

4-2c **Pacing the Writing Process**

The time you spend on each phase of the writing process varies depending on the complexity of the problem, the purpose, the audience, and your schedule. On average, you should expect to spend about 25 percent of your time prewriting, 25 percent drafting, and 50 percent revising, as shown in Figure 4.3.

These are rough guides, yet you can see that good writers spend most of their time on the final phase of revising and proofreading. Much depends, of course, on your project, its importance, and your familiarity with it. What is critical to remember, though, is that revising is a major component of the writing process even if the message is short.

It may appear that you perform one step and progress to the next, always following the same order. Most business writing, however, is not that rigid. Although writers perform the tasks described, the steps may be rearranged, abbreviated, or repeated. Some writers revise every sentence and paragraph as they go. Many find that new ideas occur after they have begun to write, causing them to back up, alter the organization, and rethink their plan. Beginning business writers often follow the writing process closely. With experience, though, they will become like other good writers and presenters who alter, compress, and rearrange the steps as needed.

FIGURE 4.3   **Scheduling the Writing Process**

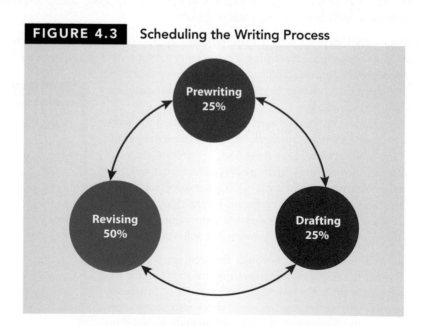

4-3 Analyzing and Anticipating the Audience

LEARNING OUTCOME

3 Identify the intended purpose and audience of a message to select the best communication channel.

Have you ever started to write a message and discovered toward the end that your purpose changed? Were you frustrated at the wasted time? If you analyze your purpose before you begin, you can avoid having to backtrack and start over. The remainder of this chapter covers the first phase of the 3-x-3 writing process: (a) analyzing the purpose for writing, (b) anticipating how the audience will react, and (c) adapting the message to the audience.

4-3a Analyzing Your Purpose

As you begin to compose a workplace message, ask yourself two important questions: (a) Why am I sending this message? and (b) What do I hope to achieve? Your responses will determine how you organize and present your information.

Your message may have primary and secondary purposes. For college work, your primary purpose may be merely to complete the assignment; secondary purposes might be to make yourself look good and earn an excellent grade. The primary purposes for sending business messages are typically to inform and persuade. A secondary purpose is to promote goodwill. You and your organization want to look good in the eyes of your audience.

Many business messages do nothing more than inform. Informational messages explain procedures, announce meetings, answer questions, and transmit findings. Such messages are usually developed directly, a strategy discussed in Chapter 5. Some business messages, however, are meant to persuade. Persuasive messages attempt to sell products, convince managers, motivate employees, and win over customers. Persuasive messages are often developed indirectly, as presented in Chapter 5 and subsequent chapters.

4-3b Anticipating and Profiling the Audience

Before beginning any message, spend a moment thinking about the audience who will receive it. What is the reader or listener like? How will that person react to the message? Although one can't always know exactly who the receiver is, it is possible to imagine some of that person's characteristics. A copywriter at a major retailer pictures his sister-in-law whenever he writes product descriptions for the catalog.

Profiling your audience is a pivotal step in the writing process. The questions in Figure 4.4 will help you understand your audience.

FIGURE 4.4 Questions to Help You Profile Your Audience

Primary Audience

- Who is my primary reader or listener?
- What are my personal and professional relationships with this person?
- How much does this person know about the subject?
- What do I know about this person's education, beliefs, culture, and abilities?
- Should I expect a neutral, positive, or negative response to my message?

Secondary Audience

- Who might see or hear this message in addition to the primary audience?
- How do these people differ from the primary audience?
- Do I need to include more background information?
- How must I reshape my message to make it understandable and accessible to others to whom it might be forwarded?

How much time you devote to answering these questions depends on your message and its context. An analytical report that you compose for management or an oral presentation before a big group would, of course, demand considerable time profiling the audience. An e-mail message to a coworker or a message to a familiar supplier might require only a few moments of planning.

Preparing a blog on an important topic to be posted to a company website would require you to think about the local, national, and international audiences that might read that message. Even posting brief personal messages at sites such as Facebook, Twitter, and Tumblr should make you think about who will read the messages. How much of your day and life do you want to share? Will customers and business partners be reading your posts?

No matter how short your message is, though, spend some time thinking about the people in your audience so that you can tailor your words to them. Remember that your receivers will be thinking, *What's in it for me?* (*WIIFM*). One of the most important writing tips you can take away from this book is remembering that every message you write should begin with the notion that your audience is thinking *WIIFM*.

4-3c Tailoring Your Message to the Audience Profile

Profiling your audience helps you make decisions about molding the message. You will determine what language is appropriate, whether you are free to use specialized technical terms, whether you should explain the background, and so on. Profiling the audience helps you decide whether your tone should be formal or informal. Profiling helps you consider whether the receiver is likely to respond positively or negatively to your message, or be neutral about it.

Another consideration in profiling your audience is the possibility of a secondary audience. Let's say, for example, that you start to write an e-mail message to your manager, Keira, describing a problem you are having. Halfway through the message, you realize that Keira will probably forward this message to her boss, the vice president. Super-efficient Keira will probably not want to rewrite what you said; instead, she may take the easy route and merely forward your e-mail. When you realize that the vice president may see this message, you decide to back up and use a more formal tone. You remove your inquiry about Keira's dog, you reduce your complaints, and you tone down your language about why things went wrong. Instead, you provide more background information, and you are more specific in identifying items the vice president might not recognize. Analyzing the task and anticipating the audience help you adapt your message so it will be effective for both primary and secondary receivers.

4-3d Choosing the Best Channel

After identifying the purpose of your message and profiling the audience, you will want to select the most appropriate communication channel. For quick messages you might decide to connect to the company's live chat program, such as that offered by Salesforce.com. It provides a complete profile for each customer as well as keyboard shortcuts and even prewritten messages. Your decision to use live chat, send an e-mail message, schedule a videoconference, or use some other channel depends on some of the following factors:

- Available technology
- Importance of the message
- Amount and speed of feedback and interactivity required
- Necessity of a permanent record
- Cost of the channel
- Degree of formality desired
- Confidentiality and sensitivity of the message
- Receiver's preference and level of technical expertise

In addition to these practical issues, you will also consider how rich the channel is. As discussed in Chapter 1, the richness of a channel involves the extent to which a channel or medium recreates or represents all the information available in the original message. A richer medium, such as a face-to-face conversation or live video chat, permits more interactivity and feedback. A leaner medium, such as a letter or an e-mail, presents a flat, one-dimensional message. Richer media enable the sender to provide more verbal and visual cues as well as to tailor the message to the audience.

4-4 Employing Expert Writing Techniques to Adapt to Your Audience

LEARNING OUTCOME

4 Discuss expert writing techniques that improve business messages.

After analyzing the purpose and anticipating the audience, writers begin to think about how to adapt a message to the task and the audience. Adaptation is the process of creating a message that suits the audience. Skilled communicators employ a number of expert writing techniques, such as those illustrated in the two versions of an e-mail in Model Document 4.1. These techniques include featuring audience benefits, cultivating a "you" view, sounding conversational but professional, and using positive, courteous expression. Additional adaptive techniques include using bias-free language and preferring plain language with familiar but vigorous words.

4-4a Focusing on Audience Benefits

Spotlighting the needs of the audience sounds like a modern idea, but actually one of America's early statesmen and authors recognized this fundamental writing principle more than 200 years ago. In describing effective writing, Ben Franklin observed, "To be good, it ought to have a tendency to benefit the reader."[16] These wise words have become a fundamental guideline for today's business communicators. Expanding on Franklin's counsel, a contemporary communication consultant gives this solid advice to his business clients: "Always stress the benefit to the audience of whatever it is you are trying to get them to do. If you can show them how you are going to save them frustration or help them meet their goals, you have the makings of a powerful message."[17] Remember, WIIFM!

> **Reality Check**
>
> **The Most Powerful Word in the Language**
>
> "When it comes to writing engaging content, 'you' is the most powerful word in the English language, because people are ultimately interested in fulfilling their own needs."[18]
>
> —Brian Clark, *founder of leading marketing blog* Copyblogger

Adapting your message to the receiver's needs means putting yourself in that person's shoes. It's called empathy. Empathic senders think about how a receiver will decode a message. They try to give something to the receiver, solve the receiver's problems, save the receiver's money, or just understand the feelings and position of that person. Which version of each of the following messages is more appealing to the audience?

Sender Focus	Audience Focus
All employees are herewith instructed to fill out the attached survey so that we can allocate our limited training resource funds to selected employees.	By filling out the attached survey, you can be one of the first employees to sign up for our limited training resource funds.
Our one-year warranty becomes effective only when we receive the owner's registration, which must be returned.	Your warranty on your mobile device begins working for you as soon as you return your owner's registration.

4-4b Cultivating the "You" View

Notice that many of the previous audience-focused messages included the word *you*. In concentrating on receiver benefits, skilled communicators naturally develop the "you" view. They emphasize second-person pronouns (*you, your*) instead of first-person pronouns (*I/we, us, our*).

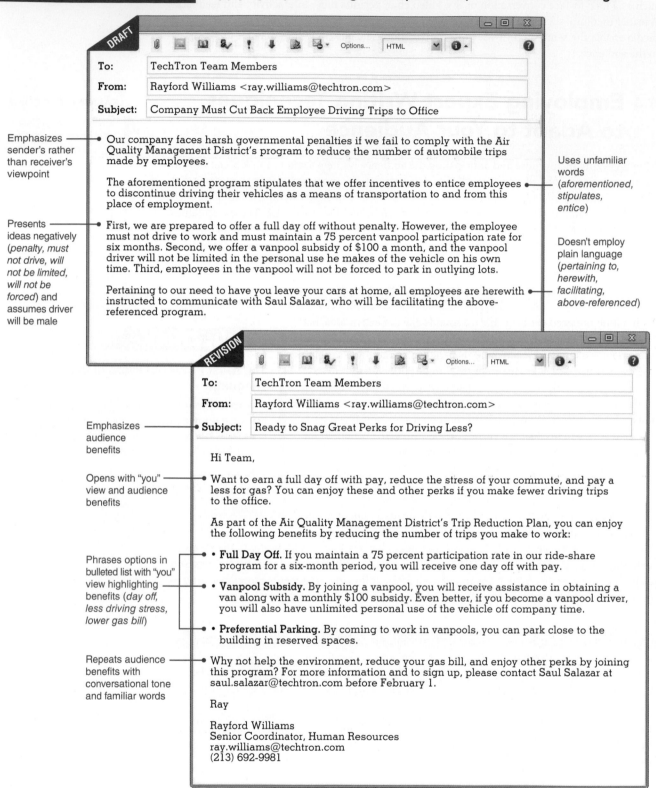

DRAFT

To:	TechTron Team Members
From:	Rayford Williams <ray.williams@techtron.com>
Subject:	Company Must Cut Back Employee Driving Trips to Office

Emphasizes sender's rather than receiver's viewpoint

Our company faces harsh governmental penalties if we fail to comply with the Air Quality Management District's program to reduce the number of automobile trips made by employees.

The aforementioned program stipulates that we offer incentives to entice employees to discontinue driving their vehicles as a means of transportation to and from this place of employment.

Uses unfamiliar words (*aforementioned, stipulates, entice*)

Presents ideas negatively (*penalty, must not drive, will not be limited, will not be forced*) **and assumes driver will be male**

First, we are prepared to offer a full day off without penalty. However, the employee must not drive to work and must maintain a 75 percent vanpool participation rate for six months. Second, we offer a vanpool subsidy of $100 a month, and the vanpool driver will not be limited in the personal use he makes of the vehicle on his own time. Third, employees in the vanpool will not be forced to park in outlying lots.

Pertaining to our need to have you leave your cars at home, all employees are herewith instructed to communicate with Saul Salazar, who will be facilitating the above-referenced program.

Doesn't employ plain language (*pertaining to, herewith, facilitating, above-referenced*)

REVISION

To:	TechTron Team Members
From:	Rayford Williams <ray.williams@techtron.com>
Subject:	Ready to Snag Great Perks for Driving Less?

Emphasizes audience benefits

Hi Team,

Opens with "you" view and audience benefits

Want to earn a full day off with pay, reduce the stress of your commute, and pay a less for gas? You can enjoy these and other perks if you make fewer driving trips to the office.

As part of the Air Quality Management District's Trip Reduction Plan, you can enjoy the following benefits by reducing the number of trips you make to work:

Phrases options in bulleted list with "you" view highlighting benefits (*day off, less driving stress, lower gas bill*)

- **Full Day Off.** If you maintain a 75 percent participation rate in our ride-share program for a six-month period, you will receive one day off with pay.

- **Vanpool Subsidy.** By joining a vanpool, you will receive assistance in obtaining a van along with a monthly $100 subsidy. Even better, if you become a vanpool driver, you will also have unlimited personal use of the vehicle off company time.

- **Preferential Parking.** By coming to work in vanpools, you can park close to the building in reserved spaces.

Repeats audience benefits with conversational tone and familiar words

Why not help the environment, reduce your gas bill, and enjoy other perks by joining this program? For more information and to sign up, please contact Saul Salazar at saul.salazar@techtron.com before February 1.

Ray

Rayford Williams
Senior Coordinator, Human Resources
ray.williams@techtron.com
(213) 692-9981

Whether your goal is to inform, persuade, or promote goodwill, the catchiest words you can use are *you* and *your*. Compare the following examples.

"I/We" View	"You" View
I need your account number before I can do anything about your claim.	Would you mind giving me your account number so that I can locate your records and help you solve this problem?
Our experienced staff has created a webinar that teaches how to use Instagram more productively.	Join an upcoming webinar to learn which of your Instagram photos are generating the most engagement to promote your business.

A recent survey revealed that *you* phrasing was more effective than *we* phrasing for conveying ideas related to interest and intent, such as in sales and marketing messages. Respondents felt more responsible for solving a problem and taking action in the *you* phrased messages. Researchers argued that *you* phrasing does a better job of unconsciously grabbing attention and transferring ownership to the receiver.[19]

Although you want to focus on the reader or listener, don't overuse or misuse the second-person pronoun *you*. Readers and listeners appreciate genuine interest; on the other hand, they resent obvious attempts at manipulation. The authors of some sales messages, for example, are guilty of overkill when they include *you* dozens of times in a direct-mail promotion. What's more, the word can sometimes create the wrong impression. Consider this statement: *You cannot return merchandise until you receive written approval.* The word *you* appears twice, but the reader may feel singled out for criticism. In the following version, the message is less personal and more positive: *Customers may return merchandise with written approval.*

Another difficulty in emphasizing the "you" view and de-emphasizing *we/I* is that it may result in an overuse of the passive voice. For example, to avoid *We will give you* (active voice), you might write *You will be given* (passive voice). The active voice in writing is generally preferred because it identifies who is doing the acting. You will learn more about active and passive voice in Chapter 5.

In recognizing the value of the "you" attitude, however, you don't have to sterilize your writing and totally avoid any first-person pronouns or words that show your feelings. You can convey sincerity, warmth, and enthusiasm by the words you choose. Don't be afraid of phrases such as *I'm happy* or *We're delighted,* if you truly are. When speaking face-to-face, you can show sincerity and warmth with nonverbal cues such as a smile and a pleasant voice tone. In letters, e-mail messages, memos, and digital messages, however, only expressive words and phrases can show your feelings. These phrases suggest hidden messages that say *You are important, I hear you,* and *I'm honestly trying to please you.*

4-4c Sounding Conversational but Professional

Most of the business messages you write replace conversation. Therefore, they are most effective when they convey an informal, conversational tone instead of a formal, pretentious tone. Just how informal you can be depends greatly on the workplace. At Google, casual seems to be preferred. In a short message to users describing changes in its privacy policies, Google wrote, "We believe this stuff matters."[21] In more traditional organizations, that message probably would have been more formal.

The dilemma for you, then, is knowing how casual to be in your writing. Should you include an **emoji**, an expressive cartoon face, to convey meaning beyond your words? See the accompanying *For the Record* to gain perspective on using emojis in the workplace. We suggest that you strive to be conversational but professional, especially until you learn what your organization prefers.

E-mail, instant messaging, chat, Twitter, and other short messaging channels enable you and your coworkers to have spontaneous conversations. Don't, however, let your messages become sloppy, unprofessional, or even dangerous. You will learn more about the dangers of e-mail and other digital channels later. At this point, though, we focus on the tone of the language.

To project a professional image, you want to sound educated and mature. The overuse of expressions such as *very, totally awesome, insanely, you know,* and *like,* as well as a reliance on unnecessary abbreviations (*BTW* for *by the way*), make a businessperson sound like a teenager.

Professional messages do not include texting-style abbreviations, slang, sentence fragments, and chitchat. We urge you to strive for a warm, conversational tone that avoids low-level diction. Levels of diction, as shown in Figure 4.5, range from unprofessional to formal.

FIGURE 4.5	Levels of Diction and Tone

Unprofessional	Conversational	Formal
badmouth	criticize	denigrate
guts	nerve	valor
pecking order	line of command	dominance hierarchy
ticked off	upset	provoked
rat on	reveal	divulge
rip off	steal	expropriate

Your goal is a warm, friendly tone that sounds professional. Although some writers are too casual, others are overly formal. To impress readers and listeners, they use big words, long sentences, legal terminology, and third-person constructions. Stay away from expressions such as *the undersigned, the writer,* and *the affected party.* You will sound friendlier with familiar pronouns such as *I, we,* and *you.* The following examples illustrate a professional yet conversational tone:

Unprofessional	Professional
Hey, boss, Gr8 news! Firewall now installed!! BTW, check with me b4 blasting the news.	Mrs. Williams, our new firewall software is now installed. Please check with me before announcing it.
Look, dude, this report is totally bogus. And the figures don't look kosher. Show me some real stats. Got sources?	Because the figures in this report seem inaccurate, please submit the source statistics.

continues

continued

Overly Formal	Conversational
All employees are herewith instructed to return the appropriately designated contracts to the undersigned.	Please return your contracts to me.
Pertaining to your order, we must verify the sizes that your organization requires prior to consignment of your order to our shipper.	We will send your order as soon as we confirm the sizes you need.

4-4d Choosing to be Positive Rather Than Negative

You can improve the clarity, tone, and effectiveness of a message by choosing positive rather than negative language. Positive language generally conveys more information than negative language. Moreover, positive messages are uplifting and pleasant to read. Positive wording tells what *is* and what *can be done* rather than what *isn't* and what *can't be done*. For example, *Your order cannot be shipped by January 10* is not nearly as informative as *Your order will be shipped January 15*. An office supply store adjacent to an ice cream parlor in Maine posted a sign on its door that reads: *Please enjoy your ice cream before you enjoy our store.* That sounds much more positive and inviting than *No food allowed!*

Using positive language also involves avoiding negative words that create ill will. Some words appear to blame or accuse your audience. For example, opening a letter to a customer with *You claim that* suggests that you don't believe the customer. Other loaded words that can get you in trouble are *complaint, criticism, defective, failed, mistake,* and *neglected.* Also avoid phrases such as *you apparently are unaware of, you did not provide, you misunderstood,* and *you don't understand.* Often you may be unconscious of the effect of these words. Notice in the following examples how you can revise the negative tone to create a more positive impression.

Negative	Positive
Our request for a fitness center will never be approved without senior management support.	Our request for a fitness center could be approved if we obtain senior management support.
You failed to include your credit card number, so we can't mail your order.	We look forward to completing your order as soon as we receive your credit card number.
Your e-mail of June 9 claims that you returned a defective headset.	Your June 9 e-mail describes a headset you returned.
Employees cannot park in Lot H until April 1.	Employees may park in Lot H starting April 1.

4-4e Expressing Courtesy

Maintaining a courteous tone involves not just guarding against rudeness but also avoiding words that sound demanding or preachy. Expressions such as *you should, you must,* and *you have to* cause people to instinctively react with *Oh, yeah?* One remedy is to turn these demands into rhetorical questions that begin with *Will you please . . . .* Giving reasons for a request also softens the tone.

Even when you feel justified in displaying anger, remember that losing your temper or being sarcastic will seldom accomplish your goals as a business communicator: to inform, to persuade, and to create goodwill. When you are irritated, frustrated, or infuriated, keep cool and try to defuse the situation. In dealing with customers in telephone conversations, use polite phrases such as *I would be happy to assist you with that, Thank you for being so patient,* and *It was a pleasure speaking with you.*

Less Courteous	More Courteous and Helpful
Jaylen, you must complete all performance reviews by April 1.	Jaylen, will you please complete all performance reviews by April 1.
Why can't you people get anything right? This is the second time I've had to write you!	Please credit my account for $250. The latest update of my online account shows that the error noted in my e-mail of January 4 has not yet been corrected.
Have you tried reading the operating manual, or am I the only one who can do that?	Let's review the operating manual together so that you can get your documents to print correctly next time.
You should organize a carpool in this department.	Organizing a carpool will reduce your transportation costs and help preserve the environment.

If you are a new or young employee who wants to fit in, don't fail to be especially courteous to older employees (generally, those over thirty) and important people in superior positions.[24] To make a great impression and show respect, use good manners in person and in writing. For example, don't be presumptuous by issuing orders or setting the time for a meeting with a superior. Use first names only if given permission to do so. Even if your boss or manager sends error-filled messages, don't let such errors creep into your writing.

4-4f Avoiding Gender, Age, and Disability Biased Language

In adapting a message to its audience, be sure your language is sensitive and bias-free. Few writers set out to be offensive. Sometimes, though, we all say things that we never thought might be hurtful. The real problem is that we don't think about the words that stereotype groups of people, such as *the boys in tech support* or *the girls in the front office.* Be cautious about expressions that might be biased in terms of gender, race, ethnicity, age, or disability.

Generally, you can avoid gender-biased language by choosing alternate language. For words involving *man* or *woman,* use plural nouns and pronouns or change to a gender-free word (*person* or *representative*). Avoid the *his or her* option whenever possible. It's wordy and conspicuous. With a little effort, you can usually find a construction that is graceful, grammatical, and unself-conscious.

Specify age only if it is relevant, and avoid expressions that are demeaning such as *spry old codger.* Avoid patronizing references such as *one of the lovely office ladies will help you.* Instead, try *one of the administrative assistants will help you.*

To avoid disability bias, do not refer to an individual's disability unless it is relevant. When necessary, use terms that do not stigmatize disabled individuals. Never use *cripple* or *crippled* when talking about a person with a disability. Moreover, don't refer to them as specially courageous, brave, or superhuman. Doing so makes it seem unexpected that they can be successful or live life like others.

Reality Check

Changing Perceptions With People-First Language

In a letter to the editor, a teacher criticized an article in *USA Today* on autism because it said "autistic child" rather than "child with autism." She championed "people-first" terminology, which avoids defining individuals by their ability or disability.[25] Can language change perceptions?

The following examples give you a quick look at a few problem expressions and possible replacements. The real key to bias-free communication, though, lies in your awareness and commitment. Be on the lookout to be sure that your messages do not exclude, stereotype, or offend people.

Gender-Biased	Improved
female doctor, woman attorney, cleaning woman	doctor, attorney, cleaner
waiter/waitress, authoress, stewardess	server, author, flight attendant
mankind, man-hour, man-made	humanity, working hours, artificial
office girl, office lady	office worker, administrative assistant
the doctor . . . he	doctors . . . they
the teacher . . . she	teachers . . . they
executives and their wives	executives and their spouses
foreman, flagman, workman, craftsman	lead worker, flagger, worker, artisan
businessman, salesman	businessperson, sales representative
Each employee had his picture taken.	Each employee had a picture taken.
	All employees had their pictures taken.

Racially or Ethnically Biased	Improved
A Hispanic accountant was hired.	An accountant was hired.
Derek Jones, an African American, applied.	Derek Jones applied.

Age-Biased	Improved
The law applied to old people.	The law applied to people over sixty-five.
Carol Cortez, 55, was transferred.	Carol Cortez was transferred.
a sprightly old gentleman	a man
a little old lady	a woman

Disability-Biased	Improved
afflicted with arthritis, suffering from arthritis, crippled by arthritis	has arthritis
confined to a wheelchair	uses a wheelchair
is mentally retarded, slow	is cognitively disabled

4-4g Preferring Plain Language and Familiar Words

In adapting your message to your audience, use plain language and familiar words that you think audience members will recognize. Don't, however, avoid a big word that conveys your idea efficiently and is appropriate for the audience. Your goal is to shun pompous and pretentious language. Instead, use *go* words. If you mean *begin*, don't say *commence* or *initiate*. If you mean *pay*, don't write *compensate*. By substituting everyday, familiar words for unfamiliar ones, as shown here, you help your audience comprehend your ideas more quickly.

Unfamiliar	Familiar
commensurate	equal
implement	begin
interrogate	question
materialize	appear
obfuscate	confuse
remuneration	pay, salary
subsequent to	after
terminate	end

At the same time, be selective in your use of jargon. **Jargon** describes technical or specialized terms within a field. These terms enable insiders to communicate complex ideas briefly, but to outsiders they mean nothing. Human resources professionals, for example, know precisely what's meant by *cafeteria plan* (a benefits option program), but most of us would be thinking about lunch. Geologists refer to *plate tectonics,* and physicians discuss *metastatic carcinomas.* These terms mean little to most of us. Such specialized language is appropriate only when the audience will understand it. In addition, don't forget to consider secondary audiences: Will those potential receivers understand any technical terms used?

4-4h Using Precise, Vigorous Words

Strong verbs and concrete nouns give receivers more information and keep them interested. Don't overlook the thesaurus (or the thesaurus program on your computer) for expanding your word choices and vocabulary. Whenever possible, use specific words, as shown here.

Imprecise, Dull	More Precise
a change in profits	a 25 percent hike in profits
	a 10 percent plunge in profits
to say	to promise, confess, understand
	to allege, assert, assume, judge
to think about	to identify, diagnose, analyze
	to probe, examine, inspect

The following checklist reviews important elements in the first phase of the 3-x-3 writing process, prewriting. As you review these tips, remember the three basics of prewriting: analyzing, anticipating, and adapting.

Checklist

Adapting a Message to Its Audience

- **Identify the message purpose.** Why are you writing, and what do you hope to achieve? Consider both primary and secondary audiences.
- **Select the most appropriate channel.** Consider the available technology, importance, feedback, interactivity, permanency, cost, formality, sensitivity, receiver's preference, and richness of the options.
- **Profile the audience.** What is your relationship with the receiver? How much does the receiver know or need to know?
- **Focus on audience benefits.** Phrase your statements from the reader's view. Concentrate on the "you" view.

- **Avoid gender, racial, age, and disability bias.** Use bias-free words (*businessperson* rather than *businessman*, *manager* rather than *Hispanic manager*, *new employee* rather than *new twenty-two-year-old employee*, *uses a wheelchair* rather than *confined to a wheelchair*).

- **Be conversational but professional.** Strive for a warm, friendly tone that is not overly formal or familiar. Avoid slang and low-level diction.

- **Express ideas positively rather than negatively.** Instead of *We can't ship until June 1*, say *We can ship on June 1*.

- **Use short, familiar words.** Avoid big words and technical terms unless they are appropriate for the audience (*end* not *terminate*).

- **Search for precise, vigorous words.** Use a thesaurus if necessary to find strong verbs and concrete nouns (*announces* instead of *says*, *brokerage* instead of *business*).

4-5 Collaborating on Team Projects

LEARNING OUTCOME

5 Explain the purpose of collaborative workplace writing and tools that facilitate it.

In today's interconnected workplace, many workers collaborate in teams to deliver services, develop products, and complete projects. It's almost assumed that progressive organizations will employ teams in some capacity to achieve their objectives. Because much of a team's work involves writing, you can expect to be putting your writing skills to work as part of a team.

4-5a When Is Team Writing Necessary?

Collaboration on team-written documents is necessary for projects that (a) are big, (b) have short deadlines, and (c) require the expertise or consensus of many people. Businesspeople sometimes also collaborate on short documents, such as memos, letters, information briefs, procedures, and policies. More often, however, teams work on big documents and presentations.

4-5b Why Are Team-Written Documents Better?

Team-written documents and presentations are standard in most organizations because collaboration has many advantages. Most important, collaboration usually produces a better product as many heads are better than one. In addition, team members and organizations benefit from team processes. Working together helps socialize members. They learn more about the organization's values and procedures. They are able to break down functional barriers, and they improve both formal and informal chains of communication. When they buy in to a project, they become part of its development. Members of effective teams are eager to implement their recommendations.

4-5c How Are Team-Written Documents Divided?

With big writing projects, teams may not actually function together for each phase of the writing process. Typically, team members gather at the beginning to brainstorm. They iron out answers to questions about the purpose, audience, content, organization, and design of their document or presentation. They develop procedures for team functioning, as you learned in Chapter 2. Then, they often assign segments of the project to individual members.

In Phase 1 of the writing process, teams work together closely as they discuss the project and establish their purpose. In Phase 2, members generally work separately when they conduct research, organize their findings, and compose a first draft. During Phase 3, some teams work together to synthesize their drafts and offer suggestions for revision. Other teams appoint one person to proofread and edit and another to prepare the final document. The revision and evaluation

FIGURE 4.6   **Sharing the Writing of Team Documents**

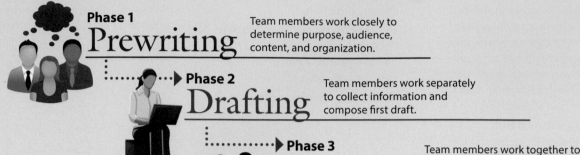

Three Phases in Team Writing

Phase 1
Prewriting
Team members work closely to determine purpose, audience, content, and organization.

Phase 2
Drafting
Team members work separately to collect information and compose first draft.

Phase 3
Revising
Team members work together to synthesize and edit, but individuals may do the final formatting and proofreading.

iadams/Fotolia LLC; denis_pc/Fotolia LLC; denis_pc/Fotolia LLC

phase might be repeated several times before the final product is ready for presentation. Sharing the entire writing process, illustrated in Figure 4.6, means that all team members contribute their skills during the three phases.

4-5d What Tools Improve Efficiency in Team Writing and Collaboration?

Increasing numbers of businesses are allowing telecommuting and remote working options for employees. To stay connected with their offices and collaborate on team projects, these employees use a vast array of devices and software. Many of these tools rely on mobile technology and cloud computing to help teams share information and work together. E-mail in the past was useful in team collaboration. However, as projects become more complex and involve people using often-incompatible devices, e-mail became a clumsy, ineffective tool. Here are a few of the many tools that teams are using to collaborate efficiently:

- **Slack.** One of the most popular messaging apps is Slack, which allows groups of people to chat with one another in both open and private conversations. Slack offers real-time conversations to help various team members make immediate decisions. It also allows files of any format to be shared and provides powerful message search. It's perfect for teams that need to be in constant communication. By creating Slack channels and setting up notifi-cations, teams boost their productivity and improve coordination of all tasks and projects.

- **Google Docs and Google Hangouts.** Although it's not the flashiest collaboration tool, Google Docs is one of the most useful. Its platform-sharing and file-storage features enable users to create and access spreadsheets, word documents, and presentations from nearly any location. Another helpful program is Google Hangouts. When team members need to be in frequent contact with each other, it provides video chat and web conferencing. Best of all, both programs are free.

- **Dropbox.** Many teams use Dropbox to share and store files. This cloud storage service enables team members to create documents on their computers and upload them to

Dropbox where other team members can edit and revise. Members can store and share photos, documents, spreadsheets, and files that are too large to transfer back and forth with e-mail. The ability to access folders from any Internet device and from any location with an Internet connection is particularly appealing to teams. Its killer feature is its automatic synchronization of files on all devices, thus saving time and streamlining collaboration.

- **Office 365.** Microsoft offers a large—and confusing—collection of collaboration tools within Office 365. This product aims to "improve collaboration by transforming the corporate intranet into a social network that cuts through hierarchies to improve executive–employee connections and eliminate barriers created by physical distance, time zones, and workers using multiple devices."[26] Office 365 provides team sites, communication sites, and hub sites, all within its SharePoint Online platform. Office 365 also provides Outlook Groups, Yammer Groups, Microsoft Teams, and Skype for Business Online.

- **Track Changes and other tools.** MS Word includes **Track Changes** and **Comment** features that enable collaborators working on the same document to identify and approve edits made by team members. See the accompanying Plugged In box for more information about using these tools.

- **Trello.** For project management, Trello is a current lightweight tool for small teams with up to ten people. It allows collaborators to create, manage, and monitor projects using checklists and task cards. Its "timestamp" feature maintains accountability within the team. Other work management tools growing in popularity are ProofHub, Asana, Workfront, Smartsheet, Planview, and Planner.

- **Wisemapping.** When teams must gather thoughts, come up with new ideas, and turn those ideas into actions, they may turn to software such as Wisemapping. This tool is a free online mind-mapping editor for individuals, educational institutions, and business organizations. It is one of many emerging mind-mapping tools that make collaboration run more smoothly.[27] You'll learn more about mind mapping and brainstorming in Chapter 5.

> ### Reality Check
>
> #### How Dependent on Collaboration Are We?
>
> "We live in an interdependent age. Very little today is the product of just one actor working alone. Collaboration, collaborators, and the technologies they choose to use are the key drivers of modern existence."[28]
>
> —Thornton May, *futurist, educator, and author, named as one of the top brains in business*

4-5e How Can Team Members Edit Documents Without Making Enemies?

A dazzling array of cloud-based tools delights team collaborators and techies. But none of these tools can repair damaged feelings when team members fail to make comments sensitively. When your team is preparing a report or presentation and members create different sections, you will probably be expected to edit or respond to the writing of others. Because no one likes to be criticized, make your statements specific, constructive, and helpful. Try the following suggestions for making edits that won't make enemies:

- Begin your remarks with a positive statement. What can you praise? Do you like the writer's conversational tone, word choice, examples, directness, or conciseness?

- Do you understand the writer's purpose? If not, be specific in explaining what you don't understand.

- Is the material logically organized? If not, how could it be improved?

- What suggestions can you make to improve specific ideas or sections?

- Make polite statements such as *I would suggest . . ., You might consider . . .,* and *How about doing this . . ..*

Zooming In

Your Turn:
Applying Your Skills at VisibleThread

You are one of the lucky applicants hired as an intern at VisibleThread. This company, introduced in the chapter-opening vignette, helps business organizations create readable documents and website content. To gauge your writing skills, training manager Fiona McBride prepared a wordy paragraph that needs serious revision. Your task is to rewrite this wordy test paragraph retaining its meaning but making it more readable. In an e-mail message addressed to *Fiona.McBride@vthread.com*, send your revision and also explain what you did to improve readability. See Chapter 8 for information on preparing e-mail messages.

Wordy Security Message

Dear Customer:

As you requested in your recent message to our marketing staff, the undersigned is transmitting to you herewith the attached information with regard to the improvement of security in your business, which we understand is causing you considerable alarm and for which you are seeking reassurance. With regard to the enhancement of your after-hours security, you should initially make a decision with regard to exactly what you contemplate must have protection.

Inasmuch as protection requires taking a number of judicious steps to inhibit crime, first and foremost defensive lighting should be installed. A consultant for lighting who happens to be currently on our staff can design both outside and inside lighting, which brings me to my second point. Exhibit security signs, due to the fact that nonprofessional thieves are often as not daunted by posted signs on windows and doors. As my final recommendation, you should install space alarms, which are sensors that look down over the areas that are to receive protection and activate bells or additional lights, thus scaring off intruders.

SUMMARY OF LEARNING OUTCOMES

1 List the steps in the communication process.

- *Communication* may be defined as the transmission of information and meaning from a sender to a receiver.

- The crucial element in this definition is *meaning*. Communication is unsuccessful if the receiver does not understand the meaning intended by the sender.

- The communication process begins when the sender has an idea. In the next step, the sender *encodes* the idea into words or gestures that convey meaning.

- The sender selects a channel and transmits the meaning. Anything that interrupts the transmission is called *noise*.

- The receiver *decodes* the message and may return *feedback* to the sender, revealing whether the message was understood.

- Barriers that may create misunderstanding include bypassing, differing frames of reference, weak language skills, and distractions.

2 Describe the goals of business writers and three phases of the writing process.

- Business writing should be purposeful, economical, and audience oriented.

- Phase 1 of the 3-x-3 writing process (prewriting) involves analyzing the message, anticipating the audience, and considering ways to adapt the message to the audience.

- Phase 2 (drafting) involves researching the topic, organizing the material, and drafting the message.

- Phase 3 (revising) includes editing, proofreading, and evaluating the message. A writing process helps a writer by providing a systematic plan describing what to do in each step of the process.

3 Identify the intended purpose and audience of a message to select the best communication channel.

- Before drafting, decide why you are creating a message and what you hope to achieve. Although many messages only inform, others also persuade.

- After identifying the purpose, visualize both the primary and secondary audiences. Doing so helps you choose the most appropriate language, tone, and content.

- Remember that receivers often think, *What's in it for me?* (WIIFM).

- Select the best channel by considering the available technology, importance of the message, the amount and speed of feedback required, the necessity of a permanent record, the cost of the channel, the degree of formality desired, the confidentiality and sensitivity of the message, and the receiver's preference and level of technical expertise.

4 Discuss expert writing techniques that improve business messages.

- Messages are often more effective if they focus on *audience benefits*, which suggests looking for ways to shape the message from the receiver's, not the sender's, view.

- Skilled communicators look at a message from the receiver's perspective, applying the "you" view without attempting to manipulate.

- Expert writing techniques include using conversational but professional language along with positive language that tells what can be done rather than what can't be done. (*You can receive a discount with the proper code* rather than *We can't authorize a discount unless you include the proper code.*)

- A courteous tone means guarding against rudeness and avoiding sounding preachy or demanding.

- Writers should also avoid language that excludes, stereotypes, or offends people (*lady lawyer, spry old gentleman,* and *confined to a wheelchair*).

- Plain language, familiar terms, strong verbs, and concrete nouns improve readability and effectiveness.

5 Explain the purpose of collaborative writing in the workplace and tools that facilitate it.

- Large projects or team efforts involving the expertise of many people often require team members to collaborate.

- During Phase 1 (prewriting) of the writing process, teams usually work together to brainstorm and work out their procedures and assignments.

- During Phase 2 (drafting), individual members research and write their portions of the project report or presentation.

- During Phase 3 (revising), teams may work together to combine and revise their drafts.

- Teams may use cloud-based collaboration tools such as Slack, Google Docs, Google Handouts, Track Changes, Dropbox, Office 365, ProofHub, Trello, and Wisemapping to collaborate effectively.

Key Terms

communication *120*

encoding *120*

channel *121*

noise *121*

receiver *121*

decoding *121*

feedback *121*

frame of reference *122*

analyzing *125*

anticipating *125*

adapting *125*

researching *125*

organizing *126*

drafting *126*

editing *126*

proofreading *126*

evaluating *126*

informational messages *127*

persuasive messages *127*

WIIFM *128*

empathy *129*

"you" view *129*

emoji *131*

jargon *136*

Critical Thinking

1. A wise observer once said that bad writing makes smart people look stupid. Do you agree or disagree? Why? (L.O. 1–4)

2. Have you ever read something complex and blamed yourself for not understanding it? Fergal McGovern, CEO of VisibleThread, argues that it's not your fault, particularly if the subject is investing. He blames turgid and dense writing. He thinks that even complex ideas can be expressed in natural, plain language. Do you agree? If so, how can writers do this? (L.O. 4)

3. The use of digital communication has overtaken face-to-face and voice-to-voice communication in the workplace. Has this shift changed the fundamental process of communication? (L.O. 1)

4. Why should business writers strive to use short, familiar, simple words? Does this dumb down business messages? (L.O. 4)

5. **Ethical Issue:** After a workplace project was completed, you were rightfully upset. You and two other team members did all of the work, but two freeloaders are sharing in the credit. This probably wouldn't have happened in college team assignments. Should you report the freeloaders to the manager?

Writing Improvement Exercises

4.1 Audience Benefits and the "You" View
(L.O. 4)

YOUR TASK Revise the following sentences to emphasize the perspective of the audience and the "you" view.

a. Because we have automated our mobile worker trip forms, we need all employees to use the SmartTrip travel reimbursement mobile app. This is the fastest way to be reimbursed.

b. We are issuing all our customers new chip-enabled credit cards to replace expired or lost cards and prevent increasingly costly payouts we have suffered from cyberfraud.

c. Our rigorous safety policy forbids us from renting power equipment to anyone who cannot demonstrate proficiency in its use.

d. We're requesting that all employees complete the attached online survey by April 1 so that we may develop a master schedule for summer vacations more efficiently.

e. To save the expense of having team trainers set up your training classes in our limited office space, we suggest offering a customized class for your employees right in your own building.

f. Our social media engineers are excited to announce a new free app called Fan Boosters that we believe will get fans to share, like, and subscribe to your content.

g. We take pride in our national policy of selling name brands at discount prices. That's why we can allow store credit, but we cannot give cash refunds on returned merchandise.

4.2 Conversational but Professional
(L.O. 4)

YOUR TASK Revise the following to make the tone conversational yet professional.

a. BTW, Madison went ballistic when the manager accused her of ripping off office supplies.

b. As per your recent request, the undersigned is happy to inform you that we are sending you forthwith the procedure manuals you requested.

c. Kindly be informed that it is necessary for you to designate the model number of the appliance before we can submit your order.

d. Pursuant to your e-mail of the 4th, please be advised that your shipment was sent March 6.

e. R head honcho wz like totally raggety kuz I wz sick n stuff n mist the team meet. Geez!

f. The undersigned respectfully reminds affected individuals that employees desirous of changing their health plans must do so before December 30.

4.3 Positive and Courteous Expression
(L.O. 4)

YOUR TASK Revise the following statements to make them more positive and courteous.

a. We regret to announce that we can offer the 50 percent discount only to the first 25 buyers, so act quickly!

b. Construction on your building is at a standstill because the contractor is unable to pour footings until the soil is no longer soggy.

c. A passport cannot be issued until an application is completed and a recent photo is included.

d. Your message of June 1 claims that the blade in your food processor malfunctioned. Although you apparently failed to read the operator's manual, we are sending you a replacement blade PLUS another manual. Next time read page 18 carefully so that you will know how to attach this blade.

e. Customers are ineligible for the 25 percent discount if they fail to provide the discount code at the time of purchase.

f. As team leader, you apparently failed to remember that you have already assigned me two gigantic and complex research tasks, and now you have dumped another big job on me—one that I can't possibly begin until after I finish the other two jobs.

4.4 Bias-Free Language (L.O. 4)

YOUR TASK Revise the following sentences to reduce bias (e.g., gender, racial, ethnic, age, disability).

a. Sports Research International hired Demarcus Jones, an African American, for the position of social media coordinator.

b. In 18 or more states, an employee has the right to view his employee record.

c. In the past a skilled assistant would proofread her boss's documents and correct any errors he made.

d. Douglas Luna is crippled with arthritis, but his crippling rarely interferes with his work.

e. Recently appointed to the commission are a lady lawyer, an Indian CPA, and two businessmen.

f. The conference in Key West offers special side trips for the wives of executives.

4.5 Plain Language and Familiar Words
(L.O. 4)

YOUR TASK Revise the following sentences to use plain language and familiar words.

a. The attorney tried to obfuscate the issue with extraneous and superfluous data.

b. Civil Service exams were once required for federal government jobs, but they were phased out subsequent to the passage of antidiscrimination laws.

c. To expedite ratification of the agreement, we beseech you to vote in the affirmative.

d. Although the remuneration for the position of social media consultant seems low, it is commensurate with other pay packages for similar positions.

e. Subsequent to the robbery, officials interrogated tellers, but the bank did not implement new procedures.

f. Although researchers dialogued with individual students on campus, subsequent group interviews proved fruitless.

4.6 Precise, Vigorous Words (L.O. 4)

YOUR TASK From the choices in parentheses, select the most precise, vigorous words.

a. If you receive two job offers at once, you can probably (*get, land, negotiate*) a better deal.

b. In the courtroom the attorney (*said, alleged, thought*) that the car was stolen.

c. If you are stressed from (*having, doing, juggling*) many tasks, look for ways to reduce your involvement.

d. Dakota's outstanding report contains (*a lot of, loads of, reams of*) helpful data.

e. The CEO said that we must (*review, change, reduce*) overtime hours to (*fix, balance, rework*) the budget.

f. Our operations manager demanded a (*substantial, 20 percent, big*) reduction in staff travel expenditures.

Activities

4.7 Document for Analysis: Improving a Negative, Discourteous, and Unprofessional Message (L.O. 4, 5)

Communication Technology / **E-Mail** / **Team**

YOUR TASK Analyze the following faulty e-mail to be sent by the vice president to all supervisors and managers. In teams or individually, discuss the tone and writing faults in this message. Your instructor may ask you to revise the e-mail so that it reflects some of the writing techniques you learned in this chapter. How can you make this e-mail

more courteous, positive, concise, precise, and audience oriented? Consider revising it as a collaboration project using Word's **Track Changes** and **Comment** features.

To: All Supervisors and Departmental Managers
From: Avianca Keller, Vice President, Employee Relations
Subject: Legally Risky Employee Evaluations

All,

Although it pains me to do this, I must warn you all that recently one of our employees filed a lawsuit against the company because of comments a supervisor made during a performance evaluation. This did not have to happen. Look, people, you must be smarter!

Because none of you are dense, here are suggestions you must share with all supervisors and managers regarding companywide evaluations:

- It goes without saying that you cannot accurately evaluate an employee's performance unless you have a system to measure that performance. That's why the obvious very first step is developing performance standards and goals for each employee. To be effective, these standards and goals must be shared with the employee. However, don't do it orally. Do it in writing.

- The performance of each employee must be monitored throughout the year. Keep a log for each worker. Note memorable incidents or projects in which he was involved. But don't just keep favorable comments. I know that many of you are understandably averse to placing negative comments in an employee's file. However, MAN UP! Even negative comments must be included as part of the evaluation process.

- Once a year each employee must be formally evaluated in a written performance appraisal—yes, I do mean written! In a face-to-face meeting, let the employee know what you think they did well and what areas the employee may be able to improve. Be specific, give deadlines, be honest, and be realistic.

Giving evaluations can be difficult. With careful preparation, however, the process can be smooth and safe. Don't allow yourself or the company to get involved in any more legal ramifications.

Avianca Keller
[Complete contact information]

4.8 Analyzing Audiences (L.O. 3)

YOUR TASK Using the questions in Figure 4.4, write a brief analysis of the audience for each of the following communication tasks. What kind of reaction should you expect from the primary reader and any secondary readers? What tone should you convey?

a. As a soon-to-graduate senior, you are writing a profile that you will post to LinkedIn. You hope it will land you a job offer.

b. As an administrator of your city water department, you must write a letter to water users explaining that the tap water may taste and smell bad; however, it poses no threats to health.

c. You are a member of an organization promoting Earth Day. You have been asked to encourage your office to save paper, and you know of several tips for doing

that. You want to persuade your boss to send a message to employees with a number of tips that you will provide.

d. You are about to send an e-mail to your regional sales manager describing your visit to a new customer who is demanding special discounts.

e. You are preparing an unsolicited sales message to a targeted group of executives promoting part-time ownership in a corporate jet plane.

f. You are planning to write an e-mail to your manager to try to persuade her to allow you to attend a leadership training program that will require two hours of weekly release time for ten weeks.

4.9 Most Annoying Business Buzzwords
(L.O. 4)

Business writing is more effective when writers avoid overused jargon or buzzwords that others find annoying, useless, and pretentious. In a recent survey of business professionals, the following phrases ranked at the top as most annoying.[29]

YOUR TASK For each of these words or phrases, write your own definition or be prepared to discuss its usefulness. Your instructor may share with you some of the responses from the survey respondents.

1. *synergy*
2. *think outside the box*
3. *take it offline*
4. *circle back*
5. *low-hanging fruit*
6. *at the end of the day*
7. *take a deep dive*
8. *you don't know what you don't know*
9. *leverage*
10. *move the needle*

4.10 Is Plain Writing a Civil Right? (L.O. 4)

E-Mail | Team

As an intern at VisibleThread, you and several other interns have been assigned the task of researching the history of the plain writing/plain language movement. Many of its principles are embodied in the business model of VisibleThread. Your training manager Fiona McBride thinks that this research will help you better understand the company goals. She found a stirring quotation from Annetta Cheek, who kicked off the Plain Language

Symposium in Washington, D.C., some years ago. Ms. Cheek claims that "plain writing is a civil right."[30] Do you agree? As part of your intern training, Ms. McBride asks you and other interns to prepare a brief history of the movement. Explain how it got started, who must comply, and whom it benefits. She also asks that you list and illustrate at least five of its guidelines with original examples. Individually or as a team, prepare a one-page report as an e-mail directed to Fiona.McBride@vthread.com but submitted to your instructor.

Test Your Workplace Etiquette IQ

New communication platforms and casual workplace environments have blurred the lines of appropriateness, leaving workers wondering how to navigate uncharted waters. Check your workplace etiquette IQ by deciding whether the following statements are true or false. Then see if you agree with the responses on p. Key-5.

1. Your cell phone rings while you are at your desk. You see immediately that it's a personal call. If you think it's going to be a short call, you should go ahead and answer.

   _____ True _____ False

2. At your office desk, it's easier to take notes from telephone calls when both hands are free. To be most efficient, you should set your phone to speaker so that your hands are always free to make notes either manually or on your computer.

   _____ True _____ False

3. In your office cubicle, you overhear Tyler, who is two cubicles away, on the phone asking when the next management council meeting is scheduled. Because you know the date, you should shout it out so that Tyler learns immediately the date of this critical meeting.

   _____ True _____ False

Chat About It

In each chapter, you will find five discussion questions related to the chapter material. Your instructor may assign these topics for you to discuss in class, in an online chat room, or on an online discussion board. Some of the discussion topics may require outside research. You may also be asked to read and respond to postings made by your classmates.

TOPIC 1: Psychologist Heidi Halvorson, presented earlier in a Reality Check, cautions communicators to think twice: "The next time you catch yourself thinking 'I didn't expressly say that to Bob, but it should be obvious . . .' STOP. Nothing is ever obvious unless you made it obvious by spelling it out." She further admonishes speakers to banish from their vocabularies the phrase "It goes without saying."[31] Think about a time when you thought you were absolutely clear, but you were misunderstood. How could you have been better understood?

TOPIC 2: After searching an alumni database, you decide to e-mail a professional who is working in the career you hope to enter. Your goal in writing this professional is to obtain firsthand information about this person's career and to receive career advice. However, you know nothing about this person. How could you profile the receiver to help you shape your message? What audience benefits could you use to persuade the receiver? What channel would you choose to deliver your message? What tone would you use?

TOPIC 3: Have you ever tried to make your writing longer than it needed to be? For example, did you count the words in what you wrote to meet a minimum word count? Do you agree with David Silverman, presented earlier in a Reality Check, that students learn to overwrite in the hope that at least some of their sentences hit the mark?

TOPIC 4: Think about a time when someone had to reveal bad news to you. Did you feel that the best communication channel was used to deliver that news? What channels are richest? Should they always be used to reveal bad news or to be persuasive?

TOPIC 5: Think back to the last time you were involved in a team project. What did the team do that resulted in an efficient working process and a successful product, or an inefficient working process and an unsuccessful product?

Adjectives and Adverbs

Review Guides 19 and 20 about adjectives and adverbs in Appendix D, Grammar and Mechanics. On a separate sheet, revise the following sentences to correct errors in adjectives and adverbs. For each error you locate, write the guide number that reflects this usage. Some sentences may have two errors. If a sentence is correct, write C. When you finish, check your answers at the end of the book.

EXAMPLE: How often do you have a once in a lifetime opportunity like this?

REVISION: How often do you have a once-in-a-lifetime opportunity like this? [Guide 20]

1. Writing concise, purposeful, and audience-centered messages is a skill that does not come natural to most people.

2. Well written business messages sound conversational but professional.

3. Many organizations use wikis to post up to the minute information about projects.

4. Most of our newly-written team documents were posted quick to the wiki.

5. We all felt badly when one member lost her laptop and had no backup.

6. The 3-x-3 writing process provides step-by-step instructions for preparing messages.

7. The written report and its bibliography were a three week project for our team.

8. Our project ran more smooth after Nazarnin reorganized the team.

9. Locally-installed online collaboration tools are easy-to-use and work well.

10. Samantha thought she had done good when she wrote her part of the team report.

CHAPTER 5

Organizing and Drafting Business Messages

LEARNING OUTCOMES

After studying this chapter, you should be able to do the following:

1 Compare two forms of research that begin Phase 2 of the 3-x-3 writing process.

2 List techniques that help writers generate and sort ideas to solve problems.

3 Demonstrate methods for organizing ideas to show relationships.

4 Write effective sentences that avoid fragments, run-ons, and comma splices.

5 Demonstrate methods for emphasizing ideas, using active and passive voice, developing parallelism, and placing modifiers correctly.

6 Explain how to create well-organized, coherent paragraphs.

Andresr/shutterstock.com

Zooming In
How a Wedding Website Grew Into a $100 Million Event Planning Business

"It all started about 15 years ago at a poker game when one of the guys announced that he was getting married, and we decided to make him a website to plan and organize the affair," said Rob Hirscheimer, cofounder of MyEvent.com.[1] What started as a one-time event eventually became one of the first wedding website builders on the Internet. Based on the idea that anyone can make a website with easy-to-use Web-based software, Rob and cofounder Mark Goldenberg brainstormed their wedding platform into a leading do-it-yourself event planning service.

Located in Montreal, MyEvent.com now provides complete Web packages that help individuals, businesses, and nonprofits organize such events as class and family reunions, personal and group fund-raisers, and corporate events. What's remarkable about its business success is that MyEvent.com has managed to remain relevant despite its small size and despite seismic upheavals in the Internet. Event planners now rely heavily on social media and emerging technologies to deliver information and interact with target audiences.

One of the most popular MyEvent.com programs is MyFunRun, which provides a step-by-step, turnkey system for schools to raise funds. Students participate in a walk, run,

or other activity, and donations arrive via e-mail, via social networks, and in person. Rather than selling candy, doughnuts, cookies, or popcorn, students engage in a healthy activity that raises funds for a good cause.

The organizations using MyEvent.com represent a wide range of events and locations. H2OpenDoors raised funds for water purification systems in third world villages. In Tacoma, Washington, the Run for Equal Justice supported legal aid for low-income people.[2] Other events include 5K Peace Fur Paws in Ontario, Canada; Walk and Wag for Veterans in Massachusetts; Battle of the Bands in Montreal; and Miles for Midwives in Brooklyn, NY.[3]

More than 150,000 users have employed MyEvent.com sites for do-it-yourself fund-raising. In the arena of crowdsourcing and crowdfunding, people can raise funds for any project or cause, such as financing a business start-up, organizing a sporting event, or soliciting funds for a sick or disabled friend. Students even attempt to crowdfund their college tuition. You'll learn more about MyEvent.com and be asked to complete a relevant task at the end of this chapter.

Critical Thinking

- In what ways would research (gathering information) have helped the founders of MyEvent.com move beyond their original wedding platform and remain relevant in the rapidly changing world of Internet commerce?

- What techniques can business communicators at MyEvent.com and other companies use to generate ideas for new products as well as to improve business processes?

- Have you experienced any crowdsourcing in your social or college activities? Have you seen it in the news?

a katz/Shutterstock.com

5-1 Organizing and Drafting Messages Begins With Research

LEARNING OUTCOME

1 Compare two forms of research that begin Phase 2 of the 3-x-3 writing process.

Businesspeople constantly make decisions, solve problems, and determine how to proceed. At MyEvent.com the owners faced significant challenges in adapting their business model to a rapidly changing social media world. Like other business leaders, the MyEvent.com owners strive to solve problems by gathering information, generating ideas, and organizing those ideas into logical messages that guide their organizations. These activities are part of the second phase of the 3-x-3

FIGURE 5.1 The 3-x-3 Writing Process

1 Prewriting	**2** Drafting	**3** Revising
Analyze: Decide on the message purpose. What do you want the receiver to do or believe?	**Research:** Gather background data by searching files and the Internet.	**Edit:** Eliminate wordy fillers, long lead-ins, redundancies, and trite business phrases. Strive for parallelism, clarity, conciseness, and readability.
Anticipate: What does the audience already know? How will it receive this message?	**Organize:** Arrange direct messages with the big idea first. For persuasive or negative messages, use an indirect, problem-solving strategy.	**Proofread:** Check carefully for errors in spelling, grammar, punctuation, and format.
Adapt: Think about techniques to present this message most effecively. Consider how to elicit feedback.	**Draft:** Prepare the first draft, using active-voice sentences, coherent paragraphs, and appropriate transitional expressions.	**Evaluate:** Will this message achieve your purpose? Is the tone pleasant? Did you encourage feedback?

writing process. You will recall that the 3-x-3 writing process, reviewed in Figure 5.1, involves three phases. This chapter focuses on the second phase of the process: researching, organizing, and drafting.

No savvy businessperson would begin drafting a message before gathering background information. We call this process **research**, a rather formal-sounding term. For our purposes, however, *research* simply means collecting information about a certain topic. This is an important step in the writing process because that information will help you shape your message. Discovering significant information after you have nearly completed a message often means starting over and reorganizing your thoughts. To avoid annoying second starts and inaccurate messages, careful writers collect information that answers several questions:

- What does the receiver need to know about this topic?
- What is the receiver to do?
- How is the receiver to do it?
- When must the receiver do it?
- What will happen if the receiver doesn't do it?

Whenever your communication problem requires more information than you have in your head or at your fingertips, you must conduct research. This research may be informal or formal.

5-1a Informal Research

Many routine tasks—such as drafting e-mails, memos, letters, informational reports, and oral presentations—require information that you can collect informally. Where can you find information before starting a project?

- **Explore your company's files.** If you are responding to an inquiry or drafting a routine message, you often can find background information such as previous correspondence in your own files or those of the company. You might consult the company wiki or other digital and manual files. You might also consult colleagues.

- **Chat with the boss.** Get information from the individual making the assignment. What does that person know about the topic? What slant should you take? What other sources would that person suggest?

- **Interview the target audience.** Consider talking with individuals at whom the message is aimed. They can provide clarifying information that tells you what they want to know and how you should shape your remarks. Suggestions for conducting more formal interviews are presented in Chapter 11.

- **Organize an informal survey.** Gather unscientific but helpful information through questionnaires, telephone surveys, or online surveys. In preparing a report predicting the success of a proposed company fitness center, for example, you might circulate a questionnaire asking for employee reactions.

5-1b Formal Research

Information for long reports and proposals may be obtained through formal research using primary or secondary sources.

- **Primary sources.** Primary data come from firsthand experience. This information might be generated from surveys, interviews, observation, and experimentation. Scientific researchers conduct experiments with controlled variables to produce information that helps solve problems. Because formal research is particularly necessary for reports, you will study resources and research techniques beginning in Chapter 11.

- **Secondary sources.** Secondary data come from reading what others have experienced or observed and written about. Books, magazines, journals, and online resources are all considered secondary sources. Most writers conducting research begin with secondary sources. These topics and research techniques are covered in Chapters 11 and 12.

5-2 Generating Ideas to Solve Problems

LEARNING OUTCOME

2 List techniques that help writers generate and sort ideas to solve problems.

Not all information for making decisions is available through research. Organizations often need to generate fresh ideas to solve problems. How can we expand our business model using social media? How can we cut costs without losing market share? Should we radically reinvent our website? For years organizations have tried to solve problems and generate ideas in group discussion using brainstorming techniques. More recently mind mapping and crowdsourcing with digital tools have expanded these collaborative methods.

5-2a Brainstorming

Traditionally, groups have generated ideas by **brainstorming**, which may be defined as the spontaneous contribution of ideas from members of a group. The process usually begins with a leader who defines the problem to be solved. That person acts as facilitator and may record the ideas voiced by the participants. The emphasis is on quantity, not quality. Some groups set a goal of 100 or more ideas. It makes no difference whether the ideas are reasonable, feasible, or silly. The goal is to lay opinions aside and think freely.

Critics charge that brainstorming in this traditional format doesn't always work. It may result in the "loudmouth meeting-hog phenomenon," in which one extrovert dominates the conversation.[4] To overcome the shortcomings of traditional brainstorming, participants may write their ideas on flip charts, on papers hung on the walls, or on post-it slips. This technique is called **brainwriting**. Either way, the facilitator helps the group discuss, organize, and rank the best ideas.

Working on a team often involves brainstorming to develop ideas that solve problems. Experts say the keys to success are defining the problem and having a good facilitator.

5-2b Mind Mapping

Like brainstorming, **mind mapping** is a process for generating and sorting ideas. However, mind mapping emphasizes visual concepts, beginning with a single concept drawn as an image in the center of a blank page. Associated words and images branch out treelike showing the relationship between the ideas and the central concept.

Some time ago at MyEvent.com, the staff decided to expand its business model to class reunions. Many schools and colleges sponsor reunions to enable classmates to reconnect and perhaps revisit their old school. But organizing such an event and following it through to a successful gathering requires skill, effort, and facilities. Who has the time and means to do that? MyEvent.com saw a perfect opportunity to enlarge its offerings. To work out details and generate ideas, staff members followed the steps for brainwriting shown in Figure 5.2. Once the best ideas for the School Reunions project were selected, the staff grouped them into a mind map such as that shown in Figure 5.2. Notice that the major categories are Operations, Benefits, Promotion, and Hub. Each of these categories has branches explaining relevant procedures and concepts related to the major concept. Mind maps serve as a visual organization chart summarizing a major event or product.

Mind mapping seems to have caught the imagination of software developers. A zillion competing online tools now promise to help teams "ideate, innovate, and even, eventually, execute."[5] Programs such as Stormboard claim to help generate 10 times more ideas than participants would in a regular meeting.[6] Stormboard groups similar ideas, removes duplicates, and detects patterns. Although most mind mapping products incorporate some form of brainstorming, many have expanded into flow charting, knowledge management, and project planning. Two mind mapping products—Bloomfire and Front & Main Honey—even function as social intranets. They provide online surveys, tips for colleagues, and "likes" for the most useful posts. Mind mapping began as a visual means of conveying ideas. This mapping concept rapidly morphed into a mass of tools enabling managers to visualize the workflow of an entire project.

5-2c Crowdsourcing

The interconnectivity of the Internet continues to spawn imaginative methods for generating ideas. Crowdsourcing describes the practice of requesting ideas or services online from unknown crowd members rather than from traditional employees or contractors.

Crowdsourcing has become an appealing and inexpensive method to build brand awareness as well to solve problems. Doritos was one of the first companies to take advantage of crowdsourcing to boost its brand. Its "Crash the Super Bowl" contest offered big bucks in prize money for fans to generate 30-second hilarious ads.[7] Similarly, Coca-Cola invited its fans to participate in a crowdsourcing contest, with a $20,000 grand prize to the winning idea for new sweeteners.[8]

FIGURE 5.2   **Mind Mapping a Product for School Reunions**

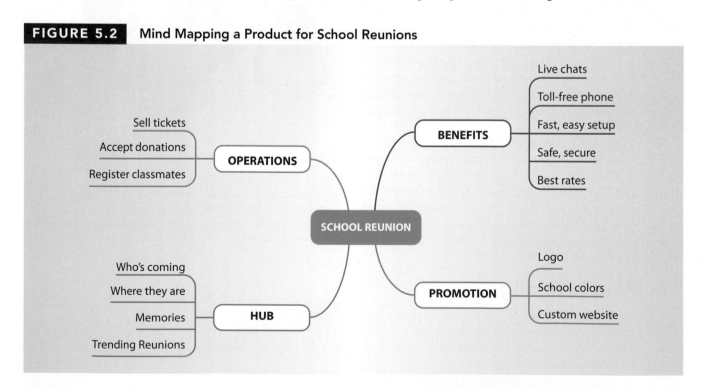

Produced through crowdsourcing, the Wizard of Oz Lego set won support from 10,000 online commenters.

Other longer-term crowdsourcing efforts seek meaningful input and collaboration in solving social issues and problems. In Europe promising young entrepreneurs met in crowdsourcing workshops, as part of the European Social Innovation Competition, to exchange ideas aimed at reducing plastic waste.[9] In the United States, computer giant Dell sponsored the Dell Social Innovation Challenge. It produced ideas such as recycling old tires to make rubber shoes for people in need. You will learn more about crowdsourcing and collaboration later in this unit.

5-3 Organizing Ideas to Show Relationships

LEARNING OUTCOME

3 Demonstrate methods for organizing ideas to show relationships.

After collecting data and generating ideas, writers must find a way to organize their information. Although some mind mapping tools claim to organize information, most business communicators will do this for themselves.

Skilled writers group similar items together. Then they place ideas in a strategic sequence that helps the reader understand relationships and accept the writer's views. Unorganized messages proceed free-form, jumping from one thought to another. Such messages fail to emphasize important points. Puzzled readers can't see how the pieces fit together, and they become frustrated and irritated. Many communication experts regard poor organization as the greatest failing of business writers. Two simple techniques can help writers organize data: the scratch list and the outline.

5-3a Creating Lists and Outlines

To develop simple messages, some writers use a digital device to make a quick scratch list of the topics they wish to cover. Next they compose a message directly from the scratch list. Most writers, though, need to organize their ideas—especially if the project is complex—into a hierarchy, such as an outline. The beauty of preparing an outline is that it gives writers a chance to organize their thoughts before becoming bogged down in word choice and sentence structure. Model Document 5.1 shows the format for a typical outline.

5-3b Typical Document Components

How you group ideas into components depends on your topic and your channel of communication. Business documents usually contain typical components arranged in traditional strategies, as shown in Figure 5.3. Notice that an e-mail, memo, or letter generally is organized with an opening, body, and closing. Instructions for writing a procedure, such as how to apply for an audit, would proceed through a number of steps. The organizational plan for

MODEL DOCUMENT 5.1   Format for an Outline

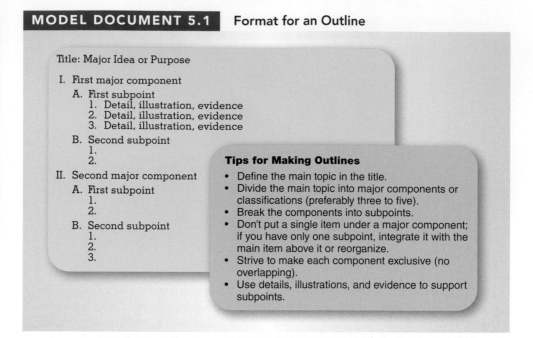

Title: Major Idea or Purpose

I. First major component
  A. First subpoint
    1. Detail, illustration, evidence
    2. Detail, illustration, evidence
    3. Detail, illustration, evidence
  B. Second subpoint
    1.
    2.
II. Second major component
  A. First subpoint
    1.
    2.
  B. Second subpoint
    1.
    2.
    3.

Tips for Making Outlines

- Define the main topic in the title.
- Divide the main topic into major components or classifications (preferably three to five).
- Break the components into subpoints.
- Don't put a single item under a major component; if you have only one subpoint, integrate it with the main item above it or reorganize.
- Strive to make each component exclusive (no overlapping).
- Use details, illustrations, and evidence to support subpoints.

an informational report usually includes an introduction, facts, and a summary. However, the plan for an analytical report includes an introduction/problem, facts/findings, conclusions, and recommendations (if requested). The plan for a proposal includes an introduction, a proposed solution, staffing, a schedule and/or costs, and authorization.

These document outlines may seem like a lot to absorb at this time. Later in this book, you will be introduced to all of the business documents outlined here, and you will learn how to expertly draft all their parts.

5-3c Structuring Ideas Into Strategies

Thus far, you have seen how to collect information, generate ideas, and prepare an outline. How you order the information in your outline, though, depends on the strategy you choose. Two organizational strategies provide plans of action for typical business messages: the direct strategy and the indirect strategy. The primary difference between the two strategies is where the main idea is placed. In the **direct strategy**, the main idea comes first, followed by details, explanation, or evidence. In the **indirect strategy**, the main idea follows the details, explanation, and evidence. The strategy you select is determined by how you expect the audience to react to the message.

Direct Strategy for Receptive Audiences. In preparing to write any message, you need to anticipate the audience's reaction to your ideas and frame your message accordingly. When you expect the reader to be pleased, mildly interested, or neutral—use the direct strategy.

FIGURE 5.3   Typical Major Components in Business Outlines

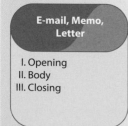
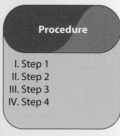

E-mail, Memo, Letter	Procedure	Informational Report	Analytical Report	Proposal
I. Opening II. Body III. Closing	I. Step 1 II. Step 2 III. Step 3 IV. Step 4	I. Introduction II. Facts III. Summary	I. Introduction/problem II. Facts/findings III. Conclusions IV. Recommendations (if requested)	I. Introduction II. Proposed solution III. Staffing IV. Schedule, costs V. Authorization

That is, put your main point—the purpose of your message—in the first or second sentence. Dianna Booher, renowned writing consultant, pointed out that typical readers begin any message by saying, "So what am I supposed to do with this information?" In business writing you have to say, "Reader, here is my point!"[11] As quickly as possible, tell why you are writing. Compare the direct and indirect strategies in the following e-mail openings. Notice how long it takes to get to the main idea in the indirect opening.

Indirect Opening	Direct Opening
As you may remember, our company has been contemplating strategies to attract better-qualified prospective job candidates. As a result, the Management Council is actively gathering information about a possible internship program that might attract college students. After considerable discussion and investigation, we have voted to launch a pilot program starting next fall. **We are asking for your help in organizing it.**	**Please help us organize a college internship pilot program that the Management Council voted to begin next fall.** Our company has been concerned with attracting better-qualified prospective job candidates. For this reason, the Management Council has been gathering information about an internship program for college students.

Explanations and details follow the direct opening. What's important is getting to the main idea quickly. This direct method, also called **frontloading**, has at least three advantages:

- **Saves the reader's time.** Many of today's businesspeople can devote only a few moments to each message. Messages that take too long to get to the point may lose their readers along the way.

- **Sets a proper frame of mind.** Learning the purpose up front helps the reader put the subsequent details and explanations in perspective. Without a clear opening, the reader may be thinking, "Why am I being told this?"

- **Reduces frustration.** Readers forced to struggle through excessive verbiage before reaching the main idea become frustrated. They resent the writer. Poorly organized messages create a negative impression of the writer.

Typical business messages that follow the direct strategy include routine requests and responses, orders and acknowledgments, nonsensitive memos, e-mails, informational reports, and informational oral presentations. All these tasks have one element in common: they do not address a sensitive subject that will upset the reader.

Indirect Strategy for Unreceptive Audiences.
When you expect the audience to be uninterested, unwilling, displeased, or perhaps even hostile, the indirect strategy is more appropriate. In this strategy you reveal the main idea only after you have offered an explanation and evidence. This approach works well with three kinds of messages: (a) bad news, (b) ideas that require persuasion, and (c) sensitive news, especially when being transmitted to superiors. The indirect strategy has these benefits:

- **Respects the feelings of the audience.** Bad news is always painful, but the trauma can be lessened by preparing the receiver for it.

- **Facilitates a fair hearing.** Messages that may upset the reader are more likely to be read when the main idea is delayed. Beginning immediately with a piece of bad news or a persuasive request, for example, may cause the receiver to stop reading or listening.

- **Minimizes a negative reaction.** A reader's overall reaction to a negative message is generally improved if the news is delivered gently.

Business messages that could be developed indirectly include e-mails, memos, and letters that refuse requests, deny claims, and disapprove credit. Persuasive requests,

Ethics ✔ Check

Let's Get Personal
A study of the language that executives use during earnings calls reveals that their words can have a distinct effect on investors. When executives use personal pronouns such as *I, we, my, ours,* and *us*, investors leave with a more positive impression—regardless of a company's results. First-person pronouns, suggested the researchers, create the impression that an executive has "more control over the past and therefore more ability to influence the future."[12] Is it unethical for an executive to use first-person pronouns to intentionally influence investors?

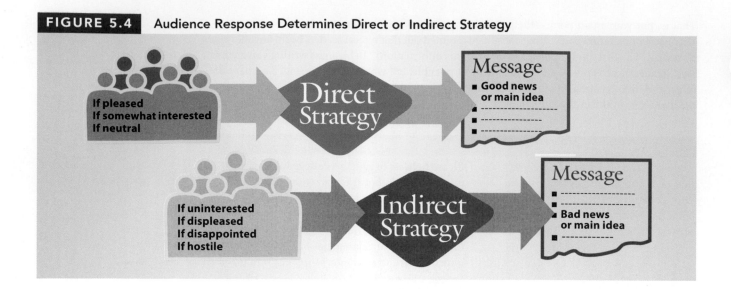

sales letters, sensitive messages, and some reports and oral presentations may also benefit from the indirect strategy. You will learn more about using the indirect strategy in Chapters 9 and 10.

In summary, business messages may be organized directly, with the main idea first, or indirectly, with the main idea delayed, as illustrated in Figure 5.4. Although these two strategies cover many communication problems, they should be considered neither universal nor absolute. Every business transaction is distinct. Some messages are mixed: part good news, part bad; part goodwill, part persuasion. In upcoming chapters you will practice applying the direct and indirect strategies in typical situations. Then, you will have the skills and confidence to evaluate communication problems and vary these strategies depending on your goals.

LEARNING OUTCOME

4 Write effective sentences that avoid fragments, run-ons, and comma splices.

5-4 Composing the First Draft With Effective Sentences

After you have researched your topic, brainstormed for fresh ideas, and selected a strategy, you're ready to begin drafting sentences. Unfortunately, at this point many writers suffer from writer's block and can't get started. However, there's no need to fret—the accompanying feature *For the Record* has many suggestions on how to overcome writer's block.

5-4a Adding Interest and Variety With Four Sentence Types

Once you begin writing, you will focus on writing effective sentences. Messages that repeat the same sentence pattern soon become boring. To avoid monotony and to add spark to your writing, use a variety of sentence types. You have four sentence types from which to choose: simple, compound, complex, and compound-complex.

Simple Sentence

Contains one complete thought (an independent clause) with a subject and predicate verb:

> Our <u>company</u> <u>lacked</u> a social media presence.

FOR THE RECORD

Troubled by Writer's Block?

It happens to every writer at one time or another. Writer's block may attack, but it can be overcome by using some of the following techniques. One excellent way to avoid getting stuck is working from an outline. Make a list of the main and minor points you want to cover. Composition is also easier if you have a quiet environment in which to concentrate. Unfortunately, increasing numbers of business offices have adopted open floorplans exposing workers to noise and distractions. Businesspeople with messages to compose must search for a quiet place, set aside a given time, and allow no calls or interruptions. This is a good technique for students as well.

As you begin writing, think about what style fits you best. Some experts suggest *free writing*. They get their thoughts down quickly and refine them in later versions. They imagine that they are talking to the reader or to an imaginary friend who is seated nearby. They don't let themselves get bogged down. If they can't think of the right word, they insert a substitute such as *find perfect word later*.

Freewriting works well for some writers, but others prefer to move more slowly and think through their ideas more deliberately. Whether you are a speedy or a deliberate writer, keep in mind that you are writing the first draft. Later you will have time to revise and polish your sentences.

Compound Sentence

Contains two complete but related thoughts. May be joined by (a) a conjunction such as *and, but*, or *or*; (b) a semicolon; or (c) a conjunctive adverb such as *however, consequently,* and *therefore*:

> Our <u>company</u> <u>lacked</u> a social media presence, <u>and</u> it hired a specialist.
> Our <u>company</u> <u>lacked</u> a social media presence; it hired a specialist.
> Our <u>company</u> <u>lacked</u> a social media presence; <u>consequently,</u> it hired a specialist.

Complex Sentence

Contains an independent clause (a complete thought) and a dependent clause (a thought that cannot stand by itself). Dependent clauses are often introduced by words such as *although, since, because, when,* and *if*. When dependent clauses precede independent clauses, they always are followed by a comma:

> Because our <u>company</u> <u>lacked</u> a social media presence, <u>it</u> <u>hired</u> a specialist.

Compound-Complex Sentence

Contains at least two independent clauses and one dependent clause:

> Because our <u>company</u> <u>lacked</u> a social media presence, <u>it</u> <u>hired</u> a specialist; however,
> our <u>brand</u> <u>required</u> time to build.

5-4b Avoiding Three Common Sentence Faults

As you craft your sentences, beware of three common traps: fragments, run-on (fused) sentences, and comma-splice sentences. If any of these faults appears in a business message, the writer immediately loses credibility.

One of the most serious errors a writer can make is punctuating a fragment as if it were a complete sentence. A **fragment** is usually a broken-off part of a complex sentence. Fragments often can be identified by the words that introduce them—words such as *although, as,* *because, even, except, for example, if, instead of, since, such as, that, which,* and *when.* These words introduce dependent clauses. Make sure such clauses always connect to independent clauses.

Fragment	Revision
Because most transactions require a permanent record. Good writing skills are critical.	Because most transactions require a permanent record, good writing skills are critical.
Even though the candidate seemed to communicate well. The recruiter requested a writing sample.	Even though the candidate seemed to communicate well, the recruiter requested a writing sample.

A second serious writing fault is the **run-on (fused) sentence**. A sentence with two independent clauses must be joined by a coordinating conjunction (*and, or, nor, but*), by a semicolon (;), or separated into two sentences. Without a conjunction or a semicolon, a run-on sentence results.

Run-On Sentence	Revision
Many job seekers prepare traditional résumés others prefer career e-portfolios.	Many job seekers prepare traditional résumés. Others prefer career e-portfolios.
	Many job seekers prepare traditional résumés; others prefer career e-portfolios.

A third sentence fault is a **comma splice**. It results when a writer joins (splices together) two independent clauses with a comma. Independent clauses may be joined with a coordinating conjunction (*and, or, nor, but*) or a conjunctive adverb (*however, consequently, therefore,* and others). Notice that clauses joined by coordinating conjunctions require only a comma. Clauses joined by a coordinating adverb require a semicolon. To rectify a comma splice, try one of the possible revisions shown here:

Comma Splice	Revisions
Be sure to include keywords from the job description, also include variations of the job title.	Be sure to include keywords from the job description, but also include variations of the job title.
	Be sure to include keywords from the job description; however, also include variations of the job title.
	Be sure to include keywords from the job description; also include variations of the job title.

5-4c Preferring Short Sentences

Because your goal is to communicate clearly, try to construct sentences that average 20 words. Some sentences will be shorter; some will be longer. The American Press Institute reports that reader comprehension drops off markedly as sentences become longer.[14] Therefore, in crafting your sentences, think about the relationship between sentence length and comprehension.

Chapter 5 Organizing and Drafting Business Messages

Instead of stringing together clauses with *and, but,* and *however,* break some of those complex sentences into separate segments. Business readers want to grasp ideas immediately. They can do that best when thoughts are separated into short sentences. On the other hand, too many monotonous short sentences will sound childish and may bore or even annoy the reader. Strive for a balance between longer sentences and shorter ones.

Sentence Length	Comprehension Rate
8 words	100%
15 words	90%
19 words	80%
28 words	50%

5-5 Mastering Four Skillful Writing Techniques

Business writers can significantly improve their messages by grasping a few skillful writing techniques. In this section we focus on emphasizing and de-emphasizing ideas, using active and passive voice strategically, using parallelism, and avoiding dangling and misplaced modifiers.

5-5a Creating Emphasis

When you are talking with someone, you can emphasize your main ideas by saying them loudly or by repeating them slowly. You could even pound the table if you want to show real emphasis! Another way you could signal the relative importance of an idea is by raising your eyebrows, shaking your head, or whispering. But when you write, you must rely on other means to tell your readers which ideas are more important than others. Emphasis in writing can be achieved primarily in two ways: mechanically and stylistically.

Achieving Emphasis Through Mechanics. To emphasize an idea in print, a writer may use any of the following devices:

Underlining	Underlining draws the eye to a word.
Italics and boldface	Using *italics* or **boldface** conveys special meaning.
Font changes	Selecting a large, small, or *different* font draws interest.
All caps	Printing words in ALL CAPS is like shouting them.
Dashes	Dashes—used sparingly—can be effective.
Tabulation	Listing items vertically makes them stand out:
	1. First item
	2. Second item
	3. Third item

Other means of achieving mechanical emphasis include the arrangement of space, color, lines, boxes, columns, titles, headings, and subheadings. Today's software and color printers provide a wonderful array of capabilities for setting off ideas. More tips on achieving emphasis are coming in Chapter 6 in which we cover document design.

Achieving Emphasis Through Style. Although mechanical devices are occasionally appropriate, more often a writer achieves emphasis stylistically. That is, the writer chooses words carefully and constructs sentences skillfully to emphasize main ideas and de-emphasize minor or negative ideas. Here are four suggestions for emphasizing ideas stylistically:

- **Use vivid, not general, words.** Vivid words are emphatic because the reader can picture ideas clearly.

General	Vivid
The way we seek jobs has changed.	The Internet has dramatically changed how job hunters search for positions.
Someone will contact you as soon as possible.	Ms. Rivera will telephone you before 5 p.m. tomorrow, May 3.

- **Label the main idea.** If an idea is significant, tell the reader.

Unlabeled	Labeled
Consider looking for a job online, but also focus on networking.	Consider looking for a job online; but, *most importantly*, focus on networking.
We shop here because of the customer service and low prices.	We like the customer service, but the *primary reason* for shopping here is the low prices.

- **Place the important idea first or last.** Ideas have less competition from surrounding words when they appear first or last in a sentence. Observe how the concept of productivity can be emphasized by its position in the sentence:

Main Idea Lost	Main Idea Emphasized
Profit-sharing plans are more effective in increasing *productivity* when they are linked to individual performance rather than to group performance.	*Productivity* is more likely to be increased when profit-sharing plans are linked to individual performance rather than to group performance.

- **Give the important idea the spotlight.** Don't dilute the effect of the main idea by making it share the stage with other words and clauses. Instead, put it in a simple sentence or in an independent clause.

Main Idea Lost	Main Idea Clear
Although you are the first trainee we have hired for this program, we had many candidates and expect to expand the program in the future. (The main idea is lost in a dependent clause.)	You are the first trainee we have hired for this program. (Simple sentence)

De-emphasizing When Necessary. To de-emphasize an idea, such as bad news, try one of the following stylistic devices:

- **Use general words.**

Emphasizes Harsh Statement	De-emphasizes Harsh Statement
Our records indicate that you were recently fired.	Our records indicate that your employment status has recently changed.

- **Place the bad news in a dependent clause connected to an independent clause that contains something positive.** In sentences with dependent clauses, the main emphasis is always on the independent clause.

Emphasizes Bad News	De-emphasizes Bad News
We cannot issue you credit at this time, but we have a special plan that will allow you to fill your immediate needs on a cash basis.	Although credit cannot be issued at this time, you can fill your immediate needs on a cash basis with our special plan.

Chapter 5 Organizing and Drafting Business Messages

- **Using the Active and Passive Voice Effectively**

In a sentence in the active voice, the subject (the actor) performs the action. In a sentence in the passive voice, the subject receives the action. Active-voice sentences are more direct because they reveal the performer immediately. They are easier to understand and usually shorter. Most business writing should be in the active voice. However, passive voice is useful to (a) emphasize an action rather than a person, (b) de-emphasize negative news, and (c) conceal the doer of an action.

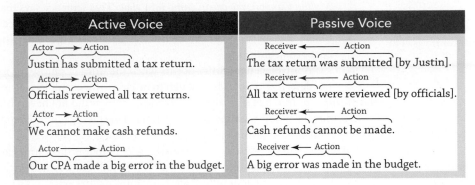

Active Voice	Passive Voice
Actor → Action Justin has submitted a tax return.	Receiver ← Action The tax return was submitted [by Justin].
Actor → Action Officials reviewed all tax returns.	Receiver ← Action All tax returns were reviewed [by officials].
Actor → Action We cannot make cash refunds.	Receiver ← Action Cash refunds cannot be made.
Actor → Action Our CPA made a big error in the budget.	Receiver ← Action A big error was made in the budget.

5-5b Creating Parallelism

Parallelism is a skillful writing technique that creates balanced writing. Sentences written so that their parts are balanced, or parallel, are easy to read and understand. To achieve parallel construction, use similar structures to express similar ideas. For example, the words *computing, coding, recording,* and *storing* are parallel because the words all end in *-ing*. To express the list as *computing, coding, recording,* and *storage* is disturbing because the last item is not what the reader expects. Try to match nouns with nouns, verbs with verbs, and clauses with clauses. Avoid mixing active-voice verbs with passive-voice verbs. Your goal is to keep the wording balanced in expressing similar ideas.

Lacks Parallelism	Illustrates Parallelism
A wedding planner is in charge of arranging the venue, the flowers, and someone to take photos.	A wedding planner is in charge of arranging the venue, the flowers, and a *photographer*. (Matches nouns.)
Our primary goals are to increase productivity, reduce costs, and the improvement of product quality.	Our primary goals are to increase productivity, reduce costs, and *improve product quality*. (Matches verbs.)
We are scheduled to meet in Tampa on January 5, we are meeting in Atlanta on the 15th of March, and in Columbus on June 3.	We are scheduled to meet in Tampa on January 5, *in Atlanta on March 15*, and in Columbus on June 3. (Matches phrases.)
Marcus audits accounts lettered A through L; accounts lettered M through Z are audited by Katherine.	Marcus audits accounts lettered A through L; *Katherine audits accounts lettered M through Z*. (Matches clauses.)
Our Super Bowl ads have three objectives: 1. We want to increase product use. 2. Introduce complementary products. 3. Our corporate image will be enhanced.	Our Super Bowl ads have three objectives: 1. *Increase* product use. 2. *Introduce* complementary products. 3. *Enhance* our corporate image. (Matches verbs in listed items.)

5-5c Dodging Dangling and Misplaced Modifiers

For clarity, modifiers must be close to the words they describe or limit. A **dangling modifier** occurs when the word or phrase the modifier describes is missing from its sentence—for example, *Driving through Malibu Canyon, the ocean came into view.* This sentence says that the ocean was driving through Malibu Canyon. Revised, the sentence contains a logical subject: *Driving through Malibu Canyon, we saw the ocean come into view.*

A **misplaced modifier** occurs when the word or phrase the modifier describes is not close enough to be clear—for example, *Firefighters rescued a dog from a burning car that had a broken leg.* Obviously, the car did not have a broken leg. The solution is to position the modifier closer to the word(s) it describes or limits: *Firefighters rescued a dog with a broken leg from a burning car.*

Introductory verbal phrases are particularly dangerous; be sure to follow them immediately with the words they logically describe or modify. Try this trick for detecting and remedying many dangling modifiers. Ask the question *Who?* or *What?* after any introductory phrase. The words immediately following should tell the reader who or what is performing the action. Try the *Who?* test on the first three danglers here:

Dangling or Misplaced Modifier	Clear Modification
Skilled at 3D printing, the Disney character was easily copied by Blake.	Skilled at 3D printing, Blake easily copied the Disney character.
Working together as a team, the project was finally completed.	Working together as a team, we finally completed the project.
To meet the deadline, all paperwork must be sent by May 1.	To meet the deadline, applicants must send all paperwork by May 1.
The recruiter interviewed candidates who had excellent computer skills in the morning.	In the morning the recruiter interviewed candidates with excellent computer skills.
As a newbie in our office, we invite you to our Friday after-hours get-together.	As a newbie in our office, you are invited to our Friday after-hours get-together.

Checklist

Drafting Effective Sentences

For Effective Sentences

- **Use a variety of sentence types.** To avoid monotony, include simple, compound, complex, and occasionally compound-complex sentences in your writing.

- **Avoid common sentence faults.** To avoid run-on sentences, do not join two clauses without appropriate punctuation. To avoid comma splices, do not join two clauses with a comma.

To avoid fragments, be sure to use periods only after complete sentences.

- **Control sentence length.** Use longer sentences occasionally, but rely primarily on short and medium-length sentences.

- **Emphasize important ideas.** Place main ideas at the beginning of short sentences for emphasis.

- **Apply active- and passive-voice verbs strategically.** Use active-voice verbs (*She sent the message* instead of *The message was sent by her*) most frequently; they immediately identify the doer. Use passive-voice verbs to emphasize an action, to be tactful, or to conceal the performer.

- **Employ parallelism.** Balance similar ideas (*biking, jogging, and walking* instead of *biking, jogging, and to walk*).

- **Eliminate dangling and misplaced modifiers.** To avoid dangling modifiers, be sure that introductory verbal phrases are followed by the words that can logically be modified (*To win the* lottery, you must purchase a ticket rather than *To win the lottery, a ticket must be purchased*). To avoid misplaced modifiers, place them close to the words they modify (*With your family, please* look over the brochure that is enclosed rather than *Please look over the brochure that is enclosed with your family*).

5-6 Building Well-Organized Paragraphs

LEARNING OUTCOME

6 Explain how to create well-organized, coherent paragraphs.

A **paragraph** is a group of sentences about one idea. The following kinds of sentences may be organized to express ideas in a well-organized paragraph:

Topic sentence:	Expresses the primary idea of the paragraph; often, but not always comes first in a paragraph.
Supporting sentence:	Illustrates, explains, or strengthens the primary idea.
Limiting sentence:	Opposes the primary idea by suggesting a negative or contrasting thought; may precede or follow the topic sentence.

Topic, supporting, and limiting sentences may be arranged in three classic paragraph plans: direct, pivoting, and indirect. Each of these plans has a specific function.

5-6a The Direct Paragraph Plan

The **direct paragraph plan** is used to define, classify, illustrate, or describe. It usually begins with the topic sentence, followed by supporting sentences. Most business messages use this paragraph plan because it clarifies the subject immediately. This plan is useful whenever you must define (a new product or procedure), classify (parts of a whole), illustrate (an idea), or describe (a process). Start with the topic sentence; then strengthen and amplify that idea with supporting ideas, as shown here:

Topic Sentence	A social audit is a report on the social performance of a company.
Supporting Sentences	Such an audit may be conducted by the company itself or by outsiders who evaluate the company's efforts to produce safe products, engage in socially responsible activities, and protect the environment. Many companies publish the results of their social audits in their annual reports. Ben & Jerry's Homemade, for example, was one of the first to devote a major portion of its annual report to its social audit. The report discusses Ben & Jerry's efforts to support environmental restoration. Moreover, it describes workplace safety, employment equality, and peace programs.

You can alter the direct plan by adding a limiting sentence if necessary. Be sure, though, that you follow with sentences that return to the main idea and support it, as shown here:

Topic Sentence	Flexible work scheduling could immediately increase productivity and enhance employee satisfaction in our entire organization.
Limiting Sentences	Such scheduling, however, is impossible for all employees. Managers would be required to maintain their regular hours.
Supporting Sentences	For many other employees, though, flexible scheduling permits extra time to manage family responsibilities. Feeling less stress, employees are able to focus their attention better at work; hence they become more relaxed and more productive.

5-6b The Pivoting Paragraph Plan

The pivoting paragraph plan is useful to compare and contrast. It usually starts with a limiting sentence that offers a contrasting or negative idea before delivering the topic sentence. Notice in the following example how two limiting sentences about drawbacks to foreign service careers open the paragraph; only then do the topic and supporting sentences describing rewards in foreign service appear. The pivoting plan is especially useful for comparing and contrasting ideas. In using the pivoting plan, be sure to emphasize the turn in direction with an obvious *but* or *however*.

Limiting Sentences	Foreign service careers are certainly not for everyone. Many representatives are stationed in remote countries where harsh climates, health hazards, security risks, and other discomforts exist.
Topic Sentence	However, careers in the foreign service offer special rewards for the special people who qualify.
Supporting Sentences	Foreign service employees enjoy the pride and satisfaction of representing the United States abroad. They enjoy frequent travel, enriching cultural and social experiences in living abroad, and action-oriented work.

5-6c The Indirect Paragraph Plan

The indirect paragraph plan is useful to explain and persuade. Indirect paragraphs usually start with the supporting sentences and conclude with the topic sentence. This plan enables you to build a rationale or a foundation of reasons before hitting the audience with a big idea—possibly one that is bad news. It enables you to explain your reasons and then in the final sentence draw a conclusion from them. In the following example, the vice president of a large accounting firm begins by describing the trend toward casual dress and concludes with a recommendation that his company alter its dress code. The indirect plan works well for describing causes followed by an effect.

Supporting Sentences	According to a recent poll, more than half of all white-collar workers are now dressing casually at work. Many high-tech engineers and professional specialists have given up suits and ties, favoring khakis and sweaters instead. In our own business, our consultants say they stand out like sore thumbs because they are attired in traditional buttoned-down styles, whereas the businesspeople they visit are usually wearing comfortable, casual clothing.
Topic Sentence	Therefore, I recommend that we establish an optional business casual policy allowing consultants to dress down, if they wish, as they perform their duties both in and out of the office.

You will learn more techniques for implementing direct and indirect writing strategies when you draft e-mails, memos, letters, reports, and other business messages as well as prepare oral presentations in coming chapters.

5-6d Developing Paragraph Coherence

Paragraphs are coherent when ideas cohere—that is, when the ideas stick together and when one idea logically leads to the next. Well-written paragraphs take the reader through a number of steps. When the author skips from Step 1 to Step 3 and forgets Step 2, the reader is lost. Several techniques will help you keep the reader in step with your ideas.

Sustain the Key Idea. Repeating a key expression or using a similar one throughout a paragraph helps sustain a key idea. In the following example, notice that the repetition of *guest* and *VIP* connects ideas.

Our philosophy holds that every customer is really a *guest*. All new employees are trained to treat *guests* in our theme parks as *VIPs*. We take great pride in respecting our guests. As *VIPs*, they are never told what they can or cannot do.

Dovetail Sentences. Sentences are dovetailed when an idea at the end of one connects with an idea at the beginning of the next. Dovetailing sentences is especially helpful with dense, difficult topics. It is also helpful with ordinary paragraphs, such as the following.

New hosts and hostesses learn about the theme park and its *facilities*. These *facilities* include telephones, food services, bathrooms, and attractions, as well as the location of *offices*. Knowledge of *offices* and the internal workings of the company is required of all staffers.

Include Pronouns. Familiar pronouns, such as *we, they, he, she,* and *it,* help build continuity, as do demonstrative pronouns, such as *this, that, these,* and *those.* These words confirm that something under discussion is still being discussed. However, be careful with such pronouns. They often need a noun with them to make their meaning clear. In the following example, notice how confusing the pronoun *this* would be if the word *training* were omitted.

All new park employees receive a two-week orientation. They learn that every staffer has a vital role in preparing for the show. *This training* includes how to maintain enthusiasm.

Employ Transitional Expressions. Transitional expressions are another excellent device for showing connections and achieving paragraph coherence. These words, some of which are shown in Figure 5.5 act as verbal road signs to readers and listeners. Transitional expressions enable the receiver to anticipate what's coming, reduce uncertainty, and speed comprehension. They signal that a train of thought is moving forward, being developed, and possibly detouring or ending. As Figure 5.5 shows, transitions can add or strengthen a thought, show time or order,

FIGURE 5.5 Transitional Expressions That Build Coherence

To Add or Strengthen	To Show Time or Order	To Clarify	To Show Cause and Effect	To Contradict	To Contrast
additionally	after	for example	accordingly	actually	as opposed to
accordingly	before	for instance	as a result	but	at the same time
again	earlier	I mean	consequently	however	by contrast
also	finally	in other words	for this reason	in fact	conversely
beside	first	put another way	hence	instead	on the contrary
indeed	meanwhile	that is	so	rather	on the other hand
likewise	next	this means	therefore	still	previously
moreover	now	thus	thus	yet	similarly

clarify ideas, show cause and effect, contradict thoughts, and contrast ideas. Look back at the examples of direct, pivoting, and indirect paragraphs to see how transitional expressions and other techniques build paragraph coherence. Remember that coherence in communication rarely happens spontaneously; it requires effort and skill.

5-6e Control Paragraph Length

Although no rule regulates the length of paragraphs, business writers recognize that short paragraphs are more attractive and readable than longer ones. Paragraphs with eight or fewer lines look inviting. Long, solid chunks of print appear formidable. If a topic can't be covered in eight or fewer printed lines (not sentences), consider breaking it up into smaller segments.

The following checklist summarizes key points in preparing meaningful paragraphs.

Checklist

Preparing Meaningful Paragraphs

- **Develop one idea.** Each paragraph should include a topic sentence plus supporting and limiting sentences to develop a single idea.

- **Use the direct plan.** To define, classify, illustrate, and describe, start with the topic sentence followed by supporting sentences.

- **Use the pivoting plan.** To compare and contrast ideas, start with a limiting sentence; then, present the topic sentence followed by supporting sentences.

- **Use the indirect plan.** To explain reasons or causes first, start with supporting sentences. Build to the conclusion with the topic sentence at the end of the paragraph.

- **Build coherence with linking techniques.** Hold ideas together by repeating key words, dovetailing sentences (beginning one sentence with an idea from the end of the previous sentence), and using appropriate pronouns.

- **Provide road signs with transitional expressions.** Use verbal signals to help the audience know where the idea is going. Words and phrases such as *moreover, accordingly, as a result,* and *therefore* function as idea pointers.

- **Limit paragraph length.** Remember that paragraphs with eight or fewer printed lines look inviting. Consider breaking up longer paragraphs if necessary.

Zooming In

Your Turn:
Applying Your Skills at MyEvent.com

As you learned at the beginning of this chapter, MyEvent.com helps individuals and organizations plan a wide array of events and activities. One platform that MyEvent.com managers plan to expand is crowdsourcing.

Your Task

As interns at MyEvent.com, you and your colleagues are in a unique position to provide useful information. You have been asked to generate ideas about how college and university students might use crowdsourcing. For what kinds of projects does crowdsourcing make sense? To learn more, conduct research to discover crowdsourcing projects that have been successful on college or university campuses. With three to five classmates, generate five or more solid ideas for crowdsourcing on college or university campuses. Organize your ideas into an e-mail message addressed to MyEvent.com in care of your instructor. Explain what your research revealed as well as listing your ideas for possible campus crowdsourcing projects. See Appendix A for message formats and Chapters 7 and 8 for tips on preparing a professional e-mail message.

SUMMARY OF LEARNING OUTCOMES

1 Compare two forms of research that begin Phase 2 of the 3-x-3 writing process.

- Informal research methods include (a) searching digital or other company files, (b) talking with the boss, (c) interviewing the target audience, and (d) conducting an informal survey.

- Formal research methods include (a) accessing electronic sources, (b) searching manually, (c) investigating primary sources, and (d) conducting scientific experiments.

2 List techniques that help writers generate and sort ideas to solve problems.

- Writers and groups may generate ideas by *brainstorming*, which involves the spontaneous contribution of ideas from members.

- When group members write their brainstorming ideas (for example, on flip charts, on papers hung on the walls, or on post-slips), it's called *brainwriting*.

- *Mind mapping*, a form of brainstorming, emphasizes visual concepts, such as words and images branching out treelike from a central concept.

- *Crowdsourcing* describes the practice of requesting ideas or services online from unknown crowd members rather than from traditional employees or contractors.

3 Demonstrate methods for organizing ideas to show relationships.

- One of the quickest ways to show relationships is to group similar ideas together.

- For simple messages, make a quick scratch list of topics, perhaps on a digital device.

- For more complex messages, organize ideas into a hierarchical outline with a main topic and three to five major components.

- Break the components into subpoints consisting of details, illustrations, and evidence.

- Place ideas in a strategic sequence that helps readers understand how the ideas are related.

- Use the direct strategy for receptive audiences; use the indirect strategy for audiences that may be uninterested, unwilling, displeased, or hostile.

4 Write effective sentences that avoid fragments, run-ons, and comma splices.

- Create interesting sentences by employing a variety of sentence types.

- Typical sentence types are (a) *simple* (one independent clause); (b) *complex* (one independent and one dependent clause); (c) *compound* (two independent clauses); and (d) *compound-complex* (two independent clauses and one dependent clause).

- Avoid *fragments* (broken-off parts of sentences), *run-ons* (two clauses fused improperly), and *comma splices* (two clauses joined improperly with a comma).

- Remember that sentences are most effective when they are short (20 or fewer words).

5 Demonstrate methods for emphasizing ideas, using active and passive voice, developing parallelism, and placing modifiers correctly.

- Emphasize an idea mechanically by using underlining, italics, boldface, font changes, all caps, dashes, tabulation, and other devices.

- Emphasize an idea stylistically by giving it the spotlight. Use vivid words, label it, make it the sentence subject, place it first or last, and remove competing ideas.

- De-emphasize ideas by using general words or by placing the idea in a dependent clause.

- For most business writing, use the active voice by making the subject the doer of the action (*the company hired the student*).

- Use the passive voice (*the student was hired*) to de-emphasize negative news, emphasize an action rather than the doer, or conceal the doer of an action.

- Employ parallelism for balanced construction (*jogging, hiking, and biking* rather than *jogging, hiking, and to bike*).

- Avoid dangling modifiers (*sitting at my computer, the words would not come*) and misplaced modifiers (*I have the report you wrote in my office*).

6 Explain how to create well-organized, coherent paragraphs.

- Use the *direct* paragraph plan to define, classify, illustrate, or describe ideas. It begins with a topic sentence followed by supporting sentences.

- Use the *pivoting* paragraph plan to compare and contrast. It starts with a limiting sentence followed by the topic and supporting sentences.

- Use the *indirect* plan to explain and persuade. It begins with supporting sentences and concludes with the topic sentence.

- Build coherence by repeating a key idea, using pronouns to refer to previous nouns, and showing connections with transitional expressions (*however, therefore, consequently*).

- Control paragraph length by striving for eight or fewer lines.

Key Terms

research *150*

brainstorming *151*

brainwriting *151*

mind mapping *151*

crowdsourcing *152*

direct strategy *154*

indirect strategy *154*

frontloading *155*

fragment *157*

run-on (fused) sentence *158*

comma splice *158*

active voice *161*

passive voice *161*

parallelism *161*

dangling modifier *162*

misplaced modifier *162*

paragraph *163*

direct paragraph plan *163*

pivoting paragraph plan *164*

indirect paragraph plan *164*

coherent *165*

dovetailed *165*

transitional expressions *165*

Critical Thinking

1. A survey from PayScale, the compensation data software website, revealed a surprising gap in perception between managers and new grads. "Overall, the majority of workers (87 percent) feel well prepared (immediately or within 3 months) for their job upon graduation from college. In contrast, only about half of managers (50 percent) feel that employees who recently graduated from college are well prepared for the workforce."[16] The skill most lacking, said the managers, was writing proficiency. What could explain this gap in perception between managers and new grads? (L.O. 1–5)

2. How can bad writing waste a businessperson's time? A researcher asked that question of workers who read business material an average of 25 hours per week (about half of which was e-mail).[17] What writing flaws do you think they named? Should new employees be trained in writing effectively on the job? (L.O. 1–5)

3. Emily, a twenty-three-year-old college graduate with a 3.5 GPA, was hired as an administrative assistant. She was a fast learner on all the software, but her supervisor had to help her with punctuation. On the ninth day of her job, she resigned, saying: "I just don't think this job is a good fit. Commas, semicolons, spelling, typos—those kinds of things just aren't all that important to me. They just don't matter."[18] For what kind of job is Emily qualified? (L.O. 1–5)

4. Why is audience analysis so important in the selection of the direct or indirect strategy of organization for a business message? (L.O. 2)

5. Ethical issue: Now that you have studied the active and passive voice, what do you think when someone in government or business says, "Mistakes were made"? Is it unethical to use the passive voice to avoid specifics? (L.O. 4)

Writing Improvement Exercises

5.1 Sentence Types (L.O. 4)

YOUR TASK For each of the following sentences, select the number that identifies its type:

1. Simple sentence
2. Compound sentence
3. Complex sentence
4. Compound-complex sentence

a. Americans pride themselves on their informality. _____

b. When Americans travel abroad on business, their informality may be viewed negatively. _____

c. Informality in Asia often equals disrespect; it is not seen as a virtue. _____

d. The order of first and last names in Asia may be reversed, and this causes confusion to Americans and Europeans. _____

e. When you are addressing someone, ask which name a person would prefer to use; however, be sure you can pronounce it correctly. _____

5.2 Sentence Faults (L.O. 4)

YOUR TASK In the following, identify the sentence fault (fragment, run-on sentence, comma splice). Then revise to remedy the fault.

a. Although they began as a side business for Disney. Destination weddings now represent a major income source.

b. About 2,000 weddings are held yearly. Which is twice the number just ten years ago.

c. You can even schedule your ceremony on the lawn outside Cinderella Castle, however, the charge starts at $75,000.

d. Limousines line up outside Disney's wedding pavilion, ceremonies are scheduled in two-hour intervals.

e. Many couples prefer a traditional wedding others request a fantasy experience.

5.3 Emphasis (L.O. 5)

YOUR TASK For each of the following sentences, circle (1) or (2). Be prepared to justify your choice.

a. Which is more emphatic? Why?

1. For many reasons hamburgers are definitely American.

2. Hot, fast, and affordable, hamburgers are a uniquely American triumph.

b. Which is more emphatic? Why?

1. The new restaurant will attract foot traffic and also serve unique burgers.

2. The new restaurant will attract foot traffic and, most important, will serve unique burgers.

c. Which is more emphatic? Why?

1. Burger King is taking its plant-based Impossible Whopper nationwide.

2. Amidst unexpected competition for vegan burgers, fast-food chain Burger King announced that it was taking its plant-based Impossible Whopper nationwide.

d. Which is more emphatic? Why?

1. Because he has experience in the restaurant business, the new CEO comes highly recommended and is expected to appear at the next meeting of the management board on January 15, which has been rescheduled because of room conflicts.

2. The new, highly recommended CEO will appear at the next meeting of the management board on January 15.

e. Which emphasizes the writer of the report?

1. Allegra wrote a report about the growth of fast casual restaurants such as Panera Bread and Chipotle Mexican Grill.

2. A report about the growth of fast casual resaurants such as Panera Bread and Chiptole Mexican Grill was written by Allegra.

f. Which places more emphasis on the seminar?

1. A training seminar for all new managers starts June 1.

2. We are pleased to announce that starting June 1 a training seminar for all new managers will include four prominent speakers who own famous restaurants.

g. Which is more emphatic? Why?

1. Three burger restaurants compete for business: (a) McDonald's, (b) Burger King, and (c) Shake Shack.

2. Three burger restaurants compete for business:

   a. McDonald's

   b. Burger King

   c. Shake Shack

5.4 Active Voice (L.O. 5)

YOUR TASK Business writing is more forceful when writers use active-voice verbs. Revise the following sentences so that verbs are in the active voice. Put the emphasis on the doer of the action. Add subjects if necessary.

Example: All job candidates are advised to write targeted résumés.

Revision: Hiring managers advise all job candidates to write targeted résumés.

a. Applying for jobs has been made easier by artificial intelligence (AI).

b. Chatbots, another form of AI, are programmed by hiring companies to conduct interviews either by text or voice.

c. Candidates were told by the counselor that their online personae were as important as their résumés.

d. Reliable data about how workers find their jobs are difficult to collect.

e. Concern was expressed about how to negotiate salary during an interview.

f. Laws are being considered to restrict asking job candidates to reveal their previous salaries.

5.5 Passive Voice (L.O. 5)

YOUR TASK When indirectness or tact is required, use passive-voice verbs. Revise the following active-voice sentences so that they are in the passive voice.

Example: Travis did not submit the proposal before the deadline.

Revision: The proposal was not submitted before the deadline.

a. The folks in Accounting made a serious error in our annual tax figures.

b. We discovered the error too late to correct the annual report.

c. The Federal Trade Commission targeted deceptive diet advertisements by weight-loss marketers.

d. We issue refunds only for the amount of the purchase; we are unable to include shipping and handling charges.

e. An embarrassing mishap was caused because someone misinterpreted the procedures.

5.6 Parallelism (L.O. 5)

YOUR TASK Revise the following sentences so that their parts are balanced.

a. (**Hint:** Match verbs.) Gone are the days when job candidates could write a résumé naming an objective, listing their skills, and then to hit the Send key.

b. (**Hint:** Match adjectives.) To be hired, an applicant must be reliable, creative, and show enthusiasm.

c. (**Hint:** Match verb phrases.) Job seekers use the Internet to find job opportunities, market themselves to companies, showcase their skills, and they hope to be able to land that dream job.

d. (**Hint:** Match adjectives.) Recent graduates are seeking jobs that are stimulating and a challenge.

e. LinkedIn can help college students by sending job alerts, by leveraging their networks, they can research a company, and LinkedIn can reduce the awkwardness of asking for recommendations.

f. A company's website might contain valuable information such as you might find current job openings, the company's mission statement might be there, and the names of key hiring managers could be available.

5.7 Dangling and Misplaced Modifiers (L.O. 5)

YOUR TASK Revise the following sentences to avoid dangling and misplaced modifiers. Retain the opening phrase.

a. When pursuing entry-level positions, salary is often a point that new grads fail to negotiate.

b. To be interviewed for a specific position, a targeted application must be submitted.

c. While interviewing applicants, questions are often asked about qualifictions.

d. After leaving the interview and walking to the parking lot, Omar's car would not start.

e. Immediately following a job interview, a thank-you note is usually written by savvy job applicants.

5.8 Costco's Polite but Firm Door Policy (L.O. 5)

The giant superstore Costco makes several requirements of its customers. Parents must keep their children with them at all times. They can't allow children to visit various food stations and wander around the warehouse on their own. Costco also asks that its customers not show up looking as if they just came from the beach. Hey, it's not too much to ask that they wear shoes and shirts while shopping. Lastly, Costco wants permission to look in the briefcases, backpacks, and packages of those entering its warehouse. It's not that Costco is snoopy; it's just too easy to slip items into big bags. Unlike other supermarkets, Costco is a private membership store and thus can make reasonable demands of its customers. But it needs help. How can it fit all of these restrictions on a concise sign at its entrance?

YOUR TASK Assume you are a staff member of a consultancy hired by Costco to draft a sign for the entrance. Individually or in teams, prepare two versions of an entrance sign—one written from a negative point of view (*don't do this, don't do that*) and one from a positive point of view. Keep your sign brief, and be sure the items are parallel. Your instructor may have you present your versions in class for discussion. Then your instructor may show you the actual entrance sign.

5.9 Organizing Paragraph Sentences (L.O. 6)

YOUR TASK Study the following list of sentences from an office memo to hospital staff.

1. *The incident report form that we previously used caused problems and confusion.*

2. *One problem was that employees often omitted important information.*

3. *The Hospital Safety Committee has revised the form used for incident reports.*

4. *Another problem was that inappropriate information was often included that might expose the hospital to liability.*

5. *The Hospital Safety Committee has scheduled a lunchtime speaker to discuss prevention of medication mistakes.*

6. *Factual details about the time and place of the incident are important, but speculation on causes is inappropriate.*

7. *The new form will be available on April 1.*

a. Which sentence should be the topic sentence? _____

b. Which sentence(s) should be developed in a separate paragraph? _____

c. Which sentences should become support sentences? _____

5.10 Revising a Pizza Promotion Paragraph (L.O. 6)

YOUR TASK Improve the organization, coherence, and correctness of the following paragraph.

We feel that the "extreme" strategy has not been developed fully in the fast-food market. Pizza Hut is considering launching a new product called The Extreme. We plan to price this new pizza at $19.99. It will be the largest pizza on the market. It will have double the cheese. It will also have double the toppings. The plan is to target millennials because pizza is their favorite food. This same target audience that would respond to an extreme product also reacts to low prices. Millennials are the fastest-growing segment in the fast-food market, and they have responded well to other marketing plans using the extreme strategy.

5.11 Constructing a Coherent Paragraph (L.O. 6)

YOUR TASK Use the following facts to construct a coherent paragraph with a topic sentence, appropriate supporting sentences, and transitional expressions.

- *The federal government will penalize medical practices that don't adopt electronic medical records (EMRs).*

- *Valley Medical Center is considering beginning converting soon.*

- *Converting paper-based records to EMRs will be complex.*

- *Converting will be technically challenging. It will probably be time-consuming and labor-intensive.*

- *Converting should bring better patient care and maybe even lower costs in the long run.*

- *The federal government provides funds to reimburse the cost of adopting the technology.*

5.12 Constructing a Coherent Teamwork Paragraph (L.O. 5)

YOUR TASK Use the following facts to construct a coherent paragraph with a topic sentence, appropriate supporting sentences, and transitional expressions.

- *Nearly all teams experience conflict. They should recognize and expect it.*
- *The most effective teams strive to eliminate destructive conflict and develop constructive conflict.*
- *Destructive conflict arises when team members take criticism personally.*
- *Destructive conflict poisons teamwork.*
- *Conflict can become constructive.*
- *Teams that encourage members to express their opinions may seem to be experiencing conflict when the opinions differ.*
- *Better decisions often result when teams listen to and discuss many views.*

Activities

5.13 Document for Analysis: Finding Faults in a Poor Message (L.O. 3–5)

`E-Mail` `Team`

YOUR TASK Study the numbered sentences in the following poorly written e-mail message. In teams or in a class discussion, identify specific sentence faults. **Hint:** You should find five sentence fragments, one dangling modifier, one passive-voice sentence, and one parallelism fault. Your instructor may ask you to revise the message to remedy these writing faults.

To: Angela Ortiz@gmail.com
From: Trent Westbrook@premierefinances.com
Subject: Taxes on Profits From eBay and Other Online Sellers

Dear Angela,

[1]As your CPA, I'm happy to respond to your request for clarification of the tax status of profits from eBay. [2]Or one of the other online sellers such as Etsy, Amazon, Shopify, and Bonanza.

[3]As you are probably already aware, you can use eBay or one of the other sellers to clean out your closets or to run a small business. [4]Tax liabilities should definitely be clarified. [5]Although no clear line separates fun from profit or a hobby from a business. [6]One thing is certain: the IRS taxes all income.

[7]A number of factors will help you determine whether your hobby is a business. [8]To use eBay safely, the following questions should be considered:

- [9]Do you run the operation in a businesslike manner? [10]That is, do you keep records, is your profit and loss tracked, and how about keeping a separate checking account?
- [11]Do you devote considerable time and effort to your selling? [12]If you spend eight or more hours a day trading on eBay. [13]The IRS would tend to think you are in a business.
- [14]Some people depend on the income from their eBay activities for their livelihood. [15]Do you?
- [16]Are you selling items for more than they cost you? [17]If you spend $5 for a garage sale vase and sell it for $50. [18]The IRS would probably consider this a business transaction.

[19]All profits are taxable. [20]Even for eBay sellers who are just playing around. [21]If you wish to discuss this further, please call me at 213-456-8901.

Trent Westbrook
[Full contact information]

5.14 Brainstorming: Solving a Problem on Campus (L.O. 1, 2)

`Team`

YOUR TASK In teams of three to five, analyze a problem on your campus such as the following: insufficient parking on campus, unavailable classes, closed campus facilities for students taking evening or weekend classes, unrealistic degree requirements, a lack of student intern programs, an inadequate registration process, too few healthy and affordable food choices, a lack of charging stations for electric vehicles, and so forth. Use brainstorming techniques to generate ideas that clarify the problem and explore its solutions. Either individually or as a team, organize the ideas into an outline with three to five main points and numerous subpoints. Assume that your ideas will become part of a message to be sent to an appropriate campus official or to your campus newspaper. Remember, however, your role as a student. Be polite, positive, and constructive—not negative, hostile, or aggressive.

5.15 Brainstorming: Solving a Problem at Work (L.O. 1, 2)

E-Mail

YOUR TASK Analyze a problem that exists where you work or go to school such as noisy work areas, an overuse of express mail services, understaffing during peak customer service hours, poor scheduling of employees, inappropriate cell phone use, an inferior or inflexible benefits package, outdated equipment, wasting time on social media instead of working, or one of the campus problems listed in **Activity 5.15.** Select a problem about which you have some knowledge. Organize the ideas into an outline with three to five main points and numerous subpoints. Be polite, positive, and constructive. E-mail the outline to your boss (your instructor). Include an introduction (such as *Here is the outline you requested in regard to . . .*). Include a closing that offers to share your outline if your boss would like to see it.

Test Your Workplace Etiquette IQ

New communication platforms and casual workplace environments have blurred the lines of appropriateness, leaving workers wondering how to navigate uncharted waters. Check your workplace etiquette IQ by deciding whether the following statements are true or false. Then see if you agree with the responses on p. Key-5.

1. On your new job, you want to show sociability by friending everyone on Facebook. To avoid favoritism, you should include managers and bosses.

   _____ True _____ False

2. You're talking with a coworker when you see an incoming text. To demonstrate your efficiency, you should answer it immediately.

   _____ True _____ False

3. You're late for a meeting. The best thing to do is text a message saying, "Sorry, I'm running 10 minutes late."

   _____ True _____ False

Chat About It

In each chapter you will find five discussion questions related to the chapter material. Your instructor may assign these topics for you to discuss in class, in an online chat room, or on an online discussion board. Some of the discussion topics may require outside research. You may also be asked to read and respond to postings made by your classmates.

TOPIC 1: In the "Let's Get Personal" Ethics Check, you learned that executives who used personal pronouns in discussing the earnings of their organizations were considered more believable than those who didn't. Are you influenced by personal pronouns? Do they make you feel that the speaker is more authentic and believable?

TOPIC 2: This chapter describes brainstorming and brainwriting as techniques for generating ideas. Explore the Internet for other methods such as *freewriting, looping, listing, clustering,* and *reporters' questions.* Select a method that appeals to you, and explain why it would be effective.

TOPIC 3: Some writers have trouble writing the opening sentence of a message. Occasionally, a quotation makes for an appropriate opening. Assume that you need to motivate an employee to achieve more at work. Find a famous quotation online about motivation that might be an appropriate opening for such a message. In addition, write a sentence that would effectively transition from this opening.

TOPIC 4: In your opinion, how many business managers know what a comma splice is? If some managers don't know what a comma splice is, then is it critical that you avoid comma splices in your writing?

TOPIC 5: If the ideal length of a sentence is 20 words, why not make all sentences that length?

Commas

Review Guides 21 through 26 about commas in Appendix D, Grammar and Mechanics. On a separate sheet, revise the following sentences to correct errors in comma usage. For each error that you locate, write the guide number that reflects this usage. The more you recognize the reasons, the better you will learn these punctuation guidelines. If a sentence is correct, write *C*. When finished, compare your responses with the key at the end of the book.

EXAMPLE: Before writing any message the writer needs to anticipate the audience's reaction.

REVISION: Before writing any **message,** the writer needs to anticipate the audience's reaction. [Guide 22]

1. More than 10,000 hungry professionals named yogurt, protein bars jerky and string cheese as the healthiest office snacks.

2. By learning to distinguish between dependent and independent clauses you can avoid serious sentence faults.

3. We hired Dalia Aljaja who was the applicant with the best qualifications as our new social media manager.

4. When you use company e-mail you must realize that your messages are monitored.

5. Active-voice verbs are best in most business messages but passive-voice verbs are useful when sensitivity is required.

6. Although the company was founded on April 15 2015 it did not show a profit until June 30 2020.

7. The new social media start-up by the way is flourishing and is expected to show a profit soon.

8. After he graduates Luke plans to move to Austin and find work there.

9. Last fall our company introduced policies regulating the use of cell phones texting and e-mail on the job.

10. The problem with many company telecommunication policies is that the policies are self-policed, and never enforced.

CHAPTER 6

Revising Business Messages

LEARNING OUTCOMES

After studying this chapter, you should be able to do the following:

1. Demonstrate techniques that achieve conciseness as part of Phase 3 of the writing process.

2. Demonstrate writing techniques that simplify and clarify business messages.

3. Explain how to enhance readability through document design.

4. Outline proofreading techniques that help you catch errors in both routine and complex documents.

5. Evaluate a message to judge its effectiveness.

G-Stock Studio/Shutterstock.com

Zooming In
Taco Bell Amazingly Ranks No. 1

Perhaps because it offers less-than-authentic food, Taco Bell stunned the public when it won the title of best Mexican restaurant chain in the United States. Observers could hardly believe the results of a nationwide Harris poll in which 77,000 Americans had ranked Taco Bell No. 1. It beat out last year's winner and arch-rival, Chipotle Grill.[1]

With 6,278 eateries in the U.S., Taco Bell serves more food than any other Mexican chain. Despite its numerous restaurants and high ranking, it continues to suffer from a limited menu and bad publicity. One of its worst crises was a lawsuit falsely accusing it of adulterating its beef with binders and extenders.[2] Undeterred, Taco Bell survived that disastrous public relations calamity, emerging with a gigantic menu hit: Doritos Locos, a cheese-flavored shell stuffed with spicy beef filling. Even this breakout menu stunner, however, could take Taco Bell only so far.

Like many *fast-service* restaurants, as it prefers to be called, Taco Bell searches for innovations that will make it stand out. A few years back, it rolled out its Cantina Bell menu, offering a gourmet selection of dishes made with upscale ingredients

and fewer calories, which seemed to appeal to antiobesity demands. Customers, however, snubbed the chain's fancy meals and low-calorie, low-fat dishes.

Searching for more hits, Taco Bell tried a menu concept centered on "American-inspired" tacos, craft beers, and alcoholic milkshakes. It tested this model in a glitzy pilot restaurant in southern California called U.S. Taco Company. Unable to secure a liquor license or many customers, it quietly closed its doors after a year.[3]

One of Taco Bell's latest menu efforts aims at vegetarians. The company proudly announced that it is the first quick-service restaurant chain to offer American Vegetarian Association (AVA) certified food options.[4] Who would have imagined that Taco Bell could sell 350 million vegetarian items a year? How about a veggie power burrito or a breakfast soft taco without bacon?

In the increasingly crowded fast-food market, customers are shifting away from the traditional burger and chicken choices. Poised to capitalize on this movement, Taco Bell must create new appealing products that respond to market trends. You will learn more about Taco Bell and be asked to complete a relevant task at the end of this chapter.

Critical Thinking

- Assume that a recently hired culinary product manager is charged with generating and implementing new menu suggestions. What role does communication skill play in this person's effectiveness in completing this task?

- Do you think a culinary product manager would make an oral or a written presentation of new menu ideas?

- Why is a writing process helpful in developing a presentation of new ideas?

6-1 Hitting the Brakes: Applying Phase 3 of the Writing Process

LEARNING OUTCOME

1 Demonstrate techniques that achieve conciseness as part of Phase 3 of the writing process.

In this hurry-up era of e-mailing, messaging, and tweeting, the idea of stopping to revise a message seems counterproductive. What? Stop to proofread and edit? Crazy idea! No time! However, sending quick but sloppy business messages not only fails to enhance productivity but also often produces the opposite result. They frequently set into motion a maddening ping-pong series of back-and-forth queries and responses seeking clarification. To avoid messages that waste time, create confusion, and reduce your credibility, you will do yourself a favor by taking time to slow down and revise—even for short messages.

The final phase of the 3-x-3 writing process focuses on editing, proofreading, and evaluating. Editing means improving the content and sentence structure of your message. Proofreading involves correcting its grammar, spelling, punctuation, format, and mechanics. Evaluating is the process of analyzing whether your message achieves its purpose. One may not expect the restaurant business to require these kinds of skills. However, the new culinary product manager at Taco Bell—and many similar businesspeople—realize that bright ideas are worth little unless they can be communicated effectively to fellow workers and management. In the communication process, revision can often mean the difference between the acceptance or rejection of ideas.

Although the drafting process differs depending on the person and the situation, this final phase should occupy a significant share of the total time you spend on a message. Writing experts, as presented earlier, recommend devoting about half the total writing time to the third phase of the writing process.[5]

Rarely is the first or even second version of a message satisfactory. Only amateurs expect writing perfection on the first try. The revision stage is your chance to make sure your message says what you mean and makes you look good. Some professional writers compose the first draft quickly without worrying about language, precision, or correctness. Then they revise and polish extensively. Other writers, however, prefer to revise as they go—particularly for shorter business documents.

Whether you revise immediately or after a break, you will want to examine your message critically. You should be especially concerned with improving its conciseness, clarity, and readability.

6-1a Revising for Conciseness

In business, time is indeed money. Translated into writing, this means that concise messages save reading time and, thus, money. In addition, messages that are written directly and efficiently are easier to read and comprehend. In the revision process, look for shorter ways to say what you mean. Examine every sentence you write. Could the thought be conveyed in fewer words? Your writing will be more concise if you slash vague expressions, purge long lead-ins, drop unnecessary fillers, reject redundancies, and eliminate empty words.

Slashing Vague Expressions. As you revise, focus on eliminating imprecise expressions. This takes conscious effort. Turning out succinct sentences and clear messages means that you will strive to trim vague expressions. For example, notice the wordiness in this sentence: *In view of the fact that sales are booming, in all probability profits will increase.* It could be said more concisely: *Because sales are booming, profits will probably increase.* Many vague, wordy expressions can be clarified and shortened as shown here and illustrated in Figure 6.1. Notice in this figure how you can revise digital documents with strikethrough formatting and color. If you are revising print documents, use popular proofreading marks.

Vague	Concise
as a means to	to
at a later date	later
at this point in time	now, presently
despite the fact that	although
due to the fact that, inasmuch as, in view of the fact that	because
feel free to	please
for the period of, for the purpose of	for

continues

Vague	Concise
in addition to the above	also
in all probability	probably
in the event that	if
in the near future	soon
in very few cases	seldom
until such time as	until
with regard to	about

Purging Long Lead-Ins. Concise sentences avoid long lead-ins with unnecessary introductory words. Consider this sentence: *We are using this e-mail to announce that we are considering a flex work schedule.* It's more concise and direct without the long lead-in. The meat of the sentence often follows the words *that* or *because,* as shown in the following:

FIGURE 6.1 Revising Digital and Print Documents

Revising Digital Documents Using Strikethrough and Color

~~This is a short note to let you know that, as~~ As you requested, I ~~made an investigation of~~ investigated several of our competitors' websites. Attached ~~hereto~~ is a summary of my findings. ~~of my investigation.~~ I was ~~really~~ most interested in ~~making a comparison of the employment of strategies for~~ comparing marketing strategies as well as ~~the use of~~ navigational graphics ~~used~~ to guide visitors through the sites. ~~In view of the fact that~~ Because we will be revising our own website ~~in the near future~~ soon, I was ~~extremely~~ intrigued by the organization, ~~kind of~~ marketing tactics, and navigation at each ~~and every~~ site I visited.

When revising digital documents, you can use simple word processing tools such as strikethrough and color. In this example, strikethroughs in red identify passages to be deleted. The strikethrough function is located on the **Font** tab. We used blue to show inserted words, but you may choose any color you prefer.

Revising Printed Documents Using Proofreading Symbols
When revising printed documents, use standard symbols to manually show your revisions.

~~This is a short note to let you know that,~~ as you requested, I ~~made an~~ investigated ~~of~~ several of our competitors' websites. Attached ~~hereto~~ is a summary of my findings. ~~of my investigation.~~ I was ~~really~~ most interested in ~~making a comparison of the employment of~~ comparing marketing strategies ~~for marketing~~ as well as ~~the use of~~ navigational graphics ~~used~~ to guide visitors through the sites. ~~In view of the fact that~~ Because we will be revising our own website soon ~~in the near future,~~ I was ~~extremely~~ intrigued by the organization, ~~kind of~~ marketing tactics, and navigation at each ~~and every~~ site I visited.

Popular Proofreading Symbols

Delete	℘
Capitalize	≡
Insert	∧
Insert comma	⋏
Insert period	⊙
Start paragraph	¶

More symbols are in Appendix C on page C1.

Wordy	Concise
This early announcement is being made at this time because it is now possible for you to sign up for vacation slots.	You may now sign up for vacation slots.
We would like to inform all customers that lower airfares may be available on our website.	Lower airfares may be available on our website.
I am writing this letter because Dr. Erin Blocher suggested that your organization was hiring trainees.	Dr. Erin Blocher suggested that your organization was hiring trainees.

Dropping Unnecessary *there is/are* and *it is/was* Fillers. In many sentences the expressions *there is/are* and *it is/was* function as **unnecessary fillers**. In addition to taking up space, these fillers delay getting to the point of the sentence. Eliminate them by recasting the sentence. Many—but not all—sentences can be revised so that fillers are unnecessary.

Wordy	Concise
There is a referee to determine the winner.	A referee determines the winner.
It was an aggregator who collected and organized the blogs.	An aggregator collected and organized the blogs.
There was a Facebook post that revealed the news.	A Facebook post revealed the news.

6-1b Rejecting Redundancies

Redundancies are expressions that repeat meaning or include unnecessary words. Saying *unexpected surprise* is like saying *surprise surprise* because *unexpected* carries the same meaning as *surprise*. Excessive adjectives, adverbs, and phrases often create redundancies and wordiness. Redundancies do not add emphasis, as some people think. Instead, they identify a writer as careless. As you revise, look for redundant expressions such as the following:

Redundant	Concise
added bonus	bonus
adequate enough	adequate
basic fundamentals	fundamentals *or* basics
collaborate together	collaborate
exactly identical	identical
each and every	each *or* every
fewer in number	fewer
final outcome	outcome
new beginning	beginning
refer back	refer
repeat again	repeat
true facts	facts

Eliminating Empty Words. Familiar phrases roll off the tongue easily, but many contain expendable parts. Be alert to these empty words and phrases: *case, degree, the fact that, factor, instance, nature,* and *quality.* Notice how much better the following sentences sound when we remove the empty words:

~~In the case of~~ Google, ~~it~~ poured money into augmented-reality glasses.

Because of the ~~degree of~~ research required, the investment was enormous.

~~We are aware of the fact that n~~New products soar when pushed by social media ~~networking~~.

Except for ~~the instance of~~ Amazon, sales sagged.

Tracy chose a career in a field that was analytical ~~in nature~~. [*OR:* Tracy chose a career in an analytical field.]

Student writing in that class is excellent ~~in quality~~.

Also avoid saying the obvious. In the following examples, notice how many unnecessary words we can omit through revision:

~~When it arrived,~~ I cashed your check immediately. (*Announcing the check's arrival is unnecessary. That fact is assumed in its cashing.*)

As consumers learn more about ingredients ~~and as they become more knowledgeable~~, they are demanding fresher foods. (*Avoid repeating information.*)

Look carefully at clauses beginning with *that, which,* and *who.* They can often be shortened without loss of clarity. Search for phrases such as *it appears that.* These phrases often can be reduced to a single adjective or adverb, such as *apparently.*

> Apparently
> ~~It appears that~~ communal working spaces are popular for ^employees ~~who work remotely~~.
> remote

> impressive
> If you are offered a new^title ~~that seems impressive~~ but it comes without a pay raise, you
> wise
> should respond with a ~~wisely considered~~ ^ answer.

> final   substantially
> The^ offer, ~~which was submitted in its final form,~~ had been ^altered ~~in many substantial ways~~.

Drafting Concise Posts for Social Media Networks. **Microblogging** is a term you probably haven't heard very often, but chances are you have posted a short message today. As its name suggests, *microblogging* consists of short messages exchanged on social media networks such as Twitter, Facebook, and Tumblr. Businesses are eagerly joining these microblogging networks to hear what's being said about them and their products. When

---

Reality Check

How to Lose a Customer Fast

"Good writing is brevity, and brevity is marketing. Want to lose me as a customer, forever, guaranteed? Have a grammar error on any form of outward communication."[6]

—Peter Shankman, *founder of Geek Factory, blogger, angel investor, author*

they hear complaints, they can respond immediately and often solve customer problems. Companies are also using microblogging to make announcements, promote goodwill, and sell their products.

Although Twitter doubled the number of characters allowed for tweets, most users still keep their messages under 140 characters because brevity is the hallmark of Twitter.

Examples of Business Twitter Messages. Regardless of what microblogging platform you choose, conciseness is critical. Your messages must be short—without straying too far from conventional spelling, grammar, and punctuation. Sound difficult? It's challenging but can be done, as shown in the following 140-character examples of business tweets:

Source: JetBlue

Replying to Customer
@JetBlue

@RMLazo13 Your flight is currently scheduled to leave at 11 a.m. Hang in there. We'll have you on your way as soon as possible

Source: British Gas

Sharing Useful Information
@BritishGas

@CleverMom Some boilers can be confusing. Please check our boiler manual to help you figure it out. Try http://po.st/BoilerManual Sarah

Source: HubSpot

Presenting Fresh Facts
@ HubSpot

72.6% of salespeople using social media actually outperformed their colleagues who were not on social media: hub.am/14ikdDS

Source: SUBWAY

Promoting Products
@SUBWAY

It's #FridayThe13th! It might be an old wive's tale but we hear a Bacon, Egg & Cheese w/Avocado counteracts bad luck.

Source: Zappos

Announcing Closure for Company Party
@Zappos

Hi all! We are closed for our annual Vendor Party! We will reopen at 7am PST tomorrow. We can still be reached at cs@zappos.com if needed.

LEARNING OUTCOME

2 Demonstrate writing techniques that simplify and clarify business messages.

Tips for Writing Concise, Effective Tweets. Your tweets and posts will be most effective if you follow these tips:

- Include only main ideas focused on useful information.
- Choose descriptive but short words.
- Personalize your message if possible.
- Draft several versions striving for conciseness, clarity, and, yes, even correctness.

6-2 Enhancing Message Clarity

"Clarity is the most important characteristic of good business writing," claims Grammar Girl podcaster Mignon Fogarty—and we agree![8] A clear message is one that is immediately understood. Today's employees, customers, and investors increasingly want to be addressed in a clear and genuine way. Fuzzy, long-winded, and unclear writing prevents comprehension. Readers understand better when information is presented clearly and concisely, as a Dartmouth study illustrates in Figure 6.2. Numerous techniques can improve the clarity of your writing including applying the KISS formula (Keep It Short and Simple), dumping trite business phrases, scrapping clichés and buzzwords, rescuing buried verbs, and restraining exuberance.

FIGURE 6.2 Conciseness Aids Clarity in Understanding Drug Facts

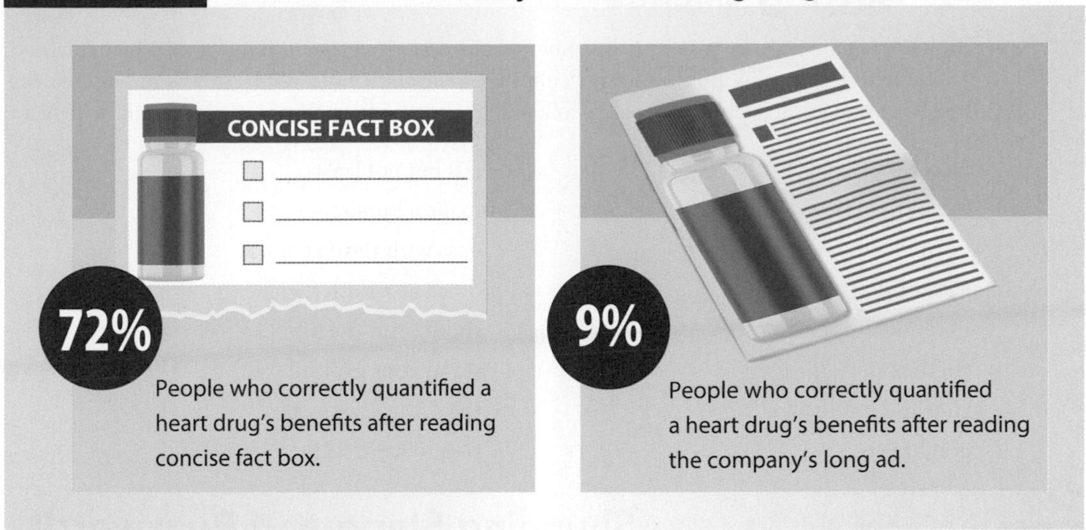

CONCISE FACT BOX

72%
People who correctly quantified a heart drug's benefits after reading concise fact box.

9%
People who correctly quantified a heart drug's benefits after reading the company's long ad.

6-2a Keeping It Short and Simple

To achieve clarity, resist the urge to show off or be fancy. Remember that your goal is not to impress a reader. As a business writer, your goal is to *express*, not *impress*. Be guided by **KISS**: *Keep it short and simple.* Avoid wordy, unclear language as shown in the following:

Wordy and Unclear	Improved
High-quality learning environments for children are a necessary precondition for facilitation and enhancement of the ongoing learning process.	To learn properly, children need good schools.
In regard to the matter of obtaining optimal results, it is essential that employees be given the implements that are necessary for their work to be completed satisfactorily.	For best results give employees the tools they need to do their work.

6-2b Dumping Trite Business Phrases

In an attempt to sound businesslike, some business writers repeat trite expressions such as those in the following lists. Your writing will sound fresher and more vigorous if you eliminate these stale, hackneyed phrases. Find more original ways to convey an idea.

Trite Phrase	Improved
as per your request	as you request
pursuant to your request	at your request
enclosed please find	enclosed is
every effort will be made	we'll try
in accordance with your wishes	as you wish
in receipt of	have received
please do not hesitate to	please
respond forthwith	respond immediately
thank you in advance	thank you
under separate cover	separately
with reference to	about

6-2c Cutting Clichés

Clichés are expressions that have become exhausted by overuse. Many cannot be explained, especially to those who are new to our culture. Clichés lack not only freshness but also clarity. Instead of repeating clichés such as the following, try to find another way to say what you mean.

below the belt	last but not least
better than new	make a bundle
beyond a shadow of a doubt	pass with flying colors
easier said than done	quick as a flash
exception to the rule	shoot from the hip
fill the bill	stand your ground
first and foremost	think outside the box
good to go	true to form

6-2d Shunning Slang and Buzzwords

Slang is composed of informal words with arbitrary and extravagantly changed meanings. These words quickly go out of fashion because they are no longer appealing when everyone begins to understand them. If you want to sound professional, avoid expressions such as *snarky, lousy, blowing the budget, bombed, trashed, screw up,* and Twitter slang such as *b/c* (because), *FOMO* (fear of missing out), *ICYMI* (in case you missed it), and *br* (best regards).

Equally unprofessional and imprecise are business buzzwords. These are technical expressions that have become fashionable and often are meant to impress rather than express. Business buzzwords to avoid include empty terms such as *optimize, incentivize, impactful, leveraging, right-size,* and *paradigm shift.* Other vague expressions to stay away from are buzzwords such as *cost effective, positioned to perform, solutions-oriented,* and *value-added services with end-to-end fulfillment.*

6-2e Rescuing Buried Verbs

Buried verbs are those that have been needlessly converted to wordy noun expressions. This happens when verbs such as *acquire, establish,* and *develop* are made into nouns such as *acquisition, establishment,* and *development.* Such nouns often end in *-tion, -ment,* and *-ance.* These nouns are sometimes called zombie nouns because they cannibalize and suck the life out of active verbs.[10] Zombie nouns increase sentence length, slow the reader, and muddy the thought. Notice how you can make your writing cleaner and more forceful by avoiding buried verbs and zombie nouns:

Buried Verbs and Zombie Nouns	Unburied Verbs
take action on	act
perform an analysis of	analyze
make an assumption	assume
reach a conclusion	conclude
give consideration to	consider
make a discovery	discover
conduct a discussion of	discuss
engage in the preparation of	prepare
create a reduction in	reduce

Boiko V/Shutterstock.com

6-2f Curbing Exuberance

Occasionally, we show our **exuberance** with overly enthusiastic words such as *very, definitely, quite, completely, extremely, really, actually,* and *totally*. These intensifiers can emphasize and strengthen your meaning. Overuse, however, sounds unbusinesslike. Punctuation marks can also display excessive exuberance. Once seldom seen in the workplace, exclamation marks are increasingly used to convey warmth and sincerity, especially in Internet messages. Whether to include them—and how many to use—depends on your workplace and its norms. See our discussion in *For the Record.*

Excessive Exuberance	Businesslike
The manufacturer was *extremely* upset to learn that its smartphones were *definitely* being counterfeited!!!	The manufacturer was upset to learn that its smartphones were being counterfeited.
We *totally* agree that we *actually* did not give his proposal a *very* fair trial.	We agree that we did not give his proposal a fair trial.

6-3 Using Document Design to Improve Readability

Want to make your readers think you are well-organized and intelligent? You can accomplish this by cleverly using document design! Doing so will also enhance the readability of your messages.

In the revision process, you have a chance to adjust formatting and make other changes so that readers grasp your main points quickly. Significant design techniques to improve readability include the appropriate use of white space, margins, typefaces, numbered and bulleted lists, and headings for visual impact.

6-3a Making White Space Work for You

Empty space on a page is called **white space**. A page crammed full of text or graphics appears busy, cluttered, and unreadable. You can make white space work for you by using headings, bulleted or numbered lists, effective margins, short sentences (20 or fewer words), and short paragraphs (eight or fewer printed lines). All of these techniques improve readability and comprehension. As you revise, think about shortening long sentences. Consider breaking up long paragraphs into shorter chunks.

6-3b Understanding Margins and Text Alignment

Margins determine the white space on the left, right, top, and bottom of a block of type. They define the reading area, provide important visual relief, and enhance readability. Business letters and memos usually have side margins of 1 to 1.5 inches.

Your word processing program probably offers four forms of margin alignment: (a) lines align only at the left, (b) lines align only at the right, (c) lines align at both left and right, and (d) lines are centered. When letter and word-spacing is adjusted so that lines are aligned at both left and right margins, the margins are said to be **justified**. The text in books, magazines, and other long works is often justified on the left and right for a formal appearance. Take a look at this book. Notice that the left and right margins are even, that is, justified. If the right margin is unjustified, as prepared in report manuscripts, it is said to be **ragged right**.

Justified text, may require more attention to word spacing and hyphenation to avoid awkward empty spaces or rivers of spaces running through a document. When right margins are ragged, they provide more white space and improve readability. Therefore, you are best served by using left-justified text and ragged-right margins without justification. Centered text is appropriate for headings and short announcements but not for complete messages.

6-3c Selecting Appropriate Typefaces

Business writers today may choose from a number of typefaces on their word processors. A typeface defines the shape of text characters. A wide range of typefaces, as shown in Figure 6.3, is available for various purposes. Some are decorative and useful for special purposes. For most business messages, however, you should choose from *serif* or *sans serif* categories.

Serif typefaces have small features at the ends of strokes. The most common serif typeface is Times New Roman. Other popular serif typefaces are Century, Georgia, and Palatino. Serif typefaces suggest tradition, maturity, and formality. They are frequently used for body text in business messages and longer documents. Because books, newspapers, and magazines favor serif typefaces, readers are familiar with them.

Sans serif typefaces include Arial, Calibri, Gothic, Tahoma, Helvetica, and Univers. These clean characters are widely used for headings, signs, and material that does not require continuous reading. Web designers often prefer sans serif typefaces for simple, pure pages. For longer documents, however, sans serif typefaces may seem colder and less accessible than familiar serif typefaces.

For less formal messages or special decorative effects, you might choose one of the happy fonts such as Comic Sans or a bold typeface such as Impact. You can simulate handwriting with a script typeface. Despite the wonderful possibilities available on your word processor, don't get carried away with fancy typefaces. All-purpose sans serif and traditional serif typefaces are most appropriate for your business messages. Generally, use no more than two typefaces within one document.

6-3d Capitalizing on Type Fonts and Sizes

Font refers to a specific style (such as *italic*) within a typeface family (such as Times New Roman). Most typeface families offer various fonts such as CAPITALIZATION, SMALL CAPS, **boldface**, *italic*, and underline, as well as less common fonts such as outline and shadow.

FIGURE 6.3	Typefaces with Different Personalities for Different Purposes

All-Purpose Sans Serif	Traditional Serif	Happy, Creative, Script, Funny	Assertive, Bold, Modern, Display	Plain Monospaced
Arial	Century	*Brush Script*	**Britannic Bold**	Courier
Calibri	Garamond	Comic Sans	**Broadway**	Letter Gothic
Helvetica	Georgia	*Gigi*	**Elephant**	Monaco
Tahoma	Goudy	Jokerman	**Impact**	Prestige Elite
Univers	Palatino	Lucinda	Bauhaus 93	
Verdana	Times New Roman	Kristen	SHOWCARD	

Font styles are a mechanical means of adding emphasis to your words. ALL CAPS, SMALL CAPS, and **boldface** are useful for headings, subheadings, and single words or short phrases in the text. ALL CAPS, HOWEVER, SHOULD NEVER BE USED FOR LONG STRETCHES OF TEXT BECAUSE ALL THE LETTERS ARE THE SAME HEIGHT, MAKING IT DIFFICULT FOR READERS TO DIFFERENTIATE WORDS. In addition, excessive use of all caps feels like shouting and irritates readers. **Boldface,** *italics*, and underlining are effective for calling attention to important points and terms. Be cautious, however, when using fancy or an excessive number of font styles. Don't use them if they will confuse, annoy, or slow down readers.

During the revision process, think about type size. Readers are generally most comfortable with 10- to 12-point type for body text. Smaller type enables you to fit more words into a space. Tiny type, however, makes text look dense and unappealing. Slightly larger type makes material more readable. Overly large type (14 points or more) looks amateurish and out of place for body text in business messages. Larger type, however, is appropriate for headings.

6-3e Using Lists for Quick Comprehension

One of the best ways to ensure rapid comprehension of ideas is through the use of numbered or bulleted lists. Lists provide high skim value. This means that readers can browse quickly and grasp main ideas. By breaking up complex information into smaller chunks, lists improve readability, understanding, and retention. They also force the writer to organize ideas and write efficiently.

In the revision process, look for ideas that could be converted to lists and use these techniques to make your lists look professional:

- **Numbered lists.** Use for items that represent a sequence or reflect a numbering system.
- **Bulleted lists.** Use to highlight items that don't necessarily show a chronology.
- **Capitalization.** Capitalize the initial word of each line.
- **Punctuation.** Add end punctuation only if the listed items are complete sentences.
- **Parallelism.** Make all the lines consistent; for example, start each with a verb.

> ### Reality Check
>
> #### Complaining of an Avalanche of Impenetrable Verbiage
>
> An advocate for plain English, former SEC chair Arthur Levitt championed readability in investor documents. He advocated using the active voice, familiar words, and graphic techniques such as boldface, headings, and lists. However, he has been only partially successful, he complains, because such efforts "get tugged into the ditch by the irresistible pull of legal jargon" with documents "buried in an avalanche of impenetrable verbiage."[12]
>
> —Arthur Levitt, *longest serving chair, U.S. Securities and Exchange Commission*

In the following examples, notice that the list on the left presents a sequence of steps with numbers. The bulleted list does not show a sequence of ideas; therefore, bullets are appropriate. Also notice the parallelism in each example. In the numbered list, each item begins with a verb. In the bulleted list, each item follows an adjective/noun sequence. Business readers appreciate lists because they focus attention. Be careful, however, not to use so many that your messages look like grocery lists.

Numbered List	Bulleted List
Our recruiters follow these steps when hiring applicants:	To attract upscale customers, we feature the following:
1. Examine the application.	• Quality fashions
2. Interview the applicant.	• Personalized service
3. Check the applicant's references.	• Generous return policy

6-3f Improving Business Messages With Headings

Headings are an effective tool for highlighting information and improving readability. They encourage the writer to group similar material together. Headings help the reader separate major ideas from details. They enable a busy reader to skim familiar or less important information.

Headings also provide a quick preview or review. They appear most often in reports, which you will study in greater detail in Chapters 11, 12, and 13. However, main headings, subheadings, and category headings can also improve readability in e-mails, memos, and letters. In the following example, they are used with bullets to summarize categories:

Category Headings

Our company focuses on the following areas in the employment process:

- **Attracting applicants.** We advertise for qualified applicants, and we also encourage current employees to recommend good people.
- **Interviewing applicants.** Our specialized interviews include simulated customer encounters as well as scrutiny by supervisors.
- **Checking references**. We investigate every applicant thoroughly. We contact former employers and all listed references.

In Model Document 6.1 the writer was able to convert a dense, unappealing e-mail into an easier-to-read version by applying document design. Notice that the all-caps font in the first paragraph makes its meaning difficult to decipher. Justified margins and lack of white space further reduce readability. In the revised version, the writer changed the all-caps font to upper- and lowercase and also used ragged-right margins to enhance visual appeal. One of the best document design techniques in this message is the use of headings and bullets to help the reader see chunks of information in similar groups. All of these improvements are made in the revision process. You can make any message more readable by applying the document design techniques presented here.

6-4 Catching Errors With Careful Proofreading

Alas, none of us is perfect, and even the best writers sometimes make mistakes. The problem, however, is not making the mistakes; the real problem is not finding and correcting them. Documents with errors affect your credibility and the success of your organization, as illustrated in Figure 6.4.

Once you have the message in its final form, it's time to proofread. Don't proofread earlier because you may waste time checking items that eventually are changed or omitted. Important messages—such as those you send to management or to customers or turn in to instructors for grades—deserve careful revision and proofreading. Even messages you post at dating sites deserve careful proofing. A survey of 5,000 singles by dating site Match revealed that 80 percent of women and 75 percent of men said they valued correct grammar highly, putting it ahead of a person's confidence and even ahead of good-looking teeth.[14]

When you finish a first draft, plan for a cooling-off period. Put the document aside and return to it after a break, preferably after 24 hours or longer. Proofreading is especially difficult because most of us read what we thought we wrote. That's why it's important to look for specific problem areas.

6-4a What to Watch for in Proofreading

Careful proofreaders check for problems in the following areas:

- **Spelling.** Now is the time to consult the dictionary. Is *recommend* spelled with one or two *c*'s? Do you mean *affect* or *effect*? Use your computer spell-checker, but don't rely on it totally.
- **Grammar.** Locate sentence subjects; do their verbs agree with them? Do pronouns agree with their antecedents? Review the grammar and mechanics principles in Appendix D if necessary. Use your computer's grammar-checker, but be suspicious; sometimes it's flat-out wrong.

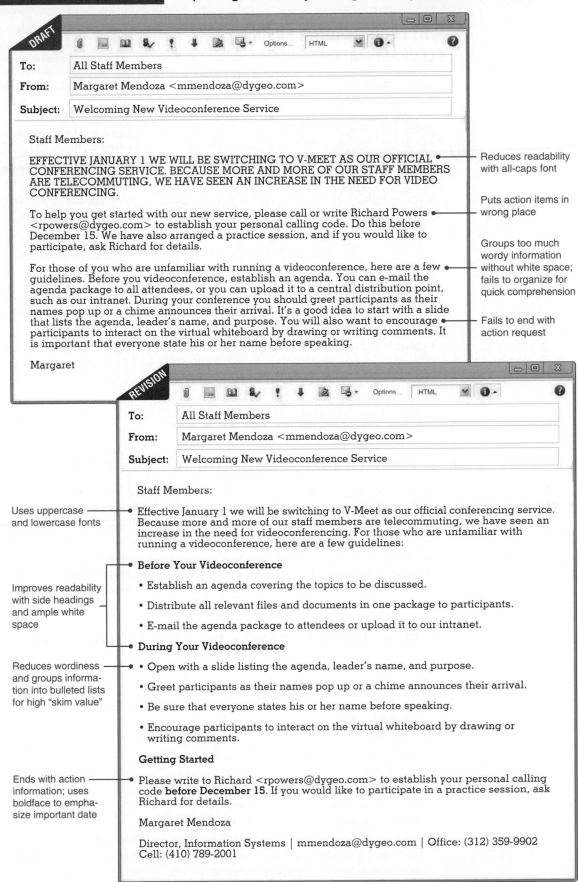

DRAFT

To: All Staff Members

From: Margaret Mendoza <mmendoza@dygeo.com>

Subject: Welcoming New Videoconference Service

Staff Members:

EFFECTIVE JANUARY 1 WE WILL BE SWITCHING TO V-MEET AS OUR OFFICIAL CONFERENCING SERVICE. BECAUSE MORE AND MORE OF OUR STAFF MEMBERS ARE TELECOMMUTING, WE HAVE SEEN AN INCREASE IN THE NEED FOR VIDEO CONFERENCING.
— Reduces readability with all-caps font

To help you get started with our new service, please call or write Richard Powers <rpowers@dygeo.com> to establish your personal calling code. Do this before December 15. We have also arranged a practice session, and if you would like to participate, ask Richard for details.
— Puts action items in wrong place

For those of you who are unfamiliar with running a videoconference, here are a few guidelines. Before you videoconference, establish an agenda. You can e-mail the agenda package to all attendees, or you can upload it to a central distribution point, such as our intranet. During your conference you should greet participants as their names pop up or a chime announces their arrival. It's a good idea to start with a slide that lists the agenda, leader's name, and purpose. You will also want to encourage participants to interact on the virtual whiteboard by drawing or writing comments. It is important that everyone state his or her name before speaking.
— Groups too much wordy information without white space; fails to organize for quick comprehension
— Fails to end with action request

Margaret

REVISION

To: All Staff Members

From: Margaret Mendoza <mmendoza@dygeo.com>

Subject: Welcoming New Videoconference Service

Staff Members:

Uses uppercase and lowercase fonts —
• Effective January 1 we will be switching to V-Meet as our official conferencing service. Because more and more of our staff members are telecommuting, we have seen an increase in the need for videoconferencing. For those who are unfamiliar with running a videoconference, here are a few guidelines:

Improves readability with side headings and ample white space —
Before Your Videoconference

• Establish an agenda covering the topics to be discussed.

• Distribute all relevant files and documents in one package to participants.

• E-mail the agenda package to attendees or upload it to our intranet.

During Your Videoconference

Reduces wordiness and groups information into bulleted lists for high "skim value" —
• Open with a slide listing the agenda, leader's name, and purpose.

• Greet participants as their names pop up or a chime announces their arrival.

• Be sure that everyone states his or her name before speaking.

• Encourage participants to interact on the virtual whiteboard by drawing or writing comments.

Getting Started

Ends with action information; uses boldface to emphasize important date —
• Please write to Richard <rpowers@dygeo.com> to establish your personal calling code **before December 15**. If you would like to participate in a practice session, ask Richard for details.

Margaret Mendoza

Director, Information Systems | mmendoza@dygeo.com | Office: (312) 359-9902
Cell: (410) 789-2001

FIGURE 6.4   Why Proofread?

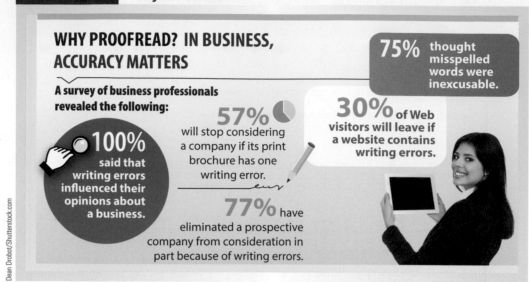

WHY PROOFREAD? IN BUSINESS, ACCURACY MATTERS

A survey of business professionals revealed the following:

100% said that writing errors influenced their opinions about a business.

57% will stop considering a company if its print brochure has one writing error.

77% have eliminated a prospective company from consideration in part because of writing errors.

30% of Web visitors will leave if a website contains writing errors.

75% thought misspelled words were inexcusable.

Dean Drobot/Shutterstock.com

- **Punctuation.** Make sure that introductory clauses are followed by commas. In compound sentences put commas before coordinating conjunctions (*and, or, but, nor*). Double-check your use of semicolons and colons.

- **Names and numbers.** Compare all names and numbers with their sources because inaccuracies are not always visible. Especially verify the spelling of the names of individuals receiving the message. Most of us immediately dislike someone who misspells our name.

- **Format.** Be sure that your document looks balanced on the page. Compare its parts with those of the standard document formats shown in Appendix A. If you indent paragraphs, be certain that all are indented.

6-4b How to Proofread Routine Documents

Most routine documents require a light proofreading. If you read on screen, use the down arrow to reveal one line at a time. This focuses your attention at the bottom of the screen. A safer proofreading method, however, is reading from a printed copy. Regardless of which method you use, look for typos and misspellings. Search for easily confused words, such as *to* for *too* and *then* for *than*. Read for missing words and inconsistencies. For handwritten or printed messages, use standard proofreading marks, shown briefly in Figure 6.1 or completely in Appendix C. For digital documents and collaborative projects, use the simple word processing tools such as strikethrough and color shown in Figure 6.1.

6-4c How to Proofread Complex Documents

Long, complex, or important documents demand careful proofreading. Apply the previous suggestions but also add the following techniques:

- Print a copy, preferably double-spaced, and set it aside for at least a day. You will be more alert after a breather.

- Allow adequate time to proofread carefully. A common excuse for sloppy proofreading is lack of time.

- Be prepared to find errors. One student confessed, "I can find other people's errors, but I can't seem to locate my own." Psychologically, we don't expect to find errors, and we don't want to find them. You can overcome this obstacle by anticipating errors and congratulating, not criticizing, yourself each time you find one.

- Read the message at least twice—once for word meanings and once for grammar and mechanics. For very long documents (book chapters and long articles or reports), read a third time to verify consistency in formatting.

- Reduce your reading speed. Concentrate on individual words rather than ideas.
- For documents that must be perfect, enlist a proofreading buddy. Have someone read the message aloud. Spell names and difficult words, note capitalization, and read punctuation.
- Use the standard proofreading marks shown in Appendix C to indicate changes.

Many of us struggle with proofreading our own writing because we are seeing the same information over and over. We tend to see what we expect to see as our eyes race over the words without looking at each one carefully. We tend to know what is coming next and glide over it. To change the appearance of what you are reading, you might print it on a different-colored paper or change the font. If you are proofing on screen, enlarge the page view or change the background color of the screen.

6-5 Evaluating the Effectiveness of Your Message

As part of applying finishing touches, take a moment to evaluate your writing. Remember that everything you write, whether for yourself or someone else, takes the place of a personal appearance. If you were meeting in person, you would be certain to dress appropriately and professionally. The same standard applies to your writing. Evaluate what you have written to be certain that it attracts the reader's attention. Is it polished and clear enough to convince the reader that you are worth listening to? How successful will this message be? Does it say what you want it to? Will it achieve your purpose? How will you know whether it succeeds?

The best way to judge the success of your communication is through feedback. For this reason you should encourage the receiver to respond to your message. This feedback will tell you how to modify future efforts to improve your communication technique.

Your instructor will also be evaluating some of your writing. Although any criticism is painful, try not to be defensive. Look on these comments as valuable advice tailored to your specific writing weaknesses—and strengths. Many businesses today spend thousands of dollars bringing in communication consultants to improve employee writing skills. You are getting the same training in this course. Take advantage of this chance—one of the few you may have—to improve your skills. The best way to improve your skills, of course, is through instruction, practice, and evaluation.

In this class you have all three elements: instruction in the writing process, practice materials, and someone to guide you and evaluate your efforts. Those three elements are the reasons this book and course may be the most valuable in your entire curriculum. Because it's almost impossible to improve your communication skills alone, take advantage of this opportunity.

The task of editing, proofreading, and evaluating, summarized in the following checklist, is hard work. It demands objectivity and a willingness to cut, cut, cut. Although painful, the process is also gratifying. It's a great feeling when you realize your finished message is clear, concise, and effective.

LEARNING OUTCOME

5 Evaluate a message to judge its effectiveness.

Checklist

Editing, Proofreading, and Evaluating

- **Slash vague expressions.** Strive to reduce wordy phrases to single words (*as a general rule* becomes *generally*; *at this point in time* becomes *now*).

- **Ditch opening fillers and long lead-ins.** Revise sentences so that they don't start with fillers (*there is, there are, it is, it was*) and long lead-ins (*this is to inform you that*).

- **Reject redundancies.** Eliminate words that repeat meanings, such as *refer back*. Watch for repetitious adjectives, adverbs, and phrases.

- **Eliminate empty writing.** Check phrases that include *case, degree, the fact that, factor,* and other words and phrases that unnecessarily increase wordiness. Avoid saying the obvious.

- **Write concisely for microblogging.** Keep your messages short without sacrificing proper spelling, grammar, and punctuation.

- **Keep the message simple.** Express ideas directly. Don't show off or use fancy language.

- **Dump trite business phrases.** Keep your writing fresh, direct, and contemporary by skipping such expressions as *enclosed please find* and *pursuant to your request.*

- **Scrap clichés and slang.** Avoid expressions that are overused and unclear (*below the belt, shoot from the hip*). Don't use slang, which is not only unprofessional but also often unclear to a wide audience.

- **Rescue buried verbs.** Keep your writing vigorous by not converting verbs to nouns (*analyze* not *make an analysis of*).

- **Restrain exuberance.** Avoid overusing intensifiers such as *really, very, definitely, quite, completely, extremely, actually, totally,* and excessive exclamation points.

- **Improve readability through document design.** Use bullets, lists, headings, capital letters, underlining, boldface, italics, and blank space to spotlight ideas and organize them.

- **Proofread for correctness.** Check spelling, grammar, and punctuation. Compare names and numbers with their sources. Double-check the format to be sure you have been consistent.

- **Evaluate your final product.** Will your message achieve its purpose? Could it be improved? How will you know whether it is successful?

Zooming In

Your Turn:
Applying Your Skills at Taco Bell

As an assistant in the communications division of Taco Bell, you have been asked to help Blake, the newly hired culinary product manager, revise a memo he has written. Assume that the CEO has asked all managers for innovative ideas. The CEO is interested in current food trends and creating exciting new menu items responding to those food trends. In his new position as culinary manager, Blake wants very much to suggest new items for Taco Bell that are in keeping with management's push for innovation and that also reflect current food trends.

Blake has prepared a rough draft of a memo summarizing his longer report, which will be presented at a management meeting next week. Although exceptionally talented in cuisine, he realizes that his writing skills are not as well developed as his cooking skills. He comes to the corporate communication department and shows your boss the first draft of his memo. Your boss is a nice guy, and, as a favor, he revises the first two paragraphs, shown in Model Document 6.2.

Your Task

The head of corporate communication has many important tasks to oversee. He hands Blake's memo to you, his assistant, and tells you to finish cleaning it up. He adds, "His ideas are right on target, but the main points are lost in wordy sentences and solid paragraphs. Revise this and concentrate on conciseness, clarity, and readability. Do you think some bulleted lists would help this memo?" Revise the remaining four paragraphs of the memo using the techniques you learned in this chapter. Prepare a copy of the complete memo, incorporating the edits shown, to submit to your boss (your instructor).

Note: This is a rough draft. The first two paragraphs show the boss's revisions. You are to finish the revision.

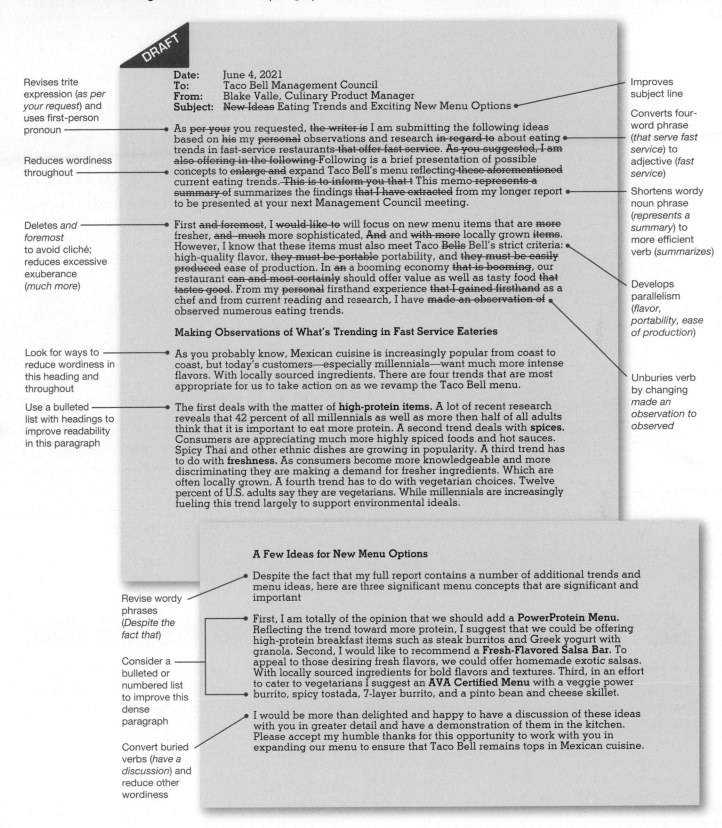

DRAFT

Date: June 4, 2021
To: Taco Bell Management Council
From: Blake Valle, Culinary Product Manager
Subject: ~~New Ideas~~ Eating Trends and Exciting New Menu Options

Revises trite expression (*as per your request*) and uses first-person pronoun

Improves subject line

As ~~per your~~ you requested, ~~the writer is~~ I am submitting the following ideas based on ~~his~~ my ~~personal~~ observations and research ~~in regard to~~ about eating trends in fast-service restaurants ~~that offer fast service.~~ ~~As you suggested, I am also offering in the following~~ Following is a brief presentation of possible concepts to ~~enlarge and~~ expand Taco Bell's menu reflecting ~~these aforementioned~~ current eating trends. ~~This is to inform you that t~~ This memo ~~represents a summary of~~ summarizes the findings ~~that I have extracted~~ from my longer report to be presented at your next Management Council meeting.

Converts four-word phrase (*that serve fast service*) to adjective (*fast service*)

Reduces wordiness throughout

Shortens wordy noun phrase (*represents a summary*) to more efficient verb (*summarizes*)

Deletes *and foremost* to avoid cliché; reduces excessive exuberance (*much more*)

First ~~and foremost~~, I ~~would like to~~ will focus on new menu items that are ~~more~~ fresher, ~~and much~~ more sophisticated, ~~And~~ and ~~with more~~ locally grown ~~items~~. However, I know that these items must also meet Taco ~~Bells~~ Bell's strict criteria: high-quality flavor, ~~they must be portable~~ portability, and ~~they must be easily produced~~ ease of production. In ~~an~~ a booming economy ~~that is booming~~, our restaurant ~~can and most certainly~~ should offer value as well as tasty food ~~that tastes good~~. From my ~~personal~~ firsthand experience ~~that I gained firsthand~~ as a chef and from current reading and research, I have ~~made an observation of~~ observed numerous eating trends.

Develops parallelism (*flavor, portability, ease of production*)

Unburies verb by changing *made an observation* to *observed*

Making Observations of What's Trending in Fast Service Eateries

Look for ways to reduce wordiness in this heading and throughout

As you probably know, Mexican cuisine is increasingly popular from coast to coast, but today's customers—especially millennials—want much more intense flavors. With locally sourced ingredients. There are four trends that are most appropriate for us to take action on as we revamp the Taco Bell menu.

Use a bulleted list with headings to improve readability in this paragraph

The first deals with the matter of **high-protein items.** A lot of recent research reveals that 42 percent of all millennials as well as more then half of all adults think that it is important to eat more protein. A second trend deals with **spices.** Consumers are appreciating much more highly spiced foods and hot sauces. Spicy Thai and other ethnic dishes are growing in popularity. A third trend has to do with **freshness.** As consumers become more knowledgeable and more discriminating they are making a demand for fresher ingredients. Which are often locally grown. A fourth trend has to do with vegetarian choices. Twelve percent of U.S. adults say they are vegetarians. While millennials are increasingly fueling this trend largely to support environmental ideals.

A Few Ideas for New Menu Options

Despite the fact that my full report contains a number of additional trends and menu ideas, here are three significant menu concepts that are significant and important

Revise wordy phrases (*Despite the fact that*)

First, I am totally of the opinion that we should add a **PowerProtein Menu.** Reflecting the trend toward more protein, I suggest that we could be offering high-protein breakfast items such as steak burritos and Greek yogurt with granola. Second, I would like to recommend a **Fresh-Flavored Salsa Bar.** To appeal to those desiring fresh flavors, we could offer homemade exotic salsas. With locally sourced ingredients for bold flavors and textures. Third, in an effort to cater to vegetarians I suggest an **AVA Certified Menu** with a veggie power burrito, spicy tostada, 7-layer burrito, and a pinto bean and cheese skillet.

Consider a bulleted or numbered list to improve this dense paragraph

I would be more than delighted and happy to have a discussion of these ideas with you in greater detail and have a demonstration of them in the kitchen. Please accept my humble thanks for this opportunity to work with you in expanding our menu to ensure that Taco Bell remains tops in Mexican cuisine.

Convert buried verbs (*have a discussion*) and reduce other wordiness

SUMMARY OF LEARNING OUTCOMES

1 Demonstrate techniques that achieve conciseness as part of Phase 3 of the writing process.

- Revise for conciseness by eliminating vague expressions (*as a general rule, at a later date, at this point in time*).

- Eliminate long lead-ins (*this is to inform you that*), fillers (*there is, there are*), redundancies (*basic essentials*), and empty words (*in the case of, the fact that*).

- Revise tweets and other posts rigorously to convey meaning in as few as 140 characters.

2 Demonstrate writing techniques that simplify and clarify business messages.

- Apply the KISS formula (Keep It Short and Simple) to improve message clarity.

- Dump trite business phrases (*as per your request, enclosed please find, pursuant to your request*).

- Cut clichés (*better than new, beyond a shadow of a doubt, easier said than done*).

- Shun slang (*snarky, lousy, bombed*) and buzzwords (*paradigm shift, incentivize*).

- Rescue buried verbs and zombie nouns (*to investigate* rather than *to conduct an investigation* and *to analyze* rather than *to perform an analysis*).

- Avoid overusing intensifiers that show exuberance (*totally, actually, very, definitely*).

3 Explain how to enhance readability through document design.

- To improve message readability and comprehension, provide ample white space, appropriate side margins, and ragged-right (not justified) margins.

- For body text use serif typefaces (fonts with small features at the ends of strokes, such as Times New Roman, Century, and Palatino); for headings and signs, use sans serif typefaces (clean fonts without small features, such as Arial, Helvetica, and Tahoma).

- Create numbered and bulleted lists to provide high skim value in messages.

- Boost visual impact and readability with headings in business messages and reports.

4 Outline proofreading techniques that help you catch errors in both routine and complex documents.

- When proofreading, be especially alert to spelling, grammar, punctuation, names, numbers, and document format.

- Proofread routine documents line by line on the computer screen or from a printed draft copy immediately after finishing.

- Proofread complex documents after a breather. Read from a printed copy, allow adequate time, reduce your reading speed, and read the document at least three times—for word meanings, grammar and mechanics, and formatting.

5 Evaluate a message to judge its effectiveness.

- Encourage feedback from the receiver of your message so that you can determine whether your communication achieved its goal.

- Be open to any advice from your instructor on how to improve your writing skills.

Key Terms

long lead-ins *179*

unnecessary fillers *180*

redundancies *180*

microblogging *181*

KISS *183*

trite *183*

clichés *184*

slang *184*

buried verbs *184*

zombie nouns *184*

exuberance *185*

white space *185*

margins *186*

justified *186*

ragged right *186*

serif *186*

sans serif *186*

font *186*

skim value *187*

headings *187*

Critical Thinking

1. A blogger has asserted that e-mail has made good writing more difficult to achieve because it invites hitting Send before you have thought through, organized, reviewed, and even rewritten your message.[15] Do you agree that good writing has become more difficult because of e-mail? (L.O. 1–5)

2. In this digital era of rapid communication, how can you justify the time it takes to stop and revise a message? (L.O. 1–5)

3. Assume you have started a new job in which you respond to customers by using boilerplate (previously constructed) paragraphs. Some of them contain clichés such as *pursuant to your request* and *in accordance with your wishes*. Other paragraphs are wordy and violate the principle of using concise and clear writing that you have learned. What should you do? (L.O. 2)

4. Most users of e-mail recognize that digital communication is undergoing exclamation-point inflation. When one female manager recently attempted to go without using exclamation points for one month, she found it difficult and time consuming to create ways to convey warmth and enthusiasm without them. She also found that messages without them prompted responses such as, "Are you mad at me?" Linguist and communication guru Deborah Tannen has found that "women (and men) expect emphasis and enthusiasm from other women, frequently in the form of exclamations or all-caps type."[16] What could managers do to convey warmth and enthusiasm without resorting to exclamation points and all caps in messages? Why do you think it is particularly important for female managers to convey warmth in their "boss messages"?

5. **Ethical Issue:** Consider the case of Taylor, who is serving as interim editor of the company newsletter. She receives an article written by the company president describing, in abstract and pompous language, the company's goals for the coming year. Taylor believes the article will need considerable revising to make it readable. Attached to the president's article are complimentary comments by two of the company vice presidents. What action should Taylor take?

Writing Improvement Exercises

6.1 Vague Expressions (L.O. 1)

YOUR TASK Revise the following to eliminate Vague expressions and other wordiness.

a. We are sending a revised proposal at this point in time due to the fact that building costs have jumped at a considerable rate.

b. In the normal course of events, we would seek additional funding; however, in view of the fact that rates have increased, we cannot.

c. In very few cases has it been advisable for us to borrow money as a means to increase our inventory.

d. Inasmuch as our Internet advertising income is increasing in a gradual manner, we might seek a loan in the amount of $50,000.

e. Despite the fact that we have had no response to our bid, we are still available in the event that you decide to proceed with your building project.

6.2 Long Lead-Ins (L.O. 1)

YOUR TASK Revise the following to eliminate long lead-ins and other wordiness.

a. This is an announcement to tell you that all computer passwords must be changed every six months for security purposes.

b. We are sending this memo to notify everyone that anyone who wants to apply for telecommuting must submit an application immediately.

c. I am writing this letter to inform you that your new account executive is Thomas Chan.

d. This is to warn you that cyber criminals are using sophisticated tools to decipher passwords in no time at all.

e. This message is to let you know that social media services can make it possible at this point in time to position your company at the forefront of online marketing opportunities.

6.3 *There is/are* and *it is/was* Fillers (L.O. 1)

YOUR TASK Revise the following to avoid unnecessary *there is/are* and *it is/was* fillers and other wordiness.

a. There is a password-checker that is now available that can automatically evaluate the strength of your password.

b. It is careless or uninformed individuals who are the most vulnerable to computer hackers.

c. There are computers in Internet cafes, at conferences, and in airport lounges that should be considered unsafe for any use that is personal.

d. A computer specialist told us that there are keystroke-logging devices that gather information typed on a computer, including passwords.

e. If there are any questions that you have about computer safety, please call us.

6.4 Redundancies (L.O. 1)

YOUR TASK Revise the following to avoid redundancies.

a. Because his laptop was small in size, he could carry it everywhere.

b. A basic fundamental of computer safety is to avoid storing your password on a file in your computer because criminals will look there first.

c. The manager repeated again his warning that any files that are large in size must be backed up.

d. Although the two files seem exactly identical, we should proofread each and every page.

e. The computer specialist combined together a PowerPoint presentation and a handout.

6.5 Empty Words (L.O. 1)

YOUR TASK Revise the following to eliminate empty words.

a. Are you aware of the fact that social media can drive brand awareness and customer loyalty?

b. Because of the surprising degree of response, the company expanded its free gift program.

c. I have before me your proposal, which was just delivered, and I will distribute it immediately.

d. The manager scheduled the meeting for 11 a.m. in the morning.

e. He plans to schedule online meetings on a monthly basis.

6.6 Condensing for Microblogging (L.O. 1)

YOUR TASK Read the following real Twitter messages. Then write a concise reply to each, preferably with 140 or fewer characters. Be selective in what you include. Your instructor may show you the actual responses (in the Instructor's Manual) that the company wrote.

a. **@HTWilson94 asks whether grocer Whole Foods stocks Whole Trade certified flowers all year long.**[17] Prepare a response (preferably 140 or fewer characters) based on the following information. Yes, at Whole Foods stores we are happy to offer Whole Trade certified flowers the entire year. We strongly advocate and support the Whole Trade movement, which strives to promote quality, premium price to the producer, better wages and working conditions, and the environment. However, we can't tell you exactly which certified flowers will be available at our stores and when. You

would have to check with your local store for its specific selection.

b. **@AmyJean64 sent Bank of America a tweet saying she was frustrated with a real estate short sale. "Have a contract on a house and cannot get them to return calls to finalize."**[18] Prepare a response based on the following information. You work for Bank of America, and you would very much like to help her, but you can't without certain information. You need her to send you the property address along with her name and phone number so that you can call to see how you can help. She should probably DM (direct message) you with this crucial information.

c. **@VickiK wrote to JetBlue: "I have booked a flt in July, CA-VT. Wondering about flying my wedding dress w/me. Is there a safe place to hang it on the plane?"**[19] Prepare a response based on the following information. We congratulate you on your coming wedding! We bet your wedding dress is beautiful. We don't have special closets on our planes and certainly nothing big enough for a wedding dress. But here's a suggestion. Have you considered having it shipped ahead of time? All the best wishes on your upcoming happy event!

d. **@ChrisC sent a message to Southwest Airlines saying, "This is extremely frustrating, how is it possible for your website to be down the entire day?"**[20] Prepare a response based on the following information. Southwest is very, very sorry! It's extremely frustrating to us also. We realize that you are accustomed to using this site to book flights. Our IT people tell us that the website functionality is getting better. We are not sure exactly what that means in terms of availability, but we are very hopeful that customers will be able to book their flights soon.

e. **@JamesR. sent a message to the delivery service UPS complaining, "Holy XXX. It's after 6 pm and UPS still hasn't delivered my pkg yet."** Prepare a response based on the following information. UPS makes every effort to deliver all packages promptly. For packages destined for offices, we must deliver by 3 p.m. However, for packages going to residences, our goal is to deliver by 7 p.m. But we can't always make it, so our drivers can sometimes run later. We're sorry about the wait.

f. **@calinelb sent a message to H&R Block: "YOU SUCK! I've been waiting for my return more than 3.5 months."**[21] Prepare a response based on the following. We are sorry that you feel that way. We certainly can't understand the reason for this long delay. We would like to look into the matter, but before we can respond, we need you to send a DM (direct message) to our customer service desk at @HRBlockAnswers. We will definitely check on this and get back to you.

6.7 Trite Business Phrases (L.O. 2)

YOUR TASK Revise the following sentences to eliminate trite business phrases.

a. Pursuant to your request, I will submit your repair request immediately.

b. Enclosed please find the list of customers to be used in our promotion.

c. As per your request, we are sending the contract under separate cover.

d. Every effort will be made to proceed in accordance with your wishes.

e. If we may help in any way, please do not hesitate to call.

6.8 Clichés, Slang, Buzzwords, and Wordiness (L.O. 2)

YOUR TASK Revise the following sentences to avoid confusing clichés, slang, buzzwords, and wordiness.

a. Our manager insists that we must think outside the box in promoting our new kitchen tool.

b. Although we got burned in the last contract, you can be sure we will stand our ground this time.

c. Beyond the shadow of a doubt, our lousy competitor will make another snarky claim that is way below the belt.

d. Team leader Sandra did not know that we were literally famished and hangry b/c someone 4got to order lunch.

e. Although I know our team is totally zonked and depressed after our comprehensive presentation bombed, this is not the time to trash each other or knock management.

6.9 Buried Verbs and Zombie Nouns (L.O. 2)

YOUR TASK Revise the following to recover buried verbs and convert zombie nouns.

a. After making an investigation, the fire department reached the conclusion that the blaze was set intentionally.

b. Our committee made a promise to give consideration to your proposal at its next meeting.

c. When used properly, zero-based budgeting can bring about a reduction in overall costs.

d. Did our department put in an application for increased budget support?

e. The budget committee has not taken action on any projects yet.

f. Homeowners must make a determination of the total value of their furnishings.

6.10 Lists, Bullets, and Headings (L.O. 3)

YOUR TASK Revise the following poorly written sentences and paragraphs using lists, bullets, and category headings, if appropriate. Improve parallel construction while reducing wordiness.

a. **Three Best Twitter Practices.** There are three simple ways you can build an online following, drive your reputation, and develop customers' trust by using these uncomplicated and simple Twitter practices. First off, share some of your photos and information about your business from behind the scenes. Sharing is so important! Next, listen. That is, you should regularly monitor the comments about your company, what's being said about your brand, and any chatter about your products. And, of course, you should respond. In real time it is necessary to respond to statements that are compliments as well as just general feedback.

b. Revise the following by incorporating a numbered list.

Computer passwords are a way of life at this point in time. In the creation of a strong password, you should remember a few things. First, you should come up with an eight-word phrase that is easy to remember, such as *my favorite uncle was a firefighter in Cleveland.* Then take each of those words and the first letter should be selected, such as *mfuwafic.* The last step for creating a really strong password is to exchange—that is, swap out— some of those letters for characters and capital letters, such as *Mf@w&%iC.*

c. Revise the following by incorporating a bulleted list with category headings.

Auto accidents account for a high number of accidental deaths. The most common causes of these accidents are due to the following causes. In all probability, the most common cause is distracted drivers. Talking on smartphones, applying makeup, texting, eating food, and reading the morning newspaper are all common ways that drivers are being distracted. Another cause is most assuredly impaired driving. Alcohol and drugs impair judgment and reaction times. This obviously results in accidents. Another cause has got to be aggressive drivers. Being an aggressive driver instead of a defensive driver puts you at risk for getting involved in an accident. Finally, road rage is a significant cause. Drivers who get angry easily and then take it out on other drivers are one of the leading causes of accidents.

d. Revise the following by incorporating a bulleted list with category headings.

There are many people today who want to improve their credit scores. Some simple tips for bumping up your score are obvious. For one thing, you should immediately fix mistakes. If you check your credit report (you should do this at least once a year) and there are errors, you can dispute these and have them investigated. Another way to improve your credit score is to pay on time. At least 35 percent of your score is a direct result of your payment history. Next, you should make an effort to lower and reduce your balances. It may be difficult, but you should keep your personal credit balances as low as possible. The less you're using, the better for your score. Finally, making a habit of keeping older accounts will improve your score. This means that you should keep your older cards so that you have a longer history to share. It also shows stability.

Activities

6.11 Document for Analysis: Ineffective E-Mail Suggestion (L.O. 1–5)

E-Mail **Team**

YOUR TASK Study the following poorly written e-mail message. In teams or in class discussion, list at least five specific weaknesses. If your instructor directs, revise to remedy vague expressions, long lead-ins, *there is/there are* fillers, trite business expressions, clichés, buried verbs, lack of parallelism, lack of plain English, and other problems.

To: Roger M. Karjala <r.m.karjala@firstbank.com>
From: Keiko Kurtz <k.kurtz@firstbank.com>
Subject: One Way to Improve Customer Relations

Mr. Karjala,

Because of the fact that you asked for suggestions on how to improve customer relations, I am submitting my idea. I am writing you this message to let you know that I think we can improve customer satisfaction easy by making a change in our counters.

Last December glass barriers were installed at our branch. There are tellers on one side and customers on the other. The barriers have air vents to be able to allow us tellers to carry on communication with our customers. Management thought that these barriers that are bullet proof would prevent and stop thieves from catapulting over the counter.

However there were customers who were surprised by these large glass partitions. Communication through them is really extremely difficult and hard. Both the customer and the teller have to raise their voices to be heard. It's even more of an inconvenience when you are dealing with a person that is elderly or someone who happens to be from another country. Beyond a shadow of a doubt, these new barriers make customers feel that they are being treated impersonally.

I did research into the matter of these barriers and made the discovery that we are the only bank in town with them. There are many other banks that are trying casual kiosks and open counters to make customers feel that they are more at home.

Although it may be easier said than done, I suggest that we actually give serious consideration to the removal of these barriers as a beginning and initial step toward improving customer relations.

Keiko Kurtz

E-mail: k.kurtz@firstbank.com

[Full contact information]

6.12 Document for Analysis: Improving Wordy Request (L.O. 1–5)

E-Mail

YOUR TASK The following wordy, inefficient, and disorganized message invites department heads to three interviewing sessions to select student interns. However, to be effective, this message needs revision. Study the message and list at least five weaknesses. Then revise to avoid excessive wordiness and repetition. Also think about how to develop an upbeat tone and improve readability. Can you reduce this sloppy 15-sentence message to six efficient sentences plus a list—and still convey all the necessary information?

To: Department Heads
From: Christina Miranda <cmiranda@cheyenne.com>
Subject: Interns

As you probably know, your management team has been discussing the possibility of having interns. We just made the decision to offer compensation to the interns in an internship program because in two fields (computer science and information systems) interns are usually paid, which is the norm. However, you may be disappointed to learn that we can offer only three internships.

In working with our nearby state university, we have narrowed the field to six excellent candidates. These six candidates will be interviewed. This is to inform you that you are invited to attend three interviewing sessions for these student candidates. Your presence is required at these sessions to help us avoid making poor selections.

Mark your calendars for the following three times. The first meeting is April 5 in the conference room. The second meeting is April 7 in Office 3 (the conference room was scheduled). On April 15 we can finish up in the conference room. All of the meetings will start at 2 p.m. In view of the fact that your projects need fresh ideas and talented new team members, I should not have to urge you to attend and be well prepared. There are six candidates that you should rank in order of your preference.

We ask that you examine the résumés of the candidates at the company website and send me your ranking lists before March 25.

Christina Miranda
[Full contact information]

6.13 Document for Analysis: Manager's Wordy Warning About Malicious Viruses (L.O. 1–5)

E-Mail

YOUR TASK Study the following ineffective message from a manager to employees and staff. It suffers from numerous wordy constructions covered in this chapter. Study the message and list at least five weaknesses. Then revise to avoid excessive wordiness and repetition.

To: Employees and Staff
From: Zach Brogdon <zbrogdon@fisher.com>
Subject: Computer Attacks

I am sending this message because an outbreak of e-mail viruses is attacking many organizations, I think it's a good time to give consideration to five incredibly important tips that are really helpful in preventing infection on your machine. Following are the tips:

Tip 1: Before opening an incoming e-mail, check the address of the person who sent the message. This is usually in the header. If it looks suspicious, don't open.

Tip 2. Look carefully at the subject line. Does it claim your account will be suspended or your account suffered an unauthorized login attempt? Attempts at urgency often are clues to malicious e-mail.

Tip 3. Do you see that the sender doesn't seem to know your name and that you are addressed anonymously as "Valued Customer"? Senders who are legitimate in all probability know your name.

Tip 4. In the matter of attachments, click only on those from senders that you know. There is danger in attachments because that's where viruses may hide or lurk.

Tip 5. Don't believe everything you see printed in an e-mail. Scammers are spectacularly clever at spoofing brands that we all know.

As a final note, if an incoming e-mail looks fishy, please use **Delete**, which will permanently delete the e-mail. Don't just delete, which does not remove it permanently. I hope these tips are useful!!

Zach B.
[Full contact information]

6.14 How Much Writing Is Required in Your Career Area? (L.O. 1–5)

The best way to learn about on-the-job writing is to talk with someone who has a job similar to the one you hope to have one day.

YOUR TASK Interview someone working in your field of study. Your instructor may ask you to present your findings orally or in a written report. Ask questions such as these: What kind of writing do you do? What kind of planning do you do before writing? Where do you get information? Do you brainstorm? Make lists? Do you compose on a computer or on a different device? How many e-mail messages do you typically write in a day? How long does it take you to compose a routine one- or two-page memo, e-mail, or letter? Do you revise? How often? Do you have a preferred method for proofreading? When you have questions about grammar and mechanics, what or whom do you consult? Does anyone read your drafts and make suggestions? Can you describe your entire composition process? Do you ever work with others to produce a document? How does this process work? What makes writing easier or harder for you? Have your writing methods and skills changed since you left school?

Test Your Workplace Etiquette IQ

New communication platforms and casual workplace environments have blurred the lines of appropriateness, leaving workers wondering how to navigate uncharted waters. Check your workplace etiquette IQ by deciding whether the following statements are true or false. Then see if you agree with the responses on p. Key-5.

1. As a manager, you learn that your employee Shelby is having exploratory surgery. Other employees ask you why Shelby is missing work. Although you would like to show concern and sympathy, it's better not to disclose personal information about employees.

_____ True _____ False

2. Although you would not enter an office with a closed door without knocking, cubicles have no doors. Therefore, it's senseless to consider knocking before entering.

_____ True _____ False

3. In a new position, you are pleasantly surprised to find that your boss is about your age and seems very friendly. The best strategy for your career is to strive to become good buddies with your boss.

_____ True _____ False

Chat About It

In each chapter you will find five discussion questions related to the chapter material. Your instructor may assign these topics for you to discuss in class, in an online chat room, or on an online discussion board. Some of the discussion topics may require outside research. You may also be asked to read and respond to postings made by your classmates.

TOPIC 1: As a new employee, you are unsure about the tone you should use in e-mail messages. To show your authenticity and warmth, you are inclined to throw in exclamation points liberally because they truly show how you feel. How can you be guided in knowing how much freedom you have in expressing yourself?

TOPIC 2: Many years ago renowned writing expert William Zinsser declared, "Clutter is the disease of American writing. We are a society strangling in unnecessary words, circular constructions, pompous frills and meaningless jargon."[22] Do you think he was too harsh? Do you believe he might feel differently about today's business writing?

TOPIC 3: When you tackle a serious writing project, do you prefer freewriting, in which you rapidly record your thoughts, or do you prefer to polish and revise as you go? What are the advantages and disadvantages of each method for you? Do you use the same method for both short and long messages?

TOPIC 4: French mathematician and philosopher Blaise Pascal is said to have excused himself wittily for the extravagant length of one of his letters by saying he had not the time to make it shorter.[23] Cicero, John Locke, Benjamin Franklin, Henry David Thoreau, Woodrow Wilson, and many other authors have made similar clever remarks when referring to the time it takes to write concisely. How do these remarks relate to the process of revision?

TOPIC 5: Are you a good proofreader? Is it easier to find other people's errors than your own? Why? What are you good at finding? What do you frequently miss?

Grammar and Mechanics Review 6

Semicolons and Colons

Review Guides 27 through 30 about semicolons and colons in Appendix D, Grammar and Mechanics. On a separate sheet, revise the following sentences to correct errors in semicolon and colon usage. Do not start new sentences. For each error that you locate, write the guide number that reflects this usage. The more you recognize the reasons, the better you will learn these punctuation guidelines. If a sentence is correct, write _C_. When finished, compare your responses with the key at the end of the book.

EXAMPLE: New products require flashy names consequently developers often hire naming specialists.

REVISION: New products require flashy **names; consequently,** developers often hire naming specialists. [Guide 27]

1. New product names must be interesting however many of the best names are already taken.

2. Although developers dreamed up a snazzy new app; it lacked an exciting name.

3. Tech specialists find it difficult to name new products, consequently they prefer hiring specialists.

4. A distinctive name helps establish the tone for a product; it acts as the primary handle for a brand.

5. Branding a product is a creative endeavor, the name becomes a product's shorthand.

6. Global names must be appealing in such faraway places as Beijing, China, Yokohama, Japan, and Dubai City, United Arab Emirates.

7. One naming expert warned companies with the following comment: "Be aware of global consequences. For example, Bimbo is the name of a Mexican baking conglomerate. However, the word in English has an unsavory meaning."

8. Company and product names are developed by combining the following three linguistic elements; morphemes, phonemes, and syntax.

9. Some English sounds (such as L, V, F, and W) are considered feminine, others (such as X, M, and Z) are viewed as masculine.

10. Among the company officers judging new names were Daniele Waters, vice president, Rachel Lohr, CFO, and Lucia Rosales, manager.

Short Workplace Messages and Digital Media

LEARNING OUTCOMES

After studying this chapter, you should be able to do the following:

1 Examine the professional usage, structure, and format of e-mails and memos in the digital era workplace.

2 Explain workplace messaging and texting including their liabilities and best practices.

3 Identify professional applications of business podcasts and the professional standards underpinning them.

4 Describe how businesses use blogs to connect with external and internal audiences.

5 Discuss business organizations' external and internal social media practices.

Be Safe. Be Free. Be Authentic: Cybersecurity Firm Averon on a Mission to Solve a Big Problem

Hardly a month goes by without news about yet another data breach. Four Chinese members of the military have been indicted for hacking credit agency Equifax in a massive stealth operation, capturing reams of sensitive consumer data.[1] Target, Home Depot, and Anthem are but a few companies attacked by bad actors. With the arrival of the Internet of Things, Americans are facing the prospect of cybercriminals targeting smart homes, security cameras, and connected vehicles. Experts tell consumers to use strong passwords, password managers, and two-factor authentication to add a layer of security by receiving a verification code. The bad news: Existing cybersecurity measures, including biometrics, are highly vulnerable. Inconvenience compounds the problem as 60 percent of online traffic now runs on mobile devices. Cumbersome password resets prompt 33 percent of online shoppers to abandon their shopping carts; 74 percent of consumers switch to a site where purchasing is easier.[2]

Enter Averon. The San Francisco-based start-up—with a world-class team of 17 serial entrepreneurs, prolific inventors, brilliant engineers, and security experts—is not a household name. In the world of cybersecurity, though, the award-winning company owning 29 patents has an outsized reputation. Co-founded in 2016 by acclaimed computer scientist Wendell Brown and venture-capital expert Lea Tarnowski, Averon has developed the world's first fully automatic and ultra-secure mobile identity verification standard that works on Wi-Fi and LTE. The revolutionary solution, Direct Autonomous Authentication (DAA), leverages existing technology that mobile carriers are using to identify, track, and bill customers through their encrypted SIM cards. The smartphone with its phone number, confirmed by the carrier in real time, serves as a stand-in for the user's identity. A SIM-based digital key means strong security and smooth user experience in any online transaction. And no more passwords! More than that, Averon's cybersecurity platform is poised to combat fake news, election tampering, financial hacking, e-mail account hijacking, and cyberterrorism, Lea Tarnowski says.[3] Users will be able to authenticate videos by identifying their source to recognize deep fakes.

Until recently Averon did not have a headquarters but now maintains offices in San Francisco and New York City. The firm relies on technology to connect its far-flung team. Members communicate by e-mail, messaging apps, and conference calls. Occasional offsite meetings bring the team together at a swanky California hotel for 2 or 3 days. You'll learn more about Averon and be asked to complete a relevant task at the end of this chapter.

Critical Thinking

- How do you feel about log-in credentials and cybersecurity? How do you handle your passwords, and do you believe they are safe? Have you ever been hacked?

- After studying teamwork in Chapter 2, you may be able to reflect on the purposes of Averon's offsite meetings. What effects might such periodic all-staff gatherings in upscale hotels have for a small dispersed team?

- Microsoft is also working on passwordless solutions but is betting on multifactor authentication (one-time codes, biometrics, hardware tokens, and more). Rob Lefferts, corporate vice president for security at Microsoft, has warned that "Cybersecurity is the central challenge of the digital age. Without it, the most basic human rights like privacy cannot exist."[4] Aside from lost privacy, what other threats may follow from weak cybersecurity?

7-1 Communicating in the Digital Age With E-Mails and Memos

We are social and mobile. Communication is rapidly evolving in this digital era. The Web has advanced from mere storage of passively consumed information to a dynamic, highly networked environment. Users are empowered, active participants who create and edit content, review products, and share information as well as media. The distinction between online and offline is becoming blurry as our virtual and real-life connectedness intertwines. As we engage socially almost all the time, our reliance on smartphones and other mobile electronic devices only keeps growing.

Messages are shorter and more frequent, and response time has become much faster. Social media platforms such as Instagram, YouTube, Facebook, and Twitter have transformed communication from one-on-one conversations to one-to-many transmissions. Social media and networking apps have also revolutionized the way we keep in touch with friends and family.

Concurrently, mobile phone ownership has skyrocketed to 96 percent of Americans who own a cellphone; smartphone ownership has shot up to 81 percent, up from 35 percent within just nine years.[5] In many businesses ever-smaller laptops, netbooks, smartphones, and tablets are making desktop computers obsolete. The powerful mobile devices access data and applications stored in the **cloud**, in remote networks, not on individual computers in an office. **Virtual private networks** (VPNs) offer secure access to organizations' information from any location in the world that provides an Internet connection. For better or for worse, businesspeople are increasingly connected 24/7.

You are probably Internet savvy, but you may need to understand how businesses use communication technologies to transmit and share information. This chapter explores short forms of workplace communication, beginning with e-mail, which many workers love to hate, and memos, which are fading away but still necessary in many organizations. Furthermore, you will learn about workplace messaging, interoffice chat applications, and comprehensive internal communication platforms. You will study business podcasts, corporate blogs, and professional social media use before exploring many contemporary cyberthreats. Familiarizing yourself with these workplace technologies and best practices can save you time, reduce blunders, and boost your credibility as a professional.

7-1a E-Mail: Going Strong at 50

For at least a decade, critics have been saying that e-mail is outdated, inefficient, and slowly dying. They complain that it takes too much time and increases stress. In the meantime, roughly 50 years after the first e-mail was sent, total e-mail traffic keeps growing 4 percent a year worldwide. More than 4 billion global e-mail users exchange almost 310 billion e-mails per day.[7] Despite social media, chat, texting, and mobile messaging of all kinds, most business messages are still sent by e-mail—not to mention that many Internet accounts require an e-mail address for sign-up.[8] Office workers receive on average 120 messages a day; globally, 125 billion business e-mails are exchanged daily.[9] Moreover, when it comes to marketing, e-mail is very much alive and kicking, as we will see in Chapter 10.

Neither social media, texting, augmented reality, and video chatting, nor phishing, hacking, and spam have diminished the high importance of e-mail in the workplace. Not even popular applications such as the interoffice chat program Slack are likely to replace e-mail anytime soon, although Slack is also an ideal collaboration tool.[10] Tech expert Alexis Madrigal is one of many staunch defenders of e-mail: "You can't kill email!" he once declared. "It's the cockroach of the Internet, and I mean that as a compliment. This resilience is a good thing."[11] Another e-mail proponent argues that e-mail is technologically far superior to social media, messaging, and collaboration platforms; he offers advice on turning e-mail into the biggest, "least-distracting," and most sophisticated social network, allowing greater privacy.[12]

E-mail has replaced paper memos for many messages inside organizations and some letters to external audiences. Most businesspeople (85 percent) now first open their e-mail on mobile devices.[13] Because you can expect to use e-mail extensively to communicate at work, it's smart to learn how to do it expertly. You may have to adjust the messaging practices you currently follow for texting, chatting, and posting on Instagram, Snapchat, or Facebook, but turning out professional e-mails is an easily attainable goal.

Tetiana Yurchenko/Shutterstock.com

Common Complaints About E-Mail.

Although e-mail is recognized as the mainstay of business communication, it's not always done well. Business journalist Suzy Welch is emphatic that sloppiness and mistakes are not an option: "You may like to write off-the-cuff, train-of-thought messages, because it's fast and easy," she says, "but no one wants to receive them, OK? No one."[14] Author Vicky Oliver insists that more than one typo per e-mail is unprofessional. She also complains about impersonal "one-line emails that are so transactional they sound like an automaton is responding."[15] Goldman Sachs CEO David Solomon is eager to hire graduates with liberal arts backgrounds because writing skills in general are increasingly harder to find, he laments.[16]

In addition to the complaints about confusing and poorly written e-mails, many people are overwhelmed with too many messages. Workers report that they spend about five hours a day reading and writing e-mail, approximately three hours on work e-mail, and two hours on personal messages.[17] Social computing expert Gloria Mark says that e-mail use is about being in control, stressing out workers who struggle in vain to bring down their clogged inboxes to zero. For a study Mark cut off participants from e-mail for a week and found significant reductions in stress levels.[18] She also discovered that white-collar workers check their e-mail 77 times a day on average—but some individuals as often as 373 times a day, substantially heightening their anxiety.[19]

Some of those messages are unnecessary, such as those that merely confirm receipt of a message or ones that express thanks. The overuse of *Reply All* adds to the inbox, irritating those who must skim and delete dozens of messages that barely relate to them. Others blame e-mail for eliminating the distinction between work life and home life. They feel pressure to be available 24/7 and respond immediately.

The Scary Permanence of Digital Messages.

Still other e-mail senders fail to recognize how dangerous e-mail can be. After deletion, e-mail files still leave trails on servers within and outside organizations. Messages are also backed up on other servers, making them traceable and recoverable by forensic experts many years later. Long-forgotten messages may turn up in court cases as damaging and sometimes costly evidence. BP engineer Brian Morel e-mailed the following note to a colleague six days before the disastrous explosion of the Deepwater Horizon oil platform off the coast of Louisiana that killed 11 workers. He said, "This has been a nightmare well which has everyone all over the place." This and other incriminating e-mails prompted BP to agree to a decade-long compensation process totaling $65 billion to settle 300 lawsuits.[21] Nevertheless, some oil-contaminated Gulf wetlands may never fully recover.[22]

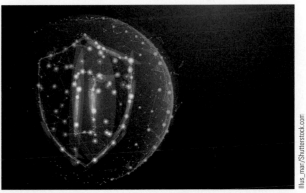

Illus_mar/Shutterstock.com

Organizations can legally monitor their staff's personal e-mail accounts too if the workers access them on the company's computer network. Moreover, if employees set up their company's e-mail on their smartphones, they have given their employer the right to remotely delete all personal data on that mobile device.[23] Even writers with nothing to hide should be concerned about what may come back to haunt them. Your best bet is to put nothing in an e-mail message that you wouldn't post on your office door. Also be sure that you know your organization's e-mail policy before sending personal messages or forwarding work-related information to your personal e-mail account. Estimates suggest that as many as a third of bosses have fired an employee for an e-mail or Internet-related violation.[24]

Despite its dark side, e-mail has many advantages and remains a prime communication channel. Therefore, it's to your advantage to learn when and how to use it efficiently and safely.

Knowing When E-Mail Is Appropriate.

Over time, e-mail has displaced much of traditional internal and external mail, and it almost never stops coming. Short informal messages now mostly travel by text, instant messenger, or chat. In comparison, e-mail is appropriate for longer, more involved, and well-organized messages that may provide or request information and respond to inquiries. It is

Ethics ✔ Check

Bcc: Sneaky and Rude?

Some workers use *Bcc* (*blind carbon copy*) to copy their friends and colleagues on e-mails when they don't want the recipient to know that a third party will also read the message. Do you believe that hiding copies from the recipient is harmless and acceptable?

Reality Check

Electronic Messages Don't Die

"Email never goes away, ever, ever, ever. The rule of thumb is if you wouldn't say it to your mother, don't put it in an email. . . . Emails are archived like crazy. They are on servers you have never heard of."[20]

—Judith Kallos, *e-mail etiquette expert*

especially effective for messages to multiple receivers and messages that must be archived (saved). An e-mail is also appropriate as a cover document when sending longer attachments and media.

E-mail, however, is not a substitute for face-to-face conversations or telephone calls. These channels are much more successful if your goal is to convey enthusiasm or warmth, explain a complex situation, present a persuasive argument, or smooth over disagreements. One expert advises delivering messages in person when they "require a human moment"—that is, when they are emotional, require negotiation, and relate to personnel.[25] Researchers have found that people are 34 times more likely to comply with in-person requests than those sent by e-mail; the scholars also established that most office workers overestimate the persuasiveness of e-mail.[26]

7-1b Composing Professional E-Mails

Professional e-mails are quite different from messages you may send to friends. Instead of casual words tossed off in haste, professional e-mails are well-considered messages that involve all three stages of the writing process. They have compelling subject lines, appropriate greetings, well-organized bodies, and complete closing information.

Draft a Compelling but Concise Subject Line.   The most important part of an e-mail is its subject line—not surprising when writers can expect that their messages will be viewed on mobile devices. To improve your chances that your e-mails will be read, avoid meaningless statements such as *Help, Urgent,* or *Meeting.* Summarize the purpose of the message clearly and make the receiver want to open the message. Try to include a verb (*Need You to Attend Las Vegas Trade Show*). In some instances the subject line can be the entire message (*Meeting Changed From May 3 to May 10*). Also be sure to adjust the subject line if the topic changes after a thread of replies emerges.

Include a Greeting.   To help recipients see the beginning of a message and to help them recognize whether they are the primary or secondary receiver, include a greeting, also called a salutation. The greeting sets the tone for the message and reflects your audience analysis. For friends and colleagues, try friendly greetings (*Hi, Sandra, Thanks, Sandra, Good morning, Sandra,* or *Greetings, Sandra*). For more formal messages and those to outsiders, include an honorific and last name (*Dear Ms. Stevens*).

Organize the Body for Readability and Tone.   In the revision phase, ask yourself how you could make your message more readable. Did you start directly? Did you group similar topics together? Could some information be presented with bulleted or numbered lists? Could you add headings—especially if the message contains more than a few paragraphs? Do you see any phrases or sentences that could be condensed? Get rid of wordiness, but don't sacrifice clarity. If a longer sentence is necessary for comprehension, then keep it. To convey the best tone, read the message aloud. If it sounds curt, it probably is.

Close Effectively.   At the end of your message, include an action statement with due dates and requests. Although complimentary closes are unnecessary, you might include a friendly closing such as *Many thanks* or *Warm regards.* Do include your name because messages without names become confusing when forwarded or when they are part of a long string of responses.

For most messages, include full contact information in a signature block that can be inserted automatically. Model Document 7.1 illustrates a typical e-mail with proper formatting.

7-1c Keeping Your Inbox in Check

Instead of letting your inbox consume your time and crimp your productivity, you can control it by observing a few time-management strategies. The most important strategy is checking your e-mail at set times, such as first thing in the morning and again after lunch or at 4 p.m. To avoid being distracted, be sure to turn off your audio and visual alerts. No fair peeking! If mornings are your best working times, check your e-mail later in the day. Discuss with your boss your schedule for responding and share it with your colleagues.

Another excellent time-saver is the two-minute rule. If you can read and respond to a message within two minutes, then take care of it immediately. For messages that require more time, add

1 Prewriting

Analyze: The purpose of this e-mail is to solicit feedback regarding a casual-dress policy.

Anticipate: The message is going to a subordinate who is busy but probably eager to be consulted in this policy matter.

Adapt: Use a direct approach beginning with the main idea. Strive for a positive, professional tone rather than an autocratic, authoritative tone.

2 Drafting

Research: Collect secondary information about dress-down days in other organizations. Collect primary information by talking with company managers.

Organize: Begin with the main idea followed by a brief explanation and questions. Conclude with an end date and a reason.

Draft: Prepare the first draft remembering that the receiver is busy and appreciates brevity.

3 Revising

Edit: Rewrite questions to ensure that they are parallel and readable.

Proofread: Decide whether to hyphenate *casual-dress policy* and *dress-down days*. Be sure commas follow introductory clauses. Check question marks.

Evaluate: Does this message encourage participatory management? Will the receiver be able to answer the questions and provide feedback as requested?

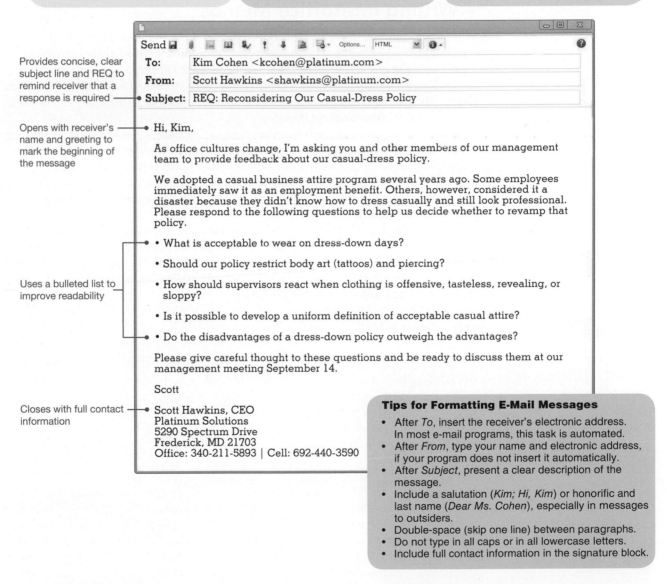

Provides concise, clear subject line and REQ to remind receiver that a response is required

Send | Options... HTML

To: Kim Cohen <kcohen@platinum.com>

From: Scott Hawkins <shawkins@platinum.com>

Subject: REQ: Reconsidering Our Casual-Dress Policy

Opens with receiver's name and greeting to mark the beginning of the message

Hi, Kim,

As office cultures change, I'm asking you and other members of our management team to provide feedback about our casual-dress policy.

We adopted a casual business attire program several years ago. Some employees immediately saw it as an employment benefit. Others, however, considered it a disaster because they didn't know how to dress casually and still look professional. Please respond to the following questions to help us decide whether to revamp that policy.

Uses a bulleted list to improve readability

• What is acceptable to wear on dress-down days?

• Should our policy restrict body art (tattoos) and piercing?

• How should supervisors react when clothing is offensive, tasteless, revealing, or sloppy?

• Is it possible to develop a uniform definition of acceptable casual attire?

• Do the disadvantages of a dress-down policy outweigh the advantages?

Please give careful thought to these questions and be ready to discuss them at our management meeting September 14.

Scott

Closes with full contact information

Scott Hawkins, CEO
Platinum Solutions
5290 Spectrum Drive
Frederick, MD 21703
Office: 340-211-5893 | Cell: 692-440-3590

Tips for Formatting E-Mail Messages

• After *To*, insert the receiver's electronic address. In most e-mail programs, this task is automated.
• After *From*, type your name and electronic address, if your program does not insert it automatically.
• After *Subject*, present a clear description of the message.
• Include a salutation (*Kim; Hi, Kim*) or honorific and last name (*Dear Ms. Cohen*), especially in messages to outsiders.
• Double-space (skip one line) between paragraphs.
• Do not type in all caps or in all lowercase letters.
• Include full contact information in the signature block.

them to your to-do list or schedule them on your calendar. To be polite, send a quick note telling the sender when you plan to respond. Blogger and podcaster Merlin Mann suggests that "Your job is not to read an email and then read it again." Instead, he recommends taking one of five steps right away: delete, delegate, respond, defer, or do.[27]

7-1d Replying Efficiently With Down-Editing

When answering e-mail, a useful skill to develop is **down-editing**. This involves inserting your responses into parts of the incoming message. After a courteous opening, your reply message will include only the parts of the incoming message to which you are responding. Delete the sender's message headers, signature, and all unnecessary parts. Your responses can be identified with your initials, if more than one person will be seeing the response. Another efficient trick is to use a different color for your down-edits. It takes a little practice to develop this skill, particularly formatting the e-mail, but the down-edited reply reduces confusion, saves writing and reading time, and makes you look savvy.

Figure 7.1 shows additional best practices for managing your e-mail.

7-1e Writing Interoffice Memos

In addition to e-mail, you should be familiar with another workplace document type, the interoffice memorandum. Although e-mail has largely replaced memos, you may still be called on to use the memo format in specific instances. Memos are necessary for important internal messages that (a) are too long for e-mail, (b) require a permanent record, (c) demand formality, or (d) inform employees who may not have access to e-mail. Within organizations, memos deliver changes in procedures, official instructions, and reports.

The memo format is particularly necessary for complex internal messages that are too long for e-mail. Prepared as memos, long messages are then delivered as attachments to e-mail cover messages. Memos seem to function better as permanent records than e-mail messages because the latter may be difficult to locate and may contain a trail of confusing replies. E-mails also may change the origination date whenever the file is accessed, thus making it impossible to know the original date of the message.

When preparing e-mail attachments, be sure that they carry sufficient identifying information. Because the cover e-mail message may become separated from the attachment, the attachment must be named thoughtfully. Preparing the e-mail attachment as a memo provides a handy format that identifies the date, sender, receiver, and subject. See Model Document 10.5 for an example of an e-mail sent with a memo attachment.

FIGURE 7.1   Best Practices for Better E-Mail

Getting Started

- Don't write if another channel—such as real-time chat, instant message, SMS, social media post, or a phone call—might work better.
- Send only content you would want published.
- Write compelling subject lines, possibly with names and dates: *Jake: Can You Present at January 10 Staff Meeting?*

Replying

- Scan all e-mails, especially those from the same person. Answer within 24 hours or say when you will.
- Change the subject line if the topic changes. Check the threaded messages below yours.
- Practice down-editing; include only the parts from the incoming e-mail to which you are responding.
- Start with the main idea.
- Use headings and lists.

Observing Etiquette

- Obtain approval before forwarding.
- Soften the tone by including a friendly opening and closing.
- Resist humor and sarcasm. Absent facial expression and tone of voice, humor can be misunderstood.
- Avoid writing in all caps, which is like SHOUTING.

Closing Effectively

- End with due dates, next steps to be taken, or a friendly remark.
- Add your full contact information including social media addresses.
- Edit your text for readability. Proofread for typos or unwanted auto-corrections.
- Double-check before hitting **Send.**

Similarities Between Memos and E-Mails. Memos have much in common with e-mails. Both usually carry nonsensitive information that may be organized directly with the main idea first. Both have guide words calling for a subject line, a dateline, and the identification of the sender and receiver. To enhance readability, both should be organized with headings, bulleted lists, and enumerated items whenever possible.

E-mails and memos both generally close with (a) action information, dates, or deadlines; (b) a summary of the message; or (c) a closing thought. An effective memo or e-mail closing might be, *Please submit your written report to me by June 15 so that we can review your data before our July planning session.* In more detailed messages, a summary of main points may be an appropriate closing. If no action request is made and a closing summary is unnecessary, you might end with a simple concluding thought (*I'm glad to answer your questions* or *This sounds like a useful project*).

You need not close messages to coworkers with goodwill statements such as those found in letters to customers or clients. However, some closing thought is often necessary to avoid sounding abrupt. Closings can show gratitude or encourage feedback with remarks such as *I sincerely appreciate your help* or *What are your ideas on this proposal?* Other closings look forward to what's next, such as *How would you like to proceed?* Avoid closing with overused expressions such as *Please let me know if I may be of further assistance*. This ending sounds mechanical and insincere.

In Model Document 7.2, notice how interoffice memos are formatted and how they can be created to improve readability with lists and white space. The accompanying checklist offers tips for creating professional e-mail messages and memos.

Checklist

Professional E-Mails and Memos

Subject Line

- **Summarize the central idea.** Express concisely what the message is about and how it relates to the reader.

- **Include labels if appropriate.** Labels such as *FYI* (*for your information*) and *REQ* (*required*) help receivers recognize how to respond.

- **Avoid empty or ambiguous words.** Don't write one-word subject lines such as *Help*, *Problem*, or *Free*.

Opening

- **State the purpose for writing.** Include the same information that is in the subject line, but expand it to a complete sentence.

- **Highlight questions.** If you are requesting information, begin with the most important question, use a polite command (*Please answer the following questions about . . .*), or introduce your request courteously.

- **Supply information directly.** If responding to a request, give the reader the requested information immediately in the opening. Explain later.

Body

- **Explain details.** Arrange information logically. For detailed topics develop separate coherent paragraphs.

- **Enhance readability.** Use short sentences, short paragraphs, and parallel construction for similar ideas.

- **Apply document design.** If appropriate, provide bulleted or numbered lists, headings, tables, or other graphic devices to improve readability and comprehension.

- **Be cautious.** Remember that e-mail messages often travel far beyond their intended audiences.

Closing

- **Request action.** If appropriate, state specifically what you want the reader to do. Include a deadline, with reasons, if possible.

- **Provide a goodwill statement or a closing thought.** When communicating outside of the company or with management, include a positive goodwill statement such as *Our team enjoyed working on the feasibility report, and we look forward to your feedback*. If no action request is necessary, end with a closing thought.

- **Avoid cliché endings.** Use fresh remarks. Stay away from overused expressions such as *If you have additional questions, please do not hesitate to call* or *Thank you for your cooperation*.

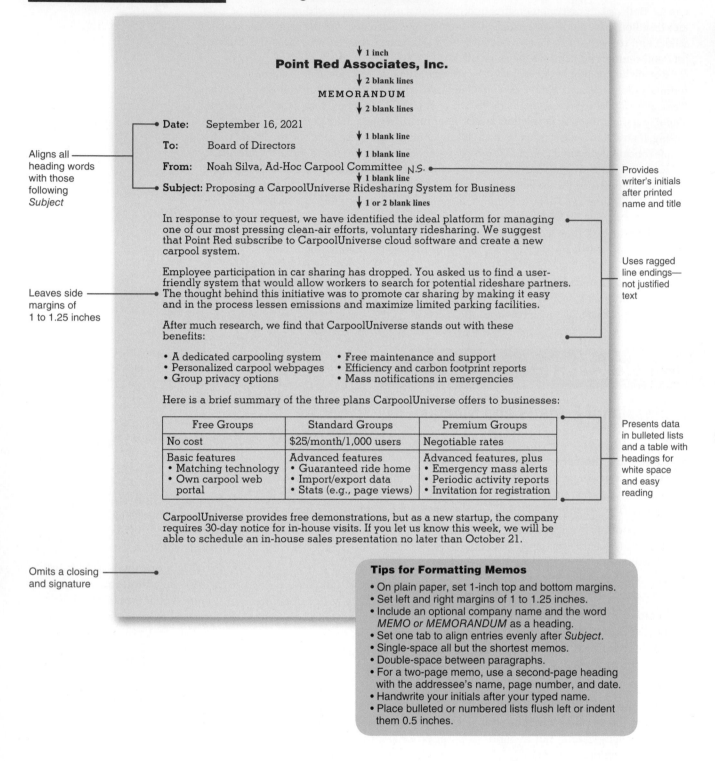

Aligns all heading words with those following *Subject*

Leaves side margins of 1 to 1.25 inches

Omits a closing and signature

↓ 1 inch
Point Red Associates, Inc.
↓ 2 blank lines
M E M O R A N D U M
↓ 2 blank lines

Date: September 16, 2021
↓ 1 blank line

To: Board of Directors
↓ 1 blank line

From: Noah Silva, Ad-Hoc Carpool Committee N.S.
↓ 1 blank line

Subject: Proposing a CarpoolUniverse Ridesharing System for Business
↓ 1 or 2 blank lines

In response to your request, we have identified the ideal platform for managing one of our most pressing clean-air efforts, voluntary ridesharing. We suggest that Point Red subscribe to CarpoolUniverse cloud software and create a new carpool system.

Employee participation in car sharing has dropped. You asked us to find a user-friendly system that would allow workers to search for potential rideshare partners. The thought behind this initiative was to promote car sharing by making it easy and in the process lessen emissions and maximize limited parking facilities.

After much research, we find that CarpoolUniverse stands out with these benefits:

- A dedicated carpooling system   • Free maintenance and support
- Personalized carpool webpages   • Efficiency and carbon footprint reports
- Group privacy options   • Mass notifications in emergencies

Here is a brief summary of the three plans CarpoolUniverse offers to businesses:

Free Groups	Standard Groups	Premium Groups
No cost	$25/month/1,000 users	Negotiable rates
Basic features • Matching technology • Own carpool web portal	Advanced features • Guaranteed ride home • Import/export data • Stats (e.g., page views)	Advanced features, plus • Emergency mass alerts • Periodic activity reports • Invitation for registration

CarpoolUniverse provides free demonstrations, but as a new startup, the company requires 30-day notice for in-house visits. If you let us know this week, we will be able to schedule an in-house sales presentation no later than October 21.

Provides writer's initials after printed name and title

Uses ragged line endings— not justified text

Presents data in bulleted lists and a table with headings for white space and easy reading

Tips for Formatting Memos

- On plain paper, set 1-inch top and bottom margins.
- Set left and right margins of 1 to 1.25 inches.
- Include an optional company name and the word *MEMO or MEMORANDUM* as a heading.
- Set one tab to align entries evenly after *Subject*.
- Single-space all but the shortest memos.
- Double-space between paragraphs.
- For a two-page memo, use a second-page heading with the addressee's name, page number, and date.
- Handwrite your initials after your typed name.
- Place bulleted or numbered lists flush left or indent them 0.5 inches.

7-2 Messaging and Texting at Work

LEARNING OUTCOME

2 Explain workplace messaging and texting including their liabilities and best practices.

Instant messaging has become a powerful communication tool in the office and on the go. It enables two or more individuals to communicate in real time by exchanging brief text-based messages. Companies large and small now provide live online chats with customer service representatives during business hours, in addition to the usual contact options, such as telephone and e-mail. Increasingly, AI-powered automated chat bots are replacing humans for routine inquiries 24/7. Facebook Messenger, WhatsApp, WeChat, Skype, and some browsers have built-in instant messaging (chat) functions. Slack is the most popular enterprise instant messaging and group chat tool.

Text messaging, or texting, is another popular means for exchanging brief messages in real time. Usually exchanged via smartphone, texting requires a short message service (SMS) supplied by a wireless service provider. A new system, rich communication services (RCS), promises advanced features such as multimedia-enhanced texts that can be customized for more appealing opt-in text alerts and mobile marketing. Increasingly, both instant and text messages are sent from mobile devices as 81 percent of Americans now own smartphones and many depend on them for Internet access.[28]

Fueled by online security and legal compliance concerns, large enterprises have bundled multiple communication and collaboration functions behind corporate firewalls. For example, Adobe Systems has developed Unicom. The Unified Communications Tool is an all-in-one internal communication platform that connects coworkers by chat, Twitter-like microblogging, an employee directory, as well as by e-mail and phone. Unicom is accessed in the office or remotely, in one easy-to-use interface, like the one presented in Figure 7.2.

FIGURE 7.2 All-in-One Messaging on an Internal Enterprise Network

To create a platform for secure and legally compliant internal communication, large companies have introduced powerful networks behind corporate firewalls that combine various capabilities in one: e-mail, chat, Twitter-like short messaging, and directory access by phone. All workers need to be professional; they are always on display. Everyone from rookie coder to CEO is on the system.

For the sake of simplicity, we will first examine short-form messaging, i.e., text messages, consumer messenger apps, and enterprise messaging tools such as Slack. Later in the chapter we will focus on enterprise-grade collaboration platforms like Unicom and their role as internal social networks.

7-2a Benefits of Instant Messaging and Texting

The major attraction of instant messaging is real-time communication with colleagues at the office or anywhere in the world—if a cell phone signal or a Wi-Fi connection is available. Facebook's Messenger and WhatsApp, Apple's iMessage, and Snapchat are popular consumer messaging apps that can also be spotted on the job. Because messaging allows people to share information immediately and make decisions quickly, its impact on business communication has been dramatic. Slack's group chat capability enables coworkers on far-flung project teams to communicate instantly or review the chat history afterward.

Like instant messaging, texting can substitute for voice calls, delivering a message between mobile phone users quickly and discreetly. Organizations around the world provide news alerts, financial information, and promotions to customers via text. Credit card accounts can be set up to notify account holders by text or e-mail of approaching payment deadlines. Embracing opt-in text marketing, Airbnb, Doordash, Lyft, Nordstrom, Subway, and hundreds of other businesses engage consumers with coupons, games, and other offers. Text alerts sent by Old Navy are shown in Figure 7.3. Marketers must follow consumer protection laws such as the Telephone Consumer Protection Act (TCPA) and the CAN-SPAM Act that restrict telemarketing and automated dialing systems, the much-hated robocalls. Some businesses, e.g., Target and Domino's Pizza, use SMS for recruitment, first by inviting applicants to opt in with a short code so that they may receive text updates at each stage of the hiring process.

FIGURE 7.3 Old Navy Uses SMS Marketing

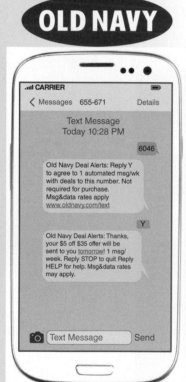

Old Navy Deal Alerts: Reply Y to agree to 1 automated msg/wk with deals to this number. Not required for purchase. Msg&data rates apply www.oldnavy.com/text

Old Navy Deal Alerts: Thanks, your $5 off $35 offer will be sent to you tomorrow! 1 msg/week. Reply STOP to quit Reply HELP for help. Msg&data rates may apply.

Old Navy encourages consumers to sign up for its mobile alert program. Once customers opt in by texting their nearest store's dedicated short code 653-689 (old-navy), they receive text messages announcing sneak peeks at new merchandise, rebates, and exclusive offers. Marketers report faster response times and increased engagement over other communication channels such as e-mail.

Source: Tatango

7-2b Risks of Messaging Apps and Texting

Despite their popularity among workers, some organizations forbid employees to use texting and instant messengers unless these tools are job-relevant and enterprise-grade. Employers consider chat and messaging yet another distraction in addition to phone calls, e-mail, and the Internet. Some organizations fear that employees using consumer-grade instant messaging apps could reveal privileged information and company records. Fearing charges of impropriety such as insider trading or interest rate manipulation following the Libor scandal, firms ranging from JPMorgan Chase, Barclays, and Citigroup to Deutsche Bank have restricted or completely banned messaging and chat apps.[29]

Compliance Requirements and Security.   The SEC and other regulators require that financial services firms track and store *all* written business communication. Banks monitor e-mails and chats on company devices and limit personal phones and messaging. However, the task may be overwhelming and onerous to some, which is why many employees are eluding oversight by communicating via encrypted apps such as WhatsApp, iMessage, and WeChat.[30] Messages on Signal or Snapchat can be set to disappear altogether, causing regulators and employers compliance headaches and fear of fraud. Bring-your-own-device (BYOD) policies may give employers access to workers' personal devices. Companies also worry about phishing (fraudulent schemes), viruses, and malware (malicious software programs). Like e-mail, any type of message and all other electronic records are subject to discovery (disclosure); that is, they can become evidence in lawsuits.

Liability Burden.   A worker's improper use of mobile devices while on company business can expose the organization to staggering legal liability. The CDC reports that even a non-fatal injury crash at work caused by distraction costs businesses on average almost $72,500. Citing growing evidence, the agency also warns that hands-free devices are just as distracting as hand-held phones.[32] When workers use messaging apps or texts to harass other workers, the employer may be culpable unless explicit rules and enforcement measures exist.

Organizations are fighting back to raise awareness and diminish liability. They are instituting detailed media use policies, now covering encrypted and ephemeral messaging apps. They also protect themselves with formal employee training and technology tools such as monitoring, filtering, and blocking.

7-2c Best Practices for Instant Messaging and Texting

Text message marketing can be highly effective if the appeal is done right. Jack in the Box reduced its reliance on e-mail campaigns by adopting SMS marketing. The fast food chain increased repeat purchases and customer engagement. Redemption rates for deals and coupons were three to five times higher than those of e-mail marketing.[33]

Aside from SMS marketing, instant messaging and texting can save time and simplify communication with coworkers and customers. However, before messaging on the job, be sure to seek approval. Because unsolicited text messages might seem invasive, ask permission first. Do not download and use third-party apps without checking with your supervisor. If your organization does allow messaging or texting for work, you can use it efficiently and professionally by following these guidelines:

- Comply with company policies: social media use, code of conduct, ethics guidelines, as well as harassment and discrimination policies.

- Don't use chats or text messages to disclose sensitive information: financial, company, customer, employee, or executive data.

- Avoid harassment and discriminatory content against classes protected by law (race, color, religion, sex, sexual orientation, national origin, age, and disability).

- Watch out for the appropriateness and security of photos, videos, and art that you link to or forward.

- As with e-mail, don't say anything that would damage your reputation or that of your organization.

- Don't text or chat driving a car. Pull over if you must read or send a message.

- Organize your contact lists to separate business contacts from family and friends.
- Avoid unnecessary chitchat, and know when to say goodbye. If personal messaging is allowed, keep it to a minimum.
- Ensure your presence status is up-to-date so that people trying to reach you don't waste their time. Make yourself unavailable when you need to meet a deadline.
- Beware of jargon, slang, and abbreviations; although they may reduce keystrokes, they can be confusing and appear unprofessional.
- Use good grammar and proper spelling.

7-2d Text Messaging and Business Etiquette

Texting is quick and unobtrusive, and for routine messages it is often the best alternative to a phone call or e-mail. Given the popularity of SMS, etiquette experts offer valuable advice.[34] Figure 7.4 summarizes the suggestions they offer for the considerate and professional use of texting.

7-2e Enterprise Messaging—Slack

As we have seen, texting and instant messaging are convenient alternatives to routine phone calls and have all but replaced e-mail for short internal communication. All the major players in tech—Facebook, Google, Apple, IBM, and Microsoft—provide instant messaging software, mostly rolled out as mobile-friendly apps, reflecting growing smartphone access. Primarily for security reasons, but also to entice businesses to commit to their complete cloud-based environment, Google, Microsoft, Adobe, and others offer popular office suite bundles that generally include personal

FIGURE 7.4 Texting Etiquette

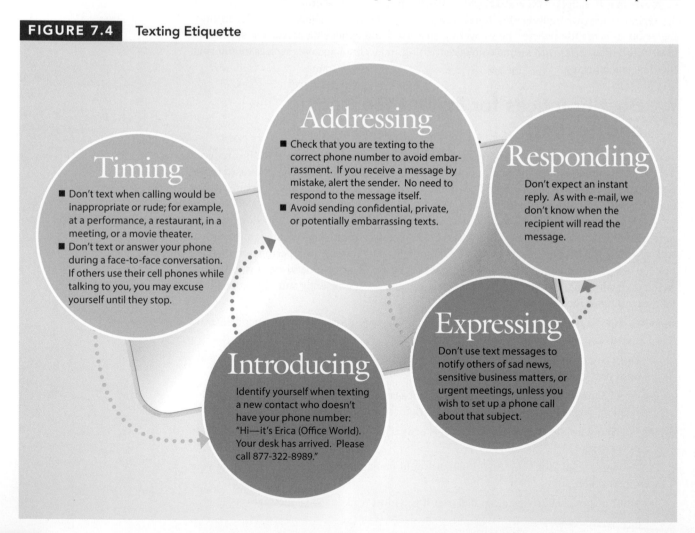

Timing
- Don't text when calling would be inappropriate or rude; for example, at a performance, a restaurant, in a meeting, or a movie theater.
- Don't text or answer your phone during a face-to-face conversation. If others use their cell phones while talking to you, you may excuse yourself until they stop.

Addressing
- Check that you are texting to the correct phone number to avoid embarrassment. If you receive a message by mistake, alert the sender. No need to respond to the message itself.
- Avoid sending confidential, private, or potentially embarrassing texts.

Responding
Don't expect an instant reply. As with e-mail, we don't know when the recipient will read the message.

Introducing
Identify yourself when texting a new contact who doesn't have your phone number: "Hi—it's Erica (Office World). Your desk has arrived. Please call 877-322-8989."

Expressing
Don't use text messages to notify others of sad news, sensitive business matters, or urgent meetings, unless you wish to set up a phone call about that subject.

productivity, communication, collaboration, and content management tools. Microsoft 365 (Skype, Teams), Google's G Suite (Hangouts), and Salesforce (Quiq) dominate the workplace. As of now, Slack is outperforming the giants.

The Upside. At 10 million daily users, Slack is popular mostly with small businesses and start-ups—so much so that it has become a verb: "Slack me" or "Yes, we Slacked."[36] Enterprise group chat apps such as Slack appeal to many workers because they declutter e-mail inboxes, simplify workplace communication, and function as digital water coolers with chat rooms (channels) to socialize in. One of Slack's main benefits is increased camaraderie as workers collaborate on main channels but also congregate in private channels to chat about mundane topics. Slack facilitates conversations across dispersed teams and time zones. Software developers, for example, tend to be heavy users. Users reviewing Slack uniformly praise its intuitive interface and ease of use for local and remote teams. They also like the seamless integration of other productivity tools with Slack, e.g., G Suite and Dropbox.[37]

Unlike e-mail, Slack is ideal for quick answers and efficient back-and-forth exchanges, but it is not suited for information dumps or lengthy discussions. Employers approve of Slack because they can securely monitor, log, and archive all communication.

The Downside. Slack critics cite three major problem areas: distraction, spillover of workplace messaging into home life, and rude behavior on the platform. Often businesses deploy Slack expecting that magically collaboration will happen without providing guidance how to use the platform. Some workers find Slack so distracting that they refuse to use it, while others cannot disengage from it. Training sessions and snoozing Slack notifications help doubters focus on work. Silencing channel notifications during downtime reduces the pressure to respond instantly and thus fosters a better work–life balance.[38] Without clear rules, workers can get overwhelmed. A recent spate of class action lawsuits has centered on the use of digital workplace and mobile apps during rest periods and outside of business hours, as Slack and similar apps are erasing the line between work and leisure.[39]

As for misconduct, the reviews are mixed. Some executives praise Slack for having a positive effect on workplace culture by providing workers with a platform to share professional and personal information. However, it's precisely the informality of Slack chat, experts say, that can also be "an incubator for misbehavior" because distinctions between professional and personal can blur.[40]

7-2f Slack Etiquette

Because Slack has the look and feel of a social media network like Facebook or Twitter, users easily slip into iMessage lingo, slang, and informal conversations. Also, chat platforms foster friendships at work, and friends tend to be casual with each other. Slack is much less formal than e-mail. To avoid the danger of accidental oversharing and forgetting you are at work, follow this "ultimate Slack etiquette guide"[41]:

- **Stay away from slang and acronyms with swear words in them.** Experts agree that swearing still has no place at work. Anticipate future readers on Slack who might dislike an ill-mannered style or rude language. Slang and trendy words grow stale quickly and aren't always understood.

- **Avoid talking about job hunting, illness, finances, or hating coworkers or your boss.** The company reads your Slack messages. It can legally access any content that passes through work devices. Keep personal issues to yourself. All chats are saved on Slack. Oversharing is forever.

Slack is ideal for quick and efficient back-and-forth exchanges. Its interface is intuitive and easy to use. Employers like Slack because they can monitor, log, and archive all communication. Some users complain that Slack is distracting.

- **Think twice about arguing**. Encrypted and ephemeral apps induce people to talk in ways they wouldn't in person through a false sense of familiarity. Slack may also enable passive-aggressive comments and even bullying. Remember you will have to look the person in the eye in the lunchroom.

- **Compliment your coworkers**. Highlight accomplishments of colleagues when deserved. In your team's main chatroom, such positive messages live on for weeks, where management may see the good work your team is doing.

- **Curb the emojis**. The occasional thumbs up or smiley face sends a friendly message, but a string of emojis is too cutesy for the workplace. Be professional; hold off on emojis in serious messages or when communicating with senior leaders at your company.

- **Use miscellaneous channels to make friends**. Aside from the main channel, companies often have miscellaneous channels for specific groups, such as remote workers. Don't share in your first week on the job, unless it's a "fun" channel for cat-lovers or NBA fanatics. Observe first.

- **Adjust your tone to your audience**. You can be colloquial with coworkers at happy hour but not with the CEO. Be professional with your boss and other executives. Leave the "LOL" for chatting with a close coworker. Follow the cues of your office.

7-3 Making Podcasts Work for Business

Professional podcasts can be elaborate productions and require quality hardware, which may explain why their use is lagging that of other corporate digital media channels. However, podcasts have their place among contemporary communication technology tools, and businesses may finally be catching on to the huge potential of podcasting as an engagement tool. In addition to discussing the role of podcasts in business today, this section includes several podcaster categories, addresses podcasters' earning strategies (monetization), identifies a few valuable business podcasts, and offers general guidelines for podcasting from seasoned practitioners.

7-3a Podcasts and Their Growing Popularity

Podcasts are digital audio programs resembling radio shows. They tend to be series of episodes that generally feature a host, sometimes two, often in an interview format. They are distributed regularly—daily, weekly, or monthly—as audio programs that can be played on demand in a Web browser or with a mobile app on various digital devices. The terms *podcast* and *podcasting* originate from combining the words *broadcasting* and *iPod*, the Apple MP3 player. Today's podcast audio can be played with many apps, most commonly in iTunes, Google Play, Spotify, and Pandora. Podcasts can cover topics as diverse as news, politics, business, sports, popular culture, and self-help. The programs can extend from short clips to 30-minute shows or much longer features. Most are pre-recorded, but some are live. Like other digital media, podcasts can be produced by individuals and organizations alike.

The growth in smartphone use and other technological advances have boosted the reach and popularity of podcasting. In the last five years alone, awareness of podcasting has grown from 50 percent to 70 percent among Americans 12 years old and up; more than half have ever listened to at least one podcast (up from a third); and 32 percent have listened to a podcast within the last month, up from 17 percent.[43] High-quality podcasts are widely available and virtually inexhaustible. Estimates suggest that 850,000 shows with more than 30 million episodes may be vying for our attention today.[44] This number is likely to keep rising. Master marketer and blogger Chris Brogan suggests that podcasting is having its heyday because Americans read fewer mainstream news sources, don't listen to terrestrial radio, and go to YouTube instead of watching TV. What's more, podcasts are easier to produce than quality video.[45]

One huge benefit of podcasting is portability. Podcasts encoded as MP3, ACC, or WMA files can be downloaded to a computer, a smartphone, a tablet, or an MP3 player to be enjoyed offline on the go. Moreover, unlike watching video that requires some focused attention, listening to a recording allows users to multitask. Busy professionals enjoy the opportunity to learn, keep informed, and be entertained while maximizing their limited time on their commute or in the gym. This flexibility also explains the growing popularity of audiobooks.

Primakov/Shutterstock.com

7-3b The Main Players in Podcasting

Podcasts can be categorized by genre (subject) and by producers and their purpose. Business is our focus; however, a clear majority of podcasts is devoted to entertainment. At 36 percent, comedy leads the weekly podcast consumption in the United States, followed by news (23 percent), society and culture (22 percent), sports (15 percent), and true crime (12 percent). Business podcasts are "consumed" only by 10 percent of weekly listeners.[46] Among podcast providers, we will focus on business organizations, podcasting entrepreneurs, news media, and podcasting in education.

Corporations and Other Businesses. Many companies are eager to jump into making a podcast series. Marketing experts estimate that half of all brands are about to launch or plan to launch their own podcasts. The advantage to companies is independence from social media algorithms and the ability to diversify their media channels. Because the investment needed for podcasting is relatively modest, businesses are encouraged to give it a try.[47]

Companies as varied as Caterpillar, IBM, and Walmart are on board with public, professionally produced podcasts. Beyond the Iron is a podcast series created by Caterpillar devoted to the company's "corporate roots and iconic products" as well as its "other brands and offerings."[48] IBM distributes a whole range of podcasts clustered around its products and tech topics. The podcasts address various audiences, external and internal, and are often paired with blogs. Some of the company's podcasts are miniseries (e.g., IBM Cloud Podcast); others are ongoing, for instance, IBM Blockchain Pulse Podcast; Making Data Simple on the IBM Big Data & Analytics Hub; and IBM Developer Podcast. Walmart Radio, the self-described "biggest retail radio show in the world,"[49] entertains employees and shoppers live in store but also publishes a series of podcast episodes featuring interviews, company news, and more.

Internally, podcasts can be used to inform, engage, and train staff. A podcast series can help convey authenticity by featuring the voices of employees and personalizing executives. Because they can broadcast repetitive information that does not require interaction, podcasts can replace costlier live teleconferences. Alternatively, teleconferences or webcasts can later be provided as podcasts to those who missed the live event. IBM is training its sales force with podcasts. The information technology company also offers highly specialized for-fee training courses as podcasts and videos behind a paywall to instruct corporate clients in the use of complex enterprise systems. Human resources policies can also be presented in the form of podcasts or videos for on-demand consumption.

Entrepreneurs and Enterprising Individuals. For the purpose of attracting listeners, it helps if the podcast host is a well-known businessperson or TV personality, whether it be sports columnist Bill Simmons or the "Matriarch of Money," Suze Orman.[50] Her Women and Money show confirms that Orman is a no-nonsense authority preaching financial literacy, and people gladly listen. Then there are those who become wealthy and Internet famous through shrewd investments and loud self-promotion on social media, entrepreneurs such as Gary Vaynerchuk and Tim Ferriss. They author best-selling self-help books, blogs, and podcasts with a loyal following.

Although he has been called a fake expert,[51] Tim Ferriss is one of America's most successful podcasters, shown in Figure 7.5. Ferriss provides podcasts on many self-improvement topics, but his interviews with businesspeople, scientists, and celebrities appear to be the most intriguing

FIGURE 7.5 A Weekly Hit Podcast: The Tim Ferriss Show

A bestselling author, Tim Ferriss is also the host of an award-winning podcast series on leadership and entrepreneurship—300+ episodes and 400 million downloads at this count. On his weekly Tim Ferriss Show, he interviews an eclectic mix of leaders, such as Disney's Bob Iger, psychologists Brené Brown and Esther Perel, filmmaker Ken Burns, or scientist and media personality Neil deGrasse Tyson. Ferriss is a master of media, whether on Instagram (1 million followers) or Twitter (1.6 million followers). He maintains a popular blog, sends out a weekly newsletter to his 1.5 million subscribers, and has been dubbed "the Oprah of audio" for his show.

Source: Spotify

feature. Countless such self-described business experts issue podcasts and amass sizable fan communities. With engaging daily episodes, founder and host John Lee Dumas ("JDL") is the creative mind behind Entrepreneurs on Fire, one of the most popular business podcasts today. JDL hosts various experts discussing topics relevant to entrepreneurs. He is selling his own success story, currently living it up in Costa Rica, and he promises this very "financial and lifestyle freedom" to his Fire Nation followers.

News and Media Organizations.

Perhaps because they already own high-value production equipment and have the necessary technical and journalistic expertise, major news organizations and media outlets podcast radio shows. National Public Radio (NPR), *Harvard Business Review, The Wall Street Journal*, and *The New York Times*, just to name a few, each distribute not one but several podcast series. The tech site Lifewire named The Daily, produced by a *New York Times* journalist team, one of the best contemporary podcasts. Other noteworthy business and tech podcasts are WSJ Secrets of Wealthy Women and WSJ's The Future of Everything. Networks from ABC to Fox podcast news, sports commentaries, and audio versions of popular TV shows.

Another notable podcast series worth exploring is the TED Radio Hour by NPR, "a narrative journey through fascinating ideas, astonishing inventions, fresh approaches to old problems, and new ways to think and create."[52] In addition to its famous TED Talks videos, the nonprofit organization produces daily TED Talks in audio format; one series serves Spanish-speaking subscribers.

Education Podcasts.

Podcasts are increasingly common in education. Instructors are catching on. Some even make their own podcasts to facilitate accessible learning for students with disabilities, add a new delivery mode benefiting auditory learners, and create an archive of lessons. To encourage teachers and students to get started in podcasting, NPR is publishing

Student Podcast Challenge. The portability of podcasts allows students to listen to instructors' lectures, interviews, sporting events, and other content anytime and anywhere. Most news outlets provide many of their shows as podcasts to enjoy on the go.

Apple's iTunes U is perhaps the best-known example of free educational programs from hundreds of renowned universities across the globe. Open University on iTunes covers a vast amount of learning resources in categories such as business and economics, engineering, history, languages, science, and many more. An Internet search reveals many options for education podcasts; an interesting one is PlayerFM. The site aggregates podcasts on a multitude of subjects and, best of all, it allows users to explore shows in English in other countries across the globe, for instance, Kenyan business podcasts or Australian breaking news.

7-3c Can Podcasts Make Money and Do They Last?

The biggest names in podcasting who command sizable audiences will attract advertisers, usually those that offer related brands and covet the listenership demographic of the show. Advertisers go where the ears are. The 2,000 most popular podcasts draw the likes of GEICO, Capital One, Progressive, Procter & Gamble brands, and TrueCar—the top five most prolific podcast advertisers among more than 9,000 brands buying podcast ads.[53] Sought-after podcasters also have sponsors and get paid for product endorsements. As a personal finance guru, Suze Orman plugs federal credit unions on her podcast website. However, promotion deals have been criticized as inevitably leading to biased recommendations.[54] Consumers should always know whether a trusted authority is being paid for endorsements.

At least one podcaster is very upfront about his total income and its origins. Dumas, the Entrepreneurs on Fire host, is displaying a real-time tally of his total monthly earnings in the top right corner on his EOFire website (almost $154,000 in a recent month). In an interview JDL disclosed five main monetization strategies: his own product, a community of 2,800 podcasters; paid endorsements; affiliate income, i.e., promoting a partner's course or venture; VIP access to JDL and other thought leaders; and consulting and speaking.[55]

7-3d How to Create a Successful Podcast

Much free advice on making podcasts is percolating on the Internet. Some clever entrepreneurs found a way to make people pay for courses on podcasting starting at $295 and up for The Podcast Host Academy. Budding podcasts producers may need to shell out as much as $2,675 for Podcast Engineering School with Chris Curran. However, if your goal is to create a less high-tech series, keep looking for free information. *PCMag* regularly runs detailed How-To instructions,[56] or follow the general tips adapted from podcast host Doree Shafrir,[57] author of *Startup*:

Consistency.   Distribute your podcast regularly. Don't skip episodes once you commit to a weekly or monthly schedule. Devoted fans will expect those episodes to arrive on time.

Topic suitable for audio and community.   Pick a topic that lends itself for audio storytelling and attracts a natural community. Ask yourself whether the audio format will work or whether the subject is better suited for writing or video. Practically no topic is too obscure or specialized for a podcast, but it needs to be interesting to a strong, well-defined fan base.

Quality recording equipment.   Produce clear audio. Listeners hate poor sound. If you don't know how to produce, hire someone who does. Other pros suggest splurging on a professional-grade microphone at a minimum, followed by a good pair of over-the-ear closed headphones. All laptops and desktops allow for recording, editing, and producing a podcast. For editing, newbies may use Audacity, a handy and free audio app. GarageBand on Apple's iOS platform is another useful app for podcast creators.

Audience building.   Obtain new listeners by mentions or guest appearances on other shows. Reach out to podcasters who discuss similar themes but also those who manage unrelated podcasts. Ask if you can be a guest or if they would plug your podcast. Use social media.

Hosting.   Use two hosts if possible. It makes for more interesting discussions, it's easier to build the audience, and it helps share the work duties.

Listener engagement.   Connect with your listeners and give them space to engage with each other. Allow for e-mail, messaging, and tweets. Create an active Facebook group for your audience.

Passion.   Make sure you're enjoying yourself. If you're not having fun, your listeners probably aren't either. Some podcasters caution that frustration is likely because creating serial episodes takes much time and effort; they point out that new podcasts are competing in a crowded market.

Of course, video is a much bigger draw on the Internet than audio. Videos range from millions of cat videos, myriad how-to instructions, and shaky user-generated smartphone footage to slick professional videos, movie previews, and entire feature films. YouTube, Vimeo, and most recently TikTok are examples of popular video hosting and sharing services. As on any other social media sites, users can upload their own creations, leave comments, and vote videos up or down. While some videos languish in obscurity, others receive millions of views, drawing advertisers and, hence, income. Most companies and brands maintain video channels as part of their overall media strategy. More coverage of YouTube is included in our discussion of social media.

LEARNING OUTCOME

4 Describe how businesses use blogs to connect with external and internal audiences.

7-4 Telling Stories With Blogs and News Sites

A **blog** is a website or social media platform with generally well-crafted articles or commentaries on topics such as new products or services, media coverage, industry news, human resources, and philanthropy. Businesses use blogs to keep customers, employees, and the public at large informed and, to some extent, interact with them. Blogs are usually written by one person, although some corporate blogs may feature multiple contributors. Originally, readers were encouraged to leave comments. Lately, though, corporate blogs have become less interactive. The two biggest advantages of external business blogs are that they can accumulate a far-flung, vast audience and allow companies to shape the brand story in a longer narrative form. Blogs are another tool for public relations and brand building—one channel in a multichannel social media strategy.

Employees and executives at companies as varied as Allstate, Caterpillar, Exxon Mobil, General Motors, Patagonia, Southwest, and Target maintain blogs. They use blogs to communicate internally with employees and externally with the public. At present, 270 (54 percent) of Fortune 500 companies in the United States maintain a public-facing corporate blog. However, direct interaction with readers may have migrated to social media sites or behind corporate firewalls because fewer than 20 percent of companies provide a comment feature on their blogs today, down from almost three fourths five years ago.[59] Some companies, such as Patagonia and Coca-Cola, have transformed their blogs to narrative posts about their brands in News or Stories sections on their websites.

Blog adoption varies across industries. Research shows that the top five sectors most likely to embrace blogs are commercial banks, specialty retailers, semiconductors and electronics makers, gas and electric utilities, and pharmaceuticals.[60] The federal government, too, has recognized the utility of blogs. The Transportation Security Administration (TSA) maintains an entertaining and informative travel- and security-related blog. One recent post was titled "To Shave, or Not to Shave, in November."[61]

FOR THE RECORD

Telling a Compelling Brand Story

Marketing experts believe that, if done right, business *storytelling* engages, inspires, and connects the audience to a brand or company. Branding guru David Aaker explains that authentic *signature stories* are more powerful than facts alone: "If I say, 'It was a drab and rainy day in mid-May, 1931, when a 28-year-old Neil McElroy, the advertising manager of PMG's Camay soap, sat down at his Royal typewriter and wrote for us perhaps the most significant memo in modern marketing history' doesn't that perk up your ears?" Moreover, authenticity is essential, Aaker says. "You don't want people to think, 'Oh, this is phony. This is contrived. This is a selling deal.'"[62] Blogs can tell compelling stories. Why has storytelling become such a potent marketing tool?

7-4a How Companies Tell Stories

Like other social networking tools, corporate blogs may create virtual communities, build brands, and develop relationships. Specifically, companies use blogs for public relations, customer relations, market research, internal communication, online communities, and recruiting. Internal blogs accessible to employees on a corporate intranet serve as information hubs, encourage discussion, create a sense of community, and foster engagement.

Public Relations and Customer Relations.   One of the prominent uses of blogs is to provide up-to-date company information to the press and the public. Blogs can be written by rank-and-file employees or by top managers. An avid longtime blogger, executive chairman Bill Marriott was among the first CEOs who started to blog more than a decade ago. Long after many of his peers abandoned their blogs, this octogenarian posts excerpts from his latest biography and writes about leadership, current events, family history, and more. Perhaps because Bill Marriott handwrites or dictates his posts in "old school" fashion, his Marriott on the Move blog feels personal and honest:

> [B]eing a technophobe like me adds a lot of steps, but I make it work because I know that it's a great way to communicate with our customers and stakeholders in this day and age. When your family's name is on the building or you are the person clearly identified with the company, everything you say or do affects the business, good or bad. In this fascinating information age, you have to be transparent.[63]

Other CEO or corporate officer blogs are also written in an accessible tone, representing the writers' own reflections and insights, not so much the streamlined stylish marketing stories of their companies, thus taking followers back to the origins of blogs as personal online journal entries.

Predictably, tech companies rely heavily on blogs. The GE Aviation blog is just one of several General Electric news and media hubs; it highlights key employees and the company's latest aerospace and flight news. The GE Digital division operates the futuristic Industrial IoT Blog. Prominent features include information about GE's many software products and its technical assistance. Occasionally a blog may be authored by unaffiliated fans or critics of a company, especially one that is so notoriously secretive as Apple. The founder of MacRumors, a former physician, has made his wildly successful site a prime destination for all things Mac over two decades and counting. The readers are highly engaged and comment freely on stories that supply generally accurate information Apple is often reluctant to release.

Many retailers blog as well. In its Best Buy Influencer Network, the electronics retailer is inviting **influencers**, loyal fans with a large social media following, to create a profile and blog on its platform. In addition to offering a secure community space, Best Buy Blogger Network is also active on Facebook. Quirky online shoe retailer Zappos in its Beyond the Box blog faithfully conjures up the image as an entrepreneurial company that strives for "The Power of WOW" by focusing on dedicated customer service. A handful of writers blog about company milestones, business topics, and community events in a conversational tone. They also casually give style tips and facilitate purchases—an unabashed focus on sales that typically is missing from blogs. The Zappos pitch to sign up for a newsletter is accompanied by a chummy nudge to bond: "Let's be friends! Subscribe to our newsletter."[64]

Business and even niche blogs can be extremely lucrative. Some consultants or techies turned bloggers pull six figures or more, depending on the number of their followers or subscribers. The greater their following, the better can bloggers monetize their writing through advertising. Well-known **brand ambassadors** such as author and podcaster Tim Ferris or former Apple exec and entrepreneur Guy Kawasaki **evangelize**, i.e., advocate for brands and are well compensated; for example, Mercedes-Benz loaned Kawasaki an AMG GTS super car. Because reader comments do not accurately measure engagement unless the number of visitors is recorded in some form, most blogs prompt readers to opt in by signing up for an e-mail newsletter or to follow their social media sites.

Engagement and Viral Marketing.

The engagement aspect of blogging appears to be waning. Starbucks shut down its long-lasting My Idea community blog it had used for crowdsourcing. The coffee retailer still solicits creative ideas from the public, just not as visibly as a running tally listing thousands of suggestions on a website. Participants were invited to share their ideas and vote the ideas of others up or down on the public blog. Some commentators were glad to see MyStarbucksIdea.com run its course because they disliked the countless negative comments and many poor or unrelated ideas. Also, when crowds vote, it's not always the best idea that wins, they felt.[65]

Similarly, Frito-Lay pulled the plug on its long-running Crash the Superbowl contest which lured thousands of fans to create a humorous Doritos commercial. Entrants competed for a $1 million prize. Finalists were subjected to a fan vote on Doritos.com, and the winning ad ran during the Super Bowl.[66] The Doritos brand's chief marketing officer Ram Krishnan explained that demographic change from millennials to Gen Z precipitated the end of the contest: "Our Doritos target is [now] Gen Z consumers and they're already content creators. You don't need a brand to play a role." In the meantime, this young target cohort may have found a new creative outlet on the hugely popular short video platform TikTok. The demographic shift corresponds with changing preferences in social media use today, which will be discussed in another section of this chapter.

Marketers realize the potential of getting the word out about their products and services in channels such as blogs and social media in general, where their messages are often picked up by well-connected brand advocates or influencers, who appeal to large audiences. The hope is that buzz will develop and even go viral. The term **viral marketing** refers to the rapid spread of messages online, much like infectious diseases that pass from person to person. Viral messages must be authentic and elicit an emotional response, but for that very reason they are difficult to orchestrate. Large companies employ teams of social media experts and marketers who scrutinize social media for buzz and positive or negative posts about their organizations and products.

Online Communities.

Like Instagram, YouTube, Snapchat, Facebook, and Twitter, company blogs and news sites can draw a loyal core following to businesses and brands. Such followers want to keep informed about company events, product updates, offers, freebies, and other news. The Coca-Cola Company has transformed its Conversations blog to a News site with rich stories about its many brands. In one article chairman and CEO James Quincey reflects on Coke's century of accomplishments as a public company. The soft drink maker also maintains interactive pages with offers to earn perks by connecting with its brands, for example, tie-ins with March Madness and AMC Theaters or games to win gift cards and vacations. A Coca-Cola smartphone app invites users to create custom Coca-Cola mixes.

Internal Communication and Recruiting.

Internally, blogs can be used to keep virtual teams on track and share updates on the road. Members in remote locations can stay in touch by smartphone and other devices, exchanging text, images, sound, and video clips. In many companies, blogs have replaced hard-copy publications in offering late-breaking news or tidbits of interest to employees. Such blogs can help build communities, prompt the sharing of expertise, and stimulate employee involvement. In addition, internal corporate blogs serve as searchable archives of company knowledge.

Public-facing blogs mirror the company culture and present an invaluable opportunity for job candidates to size up a potential employer and the people working there. The explicit purpose of Target's Pulse Blog is to "help our candidates get a sneak peek into what it's like to work at Target."[67] In addition to corporate and executive blogs, a quick Internet search yields many examples of successful niche blogs on any imaginable topic, say, on parenting, home décor, food, photography, and more.

Early blogs were attempts to show the human face of a company, its executives, as well as employees. Some continue this mission to connect on a more personal level. However, as blogs mature, fewer encourage commentary, or they require registering and logging in behind corporate firewalls. Receiving zero replies, less than a handful of polite comments, or nasty responses may have motivated businesses to make this move. In this way companies can exert greater control over their narrative and engage with fans who opt in by registering. Many blogs today publish news items written by PR professionals, and their slick posts typically remain nameless.

Plugged In

Expect Gamification and Wearables

Despite gains attributed to a strong labor market, employers struggle with worker engagement. According to a Gallup poll, 34 percent of U.S. workers are highly committed, whereas 13 percent are "actively disengaged." The remaining 53 percent are "not engaged," meaning indifferent.[68]

Gamification. To boost workers' energy, enthusiasm, and performance, companies are turning to gamification. From recruiting to training and development, organizations are adopting game-like techniques. They want to introduce fun, play, competition, and persistence (some say addiction) to job tasks and provide incentives to increase worker productivity such as badges, points, leaderboards, and score levels. Critics point out that gamification pushes workers to do more for the same pay, ending up lowering their compensation overall. They charge that some companies use gamification to exploit workers' excitement by offering them "psychic income," i.e., intangible game-like rewards, instead of bonuses or higher

KANUT PHOTO/Shutterstock.com

wages.[69] Novartis, Walt Disney Company, and others have used scoreboards and leaderboards to pit competing workers against each other. T-Mobile rewarded agents with a stint in a "money machine" blowing prize certificates.

Gamification software is here to stay because it saves employers money and appears to make employees feel more productive (89 percent) and happier (88 percent) on the job, according to a workplace study.[70] The global gamification market for marketing, sales, and HR is booming with a projected volume of $23 billion in 2022.[71]

Wearables. Wearable devices—such as heart rate monitors and skin response sensors—enable companies to monitor worker productivity and lifestyle. Much like fitness devices worn by athletes, wearables can measure brain activity, record movement, and even monitor posture. Very soon sensors will be embedded in smart work clothes; think touch-screen sleeves or collars changing color based on mood.[72] Bio-sensing wearables are entering the mining, construction, and oil and gas industries, mainly to monitor workers' health and safety.

Employers love wearables because they believe the devices can help them save on health-care costs. They feel justified in tracking workers' behavior even outside the workplace. They argue that lifestyle choices—including alcohol and caffeine intake, exercise, sleep, eating habits, and smoking—affect job performance. They want to measure stress levels and productivity. Critics fear poor morale and pushback if workers don't know how information is used and fear that their data are not private and secure. They also worry about the accuracy of the devices used.

7-4b Mastering Blogging: Seven Tips

Much advice is freely available on the Internet, but this section offers guidelines culled from experienced bloggers and communication experts that will lead you to successful online writing. As with any public writing, your posts will be scrutinized; therefore, you want to make the best impression.

Craft a Catchy but Concise Title.　The headline is what draws online readers to even click to go to your post. Some are intriguing questions or promises. Bloggers often use numbers to structure their posts. Here are some examples of blog post titles: *Six Apps You Don't Want to Miss; 9 Tips on How to Scale Your Business; Create Powerful Imagery in Your Writing; How Financially Sexy Is Your Household?* An analysis of 100 million blog post titles revealed that the most successful headline included the phrase "Will Make You," followed by "This Is Why," and "Can We Guess."[73] Success was measured by user engagement in the form of a like, share, or comment. Here are two examples: "These 3 Warren Buffett Rules Will Make You a Better Investor" and "13 Travel Tips That Will Make You Feel Smart."

Ace the Opening Paragraph.　The lead must deliver on the promise of the headline. Identify a need and propose to solve the problem. Ask a relevant question. Tell an anecdote or use an analogy to connect with the reader. Say something startling. The Direct2Dell blog author of "Do You Have What It Takes? Top 20 Most Rugged Jobs in America" opened with this:

> Have you ever scaled a 20-foot tree, hung off the side of a skyscraper, been 700 meters underground, or labored on a ship for 36 hours straight? It's hard to imagine that this is a normal day of work for some people. . . .[74]

Provide Details in the Body.　Mind the *So what?* and *What's in it for me?* questions. Use vivid examples, quotations and testimonials, or statistics. Structure the body with numbers, bullets, and subheadings. Use expressive action verbs (*buy* for *get*; *own* for *have*; *travel* or *jet* for *go*). Use conversational language to sound warm and authentic. Use contractions (*can't* for *cannot*; *doesn't* for *does not*; *isn't* for *is not*).

Consider Visuals.　Add visual interest with relevant images and diagrams. Keep paragraphs short and use plenty of white space around them. Aim to make the look simple and easy to scan.

Include Calls to Action.　Call on readers in the title to do something or provide a takeaway and gentle nudge at the end.

> Here's a tip you can use right away. You'll have vastly better copy on your website in 20 minutes by following these two simple steps:
>
> Go look at your web copy right now.
>
> Take out every word that doesn't contribute something new.
>
> Come back here and tell us about the before-and-after. I bet you'll have something to say![75]

Asking open-ended questions is another effective closing: "Those are two of XYZ Company's ideas about where business-to-business marketing is heading. How about you? Have you developed some new strategies of your own? What exciting ideas are fueling your own marketing—and how are you applying them? Let us know in the comments."

Edit and Proofread.　Follow the revision tips in Chapter 6 of this book. Cut any unneeded words, superfluous sentences, and irrelevant ideas. Fix awkward, wordy, and repetitious sentences. Edit and proofread as if your life depended on it—your reputation might. The best blogs are error free.

Respond to Posts Respectfully.　Build a positive image by posting compelling comments on other bloggers' posts. Politely and promptly reply to comments on your site. This reply to Jamie Spencer's blogging advice post[76] makes a positive comment and asks a question. The exchange is cordial, albeit marred by punctuation errors:

> ***Alice M:*** Thank you for all your helpful information. I've found this website so useful! I'm about to start my first blog. The blog is basically music reviews and I was just wondering if you knew whether I'm allowed to copy videos off YouTube for example?

FIGURE 7.6 Writing a Captivating Blog

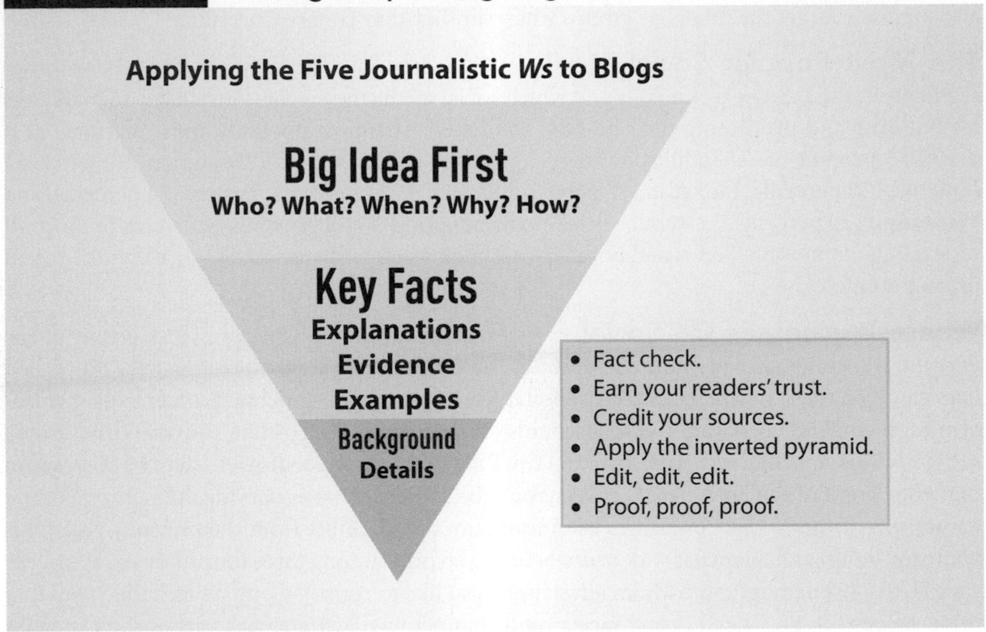

Applying the Five Journalistic *Ws* to Blogs

Big Idea First
Who? What? When? Why? How?

Key Facts
Explanations
Evidence
Examples
Background
Details

- Fact check.
- Earn your readers' trust.
- Credit your sources.
- Apply the inverted pyramid.
- Edit, edit, edit.
- Proof, proof, proof.

Jamie: As long as you use the relevant embed codes from YouTube to add videos to your site you should be ok to do that. I wouldn't recommend ripping any content from a YouTube video and then hosting it yourself, this could be a copyright issue.

If you disagree with a post, do so respectfully. Don't ramble.

Your blog posts can benefit from the journalistic pattern shown in Figure 7.6 by emphasizing the big news up front, supported with specifics and background information.

7-5 Navigating Social Networking for Business

LEARNING OUTCOME

5 Discuss business organizations' external and internal social media practices.

Popular social networking sites such as Facebook, Instagram, and Twitter are used by businesses for similar reasons and in much the same way as podcasts and blogs. Social media enable businesses to connect with customers and employees, share company news, promote goods and services, and exchange ideas. Social online communities for professional audiences (e.g., LinkedIn), discussed in Chapter 15, help recruiters find talent and encounter potential employees before hiring them. Today, LinkedIn occupies the No. 1 spot as 99 percent of businesses use the platform for business networking and recruiting.[78] Seven in ten (70 percent) of hiring managers scour social media as part of their screening processes.[79]

7-5a Tapping Into Social Media

Business interest in social networking is not surprising if we consider that online is where—in marketing speak—the consumer eyeballs are. Nearly three fourths (72 percent) of American adults use some type of social media.[80] The most avid social media users, however, are the millennials (85 percent), the cohort born 1981–1996. Their smartphone ownership is highest at 93 percent, although older age groups are gaining on them in tech adoption.[81] At the same time, millennials are now the largest generation in the workforce (35 percent).[82] No wonder,

Reality Check

Multichannel Strategy for Digital Media

"When it comes to the biggest trends in marketing today, our industry is obsessed with channels such as social, voice, and augmented reality as the means for reaching today's modern audience. And while each plays an important role in the customer journey, new research from Adobe finds a more traditional form of marketing—email—is very much holding its own among newer channels and technologies."[77]

—Giselle Abramovich, *executive editor, Enterprise Thought Leadership, Adobe*

then, that businesses are eager to connect on social media with this particular demographic but also precisely target the other age groups wherever they may congregate online.

The Most Popular Social Media.   Knowing how various cohorts and consumer segments in the U.S. use technology and which social media they favor is invaluable to marketers for building and promoting their brands. YouTube is the most popular online platform as it draws 73 percent of U.S. adults, followed by Facebook (69 percent), Instagram (37 percent), Pinterest (28 percent), LinkedIn (27 percent), Snapchat (24 percent), Twitter (22 percent), and WhatsApp (20 percent).[83] Overall, social media adoption is still growing, with a slight drop-off or leveling out among Gen X and boomer Facebook users perhaps linked to Facebook's recent privacy stumbles.

Where Businesses Go Social.   As can be expected, a whopping 95 percent of the Fortune 500 companies are now on Facebook, up six percent over the previous year. Receiving *likes* can help these businesses advertise to targeted consumer segments. With engaging word-of-mouth content, corporate Twitter accounts (96 percent in the Fortune 500) can drive e-mail subscriptions and increase sales overall. YouTube's 1 billion global users may be the reason that 90 percent of the Fortune 500 have a YouTube presence. Instagram is gaining momentum; 73 percent of the largest companies use Instagram, up 10 points from the previous year. This platform along with Snapchat is an overwhelming favorite among three fourths of young people ages 18 to 24, a demographic whom advertisers also like to court.[84] Companies understand that to be successful, they need to embrace a multichannel media strategy as part of their broader business goals.[85]

The newest kid on the block is TikTok, the quirky video-sharing platform featuring "Real People. Real Videos." Advertisers love the creativity of the wildly popular teen-dominated network and see an opportunity to win credibility with a young age group ranging from 14 to 26. Teen favorite Chipotle garnered 3.9 billion views with its viral #boorito hashtag challenge. ELF Cosmetics composed a TikTok song now appearing in 1.7 million videos. Teenage influencers like Charli D'Amelio, who has 30.6 million followers, have become early sensations.[86] However, because TikTok is owned by a Chinese company, U.S. authorities suspect it of delivering American user data to the Chinese government. Like 5G innovator Huawei, TikTok is perceived as a potential national security threat.[87]

As Figure 7.7 shows, large companies have established successful social media presences.

7-5b Enterprise Social Networking

Mirroring social media sites but securely located behind corporate firewalls, tech giant IBM has created Connections, an internal social networking platform to help organizations share knowledge, improve decision making, and foster innovation. Companies launching comprehensive enterprise networking platforms, such as Connections, Jive, or Microsoft's Yammer, are investing in what they hope will lead to greater employee engagement and productivity. The platforms promise seamless networking away from e-mail, connecting workers one-on-one, in small teams, and across the entire company in one secure environment.

Connections, for example, combines an array of functions, e.g., project management, up-to-the-minute microblogging updates across the network, profiles of people in the organization, collaborative space, crowdsourcing tools, blogging, task management, content storage, and forums. The hope is that these tools will flatten the corporate hierarchy and empower individual employees at all levels. The advantage of enterprise social media networks is that they are searchable, enabling workers to tag, follow, view activity feeds, and more. Users can access and send information much more efficiently than by e-mail alone.[88]

Nimble Damage Control and Responding to Grievances.   Insurance and financial services firm Nationwide uses internal social networking to quickly respond to disasters such as hurricanes. Agents in Florida used the platform to record customers' pressing needs during a major storm, which led to improved service in subsequent natural disasters when Nationwide trucks headed into disaster zones equipped with the right essentials.[89]

FIGURE 7.7 Most Popular Product Brands on Facebook

The biggest global social network, Facebook has reached almost 1.70 billion registered users and more than 2.50 billion monthly active users (MAU) worldwide. Since buying WhatsApp, Facebook saw the messaging app's popularity soar to 2 billion MAU. Another Facebook-owned brand, Instagram, boasts more than 1 billion global MAU; relative newcomer TikTok reports 800 million MAU; LinkedIn has 675 million registered users but only 310 million are active per month; Twitter is shedding MAU who now may number 330 million. On Facebook, the top three product brands with the most fans are Facebook itself (215 million), Samsung (160 million), and Coca-Cola (107 million).

Source: Statista, 2020; Omnicore, 2020; We Are Social, 2020

Source: Facebook

Over at IBM, after an employee posted a petition against a new company policy that would ban reimbursement for ride-sharing services such as Uber, within hours the post had drawn hundreds of comments and more than 1,200 views. IBM's social analytics picked up the network traffic, and Diane Gherson, senior vice president for human resources, responded directly to the employee on the Connections platform and explained that the company would reverse the ban. The post and the swift response to it led to positive change, and the goodwill of the unhappy employee was most likely restored.[90]

Connecting Dispersed Workers. Because social networks are about connections, they also enable companies to match up and connect dispersed employees. The Goodyear Tire & Rubber Company uses the Microsoft 365 suite that includes Yammer to ensure its associates around the world work effectively together as a team. Chief information officer Sherry Neubert explains that Goodyear's remote teams conduct meetings with Skype for Business, exchange instant messages to quickly resolve problems, and participate in enterprise social networking to contribute creative ideas.[91] The worldwide environmental movement Earth Hour uses Yammer to connect with thousands of organizers around the globe in real time, often in their native languages. Organizers share ideas and campaign materials such as ads and videos on the network.[92]

Crowdsourcing Employees to Achieve Buy-In. Internal social networks and blogs can help companies invite employee input to effect change and solve business problems. Gathering and sharing input on Yammer, the Red Robin restaurant chain motivates its workers with incentives to propose cost-saving ideas.[93] When IBM realized it had to do something about its hated performance management system, the tech firm decided to solicit employee feedback using Connections. At first the crowdsourcing initiative met with skepticism; however, during the first 24 hours of the comment period, IBM received a whopping 2,000 responses. Online debates and polling followed. Within a few months, the company developed a new evaluation system prototype, called Checkpoint, and deployed it to 375,000 employees.[94]

7-5c Social Media and Risk Management

Public-facing social networks hold great promise for businesses while also presenting potential risk. Most managers desire plugged-in employees with strong tech skills and fantasize about their brands becoming overnight sensations thanks to viral marketing. Managers like to imagine their workers as enthusiastic brand evangelists; in fact, content shared by employees seems to achieve greater engagement and re-sharing than typical brand channels do.[95] However, businesses also fret about lost productivity, reputational damage, and legal issues, e.g., violations of privacy laws, workplace harassment, and defamation. To minimize risk, companies rely on social media policies, approve and oversee employees' use of social media, and mandate training.[96]

Experts are divided on accessing private social media accounts on the job. Advocates cite authentic promotion of the business, improved morale, and new client relationship building. Skeptics denounce oversharing and the leaking of confidential information. They believe only trained social media professionals should speak for an organization.[97] Businesses vary in their approaches to personal social media use. Some, such as Zappos, take a hands-off approach and encourage employee online activity. Others, such as IBM, have crafted detailed Social Computing Guidelines that allow "incidental personal use" as long as it "is limited in duration, does not violate company policies, and does not distract us or others from the work we do."[98]

Although more than half of U.S. employers block social media at work,[99] such efforts can be circumvented when employees use their personal smartphones or other networks. Many work from home or travel. Data security scientists fear that hackers may deliver malware through Twitter, LinkedIn, Facebook, or Instagram by hijacking accounts; however, they also acknowledge that banning social media is an extreme measure that may breed resentment among current workers and deter future talent. In addition, employees may need to access social media as part of their job duties.[100] The best advice to workers is to follow company policies; assume that privacy doesn't exist, and avoid sharing sensitive information, least of all risqué photographs. Furthermore, refusing friend requests or unfriending individuals could jeopardize professional relationships. Consider the tips in Figure 7.8 if you want to use social media and keep your job.

The checklist that follows highlights some employee dos and don'ts that you should abide by to keep out of trouble on the job.

Ethics Check

Pricing Blunder Amplified Online

Arguably the world's most famous department store, Harrods suffered an embarrassing website blunder. The upscale UK retailer caused a run on its Aspinal of London designer handbags once some of these luxury items, typically costing £250 ($325) to £950 ($1,240), were advertised online for £2.13 ($2.80) to £8.08 ($10.54). The upscale department store blamed a supplier's computer pricing error for the glitch. Representatives personally contacted customers to apologize "for any inconvenience caused" but refused to deliver the merchandise at the incorrect price. Was Harrods obligated to honor the offer?

FIGURE 7.8 Guidelines for Safe Social Networking

Establish boundaries

Don't share information, images, and media online that you would not be comfortable sharing openly in the office.

Distrust privacy settings

Privacy settings don't guarantee complete protection from prying eyes. Facebook has come under fire for changing privacy settings and opening unwitting users' profiles for the world to see.

Rein in your friends

One of your 500 Facebook friends may tag you in an inappropriate photograph. Tags make pictures searchable; an embarrassing college incident may resurface years later. Always ask before tagging someone.

Beware friending

Don't reject friend requests from some coworkers while accepting them from others. Snubbed colleagues may harbor ill feelings. Don't friend your boss unless he or she friends you first. Send friend requests only once.

Expect the unexpected

Recruiters now routinely check applicants' online presence. Some employers have gone so far as to demand that candidates disclose their Facebook log-in information. Facebook and lawmakers have criticized the practice, and several state legislatures have banned it.

Checklist

Using Digital Media Like a Pro

Dos: Know Workplace Policies and Avoid Private Use of Media at Work

- **Learn your company's rules.** Some companies require workers to sign that they have read and understand Internet and digital media use policies. Being informed is your best protection.

- **Avoid sending personal e-mail, IMs, or texts from work machines and devices.** Even if your company allows personal use during lunch or after hours, keep it to a minimum. Better yet, wait to use your own electronic devices away from work.

- **Separate work and personal data.** Keep information that could embarrass you or expose you to legal liability on your personal storage devices, on hard drives, or in the cloud, never on your office computer.

- **Be careful when blogging, tweeting, or posting on social networking sites.** A rookie cop in Detroit was fired two days after posting a racist caption below a selfie in uniform on Snapchat.[101] In a tweet, a University of Tampa sociology professor called the catastrophic Hurricane Harvey "instant karma" for the Republican-leaning state of Texas. Although the professor deleted the tweet, a screenshot of it had gone viral. At first the university distanced itself from the academic, but outrage on Facebook soon prompted his firing.[102]

- **Keep sensitive information private.** Use privacy settings, but don't trust the private areas on Instagram, Facebook, Twitter, Snapchat and other social networks.

- **Stay away from pornography, sexually explicit jokes, and inappropriate screen savers.** Anything that might poison the work environment is a harassment risk and, therefore, prohibited.

Don'ts: Avoid Questionable Content, Personal Documents, and File Sharing

- **Don't spread rumors, gossip, and negative, defamatory comments.** Because all digital information is subject to discovery in court, avoid unprofessional content and conduct, including complaints about your employer, customers, and employees.

- **Don't download and share cartoons, video clips, photos, and art.** Businesses are liable for any recorded digital content regardless of the medium used.

- **Don't open attachments sent by e-mail.** Attachments with executable files or video files may carry viruses, spyware, or other malware (malicious programs).

- **Don't download free software and utilities to company machines.** Employees can unwittingly introduce viruses, phishing schemes, and other cyber bugs.

- **Don't store your music and photos on a company machine (or server), and don't watch streaming videos.** Capturing precious company bandwidth for personal use is a sure way to be shown the door, not to mention that workers are paid to work.

- **Don't share files, and avoid file-sharing services.** Clarify whether you may use G Suite and other services that offer optional file sharing. Stay away from distributors of pirated files. Clicking Google and other browser links offering first-run movies is asking for malware.

7-5d The Dark Side of Technology and Social Media

Internet access nearly for all has meant that in cyberspace users can bypass gatekeepers who filter content in the traditional print and visual media. This open marketplace of ideas online was once hailed as democratic and empowering. However, user anonymity has displaced accountability, and public discourse has descended into disrespect, hate speech, and worse. Even extreme views may reach audiences of thousands or even millions. The dangers are obvious. Fact checking often falls by the wayside, buzz becomes more important than truth,

and a few keystrokes can threaten a reputation. Americans fear for their privacy and increasingly don't trust information on social media. This section addresses several cyberthreats that affect us as businesspeople and citizens.

Privacy Fears. Our smartphones spy on us. Location services in most apps allow users to be tracked with pinpoint precision. Tracking is enabled by default and most people don't know that practically all their movements can be followed, as a disturbing *New York Times* exposé revealed.[104] Our personal data from every account or profile we create online ends up in the cloud where it exists indefinitely. Once there, our data can be hacked, viewed by unauthorized personnel, or sold to advertisers. Sometimes it ends up on the Dark Web in the hands of criminals. Sensitive financial information and our medical data are stored in networks that are frequently breached. Wearable devices track our vital signs, exercise frequency, and lifestyle patterns. The end user doesn't know where all the massive data are stored, as U.S. consumers are largely unprotected in a yet barely regulated market.

Future trends are no less worrisome to privacy advocates. The sophistication of artificial intelligence and facial recognition technology is growing. In China, a huge surveillance apparatus will soon enable the repressive regime to keep track of millions of people and identify protesters and dissidents. In the United States a small secretive company, Clearview AI, has devised a pioneering facial recognition app allowing users to match the image of an individual against all public photos of this person already existing on the Internet, revealing their identity and attached personal information in seconds. What has been a boon to law enforcement may soon land in the hands of everyday users—not just advertisers, but stalkers and other bad actors. True privacy and anonymity may be a thing of the past for consumers who use smart electronic devices, maintain social media profiles, and pay with credit cards—i.e., nearly all of us.

Disinformation and Election Tampering. Researchers tell us that social media have changed how we consume information and form opinions. More than 90 percent of users access their news online; some 50 to 68 percent of them rely solely on social media.[105] Online, people tend to seek out so-called **echo chambers** of like-minded individuals and embrace narratives that confirm their existing views while rejecting contradicting information. The resulting polarization carries with it a negative emotional charge.[106] As Pew Research suggests, such charged information environments make people vulnerable to misinformation. False news stories and doctored narratives, including targeted disinformation, i.e., propaganda originating primarily in Russia and China, confuse the public.[107] A Buzzfeed survey found that 75 percent of American adults can't spot fake news.[108]

Even more troubling, though, is stealthy interference by foreign agents who use large bot armies to disseminate fake news stories on social media and incite conflict to deepen sharp divisions among the American public. Fake news planted by bots has risen to the level of potentially tampering with U.S. elections thus undermining our democratic institutions. Bots are also used to steal social identities of people by impersonating them. Our carefree sharing on social media can provide criminals with clues.

Deepfakes, Doctored Videos. It has been said that we live in a **post-truth** era; in other words, we now exist in "circumstances in which objective facts are less influential in shaping public opinion than appeals to emotion and personal belief."[109] The urgent need for critical thinking now extends even to visual information—video content we don't question because, after all, instinctively we tend to believe what we see. Advances in AI could soon make creating fake video and audio a lot easier, permitting ever more sophisticated disinformation.

The ability to manipulate video footage to make people seem to say or do something they did not do is so worrisome to the U.S. government that it has begun to combat **deepfakes**.

Altering photos and videos to distort the truth is not new, but deepfake technology takes deception to a whole new level. Computers can be trained to synthesize facial features and create composites of realistic-looking humans. It's easy to see how such tampering could be weaponized before an election or might threaten national security; likewise, people could claim that real videos are fake.[110] Alarmingly, this is already happening as sizable Internet communities aggressively proclaim the moon landing in 1969 was staged, the Earth is flat, and the terror attacks of 9/11 were "an inside job."[111]

Incivility, Trolling, and Cyberbullying.

The anonymity of the Internet facilitates toxic behavior. Trolls are users who fake their identity, provoke skirmishes, and disrupt discussions on social media. They can be vicious bullies who thrive on denigrating others. Social media may originally have been idealized as a public square which guaranteed participants a practically unlimited freedom of expression. However, even former proponents of an unregulated Internet, such as Jack Dorsey, the Twitter founder and CEO, have second thoughts. Dorsey now admits that social media cannot be neutral, passive platforms because of threats of violence, doxxing (public shaming and harassment), and troll armies bent on silencing others.[112] Facebook too has long been criticized for allowing demagogues and bigots to go unchecked; then it banned a few of them from the site, triggering suspicions of bias.[113]

Cyberbullying is a particularly devastating form of online harassment through the sharing of embarrassing information online, persistent messaging, and other digital nastiness. Nearly all states have passed anti-bullying laws, but critics contend that social media companies aren't doing enough to combat the practice.[114] In extreme cases cyberbullying on social media, via texts, e-mails, and other electronic means has driven victims, many of them teenagers, to despair.

Data Security.

Spyware. Ransomware attacks. Phishing. Data breaches. Romance scammers on dating sites. Fake bot accounts. Hacking of connected security networks. Vulnerabilities in smart speakers and connected cars. These are but a few problems ranging from annoying to highly problematic and downright fraudulent. Businesses face a huge expenditure of time and money combatting cybercrime and ensuring safe data storage. The average total cost of a data breach stands at $3.9 million; in the most recent year, an average 25,575 records were compromised per breach, and it took 279 days on average to identify and contain the breach.[115]

One of the biggest weaknesses enabling common security threats is human. According to Pew Research, Americans' knowledge of digital topics, such as cybersecurity or the advertising business model of social media companies, is inadequate.[116] Too many Internet users are lax with their credentials and still choose the word *password* to log in, not to mention *qwerty* or the infamous number sequence *123456* that enabled 23 million victim accounts to be hacked across the globe in one recent year.[117] Instead of adopting a password manager such as LastPass to generate and keep track of strong passwords, many Internet users log in with Facebook or reuse the same password. However, the adoption of VPNs is spreading, adding a layer of security by shielding browsing activity. More people, too, prefer browsers that don't track them, such as DuckDuckGo.

Americans seem to slowly realize that their electronic devices may be keeping tabs on them and that their personal data are frequently collected without their knowledge. Convenience comes at the cost of privacy and security. Aided by fact-checking websites, people are learning that they must take news sources on the Internet with a grain of salt and not believe everything they read or see. A recent Pew study shows that Americans don't trust social media for political and election news although many primarily rely on social media for such information.[118] Growing concern has led to efforts to introduce privacy protections. The awareness seems to be spreading that technology, the Internet, and social media in particular can be a mixed blessing.

Zooming In

Your Turn:
Applying Your Skills at Averon

Communication technology frees today's workers from fixed locations. Averon's Chief Data Scientist Mark Klein sometimes dials into conference calls while riding his motorcycle in northwestern Colorado. On one of his trips, he helped finalize an Averon patent application. He also regularly checked in from a months-long 35,000-mile motorcycle ride that took him from Boulder, Colorado, to Ushuaia, Argentina, and then to Prudhoe Bay, Alaska—his shiny copper-colored HP laptop inside a solid Pelican case always at the ready. After a successful career in Silicon Valley and raising four kids, Mark Klein became a digital nomad, an inveterate traveler and trekker, as well as the envy of his friends.

However, as we have seen in this chapter, technology isn't always benign and can backfire, often as a result of human error. Averon CEO Wendell Brown still shudders when recounting how a member of the management in his previous company had accidentally sent a delicate e-mail with everyone's salary information to the entire staff. After the initial shock, the e-mail mishap turned out to be much less serious than Brown had feared. He says the incident confirmed to him that one should operate a company and treat people as though all transactions were always out in the open: "If you treat people fairly and the information did get out, it shouldn't cause much of a problem anyway, and fortunately we were in that good space."[119]

Nevertheless, Brown is adamant that all employees and interns know the challenges of e-mail correspondence. Welcoming a handful of summer interns on their first day in Averon's San Francisco office, the CEO asks them to jot down a list of the kind of information they would never include in any work correspondence and share the finished product with all staff including Mark Klein, who wants to be kept in the loop.

Your Task

In groups of two or three, decide whether to send Mark Klein an e-mail or write a memo. Decide how you will organize the e-mail or memo and include eight to ten taboo topics. Because Mark almost never visits the San Francisco office, what other channels might you choose to communicate with him? What are their advantages?

SUMMARY OF LEARNING OUTCOMES

1 Examine the professional usage, structure, and format of e-mails and memos in the digital era workplace.

- The exchange of information in organizations today is increasingly social and mobile.

- Office workers still send paper-based messages when they need a permanent record; wish to maintain confidentiality; and need to convey formal, long, and important messages.

- E-mail is the lifeblood of businesses, but messaging apps are gaining popularity; all digital workplace messages are permanent because they must be stored; they can be used in court.

- E-mail and memo subject lines summarize the central idea, which is restated in the opening. The body provides details. The closing includes (a) action information and deadlines, (b) a summary, or (c) a closing thought.

- Skilled e-mail writers take advantage of down-editing. In a reply they delete the unnecessary parts of the sender's message and insert their responses.

- Careful e-mail users write concisely and don't send content they wouldn't want published.

2 Explain workplace messaging and texting including their liabilities and best practices.

- Instant messaging and real-time chat apps such as Slack as well as texting are best suited for brief text-based exchanges.

- Benefits of messaging apps and texting are their speed, allowing quick decisions; Slack's group chat connects distant as well as local project teams; SMS marketing is growing.

- Risks include productivity losses, leaked trade secrets, and legal liability from workers' improper use of digital media; fraud, malware, and spam pose additional risks.

- Best practices include following company policies, avoiding sensitive information, not sending inappropriate digital content, and using correct grammar and spelling.

- Text messages should observe proper timing, be addressed to the correct person, and identify the sender; savvy workers don't send sensitive news or expect an instant reply.

- Slack is beloved by many as an e-mail alternative; the downsides include distraction and incivility.

3 Identify professional applications of business podcasts and the professional standards underpinning them.

- Business podcasts are digital audio files ranging from short clips to long media files.

- Applications that do not require a human presence (e.g., training videos) lend themselves to podcast recordings that users can stream or download on the go.

- Podcasts are a growing channel for informing, advising, and engaging with customers; businesses, entrepreneurs, the media, and educational organizations create podcasts.

- Some entrepreneurial podcasters are able to monetize their large, devoted following.

- Successful podcasts publish regularly, offer relevant topics, are professionally recorded, require audience building, feature a dynamic host or two, and allow listener feedback.

4 Describe how businesses use blogs to connect with external and internal audiences.

- Blogs help businesses to keep customers, employees, and suppliers informed and to receive feedback.

- Businesses tell stories with blogs to engage with their customers and the public, for public relations, to grow online communities, and for internal communication and recruiting.

- Advice for masterful blogs includes crafting a catchy title, acing the first paragraph, providing details, using visuals, including call to action, careful editing, and responding respectfully.

5 Discuss business organizations' external and internal social media practices.

- Social media such as Facebook and Twitter allow firms to share company news; exchange ideas; and connect with customers, employees, other stakeholders, and the public.

- Companies boost their brand recognition by engaging customers on the social media platforms where they congregate; enterprise social networks provide secure internal communication.

- Productivity losses, legal liability, leaking of trade secrets, and angry Internet users are potential risks of social media use at work.

- Workers should share only appropriate, work-related information, not post questionable content; they should activate and monitor their privacy options on social media sites.

- Technology and social media have a dark side, which includes threats to privacy, disinformation, deepfakes, incivility, and trolling, as well as threats to data security.

Key Terms

cloud *204*

virtual private networks (VPN) *204*

down-editing *208*

instant messaging *211*

text messaging *211*

monetization *216*

podcasts *216*

blog *220*

influencers *221*

brand ambassadors *222*

evangelize *222*

viral marketing *222*

gamification *223*

wearable devices/wearables *223*

echo chambers *230*

post-truth *230*

deepfakes *230*

trolls *231*

doxxing/doxing *231*

cyberbullying *231*

Critical Thinking

1. The eminent sociologist Zygmunt Bauman had this to say about social media: "Most people use social media not to unite, not to open their horizons wider, but on the contrary, to cut themselves a comfort zone where the only sounds they hear are the echoes of their own voice, where the only things they see are the reflections of their own face. Social media are very useful, they provide pleasure, but they are a trap."[120] Do you agree? Why or why not? How do you use social media networks? (L.O. 5)

2. You have seen that e-mail is not universally loved although it seems to be experiencing a noticeable comeback, despite the advent of real-time chat apps, texting, and other workplace short-form messaging. "Email is the last great unowned technology," said the Harvard law professor Jonathan Zittrain, "and by unowned, I mean there is no CEO of email . . . it's just a shared hallucination that works." Others believe that e-mail, though much maligned, "is still a cornerstone of the open web."[121] Interpret these statements. What points are they making, about openness in particular? (L.O. 1, 5)

3. Consider the potential impact of gamification and wearable devices on your career. How do you feel about the tracking of employees and the monitoring of your vital functions on the job and outside the workplace? Can you think of other vulnerable technologies? What advice would you give someone who is not sure how to handle invasive technologies that may threaten privacy and security? (L.O. 1–5)

4. Are conversational Internet acronyms and slang—such as *AFAIK*, *G2G*, *HIFW*, *ICYMI*, and *NSFW*—as well as all-lowercase writing acceptable in e-mail, texting, or instant messaging for business? (L.O. 2)

5. **Ethical Issue:** Some marketers and individuals aspiring to becoming influencers employ Internet bots—automated applications that run simple, repetitive tasks on the Internet—to inflate the number of likes and fans online.[122] So-called bot networks (*botnets*) operate large numbers of fake accounts on Facebook, Instagram, and Twitter. A rental agency based in Washington, D.C., went from two fans to almost 15,000 within a few days. How do you feel about companies and their brands pretending they have actual traffic on their sites and buying likes? (L.O. 5)

Activities

7.1 Document for Analysis: Poorly Organized Request Requires Revision (L.O. 1)

`E-Mail`

Ryan Abrams, Human Resources manager at Anchore, has written the following e-mail message to several line managers asking for information.

YOUR TASK Study the first draft of his poorly organized message and list its weaknesses. Then revise it to create a concise, clear message. Consider patterning your revision on Model Document 7.1 in this chapter.

To: Norberto Savala <nsavala@anchore.com>
From: Ryan.Adams <radams@anchore.com>
Subject: Need Your Input!

Norberto,

It has come to the attention of management here at Anchore that we may be missing an opportunity to find quality new employees. At a recent meeting many of us remarked about the feasibility of an internship program. Perhaps the time has come that we look into such a program. Our discussion centered on the fact that such a program could be instrumental in evaluating up-and-coming talent without making a hiring commitment.

The topic of an internship program has come up again and again, and I'm taking this opportunity to ask you to please answer some questions about whether this is a good idea or not. As our organization continues to expand, interns might make sense. But there are many points that we need to discuss, and I've put together a few questions that I think we should cover at the next management meeting. Please mark your calendar to meet on February 23 at 9 a.m. in the morning.

First, we really need to discuss whether an internship program is advantageous to us here at Anchore. In addition, what are the disadvantages? Next, what are some of the ramifications legally of hosting an internship program here in our state? Another question that enters my mind is whether we should pay interns. Do they receive college credit instead? I wonder if that serves as satisfactory compensation. Finally, we need to discuss where this program would be launched within Anchore. What departments to pilot such a program?

I hope you will give careful thought to these questions and come prepared to discuss.

Ryan

[Full contact information]

7.2 Document for Analysis: Weak Request Response Requires Your Revision (L.O. 1)

`E-Mail`

Blog writer Brian Drummond needs examples and information for a blog he plans to publish on the Online Voices platform. He writes to Nadya DeAlba, office manager at a high-tech firm, requesting information and examples. He met Ms. DeAlba at a conference and feels that she could be a willing source of information for his blog. Ms. DeAlba's advice is valuable, but her message is poorly organized, contains writing and grammar errors, and is hard to read.[123]

YOUR TASK Analyze the following poorly written message from Nadya DeAlba. Identify its weaknesses including sentence fragments, wordiness, grammar faults, misspellings, and other writing problems you have studied. Include examples. Then revise if your instructor advises. Your instructor may provide a possible revision. Remember that you can download these documents at www.cengage.com.

To: Brian Drummond <brian.drummond@gmail.com>
From: Nadya DeAlba <Nadya.dealba@techsolutions.com>
Subject: Your Request

Brian,

Thanks for this opportunity to make a contribution to your upcoming blog for Online Voices. You ask that I confine my remarks to five main and important points. Which I will try to do. However, I could share many more annoying habits that create tension in the workplace. They interrupt workflow, reduce productivity, and lead to stress. Here's my top five annoying tech habits that drive co-workers crazy. I have observed these in our open office.

The first has to do with cc abuse. Todays e-mail programs make it to easy to copy people who may be unrelated to the discussion. Before clicking the cc field, writers should ask themselves whether it's critical to ask all receivers specific questions such as who wants the vegan or the barbecue lunch. Another annoying habit is what I call "radio silence." This occurs when receivers fail to respond to e-mails within 24 hours. It's not that I expect responses to every Slack message, tweet, DM, text message, voice mail, or Facebook post. As a writer, however, it is annoying when important e-mail messages are ignored.

One of my co-workers complains about notification overload. Offices today are awash with chirps, dings, and rings of countless devices that are allowed to ring and echo through the sweeping open space. The constant ding, ding, dinging is not only annoying to the intended recipients. But also to nearby colleagues.

Another annoying habit has to do with jumbled threads. When writers do not observe the conventions of threading their comments on Slack or e-mail. The structure of the conversation becomes garbled. This really annoying behavior is one of the many tech irritants that aggravate co-workers.

A final irritant is channel hopping. I've heard a lot of complaining about co-workers who pursue the recipient from channel to channel, following an e-mail with repeated Slack messages or a text. It would be advantageous if people let there co-workers know their preferred method of staying in touch.

Hope this is helpful!

Best,

Nadya DeAlba

[Full contact information]

7.3 Document for Analysis: Live Chat at a Local Auto Dealer (L.O. 2)

`Communication Technology` `Social Media` `Web`

Read the following log of a live chat between a customer service representative and a visitor to a Baton Rouge car dealership's website.

YOUR TASK In class discuss how Jayden could have made this interaction with a customer more effective. Is his live chat with Mr. Kim professional, polite, and respectful? If your instructor directs, rewrite Jayden's responses to Mr. Kim's queries.

Dealer rep: Hey, I'm Jayden. How's it goin? Welcome to Brian Harris BMW the best dealer in Baton Rouge!

Customer: ??

Dealer rep: Im supposed to provid live assistance. What can I do you for?

Customer: I want buy car.

Dealer rep: May I have your name fist?

Customer: Kim Yoo Joon.

Dealer rep: Whoa! That's a dude's name? Okay. What kind? New inventory or preowned?

Customer: BMW. 2021 model. for family, for business.

Dealer rep: New, then, huh? Where are you from, Kim?

Customer: What car you have?

Dealer rep: We got some that will knock your socks off.

Customer: I want green car, no high gasoline burn.

Dealer rep: My man, if you can't afford the gas on these puppies, you shouldn't buy a Beemer, you know what I mean? Or ya want green color?

Chapter 7   Short Workplace Messages and Digital Media

Customer: ?

Dealer rep: Okeydoke, we got a full lineup. Which series 2, 3, 4, 5, 6, 7, or 8 Or an X3, X5, or X7? A Z4 convertible

Customer: BMW i3?

Dealer rep: Nope. That's the electric car! Oh I dont recommend those. We got two i3, one for $46, 200 and one for $49,700.

Customer: Eurepean delivery?

Dealer rep: Oh, I know zip about that. Let me find someone who does. Can I have your phone number and email?

Customer: i prefer not get a phone call yet . . . but 225-484-6356 is phone numer and yoojoonkim@t-tech.net email

Dealer rep: Awsome. Well give you a jingle back or shoot you an email pronto! Bye.

7.4 Instant Messaging: Live Chat Training at TransGlobal Airlines (L.O. 2)

Communication Technology **E-Mail** **Team** **Web**

Live chat operators who help customers by exchanging instant messages with them in real time play an important role in customer service. The goal of providing such direct communication online is to inform and troubleshoot, but also to build a lasting relationship with customers. Ideally, by being cordial, professional, and helpful, live chat operators can contribute significantly to turning customers into fans of the company or brand. Representatives must sound authentic and human. TransGlobal Airlines is training its representatives with hypothetical customer service scenarios. Following are two logs of chats by trainees who were asked to respond to a customer, Alex, in an online chat.

YOUR TASK Carefully review the logs of the conversations between Alex and Representative 1 as well as Representative 2. Individually or as a team, critique Representative 1 and Representative 2 in class or in an e-mail to your instructor summarizing your observations. Support your views with examples. For instance, you could comment on the representatives' courtesy, helpfulness, tone, or writing skills. Then, if your instructor asks you to rewrite this chat, try your hand at being Representative 3 and apply some of the lessons you have learned in this chapter and Chapter 6. **Tip:** Create a table to approximate the dialogue in an online chat. Note that sometimes the same person may write two or more comments in a row instead of waiting for a reply to the first one.

Representative 1	Representative 2
Rep: Hey, Alex, what's shakin' in Atlanta? What do you need?	**Rep:** Good day, dear sir! We are honored to serve esteemed customers like you.
Alex: Hi.	**Alex:** Hi.
Rep: Perf to have you here. Hiw can I hlep?	**Rep:** How can we be of assistance?
Alex: Your award-travel system sucks!! I'm so tired of wasting time on your website!	**Alex:** Your award-travel system sucks!! I'm so tired of wasting time on your website!
Rep: Whoa! Chill!?. Why diss our system. What trasnpired	**Rep:** We are so very sorry to hear that your customer experience is less than stellar, sir!
Alex: What happened is that I keep getting an error message just before I click Purchase. I tried many times.	**Alex:** What happened is that I keep getting an error message just before I click Purchase. I tried many times.
Alex: What point are award miles when they can't be redeemed??	**Alex:** What point are award miles when they can't be redeemed??
Rep: Where . . . what Just a sec I'm on another chat. Whats wrong?	**Rep:** Would you be so kind and describe the precise nature of your issue?
Alex: I am planning a business trip to London with some of my 500k frequent flyer miles. Whenever I choose the itinierary, fill in payment information for the taxes etc, I hit Purchase and an Error !!! pops up. I can't finish the booking. So annoying! Who has the time??	**Alex:** I am planning a business trip to London with some of my 500k frequent flyer miles. Whenever I choose the itinierary, fill in payment information for the taxes etc, I hit Purchase and an Error !!! pops up. I can't finish the booking. So annoying! Who has the time??
Rep: How v nice to be able to go to London Wow, 500k miles? I can see your search in our systm. Lemme try it for you. Leave technology to a milenial! [Pause]	**Rep:** When you visited our website, we saw your credentials and search parameters. I shall attempt to complete the booking in your stead. [Pause]
Rep: Nope! it doesn't work Sorry. System is new and has glitches.	

continues

Representative 1	Representative 2
Alex: Why on earth do you roll out something that's full of bugs, why waste my time??	**Rep:** I'm truly inconsolable, sir. It appears that I am unable to complete the transaction using our new system. I might need to escalate the problem to my supervisor.
Rep: Yasss, good question tbh. Listen I can try to get on this and will let you go now. When I make the booking I will give you a buzz first. then shoot you an email. Our tech boss has a blog for complaints. You should give him an earful there!! He says he wants to hear from our ticked off customers. Will send you the link too. Oh and I will save you money, no live booking fees.	**Alex:** Why on earth do you roll out something that's full of bugs, why waste my time??
	Rep: Please stay calm, sir. We are trying our best to serve you. As one of America's most respected airlines, we take customer service very seriously. Allow me to keep trying to complete the transaction gratis, without live booking fees. I shall telephone you and communicate via e-mail once the booking is completed. You will also receive a link that will allow you to share your experience with our CTO.
Alex: Okay. That's a relief. Thanks. I'll be awaiting your call and e-mail.	
Rep: Anything else I can do??	**Alex:** Okay. That's a relief. Thanks. I'll be awaiting your call and e-mail.
Alex: No, gotta run! Bye	**Rep:** May we do even more to provide excellent service, sir?
Rep: Cheers!	**Alex:** No, gotta run! Bye
	Rep: Have an enjoyable day, sir. Goodbye!

7.5 Instant Messaging: Practicing Your Professional Real-Time Chat Skills
(L.O. 2)

Communication Technology | **Social Media** | **Web** | **Team**

Your instructor will direct this role-playing group activity. Using instant messaging, you will simulate one of several typical business scenarios—for example, responding to a product inquiry, training a new-hire, troubleshooting with a customer, or making an appointment. For each scenario, two or more students chat professionally with only a minimal script to practice on-the-spot, yet courteous professional interactions by real-time chat. Your instructor will determine which client software or app you will need and provide brief instructions to prepare you for your role.

If you don't have instant messaging software on your computer or smart device yet, download the application first—for example, Slack, WhatsApp, Facebook Messenger, Google Hangouts, or Skype. All messaging software enables users to share photos and media files. You can make voice calls and use webcam video as well. These advanced features turn messaging apps into a simple conferencing tool and video phone. Contrary to calling landlines or cell phones, you can connect for free on Wi-Fi with people all around the world, as long as you're both on the same app. You may want to use a computer because downloading chat sessions is easier on a computer than on a smartphone.

YOUR TASK Open the messaging or chat app your instructor chooses. Follow your instructor's directions closely as you role-play the business situation you were assigned with your partner or team. The scenario involves two or more people who communicate by real-time chat.

7.6 Discovering Your Favorite Business Podcast Series (L.O. 3)

Communication Technology | **E-Mail** | **Social Media** | **Team** | **Web**

Podcasting done right is hard work. Most podcasts (80 percent) fail or no longer publish.[124] Experts advise business podcasters first to provide quality content with an authentic voice to build value, and to consider money making second.[125] To browse and learn from popular favorites, search for *iTunes Charts US Podcasts* or *Top US Podcasts Insights (Apple Podcasts Top Charts)*. These sites rank the top 100 most popular podcasts, some business-related (e.g., The $100 MBA, Freakonomics Radio, The Indicator from Planet Money, How I Built This, and HBR Ideacast). Podcast Awards, an annual ranking of favorites selected by listeners and podcasters, is another resource for finding valuable podcasts in various categories, including business, science, and technology. Past winners include the irreverent, chatty Big Girl Money show and Ellen on the Go featuring Ellen DeGeneres.

YOUR TASK Using the rankings mentioned above or other podcast sources, individually or as a small team find a highly rated business-related podcast series that sparks your interest. Scan the topics covered. Listen to several episodes and jot down notes. Evaluate the show's format (e.g., frequency of publication, duration, number of presenters or hosts, music use, interviews, formality of tone, professionalism, and other characteristics).

Categorize the content of your chosen podcast series (topics covered, invited guests, value of the information presented, your level of interest, and more). Look up the producer's credentials. Are the hosts competent subject experts? Find out what other authorities say about the podcast you selected and its producers. Then consider the overall value and credibility of the show. Would you recommend the podcast series to your classmates? Why or why not? Summarize your findings in a well-organized e-mail or classroom presentation. Alternatively, create an informative but brief social media post for an audience that doesn't know the podcast series or tweet an intriguing tidbit about the show.

7.7 Analyzing a Podcast (L.O. 3)

Communication Technology | **E-Mail** | **Social Media** | **Web**

Browsing the podcasts at iTunes, you stumble across the Quick and Dirty Tips series, specifically Money Girl, who has been dispensing financial advice since 2008. You sign up for the free podcasts that cover a variety of business topics. You can also visit the website Quick and Dirty Tips or interact with Laura D. Adams on her Money Girl Facebook page. Alternatively, examine the advice conveyed via podcast, the Web, Facebook, and Twitter by clever Grammar Girl Mignon Fogarty.

YOUR TASK Pick a Money Girl podcast that interests you. Listen to it or obtain a transcript on the website and study it for its structure. Is it direct or indirect? How is it presented? What style does the speaker adopt? How useful is the information provided? At your instructor's request, write an e-mail that discusses the podcast you analyzed. Alternatively, if your instructor allows, you could also send a very concise summary of the podcast by text message from your smartphone or tweet to your instructor. Try limiting yourself to no more than 280 characters to practice conciseness.

7.8 Creating a Simple Business Podcast (L.O. 3)

Communication Technology | **Social Media** | **Web**

Do you want to try your hand at producing a podcast? Businesses rely on a host of social media and communication technologies when reaching out to the public or internally to their workers. As you have seen, some companies produce such short audio or video clips on focused, poignant subjects. The following process describes how to create a simple podcast.

Select software. The best software for newbies is Audacity and GarageBand (Mac only). One step up is Adobe Audition. They allow recordings within a Web browser or from a smartphone. Most can also be accessed as mobile apps.

Obtain hardware. For high sound quality, you may need a sophisticated microphone and other equipment. The recording room must be properly shielded against noise, echo, and other interference. Many universities and some libraries provide recording booths.

Organize the message. Make sure your broadcast has a beginning, middle, and end. Build in some redundancy. Previews, summaries, and transitions are important to help your audience follow the message.

Choose an extemporaneous or scripted delivery. Extemporaneous delivery means that you prepare, but you use only brief notes. It usually sounds more spontaneous and natural than reading from a script, but it can also lead to undesirable redundancy, repetition, and flubbed lines.

Prepare and practice. Practice before recording. Editing audio or video is difficult and time consuming. Try to get your recording right, so that you won't have to edit much.

Publish your message. Once you post the MP3 podcast to your course website or blog, you can introduce it and request feedback.

YOUR TASK Create a short podcast about a business-related subject you care about. Producing a simple podcast does not require sophisticated equipment. With free or inexpensive recording, editing, and publishing software such as Audacity, you can inform customers, mix your own music, or host interviews. Any digital recorder can be used to create a no-frills podcast if the material is scripted and well-rehearsed.

7.9 Reviewing Corporate Blogs (L.O. 4)

Communication Technology | **E-Mail** | **Social Media** | **Web**

Here is your opportunity to view and evaluate a corporate blog. As we have seen, currently 54 percent of Fortune 500 companies, or 270 of them, have public blogs. Their use has been increasing, but some blogs have been transformed into narrative stories or company news without inviting or enabling reader comments, mainly because businesses may have relegated engagement with the public to social media networks where comments are more likely and frequent. However, the companies and their CEOs who do blog can impart valuable lessons.

YOUR TASK Within your favorite browser, search for *CEO blogs, index of corporate blogs, index of CEO blogs,* and similar phrases. You will likely end up at Top Blogs for CEOs | .CEO (www.home.ceo/top-blogs-for-ceos) with a link to Mark Cuban's blog, among others. Or you will land at Feedspot's Top 100 Corporate Blogs, Websites & Influencers, listing popular corporate blogs (e.g., Microsoft, Apple, Samsung Global Newsroom, Bayer, Toyota). Pick a company of interest to you. Note how many of the points the selected blog makes match the guidelines in this book. If your instructor directs, write a brief informational memo or e-mail summarizing your observations about the business blog, its style, the subjects covered, and so forth.

7.10 Composing a Personal Blog Entry
(L.O. 4)

Communication Technology | **E-Mail** | **Social Media** | **Web**

Review the guidelines for professional blogging in this chapter. Find a recent social media–related study or survey, and target an audience of business professionals who may wish to know more about social networking. Search for studies conducted by respected organizations and businesses such as Pew Research Center, Robert Half International, Burson-Marsteller, ePolicy Institute, and U.S. government agencies, as applicable. As you plan and outline your post, follow the advice provided in this chapter. Although the goal is usually to offer advice, you could also weigh in with your opinion regarding a controversy. For example, do you agree with companies that forbid employees to use company-owned devices and networks for social media access? Do you agree that millennials and Gen Z are losing social skills because of excessive online connectivity?

YOUR TASK Compose a one-page blog entry in MS Word and submit it in hard copy. Alternatively, post it to the discussion board on the class course-management platform, or e-mail it to your instructor, as appropriate. Because you will be drawing on other people's ideas, be careful to paraphrase correctly and not to copy from your sources. Visit Chapter 11 to review how to put ideas into your own words with integrity.

7.11 Blogging: Learning From the Best
(L.O. 4)

Communication Technology | **E-Mail** | **Social Media** | **Web**

Visit the blogs of Seth Godin, Chris Brogan, Guy Kawasaki, Bill Marriott, and other acclaimed bloggers. See what tricks of the trade you can adopt and make work for you.

YOUR TASK You may be asked to write a blog entry detailing your analysis of the professional blogs you have examined. Apply the best practices for professional business blogs outlined in this chapter. Remember to craft a catchy title that will attract browsers or, in this case, your peers in class and your instructor. Share helpful advice in easy-to-read numbered items and, if applicable, provide links to other relevant articles. To motivate readers to respond, ask questions at the end of your blog entry.

7.12 Epic Twitter Blunders (L.O. 5)

Communication Technology | **E-Mail** | **Social Media**

The modern workplace is a potential digital minefield. The imprudent use of practically any online tool—whether e-mail, real-time messaging, texting, tweeting, blogging, or posting to Instagram—can land workers in hot water and even lead to dismissal. Here are five ways Twitter can get you canned for showing poor judgment:[126]

a. **Sending hate tweets about the boss.** Example: *My idiot boss said he put in for raises. I think he lies. He is known for that. His daddy owns the company.*

b. **Lying to the boss and bragging about it.** Example: *I so lied to my boss . . . I was late but I said I forgot my badge and got away with it.*

c. **Romancing the boss (kissing and telling).** Example: *I give the boss what he wants, and the fringe benefits are amazing.*

d. **Announcing the desire to quit.** Example: *So close to quitting my job right now. Sometimes I can't [expletive] stand this place [expletive] moron assistant plant manager I'm about to deck him.*

e. **Blocking your boss.** Example: *i kept my promise . . . my boss thought she was gonna follow me on here . . . i BLOCKED her [expletive] ASAP.*

YOUR TASK Discuss each violation of Twitter best practices, or summarize in general why these tweets are potentially damaging to their authors. How could the Twitter users have handled their grievances more professionally? Should they have refrained altogether? Comment on the style of these questionable tweets. If your instructor requests, summarize your observations in an e-mail message or an online post.

7.13 Social Media: Quitting Cold Turkey?

Communication Technology | **E-Mail** | **Social Media** | **Web**

Could you give up your electronic toys for 24 hours without withdrawal symptoms? How about quitting social media cold turkey for a week? Thirty days? Would you be able to survive unplugged from all media? Headlines decrying social media addiction litter the Internet. Self-declared social media junkies detail the lessons they learned after renouncing their gadgets for a "detox," "sabbatical," "purge," or "dramatic spree." Those who go offline describe feelings of emptiness, boredom, loneliness, depression, and anxiety. Some are baffled by their digital friends reacting to their abstinence with coercion, cajoling—even scorn![127]

No wonder that a new occupation has emerged, that of a recovery consultant who works with former digital addicts. Ryan Van Cleave warns that suddenly trying to quit the compulsive use of social networking, gaming, and other digital media can lead to emotional meltdowns. He explains that young digital natives can't suddenly unplug after being plugged in since birth. Van Cleave goes so far as to say that those young people don't perceive the technology. Taking it away from them "is truly an annihilation," the consultant, a former video game addict himself, believes. He says that quitting cold turkey "feels like a powerful attack on you. It creates a powerful, unbearable sense of aloneness."[128]

YOUR TASK Discuss in a classroom debate or in a live chat the following questions: Have you ever unplugged? What was that experience like? Could you give up your smartphone, TV, car stereo, online magazines and newspapers, and computer? No texting, no Instagram, messaging, or texting for a day or longer? What would you do instead? Is there any harm in not being able to unplug? If directed by your instructor, summarize your experience with or views on giving up electronic gadgets in a compelling blog post. Follow the blogging guidelines in this chapter.

7.14 Social Media: Following the Top 10 Most Plugged-in CEOs (L.O. 5)

E-Mail | Social Media | Team | Web

If you are a budding entrepreneur and future tycoon, you may be looking to successful business leaders for inspiration. Learning about and connecting with chief executives has never been easier thanks to social media. Consulting firm Brunswick Group examined the digital profiles of 790 CEOs in the U.S. and U.K. for their social media presence on Facebook, Instagram, Twitter, and LinkedIn. Additionally, Brunswick surveyed thousands of employees in both countries for its study. After crunching 100,000+ data points, the firm established a ranking of CEOs based not only on connectedness, i.e., the presence of accounts, but their owners' active engagement. The ranking extends from the lowest score of 536 for Flutter Entertainment CEO Peter Jackson, who placed 100th, to No.1-ranked Walmart CEO Doug McMillon and his score of 829. The study also confirmed that Twitter and LinkedIn are the CEOs' preferred networking sites.[129]

Social media are "an unfiltered forum for corporate leaders to listen to their communities and to connect by sharing their successes and challenges," Nasdaq president and CEO Adena Friedman says. The fourth-ranked CEO believes that "Social media projects the human side of the corporate world."[130] The Brunswick study revealed that most workers check a CEO's social media accounts before joining a company. The candidates also consult Glassdoor, a popular platform where current and former employees submit anonymous company reviews, including otherwise hard-to-come-by salary information. A top Glassdoor score means high job approval among employees. Highly connected CEOs on average scored better than their less connected peers on Glassdoor (+5 percent) as did their companies (+3 percent).

YOUR TASK Search for the *Connected Leadership* report by Brunswick on the Web. Peruse or download a PDF copy. You will find that the top five executives are Doug McMillon (Walmart), Brent Saunders (Allergan), Ramon Laguarda (PepsiCo), Adena Friedman (Nasdaq), and Dan Schulman (PayPal). Mary Barra (GM), Hans Vestberg (Verizon), and Ed Bastian (Delta Air Lines) are also among the top 10 CEOs. Individually or as a team, pick a CEO who interests you. Analyze the executives' presence and influence on their social media networks of choice. Find out how many followers they have, how often they post, what topics they discuss (strictly business or personal), how they come across to you (approachable, friendly or formidable, tough), and more. Correlate these observations with their Glassdoor scores. Does the approval score match your CEO's Brunswick survey rating? Discuss your findings as a group or in class. If asked, summarize your research in a cogent e-mail or memo.

Test Your Workplace Etiquette IQ

New communication platforms and casual workplace environments have blurred the lines of appropriateness, leaving workers wondering how to navigate uncharted waters. Indicate whether the following statements are true or false. Then see if you agree with the responses on p. Key-5.

1. You just received an e-mail from Seth that contains important information that Kaitlyn should know. To save you the trouble of rekeying the important parts, you should take advantage of the forwarding function by sending the message on to Kaitlyn.

   _____ True _____ False

2. Because e-mail is not transmitted on letterhead stationery and is rather casual, it doesn't require you to apply the same formal standards that you use for other office correspondence.

   _____ True _____ False

3. You just returned to the office from a terrific lunch. Your spicy fish dish was tasty and enough for a second meal. Because everyone uses the office fridge to store food, it's appropriate to put it there so that you can warm it up for tomorrow's lunch.

   _____ True _____ False

Chat About It

In each chapter you will find five discussion questions related to the chapter material. Your instructor may assign these topics for you to discuss in class, in an online chat room, or on an online discussion board. Some of the discussion topics may require outside research. You may also be asked to read and respond to postings made by your classmates.

TOPIC 1: In one failed gamification effort, United Airlines planned to end bonuses rewarding at least a third of its 80,000 employees and replace them with sweepstakes. Approximately 1,400 eligible workers could have won valuable prizes such as Mercedes sedans, vacations, and cash. Why would United workers rebel online and scuttle the plan? Why might United prefer a lottery?

TOPIC 2: Describe a time when you should have had a face-to-face meeting instead of sending an electronic message. Why would the face-to-face meeting have been better?

TOPIC 3: Find an example of an e-mail or text that caused a problem for the sender because the message found its way to an unintended recipient. What problem did the situation cause?

TOPIC 4: What is your strategy to avoid sending a direct message, text, or tweet that you might regret later?

TOPIC 5: Smart connected work clothes of the future may include "mood sweaters" with skin sensors and LED-equipped collars that will change color based on wearers' feelings. Some believe such tell-tale clothes will help with nonverbal communication and team building. Can you imagine any drawbacks to color displays of your mood at the office?

Grammar and Mechanics Review 7

Apostrophes and Other Punctuation

Review Guides 31 through 38 about apostrophes and other punctuation in Appendix D, Grammar and Mechanics. On a separate sheet or on your computer, revise the following sentences to correct errors in the use of apostrophes and other punctuation. For each error you locate, write the guide number that reflects this usage. The more you recognize the reasons, the better you will learn these punctuation guidelines. If a sentence is correct, write C. When you finish, check your answers in the key at the end of the book.

EXAMPLE: Management complained that the companys computers were used to stream video.

REVISION: Management complained that the **company's** computers were used to stream video. [Guide 32]

1. In just one years time, Chynna increased her blog followers by 70 percent.

2. Max wondered whether all sales managers databases needed to be updated.

3. Even her friends resented Olivia smoking in the hallways.

4. Many followers of James blog commented on the overuse of the Reply All button.

5. Our three top sales reps, Ryan, Ashley, and Leah received substantial bonuses.

6. You must replace the ink cartridge see page 8 in the manual, before printing.

7. Success often depends on an individuals ability to adapt to change.

8. (Direct quotation) The death of e-mail, said Mike Song, has been greatly exaggerated.

9. The most helpful article was titled Ten Tools for Building Your Own Mobile App.

10. Our staffing meeting starts at 10 a.m. sharp, doesn't it.

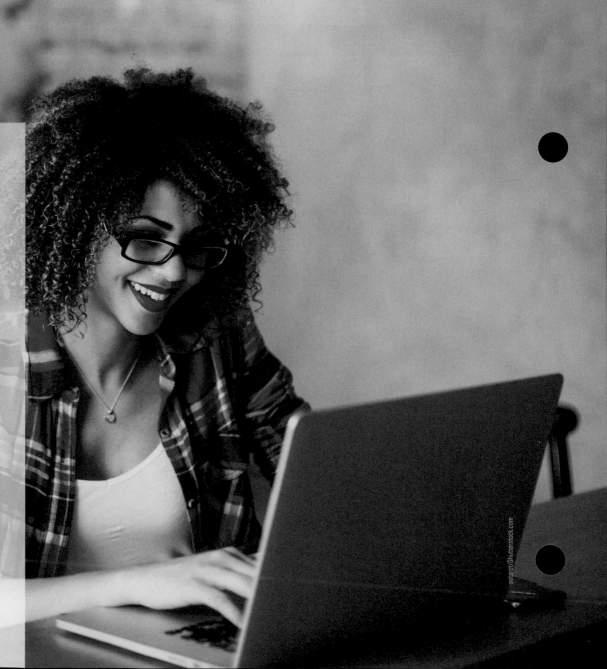

CHAPTER 8

Positive and Neutral Messages

LEARNING OUTCOMES

After studying this chapter, you should be able to do the following:

1 Applying the 3-x-3 writing process, identify the channels through which neutral and positive messages—e-mails, memos, and business letters—travel in the digital era workplace.

2 Compose direct messages that make requests, respond to inquiries via any channel, and deliver step-by-step instructions.

3 Prepare contemporary messages that make direct claims and voice complaints, including those posted online.

4 Create adjustment messages that restore customers' trust and promote further business.

5 Write special messages that convey kindness and goodwill.

astarot/Shutterstock.com

Domino's: A Technology Company That Sells Pizza?

Pizza is nearly as American as apple pie, and when it comes to ordering it, Domino's has cooked up a recipe for success by embracing digital transformation. Within a decade the pizza powerhouse revamped its operations and now uses a multichannel strategy that allows hungry customers to order in 18 different ways—from Domino's zero-click delivery app to Slack. Today 65 percent of customer orders come through digital channels. After radically changing how it does business, the international restaurant chain consistently grew and started turning a profit.[1] Sales nearly doubled within seven years; the pizza giant's shares jumped from $11 to about $260. Domino's has muscled out Pizza Hut to become the world's largest pizza chain by sales, although it has 2,000 fewer domestic outlets.[2]

Just a decade ago, however, the outlook was bleak. Domino's sales were down. A new leadership determined that, to salvage the chain, it needed to change the tired pizza recipe, the brand image, as well as the entire experience of ordering. Domino's digital transformation began. It was initiated with a crowdsourcing contest to achieve a complete turnaround. Domino's launched *Think Oven*, a Facebook platform that enabled a two-way dialogue with customers who were invited to submit suggestions to Idea Box and Current Projects. Domino's asked for help, for example, with menu items, going green, and specific topics such as new uniforms. The company solicited opinions, listened to its fans, and changed pizza recipes. It also liberally shared its technological vision with customers.[3]

When the company's leaders realized that their core customers were deeply connected to their devices, they decided that Domino's would meet them there. Customers would be able to order anywhere however they wanted.

Domino's *AnyWare* was born. The innovative ordering platform lets customers summon pizza using any channel imaginable today. Hungry pizza lovers can order by text, Twitter, and Facebook Messenger. They can use their smart TV, smart speaker such as Google or Echo, smartwatch, an in-app voice assistant, and even the Ford Sync communication system. In turn, Domino's tweets that encourage followers to order a pizza are irreverent and humorous. Facebook posts include emojis and inspire interaction. Instead of being a restaurant chain that allowed customers to order pizza online, Domino's has become an e-commerce company that happens to sell pizza.[4]

Successful businesses such as Domino's engage with customers seamlessly using the channels the fans prefer. They employ language that resonates with core target groups and tailor their messaging to customer needs. Such nimble positive and informative messaging is the bread and butter of this pizza company. You will learn more about Domino's and be asked to complete a relevant task at the end of this chapter.

Critical Thinking

- Why does Domino's employ redundancy in its methods to order its pizzas?

- What is the best way for companies such as Domino's to react to customer comments on social media?

- Why must messaging always be carefully constructed, especially on social media?

8-1 The Writing Process for Positive and Neutral Messages

LEARNING OUTCOME

1 Applying the 3-x-3 writing process, identify the channels through which neutral and positive messages—e-mails, memos, and business letters—travel in the digital era workplace.

Most workplace messages convey positive or neutral information that helps workers conduct everyday business. Because positive messages are routine and straightforward, they are direct and to the point. Such routine messages include simple requests for information or action, replies to customers, and explanations to coworkers. Other types of positive messages are instructions, direct claims, and complaints.

E-mail is the channel most frequently used, but memos and letters still matter in the digital age workplace. In addition, businesses must listen and respond to social media buzz, as Domino's does with a dedicated team at headquarters in Ann Arbor, Michigan. In some industries, memos continue to be an important channel of communication within organizations. Memos are also used as attachments sent with brief cover e-mails when formatting matters and the memo is important enough that it might be printed and displayed.

Letters are a vital paper-based channel typically used for external communication. As discussed in Chapter 7, e-mail and social media are used to communicate within organizations as well as with outside audiences. What do all these channels have in common? As shown in Chapter 1, they all require solid writing skills. In the glaring light of social media and workplace messaging of all kinds, writing skills—or the lack of them—are amplified mercilessly and can bring a career to a grinding halt.

In this book we divide business messages into three content areas: (a) **positive messages** communicating straightforward requests, replies, and goodwill, covered in this chapter; (b) **bad-news** or **negative messages** delivering refusals and bad news, covered in Chapter 9; and (c) **persuasive messages**, including sales pitches, covered in Chapter 10. This chapter focuses on routine, neutral, and positive messages. These will make up the bulk of your workplace communication. Here is a quick review of the 3-x-3 writing process to help you apply it to positive and neutral messages. You will also learn when to respond by business letter and how to format it.

8-1a Phase 1: Analyzing, Anticipating, and Adapting

In Phase 1, prewriting, you will need to spend some time analyzing your task. It is amazing how many of us are ready to start typing before engaging our minds. Too often, writers start messages without enough preparation. As you begin the writing process, ask yourself these important questions:

- **Do I really need to write this e-mail, memo, or letter?** A phone call, a Slack inquiry, or a quick visit with a coworker might solve the problem—and save the time of writing a message. On the other hand, some written messages are needed to provide a permanent record or develop a thoughtful plan.

- **Why am I writing?** Know why you are writing and what you hope to achieve. This will help you recognize the important points and decide where to place them.

- **How will the reader react?** Visualize the reader and the effect your message will have. Imagine that you are sitting and talking with your reader. Avoid speaking bluntly, failing to explain, or ignoring your reader's needs. Shape the message to benefit the reader. Remember that e-mails may very well be forwarded to someone else and that ill-conceived instant messages or social media posts can trigger very public reactions.

- **What channel should I use?** It's tempting to use e-mail for much of your correspondence. However, a phone call or face-to-face visit is a better channel choice if you need to (a) convey enthusiasm, warmth, or another emotion; (b) supply context; or (c) smooth over disagreements. A business letter is better when the matter requires (a) a permanent record, (b) confidentiality, or (c) formality. A quick chat or social media response is needed to reply to certain public posts whenever time is of the essence.

- **How can I save my reader's time?** Think of ways that you can make your message easier to comprehend at a glance. Use bullets, asterisks, lists, headings, and white space to improve readability.

Understanding Business Letters. Despite e-mail, workplace instant messaging, and social networking, in certain situations letters are still the preferred channel of communication for delivering messages *outside* an organization. Such letters go to suppliers, government agencies, other businesses, and, most important, customers. You may think that everybody is online, but with an Internet penetration rate in North America of nearly 95 percent,[5] a small portion of the U.S. population is still unplugged. Just as they are eager to connect with a majority of consumers online, businesses continue to give letters to customers a high priority because these messages, too, encourage product feedback, project a favorable image of the organization, promote future business, and signal greater formality. In addition, the sheer volume of daily e-mails can let important messages go unnoticed. Even a form letter mailed to consumers gets more attention than an e-mail does.[6]

Devina Saputri/Shutterstock.com

Whether you send a business letter will depend on the situation and the preference of your organization. Business letters are necessary when the situation calls for a permanent record. For example, when a company enters into an agreement with another company, business letters confirm the agreement and record decisions and points of understanding. Business letters deliver contracts, explain terms, exchange ideas, negotiate agreements, answer vendor questions, and maintain customer relations.

Business letters are confidential. They are less likely than electronic media to be intercepted, misdirected, forwarded, retrieved, or otherwise inspected by unintended recipients. Also, business letters presented on company stationery carry a sense of formality and importance not possible with e-mail. The Emily Post Institute calls attractive personal business letters "the single most impressive ambassador for your company." The etiquette experts point out that "A letter has a dignity that cannot be equaled by electronic mail or faxed correspondence."[7] Letters look important, as illustrated in Model Document 8.1, a customer-welcoming letter in the popular block format.

Finally, business letters deliver persuasive, well-considered messages. Letters can persuade people to change their actions, adopt new beliefs, make donations, contribute their time, and try new products. Direct-mail letters remain a powerful tool to promote services and products, boost e-commerce and retail traffic, and enhance customer relations. You will learn more about writing persuasive and sales messages in Chapter 10.

8-1b Phase 2: Researching, Organizing, and Drafting

In Phase 2, drafting, you will first want to check the files, gather documentation, and prepare your message. Make an outline of the points you wish to cover. For short messages jot down notes on the document you are answering or make a scratch list on your computer or handheld device.

For longer documents that require formal research, use the outlining techniques discussed in Chapter 5. As you compose your message, avoid amassing huge blocks of text. No one wants to read endless lines of type. Instead, group related information into paragraphs, preferably short ones. Paragraphs separated by white space look inviting. Be sure that each paragraph includes a topic sentence backed up by details and evidence. If you bury your main point in the middle of a paragraph, the reader may miss it. Also plan for revision, because excellence is rarely achieved on the first effort.

1 Prewriting

Analyze: The purpose of this direct letter is to welcome new pet owners, acknowledge their recent visit, and build goodwill.

Anticipate: The audience is a couple who own a cat, Silver, and who may appreciate reassurance that their pet will be in good hands.

Adapt: Because the message is straightforward, use the direct strategy. The letter signals greater formality, projects care, and builds goodwill.

2 Drafting

Research: No research is necessary as most of the information included in the letter would be common knowledge to the writer.

Organize: Frontload the positive welcoming greeting. Focus on the high standards of the pet clinic, establish its reputation, and detail its services.

Draft: Draft the first version with the expectation to revise.

3 Revising

Edit: Check for factual accuracy. Eliminate repetition and redundancy. Strive for concise language.

Proofread: Run a spellcheck and look for spelling errors your spellchecker won't catch (homophones). Check the format of your letter.

Evaluate: Will the recipients appreciate receiving this letter? Will the letter provide them with adequate information?

Letterhead

MORNINGSIDE VETERINARY CLINIC
2451 NE BROADWAY ST. PORTLAND, OR 97232 (503) 828-3008

Dateline

September 14, 2021

Inside address

Mr. and Mrs. Robert C. Liebert
Silver Court Apartments
2172 NE Hancock Street, Apt. E
Portland, OR 97212

Salutation

Dear Mr. and Mrs. Liebert:

Optional subject line

Subject: Welcome to Morningside Veterinary Clinic!

Body

We are grateful that you have chosen Morningside Veterinary Clinic for your pet's veterinary care. You can be sure that our attentive and sensitive hospital staff will provide you and your pet with the best veterinary care possible.

Your pet will receive the finest care at one of the few clinics in the Portland region recognized as a full member of the American Animal Hospital Association. This organization requires the very highest standards for small animal medicine and surgical care.

Our hospital also provides a wide variety of more extensive services. We offer hospitalization and intensive care for seriously ill pets. Ultrasound and X-ray facilities are available. All X-rays taken are reviewed by a board-certified veterinary radiologist.

The best way to keep your pets healthy and happy is through preventive care. One of the most important services we provide is the annual physical examination. We check all your pet's vital systems, document a baseline of health, and proactively catch any situations that need attention. Other basic services include vaccinations, deworming, dental cleaning, geriatric physicals, and toenail trims. For your convenience, your pet may be dropped off if you are unable to schedule a specific appointment time.

It was a pleasure meeting you and your adorable cat Silver. Please know that we are available anytime you have questions regarding your pet's health. We promise to do our best to practice outstanding veterinary care, communicate clearly, and earn your trust. As we discussed, please call Kathryn at (503) 828-3008 to schedule your kitty for an annual physical examination.

Complimentary close

Sincerely,

Organization name

MORNINGSIDE VETERINARY CLINIC

Gaby E. Newhose

Author's name

Gaby E. Newhouse, DVM

Reference initials

GEN:erf

Tips for Formatting Letters

- Start the date 2 inches from the top or 1 blank line below the letterhead.
- For block style, begin all lines at the left margin.
- Leave side margins of 1 to 1.5 inches depending on the length of the letter and the font size.
- Single-space the body and double-space between paragraphs.
- Use left, not right, justification.

Logo: Kalavati/Shutterstock.com

8-1c Phase 3: Editing, Proofreading, and Evaluating

Phase 3, revising, involves putting the final touches on your message. Careful and caring writers ask themselves the following questions:

- **Is the message clear?** Viewed from the receiver's perspective, are the ideas clear? Did you use plain English? If the message is passed on to others, will they need further explanation? Consider having a colleague critique your message if it is an important one.

- **Is the message correct?** Are the sentences complete and punctuated properly? Did you overlook any typos or misspelled words? Remember to use your spell-checker and grammar-checker to proofread your message before sending it.

- **Did you plan for feedback?** How will you know whether this message is successful? You can improve feedback by asking questions (such as *Are you comfortable with these suggestions?* or *What do you think?*). Remember to make it easy for the recipient to respond.

- **Will this message achieve its purpose?** The last step in the 3-x-3 writing process is evaluating the product.

8-2 Routine Request, Response, and Instruction Messages

LEARNING OUTCOME

2 Compose direct messages that make requests, respond to inquiries via any channel, and deliver step-by-step instructions.

Neutral and positive messages take the form of e-mails, memos, and letters. Brief neutral and positive messages are also delivered by instant messaging, texting, and social media posts. When you need information from a team member in another office, you might send an e-mail or dash off a Slack message. If you must explain new safety measures to rank-and-file workers who do not have company e-mail, you would write an interoffice memo for posting in a shared space such as the lunchroom. However, when you welcome a new customer or respond to a customer letter, you would prepare a letter.

Most of your business messages will involve routine requests and responses to requests, which are organized directly. Requests and replies may be transmitted in e-mails, memos, letters, or social media posts. You might, for example, receive an inquiry via Twitter, Instagram, or Facebook about an upcoming product launch. You may need to request information from a hotel as you plan a company conference. You might be answering an inquiry by e-mail from a customer about your services or products. These kinds of routine requests and replies follow a similar pattern.

8-2a Writing Requests

When you write messages that request information or action and you think your request will be received positively, start with the main idea. The most emphatic positions in a message are the opening and closing. Readers tend to look at them first. You should capitalize on this tendency by putting the most significant statement first. The first sentence of an information request is usually a question or a polite command. It should not be an explanation or justification, unless you expect resistance to the request. When the information or action requested is likely to be forthcoming, immediately tell the reader what you want.

The e-mail in Model Document 8.2 inquiring about hotel accommodations begins immediately with the most important idea: Can the hotel provide meeting rooms and accommodations for 150 people and their guests? Instead of opening with an explanation of who the writer is or why the writer happens to be writing this message, the e-mail begins directly.

If several questions must be asked, you have two choices. You can ask the most important question first, as shown in Model Document 8.2, or you can begin with a summary statement, such as *Please answer the following questions about meeting rooms and accommodations for*

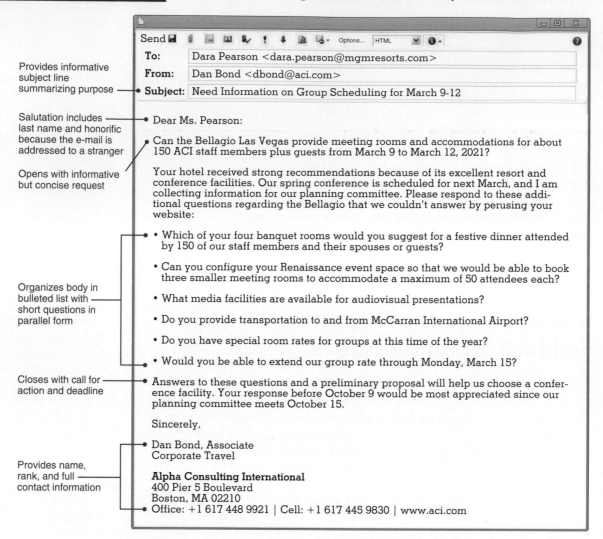

Provides informative subject line summarizing purpose

Salutation includes last name and honorific because the e-mail is addressed to a stranger

Opens with informative but concise request

Organizes body in bulleted list with short questions in parallel form

Closes with call for action and deadline

Provides name, rank, and full contact information

---

150 people from March 9 through March 12. Avoid beginning with *Will you please....* Although such a statement sounds like a question, it is actually a disguised command. Because you expect an action rather than a reply, you should punctuate this polite command with a period instead of a question mark. To avoid having to choose between a period and a question mark, just omit *Will you* and start with *Please answer.*

Providing Details.   The body of a message that requests information or action provides necessary details. Remember that the quality of the information obtained from a request depends on the clarity of the inquiry. If you analyze your needs, organize your ideas, and frame your request logically, you are likely to receive a meaningful answer that doesn't require a follow-up message. Whenever possible, focus on benefits to the reader (*To ensure that you receive the exact sweater you want, send us your color choice*). To improve readability, itemize appropriate information in bulleted or numbered lists. Notice that the questions in Model Document 8.2 are bulleted, and they are parallel. That is, they use the same balanced construction.

Closing With Appreciation and an Action Request.   In the closing of your message, tell the reader courteously what is to be done. If a date is important, set an end date to take action and explain why. Some careless writers end request messages simply with *Thank you,* forcing the reader to review the contents to determine what is expected and when. You can save the reader's time by spelling out the action to be taken. Avoid other overused endings such as *Thank you for your cooperation* (trite), *Thank you in advance for . . .* (trite and presumptuous), and *If you have any questions, do not hesitate to call me* (suggests that you didn't make yourself clear).

Showing appreciation is always appropriate, but try to do so in a fresh and efficient manner. For example, you could hook your thanks to the end date (*Thanks for taking our Qualtrics survey before May 5, when we will begin tabulation*). You might connect your appreciation to a statement developing reader benefits (*We are grateful for the information you will provide because it will help us serve you faster and better*). You could briefly describe how the information will help you (*I appreciate this information, which will enable me to . . .*). When possible, make it easy for the reader to comply with your request (*Follow the link to the fillable PDF form; once completed, your response will be automatically sent to us* or *Join our Slack workspace* IOdesignteam.slack.com *so that you can reach us quickly*).

8-2b Responding to Requests

Most of your replies to requests for information or action will be direct and favorable. A customer wants information about a product, a supplier asks to arrange a meeting, an employee inquires about a procedure, or a manager requests your input on a marketing campaign. In complying with such requests, you will want to apply the same direct strategy you used in making requests.

A customer reply e-mail that starts with an effective subject line, as shown in Model Document 8.3, helps the reader recognize the topic immediately. The subject line refers in abbreviated form to previous correspondence and/or summarizes a message (*Subject: Your June 15 Inquiry About RecordQuirk Software*). Knowledgeable business communicators use a subject line to refer to earlier correspondence so that in the first sentence, the most emphatic spot in most messages, they are free to emphasize the main idea.

In the first sentence of a direct reply e-mail, deliver the information the reader wants. Avoid wordy, drawn-out openings (*I am responding to your e-mail of December 1, in which you request information about . . .*). More forceful and more efficient is an opener that answers the inquiry (*Here is the information you wanted about . . .*). When agreeing to a request for action, announce the good news promptly (*Yes, I will be happy to speak to your business communication class about conciseness . . .*).

In the body of your response, supply explanations and additional information. Because an e-mail or e-mail thread, like other documents written for your company, may be considered a legally binding contract, be sure to check facts and figures carefully. In contexts that could be viewed as negotiations, avoid words such as *accept*, *agree*, or *agreement*.[10] Under certain circumstances in some U.S. states, an e-mail can also become an enforceable document; therefore, exercise caution when using a company e-mail address or anytime you are posting for your employer on social media. Even a simple *yes* sent by text message can be held against the sender in court.[11] If a policy or procedure needs authorization, seek approval from a supervisor or executive before writing the message.

When customers or prospective customers inquire about products or services, your response should do more than merely supply answers. Try to promote your organization and products. Be sure to present the promotional material with attention to the "you" view and to reader benefits (*You can use our standardized tests to free you from time-consuming employment screening*).

In concluding a response message, refer to the information provided or to its use. (*The attached list summarizes our recommendations. We wish you all the best in redesigning your social media presence.*) If further action is required, help the reader with specifics (*The Small Business Administration publishes many helpful booklets. Its Internet address is . . .*). Avoid signing off with clichés (*If I may be of further assistance, don't hesitate to . . .*).

The following checklist reviews the direct strategy for writing information or action requests and replying to such messages.

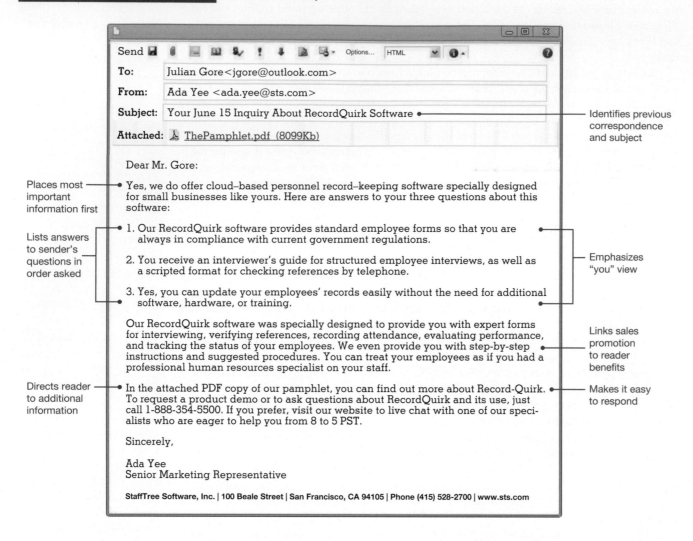

Places most important information first

Lists answers to sender's questions in order asked

Directs reader to additional information

Identifies previous correspondence and subject

Emphasizes "you" view

Links sales promotion to reader benefits

Makes it easy to respond

E-mail content:

Send | Options... | HTML

To: Julian Gore<jgore@outlook.com>

From: Ada Yee <ada.yee@sts.com>

Subject: Your June 15 Inquiry About RecordQuirk Software

Attached: ThePamphlet.pdf (8099Kb)

Dear Mr. Gore:

Yes, we do offer cloud–based personnel record–keeping software specially designed for small businesses like yours. Here are answers to your three questions about this software:

1. Our RecordQuirk software provides standard employee forms so that you are always in compliance with current government regulations.

2. You receive an interviewer's guide for structured employee interviews, as well as a scripted format for checking references by telephone.

3. Yes, you can update your employees' records easily without the need for additional software, hardware, or training.

Our RecordQuirk software was specially designed to provide you with expert forms for interviewing, verifying references, recording attendance, evaluating performance, and tracking the status of your employees. We even provide you with step-by-step instructions and suggested procedures. You can treat your employees as if you had a professional human resources specialist on your staff.

In the attached PDF copy of our pamphlet, you can find out more about Record-Quirk. To request a product demo or to ask questions about RecordQuirk and its use, just call 1-888-354-5500. If you prefer, visit our website to live chat with one of our specialists who are eager to help you from 8 to 5 PST.

Sincerely,

Ada Yee
Senior Marketing Representative

StaffTree Software, Inc. | 100 Beale Street | San Francisco, CA 94105 | Phone (415) 528-2700 | www.sts.com

Checklist

Writing Direct Requests and Responses

Requesting Information or Action

- **Open by stating the main idea.** To elicit information, ask a question or issue a polite command (*Please answer the following questions . . .*).

- **Explain and justify the request.** In the body arrange questions or information logically in parallel, balanced form. Clarify and substantiate your request.

- **Request action in the closing.** Close a request by summarizing exactly what is to be done, including dates or deadlines. Express appreciation. Avoid clichés (*Thank you for your cooperation, Thanking you in advance*).

Responding to Requests

- **Open directly.** Immediately deliver the information the receiver wants. Avoid wordy, drawn-out openings (*I have before me your request of August 5*). When agreeing to a request, announce the good news immediately.

- **Supply additional information.** In the body provide explanations and expand initial statements. In customer e-mails and letters,

promote products and the organization.

- **Conclude with a cordial statement.** Refer to the information provided or its use. If further action is required,

describe the procedures and give specifics. Avoid clichés (*If you have questions, please do not hesitate to let me know*).

Plugged In

How the GDPR Is Changing the Accountability of Internet Firms and E-Commerce

When the European Union enacted its General Data Protection Regulation (GDPR) on May 25, 2018, e-commerce businesses worldwide were scrambling to comply.[12] The purpose of the GDPR is to strengthen Europe's already strict data privacy protections. It gives European Internet users more control over what happens to their data, and businesses must be transparent about what they do with their customers' information. Existing privacy laws could not anticipate smartphones and other electronic devices collecting reams of personal user data for Google or Facebook whose

business models rely on gathering and selling information for targeted advertising. The GDPR may be a European Union law, but it affects individuals globally, not just European Internet users. It also affects U.S. businesses.

Not until the Cambridge Analytica scandal enveloped Facebook and forced CEO Mark Zuckerberg to testify before Congress did the public realize how much personal information was being shared without their knowledge and consent. The GDPR now regulates how organizations may and may not use identifiable personal data, i.e., information that can be linked to a specific user, such as an individual's name, phone number, username, IP address, or location data. Even stricter rules apply to more sensitive information such as health data, political views, and sexual orientation. Companies now need to ask customers' permission before collecting and sharing their information.

Moreover, under the GDPR, companies must notify their customers promptly of data breaches, no later than 72 hours after a cyberattack is discovered. Also, Internet companies must use simple language instead of hiding behind small print and legalese. Embedded in the GDPR is **the right to be forgotten.** Also called **the right to erasure**, it means that people have the right to access their own digital personal data and request to have it deleted or erroneous search results removed.[13] Exceptions to the right to be forgotten include information that may be in the public interest or is used to exercise the freedom of expression in legitimate news stories, for example.

Monster Ztudio/Shutterstock.com

8-2c Reacting to Customer Comments on Social Media

We live in an age when vocal individuals can start a firestorm of criticism on social media or become powerful brand ambassadors who champion certain products. Therefore, businesses must listen to social media comments about themselves and, if necessary, respond. You may ask, how do companies know when to respond, and how? After all, in the era of bots, some reviewers may not even be real, and their review may require validation.

However, social media marketing experts have developed guidelines to provide organizations with tools for strategic decision making in various situations. Figure 8.1 shows a social media response flowchart, now common in for-profit and nonprofit organizations alike. Businesses can't control the conversation without disabling fans' comments on their Facebook walls or blogs, but they can respond in a way that benefits customers, prevents the problem from snowballing, and shines a positive light on the organization.

Embracing Customer Comments. Customer reviews on social media platforms are opportunities for savvy businesses to improve their products or services and may serve as a free and efficient crowdsourced quality-control system. Companies such as JetBlue, Nike, Starbucks, T-Mobile, and Whole Foods use powerful social media monitoring software

FIGURE 8.1 Social Media Response Flowchart

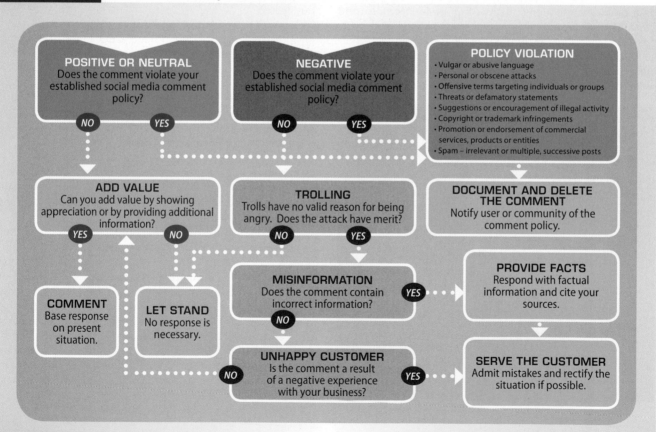

To help their employees make a prudent decision about whether and how to respond to social media posts, companies are creating decision trees and diagrams such as the one shown here.[15]

to sift through billions of posts and product reviews. The data offer real-time feedback that may help clear up supply chain bottlenecks, expose product flaws, and improve operating instructions.[16] For example, when a customer complained to Procter & Gamble that her Bounce Dryer Bar broke from its plastic base, the Bounce brand manager mailed her a cordial personal letter with a replacement. The company then fixed the problem by increasing the length of tape on the back of the dryer bar holder and improving the installation instructions.[17]

Adopting Best Practices for Replying to Social Media Posts. Marketing experts say that not every comment on social media merits a response. They recommend responding to posts only when you can add value—for example, by correcting false information or providing customer service. Additional guidelines for professional responses to customer comments are summarized in Figure 8.2.

8-2d Composing Instruction Messages

Instruction messages describe how to complete a task. You may be asked to write instructions about how to use annotation and drawing markup tools in PDFs, order supplies, file a grievance, or hire new employees. Instructions are different from policies and official procedures, which establish rules of conduct to be followed within an organization. We are most concerned with creating messages that clearly explain how to complete a task.

Like requests and responses, instruction messages follow a straightforward, direct approach. Before writing instructions for a process, be sure you understand the process completely. Practice doing it yourself. A message that delivers instructions should open with an explanation of why the procedure or set of instructions is necessary.

Creating Step-by-Step Instructions. The body of an instruction message should use plain English and familiar words to describe the process. Your messages explaining instructions will be most readable if you follow these guidelines:

- Divide the instructions into steps.
- List the steps in the order in which they are to be carried out.
- Arrange the items vertically with numbers.
- Begin each step with an action verb using the imperative (command) mood rather than the indicative mood.

FIGURE 8.2 Responding to Customers on Social Media

Be positive.	Be transparent.	Be honest.	Be timely.	Be helpful.
• Respond in a friendly, upbeat, yet professional tone. • Correct mistakes politely. • Do not argue, insult, or blame others.	• State your name and position with the business. • Personalize and humanize your business.	• Own up to problems and mistakes. • Inform customers when and how you will improve the situation.	• Respond in less than 24 hours.	• Point users to valuable information on your website or other approved websites. • Follow up with users when new information is available.

In an era of consumer-centric, omnichannel customer service, businesses must listen and be ready to respond swiftly to social media comments and complaints.

Indicative Mood	Imperative Mood
The contract must be signed immediately.	Sign the contract immediately.
The first step involves downloading the app.	Download the app first.
A survey of employees is necessary to learn what options they prefer.	Survey employees to learn the options they prefer.

In the closing of a message issuing instructions, try to tie following the instructions to benefits to the organization or individual.

If you are asked to prepare a list of instructions that is not part of a message, include a title such as *How to Add Comments to PDFs*. Include an opening paragraph explaining why the instructions are needed.

Revising a Message Delivering Instructions.

Model Document 8.4 shows the first draft of an interoffice memo written by Andre Quincy. His memo was meant to announce a new method for employees to follow in requesting equipment repairs. However, the tone was negative, the explanation of the problem rambled, and the new method was unclear. Finally, Andre's first memo was wordy and filled with clichés (*do not hesitate to call*).

In the revision Andre improved the tone considerably. The frontloaded main idea is introduced with a *please*, which softens an order. The subject line specifies the purpose of the memo. Instead of dwelling on past procedures and failures (*we are no longer using* and *many mix-ups in the past*), Andre revised his message to explain constructively how reporting should be handled.

Andre realized that his original explanation of the new procedure was confusing. To clarify the instructions, he itemized and numbered the steps. Each step begins with an action verb in the imperative (command) mood (*Log in, Indicate, Select, Identify,* and *Print*). It is sometimes difficult to force all the steps in a list into this kind of command language. Andre struggled, but he finally found verbs that worked.

Why should you go to so much trouble to make lists and achieve parallelism? Because readers can comprehend what you have said much more quickly. Parallel language also makes you look professional and efficient. The resulting document is visually appealing.

In writing messages that deliver instructions, be careful of tone. Today's managers and team leaders seek employee participation and cooperation. These goals can't be achieved, though, if the writer sounds like a dictator or an autocrat. Avoid making accusations and fixing blame. Rather, explain changes, give reasons, and suggest benefits to the reader. Assume that employees want to contribute to the success of the organization and to their own achievement. Notice in the Figure 8.4 revision that Andre tells readers that they will save time and reduce mix-ups if they follow the new method.

8-3 Direct Claims and Complaints

The wheels of commerce turn smoothly for millions of business transactions, but even the best systems are not failsafe—promised shipments are late, warrantied goods fail, and service is disappointing. When you as a customer must write to identify or correct a wrong, the message is called a claim. Straightforward claims are those to which you expect the receiver to agree readily.

Increasingly, consumers resort to telephone calls, they e-mail their claims, or—as we have seen—they vent their peeves in online posts. Large companies can afford to employ social media specialists who monitor and respond to comments. However, small and midsized businesses often have few options other than Google Alerts and their own limited forays into social networking.

Date: February 2, 2021
To: Staff Members
From: Andre Quincy, Operations Division
Subject: Repairs •──────────────────────────

We are taking this opportunity to inform you that we have recently instituted a •──
new procedure for all equipment repair requests. Effectively immediately, we
are no longer using the Equipment Repair Form that we formerly used. We want
to move everyone to an online database system. These new procedures will help •──
us repair your equipment faster and reduce the many mix-ups we suffered in the
past. You will find the new procedure at www.online-repairs.net. That's where
you log in. You should indicate the kind of equipment repair you need. It may
be a desktop, laptop, printer, copier, or other approved equipment. Then you •──
should begin the process of data entry for your specific problem by selecting
Create New Ticket. That's where you explain the problem. Following prompts
on the screen, you will also need to identify the manufacturer, model number,
and serial number. This information will appear on the new ticket, which
should be printed and attached securely to the equipment.

If you have any questions, do not hesitate to call Amanda at Extension 488. You •──
can also write to her at amanda.rodriguez@tekco.net if you can't reach her by
phone. Or you could use Slack.

Uses vague subject line

Lacks explanation of main idea in opening

Emphasizes "we" view rather than "you" view with reader benefits

Employs wordy, dense paragraph instead of numbered steps to explain new procedure

Closes with cliché expression (*do not hesitate*)

Employs informative subject line

Starts with main idea and emphasizes how the new procedure benefits the receiver

Lists easy-to-follow steps, beginning each numbered step with a verb

Closes with follow-up information and reinforces reader benefits

MEMORANDUM

Date: February 2, 2021

To: Staff Members

From: Andre Quincy, Operations Division *AQ*

• **Subject:**   New Procedure for Reporting Equipment Repair Requests

• Effective immediately, please use a new online repair database system to
report requests for equipment repairs. The following steps will return your
equipment to you more rapidly and efficiently:

1. Log in to www.online-repairs.net.

2. Indicate the kind of repair you need, such a desktop, laptop, printer, copier,
   or other approved equipment.

3. Select Create New Ticket and explain the specific problem.

4. Identify the manufacturer, model number, and serial number of the
   equipment.

5. Print the new ticket and attach it securely to the equipment.

If you have questions, call Amanda at Extension 488, write to her at amanda.
rodriguez@tekco.net, or message her on Slack. Following this new procedure
should vastly improve turnaround time and reduce mix-ups.

Tips for Writing Instructions
- Arrange steps in the order in which they should be completed.
- Start each step with an action verb in the imperative (command) mood.
- Be careful of tone in writing messages that give orders.
- Strive to show reader benefits if you are encouraging the use of the procedure.

This is why, in an age of social media, claims written as letters still play an important role even as they are being replaced by telephone calls, e-mails, and social media posts. Depending on the circumstances, letters more convincingly establish a record of what happened. Some business communicators opt for letters they can either attach to e-mail messages or fax. Regardless of the channel, straightforward claims use a direct approach. Claims that require a persuasive response are presented in Chapter 10.

8-3a Stating a Clear Claim in the Opening

Smart businesses want to hear from their customers. They know that retaining a customer is far less costly than recruiting a new customer. When you, as a customer, have a legitimate claim, you can expect a positive response from a company.

Open your claim with a compliment, a point of agreement, a statement of the problem, a brief review of action you have taken to resolve the problem, or a clear statement of the action you want. You might expect a replacement, a refund, a new product, credit to your account, correction of a billing error, free repairs, a free inspection, or cancellation of an order. When the remedy is obvious, state it immediately (*Please correct multiple charges for my single card-based cryptocurrency purchase. My VISA card was charged 17 times for the same transaction*).

When the remedy is less obvious, you might ask for a change in policy or procedure or simply for an explanation (*Because three of our employees with confirmed reservations were refused rooms September 16 in your hotel, would you please clarify your policy regarding reservations and late arrivals?*).

8-3b Supporting a Claim

In the body of a claim message, explain the problem and justify your request. Provide the necessary details so that the difficulty can be corrected without further correspondence. Avoid becoming angry or trying to fix blame. Bear in mind that the person reading your message is seldom responsible for the problem. Instead, state the facts logically, objectively, and unemotionally; let the reader decide on the causes. If you choose to send a letter by postal mail, include copies of all pertinent documents such as invoices, sales slips, catalog descriptions, and repair records. Of course, those receipts and other documents can also be scanned and attached to an e-mail.

If using paper mail, send copies and *not* your originals, which could be lost. When service is involved, cite the names of individuals you spoke to and the dates of calls. Assume that a company honestly wants to satisfy its customers—because most do. When an alternative remedy exists, spell it out (*If a refund for our return is not an option, please issue a store credit, and we will apply it to our next order*).

8-3c Concluding With an Action Request

End a claim message with a courteous statement that promotes goodwill and summarizes your action request. If appropriate, include an end date (*I hope you understand that mistakes in ordering online sometimes occur. Because I have enjoyed your prompt service in the past, I hope that you will be able to issue a refund or store credit by May 2*).

Finally, in making claims, act promptly. Delaying claims makes them appear less important. Delayed claims are also more difficult to verify. By taking the time to put your claim in writing, you indicate your seriousness. A written claim starts a record of the problem, should later action be necessary. Be sure to save a copy of your message whether paper or electronic.

8-3d Completing the Message and Revising

When Nick Arthur received a statement showing a charge for a three-year service warranty that he did not purchase, he was furious. He called the store but failed to get satisfaction. Nick decided against voicing his complaint online because he wished for a quick resolution and doubted that a social media post would be noticed by the independent retail business. He chose to write an e-mail to the customer service address featured prominently on the Maxtronics website. You can see the first draft of his direct claim e-mail in Model Document 8.5. This draft gave him a chance to vent his anger, but it accomplished little else. The tone was belligerent, and it assumed that the company intentionally mischarged him. Furthermore, it failed to tell the reader how to remedy the problem. The revision, also shown in Model Document 8.5, tempered the tone, described the problem objectively, and provided facts and figures. Most important, it specified exactly what Nick wanted to be done.

8-3e Posting Complaints and Reviews on Social Media

Social media experts advise consumers to exhaust all other options for claims and complaints with the company before venting online.[21] Just as you probably wouldn't complain to the Better Business Bureau without giving a business at least one chance to respond, you shouldn't express dissatisfaction just to let off steam. Although it may feel good temporarily to rant, most businesses want to please their customers and welcome an opportunity to right a wrong. Companies employ social media specialists who track social media platforms for chatter about their brands. These specialists analyze the conversations for opportunities to act and generate leads. This type of social data gathering to improve business strategy and customer service is called **social listening**.[22] Travelers in particular expect nearly instant replies from airlines to their gripes, even minor ones, 24/7. Delta employs more than 40 staff members who address thousands of daily tweets. At Southwest, nearly 40 employees tackle about 2,300 tweets and 1,900 Facebook posts a day. The company's Listening Center responds within minutes.[23] Travelers frequently get attention faster on social media than by calling.

Letting loose in ill-conceived online comments is a bad idea for two reasons. First, social media posts have a way of ending up in the wrong hands, making vicious complainers seem irrational. As always, think whether people you respect and prospective employers would approve. Even anonymous posts can be tracked back to the writer. No workplace wants to be associated with off-color, racist, sexist, or otherwise inappropriate comments in violation of company policy.[24] Employees who take a sick day but to go to the beach and are foolish enough to post evidence online get the boot promptly. A junior developer at a small startup was canned after he tweeted all day how much he hated the company and his job fixing software bugs.[25]

Second, businesses and professionals can take individuals to court for negative comments on digital media. A Florida man who complained on Yelp about his dog's death was sued by the animal hospital for defamation. A doctor in New York sued a patient for $1 million for posting negative reviews. A Kansas man faced a lawsuit for giving three stars to a theme park on Trip Advisor. Such so-called "strategic lawsuits against public participation" (SLAPP) are criticized as chilling to free speech. The Federal Trade Commission (FTC) is beginning to crack down on the silencing of critical reviewers under the Consumer Review Fairness Act of 2016.[26]

Gleaned from *Consumer Reports,* the tips in Figure 8.3 will allow you to exercise your right to free speech while staying safe when critiquing a product or service on social media.

Do shoppers read comments on sites such as Yelp, TripAdvisor, Angie's List, and Amazon? Most assuredly they do. A solid 36 percent of U.S. consumers *always* read user reviews when researching a product category, and a whopping 82 percent check out reviews of local businesses.[27] Even if posting does not achieve your objective, your well-written complaint or review may help others. You have a responsibility. Use it wisely.

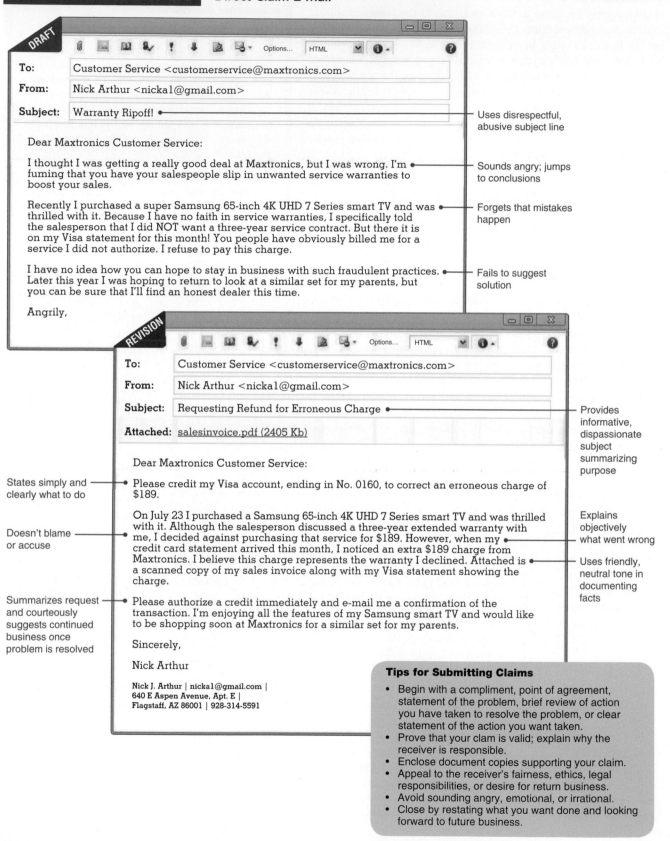

DRAFT

To: Customer Service <customerservice@maxtronics.com>

From: Nick Arthur <nicka1@gmail.com>

Subject: Warranty Ripoff! •————— Uses disrespectful, abusive subject line

Dear Maxtronics Customer Service:

I thought I was getting a really good deal at Maxtronics, but I was wrong. I'm •————— Sounds angry; jumps to conclusions
fuming that you have your salespeople slip in unwanted service warranties to
boost your sales.

Recently I purchased a super Samsung 65-inch 4K UHD 7 Series smart TV and was •————— Forgets that mistakes happen
thrilled with it. Because I have no faith in service warranties, I specifically told
the salesperson that I did NOT want a three-year service contract. But there it is
on my Visa statement for this month! You people have obviously billed me for a
service I did not authorize. I refuse to pay this charge.

I have no idea how you can hope to stay in business with such fraudulent practices. •————— Fails to suggest solution
Later this year I was hoping to return to look at a similar set for my parents, but
you can be sure that I'll find an honest dealer this time.

Angrily,

REVISION

To: Customer Service <customerservice@maxtronics.com>

From: Nick Arthur <nicka1@gmail.com>

Subject: Requesting Refund for Erroneous Charge •————— Provides informative, dispassionate subject summarizing purpose

Attached: salesinvoice.pdf (2405 Kb)

Dear Maxtronics Customer Service:

States simply and —————• Please credit my Visa account, ending in No. 0160, to correct an erroneous charge of
clearly what to do $189.

On July 23 I purchased a Samsung 65-inch 4K UHD 7 Series smart TV and was thrilled   Explains
with it. Although the salesperson discussed a three-year extended warranty with   objectively
Doesn't blame —————• me, I decided against purchasing that service for $189. However, when my   what went wrong
or accuse credit card statement arrived this month, I noticed an extra $189 charge from
Maxtronics. I believe this charge represents the warranty I declined. Attached is •————— Uses friendly,
a scanned copy of my sales invoice along with my Visa statement showing the   neutral tone in
charge. documenting
facts

Summarizes request —————• Please authorize a credit immediately and e-mail me a confirmation of the
and courteously transaction. I'm enjoying all the features of my Samsung smart TV and would like
suggests continued to be shopping soon at Maxtronics for a similar set for my parents.
business once
problem is resolved Sincerely,

Nick Arthur

Nick J. Arthur | nicka1@gmail.com |
640 E Aspen Avenue, Apt. E |
Flagstaff, AZ 86001 | 928-314-5591

Tips for Submitting Claims

• Begin with a compliment, point of agreement,
  statement of the problem, brief review of action
  you have taken to resolve the problem, or clear
  statement of the action you want taken.
• Prove that your clam is valid; explain why the
  receiver is responsible.
• Enclose document copies supporting your claim.
• Appeal to the receiver's fairness, ethics, legal
  responsibilities, or desire for return business.
• Avoid sounding angry, emotional, or irrational.
• Close by restating what you want done and looking
  forward to future business.

FIGURE 8.3 Guidelines for Writing Online Reviews and Complaints

Establish your credibility.

- Zero in on your objective and make your comment as concise as possible.
- Focus only on the facts and be able to support them.

Consider the permanence of the Internet.

- Know that your review may be posted indefinitely, even if you change your mind and modify a post later.

Check posting rules.

- Understand what's allowed by reading the terms and conditions on the site.
- Keep your complaint clean, polite, and to the point.

Accept offers to help.

- Reply if a business offers to help or discuss the problem; update your original post as necessary.

Provide balanced reviews.

- To be fair, offset criticism with positives to show that you are a legitimate consumer.
- Suggest improvements even in glowing reviews; all-out gushing is suspicious and not helpful.

Refuse payment for favorable critiques.

- Never accept payment to change your opinion or your account of the facts.
- Comply with requests for a review if you are a satisfied customer.

8-4 Adjustment Messages

LEARNING OUTCOME

4 Create adjustment messages that restore customers' trust and promote further business.

Even the best-run and best-loved businesses occasionally receive claims or complaints from consumers. When a company receives a claim and decides to respond favorably, the message is called an *adjustment.* Most businesses make adjustments promptly: they replace merchandise, refund money, extend discounts, send coupons, and repair goods. In fact, social media have shortened the response time drastically to mere minutes or hours, not days.

Businesses make favorable adjustments to legitimate claims for two reasons. First, consumers are protected by contractual and tort law for recovery of damages. If, for example, you find an insect in a package of frozen peas, the food processor of that package is bound by contractual law to replace it. If you suffer injury, the processor may be liable for damages. Second, and more obviously, most organizations genuinely want to satisfy their customers and retain their business.

In responding to customer claims, you must first decide whether to grant the claim. Unless the claim is obviously fraudulent or excessive, you will probably grant it. When you say *yes,* your adjustment message will be good news to the reader. Deliver that good news by using the direct strategy. When your response is *no*, the indirect strategy might be more appropriate. Chapter 9 discusses the indirect strategy for conveying negative news. You have three goals in adjustment messages:

- Rectifying the wrong, if one exists
- Regaining the confidence of the customer
- Promoting further business

8-4a Revealing Good News Up Front

Instead of beginning with a review of what went wrong, present the good news in an adjustment message immediately. When Leslie Bartolome-Williams responded to the claim letter from customer Daramis Services about a missing shipment, her first draft, shown at the top of

FOR THE RECORD

Making Complaints Go Away

Francesca Gino, a researcher at Harvard Business School, studies decision making, negotiation, and organizational behavior. She believes that engaged workers, if given the freedom to make their own decisions, are more creative and productive. She showcases Pal's Sudden Service, a fast-food chain in the southern United States. By empowering workers to identify and fix problems, Pal's has achieved noteworthy results: the chain's drive-through serves one car every 18 seconds. Despite a mistake-to-order ratio of 1:15 in the industry, Pal's makes only one mistake per 3,600 orders. It scores 98 percent in customer satisfaction and 97 percent in health inspections. Turnover at the assistant manager level is under 2 percent, and in 30 years, Pal's has lost only seven general managers, two of whom retired.[28] How could empowerment explain Pal's success? When would the freedom to make decisions make you happy and creative?

Model Document 8.6, was angry. No wonder. Daramis Services apparently had provided the wrong shipping address, and the goods were returned. Once Leslie and her company decided to send a second shipment and comply with the customer's claim, however, she had to give up the anger. Her goal was to regain the goodwill and the business of this customer. The improved version of her letter announces that a new shipment will arrive shortly.

If you decide to comply with a customer's claim, let the receiver know immediately. Don't begin your letter with a negative statement (*We are very sorry to hear that you are having trouble with your dishwasher*). This approach reminds the reader of the problem and may rekindle the heated emotions or unhappy feelings experienced when the claim was written. Instead, focus on the good news. The following openings for various letters illustrate how to begin a message with good news:

> *You're right! We agree that the warranty on your Whirlpool 500 Series dishwasher should be extended for six months.*

> *Shortly you will receive a new LG smartphone to replace the one that shattered when dropped recently.*

> *Please take your portable Panasonic EM835 microwave oven to Argus Appliance Repair, 360 Chapman Avenue, Orange, where it will be repaired at no cost to you.*

> *The enclosed check for $325 demonstrates our desire to satisfy our customers and earn their confidence.*

In announcing that you will make an adjustment, do so without a grudging tone—even if you have reservations about whether the claim is legitimate. Once you decide to comply with the customer's request, do so happily. Avoid halfhearted or reluctant responses (*Although the Whirlpool 500 Series dishwasher works well when used properly, we have decided to allow you to take yours to Argus Appliance Repair for repair at our expense*).

8-4b Explaining Compliance in the Message Body

In responding to claims, most organizations sincerely want to correct a wrong. They want to do more than just make the customer happy. They want to stand behind their products and services; they want to do what is right.

Dear Sir:

Your complaint letter dated May 17 has reached my desk. I assure you that we take all inquiries about missing shipments seriously. However, you failed to supply the correct address.

After receiving your complaint, our investigators looked into your problem shipment and determined that it was sent immediately after we received the order. According to the shipper's records, it was delivered to the warehouse address given on your stationery: 5261 Motor Avenue SW, Lakewood, WA 98433. Unfortunately, no one at that address would accept delivery, so the shipment was returned to us. I see from your current stationery that your company has a new address. With the proper address, we probably could have delivered this shipment.

Although we feel that it is entirely appropriate to charge you shipping and restocking fees, as is our standard practice on returned goods, in this instance we will waive those fees. We hope this second shipment finally catches up with you at your current address.

Sincerely,

Fails to reveal good news immediately and blames customer

Creates ugly tone with negative words and sarcasm

Sounds grudging and reluctant in granting claim

ACT   Allied Control Technology
4166 SE Stanley Avenue
Portland, OR 97206

Phone: (503) 777-3183
Fax: (503) 777-5167
Web: www.act-or.com

May 20, 2021

Mr. Elias Vysocky
Daramis Services
2749 Ninth Street SW
Lakewood, WA 98499

Dear Mr. Vysocky:

Subject: Your May 17 Letter About Your Purchase Order

Your second shipment of the Blu-ray players, video game consoles, and other electronics that you ordered April 19 is on its way and should arrive on May 28. Please note that we will waive the usual shipping and restocking fees.

The first shipment of this order was delivered May 3 to 5261 Motor Avenue SW, Lakewood, WA 98433. When no one at that address would accept the shipment, it was returned to us. Now that I have your letter, I see that the order should have been sent to 2749 Ninth Street SW Lakewood, WA 98499. When an order is undeliverable, we usually try to verify the shipping address by telephoning the customer. Somehow the return of this shipment was not caught by our normally painstaking shipping clerks. You can be sure that I will investigate shipping and return procedures with our clerks immediately to see if we can improve existing methods.

Your respect is important to us, Mr. Vysocky. Although our rock-bottom discount prices have enabled us to build a volume business, we don't want to be so large that we lose touch with valued customers like you. Over the years our customers' respect has made us successful, and we hope that the prompt and free redelivery of this shipment will retain yours.

Sincerely,

Leslie Bartolome-Williams

Leslie Bartolome-Williams
Distribution Manager

c Steve Richman

Uses customer's name in salutation

Announces good news immediately

Regains confidence of customer by explaining what happened and by suggesting plans for improvement

Closes confidently with genuine appeal for customer's respect

In the body of the message, explain how you are complying with the claim. In all but the most routine claims, you should seek to regain the confidence of the customer. You might reasonably expect that a customer who has experienced difficulty with a product, with delivery, with billing, or with service has lost faith in your organization. Rebuilding that faith is important for future business.

How to rebuild lost confidence depends on the situation and the claim. If procedures need to be revised, explain what changes will be made. If a product has defective parts, tell how the product is being improved. If service is faulty, describe genuine efforts to improve it. Notice in Model Document 8.6 that the writer promises to investigate shipping procedures to see whether improvements might prevent future mishaps.

Sometimes the problem is not with the product but with the way it is being used. In other instances customers misunderstand warranties or inadvertently cause delivery and billing mix-ups by supplying incorrect information. Remember that rational and sincere explanations will do much to regain the confidence of unhappy customers.

In your explanation avoid emphasizing negative words such as *trouble, regret, misunderstanding, fault, defective, error, inconvenience,* and *unfortunately.* Keep your message positive and upbeat.

8-4c Deciding Whether to Apologize

Whether to apologize is a debatable issue. Attorneys generally discourage apologies fearing that they admit responsibility and will trigger lawsuits. However, both judges and juries tend to look on apologies favorably. Thirty-six U.S. states have passed some form of an apology law that allows an expression of regret without fear that such a statement will be used as a basis for liability in court.[30] Some business writing experts advise against apologies, contending that they are counterproductive and merely remind the customer of the unpleasantness related to the claim. If, however, apologizing seems natural, do so.

People like to hear apologies. A well-timed apology is essential for repairing relationships on the job. A sincere apology shows that you value the relationship and respect the other person's perspective.[31] Don't, however, fall back on the familiar phrase, *I'm sorry for any inconvenience we may have caused.* It sounds mechanical and insincere. Instead, try something like this: *We understand the frustration our delay has caused you, We're sorry you didn't receive better service,* or *You're right to be disappointed.* If you feel that an apology is appropriate, do it early and briefly. You will learn more about delivering effective apologies in Chapter 9 when we discuss negative messages.

The primary focus of an adjustment message is on how you are complying with the request, how the problem occurred, and how you are working to prevent its recurrence.

8-4d Using Sensitive Language

The language of adjustment messages must be particularly sensitive, because customers are already upset. Here are some don'ts:

- Don't use negative words.
- Don't blame customers—even when they may be at fault.
- Don't blame individuals or departments within your organization; it's unprofessional.
- Don't make unrealistic promises; you can't guarantee that the situation will never recur.

To regain the confidence of your customer, consider including resale information. Describe a product's features and any special applications that might appeal to the customer. Promote a new product if it seems appropriate.

8-4e Showing Confidence in the Closing

End positively by expressing confidence that the problem has been resolved and that continued business relations will result. You might mention the product in a favorable light, suggest a new product, express your appreciation for the customer's business, or anticipate future business. It's often appropriate to refer to the desire to be of service and to satisfy customers. Notice how the following closings illustrate a positive, confident tone:

> *You were most helpful in informing us of this situation and permitting us to correct it. We appreciate your thoughtfulness in writing to us.*

> *Thanks for writing. Your satisfaction is important to us. We hope that this refund check convinces you that service to our customers is our No. 1 priority. Our goals are to earn your confidence and continue to justify that confidence with quality products and excellent service.*

> *For your patience and patronage, we are truly grateful.*

> *Your Acer Chromebook 514 will come in handy whether you are doing your homework, video chatting with friends, streaming music, watching movies, or playing games. What's more, you can add a Total Defense Premium Security package and a deluxe carrying bag for a little more. Take a look at the enclosed booklet detailing the big savings for essential technology on a budget. We value your business and look forward to your future orders.*

Although the direct strategy works for many requests and replies, it obviously won't work for every situation. With more practice and experience, you will be able to alter the pattern and apply the writing process to other communication problems. See the accompanying checklist for a summary of what to do when you must write claim and adjustment messages.

Checklist

Direct Claim, Complaint, and Adjustment Messages

- **Begin directly with the purpose.** Present a clear statement of the problem or the action requested such as a refund, a replacement, credit, an explanation, or the correction of an error. Add a compliment if you have been pleased in other respects.

- **Explain objectively.** In the body tell the specifics of the claim. Consider reminding the receiver of ethical and legal responsibilities, fairness, and a desire for return business. Provide copies of necessary documents.

- **Conclude by requesting action.** Include an end date, if important.

Add a pleasant, forward-looking statement. Keep a copy of the message.

- **Exercise good judgment.** Any Internet posts are permanent. Make your comments concise and focus only on the facts. Respect posting rules and be polite. Provide balanced reviews. Shun anonymity.

Messages That Make Adjustments

- **Open with approval.** Comply with the customer's claim immediately. Avoid sounding grudging or reluctant.

- **In the body win back the customer's confidence.** Explain

the cause of the problem, or describe your ongoing efforts to avoid such difficulties. Apologize if you feel that you should, but do so early and briefly. Avoid negative words, accusations, and unrealistic promises. Consider including resale and sales promotion information.

- **Close positively.** Express appreciation to the customer for writing, extend thanks for past business, anticipate continued patronage, refer to your desire to be of service, and/or mention a new product if it seems appropriate.

8-5 Goodwill Messages

Finding the right words to express feelings is often more difficult than writing ordinary business documents. Many communicators are intimidated when they must write goodwill messages expressing thanks, recognition, and sympathy. That is why writers tend to procrastinate when it comes to goodwill messages. Sending a ready-made card or picking up the telephone is easier than writing a heartfelt message. Remember, though, that the personal sentiments of the sender are always more expressive and more meaningful to readers than printed cards or oral messages. Taking the time to write gives more importance to our well-wishing. Personal notes also provide a record that can be reread, savored, and treasured.

In expressing thanks, recognition, or sympathy, you should always do so promptly. These messages are easier to write when the situation is fresh in your mind. They also mean more to the recipient. Don't forget that a prompt thank-you note carries the hidden message that you care and consider the event to be important. The best goodwill messages—whether thanks, congratulations, praise, or sympathy—should concentrate on the five Ss. Goodwill messages should be

- **Selfless.** Focus the message solely on the receiver, not the sender. Don't talk about yourself; avoid such comments as *I remember when I. . . .*

- **Specific.** Personalize the message by mentioning specific incidents or characteristics of the receiver. Telling a colleague *Great speech* is much less effective than *Great story about McDonald's marketing in Karachi.* Take care to verify names and other facts.

- **Sincere.** Let your words show genuine feelings. Rehearse in your mind how you would express the message to the receiver orally. Then transform that conversational language to your written message. Avoid pretentious, formal, or flowery language (*It gives me great pleasure to extend felicitations on the occasion of your firm's twentieth anniversary*).

- **Spontaneous.** Keep the message fresh and enthusiastic. Avoid canned phrases (*Congratulations on your promotion, Good luck in the future*). Strive for directness and naturalness, not creative brilliance.

- **Short.** Although goodwill messages can be as long as needed, try to accomplish your purpose in only a few sentences. What is most important is remembering an individual. Such caring does not require documentation or wordiness. Individuals and business organizations often use special note cards or stationery for brief messages.

8-5a Saying Thank You

In business as in our personal lives, we need to say thanks or show appreciation when someone has done us a favor or when an action deserves praise. Letters of appreciation may be written to customers for their orders, to hosts for their hospitality, to individuals for kindnesses performed, to employees for a job well done, and especially to customers who complain. After all, whether in social media posts, by e-mail, or on paper, customer gripes can be opportunities to improve your business and turn "complaints into compliments."[32]

Because the receiver will be pleased to hear from you, you can open directly with the purpose of your message. The writer of Model Document 8.7 thanks a speaker who addressed a group of marketing professionals. Although such thank-you notes can be quite short, this one is a little longer because the writer wants to lend importance to the receiver's efforts. Notice that every sentence relates to the receiver and offers enthusiastic praise. By using the receiver's name along with contractions and positive words, the writer makes the letter sound warm and conversational.

Written notes that show appreciation and express thanks are significant to their receivers. In expressing thanks, you generally write a short note on special notepaper or heavy card stock. The following messages provide models for expressing thanks for a gift, for a favor, and for hospitality.

Global Marketing Association
9654 MISSION CENTER RD., SUITE 2350-600
SAN DIEGO, CA 92109
WWW.AMERICANMARKETINGASSOCIATION.COM

October 28, 2021

Ms. Liza Hausman
Vice President, Industry Marketing
Houzz
285 Hamilton Avenue, 4th Floor
Palo Alto, CA 94301

Dear Ms. Hausman:

The San Diego chapter of the Global Marketing Association extends its sincere thanks to you for a most entertaining and enlightening presentation on October 25.

Opens directly with the purpose of message and thanks

Personalizes the message with specific references to the presentation

Your description of the unusual expansion of Houzz into India mesmerized our memers, particularly when you told us about the dizzying variety of Indian culture. We were fascinated by how India came to Houzz, not the other way around. Your Houzz site draws 40 million visitors monthly, and over time you noticed that a million customers and service providers among those monthly visitors had signed up from India. Houzz was compelled to launch a custom Indian site.

In addition to your good advice about entering the Indian market, we enjoyed your sense of humor and jokes—as you must have recognized from the uproar*ious laughter. What a great routine you do on faulty translations!

Spotlights the reader's talents

Concludes with compliments and gratitude

We are grateful, Ms. Hausman, for the stimulating and instructive evening you provided for our marketing professionals.

Cordially,

K. Dearborn

Russ K. Dearborn
Program Chair, GMA

RKD:fam

Expressing Thanks for a Gift.
When expressing thanks, tell what the gift means to you. Use sincere, simple statements.

> *Thanks, Alice, to you and the other team members for honoring me with the elegant Bohemia crystal vase at the party celebrating my retirement after twenty-five years with the company. The height and shape of the vase are perfect to hold roses and other bouquets from my garden. Each time I fill it, I'll remember your thoughtfulness in choosing this lovely gift for me.*

Sending Thanks for a Favor.
In showing appreciation for a favor, explain the importance of the gesture to you.

> *I sincerely appreciate your filling in for me last week when I was too ill to attend the planning committee meeting for the spring exhibition. Without your participation, much of my preparatory work would have been lost. Knowing that competent and generous individuals like you are part of our team, Craig, is a great comfort. Moreover, counting you as a friend is my very good fortune. I'm grateful to you.*

Extending Thanks for Hospitality.   When you have been a guest, send a note that compliments the fine food, charming surroundings, warm hospitality, excellent host, and good company.

> *Robert and I want you to know how much we enjoyed the dinner party for our department that you hosted Saturday evening. Your charming home and warm hospitality, along with the lovely dinner and sinfully delicious chocolate mousse, combined to create a truly memorable evening. Most of all, though, we appreciate your kindness in cultivating togetherness in our department. Thanks, Linda, for being such a special person.*

Recognizing Employees for Their Contributions.   A letter that recognizes specific employee contributions makes the person feel appreciated even if it is not accompanied by a bonus check.

> *Gregorio, I am truly impressed by how competently you shepherded your team through the complex AutoLive project. Thanks to your leadership, team members stayed on target and met their objectives. Your adept meeting facilitation, use of an agenda, and quick turnaround of meeting minutes kept the project on track. However, most of all I appreciate the long hours you put in to hammer out the final report.*

8-5b Replying to Goodwill Messages

Should you respond when you receive a congratulatory note or a written pat on the back? By all means! These messages are attempts to connect personally; they are efforts to reach out, to form professional and/or personal bonds. Failing to respond to notes of congratulations and most other goodwill messages is like failing to say *You're welcome* when someone says *Thank you.* Responding to such messages is simply the right thing to do. Do avoid, though, minimizing your achievements with comments that suggest you don't really deserve the praise or that the sender is exaggerating your good qualities.

Answering a Congratulatory Note.   In responding to congratulations, keep it short and simple.

> *Thanks for your kind words regarding my award, and thanks, too, for forwarding me the link to the article. I truly appreciate your warm wishes.*

Responding to Praise.   When acknowledging a pat-on-the-back note, use simple words in conveying your appreciation.

> *Your note about my work made me feel good. I'm grateful for your thoughtfulness.*

8-5c Expressing Sympathy and Sending Condolences

Most of us can bear misfortune and grief more easily when we know that others care. Notes expressing sympathy, though, are probably more difficult to write than any other kind of message. Commercial sympathy cards make the task easier—but they are far less meaningful than personal notes. Grieving friends want to know what you think—not what Hallmark's card writers think.

To help you get started, you can always glance through cards expressing sympathy. They will supply ideas about the kinds of thoughts you might wish to convey in your own words. In writing a sympathy note, (a) refer to the death or misfortune sensitively, using words that show you understand what a crushing blow it is; (b) in the case of a death, praise the deceased in a personal way; (c) offer assistance without going into excessive detail; and (d) end on a reassuring, forward-looking note. Sympathy messages may be typed, although handwriting seems more personal. In either case, use notepaper or personal stationery.

As you write your condolence note, mention the loss tactfully, recognize good qualities of the deceased, assure the receiver of your concern, offer assistance, and conclude on a reassuring note.

We are deeply saddened, Maria, to learn of the death of your husband. Bob's kind nature and friendly spirit endeared him to all who knew him. He will be missed. Although words seem empty in expressing our grief, we want you to know that your friends at Isotronics extend their profound sympathy to you. If we may help you or lighten your load in any way, you have but to call.

We know that the treasured memories of your many happy years together, along with the support of your family and many friends, will provide strength and comfort in the months ahead.

8-5d Using E-Mail for Goodwill Messages

In expressing thanks or responding to goodwill messages, handwritten notes are most impressive. However, if you frequently communicate with the receiver by e-mail and if you are sure your note will not get lost, then sending an e-mail goodwill message is acceptable, according to the Emily Post Institute.[33]

To express sympathy immediately after learning of a death or accident, you might precede a phone call or a written condolence message with an e-mail. E-mail is a fast and nonintrusive way to show your feelings. However, advises the Emily Post Institute, immediately follow with a handwritten note: "A single sincere line expressing the genuine feeling you had for the deceased is all you need to write."[34] Remember that e-mail messages are quickly gone and forgotten. Handwritten or printed messages remain and can be savored. Your thoughtfulness is more lasting if you take the time to prepare a handwritten or printed message on notepaper or personal stationery.

Checklist

Goodwill Messages

General Guidelines: The Five Ss

- **Be selfless.** Discuss the receiver, not the sender.
- **Be specific.** Instead of generic statements (*You did a great job*), include special details (*Your social media strategy to target Gen Z customers proved to be outstanding*).
- **Be sincere.** Show your honest feelings with conversational, unpretentious language (*We are all very proud of your award*).
- **Be spontaneous.** Strive to make the message natural, fresh, and direct. Avoid canned phrases (*If I may be of service, please do not hesitate . . .*).

- **Keep the message short.** Remember that, although they may be as long as needed, most goodwill messages are fairly short.

Giving Thanks

- **Cover three points in gift thank-yous.** (a) Identify the gift, (b) tell why you appreciate it, and (c) explain how you will use it.
- **Be sincere in sending thanks for a favor.** Tell what the favor means to you. Avoid superlatives and gushiness. Maintain credibility with sincere, simple statements.
- **Offer praise in expressing thanks for hospitality.** Compliment, as appropriate,

the (a) fine food, (b) charming surroundings, (c) warm hospitality, (d) excellent host, and (e) good company.
- **Be specific when recognizing employees.** To make a note of appreciation meaningful, succinctly sum up the accomplishments for which you are grateful.

Responding to Goodwill Messages

- **Respond to congratulations.** Send a brief note expressing your appreciation. Tell how good the message made you feel.
- **Accept praise gracefully.** Don't make belittling comments (*My contribution wasn't that big of a*

deal!) to reduce awkwardness or embarrassment.

Extending Sympathy

- **Refer to the loss or tragedy directly but sensitively.** In the first sentence, mention the loss and your personal reaction.

- **For deaths, praise the deceased.** Describe positive personal characteristics (*Cory was a powerful but caring leader*).

- **Offer assistance.** Suggest your availability, especially if you can do something specific.

- **End on a reassuring, positive note.** Perhaps refer to the strength the receiver finds in friends, family, colleagues, or faith.

Zooming In

Your Turn:
Applying Your Skills at Domino's

Domino's is a hyperconnected company. It certainly has been extremely successful in the last five years. Does the company's social media presence reflect this success? What are customers saying about the pizza giant on Facebook? What is its reputation on Twitter? Perhaps you are also wondering what it is like to work for the company or what type of corporate internships Domino's has to offer.

Social Media Presence

Individually or as a team, examine the company's posts and customers' comments on the pizza chain's Facebook page. What is the tone on this page? Find out whether customers seem to be happy or tend to be grousing. How do company representatives respond to comments on the Facebook page? Check the number of current followers on Facebook. Similarly, analyze Domino's Twitter feed. Record the number of followers and read enough comments to be able to generalize about the pizza chain's apparent popularity. Jot down notes about how Domino's employees reply to comments, positive or negative.

Corporate Internships

For the internship portion of this assignment, in your browser search for *internships at Domino's*. Most likely you will land on the company's corporate site and find that Domino's is reaching out to recent college grads offering them corporate internships. Explore the corporate divisions or disciplines in which internships are available and whether they are paid. Are they attractive to you? What do they entail—would you be making coffee runs, fetching sandwiches, and filing all summer? For an unvarnished look behind the corporate walls, visit Glassdoor. Find out what interns are saying about their experience and how much the internships pay, if anything.

Your Task

At your instructor's direction, summarize your observations and impressions in a memo or e-mail. In a short paragraph include your personal assessment: Would you consider an internship at Domino's? What did you find appealing about the company? What aspects of the brand still need tweaking?

SUMMARY OF LEARNING OUTCOMES

1 Applying the 3-x-3 writing process, identify the channels through which neutral and positive messages—e-mails, memos, and business letters—travel in the digital era workplace.

- When writing neutral and positive messages—e-mails, interoffice memos, or business letters—you can be direct because they convey routine, nonsensitive information.

- In Phase 1 of the writing process, determine your purpose, visualize your audience, and anticipate the reader's reaction.

- In Phase 2 collect information, make an outline, and write the first draft.

- In Phase 3 edit for clarity, proofread, and ensure skim value. Decide whether the message accomplishes its goal.

- Use business letters when a permanent record is required; when confidentiality is critical; when formality and sensitivity are essential; and when a persuasive, well-considered presentation is important.

- Write business letters on company stationery in block style with all lines starting at the left margin.

2 Compose direct messages that make requests, respond to inquiries via any channel, and deliver step-by-step instructions.

- In messages requesting information or action, state the purpose in the opening; explain the request in the body; express any questions in a parallel and grammatically balanced form; and close by telling the reader courteously what to do while showing appreciation.

- In complying with requests, deliver the good news in the opening; explain and provide additional information in the body; and write a cordial, personalized closing that tells the reader how to proceed if action is needed.

- When writing instruction messages, divide the instructions into steps; list steps in the correct order; arrange the items vertically with bullets or numbers; begin each step with an action verb using the imperative; and ensure that the instructions don't sound dictatorial.

- When responding to posts on the Internet, follow the example of businesses that strive to be positive, transparent, honest, timely, and helpful.

3 Prepare contemporary messages that make direct claims and voice complaints, including those posted online.

- When you compose a message to identify a wrong and request a correction, you are writing a *claim*; direct claims are requests to which receivers are expected to readily agree.

- Begin by describing the problem or action to be taken; in the message body explain the request without emotion; in the closing summarize the request or action to be taken. Include an end date, if applicable, and express faith in future business if the problem is resolved.

- Include copies of relevant documents to support your claim.

- Take your complaint online only after exhausting all other options with the business in question; keep your post concise and clean; focus on your objective; and be prepared to support the facts.

4 Create adjustment messages that restore customers' trust and promote further business.

- When granting a customer's claim, you are providing an *adjustment*, which has three goals: (a) rectifying the wrong, if one exists; (b) regaining the confidence of the customer; and (c) promoting further business.

- In the opening immediately grant the claim without sounding grudging. To regain the customer's trust, in the body explain what went wrong and how the problem will be corrected. However, you may want to avoid acknowledging liability for any problems.

- In the closing express appreciation; extend thanks for past business; refer to a desire to be of service; and mention a new product, if appropriate.

- If you believe that an apology should be offered, present it early and briefly.

5 Write special messages that convey kindness and goodwill.

- Make sure that messages that deliver thanks, praise, or sympathy are selfless, specific, sincere, spontaneous, and short.

- When thanking someone for a gift, tell why you appreciate it, and explain how you will use it.

- When thanking someone for a favor, convey what the favor means to you, but don't gush.

- In expressions of sympathy, mention the loss tactfully; recognize good qualities in the deceased (in the case of a death); sincerely offer assistance; and conclude on a positive, reassuring note.

Key Terms

positive messages *244*

bad news messages/negative messages *244*

persuasive messages *244*

the right to be forgotten *251*

the right to erasure *251*

claim *256*

social listening *257*

Critical Thinking

1. Whenever you navigate to any website today, you will see pop-ups forcing you to accept cookies and agree to or reject certain uses of your data. Most people don't bother to read the provisions, but they are written in relatively plain language. Users can select options restricting cookies, ad tracking, and storing of their identifiable data. American companies rushed to comply with the strict European privacy law General Data Protection Regulation (GDPR) even before it was enacted in 2018. Why does the GDPR matter in the United States, and why is it serious business? (L.O. 1, 3)

2. A writer compared letters and social media posts: "What is special about a letter is the time that is taken in creating a letter—that someone went to the trouble of finding a piece of paper, sitting down, crafting their thoughts, putting them on paper, and that they created this document really just for me. A letter is a very singular expression, it's a unique document, and for that reason, to get it in the mail feels almost like a gift. . . . It's a piece of paper that I can feel. . . . There's a physical connection."[35] How might these observations apply to business letters? What other special traits can you identify? (L.O. 1)

3. A Pew Research Center study found that 89 percent of smartphone owners had used their phones during the last social gathering they attended, but they weren't happy about it; 82 percent of respondents said their use of smartphones in social settings hurt the conversation.[36] Do you split your attention between your screen and face-to-face conversations? Do you believe it's possible to be sufficiently present while texting? (L.O. 2)

4. Why is it smart to keep your cool when making a claim, and how should you go about it? (L.O. 3)

5. **Ethical Issue:** In this chapter you learned that some businesses have used so-called SLAPP laws to sue consumers for writing negative reviews on the Internet. The acronym stands for *Strategic Lawsuit Against Public Participation*. Opponents consider such lawsuits frivolous and believe they threaten the public's free speech rights under the First Amendment. Therefore, 29 states currently have anti-SLAPP laws allowing early dismissal of meritless lawsuits brought to intimidate and silence reviewers and other public critics. Is trying to silence reviewers on social media fair, or are businesses within their rights to protect from illegitimate damaging complaints? (L.O. 3)

Writing Improvement Exercises

8.1 Analyzing Memorable Social Media Comments (L.O. 1–5)

`Social Media` `Web`

YOUR TASK Examine the following dissimilar social media posts.[37] Discuss their characteristics or, if applicable, how they could have been avoided. When appropriate, formulate a response to the post.

a. Heather applied for a job on Twitter and thought she had sent her CV. She heard from the company swiftly: *Dear Heather, you attached a Jamie Oliver for Chili Beef Recipe, not your CV.*

b. An apparent home improvement store was advertising flowerpots adorned with images of birds for only $1.19 each. A sign below the flowerpots explained the low price: *This item is reduced due to misspelling of the word* Bird. *Thank you.* The misspelling on the pots was *Brid*.

c. A young man by the name of Adam posted two pictures side by side, one showing the Tesco-branded sensitive dog shampoo, the other depicting his pink-hued Labrador retriever. His tweet read: *@Tesco Yes why on earth has your shampoo turned my dog pink?* How would you respond if you were representing Tesco?

d. On Black Friday, the day after Thanksgiving, deals and discounts are common. McDonald's sent out a strange tweet: *Black Friday **** Need copy and link ***** Thousands of responses followed on Twitter. What happened here?

e. Unilever brand Dove got itself in hot water for a Facebook ad. A looped image depicted an African American woman removing a dark brown T-shirt to reveal a very fair white woman in a pale beige T-shirt who then morphs into a third woman, likely a Latina. Explain why the post was widely criticized as tone deaf. What kind of response would you expect of Dove?

8.2 Writing Instructions (L.O. 2)

YOUR TASK Revise each of the following wordy, dense paragraphs into a set of concise instructions. Include an introductory statement or title.

a. Listening to Customers on Social Media

Customer service today is omnichannel and customer-driven, so when someone wants to reach out to you on social media, you need to be there, ready to respond. Of course, having an official response for major concerns or inquiries is an advantage. Companies must always respond and to do it quickly. Many organizations fail to respond to many (or *any*) of their social media interactions. They say they aren't exactly sure how to respond to social media comments and questions. But consistency is key when responding. It's also important to listen to the competition and to track every mention on social media to find out what people are saying about you, even if they don't know that you're listening. Measuring the effectiveness of organizations' social media response is crucial too, as is hanging out where your customers are. Social listening also means to be friendly and personable. It helps to coordinate responses with executives and others who are visible on social media.[38]

b. Making YouTube Videos

More and more amateurs are making YouTube videos, but if you have never done it before, here are some important tips. First, of course, you will need some kind of video recording device such as a smartphone, webcam, or camcorder. Another thing you will have to do is make a decision on whether or not to make a video blog, comedy skit, how-to video, or video about travel. Because nothing is perfect the first time, you should record several takes, which you can stitch together later. Next you must transfer the video files to your computer. Finally, be sure to use computer editing software to delete, improve, or change anything in your footage.

c. Customizing Your Zoom Background

Who wouldn't want to hide a messy room during a Zoom session? Millions of people were using video chat during the coronavirus pandemic as they were working and studying from home. Some discovered they could customize the video background using stock images, their own photos, or even videos. Here is how to use virtual backgrounds. Of course, one's system must have the right requirements. You should select **Virtual Background** on the menu to the left after clicking your profile and then **Settings**. People can choose a default option, e.g., an image of outer space or a green screen. Or they can upload their own background photos by clicking the plus icon on the **Virtual Background Page**. A pop-up box will let users upload a picture from their computers. By clicking the one they may want, they can see it alongside the stock pictures. To remove photos, users just need to tap the **X** in the top left corner. These instructions are for laptop and desktop computers, but mobile devices can be set up in a similar way. Zoom users shouldn't forget to experiment with a beauty filter to soften their appearance!

d. Obtaining Credit

Obtaining credit and keeping good credit can be difficult, especially for young people. Here are five suggestions that will help you obtain credit and maintain a good credit score. One thing I like to suggest first is getting a gas store card. These cards are easier to get than regular credit cards. What's great about them is that you can establish a credit history by making small payments in full and on time. To maintain good credit, you should always pay your bills on time. Delinquencies are terrible. They create the biggest negative effect on a credit score. If you already have credit cards, your balance should be paid down. If you can't afford to do that, you might take a loan from a family member or friend. If you have unused credit card accounts, don't close them. I know it sounds as if you should, but actually, canceling a card can lower your score. Don't do it! Finally, never max out your credit cards. A good rule of thumb to follow is keeping your balance below 30 percent of your credit limit.

Activities

8.3 Document for Analysis: Poor Direct Request—Planning Accessible Conference (L.O. 2)

E-Mail

As a member of the planning committee for an upcoming conference, you have been asked to draft a message requesting information about whether the venue is accessible for all participants.

YOUR TASK Analyze this message and list its writing weaknesses. Does this message apply the advice in this chapter for writing requests? If your instructor directs, revise the message using the suggestions you learned in this and previous chapters. Strive to arrange the information in an orderly bulleted list.

To: Angela.Marakot@capitalhilton.com
From: Carol.Frazier@gmail.com
Subject: Need Information
Bcc: Nanci.Masri@gmail.com; Jason.Nadir@hotmail.com; Lori.Petuno@gmail.com

`E-Mail`

Dear Angela:

How is your day going? I hope well! I need some information, and I found your name at the Capital Hilton booking site. I'm on the planning committee for our upcoming Accessibility For All (AFA) conference that we would like to hold in Washington next fall. Will you please answer the following questions that need answers? The Capital Hilton comes highly recommended.

Does your hotel provide assistive listening systems? Such as the induction-loop system that bypasses acoustical conditions and delivers sound directly to listeners? Does the hotel have accessible parking? We would need level parking nearby with drop-off availability up close to the building. In the matter of accessible restrooms, are ADA restrooms available on the meeting room floors? Some of our attendees might bring service animals. Do you provide a comfortable space for them to rest during an event? Do you also have accessible nearby toileting and watering facilities for service animals? Finally, do your meeting rooms have ample accessible electrical outlets? Do they accommodate laptops, adaptive devices, and other electronics?

Thank you.

Carol.Frazier@gmail.com
AFA Fall Conference, Washington

8.4 Document for Analysis: Direct Request—Protecting Medical Information (L.O. 2)

`E-Mail`

The following serious message requests information, but its poor organization and other writing faults prevent it from accomplishing its goal.

YOUR TASK Analyze this message and list at least five writing weaknesses. If your instructor directs, revise the message using the suggestions you learned in this and previous chapters.

To: vjgallagher@safecybernetics.com
From: scott.woo@vistalinda-internists.com
Subject: Inquiry

Dear Sir:

I am a physician in a small medical practice, and I am worried about protecting patients' medical information. Your website (**SafeCybernetics.com**) looks quite promising but

I found it overwhelming. I could not find answers to my specific questions, so I am writing this message to ask them. Could you call me within the next two days? I'm usually in surgery until 4 p.m. most days and try to leave at 6 p.m.

First, as I mentioned heretofore, my practice is small. Do you have experience in working with small medical practices? We may already have experienced a security breach. When you investigate, if you find out that privacy laws have been broken, do you report them to government agencies immediately?

We're really extremely interested in how you investigate an incident that may have taken place. If you discover a privacy breach, do you help your client make notification to his patients who are affected? Additionally, are you discreet about it?

I look forward to hearing from you.

Scott Woo, M.D.

8.5 Document for Analysis: Direct Response—Data Breach Query (L.O. 2)

`E-Mail`

The following message responds to the inquiry in **Activity 8.4**. Dr. Woo asks for information about dealing with a data breach at his medical firm. Mr. Gallagher, from Safe Cybernetics, wants to respond briefly and answer more fully in a telephone conversation with Dr. Woo. However, the following direct response is disorganized and needs revision to be effective in achieving its goal.

YOUR TASK Study the following poorly written message, list its weaknesses, and revise it if your instructor directs.

To: scott.woo@vistalinda-internists.com
From: vjgallagher@safecybernetics.com
Subject: Data Breaches

Dear Dr. Woo:

We have received your inquiry, which has been directed to me for response. I can assure you that our company can do what you want in the way of cyber security, data breach response, and incident analysis solutions. We are specialists. You asked some specific questions, such as having experience with smaller medical establishments. I can assure you that, yes, we certainly do have such experience. Even with limited resources, smaller companies will benefit from basic security awareness training in a manner related to how to properly handle, store, and the processing of patient health information.

In regard to any incident that may have already occurred, we are experienced at investigating incidents, we analyze clues, and we can quickly and defensively uncover critical information. In regard to notifying patients of any breach, we assure you that we can give discreet breach notification that is prompt and we also customize it for your business. However, I must warn you in advance that if we become aware of any wrongdoing, we must notify any applicable government or law enforcement agencies because we are obligated to do so. But I can assure you that such notification is hardly ever necessary. We can discuss your concerns more extensively by telephone. Thank you for your interest in Security Specialists.

Van Jim Gallagher
[Full contact information]

8.6 Document for Analysis: Faulty Instruction E-Mail (L.O. 2)

E-Mail

The following wordy and poorly expressed e-mail from a CEO discusses a growing problem for organizations: how to avoid the loss of valuable company data to hackers.

YOUR TASK Study the message, list its weaknesses, and then rewrite it in the form of an instruction message. Is it better to use bullets or numbers for an internal list?

To: Staff Members
From: Paul Salzman <paul.salzman@pacificsavings.com>
Subject: Vital Warning!

Valued Staff Members:

I am writing this message to let you know that, like other banks, we are extremely concerned about the possibility of hackers gaining access to sensitive information. We fear that employees will expose valuable information without realizing what they are doing. Because of our fear, we have consulted cybersecurity experts, and they gave us much good advice with new procedures to be followed. Following are some of the procedures suggested by experts:

1. Phishing links seem to be the worst problem. Any request for password information or any requests to click links should be viewed with suspicion. Never click them. Even messages that seem to be from high-level officials or the human resources department within our own company can be sophisticated, realistic fakes. Examples include a request to click a link to receive a package or to download a form from within the company.

2. Be aware of URLs. You should read all URLs from right to left. The last item is the true domain. If it is not the address of the purported sender, it is probably a phishing attempt.

3. Please don't leave out-of-office messages. These voice mails or e-mails might explain when you will be away. Such messages are a red flag to hackers telling them that your computer is vacant and not being monitored.

4. Because smartphones can be lost or stolen, don't snap photos of company documents. Phones may be lost or stolen, and our data might be compromised.

5. Although small memory devices (thumb drives) are handy and easy to use, you may be inclined to store company files or information on these drives. Don't do it. They can easily be lost, thus exposing our company information.

6. Using work e-mail addresses for social media is another problem area. When you post details about your job, hackers can figure out an organization's best target.

We want to let you all know that within the next two months, we plan to begin implementing a program that will educate and train employees with regard to what to avoid. The program will include fake phishing messages. The program will be explained and you will learn more from your managers in training workshops that are scheduled to begin January 1.

Paul Salzman, CEO
[Full contact information]

8.7 Document for Analysis: Adjustment Letter—Restretching a Sagging Canvas (L.O. 3)

When a company received an expensive office painting with sags in the canvas, it complained. The seller, Central Park Gallery, responded with the following adjustment letter. How can it be improved?

YOUR TASK Analyze the letter. List its weaknesses. If your instructor directs, revise the letter.

Current date

Ms. Sharon Nickels
2459 Drew Street
Clearwater, FL 33765

Dear Ms. Nickels:

Your letter has been referred to me for reply. You claim that the painting recently sent by Central Park Gallery arrived with sags in the canvas and that you are unwilling to hang it in your company's executive offices.

I have examined your complaint carefully, and, frankly, I find it difficult to believe because we are so careful about shipping, but if what you say is true, I suspect that the shipper may be the source of your problem. We give explicit instructions to our shippers that large paintings must be shipped standing up, not lying down. We also wrap every painting in two layers of convoluted foam and one layer of Perf-Pack foam, which we think should be sufficient to withstand any bumps and scrapes that negligent shipping may cause. We will certainly look into this.

Although it is against our policy, we will in this instance allow you to take this painting to a local framing shop for restretching. We are proud that we can offer fine works of original art at incredibly low prices, and you can be sure that we do not send out sagging canvases.

Sincerely,

8.8 Responding to Social Media Posts (L.O. 2)

`Social Media`   `Web`

YOUR TASK Decide whether to respond to the following social media posts.[39] If you believe you should respond, compose a concise Facebook reply following the guidelines in this chapter. Your instructor may also direct that you rewrite some of the posts themselves, if necessary.

a. Jackie posted this to the Grocery Barn Facebook site: *So sad!! Ran to my store to pick up Pumpkin Yippee Pie mix and it's all sold out. :(And all sold out online also! Bummer. I knew I should've bought more! LOL….*

b. Angel posted this comment on the Shoes Galore Facebook site: *I ordered a few things on the 20th and opted for next day shipping … but UPS says expected delivery date is the 30th! -:-(*

c. Tyrone wrote the following to upscale men's clothing purveyor Joss Brothers: *I first began shopping at Joss Brothers about six years ago. I had read a book on menswear called "Style" by Jamal Klein. He made mention to brass collar stays. I could not find them in Canada. I wandered into a Joss Brothers store in Michigan and asked, "You don't sell brass collar stays do you?" The salesman said, "Of course." I bought collar stays, shirts and pajamas that day. A devoted customer I became. You can imagine how happy I am that Joss Brothers has come to Canada. Bienvenue! Welcome!*

d. Katie posted this message on EsureSafe's Facebook page: *I just wanted to thank EsureSafe for all your support on a claim I filed. The service was excellent at one of your body repair shops and also, your customer service is top notch: calls, emails, and not to mention the site which gives you all details possible like pictures, status of the claim, easy contact us section, upload of files. GREAT WEBSITE and SERVICE. EsureSafe has me in GOOD HANDS, not Allstate:-)*

e. Kendra posted this request for information on the Facebook page of her favorite resort hotel, Encore at Wynn Las Vegas: *Will the pool still be open this weekend?*

8.9 Direct Request: Planning a Winter Retreat in Vail, Colorado (L.O. 2)

`E-Mail`   `Web`

Your employer, Bari Media of Columbus, Ohio, has had an excellent year, and the CEO, Stefano Bari, would like to reward the troops for their hard work with a rustic yet plush winter retreat. The CEO wants his company to host a four-day combination conference/retreat/vacation for his 55 marketing and media professionals and their spouses or significant others at some spectacular winter resort.

One of the choices is Vail, Colorado, a famous ski resort town with steep slopes and dramatic mountain views. As you investigate the options in Vail, you are captivated by the Four Seasons Resort and Residences Vail, a five-star property with an outdoor pool, indoor and outdoor hot tubs, ski-in/ski-out access, a ski concierge, two acclaimed gourmet restaurants, and an amply equipped gym and fitness center. Other amenities include an on-site spa with massage and treatment rooms, a sauna, and facial and body treatments. Bathrooms feature separate bathtubs and showers, double sinks, and bathrobes. For business travelers, the hotel offers complimentary wired high-speed Internet access, complimentary wireless Internet access, and multiline phones as well as the use of two desktop computers.

The website of the Four Seasons Resort and Residences Vail is not very explicit on the subject of business and event facilities, so you decide to jot down a few key questions. You estimate that your company will require about 50 rooms. You will also need two conference rooms (to accommodate 25 participants or more) for one and a half days. You want to know about room rates, conference facilities, A/V equipment in the conference rooms, Internet access, and entertainment options for families. You have two periods that would be possible: December 13-17 or January 10-14. You realize that both are peak times, but you wonder whether you can get a discounted group rate. You are interested in entertainment in Vail, and tours to the nearby national parks. Eagle County Airport is 36 miles away, and you would like to know whether the hotel operates a shuttle. Also, one evening the CEO will want to host a banquet for about 85 people. Mr. Bari wants a report from you by September 15.

YOUR TASK Write a well-organized direct request e-mail or letter to Kirsten Dunn, Sales Manager, Four Seasons Resort and Residences Vail, One Vail Road, Vail, CO 81657.

8.10 Direct Response: Falmouth Sail & Canvas Slammed on Yelp (L.O. 2)

Social Media / **Web**

Yelp, the social network for consumer reviews and local searches, logs approximately 104 million monthly unique mobile visitors and 74 million monthly unique desktop visitors. The platform has listed 205 million reviews at this time.[40] Many users rely on what they hope to be real reviews by real people, as the company claims. They wish to make more informed buying decisions based on Yelp reviews. Businesses would do well to monitor their status on Yelp because anything less than a four- or five-star rating might be a blemish costing them sales.

Richard Hall, owner of Falmouth Sail & Canvas in Falmouth, Maine, watches his Yelp reviews. Currently, he has six reviews, all five stars. Imagine his surprise when he recently received a rating of one star from Annabelle T.:

> Falmouth Sail & Canvas does good work, but it seems to have become a casualty of its own success. The company is unresponsive when you call and e-mail. I will take my business elsewhere because after 3 weeks, I still haven't heard about that estimate for new sails and weather cloths. I had left a voice mail message and sent an e-mail. No response. I called again and was received as if my request were outlandish when I expressed the hope of getting a quote that same week. Since then, silence. Not cool. And I am a repeat customer. ... People, fortunately there are other businesses out there!

The writer says she is a returning customer. Richard sighs because he is really shorthanded. His administrative assistant has been sick a lot lately, and inquiries have gone unanswered; communication has not been flowing well. Business is booming, and he does not have enough qualified installers; as a result, weeks elapse before his small crew gets around to completing a job. Barry searches his files and finds the job the company completed for Angela four years earlier. Falmouth had made a dodger, sail cover, and other smaller canvas items for Angela's 30-foot Catalina sailboat.

YOUR TASK Consider Richard's options. Should he respond to the one negative review? What could be the consequences of ignoring it? If you believe that Richard should respond, discuss first how. He has the disgruntled customer's e-mail, phone number, and street address. He could post a reply on Yelp to provide a commentary to the bad review. If your instructor directs, plan a strategy for Richard and respond to the customer in the way you believe is best for Richard and his business.

8.11 Direct Message: Encouraging Employees to Catch More Zs (L.O. 1, 2)

E-Mail / **Web**

Sleep deprivation is very common among executives and rank-and-file workers in most organizations. Hard-charging business leaders pull all-nighters or sleep only a few hours a night. When Tesla chief Elon Musk turned 47, he spent the full 24 hours of his birthday at work. However, sleep researchers tell us that tired workers are less effective and make more mistakes. People tend to become irritable and abusive; productivity suffers. Lack of sleep causes impulsive behavior, impairs decision making, and stifles creativity. Chronic sleep deprivation has serious repercussions for our mental, emotional, and physical health.[41]

Your human resources manager wants to spread the awareness that sleep is key to long-term health and productivity. She knows that the choice is between having a normal, full workday of high-quality work or an extremely long workday of deficient work. Getting a good night's sleep will ultimately make the staff more productive. She has read Arianna Huffington's *The Sleep Revolution*. The best-selling book details how this once driven businesswoman, author, and editor-in-chief of the *Huffington Post*—who passed out from exhaustion more than a decade ago—has become a crusader for quality shuteyes. Huffington says sleep deprivation is "the new smoking," suggesting that employers will eventually be forced recognize the harm of sleep deprivation and overwork. Then workers might be able to take walks and nap at work, perhaps.

Many businesspeople think they are indispensable and don't sufficiently delegate work to team members who could relieve their workloads. Not developing a team that could step up can lead to a dangerous spiral of unsustainable frenzy and stress. Experts believe that planning the workday with a focus on getting out of the office by a certain time and prioritizing tasks accordingly, will help disengage from work and lead to better sleep. One red flag is heavy caffeine consumption. It can mask the problem of sleep deprivation.[42]

YOUR TASK On the Internet, search for Arianna Huffington's recommendations for sound sleep hygiene. Using the steps advanced by the sleep guru and the information presented here, write a memo from HR manager Gloria Sanchez to all staff, encouraging healthy sleep habits. This memo will be sent to all employees as an e-mail attachment, posted on the intranet, and displayed in the lunchroom and other common areas.

8.12 Direct Message—Memo Relaxing Strict Dress Codes in Banking (L.O. 1, 2)

J.P. Morgan Chase, the largest U.S. bank based on assets, stunned the usually conservative financial sector when it parted with long-standing tradition and started allowing business-casual attire on most occasions, except in client meetings. The move away from pinstripes to pullovers signals a larger trend, perhaps driven by wealthy clients who are increasingly shedding their ties. Even the Chairman and CEO, Jamie Dimon, started dressing down after meetings with more casual Silicon Valley executives. Young talent, for whom banking is competing with the IT sector, may also favor more comfortable garb. A Robert Half International survey found that approximately 50 percent of senior managers stated that employees are wearing less-formal attire than they did just five years earlier. Among office workers, 31 percent said they favor a workplace with a business-casual dress code. The most common dress-code violations are overly casual clothes, followed by revealing clothing, according to the survey.[43] This suggests that workers need help understanding business-casual policies.

The J.P. Morgan memo that announced the new policy outlined the dos and don'ts. Not allowed are athletic clothing, i.e. sweatpants, leggings and yoga pants; halter tops, flip-flops, hats or hoods. "Distracting, tight, revealing or exceptionally loose or low-cut clothing" is also verboten. On the flip side, casual slacks, capris, polo shirts and dress sandals are acceptable. Jeans and sneakers aren't considered business casual in most circumstances and job sites. The key guideline is to match clients in formality of dress. "Business casual is not weekend casual," the memo states. Unacceptable attire or appearance can lead to reprimand and disciplinary action including dismissal. Critics contend that some "decoding" of ambiguous items listed in the policy, especially for women, is needed.[44] If gray capris are acceptable, how about bright floral ones? Are women wearing denim viewed differently than men? What exactly is "tasteful" jewelry? And will judging "appropriate" hairstyles be left to managers' perception of race?[45]

YOUR TASK Your boss in HR, Erin Schmidt, asks you to draft a memo modeled on J.P. Morgan's casual-dress policy for your traditional community bank, Willowbrook Financial. Mr. Hamdi, the CEO, realizes that your financial institution must go with the times. At the same time, he believes that Willowbrook employees need clear guidelines to understand the new policy and reduce ambiguity. Ms. Schmidt has instructed you to flesh out more detail in Willowbrook's policy. Consider including a table with dress code do's and don'ts.

8.13 Direct Message: Interviewing at Forrest + Partners (L.O. 2)

`E-Mail`

Nathan Forrest, founder and CEO of Forrest + Partners, is a busy architect. As he expands his business, he is looking for ecologically conscious designers who can develop sustainable architecture that minimizes the negative environmental impact of buildings. His company has an open position for an environmental architect/designer. Three candidates were scheduled to be interviewed on April 12. However, Mr. Forrest now finds he must be in Houston during that week to consult with the builders of a 112-unit planned golf course community. He asks you, his office manager, to call the candidates, reschedule for April 19 or April 20, and prepare an e-mail with the new times as well as a brief summary of the candidates' backgrounds.

Fortunately, you were able to reschedule all three candidates. Paula Larson will come on April 19 at 2 p.m. Ms. Larson specializes in passive solar energy and has two years of experience with GigaSolar, Inc. She has a bachelor's degree from the University of California, Los Angeles. Rubie Gaul has a master's degree from Arizona State University and worked for five years as an architect planner for Phoenix Builders, with expertise in sustainable building materials. She will come on April 19 at 11 a.m. Without a degree but with ten years of building experience, Sanford Clayton is scheduled for April 19 at 9 a.m. He is the owner of LEED Consulting and has experience with energy efficiency, sustainable materials, domes, and earth-friendly design. You are wondering whether Mr. Forrest forgot to include Fred Dittman, his partner, who usually helps make personnel selections.

YOUR TASK Prepare an e-mail to Mr. Forrest with all the information he needs in the most readable format. Consider using a three-column table format for the candidate information.

8.14 Instruction Message: Copying Images and Text from PDF Documents in Acrobat (L.O. 2)

`E-Mail`

As a summer intern in the Marketing Department at Dreiling Laboratory Supply, Inc., in Fairbanks, Alaska, you have been working on the company's annual catalog. You notice that staffers could save a lot of valuable time by copying and inserting images and text from the old edition into the new document. Your boss, Marketing Director Vita Landers, has received numerous inquiries from staffers asking how to copy text and images from previous editions. You know that this can be done, and you show a fellow worker how to do it using a PDF feature called **Take** a **Snapshot**. Marketing Director Landers decides that you are quite a tech-savvy student. Because she has so much confidence in you, she asks you to draft a memo or e-mail detailing the steps for copying images and text passages from portable document format (PDF) files.

You start by opening Adobe Acrobat and viewing the **Edit** pull-down menu in an open PDF document. Depending on the Acrobat version, a feature called **Take a Snapshot** can be seen. It is preceded by a tiny camera icon and a check mark when the tool is activated. To copy content, you need to select the part of the PDF document that you want to capture. The cursor will change its shape once the feature is activated. With the left mouse button, click the location where you want to start copying a passage or image. While holding down the left mouse button, you need to drag the mouse over the page to the object you want to acquire. A selected area appears that you can expand and reduce, but you shouldn't let go of the left mouse button. Once you release the left mouse button, a copy of the selected area will be made. Click **OK**. You can then paste the selected area into a blank Microsoft Office document, whether Word, Excel, or PowerPoint. You can also take a picture of an entire page.

YOUR TASK Prepare an instruction memo addressed to Marketing Department staff members for the signature of Vita Landers. Practice the steps described here in abbreviated form, and arrange all necessary instructions in a logical sequence. You may need to add steps not noted here. Remember, too, that your audience may not be as computer literate as you are, so ensure that the steps are clear and easy to follow.

8.15 Instruction E-Mail Needs Revision: Explaining the Office Move (L.O. 2)

E-Mail

The following message, which originated in an international technology company, was intended to inform new team members about their upcoming move to a different office location. But its stream-of-consciousness thinking and jumbled connections leave the receiver confused as to what is expected and how to respond.

YOUR TASK Study the complete message. Then revise it with (a) a clear introduction that states the purpose of the message, (b) a body with properly announced lists, and (c) a conclusion that includes a call to action and a deadline. Improve the organization by chunking similar material together. What questions must be answered? What tasks should be performed? Should this message show more of a *you* view? In addition, make it easy for recipients to respond. Recipients will be down-editing—that is, returning the message with their responses (in another color) interspersed among the listed items.

Hello everyone,

We'll be moving new team members into a new location next week so there are things we need you to do to be ready for the move. For one thing, let me know which Friday you want your personal items moved. The possibilities are November 12 and 19. Also, if you have an ergonomic desk or chair you want moved, let me know. By the way, we'll be sending boxes, labels, tape and a move map four or five days before the move date you choose, so let me know if this timeframe allows you enough time to pack your office tools and personal belongings. And if you are bringing office equipment from your current team to the new team, let me know. Remember that company policy allows you to take a workstation/laptop from your current team to the new workstation. So check with your admin and let me know what office equipment you will be bringing. Incidentally, your new workstation will have a monitor and peripherals.

You'll need to do some things before the movers arrive. Make sure you put foam pads around your valuable, fragile items and then box them up. This includes things such as IT plaques, glass, or anniversary glass sculptures. If the glass things break, replacing them is expensive and the cost center is responsible for replacement. You may want to move them yourself and not have the movers do it.

Another thing—make sure you pack up the contents of all gray filing cabinets because movers do not move those. Also, write on the move map the number and delivery location of whiteboards, corkboards, and rolling cabinets. Most important, make sure you add a name label to all your work tools and furniture, such as desk phones, docking stations, peripherals, monitors, tables, ergonomic desks, ergonomic chairs, etc. If you see old move labels on recycled boxes, remove them or cross them out.

Get back to me ASAP. And by the way, the movers will arrive between 4 p.m. and midnight on the move date.

Thank you

8.16 Direct Claim: Iron Gate Is a Drag (L.O. 3)

You work for Ledlow Property Management in Boise, Idaho. Your employer specializes in commercial real estate. Yesterday one of your business tenants in the tony East End neighborhood complained about problems with an iron gate you had installed by Cormier Iron Foundry just six months earlier, on August 13. Apparently, the two wings of the double wing gate have settled and don't match in height. The gate gets stuck. It takes much force to open, close, and lock the gate. The iron gate was painted, and in some spots, rust is bleeding onto the previously pristine white paint. The tenant at 4820 E Mill Station Dr., Boise, ID 83716 is a petite shop owner, who complained to you about struggling with the gate at least twice a day when opening and closing her store.

You realize that you will have to contact the installer, Cormier Iron Foundry, and request that the company inspect the gate and remedy the problem. Only six months have passed, and you recall that the warranty for the gate was for one year. To have a formal record of the claim, and because Cormier Iron Foundry does not use e-mail, you decide to write a claim letter.

YOUR TASK Address your letter to Irvin Windham at Cormier Iron Foundry, 3050 W Businesspark Ln., Unit 7, Boise, ID 83709. To jog his memory, you will enclose a copy of the company's proposal/invoice. Your business address is 290 S Fifth St., Level 2, Boise, ID 83702, phone (208) 335-5444 and fax (208) 335-5646.

8.17 Direct Claim: Disappointed? Let the Business Know (L.O. 3)

Like most consumers, you have probably occasionally been unhappy with service or with products you have used.

YOUR TASK Select a product or service that has disappointed you. Write a direct claim letter requesting a refund, replacement, explanation, or whatever seems reasonable. Generally, such letters are addressed to customer service departments. For claims about food products, be sure to include bar code identification from the package, if possible. Your instructor may ask you to mail this letter. Remember that smart companies want to know what their customers think, especially if a product could be improved. Give your ideas for improvement. When you receive a response, share it with your class.

8.18 Direct Claim: A Not-So-Smart TV (L.O. 3)

`E-Mail`

You run a popular small restaurant. Patrons have been telling you that they would like it if you installed a television in the dining area. After some hesitation, you decide to buy a late-model ultra HD 4K TV. You conduct research to compare prices and decide on a Samsung QLED Q90R 65" 4K UHD TV (QN65Q90RAFXZA). You spot the TV at Commander Electronics for $2,597.99 plus tax, the lowest price you could find for the model *PC Magazine* has selected as "Best for high-end home theaters." Although the closest Commander Electronics store is a 35-minute drive, the price is so good you decide it's worth the trip. You and one of the servers spend a good hour mounting

the new QLED TV on the wall and setting it up. It works perfectly, but the next day when you turn it on, nothing happens. You check all connections, but no matter what you do, you can't get a picture. You're irritated! You are without a TV and have wasted time hooking up the Samsung. Assuming it's just a faulty set, you pack up the TV and drive back to Commander Electronics. You have no trouble returning the item and drag a second Samsung, the same model, into your dining room.

Again you set up the TV, hook it up to the restaurant's cable receiver, and are pleased with the new purchase. Your customers seem to enjoy the TV that plays on mute with captions. But a few days later, you have no picture for a second time. Now you are fuming! Not looking forward to your third trip to Commander Electronics, you repack the Samsung television and return it. The customer service representative tries to offer you another Samsung TV, but you decline. You point out all the trouble you have been through and say you would prefer a more reliable TV from a different manufacturer that is the same size and in the same price range as the Samsung. Commander Electronics is selling a comparable LG 65-inch 4K UHD HDR Smart OLED TV (OLED65C8PUA) and carries a larger Sony 75-inch 4K Ultra HD Smart LED TV (XBR75X940E) that also fits your criteria. However, at almost $3,000 both sets cost more than you had budgeted.

You feel that after all the problems you have endured, Commander Electronics should sell you the Sony or the LG at the same price as the defective Samsung. However, when you call to discuss the matter, you learn that the local sales manager isn't authorized to make this decision. You are told to submit a written request to the regional office.

YOUR TASK Write a direct claim e-mail to Louis Estrada, Regional Manager at Commander Electronics, in Atlanta, Georgia, asking him to provide your restaurant with one of the alternative TV sets for less than the advertised price.

8.19 Adjustment: Fixing Erroneous Charge for Rental Car Upgrade (L.O. 4)

As assistant to Michael A. Dunmore, Regional General Manager at Happy Car rental company, you read a shockingly irate complaint letter from a corporate customer addressed to your boss. Sherrie McKeel, Sales Manager for Tavarez Engineering, Inc., in Austin, Texas, has angrily detailed her tribulations with your company's Chicago Midway International Airport branch.

Apparently, she and a colleague suffered long delays in obtaining their rental car. To compensate for the late car delivery, the customers received a complimentary upgrade to a vehicle with a built-in navigation and media system, a $180 value plus taxes and surcharges that would add another $70 to the customers' six-day rental. However, at the end of their rental period, their bill reflected the full cost of the upgrade to a vehicle with built-in navigation system. After multiple phone calls to the Chicago Midway International Airport branch as well as to the Happy Car corporate offices, Ms. McKeel apparently was finally able to have the $180 credited to Tavarez Engineering's business account. However, soon she realized that the $70 levy had not been credited. Irate, she now wants the remainder of the refund. Ms. McKeel has no confidence in the Chicago Midway branch and is asking your boss to intervene on her behalf and reverse the remaining $70 charge.

Mr. Dunmore asks you to investigate what has gone so terribly wrong at the Chicago Midway International Airport location. You learn that the branch is an independent franchisee, which may explain such a laxness in customer service that is unacceptable under corporate rules. In addition, you find out that the branch manager, Claude Wedeking, was traveling on company business during Ms. McKeel's six-day rental period and then left town to attend two management training seminars. Mr. Dunmore is concerned that Happy Car might lose this disappointed customer and decides to offer 20 percent discount vouchers for the engineering company's next three rentals, valid at any U.S. branch. He wants you to draft the letter and enclose the discount vouchers.

YOUR TASK Write a polite adjustment letter to Sherrie McKeel, Tavarez Engineering, Inc., 204 W Riverside Dr., Unit 110, Austin, TX 78704 to secure the customer's goodwill and future business.

8.20 Microsoft's Goodwill Letter to a Newborn (L.O. 5)

Microsoft shared with *Business Insider* the template of the goodwill letter it sends to new parents, or, more precisely, to their babies.[46]

YOUR TASK Evaluate the strengths and weaknesses of this message—in writing if your instructor assigns a written analysis.

Date

Dear [Name],

While you've been busy getting ready for the world, we've been busy doing our part to get the world ready for you.

You represent the most important thing we've all been working toward—the future.

Enclosed are some special gifts we selected just for you. The Welcome Baby Box is lovingly put together by AtWork!, a nonprofit organization whose mission is to help people with disabilities be productive, integrated, and contributing members of their communities. One of our favorite gifts is the Nanny and Webster blanket. Not only will this blanket keep you warm, but also, all profits from Nanny and Webster blankets support children's charities. Please be sure to share these gifts with your parents.

Ask your parents to familiarize themselves with the great benefits that Microsoft offers, like Back-Up Care, subsidized child care, new mothers' rooms, and family resources from the Microsoft CARES Employee Assistance Program. All can be found under Work & Life—Children & Family on **benefits. me.microsoft.com**.

We look forward to watching you grow and seeing what you'll achieve.

Sincerely,

Fred Thiele
GM, Global Benefits

8.21 Appreciating a Favor: Saying Thanks for a Recommendation (L.O. 5)

E-Mail

One of your instructors has complied with your urgent request for a letter of recommendation and has given you an enthusiastic endorsement. Regardless of the outcome of your application, you owe thanks to all your supporters. Respond promptly after receiving this favor. Also, you can assume that your instructor is interested in your progress. Let him or her know whether your application was successful.

YOUR TASK Write an e-mail or, better yet, a letter thanking your instructor. Remember to make your thanks specific so that your words are meaningful. Once you know the outcome of your application, use the opportunity to build more goodwill by writing to your recommender again.

8.22 Appreciating a Favor: Thanking a Business Etiquette Consultant (L.O. 5)

Team   Web

The etiquette and protocol expert Pamela Eyring gave an inspiring talk to your business communication class. A sought-after authority, she runs The Protocol School of Washington, a training center for etiquette consultants and protocol officers. Ms. Eyring emphasized the importance of social skills. She talked about outclassing the competition and dining like a diplomat. She addressed topics such as gift giving, business entertaining, invitations, introductions, greetings, seating arrangements, toasting, eye contact, remembering names, and conversation skills. In the table manners segment, among other topics, she discussed dining dos and don'ts, host and guest duties, seating and napkin placement, place settings and silverware savvy, eating various foods gracefully, and tipping. With characteristic poise but also humor, Ms. Eyring brought utensils, plates, and napkins to demonstrate correct place settings and table manners.

The class was thrilled to receive hands-on training from a nationally known business etiquette expert who was able to lessen their fears of making fools of themselves during business meals or at business mixers.

YOUR TASK Individually or in groups, draft a thank-you letter to Pamela Eyring, president of The Protocol School of Washington, 20 F Street NW, 7th Floor, Washington, DC 20001. Check out the company's website https://www.psow.edu, or find The Protocol School of Washington on Facebook and Instagram, where you can follow Ms. Eyring's frequent media appearances, interviews, and etiquette advice.

8.23 Cherishing Good Wishes: Saying Thank You (L.O. 5)

YOUR TASK Write a short note thanking a friend who sent you good wishes when you recently completed your degree.

8.24 Sending a Sympathy Note: To a Spouse (L.O. 5)

YOUR TASK Imagine that the spouse of a coworker recently died from an infectious disease. Write the coworker a letter of sympathy.

Test Your Workplace Etiquette IQ

New communication platforms and casual workplace environments have blurred the lines of appropriateness, leaving workers wondering how to navigate uncharted waters. Check your workplace etiquette IQ by deciding whether the following statements are true or false. Then see if you agree with the responses on p. Key-5.

1. Your office generously provides an enormous collection of Frito Lay snack and cookie packages in the break room. Because these are free and they are so delicious, it's perfectly fine to take some home for your next screening party.

_____ True _____ False

2. After completing a successful deal, you want to send a gift but the client's company has a no-gifts policy. You think, however, that it is acceptable for you to send a gourmet food basket or a subscription to a trade magazine for the entire office.

_____ True _____ False

3. When receiving a business card, you should treat it as a gift. Take a moment to study the card and perhaps remark on its distinctive design.

_____ True _____ False

Chat About It

In each chapter you will find five discussion questions related to the chapter material. Your instructor may assign these topics for you to discuss in class, in an online chat room, or on an online discussion board. Some of the discussion topics may require outside research. You may also be asked to read and respond to postings made by your classmates.

TOPIC 1: Direct mail marketers say that in the age of multitasking and myriad distractions—from social media posts, messaging, and e-mail—direct mail is special. They cite research suggesting that direct mail connects with customers on a deeper emotional level and provides a much higher response rate than "bland" e-mail. How do you feel about direct mail vs. e-mail?

TOPIC 2: Do you agree that saying sorry for a mishap in doing business is difficult? Even aside from fears of litigation, some businesspeople struggle with apologizing

properly. Have you experienced situations in which saying sorry was difficult? What makes an apology effective?

TOPIC 3: Are you the type of consumer who reads user manuals very carefully, or one who ignores instructions and prefers to figure out electronics and other gizmos by trial and error? Explain your answer. Discuss the pros and cons of following instructions in user manuals.

TOPIC 4: How do you feel about fake or paid reviews on Amazon, Yelp, Google, TripAdvisor, Angie's List, and other platforms? Do you read customer reviews before making a purchase? If yes, how long do you browse reviews on the Internet before deciding to buy?

TOPIC 5: Describe an occasion in which you should have written a goodwill message but failed to do so. Why was it difficult to write that message? What would make it easier for you to do so?

Capitalization

Review Guides 39 through 46 about capitalization in Appendix D, Grammar and Mechanics. On a separate sheet, revise the following sentences to correct capitalization errors. For each error you locate, write the guide number that reflects this usage. Sentences may have more than one error. If a sentence is correct, write C. When you finish, check your answers in the key at the end of the book.

EXAMPLE: Both the Manager and the Vice President traveled to the meeting in the west.

REVISION: Both the **manager** and the **vice president** traveled to the meeting in the **West**. [Guides 41, 43]

1. Our District Manager and Director of Operations recommended the purchase a new nordictrack treadmill for the health center.

2. The secretary of state of the united states urged members of the european union to continue to seek peace in the middle east.

3. Passengers of united airlines must exit the plane at gate 2B in terminal 4 when they reach seattle-tacoma international airport.

4. My Aunt, who lives in the south, has a big mac and a diet coke for Lunch nearly every day.

5. Our corporate Vice President and President met with several Directors on the west coast to discuss how to develop Apps for facebook.

6. Three countries with high tax rates are belgium, germany, and denmark, reported professor du-babcock, who teaches at the city university of hong kong.

7. Alyson Davis, who heads our Consumer Services Division, has a master's degree in marketing from California State University, Long Beach.

8. Please consult figure 2.3 in chapter 2 to obtain U.S. census bureau population figures for the northeast.

9. Last Summer did you see the article titled "the global consequences of using crops for fuel"?

10. Deidre plans to take courses in Management, Economics, and History in the Spring.

CHAPTER 9

Negative Messages

LEARNING OUTCOMES

After studying this chapter, you should be able to do the following:

1 Applying the 3-x-3 writing process, explain the strategies of business communicators in conveying negative news while avoiding legal liability.

2 Describe the direct and indirect strategies in conveying unfavorable news.

3 Identify the components of effective negative messages.

4 Analyze effective techniques for presenting bad news to customers and refusing requests or claims.

5 Evaluate effective techniques for delivering bad news within organizations.

The Bad News Keeps Coming: Volkswagen and *Dieselgate*

In 2013 students at West Virginia University stumbled upon "defeat device" software in VW diesel vehicles that rigged them to pass strict U.S. pollution tests. The students alerted regulators and *Dieselgate* was born. In massive ad campaigns, Volkswagen Group had touted its diesel (TDI) autos as environmentally friendly alternatives to gasoline-powered cars. Supposedly, TDIs would retain a strong resale value and meet the strictest EPA standards.[1]

The magnitude of this scandal cannot be overstated. Volkswagen was slapped with hundreds of lawsuits—from regulators, consumers, lessees, dealers, and shareholders—in the United States and in Europe. On the regulatory and judicial side alone, the carmaker has been sued by the EPA for violating the Clean Air Act, the FTC for false advertising, the Department of Justice for fraud, and the SEC for stock market manipulation. The company was forced to shell out unprecedented sums for fines, retrofits, and buybacks of its TDI vehicles—more than $31 billion at last count. VW was also compelled to buy back, scrap, or modify the 580,000 diesel cars it had sold at a premium in the United States from 2006 to 2015.[2] The company's stock initially lost 40 percent of its value.

The fallout doesn't end here. Over five years, the company was successively headed by three CEOs, each of whom was eventually indicted on various criminal charges, including cover-up, unfair competition, and fraud. The top managers pleaded ignorance of the cheating, despite likely knowing about it since 2007.[3] Five years after the first allegations became public, new charges against VW and its executives continue to be filed with no end in sight. Volkswagen Group marque Audi was also implicated in the scandal, as was supplier Bosch. Altogether 70 VW executives have been charged, nine were indicted for various crimes, and six have received prison sentences so far.[4] German automakers had bet heavily on diesel-fueled cars with tax incentives from their government but couldn't meet the strict U.S. clean-air standards unless they resorted to cheating. Volkswagen was racing to overtake Toyota as the world's largest automaker and needed to sell a lot of cars in the U.S., an underserved territory for VW, hence its aggressive "clean diesel" marketing campaign.[5]

When CEO Martin Winterkorn was ousted in the wake of the scandal, he received a $64 million golden parachute and pension payout, some of which may be clawed back if he lands in prison.[6] Observers first believed that the reputational damage to the "German national car" would be lasting and incalculable,[7] but VW stock has rebounded, and Volkswagen did become the world's largest carmaker in early 2017. Die-hard American diesel car fans have snapped up nearly all vehicles VW had bought back, repaired, and sold at steep discounts.[8] But the lawsuits keep coming, and they are bad news. You will learn more about Dieselgate and be asked to complete a relevant task at the end of this chapter.

Critical Thinking

- What should an individual or organization such as VW do when caught in an ethical impropriety or scandal?

- How do you feel about large payouts to departing managers like CEO Martin Winterkorn who are forced to step down in the aftermath of a scandal?

- Can we conclude from this scandal that the public's memory is short, or can we assume that reputational damage may linger?

9-1 Communicating Negative News Strategically

LEARNING OUTCOME

1 Applying the 3-x-3 writing process, explain the strategies of business communicators in conveying negative news while avoiding legal liability.

Bad things happen in all businesses. At Volkswagen Group, technical hurdles, ethical transgressions, and poor crisis management severely dented the automaker's carefully honed reputation. In other businesses, goods are not delivered, products fail to perform as expected, service is poor, billing gets fouled up, or customers are misunderstood. You may have to write messages ending business relationships, declining proposals, explaining service outages, describing data breaches, announcing price increases, refusing requests for donations, terminating employees, turning down invitations, or responding to unhappy customers. You might have to apologize for mistakes in orders or pricing, the rudeness of employees, overlooked appointments, substandard service, faulty accounting, defective products, or jumbled instructions. As a company representative, you may have to respond to complaints posted for the world to see on Twitter, Facebook, or complaint websites.

Handout/Getty Images News/Getty Images

The truth is that everyone occasionally must deliver bad news in business. Because bad news disappoints, irritates, and sometimes angers the receiver, such messages must be written carefully. The bad feelings associated with disappointing news can generally be reduced if the receiver (a) knows the reasons for the rejection, (b) feels that the news was revealed sensitively, and (c) believes the matter was treated seriously and fairly.

In this chapter you will learn when to use the direct strategy and when to use the indirect strategy to deliver bad news. You will study the goals of business communicators in working with unfavorable news and learn techniques for achieving those goals.

9-1a Articulating Goals in Communicating Negative News

Sending negative news is not the easiest communication task you may have, but it can be gratifying if you do it effectively. As a business communicator working with bad news, you will have many goals, the most important of which are summarized in Figure 9.1.

The goals outlined in Figure 9.1 are ambitious, and we are not always successful in achieving them all. However, many writers have found the strategies and techniques you are about to learn helpful in conveying disappointing news sensitively and safely. With experience, you will be able to vary these strategies and adapt them to your organization's specific communication tasks.

FIGURE 9.1	Goals in Conveying Unfavorable News

Explaining clearly and completely	Conveying empathy and sensitivity	Projecting a professional image	Maintaining friendly relations	Being fair
• Readers understand and, in the best case, accept the bad news. • Recipients do not have to call or write to clarify the message.	• Writers use language that respects the reader and attempts to reduce bad feelings. • When appropriate, writers accept blame and apologize without creating legal liability for the organization or themselves.	Writers stay calm, use polite language, and respond with clear explanations of why a negative message was necessary even when irate customers sound threatening and overstate their claims.	Writers demonstrate their desire to continue pleasant relations with the receivers and to regain their confidence.	Writers show that the decision was fair, impartial, and rational.

9-1b Applying the 3-x-3 Writing Process

Thinking through the entire writing process is especially important when writing bad-news messages because the way bad news is revealed often determines how it is accepted. You have probably heard people say, "I didn't mind the news so much, but I resented the way I was told!" Certain techniques can help you deliver bad news sensitively, beginning with the familiar 3-x-3 writing process.

Analyzing, Anticipating, and Adapting. In Phase 1 (prewriting), you need to analyze the bad news and anticipate its effect on the receiver. Unfortunately, some companies are tone deaf. When credit bureau Equifax exposed sensitive personal information of 143 million Americans in the biggest security breach ever, the company's response was almost worse than the actual hacking.[10] Equifax, one of the three major credit-reporting agencies, waited six weeks before announcing the data breach and then provided remedies that made consumers feel even less secure. People weren't able to establish conclusively whether they were affected. They were directed to a low-security website to register for free credit monitoring, only to be asked to sign away their legal rights.[11] In a brief video, CEO Rick Smith did apologize but came across as wooden, resorting to euphemisms such as *cybersecurity incident*, *intrusion*, and *disappointing event*. Clearly, Equifax failed to grasp the gravity of the situation and thus stoked a firestorm of consumer outrage.

When you have bad news to convey, one of your first considerations is how that message will affect its receiver. If the disappointment will be mild, announce it directly. For example, a small rate increase in a newspaper or digital subscription can be announced directly. If the bad news is serious or personal, consider techniques to reduce the pain. In the Equifax situation, the bad news was communicated in a confusing and inconsistent way; mitigation efforts failed to rebuild trust and reassure consumers.

Choose words that show that you respect the reader as a responsible, valuable person. Select the best channel to deliver the bad news. In many negative situations, you will be dealing with a customer. If your goal is retaining the goodwill of a customer, a letter on company stationery will be more impressive than an e-mail.

Researching, Organizing, and Drafting. In Phase 2 (drafting), you will gather information and brainstorm for ideas. Jot down all the reasons you have that explain the bad news. If four or five reasons prompted your negative decision, concentrate on the strongest and safest ones. Avoid presenting any weak reasons; readers may seize on them to reject the entire message. Include an ample explanation of the negative situation and avoid fixing blame.

When the U.S. Postal Service has to deliver damaged mail, it includes an explanation, such as the following: *Because the Post Office handles millions of pieces of mail daily, we must use mechanical methods to ensure prompt delivery. Damage can occur if mail is insecurely enveloped or bulky contents are enclosed. When this occurs and the machinery jams, it often damages other mail that was properly prepared.* Notice that the message offers the strongest reason for the problem, although other reasons may have been possible. Notice, too, that the explanation tactfully skirts the issue of who caused the problem.

In composing any negative message, conduct research if necessary to help you explain what went wrong and why a decision or action is necessary.

Editing, Proofreading, and Evaluating. In Phase 3 (revising), you will read over your message carefully to ensure that it says what you intend. Check your wording to be sure you are concise without sounding grumpy. If you find that you have overused certain words, use a thesaurus to find synonyms. Read your sentences to see if they sound like conversation and flow smoothly. This is the time to edit and improve coherence and tone. In bad-news messages, the tone is especially important. Readers are more likely to accept negative messages if the tone is friendly and respectful. Even when the bad news can't be changed, its effect can be reduced somewhat by the way it is presented.

In the last phase of the writing process, proofread to make sure your verbs agree with their subjects, your sentences are properly punctuated, and all words are spelled correctly. Pay attention to common mistakes (*its/it's; than/then; their/there*). Use the grammar check in your word processing program, or check your copy using a digital writing assistant, e.g., Grammarly. Finally, evaluate your message. Is it too blunt? Too subtle? Have you delivered the bad news clearly but professionally?

9-1c Conveying Negative News Without Causing Legal Liability

Before we examine the components of a negative message, let's look more closely at how you can avoid exposing yourself and your employer to legal liability in writing negative messages. Although we can't always anticipate the consequences of our words, we should be alert to three causes of legal difficulties: (a) abusive language, (b) careless language, and (c) the good-guy syndrome.

Abusive Language. Calling people names (such as *deadbeat, crook, shyster,* or *quack*) can get you into trouble. Defamation is the legal term for any false statement that harms an individual's reputation. When the abusive language is written, it is called libel; when spoken, it is slander.

To be actionable (likely to result in a lawsuit), abusive language must be (a) false, (b) damaging to one's good name, and (c) published—that is, written or spoken within the presence of others. Therefore, if you were alone with Jane Doe and accused her of accepting bribes and selling company secrets to competitors, she couldn't sue because the defamation wasn't published. Her reputation was not damaged. However, if anyone heard the words or if they were written, you might be legally liable.

Similarly, you may be prosecuted if you transmit a harassing or libelous message by e-mail or social media post. Singer and actor Courtney Love may have been the first celebrity to sue and be sued for what was then dubbed a *Twibel* case. Love won a lawsuit brought by her ex-lawyer for a tweet that had called the attorney corruptible.[12] Love was then sued by fashion designer Dawn Simorangkir for tweeting that the designer was a criminal. The singer had to fork over almost $800,000 when she lost.[13] More recently the blunt SpaceX founder and Tesla CEO Elon Musk found himself in hot water over ill-mannered tweets that maligned a British cave explorer, Vernon

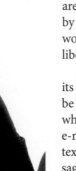

Marcos Mesa Sam Wordley/Shutterstock.com

Unsworth. But to the surprise of observers, Musk won. The lawsuit hinged on the conundrum whether social media comments are factual and hence libelous statements or opinions protected by the First Amendment. The rough-and-tumble social media world seems to give users more leeway now, but it is hardly a libel-free zone.[14]

A company may also incur liability for messages sent through its computer network by employees. For example, employers can be sued for harassment if they don't prevent misconduct. That's why most organizations are monitoring outgoing and internal e-mails and other messages. Instant messaging, live chat, and texting pose another danger for companies. Whether your message is in print or electronic, avoid making unproven charges or letting your emotions prompt abusive language.

Careless Language. As the marketplace becomes increasingly litigious, we must be certain that our words communicate only what we intend. However, even if we think our messages are harmless, in subsequent litigation they may serve to persuade a judge and jury of ill intent. A worker dashes off a casual e-mail to a coworker maligning a supervisor. An engineer expresses her concerns via an e-mail to her manager about a potential flaw in a design. These scenarios can spell trouble. Even a Post-it note tacked onto a file suggesting policy changes could appear incriminating in a legal context. Lawyers recommend phone calls and in-person meetings for voicing serious concerns about any work product and activity, thus avoiding an electronic trail.[15]

The Good-Guy Syndrome. Most of us hate to have to reveal bad news—that is, to be the bad guy. To make ourselves look better, to make the receiver feel better, and to maintain good relations, we are tempted to make statements that are legally dangerous. Alliant Techsystems, a large aerospace and defense company headquartered in Minnesota, was interviewing applicants for a technical support job. After a first interview, a recruiter for the company advised an African American candidate to remove her braids to appear more professional. The woman complied. A few interviews later, the recruiter told her that Alliant wanted to hire her. When the candidate met with the company's IT director, she was wearing her braids again. The next day she was told she would not be hired. A month later a white male was hired for the job. The rejected applicant filed an EEOC lawsuit for race discrimination and received a $100,000 settlement from Alliant. Because the victim's hairdo is culturally associated with African Americans, the EEOC found that Alliant had failed to hire the woman solely for the color of her skin, not her qualifications.[16]

Two important lessons emerge. First, business communicators act as agents of their organizations. Their words, decisions, and opinions are assumed to represent those of the organization. If you want to communicate your personal feelings or opinions, use your personal electronic gadgets on your home network, not your employer's devices, or write on plain paper (rather than company letterhead) and sign your name without title or affiliation. Even then, exercise discretion, as Chapter 7 has amply cautioned. Second, volunteering extra information can lead to trouble. Therefore, avoid supplying data that could be misused, and avoid making promises that can't be fulfilled. Don't admit or imply responsibility for conditions that caused damage or injury. Even some apologies (*We're sorry that a faulty bottle cap caused damage to your carpet*) may suggest liability.

9-2 Analyzing Negative-News Strategies

Unfavorable news in business doesn't always fall into neat categories. To successfully convey bad news, writers must carefully consider the audience, purpose, and context. Experienced business communicators understand that their approaches to negative news must be flexible.[17] However, as a business writer in training, you have at your disposal two basic strategies for delivering negative news: direct and indirect.

Which approach is better suited for your particular message? One of the first steps you will take before delivering negative news is analyzing how your receiver will react to this news. In earlier chapters we discussed applying the direct strategy to positive messages. We suggested using the indirect strategy when the audience might be unwilling, uninterested, displeased, disappointed, or hostile. In this chapter we expand on that advice and suggest additional considerations that can help you decide which strategy to use.

9-2a When to Use the Direct Strategy

The direct strategy saves time and is preferred by some who consider it to be more professional and even more ethical than the indirect strategy. The direct strategy may be more effective in situations such as the following:

- **When the bad news is not damaging**. If the bad news is insignificant (such as a small increase in cost) and doesn't personally affect the receiver, then the direct strategy makes sense.

- **When the receiver may overlook the bad news**. Changes in service, new policy requirements, legal announcements—these critical messages may require boldness to ensure attention.

- **When the organization or receiver prefers directness**. Some companies and individuals expect all internal messages and announcements—even bad news—to be straightforward and presented without frills.

- **When firmness is necessary**. Messages that must demonstrate determination and strength should not use delaying techniques. For example, the last in a series of collection letters that seek payment on an overdue account may require a direct opener.

8878 CHESTNUT RD. FRAMINGHAM, MA 01701
www.unioxfcu.com   508.288.3101

September 8, 2021

Mr. Petru Ramakrishna
30 S. Marvon Street
Phoenixville, PA 19460

Dear Mr. Ramakrishna:

Uses modified direct strategy because urgent action is needed to preven tidentity theft

We are contacting you about a potential problem involving identity theft. On August 30, names, encrypted social security numbers, birth dates, and e-mail addresses of fewer than 25 percent of accounts were compromised in an apparent hacker attack on our website. Outside data security experts are working tirelessly to identify the causes of the breach as well as prevent future intrusions into our system. Immediately upon detecting the attack, we notified the local police authorities as well as the FBI. We also alerted the three major credit-reporting agencies.

We recommend that you place a fraud alert on your credit file. A fraud alert tells creditors to contact you before they open any new accounts or change your existing accounts. Please call any one of the three major credit bureaus. As soon as one credit bureau confirms your fraud alert, the others are notified to place fraud alerts. All three credit reports will be sent to you, free of charge.

Suggests recommended steps and provides helpful information about credit-reporting agencies

Equifax	Experian	TransUnion
800-685-1111	888-397-3742	800-680-7289

Gives reasons for the recommended action, provides contact information, and offers additional pointers

Even if you do not find any suspicious activity on your initial credit reports, the Federal Trade Commission (FTC) recommends that you check your credit reports periodically. Victim information sometimes is held for use or shared among a group of thieves at different times. Checking your credit reports periodically can help you spot problems and address them quickly.

If you find suspicious activity on your credit reports or have reason to believe your information is being misused, call 518-584-5500 and file a police report. Get a copy of the report; many creditors want the information it contains to absolve you of the fraudulent debts. You also should file a complaint with the FTC at www.ftc.gov/idtheft or at 1-877-ID-THEFT (877-438-4338).

Please visit our website at www.unioxfcu.com/databreach for updates on the investigation, or call our privacy hotline at 800-358-4422. Affected customers will receive free credit-monitoring services for one year.

Ends by providing more helpful information, company phone number, and offer of one year of free credit monitoring

Sincerely,

Cyril Cenek

Cyril Cenek
Customer Service

Security breach messages provide a good example of how to employ the direct strategy in delivering bad news. Notice in Model Document 9.1 that the writer, Cyril Cenek, is fairly direct in announcing that consumer identity information was lost at Uniox Federal Credit Union.

Although he does not blurt out "your information has been compromised," the writer does announce a potential identity theft problem in the first sentence. He then explains that a hacker attack has compromised roughly a quarter of customer accounts. In the second paragraph, he recommends that credit union customer Petru Ramakrishna take specific corrective action to protect his identity and offers helpful contact information. The tone is respectful and serious.

The credit union's letter is modeled on an FTC template that was praised for achieving a balance between a direct and indirect opening.[18]

If you must write a security breach message, describe clearly what information was compromised, if known. Explain how the breach occurred, what data were stolen, and, if you know, how the thieves have used the information. Next, disclose what your company has done to repair the damage. Then list the recommended responses most appropriate for the type of data compromised. For instance, if social security numbers were stolen, urge victims to place fraud alerts and a security freeze on their credit reports; include the agencies' addresses. Designate a contact person in your organization, and work with law enforcement to ensure that your notification does not jeopardize the investigation in any way.

9-2b When to Use the Indirect Strategy

The indirect strategy does not reveal the bad news immediately. This strategy, at least theoretically, enables you to keep the reader's attention until you have been able to explain the reasons for the bad news. Some writing experts have claimed that the indirect strategy "ill suits today's skeptical, impatient, even cynical audience."[19] Others have argued the relative merits of both approaches and their effects on the receiver.[20] To be sure, in social media, bluntness seems to dominate the public debate. Directness is equated with honesty; hedging, with deceit.

Regardless, many communicators prefer to use the indirect strategy to soften negative news. Whereas good news can be revealed quickly, bad news may be easier to accept when broken gradually. Even a direct bad-news message can benefit from sandwiching the negative news between positive statements. Here are typical instances in which the indirect strategy works well:

- **When the bad news is personally upsetting**. If the negative news involves the receiver personally, such as a layoff notice, the indirect strategy makes sense. Telling an employee that he or she no longer has a job is probably best done in person and by starting indirectly and giving reasons first. When a company has made a mistake that inconveniences or disadvantages a customer, the indirect strategy also makes sense.

- **When the bad news will provoke a hostile reaction**. When your message will irritate or infuriate the recipient, the indirect method may be best. It begins with a buffer and reasons, thus encouraging the reader to finish reading or hearing the message. A blunt announcement may make the receiver stop reading.

- **When the bad news threatens the customer relationship**. If the negative message may damage a customer relationship, the indirect strategy may help salvage the customer bond. Beginning slowly and presenting reasons that explain what happened can be more helpful than directly announcing bad news or failing to adequately explain the reasons.

- **When the bad news is unexpected**. Readers who are totally surprised by bad news tend to have a more negative reaction than those who expected it. If a company suddenly closes an office or a plant and employees had no inkling of the closure, that bad news would be better received if it were revealed cautiously with reasons first.

AP Images/Julie Jacobson

FOR THE RECORD

Breaking Painful News Indirectly

Two years before his ouster, Intel chief Brian Krzanich sent an e-mail to employees announcing a "restructuring initiative." In the buffer paragraph, Krzanich described Intel's successful pivot from PC to cloud, mobile, and smart computing during his tenure. This strategy was working, he said, but it was time "to accelerate our momentum and build on our strengths." He foreshadowed "some difficult decisions" as he presented the reasons for the restructuring. Finally, in the fourth paragraph, Krzanich broke the bad news: "We expect that this initiative will result in the reduction of up to 12,000 positions globally."[21] What helps determine the choice to use the indirect strategy to deliver bad news?

Reality Check

Being Kind When Saying No

"It's important to be real and upfront with your customers but in a gentle manner. They are the most valuable part of your business, and you need to be transparent if you want them to use your product or service again. When saying no, inform them of your company policies and always offer a solution or next step, as this will show what you're doing to better the situation."[22]

—George Bousis, *founder and CEO, Raise Marketplace, Inc.*

Whether to use the direct or indirect strategy depends largely on the situation, the reaction you expect from the audience, and your goals. The direct method saves time and is preferred by some who consider it more professional and even more ethical than the indirect method. Others think that revealing bad news slowly and indirectly shows sensitivity to the receiver. By preparing the receiver, you tend to soften the impact. Moreover, although social media users may favor the direct approach, the majority of negative messages are still conveyed indirectly. As you can see in Figure 9.2, the major differences between the two strategies are whether you start with a buffer and how early you explain the reasons for the negative news.

9-2c Keeping the Indirect Strategy Ethical

You may worry that the indirect organizational strategy is unethical or manipulative because the writer deliberately delays the main idea. Now, consider the alternative. Breaking bad news bluntly can cause pain and hard feelings. By delaying bad news, you soften the blow somewhat, as well as ensure that your reasoning will be read while the receiver is still receptive. One psychologist recognized that the indirect strategy depends on a clear explanation: "If the *why* of my *no* is clear and understandable, it's less likely that the other person will take it as being a *no* to them."[23] In using the indirect strategy, your motives are not to deceive the reader or to hide the news. Rather, your goal is to be a compassionate, yet effective communicator.

The key to ethical communication lies in the motives of the sender. Unethical communicators *intend to deceive.* Although the indirect strategy provides a setting in which to announce bad news, it should not be used to avoid or misrepresent the truth. For example, the Internet is rife with bogus offers such as ineffective weight-loss supplements and skin care products promising to deliver the fountain of youth. Teeth-whitening systems Snow and iSmile fraudulently used the

FIGURE 9.2 Comparing the Direct and Indirect Strategies for Negative Messages

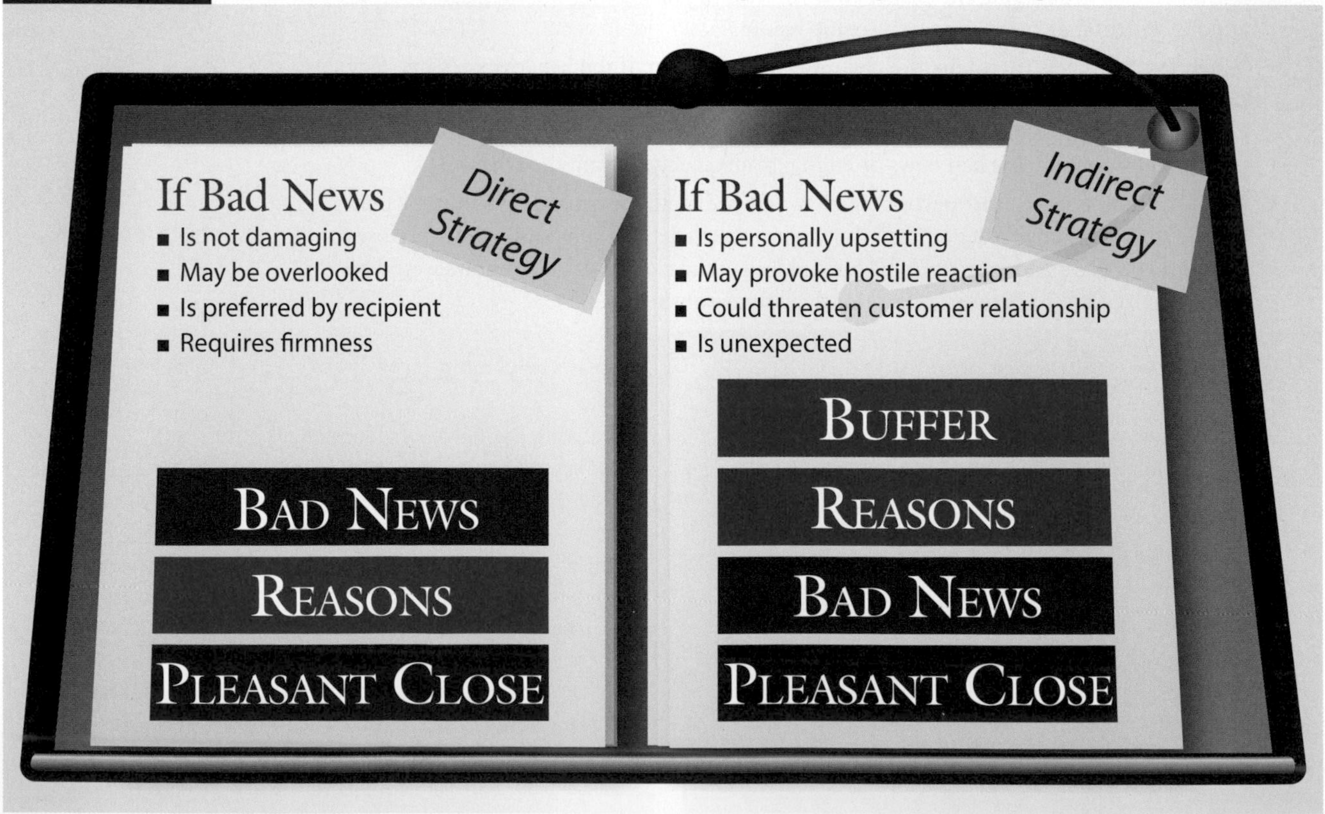

If Bad News
Is not damaging
May be overlooked
Is preferred by recipient
Requires firmness
Direct Strategy
Bad News
Reasons
Pleasant Close
If Bad News
Is personally upsetting
May provoke hostile reaction
Could threaten customer relationship
Is unexpected
Indirect Strategy
Buffer
Reasons
Bad News
Pleasant Close

FDA logo. MyPillow touted a sham sleep study. The world's largest retailer, Amazon, is promoting and profiting from falsely marketed brain supplements. These are but a few of the most recent scams, says Truth in Advertising, a nonprofit dedicated to stamping out deceptive advertising.[24] As you will see in Chapter 10, misleading, deceptive, and unethical claims are never acceptable. In fact, many of them are simply illegal.

9-3 Composing Effective Negative Messages

LEARNING OUTCOME

3 Identify the components of effective negative messages.

Even though it may be impossible to make the receiver happy when delivering negative news, you can reduce bad feelings and resentment by structuring your message sensitively. Most negative messages contain some or all of these parts: buffer, reasons, bad news, and closing. This section also discusses apologies and how to convey empathy in delivering bad news.

9-3a Opening Indirect Messages With a Buffer

A buffer is a device to reduce shock or pain. To buffer the pain of bad news, begin with a neutral but meaningful statement that makes the reader continue reading. The buffer should be relevant and concise and provide a natural transition to the explanation that follows. The individual situation, of course, will help determine what you should put in the buffer. Avoid trite buffers such as *Thank you for your letter*.

Not all business communication authors agree that buffers increase the effectiveness of negative messages. However, in many cultures softening bad news is appreciated. Following are buffer possibilities.

Best News. Start with the part of the message that represents the best news. For example, a message to customers who purchased mobile device insurance announced a progressive rate increase that was tied to the replacement value of each smart device. Only customers with very expensive handsets will experience price increases. You might start by reminding customers about the value of insuring a mobile device, *As a reminder, your MobilePeer Protection provides the benefit of a replacement device when your smartphone is accidentally damaged, including liquid damage, loss, theft, and malfunction. Although devices are becoming increasingly expensive, no changes will be made to your deductible amount or coverage.*

Compliment. Praise the receiver's accomplishments, organization, or efforts, but do so with honesty and sincerity. For instance, in a letter declining an invitation to speak, you could write, *The Karegiverz have my sincere admiration for their fund-raising projects on behalf of hungry children. I am honored that you asked me to speak Monday, November 7.*

Appreciation. Convey thanks for doing business, for sending something, for showing confidence in your organization, for expressing feelings, or simply for providing feedback. Suppose you had to draft a letter that refuses employment. You could say, *I appreciated learning about the occupational therapist program at USC and about your qualifications in our interview last Friday.* Avoid thanking the reader, however, for something you are about to refuse.

Agreement. Make a relevant statement with which both reader and receiver can agree. A letter that rejects a business loan application might read, *We both realize how much falling crude oil prices on the world market have devastated domestic oil production.*

Facts. Provide objective information that introduces the bad news. For example, in a memo announcing cutbacks in the hours of the employees' cafeteria, you might say, *During the past five years, the number of employees eating breakfast in our cafeteria has dropped from 32 percent to 12 percent.*

Reality Check

"Answer negative feedback as soon as you see it. It's an opportunity to show the human side of your business. Customers forgive if they feel their concerns are heard and taken seriously. For negative feedback, simply apologize, offer a solution or an investigation, and provide direct contact information for a human being should they wish to take it further. 'Sorry' goes a long way."[25]

—Freya Smale, *The Millennium Alliance*

Understanding. Show that you care about the reader. Notice how in this letter to customers announcing a product defect, the writer expresses concern: *We know that you expect superior performance from all the products you purchase from SupplyPlex. That's why we're writing personally about the InkMeister printer cartridges you recently ordered.*

9-3b Apologizing

You learned about making apologies in adjustment messages in Chapter 8. We expand that discussion here because apologies are often part of negative-news messages. An apology is defined as an "admission of blameworthiness and regret for an undesirable event."[26] Apologies are thought to promote healing, influence perceptions of the offending party's character, and invite victims to empathize with the offender, leading to forgiveness.[27] Apologies to customers are especially important if you or your company erred. They cost nothing, and they go a long way in soothing hard feelings.

The truth is that sincere apologies work and affect the bottom line. A study of 130 press releases shows that companies are twice as likely to pass the buck than to own up to their mistakes; however, businesses blaming external factors instead of taking responsibility for their failings tend to experience ongoing financial decline. Those who own up to their poor performance see their finances recover and improve.[28] Other research suggested that CEOs who appeared genuinely sad, not merely contrite, in videos saw their companies' stock prices rise after an apology. Conversely, leaders who smiled while apologizing were perceived as insincere, and their companies' stock prices dropped.[29]

Author John Kador recommends what he calls the Five Rs model for effective apologies in business messages[30] summarized in Figure 9.3.

Consider these poor and improved apologies:

Poor apology: We regret that you are unhappy with the price of frozen yogurt purchased at one of our self-serve scoop shops.

Improved apology: We are genuinely sorry that you were disappointed in the price of frozen yogurt recently purchased at one of our self-serve scoop shops. Your opinion is important to us, and we appreciate your giving us the opportunity to look into the problem you describe.

Poor apology: We apologize if anyone was affected.

Improved apology: I apologize for the frustration our delay caused you. As soon as I received your message, I began looking into the cause of the delay and realized that our delivery tracking system must be improved.

FIGURE 9.3   Apologizing Effectively in the Digital Age: The Five Rs

Recognition *Acknowledge the specific offense.*	**Responsibility** *Accept personal responsibility.*	**Restitution** *Explain exactly how you will fix it.*	**Remorse** *Embrace I apologize and I am sorry.*	**Repeating** *Say it won't happen again and mean it.*
• Organizations that apologize have better outcomes. • Individuals who apologize well rise higher in management and have better relationships.	• Accountability means taking reponsibility and rejecting defensiveness. • Accountability is an important skill. • The cover-up is often worse than the crime.	• A concrete explanation of what you will do to make things right is best. • The remedy should be appropriate, adequate, and satisfying.	• Apologies may become necessary unexpectedly. • We can prevent automatic defensiveness by being prepared to apologize when the need arises. • Apologies should be honest, sincere, and authentic.	• Written apologies are more formal than spoken but work similarly. • By communicating effectively over the long term, businesses gain the trust of employees, the public, as well as the media, and are therefore better equipped to weather crises successfully.

Poor apology: We are sorry that mistakes were made in filling your order.

Improved apology: You are right to be concerned. We sincerely apologize for the mistakes we made in filling your order. To prevent recurrence of this problem, we are . . . .

9-3c Showing Empathy

One of the hardest things to do in negative messages is to convey empathy. As discussed in Chapter 3, **empathy** means "understanding our emotional impact on others and making change as a result."[32] The Empathy Business, a UK-based consulting firm, offers this work-focused definition on its landing page: "We define corporate empathy, not compassion or sympathy, as the emotional impact a company has on its people—staff and customers—and society—the next generation.[33] The consultancy has established a so-called **empathy quotient** and ranked 170 large companies on metrics such as corporate culture, leadership, brand perception, ethics, carbon footprint, and social media presence. Facebook took first place, followed by Alphabet (Google), and LinkedIn.[34] Business leaders are catching on. Some U.S. employers have started providing empathy training. In a recent survey of CEOs, more than 90 percent said empathy was key to success.[35]

Here are examples of ways to express empathy in written messages:

- In writing to an unhappy customer: *We did not intentionally delay the shipment, and we sincerely regret the disappointment and frustration you must have suffered.*

- In laying off employees: *It is with great regret that we must take this step. Rest assured that I will be more than happy to write letters of recommendation for anyone who asks.*

- In responding to a complaint: *I am deeply saddened that our service failure disrupted your sale, and we will do everything in our power to . . . .*

- In showing genuine feelings: *You have every right to be disappointed. I am truly sorry that . . . .*

> ### Reality Check
>
> **Empathy Is Good for Business**
>
> "We all know empathy is the right thing to do, but empathy is not just good for the world (and our own sanity). It can also bring a competitive advantage in business. Our ability to see the world from the perspective of others is one of the most crucial tools in our business toolbox."[36]
>
> —Maria Ross, *brand strategist, author, and speaker*

9-3d Presenting the Reasons

Without sound reasons for denying a request, refusing a claim, or revealing other bad news, a message will fail, no matter how cleverly it is organized or written. Providing an explanation reduces feelings of ill will and improves the chances that readers will accept the bad news. For example, if you must deny a customer's request, as part of your planning before writing, you analyze the request and decide to refuse it for specific reasons. Where do you place your reasons? In the indirect strategy, the reasons appear before the bad news. In the direct strategy, the reasons appear immediately after the bad news.

Explaining Clearly. If the reasons are not confidential and if they will not create legal liability, you can be specific: *Growers supplied us with a limited number of patio roses, and our demand this year was twice that of last year.* In responding to a billing error, explain what happened: *After you contacted us about an error on your May statement, we realized the mistake was ours. Until our new automated billing system is fully online, we are still subject to the frailties of human error. Rest assured that your account has been credited, as you will see on your next bill.* In refusing a speaking engagement, tell why the date is impossible: *On February 19 I will be out of the country, attending a strategic planning summit.* Don't, however, make unrealistic or dangerous statements in an effort to be the good guy.

Citing Reader or Other Benefits, if Plausible. Readers are more open to bad news if in some way, even indirectly, they may benefit. When *The New York Times* announced a first-ever price hike to its 4 million digital subscribers, the e-mail included lofty words: "These rates will help us sustain and strengthen our coverage at a time when independent journalism is under great pressure. Your support allows us to go wherever the story is, no matter the danger, hardship or cost. . . . That would not be possible without subscribers like you. Thank you again for supporting *The Times* in our pursuit of the truth, without fear or favor."[37]

Readers also accept bad news more readily if they recognize that someone or something else benefits, such as other workers or the environment: *Although we would like to consider your application, we prefer to fill managerial positions from within.* Avoid trying to show reader benefits, though, if they appear insincere: *To improve our service to you, we are increasing our brokerage fees.*

Explaining Company Policy.   Readers resent blanket policy statements prohibiting something: *Company policy prevents us from making cash refunds* or *Contract bids may be accepted from local companies only* or *Company policy requires us to promote from within.* Instead of hiding behind company policy, gently explain why the policy makes sense: *We prefer to promote from within because it rewards the loyalty of our employees. In addition, we have found that people familiar with our organization instantly start contributing to our team effort.* By offering explanations, you demonstrate that you care about readers and are treating them as important individuals.

Choosing Positive Words.   Because the words you use can affect a reader's response, choose carefully. Remember that the objective of the indirect strategy is holding the reader's attention until you have had a chance to explain the reasons justifying the bad news. To keep the reader in a receptive mood, avoid expressions with punitive, demoralizing, or otherwise negative connotations. Stay away from such words as *cannot, claim, denied, error, failure, fault, impossible, mistaken, misunderstand, never, regret, rejected, unable, unwilling, unfortunately,* and *violate.*

Showing Fairness and Serious Intent.   In explaining reasons, show the reader that you take the matter seriously, have investigated carefully, and are making a reasonable decision. Receivers are more accepting of disappointing news when they feel that their requests have been heard and that they have been treated fairly. In canceling funding for a program, board members provided this explanation: *As you know, the publication of ArtWork was funded by a renewable annual grant from the National Endowment for the Arts. Recent cutbacks in federally sponsored city arts programs have left us with few funds. Because our grant has been discontinued, we have no alternative but to cease publication of ArtWork. Our board has searched long and hard for some other viable funding but was not able to find a workable path forward. Accordingly, June's issue will be our last.*

A luxury resort in French Polynesia attempted to soothe disappointed customers with a discount after an Internet price goof: *Please note that our website contained an unfortunate misprint offering $850-per-night Bora Bora bungalows at $85. Although we cannot honor that rate, we are offering a special half-price rate of $425 to those who responded.*

9-3e Cushioning the Bad News

Although you can't prevent the disappointment that bad news brings, you can reduce the pain somewhat by breaking the news sensitively. Be especially considerate when the reader will suffer personally from the bad news. A number of thoughtful techniques can cushion the blow.

Positioning the Bad News Strategically.   Instead of spotlighting it, sandwich the bad news between other sentences, perhaps among your reasons. Don't let the refusal begin or end a paragraph; the reader's eye will linger on these high-visibility spots. Another technique that reduces shock is putting a painful idea in a subordinate clause: *Although another candidate was hired, we appreciate your interest in our organization and wish you every success in your job search.* Subordinate clauses often begin with words such as *although, as, because, if,* and *since.*

Using the Passive Voice.   Passive-voice verbs enable you to depersonalize an action. Whereas the active voice focuses attention on a person (*We don't give cash refunds*), the passive voice highlights the action (*Cash refunds are not given because . . .*). Use the passive voice for the bad news. In some instances you can combine passive-voice verbs and a subordinate clause: *Although franchise scoop shop owners cannot be required to lower their frozen yogurt prices, we are happy to pass along your comments for their consideration.*

Highlighting the Positive.   As you learned earlier, messages are far more effective when you describe what you can do instead of what you can't do. Rather than *We will no longer allow credit card purchases,* try a more positive appeal: *Although credit card purchases are no longer allowed, we are now selling gasoline at discount cash prices.*

Implying the Refusal.   It is sometimes possible to avoid a direct statement of refusal. Often, your reasons and explanations leave no doubt that a request has been denied. Explicit refusals may be unnecessary and at times cruel. In this refusal to contribute to a charity, for example, the writer never actually says *no: Because we will soon be moving into new offices in Eagle Rock, all our funds are earmarked for relocation costs. We hope that next year we will be able to support your worthwhile cause.* The danger of an implied refusal, of course, is that it is so subtle that the reader misses it. Be certain that you make the bad news clear, thus preventing the need for further correspondence. If you raise hopes for possible future support, mean it.

Suggesting a Compromise or an Alternative.   A refusal is not so depressing—for the sender or the receiver—if a suitable compromise, substitute, or alternative is available. In denying permission to a group of students to visit a historical private residence, for instance, this writer softens the bad news by proposing an alternative: *Although private tours of the grounds are not given, we do open the house and its gardens for one charitable event in the fall.* You can further reduce the impact of the bad news by refusing to dwell on it. Present it briefly (or imply it) and move on to your closing.

9-3f Closing Pleasantly

After explaining the bad news sensitively, close the message with a pleasant statement that promotes goodwill. The closing should be personalized and may include a forward look, an alternative, good wishes, freebies, resale information, or a sales promotion. *Resale* refers to mentioning a product or service favorably to reinforce the customer's choice. For example, *you chose our best-selling model.*

Forward Look.   Anticipate future relations or business. A letter that refuses a contract proposal might read: *Thanks for your bid. We may be able to work with your talented staff when future projects demand your special expertise.*

Alternative Follow-Up.   If an alternative exists, end your letter with follow-through advice. For example, in a letter rejecting a customer's demand for replacement of landscaping plants, you might say: *I will be happy to give you a free inspection and consultation. Please call 301-746-8112 to arrange a date for my visit.* In a message to a prospective home buyer: *Although the lot you saw last week is now sold, we do have two excellent lots available at a slightly higher price.*

Good Wishes.   A letter rejecting a job candidate might read: *We appreciate your interest in our company, and we extend to you our best wishes in your search to find the perfect match between your skills and job requirements.*

Freebies.   When customers complain—primarily about food products or small consumer items—companies often send coupons, samples, or gifts to restore confidence and to promote future business. In response to a customer's complaint about a frozen dinner, you could write: *Your loyalty and your concern about our frozen entrées are genuinely appreciated. Because we want you to continue enjoying our healthy and convenient dinners, we are enclosing a coupon for your next nutritious Town Foods entrée that you can redeem at your local market.*

FIGURE 9.4 Delivering Bad News Sensitively

1 Buffer	**2** Reasons	**3** Bad News	**4** Closing
• Best news • Compliment • Appreciation • Agreement • Facts • Understanding • Apology	• Cautious explanation • Reader or other benefits • Company policy explanation • Positive words • Evidence that matter was considered fairly and seriously	• Embedded placement • Passive voice • Implied refusal • Compromise • Alternative	• Forward look • Information about alternative • Good wishes • Freebies • Resale • Sales promotion

Resale or Sales Promotion. When the bad news is not devastating or personal, references to resale information or promotion may be appropriate: *The rugged laptops you ordered for your field staff are unusually popular because of their rigid, robust cases. To help you locate hard-to-find accessories for these laptops, we invite you to visit our online catalog for a huge selection of USB-C hubs, Pelican cases, laptop bags, power banks, and charging stations.*

Avoid endings that sound canned, insincere, inappropriate, or self-serving. Don't invite further correspondence (*If you have any questions, do not hesitate . . .*), and don't refer to the bad news. Figure 9.4 reviews suggestions for delivering bad news sensitively.

9-4 Refusing Typical Requests and Claims

When you must refuse typical requests, you will first think about how the receiver will react to your refusal and decide whether to use the direct or the indirect strategy. If you have any doubt, use the indirect strategy. As you move forward in your career and become a professional or a representative of an organization, you may receive requests for favors or contributions. You may also be invited to speak or give presentations.

Businesses must occasionally respond to disappointed customers in print and online. In many instances disgruntled customers are turning to social media to air their grievances. They write reviews on Yelp, Amazon, TripAdvisor, Angie's List, and the Better Business Bureau, not to mention employment critiques on Glassdoor or Indeed. Gripes about products and services also appear on complaint sites such as Trustpilot in addition to Facebook, Twitter, and other social networks. Large companies have social media teams that monitor negative messages online and solve problems whenever customers voice their discontent.

9-4a Rejecting Requests for Favors, Money, Information, and Action

Requests for favors, money, information, and action may come from charities, friends, or business partners. Many are from people representing commendable causes, and you may wish you could comply. However, resources are usually limited. In a letter from Manteau Management Associates, shown in Model Document 9.2, the company must refuse a request for a donation to a charity. Following the indirect strategy, the letter begins with a buffer acknowledging the request. It also praises the good works of the charity and uses those words as a transition to the second paragraph. In the second paragraph, the writer explains why the company cannot donate. Notice that the writer reveals the refusal without actually stating it (*Because of internal restructuring and subsequent cutbacks in charitable giving, we are forced to take a much harder look at funding requests that we receive this year*). This gentle refusal makes it unnecessary to be blunter in stating the denial.

1 Prewriting

Analyze: The purpose of this letter is to reject the request for a monetary donation without causing ill will.

Anticipate: The reader is proud of her organization and the good work it pursues. She will appreciate recognition and praise for the PuppyTale Guide Dog's mission and achievements.

Adapt: The writer should strive to cushion the bad news and explain why it is necessary.

2 Drafting

Research: Collect information about the receiver's organization as well as reasons for the refusal.

Organize: Use the indirect strategy. Begin with complimentary comments, present reasons, and reveal the bad news gently or simply imply it. Close graciously.

Draft: Write the message and consider keeping a copy to serve as a form letter.

3 Revising

Edit: Be sure that the tone of the message is positive and that it suggests that the matter was taken seriously.

Proofread: Check the receiver's name and address to be sure that they are accurate. Check the letter's format.

Evaluate: Will this message retain the goodwill of the receiver despite its bad news?

manteau
Management Associates

819. Proctor Street, Suite 800
Anoka, MN 55303
WWW. manteaumanagement.com

February 16, 2021

Ms. Alexandra Milan
PuppyTale Guide Dog Foundation
7543 Spring Court
Pickerington, OH 43147

Dear Ms. Milan:

Opens with praise and compliments →
Here at Manteau Management Associates, we are pleased that over the years we were able to partner with the PuppyTale Guide Dog Foundation and assist in its admirable program that provides guide and service dogs to blind or visually impaired individuals. We appreciate your recent letter describing the exceptionally worthwhile Dogs for Vets program that offers trained animals to America's returning heroes needing service dogs. ← *Doesn't say yes or no*

Transitions with repetition of key ideas (good work and worthy projects) →
Supporting the good work and worthy projects of your organization and others, although unrelated to our business, is a luxury we have enjoyed in the past. Because of internal restructuring and subsequent cutbacks in charitable giving, we are forced to take a much harder look at funding requests that we receive this year. We feel that we must focus our charitable contributions on areas that relate more directly to our business. ← *Explains cutback in gifts, thus revealing refusal without actually stating it*

Closes graciously with praise and a forward look →
We are hopeful that in the future we will be able to again partner with the PuppyTale Guide Dog Foundation to help defray the costs of breeding, training, and placing guide and service dogs. You provide an admirable service, and Manteau salutes you.

Cordially,

MANTEAU MANAGEMENT ASSOCIATES

Victor Maquinna

Victor Maquinna
Vice President

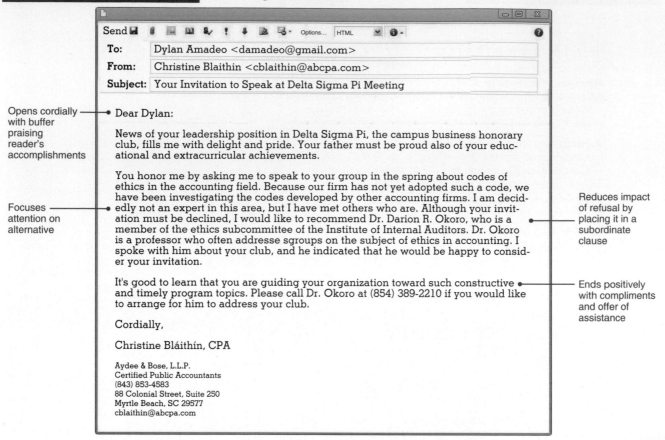

Opens cordially with buffer praising reader's accomplishments

Focuses attention on alternative

Reduces impact of refusal by placing it in a subordinate clause

Ends positively with compliments and offer of assistance

To: Dylan Amadeo <damadeo@gmail.com>

From: Christine Blaithin <cblaithin@abcpa.com>

Subject: Your Invitation to Speak at Delta Sigma Pi Meeting

Dear Dylan:

News of your leadership position in Delta Sigma Pi, the campus business honorary club, fills me with delight and pride. Your father must be proud also of your educational and extracurricular achievements.

You honor me by asking me to speak to your group in the spring about codes of ethics in the accounting field. Because our firm has not yet adopted such a code, we have been investigating the codes developed by other accounting firms. I am decidedly not an expert in this area, but I have met others who are. Although your invitation must be declined, I would like to recommend Dr. Darion R. Okoro, who is a member of the ethics subcommittee of the Institute of Internal Auditors. Dr. Okoro is a professor who often addresse sgroups on the subject of ethics in accounting. I spoke with him about your club, and he indicated that he would be happy to consider your invitation.

It's good to learn that you are guiding your organization toward such constructive and timely program topics. Please call Dr. Okoro at (854) 389-2210 if you would like to arrange for him to address your club.

Cordially,

Christine Bláithín, CPA

Aydee & Bose, L.L.P.
Certified Public Accountants
(843) 853-4583
88 Colonial Street, Suite 250
Myrtle Beach, SC 29577
cblaithin@abcpa.com

In some donation refusal letters, the reasons may not be fully explained: *Although we can't provide financial support at this time, we all unanimously agree that the Make-A-Wish Foundation contributes a valuable service to sick children.* The emphasis is on the foundation's good deeds rather than on an explanation for the refusal.

Messages that refuse requests for favors, money, information, and action can often be tactfully handled by showing appreciation for the inquiry and respect for the writer. Businesses that are required to write frequent refusals might prepare a form letter, changing a few variables as needed.

9-4b Declining Invitations

When you must decline an invitation to speak or make a presentation, you generally try to provide a response that says more than *I can't* or *I don't want to.* Unless the reasons are confidential or business secrets, try to explain them. Because responses to invitations are often taken personally, make a special effort to soften the refusal. In the e-mail shown in Model Document 9.3, an accountant must say *no* to the invitation from a friend's son to speak before the young man's college business club. This refusal starts with conviviality and compliments.

The writer then explains why she cannot accept. The refusal is embedded in a long paragraph and de-emphasized in a subordinate clause (*Although your invitation must be decline*). The reader naturally concentrates on the main clause that follows (*I would like to recommend . . .*). If no alternative is available, focus on something positive about the situation (*Although I'm not an expert, I commend your organization for selecting this topic*). Overall, the tone of this refusal is warm, upbeat, and positive.

9-4c Dealing With Disappointed Customers in Print and Online

All businesses offering products or services must sometimes deal with troublesome situations that cause unhappiness to customers. Merchandise is not delivered on time, a product fails to perform as expected, service is deficient, charges are erroneous, or customers are misunderstood. Whenever possible, these problems should be dealt with immediately and personally. Most business professionals strive to control the damage and resolve such problems in the following manner:

- Call or e-mail the individual or reply to his or her online post within 24 hours.

- Describe the problem and apologize.

- Explain why the problem occurred, what you are doing to resolve it, and how you will prevent it from happening again.

- Promote goodwill by following up with a message that documents the phone call or acknowledges the online exchange of posts.

Responding by E-Mail and in Hard Copy. Written messages are important (a) when personal contact is impossible, (b) to establish a record of the incident, (c) to formally confirm follow-up procedures, and (d) to promote good relations. Dealing with problems immediately is very important in resolving conflict and retaining goodwill.

A bad-news follow-up letter is shown in Model Document 9.4. Consultant Natalia Lelise found herself in the embarrassing position of explaining why she had released the name of her client to a salesperson. The client, Jarvis & Chantel International, had hired her firm, Maxence & Collen Consulting, to help find an appropriate service for outsourcing its payroll functions. Without realizing it, Natalia had mentioned to a potential vendor (Gragson Payroll, Inc.) that her client was considering hiring an outside service to handle its payroll. An overeager salesperson from Gragson Payroll immediately called on Jarvis & Chantel International, thus angering the client.

Natalia Lelise first called her client to explain and apologize. She was careful to control her voice and rate of speaking. She also followed up with the letter shown in Model Document 9.4. The letter not only confirms the telephone conversation but also adds the right touch of formality. It sends the nonverbal message that the writer takes the matter seriously and that it is important enough to warrant a hard-copy letter.

Many consumer problems are handled with letters, written either by consumers as complaints or by companies in response. However, e-mail and social media are now common channels for delivering complaints and negative messages.

Managing Negative News Online. The phone and e-mail remain the dominant channels for customer complaints.[39] However, today's impatient, hyperconnected consumers often take their gripes to social media sites rather than calling customer service departments. Why rely on word of mouth or send a letter to a company about poor service or a defective product when you can shout your grievance to the entire world? Internet sites, e.g., HissingKitty or GripeO, encourage consumers to quickly share complaints about stores, products, and services that fall short of their standards. Twitter, Facebook, Angie's List, TripAdvisor, Yelp, and other social media platforms allow consumers to make public their ire, often without giving the business an opportunity to fix the problem first.

> ### Reality Check
>
> #### Answering With Deliberate Speed to Customer Complaints Online
>
> "Responding within 24 hours is a good rule of thumb, depending on the situation. But be careful when handling negative reviews on social media. Once you post, it's in writing, forever. That said, addressing the customer on their turf, through their preferred mode of communication, is a good idea, but use private messages and encourage a phone conversation if it's a complicated issue."[38]
>
> —Brandie Claborn, *McAfee*

Online complaints are gaining momentum for many reasons. Consumers may receive faster responses to tweets than to customer service calls.[40] More than 50 percent of Twitter users who complain on Twitter expect an answer from customer service within an hour or less. Almost 60 percent of consumers think the response time should always be the same, including weekends.[41] Even e-mail deserves a faster response time, marketers say, of one hour or less, not the average 12-hour response time that's typical today.[42] However, according to a recent study, a whopping 62 percent of companies couldn't be bothered

MAXENCE & COLLEN CONSULTING

500 Henry Road, Suite 100
Fort Wayne, IN 46804

(260) 842-0971
www.mcconsulting.com

May 10, 2021

Mr. Reilly Ellington
Director, Administrative Operations
Jarvis & Chantel International
210 North Illinois Street, Suite 1640
Indianapolis, IN 46204

Dear Mr. Ellington:

Opens with agreement and apology

You have every right to expect complete confidentiality in your transactions with an independent consultant. As I explained in yesterday's telephone call, I am very distressed that you were called by a salesperson from Gragson Payroll, Inc. This should not have happened, and I apologize to you again for inadvertently mentioning your company's name in a conversation with a potential vendor, Gragson Payroll, Inc.

Takes responsibility and promises to prevent recurrence

All clients of Maxence & Collen Consulting are assured that their dealings with our firm are held in the strictest confidence. Because your company's payroll needs are so individual and because you have so many contract workers, I was forced to explain how your employees differed from those of other companies. Revealing your company name was my error, and I take full responsibility for the lapse. I can assure you that it will not happen again. I have informed Gragson Payroll that it had no authorization to call you directly and that its actions have forced me to reconsider using its services for my future clients.

Explains what caused the problem and how it was resolved

Closes with forward look

A number of other payroll services offer outstanding programs. I'm sure we can find the perfect partner to enable you to outsource your payroll responsibilities, thus allowing your company to focus its financial and human resources on its core business. I look forward to our next appointment when you may choose from a number of excellent payroll outsourcing firms.

Sincerely,

Natalia Lelise

Natalia Lelise
Partner

Tips for Resolving Problems and Following Up

- Whenever possible, call or see the individual involved.
- Describe the problem and apologize.
- Explain why the problem occurred.
- Take responsibility, if appropriate.
- Explain what you are doing to resolve it.
- Explain what you are doing to prevent recurrence.
- Follow up with a message that documents the personal contact.
- Look forward to positive future relations.

to answer e-mail messages from consumers and fewer than half to a third responded to tweets.[43] They may want to reconsider because 88 percent of consumers say they are less likely to buy from businesses that leave complaints on social media unanswered.[44]

Airing gripes in public also helps other consumers avoid the same problems and may improve the complainer's leverage in solving the problem. In addition, dashing off a tweet is much easier than writing a complaint e-mail or letter to a customer service department or navigating endless phone menus to reach an agent. Businesses can employ some of the following effective strategies to manage negative news on social media:

- **Recognize social media as an important feedback channel.** Instead of fearing social networks, smart companies embrace these channels as opportunities to look into the true mind-set of customers and receive free advice on how to improve.

- **Become proactive.** Social media pages help companies listen to their customers as well as spread the word about their own good deeds. Marketing experts believe that 96 percent of unhappy customers don't complain to companies directly, but they tell 15 friends about their bad experience.[45] This means anticipating trouble and exceeding consumers' expectations is key. American Airlines has set a 30-minute average response time goal for 4,500 daily tweets, but the airline's social care team is aiming to respond to the public even faster.[46] JetBlue, Virgin America, and AlaskaAir have won praise for responding in less than 5 minutes on average.[47]

- **Maintain a social media presence.** Companies that have not yet established a presence on Twitter, Facebook, Instagram, YouTube, and LinkedIn are the exception today. Wise businesses know they can benefit from interacting with their customers and the public. Companies and their brands employ an omnichannel strategy to engage consumers, i.e. customer service must also deliver on all communication channels available today to reach consumers where they are in a 24/7 world.

- **Monitor comments.** Many large companies employ social media customer service representatives to monitor online traffic and respond immediately whenever possible. At Southwest Airlines and other carriers, such social care teams listen online to what people are saying about their companies. Their policy is to engage the positive and address the negative as fast as possible, in real time ideally.

When domain registrar and Internet hosting provider GoDaddy experienced a nearly six-hour service disruption that affected the websites of more than 10 million customers, the company responded swiftly. It took to social media and used multiple channels to reassure its users. Model Document 9.5 shows a blog post by GoDaddy CEO Scott Wagner addressing the bad news head-on and apologizing to customers.[48]

An almost identical message went out by e-mail to all GoDaddy users offering a 30 percent discount on any new product or renewal to compensate for the loss of service. In addition, the company provided frequent Twitter updates. "Status Alert: Hey, all. We're aware of the trouble people are having with our site. We're working on it." Subsequently, *@GoDaddy* tweeted: "Update: Still working on it, but we're making progress. Some service has already been restored. Stick with us."[49] In a 24/7 news cycle and facing an Internet that never sleeps, companies lose if they snooze. Because the bad news didn't injure people's feelings, the company could afford to state the unfavorable news directly. GoDaddy's adept response won praise.

9-4d Handling Problems With Orders

Not all customer orders can be filled as received. Suppliers may be able to send only part of an order or none at all. Substitutions may be necessary, or the delivery date may be delayed. Suppliers may suspect that all or part of the order is a mistake; the customer may actually want something else. In writing to customers about problem orders, it is generally wise to use the direct strategy if the message has some good-news elements. However, when the message is disappointing, the indirect strategy may be more appropriate.

Let's say you represent Toyqo, a large West Coast toy manufacturer, and you are scrambling for business in a slow year. A big customer, Playvera, calls in August and asks you to hold a block of your best-selling toy, the Spacelab. Like most vendors, you require a deposit on large orders. September rolls around, and you still haven't received any money from Playvera. You must now write a tactful e-mail asking for the deposit—or else you will release the toy to other buyers. The problem, of course, is delivering the bad news without losing the customer's order and goodwill. Another challenge is making sure the reader understands the bad news. An effective message might begin with a positive statement that also reveals the facts:

> *You were smart to reserve a block of 500 Spacelabs, which we have been holding for you since August. As the holidays approach, the demand for all our learning toys, including the Spacelab, is rapidly increasing.*

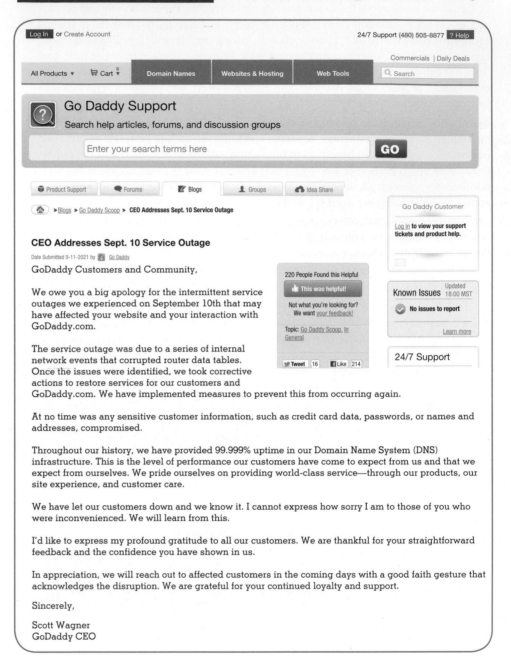

Next, the message should explain why the payment is needed and what will happen if it is not received:

> *Toy stores from Florida to California are asking us to ship these Spacelabs. One reason the Spacelab is moving out of our warehouses so quickly is its assortment of gizmos that children love, including a land rover vehicle, a shuttle craft, a hovercraft, astronauts, and even a robotic arm. As soon as we receive your deposit of $4,000, we will have this popular item on its way to your stores. Without a deposit by September 20, though, we must release this block to other retailers.*

The closing makes it easy to respond and motivates action:

For expedited service, please call our sales department at 800-358-4488 and authorize the deposit using your business credit card. You can begin showing the fascinating Toyqo toy in your stores by November 1.

9-4e Announcing Rate Increases and Price Hikes

Informing customers and clients of rate increases or price hikes can be like handling a live grenade. These messages necessarily cause consumers to recoil. With skill, however, you can help your customers understand why the rate or price increase is necessary.

The important steps in these negative messages are explaining the reasons and hooking the increase to benefits. For example, a price increase might be necessitated by higher material costs, rising taxes, escalating insurance, a driver pay increase—all reasons you cannot control. You might cite changing industry trends or technology innovations as causes of increased costs.

In developing audience benefits and building goodwill, think about how the increase will add new value or better features, make use more efficient, or make customers' lives easier. Whenever possible, give advance warning of rate increases—for example: *Because you are an important customer to us, I wanted to inform you about this right away. Our energy costs have almost doubled over the last year, forcing us to put through a 10 percent price increase effective July 1. You order these items regularly, so I thought I'd better check with you to see if it would make sense to reorder now to save you money and prevent last-minute surprises.*

Rate and price increases are typically announced by e-mail, as shown in Model Document 9.6, or in some cases by letter. Cloud storage service Cryos is growing and so are operating expenses and the need for larger, costlier server space. To soften the blow of the price hike, Cryos first announces several key benefits current Cryos Plus subscribers will enjoy: twice the storage space, syncing across all digital devices, and a rolling back feature protecting from malware and ransom attack. The price increase is mentioned after a detailed description of the benefits. Cryos breaks down the subscription rate increase to smaller monthly payments of $1.74 and the total monthly rate to a more palatable $9.99. In addition, the company suggests options such as downsizing to a basic plan.

9-4f Denying Claims

Customers occasionally want something they are not entitled to or that businesses can't grant. They may misunderstand warranties or make unreasonable demands. Because these customers are often unhappy with a product or service, they are emotionally involved. Messages that say *no* to emotionally involved receivers will probably be your most challenging communication task. As publisher Malcolm Forbes observed, "To be agreeable while disagreeing—that's an art."[50]

Fortunately, the reasons-before-refusal plan helps you be empathic and artful in breaking bad news. Obviously, in denial letters you will need to adopt the proper tone. Don't blame customers, even if they are at fault. Avoid *you* statements that sound preachy (*You would have known that cash refunds are impossible if you had read your contract*). Use neutral, objective language to explain why the claim must be refused. Consider offering resale information to rebuild the customer's confidence in your products or organization. In Model Document 9.7 the writer denies a customer's claim for the difference between the price the customer paid for speakers and the price he saw advertised locally (which would have resulted in a cash refund of $100). Although the catalog service does match any advertised lower price, the price-matching policy applies only to exact models. This claim must be rejected because the advertisement the customer submitted showed a different, older speaker model.

The e-mail to Florian Alva opens with a buffer that agrees with a statement in the customer's e-mail. It repeats the key idea of product confidence as a transition to the second paragraph. Next comes an explanation of the price-matching policy. The writer does not assume that the customer is trying to deceive. Nor does he suggest that the customer is a dummy who didn't read or understand the price-matching policy. The safest path is a neutral explanation of the policy along with

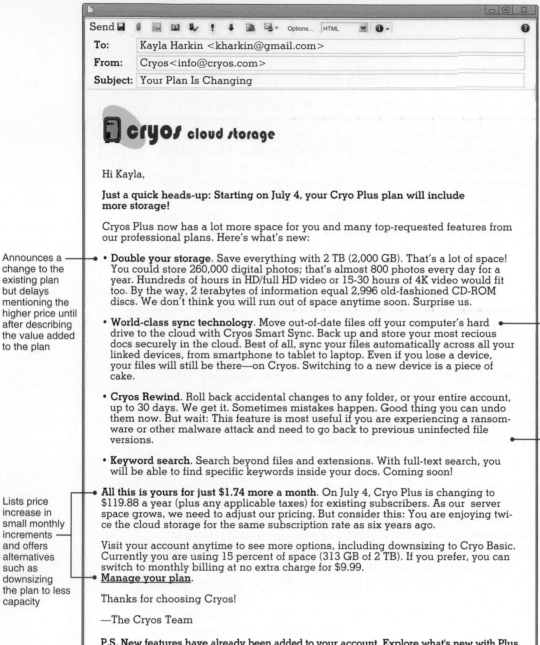

To: Kayla Harkin <kharkin@gmail.com>

From: Cryos<info@cryos.com>

Subject: Your Plan Is Changing

cryos cloud storage

Hi Kayla,

Just a quick heads-up: Starting on July 4, your Cryo Plus plan will include more storage!

Cryos Plus now has a lot more space for you and many top-requested features from our professional plans. Here's what's new:

Announces a change to the existing plan but delays mentioning the higher price until after describing the value added to the plan

- **Double your storage**. Save everything with 2 TB (2,000 GB). That's a lot of space! You could store 260,000 digital photos; that's almost 800 photos every day for a year. Hundreds of hours in HD/full HD video or 15-30 hours of 4K video would fit too. By the way, 2 terabytes of information equal 2,996 old-fashioned CD-ROM discs. We don't think you will run out of space anytime soon. Surprise us.

- **World-class sync technology**. Move out-of-date files off your computer's hard drive to the cloud with Cryos Smart Sync. Back up and store your most recious docs securely in the cloud. Best of all, sync your files automatically across all your linked devices, from smartphone to tablet to laptop. Even if you lose a device, your files will still be there—on Cryos. Switching to a new device is a piece of cake.

Focuses on customer benefits such as more storage capacity, convenient syncing, and security features

- **Cryos Rewind**. Roll back accidental changes to any folder, or your entire account, up to 30 days. We get it. Sometimes mistakes happen. Good thing you can undo them now. But wait: This feature is most useful if you are experiencing a ransomware or other malware attack and need to go back to previous uninfected file versions.

- **Keyword search**. Search beyond files and extensions. With full-text search, you will be able to find specific keywords inside your docs. Coming soon!

Lists price increase in small monthly increments and offers alternatives such as downsizing the plan to less capacity

All this is yours for just $1.74 more a month. On July 4, Cryo Plus is changing to $119.88 a year (plus any applicable taxes) for existing subscribers. As our server space grows, we need to adjust our pricing. But consider this: You are enjoying twice the cloud storage for the same subscription rate as six years ago.

Visit your account anytime to see more options, including downsizing to Cryo Basic. Currently you are using 15 percent of space (313 GB of 2 TB). If you prefer, you can switch to monthly billing at no extra charge for $9.99. <u>Manage your plan</u>.

Thanks for choosing Cryos!

—The Cryos Team

P.S. New features have already been added to your account. <u>Explore what's new with Plus.</u>

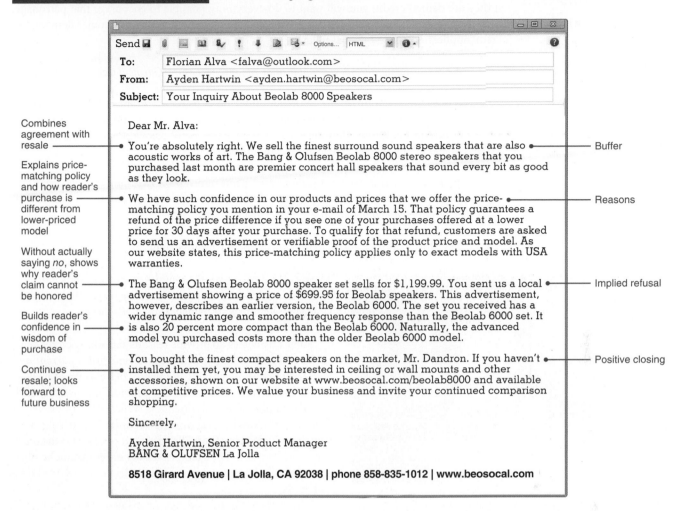

Combines agreement with resale	**Dear Mr. Alva:** You're absolutely right. We sell the finest surround sound speakers that are also acoustic works of art. The Bang & Olufsen Beolab 8000 stereo speakers that you purchased last month are premier concert hall speakers that sound every bit as good as they look. — **Buffer**
Explains price-matching policy and how reader's purchase is different from lower-priced model	We have such confidence in our products and prices that we offer the price-matching policy you mention in your e-mail of March 15. That policy guarantees a refund of the price difference if you see one of your purchases offered at a lower price for 30 days after your purchase. To qualify for that refund, customers are asked to send us an advertisement or verifiable proof of the product price and model. As our website states, this price-matching policy applies only to exact models with USA warranties. — **Reasons**
Without actually saying *no*, shows why reader's claim cannot be honored	The Bang & Olufsen Beolab 8000 speaker set sells for $1,199.99. You sent us a local advertisement showing a price of $699.95 for Beolab speakers. This advertisement, however, describes an earlier version, the Beolab 6000. The set you received has a wider dynamic range and smoother frequency response than the Beolab 6000 set. It — **Implied refusal**
Builds reader's confidence in wisdom of purchase	is also 20 percent more compact than the Beolab 6000. Naturally, the advanced model you purchased costs more than the older Beolab 6000 model.
Continues resale; looks forward to future business	You bought the finest compact speakers on the market, Mr. Dandron. If you haven't installed them yet, you may be interested in ceiling or wall mounts and other accessories, shown on our website at www.beosocal.com/beolab8000 and available at competitive prices. We value your business and invite your continued comparison shopping. — **Positive closing**

Sincerely,

Ayden Hartwin, Senior Product Manager
BANG & OLUFSEN La Jolla

8518 Girard Avenue | La Jolla, CA 92038 | phone 858-835-1012 | www.beosocal.com

precise distinctions between the customer's speakers and the older ones. The writer also gets a chance to resell the customer's speakers and demonstrate what a quality product they are. By the end of the third paragraph, it is evident to the reader that his claim is unjustified.

9-4g Refusing Credit

When customers apply for credit, they must be notified within 30 days if that application is rejected. The Fair Credit Reporting Act and Equal Credit Opportunity Act state that consumers who are denied loans must receive a notice of adverse action from the business explaining the decision. The business can refer the applicant to the credit-reporting agency, whether Experian, Equifax, or TransUnion, that provided the information upon which the negative decision was based. If you must write a letter to a customer denying credit, you have four goals in conveying the refusal:

- Avoiding language that causes hard feelings
- Retaining the customer on a cash basis
- Preparing for possible future credit without raising false expectations
- Avoiding disclosures that could cause a lawsuit

Because credit applicants are likely to continue to do business with an organization even if they are denied credit, you will want to do everything possible to encourage that patronage. Therefore, keep the refusal respectful, sensitive, and upbeat. A letter to a customer denying her credit application might begin as follows:

> *We genuinely appreciate your application of January 12 for a Garment Geeks credit account.*

To avoid possible litigation, many companies offer no explanation of the reasons for a credit refusal. Instead, they provide the name of the credit-reporting agency and suggest that inquiries be directed to it. In the following example, notice the use of passive voice (*credit cannot be extended*) and a long sentence to de-emphasize the bad news:

> *After we received a report of your current credit record from Experian, it is apparent that credit cannot be extended at this time. To learn more about your record, you may call an Experian credit counselor at (212) 356-0922.*

The cordial closing looks forward to the possibility of a future reapplication:

> *Thanks, Ms. Akakios, for the confidence you have shown in Garment Geeks. We invite you to continue shopping at our stores, and we look forward to your reapplication in the future.*

Some businesses do provide reasons explaining credit denials (*Credit cannot be granted because your firm's current and long-term credit obligations are nearly twice as great as your firm's total assets*). They may also provide alternatives, such as deferred billing or cash discounts. When the letter denies a credit application that accompanies an order, the message may contain resale information. The writer tries to convert the order from credit to cash. For example, if a big order cannot be filled on a credit basis, perhaps part of the order could be filled on a cash basis.

Whatever form the bad-news message takes, it is a good idea to have the message reviewed by legal counsel because of the litigation land mines awaiting unwary communicators in this area.

fizkes/Shutterstock.com

Internal bad news about the organization or individuals is conveyed face-to-face or in writing. The anticipated audience reaction determines whether a direct or an indirect strategy is appropriate.

LEARNING OUTCOME

5 Evaluate effective techniques for delivering bad news within organizations.

9-5 Managing Bad News Within Organizations

A tactful tone and a reasons-first approach help preserve friendly relations with customers. These same techniques are useful when delivering bad news within organizations. Interpersonal bad news might involve telling the boss that something went wrong or confronting an employee about poor performance. Organizational bad news might involve declining profits, lost contracts, harmful lawsuits, public relations controversies, and changes in policy. Whether you use a direct or an indirect strategy in delivering that news depends primarily on the anticipated reaction of the audience. Generally, bad news is better received when reasons are given first. Within organizations, you may find yourself giving bad news in person or in writing.

9-5a Delivering Bad News in Person

Whether you are an employee or a supervisor, you may have the unhappy responsibility of delivering bad news. First, decide whether the negative information is newsworthy. For example, trivial, noncriminal mistakes or one-time bad behaviors are best left alone. However, fraudulent travel claims, consistent hostile behavior, or failing projects must be reported.[51] For example, you might have to tell the boss that the team's computers picked up malware that caused them to infect the company's computer network. Similarly, as a team leader or supervisor, you might be required to confront an underperforming employee. If you know that the news will upset the receiver, the reasons-first strategy is most effective. When the bad news involves one person or a small group nearby, you should generally deliver that news in person. Here are pointers on how to do so tactfully, professionally, and safely:[52]

- **Gather all the information.** Cool down and have all the facts before marching in on the boss or confronting someone. Remember that every story has two sides.

- **Prepare and rehearse.** Outline what you plan to say so that you are confident, coherent, and dispassionate.

- **Explain: past, present, future.** If you are telling the boss about a problem such as the computer crash, explain what caused the crash, the current situation, and how and when you plan to fix it.

- **Consider taking a partner.** If you fear a shoot-the-messenger reaction, especially from your boss, bring a colleague with you. Each person should have a consistent and credible part in the presentation. If possible, take advantage of your organization's internal resources. To lend credibility to your view, call on auditors, inspectors, or human resources experts.

- **Think about timing.** Don't deliver bad news when someone is already stressed or grumpy. Experts also advise against giving bad news on Friday afternoon when people have the weekend to dwell on it.

- **Be patient with the reaction.** Give the receiver time to vent, think, recover, and act wisely.

9-5b Refusing Workplace Requests

Occasionally, managers must refuse requests from employees. In Model Document 9.8 you see the first draft and revision of a message responding to a request from a key specialist, Kevin Peterson. He wants permission to attend a conference. However, he can't attend the conference because the timing is bad; he must be present at budget planning meetings scheduled for the same two weeks. Normally, this matter would be discussed in person. However, Kevin has been traveling among branch offices, and he just hasn't been in the office recently.

The vice president's first inclination was to dash off a quick e-mail, as shown in Model Document 9.8, and tell it like it is. However, the vice president realized that this message was going to hurt and that it had possible danger areas. Moreover, the message misses a chance to give Kevin positive feedback. An improved version of the e-mail starts with a buffer that delivers honest praise (*pleased with the exceptional leadership you have provided* and *your genuine professional commitment*). By the way, don't be stingy with compliments; they cost you nothing. To paraphrase the motivational speaker Zig Ziglar, we don't live by bread alone. We need buttering up once in a while.[53] The buffer also includes the date of the meeting, used strategically to connect the reasons that follow.

The middle paragraph provides reasons for the refusal. Notice that they focus on positive elements: Kevin is the specialist; the company relies on his expertise; and everyone will benefit if he passes up the conference. In this section it becomes obvious that the request is being refused. The writer is not forced to say, *No, you may not attend.* Although the refusal is implied, the reader gets the message.

> **Reality Check**
>
> ### Sandwich the Bad News
>
> "A difficult conversation is often better received when delivered using a 'bad news sandwich,' where the 'buns' of the sandwich include positive words of praise, and the 'meat' in the middle deals with the heart of the matter. This method allows you to share good news along with hard-to-share news—ideal for those of us who dread conflict."[54]
>
> —Virginia Franco, *Virginia Franco Resumes*

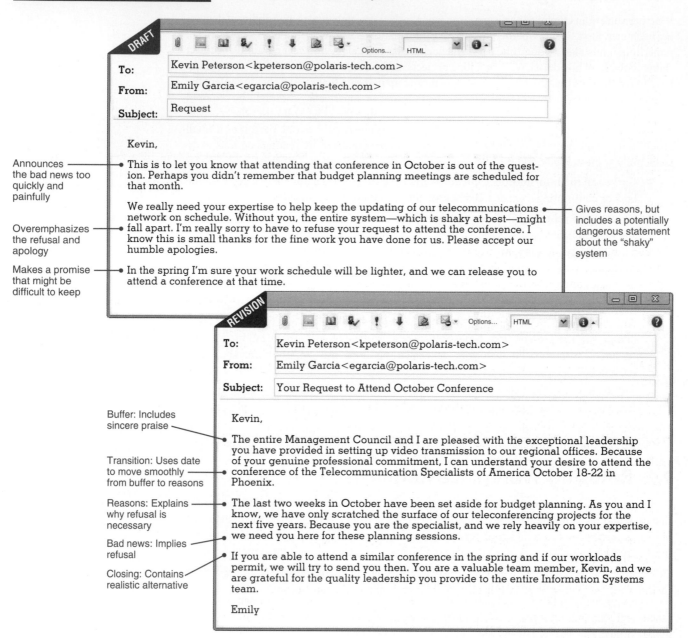

DRAFT

To: Kevin Peterson<kpeterson@polaris-tech.com>

From: Emily Garcia<egarcia@polaris-tech.com>

Subject: Request

Kevin,

Announces the bad news too quickly and painfully — This is to let you know that attending that conference in October is out of the question. Perhaps you didn't remember that budget planning meetings are scheduled for that month.

We really need your expertise to help keep the updating of our telecommunications network on schedule. Without you, the entire system—which is shaky at best—might fall apart. *Overemphasizes the refusal and apology* — I'm really sorry to have to refuse your request to attend the conference. I know this is small thanks for the fine work you have done for us. Please accept our humble apologies. — *Gives reasons, but includes a potentially dangerous statement about the "shaky" system*

Makes a promise that might be difficult to keep — In the spring I'm sure your work schedule will be lighter, and we can release you to attend a conference at that time.

REVISION

To: Kevin Peterson<kpeterson@polaris-tech.com>

From: Emily Garcia<egarcia@polaris-tech.com>

Subject: Your Request to Attend October Conference

Kevin,

Buffer: Includes sincere praise — The entire Management Council and I are pleased with the exceptional leadership you have provided in setting up video transmission to our regional offices. Because of your genuine professional commitment, I can understand your desire to attend the conference of the Telecommunication Specialists of America October 18-22 in Phoenix. — *Transition: Uses date to move smoothly from buffer to reasons*

Reasons: Explains why refusal is necessary — The last two weeks in October have been set aside for budget planning. As you and I know, we have only scratched the surface of our teleconferencing projects for the next five years. Because you are the specialist, and we rely heavily on your expertise, we need you here for these planning sessions. — *Bad news: Implies refusal*

Closing: Contains realistic alternative — If you are able to attend a similar conference in the spring and if our workloads permit, we will try to send you then. You are a valuable team member, Kevin, and we are grateful for the quality leadership you provide to the entire Information Systems team.

Emily

The closing suggests a qualified alternative (*if our workloads permit, we will try to send you then*). It also ends positively with gratitude for Kevin's contributions to the organization and with another compliment (*you're a valuable team member*). The improved version focuses on explanations and praise rather than on refusals and apologies. The success of this message depends on attention to the entire writing process, not just on using a buffer or scattering a few compliments throughout.

9-5c Announcing Bad News to Employees and the Public

In an age of social media, damaging information can rarely be contained for long. Executives can almost count on it to be leaked. Corporate officers who fail to communicate effectively and proactively may end up on the defensive and face an uphill battle trying to limit the damage. Many of the same techniques used to deliver bad news personally are useful when organizations face a crisis or must deliver bad news to various stakeholders. Smart organizations involved in a crisis prefer to communicate the news openly to employees and stockholders. A crisis might involve serious performance problems, a major relocation, massive layoffs, a management shakeup, or public controversy. Instead of letting rumors distort the truth, managers ought to explain the organization's side of the story honestly and promptly.

Morale can be destroyed when employees learn of major events affecting their jobs through the grapevine or from news accounts—rather than from management. When bad news must be delivered to individual employees, management may want to deliver the news personally. With large groups, however, this is generally impossible. Instead, organizations deliver bad news through multiple channels ranging from hard-copy and soft-copy memos to digital media. Such messages today travel over multiple channels and can take the form of intranet posts, e-mails, videos, webcasts, internal as well as external blogs, and voice mail.

The draft of the intranet blog post shown in Model Document 9.9 announces a substantial increase in the cost of employee health-care benefits. However, the message suffers from many problems. It announces jolting news bluntly in the first sentence. Worse, it offers little or no explanation for the steep increase in costs. It also sounds insincere (*We did everything possible . . .*) and arbitrary. In a final miscue, the writer fails to give credit to the company for absorbing previous health-care cost increases.

The revision of this bad-news message uses the indirect strategy and improves the tone considerably. Notice that it opens with a relevant, upbeat buffer regarding health care—but says nothing about increasing costs. For a smooth transition, the second paragraph begins with a key idea from the opening (*comprehensive package*). The reasons section discusses rising costs with explanations and figures. The bad news (*you will be paying $119 a month*) is clearly presented but embedded within the paragraph. Throughout, the writer strives to show the fairness of the company's position. The ending, which does not refer to the bad news, emphasizes how much the company is paying and what a wise investment it is.

Notice that the entire message demonstrates a kinder, gentler approach than that shown in the first draft. Of prime importance in breaking bad news to employees is providing clear, convincing reasons that explain the decision. Parallel to this internal blog post, the message was also sent by e-mail. In smaller companies in which some workers do not have company e-mail, a hard-copy memo would be posted prominently on bulletin boards and in the lunchroom.

9-5d Saying *No* to Job Applicants

Being refused a job is one of life's major rejections. Tactless letters intensify the blow (*Unfortunately, you were not among the candidates selected for . . .*).

You can reduce the receiver's disappointment somewhat by using the indirect strategy—with one important variation. In the reasons section, it is wise to be vague in explaining why the candidate was not selected. First, giving concrete reasons may be painful to the receiver (*Your grade point average of 2.7 was low compared with the GPAs of other candidates*). Second, and more important, providing extra information may prove fatal in a lawsuit. Hiring and firing decisions generate considerable litigation today. To avoid charges of discrimination or wrongful actions, legal advisors warn organizations to keep employment rejection letters general, simple, and short.

The job refusal letter shown in Model Document 9.10 is tactful but intentionally vague. It implies that the applicant's qualifications don't match those needed for the position, but the letter

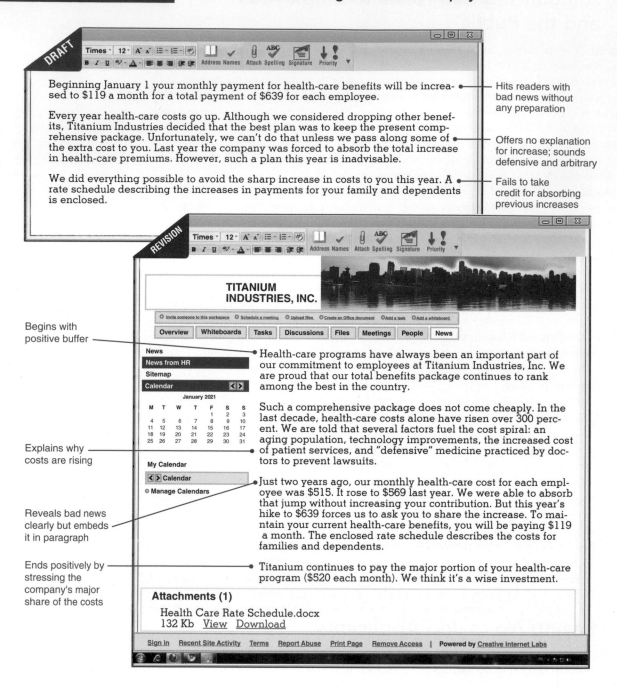

DRAFT

Beginning January 1 your monthly payment for health-care benefits will be increased to $119 a month for a total payment of $639 for each employee.

Every year health-care costs go up. Although we considered dropping other benefits, Titanium Industries decided that the best plan was to keep the present comprehensive package. Unfortunately, we can't do that unless we pass along some of the extra cost to you. Last year the company was forced to absorb the total increase in health-care premiums. However, such a plan this year is inadvisable.

We did everything possible to avoid the sharp increase in costs to you this year. A rate schedule describing the increases in payments for your family and dependents is enclosed.

- Hits readers with bad news without any preparation
- Offers no explanation for increase; sounds defensive and arbitrary
- Fails to take credit for absorbing previous increases

REVISION

TITANIUM INDUSTRIES, INC.

Invite someone to this workspace   Schedule a meeting   Upload files   Create an Office document   Add a task   Add a whiteboard

Overview Whiteboards Tasks Discussions Files Meetings People News

News
News from HR
Sitemap
Calendar

January 2021

M	T	W	T	F	S	S
				1	2	3
4	5	6	7	8	9	10
11	12	13	14	15	16	17
18	19	20	21	22	23	24
25	26	27	28	29	30	31

My Calendar
Calendar
Manage Calendars

Begins with positive buffer —

Health-care programs have always been an important part of our commitment to employees at Titanium Industries, Inc. We are proud that our total benefits package continues to rank among the best in the country.

Explains why costs are rising —

Such a comprehensive package does not come cheaply. In the last decade, health-care costs alone have risen over 300 percent. We are told that several factors fuel the cost spiral: an aging population, technology improvements, the increased cost of patient services, and "defensive" medicine practiced by doctors to prevent lawsuits.

Reveals bad news clearly but embeds it in paragraph —

Just two years ago, our monthly health-care cost for each employee was $515. It rose to $569 last year. We were able to absorb that jump without increasing your contribution. But this year's hike to $639 forces us to ask you to share the increase. To maintain your current health-care benefits, you will be paying $119 a month. The enclosed rate schedule describes the costs for families and dependents.

Ends positively by stressing the company's major share of the costs —

Titanium continues to pay the major portion of your health-care program ($520 each month). We think it's a wise investment.

Attachments (1)

Health Care Rate Schedule.docx
132 Kb View Download

Sign in   Recent Site Activity   Terms   Report Abuse   Print Page   Remove Access | Powered by Creative Internet Labs

doesn't reveal anything specific. The writer could have included this alternate closing: *We wish you every success in finding a position that exactly fits your qualifications.*

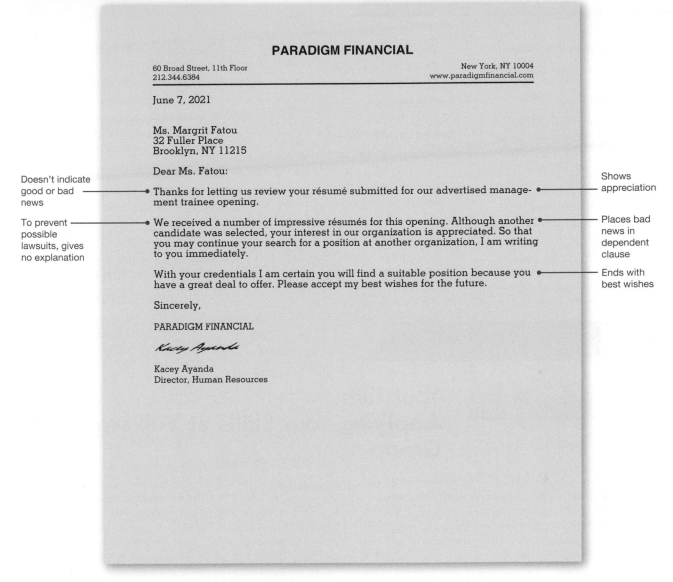

PARADIGM FINANCIAL

60 Broad Street, 11th Floor
212.344.6384

New York, NY 10004
www.paradigmfinancial.com

June 7, 2021

Ms. Margrit Fatou
32 Fuller Place
Brooklyn, NY 11215

Dear Ms. Fatou:

Thanks for letting us review your résumé submitted for our advertised management trainee opening.

We received a number of impressive résumés for this opening. Although another candidate was selected, your interest in our organization is appreciated. So that you may continue your search for a position at another organization, I am writing to you immediately.

With your credentials I am certain you will find a suitable position because you have a great deal to offer. Please accept my best wishes for the future.

Sincerely,

PARADIGM FINANCIAL

Kacey Ayanda

Kacey Ayanda
Director, Human Resources

Annotations (left):
- Doesn't indicate good or bad news
- To prevent possible lawsuits, gives no explanation

Annotations (right):
- Shows appreciation
- Places bad news in dependent clause
- Ends with best wishes

The following checklist summarizes tips on how to communicate negative news inside and outside your organization.

Checklist

Conveying Negative News

Prewrite

- Decide whether to use the direct or indirect strategy. If the bad news is minor and will not upset the receiver, open directly. If the message is personally damaging and will upset the receiver, consider techniques to reduce its pain.
- Think through the reasons for the bad news.

- Remember that your primary goal is to make the receiver understand and accept the bad news as well as to maintain a positive image of you and your organization.

Plan the Opening

- In the indirect strategy, start with a buffer. Pay a compliment to the reader, show

appreciation for something done, or mention some mutual understanding. Avoid raising false hopes or thanking the reader for something you will refuse.

- In the direct strategy, begin with a straightforward statement of the bad news.

Checklist *Continued*

Provide Reasons in the Body

- Except in credit and job refusals, explain the reasons for the negative message.
- In customer mishaps, clarify what went wrong, what you are doing to resolve the problem, and how you will prevent it from happening again.
- Use objective, nonjudgmental, and nondiscriminatory language.
- Avoid negativity (e.g., words such as *unfortunately, unwilling,*

and *impossible*) and potentially damaging statements.

- Show how your decision is fair and perhaps benefits the reader or others, if possible.

Soften the Bad News

- Reduce the impact of bad news by using (a) a subordinate clause, (b) the passive voice, (c) a long sentence, or (d) a long paragraph.
- Consider implying the refusal, but be certain it is clear.
- Suggest an alternative, such as a lower price, a different product,

a longer payment period, or a substitute. Provide help in implementing an alternative.

- Offset disappointment by offering gifts, a reduced price, benefits, tokens of appreciation, or something appropriate.

Close Pleasantly

- Supply more information about an alternative, look forward to future relations, or offer good wishes and compliments.
- Maintain a bright, personal tone. Avoid referring to the refusal.

Zooming In

Your Turn:
Applying Your Skills at Volkswagen Group

Volkswagen CEO Ferdinand Piëch, Martin Winterkorn's billionaire predecessor and mentor, bragged he elicited performance by "terrifying his engineers" and occasionally fired techs and executives who displeased him.[55] The grandson of founder Ferdinand Porsche reportedly created a "get it done or else" atmosphere at VW.[56] His protégé, CEO Winterkorn, disliked bad news. One industry analyst said, "Before anyone reports to him, they make sure they have good news.[57] E-mails from 2008 at Audi suggest a cavalier mindset after poor road tests. "We won't make it without a few dirty tricks,"[58] read one of them. Audi managers were even joking about thwarting the EPA.

When CEO Winterkorn stepped down, he stated: "I am stunned that misconduct on such a scale was possible in the Volkswagen Group. As CEO, I accept responsibility for the irregularities that have been found in diesel engines. . . . I am doing this in the interests of the company even though I am not aware of any wrongdoing on my part."[59] Winterkorn successor Matthias Müller seemed to apologize several times in two NPR interviews in 2016. He said, "We all know that we have let down customers, authorities, regulators and the

general public here in America, too." He added, "We are—I am—truly sorry for that. And I would like to apologize once again for what went wrong with Volkswagen." Müller denied, however, that VW had lied to U.S. regulators; he blamed a "misunderstanding of U.S. law." He acknowledged that "the problem" dated back approximately ten years.[60]

At his sentencing in 2017, VW executive Oliver Schmidt declared: "I made bad decisions, and for that I'm sorry." He told the judge that his loyalty to Volkswagen had led him to be "misused by my own company."[61]

Your Task

After reading this chapter, evaluate Volkswagen's handling of Dieselgate. Focus on communication, crisis management, and apologies. Consider questions such as these: What are the biggest problems at VW as evidenced by the scenario? How might corporate culture have played into the scandal? What may have led to cheating? What other options did the company have to tackle and overcome Dieselgate? Discuss these and other questions in class, in small groups, or on a discussion board. If you instructor directs, summarize your analysis in writing, either in an e-mail or a memo.

SUMMARY OF LEARNING OUTCOMES

1 Applying the 3-x-3 writing process, explain the strategies of business communicators in conveying negative news while avoiding legal liability.

- Explain clearly and completely while projecting a professional image.

- Convey empathy, sensitivity, and fairness.

- Be a mindful communicator who avoids careless and abusive language, which is defined as actionable language that is false, damaging to a person's reputation, and published (i.e., spoken in the presence of others or written).

2 Describe the direct and indirect strategies in conveying unfavorable news.

- Use the direct strategy, with the bad news first, when the news is not damaging, when the receiver may overlook it, when the organization or receiver prefers directness, or when firmness is necessary.

- Use the indirect strategy, with a buffer and explanation preceding the bad news, when the bad news is personally upsetting, when it may provoke a hostile reaction, when it threatens the customer relationship, and when the news is unexpected.

- To avoid being unethical, never use the indirect method to deceive or manipulate the truth.

3 Identify the components of effective negative messages.

- To soften bad news, start with a buffer such as the best news, a compliment, appreciation, agreement, facts, understanding, or an apology.

- Explain the reasons that necessitate the bad news, trying to cite benefits to the reader or others.

- If you apologize, do so promptly and sincerely. Accept responsibility, but don't admit blame without consulting a superior or company counsel. Aim to project empathy.

- Strive to cushion the bad news with strategic positioning by (a) sandwiching it between other sentences, (b) presenting it in a subordinating clause, (c) using passive-voice verbs, (d) accentuating the positive, (e) implying the refusal, and (f) suggesting a compromise or an alternative.

- Close pleasantly by (a) suggesting a means of following through on an alternative, (b) offering freebies, (c) extending good wishes, (d) anticipating future business, or (e) offering resale information or sales promotion.

4 Analyze effective techniques for presenting bad news to customers and refusing requests or claims.

- In rejecting requests for money, information, and action, follow the bad-news strategy: (a) begin with a buffer, (b) present valid reasons, (c) explain the bad news and possibly an alternative, and (d) close with good feelings and a positive statement.

- To deal with a disappointed customer, (a) call or e-mail the individual immediately; (b) describe the problem and apologize (when the company is to blame); (c) explain why the problem occurred, what you are doing to resolve it, and how you will prevent it from happening again; and (d) promote goodwill with a follow-up message.

- To handle negative posts and reviews online, (a) verify the situation, (b) respond quickly and constructively, (c) consider giving freebies such as refunds or discounts, (d) learn from negative comments, and (e) be prepared to accept the inevitable and move on.

- To deny claims, (a) use the reasons-before-refusal strategy, (b) don't blame customers (even when they are at fault), (c) use neutral objective language to explain why the claim must be refused, and (d) consider offering resale information to rebuild the customer's confidence in your products or organization.

- When refusing credit, avoid language that causes hard feelings, strive to retain the customer on a cash basis, and avoid disclosures that could cause a lawsuit.

5 Evaluate effective techniques for delivering bad news within organizations.

- To deliver workplace bad news in person, (a) gather all the information; (b) prepare and rehearse; (c) explain the past, present, and future; (d) consider taking a partner; (e) think about timing; and (f) be patient with the reaction.

- In announcing bad news to employees and to the public, strive to keep the communication open and honest, choose the best communication channel, and consider applying the indirect strategy, but give clear, convincing reasons.

- Be positive, but don't sugarcoat the bad news; use objective language.

- In refusing job applicants, keep messages short, general, and tactful.

Key Terms

Critical Thinking

1. Mike Michalowicz, author of *Profit First* and CEO of Provendus Group, quotes a famous American poet to illustrate how he refuses unpleasant potential clients: "Emily Dickinson said speak the truth but with slant. You don't have to say something so coldly it starts an argument. We usually tell the client we don't have resources to support your specific needs," he says.[62] Discuss this strategy, its advantages, and disadvantages. (L.O. 3)

2. At a sustainability conference, Levi Strauss CEO Chip Bergh caused a viral sensation by revealing he had never laundered his two-year-old Levi's in a washing machine. Instead, he hand-washed and line-dried his jeans every few months. His point was that jeans shouldn't be washed all the time, but people thought it meant Bergh *never* washed them. The fallout from this one quip continues even years later: "Today, if you type 'CEO Levi's' into Google, 'don't wash jeans' comes up," Bergh says. "I expect that my supposed anti-laundry stance will be mentioned in my obituary."[63] Can you think of other, more negative examples of executives' offhand public comments? (L.O. 4)

3. Consider times when you have been aware that others were using the indirect strategy in writing or speaking to you. How did you react? (L.O. 1–5)

4. Experts agree that, if possible, workers should be fired in person—not by phone, e-mail, or text message. The consensus is that the kindest way to fire someone is when the direct supervisor delivers the bad news. However, increasingly employees are getting fired by text or e-mail.[64] Make a case for and against firing workers by text or e-mail. (L.O. 1, 5)

5. **Ethical Issue**: You work for a large corporation with headquarters in a small town. Recently, you received shoddy repair work and a huge bill from a local garage. Your car's transmission has the same problems that it did before you took it in for repair. You know that a complaint letter written on your corporation's stationery would be much more authoritative than one written on plain stationery. Should you use corporation stationery?

Writing Improvement Exercises

9.1 Organizational Strategies (L.O. 1–3)

YOUR TASK Identify whether the following messages should be organized directly or indirectly. Explain briefly why.

a. A message from health-care provider CareFirst Blue-Cross BlueShield in which it must tell its 1.1 million members that their information in the form of names, birth dates, e-mail addresses, and subscriber information was compromised by hackers who obtained access to the company's website. The only good news is that member encryption prevented the cybercriminals from gaining access to social security numbers, medical claims, and financial data.

b. A letter from a theme park refusing the request of a customer who wants free tickets. The customer was unhappy that she and her family had to wait in line a very long time to ride the new Delirium thrill roller coaster.

c. An announcement to employees that a financial specialist has canceled a scheduled lunchtime talk and cannot reschedule.

d. A message from a car insurance company that it will no longer insure family members who drive the family car. Customers may expand their policies with more comprehensive coverage at a higher cost.

e. An announcement from an airline that it had to cancel most of its flights in response to the COVID-19 pandemic.

f. An e-mail from the manager denying an employee's request for special parking privileges. The employee works closely with the manager on many projects.

g. A memo from an executive refusing a manager's proposal to economize by purchasing refurbished computers. The executive and the manager both appreciate efficient, straightforward messages.

9.2 Employing Passive-Voice Verbs (L.O. 3)

YOUR TASK Revise the following sentences to present the bad news with passive-voice verbs. If possible, present the bad news positively.

a. We cannot examine new patients until we have verified their insurance coverage.

b. Company policy prevents us from offering health and dental benefits until employees have been on the job for 12 months.

c. Because we are retooling our production line, we are postponing requests for company tours until the fall.

d. Unfortunately, we cannot offer free shipping until after January 1. Act now!

e. Our retail stores will no longer accept credit cards for purchases under $5.

f. As manager, I cannot grant you the three-week vacation period you request because others have already reserved that period.

9.3 Subordinating Bad News (L.O. 3)

YOUR TASK Revise the following sentences to position the bad news in a subordinate clause. (**Hint:** Consider beginning the clause with *Although*.) Use passive-voice verbs for the bad news.

a. Your frequent flyer miles expire on December 31 because you have earned no qualifying segments during this calendar year. However, you could keep your miles if you apply for our Northeastern credit card and spend $2,000 in the next three months.

b. We appreciate your interest in our organization, but we cannot extend an employment offer to you at this time.

c. Regretfully, we cannot supply you with the cabinet hinge you requested. The manufacturer no longer offers it. A new hinge should work for you, and we are sending it to you.

d. We now offer all our catalog choices on our website, which is always current. Unfortunately, we no longer print or mail a complete print catalog. Our sustainability goals made it impossible for us to continue that practice.

e. We are sorry to report that we are unable to ship your complete order of compact fitness training stations for your hotel's gym at this point in time. However, we are able to send two Freestyle Gym compact workout stations now, and you should receive them within five days.

f. We are sorry to disappoint you, but our nine-day boat excursion to the Galápagos Islands has filled up quickly and is now fully booked. We are able to place you on a wait list that would make you only the second in line.

9.4 Implying Bad News (L.O. 3)

YOUR TASK Revise the following statements to *imply* the bad news. If possible, use passive-voice verbs and subordinate clauses to further de-emphasize the bad news.

DIRECT REFUSAL: We cannot send you a price list, nor can we sell our lawn mowers directly to customers. We sell only through authorized dealers, and your dealer is HomeCo.

IMPLIED REFUSAL: Our lawn mowers are sold exclusively through authorized dealers, and your dealer is HomeCo.

a. Because our government contract has run out, we must disband the task force managing the project. Some of you will be reassigned; unfortunately, we will also have to let a few team members go.

b. We are sorry to tell you that we cannot ship our hand-dipped chocolate-covered fresh strawberries c.o.d. Your order was not accompanied by payment, so we are not shipping it. We have it ready, though, and will rush it to its destination as soon as you call us with your credit card number.

c. Unfortunately, we find it impossible to contribute to your excellent and worthwhile fund-raising campaign this year. At present all the funds of our organization are needed to lease equipment and offices for our new branch in Clearwater. We hope to be able to support this commendable endeavor in the future.

d. Because of the holiday period, all our billboard space was used this month. Therefore, we are sorry to say that we could not give your charitable group free display space. However, next month, after the holidays, we hope to display your message as we promised.

9.5 Document for Analysis: Request Refusal—*No to Carmel-by-the-Sea*
(L.O. 1, 2, 4)

The following blunt refusal from a restaurant owner rejects a previously agreed-to favor. To avoid endangering a friendship and losing community goodwill, the writer needs to revise this message.

YOUR TASK List at least five weaknesses and suggest ways to improve this message. If your instructor directs, revise.

Current date

Mrs. Sally Segovia
Taste of the Beach
310 Ocean Avenue, Suite 304
Carmel-by-the-Sea, CA 93521

Dear Mrs. Segovia:

Unfortunately, we cannot participate in this summer's Taste of the Beach event. This may be particularly disappointing to you because, merely as a friendly gesture, I had earlier agreed to provide a selection of tasty hors d'oeuvres from my restaurant, The Zodiac. I'm sorry to let you down like this. We have participated in the past, but we just can't do it this year because our aging kitchen facilities require major and extensive remodeling.

I heard that this year's Taste of the Beach is really going to be a blast with new and old food, wine, music, and artistic offerings. How did you get so many prized vintners and all those well-known chefs, artists, and music groups to participate and perform?

This is probably quite disappointing to you (and to me) because the event supports Big Brothers Big Sisters of America. I know that BBBSA is simply the very best as a youth mentoring organization.

Let me repeat—I'm sorry we can't participate. Don't bother to beg me. But for your silent raffle we can offer you a coupon for a dinner for two. Of course, this could not be used until October when our renovations are completed.

Sincerely,

9.6 Document for Analysis: Bad News to Customers—Guard Payment Systems Was Hacked (L.O. 1, 2, 4)

`E-Mail`

The following poorly written e-mail tells customers that their e-mail addresses have been hacked. However, the message is clumsy and fails to include essential information in revealing security breaches to customers.

YOUR TASK Analyze the message and list at least seven weaknesses. If your instructor directs, revise it using the suggestions you learned in this chapter about security breach messages.

To: Detlev Max<detlev.max@alpha.com>
From: Fanny Bettino<fbettino@guardpayment.net>
Subject: Security Incident at Guard Payment Systems

Companies and individuals across the country are experiencing more and more security breaches. This is just to let you know that you are receiving this e-mail because of a recent unfortunate security breach at Guard Payment Systems. Rest assured, however, that as a customer of Guard Payment, your privacy was never at risk. We promise to guard your privacy around the clock.

Hackers last week were able to maliciously exploit a new function that we were trying to use to make the customer log-in process faster for you and our other customers. The hackers were ingenious and malicious, going to extreme lengths to gain access to some customer addresses at Guard Payment. You should now beware of scams that may result from your address being used in phishing scams. To learn more, go to http://www.fdic.gov/consumers/consumer/alerts/phishing.html.

To provide even more information about this incident, the U.S. Postal Service will bring you a letter with more information. Taking your privacy very seriously, e-mail addresses are heavily protected here at Guard Payment. Within hours of the hacker break-in, the log-in mechanism was disabled, and a new procedure was established. The user is now required to enter their e-mail address and their password before they can log in successfully. E-mail addresses were the only information the hackers got. Other information such as account information and other personal information were never risked.

We appreciate you being a Guard Payment customer.

Sincerely,

9.7 Document for Analysis: No Time Off for Infant.ly Foundation Volunteer
(L.O. 1, 2, 4, 5)

`E-Mail`

YOUR TASK Analyze the following poorly written e-mail and list its weaknesses. If your instructor directs, revise it using the suggestions you learned in this and previous chapters.

To: Kim Henning<khenning@outlaysfinancial.com)
From: Oscar Cassandra<ocassandra@outlaysfinancial.com)
Subject: Pulling Plug on Infant.ly Foundation

Hey, Kimmie, you're one in a million! But we can't give you time off to work on that charity fashion show/luncheon thingy you want to coordinate. And Outlays Financial can't make a big contribution as we've done in previous years. It's no, no, no, all the way around.

Look, we admire the work you have done for the Infant.ly Foundation. It has raised millions of dollars to make differences in the lives of babies, particularly premature ones. But we need you here! Hey, let's think about us.

With the upcoming release of our Planning Guide 3.0, we need you to interview clients. We need you to make video testimonials, and you are the one to search for stories about customer successes. Plus a gazillion other tasks! Our new website will launch in just six short weeks, and all that killer content stuff must be in final form. With the economy in the tank and our bare-bones staff, you certainly must realize that each and every team member must be here and making a difference. If our Planning Guide 3.0 doesn't make a big splash, we'll all have a lot of time off.

Due to the fact that we're the worldwide leader in on-demand financial planning and reporting software, and in view of the fact that we are about to launch our most important new product ever, you just gotta understand our position. When things get better, we might be able to return back to our past practices. But not now!

Oscar

9.8 Document for Analysis: Deflecting Request for Sensitive Info (L.O. 1, 2, 4)

E-Mail

The following e-mail responds to an e-mail request from a well-known financial blogger seeking content for her industry blog. She requests salary and commission information, as well as the gender and age of the star salespeople at PharmaCore, a large pharmaceutical firm.

YOUR TASK Revise the blunt message written by a senior executive. Yes, the request must be denied, but it can be done more tactfully so that it maintains the goodwill of this important writer.

To: Dora Wieland<dora.wieland@intheknow.com>
From: Allan Gottschalk<agottschalk@pharmacore.com>
Subject: Your Request
Attached: PharmaCore Salespeople Fact Sheet

Dear Ms. Wieland:

I am writing in response to your request for salary information for our top sales reps. We cannot release such information because that disclosure would violate our employees' privacy and lead to lawsuits. However, the

article you are researching for your blog In the Know about comparative salaries and commissions sounds fascinating and will be most interesting to your readers. As a matter of fact, we are flattered that you wish to include PharmaCore. You may be interested to know that we have many outstanding young salespeople—some are male and some are female—who command top salaries.

I cannot reveal private employee information because each of our salespeople operates under an individual salary contract. This is a result of salary negotiations several years ago. During those negotiations an agreement was reached that both sales staff members and management agreed to keep the terms of these individual contracts confidential. For obvious reasons we cannot release specific salaries and commission rates. It has been suggested, however, that we can provide you with a list with the names of our top salespeople for a period of the past five years (see attached). As a matter of fact, three of the top salespeople are currently under the age of thirty-five.

Best wishes,

9.9 Request Refusal: Walk With Love Stopped in Its Tracks (L.O. 1, 2, 4)

E-Mail   **Web**

Having enjoyed a meteoric rise, CompuBotics Incorporated prides itself on its commitment to employees who receive generous benefits and are steeped in a supportive corporate culture. This core value may have contributed to the company's high ranking among *Fortune* magazine's 50 Best Startups. The software company wants to be known for its community involvement and corporate social responsibility efforts. This is why, like most large companies, CompuBotics receives many requests for sponsorships of charity events and community projects. True to its innovative spirit, the software company has streamlined the application process by providing an online sponsorship request form on its website.

You work in Corporate Affairs/Community Relations at CompuBotics and periodically help decide which nonprofits obtain support. Just yesterday you received an e-mail from Walk With Love (WWL), the largest fundraising vehicle of the Dr. Susan Love Foundation. Since 2008, Walk With Love has raised millions of dollars to support groundbreaking breast cancer research. Both *Charity Navigator* and *Medical News Today* ranked the Dr. Susan Love Foundation the top breast cancer research organization in the U.S. for its stewardship of resources and impact. The organization hosts annual fundraising walks in Pacific Palisades, Palm Springs, and Santa Barbara, California.

The walk organizers would like CompuBotics to sponsor its fundraising walks in California taking place in less than a month, three events potentially drawing at least 6,000 participants. Your company is already funding several cancer charities and has a policy of sponsoring many causes. Naturally, no corporate giving program has infinite funds, nor can it green-light every request. CompuBotics steers clear of religious and political events. The team judging the sponsorship entries wants to ensure that each proposal reaches audiences affiliated with CompuBotics. Most important, applicants must submit their requests at least six weeks before the event.

YOUR TASK As a junior staff member in Corporate Affairs/ Community Relations, write an e-mail to Walk With Love event director Michelle Chang (*mchang@wwl.org*) refusing her initial request and explaining the CompuBotics sponsorship philosophy and submission rules.

9.10 Request Refusal: No Support for Kaboom! This Time (L.O. 1, 2, 4)

As a vice president of a financial services company, you serve many clients, and they sometimes ask your company to contribute to their favorite charities. You recently received a letter from Mia Takeshi asking for a substantial contribution to Kaboom!, a charity devoted to making playgrounds safe for everyone, including children with special needs. On visits to your office, Ms. Takeshi has told you about her organization's efforts to update existing playgrounds as well as install new play areas around the nation to make playground equipment completely safe and handicapped-accessible. She herself is active in your town as a Kaboom! volunteer, helping identify outdated playgrounds, finding sites for new playgrounds, and allocate construction funds.

You have a soft spot in your heart for children and especially for those with special needs. You sincerely want to support Kaboom! and its good work. But times are tough, and you can't be as generous as you have been in the past. Ms. Takeshi wrote a special letter to you asking you to become a Key contributor, with a pledge of $2,000.

YOUR TASK Write a refusal letter that maintains good relations with your client. Address it to Ms. Mia Takeshi, 47 Beach St., Lynchburg, VA 24502.

9.11 Request Refusal: I'm Flattered, But I Can't Speak to Your Club (L.O. 1, 2, 4)

As an assistant to Pamela Eyring, you must help her refuse an invitation to speak at Wysocki College in Boston. The business associations on campus pooled their resources and decided to invite Ms. Eyring to give a talk on campus about the importance of soft skills. A sought-after TV commentator and media personality, Ms. Eyring owns The Protocol School of Washington, a training center for etiquette consultants and protocol officers. For over two decades, she was chief of protocol at a prominent military base. Since acquiring The Protocol School of Washington, she has established herself as a frequent contributor to Reuters, *The Wall Street Journal*, *The New York Times*, *Forbes*, *Entrepreneur*, and other important publications. An authority on business etiquette, she is often featured on radio and TV programs such as the *Today Show*, CNN, and ABC Radio Network. A member of several business and professional associations, Ms. Eyring receives many invitations to speak as an authority on business etiquette and as an award-winning entrepreneur and leader. Ms. Eyring likes to speak to young students, mostly pro bono or for a nominal fee, but during the spring semester she is too busy with starting her new location in Dubai, United Arab Emirates, with organizing a meeting of the Women Presidents Organization, and with writing a book on dining like a diplomat. Ms. Eyring might be able to deliver her presentation some other time, or she could send Robert Hickey, her deputy director and senior trainer.

YOUR TASK In Ms. Eyring's name, refuse the invitation but suggest an alternative. Send your letter to Chelsea Landry, Associated Students, Wysocki College, 246 Bay State Road, Boston, MA 02215.

9.12 Bad News to Customers: Hidden French Gem Can't Deliver Gratis (L.O. 1–4)

As the owner of Croissant D'Or Patisserie in New Orleans, you have a devoted French Quarter clientele savoring your delicacies. Customers love your bakery and small café for its peaceful ambiance and cozy outdoor seating. Croissant D'Or is a hidden gem tucked away from the tourists on Bourbon Street. All your specialties are made from scratch daily and served fresh onsite. Your cupcakes are a trendy hit, but you also feature delicious French pastries, macaroons, quiches, cakes, croissants, and breads. Your bakery has a medium-sized storefront; however, most of your business comes from supplying local restaurants and coffee shops with your tantalizing treats. You own two trucks that make deliveries to customers throughout the New Orleans metropolitan area.

Although Croissant D'Or is financially successful, rising costs have severely undercut your profits over the past few months. You know that you are not the only business owner dealing with rising prices. Many of your suppliers have raised their prices over the past year. Specifically, the higher prices of wheat and sugar have resulted in a drastic increase in your production costs. Previously, you did not charge for deliveries made to your wholesale clients. However, you now feel that you have no choice but to add a delivery charge for each order to cover your increased costs and the price of gas.

YOUR TASK As the owner of Croissant D'Or Patisserie at 617 Ursulines Avenue, New Orleans, LA 70116, write a letter to your wholesale clients in which you announce a $20 charge per delivery. Try to think of a special offer to soften the blow. Address the first letter to chef Jim Richard who owns the upscale restaurant Trenasse at 444 Saint Charles Ave., New Orleans, LA 70130.

9.13 Bad News to Customers: Scheduling Snafu Could Sink Dream Wedding
(L.O. 1, 3, 4)

As the wedding planner at Eureka Springs Weddings in Arkansas, you just discovered a terrible mistake. Two weddings have been scheduled for the same Saturday in June. How could this have happened? You keep meticulous records, but six months ago, you were away for two weeks. Another employee filled in for you. She apparently didn't understand the scheduling system and lined up two weddings for the renowned Thorncrown Chapel on June 12. The month of June, of course, is the busiest month of the year. Weddings in the beautiful glass cathedral in the woods are usually booked for two years in advance, and it can handle only one wedding a day.

It's now January, and Candy Schonwald, one of the brides-to-be called to check on her arrangements. That's when you discovered the mistake. However, you didn't reveal the blunder to Candy on the telephone. From experience, you know how emotional brides can be when their plans go awry. Now you must decide what to do. Your manager has given you complete authority in scheduling weddings, and you know he would back nearly any decision you make to rectify the mistake. Unfortunately, the historic 1886 Crescent Hotel & Spa and 1905 Basin Park Hotel wedding venues are booked for June Saturdays. However, you do have some midweek openings for the unique Thorncrown Chapel in early June. If one of the brides could change to midweek, you might offer one free night in a sumptuous bridal suite at the storied 1886 Crescent Hotel & Spa to smooth ruffled feathers.

With its 6,000 square feet of glass and 425 windows, Thorncrown Chapel offers a dreamlike setting for unforgettable wedding celebrations that feel outdoors while providing the comfort of indoor air conditioning. Brides, grooms, and their guests can enjoy the palatial Crescent Hotel perched high above the Victorian Village of Eureka Springs, Arkansas, surrounded by ample green space and hidden trails.

YOUR TASK Decide what course of action to take. The two brides-to-be are Candy Schonwald, 614 Pirkle Ferry Road, Cummings, GA 30040, and Debbie Hungeling, 4590 Clairmont Road, Atlanta, GA 30346. In a memo to your instructor, explain your response strategy. If you plan a phone call, outline what you plan to say. If your instructor requests, write a letter to fax or e-mail to the customer and copy your instructor.

9.14 Claim Denial: Sorry—Smokers Must Cough Up Cash (L.O. 1–4)

Recently the Century Park Hotel embarked on a two-year plan to provide enhanced value and improved product quality to its guests. It always strives to exceed guest expectations. As part of this effort, Century Park Hotel has been refurbishing many rooms with updated finishes. The new carpet, paint, upholstery, and draperies, however, absorb the heavy odor of cigarette smoke. To protect the hotel's investment, Century Park enforces a strict nonsmoking policy for its nonsmoking rooms.

Century Park makes sure that guests know about its policy regarding smoking in nonsmoking rooms. It posts a notice in each nonsmoking room, and it gives guests a handout from the manager detailing its policy and the consequences for smoking in nonsmoking rooms. The handout clearly says, "Should a guest opt to disregard our nonsmoking policy, we will process a fee of $150 to the guest's account." For those guests who prefer to smoke, a smoking accommodation can be provided.

On May 10 Wilson M. Weber was a guest in the hotel. He stayed in a room clearly marked "Nonsmoking." After he left, the room cleaners reported that the room smelled of smoke. According to hotel policy, a charge of $150 was processed to Mr. Weber's credit card. Mr. Weber has written to demand that the $150 charge be removed. He doesn't deny that he smoked in the room. He just believes that he should not have to pay.

YOUR TASK As hotel manager, deny Mr. Weber's claim. You would certainly like to see Mr. Weber return as a Century Park Hotel guest, but you cannot budge on your smoking policy. Address your response to Mr. Wilson M. Weber, 634 Wetmore Avenue, Everett, WA 98201.

9.15 Claim Denial: Lost in Flight (L.O. 1–4)

National Airlines had an unhappy customer. Genna Morris flew from Washington, DC, to Los Angeles. The flight stopped briefly at Denver International Airport, where she got off the plane for half an hour. When she returned to her seat, her $500 prescription reading glasses were gone. She asked the flight attendant where the glasses were, and the attendant said they probably were thrown away since the cleaning crew had come in with big bags and tossed everything in them. Ms. Morris tried to locate the glasses through the airline's lost-and-found service, but she failed.

Then she wrote a strong letter to the airline demanding reimbursement for the loss. She felt that it was obvious she was returning to her seat. The airline, however, knows that an overwhelming number of passengers arriving at hubs switch planes for their connecting flights. The airline does not know who is returning. What's more, flight attendants usually announce that the plane is continuing to another city and that passengers who are returning should take their belongings. Cabin cleaning crews speed through planes removing newspapers, magazines, leftover foods, and trash. Airlines feel no responsibility for personal items left in cabins.

YOUR TASK As a staff member of the customer relations department of National Airlines, deny the customer's claim but retain her goodwill using techniques learned in this chapter. The airline never refunds cash, but it might consider travel vouchers for the value of the glasses. Remember that apologies cost nothing. Write a claim denial to Ms. Genna Morris, 1805 Panorama Drive, Bakersfield, CA 93305.

9.16 Bad News to Customers: Which Elliptical for 24-Hour Fitness? (L.O. 1–4)

You are delighted to receive a large order from Finn Valentino at 24-Hour Fitness gym. This order includes two Olympic Benches (at $349 each), three Stamina Power Towers (at $249 each), three sets of Premier Dumbbells (at $105 each), and two Titanic 20 Ellipticals (at $1,099 each).

You could ship immediately except for one problem. The Titanic 20 Elliptical, as rated by *Consumer Reports*, is intended for home use, not for gym or club use. More and more fitness lovers are purchasing ellipticals because they have better track records than treadmills and stair climbers for aerobic exercise. The Titanic 20 is definitely effective for personal use. However, this is not the model you would recommend for club use. The Titanic 90 is larger, sturdier, and safer for commercial gyms. It also has extras such as a built-in cooling fan, water bottle holder, and speakers that allow users to hook up to any MP3 player or smartphone for easy listening. You believe that Mr. Valentino should order the Titanic 90 Elliptical. It's solidly built, comes with a chest-strap heart-rate monitor, has 20 resistance levels, and features a lifetime warranty on its frame. For gym use, the Titanic 90 is clearly better. The bad news is that it is considerably more expensive at $3,100 per machine.

You get no response when you try to telephone Mr. Valentino to discuss the problem. Should you ship what you can, or hold the entire order until you learn whether he wants the Titanic 20 or the Titanic 90 Elliptical? Another option is to substitute the Titanic 90 and send only one of them. Another possibility is sending one of the home models and one of the gym models.

YOUR TASK Decide what to do and then send an e-mail to Finn Valentino (fvalentino@24hourfitness.com).

9.17 Bad News to Customers: "Human Error" Admits Rejected Students
(L.O. 1–4)

E-Mail

The University of South Florida St. Petersburg recently made a big mistake. It inadvertently welcomed 430 rejected applicants. The e-mail said, "Once again congratulations on your admission to USFSP! We are excited to welcome you to the university and are very proud of all that you have accomplished so far! I also wanted to provide you with your next steps." The message then provided instructions for students to obtain their university IDs, pay a tuition deposit, apply for housing, and more.[65]

That message was intended to be sent to the 250 students who had been accepted. Instead, it went to a subset of students whose applications were still under review or they were denied. Chancellor Martin Tadlock blamed human error in the admissions office for the mistake. "We regret it," Tadlock said in an interview. "We pride ourselves on our relationship with the community, and this doesn't represent that. It was an error and a mistake."[66]

One applicant, who had received the acceptance e-mail in error from USF St. Petersburg, Alexandria Rizzotto, was very disappointed: "I was very, very let down because I've been waiting for a final decision from them since November now."[67] What could the university do to correct this massive slip-up?

YOUR TASK For Chancellor Martin Tadlock, write an appropriate bad-news message to the students who received the message in error. Many applicants will be wondering what their real admission status is.

9.18 Bad News to Customers: Announcing a Price Increase (L.O. 1–4)

E-Mail

Select a product or service that you now use (e.g., Internet or cable service, water or electricity, propane or natural gas, smartphone or landline, car insurance). Assume that the provider must raise its rates and that you are the employee who must notify customers. Should you use a letter, e-mail, company website, or blog? Decide whether you should use the direct or indirect strategy. Gather as much information as you can about the product or service. What, if anything, justifies the increase? What benefits can be cited?

For inspiration study the example below. Netflix announced the most recent increase in its subscription price to existing customers via e-mail.

> Hi Kevin,
>
> We hope you have been enjoying your Netflix membership. We are writing to let you know about an upcoming change.
>
> Your monthly price is increasing to $12.99 on Tuesday, May 21. Why? We're hard at work improving Netflix so that you can have even more great TV shows and movies to enjoy.
>
> Here's to watching what you want, when you want, where you want.
>
> You can change your plan, or if you do not wish to continue your membership, as always you can cancel any time at netflix.com/cancel.
>
> We're here to help if you need it. Visit the Help Center for more info or contact us.
>
> —The Netflix Team

YOUR TASK Analyze the Netflix e-mail announcing the price hike. Does the message follow the practices recommended in this chapter? Prepare your own rate increase announcement. Submit it along with a memo explaining your rationale for the strategy you chose and include your analysis of the Netflix example.

9.19 Bad News to Customers: Pay Day Delayed (L.O. 1–4)

Team

Carlos Felix, a printing company sales manager, must tell one of his clients that the payroll checks her company ordered are not going to be ready by the date Carlos had promised. The printing company's job scheduler overlooked the job and didn't get the checks into production in time to meet the deadline. As a result, Carlos's client, a major insurance company, is going to miss its pay run.

Carlos meets with internal department heads. They decide on the following plan to remedy the situation: (a) move the check order to the front of the production line; (b) make up for the late production date by shipping some of the checks—enough to meet their client's immediate payroll needs—by air freight; (c) deliver the remaining checks by truck.

YOUR TASK Form groups of three or four students. Discuss the following issues about how to present the bad news to Jeanine Pradip, Carlos's contact person at the insurance company.

a. Should Carlos call Jeanine directly or delegate the task to his assistant?

b. When should Jeanine be informed of the problem?

c. What is the best procedure for delivering the bad news?

d. What follow-up would you recommend to Carlos?

Be prepared to share your group's responses during a class discussion. Your instructor may ask two students to role-play the presentation of the bad news.

9.20 Credit Refusal: Pay as You Go at Gymzo (L.O. 1–4)

As manager of Gymzo Fitness, you must refuse the application of Fiona Marin for an Extended Membership. This is strictly a business decision. You liked Fiona very much when she applied, and she seems genuinely interested in fitness and a healthy lifestyle. However, your Extended Membership plan qualifies the member for all your testing, exercise, recreation, yoga, and aerobics programs. This multiservice program is expensive for the club to maintain because of the large staff required. Applicants must have a solid credit rating to join. To your disappointment, you learned that Fiona's credit rating is decidedly negative. Her credit report indicates that she is delinquent in payments to four businesses, including Diamond Fitness Center, your principal competitor.

You do have other programs, including your Drop In and Work Out plan, which offers the use of available facilities on a cash basis. This plan enables a member to reserve space on the racquetball and handball courts. The member can also sign up for yoga and exercise classes, space permitting. Since Fiona is far in debt, you would feel guilty allowing her to plunge in any more deeply.

YOUR TASK Refuse Fiona Marin's credit application, but encourage her pay-as-you-go cash business. Suggest that she make an inquiry to the credit-reporting company Experian to learn about her credit report. She is eligible to receive a free credit report if she mentions this application. Write to Fiona Marin, 466 Circle Street, Milwaukee, WI 53204.

9.21 Bad News to Employees: Belt Tightening at TechLab (L.O. 1–3, 5)

Communication Technology

When high-tech startup TechLab first hit the technology scene, it created a big splash. Its music streaming and voice control technology promised to revolutionize the field. It attracted $500,000 in seed money, suggesting that it could hire the best talent and create amazing new products. But TechLab quickly fell off the fast track. It spent nearly $400,000 on a Bluetooth product that sold only 28 units. In addition, a botched security update resulted in the company's having to conduct a nationwide recall of one of its smart products. However, other products have been successful, and the company is not facing bankruptcy.

Initially, TechLab offered amazing perks to attract the best and brightest talent. It provided an in-house chef with free gourmet meals, unlimited snacks, on-site acupuncture, and free yoga classes. Its offices were pet-friendly, and new employees received a $10,000 cash signing bonus. To counter the long hours that the tech world notoriously demands of its workers, TechLab offered relaxation areas with table tennis and foosball tables.

Unfortunately, bad times have made it necessary for TechLab to pull back on its employee perks. Although no staff people are being laid off, the in-house chef has to go, along with on-site acupuncture, yoga classes, and the $10,000 signing bonus. However, it's still a good place to work, and camaraderie is high.

YOUR TASK As a communications trainee in the CEO's office, you have been asked to draft an intranet post or a memo to employees announcing the bad news. Explain the cutbacks that affect current employees. Employ the bad-news techniques taught in this chapter. What could soften this bad news?

9.22 Bad News to Employees: Nixing Tuition Assistance (L.O. 1-5)

Tanya Arthur, a hardworking bank teller, has sent an e-mail request asking that the company create a program to reimburse the tuition and book expenses for employees taking college courses. Although some companies have such a program, Atlantic Federal has not felt that it could indulge in such an expensive employee perk. Moreover, the CEO, Will Sebastian, is not convinced that companies see any direct benefit from such programs. Employees improve their educational credentials and skills, but what is to keep them from moving that education and those skill sets to other employers? Atlantic Federal has over 200 employees. If even a fraction of them started classes, the company could see a huge bill for the cost of tuition and books.

Because the bank is facing stiff competition and its profits are sinking, the expense of such a program makes it out of the question. In addition, it would involve administration—applications, monitoring, and record keeping. It is just too much of a hassle. When employees were hard to hire and retain, companies had to offer employment perks. With a fluctuating job market, however, such inducements are unnecessary.

YOUR TASK As director of Human Resources, send an individual e-mail response to Tanya Arthur. The answer is a definite *no*, but you want to soften the blow and retain the loyalty of this conscientious employee.

Test Your Workplace Etiquette IQ

New communication platforms and casual workplace environments have blurred the lines of appropriateness, leaving workers wondering how to navigate uncharted waters. Check your workplace etiquette IQ by deciding whether the following statements are true or false. Then see if you agree with the responses on p. Key-6.

1. You are introducing a new employee, Lucy Larios, to the office staff. The vice president shows up in the hallway. You should introduce him by saying, "Lucy, I'd like you to meet Mr. Lopez, our vice president."

   _____ True _____ False

2. You panic when you can't remember the name of someone you have met before. The best strategy is to pretend you remember the person and try to engage in small talk while searching for clues to the person's identity.

   _____ True _____ False

3. When a woman is introduced to a man, he should wait for her to extend her hand first.

   _____ True _____ False

Chat About It

In each chapter you will find five discussion questions related to the chapter material. Your instructor may assign these topics for you to discuss in class, in an online chat room, or on an online discussion board. Some of the discussion topics may require outside research. You may also be asked to read and respond to postings made by your classmates.

TOPIC 1: In an infamous incident that went viral, a passenger was brutally dragged off the plane because he wouldn't give his seat to a United employee. United CEO Oscar Munoz first said: "I apologize for having to re-accommodate these customers." Later that day Munoz falsely claimed the passenger was denied boarding and was "disruptive and belligerent." The third time around,

Munoz said: "I want you to know that we take full responsibility and we will work to make it right. It's never too late to do the right thing." He closed with "I promise you we will do better." Discuss Munoz's apology. Does the CEO show empathy and genuine contrition?

TOPIC 2: Many people say they prefer the direct approach when receiving bad news. What situational factors might cause you to use the indirect approach with these people?

TOPIC 3: Which strategies have you used to soften the blow of significant bad news with your family and friends? If you haven't, imagine situations in which such strategic thinking might be wise.

TOPIC 4: Analyze the corporate jargon for getting laid off: *realigning the workforce, reallocating resources, focusing on involuntary attrition, rightsizing the company, eliminating redundancy, rewiring for growth, smartsizing the company, redeploying workers, rebalancing human capital,* and *decruiting.* How do these terms compare to *fired, booted out, given the boot,* or *get the ax*?

TOPIC 5: You are an executive at a company that suddenly has to lay off 400 employees within three days or risk financial disaster. You have to make the cuts quickly, but you don't want to be impersonal by announcing the cuts by e-mail. How would you announce the bad news?

Grammar and Mechanics Review 9

Number Usage

Review Guides 47 through 50 about number usage in Appendix D, Grammar and Mechanics. On a separate sheet, revise the following sentences to correct errors in number usage. For each error you locate, write the guide number that reflects this usage. Sentences may have more than one error. If a sentence is correct, write C. When you finish, check your answers in the key at the end of the book.

EXAMPLE: At least 8 donors are willing to contribute 500 dollars each to the charity drive.

REVISION: At least **eight** donors are willing to contribute **$500** each to the charity drive. [Guides 47, 49]

1. Amazon employees are said to spend 2 days every 2 years working in customer service.

2. 64% of consumers have made a purchase decision based on social media content.

3. Faced with a 522 million dollar deficit, the mayor sent pink slips to fifteen thousand city employees.

4. UPS deliveries are expected before ten AM and again at four thirty PM.

5. Although tweets can now be two hundred eighty characters, about nine percent are exactly one hundred forty characters,

6. On April 15th our attorney notified all 4 managers of the lawsuit.

7. You can burn one hundred fifty calories by walking as little as thirty minutes.

8. A 5-year loan for a twenty-five thousand dollar new car with 20% down would have monthly payments of three hundred fifty-six dollars.

9. Although he expected to spend fifty dollars or less, Jake actually spent sixty five dollars for the gift.

10. In the last election, only ½ of the eligible voters turned out.

Persuasive and Sales Messages

LEARNING OUTCOMES

After studying this chapter, you should be able to do the following:

1 Identify digital age persuasion as well as time-proven techniques in persuasive messages online and in print.

2 Describe the traditional four-part AIDA strategy for creating successful and ethical persuasive messages.

3 Craft persuasive messages that request actions, make claims, and deliver complaints.

4 Write persuasive messages within organizations demonstrating your knowledge of interpersonal persuasion at work.

5 Create effective and ethical direct-mail and e-mail sales messages.

6 Apply basic persuasive techniques in developing compelling press releases.

"We created ridiculous enthusiasm for the hashtag 'Vaporized,'" bragged marketing agency Cult Collective about its Juul campaign. On its website, Cult gushed that its strategy promoting the popular e-cigarette vaporizer "aligned perfectly with those we knew would be our best customers."[1] But who exactly *were* Juul's intended customers?

The Federal Trade Commission wants to know. It's investigating whether e-cigarette startup Juul Labs used social media and influencers to appeal to minors, as vaping among teens surged by 78 percent from 2017 to 2018, and one in five high schoolers admitted to having vaped in the last 30 days, according to the CDC.[2] Regulators, parents, schools, and public health advocates are alarmed by what the Food and Drug Administration has called an "epidemic of e-cigarette use among teenagers."[3] At least three lawsuits are pending against Juul Labs for deceptively marketing its products as safe.[4] Stanford researchers found that Juul's colorful ads showing attractive twentysomethings having fun while "Juuling" appeared to mimic tobacco industry marketing in style and content. Most important, though, was that Juul "exploited social media" to reach young users, the researchers said.[5] Since its inception in 2015, Juul has rocketed past competitors to own 75 percent of the e-cigarette market.[6]

Users love the small, sleek vaporizer that produces little odor. Juul is a fad that's seemingly everywhere: "I saw everyone doing it, so I wanted to try it," said one teenager. Most of all, the "pod" flavors—e.g., fruit, crème, cucumber, or mango—appear to be a factor. A young man explained Juuling is "like having a cookies milkshake, that's what it tastes like in your mouth."[7] All fruit flavors are now banned in the United States leaving only mint and menthol to mask the harshness of the aerosol.[8] Many Juul users believe they are inhaling harmless flavored water vapor, unaware of the nicotine in the pods, each of which equals 20 regular cigarettes. Nicotine is highly addictive and particularly harmful to the developing brain. In addition, toxic metals, potentially leeching from the metal coil that's heating the e-liquid, were discovered in the aerosol users inhale.[9] Recent regulation mandates highly visible health warnings on all vaping products.

Juul strenuously denies having deliberately targeted young people: "We were completely surprised by the youth usage of the product," Ashley Gould, chief administrative officer at Juul Labs, asserted and claimed, "Juul is a switching product, not a cessation product, and it is intended for adult smokers to enable them to switch from combustible cigarettes."[10] Juul's stated mission is "improving the lives of the one billion adult smokers."[11] When e-cigarettes were first introduced, they were touted as smoking cessation devices or less harmful smoking alternatives. You will learn more about Juul and be asked to complete a relevant task at the end of this chapter.

Critical Thinking

- Why might teenagers and young adults be susceptible to Juul, and what type of appeal was the e-cigarette startup using?

- What could explain the huge success of Juul, the startup that burst onto a crowded e-cigarette scene in 2015 and within three years grabbed a 75-percent share of the vaping market?

- The marketing agency Cult Collective has removed the Juul case study from its website, and it's available only in the Internet Archive. Why may Cult have pulled the case from its e-portfolio?

10-1 Understanding Persuasion in the Contemporary Workplace

LEARNING OUTCOME

1 Identify digital age persuasion as well as time-proven techniques in persuasive messages online and in print.

Flatter corporate hierarchies, teamwork, collaboration across division walls, and blurred lines of authority characterize business today. As managers and teams are abandoning the traditional command structure, solid persuasive skills are becoming ever more important at work. Businesspeople must try to influence others.[12] Pushy hard-sell techniques are waning because today's consumers are well-informed, have many choices, and can be fickle.[13] Persuasive techniques can be used for good—or for ill, as Juul has shown. Even if we believe that the company's social media campaigns were *not* intentionally targeting young people or minors, persuaders must take responsibility for unintended consequences.

Although we are subjected daily to a barrage of print and electronic persuasive messages, we often fail to recognize the techniques of persuasion and its evil cousin, manipulation. To be smart consumers and citizens, we need to be alert to persuasive practices and how they influence behavior. Being informed is our best defense. However, trusting information sources has become trickier in the age of bots and trolls that spread disinformation and downright propaganda, often from abroad, with nefarious intent. As we have seen in Chapter 7, social media users have the tendency to congregate with like-minded people online and, as a result, may be susceptible to confirmation bias inherent in echo chambers or opinion bubbles.

You have already studied techniques for writing routine request messages that require minimal persuasion. However, this chapter focuses on messages that require deliberate and skilled persuasion in the workplace. This chapter also addresses selling, both offline and online.

10-1a Defining Persuasion

As communication scholar Richard M. Perloff defines it, persuasion is "a symbolic process in which communicators try to convince other people to change their attitudes or behaviors regarding an issue through the transmission of a message in an atmosphere of free choice."[14] Helping us understand how persuasion works, Perloff's definition has five components, which are outlined in the following sections.

Persuasion Is a Symbolic Process.
Symbols can take the form of lofty words, signs, and images infused with rich meaning—for example, words such as *liberty*, signs such as national flags, and images such as a red cross for rescue or an apple for computers. An ethical persuader understands the power of symbols and does not use them to trick others. Because people's attitudes change slowly, persuasion takes time.

Persuasion Involves an Attempt to Influence.
Persuasion involves a conscious effort to influence another person with the understanding that change is possible. For instance, when you ask your boss for permission to telecommute, you intend to achieve a specific outcome and assume that your boss can be swayed. This deliberate attempt to change another person's mind doesn't always succeed.

Persuasion Is Self-Persuasion.
Ethical communicators give others the choice to accept their arguments by making compelling, honest cases to support them. They plant the seed but do not coerce. They leave it to others to "self-influence"—that is, to decide whether to make the change. In the case of telecommuting, you would want to present to your boss clear benefits of working from home but definitely not push hard, not least because your boss has more power.

Persuasion Involves Transmitting a Message.
Persuasive messages can be verbal or nonverbal, and they can be conveyed face-to-face or via the Internet, TV, radio, and other media. Persuasive messages are not always rational. They often appeal to our emotions. Consider the car commercial playing your favorite tune and showing pristine landscapes, not a gridlocked interstate during rush hour.

Persuasion Requires Free Choice.
Although *free* is a difficult term to define, we can perhaps agree that people are free when they are not forced to comply, when they can refuse the idea suggested to them, and when they are not pressured to act against their own preferences. In fact, most people respond to pressure with what psychologists call reactance, a defensive strategy of resistance that humans adopt when feeling cornered, robbed of their autonomy, or restricted in their options by others.

Many smart thinkers have tried to explain how savvy persuaders influence others. They agree, however, that it's not easy to change entrenched views. It's a gradual, slow process. One classic model illustrating persuasion is shown in Figure 10.1. In the definitive book *Influence*,[15] Robert B. Cialdini outlined six psychological triggers that prompt us to act and believe: reciprocation, commitment, social proof, liking, authority, and scarcity. Each "weapon of automatic influence" motivates us to say *yes* or *no* without much thinking or awareness. Our complex world forces us to resort to these shortcuts. Needless to say, such automatic responses make us vulnerable to manipulation.

FIGURE 10.1 Six Psychological Triggers That Aid Human Persuasion

Reciprocation
"The Old Give and Take … and Take"

Humans seem to be hardwired to give and take. If someone does us a favor, most of us feel obligated to return the favor. This rule is so binding that it may lead to a *yes* to a request we might otherwise refuse. This explains the "gifts" that accompany requests for money.

Commitment
"Hobgoblins of the Mind"

We believe in the correctness of a difficult choice once we make it. We want to keep our thoughts and beliefs consistent with what we have already decided. Fundraisers may ask for a small amount at first, knowing that we are likely to continue giving once we start.

Social Proof
"Truths Are Us"

To determine correct behavior, we try to find out what other people think is correct. We see an action as more acceptable when others are doing it. Advertisers like to tell us that a product is "best-selling"; the message is that it must be good because others think so.

Liking
"The Friendly Thief"

We are more likely to accept requests of people we know and like or those who say they like us. Tupperware capitalizes on this impulse to buy from a friend. Strangers are persuasive if they are likable and attractive. Also, we favor people who are or appear to be like us.

Authority
"Directed Deference"

We tend to obey authority because we learn that a widely accepted system of authority is beneficial to the orderly functioning of society. People exuding authority, even con artists, can trigger our mechanical, blind compliance. Testimonials bank on this response to authority.

Scarcity
"The Rule of the Few"

We tend to regard opportunities as more valuable when their availability is restricted. Scarce items seem more appealing to us. The idea of potential loss greatly affects our decisions. Marketers may urge customers not to miss out on a "limited-time offer."

If you become aware of these gut-level mechanisms that trigger decisions, you will be able to resist unethical and manipulative persuasion more easily. Conversely, this knowledge might make you a successful persuader.

10-1b Exploring Digital Age Persuasion

The preoccupation with persuasion is not new. From the days of Aristotle in ancient Greece and Machiavelli in Renaissance Italy, philosophers, politicians, and businesspeople have longed to understand the art of influencing others. However, persuasion in the twenty-first century is different from persuasion in previous historic periods in distinct ways.[17] The most striking developments are perhaps three decades old.

The Volume and Reach of Persuasive Messages Have Exploded. Although the exact numbers are difficult to establish, experts estimate that the average American consumer today endures as many as 5,000 direct and indirect advertising impressions a day, up from around 500 daily ads 50 years ago. Some marketers believe the range of daily ad impressions and brand encounters is even higher, approximately 4,000 to 10,000.[18] Naturally, we remember only a fraction of these persuasive appeals. Marketers must work very hard to distinguish their brands from the crowd. TV, radio, the Internet, and social media blast myriad messages to the far corners of the earth. While traveling in China, you may field questions about Michael Jordan or LeBron James. Celebrities such as Beyoncé are household names all over the globe, as are brands like Coca-Cola or commodity symbols like the Nike swoosh.

Persuasive Messages Spread at Warp Speed. Take election year campaign buzz. It travels at dizzying speed. In 2016 digital organizers for primary candidate Bernie Sanders rallied his followers by text and tweet as these surrogates were reaching out to potential supporters. Within hours, 50,000 responses were logged. Climate activists, e.g., the Swedish teen Greta Thunberg, are able to mobilize millions of followers with powerful messages and images, without direct face-to-face interaction.

Ethics ✔ Check

The Perils of *Automatic Influence*

Professional persuaders try to generate "a distinct kind of automatic, mindless compliance" in people, a "willingness to say yes without thinking first," believes psychologist Robert B. Cialdini. The best-selling author of *Influence* cautions: "The ever-accelerating pace and informational crush of modern life will make . . . unthinking compliance more and more prevalent in the future. It will be increasingly important for the society, therefore, to understand the how and why of automatic influence."[16] What does this mean for you as a consumer and social media user?

Reality Check

Be Your Authentic Self

"Persuasion isn't convincing someone that you are something that you're not. Persuasion is about finding an authentic story that will change beliefs or behaviors. So don't promise innovation if you're just meeting a need. Don't tell your date you love dogs if you really don't. . . . If there's a perception gap between how you see yourself and how the person you are trying to persuade sees you, you will have a problem."[20]

—Lee Hartley Carter, *consultant and communication expert*

Organizations of All Stripes Are in the Persuasion Business. Companies big and small, ad agencies, PR firms, social activists, lobbyists, marketers, pollsters, and more, spew persuasive messages. Although outspent by corporations that can sink millions into image campaigns, activists use social networks to galvanize their followers. Savvy political campaigns use social media to solicit small donations for their candidates from huge Internet crowds. Thus, in the aggregate, they may wield an influence rivaling that of interest groups that spend millions to lobby members of Congress and sway their votes.

Persuasive Techniques Are More Subtle and Misleading. Instead of a blunt, pushy, hard-sell approach, persuaders play on emotions by using flattery, empathy, nonverbal cues, and likability appeals. They are selling an image or a lifestyle, not a product.[19] In this age of spin, the news media are increasingly infiltrated by partisan interests and spread messages masquerading as news. Sponsored content on the Web is often nearly indistinguishable from legitimate news articles next to which they are strategically and perhaps deviously placed.

Persuasion Is More Complex and Mediated by Technology. American consumers are more diverse and don't necessarily think alike. To reach them, marketers carefully study target groups and mine data to predict market segmentation. Then they highly customize, **microtarget**, their appeals to a narrow subset of the intended audience.

Technology has increased the volume of persuasion and the potential for distortion. People can "mash up" content, give it meanings the original source never intended, and blast it into the world in seconds. On the other hand, the Internet has democratized persuasion. It has empowered regular citizens armed with just a smartphone to influence public debate, affect an election, or weigh in on a business scandal.

You probably recognize how important it is not only to become a skilled persuader, but also to identify devious messages and manipulation attempts directed at you. When you want your ideas to prevail, start thinking about how to present them. Listeners and readers will be more inclined to accept what you are offering if you focus on important strategies, outlined in Figure 10.2 and further discussed throughout the chapter.

FIGURE 10.2 Effective Persuasive Techniques

Establish credibility
- Show that you are truthful, experienced, and knowledgeable.
- Use others' expert opinions and research to support your position.

Make a reasonable, specific request
- Make your request realistic, doable, and attainable.
- Be clear about your objective. Vague requests are less effective.

Tie facts to benefits
- Line up plausible support such as statistics, reasons, and analogies.
- Convert the supporting facts into specific audience benefits.

Recognize the power of loss
- Show what others stand to lose if they don't agree.
- Know that people dread losing something they already possess.

Expect and overcome resistance
- Anticipate opposition from conflicting beliefs, values, and attitudes.
- Be prepared to counter with well-reasoned arguments and facts.

Share solutions and compromise
- Be flexible and aim for a solution that is acceptable to all parties.
- Listen to people and incorporate their input to create buy-in.

10-1c Applying the 3-x-3 Writing Process to Persuasive Messages

Changing people's views and overcoming their objections are difficult tasks. Pulling it off demands planning and being perceptive. The 3-x-3 writing process provides a helpful structure for laying a foundation for persuasion. Of particular importance here are (a) analyzing the purpose, (b) adapting to the audience, (c) collecting information, and (d) organizing the message.

Analyzing the Purpose: Knowing What You Want to Achieve. The goal of a persuasive message is to convince the receiver of your ideas and motivate action. To accomplish this feat in the age of social media, persuaders seek to build relationships with their audiences. Even so, a message without a clear purpose is doomed. Too often, inexperienced writers reach the end of the first draft of a message before discovering exactly what they want the receiver to think or do.

Meet Chef James Barry and his nutritionist wife Margaret. The owners of Eat Naked Kitchen—a one-on-one whole-food coaching and lifestyle service—understand contemporary persuasive techniques. A former personal chef for celebrities, Chef James and nutrition expert Margaret recognize that all their customers want to feel special. Both know that to achieve success today, they must cultivate relationships, not just push products.[21] Margaret and James provide value by giving away free recipes, sharing cooking techniques, and offering lifestyle recommendations. They engage their well-heeled clients by maintaining a website, tweeting updates, and posting curated advice on their Facebook, Instagram, and Pinterest pages.

Eat Naked Kitchen also has a YouTube channel presenting how-to cooking tips and tricks. Margaret typically authors the opt-in advice e-newsletter such as the one shown in Model Document 10.1 and signs off with greetings on behalf of her whole family. Sales pitches are conspicuously absent, so is any mention of program cost because the audience is not price sensitive.

Adapting to the Audience to Make Your Message Heard. In addition to identifying the purpose of a persuasive message, you also need to concentrate on the receiver. Zorba the Greek wisely observed, "You can knock forever on a deaf man's door." A persuasive message is futile unless it meets the needs of its audience. In a broad sense, you want to show how your request helps the receiver achieve some of life's major goals or fulfills key needs: money, power, comfort, confidence, importance, friends, peace of mind, and recognition, to name a few.

On a more practical level, you want to show how your request solves a problem, achieves a personal or work objective, or just makes life easier for your audience. During the anxiety-inducing COVID-19 pandemic, Eat Naked Kitchen gently reminds its customers and social media followers that wholesome food and a healthy lifestyle nourish the immune system. When adapting persuasive requests to your audience, consider these questions that receivers will very likely be asking themselves:

> Why should I?
> What's in it for me?
> What's in it for you?
> Who cares?

Adapting to your audience means learning about audience members and analyzing why they might resist your proposal. It means searching for ways to connect your purpose with their needs. If completed before you begin writing, such analysis goes a long way toward overcoming resistance and achieving your goal.

Researching and Organizing Persuasive Data. Once you have analyzed the audience and considered how to adapt your message to its needs, you are ready to collect data and organize it. You might brainstorm and prepare cluster diagrams to provide a rough outline of ideas. Eat Naked Kitchen is a consultancy that arose from the success of a whole-food catering and delivery business. Chef James and his wife Margaret realized they could marry technology and their

Reality Check

Less Is More When Touting Benefits

"Even though I've been in the business of selling complex, million dollar projects to Fortune 500 companies, no matter how long the proposal itself was, I always insisted that page one include the top three reasons our solution was the best. I was always battling sales people who wanted to stack the features and benefits higher and higher. I knew that if you had the right reasons, three were enough."[22]

—Kevin Kruse, *CEO of LEADx and author of Great Leaders Have No Rules*

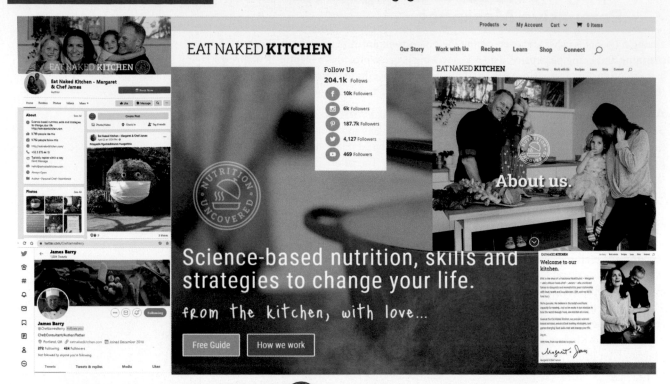

EAT NAKED **KITCHEN**

Personalizes the e-mail newsletter to connect with customers

Captures attention with references to current events, addressing the reader's concerns

Empathizes with the recipient and builds interest in boosting the immune system and removing stressors in trying times

Shifts to *we* to identify with the reader and to establish expertise

Provides link to more tips; mostly uses *you view*

Hi Linda,

With all eyes on our immune health as we battle the novel coronavirus pandemic, an often-overlooked but essential strategy is to identify those things that are taxing your immune system and systematically removing them.

Why? Well think of it this way: if you're tired and overworked, and then your boss plops a big new project on your desk, how capable are you of doing a fabulous job on that new project? Not very.

The same goes for your immune system. If it's already chronically engaged in low-level battles all day long, how well is it equipped to fight a big new battle like the coronavirus? Not very.

One of the most important things we can do right now is identify the things in our life that are engaging that immune system, and systematically removing or reducing these stressors. This is a core strategy I use with all clients - whether we're thinking of prepping for exposure to a gnarly virus or working to bring an Autoimmune disease into remission.

Here are five things you can do right now ... continue reading.

For entrepreneurs and business owners during this time....
One of the things I've found exceptionally helpful is a 2-part podcast that Brendon Burchard did called Fear, Focus and Forecasting. Part 1. Part 2.

Replay of one-day mini-summit....
Coronavirus - Voices of Reason Mini- Summit - How to Keep Yourself and Your Family Safe during the COVID-19 Pandemic. Featuring Tom Moorcroft (Infectious disease expert Margaret interviewed a couple of weeks ago); Dr. Elisa Song (Pediatrician who's written some of our favorite resources for parents during this time); Dr. Joan Rosenburg (author of 90 seconds to a Life You Love); Dr. Terry Wahls; and several other of our favorite health rock stars. The replay is free and well worth a listen.

For deeper sleep in these high anxiety times...
Weighted blankets are proving to be very therapeutic for sleep. Particularly in supporting that healing deep sleep we all need so badly! This brand is well reviewed and priced.

Here's to removing the stressors,

Margaret, Chef James and family

Follow. Share.Tag. Together we can do so much good.

Offers information and curated advice; does not engage in overt selling

Spreads good cheer; again personalizes the newsletter, signing off as a family sending greetings to the recipient's family

Positive call to action and unity; invites reader to connect on social media

Contemporary persuaders understand that audiences want to feel special and expect to have their needs met. In anxious times, most people like to feel understood. Margaret and Chef James build sincere relationships with their customers via a personalized e-newsletter and a rich social media presence that features the whole Barry family.

Eat Naked Kitchen/Margaret and Chef James

FIGURE 10.3 The AIDA Strategy for Persuasive Messages

STRATEGY	CONTENT	SECTION
Attention	Captures attention, creates awareness, makes a sales proposition, prompts audience to read on	Opening
Interest	Describes central selling points, focuses not on features of product/service but on benefits relevant to the reader's needs	Body
Desire	Reduces resistance, reassures the reader, elicits the desire for ownership, motivates action	Body
Action	Offers an incentive or gift, limits the offer, sets a deadline, makes it easy for the reader to respond, closes the sale	Closing

expertise to provide high-value individualized nutrition and lifestyle advice without the overhead of preparing and delivering wholesome food. They can serve their clients from anywhere, thanks to technology, and have settled in attractive Portland, Oregon.

The next step in a persuasive message is organizing data into a logical sequence. If you are asking for something that you know will be approved, little persuasion is required. In that case, you would make a direct request, as you studied in Chapter 8. However, when you expect resistance or when you need to educate the receiver, the indirect strategy often works better. The classic indirect strategy known by the acronym AIDA (**A**ttention, **I**nterest, **D**esire, and **A**ction) works well for many persuasive requests, not just in selling. Figure 10.3 summarizes this four-part strategy for overcoming resistance and crafting successful persuasive messages.

10-2 Applying Four Essential Principles to Successful Persuasive Messages

LEARNING OUTCOME

2 Describe the traditional four-part AIDA strategy for creating successful and ethical persuasive messages.

Although AIDA, the indirect strategy, appears to contain separate steps, successful persuasive messages actually blend the four steps into a seamless whole. Also, the sequence of the steps may change depending on the situation and the emphasis. Regardless of where they are placed, the key elements in persuasive requests are (a) gaining your audience's attention, (b) building interest by convincing your audience that your proposal is worthy, (c) eliciting desire for the offer and reducing resistance, and (d) prompting action. Figure 10.4 summarizes the tools writers use when following the AIDA strategy.

10-2a Gaining Attention

The opening statement in a persuasive request should be brief, relevant, and engaging. When only mild persuasion is necessary, the opener can be low-key and factual. If, however, your request is substantial and you anticipate strong resistance, provide a thoughtful, provocative opening. Following are some examples.

- **Problem description.** In a recommendation to employers to write more stringent smoking and vaping policies and encourage smoking cessation programs: *Compared to nonsmoking and nonvaping employees, every staff member who lights up costs you nearly $6,000 more a year in time off, smoking breaks, and health care expenses.* With this opener you have presented a capsule of the problem your proposal will help solve.

- **Unexpected statement.** In a memo preparing employees for the downside of video calling: *Zoom fatigue is real and unfortunately quite common because virtual interactions can be hard on the human brain.* Note how this opener gets readers thinking immediately.

FIGURE 10.4 The Four-Part AIDA Strategy for Persuasive Messages

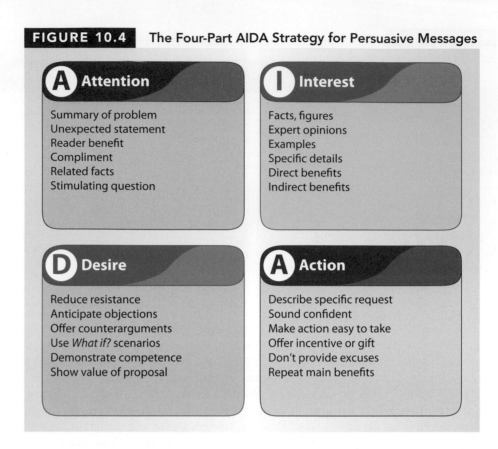

- **Reader benefit.** In a letter promoting Flex Card, a service that helps employees make credit card purchases without paying interest: *The average employee carries nearly $13,000 in revolving debt and pays $2,800 in interest and late fees. The Flex Card charges zero percent interest.* Employers immediately see the benefit of this offer to employees.

- **Compliment.** In a letter inviting a business executive to speak: *Because our members admire your best-selling leadership book and value your managerial expertise, they want you to be our keynote speaker.* In offering praise or compliments, however, be careful to avoid obvious flattery. Be sincere and don't exaggerate.

- **Related facts.** In a message to company executives who are considering prohibiting even handsfree calling by employee drivers: *A recent study showed no significant decrease in distracted driving with handsfree devices. It also revealed that the cost to the employer is more than $64,000 per crash, resulting in injuries and a whopping $657,000 on average per fatality.* This relevant fact sets the scene for the interest-building section that follows.

- **Stimulating question.** In a plea for funds to support environmental causes: *What do golden tortoise beetles, bark spiders, flounders, and Arctic foxes have in common?* Readers will be curious to find the answer to this intriguing question. (They all change color depending on their surroundings.)

10-2b Building Interest

After capturing attention, a persuasive request must retain that attention and convince the audience that the request is reasonable. To justify your request, be prepared to invest in a few paragraphs of explanation. Persuasive requests are likely to be longer than direct requests because the audience must be convinced rather than simply instructed. You can build interest and conviction through the use of the following:

- Facts and statistics
- Expert opinion
- Direct benefits
- Examples
- Specific details
- Indirect benefits

Showing how your request can benefit the audience directly or indirectly is a key factor in persuasion. If you were asking alumni to contribute money to a college emergency fund, for example, you might promote **direct benefits** such as listing the donor's name in the college magazine or sending a sweatshirt with the college logo. Another direct benefit is a tax write-off for the contribution. An **indirect benefit** might be feeling good about "paying it forward," thus helping the college and knowing that students will benefit from the gift. Nearly all charities rely in large part on indirect benefits to promote their causes.

10-2c Eliciting Desire and Reducing Resistance

The best persuasive requests anticipate audience resistance. How will the receiver object to the request? When brainstorming, try *What if?* scenarios. Let's say you want to convince management that the employees' cafeteria should switch from disposable to ceramic dishes. What if managers say the change is too expensive? What if they argue that they recycle paper and plastic? What if they contend that ceramic dishes would increase cafeteria labor and energy costs? What if they protest that ceramic is less hygienic? For each of these *What if?* scenarios, you need a counterargument.

Countering resistance and prompting desire in the receiver is important, but you must do it with finesse (*Although ceramic dishes cost more at first, they actually save money over time*). You can minimize objections by presenting your counterarguments in sentences that emphasize benefits: *Ceramic dishes may require a little more effort in cleaning, but they bring warmth and graciousness to meals. Most important, they help save the environment by requiring fewer resources and eliminating waste.* However, don't dwell on counterarguments, thus making them overly important. Finally, avoid bringing up outlandish objections that may never have occurred to the receiver in the first place.

Another factor that reduces resistance and elicits desire is credibility. Receivers are less resistant if your request is reasonable and if you are believable. When the receiver does not know you, you may have to establish your expertise, refer to your credentials, or demonstrate your competence. Even when you are known, you may have to establish your knowledge in a given area. If you are asking your manager for a flashy tablet, you might have to establish your credibility by providing information from reputable sources about the latest tablet models, their portability, memory, cost, battery life, and so on.

Some charities establish their credibility by displaying on their stationery the names of famous people who serve on their boards. The credibility of speakers making presentations is usually outlined by someone who introduces them.

10-2d Prompting Action

After gaining attention, building interest, eliciting desire, and reducing resistance, you will want to inspire the newly receptive audience to act. Knowing exactly what action you favor before you start to write enables you to point your arguments toward this important final paragraph. Here you make your recommendation as specifically and confidently as possible—without seeming pushy. A proposal from one manager to another might conclude with, *So that we can begin using the employment assessment tests by May 1, please send a return e-mail immediately.* In making a request, don't sound apologetic (*I'm sorry to have to ask you this, but . . .*), and don't supply excuses (*If you can spare the time, . . .*). Compare the following persuasive e-mail closings recommending training seminars in communication skills.

Too General

We are certain we can develop a series of training sessions that will improve the communication skills of your employees.

Too Timid

If you agree that our training proposal has merit, perhaps we could begin the series in June.

Too Pushy

Because we are convinced that you will want to begin improving the skills of your employees immediately, we have scheduled your series to begin in June.

Effective

You will see significant improvement in the communication skills of your employees. Please call me at 469-439-2201 by May 1 to give your approval so that training sessions may start in June, right after the completion of your internal restructuring.

Note how the last opening suggests a specific and easy-to-follow action. It also provides a deadline and a reason for that date. Model Document 10.2 exemplifies the AIDA persuasive strategy just discussed. Writing for her research firm, Lois Bailey seeks to persuade other companies to complete a questionnaire revealing salary data. To most organizations, salary information is strictly confidential. What can she do to convince strangers to part with such private information?

To gain attention, Lois poses two short questions that spotlight the need for salary information. To build interest and establish trust, she states that Research Bay has been collecting business data for a quarter century and has received awards. She ties her reasonable request to direct and indirect audience benefits.

10-2e Being an Ethical Persuader

Persuaders are effective only when they are believable. If receivers suspect that they are being manipulated or misled, or if they find any part of the argument untruthful, the total argument fails. Fudging on the facts, exaggerating a point, omitting crucial information, or providing deceptive emphasis may seem tempting to some business communicators, but such schemes usually backfire. Consider the case of a manager who sought to persuade employees to accept a change in insurance benefits. His memo emphasized a small perk (easier handling of claims) but de-emphasized a major increase in deductibles. Some readers missed the main point—as the manager intended. Others recognized the deception, however, and before long the manager's credibility was lost.

Persuasion becomes unethical when facts are distorted, overlooked, or manipulated with intent to deceive. Applied to language that manipulates, such distortion and twisting of the meaning is called **doublespeak**. Of course, persuaders naturally want to put forth their strongest case. However, that argument must be based on truth, objectivity, and fairness.

Consumers complain about businesses resorting to aggressive sales tactics, manipulation, and downright lies.[24] Both used-car and new-car salespeople are infamous for questionable sales techniques, but they are hardly alone. Scandals in banking and finance come to mind, involving Wells Fargo and Fisher Investments most recently—companies that drew complaints for fraudulent and shady selling methods. Even tony Aspen, Colorado, has seen its share of high-pressure tactics and overcharges. Several luxury retailers were sued by customers who ended up with $10,000 to $21,000 worth of cosmetics after enjoying free samples and spiked champagne.[25] Honest business communicators would not sacrifice their good reputation for short-term gain. Once lost, credibility is difficult to regain.

1 Prewriting

Analyze: The purpose of this letter is to persuade the reader to complete and return a questionnaire.

Anticipate: Although the reader is busy, he may respond to appeals to his professionalism and to his need for salary data in his own business.

Adapt: Because the reader may be uninterested at first and require persuasion, use the indirect strategy.

2 Drafting

Research: Study the receiver's business and find ways to relate this request to company success.

Organize: Gain attention by opening with relevant questions. Build interest by showing how the reader's compliance will help his company and others. Reduce resistance by promising confidentiality and offering free data.

Draft: Prepare a first draft with the intention to revise.

3 Revising

Edit: Revise to show direct and indirect benefits more clearly. Make sure the message is as concise as possible.

Proofread: In the first sentence, spell out *percent* rather than using the symbol. Check the use of all question marks. Start all lines at the left for a block-style letter.

Evaluate: Will this letter convince the reader to complete and return the questionnaire?

RESEARCH BAY, INC.
172 Miles Avenue, Ogden, UT 84404, www.researchbay.com
PH 801.878.2300
FAX 801.878.4359

May 18, 2021

Mr. Irvin F. Carr
Clout Wealth Management
70 West Glenlake Avenue
Muncie, IN 47302

Dear Mr. Carr:

Would you like access to more reliable salary data than Glassdoor has to offer? Has your company ever lost a valued employee to another organization that offered 20 percent more in salary for the same position?

To remain competitive in hiring and to retain qualified workers, companies rely on survey data showing current salaries. Research Bay has been collecting business data for a quarter century and has been honored by the American Management Association for its accurate data. We need your help in collecting salary data for today's workers. Information from the enclosed questionnaire will supply companies like yours with such data.

Your information, of course, will be treated confidentially. The questionnaire takes but a few moments to complete, and it can provide substantial dividends for professional organizations just like yours that need comparative salary data.

To show our gratitude for your participation, we will send you free comprehensive salary surveys for your industry and your metropolitan area. Not only will you find basic salaries, but you will also learn about bonus and incentive plans, special pay differentials, expense reimbursements, and perquisites such as a company car and credit card.

Comparative salary data are impossible to provide without the support of professionals like you. Please complete the questionnaire and return it in the prepaid envelope before June 1, our spring deadline. Participating in this survey means that you will no longer be in the dark about how much your employees earn compared with others in your industry.

Sincerely yours,

RESEARCH BAY, INC.

Lois Bailey

Lois Bailey
Director, Survey Research

Enclosures

Annotations (left margin):
- Poses two short questions related to the reader
- Presents reader benefit tied to request explanation; establishes credibility
- Anticipates and counters resistance to confidentiality and time/effort objections
- Offers free salary data as a direct benefit
- Provides deadline and a final benefit to prompt action

Annotations (right margin):
- Gains attention
- Builds interest
- Elicits desire and reduces resistance
- Appeals to professionalism, an indirect benefit
- Motivates action

LEARNING OUTCOME

3 Craft persuasive messages that request actions, make claims, and deliver complaints.

10-3 Writing Persuasive Requests, Claims, and Complaints

Persuasion is often more precise and controlled when you can think through your purpose and prepare a thoughtful message in writing. A written, rather than face-to-face, request may require more preparation but can be just as effective. Convincing someone to change a belief or to perform an action when that person is reluctant requires planning and skill—and sometimes a little luck. For example, you may ask a businessperson to make a presentation to your club. You might ask a company to encourage its employees to participate in a fundraiser. Another form of persuasion involves claims or complaints. All of these messages require skill in persuasion. AIDA, the indirect strategy, gives you a helpful structure.

10-3a Crafting Persuasive Requests

Persuading someone to do something that largely benefits you may not be the easiest task. Fortunately, many individuals and companies are willing to grant requests for time, money, information, cooperation, and special privileges. They comply for a variety of reasons. They may just happen to be interested in your project, or they may see goodwill potential for themselves. Professionals sometimes feel obligated to contribute their time or expertise to "give back." Often, though, businesses and individuals comply because they see that others will benefit from the request.

The persuasive request shown in Model Document 10.2 incorporates many of the techniques that are effective in persuasion: establishing credibility, making a reasonable and precise request, tying facts to benefits, and eliciting desire while overcoming resistance in the receiver.

10-3b Writing Persuasive Claims

Persuasive claims may involve damaged products, mistaken billing, inaccurate shipments, warranty problems, limited return policies, insurance snafus, faulty merchandise, and so on. Generally, the direct strategy is best for requesting straightforward adjustments (see Chapter 8). When you feel your request is justified and will be granted, the direct strategy is most efficient. However, if a past request has been refused or ignored, or if you anticipate reluctance, then the indirect strategy is appropriate.

Developing a Logical Argument.   Strive for logical development in a claim message. You might open with sincere praise, an objective statement of the problem, a point of agreement, or a quick review of what you have done to resolve the problem. Then you can explain precisely what happened or why your claim is legitimate. Don't provide a blow-by-blow chronology of details; just hit the highlights. Be sure to enclose copies of relevant invoices, shipping orders, warranties, and payments. Close with a clear statement of what you want done: a refund, replacement, credit to your account, or other action. Be sure to think through the possibilities and make your request reasonable.

Using a Moderate Tone.   The tone of your message is important. Don't suggest that the receiver intentionally deceived you or deliberately created the problem. Rather, appeal to the receiver's sense of responsibility and pride in the company's good name. Calmly express your disappointment in view of your high expectations of the product and of the company. Communicating your feelings without resentment is often your strongest appeal.

10-3c Composing Effective Complaints

As their name suggests, complaints deliver bad news. Some complaint messages just vent anger. However, if the goal is to change something (and why bother to write except to motivate change?), then persuasion is necessary. An effective claim message makes a reasonable and valid request, presents a logical case with clear facts, and has a moderate tone. Anger and emotion are not effective persuaders.

Jen Sims's e-mail, shown in Model Document 10.3, follows the persuasive pattern as she seeks credit for two VoIP (voice over Internet protocol) office systems. Actually, she was quite

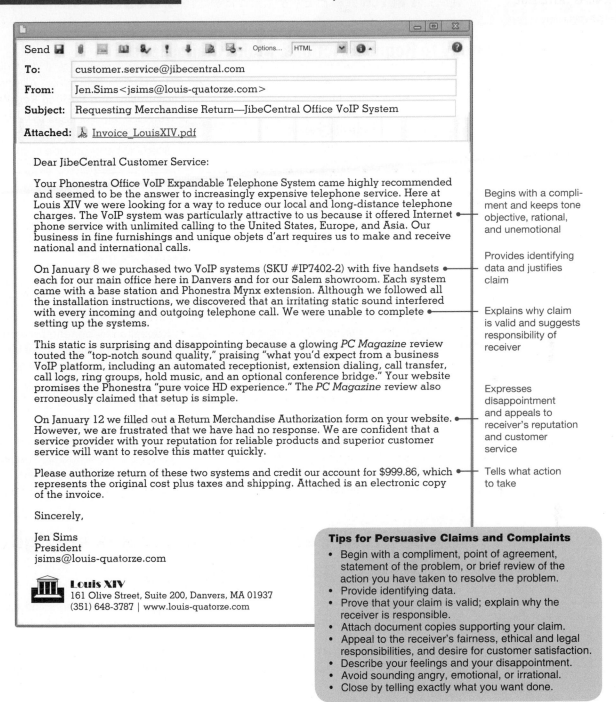

To: customer.service@jibecentral.com

From: Jen.Sims<jsims@louis-quatorze.com>

Subject: Requesting Merchandise Return—JibeCentral Office VoIP System

Attached: Invoice_LouisXIV.pdf

Dear JibeCentral Customer Service:

Your Phonestra Office VoIP Expandable Telephone System came highly recommended and seemed to be the answer to increasingly expensive telephone service. Here at Louis XIV we were looking for a way to reduce our local and long-distance telephone charges. The VoIP system was particularly attractive to us because it offered Internet phone service with unlimited calling to the United States, Europe, and Asia. Our business in fine furnishings and unique objets d'art requires us to make and receive national and international calls.

On January 8 we purchased two VoIP systems (SKU #IP7402-2) with five handsets each for our main office here in Danvers and for our Salem showroom. Each system came with a base station and Phonestra Mynx extension. Although we followed all the installation instructions, we discovered that an irritating static sound interfered with every incoming and outgoing telephone call. We were unable to complete setting up the systems.

This static is surprising and disappointing because a glowing *PC Magazine* review touted the "top-notch sound quality," praising "what you'd expect from a business VoIP platform, including an automated receptionist, extension dialing, call transfer, call logs, ring groups, hold music, and an optional conference bridge." Your website promises the Phonestra "pure voice HD experience." The *PC Magazine* review also erroneously claimed that setup is simple.

On January 12 we filled out a Return Merchandise Authorization form on your website. However, we are frustrated that we have had no response. We are confident that a service provider with your reputation for reliable products and superior customer service will want to resolve this matter quickly.

Please authorize return of these two systems and credit our account for $999.86, which represents the original cost plus taxes and shipping. Attached is an electronic copy of the invoice.

Sincerely,

Jen Sims
President
jsims@louis-quatorze.com

Louis XIV
161 Olive Street, Suite 200, Danvers, MA 01937
(351) 648-3787 | www.louis-quatorze.com

Side annotations:

Begins with a compliment and keeps tone objective, rational, and unemotional

Provides identifying data and justifies claim

Explains why claim is valid and suggests responsibility of receiver

Expresses disappointment and appeals to receiver's reputation and customer service

Tells what action to take

Tips for Persuasive Claims and Complaints

- Begin with a compliment, point of agreement, statement of the problem, or brief review of the action you have taken to resolve the problem.
- Provide identifying data.
- Prove that your claim is valid; explain why the receiver is responsible.
- Attach document copies supporting your claim.
- Appeal to the receiver's fairness, ethical and legal responsibilities, and desire for customer satisfaction.
- Describe your feelings and your disappointment.
- Avoid sounding angry, emotional, or irrational.
- Close by telling exactly what you want done.

upset because her company was counting on these new Internet systems to reduce its phone bills. Instead, the handsets produced so much static that incoming and outgoing calls were all but impossible to hear. The full setup also proved to be too complex for the small business.

What's more, Jen was frustrated that the Return Merchandise Authorization form she filled out on the company's website seemed to have sunk into a black hole in cyberspace. She had reason to be angry! However, she resolved to use a moderate tone in writing her complaint e-mail because she knew that a calm, unemotional tone would be more effective. She opted for a positive opening, a well-supported claim, and a request for specific action in the closing.

Checklist

Using the AIDA Strategy to Request Actions, Make Claims, and Deliver Complaints

Prewrite

- Determine your purpose. Know exactly what you want to achieve.
- Anticipate the reaction of your audience. Remember that the receiver is thinking, *Why should I? What's in it for me? What's in it for you? Who cares?*

Gain Attention

- Use the indirect strategy rather than blurting out the request immediately.
- Begin with a problem description, unexpected statement, reader benefit, compliment, related facts, or stimulating question to grab attention.

Build Interest

- Convince the audience that your request is reasonable.

- Develop interest by using facts, statistics, examples, testimonials, and specific details.
- Establish your credibility, if necessary, by explaining your background and expertise. Use testimonials, expert opinion, or research if necessary.
- Support your request by tying facts to direct benefits (increased profits, more efficient operations, better customer relations, money savings, a returned favor) or indirect benefits (improving the community, giving back to the profession, helping the environment).
- In claims and complaints, be objective but prove the validity of your request.

Elicit Desire and Reduce Resistance

- Anticipate objections to your request by using *What if?* scenarios and provide compelling counterarguments.
- Demonstrate credibility and competence.
- In claims and complaints, use a moderate, unemotional tone.

Motivate Action

- Make a precise request that spells out exactly what you want done. Add a deadline if necessary.
- Repeat a key benefit, provide additional details, or offer an incentive. Express appreciation.
- Be confident without seeming pushy.

LEARNING OUTCOME

4 Write persuasive messages within organizations demonstrating your knowledge of interpersonal persuasion at work.

10-4 Writing Persuasive Messages in Digital Age Organizations

As noted earlier, the lines of authority are blurry in information age workplaces, and the roles of executives have changed. The old unbending command-and-control leadership structure in companies where workers would spend a lifetime has all but vanished. Gone are managers who expect strict adherence to rigid instructions. Today's fast-paced businesses require creativity and flexibility. Wise managers foster an environment of respect, psychological safety, and autonomous decision making. Empowered by technology, rank-and-file employees are comfortable leaving micromanaging toxic bosses behind. The best talent has choices.[26]

Offering benefits such as health insurance, flexible hours, and tuition-free college, Starbucks has been successful in reducing **churn**, i.e., turnover, so common in the industry. Starbucks employees are called *partners*, suggesting equal footing but also equal responsibility for the customer experience.[27] Although Zappos has rolled back the most radical aspects of its experiment, the Amazon-owned Internet shoe seller has salvaged key elements of **holacracy**. In its purest form, holacracy is a flat organizational structure of self-managed workers, each of whom is given the power to introduce changes and make autonomous decisions to deliver "WOW service" in Zappos-speak.[28] At productivity company Evernote, the organizational structure is open and egalitarian, too. Individual offices and other perks suggesting seniority or status don't exist in the modern sweeping HQ space in Redwood City, California.[29]

This shift in authority is affecting the writing strategies and the tone of workplace persuasive messages. You may still want to be indirect if you hope to persuade your boss to do something he or she will be reluctant to do; however, your boss, in turn, is less likely to be a toxic autocrat who relies on the power of position and just issues commands. Rather, today's executives increasingly bank on persuasion to achieve buy-in from subordinates.[30]

This section focuses on messages flowing downward and upward within organizations. Horizontal messages exchanged among coworkers resemble those discussed earlier in requesting actions.

10-4a Persuading Employees: Messages Flowing Downward

Employees need to know how to perform their jobs and what is expected of them; therefore, instructions or directives moving downward from superiors to subordinates usually require little persuasion. Messages such as information about procedures, equipment, or customer service customarily use the direct strategy, with the purpose immediately stated.

However, some organizations encourage employees to join programs to stop smoking, lose weight, or start exercising. Organizations may also ask employees to participate in capacities outside their work roles—such as spending their free time volunteering for charity projects. In such cases, the four-part indirect AIDA strategy provides a helpful structure.

Because many executives today rely on buy-in instead of exercising raw power, messages flowing downward require attention to tone. Warm words and a conversational tone convey a caring attitude. Persuasive requests coming from trusted superiors are more likely to be accepted than requests from dictatorial executives who rely on threats and punishments to secure compliance. The proverbial carrot has always been more persuasive than the stick. Because the words *should* and *must* sometimes convey a negative tone, be careful in using them.

Model Document 10.4 shows an e-mail by Leticia Massey, director of HR Staffing and Training at a large bank. Her goal is to persuade employees to participate in HandsOn Suburban Chicago Day, a fund-raising and community service event that the bank sponsors. In addition to volunteering their services for a day, employees also have to pay $30 to register! You can see that this is no small persuasion task for Leticia.

Leticia decides to follow the AIDA four-part indirect strategy beginning with gaining attention. Notice, for example, that she strives to capture attention by describing specific benefits of volunteering in suburban Chicago. The second paragraph of this persuasive message builds interest by listing examples of what volunteers have accomplished during previous HandsOn Suburban Chicago events. To reduce resistance, the third paragraph explains why the $30 fee makes sense. To motivate action in the closing, Leticia saved a strong indirect benefit. The bank will chip in $30 for every employee who volunteers before the deadline. This significant indirect benefit along with the direct benefits of having fun and joining colleagues in a community activity combine to create a strong persuasive message.

10-4b Persuading the Boss: Messages Flowing Upward

Managers are just as resistant to change as others are. Convincing management to adopt a procedure or invest in a product or new equipment requires skillful communication. Providing facts, figures, and evidence is critical when submitting a recommendation to your boss. When selling an idea to management, strive to make a strong dollars-and-cents case. A request that emphasizes how the proposal saves money or benefits the business is more persuasive than one that simply announces a good deal or tells how a plan works.

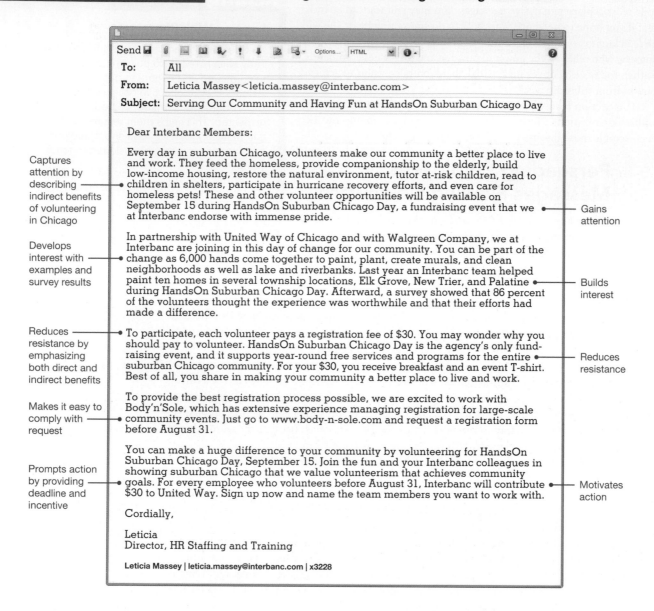

Captures attention by describing indirect benefits of volunteering in Chicago

Develops interest with examples and survey results

Reduces resistance by emphasizing both direct and indirect benefits

Makes it easy to comply with request

Prompts action by providing deadline and incentive

Gains attention

Builds interest

Reduces resistance

Motivates action

Send 🖫   Options... HTML

To: All

From: Leticia Massey<leticia.massey@interbanc.com>

Subject: Serving Our Community and Having Fun at HandsOn Suburban Chicago Day

Dear Interbanc Members:

Every day in suburban Chicago, volunteers make our community a better place to live and work. They feed the homeless, provide companionship to the elderly, build low-income housing, restore the natural environment, tutor at-risk children, read to children in shelters, participate in hurricane recovery efforts, and even care for homeless pets! These and other volunteer opportunities will be available on September 15 during HandsOn Suburban Chicago Day, a fundraising event that we at Interbanc endorse with immense pride.

In partnership with United Way of Chicago and with Walgreen Company, we at Interbanc are joining in this day of change for our community. You can be part of the change as 6,000 hands come together to paint, plant, create murals, and clean neighborhoods as well as lake and riverbanks. Last year an Interbanc team helped paint ten homes in several township locations, Elk Grove, New Trier, and Palatine during HandsOn Suburban Chicago Day. Afterward, a survey showed that 86 percent of the volunteers thought the experience was worthwhile and that their efforts had made a difference.

To participate, each volunteer pays a registration fee of $30. You may wonder why you should pay to volunteer. HandsOn Suburban Chicago Day is the agency's only fund-raising event, and it supports year-round free services and programs for the entire suburban Chicago community. For your $30, you receive breakfast and an event T-shirt. Best of all, you share in making your community a better place to live and work.

To provide the best registration process possible, we are excited to work with Body'n'Sole, which has extensive experience managing registration for large-scale community events. Just go to www.body-n-sole.com and request a registration form before August 31.

You can make a huge difference to your community by volunteering for HandsOn Suburban Chicago Day, September 15. Join the fun and your Interbanc colleagues in showing suburban Chicago that we value volunteerism that achieves community goals. For every employee who volunteers before August 31, Interbanc will contribute $30 to United Way. Sign up now and name the team members you want to work with.

Cordially,

Leticia
Director, HR Staffing and Training

Leticia Massey | leticia.massey@interbanc.com | x3228

In describing an idea to your boss, state it confidently and fairly. Don't undermine your suggestions with statements such as *This may sound crazy* or *I know we tried this once before but. . . .* Show that you have thought through the suggestion by describing the risks involved as well as the potential benefits. You may wonder whether you should even mention the downside of a suggestion. Most bosses will be relieved and impressed to know that you have considered the risks as well as the benefits to a proposal.[32] Two-sided arguments are generally more persuasive because they make you sound credible and fair. Presenting only one side of a proposal reduces its effectiveness because such a proposal seems biased, subjective, and flawed.

Persuasive messages traveling upward require a special sensitivity to tone. When asking superiors to change views or take action, use phrases such as *we suggest* and *we recommend* rather than *you must* and *we should.* Avoid sounding pushy or argumentative. Strive for a conversational, yet professional tone that conveys warmth, competence, and confidence.

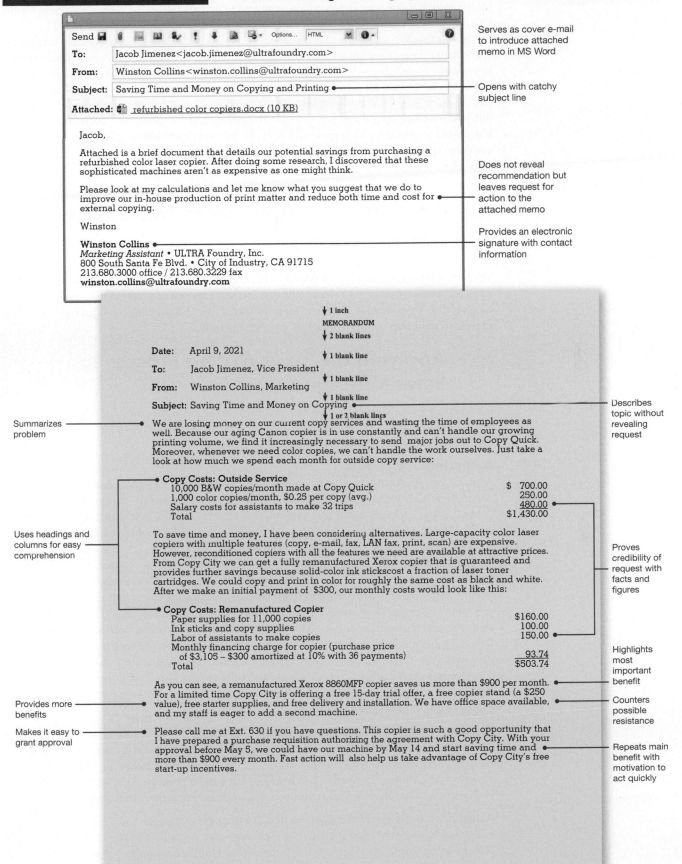

Serves as cover e-mail to introduce attached memo in MS Word

Opens with catchy subject line

Does not reveal recommendation but leaves request for action to the attached memo

Provides an electronic signature with contact information

Email portion:

Send 📧 | Options... | HTML | ❓

To: Jacob Jimenez<jacob.jimenez@ultrafoundry.com>

From: Winston Collins<winston.collins@ultrafoundry.com>

Subject: Saving Time and Money on Copying and Printing

Attached: 📎 refurbished color copiers.docx (10 KB)

Jacob,

Attached is a brief document that details our potential savings from purchasing a refurbished color laser copier. After doing some research, I discovered that these sophisticated machines aren't as expensive as one might think.

Please look at my calculations and let me know what you suggest that we do to improve our in-house production of print matter and reduce both time and cost for external copying.

Winston

Winston Collins
Marketing Assistant • ULTRA Foundry, Inc.
800 South Santa Fe Blvd. • City of Industry, CA 91715
213.680.3000 office / 213.680.3229 fax
winston.collins@ultrafoundry.com

Memo portion:

↓ 1 inch
MEMORANDUM
↓ 2 blank lines

Date: April 9, 2021
↓ 1 blank line
To: Jacob Jimenez, Vice President
↓ 1 blank line
From: Winston Collins, Marketing
↓ 1 blank line
Subject: Saving Time and Money on Copying
↓ 1 or 2 blank lines

Summarizes problem

Describes topic without revealing request

We are losing money on our current copy services and wasting the time of employees as well. Because our aging Canon copier is in use constantly and can't handle our growing printing volume, we find it increasingly necessary to send major jobs out to Copy Quick. Moreover, whenever we need color copies, we can't handle the work ourselves. Just take a look at how much we spend each month for outside copy service:

Uses headings and columns for easy comprehension

Copy Costs: Outside Service

10,000 B&W copies/month made at Copy Quick	$ 700.00
1,000 color copies/month, $0.25 per copy (avg.)	250.00
Salary costs for assistants to make 32 trips	480.00
Total	$1,430.00

Proves credibility of request with facts and figures

To save time and money, I have been considering alternatives. Large-capacity color laser copiers with multiple features (copy, e-mail, fax, LAN fax, print, scan) are expensive. However, reconditioned copiers with all the features we need are available at attractive prices. From Copy City we can get a fully remanufactured Xerox copier that is guaranteed and provides further savings because solid-color ink stickscost a fraction of laser toner cartridges. We could copy and print in color for roughly the same cost as black and white. After we make an initial payment of $300, our monthly costs would look like this:

Copy Costs: Remanufactured Copier

Paper supplies for 11,000 copies	$160.00
Ink sticks and copy supplies	100.00
Labor of assistants to make copies	150.00
Monthly financing charge for copier (purchase price of $3,105 – $300 amortized at 10% with 36 payments)	93.74
Total	$503.74

Highlights most important benefit

As you can see, a remanufactured Xerox 8860MFP copier saves us more than $900 per month. For a limited time Copy City is offering a free 15-day trial offer, a free copier stand (a $250 value), free starter supplies, and free delivery and installation. We have office space available, and my staff is eager to add a second machine.

Provides more benefits

Counters possible resistance

Makes it easy to grant approval

Please call me at Ext. 630 if you have questions. This copier is such a good opportunity that I have prepared a purchase requisition authorizing the agreement with Copy City. With your approval before May 5, we could have our machine by May 14 and start saving time and more than $900 every month. Fast action will also help us take advantage of Copy City's free start-up incentives.

Repeats main benefit with motivation to act quickly

When Marketing Assistant Winston Collins wanted his boss to authorize the purchase of a multifunction color laser copier, he knew he had to be persuasive. His memo, shown in Model Document 10.5, illustrates an effective approach.

Notice that Winston's memo isn't short. A successful persuasive message typically takes more space than a direct message because proving a case requires evidence. In the end, Winston chose to send his memo as an e-mail attachment accompanied by a polite, short e-mail because he wanted to keep the document format in MS Word intact. He also felt that the message was too long to paste into his e-mail program. The subject line announces the purpose of the message but without disclosing the actual request. The strength of the persuasive document in Model Document 10.5 is in the clear presentation of comparison figures showing how much money the company can save by purchasing a remanufactured copier.

LEARNING OUTCOME

5 Create effective and ethical direct-mail and e-mail sales messages.

10-5 Creating Effective Sales Messages in Print and Online

The best sales messages, whether delivered by direct mail or by e-mail, have much in common. They use persuasion to promote specific products and services. In this section we look at how to apply the 3-x-3 writing process to sales messages. We also present techniques developed by experts to craft effective sales messages, in print and online.

10-5a Applying the 3-x-3 Writing Process to Sales Messages

Marketing professionals analyze and perfect every aspect of a sales message to encourage consumers to read and act on the message. Like the experts, you will want to pay close attention to analysis and adaptation before writing the actual message.

Analyzing the Product. Prior to sitting down to write a sales message promoting a product, you must study the item carefully. What can you learn about its design, construction, raw materials, and manufacturing process? What can you learn about its ease of use, efficiency, durability, and applications? Be sure to consider warranties, service, price, premiums, exclusivity, and special appeals. At the same time, evaluate the competition so that you can compare your product's strengths with the competitor's weaknesses.

Now you are ready to identify your central selling point, the main theme of your appeal. In past recruiting ad campaigns, the U.S. Marine Corps often focused on themes that emphasized humanitarian aid in unstable regions. Most recently, though, the Corps highlighted "fight" as its central selling point. Dramatic battle visuals were geared to appeal to scrappy Gen Z recruits who are tough and resilient, key attributes for leathernecks. The Marines' top recruiter, Maj. Gen. Paul Kennedy, chose a streaming broadcast to reach out to athletic 18- to 24-year-old cord cutters who have overcome challenges and are fighters. "We want young, tough, smart warriors that want to continue to seek challenges," Kennedy said, "and we're seeking them from men and women from all walks of life."[33] Analyzing your product and studying the competition help you determine what to emphasize in your sales message.

Determining the Purpose of a Sales Message. Equally as important as analyzing the product is determining the specific purpose of your message. Do you want the reader to call for a free video and brochure? Listen to a podcast on your website? Fill out an order form? Send a credit card authorization? Before you write the first word of your message, know what response you want and what central selling point you will emphasize to achieve that purpose.

Adapting a Sales Message to Its Audience. Despite today's predominance of e-mail marketing over direct mail, in terms of response rates, sales letters and other direct mail pieces win by a mile. Although the USPS mail volume dropped almost 30 percent over the last

15 years, the direct mail response rates are climbing.[34] Direct mail achieves an average response rate of 9 percent from a house list (previous customers) and 4.9 percent from a prospect list, as opposed to a paltry 1 percent response rate for e-mail overall. At 15.1 percent, letter-sized direct mail generates the highest percentage of leads.[35] Marketers today are sending more tailored offers to people who appreciate receiving them. Experts believe that direct mail still is an invaluable channel in a strategic marketing mix.

The response rate can be increased dramatically by targeting the audience through selected database mailing lists. Let's say you are selling fitness equipment. A good mailing list might come from subscribers to fitness or exercise magazines, whom you would expect to have similar interests, needs, and demographics (age, income, and other characteristics). With this knowledge you can adapt the sales message to a specific audience.

10-5b Crafting Successful Sales Messages

Direct mail is usually part of multichannel or omnichannel marketing campaigns. These messages are a powerful means to make sales, generate leads, boost retail traffic, solicit donations, and direct consumers to websites. Direct mail is a great channel for personalized, tangible, three-dimensional messages that are less invasive than telephone solicitations and less reviled than unsolicited and relentless e-mail. The future of direct mail advertising seems bright, considering that a significant number of millennials (77 percent) pay attention to it, surpassing other generations. The largest cohort in the U.S. labor force, millennials are most likely to scan and read direct mail and share it with others.[37] More than a third of millennials look forward to their daily snail mail; a full 95 percent of eighteen- to twenty-nine-year-olds respond positively to receiving personal cards and letters.[38]

Studies show that physical direct mail appears to have a greater emotional impact than digital ad content. Brain scans in a USPS-sponsored neuromarketing study suggested that physical materials "leave a longer lasting impact for easy recall when making a purchase decision."[39] A UK Royal Mail study attributed the enduring effectiveness of direct mail to its tactile heft: "Giving, receiving and handling tangible objects remain deep and intuitive parts of the human experience."[40] Figure 10.5 juxtaposes the most relevant features of traditional direct-mail and digital sales messages.

10-5c Betting on Highly Targeted, Relevant Direct Mail

Professionals who specialize in traditional direct-mail campaigns have made it a science. They analyze a market, develop an effective mailing list, study the product, prepare a sophisticated campaign aimed at a target audience, and motivate the reader to act. You have probably received many direct-mail pieces, often called junk mail. These mailings typically contain a sales letter, a brochure, a price list, illustrations of the product, testimonials, and other persuasive appeals. Chances are they will keep coming, but they will be a lot more relevant to you and your spending habits.

Today's marketers take advantage of technology to connect digital leads and direct-mail appeals, resulting in a boost in effectiveness for both. They call this synergy **retargeting**, the act of targeting again the consumers who have previously visited a brand's website. Tracking technology allows advertisers to match website visitors to their name and postal address.[41] Don't be surprised, therefore, when you receive a direct mail piece from the brand whose website you have visited. Advertisers like retargeting because it links online and offline marketing. Privacy advocates are alarmed by the practice and demand stricter control over user data.[42]

Characteristics of Traditional Versus Online Sales Messages

Traditional Direct Mail (Sales Letter)	E-Commerce (E-Mail, Social Media Messages)
Creating static content (hard copy)	Creating dynamic digital content
Anticipating a single response (inquiry, sale)	Creating engagement instead of selling overtly
Resorting to "spray and pray" approach rather than building communities	Building one-to-one relationships and communities around brands
Single communication channel	Multiple communication channels
Limited response	Potentially unlimited responses
Monologue	Dialogue, potential for mass diffusion
Private response	Public, shared response
Asynchronous (delayed) response	Instant, real-time response possible
Passive	Interactive, participatory
Promoter-generated content	User-generated content
The needs of target groups must be anticipated and met in advance.	Consumers expect that brands understand their unique needs and deliver.
Direct mail is preferred for information about insurance, financial services, and health care; excellent channel for offline customers.	**Savvy brands respond nimbly to customer participation; today's sophisticated consumers dislike "hard sell."**

10-5d Considering the Value of Sales Letters

Because sales letters are generally written by specialists, you may never write one on the job. Why learn how to write a sales letter? Learning the techniques of sales writing will help you be more successful in any communication that requires persuasion and promotion. What's more, you will recognize sales strategies directed at you, which will make you a more perceptive consumer of ideas, products, and services.

Your primary goal in writing a sales message is to get someone to devote a few moments of attention to it. You may be promoting a product, a service, an idea, or yourself. In each case the most effective messages will follow the AIDA strategy and (a) gain attention, (b) build interest, (c) elicit desire and reduce resistance, and (d) motivate action. This is the same recipe we studied earlier, but the ingredients are different.

Gaining Attention in Sales Messages. One of the most critical elements of a sales message is its opening paragraph. This opener should be short (one to five lines), honest, relevant, and stimulating. Marketing pros have found that eye-catching typographical arrangements or provocative messages, such as the following, can hook a reader's attention:

- **Offer:** *Sign up now and get a free iPad to enjoy your programming on the go!*

- **Promise:** *Now you can raise your sales income by 50 percent or even more with the proven techniques found in . . . .*

- **Question:** *Why wait in the Starbucks line for a pitiful paper cup when for $20 you can have the Chiseled Chrome Coffee Cup, a handsome stylish tumbler of your own to refill every morning?*

- **Quotation or proverb:** *Automotive pioneer Henry Ford once said, "A business that makes nothing but money is a poor business."*

- **Fact:** *The Greenland Eskimos ate more fat than anyone in the world. And yet . . . they had virtually no heart disease.*

Oranzy Photography/Shutterstock.com

FOR THE RECORD

Discouraging Risky Behavior

A survey by the AAA Foundation for Traffic Safety found that 97 percent of people consider texting or e-mailing while driving a serious safety threat. However, 41 percent confessed to such risky behavior in the last 30 days. To combat this threat, the Auto Club cites sobering annual numbers of fatalities due to distracted driving (3,166 victims), but it also warns of serious costs from insufficient insurance liability limits, high fines, even punitive damages, and—most recently—points imposed on drivers who violate the laws governing handheld devices.[43] What strategy is this and is it likely to change risky behavior?

- **Product feature and its benefit:** *The Atlas sock is made from cotton, polyester, and carbonized coffee. Yup! Coffee helps filter odor, but equally important, we use pressure mapping and thermal imaging to create a ridiculously comfortable sock!*

- **Startling statement:** *Bigger houses cost less.*

- **Personalized action setting:** *It's 4:30 p.m. and you've got to make a decision. You need everybody's opinion, no matter where they are. Before you call them one at a time, call a Cisco Webex Meeting.*

Other openings calculated to capture attention include a solution to a problem, an anecdote, a personalized statement using the receiver's name, and a relevant current event.

Building Interest With Rational and Emotional Appeals.

In this phase of your sales message, you should clearly describe the product or service. In simple language emphasize the central selling points that you identified during your prewriting analysis. Those selling points can be developed using rational or emotional appeals.

Rational appeals are associated with reason and intellect. They translate selling points into references to making or saving money, increasing efficiency, or making the best use of resources. In general, rational appeals are appropriate when a product is expensive, long-lasting, or important to health, security, or financial success.

Emotional appeals relate to status, ego, and sensual feelings. Appealing to the emotions is sometimes effective when a product is inexpensive, short-lived, or nonessential. Many clever sales messages, however, combine emotional and rational strategies for a dual appeal. Consider these examples:

Rational Appeal

You can buy the things you need and want, pay household bills, and pay off higher-cost loans and credit cards—as soon as you are approved and your ChoiceCredit card account is opened.

Emotional Appeal

Leave the urban bustle behind and escape to sun-soaked Bermuda! To recharge your batteries with an injection of sun and surf, all you need is your bathing suit, a little suntan lotion, and your ChoiceCredit card.

Dual Appeal

New ChoiceCredit cardholders are immediately eligible for a $200 travel certificate and additional discounts at fun-filled resorts. Save up to 40 percent while lying on a beach in picturesque, sun-soaked Bora-Bora, the year-round resort.

A physical description of your product is not enough, however. Zig Ziglar, thought by some to be America's greatest salesperson, pointed out that no matter how well you know your product,

Ethics ✔ Check

Playing to Fear, Guilt, and Other Emotions

Direct marketers sometimes resort to scare tactics—for example, to make us purchase alarm systems or subscribe to monitoring services. They may also appeal to our compassion and guilt before the holidays in soliciting money for the less fortunate. Are such emotional appeals ethical?

no one is persuaded by cold, hard facts alone. In the end, people buy because of product benefits.[44] Your job is to translate those cold facts into warm feelings and reader benefits. A **feature** is what your product is or does; a **benefit** is how the audience can use it. Let's say a sales message promotes a hand cream made with aloe and cocoa butter extracts, along with vitamin A. Those facts become, *Nature's hand helpers—including soothing aloe and cocoa extracts, along with firming vitamin A—form invisible gloves that protect your sensitive skin against the hardships of work, harsh detergents, and constant environmental assaults.*

Reducing Resistance and Building Desire.

Marketing specialists use a number of techniques to overcome resistance and build desire. When price is an obstacle, consider these suggestions:

- Delay mentioning price until after you've created a desire for the product.
- Show the price in small units, such as the price per issue of a magazine.
- Demonstrate how the reader saves money—for instance, by subscribing for two or three years.
- Compare your prices with those of a competitor.

In addition, you need to anticipate other objections and questions the receiver may have. When possible, translate these objections into selling points (*If you are worried about training your staff members on the new software, remember that our offer includes $1,000 worth of on-site one-on-one instruction*). Be sure, of course, that your claims are accurate, and do not stretch the truth. Other techniques to overcome resistance and prove the credibility of the product include the following:

- **Testimonials:** *"I never stopped eating, yet I lost 107 pounds."* — *Tina Rivers, Greenwood, South Carolina*
- **Names of satisfied users** (with permission, of course): *Enclosed is a partial list of private pilots who enthusiastically subscribe to our service.*
- **Money-back guarantee or warranty:** *We offer the longest warranties in the business—all parts and service on-site for five years!*
- **Free trial or sample:** *We are so confident that you will like our new accounting program that we want you to try it absolutely free.*
- **Performance tests, polls, or awards:** *Our TP-3000 was named Best Internet Phone, and Etown.com voted it VoIP System of the Year.*

Motivating Action at the Conclusion of a Sales Message.

All the effort put into a sales message goes to waste if the reader fails to act. To make it easy for readers to act, you can provide a reply card, a stamped and preaddressed envelope, a toll-free telephone number, a smartphone-readable matrix bar code, a Web address, or a promise of a follow-up call. Because readers often need an extra push, consider including additional motivators or inducements, such as the following:

- **Offer a gift:** *You will receive a free iPad mini with the purchase of any new car.*
- **Promise an incentive:** *With every new paid subscription, we will plant a tree in one of America's Heritage Forests.*
- **Limit the offer:** *Call now! The first 100 customers receive free travel mugs.*
- **Set a deadline:** *You must act before June 1 to take advantage of these low prices.*
- **Guarantee satisfaction:** *We will return your full payment if you are not entirely satisfied—no questions asked.*

The final paragraph of the sales letter carries the punch line. This is where you tell readers what you want them to do and give them reasons for doing it. Most sales letters also include postscripts because they make irresistible reading. Even readers who might skim over or bypass paragraphs are drawn to a P.S. Therefore, use a postscript to reveal your strongest motivator, to add a special inducement for a quick response, or to re-emphasize a central selling point.

Although you want to be persuasive in sales letters, you must guard against overstepping legal and ethical boundaries. Information contained in sales letters has landed some writers in hot water. See the accompanying Ethical Insight box to learn how to stay out of trouble.

Ethical Insights

Legal and Ethical Quandaries in Sales Messages and Online Reviews

In promoting products and writing sales messages, be careful about the words you use and the claims you make. Watch out for paid reviews. How far can marketers go in praising and selling their products?

- **Puffery.** You might see advertisements that proclaim, *We have the perfect car for you!* or *Our coffee will blow your mind!* Called **puffery**, such promotional claims are not taken literally by reasonable consumers. Such subjective statements are accepted as puffery because they puff up, or exaggerate. They are considered **hyperbole**. Surprisingly, this kind of sales exaggeration is not illegal. However, when sales claims consist of objective statements that cannot be verified (*Our cars are the most reliable vehicles in town*), they become deceptive advertising.

- **Deceptive advertising.** If you write that your coffee is organic and responsibly sourced, you had better have evidence to support the claim. Such a claim goes beyond puffery and requires proof. This is why reputable businesses often seek certification from government or independent oversight organizations. Dietary supplements are regulated as food, not drugs, and are not subject to approval or testing as long as they make only general "structure/function claims" about how a nutrient affects the body, e.g., "calcium builds strong bones." However, manufacturers are not allowed to say their products treat diseases such as Alzheimer's or osteoporosis.[45] Goop, Gwyneth Paltrow's lifestyle company, settled a lawsuit by ten California counties for advertising women's health products without competent and reliable scientific evidence.[46]

- **Celebrities.** The unauthorized use of a celebrity's name, likeness, or nickname is not permitted in sales messages. Celebrity chef Cat Cora won a $565,000 judgment against the Fatbird restaurant group in New York for misusing Cora's name, image, and recipes without compensation.[47] Pop star Ariana Grande sued clothing company Forever 21 over Instagram posts that in her view depict a "look-alike model" dressed like the singer. The lawsuit alleged that Forever 21 was falsely insinuating an affiliation with Ariana Grande.[48] The so-called right of publicity allows claims when a person's name, likeness or voice, i.e., any identifiable traits, are used for commercial purposes without permission and/or pay.

- **Misleading promises.** Multilevel marketing companies such as Herbalife frequently invite scrutiny. In a $200 million settlement, the Federal Trade Commission forced the company to pay back consumers it had wooed with false promises of a lucrative business opportunity and big bucks from retail sales of Herbalife products. Moreover, the FTC forced the company to change its business model of rewarding distributors who buy products and recruit others to join and themselves buy products.[49] On its webpages the FTC debunks preposterous claims in ads for weight-loss supplements, warning consumers of potentially harmful drugs or chemicals not listed on the product label.[50] Devices such as electronic muscle stimulators are overseen by the U.S. Food & Drug Administration. The agency not only exposes promises that regular use will produce "rock hard abs" without working out, but it warns about "shocks, burns, bruising, skin irritation, and pain" caused by shoddy, noncompliant devices.[51]

- **Paid online reviews.** The FTC also mandates full disclosure when a merchant and a promoter have a financial relationship. Lumos Labs not only made bogus claims about the benefits of its Lumosity brain-training games, but the company also failed to disclose that it had used testimonials from customers who had received iPads, free trips, and other incentives for their reviews.[52] Skin-care brand Sunday Riley recently settled with the FTC for writing fake Sephora reviews for two years. The company got off with a warning.[53] The FTC also sued the marketer of the garcinia cambogia weight-loss supplement for using fake paid reviews to maintain a high Amazon rating and boost its sales. Fake reviews shake the public's trust. "People rely on reviews when they're shopping online," Andrew Smith, director of the FTC's Bureau of Consumer Protection, said. "When a company buys fake reviews to inflate its Amazon rating, it hurts both shoppers and companies that play by the rules."[54]

Putting Together All the Parts of a Sales Message. A direct-mail sales letter is the No. 2 preferred marketing medium right behind e-mail[55] because it can be personalized, directed to target audiences, and filled with a more complete message than other advertising media can. However, direct mail is more expensive than e-mail. That's why crafting and assembling all the parts of a sales message are so critical.

Model Document 10.6 shows a sales letter addressed to individuals and families who may need health insurance. To prompt the reader to respond to the mailing, the letter incorporates the effective four-part AIDA strategy. The writer first establishes the need for health coverage.

1 Prewriting

Analyze: The purpose is to persuade the reader to respond by calling, chatting with a representative online, or returning a reply card to obtain information.

Anticipate: The audience is individuals and families who may be interested in health insurance. The central selling point is the value and flexibility of the various health plans.

Adapt: Because readers will be reluctant, use the indirect pattern, AIDA.

2 Drafting

Research: Gather facts to promote your product and its benefits.

Organize: Gain attention by addressing the cost of health insurance. Emphasize that insurance protects assets, and focus on reader benefits. Motivate action by promising a no-obligation quote. Encourage a response with a toll-free number and an easy-reply card.

Draft: Prepare a first draft for a pilot study.

3 Revising

Edit: Use short paragraphs and short sentences. Replace *bankrupt you* with *break the bank.*

Proofread: Use bulleted list for features and benefits description. Set headings boldface, and underscore other important information. *Hyphenate easy-to-understand.* Check for any medical or bureaucratic jargon.

Evaluate: Monitor the response rate to this letter to assess its effectiveness.

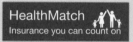

HealthMatch
Insurance you can count on

Choose our health plans if you want VALUE!

Confused about health insurance? You're not alone.

Call a licensed expert at **(877) 522-0417.**

Visit us online at **www.healthmatch.com.**

Return the completed reply card to us by mail.

June 17, 2021

Mr. Keenan Vanwinkle
96 Briarwood Drive
Hampton, VA 23646

Dear Mr. Vanwinkle:

(Addresses common fear) *(Gains attention)*
Do you think you can't afford quality health insurance? Let us try to change your mind. HealthMatch offers attractive health plans that fit a range of budgets, needs, and lifestyles. Whether you're a recent graduate, self-employed, retiring early, or working without health insurance, one of our plans could be right for you.

(Establishes need for health insurance) *(Builds interest)*
Health care needs can rise at any time in life, even in healthy and fit individuals. Anyone can succumb to an infectious disease or become sidelined by an accident. Knowing that such an event won't break the bank will give you peace of mind.

(Emphasizes central selling point and reader benefits) *(Elicits desire and reduces resistance)*
Choose from a variety of plans and benefits at affordable rates, starting at $110. Our individual and family plans feature important benefits to keep you healthy:
- Preventive care comes at no additional cost, including your annual exam!
- Generic and brand-name prescription drug coverage will save you money every time.
- Chiropractic care, acupuncture, and rehabilitation coverage will help keep you in shape.
- A range of deductible options that work for your budget will put coverage within reach.
- Optional dental, vision, and life insurance coverage will protect you from unexpected expense.

Visit our website **www.healthmatch.com** for lots of ideas on how you can achieve your wellness goals. Learn about discount programs that help you save money and achieve a healthier lifestyle—at no additional charge.

(Repeats central sales pitch in last two paragraphs) *(Motivates action)*
Compare HealthMatch plans when you're ready. No obligation. No pressure. Simple! Call us at **(877) 522-0417,** and we will answer your questions in clear, easy-to-understand language, without medical or bureaucratic jargon. We promise. No sales types will hound you, either. That's a promise too.

Stay well,

Trina Davies

Trina Davies
Director of Individual and Family Care

(Spotlights free offer in PS to prompt immediate reply)
PS Call **(877) 522-0417** today for your free quote or to apply for coverage. The first 30 callers will receive a free heart-rate monitor. We're here to help improve the health of the people we serve.

Then she develops a rational central selling point (a variety of affordable health plans for every budget offered without sales pressure and medical jargon) and repeats this selling point in all the components of the letter. This sales letter saves its strongest motivator—a free heart-rate monitor for the first 30 callers—for the high-impact P.S. line.

10-5e Writing Successful E-Mail Sales Messages

Much like traditional direct mail, e-mail marketing can attract new customers, keep existing ones, encourage future sales, cross-sell, and cut costs. However, e-marketers can create and send a promotion in half the time it takes to print and distribute a traditional message. To reach today's consumer, marketers must target their e-mails well if they wish to even get their messages opened. "Customers want to hear from you, but their expectations are rising. They increasingly demand emails that are personalized, contextual, and relevant," says one marketing specialist.[56]

Selling by E-Mail. If you will be writing online sales messages for your organization, try using the following techniques gleaned from the best-performing e-mail marketers. Although much e-marketing dazzles receivers with colorful graphics, we focus on the words involved in persuasive sales messages. Earlier in the chapter, Model Document 10.1 showing an e-mail sales message from Eat Naked Kitchen demonstrates many of the principles discussed here.

The first rule of e-marketing is to communicate only with those who have given permission. By sending messages only to opt-in folks, you greatly increase your open rate—e-mails that will be opened. E-mail users detest spam. However, receivers are highly receptive to offers tailored specifically to them. Remember that today's customer is somebody—not just anybody. Following are a few guidelines that will help you create effective e-mail sales messages:

- **Craft a catchy subject line.** Include an audience-specific location (*Emporium in Vegas Opens Soon!*); ask a meaningful question (*What's Your Dream Vacation?*); and use no more than 50 characters. Promise realistic solutions. Offer discounts or premiums.

- **Keep the main information "above the fold."** E-mails should be top heavy. Primary points should appear early in the message (before the first fold in a letter) so that they capture the reader's attention.

- **Make the message short, conversational, and focused.** Because on-screen text is taxing to read, be brief. Focus on one or two central selling points only.

- **Sprinkle testimonials throughout the copy.** Consumers' own words are the best sales copy. These comments can serve as callouts or be integrated into the copy.

- **Provide a means for opting out.** It's a legal requirement and polite business tactic to include a statement that tells receivers how to unsubscribe from the sender's marketing e-mails.

10-5f Writing Short Persuasive Messages Online

Increasingly, writers are turning to social network posts to promote their businesses, further their causes, and build their online personas. As we have seen, social media are not primarily suited for overt selling; however, tweets and other online posts can be used to influence others and to project a professional, positive social online presence.

Typically, organizations and individuals with followers post updates of their events, exploits, thoughts, and experiences. In persuasive tweets and posts, writers try to pitch offers, prompt specific responses, or draw the attention of their audiences to interesting events and media links. Figure 10.6 displays a sampling of persuasive tweets.

Note that the compact format of a tweet requires conciseness and efficiency. Don't expect the full four-part AIDA strategy to be represented in a 280-character Twitter message. Instead, you may see attention getters and calls for action, both of which must be catchy and intriguing. Regardless, many of the principles of persuasion apply even to micromessages.

Whether you actually write sales messages on the job or merely receive them, you will better understand their organization and appeals by reviewing this chapter and the tips in the following checklist:

FIGURE 10.6 Analyzing Persuasive Tweets

jonah berger ✔ @j1berger · Feb 1
Have something you want to change?
Check out my new book, The Catalyst.
All about how to change minds, organizations, and the world.
Here's more information ow.ly/UxR550y5flx

Aéropostale ✔ @Aeropostale · Apr 29
Look like sunshine, feel like sunshine. Shop now and save 60% (or more) off site wide: bit.ly/3f4UTu0

JetBlue ✔ @JetBlue · Jan 17
It's almost #BlueMonday, the gloomiest day of the year. Share your winter view with us using #JetBlueMondayContest and @JetBlue—the most creative submissions will win round-trip flights* to PHX. No purch nec 48US/DC, 18+ Ends 11:59:59pmET 1/20/20 Rules@https://bit.ly/2u3riOK

REI ✔ @REI · Apr 25
Save 50% or more on all clothing at REI Outlet! Includes jackets, pants, tops, workout wear & more, thru 4/27. Online only.

UPS ✔ @UPS · Mar 24
Moving your business online? We can help. Sign up for a free UPS My Choice® for business account to get started. #ecommerce

Arianna Huffington ✔ @ariannahuff · Feb 22
This weekend, I write about deathbed photography, beauty in Bentonville and Billie Eilish's decision to unplug. Sign up to read my Weekly Thoughts: buff.ly/38QAlBX

Bill Gates ✔ @BillGates · Jun 18, 2019
I encourage software developers, inventors, and scientists to consider how they can use their skills to fight inequity.

jonah berger ✔ @j1berger · Mar 7
Want to change minds using social media?
Check out this new podcast with @Mike_Stelzner at @SMExaminer on the Catalyst.

Los Angeles Ronald McDonald House @LosAngelesRMH · May 1
Our families are LOVING the tasty treats from @ClifBar ! Thank you for providing an easy, portable, and nutritious snack for families to enjoy throughout their busiest of days 👍 #LARMH #KeepingFamiliesClose

Apple ✔ @Apple ⌄
Introducing the new iPad Pro. The world's most advanced mobile display. Faster than most PC laptops. Featuring Wide and Ultra Wide Pro cameras and LiDAR Scanner.

Susan G. Komen ✔ @SusanGKomen · Jan 31
Did you know you can help bring an end to #breastcancer by putting your feet to the pavement? Join @The3Day and walk an inspiring 60 miles in 3 days to show your commitment. Sign up now and save $20. Hurry, early bird pricing ends February 7! bit.ly/2RFvA8f

Deloitte ✔ @Deloitte · Jan 22
Are leaders prepared to fight global financial crime in the 4IR? Join LIVE from #WEF20 as Bob Contri, Deloitte's Global Financial Services Industry Leader, leads a panel of industry experts to discuss via #Periscope 🅿:
deloi.tt/2NLy2Yw

Publix ✔ @Publix · Sep 30, 2019
The Publix Stories Podcast is back for #InternationalPodcastDay! Our Dietitians provided great info on making better choices and the benefits of family meals. Tweet us some things your family does to make better food choices. spr.ly/601418QaA

Teach For America ✔ @TeachForAmerica · Dec 23, 2019
Are you interested in gaining policy experience on the national level? Apply now to join our 2020 Capitol Hill Fellows Program, which places alumni in year-long, paid Congressional staff positions.

suzeormanshow ✔ @SuzeOrmanShow · 1h
Today's the day to listen in to another #AskSuzeAnything podcast where I'm answering your questions. Listen in!

Mashable ✔ @mashable · 4m
The end of aging: Are you ready to live to 150?

Team Robert Cialdini @RobertCialdini · Feb 18
The ability to ethically influence the decisions and behaviors of others is incredibly useful. So, how is successful ethical persuasion best achieved? You can't afford to scroll past this post. ow.ly/XfiT50ypGDe

Team Robert Cialdini @RobertCialdini · Jan 31
Happy Friday! Did you know we have a youtube channel with loads of informative and entertaining videos? Watch a video or 2 over lunch or during your commute. Have a great and safe weekend. - Team C
#influence #persuasion #watch #youtube youtube.com/influenceatwork

Guy Kawasaki ✔ @GuyKawasaki · Apr 28
How will you weather the storm? I shared The Art of Perseverance on my podcast to help you your business and answer some questions I've been getting. bit.ly/2yM45mx #remarkablepeople

Source: Twitter, Inc.

Checklist

Preparing Persuasive Direct-Mail and E-Mail Sales Messages

Prewrite

- Analyze your product or service. What makes it special? What central selling points should you emphasize? How does it compare with the competition?

- Profile your audience. How will this product or service benefit this audience?

- Decide what you want the audience to do at the end of your message.

- For e-mails, send only to those who have opted in.

Gain Attention

- Describe a product feature, present a testimonial, make a startling statement, or show the reader in an action setting.

- Offer something valuable, promise the reader a result, or pose a stimulating question.

- Suggest a solution to a problem, offer a relevant anecdote, use the receiver's name, or mention a meaningful current event.

Build Interest

- Describe the product or service in terms of what it does for the reader. Connect cold facts with warm feelings and needs.

- Use rational appeals if the product or service is expensive, long-lasting, or important to health, security, or financial success. Use emotional appeals to suggest status, ego, or sensual feelings.

- Explain how the product or service can save or make money, reduce effort, improve health, produce pleasure, or boost status.

Elicit Desire and Reduce Resistance

- Counter anticipated reluctance with testimonials, money-back guarantees, attractive warranties, trial offers, or free samples.

- Build credibility with results of performance tests, polls, or awards.

- If price is not a selling feature, describe it in small units (*only 99 cents an issue*), show it as savings, or tell how it compares favorably with that of the competition.

Motivate Action

- Close by repeating a central selling point and describing an easy-to-take action.

- Prompt the reader to act immediately with a gift, incentive, limited offer, deadline, or guarantee of satisfaction.

- Put the strongest motivator in a postscript.

- In e-mails include an opportunity to opt out.

10-6 Crafting Persuasive Press Releases

LEARNING OUTCOME

6 Apply basic persuasive techniques in developing compelling press releases.

Press (news) releases announce important information to the media, whether traditional or digital. Such public announcements can feature new products, new managers, new facilities, sponsorships, participation in community projects, awards given or received, joint ventures, donations, or seminars and demonstrations. Naturally, organizations hope that the media will pick up this news and provide good publicity. However, purely self-serving or promotional information is not appealing to magazine and newspaper editors or to TV producers. To get them to read beyond the first sentence, press release writers follow these principles:

- Open with an attention-getting lead or a summary of the important facts.

- Include answers to the five *W*s and one *H* (*who, what, when, where, why,* and *how*) in the article—but not all in the first sentence!

- Appeal to the audience of the target media. Emphasize reader benefits written in the style of the focus publication or newscast.

- Present the most important information early, followed by supporting information. Don't put your best ideas last because they may be chopped off or ignored.

- Insert intriguing and informative quotations of chief decision makers to lend the news release credibility.

- Make the document readable and visually appealing. Limit the text to one or two double-spaced pages with attractive formatting.

- Look and sound credible—no typos, no imaginative spelling or punctuation, no factual errors.

The most important ingredient of a press release, of course, is *news*. Articles that merely plug products end up in the circular file, or they languish unread on a company website. The press release in Model Document 10.7 announced the launch of a unique breast cancer research study conducted by two reputable medical organizations, Dr. Susan Love Research Foundation and City of Hope. The announcement provides an appealing headline and describes the purpose as well as the process of the massive, long-term research. The Health of Women Study is unusual in that it employs crowdsourcing and actively involves huge numbers of subjects online and by mobile devices. Moreover, data will be shared with all interested researchers and the participants themselves.

The best press releases focus on information that appeals to a targeted audience. A breast cancer study focusing on the potential causes and prevention of the disease is likely to generate keen and wide-ranging interest. The credibility of the study's sponsors discourages sensationalist coverage. Indirectly, the nonprofit organizations may also attract more research subjects and donations. Model Document 10.7 illustrates many useful techniques for creating effective press releases.

Newspapers, magazines, and digital media are more likely to publish a press release that is informative, interesting, and helpful. The websites of many organizations today provide readily available media information including press releases and photos.

MODEL DOCUMENT 10.7 Press Release With a Broad Appeal

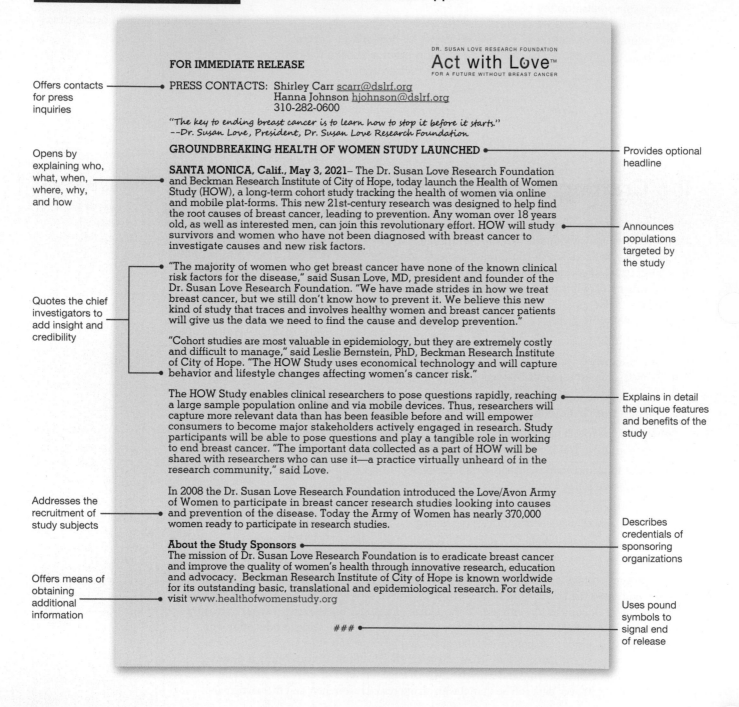

Offers contacts for press inquiries

Opens by explaining who, what, when, where, why, and how

Quotes the chief investigators to add insight and credibility

Addresses the recruitment of study subjects

Offers means of obtaining additional information

Provides optional headline

Announces populations targeted by the study

Explains in detail the unique features and benefits of the study

Describes credentials of sponsoring organizations

Uses pound symbols to signal end of release

DR. SUSAN LOVE RESEARCH FOUNDATION
Act with Love™
FOR A FUTURE WITHOUT BREAST CANCER

FOR IMMEDIATE RELEASE

PRESS CONTACTS: Shirley Carr scarr@dslrf.org
Hanna Johnson hjohnson@dslrf.org
310-282-0600

"The key to ending breast cancer is to learn how to stop it before it starts."
--Dr. Susan Love, President, Dr. Susan Love Research Foundation

GROUNDBREAKING HEALTH OF WOMEN STUDY LAUNCHED

SANTA MONICA, Calif., May 3, 2021– The Dr. Susan Love Research Foundation and Beckman Research Institute of City of Hope, today launch the Health of Women Study (HOW), a long-term cohort study tracking the health of women via online and mobile plat-forms. This new 21st-century research was designed to help find the root causes of breast cancer, leading to prevention. Any woman over 18 years old, as well as interested men, can join this revolutionary effort. HOW will study survivors and women who have not been diagnosed with breast cancer to investigate causes and new risk factors.

"The majority of women who get breast cancer have none of the known clinical risk factors for the disease," said Susan Love, MD, president and founder of the Dr. Susan Love Research Foundation. "We have made strides in how we treat breast cancer, but we still don't know how to prevent it. We believe this new kind of study that traces and involves healthy women and breast cancer patients will give us the data we need to find the cause and develop prevention."

"Cohort studies are most valuable in epidemiology, but they are extremely costly and difficult to manage," said Leslie Bernstein, PhD, Beckman Research Institute of City of Hope. "The HOW Study uses economical technology and will capture behavior and lifestyle changes affecting women's cancer risk."

The HOW Study enables clinical researchers to pose questions rapidly, reaching a large sample population online and via mobile devices. Thus, researchers will capture more relevant data than has been feasible before and will empower consumers to become major stakeholders actively engaged in research. Study participants will be able to pose questions and play a tangible role in working to end breast cancer. "The important data collected as a part of HOW will be shared with researchers who can use it—a practice virtually unheard of in the research community," said Love.

In 2008 the Dr. Susan Love Research Foundation introduced the Love/Avon Army of Women to participate in breast cancer research studies looking into causes and prevention of the disease. Today the Army of Women has nearly 370,000 women ready to participate in research studies.

About the Study Sponsors
The mission of Dr. Susan Love Research Foundation is to eradicate breast cancer and improve the quality of women's health through innovative research, education and advocacy. Beckman Research Institute of City of Hope is known worldwide for its outstanding basic, translational and epidemiological research. For details, visit www.healthofwomenstudy.org

###

Zooming In

Your Turn:
Applying Your Skills Against Vaping

As regulators started to close in and public outrage enveloped Juul, the company retreated to save its business model. Juul claimed it had never spent more than $10,000 total on influencers and soon ended the program. The e-cigarette maker did phase out most of its U.S.-based social media accounts—shuttering Facebook and Instagram and dialing down Twitter and YouTube.[57] Former CEO Kevin Burns insisted that 99 percent of all Juul-related social media content was now generated by third parties unaffiliated to his company. He blamed existing user-generated social media posts for the continued appeal of vaping to minors. Juul spokeswoman Christine Castro, concurred and said, "We have frustrations about how the product is glorified on social media."[58] In its advertising, Juul is now featuring more mature users and touting e-cigarettes as a better alternative to smoking.

Critics contend that the damage is already done because social media have taken on a life of their own, and key young people keep perpetuating the vaping fad: "Once you get kids doing it, you don't have to pay for it," Matt Myers, president of the Campaign for Tobacco-Free Kids, said. "It is 10 times dropping a rock in a still pond; the ripple just keeps going."[59]

Even after removing fruit flavors from the U.S. market—not in other markets, however—the mint and menthol flavors continue to be sold and account for 85 percent of Juul's sales in domestic retail stores. A National Youth Tobacco Survey found that more than 60 percent of high schoolers vape mint-flavored e-cigarettes, almost as many as those who used fruit-flavored pods.[60]

Your Task

The CDC has awarded a discretionary grant to your college. Participating in your school's service-learning option, you are competing with several teams to create an antivaping campaign. Create a persuasive strategy to counter the youth appeal of Juul. Tailor your campaign, and consider the most effective channels to use. Your instructor may ask you to summarize your strategy in an e-mail or memo. You may also be tasked with devising actual messages to raise awareness and make teens and young adults stop vaping.

SUMMARY OF LEARNING OUTCOMES

1 Explain digital age persuasion, identify time-proven persuasive techniques, and apply the 3-x-3 writing process to persuasive messages in print and online.

- Persuasion is the ability to use words and other symbols to influence an individual's attitudes and behaviors.

- Six psychological triggers prompt us to act and to believe: reciprocation, commitment, social proof, liking, authority, and scarcity.

- Digital age persuasion is prolific, widespread, far-reaching, and fast-moving.

- Persuasive techniques today are more subtle and misleading than those used in the past, as well as more complex and mediated by technology.

- Effective persuaders establish credibility, make a specific request, tie facts to benefits, recognize the power of loss, expect and overcome resistance, share solutions, and compromise.

- Before writing, communicators decide what they want the receiver to do or think; they adapt their message to their audience; and they collect information and organize it into an appropriate strategy. They are indirect if the audience might resist the request.

2 Describe the traditional four-part AIDA strategy for creating successful and ethical persuasive messages.

- Include four major elements to craft a persuasive message: gain attention, build interest, elicit desire while reducing resistance, and motivate action.

- Gain attention by opening with a problem, unexpected statement, reader benefit, compliment, related fact, or stimulating question.

- Build interest with facts, expert opinions, examples, details, and direct and indirect reader benefits.

- Elicit desire and reduce resistance by anticipating objections and presenting counterarguments.

- Conclude by motivating a specific action and making it easy for the reader to respond.
- As an ethical persuader, avoid distortion, exaggeration, and doublespeak when making persuasive arguments.

3 Craft persuasive messages that request actions, make claims, and deliver complaints.

- Think through your purpose and prepare a thoughtful message.
- Assume that receivers comply because they want to "give back" and because others may benefit.
- Understand that persuasive claims involve damaged products, billing mistakes, wrong shipments, warranty problems, faulty merchandise, and similar issues.
- Make a logical argument: Open with sincere praise, an objective statement of the problem, a point of agreement, or quick review of what you have done to resolve the problem.
- Use a moderate tone because anger and emotion are not effective persuaders; don't assume that the receiver intentionally deceived you.
- Appeal to the receiver's sense of responsibility and pride in the company's reputation.
- Close with a clear statement of what you want done: a refund, replacement, credit, or other action.

4 Write persuasive messages within organizations demonstrating your knowledge of interpersonal persuasion at work.

- Executives rely on persuasion and employee buy-in, not so much on the power of their position.
- When asking subordinates to volunteer for projects or to make lifestyle changes, organizations may use the AIDA strategy to persuade.
- In messages flowing downward, good writers use a conversational tone and warm words; they focus on direct and indirect benefits.
- In messages flowing upward, such as recommendations from subordinates to supervisors, providing evidence is critical; making a strong dollars-and-cents appeal whenever appropriate strengthens the argument.

- Two-sided arguments are more persuasive because they make writers sound credible and fair.

5 Create effective and ethical direct-mail and e-mail sales messages.

- Before composing sales messages, the writer must carefully analyze the product or service to establish the central selling point, determine the purpose, and adapt to the audience.
- Direct mail is part of multichannel campaigns, has a high response rate, and continues to have an emotional impact.
- Today's marketers link digital leads and direct-mail appeals to create a synergy they call *retargeting*.
- Effective sales messages begin with a short, honest, and relevant attention getter.
- Simple language is used to develop emotional and rational appeals and build interest; product features must be translated into reader benefits.
- Testimonials, money-back guarantees, and free trials can reduce resistance and elicit desire.
- A gift, incentive, or deadline can motivate action.
- E-commerce newsletters or pitches should be sent only to opt-in receivers; such e-mails begin with a catchy subject line, keep the main information "above the fold," are short and focused, convey urgency, include testimonials if available, and provide a means for unsubscribing.
- Tweets and other short persuasive social media posts can influence others and can project a professional presence; even brief posts may contain AIDA components.

6 Apply basic persuasive techniques in developing compelling press releases.

- Open with an attention-getting lead or summary of the important facts.
- Answer the questions *who, what, when, where, why,* and *how*.
- Write carefully to appeal to the audience of the target media.
- Present the most important information early, make your press release visually appealing, and make sure it looks and sounds credible.

Key Terms

opinion bubbles *326*

persuasion *326*

reactance *326*

microtarget *328*

AIDA *331*

direct benefit *333*

indirect benefit *333*

doublespeak *334*

churn *338*

holacracy *338*

retargeting *343*

rational appeals *345*

emotional appeals *345*

dual appeal *345*

feature *346*

benefit *346*

puffery *347*

hyperbole *347*

press release/news release *351*

ethos *357*

pathos *357*

logos *357*

kairos *357*

Critical Thinking

1. *Sit back in your first-class seat and sip a freshly stirred drink while letting 12 channels of superb audio wash over you—or snooze* is an example of what type of persuasive appeal? How does it compare to the following: *Take one of four daily direct flights to South America on our modern Airbus aircraft, and enjoy the most legroom of any airline. If we're ever late, you will receive coupons for free trips.* (L.O. 5)

2. The word *persuasion* turns some people off. Why? What negative connotations can it have? (L.O. 1, 5)

3. How are direct-mail sales letters and e-mail sales messages similar, and how are they different? (L.O. 5)

4. Why are magazine and newspaper editors or TV producers wary of press (news) releases from businesses and reluctant to turn them into articles? (L.O. 6)

5. **Ethical Issue:** Microtargeting is controversial. Advertisers are trying to sweettalk Internet users into allowing them to harvest their location information, browser history, and other personal behavior data. They argue it's to users' advantage to see ads tailored to their lifestyles and preferences. An even bigger problem than threats to privacy are narrowly focused political ads. Critics worry that misleading information cannot be rebutted if it's narrowly targeted. Although Facebook has been criticized not only for allowing political ads but also for not vetting them for disinformation or suspicious origin, the company is sticking to its guns. In the meantime, Google and Twitter are limiting or banning political ads outright. What are the risks of microtargeted political ads on social media? (L.O. 1, 2, 5)

Activities

10.1 Document for Analysis: A Poor Invitation to a Chef to Speak (L.O. 1–3)

The following letter from a program chair strives to persuade a well-known chef to make a presentation before a local restaurant association. But the letter is not very persuasive. How could this message be more persuasive? What reader benefits could it offer? What arguments could be made to overcome resistance? How should a persuasive message conclude?

YOUR TASK Analyze the following invitation and list its weaknesses. If your instructor directs, revise the letter.

Current date

Ms. Cassidee Dabney
Executive Chef, The Barn
Blackberry Farm
1471 West Millers Cove Road
Walland, TN 37886-2649

Dear Ms. Dabney:

We know you are a very busy hospitality professional as chef at The Barn, but we would like you to make a presentation to the Atlanta chapter of the National Restaurant Association. I was asked to write you since I am program chair.

I heard that you made a really good presentation at your local chapter in Knoxville recently. I think you gave a talk called "Avoiding the Seven Cardinal Sins in Food Service" or something like that. Whatever it was, I'm sure we would like to hear the same or a similar presentation. All restaurant operators are interested in doing what we can to avoid potential problems involving discrimination, safety at work, how we hire people, etc. As you well know, operating a fast-paced restaurant is frustrating—even on a good day. We are all in a gigantic rush from opening the door early in the morning to shutting it again after the last customer has gone. It's a rat race and easy to fall into the trap with food service faults that push a big operation into trouble.

Enclosed please find a list of questions that our members listed. We would like you to talk in the neighborhood of 45 minutes. Our June 10 meeting will be in the Carnegie Room of the St. Regis Atlanta and dinner begins at 7 p.m.

How can we get you to come Atlanta? We can only offer you an honorarium of $200, but we would pay for any travel expenses. You can expect a large crowd of restaurateurs who are known for hooting and hollering when they hear good stuff! As you can see, we are a rather informal group. Hope you can join us!

Sincerely,

10.2 Document for Analysis: Persuasive Message Flowing Upward: Sourcing Shirts in El Salvador (L.O. 1–3)

`E-Mail`

In the following message, Anton tries to convince his boss, the vice president of marketing, that their company could save money by sourcing T-shirts from El Salvador. However, his message could be improved by employing several strategies for persuasion.

YOUR TASK Analyze the following e-mail and list its weaknesses. If your instructor directs, revise the message.

To: Janelle Edwards<bryanna@ultrafit-international.com>
From: Anton Sheppard<anton@ultrafit-international.com>
Subject: Possible Chance for Saving Money

We always try our best to meet customers and sell UltraFit International equipment at numerous trade shows. But instead of expanding our visits to these trade shows, the company continues to cut back the number that we attend. And we have fewer staff members attending. I know that you have been asking us to find ways to reduce costs, but I don't think we are going about it right.

With increased airfare and hotel costs, my staff has tried to find ways to live within our very tight budget. Yet, we are being asked to find other ways to reduce our costs. I'm currently thinking ahead to the big Orlando trade show coming up in September.

One area where we could make a change is in the gift that we give away. In the past we have presented booth visitors with a nine-color T-shirt that is silk-screened and gorgeous. But it comes at a cost of $23 for each and every one of these beauties from a top-name designer.

To save money, I suggest that we try a $6 T-shirt made in El Salvador, which is reasonably presentable. It's got our name on it, and, after all, folks just use these shirts for workouts. Who cares if it is a fancy silk-screened T-shirt or a functional Salvadoran one that has "UltraFit

International" plastered on the chest? Because we give away 2,000 T-shirts at our largest show, we could save big bucks by dumping the designer shirt. But we have to act quickly. I'm sending a cheap one for you to see.

Let me know what you think.

Anton
[Full contact information]

10.3 Document for Analysis: LinkedIn Favor Request (L.O. 1–3)

`E-Mail` `Social Media`

A student chose LinkedIn to request a recommendation from his professor. The following message suffers from many writing faults, including poor tone and flawed persuasive strategy.

YOUR TASK Analyze the LinkedIn message and list at least five weaknesses. If your instructor directs, revise the message. Decide whether to use LinkedIn, of which the receiver is a member, or an e-mail to make this request.

10.4 Analyzing Tweets: Finding Persuasive Techniques in Micromessages (L.O. 1, 2, and 5)

`Communication Technology` `E-Mail` `Social Media` `Web`

As you have learned in this chapter, the time-tried AIDA sales technique is alive and well even in short Twitter messages. Of course, we can't expect to find all four parts in a single tweet.

YOUR TASK Study the following tweets and describe the persuasive techniques they employ. For additional tweets to study, especially if you have no Internet access, see Figure 10.6.

Hint: You may find that Twitter users rely on attention getters, calls for action, emotional appeals, incentives, and testimonials. They may also create urgency to stoke readers' interest. Chat about your findings in class or on your course-management platform. Your instructor may ask you to collect your own examples of persuasive tweets or other social media posts and discuss their frequency as well as effectiveness. After you have collected a sample large enough to allow you to generalize, compose an e-mail or post about your observations.

a.
Coca-Cola ✔ @CocaCola · Jan 24
Let's start a compliment thread! Comment below and tag someone who could use one. (That includes yourself. 😊) #NationalComplimentDay
💬 159   🔁 28   ♡ 263   ⬆
Source: The Coca-Cola Company

b.
Campbell Soup Co ✔ @CampbellSoupCo · Oct 28, 2019
An amazing second day at #FNCE handing out samples of some of our favorite snacks – from @swansonbroths bone broths to @V8, @GoldfishSmiles, and Campbell's Well Yes! Sipping Soups!
Source: Campbell Soup Company

c.
DirecTV ✔ @DIRECTV · May 2
Did you know vampires play baseball? 🦇🌙 Close your blinds and turn off the lights: it's time for a #TwilightWeekend with @FreeformTV.
Source: Directv, Inc.

d.
John Deere @JohnDeere18 Dec
Hurry! 0% APR for 48 Months on wide range of new John Deere construction equipment. Offer ends Jan. 5 (Canada only)
http://bit.ly/IV7Dnb
Source: Deere & Company

e.
Harley-Davidson @harleydavidson8 Nov
"When I ride there is only now, this moment. Clutch, throttle and brake. I am 100% focused." #harleywomen http://bit.ly/1d6pnW4
Source: Harley Davidson

f.
DreamWorks Animation ✔ @Dreamworks · Jan 16
It's the most epic day of the year - #AppreciateADragonDay! Celebrate with #DragonsRescueRiders on @Netflix! Join our @DreamWorksJr Facebook Group for fun ideas for the kids! facebook.com/groups/5173607...
Source: DreamWorks Animation

g.
Los Angeles Ronald McDonald House @LosAngelesRMH · May 1
Our families are LOVING the tasty treats from @ClifBar ! Thank you for providing an easy, portable, and nutritious snack for families to enjoy throughout their busiest of days 🙌 #LARMH #KeepingFamiliesClose
Source: Los Angeles Ronald McDonald House

h.
Starbucks Coffee @Starbucks15 Oct
Signed petitions from across America are bound for D.C. tonight. Add your voice: http://sbux.co/H0qPPD #cometogether
Source: Starbucks corporation

i.
Southwest Airlines @SouthwestAir23 Dec
Two days left to enter for a chance to win a Wii U video game system from @NintendoAmerica and a pair of SWA tickets! http://www.-southwest.com/Nintendo
Source: Southwest Airlines Co.

10.5 The Art of Persuasion—As Old as Aristotle's *Rhetoric* (L.O. 1)

`Social Media`   `Web`

Besides the persuasive models introduced in this chapter, many more exist. One of the oldest and best-known modes of persuasion comes from Aristotle (384–322 BC). The Greek philosopher identified four components of persuasion: **ethos**, **pathos**, **logos**, and **kairos**.[61]

Ethos describes the merit, character, and expertise of a speaker. Persuasion is possible when the audience believes that the persuader is credible and has a good reputation. For instance, we tend to believe a successful coach speaking about training methods. Testimonials in advertising by people we respect are an example of ethos.

Pathos describes an emotional appeal. It means the style of delivery—for example, when a speaker exhibits passion and uses colorful metaphors, language, attention getters, and more. When successful, pathos triggers feelings in the audience intended by the speaker, such as empathy or outrage.

Logos describes a rational appeal. It is the persuasive technique of an argument based in logic and appealing to the audience's intellect. Logos requires us to support our ideas with sound reasons, relevant statistics, and other solid evidence.

Kairos suggests that persuaders consider the timing and setting of an argument, i.e., the "right moment."

As experts point out, most persuaders skillfully weave all three tactics into a seamless, effective persuasive message.[62] In reputable publications such as *The Wall Street Journal* and *The New York Times*, and highly regarded news media such as CBS, ABC, and PBS, expect logos to dominate the generally "civilized" debate. Contributors featured in these media generally rank high on ethos. On the political fringes, however, be they left- or right-leaning, pathos dominates over logos. Similarly, expect a lot more pathos than logos in advertising.

YOUR TASK Look for persuasive messages: speeches on YouTube or opinion pieces such as editorials or blog entries. Examine them for ethos, pathos, and logos. The discussion of rational and emotional appeals in this chapter might be helpful. Jot down your observations, and bring your notes to class. If your instructor directs, submit a written interpretation discussing the ethos, pathos, and logos of a speech, an ad, or an opinion piece.

10.6 Persuasive Strategies—Applying Hugh Rank's Model (L.O. 1)

`E-Mail`   `Web`

Theorist Hugh Rank created a relatively simple model of persuasion. He believed that persuaders resort to two main strategies to reach their goals. Figure 10.7 illustrates Rank's model. Simply put, persuaders intensify their own strong points and the weaknesses of their opponent or a competing idea. Second, they downplay their own weak points and the strengths of their opponent or a competing idea.

Intensifying is achieved by repetition, association, and composition. Words and visual patterns of a key ingredient of a persuasive message are repeated to become memorable. Think jingles, recurring images, key phrases, or slogans—*It's the Real Thing* (Coca-Cola) or even the German tongue twister *Fahrvergnügen* (VW, for joy of driving). Association works by linking the idea or product with something that has emotional appeal; for example, attractive, youthful people in their pristine kitchen.

FIGURE 10.7　Hugh Rank's Persuasive Model

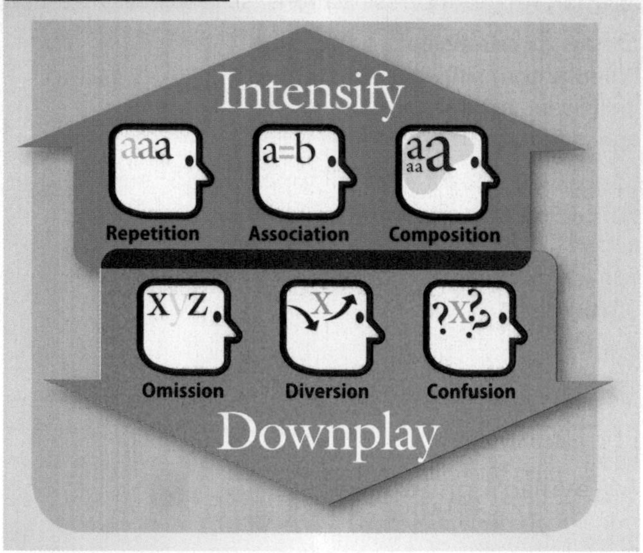

Composition can also enhance the message by contrasting it with an opposite (e.g., a cleaning product shown to work wonders on very dirty floors or clothes).

Downplaying is achieved with omission, diversion, and confusion. Omission means leaving out information that might contradict the positive message (e.g., ignoring high purchase and maintenance costs). Diversion is a tactic to cause the audience to overlook a certain negative aspect of the product or idea—for example, by pointing out fuel economy gear in a snazzy vehicle to reduce attention to its poor gas mileage overall. Confusion is used to cover up known weaknesses in one's own argument, idea, or product. In the case of a giant gas guzzler, the persuader might emphasize performance data, racing wins, and so on, to gloss over poor buyer satisfaction and a poor safety record.

YOUR TASK Look for examples to test Rank's model. Find advertising, opinion pieces, speeches, and other persuasive messages to illustrate the intensify–downplay model. In a class discussion or an e-mail to your instructor, discuss whether it is unethical to intensify or downplay, and give examples.

10.7　Persuasive Request: Suitable Suits for Interviews (L.O. 1–3)

You saw an interesting article describing a Suitable Suits program at Barnard College. Its Office of Career Development kept a closet filled with 21 crisp dark suits that students could borrow for job interviews. Students made an appointment with the office and agreed to dry clean the suits before returning them. At Barnard the program was paid for with a grant from a prominent financial firm. You think that a Suitable Suits program is worth exploring with your dean.

YOUR TASK Write a persuasive message requesting an appointment with your dean to discuss a Suitable Suits program at your school. You don't have all the answers and you are not sure how such a program would operate, but you think the idea is worth discussing. Can you convince the dean to see you? Should you write an e-mail or a letter?

10.8　Persuasive Request: Requesting a Letter of Recommendation (L.O. 1–3)

E-Mail

As a student, you will need letters of recommendation to find a job, to apply for a scholarship or grant, or to enter graduate school. Naturally, you will consider asking one or several of your college instructors. You talk to Andy, a senior you know, to find out how to get a busy professor to write you an effective letter. Andy has the following advice:

- Ask only instructors who have had the opportunity to observe your performance and may still remember you fondly. Two to five years after you attended a course of 20 to 40 students, your teachers may not recall you at all.

- Contact only professors who can sing your praises. If your grades were poor, the endorsement won't be glowing. Some instructors refuse to write recommendations for mediocre students.

Make it easy for your instructors to agree to your request and to write a solid letter promptly by following these guidelines:

- Make the first request in person, if possible. Your former instructor will be more likely to remember you.

- Introduce yourself and try to point out something memorable you did to help your professor recall your performance.

- Have a hard copy of the job description, scholarship information, grant requirements, or graduate school application ready, or direct the instructor to a website or LinkedIn.

- Carry a copy of your recent polished résumé, or promise to e-mail these documents and any other information to help your recommender recall you in a professional setting and understand what you need.

- Confirm any agreement by e-mail promptly, and set a firm yet reasonable deadline by which the letter must be received. Don't expect to get a letter if you ask at the last minute.

- Gently nudge by e-mail to remind the recommender when the deadline is approaching.

YOUR TASK Write a persuasive request by e-mail asking your instructor (or supervisor or manager) to write you a letter of recommendation for a job application, grant, scholarship, or graduate school application. Provide all relevant information to make it easy for your recommender to write a terrific letter. Explain any attachments.

10.9 Persuasive Claim: Pricy Toner for Tony Myrtle Beach Country Club (L.O. 1–3)

Nanette was new to her job as administrative assistant at the Barefoot Resort & Golf in Myrtle Beach, South Carolina. Alone in the office one morning, she answered a phone call from Chas, who said he was the country club's copier contractor. "Hey, look, Babydoll," Chas purred, "the price on the toner you use is about to go way up. I can offer you a great price on this toner if you order right now." Nanette knew that the copy machine regularly needed toner, and she thought she should go ahead and place the order to save the country club some money. Ten days later two bottles of toner arrived, and Nanette was pleased at the perfect timing. The copy machine needed it right away. Three weeks later Erika, the bookkeeper, called to report a bill from The Toner People for $960.43 for two bottles of toner. "What's going on here?" asked Erika. "We don't purchase supplies from this company, and this price is totally off the charts!"

Nanette spoke to the manager, Forrest Vartanian, who immediately knew what had happened. He blamed himself for not training Nanette. "Never ever order anything from a telephone solicitor, no matter how fast-talking or smooth he sounds," warned Forrest. He outlined an office policy for future supplies purchases. Only certain people can authorize or finalize a purchase, and purchases require a confirmed price including shipping costs settled in advance. But what to do about this $960.43 bill? The country club had already begun to use the toner, although the current copies were looking faint and streaked.

YOUR TASK As Forrest Vartanian, decide how to respond to this obvious scam. Should you pay the bill? Should you return the unused bottle? Write a persuasive claim to The Toner People, 1218 Sam Rittenberg Blvd., Suite 100, Charleston, SC 29407. Supply any details necessary.

10.10 Persuasive Claim: No Booze for Breakfast (L.O. 3)

As regional manager for a national restaurant chain, you and two other employees attended a conference in Las Vegas, Nevada. You stayed at the Aria Resort & Casino because your company recommends that employees use this hotel during annual industry meetings. Generally, your employees have liked their accommodations, and the rates have been within your company's budget.

Now, however, you are unhappy with the charges you see on your company's credit card statement from Aria

Resort & Casino. When your department's administrative assistant made the reservations, she was assured that you would receive the weekend rates and that a hot breakfast—in the hotel's Italian restaurant, Carbone—would be included in the rate. So you and the other two employees went to the restaurant and ordered a hot meal from the menu.

When you received the credit card statement, though, you saw a charge for $153 for three champagne buffet breakfasts at Carbone. You hit the ceiling! For one thing, you didn't have a buffet breakfast and certainly no champagne. The three of you got there so early that no buffet had been set up. You ordered pancakes and sausage, and for this you were billed $40 each. What's worse, your company may charge you personally for exceeding the maximum per diem rates.

In looking back at this event, you remember that other guests on your floor were having a continental breakfast in a lounge on your floor. Perhaps that's where the hotel expected all guests on the weekend rate to eat. However, your administrative assistant had specifically asked about this matter when she made the reservations, and she was told that you could order breakfast from the menu at the hotel's Italian restaurant, Carbone.

YOUR TASK You want to straighten out this problem, and you can't do it by telephone because you suspect that you will need a written record of this entire mess. Online you have tried in vain to find an e-mail address for guest relations at Aria. Write a persuasive claim to Customer Service, Aria Resort & Casino, 3730 Las Vegas Boulevard, Las Vegas, NV 89158. Should you include a copy of the credit card statement showing the charge?

10.11 Persuasive Claim: Wretched Print Job (L.O. 3)

As president of Unicorn Travel, you brought a very complex print job to the Primera Printers in Rochester, New York. It took almost 15 minutes to explain the particulars of this job to the printer. When you left, you wondered whether all of the instructions would be followed precisely. You even brought in your own special paper, which added to the cost of printing. When you got the job back (a total of 1,500 sheets of paper) and returned to your office, you discovered a host of problems. One of the pages had 300 copies made on cheap 20-pound paper. This means that the printer must have run out of your special paper and substituted something else for one of the runs. The printer also made copies of your original photos and graphics, so that all the final prints were run from second-generation prints, which reduced the quality of the graphics enormously. What's more, many of the sheets were poorly or improperly cut. In short, the job was unacceptable.

Because you were desperate to complete the job, you allowed the print shop to repeat the job using its paper supply. When you inquired about the cost, the counter person Hugh was noncommittal. He said you would have to talk to the owner, who worked in the Rochester shop. The repeat print job turned out fairly well, and you paid the full price of $782. But you are unhappy, and Hugh sensed that Primera Printers would not see Unicorn Travel again as a customer. He encouraged you to write to the owner and ask for an adjustment.

YOUR TASK Write a claim letter to Mr. Mitch Spiro, Primera Printers, 240 State Street, Rochester, NY 14608. What is a reasonable claim to make? Do you simply want to register your unhappiness, or do you want a refund? Supply any needed information.

10.12 Persuasive Organizational Message Flowing Downward: Volunteering at NuStar Energy (L.O. 4)

E-Mail

NuStar Energy in San Antonio, Texas, is big on giving back to the community. The liquids terminal and pipeline operator considers volunteering a core value and supports it with up to 60 hours (7.5 days) of paid time per worker per year. NuStar has a pet philanthropic project, the Annual Charity Golf Tournament, the proceeds of which benefit Haven of Hope, a local organization helping the homeless.

As employee relations manager of NuStar Energy, you are tasked with finding employees willing to organize the tournament, obtain sponsorships, create decorations, paint fences and other objects, assemble gift bags, direct the event, coordinate a welcome dinner for more than 1,000 guests, and more. In the last eight years NuStar has helped raise more than $27 million for Haven of Hope.[63] Although volunteers keep getting paid by their employer, participating in activities such as the golf fundraiser is not everyone's cup of tea because workers must pause important projects, or they may perhaps favor other causes. You cannot take them for granted.

YOUR TASK Write a persuasive memo or e-mail with convincing appeals that will attract as many company volunteers as possible to put on and staff the next charity golf tournament.

10.13 Persuasive Organizational Message Flowing Downward: No More Costly Shipping Charges (L.O. 4)

As office manager of a Sacramento footwear and apparel company, write a memo persuading your shipping employees to reduce express delivery fees. Your FedEx and other shipping bills have been sky high, and you feel that staff members are overusing these services to please their favorite distributors. They don't consider less expensive options, such as sharing shipping costs with the recipient.

If shipping staff members plan ahead and allow enough time, they can use UPS or FedEx ground service, which takes three to five days and is much cheaper. You wonder whether staff members consider whether the recipient would mind waiting a few days longer for the merchandise in exchange for prices remaining low. When is overnight shipment justified? You would like to reduce overnight delivery services voluntarily by 50 percent over the next two months. Unless a sizable reduction occurs, the CEO threatens severe restrictions in the future.

YOUR TASK Address your memo to all staff members. What other ways could employees reduce shipping costs?

10.14 Persuasive Organizational Message Flowing Downward: Get Into Urban Farming (L.O. 4)

E-Mail **Web**

As employee relations manager of The Clorox Company based in Oakland, California, one of your tasks is to promote Urban Farming, a global organization that has established more than 66,000 gardens in nearly 40 cities. Originating in the Detroit area, Urban Farming is a combined effort of major corporations. You must recruit 12 coworkers who will volunteer to plant gardens and teach community families about healthy eating.

Your task is to find volunteers in your company to start a community garden and in turn recruit other Clorox volunteers. The greater San Francisco area offers more than 5,000 vacant lots to choose from, and 40 gardens already exist in the region. Clorox volunteers will be expected to attend training sessions and then to supervise and instruct participating members of the community. In return, employees will receive two hours of release time per week to work on their Urban Farming projects. The program has been very successful thus far, and the interest in community gardens is strong.

YOUR TASK Learn more about Urban Farming by searching the Web. Then write a persuasive memo or e-mail with convincing appeals that will bring you 12 volunteers to work with Urban Farming.

10.15 Persuasive Message Flowing Upward: A Four-Day Workweek Sounds Divine! (L.O. 4)

E-Mail **Team** **Web**

You have heard that some companies and municipalities are switching to a four-day workweek to reduce traffic congestion, air pollution, and stressed employees. Compressing the workweek into four 10-hour days sounds pretty good to you. You would much prefer having Friday free to schedule medical appointments and take care of family business, in addition to leisurely three-day weekends.

As a manager at Nitroglow, a mineral-based skin care products and natural cosmetics company, you are convinced that the company's 200 employees could switch to a four-day workweek with many resulting benefits. For one thing, they would save on gasoline and commute time. You know that many cities and companies have already implemented a four-day workweek with considerable success. You took a quick poll of immediate employees and managers and found that 80 percent thought that a four-day workweek was a good idea. One said, "This would be great! Think of what I could save on babysitting and lunches!"

YOUR TASK With a group of other students, conduct research on the Web and discuss your findings. What are the advantages of a four-day workweek? What organizations have already tried it? What appeals could be used to persuade management to adopt a four-day workweek? What arguments could be expected, and how would you counter them? Individually or as a group, prepare a one-page persuasive e-mail or memo addressed to the Nitroglow Management Council. Decide on a goal. Do you want to suggest a pilot study? Should you meet with management to present your ideas? How about starting a four-day workweek immediately?

10.16 Persuasive Organizational Message Flowing Upward: Keep the Apples! (L.O. 4)

| E-Mail |

Omni Hotels ranks at the top in "Highest in Guest Satisfaction Among Upscale Hotel Chains," according to J. D. Power. The chain operates 60 luxury hotels and resorts in leading business gateways and leisure destinations across North America. From exceptional golf and spa retreats to dynamic business settings, each Omni showcases the local flavor of the destination while featuring four-diamond services. One signature amenity it has offered for years is a bowl of free apples in its lobbies. However, providing apples costs hundreds of thousands of dollars a year. Always seeking out efficiencies, executives are debating whether to cut out apples as a way to save money with minimal impact on guests.

Omni Hotels prides itself on delivering superior service through The Power of One, a service program that provides associates the training and authority to make decisions that exceed the expectations of guests. The entire culture of the hotel creates a positive, supportive environment that rewards associates through the Omni Service Champions program. As an Omni associate, you are disturbed that the hotel is considering giving up its free apples. You hope that executives will find other ways to trim costs, such as purchasing food in smaller amounts to reduce waste or cutting the hours of its lobby cafes.[64]

YOUR TASK In the true sense of The Power of One, you decide to express your views to management. Write a persuasive message to Richard Johnson (*rjohnson@omni.com*), Vice President, Operations, Omni Hotels, 420 Decker Drive, Irving, TX 75062. Should you write a letter or an e-mail? In a separate note to your instructor, explain your rationale for your channel choice and your message strategy.

10.17 Persuasive Organizational Message Flowing Upward: Depending on Tips (L.O. 4)

| Team |

Perched high atop a granite cliff overlooking Point Lobos on the rugged Big Sur coastline sits Pacific's Edge Restaurant, where migrating whales may be seen from every table in the dining room. Sunsets here are so spectacular that the entire dining room often breaks out in spontaneous applause. You truly enjoy working in this magical Big Sur resort setting—except for one thing. You have occasionally been "stiffed" by a patron who left no tip. You know your service is excellent, but some customers just don't get it, especially when they come from Europe, where tips are included and wait staff earns decent wages. These patrons seem to think that tips are optional and only round up a couple of dollars, if they pay anything at all. For servers, however, tips are 80 percent of their income.

What to do? Adding a mandatory "tip" of, say, 18 percent to a check is an option, but it can be problematic. First, the practice must be announced on menus or on signs visible in the restaurant. Second, the IRS treats automatic gratuities added by the restaurants as service charges, which means that payroll taxes must be withheld from them, and servers won't see the taxed tip money until payday. The IRS defines a tip as a payment added "free from compulsion" by the patrons who determine how much they wish to give.[65] Still, taxed tips paid with a delay are better than nothing.

Many restaurants print gratuity guidelines on checks, showing customers what a 15-, 20-, or even 25-percent tip would be. You also know that American Express displays a gratuity calculation on its terminals. This means that diners don't even have to do the math! But how can you educate diners tactfully that a tip is expected—and, best of all, cold hard cash is king?

YOUR TASK Because they know you are studying business communication, your fellow servers have asked you to write a letter to Gabriel Souza, General Manager,

Pacific's Edge Restaurant, Hyatt Carmel Highlands, 120 Highlands Drive, Carmel, CA 93923. They think a letter will be more effective than a conversation. First, talk with fellow servers (your classmates) about effective ways to "enlighten" patrons about tipping in California. Then develop a logical argument to present to Gabriel Souza in writing. You could ask for gratuity guidelines to be added to checks and persuade him to adopt mandatory tips in the restaurant.

10.18 The Coolest of All? Puffery in Advertising (L.O. 5)

Communication Technology | **Social Media** | **Web**

Puffery in advertising may be tacky, but it is not illegal. Few of us take claims seriously that shout, *the best pastry on the planet, the performance of a lifetime, the most accurate watch in the world, nothing outlasts an Eveready battery, anything is possible after coffee,* or *coldest beer in Colorado.* After all, such exaggerated claims, also called *hyperbole,* cannot be proven and do not fool anyone.

Serious, quantifiable claims, however, must be backed up with evidence, or they could mean litigation: "Our chicken has less fat than a hamburger. It's better for you."[66] This bold claim was investigated, and the fried chicken restaurant had to stop using it in its advertising. Yes, the fried chicken had a little less total fat than a hamburger, but it contained more harmful transfat, sodium, and cholesterol, making it higher in calories—a decidedly unhealthy alternative. As the FTC points out, a restaurant can compare itself to others, but it must tell the truth.

YOUR TASK Look for examples of puffery and find ads that would need to prove their claims. How can you tell which is which? Discuss examples in class or in an online forum set up for your class.

10.19 Selling With Audience Benefits (L.O. 1, 5)

Web

Audience benefits sell. People are more likely to be persuaded when they see a direct or indirect benefit of a product, service, idea, or cause. Features may describe a product or service, but they don't tell a story. To be persuasive, writers must convert features into benefits. They must tell the audience how they can best use the item to benefit from it.

YOUR TASK Online or offline find a product or service that you admire. Be sure to locate a detailed description of the item's unique features. Identify a suitable audience for the product or service. Create a table and in the left column list the item's features. In the right column, convert the features into benefits by matching them to the needs of your target audience.

10.20 Phony Online Reviews: Cutting Through "Opinion Spam" (L.O. 1, 2, 5)

A Cornell University study demonstrated that humans are really bad at spotting fake reviews. The study participants might as well have tossed a coin. This is why the researchers used machine learning and developed an algorithm that was said to be 90 percent accurate in flagging fake reviews of Chicago area hotels. The researchers called the tool Review Skeptic and made it available to the public.[67] The other three prominent apps designed to spot fake reviews are Fakespot, ReviewMeta, and The Review Index. Fakespot examines webpages for their trustworthiness and spits out a reliability grade; ReviewMeta works in similar ways but checks only Amazon reviews. The Review Index likewise determines whether a product score has been inflated by fake reviews.[68]

Aside from algorithms, the Cornell researchers identified these three tell-tale signs that a review is probably fake to help shoppers base their buying decisions on more solid evidence: 1) *lacks detail*: offers general praise instead of specifics; 2) *includes more first-person pronouns*: fraudsters resort to a lot of *I* and *me* to appear sincere; and 3) *contains more verbs than nouns*: genuine reviews rely more on nouns than the swindlers who use verbs to write their bogus positive (or negative) stories.[69] In addition, watch out for extremes, either very positive (five-star) or very negative (one-star) reviews that don't provide much detail. If several of them were posted at the same time, they are probably unreliable.[70]

YOUR TASK Visit Amazon, Yelp, TripAdvisor, BestBuy, or Walmart. Look up a product or service you might buy or are interested in. Pick a brand that has a number of reviews and critically examine them using the guidelines provided above. To check your accuracy, run your page through one of the apps designed to spot fakes. Compare your results with those of the review robots. Compile your notes and present your findings to the class or in writing, if your instructor directs.

10.21 Sales Message: Conquering Reactance While Promoting an Electric Car (L.O. 1, 5)

Social Media | **Team** | **Web**

Perhaps you have been eying an electric vehicle. Here is your opportunity to conduct minor research to understand your chosen EV's features and then write a direct-mail message to pitch the car to a well-defined audience. Here is information about the Nissan Leaf, for example:

The Nissan Leaf is the best-selling electric vehicle of all time; more than 400,000 cars have been delivered worldwide. Nissan completely redesigned the Leaf for the 2018 model year. In 2019 the automaker added a long-range Leaf Plus option. New features were added in 2020.

With an MSRP of $31,600, the Leaf offers an attractive price for an EV. It features a generous interior, huge cargo capacity, composed handling, and lively acceleration. However, other compact cars offer more upscale interiors and better predicted reliability ratings.

According to the EPA, the standard Leaf delivers 149 miles of range, while the Leaf Plus can travel up to 226 miles. The Leaf Plus starts at an MSRP of $38,200. These aggressive base prices are complemented by attractive lease deals.

The Leaf comes standard with an 8-inch touch screen, Android Auto, Apple CarPlay, Bluetooth, and satellite radio. Standard safety features include forward collision warning, automatic emergency braking, blind spot monitoring, rear cross traffic alert, and lane departure warning. The Leaf Plus offers a more powerful electric motor.[71]

Obviously, no one runs out to buy a car, not even after reading an eloquent sales letter. Purchases of big-ticket items typically take a long time to develop. They involve research and don't happen spontaneously. Before you can start, you will need to analyze your audience and your purpose.

YOUR TASK Choose a currently available electric car that you will pitch in a sales letter to be mailed to an audience of recent college graduates.

Your target group is defined as follows: gender neutral; mostly unmarried, no kids; late millennial and early Gen Z cohort; primarily an urban dweller with a first job out of college, receiving a steady paycheck and building credit; cares deeply about the environment and takes climate change very seriously.

Challenges you can expect: Many members of the ecologically minded age groups you're targeting don't feel the need to own a car. Walkability of their neighborhoods is more important to them. They have public transport options and may bike to work. Even the least expensive electric cars are pricier than their gasoline-burning counterparts. People contemplating electric vehicles experience range anxiety; they fear to run out of power, sometimes irrationally so. Gasoline in the United States continues to be a lot cheaper than it is in other developed countries. Tuition debt could be a crushing burden.

What is your purpose? The best you can hope for is to build awareness and potentially prompt a social media response to measure the effectiveness of your campaign,

e.g., liking a page, encouraging a post of some kind, making a TikTok video on a related topic, or similar activities. You have a budget of $2,000 to buy items that might serve as inducements to raffle off among a certain number of those who respond first, create the best submission in a contest, or visit the dealership to test drive the EV.

10.22 Sales Message: Organic Greens, Home-Delivered (L.O. 5)

E-Mail

Many consumers worry about what's in their food. They fear conventional factory farming, wish to be good stewards of the environment, and desire a sustainable lifestyle. Wholesome, organic food can increasingly be found on the shelves of mainstream supermarkets. Even big-box stores such as Costco—not just health food stores such as Mother's Market, Sprouts Farmers Market, and Whole Foods Market—are capitalizing on the farm-to-table trend. Weekly farmers' markets selling local produce and fruit are common across America.

But even busy urbanites who don't like to travel to shop can embrace healthier fare by subscribing to farm fresh veggies and fruit online for home delivery. Services such as Farm Fresh to You in California, themselves organic farmers since 1976, partner with other organic farms to offer customizable boxes with several service and delivery options. Because these co-op-type outfits benefit from economies of scale, their prices, although higher than those of conventional markets, are not exorbitant. The delivery services also offer priceless convenience. In Washington, subscribers can customize their boxes on the Fresh & Fair Farming website, or they can let the farmers select the content for them.

The advantages of receiving weekly boxes filled with healthy seasonal produce include fresh, delicious taste, wholesome food that's free from herbicides and pesticides, and less traffic by ordering a custom box online each week or less frequently. In addition, subscribers are supporting small family farms that supply local, in-season fruit and veggies instead of buying greens that are flown halfway around the world. Depending on location, subscribers receive their boxes on Tuesday or Wednesday if they order a box by 10 a.m. on Sunday. For Thursday or Friday delivery, orders must be placed by 10 a.m. on Tuesday. New members receive 20 percent off their first order.

YOUR TASK Write a sales message—a letter or an e-mail—for the signature of "Marketer-in-Chief" Martina Sabatini, Fair & Fresh Farming, 513 E Valentine Road, Glendive, MT 59330. Provide an enticing but accurate explanation of the service, and invite your reader to subscribe. Focus on audience benefits.

10.23 Sales Message: Pitching Products or Services (L.O. 5)

`E-Mail`

Identify a situation in your current job or a previous one in which a sales message is or was needed. Using suggestions from this chapter, write an appropriate sales message that promotes a product or service. Use actual names, information, and examples. If you have no work experience, imagine a business you would like to start: a window cleaning service, pet grooming, car detailing, office and house cleaning, tutoring, specialty knitting, balloon decorating, delivery service, child or elder care, gardening, lawn care, or something else.

YOUR TASK Write a sales letter or an e-mail marketing message selling your product or service to be distributed to your prospective customers. Be sure to tell them how to respond.

Consider adding graphics or photos—either your own or samples borrowed from the Internet. As long as you use them for this assignment and don't publish them online, you are not violating copyright laws.

10.24 Micromessages: AIDA Components in Tweets (L.O. 1, 2, and 5)

`Communication Technology` `Social Media` `Web`

Most persuasive micromessages incorporate some elements of sales techniques—individual AIDA components. Naturally, few of us would buy something solely on the basis of a tweet, but such micromessages are teasers or alerts, directing receivers to websites, video clips, and other media sites.

Examples:

Consider these posts and tweets; commentaries follow:

Are You a Businesswoman? Apply now to see if you qualify to join the Association of Businesswomen. Attracts attention with a question; call for action implies exclusivity of membership.

UC Davis Online MBA: Grow your network in Silicon Valley. Complete in 24 months. Bachelor's required. Establishes credibility with notable name and desirable degree; uses "you" view; sums up key information efficiently.

With our updated Android app, share collections of photos with friends and family. Enjoy! http://wo.ly/gLknQ Offers a benefit; conveys warmth (Enjoy!); provides a useful hyperlink.

Enjoy easier, smarter access to Delta with the new http://delta.com and Fly Delta apps for smartphones and iPad: http://oka.xtr.ly/m/1umh Employs "you" view; offers a benefit (easier, smarter access); prompts a response with convenient hyperlinks.

Please donate to @RedCrossAU Tasmanian Bushfires Appeal http://bit.ly/Xs4l7g All donations over $2 are tax deductible #redcross #tasfires Starts with a direct call for action; points out the benefit that contributions are tax deductible.

YOUR TASK To find persuasive posts, examine the Twitter feed of a company, nonprofit organization, brand, or businessperson for persuasive micromessages. Determine whether tweets and posts feature AIDA components such as attention getters, reader benefits, calls for action, limited-time offers, and freebies. If you can't find suitable micromessages online, use the tweets in Figure 10.6 for your analysis. Share your results in class. Analyze and critique each other's findings.

10.25 Writing Persuasive Tweets and Other Social Media Posts (L.O. 1, 5)

`Social Media` `Communication Technology` `Web`

Build your professional online persona with effective and concise micromessages and other social media posts.

YOUR TASK Brainstorm to identify a special skill you have, an event you want others to attend, a charitable cause dear to your heart, or a product you like. Applying what you have learned about short persuasive messages, write your own persuasive tweet of no more than 280 characters or create a brief persuasive Facebook post. Use Figure 10.6 as a starting point and model.

10.26 Reviewing Press Releases (L.O. 6)

`Web`

YOUR TASK Select an organization and study its press releases. For example, search the Web for *Amazon Media Room: Press Releases, FBI press release, Ben & Jerry's press releases, Mars Candy press releases, World Honda news releases, Screen Actors Guild press releases,* or an organization of your choice.

Alternatively, if you instructor directs, find three press releases published by different organizations. Evaluate their structure and other features in relation to the guidance in this chapter. Do they follow the same pattern? Which are most compelling? Can you find press releases most likely to attract the attention of reporters, or do most sound self-serving?

10.27 Press Release: We Have News for You (L.O. 6)

YOUR TASK For a company where you now work or an organization you belong to, identify a product or service that could be publicized and write a press release. You could announce a new course at your college, a new president, new equipment, or a campaign to raise funds. The press release is intended for your local newspaper or online publication.

New communication platforms and casual workplace environments have blurred the lines of appropriateness, leaving workers wondering how to navigate uncharted waters. Check your workplace etiquette IQ by deciding whether the following statements are true or false. Then see if you agree with the responses on p. Key-6.

1. As a working parent, you have two or three photos of your family that you would like to put on your office desk. You have not seen any family photos on the desks of other workers. To test the waters, you should set up your photos and see what happens.

   _____ True _____ False

2. Although you should never take company equipment or major supplies, most employees are entitled to take home small items such as paper, folders, and pens.

   _____ True _____ False

3. In interacting with superiors, you should support your boss's decisions even though you think you might have made a better decision.

   _____ True _____ False

Chat About It

In each chapter you will find five discussion questions related to the chapter material. Your instructor may assign these topics for you to discuss in class, in an online chat room, or on an online discussion board. Some of the discussion topics may require outside research. You may also be asked to read and respond to postings made by your classmates.

TOPIC 1: Traditional advertising and digital advertising have been compared to fishing with a dragnet versus spearfishing. Explain this analogy. Is it apt and what does it imply?

TOPIC 2: Consider your vast experience with TV and other advertising. Can you think of commercials or ads that seem to fall in the category of puffery or could even be considered deceptive? How do you know the difference between the two?

TOPIC 3: When have you had to persuade someone (a boss, parent, instructor, friend, or colleague) to do something or change a belief? What strategies did you use? Were they successful? How could you improve your technique?

TOPIC 4: When have you had to complain to a company, organization, or person about something that went wrong or that offended you? Share your experience. What channel did you use for your complaint? How effective was your channel choice and strategy? What would you change in your method for future complaints?

TOPIC 5: A UK study found that donors who receive thanks give again and donate even more money. Relate this finding to tangible and intangible benefits. What lessons can you learn from this insight that may apply to your own life?

Grammar and Mechanics Review 10

Confusing Words and Frequently Misspelled Words

Review the lists of confusing words and frequently misspelled words at the end of Appendix D, Grammar and Mechanics. On a separate sheet, revise the following sentences to correct word usage errors. Sentences may have more than one error. If a sentence is correct, write *C*. When you finish, check your answers in the key at the end of the book.

EXAMPLE: When sending bad news, try to accomodate a disatisfied customer with a plausible alternative.

REVISION: When sending bad news, try to **accommodate** a **dissatisfied** customer with a plausible alternative.

1. Colman complained that his capitol investments had been aversely effected.

2. The principle part of the manager's persuasive message contained a complement and valuable advise.

3. Before writing the sales message, did you allready analyse the product's major and miner appeals?

4. In responding to the irate customer, Marilyn made a conscience effort to show patients and present creditable facts.

5. Even in every day business affairs, we strive to reach farther and go beyond what is expected.

6. Before you procede with the report, please check those suprising statistics.

7. It's usally better to de-emphasize bad news then to spotlight it.

8. Incidently, passive-voice verbs can help you make a statement less personnel when neccessary.

9. Customers are more excepting of disapointing news if they are ensured that there requests were heard and treated fairly.

10. The customer's complaint illicited an immediate response that carefully presented the facts and was not to long.

Report Writing Basics

REPORT

LEARNING OUTCOMES

After studying this chapter, you should be able to do the following:

1 Apply the 3-x-3 writing process to create well-organized business reports.

2 Identify the resources and methods used in conducting primary and secondary research.

3 Outline informational and analytical report functions, strategies, and formats.

4 Explain the importance and methods of documenting report information.

5 Generate and incorporate meaningful visual aids and graphics in business reports.

Can Seventh Generation Democratize Sustainable Cleaning Products?

Vermont-based Seventh Generation seeks to inspire a consumer revolution. Its nontoxic, eco-friendly cleaning and personal care products have been so successful that corporate giant Unilever eagerly added it to its lineup of household products. Unilever is counting on Seventh Generation to deliver sustainability while making a profit. But how can this mission-driven company convince consumers that its products are worth their premium pricing?

Seventh Generation is not exactly a household name. It's based on the Great Law of the Iroquois Confederacy, which states, "In our every deliberation, we must consider the impact of our decisions on the next seven generations." Embracing this wisdom, Seventh Generation aims to transform the world into a healthy, sustainable, and equitable place for the next seven generations.[1]

To achieve this goal, the company specifically pledges that 100 percent of the materials and ingredients in its products will be sustainable, bio-based, or recycled. It aims to replace 30 percent of palm kernel oil with bio-based oils. Further, it pledges to reduce greenhouse gas emissions by 50 percent and vows that no water will be contaminated during the life cycle of any of its products.

These lofty goals, however, come at a price. Although Seventh Generation eco products are competitively priced, CEO Joey Bergstein admits that they carry a "small premium." Their pricing makes them about 10 percent more than leading conventional brands. And that is the problem. Today's price-conscious consumers may balk at slightly higher prices—even for clean, sustainable products." Recognizing the challenge, CEO Joey Bergstein pledges to find a way to democratize the concept of sustainable cleaning products. This mission "should not just be about products for the wealthy."[2] He recognizes that no clear path lies ahead to achieve these goals, but he knows "that it's imperative that we push forward to get there."

AP Images/Kevin Wolf

Critical Thinking

- Why should consumers care about nontoxic and eco-friendly products?

- Are you willing to pay as much as 1 percent, 5 percent, or even 10 percent more for nontoxic, eco-friendly products? Why or why not?

- Why do you think report writing might be important to organizations such as Seventh Generation?

11-1 Beginning With Basics: Applying the 3-x-3 Writing Process to Report Writing

LEARNING OUTCOME

1 Apply the 3-x-3 writing process to create well-organized business reports.

As a mission-driven organization, Seventh Generation is fervent in its belief that it can do well and also do good—that is, be a positive force in the world. Its ambitious goals and achievements are proudly revealed in its Corporate Consciousness Report, which is just one of the company's many messages and reports promoting its products and mission.

Not all organizations prepare corporate consciousness or responsibility reports. However, nearly all businesses create reports. Efficient reports play a critical role in helping organizations sift through data to make major decisions. Focused, in-depth reports help managers analyze the challenges they face before recommending solutions.

This chapter explores the basics of report writing by applying the 3-x-3 writing process. The chapter proceeds with information and advice for conducting primary and secondary research. Because much information will be obtained from the Internet, we offer guidance on using search

BaanTaksinStudio/Shutterstock.com

An important first step in writing a report is defining the problem and clarifying its scope, limitations, and significance.

tools, evaluating sources, and documenting findings. In organizing and presenting report data, we discuss typical report functions, organizational strategies, writing styles, and formats. The chapter concludes with suggestions for illustrating report data.

Because business reports are systematic attempts to compile often complex information, answer questions, and solve problems, the best reports are developed methodically. In earlier chapters the 3-x-3 writing process was helpful in guiding the writing of short projects such as e-mails, memos, and letters. That same process is even more necessary when writers are preparing longer projects such as reports and proposals. After all, an extensive project poses a greater organizational challenge than a short one and, therefore, requires a rigorous structure to help readers grasp the message.

How much time you spend on each step depends on your report task. A short informational report on a familiar topic might require a brief work plan, little research, and no data analysis. A complex analytical report, on the other hand, might demand a comprehensive work plan, extensive research, and careful data analysis. In this section we consider the first three steps in the process—analyzing the problem and purpose, anticipating the audience and issues, and preparing a work plan.

To illustrate the planning stages of a report, we will watch Marley Moody develop a report she's preparing for her boss, Clay Zahota, at Genzyme Laboratories. Clay asked Marley to investigate the problem of transportation for sales representatives. Currently, some Genzyme reps visit customers (mostly doctors and hospitals) using company-leased cars. A few reps drive their own cars, receiving reimbursements for use. In three months Genzyme leasing agreements for 14 cars will expire, and Clay is considering a major change. Marley's task is to investigate the choices and report her findings to Clay.

11-1a Analyzing the Problem and Purpose

The first step in writing a report is clearly understanding the problem or assignment. For complex reports, prepare a written problem statement clarifying the task. In analyzing her report task, Marley had many questions: Is the problem that Genzyme spends too much money on leased cars? Does Genzyme wish to invest in owning a fleet of cars? Is Clay unhappy with the paperwork involved in reimbursing sales reps when they use their own cars? Does he suspect that reps are submitting inflated mileage figures? Before starting research for the report, Marley talked with Clay to define the problem. She learned several dimensions of the situation and wrote the following statement to clarify the problem—both for herself and Clay.

> **Problem statement:** The leases on all company cars will expire in three months. Genzyme must decide whether to renew them or develop a new policy regarding transportation for sales reps. Expenses and paperwork for employee-owned cars seem excessive.

Marley further defined the problem by writing a specific question that she would try to answer in her report:

> **Problem question:** What plan should Genzyme follow in providing transportation for its sales reps?

Now Marley was ready to concentrate on the purpose of the report. Again, she had questions: Exactly what did Clay expect? Did he want a comparison of costs for buying and leasing cars? Should she conduct research to pinpoint exact reimbursement costs when employees drive their own cars? Did he want her to do all the legwork, present her findings in a report, and let him decide? Or did he want her to evaluate the choices and recommend a course of action? After talking with Clay, Marley was ready to write a simple purpose statement for this assignment.

Simple statement of purpose: To recommend a plan that provides sales reps with cars to be used in their calls.

Preparing a written **purpose statement** is a good idea because it defines the focus of a report and provides a standard that keeps the project on target. In writing useful purpose statements, choose action verbs telling what you intend to do: *analyze, choose, investigate, compare, justify, evaluate, explain, establish, determine*, and so on. Notice that Marley's statement begins with the action verb *recommend*.

Some reports require only a simple statement of purpose: *to investigate expanded teller hours, to select a manager from among four candidates, to describe the position of accounts supervisor*. Many assignments, though, demand additional focus to guide the project. An expanded statement of purpose considers three additional factors: scope, limitations, and significance.

Scope and Limitations.

What issues or elements will be investigated? The **scope statement** prepares the audience by clearly defining which problem or problems will be analyzed and solved. To determine the scope, Marley brainstormed with Clay and others to pin down her task. She learned that Genzyme currently has enough capital to consider purchasing a fleet of cars outright. Clay also told her that employee satisfaction is almost as important as cost-effectiveness. Moreover, he disclosed his suspicion that employee-owned cars cost Genzyme more than leased cars. Marley had many issues to sort out in setting the boundaries of her report.

What conditions affect the generalizability and utility of a report's findings? As part of the scope statement, the **limitations** further narrow the subject by focusing on constraints or exclusions. For this report Marley realized that her conclusions and recommendations might apply only to reps in her Kansas City sales district. Her findings would probably not be appropriate for reps in Seattle, Phoenix, or Atlanta. Another limitation for Marley was time. She had to complete the report in four weeks, thus restricting the thoroughness of her research.

Significance.

A **significance statement** tells why the topic is worth investigating at this time. Some topics, after initial examination, turn out to be less important than originally thought. Others involve problems that cannot be solved, making a study useless. For Marley and Clay, the problem had significance because Genzyme's leasing agreement would expire shortly and decisions had to be made about a new policy for the transportation of sales reps.

Marley decided to expand her statement of purpose to define the scope, describe the limitations of the report, and explain the significance of the problem.

Expanded statement of purpose: The purpose of this report is to recommend a plan that provides sales reps with cars to be used in their calls. The report will compare costs for three plans: outright ownership, leasing, and compensation for employee-owned cars. It will also measure employee reactions to each plan. The report is significant because Genzyme's current leasing agreement expires March 31 and an improved plan could reduce costs and paperwork. The study is limited to costs for sales reps in the Kansas City district.

After expanding her statement of purpose, Marley checked it with Clay to be sure she was on target.

11-1b Anticipating the Audience and Issues

After defining the purpose of a report, a writer must think carefully about who will read it. Concentrating solely on a primary reader is a major mistake. Although one individual may have solicited the report, others within the organization may eventually read it, including people in upper management and other departments. A report to an outside client may first be read by someone familiar with the problem and then be distributed to others less familiar with it. Moreover, candid statements to one audience may be offensive to another audience. Marley could

"My years at the United Nations made me the Grand Mistress of report writing. We wrote daily, weekly, monthly and annual reports. A couple of years in the UN and you can write reports in your sleep. Because I cared so deeply about the people I was writing about, I wanted to be sure the people in Kabul or New York who read my reports were paying attention. So I taught myself to tell a good story in every report. People pay attention and keep reading for a good story."[3]

—Marianne Elliott, *writer and human rights advocate*

make a major blunder, for instance, if she mentioned Clay's suspicion that sales reps were padding their mileage statements. If the report were made public—as it probably would be to explain a new policy—the sales reps could feel insulted that their integrity was questioned.

As Marley considered her primary and secondary readers, she asked herself these questions:

- *What do my readers need to know about this topic?*
- *What do they already know?*
- *What is their education level?*
- *How will they react to this information?*
- *Which sources will they trust?*
- *How can I make this information readable, believable, and memorable?*

Answers to these questions help writers determine how much background material to include, how much detail to add, whether to include jargon, what method of organization and presentation to follow, and what tone to use.

In the planning stages, a report writer must also break the major investigative problem into subproblems. This process, sometimes called factoring, identifies issues to be investigated or possible solutions to the main problem. In this case Genzyme must figure out the best way to transport sales reps. Each solution or issue that Marley considers becomes a factor or subproblem to be investigated. Marley came up with three tentative solutions to provide transportation to sales reps: (a) purchase cars outright, (b) lease cars, or (c) compensate employees for using their own cars. These three factors formed the outline of Marley's study.

Marley continued to factor these main points into the following subproblems for investigation:

What plan should Genzyme use to transport its sales reps?

I. Should Genzyme purchase cars outright?

   A. How much capital would be required?

   B. How much would it cost to insure, operate, and maintain company-owned cars?

   C. Do employees prefer using company-owned cars?

II. Should Genzyme lease cars?

   A. What is the best lease price available?

   B. How much would it cost to insure, operate, and maintain leased cars?

   C. Do employees prefer using leased cars?

III. Should Genzyme compensate employees for using their own cars?

   A. How much has it cost in the past to compensate employees who used their own cars?

   B. How much paperwork is involved in reporting expenses?

   C. Do employees prefer being compensated for using their own cars?

Each subproblem would probably be further factored into additional subproblems. These issues may be phrased as questions, as Marley's are, or as statements. In factoring a complex problem, prepare an outline showing the initial problem and its breakdown into subproblems. Make sure your divisions are consistent (don't mix issues), exclusive (don't overlap categories), and complete (don't skip significant issues).

11-1c Preparing a Work Plan

After analyzing the problem, anticipating the audience, and factoring the problem, you are ready to prepare a work plan. A good work plan includes the following:

- Statement of the problem (based on key background/contextual information)
- Statement of the purpose including the scope with limitations and significance

- Research strategy including a description of potential sources and methods of collecting data
- Tentative outline that factors the problem into manageable chunks
- Work schedule
- Composition of first draft
- Editing, proofreading, and evaluating

Preparing a plan encourages you to evaluate your resources, set priorities, outline a course of action, and establish a schedule. Having a plan keeps you on track and provides management with a means of measuring your progress.

A work plan gives a complete picture of a project. Because the usefulness and quality of any report rest primarily on its data, you will want to develop a clear research strategy, which includes allocating plenty of time to locate sources of information. For firsthand information you might interview people, prepare a survey, or even conduct a scientific experiment. For secondary information you will probably search electronic materials on the Internet and printed materials such as books and magazines. Your work plan describes how you expect to generate or collect data. Because data collection is a major part of report writing, the next section of this chapter treats the topic more fully.

Model Document 11.1 shows a complete work plan for a proposal pitched by social marketing company BzzAgent's advertising executive Dave Balter to his client Lee Jeans. A work plan is useful because it outlines the issues to be investigated. Notice that considerable thought and discussion and even some preliminary research are necessary to be able to develop a useful work plan.

Although this tentative outline guides the investigation, it does not determine the content or order of the final report. You may, for example, study five possible solutions to a problem. If two prove to be useless, your report may discuss only the three winners. Moreover, you will organize the report to accomplish your goal and satisfy the audience. A busy executive familiar with a topic may prefer to read the conclusions and recommendations before a discussion of the findings. If someone authorizes the report, be sure to review the work plan with that person (your manager, client, or professor, for example) before proceeding with the project.

11-2 Researching Report Data

LEARNING OUTCOME

2 Identify the resources and methods used in conducting primary and secondary research.

Research is one of the most important initial steps in writing a business report. Research may be defined as the methodical search for information relevant to the report topic. Research is usually divided into two categories. Primary research is the act of generating or gathering firsthand data. Secondary research involves the use of existing data already collected. For example, an organization preparing a survey to determine how many employees would use a proposed fitness center is conducting primary research. Reading what others have written about fitness centers is considered secondary research.

As you begin collecting data, you will answer questions about your objectives and audience: Will your readers need considerable background information? Will they value or trust statistics, case studies, or expert opinions? Will the audience want to see data from interviews or surveys? Will summaries of focus groups be useful? Should you rely on organizational data? Figure 11.1 lists five categories of data and provides questions to guide you in making your research accurate and productive.

11-2a Conducting Primary Research

Most writers of workplace and student reports begin their investigation with secondary research. However, problems that require current information often rely on primary, firsthand data, which is where we begin our discussion. Writers typically generate primary data using one of the following methods: (a) surveys, (b) interviews, (c) observation, or (d) experimentation.

Reality Check

Understanding Research

"Primary research, sometimes referred to as 'field research,' is the collection and analysis of information and data that is not already available... Secondary research, or 'desk research,' is the synthesis of information and data that has already been collected. Journals, books, import and export data, production data, and government statistics and censuses are all examples of secondary research."[4]

—Olivia Hutchinson, *consultant, worldwide marketing firm, Euromonitor International*

Statement of Problem

Many women between the ages of 22 and 35 have trouble finding jeans that fit. Lee Jeans hopes to remedy that situation with its One True Fit line. We want to demonstrate to Lee that we can create a word-of-mouth campaign that will help it reach its target audience.

Statement of Purpose

Defines purpose, scope, limits, and significance of report

The purpose of this report is to secure an advertising contract from Lee Jeans. We will examine published accounts about the jeans industry and Lee Jeans in particular. In addition, we will examine published results of Lee's current marketing strategy. We will conduct focus groups of women in our company to generate campaign strategies for our pilot study of 100 BzzAgents. The report will persuade Lee Jeans that word-of-mouth advertising is an effective strategy to reach women in this demographic group and that BzzAgent is the right company to hire. The report is significant because an advertising contract with Lee Jeans would help our company grow significantly in size and stature.

Research Strategy (Sources and Methods of Data Collection)

Describes primary and secondary data

We will gather information about Lee Jeans and the product line by examining published marketing data and conducting focus group surveys of our employees. In addition, we will gather data about the added value of word-of-mouth advertising by examining published accounts and interpreting data from previous marketing campaigns, particularly those targeted toward similar age groups. Finally, we will conduct a pilot study of 100 BzzAgents in the target demographic.

Tentative Outline

Factors problem into manageable chunks

I. How effectively has Lee Jeans marketed to the target population (women ages 22 to 35)?
   A. Historically, who has typically bought Lee Jeans products? How often? Where?
   B. How effective are the current marketing strategies for the One True Fit line?
II. Is this product a good fit for our marketing strategy and our company?
   A. What do our staff members and our sample survey of BzzAgents say about this product?
   B. How well does our pool of BzzAgents correspond to the target demographic in terms of age and geographic distribution?
III. Why should Lee Jeans engage BzzAgent to advertise its One True Fit line?
   A. What are the benefits of word of mouth in general and for this demographic in particular?
   B. What previous campaigns have we engaged in that demonstrate our company's credibility?
   C. What are our marketing strategies, and how well did they work in the pilot study?

Work Schedule

Estimates time needed to complete report tasks

Investigate Lee Jeans and One True Fit line's current marketing strategy	July 15–25
Test product using focus groups	July 15–22
Create campaign materials for BzzAgents	July 18–31
Run a pilot test with a selected pool of 100 BzzAgents	August 1–21
Evaluate and interpret findings	August 22–25
Compose draft of report	August 26–28
Revise draft	August 28–30
Submit final report	September 1

Tips for Preparing a Work Plan

- Start early; allow plenty of time for brainstorming and preliminary research.
- Describe the problem motivating the report.
- Write a purpose statement that includes the report's scope, significance, and limitations.
- Describe the research strategy including data collection sources and methods.
- Divide the major problem into subproblems stated as questions to be answered.
- Develop a realistic work schedule citing dates for the completion of major tasks.
- Review the work plan with whoever authorized the report.

FIGURE 11.1 Questions to Ask When Collecting Report Data

Background Information	Expert Opinion	Surveys, Interviews, and Observation	Statistical Data	Organizational Data
What does the audience already know?	Who are the experts? Whose opinions will the audience value?	Are credible surveys available?	How recent are the data?	Can in-house data be obtained?
Has this topic been investigated before?	Are their opinions in print?	If surveys are not available, are there questionnaires that could be modified?	What or who is the source?	Are permissions required?
Is the available data current, relevant, and credible?	Are they available for interviewing?	Would firsthand observation provide useful information?	How was the data derived?	How can data be gathered from public companies?
Will I need to add to the available data?	Are in-house experts available?	How much time or expense is necessary to generate data?	Will the statistical data be useful in its present form?	Is relevant data available from private organizations?

Surveys. A **survey** is a method of gathering information from a sample of people, usually with the goal of generalizing the results to a larger audience. Businesses and researchers in all industries and workplaces conduct surveys to help them answer important questions. Should we, for example, develop a new product to remain competitive? How can we attract the best employees? How do our customers rate our service? Maria Avila, chair of the Student Activity Fee Allocation Committee at her college, prepared a survey to gather information from students about how to spend the collected funds. Her survey, shown in Figure 11.2, illustrates several effective guidelines.

djile/Shutterstock.com

How to Develop and Conduct an Effective Survey. Surveys help businesses stay attuned to employees, customers, and markets. By using surveys, researchers can gather information economically, quickly, and efficiently whether respondents are nearby or far away. The following guidelines can help elicit the most accurate and useful survey information.

- **Choose the best media channel for conducting your survey**. Consider your time frame, budget, skills, and goals in deciding how to do it. You could conduct your survey in person, by telephone, or online. Contemporary surveys are increasingly conducted online from websites.[5] Low-cost Web-based applications such as SurveyMonkey can help you automate the collection of data. If you have 10 or fewer questions, SurveyMonkey offers its platform free. Other survey platforms are Google Forms and SurveyGizmo.

- **Select the survey population carefully**. Some surveys question a small group of people (a sample) and project the findings to a larger population. Let's say that a survey of your class reveals that nearly everyone favors reusable, refillable water bottles to reduce plastic pollution in the environment. Can you then say that all students on your campus (or in the nation) prefer refillable bottles? To be able to generalize from a survey, you must make the sample large enough. In addition, you would want to determine whether the sample represents the larger population. Serious researchers apply scientific sampling techniques.

- **Prepare a cover letter or introductory paragraph explaining the survey purpose**. Strive to show how the survey benefits the receiver or someone other than you. If appropriate, offer to send recipients a report of the findings.

- **Limit the number of questions**. Resist the temptation to ask for too much. Request only the information you will use. Don't, for example, include demographic questions (income, gender, age, and so forth) unless the information is necessary to evaluate responses.

- **Use questions that produce quantifiable answers**. Check-off, multiple choice, yes-no, and/or rank-order (scale) questions, as illustrated in Figure 11.2, provide quantifiable data that are easily tabulated. For ranking and multiple-choice questions, try to present all the possible answer choices. To be safe, add an *Other* category in case the choices seem insufficient to the respondent. Typical scale headings are *Agree strongly, Agree somewhat, Neutral, Disagree somewhat*, and *Disagree strongly*.

- **Avoid leading or ambiguous questions**. The wording of a question can dramatically affect responses. In one study when asked, "Are we spending too much, too little, or about the right amount on *assistance to the poor*?" 13 percent responded *Too much*. When the same respondents were asked, "Are we spending too much, too little, or about the right amount on *welfare*?" 44 percent responded *Too much*. Because words have different meanings for different people, strive to use objective language. If in doubt, pilot test your questions with typical respondents.

- **Tabulate the responses and analyze the findings**. Record the findings in a data sheet such as an Excel spreadsheet. Group all the answers for each question and tabulate the totals. Look for patterns that help answer the original research questions. To help readers understand the findings, create simple tables summarizing the results. You might also provide a blank copy of the questionnaire. When finished, be sure to keep all responses.

Interviews. One of the best research tools is the interview. Interviews of informed individuals can generate excellent information, particularly on topics about which little has been written. These individuals are usually experts or veterans in their fields. Consider both in-house and outside experts for business reports. Tapping these competent sources will call for in-person, telephone, or online interviews.

How to Conduct an Effective Research Interview. Regardless of how the interview is conducted, you can usually generate the most valuable data by structuring the interview with open-ended questions. Your primary goal is to hear from respondents about what they think is important about the topic and to hear it in their own words.

FIGURE 11.2 Preparing an Online Survey

1 Prewriting

Analyze: The purpose of this survey is to collect information on how students want their Student Activity funds allocated.

Anticipate: The audience will be busy students who may be initially uninterested.

Adapt: Because students may be unwilling to participate, the survey must be short and simple. Its purpose must be significant and clear. It must be easy to complete online.

2 Drafting

Research: Prepare clear, unambiguous questions with quantifiable answers. Provide logical choices.

Organize: Begin with a cover message that explains the purpose and stresses reader benefits. Organize yes-no, multiple choice, scale, and other questions concisely.

Draft: Write the first version of the questionnaire. Consider testing it on a representative audience.

3 Revising

Edit: Rewrite any questions that the pilot test revealed to be confusing. Polish your writing, choosing precise words.

Proofread: Read for correctness. Be sure that answer choices do not overlap and that they are complete. Provide an *Other* category if appropriate.

Evaluate: Is the survey clear, attractive, and easy to complete? Did you cover all necessary topics?

FIGURE 11.2   Preparing an Online Survey

Uses e-mail formatting →

Includes clear subject →

Send														Options...	HTML		

To: Tatum Tio<tatum.tio@gmail.com>

From: Maria Avila <mavila@centralstateuniversity.edu>

Subject: REQ: How Should Your Student Activity Fees Be Spent?

Dear Central State Student:

Explains the purpose of the survey from the receiver's point of view →

Please complete this online survey so that funds can be allotted to events and causes that you choose. The Student Activity Fee Allocation Committee needs your input to determine how to apportion the funds that you contribute. The primary purpose of this fee is to increase opportunities for student involvement in the educational process, particularly the out-of-class experience. In the past this fee was used for lectures, entertainment, diversity events, and student trips.

Motivates response with more "you" view →

Your responses are critical in letting us know what is most important to you for future allocations. We greatly appreciate your feedback.

Maria Avila, Chair
CSU Student Activity Fee Allocation Committee

STUDENT ACTIVITY FEE ALLOCATION COMMITTEE SURVEY

1. What year are you?
   ○ First year   ○ Sophomore   ○ Junior   ○ Senior

Presents easy-to-read format →

2. How many units are you carrying this semester?
   ○ 6 or fewer units   ○ 7-10 units   ○ 11-16 units   ○ 17 or more units

Uses questions that produce quantifiable results →

3. Have you attended any events sponsored by your Student Activity Fee?
   ○ Yes   ○ No

Allows respondents to rank responses and includes "Other" option for additional choice →

4. How should your student activity fee be spent? Please rank in order of importance to you, 1 being the most important.
   ○ Lectures and special   ○ Fitness Center equipment   ○ Entertainment
     speakers on campus   and extended hours   events

   ○ Diversity programs   ○ Support of clubs

   ○ Other (please specify) [   ]

Limits the number of responses →

5. When do you prefer entertainment events to be scheduled?
   ○ Lunchtimes   ○ Late evening   ○ Early evening   ○ Weekends

Includes few ranking questions because they take longer to answer →

6. Rank in level of importance the following entertainment events, 1 being most important.

   ○ Movie nights   ○ Dances   ○ Karaoke   ○ Cultural events

   ○ Musical and novelty performances   ○ Other [   ]

Controls responses instead of posing open-ended query →

7. Indicate your position on the following alternatives.

	Agree	Undecided	Disagree
The current Student Activity fee should be reduced or eliminated.	○	○	○
The current fee should be increased to support more and better student activities and events.	○	○	○
The current fee is about right.	○	○	○

Concludes with single open-ended question to elicit more information →

8. What would you like to see changed or improved in relation to the Student Activity fee? [   ]

Thank you for helping the Student Activity Fee Allocation Committee decide how to distribute its funds.

The following techniques can help you generate the most valuable data.

- **Locate an expert**. Ask managers and individuals who are the most knowledgeable in their areas. Check membership lists of professional organizations, and consult articles about the topic. Most people enjoy being experts or at least recommending them. You could also *crowdsource* your question in social media; that is, you could pose the query to your network to get input from your contacts.

- **Prepare for the interview**. Learn about the individual you are interviewing, and make sure you can pronounce the interviewee's name. Research the background and terminology of the topic. Let's say you are interviewing a corporate communication expert about producing an in-house newsletter. You ought to be familiar with terms such as *font* and software such as Microsoft Publisher, Adobe InDesign, and Zara. In addition, be prepared by making a list of questions that pinpoint your focus on the topic. Ask the interviewee if you may record the talk. Familiarize yourself with the recording device beforehand.

- **Maintain a professional attitude**. Call before the interview to confirm the arrangements, and then arrive on time. Be prepared to take notes if your recorder fails (and remember to ask permission beforehand if you want to record). Use your body language to convey respect.

- **Make your questions objective and friendly**. Adopt a courteous and respectful attitude. Don't get into a debating match with the interviewee, and don't interrupt. Remember that you are there to listen, not to talk! Use open-ended questions to draw experts out.

- **Watch the time**. Tell interviewees in advance how much time you expect to need for the interview. Don't overstay your appointment. If your subject rambles, gently try to draw the interviewee back to the topic; otherwise, you may run out of time before asking all your questions.

- **End graciously**. Conclude the interview with a general question, such as *Is there anything you would like to add?* Express your appreciation and ask permission to telephone later if you need to verify points.

Observation and Experimentation.

Some kinds of primary data can be obtained only through firsthand observation and investigation. If you determine that you need observational data, then you need to plan carefully. Most important is deciding what or whom you are observing and how often those observations are necessary. For example, if you want to learn more about an organization's live chat customer service, you would probably need to conduct an observation (along with interviews and perhaps even surveys). You will want to answer questions such as *How long does a typical caller wait before a chat service rep responds?* and *How many chat sessions can a service rep handle in a given amount of time?*

To observe, arrive early enough to introduce yourself and set up any equipment. If you are recording, secure permissions beforehand. In addition, take notes, not only of the events or actions but also of the settings. Changes in environment often have an effect on actions. Former Starbucks chief Howard Schultz long resisted research, advertising, and customer surveys. Instead of relying on sophisticated marketing research, Schultz would visit 25 Starbucks locations a week to learn about his customers. Faced with slowing growth in the United States and intense competition in China, Starbucks rebounded by cultivating customer loyalty in its smartphone app and rewards program.[7]

Pressmaster/Shutterstock.com

Experimentation produces data suggesting causes and effects. Informal experimentation might be as simple as a pretest and posttest in a college course. Did students learn in the course? Scientists and professional researchers undertake more formal experimentation. They control variables to test their effects. Assume, for example, that Hershey's wants to test the hypothesis (a tentative assumption) that chocolate provides an emotional lift. An experiment testing the hypothesis would separate depressed people into two groups: the chocolate eaters (the experimental group) and the chocolate deprived (the control group). Such experiments are not done haphazardly, however. Valid experiments require sophisticated research designs with careful matching of control and experimental groups.

11-2b Conducting Secondary Research

Instead of collecting and analyzing primary data, most report writers begin with secondary research. With the sheer volume and breadth of data publicly available today, you are likely to find that something has already been written about your topic. Why reinvent the wheel?

Reviewing secondary sources can save time and effort because typically the data have already been organized and stored in an electronic format. But where to begin? Following is information about the most valuable secondary resources, including books, library databases, periodicals, and encyclopedias.

Books and E-Books. Print and e-books provide excellent historical, in-depth data. Check the book's table of contents or index to find information relevant to your project. You may also find helpful citations to other resources in the book's bibliography. Although books can become swiftly outdated, they provide a broad background.

By the way, if you are an infrequent library user, begin your research by talking with a reference librarian about your project. Librarians won't do your research for you, but they will steer you in the right direction. Many librarians help you understand their computer, cataloging, and retrieval systems by providing advice, brochures, handouts, and workshops. As one wise person observed, "Google can bring you back 100,000 answers; a librarian can bring you back the right one."[9]

Library Databases. Most writers conducting secondary research quickly turn to library databases because they are fast and easy to use. You can use your computer to conduct detailed searches without ever leaving your office, home, or dorm room.

A database is a collection of searchable information stored digitally so that it is accessible by computer or mobile electronic devices. Libraries subscribe to databases that provide bibliographic information (titles of documents and brief abstracts) and links to full-text documents. Library databases contain a rich array of magazine, newspaper, and journal articles, as well as newsletters, business reports, company profiles, government data, reviews, and directories. The five databases most useful to business writers are ABI/INFORM Complete Collection (ProQuest), EBSCO (Business Source Premier), JSTOR Business, Factiva (Dow Jones), and LexisNexis Academic. Figure 11.3 shows the EBSCO and ABI/INFORM search menus.

Periodicals. Publications that are produced on a set schedule are called periodicals. Three kinds of periodicals may be helpful in your research:

- **Scholarly journals** publish peer-reviewed articles usually written by academics, experts, or researchers. The in-depth articles are likely to be scientifically valid, contain original research, and reach reasonable conclusions. Examples include *The Journal of Business and Professional Communication*, *Journal of Management*, and *Technology and Culture*.

- **Trade publications** offer practical articles written to appeal to individuals interested in a specific trade or industry. Examples include *Advertising Age*, *Beverage and Industry*, and *Women's Wear Daily*. Although trade publication articles are not peer-reviewed, they provide specialized information that may not be available elsewhere.

- **Newspapers, magazines, and other popular periodicals** include *The New York Times*, *Sports Illustrated*, and *People*. Their primary purpose is to produce a profit, entertain, persuade, or inform the general public. Newspapers and magazines are excellent for up-to-date information on current events and for opinion pieces. However, like trade publications, articles in popular periodicals are not peer-reviewed. Therefore, they must be cited cautiously in reports.

In conducting digital research, one must be selective, guarding against distractions and information overload.

FIGURE 11.3 Library Database Search Result

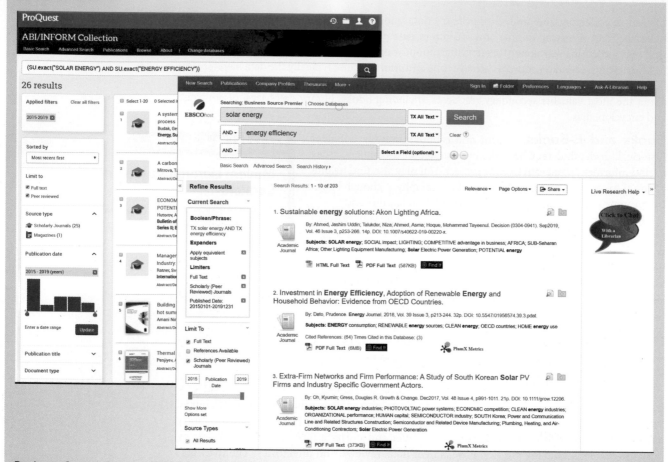

Business Source Premier (EBSCO) provides full text for more than 2,300 periodicals, including 1,100 peer-reviewed journals. ABI/INFORM (ProQuest) indexes more than 6,800 journals and features more than 5,510 full-text documents about business topics. Users can access newspapers, magazines, reports, dissertations, book reviews, scholarly journals, and trade publications. Figure 11.3 shows that the search terms *solar energy* and *energy efficiency* brought up 203 full-text, peer-reviewed search results in EBSCO and only 26 full-text, peer-reviewed search results in ABI/INFORM after a more focused search. When retrieving too many results, savvy researchers further narrow their search to retrieve a more manageable number.

Source: EBSCO PUBLISHING

Wikipedia and Other Encyclopedias. College-level research requires you to use general encyclopedia information only as a starting point for more in-depth research. That means you will not cite nor copy from Wikipedia, general encyclopedias, search engines, or similar reference works in your writing. Because most online encyclopedias are crowdsourced, their information is too uneven in quality and too general. However, these information-packed sites often provide references (bibliographies) that you can employ in your research. Locate the original sources of information rather than the condensed reference articles. Both the American Psychological Association (APA) and the Modern Language Association (MLA) favor the use of original source material.

11-2c Searching the Internet

Finding what you are seeking on the Internet is hopeless without powerful search tools such as browsers and search engines. When you enter a search term, you usually do so in a **browser** such as (Google) Chrome, (Mozilla) Firefox, (Apple) Safari, or (Microsoft) Edge. A browser is a software application that connects to servers and displays their webpages. When you enter keywords or search terms into a browser, a **search engine** scans hundreds of millions of webpages to locate the desired content. Some of the best-known search engines are Google, Bing, Baidu, and DuckDuckGo.

How does a search engine work? Using your keywords, it sends out software robots, known as spiders or crawlers, to locate the requested content. These bots scour the Web searching for documents, images, videos, PDFs, and other files. The search engine then sorts and organizes the content and ranks it from most to least relevant. Your Web browser allows you to see the results of this search. Most search engines list the results based on how frequently users access them. Therefore, you shouldn't just rely on the links on top of the first browser page.

Applying Internet Search Strategies and Techniques. It's easy to use Google casually to find a restaurant menu or trivia answers. However, using the Internet to find factual, rigorous, reliable data requires skill. The following tips can help you conduct serious secondary research efficiently and effectively.

- **Define your search question**. Before logging on, frame your search in a question. A building contractor might ask, "Is it worth it to *go green* in constructing an apartment complex?"

- **Choose effective keywords**. Analyze your topic and distill it into four or five words. The building contractor might search for *green building, ecofriendly construction, sustainability costs*, and *LEED certification*.

- **Use natural language questioning**. Most search engines today also respond to natural language questioning. Relying on artificial intelligence, search engines understand questions as people speak them. No longer restricted to keyword searches, a contractor seeking information might ask, "What is the return on investment (ROI) for going green in constructing an apartment complex?" Today's search engines might respond with solid hits or with a number of related questions to be searched, thus expanding the possibilities.

- **Try scholarly Web searches**. For academic topics, use Google Scholar and Google's Advanced Search for more nuanced results. Both tools allow you to focus and limit your search very precisely.

- **Employ Boolean search strategies**. The most skilled researchers save time by narrowing their searching with these Boolean operators:

AND	Identifies only documents containing all specified words: **green building** AND **ROI**
OR	Identifies documents containing at least one of the specified words: **green building** OR **ecofriendly construction** OR **sustainability**
NOT	Excludes documents containing the specified word: **green construction** NOT **color**
NEAR	Finds documents containing target words or phrases within a specified distance, for instance, within ten words: **green building** NEAR **costs**

- **Enclose keywords in quotation marks**. When search terms are enclosed in quotation marks, the search engine can go straight to an exact match. Using quotation marks eliminates many marginal hits.

- **Bookmark everything interesting**. Even if you are not sure you will use it, bookmark anything that just might be helpful. Removing a bookmark is easy, but tracking down a lost reference can be maddening. Refer to the accompanying Plugged In to help you keep track of your research data.

- **Keep trying**. If a search produces no results, check your spelling. If you are using Boolean operators, check the syntax of your queries. Try synonyms and variations on words. If your search procures too many hits, try to be more specific. Think of words that uniquely identify what you are looking for. Use as many relevant keywords as possible.

Evaluating the Credibility of Internet Sources. Most Internet users tend to assume that any information located by a search engine has somehow been evaluated as part of a valid selection process. Wrong! Unlike library-based research, information at many sites has not undergone the editing or scrutiny of scholarly publication procedures. Anyone can publish anything, truthful or not. That's what makes the Internet treacherous.

Ethics ✓ Check

Jail Time for Fraudulent Researchers?

Australian researcher Bruce Murdoch admitted that his breakthrough findings for Parkinson's disease were false. A judge concluded that there was no evidence that the neuroscientist had conducted the clinical trial on which his published findings were based. Murdoch admitted that he had even forged consent forms for participants, one of whom was dead at the time of the study.[10] Should researchers go to jail for fabricating data in their studies?

Plugged In

Staying on Top of Research Data

In collecting search results, you can easily lose track of websites and articles you quoted. To document Web data that may change, as well as to manage all your other sources, you need a plan for saving the information. At the very least, you will want to create a *working bibliography* or list of *references* in which you record the URL of each electronic source. These techniques can help you stay in control of your data:

- **Saving sources to a local drive or USB flash drive** has advantages, including being able to open the document in a browser even if you don't have access to the Internet. More important, saving sources to disk or memory stick preserves information that may not be available later. Using either the **File** and **Save As** or the **File** and **Save Page As** menu command in your browser, you can store the information permanently. Save images and other kinds of media by either right-clicking or command-clicking on the item, and selecting **Save Picture As** or **Save Image As**. Sometimes e-mail can be a useful retrieval method. Many databases and online magazines permit you to e-mail information and sometimes the entire article to your account.

- **Copying and pasting** information you find on the Web into Microsoft Word is an easy way to save and store it. Copy and paste the URL into the file as well, and record the URL in your working bibliography. You can save most files as PDFs simply by choosing the **Print** command and selecting Adobe PDF in the **Printer** window of the **Print** menu. You can keep your PDF documents as electronic files or print paper copies later.

- **Printing** at least some pages remains a handy way to gather and store information. Doing so enables you to have copies of important data that you can annotate or highlight. Make sure the title of the article or the URL prints with the document (usually on the bottom of the page). If not, write it on the page.

- **Bookmarking favorites** is an option within browsers to enable you to record and store the URLs of important sources. The key to using this option is creating folders with relevant names and choosing concise and descriptive names for bookmarks.

- **Cloud storage and note-taking apps** can help you keep track of documents, quotes, clippings, images, or URLs. Cloud storage accounts such as Dropbox, Google Drive, Microsoft OneDrive, or iCloud let you access your files from any electronic device. The most popular note-taking apps are Evernote and Microsoft OneNote. Their biggest advantage for researchers is that documents archived in these apps are searchable. They can be tagged, annotated, and edited.

Information on the Web is much less reliable than information from traditional sources. Blogs and discussion forum entries illustrate this problem. They change constantly and may disappear fast, so that your source can't be verified. Many don't provide any references or reveal sources that are either obscure or suspect. Academic researchers prefer lasting, scholarly sources.

To use the Internet meaningfully, you must scrutinize what you find and check who authored and published it. Here are specific criteria to consider as you examine a site:

- **Currency**. What is the date of the Web page? Is some of the information obviously out-of-date? If the information is time sensitive and the site has not been updated recently, the site is probably not reliable.

- **Authority**. Who publishes or sponsors this Web page? What makes the presenter an authority? Is information about the author or creator available? Is a contact address available for the presenter? Learn to be skeptical about data and assertions from individuals and organizations whose credentials are not verifiable.

- **Content**. Is the purpose of the page to entertain, inform, convince, or sell? How would you classify this page (e.g., news, personal, advocacy, reference)? Who is the intended audience, based on content, tone, and style? Can you judge the overall value of the content compared with the other resources on this topic?

- **Accuracy**. Do the facts seem reliable? Are there errors in spelling, grammar, or usage? Do you see any evidence of bias? Are references provided? Errors and missing references should alert you that the data may be questionable.

FOR THE RECORD

The Short Life of Electric Scooters

Suddenly electric scooters multiplied on sidewalks and street corners across the country. Bird and Lime, two companies pushing the shareable dockless vehicles, seemingly had hit upon a potentially huge market. Electric scooters could transform urban transportation. But had the investors done the research necessary to ensure acceptance and profitability? In many cities, vandals, pedestrians, and infuriated merchants rebelled by destroying unwanted scooters littering walkways. Scooter companies were accused of dumping the vehicles while ignoring local regulations. Although the companies may become profitable, some researchers expect to see many go bankrupt.[11] What kinds of primary and secondary research could have prevented the backlash and potential bankruptcy?

11-3 Understanding Typical Report Functions, Organization, Writing Styles, and Formats

Business reports range widely in length, purpose, and delivery mode. Some are short, informal bulleted lists with status updates. Others are formal 100-page financial forecasts. Report findings may be presented orally in a meeting or shared online. Reports today are delivered digitally in e-mail messages, PDF (portable document format) files, websites, or in slide decks. Report files can be accessed on a company's intranet or saved on cloud servers off-site. Although reports vary greatly in many characteristics, they all have one or more of the following purposes: *to convey information, answer questions,* and *solve problems.*

11-3a Functions

In terms of functions, most business reports fit into one of two broad categories, informational reports and analytical reports.

Informational Reports. Informational reports present data without analysis or recommendations. For such reports, writers collect and organize facts, but they do not analyze the facts for readers. A trip report describing an employee's visit to a trade show, for example, presents information. Weekly bulleted status reports distributed by e-mail to a team would present the activities of each group member and are shared with supervisors. Other reports that present information without analysis are monthly sales reports, progress reports, and government compliance reports.

Analytical Reports. In addition to reporting data and findings, analytical reports provide analysis and conclusions. If requested, writers also supply recommendations. Analytical reports may intend to persuade readers to act or change their beliefs. For example, if you were writing a yardstick report that compares several potential manufacturing locations for a new automobile plant, you would compare the locations using the same criteria and then provide a recommendation. Other reports that provide recommendations are feasibility studies (e.g., for expansion opportunities) and justification reports (e.g., for buying equipment or changing procedures).

To distinguish among findings, conclusions, and recommendations, consider the example of an audit report. The auditor compiles facts and figures—the findings of the report—to meet the purpose or objective of the audit. Drawing inferences from the findings, the auditor arrives at conclusions. With the audit objectives in mind, the auditor may then propose corrective steps or actions as part of the recommendations.

11-3b Organizational Strategies

Like other business messages, reports may be organized directly or indirectly. The reader's anticipated reaction and the content of a report determine its organizational strategy, as illustrated in Figure 11.4. In long reports, such as corporate annual reports, some parts may be developed directly, whereas other parts are arranged indirectly.

Direct Strategy.   When you place the purpose for writing close to the beginning of a report, the organizational strategy is direct. Informational reports, such as the short report shown in Model Document 11.2, are usually arranged directly. They open with an introduction, which is followed by the facts and a summary. In Model Document 11.2 Noah Prewarski responds to a request for information about a legal services plan offered by Alliance Legal Plans. The report opens with an introduction that provides details about two kinds of plans. Following is information about a plan's services and benefits for both employees and employers. The report ends with a summary and a complimentary close. Notice that side headings promote readability by breaking up large chunks of text into convenient and inviting segments.

Analytical reports may also be organized directly, especially when readers are supportive of or familiar with the topic. Many busy executives prefer this strategy because it gives them the results of the report immediately. They don't have to spend time wading through the facts, findings, discussion, and analyses to get to the two items they are most interested in—the conclusions and recommendations. Model Document 11.3 illustrates such an arrangement in a short analytical report in memo format. Sebastian Lugo, an investigator for Environmental Consultants, describes

---

FIGURE 11.4   **Audience Analysis and Report Organization**

If readers are informed | If readers are eager to have results first | If readers are supportive

Direct Strategy

Informational Report
- **Introduction/Background**
- **Facts/Findings**
- **Summary**

Analytical Report
- **Introduction/Problem**
- **Conclusions/Recommendations**
- **Facts/Findings**
- **Discussion/Analysis**

If readers need to be educated | If readers need to be persuaded | If readers may be disappointed or hostile

Indirect Strategy

Analytical Report
- **Introduction/Problem**
- **Facts/Findings**
- **Discussion/Analysis**
- **Conclusions/Recommendations**

---

environmental hazards of a property that Mountain View Realty has just listed. The realtor is familiar with the investigation and eager to learn the recommendations. Therefore, the memo is organized directly. You should be aware, though, that unless readers are familiar with the topic, they may find the direct strategy confusing. Many readers prefer the indirect strategy because it seems logical and mirrors the way they solve problems.

Indirect Strategy.   The organizational strategy is indirect when the conclusions and recommendations, if requested, appear at the end of the report. Such reports usually begin with an introduction or description of the problem, followed by facts and interpretations from the writer. They end with conclusions and recommendations. This strategy is helpful when readers are unfamiliar with the problem. This strategy is also useful when readers must be persuaded or when they may be disappointed in or hostile toward the report's findings. The writer is more likely to retain the reader's interest by first explaining, justifying, and analyzing the facts and then making recommendations. This strategy also seems most rational to readers because it follows the normal thought process: problem, alternatives (facts), solution.

MODEL DOCUMENT 11.2   **Short Informational Report – Letter Format**

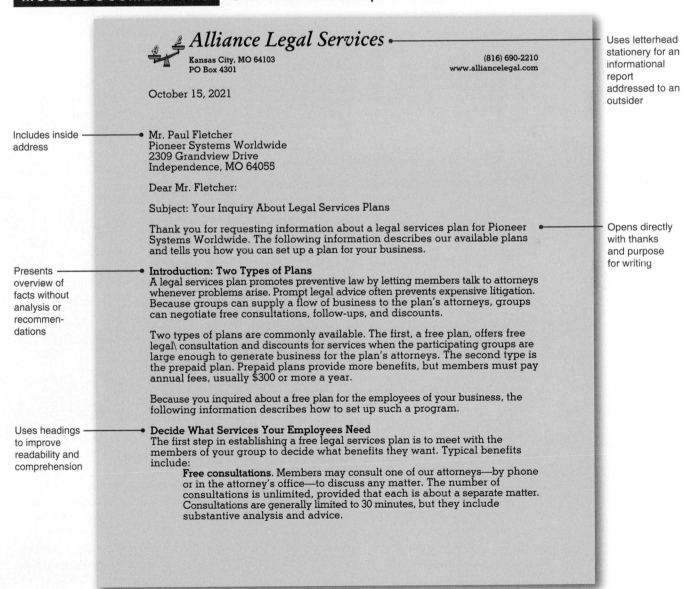

Uses letterhead stationery for an informational report addressed to an outsider

Alliance Legal Services

Kansas City, MO 64103
PO Box 4301

(816) 690-2210
www.alliancelegal.com

October 15, 2021

Includes inside address

Mr. Paul Fletcher
Pioneer Systems Worldwide
2309 Grandview Drive
Independence, MO 64055

Dear Mr. Fletcher:

Subject: Your Inquiry About Legal Services Plans

Thank you for requesting information about a legal services plan for Pioneer Systems Worldwide. The following information describes our available plans and tells you how you can set up a plan for your business.

Opens directly with thanks and purpose for writing

Presents overview of facts without analysis or recommendations

Introduction: Two Types of Plans
A legal services plan promotes preventive law by letting members talk to attorneys whenever problems arise. Prompt legal advice often prevents expensive litigation. Because groups can supply a flow of business to the plan's attorneys, groups can negotiate free consultations, follow-ups, and discounts.

Two types of plans are commonly available. The first, a free plan, offers free legal\ consultation and discounts for services when the participating groups are large enough to generate business for the plan's attorneys. The second type is the prepaid plan. Prepaid plans provide more benefits, but members must pay annual fees, usually $300 or more a year.

Because you inquired about a free plan for the employees of your business, the following information describes how to set up such a program.

Uses headings to improve readability and comprehension

Decide What Services Your Employees Need
The first step in establishing a free legal services plan is to meet with the members of your group to decide what benefits they want. Typical benefits include:

Free consultations. Members may consult one of our attorneys—by phone or in the attorney's office—to discuss any matter. The number of consultations is unlimited, provided that each is about a separate matter. Consultations are generally limited to 30 minutes, but they include substantive analysis and advice.

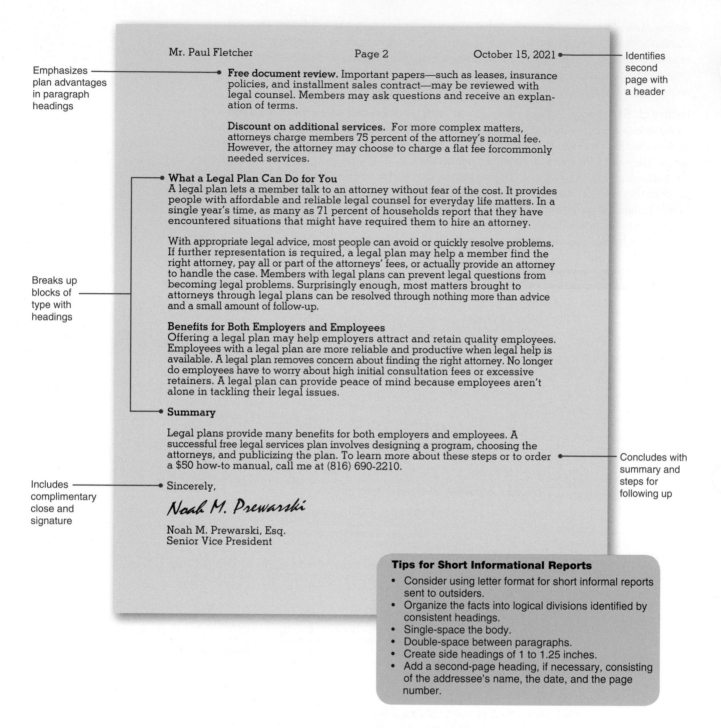

Identifies second page with a header

Emphasizes plan advantages in paragraph headings

Free document review. Important papers—such as leases, insurance policies, and installment sales contract—may be reviewed with legal counsel. Members may ask questions and receive an explanation of terms.

Discount on additional services. For more complex matters, attorneys charge members 75 percent of the attorney's normal fee. However, the attorney may choose to charge a flat fee forcommonly needed services.

Breaks up blocks of type with headings

What a Legal Plan Can Do for You
A legal plan lets a member talk to an attorney without fear of the cost. It provides people with affordable and reliable legal counsel for everyday life matters. In a single year's time, as many as 71 percent of households report that they have encountered situations that might have required them to hire an attorney.

With appropriate legal advice, most people can avoid or quickly resolve problems. If further representation is required, a legal plan may help a member find the right attorney, pay all or part of the attorneys' fees, or actually provide an attorney to handle the case. Members with legal plans can prevent legal questions from becoming legal problems. Surprisingly enough, most matters brought to attorneys through legal plans can be resolved through nothing more than advice and a small amount of follow-up.

Benefits for Both Employers and Employees
Offering a legal plan may help employers attract and retain quality employees. Employees with a legal plan are more reliable and productive when legal help is available. A legal plan removes concern about finding the right attorney. No longer do employees have to worry about high initial consultation fees or excessive retainers. A legal plan can provide peace of mind because employees aren't alone in tackling their legal issues.

Summary

Legal plans provide many benefits for both employers and employees. A successful free legal services plan involves designing a program, choosing the attorneys, and publicizing the plan. To learn more about these steps or to order a $50 how-to manual, call me at (816) 690-2210.

Concludes with summary and steps for following up

Includes complimentary close and signature

Sincerely,

Noah M. Prewarski

Noah M. Prewarski, Esq.
Senior Vice President

Tips for Short Informational Reports

- Consider using letter format for short informal reports sent to outsiders.
- Organize the facts into logical divisions identified by consistent headings.
- Single-space the body.
- Double-space between paragraphs.
- Create side headings of 1 to 1.25 inches.
- Add a second-page heading, if necessary, consisting of the addressee's name, the date, and the page number.

11-3c Informal and Formal Writing Styles

Like other business messages, reports can range from informal to formal, depending on their purpose, audience, and setting. An **informal writing style** is conversational. It is appropriate for familiar audiences and noncontroversial topics. Characterized by a friendly tone, first-person pronouns, and shorter sentences, an informal writing style is often used for short internal business reports.

A **formal writing style** is characterized by objectivity, authority, and impartiality. It is appropriate for proposals and long research reports. A report from a consultant informing executives about the feasibility of moving to a new location would tend to be formal.

An office worker once called a grammar hotline service with this problem: "We've just sent a report to our headquarters, and it was returned with this comment, 'Put it in the third person.'" What does it mean "to put it in the third person"? The hotline experts explained that management

Applies memo format for short, informal internal report; could also be sent as attachment to an e-mail message

Environmental Consultants
Interoffice Memo

Date: February 15, 2022
To: Kennedy de la Rocha
From: Sebastian Lugo *SL*
Subject: Investigation of Plains Realty Commercial Site

For Plains Realty, Inc., I've completed my preliminary investigation of its property listing. The following recommendations are based on my physical inspection of the site, official records, and interviews with officials and persons knowledgeable about the site.

Uses first paragraph as introduction

Recommendations

To reduce its potential environmental liability, Plains Reality should take the following steps in regard to its commercial listing at 3201 Highlands Plaza Drive:

Presents recommendations first (direct pattern) because reader is supportive and familiar with topic

- Conduct an immediate asbestos survey at the site, including inspection of ceiling insulation materials, floor tiles, and insulation around a gas-fired heater vent pipe in the building.

- Prepare an environmental audit of the generations of hazardous waste currently operating at the site, including Plains Technology.

- Obtain lids for the dumpsters situated in the parking areas and ensure that the lids are kept closed.

Findings and Analyses

Combines findings and analyses

My preliminary assessment of the site and its immediate vicinity revealed rooms with damaged floor tiles on the first and second floors of 3201 Highlands Plaza Drive. Apparently, in recent remodeling efforts, these tiles had been cracked and broken. Examination of the ceiling and attic revealed further possible contamination from asbestos. Additionally, the insulation for the hot-water tank was in poor condition.

Located on the property is Plains Technology, a possible hazardous waste generator. Although I could not examine its interior, this company has the potential for producing hazardous material contamination.

In the parking area, large dumpsters collect trash and debris from several businesses. These dumpsters were uncovered, thus posing a risk to the general public.

Discusses how to implement the recommended actions

In view of the construction date of the structures on this property, asbestos-containing building materials might be present. Moreover, this property is located in an industrial part of the city, further prompting my recommendation for a thorough investigation. Plains Realty can act immediately to eliminate one environmental concern: covering the dumpsters in the parking area.

I would be happy to investigate further if you think it is necessary.

Tips for Short Analytical Reports

- Use memo format for short (ten or fewer pages) informal reports within an organization.
- Leave side margins of 1 to 1.25 inches.
- If printed, sign your initials on the *From* line.
- If sent as an e-mail attachment, compose a short cover message introducing the attachment.
- Use an informal, conversational writing style.
- For direct analytical reports, put the recommendations first. For indirect reports, put the recommendations last.

---

apparently wanted a more formal writing style, using third-person constructions (*the company* or *the researcher* instead of *we* or *I*). However, formal report writers today are increasingly using contractions and active-voice verbs. They try to avoid awkward third-person references to themselves as *the researchers* or *the authors* because it sounds stilted and outdated. Figure 11.5, which compares the characteristics of formal and informal report-writing styles, can help you decide which style is appropriate for your reports.

FIGURE 11.5 Report-Writing Styles

	Informal Writing Style	Formal Writing Style
Appropriate Use	• Short, routine reports • Reports for familiar audiences • Noncontroversial reports • Internal use reports • Internal announcements and invitations	• Lengthy, formal reports and proposals • Research studies • Controversial or complex reports • External use reports • Formal invitations
Overall Effect	• Friendly tone • Relationship building • Casual	• Objectivity and accuracy • Sense of professionalism and fairness • Professional distance between writer and reader
Writing Style Characteristics	• Use of first-person pronouns (*I, we, me, my, us, our*) • Use of contractions (*can't, don't*) • Emphasis on active-voice verbs (*I conducted the study*) • Shorter sentences • Familiar words • Conversational language	• Use of third-person (*the researcher, the writer*), depending on the circumstances. • Absence of contractions (*cannot, do not*) • Use of passive-voice verbs (*the study was conducted*) • Professional, respectful language • Absence of humor and figures of speech • Elimination of "editorializing" (author's opinions and perceptions)

11-3d Typical Report Formats

Reporting in organizations remains a key need in business today. Many types of reports coexist and vary greatly by sector or industry. The format of a report depends on its length, topic, audience, and purpose. After considering these elements, you will probably choose from among the following formats.

Digital Formats and PDF Files.   Writers routinely save and distribute reports as portable document format (PDF) files. This file type, invented by Adobe, condenses documents while preserving the formatting and graphics. A report created with Microsoft Word, Excel, or PowerPoint can easily be saved as a PDF file. A PDF report might include links to external websites, a nice advantage over printed reports. Web-based reports may feature engaging multimedia effects, such as interactive charts and video.

Digital Slide Decks.   Many business writers deliver their report information in a digital slideshow, also called a slide deck. These slides can be sent by e-mail, posted on the Web, or accessed on a company intranet. When used in reporting, slide decks may have more text than typical presentation slides. Photographs, tables, charts, and other visuals make slide decks more inviting to read than print pages of dense report text. Not surprisingly, communicators in marketing, technology, media, entertainment, and consulting are fond of using slide deck reports to summarize their statistics and other findings. Figure 11.6 illustrates a Facebook slide deck reporting topics and trends recently gaining momentum. The slides present the key elements of a report: introduction, methodology, concise descriptions, statistics, and even footnotes. From the conversation of Facebook users, this report documents developments in people's attitudes, expectations, and behaviors. This valuable information is of particular interest to Facebook advertisers as well as to other marketers looking for future consumer trends and behavior.

Infographics.   Infographics, short for information graphics, are visual representations of data or information. They can display complex information quickly and clearly, and they are easier to understand than written text. Infographics are also affordable and easily shared on social media platforms. In fact, good infographics can go viral when viewers embed and spread the word about them in their blogs and on their social media networks. Infographics can tell compelling stories that help all types of businesses attract and inform consumers. To learn more about infographics, refer to the Plugged In article on page 399.

FIGURE 11.6 Facebook Slide Deck

Facebook presents the culmination of a year's research and insights in a visually appealing slide deck. The report validates the findings of its research tracking conversations of its users in six categories: Art and Design, Beauty and Fashion, Entertainment, Food and Drink, Mind and Body, and Travel and Leisure. The slide deck follows a typical report format with a title page, table of contents, introduction, executive letter, methodology, and sections devoted to findings including statistics and charts—all properly footnoted.

E-Mail and Memo Formats. Many reports are attached to e-mails, posted online, or, if short, embedded in the body of e-mails. For short informal reports that stay within organizations, the memo format may still be appropriate. Memo reports begin with essential background information, using standard headings: *Date, To, From,* and *Subject,* as shown in Model Document 11.3. Memo reports differ from regular memos in length, use of headings, and deliberate organization. Today, memo reports are rarely distributed in hard copy; more likely they are shared electronically as PDF files.

Forms and Templates. Office workers use digital forms that are usually made available on the company intranet or the Internet. Such electronic templates are suitable for repetitive data, such as monthly sales reports, performance appraisals, merchandise inventories, and personnel and financial reports. Employees can customize and fill in the templates and forms. Then they distribute them electronically or print them. Using standardized formats and headings saves a writer time and ensures that all necessary information is included.

Letter Format. The letter format for short informal reports (usually eight or fewer pages) addressed outside an organization can still be found in government agencies, real estate, and accounting firms. Prepared on office stationery, a letter report contains a date, inside address, salutation, and complimentary close, as shown in Model Document 11.2. Although they may carry information similar to that found in correspondence, letter reports usually are longer and show more careful organization than typical letters. They also include headings to guide the reader through the content and may come with attachments. Like memo reports, letter reports are also likely to be sent to clients as PDF files.

Manuscript Format.   For longer, more formal reports, business writers use the manuscript format. These reports are usually printed on plain paper without letterhead or memo forms. They too can be shared digitally as PDF files. They begin with a title followed by systematically displayed headings and subheadings. You will see examples of proposals and formal reports using the manuscript format in Chapter 13.

LEARNING OUTCOME

4 Explain the importance and methods of documenting report information.

11-4 Documenting Information

In writing business reports, you will often build on the ideas and words of others. In Western culture, whenever you borrow the ideas of others, you must give credit to your information sources. This is called documentation.

11-4a The Purposes of Documentation

As a careful writer, you should take pains to document report data properly for the following reasons:

- **To strengthen your argument**. Including good data from reputable sources will convince readers of your credibility and the logic of your reasoning.
- **To protect yourself against charges of plagiarism**. Acknowledging your sources keeps you honest. Plagiarism, which is unethical and in some cases illegal, is the act of using others' ideas without proper documentation.
- **To instruct the reader**. Citing references enables readers to pursue a topic further and make use of the information themselves.
- **To save time**. The world of business moves so quickly that words and ideas must often be borrowed—which is very acceptable when you give credit to your sources.

11-4b Intellectual Theft: Plagiarism

Plagiarism of words or ideas is a serious offense and can lead to loss of a job. Famous historians, politicians, journalists, and even college professors have suffered grave consequences for copying from unnamed sources.[12] Your instructor may use a commercial plagiarism detection service such as Turnitin, which cross-references much of the information on the Web, looking for documents with identical phrasing. The result, an "originality report," shows the instructor whether you have been accurate and honest.

You can avoid charges of plagiarism as well as add clarity to your work by knowing what to document and by developing good research habits. First, however, let's consider the differences between business and academic writing with respect to documentation.

11-4c Academic Documentation and Business Practices

In the academic world, documentation is critical. Especially in the humanities and sciences, students are taught to cite sources by using quotation marks, parenthetical citations, footnotes, and bibliographies. College term papers require full documentation to demonstrate that a student has become familiar with respected sources and can cite them properly in developing an argument. Giving credit to the authors is extremely important. Students who plagiarize risk a failing grade in a class and even expulsion from school.

In business, however, documentation and authorship are sometimes viewed differently. Business communicators on the job may find that much of what is written does not follow the standards they learned in school. In many instances, individual authorship is unimportant. For example, employees may write for the signature of their bosses. The writer receives no credit. Similarly, teams turn out documents for which none of the team members receive individual credit. Internal business reports, which often include chunks of information from previous reports, also don't give credit. Even information from outside sources may lack detailed documentation. However, if facts are questioned, business writers must be able to produce their source materials.

Although both internal and external business reports are not as heavily documented as school assignments or term papers, business communication students are well advised to learn proper documentation methods. In the workplace, stealing the ideas of others and passing them off as one's own can be corrosive to the business because it leads to resentment and worse. One writer suggests that in addition to causing businesses to lose the public's trust, unethical practices undermine free markets and free trade.[13] Moreover, copyright and trademark violations are criminal offenses and can lead to severe punishment.

11-4d What to Document

When you write reports, especially in college, you are continually dealing with other people's ideas. You are expected to conduct research, synthesize ideas, and build on the work of others. But you are also expected to give proper credit for borrowed material. To avoid plagiarism, you must give credit whenever you use the following:[14]

- Another person's ideas, opinions, examples, or theory
- Any facts, statistics, graphs, and drawings that are not common knowledge
- Quotations of another person's actual spoken or written words
- Paraphrases of another person's spoken or written words
- Visuals, images, and any kind of electronic media

Information that is common knowledge requires no documentation. For example, the statement *The Wall Street Journal is a popular business newspaper* would require no citation. Statements that are not common knowledge, however, must be documented. For example, the following statement would require a citation because most people do not know this fact: *Phoenix, Arizona, is the nation's fastest-growing U.S. city with a population of 50,000 or more.*[15] More important, someone went through the trouble and expense of assembling this original work and now *owns* it. Cite sources for such proprietary information—in this case, statistics reported by a newspaper or magazine. You probably know to use citations to document direct quotations, but you must also cite ideas that you summarize in your own words.

When in doubt about common knowledge, check to see whether the same piece of information is available in at least three sources in your topic's specific field and appears without citation. If what you borrow doesn't fall into one of the five categories listed earlier for which you must give credit, you are safe in assuming it is common knowledge. Copyright and intellectual property are discussed in greater detail later in this chapter.

11-4e Good Research Habits

As they gather sources, report writers have two methods available for recording the information they find. The time-honored manual method of notetaking works well because information is recorded on separate cards, which can then be conveniently arranged in the order needed to develop a thesis or argument. Today, however, writers prefer to do their research online. Traditional notetaking may seem antiquated and laborious in comparison. Let's explore both methods.

Paper Note Cards. To make sure you know whose ideas you are using, train yourself to take excellent notes. If possible, know what you intend to find before you begin your research so that you won't waste time on unnecessary notes. Here are some pointers on taking good notes:

- Record all major ideas from various sources on separate note cards.
- Include all publication information (author, date, title, and so forth) along with precise quotations.

- Consider using one card color for direct quotes and a different color for your paraphrases and summaries.
- Put the original source material aside when you are summarizing or paraphrasing.

Digital Records. Instead of recording facts on note cards, savvy researchers take advantage of digital media tools, as noted earlier in the Plugged In box titled "Staying on Top of Research Data" on page 382. Beware, however, of the risk of cutting and pasting your way into plagiarism. Here are some pointers on taking good virtual notes:

- Begin your research by setting up a folder on your local drive or cloud-based storage site. On the go, you can access these files with any mobile electronic device, or you can use a USB flash drive to carry your data.
- Create subfolders for major sections, such as introduction, body, and closing.
- When you find facts on the Web or in research databases, highlight the material you want to record, copy it, and paste it into a document in an appropriate folder.
- Develop the habit of recording bibliographic information in the documentation format your report will follow. Include author(s), publication date, title, and "Retrieved from" address so that it will be handy for your references or works-cited lists.
- Consider archiving in cloud storage or on a USB flash drive those Web pages or articles used in your research in case the data must be verified.

11-4f The Fine Art of Paraphrasing

In writing reports and using the ideas of others, you will probably rely heavily on **paraphrasing**, which means restating an original passage in your own words and in your own style. To do a good job of paraphrasing, follow these steps:

1. Read the original material intently to comprehend its full meaning.
2. Write your own version without looking at the original.
3. Avoid repeating the grammatical structure of the original and merely replacing words with synonyms.
4. Reread the original to be sure you covered the main points but did not borrow specific language.

To better understand the difference between plagiarizing and paraphrasing, study the following passages. Notice that the writer of the plagiarized version uses the same grammatical construction as the source and often merely replaces words with synonyms. Even the acceptable version, however, requires a reference to the source author.

Source
Once Web enterprises figured out their business models and how to securely process credit cards, clicks turned to dollars, forging some of the most powerful companies in the world, companies that have since become titans in distribution, media, and even space travel.[16]

Plagiarized version
When Web businesses finally developed their business models and learned how to safely transact credit cards online, they were able to convert clicks to big bucks and create many of the most successful enterprises in the world, enterprises that have become leaders in media, distribution, and even space exploration.

Acceptable paraphrase
The ability to securely process credit cards online enabled Web entrepreneurs to convert clicks to profits, thus propelling the growth of many of today's most successful enterprises in media, distribution, and even space exploration.[17]

11-4g When and How to Quote

On occasion, you will want to use the exact words of a source, but beware of overusing quotations. Documents that contain pages of spliced-together quotations suggest that writers have few ideas of their own. Wise writers and speakers use direct quotations for three purposes only:

- To provide objective background data and establish the severity of a problem as seen by experts
- To repeat identical phrasing because of its precision, clarity, or aptness
- To duplicate exact wording before criticizing

When you must use a long quotation, try to summarize and introduce it in your own words. Readers want to know the gist of a quotation before they tackle it. For example, to introduce a quotation describing the impact of secure credit cards, you could precede the quotation with your words: *In describing the explosive growth of online enterprises as a result of secure online credit cards, in her book Broad Band, Evans observed that. . . .* To introduce quotations or paraphrases, use wording such as the following:

> *According to Evans, . . .*
>
> *Evans argues that . . .*
>
> *In her book, Evans reported . . .*

Use quotation marks to enclose exact quotations, as shown in the following. The Internet, a *"technology that began as a networked hypertext system for particle physicists," writes Clare Evans, "became the world's gossip page, multimedia art gallery, and library, in a feverish burst of cultural activity the likes of which the world has never seen"* (2018, p. 204).

11-4h Copyright Information

The **U.S. Copyright Act of 1976** protects authors—literary, dramatic, and artistic—of published and unpublished works. The word **copyright** refers to "the right to copy," and a key provision is **fair use**. Under fair use, individuals have limited use of copyrighted material without needing to acquire permission. These uses are for criticism, comment, news reporting, teaching, scholarship, and research. Unfortunately, the distinctions between fair use and infringement are not clearly defined.

Four-Factor Test to Assess Fair Use. What is fair use? Actually, it is a shadowy territory with vague and often disputed boundaries—now even more so with the addition of cyberspace. Courts use four factors as a test in deciding disputes over fair use:

- **Purpose and character of the use, particularly whether for profit**. Courts are more likely to allow fair use for nonprofit educational purposes than for commercial ventures.
- **Nature of the copyrighted work**. When information is necessary for the public good—such as medical news—courts are more likely to support fair use.
- **Amount and substantiality of portion used**. Copying a 200-word passage from a 200,000-word book might be allowed but not 200 words from a 1,000-word article or a substantial part of a shorter work. A total of 300 words is mistakenly thought by many to be an acceptable limit for fair use, but courts have not upheld this figure. Don't rely on it.
- **Effect of the use on the potential market**. If use of the work may interfere with the author's potential profit from the original, fair use copying would not be allowed.

How to Avoid Copyright Infringement. Whenever you borrow words, charts, graphs, photos, music, and other media—in short, any **intellectual property**—be sure you know what is legal and acceptable. The following guidelines will help:

- **Assume that all intellectual property is copyrighted**. Nearly everything created privately and originally after 1989 is copyrighted and protected whether or not it has a copyright notice.

- **Realize that Internet items and resources are NOT in the public domain**. No modern intellectual or artistic creation is in the **public domain** (free to be used by anyone) unless the owner explicitly says so.
- **Observe fair-use restrictions**. Be aware of the four-factor test. Avoid appropriating large amounts of outside material.
- **Ask for permission**. You are always safe if you obtain permission. Write to the source, identify the material you wish to include, and explain where it will be used. Expect to pay for permission.
- **Don't assume that a footnote is all that is needed**. Including a footnote to a source prevents plagiarism but not copyright infringement. Anything copied beyond the boundaries of fair use requires permission.

For more information about *copyright law, fair use, public domain*, and *work for hire*, you can search the Web with these keywords.

11-4i Citation Formats

You can direct readers to your sources with parenthetical notes inserted into the text and with bibliographies. The most common **citation formats** are those presented by the MLA and the APA. Learn more about how to use these formats in Appendix B.

LEARNING OUTCOME

5 Generate and incorporate meaningful visual aids and graphics in business reports.

11-5 Creating Meaningful Graphics

Whether you are presenting a business report in person, in print, or digitally, you can create visual interest and clarify the data with meaningful graphics. If your report contains complex data and numbers, you may want to consider graphics such as tables and charts. By simplifying complex ideas and emphasizing key data, well-constructed graphics make key information easier to remember. However, the same data can be shown in many forms, for example, in a chart, table, or graph. The following guidelines will help you match the graphic with your objective and how to incorporate it into your report.

11-5a Matching Graphics and Objectives

In developing the best graphics, you must decide what data you want to highlight and which graphics are most appropriate given your objectives. Tables? Bar charts? Pie charts? Line charts? Surface charts? Flowcharts? Organization charts? Pictures? Figure 11.7 summarizes appropriate uses for each type of graphic. The following sections discuss each type in more detail.

Tables. Probably the most frequently used graphic in reports is the **table**. Because a table presents quantitative or verbal information in systematic columns and rows, it can clarify large quantities of data in small spaces. The disadvantage is that tables do not readily display trends. You may have made rough tables to help you organize the raw data collected from questionnaires or interviews. In preparing tables for your readers or listeners, however, you need to pay more attention to clarity and emphasis. Following are tips for making effective tables, one of which is provided in Figure 11.8.

Place titles and labels at the top of the table.

Arrange items in a logical order (alphabetical, chronological, geographical, highest to lowest), depending on what you need to emphasize.

Provide clear headings for the rows and columns.

Identify the units in which figures are given (percentages, dollars, units per worker hour) in the table title, in the column or row heading, with the first item in a column, or in a note at the bottom.

FIGURE 11.7   Matching Graphics to Objectives

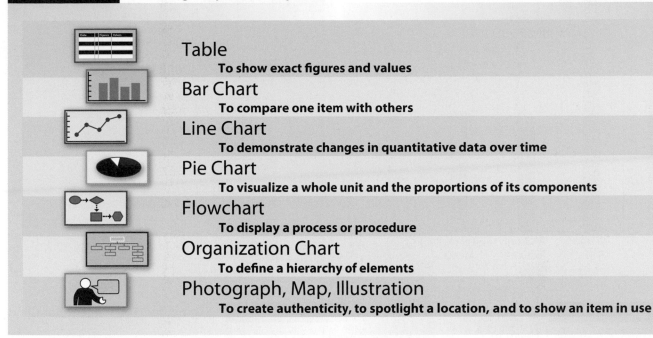

Table
To show exact figures and values

Bar Chart
To compare one item with others

Line Chart
To demonstrate changes in quantitative data over time

Pie Chart
To visualize a whole unit and the proportions of its components

Flowchart
To display a process or procedure

Organization Chart
To define a hierarchy of elements

Photograph, Map, Illustration
To create authenticity, to spotlight a location, and to show an item in use

- Use *N/A* (*not available*) for missing data.
- Make long tables easier to read by shading alternate lines or by leaving a blank line after groups of five.
- Place tables as close as possible to the place where they are mentioned in the text.

As illustrated in Figure 11.8, tables are especially suitable for showing exact figures in systematic rows and columns. The table in our figure is particularly useful because it presents data about the MPM Entertainment Company over several years, making it easy to compare several divisions. Figures 11.9 through 11.12 highlight additional data shown in the MPM Entertainment Company table. These figures illustrate four types of **bar charts**: vertical, horizontal, grouped, and segmented 100 percent bar charts, each of which creates a unique effect.

FIGURE 11.8   Table Summarizing Precise Data

Figure 1
MPM ENTERTAINMENT COMPANY
Income by Division (in millions of dollars)

	Theme Parks	Motion Pictures	Streaming Media	Total
2019	$15.8	$39.3	$11.2	$66.3
2020	18.1	17.5	15.3	50.9
2021	23.8	21.1	22.7	67.6
2022	32.2	22.0	24.3	78.5
2023 (projected)	35.1	21.0	26.1	82.2

Source: Industry Profiles (New York: DataPro, 2023) 225.

Bar Charts.   Although they lack the precision of tables, bar charts enable you to make emphatic visual comparisons by using horizontal or vertical bars of varying lengths. Bar charts are useful for comparing related items, illustrating changes in data over time, and showing segments as a part of the whole. Note how the varied bar charts present information in differing ways.

Many techniques for constructing tables also hold true for bar charts. Here are a few additional tips:

- Keep the length and width of each bar and segment proportional.
- Include a total figure in the middle or at the end of the bar if the figure helps the reader and does not clutter the chart.
- Start dollar or percentage amounts at zero.
- Place the first bar at some distance (usually half the amount of space between bars) from the *y*-axis.
- Avoid showing too much information, to avoid clutter and confusion.
- Place each bar chart as close as possible to the place where it is mentioned in the text.

FIGURE 11.9   Vertical Bar Chart

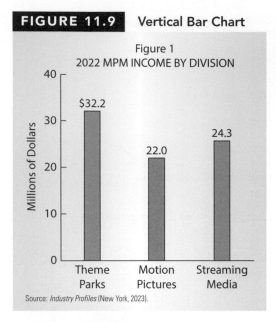

Figure 1
2022 MPM INCOME BY DIVISION

Source: *Industry Profiles* (New York, 2023).

FIGURE 11.10   Horizontal Bar Chart

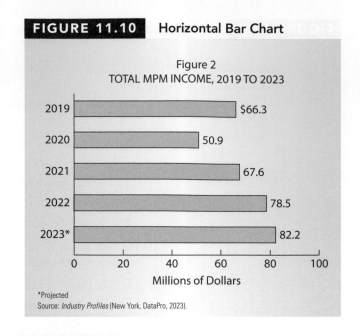

Figure 2
TOTAL MPM INCOME, 2019 TO 2023

*Projected
Source: *Industry Profiles* (New York, DataPro, 2023).

FIGURE 11.11   Grouped Bar Chart

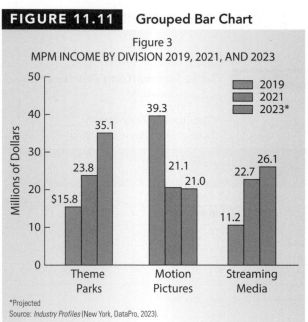

Figure 3
MPM INCOME BY DIVISION 2019, 2021, AND 2023

*Projected
Source: *Industry Profiles* (New York, DataPro, 2023).

FIGURE 11.12   Segmented 100 Percent Bar Chart

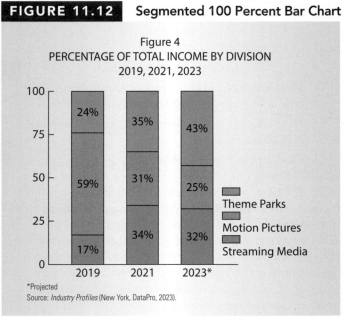

Figure 4
PERCENTAGE OF TOTAL INCOME BY DIVISION
2019, 2021, 2023

*Projected
Source: *Industry Profiles* (New York, DataPro, 2023).

Line Charts.   The major advantage of **line charts** is that they show changes over time, thus indicating trends. The vertical axis is typically the dependent variable, and the horizontal axis is the independent one. Simple line charts (Figure 11.13) show just one variable. Multiple line charts compare items, such as two or more data sets, using the same variable (Figure 11.14). Segmented line charts (Figure 11.15), also called surface charts, illustrate how the components of a whole change over time. To prepare a line chart, remember these tips:

- Begin with a grid divided into squares.
- Arrange the time component (usually years) horizontally across the bottom; arrange values for the other variable vertically.
- Draw small dots at the intersections to indicate each value at a given year.
- Connect the dots and add color if desired.
- To prepare a segmented (surface) chart, plot the first value (say, streaming media income) across the bottom; add the next item (say, motion picture income) to the first figures for every increment; for the third item (say, theme park income), add its value to the total for the first two items. The top line indicates the total of the three values.

FIGURE 11.13 Simple Line Chart

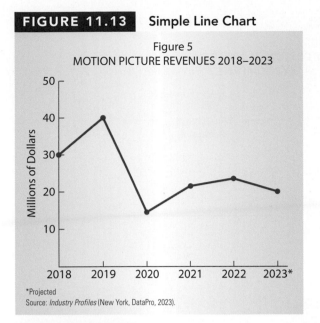

Figure 5
MOTION PICTURE REVENUES 2018–2023

*Projected
Source: *Industry Profiles* (New York, DataPro, 2023).

FIGURE 11.14 Multiple Line Chart

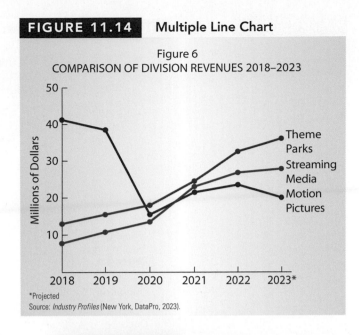

Figure 6
COMPARISON OF DIVISION REVENUES 2018–2023

*Projected
Source: *Industry Profiles* (New York, DataPro, 2023).

FIGURE 11.15 Segmented Line (Area) Chart

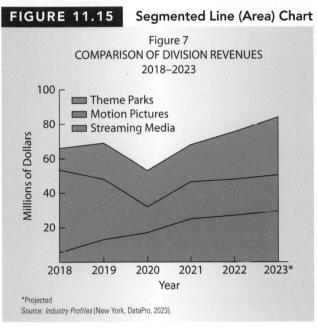

Figure 7
COMPARISON OF DIVISION REVENUES
2018–2023

*Projected
Source: *Industry Profiles* (New York, DataPro, 2023).

FIGURE 11.16 Pie Chart

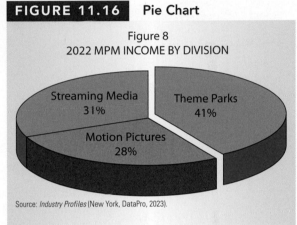

Figure 8
2022 MPM INCOME BY DIVISION

Source: *Industry Profiles* (New York, DataPro, 2023).

Pie Charts. **Pie charts,** or circle graphs, enable readers to see a whole and the proportion of its components, or wedges. Although less flexible than bar or line charts, pie charts are useful for showing percentages, as Figure 11.16 illustrates. They are very effective for lay, or nonexpert, audiences. Notice that a wedge can be exploded, or popped out, for special emphasis, as seen in Figure 11.16. Microsoft Excel and other spreadsheet programs provide a selection of three-dimensional pie charts. For the most effective pie charts, follow these suggestions:

- Make the biggest wedge appear first. Computer spreadsheet programs correctly assign the biggest wedge first (beginning at the 12 o'clock position) and arrange the others in order of decreasing size as long as you list the data representing each wedge on the spreadsheet in descending order.

- Include, if possible, the actual percentage or absolute value for each wedge.

- Use four to six segments for best results; if necessary, group small portions into a wedge called *Other.*

- Draw radii from the center.

Chapter 11 Report Writing Basics

FIGURE 11.17   Flowchart

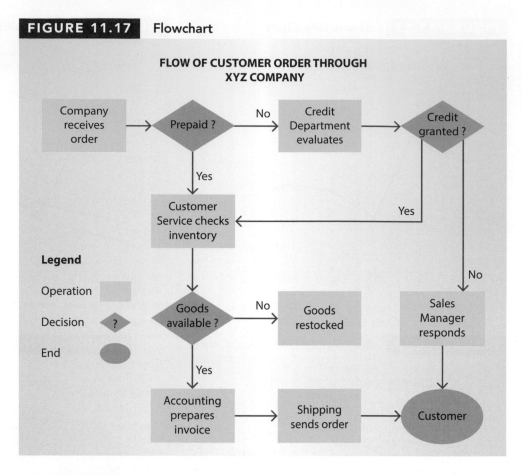

FLOW OF CUSTOMER ORDER THROUGH XYZ COMPANY

- Distinguish wedges with color, shading, or cross-hatching.
- Keep all the labels horizontal.

Flowcharts.   Procedures are simplified and clarified by diagramming them in a flowchart, as shown in Figure 11.17. Whether you need to describe the procedure for handling a customer's purchase, highlight steps in solving a problem, or display a problem with a process, flowcharts help the reader visualize the process. Traditional flowcharts use the following symbols:

- Ovals to designate the beginning and end of a process
- Diamonds to designate decision points
- Rectangles to represent major activities or steps

Organization Charts.   Many large organizations are so complex that they need charts to show the chain of command, from the boss down to the line managers and employees. Organization charts provide such information as who reports to whom, how many subordinates work for each manager (the span of control), and what channels of official communication exist. These charts may illustrate a company's structure—for example, by function, customer, or product. They may also be organized by the work being performed in each job or by the hierarchy of decision making.

Photographs, Maps, and Illustrations.   Some business reports include photographs, maps, and illustrations to serve specific purposes. Photos, for example, add authenticity and provide a visual record. An environmental engineer may use photos to document hazardous waste sites. Maps enable report writers to depict activities or concentrations geographically, such as dots indicating sales reps in states across the country. Illustrations and diagrams are useful in indicating how an object looks or operates. A drawing showing the parts of a printer with labels describing their functions, for example, is more instructive than a photograph or verbal description.

With today's smart visualization tools as described in the accompanying Plugged In box, high-resolution photographs, maps, and illustrations can be inserted into business reports, or accessed through hyperlinks within electronically delivered documents. Online they can be animated or appear in clusters as they do in infographics.

Plugged In

Infographics: More Than Pretty Pictures

An **infographic** combines words, figures, and graphics to transform complex information quickly and clearly using visually appealing pictures. More than compelling pictures, infographics are designed with a purpose. They offer a visual shorthand to deliver a message that presents information with few words. Many infographics include a call to action. The food safety infographic shown here carries information on the risk of mechanically tenderized beef. After describing the process of tenderizing beef, it explains the risk. The call to action describes how to cook steaks and roasts safely.

Infographics have many exciting purposes in conveying business information. They can be used to build an argument, to enliven statistics, to illustrate work-flow charts, to provide a timeline, to explain the sequence and steps in a process, to compare and contrast places and cultures, to show how multiple paths can lead to similar conclusions, to present interactivity in explaining novel ideas, and even to enhance employment résumés.

With today's innovative software, amateur designers can create their own infographics by combining facts, statistics, and graphics. The most effective designs begin with an engaging title followed by hard data usually in the form of statistics. Some of the best low-priced or free tools for beginning designers include Piktochart, Biteable, Mural, BeFunky, and Visme.

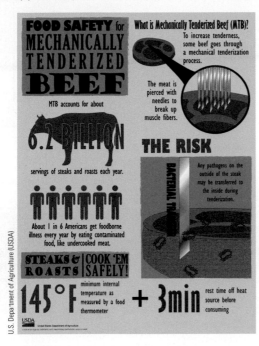

U.S. Department of Agriculture (USDA)

11-5b Incorporating Graphics in Reports

Used appropriately, graphics make reports more interesting and easier to understand. In putting graphics into your reports, follow these suggestions for best effects:

- **Evaluate the audience.** Consider the reader, the content, your schedule, and your budget. Graphics take time and can be costly to print in color, so think carefully before deciding how many graphics to use. Six charts in an internal report to an executive may seem like overkill; however, in a long technical report to outsiders, six may be too few.

- **Use restraint.** Don't overuse color or decorations. Although color can effectively distinguish bars or segments in charts, too much color can be distracting and confusing. Remember, too, that colors themselves sometimes convey meaning: red suggests deficits or negative values; blue suggests calmness and authority; and yellow may suggest warning.

- **Be accurate and ethical.** Double-check all graphics for accuracy of figures and calculations. Be certain that your visuals aren't misleading—either accidentally or intentionally. Manipulation of a chart scale can make trends look steeper and more dramatic than they really are. Moreover, be sure to cite sources when you use someone else's facts. The Ethical Insight box discusses in more detail how to make ethical charts and graphs.

- **Introduce a graph meaningfully.** Refer to every graphic in the text, and place the graphic close to the point where it is mentioned. Most important, though, help the reader understand the significance of the graphic. You can do this by telling your audience what to look for or by summarizing the main point of the graphic. Don't assume the reader will automatically reach the same conclusions you reached from a set of data. Instead of saying, *The* *findings are shown in Figure 3*, tell the reader what to look for: *Two thirds of the responding employees, as shown in Figure 3, favor a flextime schedule*. The best introductions for graphics interpret them for readers.

- **Choose an appropriate caption or title style**. Like reports, graphics may use talking titles or generic, descriptive titles. Talking titles are more persuasive; they tell the reader what to think. Descriptive titles describe the facts more objectively.

Talking Title	Descriptive Title
Rising Workplace Drug Testing Unfair and Inaccurate	Workplace Drug Testing Up 277 Percent
College Students' Diets Clogged With Fat	College Students and Nutrition

Ethical Insights

Creating Accurate Graphics

Graphical data must be represented in the same ethical, honest manner required for all other messages. Remember that the information shown in your charts and graphics will be used to inform others or help them make decisions.

Chart data can be distorted in many ways. Figure 1 shows advertising expenses displayed on an appropriate scale. Figure 2 shows the same information, but the horizontal scale, from 2017 to 2022, has been lengthened. Notice that the data have not changed but the increases and decreases are smoothed out, so changes in expenses appear to be slight. In Figure 3, the vertical scale is taller and the horizontal scale is shortened, resulting in what appear to be sharp increases and decreases in expenses.

To avoid misrepresenting data, keep the following pointers in mind when designing your graphics:

- Design the chart so that it focuses on the appropriate information.

- Don't misrepresent data by plotting in misleading intervals, as shown in Figures 2 and 3.
- Don't bury critical information by including too much data in one graphic.

Career Application

Locate one or two graphics in a newspaper, magazine article, or business report. Analyze the strengths and weaknesses of each graphic. Is the information presented accurately? Select a bar or line chart. Sketch the same chart but change the vertical or horizontal scales on the graphic. How does the message or the chart change?

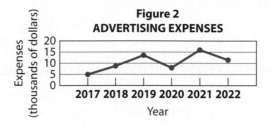

Figure 2
ADVERTISING EXPENSES

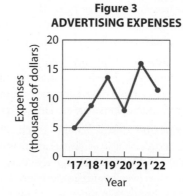

Figure 1
ADVERTISING EXPENSES

Figure 3
ADVERTISING EXPENSES

Zooming In

Your Turn:
Applying Your Skills at Seventh Generation

Your Turn at Seventh Generation

Assume you are an intern at Seventh Generation working for the senior public relations manager. She has been asked to make a presentation at the fall meeting of the New England Association of Chambers of Commerce. Her topic will focus on nonprofit B corporations and their goal of using business as a force for good. She wants to avoid promoting Seventh Generation or its products. Instead, she plans to explain the certification process involved in becoming a B corporation and why having this certification benefits society as well as businesses. She knows that you may be unfamiliar with B corporations. However, she also knows that you have just completed college courses in which you learned to conduct Internet research. Your task is intended to expand your knowledge as well as provide facts for her presentation.

Your Task

Locate at least seven Internet articles on the topic of B corporations. What are they, why are they important, and how does a company become certified? Prepare an annotated bibliography that includes a brief synopsis of each article. Your boss might want to distribute the bibliography to the audience at her talk. To make it look professional, list each article using APA citation format. Refer to Appendix C for examples. For additional examples, look at the Notes section for all references in this textbook. Prepare your list as part of a memo report addressed to your instructor. Here are two sample citations:

- Stammer, R. (2016, June 12). It pays to become a B corporation. Retrieved from https://hbr.org

Richard Stammer's article in the *Harvard Business Review* describes why he decided to seek B-corporation certification for his local company, Cabot Creamery Cooperative. He notes that several Nielsen studies indicate that consumers will pay more for products coming from companies with a demonstrated commitment to sustainability. The article describes other reasons for certification, and it notes many well-known companies that are B corporations, a few of which are Ben & Jerry's, Fetzer Vineyards, and Patagonia.

- Weinreb, S. (2018, April 30). Mission driven business? Here's why to become a B corp, according to four certified companies. Retrieved from https://www.forbes.com

This article in *Forbes* is especially useful because it explains many benefits from becoming certified as a B corp. One benefit is that the certification sets high standards for companies to comply. It provides benchmarks for local purchasing, carbon emissions, and fair labor. Among the many financial, social, and community-driven reasons a business would seek B corp certification is the fact that consumers would recognize what businesses to trust and buy from. It's a seal of approval.

SUMMARY OF LEARNING OUTCOMES

1 Apply the 3-x-3 writing process to create well-organized business reports.

- In applying the 3-x-3 writing process, report writers begin by preparing a problem statement, which may include the scope, significance, and limitations of the project.

- After analyzing the audience and defining major issues, report writers prepare a work plan, including a tentative outline and work schedule.

- Next, data must be collected, organized, interpreted, and illustrated.

- After composing the first draft, report writers edit (often many times), proofread, and evaluate.

2 Identify the resources and methods used in conducting primary and secondary research.

- One of the most important steps in writing business reports is conducting research, which is the methodical gathering of information.

- Primary research is the act of generating or gathering firsthand data. Secondary research involves the use of existing data already collected.

- Researchers generate primary data through surveys (in-person, online, and print), interviews, observation, and experimentation.

- Surveys are most efficient for gathering information from large groups of people; interviews are useful when working with experts in the field.

- Experimentation may produce data suggesting cause and effect; valid experiments require sophisticated research designs and careful matching of experimental and control groups.

- Secondary data may be located by searching in books, periodicals (scholarly articles, trade publications, newspapers, magazines), encyclopedias, and online databases.

- One of the most effective was to conduct secondary research is by browsing the Internet with search engines, but the retrieved information must be scrutinized for currency, authority, content, and accuracy.

3 Outline informational and analytical report functions, strategies, and formats.

- Informational reports—such as monthly sales reports, status updates, and compliance reports—present data without analysis or recommendations.

- Analytical reports provide findings, analyses, conclusions, and recommendations when requested. Examples include justification, recommendation, feasibility, and yardstick reports.

- Audience reaction and content determine whether a report is organized directly or indirectly.

- Reports organized directly reveal the purpose and conclusions immediately; reports organized indirectly place the conclusions and recommendations last.

- Reports written in a formal style use third-person constructions, avoid contractions, and may include passive-voice verbs. Informal reports use first-person constructions, contractions, shorter sentences, familiar words, and active-voice verbs.

- Reports may appear in various formats: e-mail, letter, memo, manuscript, template, infographic, or slide deck. They may be shared electronically or in hard copy.

4 Explain the importance and methods of documenting report information.

- Documenting sources means giving credit to information sources to avoid plagiarism, strengthen an argument, and instruct readers.

- Although documentation is less strict in business reports than in academic writing, business writers need to learn proper techniques to verify their sources and avoid plagiarism.

- Report writers should document others' ideas, facts that are not common knowledge, quotations, and paraphrases; good notetaking is essential to giving accurate credit to sources.

- Paraphrasing involves putting another's ideas into one's own words.

- Quotations may be used to provide objective background data, to repeat memorable phrasing, and to duplicate exact wording before criticizing.

5 Generate and incorporate meaningful visual aids and graphics in business reports.

- Graphics clarify data, add visual interest, and make complex data easy to understand.

- Tables show quantitative information in systematic columns and rows; they require meaningful titles, bold labels, and a logical arrangement (alphabetical, chronological, etc.).

- Bar charts and line charts enable data to be compared visually; line charts are especially helpful in showing changes over time.

- Pie charts show a whole and the proportion of its components; flowcharts diagram processes and procedures.

- Infographics combine images and graphic elements to illustrate information in an easy-to-understand format.

- Report writers work carefully to avoid distorting visual aids.

Key Terms

Critical Thinking

1. Why do researchers trust the reliability of information obtained from scholarly journals, major newspapers, and well-known magazines? Why should researchers use caution when accessing information from anonymous blogs, Wikipedia, and other crowdsourced content? (L.O. 3)

2. An infographic is far more effective at conveying statistics than any bar graph or pie chart, claims Dallas marketing firm Frozen Fire.[19] Do you agree or disagree? How could infographics be useful in your field? (L.O. 5).

3. Some people say that business reports never contain footnotes. If you were writing your first report for a business and you did considerable research, what would you do about documenting your sources? (L.O. 4)

4. Of what use is a business report that is merely informational? That is, it does not present analysis, conclusions, or recommendations. (L.O. 3)

5. **Ethical Issue:** Consider this logical appeal under the heading "Reasons Students Hate Writing Essays or Term Papers" and evaluate its validity and ethics:

   Three term papers due tomorrow with three major tests from three of the classes as well as a long math assignment. What should a student do? This problem while in [sic] exaggeration often happens to students. It is like all the teachers decide to overwhelm the students in their classes with not only tests on the same day but also term papers, essays, or other writing assignments. This is the reason most students hate writing term papers or other types of writing. Other reasons for disliking writing assignments are poor English classes in high school, often instructors fail to explain different writing styles, unsure of topics to write, and instructors fail to read the writing assignments.[. . .] Don't be afraid to reach out and get help if it's needed! CustomPapers.com can assist you.[20]

Activities

11.1 Problem, Purpose, and Scope Statements (L.O. 1)

YOUR TASK The following situations require reports. For each situation write (a) a concise problem question, (b) a simple statement of purpose, and (c) a scope statement with limitations if appropriate.

a. Foot Locker must collect data on its core customers—12- to 25-year-old sneakerheads—who want tomorrow's shoes today. The company seeks to transform itself from a 45-year-old brick-and-mortar enterprise into a nimble, tech-driven business able to respond immediately to the latest trends. First, however, it must better understand its customers and how to reach them.[21]

b. Customers placing telephone orders for outdoor gear and apparel clothing at Patagonia usually order only one or two items. The company wonders whether it can train telephone service reps to motivate customers to increase the number of items ordered per call.

c. A third of millennials are reportedly permanently deleting their social media accounts, with Facebook among the first to go.[22] As a business owner who regularly advertises on social media platforms, you want to compare the revenue you receive from targeted ads on Twitter, Instagram, Snapchat, and Pinterest against the results you usually see with Facebook ads.

d. Valley View Elementary school worries about the increasing morning chaos of cars and busses. Parents dropping off children form long lines backing up traffic, while crossing guards herd children through the dangerous gridlock. Major problems are the single entrance and exit, along with buses making wide turns. Valley View hires a consultant to study the problem and make recommendations.

e. Cities around the country enacted strict regulations banning trans fats in restaurant fare. Food processors nationwide are wondering whether they need to make changes before being forced to switch to nonhydrogenated fats by law. Food and Drug Administration regulations have already changed the definitions of common terms such as *fresh*, *fat free*, *low in cholesterol*, and *light*. The Old World Bakery worries that it may have to change its production process and rewrite all its package labels. With an FDA compliance deadline looming, Old World doesn't know whether to hire a laboratory or a consultant for this project.[23]

11.2 Problem and Purpose Statements
(L.O. 1)

YOUR TASK Identify a problem in your current job or a previous job, such as inadequate use of technology, inefficient procedures, spotty customer service, poor product quality, low morale, or a personnel problem. Assume that your boss agrees with your criticism and asks you to prepare a report. Write (a) a two- or three-sentence statement describing the problem, (b) a problem question, and (c) a simple statement of purpose for your report.

11.3 Data Categories and Research
Questions (L.O. 1)

Researchers must identify or generate credible but also relevant data that will be suitable for their research tasks.

YOUR TASK In conducting research for the following reports, name one or more categories of data you will need, such as background information, expert opinion, survey data, statistics, and organizational data. Using

Figure 11.2, what questions should you ask to determine whether that set of data is appropriate?

a. A report examining the effectiveness of current sustainability efforts in the home construction industry

b. A report about the feasibility of an employer-provided preschool day-care program

c. A report by a state boating and waterways commission providing information on the state marinas as they were operated during the most recent fiscal year

d. A report on business attire in banking that you must submit to your company's executives, who want to issue a formal professional dress code on the job

e. A report by the Agricultural Research Service of the U.S. Department of Agriculture on the nutritional value of oats

11.4 Preparing a Work Plan (L.O. 2)

Any long report project requires a structured work plan.

YOUR TASK Select a report topic from activities presented at the ends of Chapters 12 and 13. For that report prepare a work plan that includes the following:

a. Statement of the problem

b. Expanded statement of purpose (including scope, limitations, and significance)

c. Research strategy to answer the questions

d. Tentative outline of key questions to answer

e. Work schedule (with projected completion dates)

11.5 Conducting Primary Research by Exploring Campus Food Delivery Options (L.O. 2)

Communication Technology | **E-Mail** | **Team** | **Web**

Hungry students bored with dining hall menus are increasingly using food delivery apps such as GrubHub or UberEats.[24] However, delivery fees and wait time can make the experience less than appealing. Your University Business Club (UBC) sees an opportunity to put its business expertise to work by sponsoring a small student-run restaurant in the campus food court. But what food should it dish out? Is it true that college students overwhelmingly prefer food high in salt, sugar, and fat? Your fellow club members have chosen you to create an online survey to poll fellow students, staff, and faculty about their preferences. You hope to generate data that will support the feasibility of the eatery and help UBC create winning menu choices.

The main provider of online survey software, SurveyMonkey, makes creating questionnaires fast, fun, and easy. After signing up for the free no-frills basic plans, you can create brief online questionnaires and e-mail the links to your targeted respondents. The programs analyze and display the results for you—at no charge.

YOUR TASK In pairs or teams of three, design a basic questionnaire to survey students on your campus about food options in the campus cafeteria. Visit SurveyMonkey, which offers a free basic plan limited to 10 questions. After creating the online survey, e-mail the survey link to as many members of the campus community as possible. For a smaller sample, start by polling students in your class. Interpret the results. As a team, write a memo that you will e-mail to the campus food services administrator advocating for a student-run eatery featuring the top-scoring national or regional foods.

Your instructor may ask you to complete this activity as a report or proposal assignment after you study Chapters 12 and 13. If so, write a feasibility report or proposal for the campus food services administrator and support your advocacy with the survey results.

11.6 Secondary Research: Where Are Teens Heading After Facebook? (L.O. 2)

Communication Technology | **E-Mail** | **Web**

As an assistant market researcher, you have been asked by your boss, Kym Koenig, to explore marketing opportunities targeting teens. Understanding teen preferences in this notoriously fickle consumer group is key to success of any promotional or ad campaign. Recent studies suggest that, although some teens still use Facebook, they prefer to spend their time on Instagram, Snapchat, YouTube, or TikTok. They also love to try new apps recommended by friends. Most important, 95 percent of teens have a smartphone or access to one, and 45 percent admit that they are online nearly constantly.

For a full picture to emerge, you will need to consult several recent studies. The best candidates for your research are surveys by Pew Research Center, Common Sense Media, and similar reputable sources of data.

YOUR TASK Ms. Koenig has requested a brief informational e-mail report summarizing your main findings. Paraphrase correctly and don't just copy from the online source. She may ask you later to analyze more comprehensive data in an analytical report and create a media use profile of American teens and young adults. You may be called on to create graphs to illustrate your findings.

11.7 Experimenting With Secondary Sources (L.O. 2)

Web

Secondary sources can provide quite different information depending on your mode of inquiry.

YOUR TASK Use Google or another search engine that supports Boolean searches to investigate a topic such as carbon footprint, sustainability, or any other business topic of interest to you. Explore the same topic using (a) keywords and (b) Boolean operators. Which method produces more relevant hits? Save two relevant sources from each search using two or more of the strategies presented in this chapter. Remember to include the URL for each article.

In a memo to your instructor, list the bibliographical information from all sources and explain briefly which method was most productive.

11.8 Report Functions, Strategies, and Formats (L.O. 3)

YOUR TASK For the following reports, (a) name the report's primary function (informational or analytical), (b) recommend the direct or indirect strategy of development, and (c) suggest a report format.

a. A report prepared by an outside consultant responding to an elementary school's request for recommendations to reduce the morning drop-off gridlock of parent cars and school busses

b. A report to a grant-funding organization asking for continued funding for the humane removal and relocation of wildlife from homes and commercial buildings

c. A report submitted by a sales rep to her division head describing her weekly client visits and contacts

d. A report in the leisure industry put together by consultants who compare the potential of a future theme park at three different sites

e. A progress report from an intern at NASA's Employee and Organizational Excellence Branch to her mentor and the management

f. A report from a national shipping company telling state authorities how it has improved its safety program so that its trucks now comply with state regulations (the report describes but doesn't interpret the program)

11.9 The New World of Colorful Annual Reports (L.O. 1, 3, and 5)

Team | **Web**

All publicly traded companies must provide financial information annually to inform shareholders, investors, and the government of their financial health. Companies may present their financial information in two kinds of reports. The Securities and Exchange Commission requires a 10-K report in generic format with strict guidelines on what must be included. These largely financial reports are usually lengthy chunks of colorless text. A second kind of annual report is often a shorter version of the 10-K that presents financial and other information with glitzy, creative infographics, charts, and photographs promoting the company's brand and achievements.

YOUR TASK Individually or in teams of three or four, conduct research analyzing annual reports. Each team member should analyze at least two annual reports, using the characteristics listed here. Then as a team, compare your findings and summarize them in an informational memo report to your instructor or in a class presentation. A good place to find easy-to-view reports is at **annualreports.com**. For each annual report, discuss the following characteristics:

a. **Function/purpose:** Is the report primarily informational or analytical? How does it provide facts? Does it promote the company? Does it strive to persuade readers with a call to action? In your opinion, was it more promotional or factual?

b. **Audience:** Who is the intended audience—shareholders, potential investors, government regulators, customers, others? Explain.

c. **Writing Style:** Is the text formal as in scholarly papers or is it informal and conversational? Give examples.

d. **Format:** How is the report presented? Does it look like a memo, letter, or manuscript? Does it look more like a Web page?

e. **Visualization techniques:** Does the report present information in photographs, charts, and infographics? Discuss examples.

f. **Overall effectiveness:** Did the report fulfill its purpose?

11.10 Plagiarism, Paraphrasing, and Citing Sources (L.O. 4)

One of the biggest challenges for student writers is paraphrasing secondary sources correctly to avoid plagiarism.

YOUR TASK For each of the following, read the original passage. Analyze the paraphrased version. List the weaknesses in relation to what you have learned about plagiarism and the use of references. Then write an improved version.

a. Original Passage

The abbreviation AI is used to refer both to present-day technology like Siri, Google Translate, and IBM's Watson and to transformative future technologies that surpass human capabilities in all areas. That means surveying people about "risks from AI" is a fraught project—some of them will be thinking about Facebook's News Feed, and some of them, like Stephen Hawking, about technologies that exceed our intelligence "by more than ours exceeds that of snails."[25]

Paraphrased Passage

The term AI [Artificial Intelligence] is used to describe current technologies like Siri, Google Translate, and IBM's Watson. It also refers to future technologies that may exceed our ability to understand them. That means that asking people what they think about "risks from AI" is a worrisome project. Some may think about Facebook's News Feed, and others, such as Stephen Hawking, will imagine technologies that surpass our intelligence "by more than ours exceeds that of snails."

b. Original Passage

Lurking behind chartjunk is contempt both for the information and for the audience. Chartjunk promoters imagine that numbers and details are boring, dull, and tedious, requiring ornament to enliven. Cosmetic decoration, which frequently distorts the data, will never salvage an underlying lack of content. If the numbers are boring, then you've got the wrong numbers. Credibility vanishes in clouds of chartjunk; who would trust a chart that looks like a video game?[26]

Paraphrased Passage

Chartjunk creators hold the information they are conveying and their audience in contempt because they believe that statistical details are dull, unimaginative, and tedious and need to be spruced up with decorations. Purely ornamental design elements distort the data and cannot cover up a lack of content. If the statistics are boring, then they are the wrong statistics. Chartjunk kills credibility. Readers cannot trust a chart that looks like a video game.

c. Original Passage

American Dream, the most expensive U.S. mall ever built, opened Friday. It is the first in the United States to devote more space to entertainment, restaurants, and theme-park rides than to traditional retail. Given that more than a few people have declared the mall dead, the entire industry is glued to the spectacle to see if its formula could save the American shopping center from oversupply and the rise of online shopping.[27]

Paraphrased Passage

The most expensive U.S. mall ever built, American Dream, opened Friday. It is the first in this country to give more space to theme-park rides, entertainment, and restaurants than it gives to traditional retail. The complete industry is fascinated by the spectacle to see if its model could save the American shopping center from online shopping and oversupply.

11.11 Who Gets Hurt? Examining Infamous Plagiarism Scandals (L.O. 4)

`Team` `Web`

Have you ever wondered who gets hurt when students, teachers, journalists, scientists, and other authors are dishonest researchers and writers? Occasionally we read about people who plagiarize their work, try to cheat their way through college, invent news features, copy from others, or fabricate research results. One of the most notorious medical miscreants was Japanese anesthesiologist Yoshitaka Fujii, who wrote 172 bogus scientific papers, 126 of which were based on imaginary research studies.

Two other shocking cases in medical research rival Fujii's fabrications in gravity and scope. Former British surgeon Andrew Wakefield published an article in the reputable medical journal *The Lancet* that seemed to provide evidence that a common immunization against measles, mumps, and rubella (MMR) could cause autism. Wakefield had fabricated evidence and was found guilty of professional misconduct. He lost his license to practice as a medical doctor. His fraudulent research, however, caused a precipitous drop in vaccinations in the United Kingdom and Ireland. In the words of one pediatrician, "That paper killed children."[28] Despite the efforts of the World Health Organization and countless health providers, many parents still refuse to vaccinate their kids, causing the spread of diseases that had been eradicated in the United States and abroad.[29]

A Harvard researcher's purposely nonsensical research paper, consisting of randomly generated text accompanied by two fake authors, was accepted by 17 of 37 medical journals. Journals publishing such bogus research are called predatory publishers. A prominent bioethicist calls such practices "publication pollution."[30]

YOUR TASK If your instructor directs, individually or as a team, investigate the cases of Andrew Wakefield, Joachim Boldt, Stephen Ambrose, Jayson Blair, Doris Kearns Goodwin, Jonah Lehrer, Kaavya Viswanathan, or other infamous plagiarists. Alternatively, you could focus on the case of 200 professors from 50 universities implicated in a massive publishing scam in South Korea.[31] Consider the authors' transgressions, their excuses, and the consequences of their actions. As a team, gather your individual research results, compare notes, and summarize your insights in a memo report to your instructor. This assignment could also be turned into a longer report as presented in Chapters 12 and 13 if the investigation is expanded to include more detailed discussions and more cases.

11.12 Selecting Graphics (L.O. 5)

YOUR TASK Identify the best graphics forms to illustrate the following data.

a. Figure showing the tracking and fulfillment of an e-commerce order

b. Annual restaurant industry sales figures for meatless hamburgers

c. Government unemployment data by industry and sector, in percentages

d. Figures showing the distribution of the coronavirus Covid-19 in humans by state

e. Figures showing the process of delivering water to a metropolitan area

f. Information showing which states in the United States have enacted laws banning handheld phone conversations while driving

g. Figures showing what proportion of every state tax dollar is spent on education, social services, transportation, debt, and other expenses

h. Academic, administrative, and operation divisions of a college, from the president to department chairs and division managers

i. Figures comparing the sales of smartphones, tablets, and laptops over the past five years

11.13 Creating a Bar Chart and Writing a Title (L.O. 5)

Web

YOUR TASK Create a bar chart comparing the current number of Internet users (by millions) in the following eight countries: United States, India, Japan, Brazil, Indonesia, China, United Kingdom, and Russia. Find statistics within the last year and name the source of your information. Arrange the bars according to the country with the highest number of users to the lowest. Add a chart title and appropriate labels.

11.14 Creating a Line Chart (L.O. 5)

YOUR TASK Prepare a line chart showing the sales of Sidekick Athletic Shoes, Inc., for these years: 2021, $6.7 million; 2020, $5.4 million; 2019, $3.2 million; 2018, $2.1 million; 2017, $2.6 million; 2016, $3.6 million. In the chart title, mention the trend you see in the data.

11.15 Searching for Data Visualization and Infographics in Annual Reports (L.O. 5)

E-Mail   Web

Annual reports are infamous for being anything but fascinating reading even for the most ardent investors.

YOUR TASK Search annual reports filed by Fortune 500 companies, and examine to what extent they have embraced infographics. Critique their readability, clarity, and effectiveness in visualizing data. How were the visuals introduced in the text? What suggestions would you make to improve them? Can you detect any effort to present financials and other data in visually appealing, unconventional ways? In an e-mail or memo to your instructor, evaluate the use and effectiveness of graphics in three to five corporate annual reports.

11.16 Seeking Business Infographics
(L.O. 1, 4, and 5)

Web

YOUR TASK On the Web or in print, find an infographic that visualizes intriguing business-relevant data. Look for sources within or below the infographic. Are they indicated? If yes, are they credible? How much hard statistical information is provided in relation to the space the infographic occupies? Does the infographic meet its objective: is the information clearly presented, easy to read, and insightful? Report your findings orally or in writing. Be prepared to show your chosen infographic to the class. **Tip:** When searching for images, use Google Images, Bing Images, or Yahoo Images.

Test Your Workplace Etiquette IQ

New communication platforms and casual workplace environments have blurred the lines of appropriateness, leaving workers wondering how to navigate uncharted waters. Check your workplace etiquette IQ by deciding whether the following statements are true or false. Then see if you agree with the responses on p. Key-6.

1. If your cell phone rings in today's workplace, answer it and head toward the nearest empty conference room or phone room to conduct your conversation.

_____ True _____ False

2. If you have been invited to attend a meeting of a group you have never met before, you should enter the room and take an empty seat without causing a fuss.

_____ True _____ False

3. Giving a personal gift to your boss is acceptable if the gift is tasteful and expensive.

_____ True _____ False

Chat About It

In each chapter, you will find five discussion questions related to the chapter material. Your instructor may assign these topics for you to discuss in class, in an online chat room, or on an online discussion board. Some of the discussion topics may require outside research. You may also be asked to read and respond to postings made by your classmates.

TOPIC 1: As you know, college students are required to locate information and then analyze and present their findings either orally or in writing. A recent survey of college librarians, however, revealed that only 23 percent of first-year students at two-year institutions and 30 percent of first-year students at four-year schools were prepared to conduct college-level research.[32] In your first year of school, did you feel you were properly prepared? Since then, have your skills improved? How do you feel about your current strengths and weaknesses in researching?

TOPIC 2: Research suggests that colleges with strong, explicit ethics codes and zero tolerance of cheating have the lowest incidence of academic dishonesty. Find the student handbook on your portal (or check the university catalog) for rules of conduct regarding cheating. Are they clear? Does your school make students pledge not to cheat? How do you feel about such efforts?

TOPIC 3: The Internet has brought the paper mills to the masses. Some students pay to have their papers written by shady authors online. Discuss the views in your class regarding this practice and how it could be harmful to honest students. Is any harm done to colleges and universities? Society?

TOPIC 4: Do you believe that a survey of 1,000 people can reveal what an entire country thinks?

TOPIC 5: Is plagiarism worth the risk of being caught? Why or why not?

Total Review

The first nine chapters reviewed specific guides from Appendix D, Grammar and Mechanics. The exercises in this and the remaining chapters are total reviews, covering all of the grammar and mechanics guides plus confusing words and frequently misspelled words.

Each of the following sentences has **three** errors in grammar, punctuation, capitalization, usage, or spelling. On a separate sheet, write a correct version. Avoid adding new phrases, starting new sentences, or rewriting in your own words. When finished, compare your responses with the key at the end of the book.

EXAMPLE: Networking is said to be the key to finding a job, however, its easier said then done.

REVISION: Networking is said to be the key to finding a **job**; however, **it's** easier said **than** done.

1. Many jobs in todays digital workplace are never advertised, there part of the hidden job market.

2. Some job seekers paid six hundred dollars each to attend twelve sessions that promised expert job-searching advise.

3. One creditable study revealed that thirty percent of jobs go to companies inside candidates.

4. To excel at networking a candidate must have a easy to remember e-mail address.

5. My friend wondered if I had all ready prepared a thirty second elevator speech?

6. When Kaitlyn and myself were collecting data for the report we realized that twitter and Facebook could be significant.

7. Todays workers must brush up their marketable skills otherwise they may not find another job after being laid off.

8. Being active on LinkedIn and building an impressive Internet presence is important, but the looseness of these connections mean you shouldn't expect to much from them.

9. Just between you and I, one of the best strategys in networking are distributing business cards with your personal tagline.

10. On January 1st our company President revealed that we would be hiring thirty new employees, which was excellent news for everyone.

LEARNING OUTCOMES

After studying this chapter, you should be able to do the following:

1 Analyze statistical data and other information using tables, measures of central tendency (mean, median, and mode), and decision matrices.

2 Develop meaningful conclusions and practical report recommendations after valid analysis.

3 Organize report data logically while providing reader cues to aid comprehension.

4 Write short informational reports that describe routine tasks.

5 Compose short analytical reports that solve business problems.

KorArkaR/Shutterstock.com

Zooming In — Measuring Data the Netflix Way

Since Netflix began its DVD-by-mail service in 1997, the media-services provider and production company has done things its own way. Perhaps its most significant move was to upend "appointment TV," whereby viewers could watch only their favorite shows when they aired. Instead, Netflix developed a streaming platform on which subscribers could view any program from Netflix's library whenever they wished. Unlike traditional TV, Netflix's business model did not obligate it to report viewership numbers—ratings that report the number of people watching a show at a given time and that networks used to sell airtime for commercials. Netflix runs no commercials thus making standard measures such as viewership data irrelevant.

Instead, the entertainment company reports subscriber growth, the same metric Wall Street uses to evaluate and value Netflix.[1] Those impressive numbers reveal a huge increase from 7.48 million U.S. viewers in 2007 to more than 167 million across the globe in 2019.[2] Regardless, the company's lack of transparency in reporting viewership metrics is a recurring theme among its critics.

At the root of the complaints is the way Netflix measures a view. Until recently, Netflix counted a view as a subscriber watching 70 percent of one episode of a series or 70 percent of a film. The company recently changed that measure to a viewer watching programming for at least two minutes.[3] The new low-threshold metric resulted in another flurry of criticism, but Netflix's response was to brush off detractors claiming that such a manipulation of data makes it meaningless. Netflix argues that releasing more specific data could negatively affect the viability of shows that were never meant to attract large audiences. The company also maintains that providing content geared to niche audiences attracts new subscribers, which is the entertainment giant's ultimate goal.

Moving forward, the company faces increasing competition for membership from streaming services such as Amazon Prime Video, Hulu, Disney+, and Apple TV+. To hold on to its dominance in the lucrative market, Netflix has begun sparingly to release detailed viewership data on its top-rated shows hoping to create buzz. Still, naysayers claim that even those data are unreliable because they are not verified by an independent entity. In Hollywood, though, regardless of how Netflix measures viewership, its most recent 24 Oscar nominations seem to indicate that the company is doing something very, very right.

Critical Thinking

- Why is the number of subscribers a better measure of Netflix's success instead of traditional television metrics that focus on viewership of specific shows?

- What other factors might influence Netflix to withhold data on viewership compared with network TV?

- Netflix has recently hired the independent TV rating service Nielsen to collect data on selected Netflix programming. Why is vetting by an outside source important?

12-1 Interpreting Digital Age Data

LEARNING OUTCOME

1 Analyze statistical data and other information using tables, measures of central tendency (mean, median, and mode), and decision matrices.

Given the easy access to many sources of digitized information on the Internet and in research databases, collecting information is easier than ever. However, making sense of the data you collect is much harder, especially when a search can generate massive amounts of statistics, articles, and viewpoints. Raw data become meaningful through the process of sorting, analyzing, combining, and recombining. Examining what each piece of information suggests by itself—and in relation to other data—reveals meanings, relationships, and, in turn, answers to research questions that shape important decisions. Even pioneering companies such as Netflix that deviate from performance metrics typical in their industries need reliable data to weather changing economic times and adapt to changing business models. Information helps businesses stay abreast of trends inside and outside of their organizations.

This chapter focuses on analyzing and organizing data, drawing conclusions, providing reader cues, and writing informal business reports—all key in allowing business leaders to make sound decisions in the digital age.

12-1a Tabulating and Analyzing Data

After collecting numerical data and other information, you must tabulate and analyze them. Fortunately, several techniques can help you simplify, summarize, and classify large amounts of data. The most helpful summarizing techniques are tables, statistical concepts (mean, median, and mode), correlations, grids, and decision matrices.

Tables. Tables usually help researchers summarize and simplify data. Using columns and rows, tables make quantitative information easier to comprehend. After assembling your data, you will want to prepare preliminary tables to enable you to see what the information means. Here is a table summarizing the response to one question from a campus survey about student parking:

Question: Should student fees be increased to build parking lots?

	Number	Percentage	
Strongly agree	76	11.5	} **To simplify the table, combine these items.**
Agree	255	38.5	**50 percent support the proposal**
No opinion	22	3.3	
Disagree	107	16.1	} **To simplify the table, combine these items.**
Strongly disagree	203	30.6	**46.7 (nearly 47) percent oppose the proposal**
Total	**663**	**100.0**	

Notice that this preliminary table includes a total number of responses and a percentage for each response. (To calculate a percentage, divide the figure for each response by the total number of responses and then multiply the result by 100.)

Sometimes data become more meaningful when cross-tabulated. This process allows us to analyze two or more variables together. By breaking down our student survey data into male and female responses, shown in the following table, we make an interesting discovery.

Question: Should student fees be increased to build parking lots?

	Total		Male			Female		
	Number	Percentage	Number	Percentage		Number	Percentage	
Strongly agree	76	11.5	8	2.2	} = **17.5 percent**	68	22.0	} = **87 percent**
Agree	255	38.5	54	15.3	**SUPPORT**	201	65.0	**SUPPORT**
No opinion	22	3.3	12	3.4		10	3.2	
Disagree	107	16.1	89	25.1	} = **79.1 percent**	18	5.8	} = **9.8 percent**
Strongly disagree	203	30.6	191	54.0	**OPPOSE**	12	4.0	**OPPOSE**
Total	**663**	**100.0**	**354**	**100.0**		**309**	**100.0**	

Although 50 percent of all student respondents supported the proposal, among females the approval rating was much higher. You naturally wonder why such a disparity exists. Are female students unhappier than male students with the current parking situation? If so, why? Is safety a reason? Are male students more concerned with increased fees than female students are?

By cross-tabulating the findings, you sometimes uncover data that may help answer your problem question or that may prompt you to explore other possibilities. Do not, however,

FIGURE 12.1   Converting Survey Data Into Finished Tables

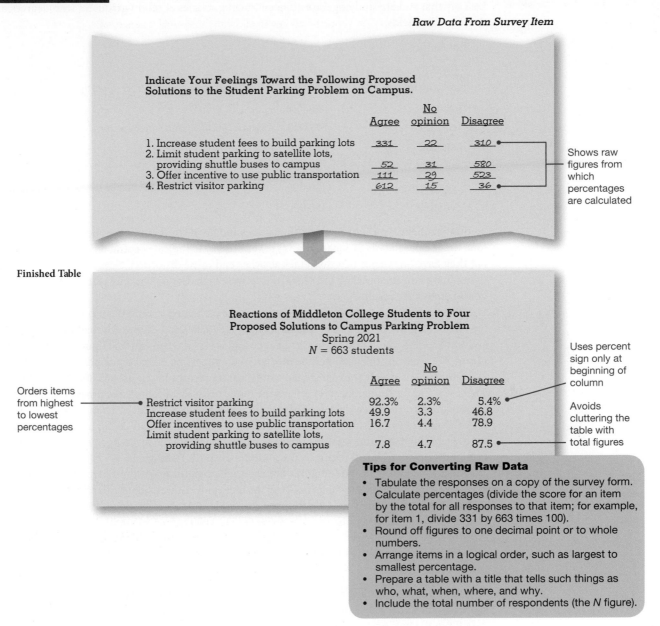

Raw Data From Survey Item

Indicate Your Feelings Toward the Following Proposed Solutions to the Student Parking Problem on Campus.

	Agree	No opinion	Disagree
1. Increase student fees to build parking lots	331	22	310
2. Limit student parking to satellite lots, providing shuttle buses to campus	52	31	580
3. Offer incentive to use public transportation	111	29	523
4. Restrict visitor parking	612	15	36

Shows raw figures from which percentages are calculated

Finished Table

Reactions of Middleton College Students to Four Proposed Solutions to Campus Parking Problem
Spring 2021
N = 663 students

	Agree	No opinion	Disagree
Restrict visitor parking	92.3%	2.3%	5.4%
Increase student fees to build parking lots	49.9	3.3	46.8
Offer incentives to use public transportation	16.7	4.4	78.9
Limit student parking to satellite lots, providing shuttle buses to campus	7.8	4.7	87.5

Orders items from highest to lowest percentages

Uses percent sign only at beginning of column

Avoids cluttering the table with total figures

Tips for Converting Raw Data

- Tabulate the responses on a copy of the survey form.
- Calculate percentages (divide the score for an item by the total for all responses to that item; for example, for item 1, divide 331 by 663 times 100).
- Round off figures to one decimal point or to whole numbers.
- Arrange items in a logical order, such as largest to smallest percentage.
- Prepare a table with a title that tells such things as who, what, when, where, and why.
- Include the total number of respondents (the N figure).

undertake **cross-tabulation** unless it serves more than merely satisfying your curiosity. Tables also help you compare multiple data collected from questionnaires and surveys. Figure 12.1 shows, in raw form, responses to several survey items. To convert these data into a more usable form, you need to calculate percentages for each item. Then you can arrange the responses in some rational sequence, such as largest percentage to smallest.

Once the data are displayed in a table, you can more easily draw conclusions. As Figure 12.1 shows, Middleton College students apparently are not interested in public transportation or shuttle buses from satellite lots. They want to park on campus and restrict visitor parking; and only half are willing to pay for new parking lots.

Measures of Central Tendency.   Tables help you organize data, and the three Ms—mean, median, and mode—help you describe data. These statistical terms are all occasionally used loosely to mean "average." To be safe, though, you should learn to apply these statistical terms precisely.

When people say **average**, they usually intend to indicate the **mean**, or arithmetic average. Let's say that you are studying the estimated starting salaries of recent graduates with degrees in the following fields:

Education	$ 65,000	
Sociology	65,000	
Humanities	65,000	*Mode (figure occurring most frequently)*
Biology	70,000	
Health sciences	79,000	*Median (middle point in continuum)*
Business	83,000	*Mean (arithmetic average)*
Law	90,000	
Engineering	100,000	
Medicine	130,000	

To find the mean, you simply add all the salaries and divide by the total number of items. Therefore, the mean salary is $83,000. Means are very useful to indicate central tendencies of figures, but they have one major flaw: extremes at either end cause distortion. Notice that the $130,000 figure makes the mean salary of $83,000 deceptively high. Use means only when extreme figures do not distort the result.

The **median** represents the midpoint in a group of figures arranged from lowest to highest (or vice versa). In our list of salaries, the median is $79,000. In other words, half the salaries are above this point, and half are below it. The median is useful when extreme figures may warp the mean. You are likely to encounter the median in the reporting of real estate prices.

The **mode** is simply the value that occurs most frequently. In our list $65,000 (for education, sociology, and the humanities) represents the mode because it occurs three times. The mode has the advantage of being easily determined—just a quick glance at a list of arranged values reveals it. Although researchers use mode infrequently, knowing the mode is useful in some situations; for example, to determine a group's preferences. To remember the meaning of *mode*, think about fashion: the most frequent response, the mode, is the most fashionable.

Mean, median, and mode figures are especially helpful when the range of values is also known. Range represents the span between the highest and lowest values. To calculate the range, you simply subtract the lowest figure from the highest. Among starting salaries for graduates in the fields listed earlier, the range is $65,000 ($130,000 minus $65,000). Knowing the range enables readers to put mean and median figures into perspective. This knowledge also prompts researchers to wonder why such a range exists, thus stimulating hunches and further investigation to solve problems.

Correlations. In tabulating and analyzing data, you may see relationships between two or more variables that help explain the findings; such relationships are called **correlations**. If your data for graduates' starting salaries also included years of education, you would doubtless notice that graduates with more years of education received higher salaries. A correlation may exist between years of education and starting salary.

Intuition suggests correlations that may or may not prove to be accurate. Is there a causal relationship between studying and good grades? Between electronic gadget use by supervising adults and increased injuries of children? Between the rise and fall of hemlines and the rise and fall of the stock market (as some newspaper writers have suggested)? The business researcher who sees a correlation needs to ask why and how the two variables are related. In this way, apparent correlations stimulate investigation and present possible solutions to be explored.

In reporting correlations, you should avoid suggesting that a cause-and-effect relationship exists when none can be proved. Only sophisticated research methods can statistically prove correlations. Instead, present a correlation as a possible relationship (*The data suggest that beginning salaries are related to years of education*). Cautious statements followed by explanations gain you credibility and allow readers to make their own decisions.

Grids. Another technique for analyzing raw data—especially verbal data—is the **grid**. Let's say you have been asked by the CEO to collect opinions from all vice presidents about the CEO's

DRY, HOT AND SUNNY
SUMMER WEATHER

ICE CREAM

causation

correlation

causation

SUNBURN

desdemona72/Shutterstock.com

four-point plan to build cash reserves. The grid shown in Figure 12.2 enables you to summarize the vice presidents' reactions to each point. Notice how this complex verbal information is transformed into concise, manageable data; readers can see immediately which points are supported and which are opposed. Imagine how long you could have struggled to comprehend the meaning of this verbal information without a grid.

Arranging data in a grid also works for projects such as feasibility studies and yardstick reports that compare many variables. *Consumer Reports* often uses grids to display test results. In addition, grids help classify employment data. For example, suppose your boss asks you to recommend one individual from among many job candidates. You could arrange a grid with names across the top and distinguishing characteristics—experience, skills, education, and other employment interests—down the left side. Summarizing each candidate's points offers a helpful tool for drawing conclusions and writing a report.

Decision Matrices. A **decision matrix** is a special grid that helps managers make the best choice among complex options. Designed to eliminate bias and poor judgment, decision matrices are helpful in many fields. Assume you need to choose the most appropriate tablet for your sales representatives. You are most interested in four criteria: screen resolution, battery life, price, and

FIGURE 12.2 Grid to Analyze Complex Verbal Data About Building Cash Reserves

	Point 1	Point 2	Point 3	Point 4	Overall Reaction
VICE PRESIDENT 1	Disapproves. "Too little, too late."	Strong support. "Best of all points."	Mixed opinion. "Must wait and see market."	Indifferent.	Optimistic, but "hates to delay expansion for six months."
VICE PRESIDENT 2	Disapproves. "Creates credit trap."	Approves.	Strong disapproval.	Approves. "Must improve receivable collections."	Mixed support. "Good self-defense plan."
VICE PRESIDENT 3	Strong disapproval.	Approves. "Key to entire plan."	Indifferent.	Approves, but with "caveats."	"Will work only with sale of unproductive fixed assets."
VICE PRESIDENT 4	Disapproves. "Too risky now."	Strong support. "Start immediately."	Approves, "but may damage image."	Approves. "Benefits far outweigh costs."	Supports plan. Suggests focus on Pacific Rim markets.

storage space. You want to compare these features in four highly rated business tablet models. Figure 12.3 shows a simple decision matrix to help you make the choice. In Table 1, you evaluate each of the desired features on a scale of 1 to 5. Because the Apple iPad Pro 12.9 has one of the highest pixel displays currently on the market, you give it a score of 5 for resolution. However, at more than $1,100, it is expensive, so you give it a score of 1 in the price category.

You could add up the points for each tablet and pick the winner: the Apple iPad Pro with 14 points. However, this score doesn't reflect your needs or priorities. Weights will help you decide by boosting the relevance of your most important criteria. For example, you decide to assign a value of 7 to battery life and storage space of the tablets because these two aspects are of relative importance, but not as important as price, given the number of tablets your company will need to purchase. Therefore, you assign a value of 10 to price. Then you multiply the scores in Table 1 with the weights and total them, as shown in Table 2. According to the weighted matrix and the rating system used, the Samsung Galaxy Tab S6 should be purchased for the sales reps because it received the highest score of 92. Although it beats the Apple iPad Pro 12.9" by only one point in your weighted matrix, it is significantly more affordable (your most important consideration) and is likely to perform similarly.

FIGURE 12.3 **Decision Matrix Used to Choose a Business Tablet for Sales Reps**

Unweighted Decision Matrix—Table 1					
Features:	Screen Resolution	Battery Life	Price	Storage	Total
Tablet Options					
Lenovo Yoga Book C630 (1920x1080p; 25 hrs; $859; 128 GB)	2	5	2	2	(11)
Microsoft Surface Go (1800x1200p; 7 hrs; $429; 128 GB	3	1	5	2	(11)
Apple iPad Pro 12.9" (2732x2048p; 11 hrs; $1150; 256 GB)	**5**	**4**	**1**	**4**	**(14)**
Samsung Galaxy Tab S6 (2560x1440p ; 9 hrs ; $629; 256 GB)	4	2	3	4	(13)

Weighted Decision Matrix—Table 2					
Features:	Screen Resolution	Battery Life	Price	Storage	Total
Tablet Options Weights:	**5**	**7**	**10**	**7**	
Lenovo Yoga Book C630 (1920x1080p; 25 hrs; $859; 128 GB)	10	35	20	14	79
Microsoft Surface Go (1800x1200p; 7 hrs; $429; 128 GB)	15	7	50	14	86
Apple iPad Pro 12.9" (2732x2048p; 11 hrs; $1150; 256 GB)	25	28	10	28	91
Samsung Galaxy Tab S6 (2560x1440p ; 9 hrs ; $629 ; 256 GB)	**20**	**14**	**30**	**28**	**92**

Tips for Creating a Decision Matrix
- **Select the most important criteria.** For a tablet, the criteria were screen resolution, battery life, price, and storage.
- **Create a matrix.** List each tablet brand (Lenovo, Microsoft, Apple, and Samsung) down the left side. Place the features across the top of the columns.
- **Evaluate the criteria.** Use a scale of 1 (lowest) to 5 (highest). Rate each feature for each option, as shown in Table 1.
- **Assign relative weights.** Decide how important each feature is, and give it a weight.
- **Multiply the scores.** For each feature in Table 1, multiply by the weights in Table 2 and write the score in the box.
- **Total the scores.** The total reveals the best choice.

12-2 Drawing Conclusions and Making Recommendations

LEARNING OUTCOME

2 Develop meaningful conclusions and practical report recommendations after valid analysis.

The sections devoted to conclusions and recommendations are the most widely read portions of a report. Knowledgeable readers go straight to the conclusions to see what the report writer thinks the data mean. Because conclusions summarize and explain the findings, they represent the heart of a report.

Your value in an organization rises considerably if you can analyze information logically, draw conclusions, and show how the data answer questions and solve problems. Responding to a growing demand for sustainable electronics, Dutch entrepreneur Bas van Abel developed the Fairphone, a fair-trade device. This easy-to-fix, upgradable, modular smartphone (now available in a third-generation model) is ethically sourced and was built from components designed to be reused to reduce e-waste. So far, van Abel's startup has sold 160,000 units in Europe to people concerned about the environment and ethics—not so much about the latest bells and whistles. Smartphone manufacturers have incurred criticism for sourcing conflict metals extracted under dangerous, toxic working conditions frequently by children. With its rapid obsolescence cycles, the industry is generating huge amounts of electronic waste, mainly because the units cannot be easily upgraded and repaired.[6] Solving such problems requires research. Drawing logical conclusions from data is crucial to business success.

12-2a Analyzing Data to Arrive at Conclusions

Any set of data can produce a variety of meaningful conclusions. Always bear in mind, though, that the audience for a report wants to know how these data relate to the problem being studied. What do the findings mean in terms of solving the original report problem?

For example, the American Trucking Associations (ATA) recognized a serious problem many of its members—more than 37,000 U.S. motor carriers—were facing. Large trucking companies with more than $30 million in revenue per year reported a whopping annual turnover rate of 96 percent among their drivers. Smaller carriers saw a turnover rate of 76 percent. These disturbing numbers persisted, despite significant increases to mileage-based pay. What was happening?

To find answers, ATA sponsored a survey of one trucking firm, CarrierAdvantage. The researchers sought answers to this question: What was causing the high turnover rate among truck drivers? The resulting survey revealed that the average annual miles for drivers had fallen 11 percent, from 124,200 to 108,800 within the most recent year. This drop in mileage might be attributed to the Amazon effect as shippers started changing their freight distribution models to shorten distances between warehouses and customers to match Amazon's same-day and next-day delivery. Additional research of CarrierAdvantage drivers showed that they were

---

FOR THE RECORD

Trader Joe's Navigates Success Using Data

Since Trader Joe's opened its first store in 1967, the nautical-themed grocery chain has attracted a loyal following of shoppers who gobble up its good values. Staff called *crew members* wear bright, tropical patterned shirts and are known for being helpful and well-informed. With more than 500 stores in 42 states, Trader Joe's constantly collects data on which products fly off the shelves and which ones sit, quickly relegating the laggards to the gangplank. Monitoring inventory data to arrive at conclusions about reorders allows the German-owned grocery chain to focus on providing customers with high quality and affordable products, many of which carry the store's private label offerings—without loyalty programs or other marketing gimmicks.

Joe Raedle/Getty Images News/Getty Images

unhappy with their pay during the same period. Dissatisfaction with wages is a top predictor of turnover.[7]

A sample of possible conclusions that a writer might draw from these findings is shown in Model Document 12.1. Notice that each conclusion relates to the initial report problem. Although only a few possible findings and conclusions are shown here, you can see that the conclusions try to explain the causes for the high turnover rates among drivers. Many report writers would expand the conclusion section by explaining each item and citing supporting evidence. Even for simplified conclusions, such as those shown in Model Document 12.1, you will want to list each item separately and use parallel construction (balanced sentence structure).

Although your goal is to remain objective, drawing conclusions naturally involves a degree of subjectivity. Your goals, background, and frame of reference all color the inferences you make. All writers interpret findings from their own perspectives, but they should not manipulate them to achieve a preconceived purpose. You can make your report conclusions more objective by using consistent evaluation criteria. Let's say you are comparing computers for an office equipment purchase. If you evaluate each by the same criteria (such as price, specifications, service, and warranty), your conclusions are more likely to be bias-free.

MODEL DOCUMENT 12.1   Report Conclusions and Recommendations on Intranet Screen

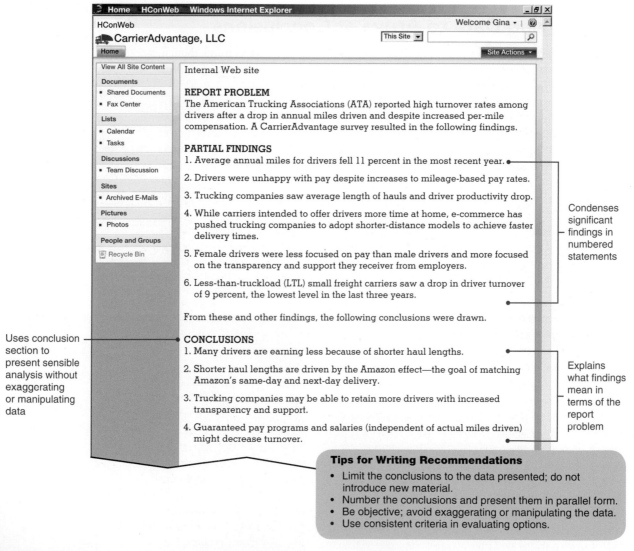

© Cengage Learning 2015; Courtesy of Mary Ellen Guffey and Dana Loewy; Used with permission from Microsoft.

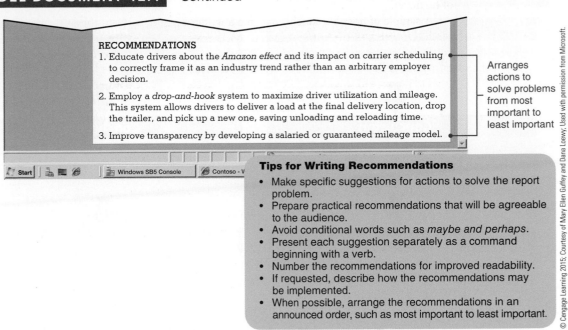

RECOMMENDATIONS

1. Educate drivers about the *Amazon effect* and its impact on carrier scheduling to correctly frame it as an industry trend rather than an arbitrary employer decision.

2. Employ a *drop-and-hook* system to maximize driver utilization and mileage. This system allows drivers to deliver a load at the final delivery location, drop the trailer, and pick up a new one, saving unloading and reloading time.

3. Improve transparency by developing a salaried or guaranteed mileage model.

Arranges actions to solve problems from most important to least important

Tips for Writing Recommendations

- Make specific suggestions for actions to solve the report problem.
- Prepare practical recommendations that will be agreeable to the audience.
- Avoid conditional words such as *maybe and perhaps*.
- Present each suggestion separately as a command beginning with a verb.
- Number the recommendations for improved readability.
- If requested, describe how the recommendations may be implemented.
- When possible, arrange the recommendations in an announced order, such as most important to least important.

You also need to avoid the temptation to sensationalize or exaggerate your findings or conclusions. Be careful of words such as *many, most,* and *all*. Instead of *many of the respondents felt* . . . you might more accurately write *some of the respondents felt. . . .* Examine your motives before drawing conclusions. Do not let preconceptions or wishful thinking color your reasoning.

12-2b **Preparing Report Recommendations**

Recommendations evolve from the interpretation of the findings and conclusions. Conclusions explain what the problem is, whereas recommendations tell how to solve it. Typically, business readers prefer specific, practical recommendations. They want to know exactly how to implement the suggestions. The specificity of your recommendations depends on your authorization. What are you commissioned to do, and what does the reader expect? In the planning stages of your report project, you anticipate what the reader wants in it. Use your intuition and your knowledge of the audience to determine how comprehensive your recommendations should be.

Shown in Model Document 12.1 are the recommendations drawn from the findings of the CarrierAdvantage survey seeking answers to the high turnover rate among drivers. The actual report would include specifics and ideas for implementing each recommendation. For example, the recommendation to introduce salaries or minimum mileage payments would be further explained with support, including numbers based on current industry trends.

A good report provides practical recommendations that are helpful and relevant to the audience. In the driver turnover survey, for example, findings showed that e-commerce was forcing carriers to increase efficiency if they wanted to remain competitive. A drop-and-hook system might end inefficiency and make optimal use of delivery drivers' time, potentially reducing their frustration. If possible, make each recommendation a command. Note in Model Document 12.1 that each recommendation begins with a verb. This structure sounds forceful and confident and helps the reader comprehend the information quickly. Avoid hedging words such as *maybe* and *perhaps*; they reduce the strength of recommendations.

Experienced writers may combine recommendations and conclusions. In short reports writers may omit conclusions and move straight to recommendations. An important point about recommendations is that they include practical suggestions for solving the report problem. Furthermore, they are always the result of logical analysis. Consider the examples from the driver turnover survey summarized in Figure 12.4.

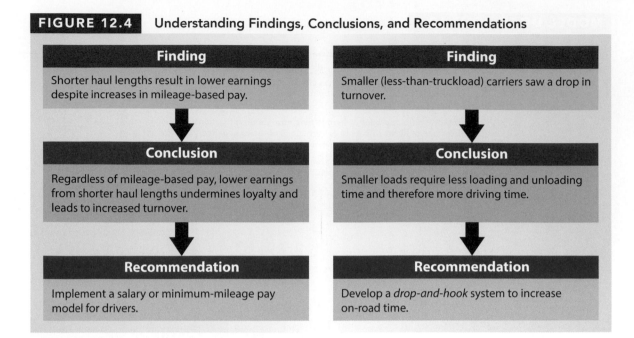

FIGURE 12.4 Understanding Findings, Conclusions, and Recommendations

Finding	Finding
Shorter haul lengths result in lower earnings despite increases in mileage-based pay.	Smaller (less-than-truckload) carriers saw a drop in turnover.
Conclusion	**Conclusion**
Regardless of mileage-based pay, lower earnings from shorter haul lengths undermines loyalty and leads to increased turnover.	Smaller loads require less loading and unloading time and therefore more driving time.
Recommendation	**Recommendation**
Implement a salary or minimum-mileage pay model for drivers.	Develop a *drop-and-hook* system to increase on-road time.

LEARNING OUTCOME

3 Organize report data logically while providing reader cues to aid comprehension.

12-3 Organizing Data

After collecting sets of data, interpreting them, drawing conclusions, and thinking about the recommendations, you are ready to organize the parts of the report into a logical framework. Poorly organized reports lead to frustration. Readers will not understand, remember, or be persuaded. Wise writers know that reports rarely "just organize themselves." Instead, the report author must impose organization on the data and provide cues so the reader can follow the logic of the writer.

Informational reports, as you learned in Chapter 11, generally present data without interpretation. As shown in Figure 12.5, informational reports typically consist of three parts. **Analytical reports**, which generally analyze data and draw conclusions, typically contain four parts. However, the parts in analytical reports do not always follow this sequence. For readers who know about the project, are supportive, or are eager to learn the results quickly, the direct strategy is appropriate. Conclusions and recommendations, if requested, appear up front. For readers who must be educated or persuaded, the indirect strategy works better. Conclusions and recommendations appear last, after the findings have been presented and analyzed.

Although every report is unique, the overall organizational strategies described here generally hold true. The real challenge, though, lies in (a) organizing the facts/findings and discussion/analysis sections and (b) providing reader cues.

FIGURE 12.5 Organizational Strategies for Informational and Analytical Reports

Informational Reports	Analytical Reports	
Direct Strategy	**Direct Strategy**	**Indirect Strategy**
I. Introduction/background	I. Introduction/problem	I. Introduction/problem
II. Facts/findings	II. Conclusions/recommendations	II. Facts/findings
III. Summary/conclusion	III. Facts/findings	III. Discussion/analysis
	IV. Discussion/analysis	IV. Conclusions/recommendations

12-3a Ordering Information Logically

Whether you are writing informational or analytical reports, you must structure the data you have collected. Five common organizational methods are by time, component, importance, criteria, and convention. Regardless of the method you choose, be sure that it helps the reader understand the data. Reader comprehension, not writer convenience, should govern organization. Additional examples of organizational principles are presented in Chapter 14.

Time. Ordering data by time means establishing a chronology of events. Agendas, minutes of meetings, progress reports, and procedures are usually organized by time. For example, a report describing an eight-week training program would most likely be organized by weeks. A plan for the step-by-step improvement of customer service would be organized by steps. A monthly trip report submitted by a sales rep might describe customers visited during Week 1, Week 2, and so on.

Beware of overusing chronologies (time) as an organizing method for reports, however. Although this method is easy and often mirrors the way data are collected, chronologies—like the sales rep's trip report—tend to be boring, repetitious, and lacking in emphasis. Readers cannot always pick out what is important.

Component. Especially for informational reports, data may be organized by components such as location, geography, division, product, or part. For instance, a report detailing company expansion might divide the plan into West Coast, East Coast, and Midwest expansion. The report could also be organized by divisions: personal products, consumer electronics, and household goods. A report comparing profits among makers of athletic shoes might group the data by company: Nike, Adidas, Sketchers, New Balance, ASICS, and so forth. Organization by component works best when the classifications already exist.

Importance. Organization by importance involves beginning with the most important item and proceeding to the least important—or vice versa. For example, a report discussing the reasons for declining product sales would present the most important reason first followed by less important ones. Describing the reasons for high driver turnover, consultants interpreting the survey findings for trucking company CarrierAdvantage might begin by discussing the Amazon effect exerting pressure on the industry. Using importance to structure findings involves a value judgment. The writer must decide what is most important, always keeping in mind the readers' priorities and expectations. Busy readers appreciate seeing important points first; they may skim or skip other points.

On the other hand, building to a climax by moving from least important to most important enables the writer to focus attention at the end. Thus, the reader is more likely to remember the most important item. Of course, the writer also risks losing the reader's attention along the way.

Criteria. Establishing criteria by which to judge helps writers to treat topics consistently. Let's say your report compares health plans A, B, and C. For each plan you examine the same standards: cost per employee, amount of deductible, and patient benefits. The resulting data could then be organized either by plans or by criteria, as Figure 12.6 illustrates:

Although you might favor organizing the data by plans (because that is the way you collected the data), the better way is by criteria. When you discuss patient benefits, for example, you would examine all three plans' benefits together. Organizing a report around criteria helps readers make comparisons, instead of forcing them to search through the report for similar data.

Convention. Many operational and recurring reports are structured according to convention. That is, they follow a prescribed plan that everyone understands. For example, an automotive parts manufacturer might ask all sales reps to prepare a weekly report with these headings: *Competitive observations* (competitors' price changes, discounts, new products, product problems, distributor changes, product promotions), *Product problems* (quality, performance, needs), and *Customer service problems* (delivery, mailings, correspondence, social media, Web traffic). Management gets exactly the information it needs in an easy-to-read form.

Like operating reports, proposals are often organized conventionally. They might use such groupings as background, problem, proposed solution, staffing, schedule, costs, and authorization.

FIGURE 12.6 Ordering Information Logically by Using Criteria

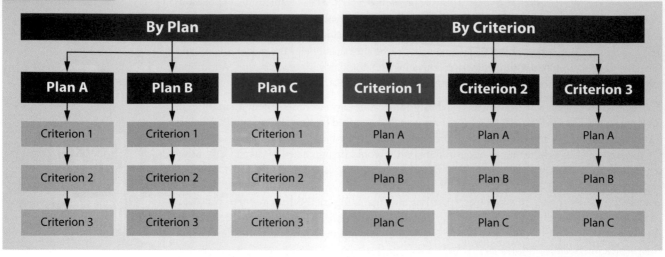

As you might expect, reports following these conventional, prescribed structures greatly simplify the task of organization. Proposals and long reports are presented in Chapter 13.

12-3b Providing Reader Cues

When you finish organizing a report, you probably see a neat outline in your mind: major points supported by subpoints and details. Readers, however, do not know the material as well as you do; they cannot see your outline. To guide them through the data, you need to provide the equivalent of a map and road signs. For both formal and informal reports, devices such as introductions, transitions, and headings prevent readers from getting lost.

Introduction.   One of the best ways to point a reader in the right direction is to provide a report introduction that does three things:

- Tells the purpose of the report
- Describes the significance of the topic
- Previews the main points and the order in which they will be developed

The following paragraph includes all three elements in introducing a report on computer security:

> *This report examines the security of our current IT infrastructure and presents sugges-tions for improving security. Lax computer security could mean loss of information, loss of business, and damage to our equipment and systems. Because many employees are still our biggest liability for using weak passwords, we must make major changes. To improve security, I will present three recommendations: (a) begin using dongles that limit access to our computer system, (b) alter log-on and log-off procedures to include two-factor authen-tication, and (c) move central computer operations to a more secure area.*

This opener tells the purpose (examining computer security), describes its significance (loss of information and business, damage to equipment and systems), and outlines how the report is organized (three recommendations). Good openers in effect set up a contract with the reader. The writer promises to cover certain topics in a specified order. Readers expect the writer to fulfill the contract. They want the topics to be developed as promised—using the same wording and presented in the order mentioned. For example, if in your introduction you state that you will discuss the use of *dongles* (USB security devices), do not change the heading for that section to *security keys*. Remember that the introduction provides a map to a report; switching the names on the map will ensure that readers get lost. To maintain consistency, delay writing the introduction until you have completed the report. Long, complex reports may require introductions, brief internal summaries, and previews for each section.

Transitions. Expressions such as *on the contrary, at the same time*, and *however* show relationships and help reveal the logical flow of ideas in a report. These transitional expressions enable writers to tell readers where ideas are headed and how they relate. Notice how abrupt the following three sentences sound without any transition: Many tablets are available on the market today. [For example,] Apple alone is selling five iPad versions. [In addition,] Samsung, Google, and Amazon offer tablets with excellent reviews and varying price ranges.

The following transitional expressions (see Chapter 5, Figure 5.5, for a complete list) enable you to show readers how you are developing your ideas:

To present additional thoughts: *additionally, again, also, moreover, furthermore*

To suggest cause and effect: *accordingly, as a result, consequently, therefore*

To contrast ideas: *at the same time, but, however, on the contrary, though, yet*

To show time and order: *after, before, first, finally, now, previously, then, to conclude*

To clarify points: *for example, for instance, in other words, that is, thus*

In using these expressions, recognize that they do not have to sit at the head of a sentence. Listen to the rhythm of the sentence, and place the expression where a natural pause occurs. If you are unsure about the placement of a transitional expression, position it at the beginning of the sentence. Used appropriately, transitional expressions serve readers as guides; misused or overused, they can be as distracting and frustrating as too many road signs on a highway.

Headings. Good headings are another structural cue that assists readers in comprehending the organization of a report. They highlight major ideas, allowing busy readers to see the big picture at a glance. Moreover, headings provide resting points for the mind and for the eye, breaking up large chunks of text into manageable and inviting segments.

Report writers may use functional or talking headings (see examples in Figure 12.7). Functional headings show the outline of a report but provide little insight for readers. Functional headings are useful for routine reports. They are also appropriate for sensitive topics that might provoke emotional reactions. By keeping the headings general, experienced writers hope to minimize reader opposition or reaction to controversial subjects.

Talking headings provide more information and spark interest. Unless carefully written, however, talking headings can fail to reveal the organization of a report. With some planning, though, headings can combine the best attributes of both functional and talking, as Figure 12.7 shows.

The best strategy for creating helpful talking headings is to write a few paragraphs first and then generate a talking heading that covers both paragraphs. To create the most effective headings, follow a few basic guidelines:

- **Use appropriate heading levels**. The position and format of a heading indicate its level of importance and relationship to other points. Model Document 12.2 illustrates and discusses a commonly used heading format for business reports. For an overview of alphanumeric and decimal outlines, see Figures 5.3 and 5.4 in Chapter 5.

- **Capitalize and emphasize carefully**. Most writers use all capital letters (without underlines) for main titles, such as report, chapter, and unit titles. For first- and second-level headings, they capitalize only the first letter of main words such as nouns, verbs, adjectives,

FIGURE 12.7 Distinguishing Among Functional, Talking, and Combination Headings

Functional Headings
- Background
- Findings
- Personnel
- Production Costs

Talking Headings
- More Colleges Offer Sustainability Courses
- Survey Shows Support for Campus Recycling Program

Combination Headings
- Introduction: Students Increasingly Proactive about Sustainability
- Sustainability Recommendation: Switching to Drought-Resistant Landscaping

adverbs, names, and so on. Articles (*a, an, the*), conjunctions (*and, but, or, nor*), and prepositions with three or fewer letters (*in, to, by, for*) are not capitalized unless they appear at the beginning or end of the heading. For additional emphasis, most writers use a bold font, as shown in Model Document 12.2.

- **Try to balance headings within levels**. Although it may not be always possible, attempt to create headings that are grammatically similar at a given level. For example, *Developing Product Teams* and *Presenting Plan to Management* are balanced, but *Development of Product Teams* and *Presenting Plan to Management* are not.

- **For short reports use first-level or first- and second-level headings**. Many business reports contain only one or two levels of headings. For such reports use first-level headings (centered, bolded) and, if needed, second-level headings (flush left, bolded). See Model Document 12.2.

MODEL DOCUMENT 12.2   Levels of Headings

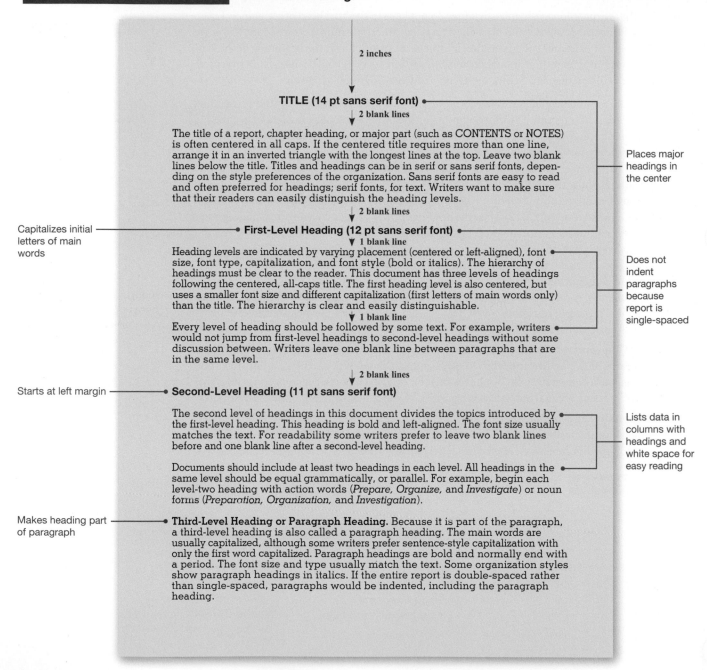

2 inches

TITLE (14 pt sans serif font)

↓ 2 blank lines

The title of a report, chapter heading, or major part (such as CONTENTS or NOTES) is often centered in all caps. If the centered title requires more than one line, arrange it in an inverted triangle with the longest lines at the top. Leave two blank lines below the title. Titles and headings can be in serif or sans serif fonts, depending on the style preferences of the organization. Sans serif fonts are easy to read and often preferred for headings; serif fonts, for text. Writers want to make sure that their readers can easily distinguish the heading levels.

↓ 2 blank lines

First-Level Heading (12 pt sans serif font)

▼ 1 blank line

Heading levels are indicated by varying placement (centered or left-aligned), font size, font type, capitalization, and font style (bold or italics). The hierarchy of headings must be clear to the reader. This document has three levels of headings following the centered, all-caps title. The first heading level is also centered, but uses a smaller font size and different capitalization (first letters of main words only) than the title. The hierarchy is clear and easily distinguishable.

▼ 1 blank line

Every level of heading should be followed by some text. For example, writers would not jump from first-level headings to second-level headings without some discussion between. Writers leave one blank line between paragraphs that are in the same level.

↓ 2 blank lines

Second-Level Heading (11 pt sans serif font)

The second level of headings in this document divides the topics introduced by the first-level heading. This heading is bold and left-aligned. The font size usually matches the text. For readability some writers prefer to leave two blank lines before and one blank line after a second-level heading.

Documents should include at least two headings in each level. All headings in the same level should be equal grammatically, or parallel. For example, begin each level-two heading with action words (*Prepare, Organize,* and *Investigate*) or noun forms (*Preparation, Organization,* and *Investigation*).

Third-Level Heading or Paragraph Heading. Because it is part of the paragraph, a third-level heading is also called a paragraph heading. The main words are usually capitalized, although some writers prefer sentence-style capitalization with only the first word capitalized. Paragraph headings are bold and normally end with a period. The font size and type usually match the text. Some organization styles show paragraph headings in italics. If the entire report is double-spaced rather than single-spaced, paragraphs would be indented, including the paragraph heading.

Capitalizes initial letters of main words

Starts at left margin

Makes heading part of paragraph

Places major headings in the center

Does not indent paragraphs because report is single-spaced

Lists data in columns with headings and white space for easy reading

- **Include at least one heading per report page, but don't end the page with a heading**. Headings increase the readability and attractiveness of report pages. Use at least one per page to break up blocks of text. Move a heading that is separated from the text that follows from the bottom of the page to the top of the following page.
- **Apply punctuation correctly**. Omit end punctuation in first- and second-level headings. End punctuation is required in third-level headings because they are capitalized and punctuated like sentences. Proper nouns (names) are capitalized in third-level headings as they would be in a sentence.
- **Keep headings short but clear**. One-word headings are emphatic but not always clear. For example, the heading *Budget* does not adequately describe figures for a summer project involving student interns for an oil company in Texas. Try to keep your headings brief (no more than eight words), but make sure they are understandable. Experiment with headings that concisely tell who, what, when, where, and why.

12-4 Writing Short Informational Reports

LEARNING OUTCOME

4 Write short informational reports that describe routine tasks.

Now that you are familiar with the basics of gathering, interpreting, and organizing data, you are ready to enter that information into short informational or analytical reports. Informational reports often describe periodic, recurring activities (such as monthly sales or weekly customer calls) as well as situational, nonrecurring events (such as trips, conferences, and special projects). Short informational reports may also take the form of summaries of longer publications. Most informational reports have one thing in common: a neutral or receptive audience. The readers of informational reports do not have to be persuaded; they simply need to be informed.

You can expect to write many informational reports as an entry-level or middle- management employee. These reports generally deliver nonsensitive data and are therefore written directly. Although the writing style is usually conversational and informal, the report contents must be clear to all readers. All headings, lists, and graphics should help the reader grasp major ideas immediately.

The principles of conciseness, clarity, courtesy, and correctness discussed in earlier chapters apply to report writing as well. Your ability to write effective reports can boost your visibility in an organization and result in advancement. The following pointers on design features and techniques can assist you in improving your reports.

12-4a Effective Document Design

Desktop publishing packages, sophisticated word processing programs, and high-quality laser printers now make it possible for you to turn out professional-looking documents and promotional materials. Resist the temptation, however, to overdo it by incorporating too many features in one document. The top ten design tips summarized in Figure 12.8 will help you apply good sense and solid design principles in "publishing" your documents.

Reality Check

Putting Readers at the Center of Report Writing

"[Sharing financial information] is much more than presenting balance sheets or profit/loss statements. Instead, it is trying to understand how each team measures success in terms of what outcomes they're trying to achieve. If I know that abc or xyz is important to a certain team, I go to the drawing board and figure out how to best present data that they're going to embrace."[8]

—Brad Dudding, *Chief Impact Officer at The Bail Project*

12-4b Summaries

A summary compresses the main points from a book, report, article, website, meeting, or convention. A summary saves time by reducing a report or article by 85 to 95 percent. Employees are sometimes asked to write summaries that condense technical reports, periodical articles, or books so that their staff or superiors may grasp the main ideas quickly. As a student, you may be asked to write summaries of articles, chapters, or books to sharpen your writing skills and to confirm your knowledge of reading assignments. In writing a summary, follow these general guidelines:

- Present the goal or purpose of the document being summarized. Why was it written?
- Highlight the research methods (if appropriate), findings, conclusions, and recommendations.

FIGURE 12.8 The Top Ten Tips for Designing Better Documents

① Analyze your audience.

Give readers what they need. Avoid flashiness in traditional documents. Use headings and lists to suit a busy audience.

② Avoid amateurish effects.

Strive for simple, clean, and forceful effects. Do not overwhelm readers with cluttered documents.

③ Choose an appropriate font size.

Use body text that is 11 to 12 points tall. Larger type looks amateurish. Smaller type is hard to read.

④ Use a consistent type font.

Stay with a single family of type within one document. For emphasis and contrast, vary the font size and weight with bold, italic, and other selections.

⑤ Do not justify right margins.

Opt for ragged-right margins to add white space. More deliberate readers find ragged-right text more legible.

⑥ Separate paragraphs and sentences properly.

Skip a line between single-spaced paragraphs. Indent five spaces in double-spaced text. Don't skip a line. Be consistent.

⑦ Design readable headings.

For high readability, show most headings in upper- and lowercase and choose sans-serif type such as Arial or Calibri.

⑧ Strive for an attractive page layout.

Balance print and white space. Provide a focal point three lines above the center of the page. Expect readers to scan a page in a Z pattern.

⑨ Use graphics and clip art with restraint.

You can import, copy, or scan charts, drawings, photos, and clip art into documents. Use only images that are well drawn, relevant, and appropriately sized.

⑩ Develop expertise.

Use the desktop publishing capabilities of your current word processing program, or learn software such Microsoft Publisher, Adobe InDesign, or Canva.

- Omit illustrations, examples, and references.
- Organize for readability by including headings and bulleted or enumerated lists.
- Include your reactions or an overall evaluation of the document if asked to do so.

An **executive summary** summarizes a long report, proposal, or business plan. It concentrates on what management needs to know from a longer report. How to prepare an executive summary is covered in Chapter 13.

12-4c Trip, Convention, and Conference Reports

Employees sent on business trips or to conventions and conferences typically must submit reports when they return. Organizations want to know that their money was well spent in funding the travel. These reports inform management about new procedures, equipment, and laws as well as supply information affecting products, operations, and service.

The hardest parts of writing these reports are selecting the most relevant material and organizing it coherently. Generally, it is best not to use chronological sequencing (*in the morning we did X, at lunch we heard Y, and in the afternoon we did Z*). Instead, you should focus on three to five topics in which your reader will be interested. These items become the body of the report. Then simply add an introduction and a closing, and your report is organized. Here is a general outline for trip, conference, and convention reports:

- Begin by identifying the event (exact date, name, and location) and previewing the topics to be discussed.
- Summarize in the body three to five main points that might benefit the reader.
- Itemize your expenses, if requested, on a separate sheet.
- Close by expressing appreciation, suggesting action to be taken, or synthesizing the value of the trip or event.

Adelyn Richards was recently hired as marketing specialist in the Marketing Department of SmartBaud, a wireless devices and consumer electronics store in Phoenix, Arizona. Recognizing her lack of experience in online customer service, the marketing manager gave her permission to attend a two-day training conference titled Social Customer Service. Her boss, Dan Preston, encouraged Adelyn to attend, saying, "We are serious about increasing our social media involvement, and we want to build solid relationships with our customers while promoting our products. Come back and tell us what you learned." When she returned, Adelyn wrote the conference report shown in Model Document 12.3. Here is how she described its preparation: "I know my boss values brevity, so I worked hard to make my report no more than a page. The conference saturated me with great ideas, far too many to cover in one brief report. So, I decided to discuss two topics that would most benefit our staff. By the third draft, I had compressed my ideas into a manageable size without sacrificing any of the meaning."

MODEL DOCUMENT 12.3   Conference Report

Date: March 16, 2021

To: Dan Preston, Marketing Manager

From: Adelyn Richards, Marketing Specialist AR

Subject: Conference on Social Customer Service–February 2021

I attended the Social Customer Service conference in Tucson, Arizona, on February 25-26, sponsored by Social Partners, Inc. The conference emphasized the importance of delivering excellent customer service in social spaces (social media gathering places). As we prepare to increase our social media involvement, this report summarizes two topics that would benefit our employees: (a) the rising expectations of customers in social media networks, and (b) the role of customer service specialists.

Identifies the topic and previews the report's contents

Customer Expectations of Social Marketers

Conference presenters emphasized the following customer service expectations:
- Customers expect social business connections to be helpful and friendly —always.
- Online customers expect that you're listening and will remember what they said to you last time.
- Before buying, customers are powerfully influenced by user reviews, Facebook comments, Twitter feeds, and forum messages.
- Customers expect honest and prompt responses when they have complaints.

Sets off major topics with bold headings in the same font

The Role of Social Marketers

Whether a company hires a social media management service or uses in-house personnel, the responsibilities of social customer service specialists are the same:
- Monitor customer feedback and respond promptly to questions and complaints.
- Check social media platforms for mention of their businesses. Send text message responses to the right people immediately.
- Examine the company's Facebook activity and create dialogue on Twitter.
- When problems occur, own up to them and explain publicly what you're doing to make things right.

Covers the main ideas that will benefit the reader

Conference Highlights

Companies realize the importance of communicating with customers promptly and personally, especially in social spaces. Since our company is heavily invested in social media platforms, the conference topics seemed especially relevant. I would be happy to share highlights from the conference at our next management meeting. Let me know what date and time work best.

Concludes with an offer to share information

12-4d Periodic (Activity) Reports

Most businesses—especially larger ones—require *periodic reports* (sometimes called *activity reports*) to keep management informed of operations. These recurring reports are written at regular intervals—weekly, monthly, yearly—so that management can monitor business strategies and, if necessary, remedy any problems. Some periodic reports simply contain figures, such as sales volume, the number and kind of customer service calls, shipments delivered, accounts payable, and personnel data. More challenging periodic reports require descriptions and discussions of activities. In preparing a narrative description of their activities, employees writing periodic reports usually do the following:

- Summarize regular activities and events performed during the reporting period.
- Describe irregular events deserving the attention of management.
- Highlight special needs and problems.

Managers naturally want to know that routine activities are progressing normally. Employees today enjoy a great deal of independence and shoulder much responsibility as a result of flattened hierarchies on the job. They often work flexible hours in far-flung locations. Keeping track of their activities and the tasks they were assigned is crucial in such an environment. Routine reports are typically sent by e-mail and may take the form of efficient bulleted lists without commentary.

Model Document 12.4 shows a weekly activity report prepared by Taylor Xin, a senior Web producer at the information technology firm Sphere1 IT in Silicon Valley. Taylor is responsible for her firm's Web presence in Asian countries or territories, mainly Japan, China, Hong Kong, and

MODEL DOCUMENT 12.4   Periodic (Activity) Report

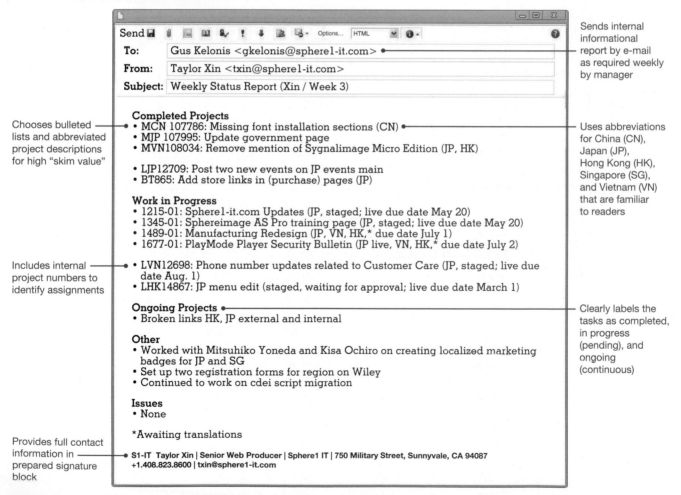

Sends internal informational report by e-mail as required weekly by manager

Chooses bulleted lists and abbreviated project descriptions for high "skim value"

Includes internal project numbers to identify assignments

Provides full contact information in prepared signature block

Uses abbreviations for China (CN), Japan (JP), Hong Kong (HK), Singapore (SG), and Vietnam (VN) that are familiar to readers

Clearly labels the tasks as completed, in progress (pending), and ongoing (continuous)

To: Gus Kelonis <gkelonis@sphere1-it.com>
From: Taylor Xin <txin@sphere1-it.com>
Subject: Weekly Status Report (Xin / Week 3)

Completed Projects
- MCN 107786: Missing font installation sections (CN)
- MJP 107995: Update government page
- MVN108034: Remove mention of Sygnalimage Micro Edition (JP, HK)

- LJP12709: Post two new events on JP events main
- BT865: Add store links in (purchase) pages (JP)

Work in Progress
- 1215-01: Sphere1-it.com Updates (JP, staged; live due date May 20)
- 1345-01: Sphereimage AS Pro training page (JP, staged; live due date May 20)
- 1489-01: Manufacturing Redesign (JP, VN, HK,* due date July 1)
- 1677-01: PlayMode Player Security Bulletin (JP live, VN, HK,* due date July 2)

- LVN12698: Phone number updates related to Customer Care (JP, staged; live due date Aug. 1)
- LHK14867: JP menu edit (staged, waiting for approval; live due date March 1)

Ongoing Projects
- Broken links HK, JP external and internal

Other
- Worked with Mitsuhiko Yoneda and Kisa Ochiro on creating localized marketing badges for JP and SG
- Set up two registration forms for region on Wiley
- Continued to work on cdei script migration

Issues
- None

*Awaiting translations

S1-IT Taylor Xin | Senior Web Producer | Sphere1 IT | 750 Military Street, Sunnyvale, CA 94087
+1.408.823.8600 | txin@sphere1-it.com

Vietnam. In her weekly reports to her supervisor, Gus Kelonis, Taylor neatly divides her projects into three categories: *completed, in progress*, and *ongoing. In progress* means the task is not yet completed or is pending. *Ongoing* refers to continuous tasks such as regular maintenance. Gus, the manager, then combines the activity reports from all his subordinates into a separate periodic report detailing the department's activities to send to his superiors.

Taylor justifies the use of jargon, the lack of a salutation and complimentary close, and ultra-short bulleted items as follows: "We e-mail our reports internally, so some IT jargon can be expected. The readers will understand it. Gus and upper management all want reporting to be brief and to the point. Bullets fit us just fine." Periodic reports ensure that information within the company flows steadily and that supervisors know the status of current and pending projects. This efficient information flow is all the more important because Taylor works at home two days a week to spend time with her young children. Several of her coworkers also telecommute.

12-4e Progress and Interim Reports

Continuing projects often require progress or interim reports to describe their status. These reports may be external (advising customers about the headway of their projects) or internal (informing management of the status of activities). Progress reports typically follow this pattern of development:

- Specify in the opening the purpose and nature of the project.
- Provide background information if the audience requires filling in.
- Describe the work completed.
- Explain the work currently in progress, including personnel, activities, methods, and locations.
- Describe current problems and anticipate future problems and possible remedies.
- Discuss future activities and provide the expected completion date.

As a location manager for Angel City Productions, Ellie Harper frequently writes progress reports, such as the one shown in Model Document 12.5. Producers want to know what she is doing, and a phone call does not provide a permanent record. Here is how she described the reasoning behind her progress report: "I usually include background information in my reports because a director does not always know or remember exactly what specifications I was given for a location search. Then I try to hit the high points of what I have completed and what I plan to do next, without getting bogged down in tiny details. Although it would be easier to skip them, I have learned to be up front with any problems I anticipate. I do not tell how to solve the problems, but I feel duty-bound to at least mention them."

Christopher Penler/Shutterstock.com

FOR THE RECORD

Spotify Is All Grown Up and That Means Reporting
Music-streaming service Spotify is part of the industry trend of providing both free and paid access to a huge inventory of music. Unlike Internet radio app Pandora, however, Spotify allows listeners to choose an unlimited number of songs to share with friends or to listen to at any time. The Swedish-based service partners with broadcasters, festivals, blogs, and nongovernmental organizations to bring music to their constituents. As a public company, Spotify must issue regular financial reports. Its July 2019 quarterly report, for example, includes information about user data, financial metrics, and new products and services.[9] What types of information would business communicators need to include in these reports?

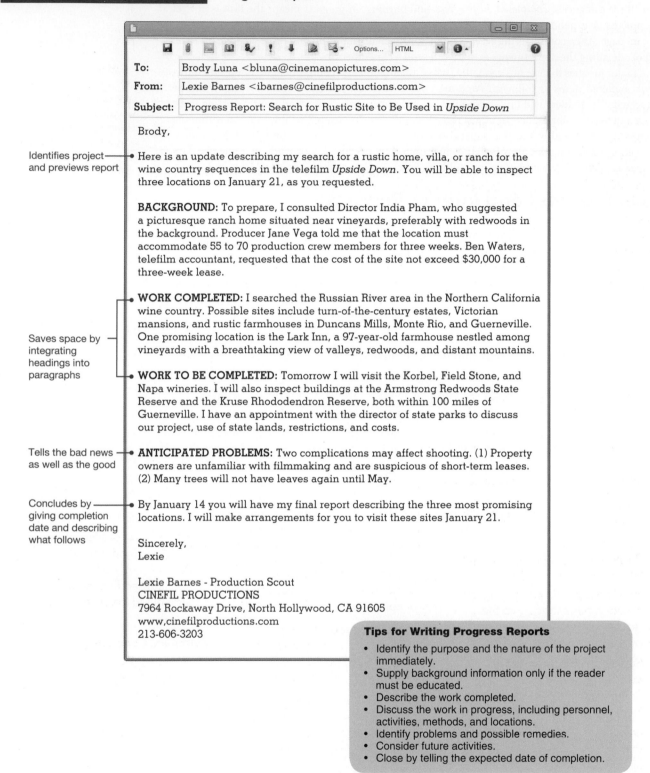

Identifies project and previews report

To: Brody Luna <bluna@cinemanopictures.com>

From: Lexie Barnes <ibarnes@cinefilproductions.com>

Subject: Progress Report: Search for Rustic Site to Be Used in *Upside Down*

Brody,

Here is an update describing my search for a rustic home, villa, or ranch for the wine country sequences in the telefilm *Upside Down*. You will be able to inspect three locations on January 21, as you requested.

BACKGROUND: To prepare, I consulted Director India Pham, who suggested a picturesque ranch home situated near vineyards, preferably with redwoods in the background. Producer Jane Vega told me that the location must accommodate 55 to 70 production crew members for three weeks. Ben Waters, telefilm accountant, requested that the cost of the site not exceed $30,000 for a three-week lease.

Saves space by integrating headings into paragraphs

WORK COMPLETED: I searched the Russian River area in the Northern California wine country. Possible sites include turn-of-the-century estates, Victorian mansions, and rustic farmhouses in Duncans Mills, Monte Rio, and Guerneville. One promising location is the Lark Inn, a 97-year-old farmhouse nestled among vineyards with a breathtaking view of valleys, redwoods, and distant mountains.

WORK TO BE COMPLETED: Tomorrow I will visit the Korbel, Field Stone, and Napa wineries. I will also inspect buildings at the Armstrong Redwoods State Reserve and the Kruse Rhododendron Reserve, both within 100 miles of Guerneville. I have an appointment with the director of state parks to discuss our project, use of state lands, restrictions, and costs.

Tells the bad news as well as the good

ANTICIPATED PROBLEMS: Two complications may affect shooting. (1) Property owners are unfamiliar with filmmaking and are suspicious of short-term leases. (2) Many trees will not have leaves again until May.

Concludes by giving completion date and describing what follows

By January 14 you will have my final report describing the three most promising locations. I will make arrangements for you to visit these sites January 21.

Sincerely,
Lexie

Lexie Barnes - Production Scout
CINEFIL PRODUCTIONS
7964 Rockaway Drive, North Hollywood, CA 91605
www.cinefilproductions.com
213-606-3203

Tips for Writing Progress Reports

- Identify the purpose and the nature of the project immediately.
- Supply background information only if the reader must be educated.
- Describe the work completed.
- Discuss the work in progress, including personnel, activities, methods, and locations.
- Identify problems and possible remedies.
- Consider future activities.
- Close by telling the expected date of completion.

© Cengage Learning 2015; Courtesy of Mary Ellen Guffey and Dana Loewy; Used with permission from Microsoft.

12-4f Investigative Reports

Investigative reports deliver data for specific situations—without offering interpretations or recommendations. These nonrecurring reports are generally arranged using the direct strategy with three segments: introduction, body, and summary. The body—which includes the facts, findings, or discussion—may be organized by time, component, importance, criteria, or convention. What is important is dividing the topic into logical segments—say, three to five areas that are roughly equal and do not overlap.

The subject matter of the report usually suggests the best way to divide or organize it. Cassie Rivas, an information specialist for a health-care consulting firm in Durham, North Carolina, received the task of researching and writing an investigative report for St. Joseph's Hospital. Her assignment: study the award-winning patient service program at Grand Oak Medical Center and report how it improved its patient satisfaction rating from 6.2 to 7.8 in just one year. Cassie collected data and then organized her findings into four parts: management training, employee training, patient services, and follow-up program. Although we do not show Cassie's complete report here, you can see a similar informational report in Chapter 11, Model Document 11.2.

Whether you are writing a periodic, trip, conference, progress, or investigative report, you will want to review the suggestions in the following checklist.

Checklist

Writing Informational Reports

Introduction

- **Begin directly.** Identify the report and its purpose.

- **Provide a preview.** If the report is over a page long, give the reader a brief overview of its organization.

- **Supply background data selectively.** When readers are unfamiliar with the topic, briefly fill in the necessary details.

- **Divide the topic.** Strive to group the facts or findings into three to five roughly equal segments that do not overlap.

Body

- **Arrange the subtopics logically.** Consider organizing by time, component, importance, criteria, or convention.

- **Use clear headings.** Supply functional or talking headings (at least one per page) that describe each important section.

- **Determine the degree of formality.** Use an informal, conversational writing style unless the audience expects a more formal tone.

- **Enhance readability with graphic highlighting.** Make liberal use of bullets, numbered and lettered lists, headings, underlined items, and white space.

Summary/Concluding Remarks

- **When necessary, summarize the report.** Briefly review the main points and discuss what action will follow.

- **Offer a concluding thought.** If relevant, express appreciation or a willingness to provide further information.

12-5 Preparing Short Analytical Reports

Analytical reports differ significantly from informational reports. Although the authors of both seek to collect and present data clearly, writers of analytical reports also evaluate the data and typically try to persuade the reader to accept the conclusions and act on the recommendations. Informational reports emphasize facts; analytical reports emphasize reasoning and conclusions. This section describes three common types of analytical business reports: (a) justification/recommendation reports, (b) feasibility reports, and (c) yardstick reports. These reports involve collecting and analyzing data, evaluating the results, drawing conclusions, and making recommendations.

For some situations you may organize analytical reports directly with the conclusions and recommendations near the beginning. Directness is appropriate when the reader has confidence in the writer, based on either experience or credentials. Frontloading the recommendations also works when the topic is routine or familiar and the reader is supportive.

Directness can backfire, though. If you announce the recommendations too quickly, the reader may immediately object to a single idea. Once the reader has an unfavorable mind-set, changing it may be difficult or impossible. A reader may also believe that you have oversimplified or disregarded something noteworthy if you provide your recommendations first. When you must lead the reader through the process of discovering the solution, use the indirect strategy: present conclusions and recommendations last.

Most analytical reports answer questions about specific problems and aid in decision making (e.g., *How can we use social media most effectively? Should we close the Brownsville plant? How can we improve customer service?* Analytical reports provide conclusions that help management answer these questions.

12-5a Justification/Recommendation Reports

Both managers and employees must occasionally write reports that justify or recommend actions, such as buying equipment, changing a procedure, hiring an employee, consolidating departments, or investing funds. These reports may also be called **internal proposals** because their persuasive nature is similar to that of external proposals (presented in Chapter 13). Large organizations sometimes prescribe how these reports should be organized and formatted; they often use forms with conventional headings. When you are free to select an organizational plan yourself, however, let your audience and topic determine your choice of the direct or indirect strategy.

Direct Strategy. For nonsensitive topics and recommendations that will be agreeable to readers, you can organize directly according to the following order:

- Identify the problem or need briefly.
- Announce the recommendation, solution, or action concisely and with action verbs.
- Explain more fully the benefits of the recommendation or steps necessary to solve the problem.
- Include a discussion of pros, cons, and costs.
- Conclude with a summary specifying the recommendation and necessary action.

Indirect Strategy. When a reader may oppose a recommendation or when circumstances suggest caution, do not rush to reveal your recommendation. Consider using the following sequence for an indirect approach to your recommendations:

- Refer to the problem in general terms, not to your recommendation, in the subject line.
- Describe the problem or need your recommendation addresses. Use specific examples, supporting statistics, and authoritative quotes to lend credibility to the seriousness of the problem.
- Discuss alternative solutions, beginning with the least likely to succeed.
- Present the most promising alternative (your recommendation) last.
- Show how the advantages of your recommendation outweigh its disadvantages.
- Summarize your recommendation. If appropriate, specify the action it requires.
- Ask for authorization to proceed, if necessary.

Noel Navarro, an executive assistant at a large petroleum and mining company in Grand Prairie, Texas, received a challenging research assignment. Her boss, the director of Human Resources and

Welfare, asked her to investigate ways to persuade employees to quit smoking. Here is how she described her task: "We banned smoking many years ago inside our buildings and on the premises, but we never tried very hard to get smokers to actually kick their habits. My job was to gather information about the problem and learn how other companies have helped workers stop smoking. The report would go to my boss, but I knew he would pass it along to the management council for approval."

Continuing her explanation, Noel said, "If the report were just for my boss, I would put my recommendation right up front, because I'm sure he would support it. However, the management council may need to be persuaded because of the costs involved—and because some of them are smokers. Therefore, I put the alternative I favored last. To gain credibility, I footnoted my sources. I had enough material for a ten-page report, but I kept it to two pages in keeping with our company report policy." Noel chose MLA style to document her sources. A long report that uses the APA style is shown in Chapter 13.

Noel single-spaced her report, shown in Model Document 12.6, because her company prefers this style. Some companies prefer the readability of double-spacing. Be sure to check with your organization for its preference before printing your reports.

MODEL DOCUMENT 12.6 Justification/Recommendation Report, MLA Style

Date: November 18, 2021

To: Keith Kunin, Vice President, Human Resources

From: Noel Navaro, Executive Assistant

Subject: Analysis of Employee Smoking Cessation Programs

At your request, I have examined measures that encourage employees to quit smoking. As company records show, approximately 23 percent of our employees still smoke, despite the antismoking and clean-air policies we adopted in 2019. To collect data for this report, I studied professional and government publications; I also inquired at companies and clinics about stop-smoking programs.

Introduces purpose of report, tells method of data collection, and previews organization

Avoids revealing recommendation immediately

This report presents data describing the significance of the problem, three alternative solutions, and a recommendation based on my investigation.

Uses headings that combine function and description

Significance of Problem: Health Care and Productivity Losses

Employees who smoke are costly to any organization. The following statistics show the effects of smoking for workers and for organizations:

- Absenteeism is 40 to 50 percent greater among smoking employees.
- Accidents are two to three times greater among smokers.
- Bronchitis, lung and heart disease, cancer, and early death are more frequent among smokers (Arhelger, 2019, p. 4).

Documents data sources for credibility, uses APA style citing author and year in the text

Although our clean-air policy prohibits smoking in the building, shop, and office, we have done little to encourage employees to stop smoking. Many workers still go outside to smoke at lunch and breaks. Other companies have been far more proactive in their attempts to stop employee smoking. Many companies have found that persuading employees to stop smoking was a decisive factor in reducing their health insurance premiums. Following is a discussion of three common stop-smoking measures tried by other companies, along with a projected cost factor for each (Rindfleisch, 2018, p. 4).

Discusses least effective alternative first

Alternative 1: Literature and Events

The least expensive and easiest stop-smoking measure involves the distribution of literature, such as "The Ten-Step Plan" from Smokefree Enterprises and government pamphlets citing smoking dangers. Some companies have also sponsored events such as the Great American Smoke-Out, a one-day occasion intended to develop group spirit in spurring smokers to quit. "Studies show, however," says one expert, "that literature and company-sponsored events have little permanent effect in helping smokers quit" (Mendel, 2017, p. 108).

Cost: Negligible

Keith Kunin   November 18, 2021   Page 2

Alternative 2: Stop-Smoking Programs Outside the Workplace

Local clinics provide treatment programs in classes at their centers. Here in Dallas we have the Smokers' Treatment Center, ACC Motivation Center, and New-Choice Program for Stopping Smoking. These behavior-modification stop-smoking programs are acknowledged to be more effective than literature distribution or incentive programs. However, studies of companies using off-workplace programs show that many employees fail to attend regularly and do not complete the programs.

> Cost: $1,200 per employee, three-month individual program ●——————— Highlights costs for
> (Your-Choice Program)   easy comparison
> $900 per employee, three-month group session

Alternative 3: Stop-Smoking Programs at the Workplace

Many clinics offer workplace programs with counselors meeting employees in ●——— Arranges
company conference rooms. These programs have the advantage of keeping a   alternatives so that
firm's employees together so that they develop a group spirit and exert pressure   most effectiveis last
on each other to succeed. The most successful programs are on company
premises and also on company time. Employees participating in such programs
had a 72 percent greater success record than employees attending the same stop-
smoking program at an outside clinic (Honda, p. 35). A disadvantage of this
arrangement, of course, is lost work time—amounting to about two hours a
week for three months.

> Cost: $900 per employee, two hours per week of release time for
> three months

Conclusions and Recommendation ●——————————————————— Summarizes
                                                                                         findings and ends
Smokers require discipline, counseling, and professional assistance to kick the   with specific
nicotine habit, as explained at the American Cancer Society website ("Guide   recommendation
to Quitting Smoking,"). Workplace stop-smoking programs on company time
are more effective than literature, incentives, and off-workplace programs. If
our goal is to reduce health care costs and lead our employees to healthful lives,
we should invest in a workplace stop-smoking program with release time for   Reveals
smokers. Although the program temporarily reduces productivity, we can expect   recommendation
to recapture that loss in lower health care premiums and healthier employees.   only after
                                                                                    discussing all
Therefore, I recommend that we begin a stop-smoking treatment program on ●———   alternatives
company premises with two hours per week of release time for participants for
three months.

Keith Kunin   November 18, 2021   Page 3

Lists all references ————————————————————● **Works Cited**
in MLA Style

Magazine ————————————● Arhelger, Zack. "The End of Smoking." *The World of Business*, 5 Nov. 2020,
                                          pp. 3–8.

Website article ————————● "Guide to Quitting Smoking." *The American Cancer Society.org*, 27 Oct.
                                          2020, http://www.cancer.org/healthy/stayawayfromtobacco/
                                          guidetoquittingsmoking/guide-to-quitting-smoking-toc

Journal article ————————● Honda, Emeline M. "Managing Anti-Smoking Campaigns: The Case for
                                          Company Programs." *Management Quarterly*, vol. 32, 2019, pp. 29–47.

Book ————————————————● Mendel, I. A. *The Puff Stops Here.* Science Publications, 2019.

Newspaper article ————————● Rindfleisch, Terry. "Smoke-Free Workplaces Can Help Smokers Quit,
                                          Expert Says." *Evening Chronicle*, 4 Dec. 2020, pp. 4+.

12-5b Feasibility Reports

Feasibility reports examine the practicality and advisability of following a course of action. They answer this question: Will this plan or proposal work? Feasibility reports typically are internal reports written to advise on matters such as consolidating departments, offering a wellness program to employees, or hiring an outside firm to handle a company's accounting or social media presence. These reports may also be written by consultants called in to investigate a problem. The focus of these reports is on the decision: rejecting or proceeding with the proposed option. Your role as a report writer is usually not to persuade the reader to accept the decision; your role is to present information objectively. In writing feasibility reports, consider these suggestions:

- Announce your decision immediately.
- Provide a description of the background and problem necessitating the proposal.
- Discuss the benefits of the proposal.
- Describe the problems that may result.
- Calculate the costs associated with the proposal, if appropriate.
- Show the time frame necessary for implementing the proposal.
- Conclude with an action request if appropriate.

Brenda Tchakerian, human resources manager for a large financial services firm in St. Louis, Missouri, wrote the feasibility report shown in Model Document 12.7. Because she discovered that the company was losing time and money as a result of personal e-mail and Internet use by employees, she talked with Damian Gorman, vice president, about employee-monitoring software. Rather than take time away from Brenda's regular duties to have her investigate software programs, the vice president suggested that she hire a consultant to analyze the situation and present a plan. When the consultant's work was completed, the vice president wanted to know whether the consultant's plan was feasible. Although Brenda's feasibility report is only one page long, it provides all the necessary information: background, benefits, employee acceptance, costs, and time frame.

12-5c Yardstick Reports

Yardstick reports examine problems with two or more solutions. To determine the best solution, the writer establishes criteria by which to compare the alternatives. The criteria then act as a yardstick against which all the alternatives are measured, as shown in Model Document 12.8. The yardstick approach is effective for companies that must establish specifications for equipment purchases and then compare each manufacturer's product with the established specs. The yardstick approach is also effective when exact specifications cannot be established.

For example, a yardstick report might help a company choose an attractive job perk. Perks are nontraditional benefits that appeal to employees, e.g., free food and beverages, flexible scheduling and telecommuting options, on-site gyms, and fitness classes. A yardstick report may help a company pick an appropriate job perk. To encourage long-term wellness, the company might consider offering employees discounted fitness club memberships, on-site yoga classes, or ergonomic workstations. The yardstick report would describe and compare the three alternatives in terms of (a) costs, (b) long-term benefits, and (c) expected participation level. After surveying employees and researching companies offering similar benefits, report writers would compare the alternatives and recommend the most workable job perk.

The real advantage to yardstick reports is that alternatives can be measured consistently using the same criteria. Writers using a yardstick approach typically do the following:

- Begin by describing the problem or need.
- Explain possible solutions and alternatives.
- Establish criteria for comparing the alternatives; tell how the criteria were selected or developed.
- Discuss and evaluate each alternative in terms of the criteria.
- Draw conclusions and make recommendations.

RUIZ FINANCIAL SERVICES LLP
MEMORANDUM

Date: October 4, 2021

To: Damian Gorman, Vice President

From: Brenda Tchakerian, Director, Human Resources *B.T.*

Subject: Feasibility of Implementation of Internet Monitoring Program

Explains reason for report and outlines its organization

As you suggested, we hired a consultant to investigate the feasibility of implementing a plan to monitor employee Internet use. The consultant reports that such a plan is workable and could be fully implemented by February 1. This report discusses the background, benefits, problems, costs, and time frame of the plan.

Reveals decision immediately

Background: Current Misuse of Internet Privileges. Currently we allow employees Internet access for job-related tasks. Many use social media—specifically, Facebook, Twitter, and LinkedIn—to communicate with clients and the public. However, some employees use this access for personal reasons, resulting in lowered productivity, higher costs, and a strain on the network. Therefore, we hired an outside consultant who suggested an Internet-monitoring program.

Describes problem and background

Evaluates positive and negative aspects of proposal objectively

Benefits of Plan: Appropriate Use of Social Media and the Internet. The proposed plan calls for installing Internet-monitoring software such as NetGuard or eMonitor. We would fully disclose to employees that this software will be tracking their online activity. We would also teach employees what social media and Internet use is appropriate. In addition to increased productivity, lowered costs, and improved network performance, this software will also help protect our company against loss of intellectual property, trade secrets, and confidential information.

Employee Acceptance. One of the biggest problems will be convincing employees to accept this new policy without feeling that their privacy is being violated. However, proper training will help employees understand the appropriate use of social media and the Internet.

Costs. Implementing the monitoring plan involves two direct costs. The first is the initial software cost of $500 to $1,100, depending on the package we choose. The second cost involves employee training and trainer fees. However, the expenditures are within the project's budget.

Presents costs and schedule; omits unnecessary summary

Time Frame. Selecting the software package will take about two weeks. Preparing a training program will require another three weeks. Once the program is started, the breaking-in period will take at least three months. By February 1 the Internet-monitoring program will be fully functional resulting in increased productivity, decreased costs, lowered liability, and improved network performance.

Please let me know by October 15 whether you would like additional information about monitoring social media and Internet programs.

Concludes with action request

Alexis Broussard, benefits administrator for computer manufacturer CompuTech, was called on to write the report comparing outplacement agencies illustrated in Model Document 12.8. These agencies counsel discharged employees and help them find new positions; fees are paid by the former employer. Alexis knew that times were bad for CompuTech and that extensive downsizing would take place in the next two years. Her task was to compare outplacement agencies and recommend one to management.

After collecting information, Alexis found that her biggest problem was organizing the data and developing a system for making comparisons. All the outplacement agencies she investigated seemed to offer the same basic package of services.

With the information she gathered about three outplacement agencies, she made a big grid listing the names of the agencies across the top. Down the side she listed general categories—such as services, costs, and reputation. Then she filled in the information for each agency. This grid, which began to look like a table, helped her organize all the pieces of information. After studying the grid, she saw that all the information could be grouped into four categories: counseling services, administrative and research assistance, reputation, and costs. She made these the criteria she would use to compare agencies.

Next, Alexis divided her grid into two parts, which became Table 1 and Table 2. In writing the report, she could have made each agency a separate heading, followed by a discussion of how it measured up to the criteria. Immediately, though, she saw how repetitious that would become. Therefore, she used the criteria as headings and discussed how each agency met each criterion—or failed to meet it. Making a recommendation was easy once Alexis had made the tables and could see how the agencies compared.

MODEL DOCUMENT 12.8 **Yardstick Report**

Date: March 2, 2021
To: Vinay P. Devaki, Director, Operations
From: Alexis Broussard, Benefits Administrator *A B*
Subject: Choosing Outplacement Plan

Here is the report you requested investigating the possibility of Compu Tech's use of outplacement services. It discusses the problem of counseling services for discharged staff and establishes criteria for selecting an outplacement agency. It then evaluates three prospective agencies and presents a recommendation based on that evaluation.

Introduces purpose and gives overview of report organization

Problem: Counseling Discharged Staff

Discusses background briefly because readers already know the problem

In an effort to reduce costs and increase competitiveness, Compu Tech will begin a program of staff reduction that will involve releasing up to 20 percent of our workforce over the next 12 to 24 months. Many of these employees have been with us for ten or more years, and they are not being released for performance faults. These employees deserve a severance package that includes counseling and assistance in finding new careers.

Solution and Alternatives: Outplacement Agencies

Uses dual headings, giving function and description

Numerous outplacement agencies offer discharged employees counseling and assistance in locating new careers. This assistance minimizes not only the negative feelings related to job loss but also the very real possibility of litigation. Potentially expensive lawsuits have been lodged against some companies by unhappy employees who felt they were unfairly released.

Announces solution and the alternatives it presents

In seeking an outplacement agency, we should find one that offers advice to the sponsoring company as well as to dischargees. The law now requires certain procedures, especially in releasing employees over forty. CompuTech could unwittingly become liable to lawsuits because our managers are uninformed of these procedures. I have located three potential outplacement agencies appropriate to serve our needs: Gray & Associates, Right Access, and Careers Plus.

Establishing Criteria for Selecting Agency

Tells how criteria were selected

In order to choose among the three agencies, I established criteria based on professional articles, discussions with officials at other companies using outplacement agencies, and interviews with agencies. Here are the four groups of criteria I used in evaluating the three agencies:

1. <u>Counseling services</u>—including job search advice, résumé help, crisis management, corporate counseling, and availability of full-time counselors
2. <u>Administrative and research assistance</u>—including availability of admin-istrative staff, librarian, and personal computers
3. <u>Reputation</u>—based on a telephone survey of former clients and listing with a professional association
4. <u>Costs</u>—for both group programs and executive services

Creates four criteria for use as yardstick in evaluating alternatives

Director Devaki   Page 2   March 2, 2021

Discussion: Evaluating Agencies by Criteria

Each agency was evaluated using the four criteria just described. Data comparing the first three criteria are summarized in Table 1.

Table 1
A COMPARISON OF SERVICES AND REPUTATIONS
FOR THREE LOCAL OUTPLACEMENT AGENCIES

(marginal note: Places table close to spot where it is first mentioned)

	Gray & Associates	Right Access	Careers Plus
Counseling services			
Résumé advice	Yes	Yes	Yes
Crisis management	Yes	No	Yes
Corporate counseling	Yes	No	No
Full-time counselors	Yes	No	Yes
Administrative, research assistance			
Administrative staff	Yes	Yes	Yes
Librarian, research library	Yes	No	Yes
Personal computers	Yes	No	Yes
Listed by National Association of Career Consultants	Yes	No	Yes
Reputation (telephone survey of former clients)	Excellent	Good	Excellent

(marginal note: Summarizes complex data in table for easy reading and reference)

Counseling Services
All three agencies offered similar basic counseling services with job-search and résumé advice. They differed, however, in three significant areas.

Right Access does not offer crisis management, a service that puts the discharged employee in contact with a counselor the same day the employee is released. Experts in the field consider this service especially important to help the dischargee begin "bonding" with the counselor immediately. Immediate counseling also helps the dischargee learn how to break the news to family members. Crisis management can be instrumental in reducing lawsuits because dischargees immediately begin to focus on career planning instead of concentrating on their pain and need for revenge. Moreover, Right Access does not employ full-time counselors; it hires part-timers according to demand. Industry authorities advise against using agencies whose staff members are inexperienced and employed on an "asneeded" basis.

(marginal note: Highlights the similarities and differences among the alternatives)

In addition, neither Right Access nor Careers Plus offers regular corporate counseling, which I feel is critical in training our managers to conduct terminal interviews. Careers Plus, however, suggested that it could schedule special work-shops if desired.

Administrative and Research Assistance
Both Gray & Associates and Careers Plus offer complete administrative services and personal computers. Dischargees have access to staff and equipment to assist them in their job searches. These agencies also provide research libraries, librarians, and databases of company information to help in securing interviews.

(marginal note: Does not repeat obvious data from table)

Director Devaki   Page 3   March 2, 2021

Reputation

Discusses objectively how each agency meets criteria

To assess the reputation of each agency, I checked its listing with the National Association of Career Consultants. This is a voluntary organization of outplacement agencies that monitors and polices its members. Gray & Associates and Careers Plus are listed; Right Access is not.

For further evidence I conducted a telephone survey of former agency clients. The three agencies supplied me with names and telephone numbers of companies and individuals they had served. I called four former clients for each agency. Most of the individuals were pleased with the outplacement services they had received. I asked each client the same questions so that I could compare responses.

Costs

All three agencies have two separate fee schedules, summarized in Table 2. The first schedule is for group programs intended for lowerlevel employees. These include offsite or on-site single-day workshop sessions, and the prices range from $1,200 a session (at Right Access) to $1,700 per session (at Gray & Associates). An additional fee of $50 to $60 is charged for each participant.

Selects most important data from table to discuss

The second fee schedule covers executive services. The counseling is individual and costs from 10 percent to 18 percent of the dischargee's previous year's salary. Since CompuTech will be forced to release numerous managerial staff members, the executive fee schedule is critical. Table 2 shows fees for a hypothetical case involving a manager who earns $100,000 a year.

Table 2
A COMPARISON OF COSTS FOR THREE AGENCIES

	Gray & Associates	Right Access	Careers Plus
Group programs	$1,700/session $55/participant	$1,200/session $50/participant	$1,600/session $60/participant
Executive services	15% of previous year's salary	10% of previous year's salary	18% of previous year's salary plus $1,000 fee
Manager at $100,000/year	$15,000	$10,000	$19,000

Conclusions and Recommendations

Gives reasons for making recommendation

Although Right Access charges the lowest fees, it lacks crisis management, corporate counseling, full-time counselors, library facilities, and personal computers. Moreover, it is not listed by the National Association of Career Consultants. Therefore, the choice is between Gray & Associates and Careers Plus. Because they offer similar services, the deciding factor is costs. Careers Plus would charge $4,000 more for counseling a manager than would Gray & Associates. Although Gray & Associates has fewer computers available, all other elements of its services seem good. Therefore, I recommend that CompuTech hire Gray & Associates as an outplacement agency to counsel discharged employees.

Narrows choice to final alternative

Checklist

Writing Analytical Reports

Introduction

- **Identify the purpose of the report.** Explain why the report is being written.
- **Describe the significance of the topic.** Explain why the report is important.
- **Preview the organization of the report.** Especially for long reports, explain how the report will be organized.
- **Summarize the conclusions and recommendations for receptive audiences.** Use the direct strategy only if you have the confidence of the reader.

Findings

- **Discuss pros and cons.** In recommendation/justification reports, evaluate the advantages and disadvantages of each alternative. For unreceptive audiences consider placing the recommended alternative last.
- **Establish criteria to evaluate alternatives.** In yardstick reports, create criteria to use in measuring each alternative consistently.
- **Support the findings with evidence.** Supply facts, statistics, expert opinion, survey data, and other proof from which you can draw logical conclusions.
- **Organize the findings for logic and readability.** Arrange the findings around the alternatives or the reasons leading to the conclusion. Use headings, enumerations, lists, tables, and graphics to focus emphasis.

Conclusions/Recommendations

- **Draw reasonable conclusions from the findings.** Develop conclusions that answer the research question. Justify the conclusions with highlights from the findings.
- **Make recommendations, if asked.** For multiple recommendations prepare a list. Use action verbs. Explain fully the benefits of the recommendation or steps necessary to solve the problem or answer the question.

Zooming In

Your Turn:
Applying Your Skills at Netflix

Streaming has become so popular worldwide that it is projected to be a $70.5 billion industry by 2021.[12] To maintain its position as a market leader, Netflix must continually vie for subscribers, and part of its strategy is to offer a wide selection of content. Although its library of previously aired TV shows and movies continues to draw the most views, Netflix has started producing its own content, including documentaries, drama and comedy series, children's shows, anime series, and feature films. Most recently, Netflix released 371 series and movies adding up to 1,178 original shows in one year alone.[13]

Netflix understands that some of its programming will appeal only to a small audience segment; therefore, to augment that strategy, Netflix has amped up its original programming arm. Its goal is to attract luminaries such as former President and Mrs. Obama, film star Salma Hayek, and Broadway darling Darren Criss, all of whom bring cachet to the brand, attract new subscribers, and retain its current subscriber base. Doing so has caused Netflix to reexamine its policies about releasing viewership data because top-tier stars require hard numbers before signing on. Why else would they choose Netflix when many other attractive contenders exist?

Your Task

As an intern in the Netflix marketing department, you are charged with writing a yardstick report comparing the subscriber figures, subscription prices, size of catalog, and the impact of the most popular streamed titles among the major streaming services: Netflix, Prime Video, Apple TV, Hulu, HBO Max, and Disney+. Look for trends; for example, Disney+ soared in popularity after its launch, exceeding all projections. Are subscriber numbers at Netflix and its competitors growing, flattening, or dropping? Establish other criteria that could potentially help Netflix size up its competition. The goal of your report is to assess the competing services' position in the market relative to Netflix's.

SUMMARY OF LEARNING OUTCOMES

1 Analyze statistical data and other information using tables, measures of central tendency (mean, median, and mode), and decision matrices.

- To make sense of report information, writers sort it into tables or analyze it by mean (the arithmetic average), median (the midpoint in a group of figures), and mode (the most frequent response); range represents a span between the highest and lowest figures.

- Grids help organize complex data into rows and columns.

- A decision matrix, a special grid with weights, assists decision makers in choosing objectively among complex options.

- Writers need to maintain accuracy in applying statistical techniques to gain and maintain credibility with their readers.

2 Develop meaningful conclusions and practical report recommendations after valid analysis.

- Writers explain what the survey data mean in a conclusion—especially in relation to the original report problem; they interpret key findings and may attempt to explain what caused the problem.

- Reports that call for recommendations require writers to make specific suggestions for actions that can solve the report problem.

- Recommendations should be feasible, practical, and potentially agreeable to the audience; they should relate to the initial report problem.

- Recommendations may be combined with conclusions.

3 Organize report data logically while providing reader cues to aid comprehension.

- Reports may be organized in many ways, including by (a) time (establishing a chronology), (b) component (discussing a problem by geography, division, or product), (c) importance (arranging data from most important to least important, or vice versa), (d) criteria (comparing items by standards), or (e) convention (using an already established grouping).

- To help guide the reader through the text, introductions, transitions, and headings serve as cues.

4 Write short informational reports that describe routine tasks.

- Typical informational reports include periodic, trip, convention, progress, and investigative reports.

- The introduction in informational reports previews the purpose and supplies background data, if necessary.

- The body of an informational report is generally divided into three to five segments that may be organized by time, component, importance, criteria, or convention; clear headings make the body easy to scan. Unless formality is expected, an informal, conversational style is used.

- In the conclusion writers review the main points and discuss actions that will follow; the report may conclude with a final thought, appreciation, or an offer to provide more information.

- Like all professional documents, a well-written report cements the writer's credibility with the audience; writers need to apply all the writing techniques addressed in Chapters 4, 5, and 6.

5 Compose short analytical reports that solve business problems.

- Typical analytical reports include justification/recommendation reports, feasibility reports, and yardstick reports.

- Justification/recommendation reports organized directly identify a problem, immediately announce a recommendation or solution, discuss its merits, and explain the action to be taken.

- Justification/recommendation reports organized indirectly describe a problem, discuss alternative solutions, prove the superiority of one solution, and ask for authorization to proceed with that solution.

- Feasibility reports, generally organized directly, study the advisability of following a course of action; they describe the background of, advantages and disadvantages of, costs of, and time frame for implementing the proposal.

- Yardstick reports compare two or more solutions to a problem by measuring each against a set of established criteria, thus ensuring consistency. Yardstick reports usually describe a problem, explain possible solutions, establish criteria for comparing alternatives, evaluate each alternative in terms of the criteria, draw conclusions, and make recommendations.

Key Terms

cross-tabulation *413*	mode *414*	Amazon effect *417*
average *414*	correlations *414*	analytical reports *420*
mean *414*	grid *414*	executive summary *426*
median *414*	decision matrix *415*	internal proposals *432*

Critical Thinking

1. Grids and decision matrices can be very helpful to consumers, as well as businesses, in making decisions. How might you have used a decision matrix in choosing which college to attend or which cell phone or other electronic device to purchase? What factors would you have included in your matrix? (L.O. 1)

2. Digital technologies are allowing, even forcing, businesses to examine how they can improve their internal and external reporting. In what ways are artificial intelligence (AI) and other technologies driving the future of reporting, and what are some of the specific benefits? (L.O. 1-5)

3. In writing report recommendations, what considerations and strategies can help you increase the chances of their being implemented? (L.O. 2)

4. What are the differences between periodic (activity) reports and progress (interim) reports? What type of information can you typically expect in each? (L.O. 4)

5. **Ethical Issue:** When it comes to financial reporting, transparency and ethical compliance have been at the forefront of shareholder discussions in many businesses, especially because non-compliance cases at leading firms have made headlines time and again. With the aid of digital technology, employees may now contribute to these discussions as well while protecting their anonymity. Alethia (which means "truth and disclosure" in Greek) is a digital communication app launched by United Arab Emirates-based firm AQ&P that provides an online dashboard for an employee to report potentially fraudulent activity to internal compliance functions without the fear of being labeled a whistleblower.[14] Although this technology provides the benefit of increasing organizational transparency and accountability, what concerns might potential whistleblowers still have? What reservations might companies have about investing in the technology? (L.O. 2)

Activities

12.1 Analyzing Survey Results (L.O. 1)

Team

Your business communication class at Middleton College was asked by the college bookstore manager, Dean Adams, to conduct a survey. Mindful of campus sustainability initiatives, Adams wants to learn students' reactions to eliminating plastic bags, of which the bookstore gives away 45,000 annually. Students answered questions about a number of proposals, resulting in the following raw data:

For major purchases (textbooks, apparel, and other larger items) the bookstore should:

	Agree	Undecided	Disagree
1. Continue to provide plastic bags	132	17	411
2. Provide no bags; encourage students to bring their own bags	414	25	121
3. Provide no bags; offer cloth bags at a reduced price (about $3)	357	19	184
4. Give a cloth bag with each major purchase, the cost to be included in registration fees	63	15	482

YOUR TASK In groups of four or five, do the following:

a. Convert the data into a table (see Figure 12.1) with a descriptive title. Arrange the items in a logical sequence.

b. How could these survey data be cross-tabulated? Would cross-tabulation serve any purpose?

c. Given the conditions of this survey, name at least three conclusions that researchers could draw from the data.

d. Prepare three to five recommendations to be submitted to Mr. Adams. How could the bookstore implement them?

e. Role-play a meeting in which the recommendations and implementation plan are presented to Mr. Adams. One student plays the role of Mr. Adams; the remaining students play the role of the presenters.

12.2 Making Sense of the Three Ms (L.O. 1)

Your boss at Star Key Real Estate Associates, Jacqueline Rialjo, has asked for your help in analyzing the market in a nearby neighborhood. Nine homes recently sold in the following order and for these amounts: $360,000; $460,000; $360,000; $380,000; $360,000; $420,000; $380,000; $520,000; and $360,000.

YOUR TASK Compute the mean, median, and mode for the recently sold homes. Explain your analysis as well as the characteristics of each type of "average."

12.3 Telling Conclusions From Recommendations (L.O. 2)

Experts believe that many essential study techniques popular with students—such as highlighting key words or phrases in a text with a marker—are not as effective as many learners assume. For example, if a text contains too many important points or the ideas in it are too complex to be expressed in a brief phrase, highlighting is not an effective study technique.[15] One author, Benedict Carey, argues that people fail tests because study aids like highlighting create a misperception that the material learned *now* is committed to memory and will be recalled in the exam. Carey calls this misperception the *fluency illusion*. We become poor judges of what we need to study and practice again. Ironically, it's testing itself that makes us better at retaining knowledge.[16]

YOUR TASK Based on the preceding facts, indicate whether the following statements are conclusions or recommendations:

a. A test is not only a measurement tool; it alters what we remember and *changes* how we subsequently organize that knowledge in our minds.

b. Although it is a common learning technique, imitating the style of famous writers is not always an effective study tool.

c. Instructors need to teach study skills to help students maximize their use of time and outcomes.

d. Highlighting text has little to offer in the way of subsequent performance.

e. Students should identify the main ideas in the text *before* highlighting to benefit from this technique.

f. Reading, notetaking, and highlighting are not as effective as reading, memorizing, and reciting—time-honored techniques largely absent in classrooms today.

g. Students should consider techniques they have never tried before; for example, interleaved practice, which mixes different types of material or problems in a single study session.

12.4 Can't Pick a Laptop? Fire Up a Decision Matrix (L.O. 1, 2)

You want to buy an affordable laptop for your college work and consider price the most important feature. With so many options on the market, you know that you'll have to do your research.

YOUR TASK Study Figure 12.3 and change the weights in Table 2 to reflect your emphasis on affordability, to which you will assign a factor of 10 because it is twice as important to you as unit weight, which receives a factor of 5. The hard drive size is likewise secondary to you, so you give it a 5 also. Last, you change battery life to a factor of 7 from 10 because it is less important than price, but more important than unit weight and hard drive size. Calculate the scores to determine which laptop is best for you.

12.5 Which Car to Buy? Taking a Decision Matrix for a Spin (L.O. 1, 2)

Kyle, an outrigger canoe racer, needs to buy a new car. He wants a vehicle that will carry his disassembled boat and outrigger. At the same time, he will need to travel long distances on business. His passion is soft-top sports cars, but he is also concerned about gas mileage. These four criteria are impossible to find in one vehicle. Kyle has the following choices:

- Station wagon
- SUV with or without a sunroof
- Four-door sedan, a high-miles-per-gallon family car
- Sports car, convertible

He wants to consider the following criteria:

- Price
- Ability to carry cargo such as a canoe
- Fuel efficiency
- Comfort over long distances
- Good looks and fun
- Quality build/manufacturer's reputation

YOUR TASK Follow the steps outlined in Figure 12.3 to determine an assessment scale and to assign a score to each feature. Then, consider which weights are probably most important to Kyle, given his needs. Calculate the totals to find the vehicle that's most suitable for Kyle.

12.6 Organizing Report Data (L.O. 3)

Team

YOUR TASK In groups of three to five, discuss how the findings in the following reports could be best organized (i.e., by time, component, importance, criteria, or convention).

a. A set of guidelines for businesses described in a recommendation report detailing four stages of emergency response to a global pandemic

b. A city's building division website reporting permits issued during a specific date range

c. A report comparing the benefits of buying or leasing a fleet of electric vehicles. The report presents data on depreciation, upfront cost, maintenance, battery life, range on one charge, and other factors.

d. A progress report written by a team of engineers to keep their supervisor informed at each of the five project stages

e. An employee performance appraisal submitted annually

f. A recommendation report to be submitted to management presenting four building plans to improve access to your building, in compliance with federal regulations. The plans range considerably in feasibility and cost.

g. An investigative report describing a company's expansion plans in India and China

h. A report comparing the sales volumes of the agents of a large national realtor based on the number of listings taken, number of listings sold, total sales in the agents' market areas, and more.

12.7 Engaging Readers With Report Headings (L.O. 3)

YOUR TASK Identify the following report headings and titles as *functional*, *talking*, or *combination*. Discuss the usefulness and effectiveness of each.

a. Guarding Against Online Identity Theft

b. Project Costs

c. Disadvantages

d. Using the Intranet to Convey Employee Benefits

e. Case Study: America's Most Sustainable College Campuses

f. Recommendations: Identifying Non-Compliance Risks

g. Comparing Costs of AI Recruiting Platforms

h. Budget

12.8 Writing an Executive Summary for Your Supervisor (L.O. 4)

Web

Like many executives, your boss is too rushed to read long journal articles. She asks you to submit one summary to her every month on an article of interest to help her stay abreast of relevant research in various business disciplines.

YOUR TASK In your field of study, select a professional journal, such as the *Journal of Marketing*, *Journal of Management*, *Journal of Accountancy*, or *Harvard Business Review*. Using a research database or a Web search, look for articles in your target journal. Select an interesting article that is approximately 2,000 words long, and write an executive summary in memo format. Include an introduction that might begin with *As you requested, I am submitting this executive summary of ....* Identify the author, article title, journal, and date of publication. Start with the main idea of the study or article. Summarize three or four of the most important findings of the study or article in approximately 200 words, or 10 percent of the original article. Use descriptive rather than functional headings. Your boss would also like a concluding statement indicating your response to the article in a separate paragraph below your summary. Address your memo to Joyce Fields.

12.9 Periodic Report: Keeping the Boss in the Loop (L.O. 4)

E-Mail

Because your boss often travels for work, he has asked to be informed of your activities and accomplishments and any problems you are encountering.

YOUR TASK For a job or internship that you currently hold or held in the past, describe your regular activities, discuss irregular events that management should be aware of, and highlight any particular needs or problems you are having. If you aren't currently working, communicate to your instructor your weekly or monthly activities related to your classes and campus activities. Establish components or criteria such as those in the bulleted e-mail in Model Document 12.4. Write an e-mail report just like it or use the memo format. Address the memo or the e-mail report to your boss or, alternatively, to your instructor.

12.10 Progress Report: How Is That Project Coming? (L.O. 4)

E-Mail **Team**

Consider a research project, service-learning assignment, or an experiential learning opportunity you are currently completing. Perhaps you are doing research for the long report assignment in Chapter 13 or another course. In any case, you will want to keep your instructor informed of your progress.

YOUR TASK Write a progress report informing your instructor of your work. Briefly describe the project (its purpose, scope, limitations, and methodology), assigned team member roles, work completed, work yet to be completed, problems encountered, future activities, and expected completion date. Address the e-mail report to your instructor. Emulate the e-mail progress report shown in Model Document 12.5.

12.11 Progress Report: Closing in on Your Goal? (L.O. 4)

You have promised your parents (or spouse, partner, relative, or friend) that you would submit a progress report at this time.

YOUR TASK Prepare a progress report in letter format in which you do the following: (a) describe your headway toward your educational goal (such as employment, degree, or certificate); (b) summarize the work you have completed thus far; (c) discuss the work currently in progress, including your successes and anticipated obstacles; and (d) outline what you have left to complete.

12.12 Investigative Report: Scoping Out the Competition (L.O. 4)

Web

As a junior sales associate working for Irv Seaver BMW Motorcycles in Orange, California, you wonder what your sales will look like as the COVID-19 pandemic thrusts the country into a severe downturn. Until the global pandemic hit, BMW motorcycles had enjoyed nine years of continuous healthy growth in all regions of the world except North America. Closing in on its annual sales target of 200,000 units, BMW Motorrad has cemented its third place among the biggest premium motorcycle makers behind Honda and Harley-Davidson.[17]

In the meantime, the pandemic has hit Harley-Davidson at a vulnerable time. The biggest manufacturer of large premium bikes has suffered plummeting sales numbers for five years in a row, with international shipments down to the lowest level in a decade.[18] Within three years the company's stock price has dropped 42 percent. Some believe the worrisome trend is a sign of a structural decline in the U.S. motorcycle market and changing demographics. Young consumers appear unimpressed by the brand, not even after the launch of its first-ever electric motorcycle—a model far removed from its core business.[19]

After all, the iconic manufacturer's core target audience has traditionally been white, male, and middle-aged. This is why Harley-Davidson is now trying to appeal to women riders and a younger generation of would-be bikers. You bring up this topic with your boss, Dale Diaz, and he asks you to find out what exactly Harley-Davidson is doing.

YOUR TASK Visit the Harley-Davidson USA website and study how the legendary motorcycle manufacturer is targeting females and younger riders. Write an informational report in memo form addressed to Dale Diaz. Which of its motorcycles does your competitor promote as ideal for women, and why? How about apparel? What other ways has Harley-Davidson found to attract new riders? Is the company succeeding?

12.13 Investigative Report: Going Global (L.O. 4)

Intercultural **Team** **Web**

Because your company is fast expanding in various regions of the world, the VP of human resources has asked you, the department interns, to research material for a cross-cultural communication training program she is developing. Specifically, she would like to incorporate information about written and verbal communication styles, meeting etiquette, social customs, and time orientation in Asia, the Middle East, and Europe and how they compare to U.S. practices.

Assume that your boss will assign different countries to several interns and recent hires. Choose a country that interests you and conduct a Web search. For example, in a Google search, input terms such as *business etiquette*, *business etiquette abroad*, and *intercultural communication*. You could visit websites such as the popular, informative etiquette and business guides for specific countries by Kwintessential Ltd. Also consider Country-Watch and the Central Intelligence Agency's (CIA) *The World Factbook*.

YOUR TASK As an intern or a new-hire, write a memo report about one country that is considerably different from the United States and that offers new business opportunities. Address your report to Tamara Mayo, VP of human resources. Confine your research to what U.S. managers need to know about business etiquette in that culture. You should investigate social customs such as greetings, attire, gift giving, formality, business meals, attitudes toward time, and communication styles to help your boss avoid etiquette blunders. The purpose of your report is to promote business, not tourism. Compare your results with those of other students and, if directed, compile them in an informational team report.

12.14 Informational or Analytical Report: Examining Tweets and Other Social Media Posts (L.O. 4, 5)

E-Mail | **Social Media** | **Web**

Select a Fortune 500 company that appeals to you, and search recent tweets and Facebook posts about it. Soon you will recognize trends and topic clusters that may help you organize the report content by criteria. For example, if you use the hashtag to conduct a subject search on Coca-Cola (i.e., #Coca-Cola), you will obtain a huge number of tweets about the company and brand. They will range from fan posts, buying tips, exhortations to recycle plastic, and specious cleaning tips involving Coke all the way to urban legends (e.g., the acid in Coke will completely dissolve a T-bone steak in two days). Many returned tweets will be only marginally interesting because they show up just because #Coca-Cola is mentioned.

If you explore Facebook, you will mostly find official pages and fan sites, most of which display favorable posts. You would have to look hard to find negative posts, partly because companies moderate discussions and often remove offensive posts according to their user agreements.

YOUR TASK Write either an informational or analytical report about the company you chose. In an informational report to your instructor, you could summarize your findings in memo form or as an e-mail. Describe how the tweets about the company are trending. Are they overwhelmingly positive or negative? Organize the report around the subject areas you identify (criteria). Alternatively, you could write an analytical report detailing the strategies your chosen company adopts in responding to tweets and Facebook posts. Your analytical report would evaluate the organization's social media responses and provide specific examples to support your claims.

12.15 Informational Report: Researching Potential Employers (L.O. 4)

Web

You are preparing a targeted résumé and cover message for a Fortune 500 company. You've spoken with a friend who works there, but you now want to do your own research.

YOUR TASK If available, use your campus library's research database to access Hoover's and other resources

for company records and other facts. Then take a look at the company's website; check its background, news releases, and annual report. Learn about its major product, service, or emphasis. Find its Fortune 500 ranking, its current stock price (if listed), and its high and low range for the year. Look up its profit-to-earnings ratio. Track its latest marketing plan, promotion, or product. Identify its home office, major officers, and number of employees. In a memo report to your instructor, summarize your research findings. Explain why this company would be a good or bad employment choice for you.

12.16 Justification/Recommendation Report: Cash Available for Philanthropy (L.O. 5)

Web

Great news! MegaTech, the startup company where you work, has become enormously successful. Now the owner wants to support some kind of philanthropic program. He does not have time to check out the possibilities, so he asks you, his assistant, to conduct research and report to him and the board of directors.

YOUR TASK The owner wants you to investigate the philanthropic projects at 20 high-profile companies of your choice. Visit their websites and study programs such as volunteerism, cause-related marketing, matching funds, and charitable donations. In a recommendation report, discuss five of the best programs and recommend one that could serve as a philanthropic project model for your company.

12.17 Feasibility Report: International Student Club on Campus (L.O. 5)

Intercultural

To fulfill a senior project in your department, you have been asked to submit a letter report to the dean evaluating the feasibility of starting an organization of international students on campus.

YOUR TASK Find out how many international students are on your campus, what nations they represent, how one goes about starting an organization, and whether a faculty sponsor is needed. Assume that you conducted an informal survey of international students. Of the 39 who filled out the survey, 31 said they would be interested in joining.

12.18 Feasibility Report: Encouraging Healthy Habits (L.O. 5)

Your company is considering ways to promote employee fitness and morale.

YOUR TASK Select a fitness/teambuilding program that seems reasonable for your company. Consider a softball league, bowling teams, a basketball league, lunchtime walks, lunchtime fitness speakers and demos, company-sponsored health club memberships, a workout room, a fitness center, or a fitness director. Assume that your boss has tentatively agreed to the program you select and has asked you to write a memo report investigating its feasibility.

12.19 Yardstick Report: Office Equipment Options (L.O. 5)

You recently complained to your boss that you were unhappy with a piece of equipment you use (printer, computer, copier, scanner, or the like). After some thought, the boss decided that your complaint is valid and told you to go shopping.

YOUR TASK Compare at least three manufacturers' models and recommend one. Because the company will be purchasing ten or more units, and because several managers must approve the purchase, write a careful report documenting your findings. Establish at least five criteria for comparing the models. Submit a memo report to your boss. If your instructor directs, prepare a decision matrix with reasonable weights assigned to significant attributes.

12.20 Yardstick Report: Improving Workplace Procedures (L.O. 5)

YOUR TASK Identify a problem or procedure that must be changed at your work or in an organization you know. Consider challenges such as poor scheduling of employees, outdated equipment, slow order processing, failure to encourage employees to participate fully, restrictive rules, inadequate training, or disappointed customers. Consider several solutions or courses of action (retaining the present status could be one alternative). Develop criteria that you could use to evaluate each alternative. Write a report measuring each alternative by the yardstick you have created. Recommend a course of action to your boss or to the organization head.

Self-Contained Report Activities

No Additional Research Required

12.23 Justification/Recommendation Report: Speedier Service at Giovanni's Family Pizza (L.O. 5)

You are a trusted employee working for Giovanni LaRosa, owner of Giovanni's Family Pizza, a small, casual pizza shop he founded 27 years ago. Its signature items are eight-inch-diameter individual pizzas. The pizza shop also serves calzones, hoagies, pasta, desserts, and assorted beverages. Here, you always have a choice.

The pizza shop is located in the warehouse district of Indianapolis, where it originally served truckers who delivered their meat, fruits, and vegetables in the middle of the night and then whisked off to the next city. Truckers loved the satisfying and filling pizza because it provided them with lots of energy on those tedious late-night runs. Later the pizza shop caught on with the nightclub crowd and with students who studied late. The shop opens at 6 p.m. and closes at 6 a.m.

The concept was a resounding success. However, success brings competition. Three imitators opened their pizza shops within a five-mile radius of Giovanni's Family Pizza. You know that the family has been using the same delivery system for years, and you know service could be faster. You also notice that new pizza shops are receiving orders via smartphones.

The current system at Giovanni's begins with a counter clerk recording the customer's order and table number on a ticket. The customer pays, and the counter person gives the order to the pizza makers. The pizza makers remove the dough from the refrigerator, shape it, add the sauce and other ingredients, put the pie in the oven, and remove it from the oven when baked. The counter clerk then takes the order to the customer's table. Giovanni's Family Pizza has three counter clerks, two pizza makers, and one cash register that the counter clerks share. It takes two minutes to prep a pizza before it can go in the oven. The pizza shop uses an outdated Rankin Model D85 pizza deck oven, which cooks a pizza in seven minutes.

You think the entire system is inefficient, and when you discuss the problem with Mr. LaRosa, he says, "Although the original ways are familiar to me, I see that the time for improvement has come."

You suggest observing the three competitors' systems of serving customers to understand why their service is faster. Currently, the average time it takes a customer to receive an order at Giovanni's 16 minutes. The following are notes from your observations of the competitors.

DeNunzio Pizza
- Similar menu
- Orders are taken using an electronic system that includes the customer's number

- Customers pay immediately
- Customers pick up their orders after their numbers have been called
- Two counter clerks at one register; two pizza makers
- Preprepared dough; prep time: one minute
- One state-of-the art Elite Chef Model BFE-28 convection oven—five minutes to cook a pizza
- Average time a customer waits to receive an order: ten minutes

Capriotti's

- Similar menu
- Order takers call out the menu item as the order is taken
- Customers pay immediately
- Customers wait at the counter to pick up their orders
- Three counter employees at three registers; two pizza makers
- Preprepared dough; prep time: one minute
- One state-of-the art Elite Chef Model BFE-28 convection oven—five minutes to cook a pizza
- Average time a customer waits to receive an order: eight minutes

Rusty's Pizza Shop

- Similar menu
- Tickets are used to record the customers' orders
- Customers pay immediately
- Counter staff employees take the order to customers' tables
- Three counter staff employees, two pizza makers, and one cash register
- Pizza prep the same as Giovanni's: two minutes
- One DeLong Model FC30 pizza deck oven—six minutes to cook a pizza
- Average time a customer waits to receive an order: 15 minutes

YOUR TASK Now it is up to you to analyze the data you have collected. In a short memo report to Giovanni LaRosa, present your findings, discuss your conclusions, and make recommendations, including a recommendation on how Giovanni's might gain a competitive edge by enabling its customers to use some of the most recent technology to order their food. You may want to present the data using visual aids, but you also realize that you must emphasize the important findings by presenting them in an easy-to-read list.

12.24 Feasibility Report: Advisability of Hiring a Social Media Consultant
(L.O. 5)

You are the vice president of marketing for Scents Are Us, a manufacturer and distributor of scented flameless candles and candle warmers. The president, Kim Johnson, feels that the company could do a better job of listening to and connecting with its customers. Kim knows that the company's two main competitors are gaining ground in brand awareness and sales. She also knows that, although Scents Are Us created a Facebook page, she wants the company to develop a broader social media strategy. Kim thinks it might be wise to hire a social media consultant to help Scents Are Us in this effort, and she wants your advice.

To provide Kim with an informed recommendation, you decide to conduct research to answer the following questions:

1. Is the company collecting social media data (tracking number of mentions, number of followers, and so on), and is the company using the data?

2. Does the Marketing Department have employees with the talent to implement this strategy without a consultant's help?

3. If it has the talent, does the department have the time to implement this strategy?

4. How long will it take to implement this strategy?

5. What social media tools should the company use? What services do consultants provide?

6. What is the cost of hiring a social media expert?

7. What are the disadvantages of hiring a consultant?

8. What could go wrong if the company hires a consultant?

As vice president of marketing, you already know answers to many of these questions, but Kim, understandably, does not.

Following are the results of your research. The company collects data from Facebook, but it doesn't analyze that data for decision making. Two of the Marketing Department's 12 employees have some social media knowledge and skills, but no employee has enough knowledge and skill to implement a social media strategy. What's more, not one of your employees is able to devote 40 hours a week to such an effort.

The estimated implementation time for a social media strategy is two months. Many social media consultants recommend implementing a wide range of tools, including Facebook, Instagram, Twitter, Pinterest, and blogging. The average fees for these social media consulting services appear in the following table.

Average Fees for Social Media Consulting Services

Tool	Setup Charge	Monthly Charges
Facebook	$950 for initial page setup	$1,450 for monthly content management
Twitter and Pinterest	$800 for account setup	$950 for monthly account management
Instagram	$500 for account setup	$1,050 for monthly account management
Blogging	$1,950 for design and template creation	$1,850 per month for writing and editing content for the blog (one post per week)

A consultant also has the time to uncover what social media tools and strategies other companies are using.

You have identified two main disadvantages of hiring a social media consultant. First, the consultant will not be an expert in your company or its products. You'll have to combine the consultant's knowledge of social media tools with your knowledge of the scented candle business. Second, it's impossible to accurately predict the return on investment of these services. The best you can do is monitor costs and make sure you receive the services the company has paid for.

Reading about various social media fiascos, such as Wendy's sassy back-and-forth Twitter exchange about its claim that it used "fresh, never frozen" beef, taught you that it's unwise to respond negatively on social media. Yet, it's also dangerous to remain silent when damaging messages appear or to remove negative comments on your Facebook page. Wise organizations train their social media monitors to plan for problems and strive to avoid alienating customers. Removing negative comments on your site can create a major blunder in a social media campaign. To avoid these problems, the company can make one employee responsible for participating in Twitter conversations, hold worst-case scenario meetings, prohibit the removal of negative comments without permission, and implement other best practices.

YOUR TASK Write a one- to three-page memo report to the president. Make clear your decision regarding whether to hire a consultant, and determine where in the report to announce it. Include all the results of your research in the report, condensing it to stay within the page-length limit. Format the report for easy reading.

12.25 Yardstick Report: Selecting the Best Social Media Manager Candidate
(L.O. 5)

You have worked long and hard to become the chief marketing officer (CMO) of a global retailer, Fast Fashion, with revenues of more than $5 billion. Fast Fashion offers casual and career apparel and accessories at value prices for women ages twenty-five to thirty-five. It operates approximately 3,800 stores in the United States, Europe, Puerto Rico, and Canada.

Because you recognize the growth and future impact of social media, you work with the chief executive officer (CEO) and human resources (HR) director to fund and develop a new position for the company, social media manager. Your goal is to find the perfect candidate to promote the company brand and—as all businesses hope—build customer engagement through social media. With HR, you develop the job description and advertise the job, screen applications, and select three candidates to interview. Although their strengths and weaknesses differ, all three meet the job requirements, have excellent references, and are impressive interviewees. With résumés,

Job Description

At Fast Fashion, talented people are our greatest asset. We offer a competitive compensation package and excellent benefits.

Job Title and Overview:

Manager, Social Media—Fast Fashion. The Social Media Manager is responsible for the content and communication strategy across all social platforms—driving brand awareness, increasing product purchases, and promoting the company's image.

Required Qualifications and Functions (Weighted):

- Bachelor's degree in marketing, communication, computer systems, or a related field

- Three years or more of social media marketing work in a multiunit retail company, preferably in apparel (20%)

- Experienced in building an audience on relevant social media channels through daily publishing and recommending of social content and trends based on social listening (40%)

- Demonstrated superb written, verbal, and visual communication; positive, energetic personality; and ability to direct cross-functional teams and juggle multiple projects (20%)

- Strong analytical, organizational, and creative problem-solving skills; able to work with the internal teams on postevent and return-on-investment (ROI) analyses (20%)

interview notes, and the job description in hand, you sit down at your desk to develop a decision matrix and list the pros and cons of each candidate to write a report for the CEO, concluding with your recommendation.

Candidate 1: Shawna Jackson

Shawna has a BS degree in mass communication from a state university. She earned a 3.0/4.0 cumulative GPA, worked part-time as night manager in women's apparel at Walmart while in college, and participated in extra-curricular volunteer activities in the community provided by student organizations in her major. Since graduating three years ago, Shawna has worked as assistant to the social media director of a national home furnishings retail chain. In the interview Shawna appeared a bit nervous and shy but warmed up when she showed her portfolio. Her portfolio includes samples of work in a wide range of social media channels, including Facebook, Pinterest, Snapchat, and Instagram. It illustrates her strong written, visual, and technological skills.

Candidate 2: John Andrews

John graduated at the top of his class with a BS degree in computer information systems from a private college. While in college, he worked 30 hours a week in the campus Computer Services Department. Upon graduation, he worked for a major electronics retailer for three years, starting as the technology department manager and moving up to store manager. He left this management position to start his own company, in which he oversaw the marketing of products and services through websites, social media, and text messages. For two years John built his entrepreneurial business and recently sold it. Ready to use his business knowledge in a large corporation, he wants to focus on social media in a corporation that offers opportunities for promotion and growth, and fulfill his desire to run a business. During the interview, John shared his salary history, revealing that he made much more than this position offers. He seems to be a confident and extroverted interviewee.

Candidate 3: Lauren Chin

Lauren earned a BS degree in fashion merchandising from a state university, graduating with a 3.5/4.0 cumulative GPA. She worked in Nordstrom's Executive Trainee Program for two years in apparel merchandising at corporate headquarters. While there, she recognized that she loved her social time online as much as she disliked her time developing and analyzing quantitative merchandising reports. Ready for a change, she returned to college to complete a master's degree in digital media. Lauren worked part-time in apparel retailing chains while in college. For three years she has operated a blog with a growing number of followers. Lauren is active on Facebook, Pinterest, and Instagram. In the interview she appeared relaxed and well versed in using new and growing social media channels.

YOUR TASK Write a memo report of three to five pages. Complete the decision matrix with the weights provided, and include it in your report. No weight is necessary for education, as all candidates fulfill this requirement. For each criterion in the decision matrix, provide one of three rankings for each candidate with a score of 3 as the highest, 2 as the second highest, and 1 for the candidate who ranks the lowest. For example, if you believe Shawna has the highest level of social media marketing experience and Lauren has the lowest level, you would post 3 for Shawna, 2 for John, and 1 for Lauren. Multiply each weight by the ranking, repeat for the other criteria, and then add the results to compute a total. From your decision matrix, draw conclusions and then make recommendations in your yardstick report. Overall, which candidate is best for the position, and why?

Decision Matrix

Candidates	Demonstrated ability to lead teams and to juggle multiple projects (20%)	Quality and quantity of knowledge and work experience in social media (40%)	Strong analytical, organizational, and creative problem-solving skills (20%)	Social media marketing experience with a multiunit retail company (20%)	Total
Shawna Jackson					
John Andrews					
Lauren Chin					

New communication platforms and casual workplace environments have blurred the lines of appropriateness, leaving workers wondering how to navigate uncharted waters. Check your workplace etiquette IQ by deciding whether the following statements are true or false. Then see if you agree with the responses on p. Key-6.

1. Noah is out of the office, but you just had a brilliant idea to share with him. You should call and leave a voice-mail message so that he can hear it when he returns.

_____ True _____ False

2. You're sick and must miss work tomorrow. Because you don't feel well, it's acceptable to text your boss to say you won't be in.

_____ True _____ False

3. As a manager, you are upset because your employee Mike is habitually late for meetings. You would like to reprimand him in front of everyone to serve as a lesson, but the better plan is to speak to him privately.

_____ True _____ False

Chat About It

In each chapter you will find five discussion questions related to the chapter material. Your instructor may assign these topics for you to discuss in class, in an online chat room, or on an online discussion board. Some of the discussion topics may require outside research. You may also be asked to read and respond to postings made by your classmates.

TOPIC 1: Provide a simple example that illustrates the differences among findings, conclusions, and recommendations when analyzing data.

TOPIC 2: Some research studies have revealed that young people experience anxiety and feelings of isolation as a result of their social media use. Other studies report that young people believe social media use has helped them make personal connections and develop professionally. In your experience, does social media seem to enhance or hinder your personal relationships? How about your professional growth? Explain each.

TOPIC 3: In an analysis of employee salaries within a company or industry, which value might be the most valuable in determining the salary commonly paid: mean, median, or mode? Why?

TOPIC 4: You are preparing to write a report detailing your company's plan to expand globally. What might be the best strategy to organize the information? What classifications may help you arrange the information logically?

TOPIC 5: Psychologists are telling us that procrastination is addictive because it provides an adrenaline rush. Mark Twain offered this humorous remedy: "Eat a live frog first thing in the morning and nothing worse will happen to you the rest of the day."[20] Are you an adrenaline junkie or do you approach work tasks early and systematically? How do you keep motivated? How could one break the habit of task avoidance short of eating a live frog?

Total Review

The first nine chapters reviewed specific guides from Appendix D, Grammar and Mechanics. The exercises in this and the remaining chapters are total reviews, covering all of the grammar and mechanics guides plus confusing words and frequently misspelled words.

Each of the following sentences has **three** errors in grammar, punctuation, capitalization, usage, or spelling. On a separate sheet, write a correct version. Avoid adding new phrases, starting new sentences, or rewriting in your own words. When finished, compare your responses with the key at the end of the book.

EXAMPLE: The auditors report, which the manager and myself read closely, contained the following three main flaws, factual inaccuracies, omissions, and incomprehensible language.

REVISION: The **auditor's** report, which the manager and **I** read closely, contained the following three main **flaws:** factual inaccuracies, omissions, and incomprehensible language.

1. Among the oddly named towns in the United States are: What Cheer, Iowa, Peculiar, Missouri, and Cheesequake, New Jersey.

2. After our supervisor and her returned from their meeting at 2:00 p.m., we were able to sort the customers names more quickly.

3. 6 of the 18 workers in my department were fired, as a result we had to work harder to achieve our goals.

4. Jeffreys presentation to a nonprofit group netted him only three hundred dollars, which is a tenth of his usual honorarium but he believes in pro bono work.

5. Of all the discoveries and inventions in human history the 4 greatest are said to be these speech, fire, agriculture, and the wheel.

6. Our latest press release written by our corporate communication department announces the opening of three Asian offices.

7. In his justification report dated September first, Justin argued that expansion to twelve branch offices could boost annual revenue to 22 million dollars.

8. The practicality and advisability of opening 12 branch offices are what will be discussed in the consultants feasability report.

9. 3 categories of Apps (social media, productivity, and entertainment—are most popular for installing on smartphones.

10. Because some organizations prefer single spaced reports be sure to check with your organization to learn it's preference.

CHAPTER 13

Proposals, Business Plans, and Formal Business Reports

LEARNING OUTCOMES

After studying this chapter, you should be able to do the following:

1 Explain the importance and purpose of informal proposals and their basic components.

2 Discuss the components of formal and grant proposals.

3 Identify the components of typical business plans.

4 Describe how the components of the front matter in formal business reports support the purpose of the report.

5 Explain how the body and back matter of formal business reports serve the purpose of the report.

6 Specify final writing tips that aid authors of formal business reports.

S_L/Shutterstock.com

Bold Proposals Helped Propel SpaceX Ahead of the Competition

Fresh off a triumphant launch of its Crew Dragon capsule carrying two astronauts to the International Space Station (ISS), SpaceX has beaten the venerable giant Boeing for primacy in NASA's Commercial Crew Program. The relative upstart, once dismissed as a long shot, succeeded spectacularly with 40 percent of the $6.8 billion contract NASA had awarded, whereas rival Boeing pocketed 60 percent, yet has suffered a series of setbacks.[1] Founded in 2002 by its mercurial CEO, Elon Musk, Space Exploration Technologies Corporation (SpaceX for short) has quickly become a nimble, scrappy player in the challenging and capital-intensive aerospace industry. The 8,000 employees-strong Hawthorne, California–based company has ended the sole reliance of the United States on Russian launches to the ISS.

Elon Musk, who also cofounded PayPal and Solar City and simultaneously runs Tesla Motors, is a relentless, hard-driving boss. An extraordinary mind, Musk is infamous for putting in 100+ work hours a week and sleeping on the factory floor when one of his companies must solve problems or meet deadlines. He exhibits a fierce, crushing temper and expects unflagging commitment from his many brilliant engineers. At times Musk has exhibited poor judgment, for example when he fired off an ill-conceived tweet that, as the SEC ruled, amounted to stock manipulation or when he lit up a joint in a podcast streamed on the Internet, thus prompting a full safety review of SpaceX by NASA. Considered by many a real-life Iron Man, Musk is an inventor and business magnate known for his bold vision of the future, most prominently of space travel to Mars by 2024. As with production delays of Tesla cars, though, Musk has at times failed to deliver on his audacious projections.

Eager to compete for lucrative defense contracts, Musk sued the Air Force and has since won a handful of Pentagon launches—in addition to sending more than a hundred commercial satellites and other payloads into orbit in the last decade.[2] How was SpaceX able to win valuable government contracts? Certainly, the company's breakthrough technical expertise and cost efficiency enabled by reusability were decisive factors. Boeing's Starliner will cost an average $90 million per astronaut, compared with $55 million per seat on SpaceX's Dragon. SpaceX's strict adherence to the space agency's rigorous RFP standards and killer proposals have clinched the lucrative deals. Such success is the culmination of lengthy, intense effort, which makes projecting the budget accurately for the long term extremely difficult. Musk has acknowledged that SpaceX has exceeded NASA's "firm-fixed price" contract by spending hundreds of millions of dollars of its own money for building and testing the Crew Dragon spacecraft.[3] You will learn more about SpaceX and be asked to complete a relevant task at the end of this chapter.

Critical Thinking

- Why are proposals vitally important to a company such as SpaceX?

- How are proposals at SpaceX similar to and different from proposals or long reports written by students?

- How can team members maintain consistency and meet deadlines when writing important, time-constrained, multivolume documents such as formal proposals?

13-1 Writing Informal Proposals

LEARNING OUTCOME

1 Explain the importance and purpose of informal proposals and their basic components.

Proposals can mean life or death for an organization. Why are they so important? Let's begin by defining what they are. A **proposal** may be defined as a written offer to solve a problem, provide a service, or sell equipment. Profit-making organizations, such as SpaceX, depend on proposals to compete for business. A well-written proposal can generate billion-dollar contracts resulting in millions of dollars of income. Smaller organizations also depend on proposals to sell their products and services. Equally dependent on proposals are many nonprofit organizations. Their funding depends on grant proposals, to be discussed shortly.

Some proposals are internal, often taking the form of justification and recommendation reports. You learned about these persuasive reports in Chapter 12. Most proposals, however, are external, such as those written at SpaceX. These proposals respond to requests for proposals (RFPs). When government organizations or businesses know exactly what they want, they prepare a **request for proposals (RFP)**, specifying their requirements. Government agencies such as NASA as well as private businesses use RFPs to solicit competitive bids from vendors. RFPs ensure that bids are comparable and that funds are awarded fairly, using consistent criteria.

Proposals may be further divided into two categories: solicited and unsolicited. Most proposals are solicited. For example, the California city of Hermosa Beach announced that it was seeking bids for an audiovisual system to be installed at its city council chambers meeting room. This solicited RFP included details of how and where the application should be made.[4] Enterprising companies looking for work or a special challenge might submit an unsolicited proposal. The Center for the Advancement of Science in Space (CASIS), which runs the International Space Station U.S. National Laboratory, welcomes innovative unsolicited proposals to develop groundbreaking technologies and products.[5] Although many kinds of proposals exist, we'll focus on informal, formal, and grant proposals.

13-1a Components of Informal Proposals

Informal proposals may be presented in manuscript format (usually no more than ten pages) with a cover page, or they may take the form of short (two- to four-page) letters. Sometimes called letter proposals, they usually contain six principal components: introduction, background, proposal, staffing, budget, and authorization. As you can see in Figure 13.1, both informal and formal proposals contain these six basic parts.

Model Document 13.1 illustrates a letter proposal to a Nebraska dentist who sought to improve patient satisfaction. Notice that it contains all six components of an informal proposal.

Introduction. Most proposals begin by briefly explaining the reasons for the proposal and highlighting the writer's qualifications. To make your introduction more persuasive, you should strive to provide a hook, such as the following:

- Hint at extraordinary results with details to be revealed shortly.
- Promise low costs or speedy results.
- Mention a remarkable resource (well-known authority, new computer program, well-trained staff) available exclusively to you.
- Identify a serious problem (worry item) and promise a solution, to be explained later.
- Specify a key issue or benefit that you feel is the heart of the proposal.

FIGURE 13.1   Components of Informal and Formal Proposals

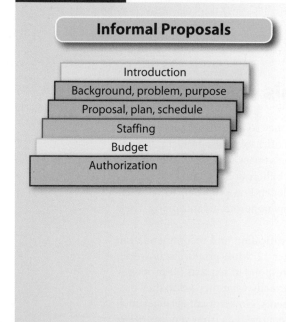

Informal Proposals

- Introduction
- Background, problem, purpose
- Proposal, plan, schedule
- Staffing
- Budget
- Authorization

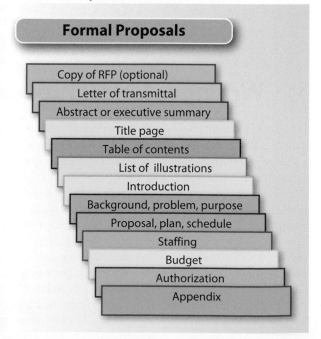

Formal Proposals

- Copy of RFP (optional)
- Letter of transmittal
- Abstract or executive summary
- Title page
- Table of contents
- List of illustrations
- Introduction
- Background, problem, purpose
- Proposal, plan, schedule
- Staffing
- Budget
- Authorization
- Appendix

1 Prewriting

Analyze: The purpose of this letter proposal is to persuade the reader to accept this proposal.

Anticipate: The reader expects this proposal but must be convinced that this survey project is worth its hefty price.

Adapt: Because the reader will be resistant at first, use a persuasive approach that emphasizes benefits.

2 Drafting

Research: Collect data about the reader's practice and other surveys of patient satisfaction.

Organize: Identify four specific purposes (benefits) of this proposal. Specify the survey plan. Promote the staff, itemize the budget, and ask for approval.

Draft: Prepare a first draft, expecting to improve it later.

3 Revising

Edit: Revise to emphasize benefits. Improve readability with functional headings and lists. Remove jargon and wordiness.

Proofread: Check spelling of client's name. Verify dates and calculation of budget figures. Recheck all punctuation.

Evaluate: Is this proposal convincing enough to sell the client?

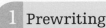

6300 O Street
Lincoln, NE 68510
(402) 747-6300
www.corepoll.com

May 28, 2021

Caroline Foley, DDS
7880 Cobblestone Street
Lincoln, NE 68506

Dear Dr. Foley:

(Uses opening paragraph in place of introduction) Understanding the views of your patients is the key to meeting their needs. *(Grabs attention with hook that focuses on key benefit)* CorePoll Research is pleased to propose a plan to help you become even more successful by learning what patients expect of your practice, so that you can improve your services.

Background and Goals

We know that you have been incorporating a total quality management system in your practice. Although you have every reason to believe that your patients are pleased with your services, you may want to give them an opportunity to discuss what they like and possibly don't like about your office. Specifically, your purposes are to survey your patients to (a) determine the level of their satisfaction with you and your staff, (b) elicit their suggestions for improvement, (c) learn more about how they discovered you, and (d) compare your preferred and standard patients. *(Identifies four purposes of survey)*

Proposed Plan *(Announces heart of proposal)*

On the basis of our experience in conducting many local and national customer satisfaction surveys, CorePoll proposes the following plan: *(Describes procedure for solving problem or achieving goals)*

Survey. We will develop a short but thorough questionnaire probing the data you desire. Although the survey instrument will include both open-ended and close-ended questions, it will concentrate on the latter. Close-ended questions enable respondents to answer easily; they also facilitate systematic data analysis. The questionnaire will gauge patients' views of courtesy, professionalism, billing accuracy, friendliness, and waiting time. After you approve it, the questionnaire will be sent to a carefully selected sample of 300 patients whom you have separated into groupings of preferred and standard. *(Divides total plan into logical segments for easy reading)*

Analysis. Survey data will be analyzed by demographic segments, such as patient type, age, and gender. Using state-of-the art statistical tools, our team of seasoned experts will study (a) satisfaction levels, (b) the reasons for satisfaction or dissatisfaction, and (c) the responses of your preferred compared to standard patients. Moreover, our team will give you specific suggestions for making patient visits more pleasant.

Report. You will receive a final report with the key findings clearly spelled out, Dr. Foley. Our expert staff will draw conclusions based on the results. The report will include tables summarizing all responses, divided into preferred and standard clients.

Includes second-page heading

Dr. Caroline Foley Page 2 May 28, 2021

Schedule. With your approval, the following schedule has been arranged for your patient satisfaction survey:

Questionnaire development and mailing	August 2–6
Deadline for returning questionnaire	August 16
Data tabulation and processing	August 16–18
Completion of final report	September 3

Uses past-tense verbs to show that work has already started on the project

Staffing

Promotes credentials and expertise of key people

CorePoll is a nationally recognized, experienced research consulting firm specializing in survey investigation. I have assigned your customer satisfaction survey to Joel Palmer, PhD, our director of research. Dr. Palmer was trained at Emory University and has successfully supervised our research program for the past nine years. Before joining CorePoll, he was a marketing analyst with T-Mobile.

Builds credibility by describing outstanding staff and facilities

Assisting Dr. Palmer will be a team headed by Elizabeth Avila, our vice president for operations. Ms. Avila earned a BS degree in computer science and an MA degree in marketing from the University of Florida. She supervises our computer-aided telephone interviewing (CAT) system and manages our 30-person professional staff.

Budget

Itemizes costs carefully because a proposal is a contract offer

	Estimated Hours	Rate	Total
Professional and administrative time			
Questionnaire development	3	$175/hr.	$ 525
Questionnaire mailing	4	50/hr.	200
Data processing and tabulation	12	50/hr.	600
Analysis of findings	15	175/hr.	2,625
Preparation of final report	5	175/hr.	875
Mailing costs			
300 copies of questionnaire			150
Postage and envelopes			300
Total costs			$5,275

Authorization

Closes by repeating key qualifications and main benefits

We are convinced, Dr. Foley, that our professionally designed and administered patient satisfaction survey will enhance your practice. CorePoll Research can have specific results for you by September 3 if you sign the enclosed duplicate copy of this letter and return it to us with a retainer of $2,500 so that we may begin developing your survey immediately. The rates in this offer are in effect only until October 1.

Makes response easy

Provides deadline

Sincerely,

Antoine Gibson

Antoine Gibson
Senior Researcher

AG:mem
Enclosure

Reality Check

Combating Writer's Block

"To conquer writer's block, begin with a bulleted list of what the customer is looking for. The list is like a road map; it gets you started and keeps you headed in the right direction."[7]

—Mary Piecewicz, *former Hewlett-Packard proposal manager*

Although writers may know what goes into the proposal introduction, many face writer's block before they get started. Proposal expert Tom Sant recommends a method he calls **cognitive webbing** to overcome the paralyzing effects of writer's block and arrive at a proposal writing plan. Dr. Sant tells proposal writers to (a) identify the outcome the client seeks, (b) brainstorm by writing down every idea and detail that will help the client achieve that objective, and (c) prioritize by focusing on the client's most pressing needs.[8] You may have brainstormed using a similar technique, mind mapping, presented in Chapter 5, to generate ideas for your papers. Like brainstorming, mind mapping involves generating ideas around a single word and grouping those ideas into major and minor categories, thus creating a web of relationships.

In the proposal introduction shown in Model Document 13.1, Antoine Gibson focused on what the customer wanted. The researcher analyzed the request of Nebraska dentist Caroline Foley and decided that she was most interested in specific recommendations for improving service to her patients. However, Antoine did not hit on this hook until he had written a first draft and had come back to it later. It's not a bad idea to put off writing the proposal introduction until after you have completed other parts. In longer proposals the introduction also describes the scope and limitations of the project, as well as outlining the organization of the material to come.

Background, Problem, and Purpose.   The background section identifies the problem and discusses the goals or purposes of the project. In an unsolicited proposal, your goal is to convince the reader that a problem exists. Therefore, you must present the problem in detail, discussing such factors as revenue losses, failure to comply with government regulations, or loss of customers. In a solicited proposal, your aim is to persuade the reader that you understand the problem completely and that you have a realistic solution. If you are responding to an RFP, follow the requirements precisely, and use the company's language in your description of the problem. For example, if the RFP asks for the *design of a maintenance program for wireless communication equipment*, don't call it a *customer service program for wireless products*. The background section might include segments titled *Statement of Need*, *Basic Requirements*, *Most Critical Tasks*, or *Important Secondary Problems*.

Proposal, Plan, and Schedule.   In the proposal section itself, you should discuss your plan for solving the problem. In some proposals this is tricky because you want to disclose enough of your plan to secure the contract without giving away so much information that your services aren't needed. Without specifics, though, your proposal has little chance, so you must decide how much to reveal.

The proposal section often includes the implementation plan. If research is involved, state what methods you will use to gather the data. Remember to be persuasive by showing how your methods and products will benefit the reader. For example, show how the initial investment will pay off later. The proposal might even promise specific **deliverables**—tangible items your project will produce for the customer. A proposal deliverable might be a new website design or an online marketing plan. To add credibility, also specify how the project will be managed and how its progress will be audited. Most writers also include a schedule or timetable of activities showing the proposal's benchmarks for completion.

Staffing.   The staffing section of a proposal describes the staff qualifications for implementing the proposal as well as the credentials and expertise of the project leaders. In other words, it attests to the size and qualifications of the staff. The staffing section is a good place to endorse and promote your staff and to demonstrate to the client that your company can do the job. As a result, the client sees that qualified people will be on board to implement the project. Résumés may even be included in this section. Although the full résumés of key people might be attached to a proposal, busy decision makers will appreciate a summary of the relevant highlights of staff members who may be involved. Each summary might describe that person's expertise, certifications, and a few examples of experience on similar projects.[10]

Budget.   A central item in most proposals is the **budget**, a list of proposed project costs. You need to prepare this section carefully because it represents a contract; much like SpaceX, you cannot raise the price later—even if your costs increase. You can—and should—protect yourself from rising costs with a deadline for acceptance. In the budget section, some writers itemize hours and costs; others present a total sum only. In the proposal shown in Model Document 13.1, Antoine Gibson decided to justify the budget for his firm's patient satisfaction survey by itemizing the costs. However, the budget for a proposal to conduct a one-day seminar to improve employee communication skills might be a lump sum. Whether the costs are itemized or presented as a lump sum depends on the reader's needs and the proposal's goals.

Conclusion and Authorization. The closing section should remind the reader of the proposal's key benefits and make it easy for the reader to respond. It might also include a project completion date as well as a deadline beyond which the proposal offer will no longer be in effect. Writers of informal proposals often refer to this as a request for approval or authorization. The conclusion of the proposal in Figure 13.2 states a key benefit as well as a deadline for approval.

13-2 Preparing Formal Proposals

Formal proposals differ from informal proposals not in style but in size and format. Formal proposals respond to big projects and may range from 5 to 200 or more pages. Because proposals are vital to the success of many organizations, larger businesses may maintain specialists who do nothing but write proposals. Smaller firms rely on in-house staff to write proposals. Proposals use standard components that enable companies receiving bids to "compare apples with apples." Writers must know the parts of proposals and how to develop those parts effectively.

13-2a Components of Formal Proposals

To help readers understand and locate the parts of a formal proposal, writers organize the project into a typical structure, as shown in Figure 13.1. In addition to the six basic components described for informal proposals, formal proposals may contain some or all of the following front matter and back matter components.

Copy of the RFP. A copy of the RFP may be included in the front matter of a formal proposal. Large organizations may have more than one RFP circulating, in which case identification is necessary.

Letter of Transmittal. A letter of transmittal, usually bound inside formal proposals, addresses the person who is designated to receive the proposal or who will make the final decision. The letter describes how you learned about the problem or confirms that the proposal responds to the enclosed RFP. This persuasive letter briefly presents the major features and benefits of your proposal. Here, you should assure the reader that you are authorized to make the bid and mention the time limit for which the bid stands. You may also offer to provide additional information and ask for action, if appropriate.

Abstract or Executive Summary. An abstract is a brief summary (typically one page) of a proposal's highlights intended for specialists or technical readers. An executive summary also reviews the proposal's highlights, but it is written for managers and should be less technically oriented. An executive summary tends to be longer than an abstract, up to 10 percent of the original text. In reports and proposals, the executive summary typically represents a nutshell version of the entire document and addresses all its sections or chapters. Formal proposals may contain either an abstract or an executive summary, or both. For more information about writing executive summaries and abstracts, use a search engine such as Google.

Title Page. The title page includes the following items, generally in this order: title of proposal, name of client organization, RFP number or other announcement, date of submission, and the authors' names and/or the name of their organization.

Table of Contents. Because most proposals don't contain an index, the table of contents becomes quite important. A table of contents should include all headings and their beginning page numbers. Items that appear before the contents (copy of RFP, letter of transmittal, abstract, and title page) typically are not listed in the contents. However, any appendixes should be listed.

List of Illustrations. Proposals with many tables and figures often contain a list of illustrations. This list includes each figure or table title and its page number. If you have just a few figures or tables, however, you may omit this list.

Appendix(es). Ancillary material of interest to only some readers goes in an appendix. Appendix A might include résumés of the principal investigators or testimonial letters. Appendix B might include examples or a listing of previous projects. Other appendixes could include audit procedures, technical graphics, or professional papers cited in the body of the proposal.

13-2b Grant Proposals

A **grant proposal** is a formal proposal submitted to a government or civilian organization that explains a project, outlines its budget, and requests money in the form of a grant. Every year the U.S. government, private foundations, and public corporations make available billions of dollars in funding for special projects. These funds, or grants, require no repayment, but the funds must be used for the purposes outlined in the proposal. Grants are often made to charities, educational facilities, and especially nonprofits. Securing funding can mean life or death for nonprofits and other organizations.

Organizations such as McDonald's offer millions of dollars in grants to support health care. In the past 25 years, the Ronald McDonald House Charities (RMHC) has awarded more than $100 million in funding through its Global Grants Program to promote children's health and well-being worldwide. Most recently its grants program focused on oral health needs of children ages 0 to 6 in the U.S. and on reducing maternal and child mortality in the first six months of life in Africa, South Asia, and Latin America.[11] From treating pediatric cancer in Poland to ophthalmology in Thailand and neonatal care in South Africa, RMHC takes a holistic approach to providing health care.

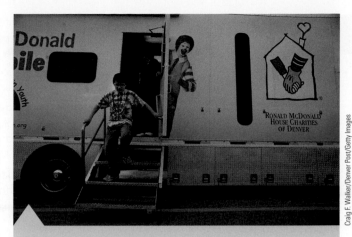

Costing about $500,000 each, Ronald McDonald Care Mobiles depend on grant funding to deliver health education, immunizations, dental care, and other treatments to families where children need it most.

Many of the parts of a grant proposal are similar to those of a formal proposal. A grant proposal includes an abstract and needs statement that explains a problem or situation that the grant project proposes to address. The body of the proposal explains that the problem is significant enough to warrant funding and that the proposal can solve the problem. The body also describes short- and long-term goals, which must be reasonable, measurable, and attainable within a specific time frame. An action plan tells what will be done by whom and when. The budget outlines how the money will be spent. Finally, a grant proposal presents a plan for measuring progress toward completion of its goal.

Skilled grant writers are among the most in-demand professionals today. A grant writer is the vital connecting link between a funder and a grant seeker. Large projects may require a team of writers to produce various sections of a grant proposal. Then one person does the final editing and proofreading. Effective grant proposals require careful organization, planning, and writing. Skillful writing is particularly important because funding organizations may receive thousands of applications for a single award.

Well-written proposals win contracts and sustain the business life of many companies, individuals, and nonprofit organizations. The following checklist summarizes key elements to remember in writing proposals.

Checklist

Writing Proposals

Introduction

- **Indicate the purpose.** Specify why you are making the proposal.

- **Develop a persuasive hook.** Suggest excellent results, low costs, or exclusive resources.

Identify a serious problem, or name a key issue or benefit.

Background, Problem, and Purpose

- **Provide the necessary background.** Discuss the

significance of the proposal and the goals or purposes that matter to the client.

- **Introduce the problem.** For unsolicited proposals convince the reader that a problem exists. For solicited proposals show that you fully understand the customer's problem and its ramifications.

Proposal, Plan, and Schedule

- **Explain the proposal.** Present your plan for solving the problem or meeting the need.

- **Discuss plan management and evaluation.** If appropriate, tell how the plan will be implemented and evaluated.

- **Outline a timetable.** Furnish a schedule showing what will be done and when.

Staffing

- **Promote the qualifications of your staff.** Explain the specific credentials and expertise of the key personnel for the project.

- **Mention special resources and equipment.** Show how your support staff and resources are superior to those of the competition.

Budget

- **Show project costs.** For most projects itemize costs. Remember, however, that proposals are contracts.

- **Include a deadline.** Here or in the conclusion, present a date beyond which the bid figures are no longer valid.

Authorization

- **Ask for approval.** Make it easy for the reader to authorize the project (for example, *Sign and return the enclosed duplicate copy*).

13-3 Creating Effective Business Plans

Another form of proposal is a business plan. Let's say you want to start your own business. Unless you can count on the Bank of Mom and Dad, you will need financial backing such as a bank loan, seed money from an individual angel investor, or funds supplied by venture capitalists. A business plan is critical for securing financial support of any kind. Such a plan also ensures that you have done your homework and know what you are doing in launching your business. It provides you with a detailed road map to chart a course to success.

Creating a business plan for an entirely new concept is hard work and takes time. Estimates range from 100 to 200 hours.[13] Consultants can probably do it in less time, but they may be pricey. Costs generally start at $1,500 for simple projects and may range as high as $25,000 to $50,000 for corporate jobs.[14] Budding entrepreneurs often prefer to save the cash and do it themselves using software programs designed for the purpose. Business.org ranked the following best software programs for writing business plans: Live Plan (best overall); BizPlanBuilder (most user friendly); GoSmallBiz.com (best for nonprofits); and Business Plan Pro (best for customer support).[15] However, no business plan app can provide a cookie-cutter plan that works for everyone.

Reality Check

Study: Three Months to Write a Successful Business Plan

"We found that the optimal time to spend on the plan was three months. This increased the chances of creating a viable venture by 12%. Spending any longer than this was futile, mostly because the information used to inform the plan loses its currency. Spending just a month or two on the plan was just as bad. If the choice was between quickly writing a plan or not writing a plan, the entrepreneur was better off not writing a plan at all."[12]

—Francis J. Greene & Christian Hopp, *researchers, professors of entrepreneurship*

13-3a Components of Typical Business Plans

For people who are serious about starting a business, the importance of a comprehensive, thoughtful business plan cannot be overemphasized, says the Small Business Administration. A **business plan** may be defined as a description of a proposed company that explains how it expects to achieve its marketing, financial, and operational goals. If you are considering becoming an entrepreneur, your business plan is more likely to secure the funds it needs if it is carefully written and includes the following elements.

FOR THE RECORD

Student Entrepreneur Competition

Every year, young entrepreneurs participating in the New Venture Competition offered at the University of California, Santa Barbara, work with local business mentors to compete for a share of $40,000 in prize money and the chance to launch their business. Students make 60- to 90-second investor pitches and write comprehensive business plans. Past competition winners have started successful companies including Allthenticate, a device-based digital security solution; Phone Halo, which produces a tracking device; and Inogen, a firm that created and markets a compact oxygen delivery system.[16] Why is the executive summary often the most important section of a business plan?

Letter of Transmittal.   A letter of transmittal provides contact information for all principals and explains your reason for writing. If you are seeking venture capital or an angel investor, the transmittal letter may become a pitch letter. In that case you would want to include a simple description of your idea and a clear statement of what's in it for the investor. The letter should include a summary of the market, a brief note about the competition, and an explanation of why your business is worthy of investment.

Mission Statement.   A business plan mission statement explains the purpose of your business and why it will succeed. Because potential investors will be looking for this mission statement, consider highlighting it with a paragraph heading (*Mission Statement*) or use bolding or italics. Some consultants say that you should be able to write your mission statement in eight or fewer words.[17] Others think that one or two short paragraphs might be more realistic. Many Fortune 500 companies have created mission statements that are both inspirational and concrete. For example, Starbucks states its mission simply but graphically: "To inspire and nurture the human spirit—one person, one cup and one neighborhood at a time." As illustrated in Figure 13.2, mission statements should be simple, concise, memorable, and unique.

Executive Summary.   Your executive summary, which is written last, highlights the main points of your business plan and should not exceed two pages. It should conclude by introducing the parts of the plan and asking for financial backing. Some business plans combine the mission statement and executive summary.

Table of Contents and Company Description.   List the page numbers and topics included in your plan. Identify the form of your business (proprietorship, partnership, or corporation) and its type (merchandising, manufacturing, or service). For existing companies, describe the company's founding, growth, sales, and profit.

Product or Service Description.   In jargon-free language, explain what you are providing, how it will benefit customers, and why it is better than existing products or services. For start-ups, explain why the business will be profitable. Investors aren't always looking for a unique product or service. Instead, they are searching for a concept whose growth potential distinguishes it from others competing for funds.

Market Analysis.   Discuss market characteristics, trends, projected growth, customer behavior, complementary products and services, and barriers to entry. Identify your customers and how you will attract, hold, and increase your market share. Discuss the strengths and weaknesses of your direct and indirect competitors.

Operations and Management.   Explain specifically how you will run your business, including location, equipment, personnel, and management. Highlight experienced and

> ## Reality Check
>
> ### Don't Skimp on Your Business Plan
>
> "The best business plan is one you do yourself. . . . Consider hiring somebody from the outside only if you have the budget for it. . . . Cheap business plan writing strikes me as about as good an idea as cheap surgery, cheap dentistry, or discount sushi."[18]
>
> —Tim Berry, *founder and chairman of Palo Alto Software, maker of Business Plan Pro*

FIGURE 13.2 Creating Winning Mission Statements

Definition

A mission statement describes the reason an organization or program exists.

GOALS should be:

- Easily understood
- Free of complex words and buzz words
- Concise, memorable, and simple
- Unique in distinguishing a business or program

QUESTIONS TO PONDER

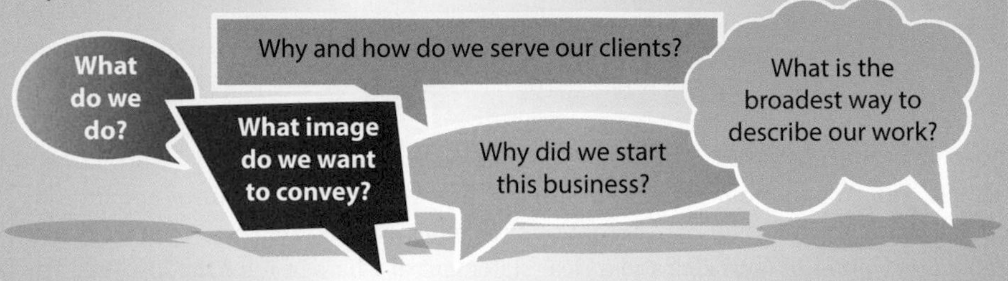

- What do we do?
- Why and how do we serve our clients?
- What image do we want to convey?
- Why did we start this business?
- What is the broadest way to describe our work?

EXAMPLES

Nonprofit Organizations

Wounded Warrior Project: To honor and empower wounded warriors

The Humane Society: Celebrating Animals, Confronting Cruelty

Charity Water: We're a nonprofit organization bringing clean, safe drinking water to people in developing countries.

Make-A-Wish: We grant the wishes of children with life-threatening medical conditions to enrich the human experience with hope, strength and joy.

Fortune 500 Companies

Nike: To bring inspiration and innovation to every athlete in the world

LinkedIn: Create economic opportunity for every member of the global workforce

Prezi: To reinvent how people share knowledge, tell stories, and inspire their audiences to act

Amazon: To be the most customer centric company in the world, where people can find and discover anything they want to buy online

Ethics ✔ Check

Honesty Is Key

A business plan's purpose is to help manage a company and raise capital; hence, it is a persuasive document that must be accurate and honest. Whether the goal is to persuade a lender or investors or whether it is the blueprint for running operations, the business plan must be realistic. What are the risks of fudging numbers or sugarcoating potential challenges?

well-trained members of the management team and your advisors. Many investors consider this the most important factor in assessing business potential. Can your management team implement this business plan?

Financial Analysis. Outline a realistic start-up budget that includes fees for legal and professional services, occupancy, licenses and permits, equipment, insurance, supplies, advertising and promotions, salaries and wages, accounting, income, and utilities. Also present an operating budget that projects costs for personnel, insurance, rent, depreciation, loan payments, salaries, taxes, repairs, and so on. Explain how much money you have, how much you will need to start up, and how much you will need to stay in business.

Appendixes. Provide necessary extras such as managers' résumés, promotional materials, and product photos in appendixes. Most appendixes contain tables that exhibit the sales forecast, a personnel plan, anticipated cash flow, profit and loss, and a balance sheet.

13-3b Sample Business Plans on the Internet

Writing a business plan is easier if you can see examples and learn from experts' suggestions. On the Internet you will find many sites devoted to business plans. Some sites want to sell you something; others offer free advice. One of the best websites, that of Palo Alto Software (search for *Palo Alto 500+ free business plans*), does try to sell business plans and software. However, in addition to templates and useful advice from experts, the site provides more than 500 free samples of business plans ranging from bar and nightclub to wedding consultant businesses. These simple but helpful plans illustrate diverse business start-ups.

At the Small Business Administration site, you will find more advice for writing business plans (search for *SBA write your business plan*). Two kinds of plans are outlined: traditional and lean. With nine sections, the traditional plan appeals to a detail-oriented person. It includes financial information and high-level growth plans if you plan to seek financing. The lean plan is relatively simple, using only a few elements to describe your company's proposed value, infrastructure, customers, and finances. The site provides samples of both plans for small businesses.

13-4 Writing Formal Business Reports

LEARNING OUTCOME

4 Describe how the components of the front matter in formal business reports support the purpose of the report.

A **formal report** may be defined as a document in which a writer analyzes findings, draws conclusions, and makes recommendations intended to solve a problem. Formal business reports are similar to formal proposals in length, organization, and tone. Instead of making an offer, however, formal reports represent the product of thorough investigation and analysis. They convey ordered information to decision makers in business, industry, government, and education. In many ways formal business reports are extended versions of the analytical business reports presented in Chapter 12. If you are preparing a formal business report, be sure to review the work plan that appears in Model Document 11.1 in Chapter 11.

Informal and formal business reports have similar components, as shown in Figure 13.3, but, as might be expected, formal reports have more sections.

FIGURE 13.3 Components of Informal and Formal Reports

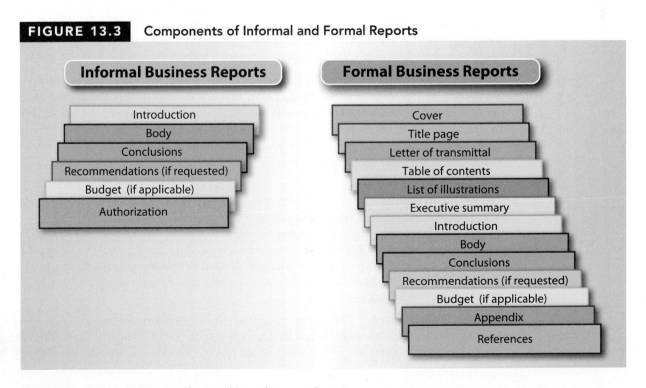

Informal Business Reports
- Introduction
- Body
- Conclusions
- Recommendations (if requested)
- Budget (if applicable)
- Authorization

Formal Business Reports
- Cover
- Title page
- Letter of transmittal
- Table of contents
- List of illustrations
- Executive summary
- Introduction
- Body
- Conclusions
- Recommendations (if requested)
- Budget (if applicable)
- Appendix
- References

13-4a Front Matter Components of Formal Business Reports

A number of front matter and back matter items lengthen formal reports but enhance their professional tone and serve their multiple audiences. Formal reports may be read by many levels of managers, along with technical specialists and financial consultants. Therefore, breaking a long, formal report into small segments makes its information more accessible and easier to understand for all readers. The segments in the front of the report, called front matter or preliminaries, are discussed in this section. They are also illustrated in Model Document 13.2, the model formal report shown later in the chapter. This analytical report studies the economic impact of an industrial park on Flagstaff, Arizona, and recommends increasing the city's revenues.

Cover.   Traditional formal reports are usually enclosed in vinyl or heavy paper binders to protect the pages and to create a professional, finished appearance. Some companies have binders imprinted with their name and logo. The title of the report may appear through a cut-out window or may be applied with an adhesive label. Formal reports provided digitally may present an attractive title with the company logo.

Title Page.   A report title page, as illustrated in the Model Document 13.2 model report, begins with the name of the report typed in uppercase letters (no underscore and no quotation marks). Next comes *Presented to* (or *Submitted to*) and the name, title, and organization of the individual receiving the report. Lower on the page is *Prepared by* (or *Submitted by*) and the author's name plus any necessary identification. The last item on the title page is the date of submission. All items after the title are typed in a combination of upper- and lowercase letters.

Letter or Memo of Transmittal.   Generally written on organization stationery, a letter or **memorandum of transmittal** introduces a formal report. You will recall that letters are sent to external audiences; and memos, to internal audiences. A transmittal letter or memo uses the direct strategy and is usually less formal than the report itself (for example, the letter or memo may use contractions and the first-person pronouns *I* and *we*). The transmittal letter or memo typically (a) announces the topic of the report and tells how it was authorized; (b) briefly describes the project; (c) highlights the report's findings, conclusions, and recommendations, if the reader is expected to be supportive; and (d) closes with appreciation for the assignment, instruction for the reader's follow-up actions, acknowledgement of help from others, or offers of assistance in answering questions. If a report is going to various readers, a special transmittal letter or memo should be prepared for each, anticipating how each reader will use the report.

Table of Contents.   The table of contents shows the headings in the report and their page numbers. It gives an overview of the report topics and helps readers locate them. You should wait to prepare the table of contents until after you have completed the report. For short reports you should include all headings. For longer reports you might want to list only first- and second-level headings. Leaders (spaced or unspaced dots) help guide the eye from the heading to the page number. Items may be indented in outline form or typed flush with the left margin.

List of Illustrations.   For reports with several figures or tables, you may wish to include a list to help readers locate them. This list may appear on the same page as the table of contents, space permitting. For each figure or table, include a title and page number. Some writers distinguish between tables and all other illustrations, which they call figures. If you make the distinction, you should prepare separate lists of tables and figures. Because the formal report in Model Document 13.2 has few illustrations, the writer labeled them all *figures*, a method that simplifies numbering.

Executive Summary.   The purpose of an executive summary is to present an overview of a longer report to people who may not have time to read the entire document. Generally, an executive summary is prepared by the author of the report. However, occasionally you may be asked to write an executive summary of a published report or article written by someone else. In either case, your goal is to summarize the important points. The best way to prepare an executive summary is to do the following:

- **Look for strategic words and sentences**. Read the completed report carefully. Pay special attention to the first and last sentences of paragraphs, which often contain summary statements. Look for words that enumerate (*first, next, finally*) and words that express causation (*therefore, as a result*). Also, look for words that signal essentials (*basically, central, leading, principal, major*) and words that contrast ideas (*however, consequently*).

- **Prepare an outline with headings**. At a minimum, include headings for the purpose, findings, and conclusions/recommendations. What kernels of information would your reader want to know about these topics?

- **Fill in your outline**. Some writers cut and paste important parts of the text. Then they condense with careful editing. Others find it more efficient to create new sentences as they prepare the executive summary.

- **Begin with the purpose**. The easiest way to begin an executive summary is with the words *The purpose of this report is to . . . .* Experienced writers may be more creative.

- **Follow the report sequence**. Present all your information in the order in which it is found in the report.

- **Eliminate nonessential details**. Include only main points. Do not include anything not in the original report. Use minimal technical language.

- **Control the length**. An executive summary is usually no longer than 10 percent of the original document. Thus, a 100-page report might require a 10-page summary. A 10-page report might need only a 1-page summary—or no summary at all. The executive summary for a long report may also include graphics to highlight main points.

To see a representative executive summary, look at Model Document 13.2. Although it is only one page long, this executive summary includes headings to help the reader see the main divisions immediately. Let your organization's practices guide you in determining the length and format of an executive summary.

Introduction.   Formal reports begin with an introduction that sets the scene and announces the subject. Because they contain many parts that serve different purposes, formal reports are somewhat redundant. The same information may be included in the letter of transmittal, summary, and introduction. To avoid sounding repetitious, try to present the data slightly differently. However, do not skip the introduction because you have included some of its information elsewhere. You cannot be sure that your reader saw the information earlier. A good report introduction typically covers the following elements, although not necessarily in this order:

- **Background**. Describe events leading up to the problem or need.

- **Problem or purpose**. Explain the report topic, and specify the problem or need that motivated the report.

- **Significance**. Tell why the topic is important. You may wish to quote experts or cite newspapers, journals, books, Web resources, and other secondary sources to establish the importance of the topic.

- **Scope**. Clarify the boundaries of the report, defining what will be included or excluded.

- **Organization**. Orient readers by giving them a road map that previews the structure of the report.

Beyond these minimal introductory elements, consider adding any of the following information that may be relevant to your readers:

- **Authorization**. Identify who commissioned the report. If no letter of transmittal is included, also tell why, when, by whom, and to whom the report was written.

- **Literature review**. Summarize what other authors and researchers have published on this topic, especially for academic and scientific reports.

- **Sources and methods**. Describe your secondary sources (periodicals, books, databases). Also explain how you collected primary data, including the survey size, sample design, and statistical programs you used.
- **Definitions of key terms**. Define words that may be unfamiliar to the audience. Also define terms with special meanings, such as *small businesses* when it specifically means businesses with fewer than 30 employees.

LEARNING OUTCOME

5 Explain how the body and back matter of formal business reports serve the purpose of the report.

13-5 Body and Back Matter Components of Formal Business Reports

The body of a formal business report is the "meat" of the document. In this longest and most substantive section of the text, the author or team discusses the problem and findings, before reaching conclusions and making recommendations. Extensive and bulky materials that don't fit in the text belong in the appendix. Although some very long reports may have additional components, the back matter usually concludes with a list of sources. Figure 13.3 shows the parts of typical reports, the order in which they appear, and elements usually found only in formal reports.

Because formal business reports can be long and complex, they usually include more sections than routine informal business reports do. These components are standard and conventional; that is, the audience expects to see them in a professional report. Documents that conform to such expectations are easier to read and deliver their message more effectively. You will find most of the components addressed here in the formal report in Model Document 13.2, the formal analytical report studying the economic impact of an industrial park on Flagstaff, Arizona.

Body. The principal section in a formal report is the body. It discusses, analyzes, interprets, and evaluates the research findings or solution to the initial problem. This is where you show the evidence that justifies your conclusions. Organize the body into main categories following your original outline or using one of the organizational methods described in Chapter 12 (i.e., time, component, importance, criteria, or convention).

Although we refer to this section as the body, it does not carry that heading. Instead, it contains clear headings that explain each major section. Headings may be functional or talking. Functional heads (such as *Results of the Survey*, *Analysis of Findings*, or *Discussion*) help readers identify the purpose of the section but do not reveal what is in it. Such headings are useful for routine reports or for sensitive topics that may upset readers. Talking heads (for example, *Anatomy of a Market Crash* or *Your Money as a Force for Good*) are more informative and interesting, but they do not help readers see the organization of the report. The formal report in Model Document 13.2 uses combination headings; as the name suggests, they combine functional heads for organizational sections (*Introduction*, *Conclusions and Recommendations*) with talking heads that reveal the content. The headings divide the body into smaller parts.

Conclusions. This important section tells what the findings mean, particularly in terms of solving the original problem. Some writers prefer to intermix their conclusions with the analysis of the findings—instead of presenting the conclusions separately. Other writers place the conclusions before the body so that busy readers can examine the significant information immediately. Still others combine the conclusions and recommendations. Most writers, though, present the conclusions after the body because readers expect this structure. In long reports this section may include a summary of the findings. To improve comprehension, you may present the conclusions in a numbered or bulleted list. See Chapter 12 for more suggestions on drawing conclusions.

Recommendations. When asked, you should submit recommendations that make precise suggestions for actions to solve the report problem. Recommendations are most helpful when they are practical, reasonable, feasible, and ethical. Naturally, they should evolve from the findings and conclusions. Do not introduce new information in the conclusions or recommendations sections. As with conclusions, the position of recommendations is somewhat flexible. They may be combined with conclusions, or they may be presented before the body, especially when the audience is eager and supportive. Generally, though, in formal reports they come last.

Recommendations require an appropriate introductory sentence, such as *The findings and conclusions in this study support the following recommendations*. When making many recommendations, number them and phrase each as a command, such as *Begin an employee fitness program with a workout room available five days a week*. If appropriate, add information describing how to implement each recommendation. Some reports include a timetable describing the who, what, when, where, why, and how for putting each recommendation into operation. Chapter 12 provides more information about writing recommendations.

Appendix(es). Incidental or supporting materials belong in **appendixes** at the end of a formal report. These materials are relevant to some readers but not to all. They may also be too bulky to include in the text. Appendixes may include survey forms, copies of other reports, tables of data, large graphics, and related correspondence. If multiple appendixes are necessary, they are named *Appendix A, Appendix B*, and so forth.

Works Cited or References. If you use the MLA (Modern Language Association) citation format, list all sources of information alphabetically in a section titled **Works Cited**. If you use the APA (American Psychological Association) format, your list is called **References**. Your listed sources must correspond to in-text citations in the report whenever you are borrowing words or ideas from published and unpublished resources.

Regardless of the documentation format, you must include the author, title, publication, date of publication, page number, and other significant data for all ideas or quotations used in your report. For digital references include the preceding information plus the Internet address, or URL, leading to the citation. For model citations, examine the list of references at the end of Model Document 13.2. In addition, Appendix B of this textbook contains documentation models and information.

13-6 Final Writing Tips

LEARNING OUTCOME

6 Specify final writing tips that aid authors of formal business reports.

Formal business reports are not undertaken lightly. They involve considerable effort in all three phases of writing, beginning with analysis of the problem and anticipation of the audience (as discussed in Chapter 4). Researching the data, organizing it into a logical presentation, and composing the first draft (Chapter 5) make up the second phase of writing. Editing, proofreading, and evaluating (Chapter 6) are completed in the third phase. Although everyone approaches the writing process somewhat differently, the following tips offer advice in problem areas faced by most writers of formal reports:

- **Allow sufficient time**. The main reason given by writers who are disappointed with their reports is "I just ran out of time." Develop a realistic timetable and stick to it.

- **Finish data collection**. Do not begin writing until you have collected all the data and drawn the primary conclusions. Starting too early often results in having to backtrack. For reports based on survey data, complete the tables and figures first.

- **Work from a good outline**. A big project such as a formal report needs the order and direction provided by a clear outline, even if the outline has to be revised as the project unfolds.

- **Create a proper writing environment**. You will need a quiet spot where you can spread out your materials and work without interruption. Formal reports demand blocks of concentration time.

- **Use the features of your computer wisely**. Your word processor enables you to keyboard quickly; revise easily; and check spelling, grammar, and synonyms readily. A word of warning, though: save your document often and keep backup copies in the cloud, on disks, or on other devices. Print out important materials so that you have a hard copy. Take these precautions to guard against the grief caused by lost files, power outages, and computer malfunctions.

- **Write rapidly; revise later**. Some experts advise writers to record their ideas quickly and save revision until after the first draft is completed. They say that quick writing avoids

Ethics ✓ Check

One for All, All for One

If one of your teammates cowriting a formal report with you has been found to have plagiarized a portion of your writing project, typically the instructor will punish the entire group, assuming ownership by the entire team. After all, researchers are expected to deliver a product that they have jointly prepared. Is this fair?

wasted effort spent in polishing sentences or even sections that may be cut later. Moreover, rapid writing encourages fluency and creativity. However, a quick-and-dirty first draft does not work for everyone. Many business writers prefer a more deliberate writing style, so consider this advice selectively and experiment to find the method that works best for you.

- **Save difficult sections**. If some sections are harder to write than others, save them until you have developed confidence and a rhythm from working on easier topics.

- **Be consistent in verb tense**. Use past-tense verbs to describe completed actions (for example, *the respondents said* or *the survey showed*). Use present-tense verbs, however, to explain current actions (*the purpose of the report is, this report examines, the table shows*). When citing references, use past-tense verbs (*Jones reported that*). Do not switch back and forth between present- and past-tense verbs in describing related data.

- **Generally avoid *I* and *we***. To make formal reports seem as objective and credible as possible, most writers omit first-person pronouns. This formal style sometimes results in the overuse of passive-voice verbs (for example, *periodicals were consulted* and *the study was conducted*). Look for alternative constructions (*periodicals indicated* and *the study revealed*). It is also possible that your organization may allow first-person pronouns, so check before starting your report.

- **Let the first draft sit**. After completing the first version, put it aside for a day or two. Return to it with the expectation of revising and improving it. Don't be afraid to make major changes.

- **Revise for clarity, coherence, and conciseness**. Read a printed copy out loud. Do the sentences make sense? Do the ideas flow together naturally? Can wordiness be cut out? Make sure that your writing is so clear that a busy manager does not have to reread any part. See Chapter 6 for specific revision suggestions.

- **Proofread the final copy three times**. First, read a printed copy slowly for word meanings and content. Then read the copy again for spelling, punctuation, grammar, and other mechanical errors. Finally, scan the entire report to check its formatting and consistency (page numbering, indenting, spacing, headings, and so forth).

13-6a Putting It All Together

Formal reports in business generally aim to study problems and recommend solutions. Keyla T. Wright, senior research consultant with Pueblo Development Company, was asked to study the economic impact of a local industrial park on the city of Flagstaff, Arizona, resulting in the formal report shown in Model Document 13.2.

The city council hired the consultants to evaluate Coconino Industrial Park and to assess whether future commercial development would stimulate further economic growth. Keyla Wright subdivided the economic impact into three aspects: Revenues, Employment, and Indirect Benefits. The report was compiled from survey data as well as from secondary sources that Sophia consulted.

Keyla's report illustrates many of the points discussed in this chapter. Although it is a good example of the typical report format and style, it should not be viewed as the only way to present a report. Wide variation exists in business and academic reports.

The following checklist summarizes the report process and report components in one handy list.

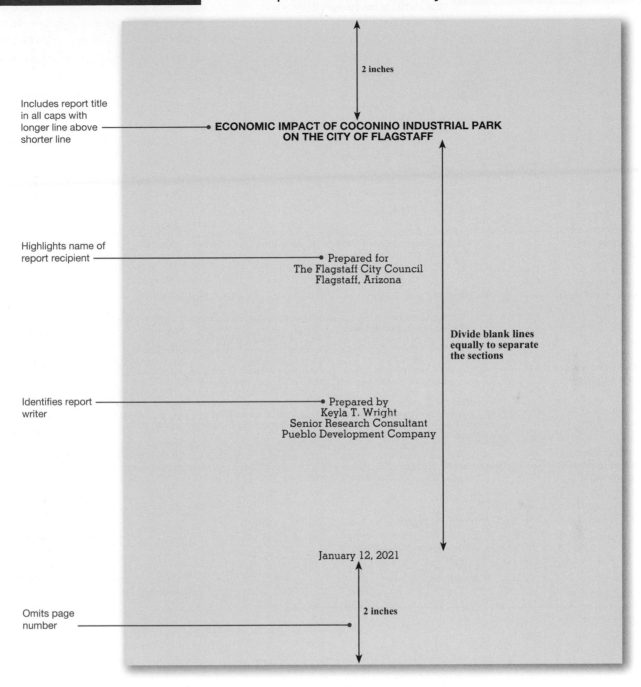

Includes report title in all caps with longer line above shorter line

2 inches

ECONOMIC IMPACT OF COCONINO INDUSTRIAL PARK ON THE CITY OF FLAGSTAFF

Highlights name of report recipient

Prepared for
The Flagstaff City Council
Flagstaff, Arizona

Divide blank lines equally to separate the sections

Identifies report writer

Prepared by
Keyla T. Wright
Senior Research Consultant
Pueblo Development Company

January 12, 2021

Omits page number

2 inches

PUEBLO DEVELOPMENT COMPANY
154 Hall Road, Suite 110   www.pueblodevco.com
Phoenix, AZ 85021   928.851.3348

January 12, 2021

City Council
City of Flagstaff
211 West Aspen Avenue
Flagstaff, AZ 86001

Dear Council Members:

Announces report and identifies authorization → The attached report, requested by the Flagstaff City Council in a letter to Goldman-Lyon & Associates dated October 20, describes the economic impact of Coconino Industrial Park on the city of Flagstaff. We believe you will find the results of this study useful in evaluating future development of industrial parks within the city limits.

Gives broad overview of report purposes → This study was designed to examine economic impact in three areas:

- Current and projected tax and other revenues accruing to the city from Coconino Industrial Park
- Current and projected employment generated by the park
- Indirect effects on local employment, income, and economic growth

Describes primary and secondary research → Primary research consisted of interviews with 15 Coconino Industrial Park (CIP) tenants and managers, in addition to a 2019 survey of over 5,000 CIP employees. Secondary research sources included the Annual Budget of the City of Flagstaff, county and state tax records, government publications, periodicals, books, and online resources. Results of this research, discussed more fully in this report, indicate that Coconino Industrial Park exerts a significant beneficial influence on the Flagstaff metropolitan economy.

Offers to discuss report; expresses appreciation → We would be pleased to discuss this report and its conclusions with you at your request. My firm and I thank you for your confidence in selecting our company to prepare this comprehensive report.

Sincerely,

Keyla T. Wright

Keyla T. Wright
Senior Research Consultant

KTW:mef
Attachment

Uses Roman numerals for prefatory pages → ii

TABLE OF CONTENTS

LIST OF FIGURES

iii

EXECUTIVE SUMMARY

Opens directly with major research findings

The city of Flagstaff can benefit from the development of industrial parks like the Coconino Industrial Park. Both direct and indirect economic benefits result, as shown by this in-depth study conducted by Pueblo Development Company. The study was authorized by the Flagstaff City Council when Goldman-Lyon & Associates sought the City Council's approval for the proposed construction of a G-L industrial park. The City Council requested evidence demonstrating that an existing development could actually benefit the city.

Identifies data sources

Our conclusion that the city of Flagstaff benefits from industrial parks is based on data supplied by a survey of 5,000 Coconino Industrial Park employees, personal interviews with managers and tenants of CIP, city and state documents, and professional literature.

Summarizes organization of report

Analysis of the data revealed benefits in three areas:

- **Revenues.** The city of Flagstaff earned over $3 million in tax and other revenues from the Coconino Industrial Park in 2019. By 2028 this income is expected to reach $5.4 million (in constant 2019 dollars).

- **Employment.** In 2019, CIP businesses employed a total of 7,035 workers, who earned an average wage of $56,579. By 2028, CIP businesses are will expected to employ directly nearly 15,000 employees who earn salaries totaling over $998 million.

- **Indirect benefits.** Because of the multiplier effect, by 2028 Coconino Industrial Park will directly and indirectly generate a total of 38,362 jobs in the Flagstaff metropolitan area.

Condenses recommendations

On the basis of these findings, it is recommended that development of additional industrial parks be encouraged to stimulate local economic growth. The city would increase its tax revenues significantly, create much-needed jobs, and thus help stimulate the local economy in and around Flagstaff.

iv

INTRODUCTION: COCONINO AND THE LOCAL ECONOMY

This study was designed to analyze the direct and indirect economic impact of Coconino Industrial Park on the city of Flagstaff. Specifically, the study seeks answers to these questions:

Uses a bulleted list for clarity and ease of reading

- What current tax and other revenues result directly from this park? What tax and other revenues may be expected in the future?

- How many and what kinds of jobs are directly attributable to the park? What is the employment picture for the future?

Lists three problem questions

- What indirect effects has Coconino Industrial Park had on local employment, incomes, and economic growth?

BACKGROUND: THE ROLE OF CIP IN COMMERCIAL DEVELOPMENT

Describes authorization for report and background of study

The development firm of Goldman-Lyon & Associates commissioned this study of Coconino Industrial Park at the request of the Flagstaff City Council. Before authorizing the development of a proposed Goldman- Lyon industrial park, the city council requested a study examining the economic effects of an existing park. Members of the city council want- ed to determine to what extent industrial parks benefit the local community, and they chose Coconino Industrial Park as an example.

For those who are unfamiliar with it, Coconino Industrial Park is a 400-acre industrial park located in the city of Flagstaff about 4 miles from the center of the city. Most of the land lies within a specially designated area known as Redevelopment Project No. 2, which is under the jurisdiction of the Flagstaff Redevelopment Agency. Planning for the park began in 2005; construction started in 2007.

The original goal for Coconino Industrial Park was development for light industrial users. Land in this area was zoned for uses such as warehousing, research and development, and distribution. Like other communities, Flagstaff was eager to attract light industrial users because such businesses tend to employ a highly educated workforce, are relatively quiet, and do not pollute the environment

Includes APA citation with author name and date

(Cohen, 2020). The city of Flagstaff recognized the need for light industrial users and widened an adjacent highway to accommodate trucks and facilitate travel by workers and customers coming from Flagstaff.

1

The park now contains 14 building complexes with over 1.25 million square feet of completed building space. The majority of the buildings are used for office, research and development, marketing and distribution, or manufacturing uses. Approximately 50 acres of the original area are yet to be developed.

Provides
specifics for
data sources

Data for this report came from a 2019 survey of over 5,000 Coconino Industrial Park employees; interviews with 15 CIP tenants and managers; the annual budget of the city of Flagstaff; county and state tax records; and current books, articles, journals, and online resources. Projections for future revenues resulted from analysis of past trends and "Estimates of Revenues for Debt Service Coverage, Redevelopment Project Area 2" (Miller, 2019, p. 79).

Uses
combination
heads

DISCUSSION: REVENUES, EMPLOYMENT, AND INDIRECT BENEFITS

Previews
organization
of report

The results of this research indicate that major direct and indirect benefits have accrued to the city of Flagstaff and surrounding metropolitan areas as a result of the development of Coconino Industrial Park. The research findings presented here fall into three categories: (a) revenues, (b) employment, and (c) indirect benefits.

Revenues

Coconino Industrial Park contributes a variety of tax and other revenues to the city of Flagstaff, as summarized in Figure 1. Current revenues are shown, along with projections to the year 2028. At a time when the economy is unstable, revenues from an industrial park such as Coconino can become a reliable income stream for the city of Flagstaff.

Places figure
close to
textual
reference

Figure 1

**REVENUES RECEIVED BY THE CITY OF FLAGSTAFF
FROM COCONINO INDUSTRIAL PARK**

Current Revenues and Projections to 2028

	2019	2028
Sales and use taxes	$1,966,021	$3,604,500
Revenues from licenses	532,802	962,410
Franchise taxes	195,682	220,424
State gas tax receipts	159,420	211,134
Licenses and permits	86,213	201,413
Other revenues	75,180	206,020
Total	$3,015,318	$5,405,901

Source: Arizona State Board of Equalization Bulletin. Phoenix: State Printing Office, 2020, p. 28.

2

Sales and Use Revenues

As shown in Figure 1, the city's largest source of revenues from CIP is the sales and use tax. Revenues from this source totaled $1,966,021 in 2016, according to figures provided by the Arizona State Board of Equalization (2020, p. 28). Sales and use taxes accounted for more than half of the park's total contribution to the total income of $3,015,318.

Other Revenues

Other major sources of city revenues from CIP in 2019 include alcohol licenses, motor vehicle in lieu fees, trailer coach licenses ($532,802), franchise taxes ($195,682), and state gas tax receipts ($159,420). Although not shown in Figure 1, other revenues may be expected from the development of recently acquired property. The U.S. Economic Development Administration has approved a grant worth $975,000 to assist in expanding the current park eastward on an undeveloped parcel purchased last year. Revenues from leasing this property may be sizable.

Projections

Total city revenues from CIP will nearly double by 2028, producing an income of $5.4 million. This estimate is based on an annual growth rate of 0.65 percent, as projected by the Bureau of Labor Statistics.

Employment

One of the most important factors to consider in the overall effect of an industrial park is employment. In Coconino Industrial Park the distribution, number, and wages of people employed will change considerably in the next six years.

Distribution

A total of 7,035 employees currently work in various industry groups at Coconino Industrial Park. The distribution of employees is shown in Figure 2. The largest number of workers (58 percent) is employed in manufacturing and assembly operations. The next largest category, computer and electronics, employs 24 percent of the workers. Some overlap probably exists because electronics assembly could be inclded in either group. Employees also work in publishing (9 percent), warehousing and storage (5 percent), and other industries (4 percent).

Although the distribution of employees at Coconino Industrial Park shows a wide range of employment categories, it must be noted that other industrial parks would likely generate an entirely different range of job categories.

Annotations (left margin):
- Continues interpreting figures in table
- Includes ample description of electronic reference
- Sets stage for next topic to be discussed

3

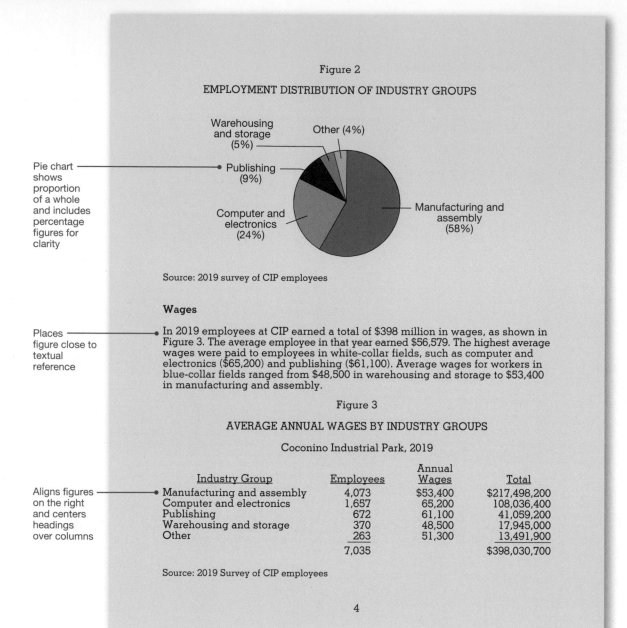

Figure 2

EMPLOYMENT DISTRIBUTION OF INDUSTRY GROUPS

Warehousing and storage (5%)

Other (4%)

Pie chart shows proportion of a whole and includes percentage figures for clarity

Publishing (9%)

Computer and electronics (24%)

Manufacturing and assembly (58%)

Source: 2019 survey of CIP employees

Wages

Places figure close to textual reference

In 2019 employees at CIP earned a total of $398 million in wages, as shown in Figure 3. The average employee in that year earned $56,579. The highest average wages were paid to employees in white-collar fields, such as computer and electronics ($65,200) and publishing ($61,100). Average wages for workers in blue-collar fields ranged from $48,500 in warehousing and storage to $53,400 in manufacturing and assembly.

Figure 3

AVERAGE ANNUAL WAGES BY INDUSTRY GROUPS

Coconino Industrial Park, 2019

Aligns figures on the right and centers headings over columns

Industry Group	Employees	Annual Wages	Total
Manufacturing and assembly	4,073	$53,400	$217,498,200
Computer and electronics	1,657	65,200	108,036,400
Publishing	672	61,100	41,059,200
Warehousing and storage	370	48,500	17,945,000
Other	263	51,300	13,491,900
	7,035		$398,030,700

Source: 2019 Survey of CIP employees

4

Projections

Clarifies information and tells what it means in relation to original research questions

By 2028 Coconino Industrial Park is expected to more than double its number of employees, bringing the total to over 15,000 workers. The total payroll in 2028 will also more than double, producing over $998 million (using constant 2016 dollars) in salaries to CIP employees. These projections are based on a 9 percent growth rate (Miller, 2019, p. 78), along with anticipated increased employment as the park reaches its capacity.

Future development in the park will influence employment and payrolls. One CIP project manager stated in an interview that much of the remaining 50 acres is planned for medium-rise office buildings, garden offices, and other structures for commercial, professional, and personal services (I. M. Novak, personal communication, November 30, 2019). Average wages for employees are expected to increase because of an anticipated shift to higher-paying white-collar jobs. Industrial parks often follow a similar pattern of evolution (Badri, Rivera, & Kusak, 2017, p. 41). Like many industrial parks, CIP evolved from a warehousing center into a manufacturing complex.

Combines conclusions and recommendations

CONCLUSIONS AND RECOMMENDATIONS

Analysis of tax revenues, employment data, personal interviews, and professional literature leads to the following conclusions and recommendations about the economic impact of Coconino Industrial Park on the city of Flagstaff:

1. Sales tax and other revenues produced over $3 million in income to the city of Flagstaff in 2019. By 2028 sales tax and other revenues are expected to produce $5.4 million in city income.

Uses a numbered list for clarity and ease of reading

2. CIP currently employs 7,035 employees, the majority of whom are working in manufacturing and assembly. The average employee in 2019 earned $56,579.

3. By 2028 CIP is expected to employ more than 15,000 workers producing a total payroll of over $998 million.

4. Employment trends indicate that by 2028 more CIP employees will be engaged in higher-paying white-collar positions.

On the basis of these findings, we recommend that the City Council of Flagstaff authorize the development of additional industrial parks to stimulate local economic growth. The direct and indirect benefits of Coconino Industrial Park strongly suggest that future commercial development would have a positive impact on the Flagstaff community and the surrounding region as population growth and resulting greater purchasing power would trigger higher demand.

As the Coconino example shows, gains in tax revenue, job creation, and other direct and indirect benefits would follow the creation of additional industrial parks in and around Flagstaff.

5

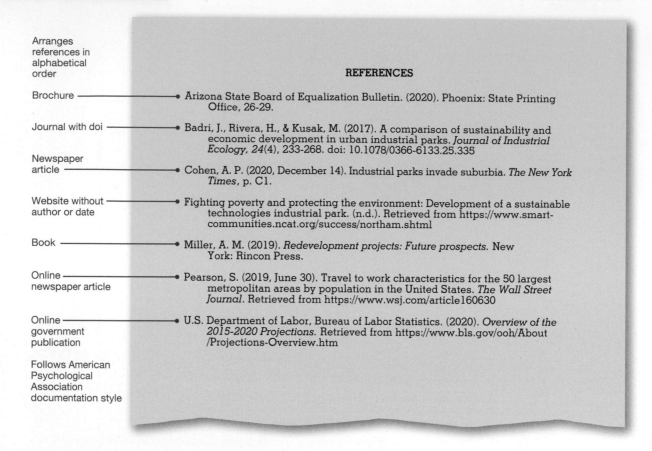

Arranges references in alphabetical order

Brochure

Journal with doi

Newspaper article

Website without author or date

Book

Online newspaper article

Online government publication

Follows American Psychological Association documentation style

REFERENCES

Arizona State Board of Equalization Bulletin. (2020). Phoenix: State Printing Office, 26-29.

Badri, J., Rivera, H., & Kusak, M. (2017). A comparison of sustainability and economic development in urban industrial parks. *Journal of Industrial Ecology, 24*(4), 233-268. doi: 10.1078/0366-6133.25.335

Cohen, A. P. (2020, December 14). Industrial parks invade suburbia. *The New York Times*, p. C1.

Fighting poverty and protecting the environment: Development of a sustainable technologies industrial park. (n.d.). Retrieved from https://www.smart-communities.ncat.org/success/northam.shtml

Miller, A. M. (2019). *Redevelopment projects: Future prospects.* New York: Rincon Press.

Pearson, S. (2019, June 30). Travel to work characteristics for the 50 largest metropolitan areas by population in the United States. *The Wall Street Journal*. Retrieved from https://www.wsj.com/article160630

U.S. Department of Labor, Bureau of Labor Statistics. (2020). *Overview of the 2015-2020 Projections.* Retrieved from https://www.bls.gov/ooh/About/Projections-Overview.htm

Checklist

Preparing Formal Business Reports

Report Process

- **Analyze the report and purpose.** Develop a problem question (*Could expanded development of the Coconino Industrial Park benefit the city of Flagstaff?*) and a purpose statement (*The purpose of this report is to investigate the expansion of Coconino Industrial Park and possible benefits accruing to the city of Flagstaff in the area of revenues, employment, and other indirect benefits*).

- **Anticipate the audience and issues.** Consider primary and secondary audiences. What do they already know? What do they need to know? Divide the major problem into subproblems for investigation.

- **Prepare a work plan.** Include problem and purpose statements, as well as a description of the sources and methods of collecting data. Prepare a tentative project outline and work schedule with anticipated dates of completion for all segments of the project.

- **Collect data.** Begin by searching secondary sources (electronic sources, books, magazines, journals, newspapers) for information on your topic. Then, if necessary, gather primary data by surveying, interviewing, observing, and experimenting.

- **Document data sources.** Establish a system for keeping track of your sources. When saving files from business databases or the Internet, be sure to record the complete publication information. Some researchers prepare electronic folders or note cards citing all references (author, date, source, page, and quotation). Select a documentation format and use it consistently.

- **Interpret and organize the data.** Arrange the collected information in tables, grids, or outlines to help you visualize relationships and interpret meanings. Organize the data into an outline (see Chapter 5).

- **Prepare graphics.** Make tables, charts, graphs, and illustrations—but only if they serve a function. Use graphics to help clarify, condense, simplify, or emphasize your data (see Chapter 11).

- **Compose the first draft.** At a computer write the first draft from your outline. Use appropriate headings as well as transitional expressions (such as *however, on the contrary*, and *in addition*) to guide the reader through the report.

- **Revise and proofread.** Revise to eliminate wordiness, ambiguity, and redundancy. Look for ways to improve readability, such as bulleted or numbered lists. Proofread three times for (a) word and content meaning; (b) grammar, punctuation, and usage errors; and (c) formatting.

- **Evaluate the product.** Examine the final report. Will it achieve its purpose? Encourage feedback so that you can learn how to improve future reports.

Report Components

- **Title page.** Balance the following lines on the title page: (a) name of the report (in all caps);

(b) name, title, and organization of the individual receiving the report; (c) author's name, title, and organization; and (d) date submitted.

- **Letter of transmittal.** Announce the report topic and explain who authorized it. Briefly describe the project and preview the conclusions if the reader is supportive. Close by expressing appreciation for the assignment, suggesting follow-up actions, acknowledging the help of others, or offering to answer questions.

- **Table of contents.** Show the number of the page where each report heading appears in the report. Connect the page numbers and headings with leaders (spaced dots) using your word processing software.

- **List of illustrations.** Include a list of tables, illustrations, or figures showing the title of the item and its page number. If space permits, put these lists on the same page with the table of contents.

- **Executive summary.** Summarize the report purpose, findings, conclusions, and recommendations. Gauge the length of the summary by the length of the report and by your organization's practices.

- **Introduction.** Explain the problem motivating the report; describe its background and

significance. Clarify the scope and limitations of the report. Optional items include a review of the relevant literature and a description of data sources, methods, and key terms. Close by previewing the report's organization.

- **Body.** Discuss, analyze, and interpret the research findings or the proposed solution to the problem. Arrange the findings in logical segments following your outline. Use clear, descriptive headings.

- **Conclusions and recommendations.** Explain what the findings mean in relation to the original problem. If requested, make enumerated recommendations that suggest actions for solving the problem.

- **Appendix(es).** Include items of interest to some, but not all, readers, such as questionnaires, transcripts of interviews, data sheets, and other information that is not essential to explain your findings, but that supports your analysis. Add large graphics—pictures, maps, figures, tables, charts, and graphs—that are not discussed directly in the text.

- **Works cited or references.** If footnotes are not provided in the text, list all references in a section called *Works Cited* or *References*.

Zooming In

Your Turn:
Applying Your Skills at SpaceX

Proposals and reports are often written in teams to accomplish serious business purposes. Both require research, and sometimes resources are unavailable. As an intern for James Gleeson, communications director at SpaceX, you have been asked to help him develop materials to fine-tune SpaceX reports and proposals. He suggests two possible tasks:

1. A short (three- to five-page) business report recommending a structured writing process to be used for team-written company documents

2. A memo evaluating two to four proposal consulting companies that might be able to help SpaceX teams write good proposals when the company's proposal specialists are unavailable

Your Task

Select one of the suggested tasks. For Task 1, in a two- or three-person team, plan the report and have each team member prepare an outline of his or her assigned section. As a team, review and improve the outlines with written comments and annotations. For Task 2, individually research, plan, and write a one- to two-page memo.

SUMMARY OF LEARNING OUTCOMES

1 Explain the importance and purpose of informal proposals and their basic components.

- Proposals are important to organizations because they generate business or funding.

- A proposal is a written offer to solve problems, provide services, or sell equipment.

- Requests for proposals (RFPs) specify what a proposal should include.

- Standard parts of informal proposals include (a) a persuasive introduction explaining the purpose of the proposal; (b) background identifying the problem and project goals; (c) a proposal, plan, or schedule outlining the project; (d) a section describing staff qualifications; (e) expected costs; and (f) a request for approval or authorization.

2 Discuss the components of formal and grant proposals.

- Formal proposals may include additional parts not found in informal proposals: (a) a copy of the RFP (request for proposals); (b) a letter of transmittal; (c) an abstract or executive summary; (d) a title page; (e) a table of contents; (f) a list of illustrations; and (g) an appendix.

- A grant proposal is a formal document submitted to a government agency or funding organization that explains a project, outlines its budget, and requests grant money that requires no repayment.

- Grants are made to charities, educational facilities, and especially nonprofits.

3 Identify the components of typical business plans.

- A business plan describes a proposed business and explains how it expects to achieve its marketing, financial, and operational goals.

- Typical business plans include a letter of transmittal, mission statement, executive summary, table of contents, company description, product or service description, market analysis, description of operations and management, financial analysis, and appendixes.

- Start-up businesses seeking financial backing must pay particular attention to the product or service description as well as the operations and management analyses. Start-ups must prove growth potential and present a team capable of implementing the business plan.

4 **Describe how the components of the front matter in formal business reports support the purpose of the report.**

- In a formal report, the author analyzes findings, draws conclusions, and makes recommendations intended to solve a problem.

- The front matter may include a cover, title page, letter or memo of transmittal, table of contents, list of illustrations, and an executive summary that explains key points.

- In the introduction the writer typically discusses the significance, scope, and organization of the report as well as its authorization, relevant literature, sources, methods of research, and definitions of key terms.

5 **Explain how the body and back matter of formal business reports serve the purpose of the report.**

- The body of the report discusses, analyzes, interprets, and evaluates the research findings or solution to a problem.

- The conclusion states what the findings mean and how they relate to the report's purpose.

- The recommendations explain how to solve the report problem.

- The last portions of a formal report are the appendix(es) and references or works cited.

6 **Specify final writing tips that aid authors of formal business reports.**

- Before writing, develop a realistic timetable and collect all necessary data.

- While writing, work from a good outline, compose in a quiet environment, and use the features of your computer wisely.

- Remember that some writers like to write rapidly, intending to revise later; other writers prefer a more deliberate writing style, perfecting their prose as they go.

- As you write, use verb tenses consistently and generally avoid *I* and *we*.

- After completing the first draft, wait a few days before you edit to improve clarity, coherence, and conciseness; proofread the final copy three times.

Key Terms

proposal *455*
request for proposals (RFP) *455*
letter proposals *456*
cognitive webbing *458*
deliverables *459*
budget *459*
formal proposal *460*
letter of transmittal *460*
abstract *460*

executive summary *460*
title page *460*
table of contents *460*
list of illustrations *460*
appendix *460*
grant proposal *461*
business plan *462*
mission statement *463*
formal report *465*

memorandum of transmittal *466*
body *468*
appendixes *469*
MLA *469*
Works Cited *469*
APA *469*
References *469*
contract cheating *484*

Critical Thinking

1. Why are highly capable grant writers among the most sought-after professionals today? What activities does their work entail? (L.O. 2)

2. Is it true that business reports shouldn't contain footnotes? If you were writing your first business report and did considerable research, what would you do about documenting your sources? (L.O. 5)

3. If you were to read credible reports showing that streaming (think films and gaming) is very bad for the environment because the growing electricity needs of

huge data centers are nearly exhausting power production, would you change your behavior? Why or why not? (L.O. 5, 6)

4. If you were about to launch a new business, would you write your business plan from scratch or use a software program? What are the pros and cons of each method? (L.O. 3)

5. **Ethical Issue:** Plagiarism detection software such as Turnitin makes cheating by copying easy to spot. This explains why ghostwritten assignments are booming

online. The old paper mills have morphed into global enterprises and brazenly market their services in slick YouTube videos but also offline. Students cite time pressure and stress as reasons for resorting to contract cheating. Some rationalize buying written-to-order papers online by falling back on the old saw that "everyone is doing it." In a recent NPR story, a student made this argument: "Technically, I don't think it's cheating. Because you're paying someone to write an essay, which they don't plagiarize, and they write everything on their own." When pressed, the student acknowledged that perhaps it's "a difficult question to answer," verging on "a gray area" or being "on the edge, kind of."[19] What is your take on this type of growing academic dishonesty? Is it really common?

Activities

13.1 Proposal: Never too Soon to Plan for Retirement (L.O. 1)

As a financially savvy business student, you know about the magic of compound interest. Conventional wisdom and Suze Orman tell us that college grads will have a tidy sum as seniors if they start socking away for retirement even a small sum each month and letting it grow in stock mutual funds for three to five decades.

Unlike you, few of your peers worry about retirement savings; they are busy looking for a good job fresh out of college. Now, imagine you are working for a small but growing construction company. Your boss insists he can't afford to offer an IRA or 401(k) plan to you and the other ten employees. You do some digging and find that providing a SIMPLE IRA (Savings Incentive Match Plan for Employees Individual Retirement Account) would generate tax savings for your boss's small company, not to mention give you a head start on investing in mutual funds.

YOUR TASK Search for articles that explain SIMPLE IRA rules. Check out the Department of Treasury, Internal Revenue Service website. Once you are well informed about the plan, think through your persuasive strategy. What arguments are most likely to sway your boss? Write a memo proposal to your boss (use your current supervisor's or your instructor's name) arguing for the benefits of introducing a SIMPLE IRA. Apply what you have learned about unsolicited informal proposals in this chapter.

13.2 Proposal: Be a Problem Solver at Work (L.O. 1)

Most managers welcome workers who are able to spot problems before they turn into serious risks. Drawing on your internship and work experience, can you identify a problem that could be solved with a small to moderate financial investment? Look for issues such as a lack of lunch or break rooms for staff; badly needed health initiatives such as gyms or sport club memberships; replacing low-gas-mileage, high-emission company vehicles; or introducing a recycling program.

YOUR TASK Discuss with your instructor the workplace problem you have identified. Make sure you choose a relatively weighty problem that can be lessened or eliminated with a minor expenditure. Be sure to include a cost–benefit analysis. Address your unsolicited letter or memo proposal to your current or former boss and copy your instructor.

13.3 Proposal: Are You a Tycoon in the Making? (L.O. 1)

Web

Perhaps you have fantasized about one day owning your own company, or maybe you have already started a business. Proposals are offers to a very specific audience whose business you are soliciting. Think of a product or service that you like or know something about. Search the Internet or research databases, and study the market so that you understand going rates, prices, and costs. Search the Small Business Administration's website for valuable tips on how to launch and manage a business.

YOUR TASK Choose a product or service you would like to offer to a particular audience, such as a dating consulting service, a window cleaning business, a bakery specializing in your favorite cakes, an online photography business, a distributor of e-bikes, or a new specialized hair care line. Discuss products and services as well as target audiences with your instructor. Write an informal letter proposal promoting your chosen product or service.

13.4 Proposal: Helping a Friend Find Examples to Study (L.O. 1, 2)

Web

Many new companies with services or products to offer would like to land corporate or government contracts. However, they are intimidated by the proposal and RFP processes. Your friend Joselyn, who has started her own designer uniform company, has asked you for help. Her goal is to offer her colorful yet functional uniforms to hospitals and clinics. Before writing a proposal, however, she wants to see examples and learn more about the process.

YOUR TASK Search the Internet to find at least two examples of business proposals. Try search terms such as *small business proposals* or *small business proposal examples*. Don't waste time on sites that want to sell templates or books. Find actual examples. Then prepare a memo to Joselyn in which you do the following:

a. Identify two sample business proposals.

b. Outline the parts of each proposal.

c. Compare the strengths and weaknesses of each proposal.

d. Draw conclusions. What can Joselyn learn from these examples?

13.5 Proposal: Pitching Ortopedica Sports Medicine (L.O. 1)

`Team`

Sports medicine is increasingly popular, especially in university towns. A new medical clinic, Ortopedica Sports Medicine, is opening its doors in your community. A friend recommended your small business to the administrator of the clinic, and you received a letter asking you to provide information about your service. The new medical clinic specializes in sports medicine, physical therapy, and cardiac rehabilitation services. It is interested in retaining your company, rather than hiring its own employees to perform the service your company offers.

YOUR TASK Working in teams, first decide what service you offer. It could be landscaping, uniforms, uniform laundering, general cleaning, a cloud-based storage system, online medical supplies, patient transportation, supplemental hospice care, temporary office support, social media guidance, or food service. As a team, develop a letter proposal outlining your plan, staffing, and budget. Use persuasion to show why contracting your services is better than hiring in-house employees. In the proposal letter, request a meeting with the administrative board. In addition to a written proposal, you may be expected to make an oral presentation that includes visual aids and/or handouts. Send your proposal to Dr. Sven Rasmussen, Director, Ortopedica Sports Medicine. Supply a local address.

13.6 Grant Writing: Nonprofits' Lifeblood (L.O. 1, 2)

`Web`

Nonprofit organizations are always seeking grant writers, and you would like to gain experience in this area. You've heard that they earn high salaries, and one day you might even decide to become a professional grant/proposal writer. However, you first need experience. You saw a website by The Actors Theatre Workshop advertising for a grant writer to "seek funding for general operating expenses and program-related funding." A grant writer would "develop proposals, generate boilerplates for future applications, and oversee a writing team." This listing sounds good, but you need a local position.

YOUR TASK Search the Internet for local nonprofits. Alternatively, your instructor may already know of local groups seeking grant writers, such as a United Way member agency, an educational institution, or a faith-based organization. Perhaps your university maintains a service-learning or experiential learning program. Talk with your instructor about an assignment. Your instructor may ask you to submit a preliminary memo report outlining ten or more guidelines you expect to follow when writing proposals and grants for nonprofit organizations.

13.7 Service Learning: Better Your Community! (L.O. 1, 2, 4, and 5)

`E-Mail` `Web`

Your school may be one that encourages service learning, a form of experiential learning. You could receive credit for a project that bridges academic and nonacademic communities. Because writing skills are in wide demand, you may have an opportunity to simultaneously apply your skills, contribute to the community, and expand your résumé. The National Service-Learning Clearinghouse describes service learning as "a teaching and learning strategy that integrates meaningful community service with instruction and reflection to enrich the learning experience, teach civic responsibility, and strengthen communities."[20] The Internet offers many sites devoted to examples of students engaging in service-learning projects.

YOUR TASK Research possible service-learning projects in this class or another. Your instructor may ask you to submit a memo or e-mail message analyzing your findings. Describe at least four completed service-learning projects that you found on the Web. Draw conclusions about what made them successful or beneficial. What kinds of similar projects might be possible for you or students in your class? Your instructor may use this as a research project or turn it into a hands-on project by having you find a service organization in your community that needs trained writers.

13.8 Business Plans: Examining Mission Statements (L.O. 3)

`E-Mail`

Large and small businesses develop mission statements to explain their purposes. Some statements are excellent; others, less so.

YOUR TASK Analyze the following selection of Fortune 500 company descriptions and mission statements.[21] In a class discussion or an e-mail to your instructor, (a) list four goals of mission statements (see Figure 13.2), (b) list five questions to be answered in preparing mission statements, (c) explain which of the following statements fulfill the goals of winning mission statements discussed in Figure 13.2, and (d) tell how the following statements could be improved.

Company	Mission Statement
1. The BMW Group is the world's leading provider of premium products and premium services for individual mobility. The BMW brand stands for one thing: sheer driving pleasure.	Sporting and dynamic performance combined with superb design and exclusive quality.
2. Dunkin' (formerly Dunkin' Donuts) is an American multinational coffeehouse and donut company.	Make and serve the freshest, most delicious coffee and donuts quickly and courteously in modern, well-merchandised stores.
3. Eaton Corporation supplies parts for fluid power, electrical systems, automobiles, and trucks.	We are committed to attracting, developing, and keeping a diverse workforce that reflects the nature of our global business.
4. Graybar Electric Company acquires, stores, and distributes electrical, data, and communication components such as wire, cable, and lighting products.	We are a vital link in the supply chain, adding value with efficient and cost-effective service and solutions for our customers and our suppliers.
5. Harley-Davidson, Inc., manufactures motorcycles with more than 32 models of touring and custom Harleys plus motorcycle accessories, motorcycle clothing apparel, and engines.	We fulfill dreams through the experience of motorcycling, by providing to motorcyclists and to the general public an expanding line of motorcycles and branded products and services in selected market segments.
6. IBM provides computer hardware such as mainframes, servers, storage systems, printing systems, and semiconductors, as well as software related to business integration, networking, operating systems, systems management, and so forth.	To lead in the creation, development, and manufacture of the industry's most advanced information technologies, including computer systems, software, networking systems, storage devices, and microelectronics. And our worldwide network of IBM solutions and services professionals translates these advanced technologies into business value for our customers. We translate these advanced technologies into value for our customers through our professional solutions, services and consulting businesses worldwide.

13.9 Business Plan: Baby Sharks, Get Ready for the Shark Tank (L.O. 3)

Team | Web

Business plans at many schools are more than classroom writing exercises. They have won regional, national, and worldwide prizes. Although some contests are part of MBA programs, other contests are available for undergraduates. As part of a business plan project, you and your team are challenged to come up with an idea for a new business or service. For example, you might want to offer a lunch service with fresh sandwiches or salads delivered to office workers' desks. You might propose building a better website for an organization. You might want to start a document preparation business that offers production, editing, and printing services. You might have a terrific idea for an existing business to expand with a new product or service.

YOUR TASK Working in teams, explore entrepreneurial ventures based on your experience and expertise.

Conduct team meetings to decide on a product or service, develop a work plan, assign responsibilities, and create a schedule. Your goal is to write a business plan that will convince potential investors (sometimes your own management) that you have an excellent business idea and that you can pull it off. Check out sample business plans on the Internet. The two deliverables from your project will be your written business plan and an oral presentation. Your written plan should include a cover, transmittal document (letter or memo), title page, table of contents, executive summary, proposal (including introduction, body, and conclusion), appendix items, glossary (optional), and sources. In the body of the document, be sure to explain your mission and vision, the market, your marketing strategy, operations, and financials. Address your business plan to your instructor.

* A complete instructional module for this activity is available at the instructor premium website. Under the tab Teaching Modules, click Business Plan.

13.10 Executive Summary: In a Nutshell, Boil it Down 10 Percent (L.O. 2, 5)

Communication Technology | **E-Mail** | **Web**

Being able to distill information quickly and accurately is an important study skill. Academic, peer-reviewed articles provide you with an abstract, but an abstract just gives you a *general* idea whether the article is worth skimming or reading. An executive summary of a business report, however, is a document that—while concise—should provide enough information to allow executives to act on it without necessarily having to read every word of the report. If you are asked to summarize a news article, for example, you need to provide the gist of it to the reader who then ought to be able to clearly understand the original without having to read it.

As a rule of thumb, executive summaries tend to be nutshell versions, boiled down to approximately 10 percent, of the original. A 100-page report might result in an executive summary of up to ten pages. If the report has five sections, the executive summary needs to address each of these sections, too. Think of the executive summary as a miniature version of the original document, following the structure but leaving out details, examples, and other supporting information. Another benefit of being able to summarize skillfully is that you verify your understanding of the concepts in your reading. If you can't summarize the original accurately from memory, in your own words, you probably need to reread it to understand it better.

YOUR TASK To practice the important skill of summarizing, pick a substantial news analysis or feature article in a reputable business publication, i.e., *The Wall Street Journal, The Economist, Bloomberg Businessweek, Money, Forbes, The Financial Times*, or the business sections of big U.S. dailies (e.g., *The New York Times, The Washington Post*, or *U.S. News & World Report*). Choose an article of length and substance, at least 2,000 words long. Tip: If you access the article in a research database, a word count will be provided for you. Write an executive summary, retaining the basic structure of the original, choosing precise, specific words for conciseness, while omitting details and examples that only serve as supporting evidence or explanation. Do not distort the meaning or inject your own opinion. Your summary can be up to 200 words long, i.e., two short paragraphs. Provide the source and other citation information for your instructor with an introductory statement such as *As you requested, I am submitting this executive summary of . . . .* Submit your executive summary as a memo, e-mail, or discussion board post, following your instructor's directions.

13.11 Unsolicited Proposal: Cash Infusion Needed (L.O. 1)

Team

Let's say you are a member of a campus business club, such as the Society for the Advancement of Management (SAM), the American Marketing Association (AMA), the American Management Association (AMA), the Accounting Society (AS), the Finance Association (FA), or the Association of Information Technology Professionals (AITP). Your organization has managed its finances well, and therefore, it is able to fund monthly activities. However, membership dues are insufficient to cover any extras. Identify a need such as a hardware or software purchase, a special one-time event that would benefit a great number of students, or officer training and travel to a national conference.

YOUR TASK Request one-time funding to cover what you need by writing an unsolicited letter or memo proposal to your assistant dean, who oversees student business clubs. Identify your need or problem, show the benefit of your request, support your claims with evidence, and provide a budget (if necessary).

13.12 Unsolicited Proposal: Protecting Gadgets in the Dorm (L.O. 1, 2)

Team | **Web**

As an enterprising college student, you recognized a problem as soon as you arrived on campus. Dorm rooms filled with pricey digital doodads were very attractive to thieves. Some students move in with more than $3,000 in gear, including laptops, tablets, flat-screen TVs, digital cameras, video game consoles, smartphones, and piles of other digital delights. You solved the problem by buying an extra-large steel footlocker in which to stash your valuables. However, shipping the footlocker was expensive (nearly $100), and you had to wait for it to arrive from a catalog company. Your bright idea is to propose to the Associated Student Organization (ASO) that it allow you to offer these steel footlockers to students at a reduced price and with campus delivery. Your footlocker, which you found by searching the Internet, is extremely durable and works great as a coffee table, nightstand, or card table. It comes with a smooth interior liner and two compartments.

YOUR TASK Working individually or with a team, imagine that you have made arrangements with a manufacturer to act as an intermediary selling footlockers on your campus at a reduced price. Search the Internet for manufacturers and make up your own figures. How can you get the ASO's permission to proceed? Give that organization a cut? For books and supplies, for example, campus book-stores like a 25-percent margin. Use your imagination in deciding how this plan might work on a college campus. Then prepare an unsolicited proposal to your ASO. Outline the problem and your goals of protecting students' valuables and providing convenience. Scour the Internet for statistics regarding on-campus burglaries. Such figures should help you develop one or more persuasive hooks. Then explain your proposal, project possible sales, discuss a timetable, and describe your staffing. Submit your proposal to Anthony Johnson, president, Associated Student Organization.

13.13 Formal Business Report: Planning an International Launch (L.O. 4–6)

Intercultural / **Team** / **Web**

U.S. businesses are expanding into foreign markets with manufacturing plants, sales offices, and branches abroad. Many Americans, however, have little knowledge of or experience with people from other cultures. To prepare for participation in the global marketplace, you are to collect information for a report focused on an Asian, Latin American, European, or African country where English is not regularly spoken. Before selecting the country, though, consult your campus international student program for volunteers who are willing to be interviewed. Your instructor may make advance arrangements with international student volunteers.

YOUR TASK In teams of three to five, collect information about your target country from research databases, the Internet, and other sources. Then invite an international student representing your target country to be interviewed by your group. Alternatively, you could interview a faculty member who hails from another country. Prepare and know your interview questions and be courteous; people like to talk about themselves, but no one wants to waste time.

As you conduct primary and secondary research, investigate the topics listed in Figure 13.4. Confirm what you learn in your secondary research by talking with your interviewee. When you complete your research, write a report for the CEO of your company (make up a name and company). Assume that your company plans to expand its operations abroad. Your report should advise the company's executives of the social customs, family life, attitudes, religions, education, and values of the target country. Remember that your company's interests are business oriented; do not dwell on tourist information. Write your report individually or in teams.

13.14 Proposals, Business Plans, and Formal Reports: Find Topics to Write About (L.O. 1–6)

Team / **Web**

A list of more than 100 report topics is available at the accompanying student site. The topics are divided into the following categories: accounting, finance, personnel/human resources, marketing, information systems, management, and general business/education/campus issues. You can collect information for many of these reports by using electronic databases and the Internet. Your instructor may assign them as individual or team projects. All involve critical thinking in organizing information, drawing conclusions, and making recommendations. The topics are appropriate for proposals, business plans, and formal business reports. Also, a number of self-contained report activities that require no additional research are provided at the end of Chapter 12.

YOUR TASK As directed by your instructor, select a topic from the report list at the accompanying student site.

| **FIGURE 13.4** | Intercultural Interview Topics and Questions |

Social Customs

- How do people react to strangers? Are they generally friendly? Hostile? Reserved?

- How do people greet each other?

- What are the appropriate manners when you enter a room? Bow? Nod? The COVID-19 pandemic has all but nixed handshaking.

- How are names used for introductions? Is it appropriate to inquire about one's occupation or family?

- What are the attitudes toward touching?

- How does one express appreciation for an invitation to another's home? Bring a gift? Send flowers? Write a thank-you note? Are any gifts taboo?

- Are there any customs related to how or where one sits?

- Are any facial expressions or gestures considered rude?

- What is the attitude toward punctuality in social situations? In business situations?

- What are acceptable eye contact patterns?

- What gestures indicate agreement? Disagreement?

Family Life

- What is the basic unit of social organization? Basic family? Extended family?

- Do women work outside of the home? In what occupations?

FIGURE 13.4 *Continued*

Housing, Clothing, and Food

- Are there differences in the kinds of housing used by different social groups? Differences in location? Differences in furnishings?
- What occasions require special clothing?
- Are some types of clothing considered taboo?
- What is appropriate business attire for men? For women?
- How many times a day do people eat? What are some of the staples, i.e., typical foods?
- What types of places, food, and drink are appropriate for business entertainment? Where is the seat of honor at a table?

Class Structure

- Into what classes is society organized?
- Do racial, religious, or economic factors determine social status?
- Are there any minority groups? What is their social standing?

Political Patterns

- Are there any immediate threats to the political survival of the country?
- How is political power manifested?
- What channels are used for expressing political opinions?
- What information media are important?
- Is it appropriate to talk politics in social situations?

Religion and Folk Beliefs

- To which religious groups do people belong? Is one predominant?

- Do religious beliefs influence daily activities?
- Which places are considered sacred? Which objects? Which events?
- How do religious holidays affect business activities?

Economic Institutions

- What are the country's principal products?
- Are workers organized in unions?
- How are businesses owned? By family units? By large public corporations? By the government?
- What is the standard work schedule?
- Is it appropriate to do business by telephone? By computer?
- How has technology affected business procedures?
- Is participatory management used?
- Are there any customs related to exchanging business cards?
- How is status shown in an organization? Private office? Secretary? Furniture?
- Are businesspeople expected to socialize before conducting business?

Value Systems

- Is competitiveness or cooperation more prized?
- Is thrift or enjoyment of the moment more valued?
- Is politeness more important than honesty?
- What are the attitudes toward education?
- Do women own or manage businesses? If so, how are they treated?
- What are your people's perceptions of Americans? Do Americans offend you? What has been hardest for you to adjust to in the United States? How could Americans make this adjustment easier for you?

Test Your Workplace Etiquette IQ

New communication platforms and casual workplace environments have blurred the lines of appropriateness, leaving workers wondering how to navigate uncharted waters. Check your workplace etiquette IQ by deciding whether the following statements are true or false. Then see if you agree with the responses on p. Key-6.

1. In your office you rarely drink the coffee or eat the pastries that are often available. Although everyone is expected to contribute to these office treats, you are justified in refusing because you seldom partake of the

goodies and you feel that it is not your obligation to support the snacking habits of others.

_____ True _____ False

2. Office casual means you can be comfortable and wear your Saturday clothes to work.

_____ True _____ False

3. If a group of businesspeople is approaching a door, the first male should hold the door for any woman in the group.

_____ True _____ False

Chat About It

In each chapter you will find five discussion questions related to the chapter material. Your instructor may assign these topics for you to discuss in class, in an online chat room, or on a discussion board. Some of the discussion topics may require outside research. You may also be asked to read and respond to postings made by your classmates.

TOPIC 1: Should companies take a stand on controversial topics of the day or remain as neutral as possible? Do you make any buying decisions based on how a company or brand is expressing support for causes that are dear to you? Would an endorsement by Katy Perry, Avril Lavigne, or Sean "Diddy" Combs make a difference in your purchases?

TOPIC 2: What category of proposal, solicited or unsolicited, is more likely to succeed, and why?

TOPIC 3: Why do experts refer to a business plan as a living document? Some have said that a business plan needs constant review and adjustment. What might account for such a short shelf life?

TOPIC 4: Discuss the pros and cons of the following two methods for completing the outline of the executive summary of a formal report: (a) cutting and pasting existing report sentences, or (b) creating new sentences.

TOPIC 5: Is it ethical for a student team to substantially revise a report from a team that wrote about the same topic during the previous semester? What does your school say about such a practice?

Grammar and Mechanics Review 13

Total Review

Each of the following sentences has **three** errors in grammar, punctuation, capitalization, usage, or spelling. On a separate sheet, write a correct version. Avoid adding new phrases, starting new sentences, or rewriting in your own words. When finished, compare your responses with the key at the end of the book.

EXAMPLE: During the Winter I will enroll in Management, English composition, and Accounting.

REVISION: During the **winter** I will enroll in **management**, English composition, and **accounting**.

1. If you face writers block you should review your 3 main reasons for writing.

2. Our Manager and CEO both worked on the thirty page proposal. Which was due immediately.

3. Supervisors in 2 departments' complained that there departments should have been consulted.

4. The RFP and it's attachments arrived to late for my manager and I to complete the necessary research.

5. Although we worked everyday on the proposal, we felt badly that we could not meet the May 15th deadline.

6. Daryl had 3 Interviews, and in each one he was asked to demonstrate his critical thinking, and communication skills.

7. Although short a successful mission statement should capture your businesses goals and values. In a few succinct sentences.

8. A proposal budget cannot be changed if costs raise later, consequently, it must be written careful.

9. Entrepreneur Stephanie Rivera publisher of a urban event callendar, relies on social media to broadcast her message.

10. Stephanie asked Jake and myself to help her write a business plan. That would guide her new company and garner perminent funding.

LEARNING OUTCOMES

After studying this chapter, you should be able to do the following:

1 Discuss two important first steps in preparing for business presentations.

2 Explain how to organize your business presentation and design contemporary visual aids to build audience rapport.

3 Create a memorable error-free multimedia presentation that shows a firm grasp of basic visual design principles.

4 Describe delivery techniques for use before, during, and after a presentation to keep the audience engaged.

5 Organize presentations for intercultural audiences and in teams.

6 List techniques for improving telephone skills to project a positive image.

Jean-luc Doumont: A Globe-Trotting Engineer Teaches Speaking Skills

Hooking an audience and capturing its attention is crucial to effective presentations. To do so, presenters must be clear, understandable, and engaging from the onset, says Belgium-based Jean-luc Doumont. An engineer with a PhD in physics from Stanford University, Doumont teaches presentation skills at institutions and businesses across the globe. One of his core beliefs is that presenters must be aware of the difference between the "what," or information the speaker will provide, and the "so what," the message that explains why the audience should care about that information. Being audience-centered makes a presentation about the audience, not the speaker. "Show respect for the audience and don't waste their time," Doumont says.[1]

Doumont divides presentation preparation into five steps. *Planning* defines the presentation's purpose and audience as well as any time and space constraints. *Designing* concentrates on developing content with an introduction, body, and conclusion. An introduction must go beyond the attention-grabbing hook and preview three to five main points that will be discussed later. The body should contain support for these points and smooth transitions between them. The talk should conclude by recapping key points and then reminding the audience of the main take-away.

The *creating slides* step is optional, Doumont says. "Do your slides right . . . or don't do slides at all," he advises.[2] Limit each slide to one message that you make verbally. *Delivering* the presentation is key to its success. Doumont considers delivery a performance that requires practice. He recommends against reciting an entire presentation from memory to avoid sounding canned. Instead, he suggests memorizing an outline and recreating the words spoken during practice sessions to sound extemporaneous. Look at everyone in the audience, move from behind the podium, and make deliberate gestures. Project confidence by controlling your body.

Some speakers consider the last element of delivering effective presentations intimidating. *Answering questions*, however, is essential to a successful presentation. Be honest, and remain calm and professional. Repeat or rephrase the question while addressing the answer to the entire audience. By following these steps and remembering your audience at all times, you will give your listeners what they need to act on the information you have delivered.[3]

Critical Thinking

- Why is being audience-centric and focusing on the purpose crucial to successful business presentations?

- Why does Jean-luc Doumont say, "Do your slides right . . . or don't do them at all"?

- How can you build rapport with your audience?

14-1 Creating Effective Business Presentations

LEARNING OUTCOME

1 Discuss two important first steps in preparing for business presentations.

It's called **glossophobia** by experts and means fear of public speaking. Many of us suffer bouts of intense anxiety at the prospect of having to speak or present in front of an audience. We admire public personalities such as Tony Robbins, Earvin "Magic" Johnson, Suze Orman, Oprah Winfrey, or best-selling author Malcolm Gladwell, who speak in front of multitudes with apparent ease. Don't be fooled. As you will see, making a business presentation look seamless requires many hours of intense preparation and practice.

At some point all businesspeople have to inform others or sell an idea. Such informative and persuasive presentations are often conveyed in person and involve audiences of various sizes. The good news is that you can conquer the fear of public speaking and hone your skills with instruction and practice. Following the tips provided by Jean-luc Doumont and provided in this chapter will help you improve your presentation skills. Good speakers are made, not born.

14-1a Speaking Skills and Your Career

The savviest future businesspeople take advantage of opportunities in college to develop their speaking skills. As you have seen in Chapters 1 and 2, social and emotional skills play an important role in a successful career: Interpreting information through speaking, listening, and observing are part of the skill set that will robot-proof your career.[4] In one much-cited survey, 39 percent of managers found new graduates lacking in public speaking; 46 percent would like to see better overall communication skills.[5] Speaking skills are useful at every career stage. You might, for example, have to make a sales pitch before customers, speak to a professional gathering, or describe your company's expansion plans to your banker.

When you are in the job market, remember that speaking skills rank high on recruiters' wish lists. According to an annual survey of career services professionals, almost 70 percent of the respondents named verbal communication as a key attribute they seek in an applicant's résumé; being well-spoken ranks among the top ten employability skills.[6] A Harris poll for presentation software service Prezi revealed that 70 percent of professionals who give presentations consider them "critical to their success at work."[7] Professionals with public speaking skills are well compensated. Top executives, media relations managers, trade relations managers, or PR specialists command average base salaries of $530,500 a year.[8]

This chapter prepares you to use speaking skills in making professional oral presentations, whether alone or as part of a team, whether face-to-face or virtually. Before we dive into the specifics of how to become an excellent presenter, the following section addresses the types of business presentations you may encounter in your career.

Reality Check

Public Speaking: A Career-Critical Skill

"Poor presentation skills mean that leaders fail to inspire their teams, products fail to sell, entrepreneurs fail to attract funding, and careers fail to soar. That seems like a big price to pay for neglecting such a basic skill that anyone can improve upon."[9]

—Carmine Gallo, communication coach, keynote speaker, author

FIGURE 14.1   Types of Business Presentations

Briefing
- Overview or summary of an issue, proposal, or problem
- Delivery of information, discussion of questions, collection of feedback

Report
- Oral equivalent of business reports and proposals
- Informational or persuasive oral account, simple or elaborate

Podcast
- Audio recording distributed by app or on a website
- Opportunity to launch products, introduce and train employees, and sell products and services

Virtual Presentation
- Collaboration facilitated by technology (smartphone app or Web application)
- Real-time meeting online with remote colleagues

Webinar
- Web-based presentation, lecture, workshop, or seminar
- Digital transmission with or without video to train employees, interact with customers, or promote products

14-1b Understanding Presentation Types

A common part of a business professional's life is making presentations. Some presentations are informative, whereas others are persuasive. Some are face-to-face; others, virtual. Some are performed before big audiences, whereas others are given to smaller groups. Some presentations are elaborate; others are simple. Figure 14.1 shows a sampling of business presentations you may encounter in your career.

14-1c Knowing Your Purpose

Regardless of the type of presentation, you must prepare carefully to ensure that it is effective. The most important part of your preparation is deciding what you want to accomplish. Do you want to sell a health-care program to a prospective client? Do you want to persuade management to increase the social media marketing budget? Whether your goal is to persuade or to inform, you must have a clear idea of where you are going. At the end of your presentation, what do you want your listeners to remember or do?

Sheri Valdez, a loan officer at Credit Federation, faced such questions as she planned a talk for a class in small business management. Sheri's former business professor had asked her to return to campus and give the class advice about borrowing money from banks to start new businesses. Because Sheri knew so much about this topic, she found it difficult to extract a specific purpose statement for her presentation. After much thought she narrowed her purpose to this: *To inform potential entrepreneurs about three important factors that loan officers consider before granting start-up loans to launch small businesses.* Her entire presentation focused on ensuring that the class members understood and remembered three principal ideas.

14-1d Knowing Your Audience

As in any type of communication, a second key element in preparation is analyzing your audience, anticipating the reactions of audience members, and adjusting to their needs if necessary. Audiences may fall into four categories, as summarized in Figure 14.2. By anticipating your audience, you have a better idea of how to organize your presentation. A friendly audience, for example, will respond to humor and personal experiences. A hostile audience requires an even, controlled delivery style with objective data and expert opinion. Whatever type of audience you will face, remember to plan your presentation so that it focuses on audience benefits. People in your audience will want to know what's in it for them.

Other elements, such as age, gender, education level, experience, and the size of the audience, will affect your style and message. Analyze the following questions to determine your organizational pattern, delivery style, and supporting material.

- How will this topic appeal to this audience?
- How can I relate this information to my listeners' needs?
- How can I earn respect so that they accept my message?
- What would be most effective in making my point? Facts? Statistics? Personal experiences? Expert opinion? Humor? Cartoons? Graphic illustrations? Demonstrations? Case histories? Analogies?
- What measures must I take to ensure that this audience remembers my main points?

If you have agreed to speak to an audience with which you are unfamiliar, ask for the names of a half-dozen people who will be in the audience. Contact them and learn about their backgrounds and expectations for the presentation. This information can help you answer questions about what they want to hear and how deeply you should explore the subject. You will want to thank these people when you start your talk. Doing this kind of homework will impress the audience.

Reality Check

Telling Stories to Engage

"Engaging your audience can mean telling stories with which people can identify, using illustrations or exercises that engage all their senses, asking rhetorical questions, using 'you' rather than 'I' phrasing, polling the audience for their opinion, telling hero stories about audience members, and so forth."[10]

—Dianna Booher, communication consultant and author

FIGURE 14.2   Succeeding With Four Audience Types

Audience Members	Organizational Pattern	Delivery Style	Supporting Material
Friendly			
They like you and your topic.	Use any pattern. Try something new. Involve the audience.	Be warm, pleasant, and open. Use eye contact and smiles.	Include humor, personal examples, and experiences.
Neutral			
They are calm, rational; their minds are made up, but they think they are objective.	Present both sides of the issue. Use pro/con or problem/solution patterns. Save time for audience questions.	Be controlled. Do nothing showy. Use confident, small gestures.	Use facts, statistics, expert opinion, and comparison and contrast. Avoid humor, personal stories, and flashy visuals.
Uninterested			
They have short attention spans; they may be there against their will.	Be brief—include no more than three points. Avoid topical and pro/con patterns that seem lengthy to the audience.	Be dynamic and entertaining. Move around. Use large gestures.	Use humor, cartoons, colorful visuals, powerful quotations, and startling statistics.
CAUTION! Avoid darkening the room, standing motionless, providing handouts, using dull visuals, or asking the audience to participate.			
Hostile			
They want to take charge or to ridicule the speaker; they may be defensive, emotional.	Organize using a noncontroversial pattern, such as a topical, chronological, or geographical strategy.	Be calm and controlled. Speak evenly and slowly.	Include objective data and expert opinion. Avoid anecdotes and humor.
CAUTION! Avoid a question-and-answer period, if possible; otherwise, use a moderator or accept only written questions.			

LEARNING OUTCOME

2 Explain how to organize your business presentation and design contemporary visual aids to build audience rapport.

14-2 Organizing Content and Using Visual Aids to Connect With Audiences

After determining your purpose and analyzing the audience, you are ready to collect information and organize it logically. Good organization and intentional repetition are the two most powerful keys to audience comprehension and retention. In fact, many speech experts recommend the following admittedly repetitious, but effective, plan:

- **Step 1:** Tell them what you are going to tell them.
- **Step 2:** Tell them.
- **Step 3:** Tell them what you have told them.

In other words, repeat your main points in the introduction, body, and conclusion of your presentation. Although it is redundant, this strategy is necessary in oral presentations. Let's examine how to construct the three parts of an effective presentation: introduction, body, and conclusion.

14-2a Capturing Attention in the Introduction

How many times have you heard a speaker begin with *It's a pleasure to be here*, or *I'm honored to be asked to speak*, or the all-too-common *Today I'm going to talk about . . . .* Boring openings such as these get speakers off to a dull start. Avoid such banalities by striving to accomplish three goals in the introduction to your presentation:

- Capture listeners' attention and get them involved.
- Identify yourself and establish your credibility.
- Preview your main points.

If you are able to appeal to listeners and involve them in your presentation right from the start, you are more likely to hold their attention until the finish. Consider some of the same techniques that you used to open sales letters: a question, a startling fact, a joke, a story, or a quotation. Some speakers achieve involvement by opening with a question or command that requires audience members to raise their hands or stand up. Additional techniques to gain and keep audience attention are presented in the accompanying Career Coach box.

Career Coach

Gaining and Keeping Audience Attention

Experienced speakers know how to capture the attention of an audience and how to maintain that attention throughout a presentation. You can spruce up your presentations by trying these twelve proven techniques.

- **A promise**. Begin with a realistic promise that keeps the audience expectant (for example, *By the end of this presentation, you will know how you can increase your sales by 50 percent!*).
- **Drama**. Open by telling an emotionally moving story or by describing a serious problem that involves the audience. Throughout your talk include other dramatic elements, such as a long pause after a key statement. Change your vocal tone or pitch. Professionals use high-intensity emotions such as anger, joy, sadness, and excitement.
- **Eye contact**. As you begin, command attention by surveying the entire audience to take in all listeners. Give yourself two to five seconds to linger on individuals to avoid fleeting, unconvincing eye contact. Don't just sweep the room and the crowd.
- **Movement**. Leave the lectern area whenever possible. Walk around the conference table or down the aisles of the presentation room. Try to move toward your audience, especially at the beginning and end of your talk.
- **Questions**. Keep listeners active and involved with rhetorical questions. Ask for a show of hands to get each listener thinking. The response will also give you a quick gauge of audience attention.
- **Demonstrations**. Include a member of the audience in a demonstration (for example, *I'm going to show you exactly how to implement our four-step customer courtesy process, but I need a volunteer from the audience to help me*).
- **Samples/props**. If you are promoting a product, consider using items to toss out to the audience or to award as prizes to volunteers. You can also pass around product samples or promotional literature. Be careful, though, to maintain control.
- **Visuals**. Give your audience something to look at besides yourself. Use a variety of visual aids in a single session. Also consider writing the concerns expressed by audience members on a flipchart or on a whiteboard or Smart Board as you go along.
- **Attire**. Enhance your credibility with your audience by dressing professionally for your presentation. Professional attire will help you look competent and qualified, making your audience more likely to listen and take you seriously.
- **Current events/statistics**. Mention a current event or statistic (the more startling, the better) that is relevant to your topic and to which the audience can relate.
- **A quote**. Quotations, especially those made by well-known individuals, can be powerful attention-getting devices. The quotation should be pertinent to your topic, short, and interesting.
- **Self-interest**. Review your entire presentation to ensure that it meets the critical *What's-in-it-for-me* audience test. Remember that people are most interested in things that benefit them.

To establish your credibility, you need to describe your position, knowledge, education, or experience—whatever qualifies you to speak. The way you dress, the self-confidence you display, and your direct eye contact can also build credibility. In addition, try to connect with your audience. Listeners respond particularly well to speakers who reveal something of themselves and identify with them. A consultant addressing office workers might reminisce about how she started as an administrative assistant; a CEO might tell a funny story in which the joke is on him. With American audiences, use humor if you can pull it off (not everyone can); self-effacing humor may work best.

After capturing your audience's attention and effectively establishing your credibility, you will want to preview the main points of your topic, perhaps with a visual aid.

Take a look at Sheri Valdez's introduction, shown in Model Document 14.1, to see how she integrated all the elements necessary for a good opening.

14-2b Organizing the Body of the Presentation

The most effective oral presentations focus on a few principal ideas. Therefore, the body of your short presentation (20 minutes or shorter) should include a limited number of main points—say, two to four. Develop each main point with adequate, but not excessive, explanation and details. Too many details can obscure the main message, so keep your presentation simple and logical. Remember, listeners have no pages to refer to should they become confused.

When Sheri Valdez began planning her presentation, she realized immediately that she could talk for hours on her topic. She also knew that listeners are not good at separating major and minor points. Therefore, instead of drowning her listeners in information, she sorted out a few main ideas. In the banking industry, loan officers generally ask the following three questions of each budding entrepreneur: (a) Are you ready to hit the ground running in starting your business? (b) Have you done your homework? and (c) Have you made realistic projections of sales, cash flow, and equity investment? These questions would become her main points, but Sheri wanted to streamline them further so that her audience would be sure to remember them. She encapsulated the questions in three words: *experience, preparation*, and *projection*. As you can see in Model Document 14.1, Sheri prepared a sentence outline showing these three main ideas. Each is supported by examples and explanations.

How to organize and sequence main ideas may not be immediately obvious when you begin working on a presentation. The following methods, which review and amplify those discussed in Chapter 12, provide many possible strategies and examples to help you organize a presentation:

- **Chronology**. A presentation describing the history of a problem, organized from the first sign of trouble to the present.
- **Geography/space**. A presentation about the changing diversity of the workforce, organized by regions in the country (East Coast, West Coast, and so forth).
- **Topic/function/conventional grouping**. A presentation discussing on-time performance, organized by names of airlines.
- **Comparison/contrast (pro/con)**. A presentation comparing e-marketing with traditional direct mail.
- **Journalistic pattern (the six Ws)**. A presentation describing the prevention of identity theft and how to recover after identity thieves strike. Organized by *who, what, when, where, why*, and *how*.
- **Value/size**. A presentation describing fluctuations in housing costs, organized by home prices.
- **Importance**. A presentation describing five reasons a company should move its headquarters to a specific city, organized from the most important reason to the least important.
- **Problem/solution**. A presentation offering a solution to a problem of declining sales, such as reducing staff.
- **Simple/complex**. A presentation explaining genetic modification of plants such as corn, organized from simple seed production to complex gene introduction.

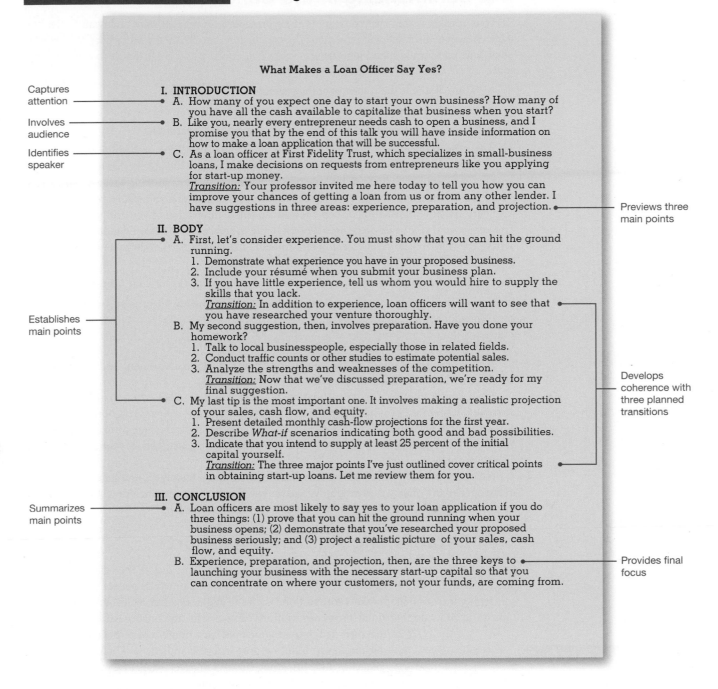

What Makes a Loan Officer Say Yes?

Captures attention

Involves audience

Identifies speaker

I. INTRODUCTION
  A. How many of you expect one day to start your own business? How many of you have all the cash available to capitalize that business when you start?
  B. Like you, nearly every entrepreneur needs cash to open a business, and I promise you that by the end of this talk you will have inside information on how to make a loan application that will be successful.
  C. As a loan officer at First Fidelity Trust, which specializes in small-business loans, I make decisions on requests from entrepreneurs like you applying for start-up money.
      Transition: Your professor invited me here today to tell you how you can improve your chances of getting a loan from us or from any other lender. I have suggestions in three areas: experience, preparation, and projection.

Previews three main points

II. BODY
  A. First, let's consider experience. You must show that you can hit the ground running.
      1. Demonstrate what experience you have in your proposed business.
      2. Include your résumé when you submit your business plan.
      3. If you have little experience, tell us whom you would hire to supply the skills that you lack.
          Transition: In addition to experience, loan officers will want to see that you have researched your venture thoroughly.
  B. My second suggestion, then, involves preparation. Have you done your homework?
      1. Talk to local businesspeople, especially those in related fields.
      2. Conduct traffic counts or other studies to estimate potential sales.
      3. Analyze the strengths and weaknesses of the competition.
          Transition: Now that we've discussed preparation, we're ready for my final suggestion.
  C. My last tip is the most important one. It involves making a realistic projection of your sales, cash flow, and equity.
      1. Present detailed monthly cash-flow projections for the first year.
      2. Describe *What-if* scenarios indicating both good and bad possibilities.
      3. Indicate that you intend to supply at least 25 percent of the initial capital yourself.
          Transition: The three major points I've just outlined cover critical points in obtaining start-up loans. Let me review them for you.

Establishes main points

Develops coherence with three planned transitions

Summarizes main points

III. CONCLUSION
  A. Loan officers are most likely to say yes to your loan application if you do three things: (1) prove that you can hit the ground running when your business opens; (2) demonstrate that you've researched your proposed business seriously; and (3) project a realistic picture of your sales, cash flow, and equity.
  B. Experience, preparation, and projection, then, are the three keys to launching your business with the necessary start-up capital so that you can concentrate on where your customers, not your funds, are coming from.

Provides final focus

- **Best case/worst case**. A presentation analyzing whether two companies should merge, organized by the best-case result (improved market share, profitability, employee morale) as opposed to the worst-case result (devalued stock, lost market share, poor morale).

In the presentation shown in Model Document 14.1, Sheri arranged the main points by importance, placing the most important point last where she believes it has maximum effect. When organizing any presentation, prepare a little more material than you think you will actually need. Savvy speakers always have something useful in reserve such as an extra handout, slide, or idea—just in case they finish early. At the same time, most speakers go about 25 percent over the time they spent practicing at home in front of the mirror. If your speaking time is limited, as it usually is in your classes, aim for less than the limit when rehearsing, so that you don't take time away from the next presenters.

14-2c Summarizing in the Conclusion

Nervous speakers often rush to wrap up their presentations because they can't wait to flee the stage. However, listeners will remember the conclusion more than any other part of a speech. That's why you should spend some time to make it as effective as you can. Strive to achieve three goals:

- Summarize the main themes of the presentation.
- Leave the audience with a specific and memorable take-away.
- Include a statement that allows you to exit the podium gracefully.

A conclusion is like a punch line and must stand out. Think of it as the high point of your presentation, a valuable kernel of information to take away. The valuable kernel of information, or take-away, should tie in with the opening or present a forward-looking idea. Avoid merely rehashing, in the same words, what you said before, but ensure that you will leave the audience with very specific information or benefits and a positive impression of you and your company. The take-away is the value of the presentation to the audience and the benefit audience members believe they have received. The tension that you built in the early parts of the talk now culminates in the close. Compare these poor and improved conclusions:

Poor conclusion: Well, I guess that's about all I have to say. Thanks for your time.

Improved: In bringing my presentation to a close, I will restate my major purpose . . . .

Improved: In summary, my major purpose has been to . . . .

Improved: In conclusion, let me review my three major points. They are . . . .

Notice how Sheri Valdez, in the conclusion shown in Model Document 14.1, summarized her three main points and provided a final focus to listeners.

If you are promoting a recommendation, you might end as follows: *In conclusion, I recommend that we retain Envoy Marketing to conduct a telemarketing campaign beginning September 1 at a cost of X dollars. To do so, I suggest that we (a) finance this campaign from our operations budget, (b) develop a persuasive message describing our new product, and (c) name Lucia Roy to oversee the project.*

In your conclusion you could use an anecdote, an inspiring quotation, or a statement that ties in the opener and offers a new insight. Whatever you choose, be sure to include a closing thought that indicates you are finished without having to say lamely, *That's it!*

14-2d Establishing Audience Rapport

Excellent speakers are skilled at building audience rapport. This means they establish a connection with the audience, creating a harmonious relationship in which people feel they have something in common. Speakers form a bond with the audience, often entertaining as well as informing. How do they do it? From observations of successful and unsuccessful speakers, we have learned that the good ones use a number of verbal and nonverbal techniques to build rapport with the audiences. Their helpful techniques include providing effective imagery, supplying verbal signposts, and using body language strategically.

Effective Imagery. You will lose your audience quickly if you fill your talk with abstractions, generalities, and dry facts. To enliven your presentation and enhance comprehension, try using some of the techniques shown in Figure 14.3. However, beware of exaggeration or distortion. Keep your imagery realistic and credible.

Verbal Signposts. Speakers must remember that listeners, unlike readers of a report, cannot control the rate of presentation or read back through pages to review main points. As a result, listeners get lost easily. Knowledgeable speakers help the audience recognize the organization and main points in an oral message with verbal signposts.

FIGURE 14.3 Effective Imagery Engages the Audience

Metaphor	**Comparison between dissimilar things without the words *like* or *as***
	• Our competitor's CEO is a snake when it comes to negotiating. • My desk is a garbage dump.

Analogy	**Comparison of similar traits between dissimilar things**
	• Product development is similar to conceiving, carrying, and delivering a baby. • Downsizing is comparable to an overweight person's regimen of dieting and exercising.

Personalized Statistics	**Statistics that affect the audience**
	• Look around you. Only three out of five graduates will find a job right after graduation. • One typical meal at a fast food restaurant contains all the calories you need for an entire day.

Worst- or Best-Case Scenario	**The worst or best that could happen**
	• If we don't back up now, a crash could wipe out all customer data. • If we fix the system now, we can expand our customer files and also increase sales.

Personal Anecdote	**A personal story**
	• Let me share a few personal blunders online and what I learned from my mistakes. • I always worried about my pets while I was away. That's when I decided to start a pet hotel.

Simile	**Comparison that includes the words *like* or *as***
	• Our critics used our report like a drunk uses a lamppost—for support rather than illumination. • She's as happy as someone who just won the lottery.

They keep listeners on track by including helpful previews, summaries, and transitions such as these:

- **Previewing**
  The next segment of my talk presents three reasons for . . . .
  Let's now consider the causes of . . . .

- **Summarizing**
  Let me review with you the major problems I have just discussed . . . .
  You see, then, that the most significant factors are . . . .

- **Switching directions**
  Thus far we have talked solely about . . . ; now let's move to . . . .
  I have argued that . . . and . . . , but an alternate view holds that . . . .

You can further improve any oral presentation by including appropriate transitional expressions such as *first, second, next, then, therefore, moreover, on the other hand, on the contrary,* and *in conclusion.* These transitional expressions, which you learned about in Chapter 5 (see Figure 5.5), build coherence, lend emphasis, and tell listeners where you are headed. Notice in Sheri Valdez's outline in Model Document 14.1 the specific transitional elements designed to help listeners recognize each new principal point.

Nonverbal Messages. Although what you say is most important, the nonverbal messages you send can also have a powerful effect on how well your audience receives your message. How you look, how you move, and how you speak can make or break your presentation. The following suggestions focus on nonverbal tips to ensure that your verbal message resonates with your audience.

- **Look terrific!** Like it or not, you will be judged by your appearance. For everything but small in-house presentations, be sure you dress professionally. The rule of thumb is that you should dress at least as well as the best-dressed person in the audience.

- **Animate your body.** Be enthusiastic and let your body show it. Stand with good posture to show confidence. Emphasize ideas to enhance points about size, number, and direction. Use a variety of gestures, but, if you want them to look natural, don't plan them in advance.

- **Punctuate your words.** You can keep your audience interested by varying your tone, volume, pitch, and pace. Use pauses before and after important points. Allow the audience to take in your ideas.

- **Get out from behind the podium.** Avoid standing rigidly behind a podium. Movement makes you look natural and comfortable, unless you pace nervously. You might pick a few places in the room to walk to calmly. Even if you must stay close to your visual aids, make a point of leaving them occasionally so that the audience can see your whole body.

- **Vary your facial expression.** Begin with a smile, but change your expressions to correspond with the thoughts you are voicing. You can shake your head to show disagreement, roll your eyes to show disdain, look heavenward for guidance, or wrinkle your brow to show concern or dismay. This advice to be an animated speaker applies to most North American audiences. Later you will learn to adapt your presentation style to intercultural audiences who may be accustomed to a more measured delivery.

Whenever possible, beginning presenters should have an experienced speaker watch them and give them tips as they rehearse. Your instructor is an important coach who can provide you with invaluable feedback. In the absence of helpers, record yourself and watch your nonverbal behavior on camera. Are you doing what it takes to build rapport?

14-2e Understanding Contemporary Visual Aids

Before you make a business presentation, consider this wise proverb: "Tell me, I forget. Show me, I remember. Involve me, I understand." Your goals as a speaker are to make listeners understand, remember, and act on your ideas. To get them interested and involved, include effective visual aids. Some experts claim that we acquire 85 percent of all our knowledge visually: "Professionals everywhere need to know about the incredible inefficiency of text-based information and the incredible effects of images," says developmental molecular biologist John Medina, who urges readers to "toss your PowerPoint presentations."[12] Information conveyed in images is more memorable than text alone; scientists call this phenomenon **pictorial superiority**.[13] Therefore, an oral presentation that incorporates effective visual aids is far more likely to be understood and retained than one lacking a visual component.

Good visual aids serve many purposes. They emphasize and clarify main points, thus improving comprehension and retention. They increase audience interest, and they make the presenter appear more professional, better prepared, and more persuasive. Well-designed visual aids illustrate and emphasize your message more effectively than words alone; therefore, they may help shorten a meeting or achieve your goal faster. Visual aids are particularly helpful for inexperienced speakers because the audience concentrates on the visual aid rather than on the speaker. However, experienced speakers work hard at not being eclipsed or upstaged by their slideshows. Good visual aids also serve to jog the memory of a speaker, thus improving self-confidence, poise, and delivery.

Types of Visual Aids. Speakers have many forms of visual media at their fingertips if they wish to enhance their presentations. Figure 14.4 describes the pros and cons of a number of visual aids, both high-tech and low-tech, that can guide you in selecting the best one for any

FIGURE 14.4 Pros and Cons of Visual Aid Options

Media: High Tech	Pros	Cons
Multimedia slides	Create professional appearance with many color, art, graphic, and font options. Allow users to incorporate video, audio, and hyperlinks. Offer ease of use and transport via removable storage media, Web download, or e-mail attachment. Are inexpensive to update.	Present potential incompatibility issues. Require costly projection equipment and practice for smooth delivery. Tempt user to include razzle-dazzle features that may fail to add value. Can be too one-dimensional and linear.
Zoom presentations	Enable presenter to zoom in on and out of content to show the big picture or specific details in nonlinear, 3D quality. Provide attractive templates. Allow users to insert rich media. Offer an interactive, cinematic, and dynamic experience.	Require Internet access because they are cloud based. Don't allow editing of images. Offer limited font choices. Can be difficult to operate for some presenters used to individual slides; can make moving around the canvas challenging. Zooming can be distracting and even nauseating.
Video	Gives an accurate representation of the content; strongly indicates forethought and preparation.	Creates potential for compatibility issues related to computer video formats. Is generally expensive to create and update.
Media: Low Tech		
Handouts	Encourage audience participation. Are easy to maintain and update. Enhance recall because audience keeps reference material.	Increase risk of unauthorized duplication of speaker's material. Can be difficult to transport. May cause speaker to lose audience's attention.
Flipcharts or whiteboards	Provide inexpensive option available at most sites. Enable users to (a) create, (b) modify or customize on the spot, (c) record comments from the audience, and (d) combine with more high-tech visuals in the same presentation.	Require graphics talent. Can be difficult for larger audiences to see. Can be cumbersome to transport. Easily wear with use.
Props	Offer a realistic reinforcement of message content. Increase audience participation with close observation.	Lead to extra work and expense in transporting and replacing worn objects. Are of limited use with larger audiences.

speaking occasion. Two of the most popular visuals for business presentations are multimedia slides and handouts. Zoom presentations, an alternative to multimedia slides, are also growing in popularity.

Multimedia Slides. With today's excellent slide presentation software—such as Microsoft PowerPoint, Apple Keynote, Google Slides, and many other fine cloud-based presentation apps—you can create or enhance dynamic, colorful presentations with your desktop, laptop, tablet, or smartphone. The most popular alternatives to PowerPoint are Keynote, Prezi, Canva, LibreOffice, Google Slides, and WPS Office Free. The output from these programs is generally shown on a computer screen, a smart TV, an LCD (liquid crystal display) or LED (light emitting diode display), and a projection screen.

With a little expertise and minimal equipment, you can create multimedia presentations that include audio, video, images, animation, and hyperlinks, as described shortly in the discussion of multimedia presentations. Multimedia slides can also be created by cloud-based apps that are either free with limited functionality or require a tiered subscription as software as a service (SaaS) applications. MS PowerPoint, too, is now in the cloud as part of Office 365. Check whether your college has an education license with the big software companies, e.g., Microsoft and Adobe. You might be able to use their latest apps free of charge while you are a student.

Handouts. You can enrich and complement your presentations by distributing pictures, outlines, brochures, articles, charts, summaries, or other supplements. Speakers who use presentation software often prepare a set of their slides along with notes to hand out to viewers. Timing the distribution of any handout, though, is tricky. To avoid distractions and to keep control, announce and discuss handouts during the presentation, but delay distributing them until after you finish.

Prezi Zoom Presentations. Many business presenters feel limited by multimedia slides, which tend to be linear. As a result, some communicators prefer more dynamic visual aids. Using software such as Prezi, a cloud-based presentation and storytelling tool, they work with a single large canvas that enables the speaker to zoom in on and out of text blocks or images to help the audience understand and remember content, details, and relationships. Prezi zoom presentations allow presenters to communicate their ideas in a more exciting, creative way. Audience members also seem to appreciate the cinematic, interactive quality of these presentations. Figure 14.5 shows what a typical Prezi canvas looks like during the design process. Hyatt, TED, Vodafone, and Avon are just a few among the many businesses that have adopted the software. Prezi the company claims to support more than 100 million users.

| FIGURE 14.5 | Prezi Canvas |

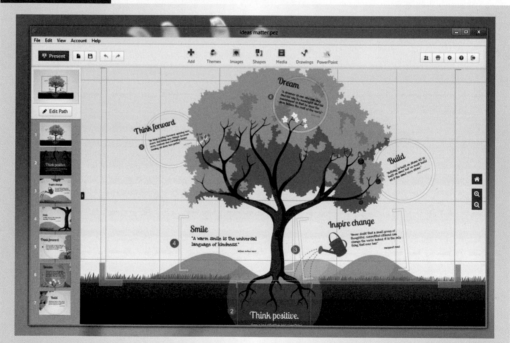

Prezi uses one canvas for a presentation rather than individual slides arranged in a linear fashion. Here is an example of the main canvas of a zoom presentation. Clicking on any section of this canvas will zoom in on detailed information. For example, if you click on the area around the tree roots, you will zoom in on a quote about thinking positively, as shown in the thumbnail images in the left pane.

Source: http://prezi-a.akamaihd.net/presskit/Prezi%20Desktop/PreziDesktop_Windows.png

Moving Beyond Bullet Points. Slideshows created using PowerPoint in particular are a staple of business presentations. However, overuse or misuse may be the downside of the ever-present PowerPoint slideshow. Over more than three decades of the software program's existence, millions of poorly created and badly delivered presentations have tarnished PowerPoint's reputation as an effective communication tool. Of course, tools are helpful only when used properly.

More than a decade ago, several communication experts set out to show businesspeople how they can move beyond bullet points to avoid "chartjunk" and "PowerPoint Phluff." The experts recommended creating slideshows that tell a story and send a simple, yet powerful message with less text and more images.[14] Presentation guru Garr Reynolds urges readers to unleash their creativity: "Do not rely on technology or other people to make your choices. Most of all, do not let mere habit—and the habits of others—dictate your decisions on how to prepare, design, and ultimately deliver your presentations."[15]

However, not all content—think complex financial or technical data—is equally suitable to being presented in images, as attractive as such slideshows may be. Communication consultant Nancy Duarte believes that such data don't belong on slides in the first place but should be provided on handouts. In her classic book *Slide:ology*, she too advocates for simplicity and clarity.

Expect a learning curve if you are new to presentation programs. Even much-touted alternatives to PowerPoint, such as Prezi, Canva, and Google Slides, require some knowledge of the solid design principles covered in the next section. Figure 14.6 shows some of the tools that Canva provides to create a visually rich presentation. The goal is to abandon boring bulleted lists.

FIGURE 14.6 Canva Presentation

Like most applications today, the basic version of Canva is a free cloud-based presentation software. Like PowerPoint, it allows users to create slides, but it takes the emphasis off bullet points. Canva's strength is in offering appealing slide templates, ready-made customizable graphic design elements, and many tools to help users create visually rich slides and social media graphics, such as eye-catching YouTube thumbnails, Instagram stories, or Facebook covers.

Source: Canva

LEARNING OUTCOME

3 Create a memorable
error-free multimedia
presentation that shows a
firm grasp of basic visual
design principles.

14-3 Preparing Engaging Multimedia Presentations

When operated by proficient designers and skillful presenters, PowerPoint, Keynote, or Prezi can add visual impact to any presentation. In the sections that follow, you will learn to create an impressive multimedia presentation with the most widely used presentation software program, PowerPoint. You will also learn about Prezi zoom presentations as an alternative to PowerPoint slides. With any software program, of course, gaining expertise requires an investment of time and effort. You could take a course, or you could teach yourself through an online tutorial. Another way to master PowerPoint or Prezi is to read a book such as Doug Lowe's *PowerPoint for Dummies* or take an online tutorial on the Prezi website. YouTube and LinkedIn-owned Lynda learning site offer many free presentation tips and tricks.

14-3a Applying the 3-x-3 Writing Process to Multimedia Presentations

Some presenters prefer to create their visuals first and then develop the narrative around their visuals. Others prefer to prepare their content first and then create the visual component. The risk associated with the first approach is that you may be tempted to spend too much time making your visuals look good and not enough time preparing your content. Remember that great-looking slides never compensate for thin content.

The following sections explain how to adjust your visuals to the situation and your audience. We review the three phases of the writing process and show how they can help you develop a visually appealing PowerPoint, Keynote, Canva, or Prezi presentation. In the first phase (prewriting), you analyze, anticipate, and adapt. In the second phase, you research, organize, compose, and design. In the third phase, you edit, proofread, and evaluate.

14-3b Analyzing the Situation and Purpose

Making the best design choices for your presentation depends greatly on your analysis of the situation and the purpose of your slideshow. Will your slides be used during a live presentation? Will they be part of a self-running presentation such as in a store kiosk? Will they be saved on a server so that users can watch the presentation online at their convenience? Will they be sent as a PowerPoint show or a PDF slide deck to a client instead of a hard-copy report? Will your presentation mainly run on smartphones or tablets?

If you are e-mailing the presentation or posting it online as a self-contained file or slide deck, it should feature more text than one that you would deliver orally. If, on the other hand, you are creating slides for a live presentation, you will likely rely more on images than on text.

14-3c Adjusting Slide Design to Your Audience

Think about how you can design your presentation to get the most positive response from your audience. Audiences respond, for example, to the colors, images, and special effects you use. Primary ideas are generally best conveyed with bold colors such as blue, green, and purple. Because the messages that colors convey can vary from culture to culture, presenters must choose colors and other design elements carefully.

The Meaning of Color. In the United States, blue is the color of credibility, tranquility, conservatism, and trust. Therefore, it is the background color of choice for many business presentations and social media sites. Green relates to interaction, growth, money, and stability. It can work well as a background or an accent color. Purple can also work as a background or accent color. It conveys spirituality, royalty, dreams, and humor.[16] As for text, adjust the color to provide high contrast so that it is readable. White or yellow, for example, usually works well on dark backgrounds.

Adapt the slide colors based on where you will give the presentation. Use light text on a dark background for presentations in darkened rooms. Use dark text on a light background for presentations in lighted rooms. Avoid using a dark font on a dark background, such as red text on a dark blue background. In the same way, avoid using a light font on a light background, such as white text on a pale blue background.

The Power of Images.

Adapt the amount of text on your slide to how your audience will use the slides. The traditional guideline for slide design is to follow the **6-x-6 rule**: "Six bullets per screen, max; six words per bullet, max."[17] You may find, however, that breaking this rule is sometimes necessary, particularly when your users will be viewing the presentation on their own with no speaker assistance. For most purposes, though, strive to break free from bulleted lists whenever possible and minimize the use of text.

When using presentation software such as PowerPoint, try to avoid long, boring bulleted lists. You can alter layouts by repositioning, resizing, or changing the fonts for the placeholders in which your title, bulleted list, organization chart, video clip, photograph, or other elements appear. Figure 14.7 shows how to make your slides visually more appealing and memorable even with relatively small changes. The advice illustrated here comes from communication consultant Carmine Gallo.[18]

Notice that the bulleted items on the Before Revision slide in Figure 14.7 are not parallel. The wording looks as if the author had been brainstorming or freewriting a first draft. The first and the last bullet points are needlessly long; the first two bullets repeat "Great presenters." On the After Revision slide, the former bullets almost serve as captions that accompany illustrations. Notice that the captions are short and well within the 6-x-6 rule, although they are complete sentences. The illustrations in the revised slide add interest and highlight the message. You may use icons and stock photos that you download from the Internet for personal or school use without penalty, or consider taking your own digital pictures.

You can also use other PowerPoint features, such as SmartArt, to add variety and pizzazz to your slides. Converting pure text and bullet points to graphics, charts, and other images will keep your audience interested and help them retain the information you are presenting. The newer versions of PowerPoint now offer helpful design assistance, converting bullets into more attractive slides.

FIGURE 14.7   Using Images and Illustrations for Greater Impact

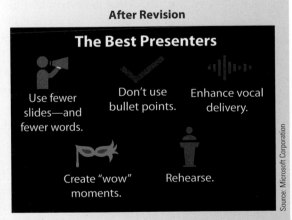

Source: Microsoft Corporation

The slide on the left contains bullet points that are not parallel. Two unnecessarily repeat "Great presenters." The first and the last bullets are needlessly long. The contrast of white on gray is poor. In the revised slide, the title avoids the overused word "great." The short sentences begin with a verb for parallelism and an emphasis on action. The icons add interest.

The Impact of Special Effects.   Just as you anticipate audience members' reactions to color, you can usually anticipate their reactions to special effects. Using animation and sound effects—flying objects, swirling text, clashing cymbals, and the like—only because they are available is not a good idea. Special effects distract your audience, drawing attention away from your main points. You should add animation features only if doing so helps convey your message or adds interest to the content. When your audience members leave, they should be commenting on the ideas you conveyed—not on the wild swivels and sound effects. The zooming effect of Prezi presentations can add value to your presentation as long as it helps your audience understand connections and remember content. The motion should not make your listeners dizzy, however.

14-3d Building Your Business Presentation

After considering design principles and their effects, you are ready to start putting together your presentation. In this section you will learn how to organize and compose your presentation, which templates to choose, and how to edit, proofread, and evaluate your work.

Organizing Your Presentation.   When you prepare your presentation, translate the major headings in your outline into titles for slides. Then build bullet points using short phrases. In Chapters 5 and 6 you learned to improve readability by using document design techniques including bullets, lists, and headings. In preparing a PowerPoint, Keynote, or Prezi presentation, you will use those same techniques.

The slides (or canvas) you create to accompany your spoken ideas can be organized with visual elements that will help your audience understand and remember what you want to communicate. Let's say, for example, that you have three points in your presentation. You can create a blueprint slide that captures the three points in a visually appealing way, and then you can use that slide several times throughout your presentation. Near the beginning, the blueprint slide provides an overview of your points. Later, it provides transitions as you move from point to point. For transitions, you can direct your audience's attention by highlighting the next point you will be talking about. Finally, the blueprint slide can be used near the end to provide a review of your key points.

Composing Your Presentation.   During the composition stage, many users fall into the trap of excessive formatting and programming. They waste precious time fine-tuning their slides or canvas and don't spend enough time on what they are going to say and how they will say it. To avoid this trap, set a limit for how much time you will spend making your slides or canvas visually appealing. Your time limit will be based on how many "bells and whistles" (a) your audience expects and (b) your content requires to make it understandable.

Remember that not every point and not every thought requires a visual. In fact, it's smart to switch off the presentation occasionally and direct the focus to yourself. Darkening the screen while you discuss a point, tell a story, give an example, or involve the audience will add variety to your presentation.

Create a slide or canvas only if it accomplishes at least one of the following purposes:

- Generates interest in what you are saying and helps the audience follow your ideas
- Highlights points you want your audience to remember
- Introduces or reviews your key points
- Provides a transition from one major point to the next
- Illustrates and simplifies complex ideas

Consider perusing the Help articles built into your presentation software, purchasing one of many inexpensive guides to electronic slide presentations, or learning from online teaching manuals and tips. Your presentations will be more appealing, and you will save time if you know, for example, how to design with master slides and how to create your own templates. In a later section of this chapter, you will find very specific steps to follow as you create your presentation.

Working With Templates.   All presentation programs require you to (a) select or create a template that will serve as the background for your presentation and (b) make each individual slide by selecting a layout that best conveys your message. Novice and even advanced users often use existing templates because they are designed by professionals who know how to combine harmonious colors, borders, bullet styles, and fonts for pleasing visual effects. If you prefer, you can alter existing templates so they better suit your needs. Adding a corporate logo, adjusting the color scheme to better match the colors used on your organization's website, or selecting a different font are just some of the ways you can customize existing templates. One big advantage of templates is that they get you started quickly.

Be careful, though, of what one expert calls visual clichés.[19] Overused templates and clip art that come preinstalled with PowerPoint, Canva, and Prezi can weary viewers who have seen them repeatedly in presentations. Instead of using a standard template, search for *PowerPoint template*, *Keynote template*, or *Prezi template* in your favorite search tool. You will see hundreds of templates available as free downloads. Unless your employer requires that presentations all have the same look, your audience will appreciate fresh templates that complement the purpose of your presentation and provide visual variety.

Revising and Proofreading Your Presentation.   Use the PowerPoint slide sorter view to rearrange, insert, and delete slides during the revision process. You can use the Prezi editor to make any necessary changes to your canvas. This is the time to focus on making your presentation as clear and concise as possible. If you are listing items, be sure they all use parallel grammatical form. Figure 14.8 shows how to revise a PowerPoint slide to improve it for conciseness, parallelism, and other features. Study the design tips described in the first slide and determine which suggestions the author did not follow. Then compare it with the revised slide.

As you are revising, check carefully to find spelling, grammar, punctuation, and other errors. Use the PowerPoint, Keynote, or Prezi spell-check feature, but don't rely on it solely. Careful proofing, preferably from a printed copy of the slideshow, is a must. Nothing is as embarrassing as projecting errors on a huge screen in front of an audience. Also, check for consistency in how you capitalize and punctuate points throughout the presentation.

Evaluating Your Presentation.   The final stage in applying the 3-x-3 writing process to developing a PowerPoint, Keynote, Canva, or Prezi presentation involves evaluation. Is your message presented in a visually appealing way? Have you tested your slides on the equipment and in the room you will be using during your presentation? Do the colors you selected work in this new setting? Are the font styles and sizes readable from the back of the room? Figure 14.9 shows examples of PowerPoint slides that incorporate what you have learned in this discussion.

FIGURE 14.8   Designing More Effective Slides

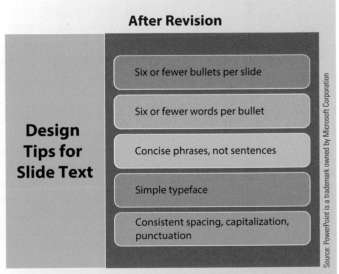

The slide on the left uses a difficult-to-read font style on a busy background. In addition, the slide includes too many words per bullet and violates most of the slide-making rules it covers. After revision, the slide on the right provides an appealing color combination, uses short phrases in a readable font style, and creates an attractive list using PowerPoint design features.

FIGURE 14.9 **PowerPoint Slides That Illustrate Multimedia Presentations**

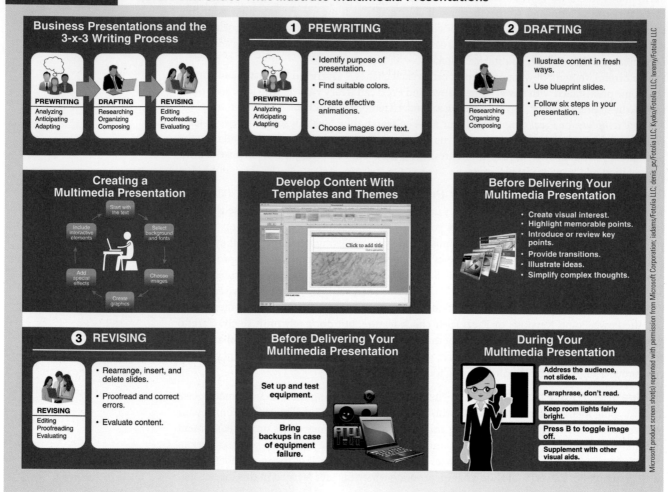

The blue background and the matching hues in the slideshow shown in Figure 14.9 are standard choices for many business presentations. With an unobtrusive dark background, white fonts are a good option for maximum contrast and, hence, readability. The creator of the presentation varied the slide design to break the monotony of bulleted or numbered lists. Images and sparsely animated diagrams add interest and zing to the slides.

14-3e Preparing and Anticipating

Solid preparation and anticipating your talk are crucial. One expert, Carmine Gallo, advises presenters to put in "the hours of deliberate practice that will make them shine." He cites famous speakers, such as Martin Luther King, Jr., who "have put in the time to go from good to great."[20] Solid preparation will boost your confidence. Allow plenty of time before your presentation to set up and test your equipment. Confirm that the places you plan to stand are not in the line of the projected image. Audience members don't appreciate having part of the slide displayed on your body. Make sure that all video or Web links are working and that you know how to operate all features the first time you try.

No matter how much time you put into preshow setup and testing, you still have no guarantee that all will go smoothly. Therefore, always bring backups of your presentation. Transferring your presentation to a USB flash drive that could run from any available computer might prove useful. Copying your digital file to the cloud (e.g., Dropbox or Google Drive) or sending it to yourself as an e-mail attachment is also a good strategy, as long as you can be sure you will have Internet access. If all fails, handouts of your presentation provide good substitutes as well.

Some presenters allow their PowerPoint slides, Keynote slides, or Prezi canvases to upstage them. Advertising mogul David Ogilvy once observed, "Most people use PowerPoint like a drunk uses a lamppost—for support rather than for illumination."[21] Although multimedia presentations can supply terrific sizzle, they cannot replace the steak. In developing a presentation, don't expect your visuals to carry the show. You can avoid being upstaged by not relying totally on your slides or canvas. Remember that you are still the main attraction!

14-3f Seven Steps to a Powerful Multimedia Presentation

We have now discussed many suggestions for making effective PowerPoint, Keynote, and Prezi presentations, but you may still be wondering how to put it all together. Figure 14.10 presents a step-by-step process for creating a powerful multimedia presentation:

FIGURE 14.10   Seven Steps to a Powerful Multimedia Presentation

1   Start with the text.

What do you want your audience to believe, do, or remember? Organize your ideas into an outline with major and minor points.

2   Select background and fonts.

Choose a template or create your own. Focus on consistent font styles, sizes, colors, and backgrounds. Try to use no more than two font styles in your presentation. The point size should be between 24 and 36, and title fonts should be larger than text font.

3   Choose images that help communicate your message.

Use relevant clip art, infographics, photographs, maps, or drawings to illustrate ideas. Access Microsoft Office 365 from within PowerPoint and choose from thousands of images and photographs, most of which are in the public domain and require no copyright permissions. Before using images from other sources, determine whether permission from the copyright holder is required. Canva, Prezi, and other apps also offer these features.

4   Create graphics.

When possible, transform boring bulleted items into appealing graphics and charts. PowerPoint's SmartArt feature can be used to create organization charts, cycles and radials, time lines, pyramids, matrixes, and Venn diagrams. Use PowerPoint's Chart feature to develop types of charts including line, pie, and bar charts. In PowerPoint follow the guidance of the built-in Designer feature that will "suggest" design options.

5   Add special effects.

To keep the audience focused, use animation and transition features to control when text or objects appear. With motion paths, 3D, and other animation options, you can move objects to various positions on the slide and zoom in on and out of images and text on your canvas. To minimize clutter, you can dim or remove them once they have served their purpose. But use with care! Some experts discourage the use of special effects.

6   Create hyperlinks.

Make your presentation more interactive and intriguing by connecting to videos, spreadsheets, or websites.

7   Move your presentation online.

Make your presentation available by posting it to the Internet or an organization's intranet. Even if you are giving a face-to-face presentation, attendees appreciate electronic handouts if you don't want to give away your entire slideshow. To discourage copying, convert your presentations to PDF documents—if needed with a watermark and in black and white. Your multimedia presentation can be shared in a Web conference or broadcast. Slide presentations can also be converted to video, still photos, decks, and other formats.

FOR THE RECORD

Nonprofit Making a Difference in Rural Zimbabwe

When the founders of the microlending nonprofit organization Kiva make business presentations around the world, audiences respond with enthusiastic applause and even tears. Kiva's online lending platform connects personal lenders with poverty-stricken individuals in developing nations, enabling villagers to start tomato farms, carpet kiosks, and other small ventures that improve their lives. Kiva's presentations include heartwarming stories and videos about village entrepreneurs to show that small loans can make a big difference.[22] What tips can communicators follow to deliver powerful, inspirational presentations?

14-4 Refining Delivery, Rehearsing, and Performing Your Talk

Once you have organized your presentation and prepared visuals, you are ready to practice delivering it. You will feel more confident and appear more professional if you know more about various delivery methods and techniques to use before, during, and after your presentation.

14-4a Choosing a Delivery Method

Inexperienced speakers often hold on to myths about public speaking. They may believe that they must memorize an entire presentation or read from a manuscript to be successful. Let's debunk the myths and focus on effective delivery techniques.

Avoid Memorizing Your Presentation. Unless you are an experienced performer, you will sound robotic and unnatural if you try to recite your talk by heart. What's more, forgetting your place can be disastrous! That is why we don't recommend memorizing an entire oral presentation. However, memorizing significant parts—the introduction, the conclusion, and perhaps a meaningful quotation—can make your presentation dramatic and impressive.

Don't Read From Your Notes. Reading your business presentation to an audience from notes or a manuscript is boring, and listeners will quickly lose interest. Because reading suggests that you don't know your topic well, the audience loses confidence in your expertise. Reading also prevents you from maintaining eye contact. You can't see audience reactions; consequently, you can't benefit from feedback.

Deliver Your Presentation Extemporaneously. The best plan for delivering convincing business presentations, by far, is extemporaneous delivery, especially when you are structuring your talk with a multimedia presentation such as a PowerPoint slideshow, Keynote presentation, Google Slides, Adobe Presenter, or Prezi canvas. **Extemporaneous** delivery means speaking freely, generally without notes, after preparing and rehearsing. You comment on the multimedia visuals you have prepared. Reading from notes or a manuscript in addition to a PowerPoint slideshow, Keynote slides, or a Prezi canvas will damage your credibility. Unlike extemporaneous delivery, **impromptu** speaking describes improvised, unrehearsed, spontaneous spur-of-the-moment delivery.

Know When Notes Are Appropriate.　If you give a talk without multimedia technology, you may use note cards or an outline containing key sentences and major ideas, but beware of reading from a script. By preparing and then practicing with your notes, you can use them while also talking to your audience in a conversational manner. Your notes should be neither entire paragraphs nor single words. Instead, they should contain a complete sentence or two to introduce each major idea. Below the topic sentence(s), outline subpoints and illustrations. Note cards will keep you on track and prompt your memory but only if you have rehearsed the presentation thoroughly.

14-4b Combating Stage Fright

Even pros experience some stage fright when performing before an audience. World-renowned singer-songwriter Adele is terrified of huge arenas and has said she may never tour again: "I have anxiety attacks, constant panicking on stage; my heart feels like it's going to explode because I never feel like I'm going to deliver, ever."[24] Celebrated soprano Renee Fleming confessed in her biography, "Stage fright makes you feel as if you will die if you go out on the stage."[25] And Laurence Olivier, considered one of the greatest actors of the twentieth century, acquired performance anxiety late in life. It filled him with dread. Performing in a London theater, he had a manager push him onstage every night.[26]

Being afraid is quite natural and results from actual physiological changes occurring in your body. Faced with a frightening situation, your body responds with the **fight-flight-freeze response**, discussed more fully in the accompanying Career Coach box. You can learn to control and reduce performance anxiety as well as to incorporate techniques for effective speaking, by using the following strategies and techniques before, during, and after your presentation.

iStock.com/Mikolette

14-4c Before Your Presentation

Speaking in front of a group will be less daunting if you allow for adequate preparation, sufficient practice, and rehearsals. Interacting with the audience and limiting surprises such as malfunctioning equipment will also enhance your peace of mind. Review the following tips for a smooth start:

Prepare Thoroughly.　One of the most effective strategies for reducing stage fright is knowing your subject thoroughly. Research your topic diligently and prepare a careful sentence outline. Those who try to wing it usually suffer the worst butterflies—and give the worst presentations.

Rehearse Repeatedly.　When you rehearse, practice your entire presentation. In PowerPoint you may print out speaker's notes, an outline, or a handout featuring miniature slides, which are excellent for practice. If you don't use an electronic slideshow, place your outline sentences on separate note cards. You may also wish to include transitional sentences to help you move to the next topic as you practice. Rehearse alone or before friends and family. Also consider making an audio or video recording of your rehearsals so you can evaluate your effectiveness.

Time Yourself.　Most audiences tend to get restless during longer talks. Therefore, try to complete your presentation in 20 minutes or less. If you have a time limit, don't go over it. Set a simple kitchen timer or the timer app on your smartphone during your rehearsal to keep track of time. Better yet, use the PowerPoint function Rehearse Timings in the Slide Show tab to measure the length of your talk as you practice. Other presentation software packages offer similar features.

Dress Professionally.　Dressing professionally for a presentation will make you look more credible to your audience. You will also feel more confident. If you are not used to professional attire, practice wearing it so that you appear comfortable during your presentation.

How to Conquer Stage Fright

Ever get nervous before making a presentation? Everyone does! And it's not all in your head, either. When you face something threatening or challenging, your body reacts in what psychologists call the fight-flight-freeze response. This physical reflex provides your body with increased energy to deal with threatening situations. It also creates those sensations—dry mouth, sweaty hands, increased heartbeat, and stomach butterflies—that we associate with stage fright. The fight-flight-freeze response arouses your body for action—in this case, making a presentation.

Because everyone feels some form of apprehension before speaking, it's impossible to eliminate the involuntary physiological symptoms altogether. However, you can reduce their effects with the following techniques:

- **Breathe deeply**. Use deep breathing to ease your fight-flight-freeze symptoms. Inhale to a count of ten, hold this breath to a count of ten, and exhale to a count of ten. Concentrate on your counting and your breathing; both activities reduce your stress.

- **Convert your fear**. Don't view your sweaty palms and dry mouth as evidence of fear. Reframe them as symptoms of exuberance, excitement, and enthusiasm to share your ideas.

- **Know your topic and come prepared**. Feel confident about your topic. Select a topic that you know well and that is relevant to your audience. Prepare thoroughly and practice extensively.

- **Use positive self-talk**. Remind yourself that you know your topic and are prepared. Tell yourself that the audience is on your side—because it is! Moreover, most speakers appear to be more confident than they feel. Make this apparent confidence work for you.

- **Take a sip of water**. Drink some water to alleviate your dry mouth and constricted voice box, especially if you're talking for more than 15 minutes.

- **Shift the spotlight to your visuals**. At least some of the time the audience will be focusing on your slides, transparencies, handouts, or whatever you have prepared—and not totally on you.

- **Ignore any stumbles**. If you make a mistake, ignore the stumble and keep going. Don't apologize or confess your nervousness. The audience will forget any mistakes quickly—or not even notice.

- **Feel proud when you finish**. You will be surprised at how good you feel when you finish. Take pride in what you have accomplished, and your audience will reward you with applause and congratulations. Your body, of course, will call off the fight-flight-freeze response and return to normal!

Check the Room and the Equipment. If you are using a computer, a projector, or sound equipment, be certain they are operational. Before you start, check electrical outlets and the position of the viewing screen. Ensure that the seating arrangement is appropriate to your needs.

Greet Members of the Audience. Try to make contact with a few members of the audience when you enter the room, while you are waiting to be introduced, or when you walk to the podium. Your body language should convey friendliness, confidence, and enjoyment.

Practice Stress Reduction. If you feel tension and fear while you are waiting your turn to speak, use stress-reduction techniques, such as deep breathing. Additional techniques to help you conquer stage fright are presented in the accompanying Career Coach box.

14-4d During Your Presentation

To stay in control during your talk, to build credibility, and to engage your audience, follow these time-tested guidelines for effective speaking:

Start With a Pause and Present Your First Sentence From Memory. When you first approach the audience, take a moment to make yourself comfortable. Establish your control of the situation. By memorizing your opening, you can immediately develop rapport with the audience through eye contact. You will also sound confident and knowledgeable.

Maintain Eye Contact. If the size of the audience overwhelms you, pick out two individuals on the right and two on the left. Talk directly to these people. Don't ignore listeners

FOR THE RECORD

Practicing for Presentations With Ummo

You may know Apple's trademarked slogan *There's an app for that.* Now imagine that an app could help you lower your public speaking anxiety and eliminate annoying fillers such as *um, uh, er, basically,* or *you know.* One such app is Ummo. When activated as a presentation begins, it tracks users' speech patterns, pace, and volume. It logs pauses and fillers. A handy transcript can be displayed on screen showing the problem areas that will require more practice. To improve, users can set a beep to alert them to pesky speech mannerisms.[27] Why is it a good idea to work on improving speech habits?

in the back of the room. Even when presenting to a large audience, try to make genuine, not fleeting eye contact with as many people as possible during your presentation.

Control Your Voice and Vocabulary.   This means speaking in moderated tones but loudly enough to be heard. Eliminate verbal static, such as *ah, er, like, you know,* and *um.* Silence is preferable to meaningless fillers when you are thinking of your next idea. Certain apps can help train you to lose the pesky fillers in your speech. See For the Record in this chapter.

Show Enthusiasm.   If you are not excited about your topic, how can you expect your audience to be? Show passion for your topic through your tone, facial expressions, and gestures. Adding variety to your voice also helps to keep your audience alert and interested.

Skip the Apologies.   Avoid weak openings, such as *I know you have heard this before, but we need to review it anyway.* Or: *I had trouble with my computer and the slides, so bear with me.* Unless the issue is blatant, such as not being able to load the presentation or make the projector work, apologies are counterproductive. Focus on your presentation.

Slow Down and Know When to Pause.   Many novice speakers talk too rapidly, displaying their nervousness and making it very difficult for audience members to understand their ideas. Put the brakes on and listen to what you are saying. Pauses give the audience time to absorb an important point. Silence can be effective especially when you are transitioning from one point to another.

Move Naturally.   If you have a lectern, don't hide behind it. Move about casually and naturally. Avoid fidgeting with your clothing, hair, or items in your pockets. Do not roll up your sleeves or put your hands in your pockets. Learn to use your body to express a point.

Control Visual Aids With Clickers, Pointers, and Blank Screens.   Discuss and interpret each visual aid for the audience. Move aside as you describe it so that people can see it fully. Learn to use a clicker to advance your slides remotely. Use a laser pointer if necessary, but steady your hand if it is shaking. Dim the slideshow when not discussing the slides. In Slide Show view in PowerPoint, press *B* on the keyboard to blacken the screen or *W* to turn the screen white. In Prezi, remember to zoom back out when necessary.

Avoid Digressions.   Stick to your outline and notes. Don't suddenly include clever little anecdotes or digressions that occur to you on the spot. If it is not part of your rehearsed material, leave it out so you can finish on time.

Summarize Your Main Points and Drive Home Your Message.   Conclude your presentation by reiterating your main points or by emphasizing what you want the audience to think or do. Once you have announced your conclusion, proceed to it directly.

14-4e After Your Presentation

As you are concluding your presentation, handle questions and answers competently and provide handouts, if appropriate. Try the following techniques:

Distribute Handouts. If you prepared handouts with data the audience will not need during the presentation, pass them out when you finish to prevent any distraction during your talk.

Encourage Questions but Keep Control. If the situation permits a question-and-answer period, announce it at the beginning of your presentation. Then, when you finish, ask for questions. Set a time limit for questions and answers. If you don't know the answer to a question, don't make one up or panic. Instead offer to find the answer within a day or two. If you make such a promise, be sure to follow through. Don't allow one individual to dominate the Q & A period. Keep the entire audience involved.

Repeat Questions. Although you may have heard the question, some audience members may not have. Begin each answer by repeating the question. This also gives you thinking time. Then, direct your answer to the entire audience.

Reinforce Your Main Points. You can use your answers to restate your primary ideas (*I'm glad you brought that up because it gives me a chance to elaborate on . . .*). In answering questions, avoid becoming defensive or debating the questioner.

Avoid Yes, but Answers. The word *but* immediately cancels any preceding message. Try replacing it with *and*. For example, *Yes, X has been tried. And Y works even better because . . . .*

End With a Summary and Appreciation. To signal the end of the session before you take the last question, say something like *We have time for just one more question.* As you answer the last question, try to work it into a summary of your main points. Then, express appreciation to the audience for the opportunity to talk with them.

Checklist

Preparing and Organizing Business Presentations

Getting Ready to Speak

- **Identify your purpose.** Decide what you want your audience to believe, remember, or do when you finish. Aim all parts of your talk toward this purpose.

- **Analyze the audience.** Consider how to adapt your message (its organization, appeals, and examples) to your audience's knowledge and needs.

Organizing the Introduction

- **Connect with the audience.** Capture the audience's attention by opening with a promise, story, startling fact, question, quote, relevant problem, or self-effacing joke.

- **Establish your authority.** Demonstrate your credibility by identifying your position, expertise, knowledge, or qualifications.

- **Preview your main points.** Introduce your topic and summarize its principal parts.

Organizing the Body

- **Develop two to four main points.** Streamline your topic so that you can concentrate on its major issues.

- **Arrange the points logically.** Sequence your points chronologically, from most important to least important, by comparison and contrast, or by some other strategy.

- **Prepare transitions.** Between major points write bridge statements that connect the previous item to the next one. Use transitional expressions as verbal signposts (*first, second, then, however, consequently, on the contrary,* and so forth).

- **Have extra material ready.** Be prepared with more information and visuals in case you have additional time to fill.

Organizing the Conclusion

- **Review your main points.** Emphasize your main ideas in the closing so your audience will remember them.

- **Provide a strong, final focus.** Tell how your listeners can use this information, why you have spoken, or what you want them to do. End with a specific audience benefit or thought-provoking idea (a take-away), not just a lame rehash.

Designing Visual Aids

- **Select your media carefully.** Consider the pros and cons of each alternative.

- **Highlight main ideas.** Use visual aids to illustrate major concepts only. Keep them brief and simple.

- **Try to replace bullets whenever possible.** Use flowcharts, diagrams, timelines, images, and so forth, to substitute for bulleted lists when suitable.

- **Use visual aids skillfully.** Talk to the audience, not to the visuals. Paraphrase their content.

Developing Multimedia Presentations

- **Learn to use your presentation software.** Study template and layout designs to see how you can adapt them to your purposes.

- **Select colors based on the light level in the room.** Consider how mixing light and dark fonts and backgrounds affects their visibility. Use templates and preset layouts if your presentation software is new to you.

- **Use bulleted points for major ideas.** Make sure your points are parallel, and observe the 6-x-6 rule.

- **Include multimedia options that will help you convey your message.** Use moderate animation features and hyperlinks to make your talk more interesting and to link to files with related content in the same document, in other documents, or on the Internet. Use Prezi's zooming feature to help audience members narrow in on details.

- **Make speaker's notes.** Jot down the narrative supporting each visual, and use these notes to practice your presentation. Do not read from notes while speaking to an audience, however.

- **Maintain control.** Don't let your slides or canvas upstage you. Engage your audience by using additional techniques to help them visualize your points.

14-5 Developing Intercultural and Team Presentations

LEARNING OUTCOME

5 Organize presentations for intercultural audiences and in teams.

Most of the information presented thus far assumes you are a single presenter before a traditional audience. However, in this hyperconnected world of work, presentations take on myriad forms and purposes. Now we'll explore effective techniques for adapting presentations to intercultural audiences and participating in team presentations.

14-5a Adapting Presentations to Intercultural Audiences

In our globalized business world, adjusting to a multicultural audience can be challenging. Rarely will you encounter only one ethnic or national group when speaking, whether domestically or overseas. Of course, every good speaker adapts to the audience, but intercultural presentations call for special adjustments and sensitivity. Most people understand that they must speak slowly, choose simple English, avoid jargon and clichés, use short sentences, and pause frequently when communicating with nonnative speakers of English.

Beyond these basic language adaptations, however, more fundamental sensitivity is often necessary. In organizing a presentation for an intercultural audience, you may need to anticipate and adapt to various speaking conventions, values, and nonverbal behaviors. You may also need to contend with a reluctance to voice opinions openly.

Reality Check

Presentation Style and Multicultural Audiences

"In the United States, an expressive leader is often seen as charismatic and powerful. But in other countries—like Japan, for instance—power is more commonly associated with a reserved bearing. Even closer to home, in Canada, American leadership style can seem a little too bold and too aggressive. To maximize your presence and authority, maintain a balance between composure and expressiveness."[28]

—Anett Grant, *author and CEO of Executing Speaking, Inc.*

Understanding Different Values and Nonverbal Behaviors.

In addressing intercultural audiences, anticipate expectations and perceptions that may differ significantly from what you may consider normal. Remember, for example, that the North American emphasis on getting to the point quickly is not equally prized across the globe. Therefore, think twice about delivering your main idea up front. Many people (notably those in Japanese, Latin American, and Arabic cultures) consider such directness to be brash and inappropriate. Remember that others may not share our cultural emphasis on straightforwardness.

When working with an interpreter or speaking before individuals whose English is limited, you must be very careful about your language. For example, you will need to express ideas in small chunks to give the interpreter time to translate. You may need to slow down as you speak and stop after each thought to allow time for the translation that will follow. Even if your presentation or speech is being translated simultaneously, remember to speak slowly and to pause after each sentence to ensure that your message is rendered correctly in the target language.

The same advice is useful in organizing presentations. You may want to divide your talk into distinct topics, developing each separately and encouraging a discussion period after each one. Such organization enables participants to ask questions and digest what has been presented. This technique is especially effective in cultures in which people communicate in "loops." In the Middle East, for example, Arab speakers "mix circuitous, irrelevant (by American standards) conversations with short dashes of information that go directly to the point." Presenters who are patient, tolerant, and "mature" (in the eyes of the audience) will make the sale or win the contract. Trust must be earned.[29]

Match your presentation and your nonverbal messages to the expectations of your audience. In Germany, for instance, successful presentations tend to be dense with facts and precise statistics. Americans might say "roughly 30 percent," whereas a German presenter might say "30.4271 percent." Similarly, constant smiling is not as valued in Europe as it is in North America. Many Europeans distrust a speaker who is cracking jokes, smiling, or laughing in a business presentation. Rather, many expect a rational—that is, serious—fact-based delivery.

American-style enthusiasm is often interpreted abroad as hyperbolic exaggeration or, worse, as dishonesty and can lead to misunderstandings. If an American says "Great job!" to offer praise, a Spanish counterpart might believe that the American has approved the project. "When Europeans realize there's no commitment implied," warned an intercultural consultant, "they might feel deceived or that the American is being superficial."[30]

Remember, too, that some cultures prefer greater formality than Americans exercise. When communicating with people from such cultures, instead of first names, use only honorifics (*Mr.* or *Ms.*) and last names, as well as academic or business titles—such as *Doctor* or *Director*.

Adjusting Visual Aids to Intercultural Audiences.

Although you may have to exercise greater caution with culturally diverse audiences, you still want to use visual aids to help communicate your message. Find out from your international contact whether you can present in English or will need an interpreter. In many countries listeners are too polite or too proud to speak up when they don't understand a speaker. One expert advises explaining important concepts in several ways using different words and then requesting members of the audience to relay their understanding of what you have just said back to you. Another expert suggests packing more text on PowerPoint slides and staying closer to its literal meaning. After all, most nonnative speakers of English understand written text much better than spoken English. In the United States, presenters may spend 90 seconds on a slide, whereas in other countries they may need to slow down to two minutes per slide.[31]

To ensure clarity and show courtesy, provide handouts in both English and the target language. Never use numbers without projecting or writing them out for all to see. If possible, say numbers in both languages, but only if you can pronounce or even speak the target language well enough to avoid embarrassment. Distribute translated handouts, summarizing your important information, when you finish. For a detailed discussion of intercultural communication, see Chapter 3.

14-5b Preparing Team Presentations

For many reasons increasing numbers of organizations are using teams, as discussed in Chapter 2. The goal of some teams is a business presentation to pitch a new product or to win a high-stakes contract. Before Apple CEO Tim Cook and his team roll out one of their hotly anticipated new electronic gadgets, you can bet that team members spend months preparing so that the presentation flows smoothly. The same is true of most new product launches or major announcements. Teams collaborate to make sure the presentation meets its objectives.

Other teams form as needed to tackle challenges efficiently and fast. Spanish clothing chain Zara is famous for bringing leading-edge, yet inexpensive fashion trends to the consumer within weeks, not months like its competitors. Nimble cross-functional teams "can quickly innovate across organizational boundaries," making the company a lot more responsive than traditional organizations.[32] The outcome of any team effort is often (a) a written report, (b) a multimedia slideshow or presentation, or (c) an oral presentation delivered live. The boundaries are becoming increasingly blurred between flat, two-dimensional hard-copy reports and multimedia, hyperlinked slideshows and zoom presentations. Both hard-copy reports and multimedia presentations are delivered to clients in business today.

Whether your team produces written reports, multimedia presentations, or oral presentations, you generally have considerable control over how each project is organized and completed. If you have been part of any team efforts before, you also know that such projects can be very frustrating—particularly when some team members don't carry their weight or when members cannot resolve conflict. On the other hand, team projects can be harmonious and productive when members establish ground rules and follow guidelines related to preparing, planning, and collecting information as well as for organizing, rehearsing, and evaluating team projects.

When Apple CEO Tim Cook continues the tradition started by the late Steve Jobs and headlines one of his spectacular product launches, the world is listening. Striking graphics and Cook's commentary work together seamlessly. Making his keynote presentations look effortless requires countless hours of practice and rehearsals.

Preparing to Work Together. Before any group begins to talk about a specific project, members should establish basic ground rules. One of the first tasks is naming a leader to call and manage meetings, a recorder to track group decisions, and an evaluator to determine whether the group is on target and meeting its goals. The group should decide whether it will be governed by consensus (everyone must agree), by majority rule, or by some other method. These ground rules should be put in writing much like a contract. A team charter, signed by all team members, can be used in an academic setting to spell out responsibilities, specific roles, deadlines, meeting frequency, communication, and any penalties.

When teams first organize, they should also consider the value of conflict. By bringing conflict into the open and encouraging healthy confrontation, teams can prevent personal resentment and group dysfunction. Confrontation can actually create better final products by promoting new ideas and avoiding groupthink. Conflict is most beneficial when team members can air their views fully. Another important topic to discuss during team formation is how to deal with team members who are not pulling their share of the load. Teams should decide whether they will "fire" members who are not contributing or take some other action in dealing with slackers.

The most successful teams make meetings a top priority. They compare schedules to set up the best meeting times, and they meet often, either in person or virtually. They avoid other responsibilities that might disrupt these meetings. Today's collaboration software and mobile apps make teamwork efficient and productive. Team members can use tools such as Google Slides and Google Drive, Dropbox, or Keynote to jointly create and edit documents and presentations in the cloud. Prezi too allows team members to invite others to collaborate live on a Prezi canvas. Team members receive an invitation link and can work on presentations from anywhere at any time of day, synchronously or asynchronously.

Planning and Preparing the Document or Presentation.
Once teams have established ground rules, members are ready to discuss the target document or presentation. During these discussions, they must be sure to keep a record of all decisions. They should establish the specific purpose for the document or presentation and identify the main issues involved. They must decide on the final format. For a collaborative business report, they should determine what parts to include, such as an executive summary, figures, and an appendix.

Team members should consider how the report or presentation will be delivered—in person, online, or by e-mail. For a team oral presentation, they should decide on its parts, length, and graphics. For either written or oral projects, they should profile the audience and focus on the questions audience members would want answered. If the report or presentation involves persuasion, they must decide what appeals would achieve the team's purpose.

Next, the team should develop a work plan (see Chapter 11), assign jobs, and set deadlines. If time is short, members should work backward from the due date. For oral presentations, teams must schedule time for content and creative development as well as for a series of rehearsals. The best-planned presentations can fall apart if they are poorly rehearsed.

For oral presentations, all team members should have written tasks. These tasks should detail each member's specific responsibilities for researching content, producing visuals, developing handouts, building transitions between segments, and showing up for rehearsals. For written reports, members must decide how the final document will be composed: individuals working separately on assigned portions, one person writing the first draft, the entire group writing the complete document together, or some other method. Team members will be responsible for collecting information; organizing, writing, and revising; and editing, rehearsing, and evaluating the document or presentation.

Collecting Information.
One of the most challenging jobs for team projects is generating and collecting information. Unless facts are accurate, the most beautiful report or the most high-powered presentation will fail. Team members should brainstorm for ideas, assign topics, and decide who will be responsible for gathering what information. Establishing deadlines for collecting information is important if a team is to remain on schedule. Team members should also discuss ways to ensure the accuracy of the information collected.

Organizing, Writing, and Revising.
When a project progresses into the organizing and writing stages, a team may need to modify some of its earlier decisions. Members may review the proposed organization of the document or presentation and adjust it if necessary. In composing the first draft of a written report or presentation, team members will probably write separate segments. As they work on these segments, they should use the same presentation software to facilitate combining files. They can also use Google Drive, Google Slides, Dropbox, and other tools to edit and store documents.

As individuals work on separate parts of a written report, the team should decide on one person (probably the best writer) to coordinate all the parts. The writer strives for a consistent style, format, and feel in the final product. For oral presentations, team members must try to make logical connections between segments. Each presenter builds a bridge to the next member's topic to create a smooth transition. Team members should also select and use the same template. Only one person ought to make global changes in color, font, and other formatting.

Editing, Rehearsing, and Evaluating.
The last stage in a collaborative project involves editing, rehearsing, and evaluating. For a written report, one person should assume the task of merging the various files, running a spell-checker, and examining the entire document for consistency of design, format, and vocabulary. That person is responsible for finding and correcting grammatical and mechanical errors. Then the entire group meets as a whole to evaluate the final document. Does it fulfill its purpose and meet the needs of the audience?

For oral presentations, one person should also merge all the files and be certain that they are consistent in design, format, and vocabulary. Teams making presentations should practice together several times. If that is not feasible, experts say that teams must schedule at least one full real-time rehearsal with the entire group. As professional speaker and coach Carmine Gallo tells it, legendary speakers rehearse "endlessly and fastidiously" to sound natural, authentic, animated, and conversational.[34] Whenever possible, the team should practice in a room that is similar to the location of the talk. Video recording one of the rehearsals will give each presenter the opportunity to critique his or her own performance. Scheduling a dress rehearsal with an audience at least two days before the actual presentation is helpful. Team members should also practice fielding questions.

Successful group documents emerge from thoughtful preparation, clear definitions of contributors' roles, commitment to a group-approved plan, and a willingness to take responsibility for the final product. More information about writing business reports appeared in previous chapters of this book.

14-6 Adopting Smartphone Best Practices for Business

LEARNING OUTCOME

6 List techniques for improving telephone skills to project a positive image.

The skill of presenting yourself well on the telephone is still very important in today's workplace. Despite the continuing reliance on e-mail, the telephone remains an extremely important piece of equipment, whether in offices or on the go, thanks to mobile technology. This section focuses on traditional telephone techniques as well as cell phone and voice mail etiquette—all opportunities for making a good impression. As a business communicator, you can be more productive, efficient, and professional by following some simple suggestions.

14-6a Making Telephone Calls Professionally

Before making a telephone call, decide whether the intended call is really necessary. Could you find the information yourself? If you wait a while, will the problem resolve itself? Perhaps your message could be delivered more efficiently by some other means. Some companies have found that telephone calls are often less important than the work they interrupt. Alternatives to telephone calls include instant messaging, texting, e-mail, and calls to automated voice mail systems. If you must make a telephone call, consider using the following suggestions to make it fully productive:

mimagephotography/Shutterstock.com

- **Plan a mini-agenda**. Have you ever been embarrassed when you had to make a second telephone call because you forgot an important point the first time? Before placing a call, jot down notes regarding all the topics you need to discuss.

- **Use a three-point introduction**. When placing a call, immediately (a) name the person you are calling, (b) identify yourself and your affiliation, and (c) give a brief explanation of your reason for calling. For example: *May I speak to Gino Suarez? This is Gwyn Roundtree of Waldman Enterprises, and I'm seeking information about a software program called ZoneAlarm Internet Security.*

- **Be brisk if you are rushed**. For business calls when your time is limited, avoid questions such as *How are you?* Instead, say, *Emily, I knew you would be the only one who could answer these two questions for me.* Another efficient strategy is to set a contract with the caller: *Look, Emily, I have only ten minutes, but I really wanted to get back to you.*

- **Be cheerful and accurate**. Let your voice show the same kind of animation that you radiate when you greet people in person. In your mind try to envision the individual answering the telephone. A smile can certainly affect the tone of your voice, so smile at that person.

- **Be professional and courteous**. Remember that you are representing yourself and your company when you make phone calls. Use professional vocabulary and courteous language. Say *thank you* and *please* during your conversations. Don't eat, drink, or chew gum while talking on the phone, which can often be heard on the other end. Don't shuffle papers, loudly close drawers, or make noise of any kind.

- **Bring it to a close**. The responsibility for ending a call lies with the caller. This is sometimes difficult to do if the other person rambles on. You may need to use suggestive closing language, such as the following: (a) *I have certainly enjoyed talking with you*; (b) *I have learned what I needed to know, and now I can proceed with my work*; (c) *Thanks for your help*; (d) *I must go now, but may I call you again in the future if I need . . . ?* or (e) *Should we talk again in a few weeks?*

- **Avoid telephone tag**. If you call someone who's not in, ask when it would be best to call again. State that you will call at a specific time—and do it. If you ask a person to call you, give a time when you can be reached—and then be sure you are available at that time.

- **Leave complete voice mail messages**. Always enunciate clearly and speak slowly when giving your telephone number or spelling your name. Be sure to provide a complete message, including your name, your telephone number, and the time and date of your call. Explain your purpose so that the receiver can be ready with the required information when returning your call.

14-6b Receiving Telephone Calls Professionally

With a little forethought you can present a professional image and make your telephone a productive, efficient work tool. Developing good telephone manners and techniques, such as the following, will also reflect well on you and on your organization.

- **Identify yourself immediately**. In answering your telephone or someone else's, provide your name, title or affiliation, and, possibly, a greeting. For example, *Gino Suarez, Meta-Digital. How may I help you?* Force yourself to speak clearly and slowly. Remember that the caller may be unfamiliar with what you are saying and fail to recognize slurred syllables.

- **Be responsive and helpful**. If you are in a support role, be sympathetic to callers' needs. Instead of *I don't know*, try *That's a good question; let me investigate*. Instead of *We can't do that*, try *That's a tough one; let's see what we can do*. Avoid *No* at the beginning of a sentence. It sounds especially abrasive and displeasing because it suggests total rejection.

- **Practice telephone confidentiality**. When answering calls for others, be courteous and helpful, but don't give out confidential information. Better to say, *She's away from her desk* or *He's out of the office* than to report a colleague's exact whereabouts. Also, be tight-lipped about sharing company information with strangers.

- **Take messages carefully**. Few things are as frustrating as receiving a potentially important phone message that is illegible. Repeat the spelling of names and verify telephone numbers. Write messages legibly and record their time and date. Promise to give the messages to intended recipients, but don't guarantee return calls.

- **Leave the line respectfully**. If you must put a call on hold, let the caller know and give an estimate of how long you expect the call to be on hold. Give the caller the option of holding (e.g., *Would you prefer to hold, or would you like me to call you back?*).

14-6c Using Smartphones in Business

Business is unthinkable without cell phones. We're mobile and always on: The vast majority of Americans (96 percent) own a cell phone today. Smartphone ownership stands at 81 percent, up from 35 percent just a decade ago. Almost 40 percent of U.S. adults primarily access the Internet using their smartphone, and more than a quarter no longer subscribe to broadband at home.[36] Over half of U.S. children now own a smartphone by the age of 11.[37] Aside from posture problems resulting from the so-called **text neck** as we hang our heads while staring at screens, smartphones also make us antisocial, experts say.[38] No wonder! Most U.S. adults on average spend 10 hours per day consuming various electronic media, according to Nielsen.[39]

Constant connectivity is posing new challenges in social settings and is perceived as distracting to group dynamics, a Pew study found.[40] However, people's views on acceptable cell phone use vary. More than three quarters don't object to using a cell phone while walking down the street, on public transport, and when waiting in line. Even in restaurants, smartphone use is acceptable to 38 percent. However, respondents strongly condemned cell phone use during meetings, in movie theaters, and in places of worship. Although Americans view cell phones as distracting and annoying, many *do* access their own devices in group settings.

Because so many people depend on their smartphones, it's important to understand proper use and etiquette. Most of us have experienced thoughtless and rude cell phone behavior. Researchers say that the rampant use of mobile electronic devices has increased workplace incivility. Most employees consider texting and compulsive e-mail checking while working and during meetings disruptive, even insulting. Employers may question workers' commitment and productivity if they are among the 20 percent who check their phones at least once every 20 minutes at work.[41] To avoid offending, smart business communicators practice professional cell phone etiquette, as outlined in Figure 14.11.

14-6d Making the Best Use of Voice Mail

Because telephone calls can be disruptive, many businesspeople make extensive use of voice mail to intercept and screen incoming calls on their landlines and smartphones. Here are some ways to make voice mail work most effectively for you.

On the Receiver's End. Your voice mail should project professionalism and provide an easy way for your callers to leave messages for you. Here are some voice mail etiquette tips:

- **Don't overuse voice mail**. Don't use voice mail to avoid taking phone calls. It is better to answer calls yourself than to let voice mail messages build up.

- **Prepare a professional, concise, friendly greeting**. Make your voice mail greeting sound warm and inviting, both in tone and content. Identify yourself, thank the caller, and briefly explain that you are unavailable. Invite the caller to leave a message or, if appropriate, to call back. Here's a typical voice mail greeting: *Hi! This is Jenny Schwartz of Kerberos Software, and I appreciate your call. I'm either working with customers or talking on another line at the moment. Please leave your name, number, and reason for calling so that I can be prepared when I return your call.*

- **Respond to messages promptly**. Check your messages regularly, and try to return all voice mail messages within one business day.

- **Plan for vacations and other extended absences**. If you will not be picking up voice mail messages for an extended period, let callers know how they can reach someone else if needed.

On the Caller's End. When leaving a voice mail message, follow these tips:

- **Be prepared to leave a message**. Before calling someone, be prepared for voice mail. Decide what you are going to say and what information you will include in your message. If necessary, write your message down before calling.

FIGURE 14.11 Courteous and Responsible Cell Phone Practices

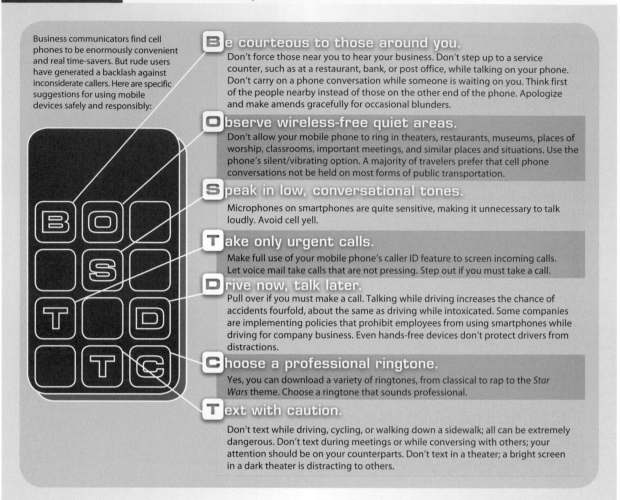

Business communicators find cell phones to be enormously convenient and real time-savers. But rude users have generated a backlash against inconsiderate callers. Here are specific suggestions for using mobile devices safely and responsibly:

Be courteous to those around you.
Don't force those near you to hear your business. Don't step up to a service counter, such as at a restaurant, bank, or post office, while talking on your phone. Don't carry on a phone conversation while someone is waiting on you. Think first of the people nearby instead of those on the other end of the phone. Apologize and make amends gracefully for occasional blunders.

Observe wireless-free quiet areas.
Don't allow your mobile phone to ring in theaters, restaurants, museums, places of worship, classrooms, important meetings, and similar places and situations. Use the phone's silent/vibrating option. A majority of travelers prefer that cell phone conversations not be held on most forms of public transportation.

Speak in low, conversational tones.
Microphones on smartphones are quite sensitive, making it unnecessary to talk loudly. Avoid cell yell.

Take only urgent calls.
Make full use of your mobile phone's caller ID feature to screen incoming calls. Let voice mail take calls that are not pressing. Step out if you must take a call.

Drive now, talk later.
Pull over if you must make a call. Talking while driving increases the chance of accidents fourfold, about the same as driving while intoxicated. Some companies are implementing policies that prohibit employees from using smartphones while driving for company business. Even hands-free devices don't protect drivers from distractions.

Choose a professional ringtone.
Yes, you can download a variety of ringtones, from classical to rap to the *Star Wars* theme. Choose a ringtone that sounds professional.

Text with caution.
Don't text while driving, cycling, or walking down a sidewalk; all can be extremely dangerous. Don't text during meetings or while conversing with others; your attention should be on your counterparts. Don't text in a theater; a bright screen in a dark theater is distracting to others.

- **Leave a concise, thorough message**. When leaving a message, always identify yourself using your complete name and affiliation. Mention the date and time you called and a brief explanation of your reason for calling. Always leave a complete phone number, including the area code. Tell the receiver the best time to return your call. Don't ramble.

- **Speak slowly and clearly**. You want to make sure that your receiver will be able to understand your message. Speak slowly and pronounce your words carefully, especially when providing your phone number. The receiver should be able to write information down without having to replay your message.

- **Be careful with confidential information**. Don't leave confidential or private information in a voice mail message. Remember that anyone could gain access to this information.

Zooming In

Your Turn:
Applying Your Skills at an NGO

You love your new internship planning special projects for a nongovernmental organization (NGO) that sends medical supplies to the needy in developing countries. At a recent staff meeting, many account representatives expressed the desire to learn how to make better presentations to donors. Your supervisor has asked you to find someone who can give the staff members a workshop designed to teach presentation skills. You recently heard Jean-luc Doumont speak at your college and think he'd be a perfect fit for your NGO. To illustrate what you learned from Doumont as a way to persuade your boss to hire him, you decide to create a PowerPoint presentation instead of a written document.

Your Task

In teams of three or four, research Jean-luc Doumont at http://www.principiae.be and peruse a YouTube video featuring Doumont discussing effective slides at https://www .youtube.com/watch?v=meBXuTIPJQk. With your group, create a short presentation geared to your audience—your supervisor—that will convince her to hire Doumont.

SUMMARY OF LEARNING OUTCOMES

1 Discuss two important first steps in preparing for business presentations.

- Speaking skills rank high on employers' wish lists and are crucial to career success.

- Presentations can be informative or persuasive, face-to-face or virtual, performed in front of big audiences or smaller groups, and elaborate or simple.

- Business professionals give a variety of business presentations including briefings, reports, podcasts, virtual presentations, and webinars.

- Once speakers know what they want to accomplish with their presentation, they must identify the purpose and the audience, so that they can aim the entire presentation toward their goal and adjust their message and style to the audience's knowledge and needs.

2 Explain how to organize your business presentation and design contemporary visual aids to build audience rapport.

- The introduction should capture the listener's attention, identify the speaker, establish credibility, and preview the main points.

- The body should discuss two to four main points, with appropriate explanations, details, and verbal signposts to guide listeners.

- The conclusion should review the main points, provide a memorable take-away, and allow the speaker to leave the podium gracefully.

- Speakers establish rapport with their audiences by using effective imagery, useful verbal signposts or transitions, and appropriate nonverbal behavior.

- Contemporary visual aids—such as multimedia slides, handouts, and zoom presentations—illustrate and emphasize main points, draw audience interest, and make the presenter look more professional, better prepared, and more persuasive.

- Whenever possible, savvy speakers move beyond boring bulleted text and choose vivid images.

3 Create a memorable error-free multimedia presentation that shows a firm grasp of basic visual design principles.

- Before creating a presentation, effective speakers analyze its purpose, delivery, and distribution.

- Expert presenters adjust their slide design to their audiences and demonstrate that they understand the meaning of color, the power of images, and the impact of special effects.

- When composing a talk, presenters organize their work by translating the major headings in the outline into slide titles and avoid formatting and fine-tuning their slides prematurely.

- For a quick start, speakers use templates, but they avoid visual clichés—that is, overused visuals.

- The final stage of creating a slideshow requires revising and proofreading as well as evaluating.

- Presenters must anticipate potential technical difficulties, rehearse, and create backups of their presentations.

4 Describe delivery techniques for use before, during, and after a presentation to keep the audience engaged.

- Effective public speaking techniques include avoiding memorizing, refraining from reading from notes, and delivering the presentation extemporaneously (speaking freely, without notes).

- When speaking without slides, presenters may use note cards or rough outlines to stay on track.

- Stage fright is lessened by breathing deeply, converting fear, preparing well, using positive self-talk, sipping water, shifting focus to the visuals, ignoring stumbles, and feeling proud at the end.

- Before the talk, speakers prepare a sentence outline, rehearse repeatedly, time themselves, dress professionally, check the room, greet audience members, and practice stress reduction.

- During the talk, speakers present the first sentence from memory, maintain eye contact, control their voice, show enthusiasm, skip apologies, pace themselves, use pauses, move naturally, control visuals competently, avoid digressions, and summarize their main points.

- After the talk, savvy presenters distribute handouts and answer questions; they repeat questions, reinforce main points, avoid *yes, but* answers; and end with a summary and appreciation.

5 Organize presentations for intercultural audiences and in teams.

- Businesspeople adapt language to intercultural audiences and understand different conventions.

- In nonnative environments, presenters speak slowly, use simple English, avoid directness, break the presentation into short chunks, respect formality, and adapt visuals to their audiences.

- Teams of presenters should name a leader; discuss decision making; work out a schedule; consider the value of conflict; determine how to rein in uncooperative members; and decide on the purpose, form, and procedures for preparing the final document or presentation.

- Teams collect information, brainstorm ideas, assign topics, establish deadlines, and plan meetings to discuss drafts.

- Teams coordinate their assigned contributions and edit, rehearse, and evaluate their presentations.

6 List techniques for improving telephone skills to project a positive image.

- Efficient callers plan a mini-agenda, use a three-point introduction (name, affiliation, and purpose), practice sounding cheerful and courteous, and use closing language.

- Savvy businesspeople avoid telephone tag by leaving complete voice mail messages.

- In answering calls, workers identify themselves immediately, show a helpful attitude, don't give out confidential information when answering for others, and take careful messages.

- Workers need to follow proper etiquette when using their smartphones for business.

- Skilled businesspeople prepare a concise, friendly voice mail greeting, respond to messages promptly, and plan for extended absences.

- Callers should be prepared to leave a concise message, speak slowly and clearly, and not reveal confidential information.

Key Terms

glossophobia *493*

take-away *500*

rapport *500*

pictorial superiority *502*

software as a service (SaaS) *504*

6-x-6 rule *507*

extemporaneous *512*

impromptu *512*

fight-flight-freeze response 513

text neck 523

Critical Thinking

1. Why should even veteran speakers plan their presentations when addressing a business audience instead of just "winging it"? (L.O. 1–4)

2. Corporate communication consultant Dianna Booher believes that enthusiasm is infectious and "boredom is contagious."[42] What does this mean for you as a presenter? (L.O. 2, 3)

3. Why do many communication consultants encourage businesspeople to move beyond bullet points? What do they recommend instead, and why? (L.O. 2, 3)

4. Name at least five effective techniques for reducing stage fright. (L.O. 4)

5. Etiquette expert Jacqueline Whitmore offers this advice to aspiring speakers: "A long, dry presentation of facts is sure to be a yawn-inducer, so consider your presentation as a conversation with your audience. . . . Ask questions, incorporate teambuilding exercise, and ask for volunteers to come up to the front to help you demonstrate a point. . . . Ask the group to stand, clap, or raise their hands, and give you frequent feedback. And remember, a little humor goes a long way."[43] Consider what you've learned in this chapter. Is this good advice for all audiences? (L.O. 5)

6. **Ethical Issue:** Deborah Grayson Riegel, a communication skills expert, has this to say about team presentations: "I've found that group presentations tend to fall into the trap of creating a feeling of shared accountability ('we're all in this together') that translates into a reality of no accountability ('I'm sure someone else will test that the A/V set up is working'). This means that core elements of presentation planning, design and delivery often fall through the cracks, resulting in a mishmash of uncoordinated—and sometimes competing— objectives, repeated or missing information, wildly different styles in graphics, and the likelihood that the presentation will run significantly under- or over-time. Add to that the feelings of frustration and resentment that people working in teams often feel about carrying more weight than their partners, and a team presentation is often a recipe for disaster." Can you relate? How can you ensure successful team presentations? (L.O. 5)

Activities

14.1 Studying Iconic Speeches (L.O. 1–3)

`Web`

YOUR TASK Select a speech by a significant businessperson or a well-known public figure. Consider watching the following iconic political speeches, thought to be among the best in the twentieth century: Martin Luther King Jr.'s "I Have a Dream" speech, President Kennedy's inaugural address, and Franklin Delano Roosevelt's Pearl Harbor Address to the Nation.[44] If you prefer business tycoons dispensing advice, search for the best-known commencement speeches—for example, Steve Jobs's legendary "Stay Hungry, Stay Foolish" Stanford address, Salman Khan's "Live Your Life Like It's Your Second Chance" speech at MIT, or Sheryl Sandberg's "Rocketship" commencement speech at Harvard Business School. Transcripts of these and other well-known speeches are also available online.[45] Write a memo report or give a short presentation to your class critiquing the speech in terms of the following:

a. Effectiveness of the introduction, body, and conclusion

b. Evidence of effective overall organization

c. Use of verbal signposts to create coherence

d. Emphasis on two to four main points

e. Effectiveness of supporting facts (use of examples, statistics, quotations, and so forth)

f. Focus on audience benefits

g. Enthusiasm for the topic

h. Body language and personal mannerisms

14.2 Audience Analysis First (L.O. 1, 2)

YOUR TASK Select a recent issue of *Fortune, The Wall Street Journal, Bloomberg Businessweek, The Economist,* or another business periodical approved by your instructor. Based on an analysis of your peer audience, select an article that will appeal to them and that you can relate to their needs. Submit to your instructor a one-page summary that includes (a) the author, article title, source, issue date, and page reference; (b) a one-paragraph article summary; (c) a description of why you believe the article will appeal to your classmates; and (d) a summary of how you can relate the article to their needs. Your instructor may make this a topic for a class presentation.

14.3 Seeking Inspiration and Charisma: Hiring a Speaker (L.O. 1)

`Communication Technology` `Social Media`
`Team` `Web`

Have you ever wondered why famous entrepreneurs, politicians, athletes, and other celebrities command high speaking fees? How much are they really making per appearance, and what factors may justify their exorbitant fees? You may also wonder how a motivational speaker or corporate trainer might benefit you and your class or your campus community. Searching for and selecting an expert is easy online with several commercial speaker bureaus vying for clients. All bureaus provide detailed speaker bios, areas of expertise, and fees. One even features video previews of its clients.

The preeminent agencies for booking talent are All American Speakers Bureau, BigSpeak Speakers Bureau, Speakerpedia, and Brooks International Speakers & Entertainment Bureau. Speakerpedia represents the likes of real estate mogul Barbara Corcoran, investor Mark Cuban, Netflix founder and CEO Reed Hastings, and futurist Samantha Radocchia. Brooks International features casino mogul Stephen Wynn, entrepreneur and philanthropist Richard Branson, and polar explorer Robert Swan, among others.

YOUR TASK Imagine that you have a budget of up to $100,000 to hire a well-known public speaker. In teams or individually, select a business-related category of speaker by visiting one of the speaker bureaus online. For example, choose several prominent personal finance gurus (Suze Orman, Terry Savage, and others) or successful entrepreneurs and venture capitalists (e.g., Elon Musk, Richard Branson, Jack Dorsey). Other categories are motivational speakers, philanthropists, and famous economists. Study their bios for clues about their expertise and accomplishments.

Comparing at least three speakers, come up with a set of qualities that apparently make these individuals sought-after speakers. Consider how those qualities could enlighten you and your peers. To enrich your experience and enhance your knowledge, watch videos of your chosen speakers on YouTube or the TED website, if available. Check talent agencies, personal websites, and Facebook for further information. Write a memo report about your speaker group, or present your findings orally, with or without a slide presentation. If your instructor directs, recommend your favorite speaker and give reasons for your decision.

14.4 Following a Business Tycoon on Twitter (L.O. 1)

`Communication Technology` `Social Media` `Web`

YOUR TASK On Twitter, in the Search window on top of the page, enter the name of the businessperson whose tweets you wish to follow. Bill Gates, Jeff Bezos, Tim Cook, Warren Buffett, Jack Ma, Martha Stewart, and other well-known businesspeople are avid Twitter users. Over the course of a few days, read the tweets of your favorite. After a while, you should be able to discern some trends and areas of interest. Note whether and how your subject responds to queries from followers. What are his or her favorite topics? Report your findings to the class, verbally with notes or using PowerPoint or Prezi. If you find particularly intriguing tweets and links, share them with the class.

14.5 Speaking Anxiety Be Banned! (L.O. 4)

`E-Mail` `Team`

What scares you the most about making a presentation in front of your class? Being tongue-tied? Fearing all eyes on you? Messing up? Forgetting your ideas and looking unprofessional?

YOUR TASK Discuss the previous questions as a class. Then, in groups of three or four, talk about ways to overcome these fears. Your instructor may ask you to write a memo, an e-mail, or a discussion board post (individually or collectively) summarizing your suggestions, or you may break out of your small groups and report your best ideas to the entire class.

14.6 Will You Get by Without Speaking in Your Field? Not Likely (L.O. 1, 4)

`Team`

YOUR TASK Interview one or two individuals in your professional field. How is oral communication important in this profession? Does the need for oral skills change as one advances? What suggestions can these people make to newcomers to the field for developing proficient oral communication skills? Discuss your findings with your class.

14.7 Outlining an Oral Presentation (L.O. 1, 2)

One of the hardest parts of preparing an oral presentation is developing the outline.

YOUR TASK Select an oral presentation topic from the list in **Activity 14.15**, or suggest an original topic. Prepare an outline for your presentation using the following format:

Title
Purpose

	I. INTRODUCTION
State your name	A.
Gain attention and involve audience	B.
Establish credibility	C.
Preview main points	D.
Transition	
	II. BODY
Main point	A.
Illustrate, clarify, contrast	1.
	2.
	3.
Transition	
Main point	B.
Illustrate, clarify, contrast	1.
	2.
	3.
Transition	
Main point	C.
Illustrate, clarify, contrast	1.
	2.
	3.
Transition	
	III. CONCLUSION
Summarize main points	A.
Provide final focus or take-away	B.
Encourage questions	C.

14.8 Life After Death by PowerPoint and Beyond (L.O. 1–3)

Web

YOUR TASK Watch Don McMillan's now famous YouTube classic "Life After Death by PowerPoint." Which specific PowerPoint sins is McMillan satirizing? Write a brief summary of the short clip for discussion in class. With your peers discuss whether the bad habits the YouTube video parodies correspond with design principles introduced in this chapter.

14.9 Examining a TED Talk (L.O. 1–3)

Communication Technology   **E-Mail**   **Web**

Communication consultant Nancy Duarte dispenses this useful piece of advice in her classic guide to business presentations, *Slide:ology*: "Keep yourself visually and conceptually fed by watching films, visiting museums, and reading design-related publications."[46] Duarte suggests that we can develop expertise by learning from and emulating outstanding examples.

To learn from the presentation skills of the best speakers today, visit the TED channel on YouTube or the TED website. Watch one or more of the 2,400+ TED talks (motto: Ideas worth spreading) available online. Standing at more than one billion views worldwide, the presentations cover topics from the fields of technology, entertainment, and design (TED).

YOUR TASK If your instructor directs, select and watch one of the TED talks and outline it. You may also be asked to focus on the speaker's presentation techniques based on the guidelines you have studied in this chapter. Jot down your observations either as notes for a classroom discussion or to serve as a basis for an informative memo or e-mail. If directed by your instructor, compose a concise yet informative tweet directing Twitter users to your chosen TED talk and commenting on it.

14.10 Showcasing Your Job (L.O. 1–3)

Communication Technology

Could you describe the multiple tasks you perform at work or when volunteering in a five-minute PowerPoint, Keynote, or Prezi presentation?

Your instructors, for example, may wear many hats. Most academics (a) teach; (b) conduct research to publish; and (c) serve the department, college, university, and community. Can you see how those aspects of their profession lend themselves to an outline of primary slides (teaching, publishing, service) and second-level slides (instructing undergraduate and graduate classes, presenting workshops, and giving lectures under the teaching label)?

YOUR TASK Now it's your turn to introduce the duties you perform (or performed) in a current or past job, volunteer activity, or internship in a brief, simple, yet well-designed slide presentation. Your goal is to inform your audience of your job duties in a three- to five-minute talk. Use animation features and graphics where appropriate.

14.11 Preparing the Perfect Elevator Pitch
(L.O. 1–3)

"Can you pass the elevator test?" asks presentation whiz Garr Reynolds in a new twist on the familiar scenario.[47] He suggests that this technique will help you sharpen your core message. In this exercise, you need to pitch your idea in a few brief moments instead of the 20 minutes you had been granted with your vice president of product marketing. You arrive at her door for your appointment as she is leaving, coat and briefcase in hand. Something has come up.

This meeting is a huge opportunity for you if you want to get the OK from the executive team. Could you sell your idea during the elevator ride and the walk to the parking lot? Reynolds asks. Although this scenario may never happen, you will possibly be asked to shorten a presentation, say, from an hour to 30 minutes or from 20 minutes to 5 minutes. Could you make your message tighter and clearer on the fly?

YOUR TASK Take a business idea you may have, a familiar business topic you care about, or a promotion or raise you wish to request. Create an impromptu two- to five-minute speech making a good case for your core message. Even though you won't have much time to think about the details of your speech, you should be sufficiently familiar with the topic to boil it down and yet be persuasive.

14.12 Practicing Phone Skills by Role-Playing (L.O. 6)

YOUR TASK Your instructor will divide the class into pairs. For each scenario take a moment to read and rehearse your role silently. Then play the role with your partner. If time permits, repeat the scenarios, changing roles.

Partner 1	Partner 2
a. You are the personnel manager of Technowire, Inc. Call Sheri Darbonne, office manager at Computer.ly. Inquire about a job applicant, Eden Collado, who listed Ms. Darbonne as a reference. Respond to Partner 2.	a. You are the receptionist for Computer.ly. The caller asks for Sheri Darbonne, who is home sick today. You don't know when she will be able to return. Answer the call appropriately.
b. Call Ms. Darbonne again the following day to inquire about the same job applicant, Eden Collado. Ms. Darbonne answers today, but she talks on and on, describing the applicant in great detail. Tactfully end the conversation.	b. You are now Ms. Darbonne, office manager. Describe Eden Collado, an imaginary employee. Think of someone with whom you have worked. Include many details, such as her ability to work with others, her appearance, her skills at computing, her schooling, her ambition, and so forth.
c. You are now the receptionist for Bruno Haider of Importiva. Answer a call for Mr. Haider, who is working in another office, at Extension 134, where he will accept calls.	c. You are now an administrative assistant for attorney Carson Michaelsen. Call Bruno Haider to verify a meeting date Mr. Michaelsen has with Mr. Haider. Use your own name in identifying yourself.
d. You are now Bruno Haider, owner of Importiva. Call your attorney, Carson Michaelsen, about a legal problem. Leave a brief, incomplete message.	d. You are now the receptionist for attorney Carson Michaelsen. Mr. Michaelsen is skiing in Telluride and will return in two days, but he doesn't want his clients to know where he is. Take a message.
e. Call Mr. Michaelsen again. Leave a message that will prevent telephone tag.	e. Take a message again as the receptionist for attorney Carson Michaelsen.

14.13 Professional Phone and Voice Mail Manners (L.O. 6)

YOUR TASK Practicing the phone skills you learned in this chapter, leave your instructor a professional voice mail message. Prepare a mini-agenda before you call. Introduce yourself. If necessary, spell your name and indicate the course and section. Speak slowly and clearly, especially when leaving your phone number. Think of a comment you could make about an intriguing fact, a peer discussion, or your business communication class. Be courteous: Include a polite greeting, and end the call on a gracious note.

14.14 Texting Like a Pro (L.O. 6)

Communication Technology

Much like professional e-mail and phone skills, texting in business is often markedly different in style and tone from the messages you may be exchanging with friends.

YOUR TASK Send a professional text message to your instructor or to another designated partner in class responding to one of the following scenarios: (a) Explain why you must be late to an important meeting; (b) request permission to purchase a piece of important equipment for the office; or (c) briefly summarize what you have learned in your latest staff development seminar (use a key concept from one of your business classes). Use the recipient's e-mail address to send your text. Do not use abbreviations or smiley faces.

14.15 Selecting Business Presentation Topics (L.O. 1–5)

Team

YOUR TASK Select a topic from the following list or from the report topics in the activities at the ends of Chapters 11 and 12. An expanded list of report topics is available at your Student Companion Website. Individually or as a team, prepare a short oral presentation. Consider yourself an expert or a team of experts called in to explain some aspect of the topic before a group of interested people. Because your time is limited, prepare a concise yet forceful presentation with effective visual aids.

If this is a group presentation, form a team of three or four members and conduct thorough research on one of the following topics, as directed by your instructor. Follow the tips on team presentations in this chapter. Divide the tasks fairly, meet for discussions and rehearsals, and crown your achievement with a 10- to 15-minute presentation to your class. Make your multimedia presentation interesting and dynamic.

a. How are businesses using Facebook, Instagram, Twitter, or LinkedIn? Is their social media presence effective? Cite specific examples in your chosen field.

b. Which is financially more beneficial to a business, leasing or buying company cars?

c. Tablet computers and other mobile devices are eroding the market share previously held by laptops and netbooks. Which brands are businesses embracing, and why? Which features are a must-have for businesspeople?

d. What kind of marketing works best with students on college campuses? Word of mouth? Internet banner advertising? Social media? Free samples? How do students prefer to get information about goods and services?

e. How can your organization appeal to its members to prevent them from texting while driving or from driving under the influence?

f. Some brands are not afraid to poke fun at themselves. Take Buick, maker of vehicles many associate with older drivers. The company leveraged this perception into a discussion of what Buick is today in a successful series of "Experience the New Buick" ads. Find three or more examples of companies admitting weaknesses, and draw conclusions from their strategies. Would you recommend this as a smart marketing ploy?

g. How can students and other citizens contribute to conserving gasoline and other fossil fuel to save money and help slow global climate change?

h. What is the career outlook in a field of your choice? Consider job growth, compensation, and benefits. What kind of academic or other experience is typically required in your field?

i. What is the economic outlook for a given product, such as electric cars, laptop computers, digital cameras, fitness equipment, or a product of your choice?

j. What kinds of workers can most easily work from home? Examine how the COVID-19 pandemic has changed telecommuting.

k. What are the Webby Awards, and what criteria do the judges use to evaluate websites? Alternatively, examine the Clio Awards or Cannes Lions Awards. Consider evaluation criteria and several of the most recent winners.

l. What franchise would offer the best investment opportunity for an entrepreneur in your area?

m. What should a guide to proper smartphone etiquette include?

n. Why should a company have a written e-mail, Web use, and social media policy?

o. Where should your organization hold its next convention?

p. What is the outlook for real estate (commercial or residential) investment in your area?

q. What do the personal assistants for celebrities do, and how does one become a personal assistant? (Investigate the Association of Celebrity Personal Assistants.)

r. What kinds of gifts are appropriate for businesses to give clients and customers during the holiday season?

s. What rip-offs are on the Federal Trade Commission's list of top ten consumer scams, and how can consumers avoid falling for them?

t. How can your organization or institution improve its image?

u. What are the pros and cons of using Prezi zoom presentations? Would they be appropriate in your field?

v. How can consumers protect themselves against identity theft?

w. How could people be persuaded to start saving for retirement, considering the magic of compound interest, which allows even small contributions to grow substantially over long periods of time? How could very young people who may not give much thought to retiring be motivated to start?

x. What are the differences among casual, business casual, and business formal attire?

y. What is a sustainable business? What can companies do to become sustainable?

z. What smartphone apps are available that will improve a businessperson's productivity?

New communication platforms and casual workplace environments have blurred the lines of appropriateness, leaving workers wondering how to navigate uncharted waters. Check your workplace etiquette IQ by deciding whether the following statements are true or false. Then see if you agree with the responses on p. Key-6.

1. At a business lunch, it is permissible to discuss topics such as sex, politics, or religion only if you know the other guests very well.

   _____ True _____ False

2. If a man has been invited to a business lunch by a businesswoman, he should offer to pay for his own lunch even if the host has made it clear that she is paying.

   _____ True _____ False

3. When you are a guest at a business dinner, you should not order expensive dishes, liquor, appetizers, or desserts unless the host does.

   _____ True _____ False

Chat About It

In each chapter you will find five discussion questions related to the chapter material. Your instructor may assign these topics for you to discuss in class, in an online chat room, or on an online discussion board. Some of the discussion topics may require outside research. You may also be asked to read and respond to postings made by your classmates.

TOPIC 1: In her best-selling book, the classic *Slide:ology*, Nancy Duarte says this about presentations: "Save the decorations for the holidays." What does she mean and how does this piece of advice apply to business presentations?

TOPIC 2: Remember some of the speeches or oral presentations you have witnessed. What were some of the elements that made them stand out, whether positively or negatively?

TOPIC 3: Why do some presenters avoid making steady eye contact? What might these individuals do to correct this problem?

TOPIC 4: Survey your class informally to find out what you and your classmates consider acceptable smartphone use in various settings—when walking down the street, in a restaurant, in a place of worship, in class, on a date, and more.

TOPIC 5: The American writer and humorist Mark Twain once said: "It usually takes me more than three weeks to prepare a good impromptu speech." *Impromptu*, as we have seen, describes delivery that's spontaneous, improvised, and not prepared beforehand. What is Mark Twain saying?

Grammar and Mechanics Review 14

Total Review

Each of the following sentences has a total of **three** errors in grammar, punctuation, capitalization, usage, or spelling. On a separate sheet, write a correct version. Avoid adding new phrases, starting new sentences, or rewriting in your own words. When finished, compare your responses with those in the key at the end of the book.

EXAMPLE: In the body of a short presentation speakers should focus on no more than 3 principle points.

REVISION: In the body of a short **presentation,** speakers should focus on no more than **three principal** points.

1. A poll of two thousand five hundred employees revealed that 4/5 of them said they feared giving a presentation more then anything else they could think of.

2. The CEOs assistant scheduled my colleague and I for a fifteen minute presentation to explain the new workplace sustainability initiative.

3. PowerPoint presentations, claims one expert should be no longer then twenty minutes and have no more than ten slides.

4. The introduction to a presentation should accomplish 3 goals, (a) capture attention, (b) establish credibility and (c) preview main points.

5. My accountant and me are greatful to be asked to make a short presentation, however, we may not be able to cover the entire budget.

6. A list with forty tips for inexperienced speakers are found in the article titled "Quick Tips For Speakers."

7. In the Spring our companies stock value is expected to raise at least 10 percent.

8. The Director of operations made a twenty-minute presentation giving step by step instructions on achieving our sustainability goals.

9. The appearance and mannerisms of a speaker definately effects a listeners evaluation of the message.

10. Because the bosses daughter was a dynamic speaker who had founded a successful company she earned at least twenty thousand dollars for each presentation.

Employment Communication

CHAPTER 15

The Job Search, Résumés, and Cover Letters in the Digital Age

LEARNING OUTCOMES

After studying this chapter, you should be able to do the following:

1 Describe how technology is altering the four major steps in a job search.

2 List search strategies that explore the open job market.

3 Identify search strategies that unlock the hidden job market.

4 Explain how to organize your qualifications and skills into effective résumé categories.

5 Describe digital tools that can enhance your job search and résumé.

6 Analyze the importance and construction of cover messages.

Zooming In Is Job Searching Like Dating?

Prominent career coach and prolific job-search thought leader Amanda Augustine sees many similarities in job searching and dating. In an interview with Mary Ellen Guffey, Augustine explained that, in both job seeking and dating, it's all about finding the right one—someone who shares your values but also brings out the best in you.

Just how does a candidate find that perfect job match? With the right approach, it's not as difficult as you might think, says Augustine. First, decide what you have to offer and what you want. Once you have clarified your goals, begin your job search. Your two main paths for locating job openings are online searching and networking. Nearly all candidates begin with an online search, but rather than sending your résumé to an online black hole, she emphasizes networking. Nearly 60 percent of jobs are gained through networking, which may open the door to the hidden job market by revealing unlisted jobs.

You may protest that you're in college and have no network. Not true, she retorts. Even college students have networking opportunities. You can develop network connections by including your friends, relatives, professors, and classmates. Let them know your qualifications and what you are seeking. One frequently overlooked resource for successful networking is your school's alumni. Reach out to people who graduated from your school. Amazingly, 90 percent of hiring managers, says Augustine, would prefer to hire a fellow alum if given the option. In expanding your network, attend local events in your field; listen to learn current trends and issues.

Referrals are equally important. You are ten times more likely to land a job when your application is accompanied by an employee referral. How can you obtain a referral? Before applying for a position, examine carefully your network to learn if you know anyone who currently works or previously worked at your target organization. An insider might provide not only a referral opportunity but also valuable information about the company culture and its hiring process.

When asked about job trends, Augustine noted that location is not as critical as it once was. Today's flexible work arrangements allow you to live and work almost anywhere you have an Internet connection. This greatly expands your job-search horizons; no longer are you confined to local listings. Another significant job trend, she says, is branding. Once you launch a job search, you become a marketer. Today's most successful candidates develop a brand that distinguishes them from other candidates.

Whether you are a traditional or nontraditional student, getting a job is of paramount interest near the end of your schooling. Developing your brand and expanding your personal network are critical steps in a successful job search.

Critical Thinking

- Amanda Augustine feels strongly that networking is the most effective way to find a job. What if you don't like networking and are uncomfortable pushing yourself into awkward conversations that you find distressing?

- What do you know about the hidden job market, and how does networking help a new grad find a job in this elusive market?

- Career expert Amanda Augustine encourages job applicants to develop their own "brands." You may object that you are not a car or a line of sneakers. What does "branding" mean to you, and why is it essential in a competitive job market?

15-1 Technology Shapes Today's Job Searching

LEARNING OUTCOME

1 Describe how technology is altering the four major steps in a job search.

In many ways, searching for a job is like dating, as employment specialist Amanda Augustine described in the Zooming In feature. As a candidate, you are searching for the right fit. Employers, too, are eager to find a perfect match. Whether you are actively looking for a position now or hope to do so later, becoming aware of job trends, requirements, and technology tools is essential for students. Why now? Doing so enables you to tailor your education, experience, and training to be most effective when you enter the market. This chapter presents the latest information regarding job searching, résumé writing, and cover messages to give you an advantage in a job market that is more competitive, more mobile, and more dependent on technology than ever before.

15-1a Emerging Trends in Digital Age Job Hunting

A successful job search today requires a blend of old and new job-hunting skills. Traditional techniques are still effective, but savvy job candidates must also be ready to act on emerging trends, some of which are presented in Figure 15.1. Job boards, social networks, and mobile technologies have all become indispensable tools in hunting for a job. Surprisingly, however, even in the digital age, networking and referrals are often the way many candidates find a job.

In any economic climate, employers need skilled workers to fill the strong demand for products and services. Businesses can't survive without workers. In the current complex and ever-changing economy, jobs are available, but competition is intense. A recent study of 2,500 recent grads by Cengage and Wakefield Research revealed that "although 93 percent of grads believe they'll land a job related to their college major, only 60 percent who graduated in the past 12 months managed to do so."[1] This chapter aims to guide you through the complex job-search process and help you land a dream job in your field of study.

FIGURE 15.1 | What You Need to Know About the Latest Trends in Job Searching

It's all digital.
Today's candidates search job boards, apply online, research employers, e-mail their résumés, and develop a personal online brand.

A positive social media presence is a must!
Those who haven't developed a social media presence may be left in the dust.

Mobile technologies are on the rise.
Candidates use apps to receive job listings and respond rapidly to openings; recruiters use mobile devices to post jobs, contact candidates, and forward résumés to company colleagues.

Networking—it's all about whom you know and who knows you.
Recruiters say their best job candidates come from referrals. Now, more than ever, candidates need to be proactive in making professional connections.

Interpersonal skills in high demand.
Increasingly, employers demand critical thinking, writing, speaking, and team skills, also called "soft skills."

Résumés must please skimmers and scanners.
Overwhelmed with candidates, recruiters hurriedly skim résumés preselected by scanning devices using artificial intelligence.

15-1b Mobile Technology Dominates Job Searching

Technology has become an integral part of the job-search process for both candidates and organizations. Nearly every job hunter today has at least one mobile device, and the number of apps for these devices is overwhelming. You can download apps to plan your career, organize the job-search process, scour numerous job boards, receive immediate job alerts, and even arrange lunch dates to network and meet others in your field. Working from a smartphone, you can create, store, and send a résumé at the beach, on the train, or whenever a promising opening pops up.

Organizations Rely on Technology. Beyond mobile devices, technology has greatly affected the way organizations announce jobs, select candidates, screen résumés, and conduct interviews. Companies of all sizes now employ applicant tracking systems (ATS) to automatically post openings, select résumés, rank candidates, and generate interview requests. Automated texting enables candidates to be better informed about the status of their applications. With all the digital options in job searching, candidates more than ever need guidance in crafting their job search and résumés. Tips in this chapter will help you to adapt your job search and résumé to take advantage of tracking systems and other technologies flooding the job-search market.

Just as candidates are eager to find the right fit, organizations are eager to hire people who will fit into their culture. A candidate today should be prepared for a longer interview process, perhaps enduring as many as four different interviews as companies strive to find the perfect someone who fits their culture.

Has Technology Killed the Résumé? The résumé is still important, but it may not be the document that introduces you as a job seeker. Instead, the résumé may come only after you have established a real-world relationship. What's more, chances are that your résumé and cover message will be read digitally rather than in print. Although some attention-grabbing publications scream that the print résumé is dead, the truth is that every job hunter needs one. Whether offered online or in print, your résumé should be always available and current. Later in this chapter we'll present résumé styles, formats, and online posting tips.

15-1c Four-Step Process Guides Job Search

It's natural to think that the first step in finding a job is writing a résumé. However, that's a mistake. The job-search process begins long before you are ready to prepare your résumé. Regardless of the kind of employment you seek, you must invest time and effort in getting ready. As illustrated in Figure 15.2, your best plan for completing a successful job search involves a four-step process: (1) analyzing yourself, (2) exploring the open and hidden job markets, (3) creating a customized résumé package, and (4) knowing the hiring process.

Opening Your Job Search With Self-Analysis. Despite the decided movement toward all things digital, many aspects of job searching still revolve around you. The first step in a job search is analyzing your interests and goals and evaluating your qualifications. This means looking inside yourself to explore what you like and dislike so that you can make good employment choices. For guidance in choosing a career that eventually proves to be satisfying, ask yourself the following questions:

- What are you passionate about? Can you turn this passion into a career?
- Do you enjoy working with people, data, or things?
- How important are salary, benefits, technology support, and job stimulation?
- Must you work in a specific city, geographic area, or climate?
- Are you looking for security, travel opportunities, money, power, or prestige?
- How would you describe the perfect job, boss, and coworkers?

If you need assistance in your self-analysis, numerous online tools help measure personalities, interests, skills, and values. One of the best known is the **Myers–Briggs Type Indicator**. It divides

FIGURE 15.2 Four Steps in an Effective Job Search

1

Analyze Yourself

- Identify your interests and goals.
- Assess your qualifications.
- Explore career opportunities.

2

Explore the Open and Hidden Job Markets

- Search online job boards and beyond.
- Prospect for jobs on social media.
- Begin building your personal network.
- Create your personal brand.

3

Create a Customized Résumé and Cover Letter

- Choose a résumé style.
- Tailor your résumé to each targeted position.
- Maximize the potential rank of your résumé.
- Prepare a LinkedIn profile.

4

Know the Hiring Process

- Submit your résumé, application, e-portfolio, or video.
- Undergo screening and hiring interviews.
- Accept an offer or reevaluate your progress.

people into four temperaments (guardian, idealist, rational, and artisan). A similar tool is **Big Five**, which groups people into five personality types (openness, conscientiousness, extraversion, agreeableness, and neuroticism).

Taking Stock of Your Qualifications.

Once you have analyzed your interests and goals, it's time to take a hard look at your qualifications. Remember that today's job market is fiercely competitive. How will your qualifications stack up against those of other candidates? What assets can you offer? Your responses to the following questions will target your thinking as well as prepare a foundation for your résumé. Always keep in mind, though, that employers seek more than empty assurances; they will want proof of your qualifications.

- What technology skills can you present? What specific software programs are you familiar with, what Internet experience do you have, and what social media skills can you offer?

- Do you communicate well in speech and in writing? Do you know another language? How can you verify these talents?

- What other skills have you acquired in school, on the job, or through activities? How can you demonstrate these skills?

- Do you work well with people? Do you enjoy teamwork? What proof can you offer? Consider extracurricular activities, clubs, class projects, and jobs.

- Are you a leader, self-starter, or manager? What evidence can you offer? What leadership roles have you held?

- Do you learn quickly? Can you think critically? How can you demonstrate these characteristics?

Preparing for Career Opportunities.

The job picture in the United States remains extraordinarily dynamic and flexible. In a U.S. Bureau of Statistics 37-year longitudinal survey, individuals between the ages of 28 and 52 averaged 12.3 jobs with nearly half of these jobs held before the age of 25.[2] If the past is any indication of the future, you can expect to have as many as six different jobs before you reach 25. Older workers can also expect to hold many different positions during their working lives. Not only are people changing jobs, but they often are working in new ways: flexibly, remotely, and part time in the gig economy. In the past workers expected to develop skills and remain in their careers for life. Today, continuous education and training are required to remain relevant and employable.

Because you can expect to hold numerous jobs in your future, now is the time to explore career opportunities so that you can make the best decisions when job possibilities arise. Where can you find the best career data? Here are some suggestions:

- **Visit your campus career center**. Most campus career centers have literature, inventories, career-related software programs, and employment or internship databases that allow you to explore such fields as accounting, finance, office technology, information systems, and hotel management.

- **Search for career apps**. Many job-search sites—such as Indeed, Monster, and CareerBuilder—offer career-planning information and resources. One popular Apple app is PathSource, a tool that suggests careers, gives salaries, and helps you build a résumé.

- **Check government data**. Consult O*NET Online (*Occupational Outlook Information Network*), available from the U.S. Department of Labor. It provides detailed descriptions of the world of work and helps you explore careers in industry, science, education, the military, and other fields.

- **Take a summer job, internship, or part-time position in your field**. Nothing is better than trying out a career. Many companies offer internships and temporary or part-time jobs to begin training college students and to develop relationships with them. An amazing number of interns are hired into full-time positions—57 percent in one study.[3]

- **Interview someone in your chosen field**. People are usually flattered when asked to describe their careers. Inquire about needed skills, required courses, financial and other rewards, benefits, working conditions, future trends, and entry requirements.

- **Volunteer with a nonprofit organization**. Many colleges and universities encourage service learning. In volunteering your services, you can gain valuable experience, and nonprofits appreciate the expertise and fresh ideas that students bring.

- **Monitor the classified ads**. Early in your college career, begin monitoring want ads and the websites of companies in your career area. Check job availability, qualifications sought, duties, and salary ranges. Don't wait until you are about to graduate to explore the job market.

Reality Check

Get Experience First

"Students need to build practical skills much earlier than in the past," says Lesley Mitler, career coach for young adults. She urges her clients "to do two to four internships before graduating to acquire the analytical, technical and interpersonal skills they may not learn in class."[4]

—Lesley Mitler, *co-founder, Early Stage Careers*

15-2 Exploring the Open Job Market

LEARNING OUTCOME

2 List search strategies that explore the open job market.

Candidates for jobs will quickly become aware of two distinct job markets. The open job market consists of jobs that are advertised or publicly listed. The hidden job market consists of jobs that are never advertised or listed. Some analysts and authors claim that between 50 and 80 percent of all jobs are never listed or are filled before they even make it to online job boards or advertisements.[5] Those openings are in the hidden job market, which we will explore shortly. First, let's start where most job seekers begin—in the open job market.

15-2a Surveying the Big Boards and Beyond

Job seekers generally start their job search by visiting the big job boards. Sadly, searching well-known job boards such as Monster and Indeed is a common, but not always rewarding, approach. Both recruiters and job seekers have valid complaints. Corporate recruiters readily post job openings at job boards, but these recruiters moan that such ads bring a flood of candidates, many unsuited for the listed jobs. Job candidates grumble that job board listings are frequently outdated and fail to produce leads.

To many candidates, Internet job boards seem like a giant swamp that swallows résumés. Yet job boards can provide valuable job-search information such as résumé, interviewing, and salary tips. Job boards also serve as a jumping-off point in most searches. They inform candidates about the kinds of jobs available and the skill sets required. Some professionals, however, believe that job boards may be on their way out.[6] Social media sites have taken the recruitment world by storm, and savvy millennials and others are eagerly turning to LinkedIn, Facebook, and Twitter to search for jobs. Still, many job seekers will begin their search with job boards.

Four Top Job Sites. Although job hunters and recruiters complain about them, job boards provide listings and valuable information. Following are four of the best job sites for both traditional and nontraditional college students:

- **Indeed** offers millions of job postings in one place. Whether you are looking for your first real job, changing careers, or seeking career advancement, Indeed presents extensive listings from company career pages.
- **CareerBuilder** lets you filter by several criteria such as location, degree required, and pay range.
- **Monster** permits you to upload your résumé and offers company profiles, a résumé review service, and a mobile app.
- **CollegeRecruiter** strives to be the premier information and job source for recent grads who are seeking employment, continuing education, or business opportunities. It focuses on positions that generally require zero to three years of work experience.

Niche Sites for Specialized Fields. If you seek a job in a particular field, look for a niche site, such as **Dice** for technology jobs, **Advance Healthcare Network** for jobs in the medical field, and **Accountemps** for temporary accounting positions. Niche websites also exist for job seekers with special backgrounds or needs, such as **GettingHired** for disabled workers and **Workforce50** for older workers. If you are looking for a short-term job, check out **CoolWorks**, which specializes in seasonal employment. If you yearn for a government job, try **USAJOBS**, a website for students and recent graduates interested in federal service.

Company Websites for the Best Leads. Although you may start by searching job boards and niche sites, probably the best way to find a job online is at a company's own website. Many companies post job openings only at their own sites to avoid being inundated by the hordes of applicants—many unqualified—responding to postings at online job boards. A company's website is the first place to go if you have a specific employer in mind. You might find vision and mission statements, a history of the organization, and the names of key hiring managers. Possibly you will see a listing for a position that doesn't fit your qualifications. Even though you're not right for this job, you have discovered that the company is hiring. Don't be afraid to send a résumé and cover message expressing your desire to be considered for future jobs.

Newspapers, Career Fairs, and Other Sources. Despite the rush to social media and mobile technology, some organizations still list openings in newspapers. Don't overlook this possibility, especially for local jobs. Craigslist can be a haven for people looking for part-time or even full-time work. Plenty of jobs can also be found through career fairs and university and college alumni contacts.

15-2b Gaining an Edge With Mobile Apps

Job seekers are eagerly embracing smartphone apps to gain an edge in the job search. With many of the following mobile apps, you can access and vet job openings as soon as they are listed—even when you are on the go. Like its full website, the **Indeed Job Search** app lets you filter your search results based on your field, desired salary, and location. **Intro** is an app that connects you to people in your field or in your social media network. **JobAware** allows you to integrate all your Internet job-search activity including LinkedIn. **JobCompass** helps you narrow the search to your zip code. **LinkUp Job Search Engine, Monster, Reach, Simply Hired, Snagajob**, and **Switch** all offer mobile links to job listings from a variety of sources.[7]

When posting job-search information online, it's natural to want to put your best foot forward and openly share information that will get you a job. The challenge is to strike a balance between supplying enough information and protecting yourself. To avoid some of the risks involved, study the cautions described in Figure 15.3.

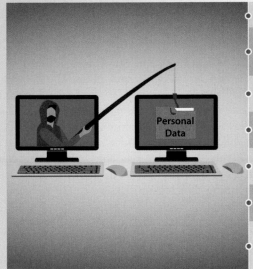

Use reputable, well-known sites and never pay to post your résumé.

Don't divulge personal data such as your date of birth, social security number, or home address. Use your city and state or region in place of your home address.

Set up a separate e-mail account with a professional-sounding e-mail address for your job search.

Post privately if possible. Doing so means that you can control who has access to your e-mail address and other information.

Keep careful records of every site on which you posted. At the end of your job search, remove all posted résumés.

Don't include your references or reveal their contact information without permission.

Don't respond to blind job postings (those without company names or addresses). Unfortunately, scammers use online job boards to post fake job ads to gather your personal information.

15-3 Unlocking the Hidden Job Market

LEARNING OUTCOME

3 Identify search strategies that explore the hidden job market.

Not all available positions are announced or advertised in the open job market. As mentioned earlier, between 50 and 80 percent of jobs are estimated to be in the hidden job market. Companies prefer to avoid publicizing job announcements openly for many reasons. They don't welcome the deluge of unqualified candidates. What's more, companies dislike hiring unknown quantities. Career coach Donald Asher, author of *Cracking the Hidden Job Market*, sets this scene: Imagine you are a hiring manager facing hundreds of résumés on your desk and a coworker walks in with the résumé of someone she vouches for. Which résumé do you think hits the top of the stack?[8] Companies prefer known quantities.

The most successful job candidates seek to transform themselves from unknown into known quantities through networking. Many jobs today are found through referrals and person-to-person contacts. That's because people trust what they know. Therefore, your goal is to become known to a large network of people, and this means going beyond close friends.

15-3a Building a Personal Network

Because most candidates find jobs today through networking, be prepared to work diligently to build your personal networks. Just what is **networking**? In the context of job searching, networking means developing a supportive system of individuals with a common interest who are willing to share information and services. If you are looking for a job, networking involves meeting people and talking to them about your field or industry so that you can gain information and possibly open doors to job vacancies.

Not only are many jobs never advertised, but some positions aren't even contemplated until the right person appears. One recent college grad underwent three interviews for a position, but the company hired someone else. After being turned down, the grad explained why she thought she was perfect for this company but perhaps in a different role. Apparently, the hiring manager agreed and decided to create a new job (in social media) because of the skills, personality, and perseverance of this determined young grad. Traditional networking pays off, but it requires dedication. Here are three steps that will help you establish your own network:

Step 1: Develop a contact list. Make a list of anyone who would be willing to talk with you about finding a job. Figure 15.4 suggests possibilities. Even if you haven't talked with people in years, reach out to them in person or online. Consider asking your campus career center for alumni willing to talk with students. Also dig into your social networking circles, which we will discuss shortly.

Step 2: Make contacts in person and online. Call the people on your list or connect online. To set up a meeting in person, say, *Hi,_____. I'm looking for a job and I wonder if you could help me out. When could I come over to talk about it?* During your visit be friendly, well organized, polite, and interested in what your contact has to say. Provide a copy of your résumé, and try to keep the conversation centered on your job search. Your goal is to get two or more referrals. In pinpointing your request, ask, *Do you know of anyone who might have an opening for a person with my skills?* If the person does not, ask, *Do you know of anyone else who might know of someone?*

Step 3: Follow up on your referrals. Call or contact the people on your list. You might say something like, *Hello. I'm Stacy Rivera, a friend of Jason Tilden. He suggested that I ask you for help. I'm looking for a position as a marketing trainee, and he thought you might be willing to spare a few minutes and steer me in the right direction.* Don't ask for a job. During your referral interview, ask how the individual got started in this line of work, what he or she likes best (or least) about the work, what career paths exist in the field, and what problems a newcomer must overcome. Most important, ask how a person with your background and skills might get started in the field. Send an informal thank-you note to anyone who helps you in your job search, and stay in touch with the most promising people. Ask whether you could stay in contact every three weeks or so during your job search.

Unfortunately, many new grads are reluctant to engage in traditional person-to-person networking because it feels pushy, and it requires considerable effort. They are much more comfortable with networking through social media sites.

FIGURE 15.4	Whom to Contact in Networking

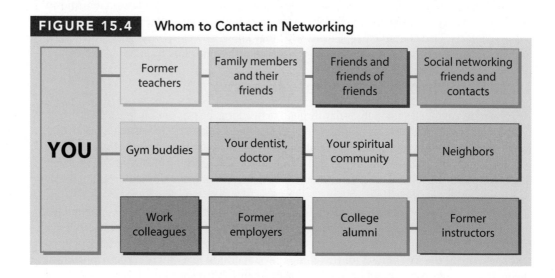

15-3b Targeting Social Media in a Job Search

As digital technology saturates our lives, job candidates have powerful tools at their disposal: social media networks. One of the most important networks is LinkedIn, which has become critical in a job search. If you just send out your résumé blindly, not much will happen. However, if you have a referral, your chances of landing an interview multiply. Social media are a principal path to developing those coveted referrals.

Letting LinkedIn Help You Find a Job. If you are seriously looking for a job, it's extremely important that you create a LinkedIn profile. This social media site dominates the world of job searching and recruiting. As discussed in Chapter 7, polls have shown that as many as 95 percent of recruiting and staffing professionals use LinkedIn to locate and vet job candidates.[9] Critics, however, complain that people post their profiles at LinkedIn and then fail to update them. Résumés posted on Facebook and Instagram may be more active.[10] Regardless, LinkedIn is truly the place to find and be found—especially for new grads. Developing an online presence at LinkedIn enables you to post information about yourself in one central place where it's available to potential employers, graduate schools, future colleagues, and people you will want to stay connected to. A LinkedIn page tells the working world that you are a professional, and it remains significant even after you obtain a position. However, your LinkedIn page must be updated regularly!

One of the best ways to use LinkedIn is to search for a company in which you are interested. Try to find company employees who are connected to other people you know. Then use that contact as a referral when you apply. You can also send an e-mail to everyone in your LinkedIn network asking for help or for people they could put you in touch with. Don't be afraid to ask an online contact for advice on getting started in a career and for suggestions to help a newcomer break into that career. Another excellent way to use a contact is to have that person look at your résumé and help you tweak it. Like Facebook, LinkedIn has status updates, and it's critical to update yours regularly so that your connections know what is happening in your career search and afterward.

Sadly, some young people dislike LinkedIn because they say it's bland, boring, and restrictive.[12] Admittedly, it's not a "fun" social media site and it does have rules, but LinkedIn can aid your job search in at least five ways, as shown in Figure 15.5. Because LinkedIn functions in many ways as a résumé, you will find tips for preparing your LinkedIn page in our discussion of résumés coming up shortly.

metamorworks/Shutterstock.com

What About Facebook, Twitter, and Instagram? In addition to LinkedIn, job seekers will find employment opportunities on other social media sites, such as Facebook, Twitter, and Instagram. If you are in the market for a job, these sites are places where you can showcase your skills, highlight your experience, and possibly land that dream job. Because organizations may post open jobs to their Facebook or Twitter pages prior to advertising them elsewhere, you might gain a head start on applying by following these organizations on their social media sites. If you have a Facebook account, examine your profile and decide what you want prospective employers to see—or not see. Create a simple profile with minimal graphics, widgets, and photos. Post only content relevant to your job search or career, and choose your friends wisely.

Employers often visit social media sites to check the online presence of a candidate. They check social media to keep tabs on and vet candidates before the interview. Make sure your social networking accounts represent you professionally. You can make it easy for your potential

FIGURE 15.5   Harnessing the Power of LinkedIn

Five Ways LinkedIn Can Help You Find a Job

1. **Receiving Job Alerts.** LinkedIn notifies you of recommended jobs.

2. **Leveraging Your Network.** You may start with two connections, but you can leverage those connections to thousands.

3. **Researching a Company.** Before applying to a company, you can check it out on LinkedIn and locate valuable inside information.

4. **Getting Recommendations.** LinkedIn helps you take the awkwardness out of asking for recommendations. It's so easy!

5. **Helping Companies Find You.** Many companies are looking for skilled college grads, and your strong profile on LinkedIn can result in inquiries.

employer to learn more about you by including an informative bio in your Twitter or Facebook profile that has a link to your LinkedIn profile. Posting thoughtful blog posts and tweets on topics related to your career goal makes you even more discoverable.

15-3c Building Your Personal Brand

A large part of your job-search strategy involves creating a brand for yourself. You may be thinking, *Who me? A brand?* Yes, absolutely! Even college grads should seriously consider branding because finding a job in a competitive market is tough. Before you get into the thick of the job hunt, focus on developing your brand so that you know what you want to emphasize.

Personal branding involves deciding what makes you special and desirable in the job market. What is your unique selling point? What special skill set or trait makes you stand out among all job applicants? What would your instructors or employers say is your greatest strength? Think about your intended audience. What are you promoting about yourself?

FOR THE RECORD

What Next? Facebook for Jobs!

Employers routinely refer to job applicants' social media sites to discover indiscretions. Perhaps less commonly known, however, is that Facebook now allows employers to post jobs directly to their pages. This enables employers to run the postings as ads and target potential employees. The good news for job hunters is that many already have Facebook accounts and can fill out job applications automatically with their profile information. Be aware, however, that when using Facebook as part of a job search, candidates must be extremely careful to separate personal friends from professional contacts. The professional contacts list becomes a way for job seekers to reach out by posting industry-related content and personal work-related status updates. How can you build your personal brand on Facebook?[13]

Experts suggest that you create a tagline that describes what you do, who you are, and what's special about you. A nurse wrote this fetching tagline:

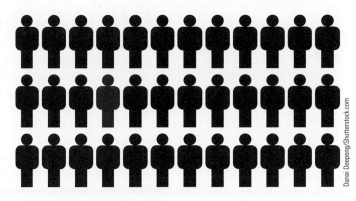

Tireless, caring Registered Nurse who helps pediatric cancer patients and their families feel at ease throughout treatment and recovery

If you prefer a shorter tagline for your business card, consider the sample taglines for new grads in Figure 15.6. It's OK to shed a little modesty and strut your stuff. However, do keep your tagline simple, short, and truthful so that it's easy to remember. Does your tagline makes you stand out from the crowd?

Once you have a tagline, prepare a professional-looking business card with your name and tagline. Include an easy-to-remember e-mail address such as *firstname.lastname@domain.com*. Despite digital alternatives, many businesspeople maintain that printed cards add a personal touch, are easy to carry, and make you look professional. If you prefer a digital version, consider using CardDrop, an app that creates a digital business card to use to connect with new contacts and help you be remembered.

Now that you have your tagline and business card, work on an elevator speech. This is a pitch that you can give in 60 seconds or less describing who you are and what you can offer. Tweak your speech for your audience, and practice until you can say it naturally. Here are suggestions to help you prepare your own authentic elevator speech depending on your situation:

Hi, my name is _____, and I am about to graduate from _____ with a major in _____. I'm looking to _____ because I enjoy _____. Recently I _____ where I was able to develop skills such as _____. I'm most confident about my skills in _____. I'm inspired by the field (or position) of _____ because _____ . My ultimate aim is to _____. I'm looking for a position in _____. Do you have any suggestions or advice on how I can _____?

FIGURE 15.6 **Branding YOU**

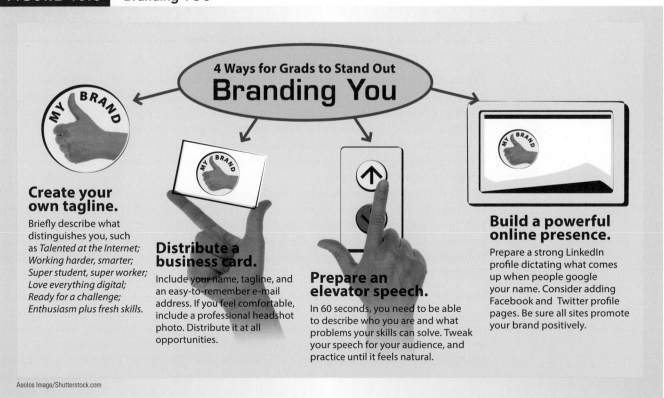

Aeolos Image/Shutterstock.com

LEARNING OUTCOME

4 Explain how to organize your qualifications and skills into effective résumé categories.

15-4 Customizing Your Résumé

In today's highly competitive job market, you must customize your résumé for every position you seek. The competition is so stiff that you cannot get by with a generic, one-size-fits-all résumé. Although you can start with a basic résumé, you should customize it to fit each company and position if you want it to stand out from the crowd.

In this digital era, the Internet has made it exceedingly simple to apply for jobs. Result: Recruiters are swamped with applications. You now have between 5 and 10 seconds to catch the recruiter's eye—if your résumé is even read by a person. It may very well first encounter an **applicant tracking system (ATS)**. This software helps businesses automatically post openings, screen résumés, rank candidates, and generate interview requests. These automated systems make writing your résumé doubly challenging. Although your goal is to satisfy a recruiter or hiring manager, that person may never see your résumé unless it is selected by the ATS. Because so many organizations are using ATS software today, this chapter provides you with the latest advice on how to get your résumé ranked highly—so that it will then proceed to a real human being who will call you for an interview.

15-4a Selecting a Résumé Style

The first step in preparing a winning, customized résumé that appeals to both the human reader and the ATS screening device is to decide what style to use. Résumés usually fall into two categories: chronological and functional. This section presents basic information as well as insider tips on how to choose an appropriate résumé style, determine its length, and arrange its parts. You will also learn about adding a summary of qualifications, which many busy hiring managers readily welcome. In the upcoming pages, we present numerous examples for you to use as models.

What Is a Chronological Résumé?   The most popular résumé format is the chronological format, shown in Model Documents 15.3, 15.4, 15.6. The chronological résumé lists work history job by job but in reverse order, starting with the most recent position. Recruiters favor the chronological format because they are familiar with it and because it quickly reveals a candidate's education and experience. The chronological style works well for candidates who have experience in their field of employment and for those who show steady career growth, but it is less helpful for people who have changed jobs frequently or who have gaps in their employment records. For college students and others who lack extensive experience, the functional résumé format may be preferable.

What Is a Functional Résumé?   The functional résumé, shown in Model Document 15.5 on page 558, focuses on a candidate's skills rather than on past employment. Like a chronological résumé, a functional résumé begins with the candidate's name, contact information, job objective, and education. Instead of listing jobs, though, the functional résumé groups skills and accomplishments in special categories, such as Supervisory and Management Skills or Retailing and Marketing Experience. This résumé style highlights accomplishments and can de-emphasize a negative employment history.

People who have changed jobs frequently, who have gaps in their employment records, or who are entering an entirely different field may prefer the functional résumé. Recent graduates with little or no related employment experience often find the functional résumé useful. Older job seekers who want to downplay a long job history and job hunters who are afraid of appearing overqualified may also prefer the functional format. Be aware, though, that online job boards may insist on the chronological format.

How Long Should a Résumé Be?   Experts disagree on how long a résumé should be. Conventional wisdom has always held that recruiters prefer one-page résumés. However, recruiters who are serious about candidates often prefer the kind of details that can be provided in a two-page or longer résumé. What's more, with today's digital résumés, length is no longer restricted. The best advice is to make your résumé as long as needed to present your skills to recruiters and hiring managers. Individuals with more experience will naturally have longer résumés. Those with fewer than ten years of experience, those making a major career change, and those who have had only one or two employers will likely have one-page résumés. Those with ten years or more of related experience may have two-page résumés. Finally, some senior-level managers and executives with a lengthy history of major accomplishments might have résumés that are three pages or longer.[14]

15-4b Organizing Your Information Into Effective Résumé Categories

Although résumés have standard categories, their arrangement and content should be strategically planned. A customized résumé emphasizes skills and achievements aimed at a specific job or company. It shows a candidate's most important qualifications first, and it de-emphasizes weaknesses. In organizing your qualifications and information, try to create as few headings as possible; more than six looks cluttered. No two résumés are ever exactly alike, but most writers include all or some of these categories: Main Heading, Career Objective, Summary of Qualifications, Education, Experience, Capabilities and Skills, and Awards and Activities.

Main Heading. Your résumé, whether chronological or functional, should start with an uncluttered and simple main heading. The first line should always be your name; add your middle initial for an even more professional look. Format your name so that it stands out on the page. Following your name, include your e-mail address and social media handles, if relevant. Some candidates omit their street addresses to protect their privacy and for safety reasons. Your telephone listing should be one where you can receive text and voice mail messages. The outgoing message at this number should be in your voice, it should state your full name, and it should be concise and professional. If you include your cell phone number and are expecting an important call from a recruiter, pick up only when you are in a quiet environment and can concentrate.

For your e-mail address, be sure it sounds professional instead of something like *toosexy4you@gmail.com* or *sixpackguy@yahoo.com*. Also be sure that you are using a personal e-mail address. Putting your work e-mail address on your résumé announces to prospective employers that you are using your current employer's resources to look for another job. If you have a LinkedIn profile or a website where an e-portfolio or samples of your work can be viewed, include the links in the main heading.

Career Objective or Job Title. Although experts disagree about whether to include an objective or a job title on a résumé, nearly all agree that if you do, it should be very specific. A well-written objective—customized for the job opening—makes sense, especially for new grads with fresh training and relevant skills. Strive to include strategic keywords from the job listing because these will help tracking systems select your résumé. Focus on what you can contribute to the organization, not on what the organization can do for you.

> **Poor objective:** To obtain a position with a well-established organization that will lead to a lasting relationship in the field of marketing. (Sounds vague and self-serving.)

> **Improved objective:** To obtain a position that capitalizes on my recent training in business writing and marketing to boost customer contacts and expand brand penetration using my social media expertise. (Names specific skills and includes many nouns that might snag the attention of an ATS.)

If you decide to use a job title instead of an objective, consider including the words *Target Job Title* as shown here:

Target Job Title: Medical Administrative Assistant

Using a customized objective or a job title makes it clear that you have taken the time and made the effort to prepare your résumé for the position. If you decide to omit a career objective, be sure to discuss your career goals in your cover message.

Optional Summary of Qualifications.   Over the past decade, the biggest change in résumés has been a switch from a career objective to a **summary of qualifications** at the top. Also called a *Résumé Summary* or *Profile Statement*, this list presents a snapshot of your most notable work experience, achievements, and skills.[16] Once a job is advertised, a hiring manager may receive hundreds or even thousands of résumés. A summary ensures that your most impressive qualifications are not overlooked by a recruiter who is skimming résumés quickly. A summary also enables you to present a concentrated list of many relevant keywords for a tracking system to pick up, thus boosting your chance of selection. Additionally, because résumés today may be viewed on tablets and smartphones, the summary spotlights your most compelling qualifications in a highly visible spot.

Your summary might consist of a list of three to eight bulleted statements proving that you are the ideal candidate for the position. When formulating these statements, consider your experience in the field, your education, your unique skills, awards you have won, certifications you hold, and any other accomplishments. Strive to quantify your achievements wherever possible. Target the most important qualifications an employer will be looking for in the person hired for this position. Focus on nouns that might be selected as keywords by a tracking system. Examples of qualifications summaries appear in Model Documents 15.3 and 15.5.

Education.   The next component in a chronological résumé is your education—if it is more noteworthy than your work experience. In this section you should include the name and location of schools, dates of attendance, major fields of study, and degrees received. By the way, once you have attended college. you needn't list high school information on your résumé.

Your grade point average (GPA) and/or class ranking may be important to prospective employers in certain fields. In accounting, education, finance, health, and law, GPA is an important qualification. A high GPA is generally proof that you can complete tasks, are organized, and can handle stress. If your GPA is not stellar, one way to enhance it is to calculate it in your major courses only (for example, *3.6/4.0 in major*). Doing so is not unethical if you clearly show that your GPA is in the major only.

Under Education you might be tempted to list all the courses you took, but such a list makes for dull reading and consumes valuable space. Include a brief list of courses only if you can relate them to the position sought. When relevant, include certificates earned, seminars attended, workshops completed, scholarships awarded, and honors earned. If your education is incomplete, include such statements as *BS degree expected 6/22* or *80 units completed in 120-unit program*. Title this section Education, Academic Preparation, or Professional Training. If you are preparing a functional résumé, you will probably put the Education section below your skills summary, as in Model Document 15.5.

Work Experience or Employment History.   When your work or volunteer experience is significant and relevant to the position sought, this information should appear before your education. List your most recent employment first and work backward, including only those jobs that you think will help you win the targeted position. A job application form may demand a full employment history, but your résumé may be selective. Be aware, though, that time gaps in your employment history will probably be questioned in the interview. For each position show the following:

- Employer's name, city, and state
- Dates of employment (month and year)
- Most important job title
- Significant duties, activities, accomplishments, and promotions

Be sure to include relevant volunteer work. A survey conducted by LinkedIn revealed that 41 percent of LinkedIn hiring managers consider volunteer work experience as respectable as paid work experience when evaluating candidates.[18]

Your employment achievements and job duties will be easier to read if you place them in bulleted lists. Rather than list every single thing you have done, customize your information so that it relates to the targeted job. Your bullet points should be concise but not complete sentences, and they usually do not include personal pronouns (*I, me, my*). Strive to be specific:

Poor:	Worked with customers
Improved:	Developed superior customer service skills by successfully interacting with 40+ customers daily

Whenever possible, quantify your achievements:

Poor:	Did equipment study and report
Improved:	Conducted research and wrote final study analyzing equipment needs of 100 small businesses in Houston
Poor:	Was successful in sales
Improved:	Personally generated orders for sales of $90,000 annually

In addition to technical skills, employers seek individuals with communication, management, and interpersonal capabilities. This means you will want to select work experiences and achievements that illustrate your initiative, dependability, responsibility, resourcefulness, flexibility, and leadership. Employers also want people who can work in teams.

Poor:	Worked effectively in teams
Improved:	Enjoyed collaborating with five-member interdepartmental team in developing ten-page handbook for temporary workers
Poor:	Joined in team effort on campus
Improved:	Headed 16-member student government team that conducted the most successful voter registration in campus history

Statements describing your work experience should include many nouns relevant to the job you seek. These nouns may match keywords sought by the ATS. To appeal to human readers, your statements should also include action verbs, such as those in Figure 15.7. Starting each of your bullet points with an action verb helps ensure that your bulleted lists are parallel.

Capabilities and Skills.   Recruiters want to know specifically what you can do for their companies. List your special skills, including many nouns that relate to the targeted position. Highlight your familiarity with the Internet, searches, software programs, apps, social media platforms, office equipment, and other communication technology tools. Use expressions such as *proficient in, competent in, experienced in*, and *ability to*, as illustrated in the following:

Poor:	Have payroll experience
Improved:	Proficient in preparing federal, state, and local payroll tax returns as well as franchise and personal property tax returns
Poor:	Trained in computer graphics
Improved:	Certified in graphic design including infographics through an intensive 350-hour classroom program
Poor:	Have writing skills
Improved:	Competent in writing, editing, and proofreading reports, tables, letters, memos, e-mails, manuscripts, and business forms

FIGURE 15.7   Action Verbs for a Powerful Résumé

Communication Skills	Teamwork, Supervision Skills	Management, Leadership Skills	Research Skills	Clerical, Detail Skills	Creative Skills
clarified	advised	analyzed	assessed	activated	acted
collaborated	coordinated	authorized	collected	approved	conceptualized
explained	demonstrated	coordinated	critiqued	classified	designed
interpreted	developed	directed	diagnosed	edited	fashioned
integrated	evaluated	headed	formulated	generated	founded
persuaded	expedited	implemented	gathered	maintained	illustrated
promoted	facilitated	improved	interpreted	monitored	integrated
resolved	guided	increased	investigated	proofread	invented
summarized	motivated	organized	reviewed	recorded	originated
translated	set goals	scheduled	studied	streamlined	revitalized
wrote	trained	strengthened	systematized	updated	shaped

You will also want to highlight exceptional aptitudes, such as working well under stress, learning computer programs quickly, and interacting with customers. If possible, provide details and evidence that back up your assertions. Include examples of your writing, speaking, management, organizational, interpersonal, and presentation skills—particularly those that are relevant to your targeted job. For recent graduates, this section can be used to give recruiters evidence of your potential and to highlight successful college projects.

Awards, Honors, and Activities.   If you have three or more awards or honors, highlight them by listing them under a separate heading. If not, put them in the Education or Work Experience section, if appropriate. Include awards, scholarships (financial and other), fellowships, dean's list, honors, recognition, commendations, and certificates. Be sure to identify items clearly. Your reader may be unfamiliar, for example, with Greek organizations, honors, and awards; tell what they mean.

> **Poor:**   Recipient of Star award
>
> **Improved:**   Recipient of Star award given by Pepperdine University to outstanding graduates who combine academic excellence and extracurricular activities

It's also appropriate to include school, community, volunteer, and professional activities. Employers are interested in evidence that you are a well-rounded person. This section provides an opportunity to demonstrate leadership and interpersonal skills. Strive to use action statements.

> **Poor:**   Treasurer of business club
>
> **Improved:**   Collected dues, kept financial records, and paid bills while serving as treasurer of 35-member business management club

Personal Data.   Résumés in the United States omit personal data, such as birth date, marital status, height, weight, national origin, health, disabilities, and religious affiliation. Such information doesn't relate to genuine occupational qualifications, and recruiters are legally barred from asking for such information. Some job seekers do, however, include hobbies or interests (such as skiing or photography) that might grab the recruiter's attention or serve as conversation starters. For example, let's say you learn that your hiring manager enjoys distance running. If you

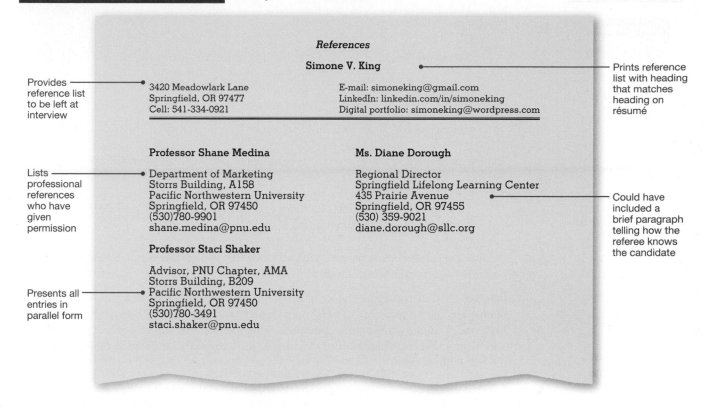

Provides reference list to be left at interview

Lists professional references who have given permission

Presents all entries in parallel form

Prints reference list with heading that matches heading on résumé

Could have included a brief paragraph telling how the referee knows the candidate

References

Simone V. King

3420 Meadowlark Lane
Springfield, OR 97477
Cell: 541-334-0921

E-mail: simoneking@gmail.com
LinkedIn: linkedin.com/in/simoneking
Digital portfolio: simoneking@wordpress.com

Professor Shane Medina

Department of Marketing
Storrs Building, A158
Pacific Northwestern University
Springfield, OR 97450
(530)780-9901
shane.medina@pnu.edu

Professor Staci Shaker

Advisor, PNU Chapter, AMA
Storrs Building, B209
Pacific Northwestern University
Springfield, OR 97450
(530)780-3491
staci.shaker@pnu.edu

Ms. Diane Dorough

Regional Director
Springfield Lifelong Learning Center
435 Prairie Avenue
Springfield, OR 97455
(530) 359-9021
diane.dorough@sllc.org

have run a marathon, you may want to mention it. Many executives play tennis or golf, two sports highly suitable for networking. You could also indicate your willingness to travel or to relocate, since many companies will be interested.

References?   Listing references directly on a résumé takes up valuable space. Moreover, references are not normally instrumental in securing an interview—few companies check them before the interview. Instead, recruiters prefer that you bring to the interview a list of individuals willing to discuss your qualifications. Therefore, you should prepare a separate list, such as that in Model Document 15.1, when you begin your job search. Consider three to five individuals, such as instructors, your current employer or previous employers, colleagues or subordinates, and other professional contacts. Ask whether they would be willing to answer inquiries regarding your qualifications for employment. Be sure, however, to provide them with an opportunity to refuse. No reference is better than a negative one. Better yet, to avoid rejection and embarrassment, ask only those contacts who you are confident will give you a glowing endorsement.

Do not include personal or character references, such as friends, family, or neighbors, because recruiters rarely consult them. One final note: Most recruiters see little reason for including the statement *References furnished upon request.* It is unnecessary and takes up precious space.

15-4c Creating a LinkedIn Profile Résumé

LinkedIn is one of the first places hiring managers and recruiters go to look for candidates. Preparing a LinkedIn profile takes a little effort, but it's well worth the investment. To ease your task, LinkedIn provides a template with standard résumé categories in which you insert your qualifications. Compared with a print résumé, LinkedIn has many advantages. You have ample space to expand the description of your skills and qualifications. Your LinkedIn page also allows you to be more conversational and personal than you can be within the confines of a restricted résumé. You can even use the pronoun *I* to tell your story more naturally and passionately. Include your LinkedIn URL such as **www.linkedin.com/in/simoneking**.

Headline.   To stand out, prepare an informative headline that appears below your name. It should include keywords in your field and a brief description of what you want, such as the following:

Marketing Grad and Social Media Branding Specialist Seeking Internship

Recent Grad With Billing and Coding Training in Medical Insurance Field

Seeking Recruiter/Human Resources Assistant Position in Health Services Field

Finance and Management Grad Looking for Position as Analyst Trainee

Some experts suggest that you write an even longer headline that takes full advantage of the 120-character LinkedIn space to sell yourself. Check out this recent grad's headline:

Communication Graduate, Specializing in Millennials, Mobile Marketing. Interested in Survey Research and Data Analysis

Because the headline is important, LinkedIn won't let you leave it blank. Use the headline to promote your most enticing expertise.

Photo.   To increase your chance of being selected, definitely include a photo. Profiles with photos are known to score 14 times more views than those without. Your photo should be a head-and-shoulder shot in work-appropriate attire. Should you smile? A recent study by New York University researchers revealed that people who looked a "little" happy in their photos made the best impression.[19]

Profile.   In your profile/summary, use keywords and phrases that might appear in job descriptions. Weave them into an engaging story about your career goals and what motivates you. Whenever possible, include quantifiable achievements and specifics that reveal your skills. Unsurprisingly, listing your skills at LinkedIn makes you 13 times more likely to be viewed.[20] You can borrow much of this information from your résumé, but don't make it sound like a résumé. In the Work Experience and Education fields, include all your experience, not just your current position.

Recommendations.   Encourage your instructors and employers to recommend you. Having recommendations in your profile makes you look more credible, trustworthy, and reliable. Career coach Susan Adams even encourages job seekers to offer to write the draft for the recommender; in the world of LinkedIn, she says, this is perfectly acceptable.[21] Model Document 15.2 shows a portion of a recent graduate's LinkedIn page.

Reality Check

The Fastest Way to Lose a Job

"If you lie on your résumé, land the job, and your employer later discovers you can't actually maneuver an Excel sheet or code in JavaScript, there is a good chance that they'll be within their legal right to terminate your employment."[22]

—Lauren Kreps, *e-mail marketing consultant, Shake Law, Inc.*

15-4d Perfecting Your Résumé and Keeping It Honest

With so much riding on this document, look for ways to polish and improve your résumé. For example, consider consolidating headings. By condensing your information into as few headings as possible, you will produce a clean, professional-looking document. Study other résumés for valuable formatting ideas. Ask yourself what graphic highlighting techniques you can use to improve readability such as capitalization, underlining, indenting, and bulleting. Experiment with headings and styles to achieve a pleasing, easy-to-read message. Moreover, look for ways to eliminate wordiness. For example, instead of *Supervised two employees who worked at the counter*, try *Supervised two counter employees*. Review Chapter 4 for more tips on writing concisely.

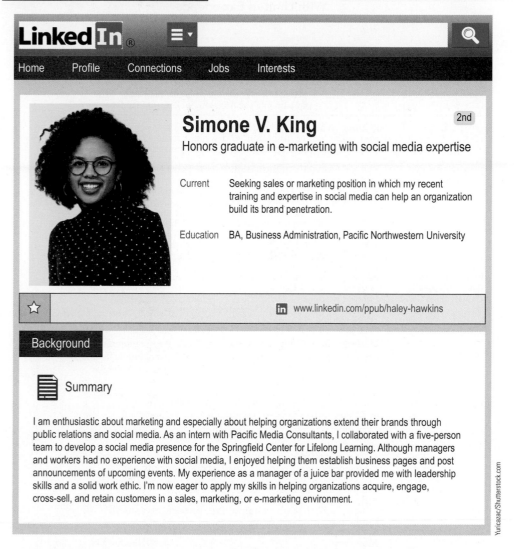

At LinkedIn Simone King presents a more personal description of her background, education, and experience than on her résumé. She includes a photo and a headline, "Honors graduate in e-marketing with social expertise." Her summary briefly describes her skills and experience, but one expert warns candidates not to cut corners on the summary statement. Describe what motivates you and use first-person pronouns, unlike what you would do on a résumé. LinkedIn gives you a chance to be more conversational than you can be in a résumé. You may be asked to present this same kind of personalized résumé information at job boards.

A résumé is expected to showcase a candidate's strengths and minimize weaknesses. For this reason, recruiters expect a certain degree of self-promotion. Some résumé writers, however, step over the line that separates honest self-marketing from deceptive half-truths and flat-out lies. Distorting facts on a résumé is unethical; lying may be illegal. Most important, either practice can destroy a career. In the Ethical Insight feature on page 560, learn more about how to keep your résumé honest and about the consequences of fudging the facts.

Simone V. King

3420 Meadowlark Lane
Springfield, OR 97477
Cell: 541-334-0921

E-mail: simoneking@gmail.com
LinkedIn: www.linkedin.com/in/simoneking
Digital portfolio:https://simoneking.wordpress.com

OBJECTIVE

Position in sales, marketing, or e-marketing in which my marketing, communication, and social media expertise helps an organization expand its brand penetration.

SUMMARY OF QUALIFICATIONS

- Graduated with honors from Pacific Northwestern University
- Applied e-marketing and public relations skills as an intern
- Experienced in Twitter, Facebook, and Instagram
- Keep current with social networking technologies
- Developed strong work ethic with part-time jobs that financed more than 50 percent of my education
- Honed leadership skills as vice president of award winning chapter of American Marketing Association

EDUCATION AND RELATED COURSE WORK

BA in Business Administration, Pacific Northwestern University, Cum Laude   **May, 2021**
  Major: Business Administration, e-marking emphasis
  Minor: Organizational Communication
  GPA: Major, 3.7; overall 3.5 (A = 4.0)

Marketing Research and Analysis   Marketing Communication
Social Relations in the Workplace   Professional Public Relations
Writing for the Web and Social Media   Organizational Behavior

PROFESSIONAL EXPERIENCE

Social Media Intern   09/2020–02/2021
Pacific Media Consultants, Springfield, Oregon
- Collaborated with 5-person team to develop social media presence for Center for Lifelong Learning
- Introduced clients to LinkedIn and established Facebook and Twitter accounts for LifeLong Learning staff
- Demonstrated how to boost social media presence with announcements and tweets of upcoming activities
- Prepared brochure, handouts, name tags, and press kit to promote a Saturday community event
- Handled over 40 client calls with the account management team, ranging from project checkins to inbound client inquiries

Manager   06/2018–08/2020
Juice Zone, Eugene, Oregon
- Developed management skills in assuming all responsibilities in absence of store owners including finances and scheduling
- Supervised daily store operations, maintained store security, and managed a team of 5 to 10 employees

HONORS ACTIVITIES

- Received Brooks Award as the outstanding graduate in marketing based on academic excellence and community service
- Served as vice president of local chapter of the American Marketing Association, providing monthly marketing forums, events, and competitions

SOFIA M. MONTANO

Cell: 916-440-3981 | E-mail: ssofiamontano@cox.com | LinkedIn: www.linkedin.com/in/sofiamontano

TARGET POSITION

Responds to specific job advertisement

A clinical psychology internship with Sacramento Child Protective Services

EDUCATION AND RELATED COURSE WORK

Sacramento State University
Bachelor of Arts, Psychology
Overall GPA 3.6; Psychology GPA 3.8

Expected graduation: June 2021

Relevant Courses:

Educational Psychology	Ethnic Identity Development
Assessment and Treatment of Behavior Problems	Development Psychology
	Health Psychology
Advanced Applied Behavioral Analysis	

Highlights courses related to skills named in advertisement

INTERNSHIP EXPERIENCE

Case Management Support Intern Family   09/2020–02/2021
Preservation and Support Services, Sacramento

Uses present tense verbs for current tasks

- Counsel families on eligibility for the Housing Choice Voucher Program
- Ensure completion of documentation to comply with program specifications
- Work with Client Service Tracker database software to facilitate care coordination
- Serve as liaison for the Housing Choice Voucher Program within Family Preservation and Support Services
- Able to converse with clients in Spanish and English
- Comfortable in iOS and Android environments

WORK EXPERIENCE   08/2018–08/2020

Limits résumé categories to five main areas

Customer Service Assistant
Career Center
Sacramento State University

- Worked 10 to 15 hours per week while in college and maintained a 3.6 GPA
- Developed customer service skills assisting guests visiting the Career Center
- Assisted students, campus staff, and employees with a variety of inquiries, answered incoming telephone calls, and greeted walk-in traffic
- Collaborated with small diverse groups to plan large-scale events such as a campus-wide Career Center Open House for 1,500+ visitors
- Worked independently to research the best career websites for college students, concluding with a five-page report to the director

Describes experience specifically

HONORS

- Dean's List, Spring and Fall, 2020-2021
- Elected to Phi Chi Honor Society
- Recipient of Applied Behavior Consultants Scholarship based on outstanding scholarship and departmental service

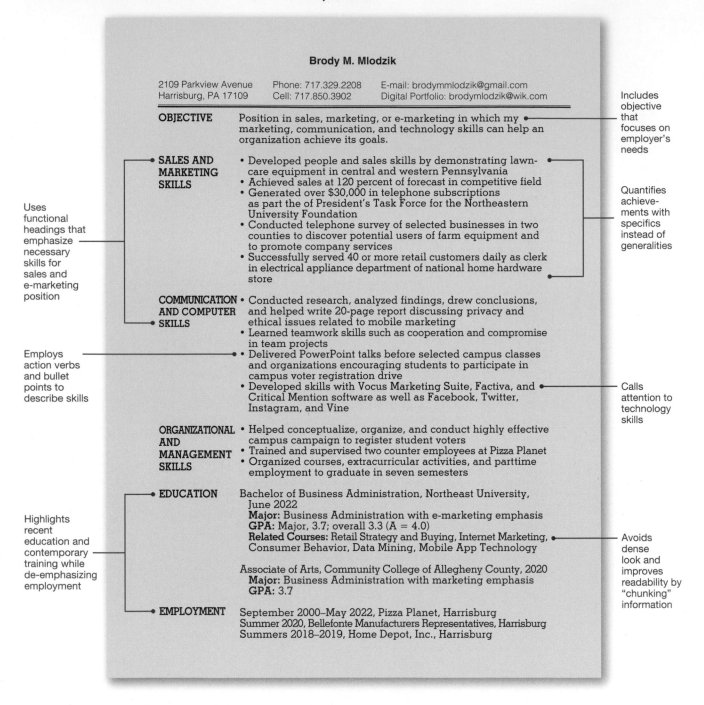

Brody M. Mlodzik

2109 Parkview Avenue   Phone: 717.329.2208   E-mail: brodymmlodzik@gmail.com
Harrisburg, PA 17109   Cell: 717.850.3902   Digital Portfolio: brodymlodzik@wik.com

Includes objective that focuses on employer's needs

OBJECTIVE Position in sales, marketing, or e-marketing in which my marketing, communication, and technology skills can help an organization achieve its goals.

SALES AND MARKETING SKILLS
- Developed people and sales skills by demonstrating lawn-care equipment in central and western Pennsylvania
- Achieved sales at 120 percent of forecast in competitive field
- Generated over $30,000 in telephone subscriptions as part the of President's Task Force for the Northeastern University Foundation
- Conducted telephone survey of selected businesses in two counties to discover potential users of farm equipment and to promote company services
- Successfully served 40 or more retail customers daily as clerk in electrical appliance department of national home hardware store

Uses functional headings that emphasize necessary skills for sales and e-marketing position

Quantifies achievements with specifics instead of generalities

COMMUNICATION AND COMPUTER SKILLS
- Conducted research, analyzed findings, drew conclusions, and helped write 20-page report discussing privacy and ethical issues related to mobile marketing
- Learned teamwork skills such as cooperation and compromise in team projects
- Delivered PowerPoint talks before selected campus classes and organizations encouraging students to participate in campus voter registration drive
- Developed skills with Vocus Marketing Suite, Factiva, and Critical Mention software as well as Facebook, Twitter, Instagram, and Vine

Employs action verbs and bullet points to describe skills

Calls attention to technology skills

ORGANIZATIONAL AND MANAGEMENT SKILLS
- Helped conceptualize, organize, and conduct highly effective campus campaign to register student voters
- Trained and supervised two counter employees at Pizza Planet
- Organized courses, extracurricular activities, and parttime employment to graduate in seven semesters

EDUCATION Bachelor of Business Administration, Northeast University, June 2022
Major: Business Administration with e-marketing emphasis
GPA: Major, 3.7; overall 3.3 (A = 4.0)
Related Courses: Retail Strategy and Buying, Internet Marketing, Consumer Behavior, Data Mining, Mobile App Technology

Associate of Arts, Community College of Allegheny County, 2020
Major: Business Administration with marketing emphasis
GPA: 3.7

Highlights recent education and contemporary training while de-emphasizing employment

Avoids dense look and improves readability by "chunking" information

EMPLOYMENT September 2000–May 2022, Pizza Planet, Harrisburg
Summer 2020, Bellefonte Manufacturers Representatives, Harrisburg
Summers 2018–2019, Home Depot, Inc., Harrisburg

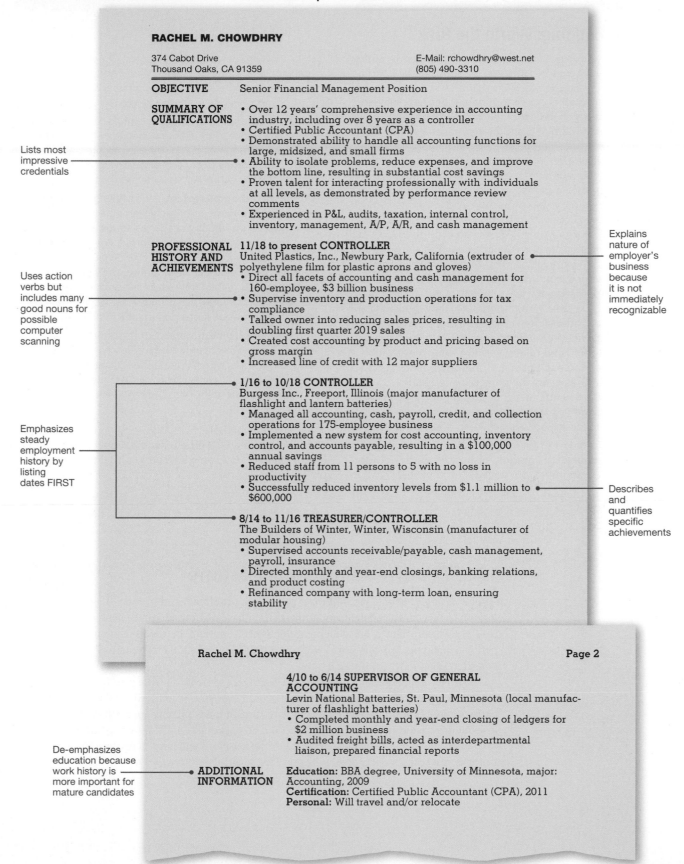

RACHEL M. CHOWDHRY

374 Cabot Drive
Thousand Oaks, CA 91359

E-Mail: rchowdhry@west.net
(805) 490-3310

OBJECTIVE   Senior Financial Management Position

SUMMARY OF QUALIFICATIONS
- Over 12 years' comprehensive experience in accounting industry, including over 8 years as a controller
- Certified Public Accountant (CPA)
- Demonstrated ability to handle all accounting functions for large, midsized, and small firms
- Ability to isolate problems, reduce expenses, and improve the bottom line, resulting in substantial cost savings
- Proven talent for interacting professionally with individuals at all levels, as demonstrated by performance review comments
- Experienced in P&L, audits, taxation, internal control, inventory, management, A/P, A/R, and cash management

Lists most impressive credentials

PROFESSIONAL HISTORY AND ACHIEVEMENTS   **11/18 to present CONTROLLER**
United Plastics, Inc., Newbury Park, California (extruder of polyethylene film for plastic aprons and gloves)
- Direct all facets of accounting and cash management for 160-employee, $3 billion business
- Supervise inventory and production operations for tax compliance
- Talked owner into reducing sales prices, resulting in doubling first quarter 2019 sales
- Created cost accounting by product and pricing based on gross margin
- Increased line of credit with 12 major suppliers

Explains nature of employer's business because it is not immediately recognizable

Uses action verbs but includes many good nouns for possible computer scanning

1/16 to 10/18 CONTROLLER
Burgess Inc., Freeport, Illinois (major manufacturer of flashlight and lantern batteries)
- Managed all accounting, cash, payroll, credit, and collection operations for 175-employee business
- Implemented a new system for cost accounting, inventory control, and accounts payable, resulting in a $100,000 annual savings
- Reduced staff from 11 persons to 5 with no loss in productivity
- Successfully reduced inventory levels from $1.1 million to $600,000

Emphasizes steady employment history by listing dates FIRST

Describes and quantifies specific achievements

8/14 to 11/16 TREASURER/CONTROLLER
The Builders of Winter, Winter, Wisconsin (manufacturer of modular housing)
- Supervised accounts receivable/payable, cash management, payroll, insurance
- Directed monthly and year-end closings, banking relations, and product costing
- Refinanced company with long-term loan, ensuring stability

Rachel M. Chowdhry   Page 2

4/10 to 6/14 SUPERVISOR OF GENERAL ACCOUNTING
Levin National Batteries, St. Paul, Minnesota (local manufacturer of flashlight batteries)
- Completed monthly and year-end closing of ledgers for $2 million business
- Audited freight bills, acted as interdepartmental liaison, prepared financial reports

De-emphasizes education because work history is more important for mature candidates

ADDITIONAL INFORMATION
Education: BBA degree, University of Minnesota, major: Accounting, 2009
Certification: Certified Public Accountant (CPA), 2011
Personal: Will travel and/or relocate

Ethical Insights

Résumé Padding: Worth the Risk?

Given today's competitive job market, it might be tempting to pad your résumé. Résumé padding means adding false or exaggerated information to boost your credentials for a job. Unfortunately, this happens more often than we might think. A CareerBuilder survey of 2,532 hiring and human resources managers revealed that 56 percent have caught a lie on a résumé.[23]

Candidates may embellish their skills or background information to qualify for a position, but it's a risky game. Background checks are much easier now with the Internet and specialists who sniff out untruths. What's more, puffing up your qualifications may be unnecessary. The same CareerBuilder survey revealed that 42 percent of employers would consider a candidate who met only three out of five key qualifications for a job.[24]

After they have been hired, candidates may think they are safe—but organizations often continue the checking process. If hiring officials find a discrepancy in a GPA or prior experience and the error is an honest mistake, they meet with the new-hire to hear an explanation. If the discrepancy wasn't a mistake, they will likely fire the person immediately.

No job seeker wants to be in the unhappy position of explaining résumé errors or defending misrepresentation. Avoiding the following actions can keep a job candidate off the hot seat:

- **Enhancing education, grades, or honors.** Some job candidates claim degrees from colleges or universities when in fact they merely attended classes. Others increase their grade point averages or claim fictitious honors. Any such dishonest reporting is grounds for dismissal when discovered.

- **Inflating job titles and salaries.** Wishing to elevate their status, some applicants misrepresent their titles or increase their past salaries. For example, one technician called himself a programmer when he had actually programmed only one project for his boss. A mail clerk who assumed added responsibilities conferred upon herself the title of supervisor.

- **Puffing up accomplishments.** Job seekers may inflate their employment experience or achievements. One clerk, eager to make her photocopying duties sound more important, said that she assisted the *vice president in communicating and distributing employee directives*. Similarly, guard against taking sole credit for achievements that required many people. When recruiters suspect dubious claims on résumés, they nail applicants with specific—and often embarrassing—questions during their interviews.

- **Altering employment dates.** Some candidates extend the dates of employment to hide unimpressive jobs or positions they lost. Others try to hide periods of unemployment and illness. Although their employment histories have no gaps, their résumés are dishonest and represent potential booby traps.

If you do get a job based on dishonesty, you could find yourself over your head in completing the required tasks, and the fear of being discovered would be a constant burden. It's simply not worth the risk.

15-4e Proofreading Your Résumé

After revising your résumé, you must proofread, proofread, and proofread again for spelling, grammar, mechanics, content, and format. Then have a knowledgeable friend or relative proofread it yet again. This is one document that must be perfect. Because the job market is so competitive, one typo, one misspelled word, or a single grammatical error could eliminate you from consideration.

By now you may be thinking that you'd like to hire someone to write your résumé. Don't! First, you know yourself better than anyone else could know you. Second, you will end up with either a generic or a one-time résumé. A generic résumé in today's highly competitive job market will lose out to a customized résumé nine times out of ten. Equally useless is a one-time résumé aimed at a single job. What if you don't get that job? Because you will need to revise your résumé many times as you seek a variety of jobs, be prepared to write (and rewrite) it yourself.

15-5 Using Digital Tools to Boost Your Job Search

LEARNING OUTCOME

5 Describe digital tools that can enhance your job search and résumé.

Just as electronic media have changed the way candidates seek jobs, these same digital tools are transforming the way employers select qualified candidates. As mentioned earlier, the first reader of your résumé may very well be an ATS. As many as 98 percent of large companies and scores of smaller companies are now employing these systems.[25] Why have they become so popular? In this digital era, the process of applying for jobs has become so effortless that organizations are flooded with résumés. Screening systems whittle down the cumbersome applicant pool to just a handful of qualified applicants for the human hiring managers to review more closely. The sad truth for applicants, however, is that up to 75 percent of résumés may not make it past the ATS screening.[26]

TaLaNoVa/Shutterstock.com

15-5a Maximizing the Rank of Your Résumé

The higher your résumé ranks when it is evaluated by an ATS, the more likely it will be reviewed by a recruiter or hiring manager. In the past candidates tried to game the system by stuffing their résumés with keywords. Newer screening systems are not so easily fooled. Although keywords are important, "the system looks for relevance of the key word to your work history and education," advises job-search authority Quint Careers.[27] In addition to including the right keywords in context, your résumé must qualify in other ways to be selected. The following techniques, in addition to those cited earlier, can boost the probability that your résumé will rank high enough to qualify for review by a human reader.

- **Include specific keywords or phrases in context**. Study carefully any advertisements and job descriptions for the position you want. Describe your experience, education, and qualifications in terms associated with the job advertisement or job description for this position. However, don't just plop a keyword into your résumé; use it in context to ensure ATS recognition (e.g., *collaborated within four-member team to create a pilot business plan*).

- **Focus on nouns**. Although action verbs will make your résumé appeal to a recruiter, the applicant tracking system will often be looking for nouns in three categories: (a) a job title, position, or role (e.g., *accountant, Web developer, team leader*); (b) a technical skill or specialization (e.g., *Javascript, C, Python*); and (c) a certification, a tool used, or specific experience (e.g., *Certified Financial Analyst, Chartered Financial Analyst*).

- **Use variations of the job title**. Tracking systems may seek a slightly different job title from what you list. To be safe, include variations and abbreviations (e.g., *occupational therapist, certified occupational therapist*, or *COTA*). If you don't have experience in your targeted area, use the job title you list in your objective.

- **Concentrate on the Skills section**. A majority of keywords sought by employees relate to specialized or technical skill requirements. Therefore, be sure the Skills section of your résumé is loaded with nouns that describe your skills and qualifications.

- **Keep the formatting simple**. Stay away from logos, pictures, symbols, and shadings.

- **Use conventional headings**. Include familiar headings such as *Skills, Qualifications*, and *Education*. ATS software may not recognize headings such as *Professional Engagement* or *Core Competencies*.

15-5b Spotlighting Your Qualifications in a Career E-Portfolio

With the workplace becoming increasingly digital, you have yet another tool to display your qualifications to prospective employers. A **career e-portfolio** is a collection of electronic files, images, multimedia, blog entries, and hyperlinks that demonstrate a writer's talents, accomplishments, and technical skills.

What Goes in a Career E-Portfolio?
A career e-portfolio may include a copy of your career-specific résumé, reference letters, commendations for special achievements, awards, certificates, work samples, a complete list of your courses, thank-you letters, and other items that tout your accomplishments. An e-portfolio could also offer links to digital copies of your artwork, film projects, videos, blueprints, documents, photographs, multimedia files, and blog entries that might otherwise be difficult to share with potential employers.

Displaying a variety of resources in one place, e-portfolios have many advantages, as seen in Figure 15.8. When they are posted on websites, they can be viewed at an employer's convenience. Let's say you are talking on the phone with an employer in another city who wants to see a copy of your résumé. You can simply text or message a link to the website where your résumé resides. E-portfolios can also be seen by many individuals in an organization without circulating a paper copy. However, the main reason for preparing an e-portfolio is to show off your talents and qualifications more thoroughly than you can in a print résumé.

Some recruiters may be skeptical about e-portfolios because they fear that such presentations will take more time to view than paper-based résumés do. As a result, nontraditional job applications may end up at the bottom of the pile or be ignored. That's why some applicants submit a print résumé in addition to an e-portfolio.

Where Are E-Portfolios Posted?
You have many options when you are ready to post your e-portfolio. Some schools as well as learning management systems make website space available for student e-portfolios. A few well-known public places for posting student e-portfolios are WordPress, Wix, Weebly, and Rubio. In addition, institutions may provide instruction and resources for scanning photos, digitizing images, and preparing graphics. Savvy candidates may also provide employers with links to their e-portfolios at Google Docs, Box, or Dropbox.

FIGURE 15.8 Making a Career E-Portfolio

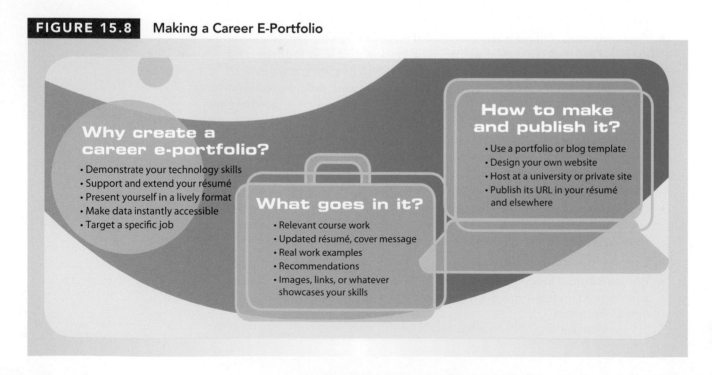

Why create a career e-portfolio?
- Demonstrate your technology skills
- Support and extend your résumé
- Present yourself in a lively format
- Make data instantly accessible
- Target a specific job

What goes in it?
- Relevant course work
- Updated résumé, cover message
- Real work examples
- Recommendations
- Images, links, or whatever showcases your skills

How to make and publish it?
- Use a portfolio or blog template
- Design your own website
- Host at a university or private site
- Publish its URL in your résumé and elsewhere

15-5c Expanding Your Employment Chances With a Video Résumé

Still another way to expand your employment possibilities is with a **video résumé**. Video résumés enable job candidates to present their experience, qualifications, and interests in video form. This format has many benefits. It allows candidates to demonstrate their public speaking, interpersonal, and technical skills more impressively than they can in traditional print résumés. Both employers and applicants can save recruitment and travel costs by using video résumés. Instead of flying distant candidates to interviews, organizations can see them digitally.

Video résumés are becoming more prevalent with the popularity of YouTube, inexpensive webcams, and widespread broadband. With simple edits on a computer, you can customize a video message to a specific employer and tailor your résumé for a particular job opening. In making a video résumé, dress professionally in business attire, just as you would for an in-person interview. Keep your video to three minutes or less. Explain why you would be a good employee and what you can do for the company that hires you. By the way, video résumés are not prohibited under federal equal employment opportunity laws.[28]

Before committing time and energy to a video résumé, decide whether it is appropriate for your career field. Such presentations make sense for online, media, social, and creative professions. Traditional organizations, however, may be less impressed. Done well, a video résumé might give you an edge. Done poorly, however, it could bounce you from contention. Paper résumés still do a good job of condensing your achievements. A video résumé, however, can show off strengths such as warmth, clear communication, charisma, humor, and conversational chatter. Check out dazzling video résumés at **biteable.com**.

15-5d How Many Résumés and What Format?

At this point you may be wondering how many résumés you should make, and what format they should follow. The good news is that you need only one basic résumé that you can customize for various job prospects and formats.

Preparing a Basic Print-Based Résumé.   The one basic résumé you should prepare is a print-based traditional résumé. It should be attractively formatted to maximize readability. This résumé is useful (a) during job interviews, (b) for person-to-person networking situations, (c) for recruiters at career fairs, and (d) when you are competing for a job that does not require an electronic submission.

You can create a basic, yet professional-looking résumé by using your word processing program. Our collection of résumé examples in this chapter provides ideas for simple layouts that are easily duplicated and adapted. You can also examine résumé templates for design and format ideas. Their inflexibility, however, may be frustrating as you try to force your skills and experience into a predetermined template sequence.

Converting a Plain-Text Résumé for Digital Submission.   After preparing a basic résumé, you can convert it to a plain-text résumé so that it is ready for e-mailing. Parts of it will also be available for uploading to online submission forms. Many job-board sites and most government employers require job candidates to complete official application forms. Even if your résumé contains the same information, an application form is often required for legal and data processing as well as for employer convenience.

Some employers prefer that résumé information be submitted in **plain-text format**. This is a format that contains only standard keyboard characters. It will have no special formatting such as bold, underlining, italics, and larger font sizes. Plain-text documents are preferred because they avoid possible e-mail viruses and word processing incompatibilities. To make a plain-text résumé, convert your basic résumé into a new document in which you do the following:

- Use basic fonts such as Helvetica or Arial. Eliminate the use of italics, boldface, and underlining, which cause some scanners to glitch or choke.
- Consider using capital letters rather than boldface type to emphasize words—but don't overdo the caps.

- Remove images, designs, colors, and any characters not on a standard keyboard.

- Punctuate and capitalize correctly so that the software knows where to begin and end a field. Avoid lowercase expression frequently seen in texting.

- If you use a header or footer feature to place your name at the top of your résumé, be sure that your name and contact information also appear in the body of the résumé.

- In Microsoft Word, save the document with *Plain Text* (**.txt*) as the file type.

- Send yourself a copy embedded within an e-mail message to check its appearance. Also send it to a friend to try it out.

15-5e Submitting Your Résumé

The format you choose for submitting your résumé depends on what is required. If you are responding to a job advertisement, be certain to read the listing carefully to learn how the employer wants you to submit your résumé. Not following the prospective employer's instructions can eliminate you from consideration before your résumé is even reviewed. If you have any doubt about what format is desired, send an e-mail inquiry to a company representative, or call and ask. Most organizations request one of the following submission formats:

- **Word document.** Some organizations ask candidates to send their résumés and cover messages by surface mail. Others request that résumés be submitted as Word documents attached to e-mail messages, despite the fear of viruses.

- **Plain-text document.** As discussed earlier, many employers expect applicants to submit résumés and cover letters as plain-text documents. This format is also widely used for posting to an online job board or for sending by e-mail. Plain-text résumés may be embedded within or attached to e-mail messages.

- **PDF document.** For safety reasons some employers prefer PDF (portable document format) files. A PDF résumé looks exactly like the original and cannot be altered. Most computers have Adobe Acrobat Reader installed for easy reading of PDF files. Converting your résumé to a PDF file can be done by saving it as a PDF file, which preserves all formatting.

- **Company database.** Larger organizations and the government may prefer that you complete an online form with your résumé information. This enables them to plug your data into their template categories for rapid searching. You might be able to cut and paste the information from your résumé into the form; however, uploading the information is less likely to choke a scanning device than pasting it in.[29]

Because your résumé is probably the most important message you will ever write, you will revise it many times. With so much information in concentrated form and with so much riding on its outcome, your résumé demands careful polishing, proofreading, and critiquing. The following checklist will help you review the primary steps in creating and submitting a customized résumé.

Checklist

Creating and Submitting a Customized Résumé

Preparation

- **Analyze your strengths.** Determine what aspects of your education, experience, and personal characteristics will be assets to prospective employers.

- **Research job listings.** Learn about available jobs, common qualifications, and potential employers. The best résumés are customized for specific jobs with specific companies.

Heading, Objective, and Summary of Qualifications

- **Identify yourself.** List your name, address, telephone numbers, and possibly links to your e-portfolio and LinkedIn profile.

- **Include a career objective for a targeted job.** Use an objective only if it is intended for a specific job (*Objective: Junior cost accountant position in the petroleum industry*).

- **Prepare a summary of qualifications.** Include a list of three to eight bulleted statements that highlight your qualifications for the targeted position.

Education

- **Name your degree, date of graduation, and institution.** Emphasize your education if your experience is limited.

- **List your major and GPA.** Give information about your studies, but don't inventory all your courses.

Work Experience

- **Itemize your jobs.** Start with your most recent job. Give the employer's name and city, dates of employment (month, year), and most significant job title.

- **Describe your experience.** Use action verbs and keyword nouns to summarize achievements and skills relevant to your targeted job.

- **Promote your soft skills.** Give evidence of communication, management, and interpersonal talents. Employers want more than empty assurances; try to quantify your skills and accomplishments (*Developed teamwork skills while collaborating within six-member task force in producing 20-page mission statement*).

Special Skills, Achievements, and Awards

- **Highlight your technology skills.** Remember that nearly all employers seek employees who are proficient in using the Internet, e-mail, word processing, social media, spreadsheets, and presentation programs. Add your proficiency in relevant software programs.

- **Show that you are a well-rounded individual.** List awards, experiences, and extracurricular activities—particularly if they demonstrate leadership, teamwork, reliability, loyalty, industry, initiative, efficiency, and self-sufficiency.

Final Tips

- **Look for ways to condense your data.** Omit all street addresses except your own. Consolidate your headings. Study models and experiment with formats to find the most readable and efficient groupings.

- **Omit references.** Have a list of references available for the interview, but don't include them or refer to them on your résumé unless you have a reason to do so.

- **Resist the urge to inflate your qualifications.** Be accurate in listing your education, grades, honors, job titles, employment dates, and job experience.

- **Proofread, proofread, proofread!** Make this important document perfect by proofreading at least three times. Ask a friend to check it, too.

Submitting

- **Follow instructions for submitting.** Learn whether the employer wants candidate information in a hard copy print résumé, e-mail résumé, plain-text version, PDF file, company database, or some other format.

- **Practice sending a plain-text résumé.** Before submitting a plain-text résumé, try sending it to yourself or friends. Perfect your skill in achieving an attractive format.

15-6 Cover Messages—Do They Still Matter?

LEARNING OUTCOME

6 Analyze the importance and construction of cover messages.

A cover message, also known as a **cover letter** or **letter of application**, has always been a graceful way of introducing your résumé. However, with the steady movement toward online recruiting and digitized ATS, cover letters are losing significance for recruiters. A recent survey by JobVite revealed that only 26 percent of recruiters thought the cover letter was important.[30] Recruiters may skip over cover messages because they are involved only with initial screening. Hiring managers, on the other hand, present a different story. They often seek as much information as they can obtain to avoid expensive bad hires. Cover letters may reveal key information missing in a résumé. Hiring managers are eager to learn whether the candidate will fit into the company culture.[31]

15-6a Creating a Customized Cover Message

For new grads to compete in a job market saturated by degree holders, it's increasingly important to find a way to stand out.[33] Cover messages give you the opportunity to set yourself apart. A well-written cover message can reveal to employers your ability to put together complete sentences and to sound intelligent. A cover message also can be more personal and strengthen a weak résumé by showing how your special talents relate to the opening.

Although some hiring managers favor cover messages, they disagree about their length. Some prefer short messages with no more than two paragraphs embedded in an e-mail message. Other recruiters desire longer messages that supply more information, thus giving them a better opportunity to evaluate a candidate's qualifications and writing skills. These recruiters argue that hiring and training new employees is expensive and time consuming; therefore, they welcome extra data to guide them in making the best choice the first time. Follow your judgment in writing a brief or a longer cover message.

Regardless of its length, a cover message should have three primary parts: (a) an opening that captures attention, introduces the message, and identifies the position; (b) a body that sells the candidate and focuses on the employer's needs; and (c) a closing that requests an interview and motivates action. When putting your cover message together, remember that the biggest mistake job seekers make when writing cover messages is being too generic. You should, therefore, write a personalized, customized cover message for every position that interests you.

Gaining Attention in the Opening.

Your cover message will be more appealing—and more likely to be read—if it begins by addressing the reader by name. Rather than sending your message to the *Hiring Manager* or *To Whom It May Concern*, try to identify the name of the appropriate individual by studying the company's website. You could also call the human resources department and ask the name of the person in charge of hiring. Another possibility is using LinkedIn to find someone working in the same department as the position in the posted job. This person may know the name of the hiring manager. If you still cannot find the name of any person to address, you might replace the salutation of your letter with a descriptive subject line such as *Application for Marketing Specialist Position*.

How you open your cover message depends largely on whether the application is solicited or unsolicited. If an employment position has been announced and applicants are being solicited, you can use a direct approach. If you do not know whether a position is open and you are prospecting for a job, use an indirect approach. Whether direct or indirect, the opening should attract the attention of the reader. Strive for openings that are more imaginative than *Please consider this letter an application for the position of . . .* or *I would like to apply for . . . .*

Openings for Solicited Jobs.

When applying for a job that has been announced, consider some of the following techniques to open your cover message:

- **Refer to the name of an employee in the company**. Remember that employers always hope to hire known quantities rather than complete strangers.

    Kennedy Harris, a member of your Customer Service Department, told me that Thomson & Associates is seeking a customer service trainee. The enclosed summary of my qualifications demonstrates my preparation for this position.

    At the suggestion of Tiffany Weinstein, in your Legal Services Department, I submit my qualifications for the position of staffing coordinator.

    Amarjit Singh, placement director at Southwest University, told me that Dynamic Industries has an opening for a technical writer with knowledge of Web design and graphics.

- **Refer to the source of your information precisely**. If you are answering an advertisement, include the exact position advertised and the name and date of the publication. If you are responding to a position listed on an online job board, include the website name and the date the position was posted.

  From your company's website, I learned about your need for a sales representative for the Ohio, Indiana, and Illinois regions. I am very interested in this position and am confident that my education and experience are appropriate for the opening.

  My talent for interacting with people, coupled with more than five years of customer service experience, make me an ideal candidate for the director of customer relations position you advertised on the CareerJournal website on August 3.

- **Refer to the job title, and describe how your qualifications fit the requirements**. Hiring managers are looking for a match between an applicant's credentials and the job needs.

  Ceradyne Company's marketing assistant opening is an excellent match with my qualifications. As a recent graduate of Southern University with a major in marketing, I offer solid academic credentials as well as industry experience gained from an internship at Flotek Industries.

  Would an honors graduate with a degree in recreation and two years of part-time experience organizing social activities for a convalescent hospital qualify for your position of activity director?

  Because of my specialized training in finance and accounting at Michigan State University, I am confident that I have the qualifications you described in your advertisement for a staff accountant trainee.

Openings for Unsolicited Jobs.   If you are unsure whether a position actually exists, you might use a more persuasive opening. Because your goal is to convince this person to read on, try one of the following techniques:

- **Demonstrate an interest in and knowledge of the reader's business**. Show the hiring manager that you have done your research and that this organization is more than a mere name to you.

  Because Signa HealthNet, Inc., is organizing a new information management team for its recently established group insurance division, could you use the services of a well-trained information systems graduate who seeks to become a professional systems analyst?

  I read with great interest the article in Forbes *announcing the upcoming launch of US Bank. Congratulations on this new venture and its notable $50 million in loans precharter! The possibility of helping your bank grow is exciting, and I would like to explore a potential employment match that I am confident will be mutually beneficial.*

- **Show how your special talents and background will benefit the company**. Human resources managers need to be convinced that you can do something for them.

  Could your rapidly expanding publications division use the services of an editorial assistant who offers exceptional language skills, an honors degree from the University of Mississippi, and two years' experience in producing a campus literary publication?

In applying for an advertised job, Tracy Karacia wrote the solicited cover letter shown in Model Document 15.7. Notice that the opening of her message identifies the position advertised on the company's website so that the reader knows exactly what advertisement Tracy means. Using features on her word processing program, Tracy designed her own letterhead that uses her name and looks like professionally printed letterhead paper.

More challenging are unsolicited cover messages, such as the letter of Jared L. Chen shown in Model Document 15.8. Because he hopes to discover or create a job, his opening must grab the reader's attention immediately. To do that, he capitalizes on company information appearing in an online article. Jared purposely kept his cover letter short and to the point because he anticipated that a busy executive would be unwilling to read a long, detailed letter. Jared's unsolicited letter

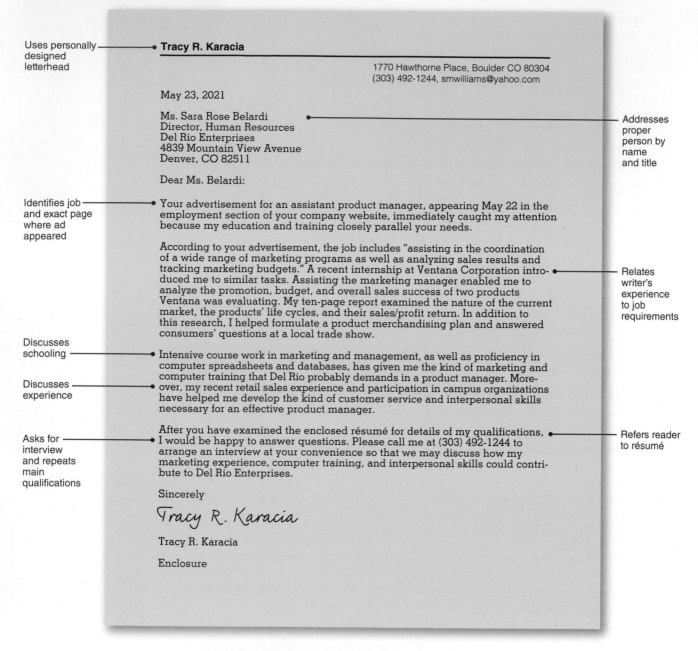

Uses personally designed letterhead

Tracy R. Karacia

1770 Hawthorne Place, Boulder CO 80304
(303) 492-1244, smwilliams@yahoo.com

May 23, 2021

Ms. Sara Rose Belardi
Director, Human Resources
Del Rio Enterprises
4839 Mountain View Avenue
Denver, CO 82511

Addresses proper person by name and title

Dear Ms. Belardi:

Identifies job and exact page where ad appeared

Your advertisement for an assistant product manager, appearing May 22 in the employment section of your company website, immediately caught my attention because my education and training closely parallel your needs.

According to your advertisement, the job includes "assisting in the coordination of a wide range of marketing programs as well as analyzing sales results and tracking marketing budgets." A recent internship at Ventana Corporation introduced me to similar tasks. Assisting the marketing manager enabled me to analyze the promotion, budget, and overall sales success of two products Ventana was evaluating. My ten-page report examined the nature of the current market, the products' life cycles, and their sales/profit return. In addition to this research, I helped formulate a product merchandising plan and answered consumers' questions at a local trade show.

Relates writer's experience to job requirements

Discusses schooling

Discusses experience

Intensive course work in marketing and management, as well as proficiency in computer spreadsheets and databases, has given me the kind of marketing and computer training that Del Rio probably demands in a product manager. Moreover, my recent retail sales experience and participation in campus organizations have helped me develop the kind of customer service and interpersonal skills necessary for an effective product manager.

Asks for interview and repeats main qualifications

After you have examined the enclosed résumé for details of my qualifications, I would be happy to answer questions. Please call me at (303) 492-1244 to arrange an interview at your convenience so that we may discuss how my marketing experience, computer training, and interpersonal skills could contribute to Del Rio Enterprises.

Refers reader to résumé

Sincerely

Tracy R. Karacia

Tracy R. Karacia

Enclosure

prospects for a job. Some job candidates feel that such letters may be even more productive than efforts to secure advertised jobs because prospecting candidates face less competition and show initiative. Notice that Jared's letter in Model Document 15.8 as well as that of Tracy Karacia above, uses a personal business letter format with the return address above the date.

15-6b Promoting Your Strengths in the Message Body

Once you have captured the attention of the reader and identified your purpose in the letter opening, you should use the body of the letter to plug your qualifications for this position. If you are responding to an advertisement, you will want to explain how your preparation and experience fulfill the stated requirements. If you are prospecting for a job, you may not know the exact requirements. Your employment research and knowledge of your field, however, should give you a reasonably good idea of what is expected for the position you seek.

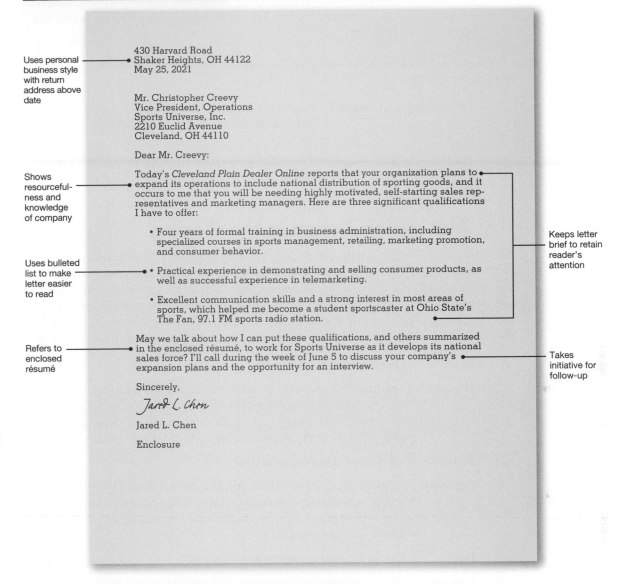

Uses personal business style with return address above date

Shows resourcefulness and knowledge of company

Uses bulleted list to make letter easier to read

Refers to enclosed résumé

Keeps letter brief to retain reader's attention

Takes initiative for follow-up

430 Harvard Road
Shaker Heights, OH 44122
May 25, 2021

Mr. Christopher Creevy
Vice President, Operations
Sports Universe, Inc.
2210 Euclid Avenue
Cleveland, OH 44110

Dear Mr. Creevy:

Today's *Cleveland Plain Dealer Online* reports that your organization plans to expand its operations to include national distribution of sporting goods, and it occurs to me that you will be needing highly motivated, self-starting sales representatives and marketing managers. Here are three significant qualifications I have to offer:

- Four years of formal training in business administration, including specialized courses in sports management, retailing, marketing promotion, and consumer behavior.

- Practical experience in demonstrating and selling consumer products, as well as successful experience in telemarketing.

- Excellent communication skills and a strong interest in most areas of sports, which helped me become a student sportscaster at Ohio State's The Fan, 97.1 FM sports radio station.

May we talk about how I can put these qualifications, and others summarized in the enclosed résumé, to work for Sports Universe as it develops its national sales force? I'll call during the week of June 5 to discuss your company's expansion plans and the opportunity for an interview.

Sincerely,

Jared L. Chen

Jared L. Chen

Enclosure

It is also important to stress reader benefits. In other words, you should describe your strong points in relation to the needs of the employer. Hiring officers want you to tell them what you can do for their organizations. This is more important than telling what courses you took in college or what duties you performed in your previous jobs.

Poor: I have completed courses in business communication, report writing, and technical writing.

Improved: Courses in business communication, report writing, and technical writing have helped me develop the research and writing skills required of your technical writers.

In the body of your letter, you may choose to discuss relevant personal traits. Employers are looking for candidates who, among other things, are team players, take responsibility, show initiative, and learn easily. Don't just list several personal traits, though; instead, include documentation that proves you possess these traits. Notice how the following paragraph uses action verbs to paint a picture of a promising candidate:

In addition to developing tech`nical and academic skills at Florida Central University, I have gained interpersonal, leadership, and organizational skills. As vice president of the business students' organization, Gamma Alpha, I helped organize and supervise two successful *fund-raising events. These activities involved conceptualizing the tasks, motivating others to help, scheduling work sessions, and coordinating the efforts of 35 diverse students. I enjoyed my success with these activities and look forward to applying my experience in your management trainee program.*

Finally, in this section or the next, refer the reader to your résumé. Do so directly or as part of another statement.

Direct reference to résumé: Please refer to the attached résumé for additional information regarding my education, experience, and skills.

Part of another statement: As you will notice from my enclosed résumé, I will graduate in June with a bachelor's degree in business administration.

15-6c Motivating Action in the Closing

After presenting your case, you should conclude by asking confidently for an interview. Don't ask for the job. To do so would be presumptuous and naïve. In requesting an interview, you might suggest reader benefits or review your strongest points. Sound sincere and appreciative. Remember to make it easy for the reader to agree by supplying your telephone number and the best times to call you. In addition, keep in mind that some hiring officers prefer that you take the initiative to call them. Avoid expressions such as *I hope*, which weaken your closing. Here are possible endings:

Poor: I hope to hear from you soon.

Improved: This brief description of my qualifications and the additional information on my résumé demonstrate my readiness to put my accounting skills to work for McLellan and Associates. Please call me at (405) 488-2291 before 10 a.m. or after 3 p.m. to arrange an interview.

Poor: I look forward to a call from you.

Improved: To add to your staff an industrious, well-trained administrative assistant with proven Internet and communication skills, call me at (350) 492-1433 to arrange an interview. I look forward to meeting with you to discuss further my qualifications.

Poor: Thanks for looking over my qualifications.

Improved: I look forward to the opportunity to discuss my qualifications for the financial analyst position more fully in an interview. I can be reached at (213) 458-4030.

15-6d Sending Your Résumé and Cover Message

How you submit your résumé depends on the employer's instructions, which usually involve one of the following methods:

- Submit both your cover message and résumé in an e-mail message. Convert both to plain text.
- Send your cover message in an e-mail and attach your résumé (plain text, Word document, or PDF).
- Send a short e-mail message with both your cover message and résumé attached.
- Send your cover message and résumé as printed Word documents by U.S. mail.

Serious job candidates will take the time to prepare a professional cover message. If you are e-mailing your résumé, use the same cover message you would send by surface mail, but shorten it a bit, as illustrated in Model Document 15.9. Just below your name, include your address, e-mail address, and phone number. For résumés submitted as PDF files, send the cover message as a PDF also.

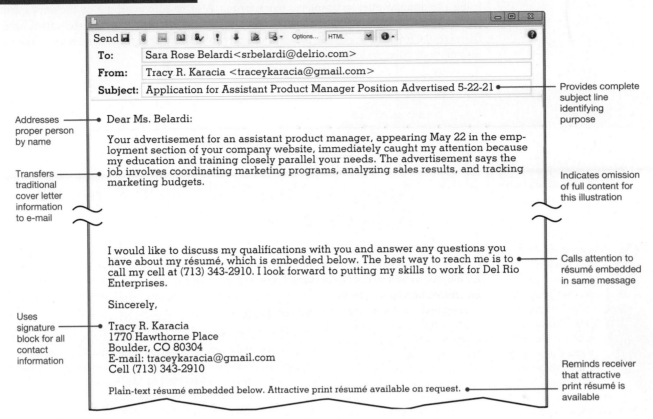

Provides complete subject line identifying purpose

Addresses proper person by name

Transfers traditional cover letter information to e-mail

Indicates omission of full content for this illustration

Calls attention to résumé embedded in same message

Uses signature block for all contact information

Reminds receiver that attractive print résumé is available

To: Sara Rose Belardi<srbelardi@delrio.com>

From: Tracy R. Karacia <traceykaracia@gmail.com>

Subject: Application for Assistant Product Manager Position Advertised 5-22-21

Dear Ms. Belardi:

Your advertisement for an assistant product manager, appearing May 22 in the employment section of your company website, immediately caught my attention because my education and training closely parallel your needs. The advertisement says the job involves coordinating marketing programs, analyzing sales results, and tracking marketing budgets.

I would like to discuss my qualifications with you and answer any questions you have about my résumé, which is embedded below. The best way to reach me is to call my cell at (713) 343-2910. I look forward to putting my skills to work for Del Rio Enterprises.

Sincerely,

Tracy R. Karacia
1770 Hawthorne Place
Boulder, CO 80304
E-mail: traceykaracia@gmail.com
Cell (713) 343-2910

Plain-text résumé embedded below. Attractive print résumé available on request.

15-6e Final Tips for Successful Cover Messages

As you revise your cover message, notice how many sentences begin with *I*. Although it is impossible to talk about yourself without using *I*, you can reduce "I" domination with a number of thoughtful techniques. Make activities and outcomes, and not yourself, the subjects of sentences. Sometimes you can avoid "I" domination by focusing on the "you" view. Another way to avoid starting sentences with *I* is to move phrases from within the sentence to the beginning.

Poor:	*I took classes in business communication and computer applications.*
Improved:	Classes in business communication and computer applications prepared me to . . . . (Make activities the subject.)
Poor:	*I enjoyed helping customers, which taught me to . . . .*
Improved:	*Helping customers was a real pleasure and taught me to . . . .* (Make outcomes the subject.)
Poor:	*I am a hardworking team player who . . . .*
Improved:	*You are looking for a hardworking team player who . . . .* (Use the "you" view.)
Poor:	*I worked to support myself all through college, thus building . . . .*
Improved:	*All through college, I worked to support myself, thus building . . . .* (Move phrase to the beginning to avoid starting sentence with *I*.)

Strive for a comfortable style. In your effort to avoid sounding self-centered, don't write unnaturally.

Like your résumé, your cover message must look professional and suggest quality. This means using a traditional letter style, such as block format. Also, be sure to print it on the same quality paper as your résumé. As with your résumé, proofread it several times yourself; then have a friend read it for content and mechanics. Don't rely on spell-check to find all the errors. Like your résumé, your cover message must be perfect.

Zooming In

Your Turn:
Applying Your Skills With Amanda Augustine

As an intern to career coach Amanda Augustine, you are a good source of information about how first-time job seekers view the job search. She wants your input for an article she plans to write that targets recent college graduates, both traditional and nontraditional. She wonders about the following: Do students give much thought to job searching and résumé writing before they graduate and enter the job market? How do students view networking in general and social networking sites as they relate to finding jobs? Ms. Augustine suggests that you query your current and former classmates and get back to her. She would like to use the information you develop to write a meaningful article with advice for new grads.

Your Task

In groups of three to four, address the topics Ms. Augustine has brought up. Ask each student to contribute at least two responses. Individually or as a group, summarize your findings in an e-mail report addressed to Ms. Augustine but delivered to your instructor. Treat this message as a short report, dividing it into logical sections with headings.

SUMMARY OF LEARNING OUTCOMES

1 Describe how technology is altering the four major steps in a job search.

- The four steps in a job search include the following: analyzing yourself, exploring the open and hidden job markets, creating a customized résumé and cover message, and knowing the hiring process.

- Recognize that searching for a job in this digital age now includes such indispensable tools as job boards, social networks, and mobile technologies.

- Start the process by learning about yourself, your field of interest, and your qualifications. How do your skills match what employers seek?

- To investigate career opportunities, visit a campus career center, search for apps and online help, take a summer job, interview someone in your field, volunteer, or join professional organizations.

- Identify job availability, the skills and qualifications required, duties, and salaries.

2 List search strategies that explore the open job market.

- In searching the open job market—that is, jobs that are listed and advertised—explore the big job boards, such as Indeed, CareerBuilder, Monster, and CollegeGrad.

- To find a job with a specific company, go directly to that company's website and check its openings and possibilities.

- For jobs in specialized fields, search some of the many niche sites, such as Dice for technology positions or CoolWorks for seasonal employment.

- Take advantage of mobile apps to access and vet job openings as soon as they are listed.

- Protect yourself when using online job boards by posting privately, not revealing personal information, keeping careful records, and avoiding blind job postings.

3 Identify search strategies that unlock the hidden job market.

- Estimates suggest that as many as 80 percent of jobs are in the hidden job market—that is, never advertised. Successful job candidates find jobs in the hidden job market through networking.

- An effective networking procedure involves (a) developing a contact list, (b) reaching out to these contacts in person and online in search of referrals, and (c) following up on referrals.

- Because electronic media and digital tools continue to change our lives, savvy candidates use social media networks—especially LinkedIn—to extend their networking efforts.

- Invaluable in a job search, LinkedIn enables candidates to receive job alerts, leverage their networks, research companies, get recommendations, and help companies locate them online.

- Effective networking strategies include building a personal brand, preparing a professional business card with a tagline, composing a 60-second elevator speech that describes what you can offer, and building a powerful online presence.

4 Explain how to organize your qualifications and skills into effective résumé categories.

- Because of intense competition, you must customize your résumé to appeal to an applicant tracking system (ATS) as well as to a human reader.

- Chronological résumés, which list work and education by dates, rank highest with recruiters. Functional résumés, which highlight skills instead of jobs, may be helpful for people with little experience, those changing careers, and those with negative employment histories.

- Arrange your skills and achievements to aim at a particular job or company.

- Study models to effectively arrange the résumé main heading and the optional career objective, summary of qualifications, education, work experience, capabilities, awards, and activities sections.

- The most effective résumés include action verbs to appeal to human readers and job-specific nouns that become keywords selected by ATS.

- Prepare a LinkedIn page with a headline, photo, profile, and information about your education, skills,

and experience. Encourage your instructors and employers to post recommendations.

5 Describe tools that can enhance your job search and résumé.

- To maximize the rank of your résumé when it is evaluated by an automated tracking system, include specific keywords such as nouns that name job titles, technical skills, and tools used or specific experience.

- Consider preparing a career e-portfolio to showcase your qualifications. This collection of digital files can feature your talents, accomplishments, and technical skills. It may include examples of academic performance, photographs, multimedia files, and other items beyond what can be shown in a résumé.

- A video résumé enables you to present your experience, qualifications, and interests in video form.

- Start with a basic print-based résumé from which you can make a plain-text résumé stripped of formatting to be embedded within e-mail messages and submitted online.

- Decide whether you should submit your résumé as a Word, plain-text, or PDF document. You may also be asked to enter your information into a company database.

6 Analyze the importance and construction of cover messages.

- Although ATS may accept only a résumé, cover messages still play a significant role in the job application process, especially to hiring managers.

- Cover messages help recruiters make decisions, and they enable candidates to set themselves apart from others.

- In the opening of a cover message, gain attention by addressing the receiver by name and identifying the job. You might also identify the person who referred you.

- In the body of the message, build interest by stressing your strengths in relation to the stated requirements. Explain what you can do for the targeted company.

- In the body or closing, refer to your résumé, request an interview, and make it easy for the receiver to respond.

- If you are submitting your cover message by e-mail, shorten it a bit and include your complete contact information in the signature block.

Key Terms

Critical Thinking

1. When asked if they would pass up a traditional job for full-time gig work, 53 percent of Generation Z (ages 16–25) respondents in a global study said yes.[34] Commissioned by the Workforce Institute of Kronos, this study, titled "Gen Z and the Gig Economy: It's Time to Gig in or Get Out," surveyed 3,400 individuals around the world. What is it about gig work that appeals to young people and others? What disadvantages do you see? (L.O. 1–4)

2. "If you are starting your job search with Monster.com, CareerBuilder, or similar search tools, then you are starting at the end of the chain," claims job-search author Ryan Guina.[35] What do you think he means? (L.O. 2, 3)

3. Why do you think some businesses avoid advertising job openings? If jobs are unlisted, how can candidates locate them? (L.O. 3)

4. LinkedIn has 675 million registered users, but only 310 million are active each month. Although it is highly recommended that new grads complete a LinkedIn profile, some critics charge that LinkedIn is a waste of time because it has become bogged down with spam connection requests, posturing, and users' attempts to market products instead of building relationships, as originally intended.[36] As a job candidate, would you post your résumé information at LinkedIn? Why or why not? How could candidates make better use of LinkedIn? (L.O. 4)

5. **Ethical Issue**: Phantom job listings are announcements for jobs that have already been filled through informal networking processes. The public job posting is necessary to comply with human resources department rules that mandate the advertising of open positions. Sometimes the job has been filled by an internal candidate who already had the position nailed down. Although not required by law, management policies and human resources departments at many companies demand that hiring managers list all openings on job boards or career sites. Often, hiring managers have already selected candidates for these phantom jobs. Do you believe it is ethical to advertise jobs that are not really available?[37]

Activities

15.1 Document for Analysis: Poorly Written Résumé (L.O. 4)

One effective way to improve your writing skills is to critique and edit the résumé of someone else.

YOUR TASK Analyze the following poor résumé. List at least eight weaknesses. Your instructor may ask you to revise sections of this résumé before showing you an improved version.

Résumé
Annalise Ortez-Villa
1340 East Phillips Ave., Apt. D Littleton, CO 80126
Phone 455-5182 | E-Mail: Hotchilibabe@gmail.com | LinkedIn

OBJECTIVE

I'm dying to become an accounting associate in the "real world" with a big profitable company that will help me get the experience I need to become a CPA.

SKILLS

Microsoft Word, MS Outlook, Powerpoint, Excel, spreadsheets Excel; experienced with QuickBooks, great composure in stressful situations; 3 years as leader and supervisor and 4 years in customer service

EDUCATION

Arapahoe Community College, Littleton, Colorado. AA degree, Fall 2018

Now I am pursuing a BA in Accounting at CSU-Pueblo, majoring in Accounting; my minor is Finance. Completed

64 units of upper-level units. My expected degree date is June 2021; I recieved a Certificate of Completion in Entry Level Accounting in December 2018. My overall GPA is 3.5 on a 4.0 = A system.

I graduated East High School, Denver, CO in 2014.

Highlights:

- Named Line Manger of the Month at Target, 10/2017 and 03/2018
- Obtained a Certificate in Entry Level Accounting, June 2018
- Chair of Accounting Society, Spring and fall 2020
- Dean's Honor List, Fall 2020
- Financial advisor training completed through Primerica (May 2019)
- Webmaster for M.E.Ch.A, Spring 2020

Part-Time Employment
Financial Consultant, 2019 to present

I worked only part-time (January 2019-present) for Primerica Financial Services, Pueblo, CO to assist clients in refinancing a mortgage or consolidating a current mortgage loan and also to advice clients in assessing their need for life insurance.

Target, Littleton, CO. As line manager, from September 2017 - August 2018, I supervised 12 cashiers and front-end associates. I helped to write schedules, disciplinary action notices, and performance appraisals. I also kept track of change drawer and money exchanges; occasionally was manager on duty for entire store. Named line manager of the month August 2017 and March 2018.

Mr. K's Floral Design of Denver. I taught flower design from August, 2016 to September, 2017. I supervised 5 florists, made floral arrangements for big events like weddings, send them to customers, and restocked flowers.

15.2 Document for Analysis: Poor Cover Letter (L.O. 6)

The following cover letter accompanies Annalise Ortez-Villa's résumé (**Activity 15.1**).

YOUR TASK Analyze each section of the following cover letter and list its weaknesses. Your instructor may ask you to revise this letter before showing you an improved version.

To Whom It May Concern:

I saw your accounting associate position listing yesterday and would like to apply right away. It would be so exiting to work for your esteemed firm! This position would really give me much needed real-world experience and help me become a CPA.

I have all the qualifications you require in your add and more. I am a senior at Colorado State University-Pueblo and an Accounting major (with a minor in Finance) and have completed 64 units of upper-level course work. Accounting and Finance are my passion and I want to become a CPA and a financial advisor. I have taken eight courses in accounting and now work as a part-time financial advisor with Primerica Financial Services in Pueblo. I should also tell you that I was at Target for four years. I learned alot, but my heart is in accounting and finance.

I am a team player, a born leader, motivated, reliable, and I show excellent composure in stressful situations, for example, when customers complain. I put myself through school and always carry at least 12 units while working part time.

You will probably agree that I am a good candidate for your accounting position, which I understand should start about July 1. I feel that my motivation, passion, and strong people skills will serve your company well.

Sincerely,

15.3 Opening Your Job Search With Self-Analysis (L.O. 1)

E-Mail

YOUR TASK In an e-mail or a memo addressed to your instructor, answer the questions in the section "Opening Your Job Search With Self-Analysis" on page 539. Draw a conclusion from your answers. What kind of career, company, position, and location seem to fit your self-analysis?

15.4 Taking Stock of Your Qualifications (L.O. 1–3)

YOUR TASK Prepare four worksheets that inventory your qualifications in these areas: employment; education; capabilities and skills; and awards, honors, and activities. Use active verbs when appropriate and specific nouns that describe job titles and skills.

a. **Employment**. Begin with your most recent job or internship. For each position list the following information: employer; job title; dates of employment; and three to five duties, activities, or accomplishments. Emphasize activities related to your job goal. Strive to quantify your achievements.

b. **Education**. List degrees, certificates, and training accomplishments. Include courses, seminars, and skills that are relevant to your job goal. Calculate your grade point average in your major.

c. **Capabilities and skills**. List all capabilities and skills that qualify you for the job you seek. Use words and phrases such as *skilled, competent, trained, experienced, and* *ability to*. Also list five or more qualities or interpersonal skills necessary for success in your chosen field. Write action statements demonstrating that you possess some of these qualities. Empty assurances aren't good enough; try to show evidence (*Developed teamwork skills by working on a committee of eight to produce a . . .*).

d. **Awards, honors, and activities**. Explain any awards so that the reader will understand them. List campus, community, and professional activities that suggest you are a well-rounded individual or possess traits relevant to your target job.

15.5 Building Your Future by Choosing a Career Path (L.O. 1)

`Web`

Many people know amazingly little about the work done in various occupations and the training requirements.

YOUR TASK Visit O*Net Online at **https://www.onetonline.org**, prepared by the Bureau of Labor Statistics (BLS), to learn more about an occupation of your choice. This is the nation's premier source for career information. It provides detailed descriptions of the world of work for use by job seekers, workforce development and HR professionals, students, and researchers.

The career profiles featured cover hundreds of occupations and describe what people in these occupations do, the work environment, how to get these jobs, how much they earn, and more. The listings range alphabetically from Actuaries to Wind Tunnel Service Technicians. Did you know that the median salary for a wind tunnel technician is $54,370? Not bad, right?

Find the description of a position for which you could apply in two to five years. Learn about what workers do on the job, working conditions, training and education needed, earnings, and expected job prospects. Print two or more pages from the occupational listings that describe employment in the area in which you are interested. If your instructor directs, attach these copies to the cover letter you will write in **Activity 15.9**.

15.6 Searching the Job Market (L.O. 1)

`Web`

Where are the jobs? Even though you may not currently be in the job market, become familiar with the kinds of available positions because job awareness should be an important part of your education.

YOUR TASK Clip or print a job advertisement or announcement from (a) a social media site, (b) the classified section of a newspaper, (c) a job board on the Web, (d) a company

website, or (e) a professional association listing. Select an advertisement or announcement describing the kind of employment you are seeking now or plan to seek when you graduate. Save this advertisement or announcement to attach to the résumé and cover letter you will write in **Activity 15.8 and Activity 15.9.**

15.7 Learning About Posting a Résumé Online

`Team` `Web`

The world of online job boards is a little bewildering at first. Luckily, you can learn how to do it with a little research. Some job boards provide instructions for posting résumés. You can also find blog articles that offer excellent tips on how to post online.

YOUR TASK Individually or in teams, conduct research about posting résumés online. Find answers to questions such as these: What are the most reputable sites for posting, how can you protect your résumé while keeping it visible to employers, and can anyone apply for a listed job? What tips do you find that will aid candidates in posting their résumés online? In teams of three to five, discuss the answers to the questions raised. In class discussion or in an e-mail to your instructor, describe your team findings.

15.8 Writing Your Résumé (L.O. 4)

YOUR TASK Using the data you developed in **Activity 15.4**, write your résumé. Aim it at the full-time job, part-time position, or internship that you located in **Activity 15.7**. Attach the job listing to your résumé. Also prepare a list of references. Revise your résumé until it is perfect.

15.9 Preparing Your Cover Message (L.O. 6)

`E-Mail`

YOUR TASK Using the job listing you found for **Activity 15.6**, write a cover message introducing your résumé. Decide whether it should be a letter or an e-mail. Again, revise until it is perfect.

15.10 Using LinkedIn in Your Job Search (L.O. 2)

`Social Media` `Web`

Despite criticism, LinkedIn is the acknowledged No. 1 site for job seekers and recruiters. It's free and easy to join. Even if you are not in the job market yet, becoming familiar with LinkedIn can open your eyes to the kinds of information employers seek and also give you practice in filling in templates such as those that ATS employ.

YOUR TASK To become familiar with LinkedIn, set up an account and complete a profile. This consists of a template with categories to fill in. The easiest way to begin is to view a LinkedIn video taking you through the steps of creating a profile. Search for *LinkedIn Profile Checklist*. In colorful subsections, it discusses how to fill in information in categories such as the following:

- **Photo**. Have a friend or a professional take a photo that shows your head and shoulders. No selfies! Wear work-appropriate attire and a smile. See examples in the LinkedIn Profile Checklist.

- **Headline**. Use a tagline to summarize your professional goals.

- **Summary**. Explain what motivates you, what you are skilled at, and where you want to go in the future.

- **Experience**. List the jobs you have held and be sure to enter the information precisely in the template categories. You can even include photos and videos of your work.

You can fill in other categories such as Organizations, Honors, and Publications. After completing a profile, discuss your LinkedIn experience with classmates. If you already have an account set up, discuss how it operates and your opinion of its worth. How can LinkedIn help students now and in the future?

15.11 Consider a Twitter Mini Résumé as a LinkedIn Alternative (L.O. 4, 5)

`Communication Technology` `Social Media` `Web`

Twitter may not be the first social media site you consider for posting your résumé. Savvy candidates, however, know that Twitter has one major advantage over more obvious sites such as LinkedIn and Facebook. Twitter is an unsaturated market where your brand and mini résumé could separate you from the crowd. Everyone wants to read less, including hiring managers. In up to 280 characters, your main selling points in a mini Twitter résumé would be an appealing, easy read. The résumé of Alya Salib presents just enough information to tantalize a hiring manager looking for someone who fits her profile. In preparing a more professional Twitter résumé, include the job title you are seeking, your strongest and most relevant skills, and where you are now or wish to relocate. Refer readers to your full information at LinkedIn or your website. To explore examples, conduct a Google search for *Twitter resumes*. Following are a few examples of content. Can you do better?

- Copywriter for print/online. Photo editor. Fashion/luxury market. LinkedIn.comin [name]

- Recent grad. Intern experience in marketing/communications in NYC. Will relocate.

- Data analyst. Coffee lover. Full-time cat mom. Database extraordinaire. Ref: Acct mgr @ABCLtd.

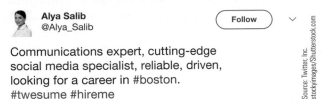

Alya Salib
@Alya_Salib   `Follow` ⌄

Communications expert, cutting-edge social media specialist, reliable, driven, looking for a career in #boston. #twesume #hireme

YOUR TASK Compose three possible mini Twitter résumés using your information. Your instructor may ask you to present them for discussion in class or in your chat group.

15.12 Analyzing and Building Student E-Portfolios (L.O. 5)

`Communication Technology` `Team` `Web`

Take a minute to conduct a Google search on your name. What comes up? Are you proud of what you see? If you want to change that information—and especially if you are in the job market—think about creating a career e-portfolio. Building such a portfolio has many benefits. It can give you an important digital tool to connect with a large audience. It can also help you expand your technology skills, confirm your strengths, recognize areas in need of improvement, and establish goals for improvement. Many students are creating e-portfolios with the help of their schools.

YOUR TASK NO. 1 Before attempting to build your own career e-portfolio, take a look at those of other students. Use the Google search term *student career e-portfolio* to see lots of samples. Your instructor may assign you individually or as a team to visit specific digital portfolio sites and summarize your findings in a memo or a brief oral presentation. You could focus on the composition of the site, page layout, links provided, software tools used, colors selected, or types of documents included.

YOUR TASK NO. 2 Next, examine websites that provide tutorials and tips on how to build career e-portfolios. Your instructor may have you individually or as team write a memo summarizing tips on how to create an e-portfolio and choose the types of documents to include. Alternatively, your instructor may ask you to create a career e-portfolio.

Test Your Workplace Etiquette IQ

New communication platforms and casual workplace environments have blurred the lines of appropriateness, leaving workers wondering how to navigate uncharted waters. Check your workplace etiquette IQ by deciding whether the following statements are true or false. Then see if you agree with the responses on p. Key-6.

1. You're currently employed but have decided to move on. As you begin the job search, you should share your decision only with coworkers who can help you find another position and who promise to keep your goal secret.

_____ True _____ False

2. If you are keen on a specific job, you should apply to the same job multiple times in the same week to guarantee that your name and résumé keep popping up on the company's radar.

_____ True _____ False

3. The safest way to avoid a cell phone blunder during a job interview is to not take your phone with you at all. If you leave it locked in your car, you will not be tempted to look at it. Remember that you may be observed from the moment you walk into the building and being glued to your phone could present a less-than-favorable impression.

_____ True _____ False

Chat About It

In each chapter you will find five discussion questions related to the chapter material. Your instructor may assign these topics for you to discuss in class, in an online chat room, or on an online discussion board. Some of the discussion topics may require outside research. You may also be asked to read and respond to postings made by your classmates.

TOPIC 1: A recent survey of millennial managers revealed that 75 percent of respondents felt that constantly changing jobs advanced their careers. This survey of 1,000 managers and mid- to executive-level executives between the ages of 18 and 36 was conducted by employee experience platform Akumina "to understand the needs of millennials in the rapidly changing workplace."[38] How do you think changing jobs frequently advances one's career? Does this seem ethical?

TOPIC 2: A study by career website The Ladders found that candidates need to apply to a job within 72 hours after it has been posted online. After that, chances of being hired drop by more than 50 percent. Does this sound reasonable to you? How could job candidates apply so quickly?

TOPIC 3: Why do you think it is important to customize your résumé for each employer and each job for which you apply? How do you think employers will respond to a customized résumé versus a generic résumé? Is creating a customized résumé for each position worth your time and effort? Share your opinions with your classmates.

TOPIC 4: In your opinion, what is the difference between honest self-marketing and deception? What are some examples from your experience?

TOPIC 5: A blogger recently wrote that "cover letters probably don't matter, but you still need one." How can you justify cover letters?

Grammar and Mechanics Review 15

Total Review

Each of the following sentences has **three** errors in grammar, punctuation, capitalization, usage, or spelling. On a separate sheet, write a correct version. Avoid adding new phrases or rewriting sentences in your own words. When finished, compare your responses with the key at the end of the book.

EXAMPLE: If I was you I would shorten my résumé to 1 page and include a summary of qualifications.

REVISION: If I **were you**, I would shorten my résumé to **one** page and include a summary of qualifications.

1. When searching for jobs candidates discovered that the résumé is more likely to be used to screen candidate's then for making hiring decisions.

2. If you have 10 or fewer years' of experience, its customary to prepare a one-page résumé.

3. To conduct a safe online job search, you should: (a) Use only reputable job boards, (b) keep careful

records, and (c) limit the number of sites on which you post your résumé.

4. Todays employers use sights such as Facebook to learn about potential employees. Which means that a job seeker must maintain a professional online presence.

5. Although action verbs make a résumé appeal to a recruiter, applicant tracking systems often looks for nouns in three categories (a) job titles, (b) technical skills and (c) certification.

6. Luca wondered whether it was alright to ask his professor for employment advise?

7. At last months staff meeting team members examined several candidates résumés.

8. Rather then schedule face to face interviews the team investigated videoconferencing.

9. 11 applicants will be interviewed on April 10th, consequently, we may need to work late to accommodate them.

10. Although as many as twenty-five percent of jobs are found on the Internet the principle source of jobs still involves networking.

Interviewing and Following Up

LEARNING OUTCOMES

After studying this chapter, you should be able to do the following:

1 Explain current trends as well as the purposes, sequence, and types of job interviews.

2 Describe how to prepare *before* a job interview.

3 Describe what to do *during* an interview.

4 Describe what to do *after* an interview.

5 Prepare additional employment documents.

Zooming In

Thorough Preparation Triggers Interview Success

When it comes to stressful life experiences, job interviews rank pretty close to the top. Don Georgevich, a leading authority on interviewing and résumé writing, says it's perfectly normal to be anxious and insecure. However, with the right kind of preparation, you can greatly reduce your fears and convert that anxiety into enthusiastic energy.

The author of three top-selling career books—plus e-tools, blogs, YouTube videos, and Internet articles—Georgevich has special advice directed at those who are unaccustomed to the job-search process. "For new grads, being aware of recent trends and preparing diligently for the interview is crucial," he stressed in a telephone interview with Mary Ellen Guffey. "The more you study the company and the job description, combined with how you believe your skills and experiences fit the targeted organization, the more prepared you will be. You can even predict what to expect in a typical interview because interviewers tend to repeat common questions."

When asked how new grads and career changers can gain traction in a dynamic, highly competitive job market, Georgevich stressed demonstrating transferable skills. For example, candidates can say, "I have [blank] skills and I can use them to do [blank] for you." Job seekers need to connect the dots for employers and show how their qualifications fit the targeted position. "All too often," he said, "job seekers leave it up to the interviewer to figure out what they are good at doing instead of taking a proactive stance."

Courtesy of Don Georgevich

A recent trend is video interviewing, either for initial screening or to choose among final candidates. "Keep in mind," Georgevich said, "that an employer will be reviewing videos from many candidates. To make yours stand out, start off with an eye-opening statement, such as 'In this video I'm going to show why I'm the only person you need to consider for this position.' Then proceed to show that you understand the company, its products, and its pains."

Companies today are putting candidates through many layers of interviewing to avoid a bad hire. Because the hiring process is more stretched out, it's more important than ever to follow up with the hiring manager to avoid being forgotten. Your goal is to stay in close contact without being a pest. To follow up, call about once every seven to ten days after your interview. Recent graduates, Georgevich said, seem to prefer only e-mail or text follow-ups, but he highly recommends a phone call to make a personal connection and achieve greater authenticity. From the beginning to the end of the process, the hiring manager wants to discover whether you are a good culture fit and whether you are truly invested in the company.[1] You will learn more about working with Don Georgevich and be asked to complete a relevant task later in this chapter.

Critical Thinking

- Can novice job seekers predict what a job interview will involve?

- How is interviewing a two-way street? What does this mean for job candidates?

- How can job seekers show recruiters or hiring managers that they are invested in a position during the job interview?

16-1 Sharpening Your Interview Skills

LEARNING OUTCOME

1 Explain current trends as well as the purposes, sequence, and types of job interviews.

Whether you are completing your education or are in the workforce and striving to improve your career, a job interview can be life changing. Because employment is a major part of everyone's life, the job interview takes on enormous importance. An excellent résumé, an engaging cover letter, and good references will help you secure an interview. None of these, however, will automatically get you hired. Only when you talk directly to the hiring manager will an organization be motivated to hire you.

Despite the importance of the interview, too many candidates fail to prepare sufficiently. As career coach Don Georgevich pointed out in the Zooming In feature, preparation is critical to successful interviewing. Careful preparation can also greatly reduce interview stress. Most candidates fear interviews almost as much as making a speech or going on a first date. The truth is that the more you learn about the process and the more prepared you are, the less stress you will feel. Moreover, a job interview is a two-way street. It is not just about being judged by the employer. You, the applicant, will be using the job interview to evaluate the employer. Do you really want to work for this organization?

To be successful in a competitive job market, you must keep up with the latest trends and techniques that recruiters use to choose the best candidates. Figure 16.1 describes seven hot trends facing job candidates. This chapter offers the latest tips as well as traditional techniques that will improve your interviewing skills and boost your confidence. You will learn how to gather information about a prospective employer, how to project a professional image, how to reduce nervousness during an interview, and how to prepare for video interviews.

Because today's recruiters regularly check social media and the Internet to vet applicants, this chapter presents valuable advice on using social media safely and skillfully. Additionally, you will find typical interview questions, possible responses, and advice on how to cope with

FIGURE 16.1   Hot Trends in Interviewing

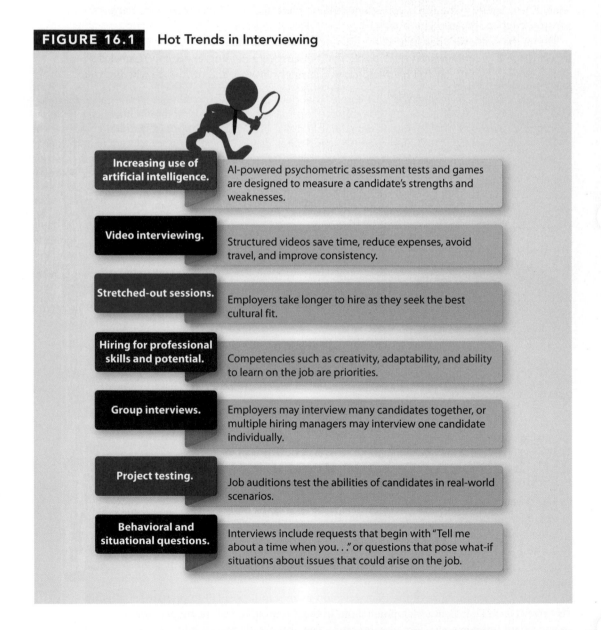

Increasing use of artificial intelligence. AI-powered psychometric assessment tests and games are designed to measure a candidate's strengths and weaknesses.

Video interviewing. Structured videos save time, reduce expenses, avoid travel, and improve consistency.

Stretched-out sessions. Employers take longer to hire as they seek the best cultural fit.

Hiring for professional skills and potential. Competencies such as creativity, adaptability, and ability to learn on the job are priorities.

Group interviews. Employers may interview many candidates together, or multiple hiring managers may interview one candidate individually.

Project testing. Job auditions test the abilities of candidates in real-world scenarios.

Behavioral and situational questions. Interviews include requests that begin with "Tell me about a time when you. . ." or questions that pose what-if situations about issues that could arise on the job.

illegal inquiries and salary matters. Moreover, you will receive pointers on significant questions you can ask during an interview. Finally, you will learn how to follow up successfully after an interview.

Yes, job interviews can be intimidating and stressful. However, you can expect to ace an interview when you know what's coming and prepare thoroughly. Remember, preparation often determines who gets the job. First, though, you need to know the purposes of employment interviews, the typical sequence of events, and the types of interviews you might encounter in your job search.

16-1a Purposes and Sequencing of Employment Interviews

An interview has several purposes for you as a job candidate. It is an opportunity to (a) convince the employer of your potential, (b) learn more about the job and the company, and (c) expand on the information in your résumé. This is the time for you to gather information to determine whether you would fit into the company culture. You should also be thinking about whether this job suits your career goals.

From the employer's perspective, the interview is an opportunity to (a) assess your abilities in relation to the requirements for the position; (b) discuss your training, experience, knowledge, and abilities in more detail; (c) see what drives and motivates you; and (d) decide whether you would fit into the organization. Interviews are getting longer as employers seek to learn whether the candidate will fit into their culture.

The hiring process often follows a six-stage sequence, as illustrated in Figure 16.2. Following the application, interviews proceed from screening to hiring interviews.

16-1b Screening Interview

A **screening interview** does just that—it screens candidates to eliminate those who fail to meet minimum requirements. Companies use screening interviews to save time and money by weeding out lesser-qualified candidates before scheduling final face-to-face or video interviews. Although initial screening interviews may be conducted during job fairs or on college campuses, they usually take place by telephone or video.

During an initial screening interview, the interviewer will probably ask you to provide details about the education and experience listed on your résumé; therefore, you must be prepared to promote your qualifications. If you do well on the initial interview, you may be invited to a secondary screening interview. This interview may be conducted by a human resources specialist with more specific questions relating to the open position. It could be a telephone or a video interview scheduled on Skype, Zoom, Google Hangouts, or another chat app. The interviewer is trying to decide whether you are a strong enough candidate to be interviewed by a hiring manager.

FIGURE 16.2   Six Stages of the Hiring Process

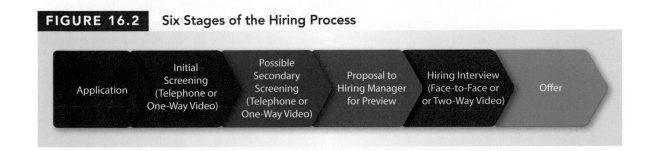

Application | Initial Screening (Telephone or One-Way Video) | Possible Secondary Screening (Telephone or One-Way Video) | Proposal to Hiring Manager for Preview | Hiring Interview (Face-to-Face or or Two-Way Video) | Offer

16-1c Hiring/Placement Interview

The most promising candidates selected from screening interviews are invited to a **hiring/placement interview**. Hiring managers want to learn whether candidates are motivated, qualified, and a good fit for the position. Their goal is to learn how the candidate would fit into their organization. Conducted in depth, a hiring/placement interview may take many forms, such as the following:

One-on-One Interview. In a **one-on-one interview**, which is most common, you can expect to sit down with a company representative and talk about the job and your qualifications. If the representative is the hiring manager, questions will be specific and job related. If the representative is from human resources, the questions will probably be more general.

Panel Interview. A **panel interview** is typically conducted by people who will be your supervisors and colleagues. Usually seated around a table, interviewers take turns asking questions. Panel interviews are advantageous because they save the company time and money, and they show you how the staff works together. If possible before these interviews, try to gather basic biographical information about each panel member. This information may be available on the company website or LinkedIn. When answering questions, maintain eye contact with the questioner as well as with the others. Expect to repeat information you may have given in earlier interviews. Take paper-and-pen notes during the interview so that you can remember each person's questions and what was important to that individual. Don't take notes on a laptop or other digital device as interviewers may think you are checking incoming texts.

Group Interview. A **group interview** is one in which a company interviews several candidates for the same position at the same time. Some employers use this technique to evaluate leadership skills and communication styles. During a group interview, stay focused on the interviewer, and treat the other candidates with respect. Even if you are nervous, try to remain calm, take your time when responding, and express yourself clearly. The key during a group interview is to make yourself stand out from the other candidates in a positive way.

Sequential Interview. In a **sequential interview**, you meet individually with two or more interviewers one-on-one over the course of several hours or days. It is not uncommon for a job candidate to endure three or more interviews over an extended period of time. For example, you may meet with human resources representatives, the hiring manager, and potential future supervisors and colleagues in your division or department. You must listen carefully and respond positively to all interviewers. Promote your qualifications to each one; don't assume that any interviewer knows what was said in a previous interview. Keep your responses fresh, even when repeating yourself many times over. Subsequent interviews also tend to be more in-depth than first interviews, which means that you need to be even more prepared and know even more about the company.

Video Interview. Perhaps the hottest trend in interviewing is the rush to video interviews. A **one-way video interview** is one in which a candidate responds to a list of scripted questions prepared by the hiring organization. When convenient, the candidate creates a video recording of the answers. The interviewer can view the job seeker, but the job seeker cannot see the interviewer. One-way interviewing benefits employers by cutting the time needed to meet lots of candidates. One-way interviewing also benefits candidates by enabling them to be interviewed at their leisure without traveling to distant locations. Candidates can practice and perfect their responses by rerecording.

A **two-way video interview**, sometimes called a **live video interview**, is like regular face-to-face interviewing, but it is typically conducted through video chat. A key advantage of two-way interviewing is that it provides an interactive forum enabling hiring companies to better assess a candidate's communication skills, body language, and personality. Preparing for either a one-way or a two-way video interview is extremely important; check out the accompanying Plugged In for tips to help you succeed.

No matter what interview structure you encounter, you will feel more comfortable if you know what to do before, during, and after the interview.

How to Ace a Video Job Interview

Both one-way and two-way video interviews enable job seekers to connect with potential employers without traveling. Because video interviews present many potential pitfalls, preparation is essential. The following tips can increase your confidence and help you ace such an interview.

Do your homework. Using the Internet, learn all that you can about the target company including its competitors, products, and goals.

Plan your answers. For one-way interviews, you have the questions in advance giving you a marvelous opportunity to prepare perfect responses. For two-way interviews, practice your answers to typical questions until you can recite them flawlessly by looking straight into the camera.

Check your tech. Be sure you know how your webcam and microphone work so that your audio and video are clear and free of glitches. Position the camera at eye level. Close any unnecessary web browser tabs and applications.

Look at your lighting. Place lights behind your computer and overhead so that your face is not in the shadows.

Control your surroundings. The room you sit in should be neat, attractive, and quiet. Avoid distractions such as barking dogs, crying children, flushing toilets, or ringing cell phones.

Dress to impress. Just as you would prepare for a face-to-face interview, be well groomed. If you are interviewing for a professional position, wear a suit. Avoid distracting prints, disturbingly bright colors, and loud jewelry.

Practice, practice, practice. Know your answers well enough to be natural and comfortable in saying them, but avoid sounding mechanical. This requires lots and lots of practice.

Be the best you can be. Sit up straight, look interested by leaning forward slightly, and don't let your eyes drop, suggesting you are reading from a script. Don't mumble or fidget. Project an upbeat attitude by using positive rather than negative words. Focus on answers and stories that illustrate your competence with the smart skills listed in the job description.

16-2 **Before the Interview**

LEARNING OUTCOME

2 Describe how to prepare *before* a job interview.

Once you have sent out at least one résumé or filled out at least one job application, you must consider yourself an active job seeker. Being active in the job market means that you should be prepared to be contacted by potential employers. As discussed earlier, employers often use screening interviews to narrow the list of candidates. If you do well in the screening interview, you will be invited to an in-person or video meeting. Screening interviews should not be taken lightly.

16-2a **Preparing for a Screening Telephone Call**

Even with the popularity of texting and e-mail, most employers contact job applicants by phone to set up interviews. Employers can judge how well applicants communicate by hearing their voices and expressions over the phone. Once you are actively looking for a job, anytime the phone rings, it could be a potential employer. Do not make the mistake of letting an unprofessional voice mail message or a lazy roommate or a sloppy cell phone manner ruin your chances. To make the best impression, try these tips:

- On your answering machine device, make sure that your outgoing message is concise and professional, with no distracting background sounds. It should be in your own voice and include your full name for clarity. You can find more tips for creating professional telephone messages in Chapter 14.

- Tell those who might answer your phone at home about your job search. Explain to them the importance of acting professionally and taking complete messages. Family members or roommates can affect the first impression an employer has of you.

- If you have children, prevent them from answering the phone during your job search. Children of all ages are not known for taking good messages!

- If you listed your cell phone number on your résumé or elsewhere, don't answer unless you are in a good location to carry on a conversation with an employer. It is hard to pay close attention when you are driving down the highway or eating in a noisy restaurant!
- Use voice mail to screen calls. By screening incoming calls, you can be totally in control when you return a prospective employer's call. Organize your materials and ready yourself psychologically for the conversation.

16-2b Making the First Conversation Impressive

Whether you answer the phone directly or return an employer's call, make sure you are prepared for the conversation. Remember that this is the first time the employer has heard your voice. How you conduct yourself on the phone will create a lasting impression. To make that first impression a positive one, follow these tips:

- Keep a list on your cell phone or near the telephone of positions for which you have applied.
- Treat any call from an employer just like an interview. Use a professional tone and businesslike language. Be polite and enthusiastic, and sell your qualifications.
- If caught off guard by the call, ask whether you can call back in a few minutes. Take that time to organize your materials and yourself.
- Have a copy of the job description and your résumé available so that you can answer any questions that come up. Also have your list of references, a calendar, and a notepad handy.
- Be prepared for a screening interview. As discussed earlier, this might occur during the first phone call.
- Take good notes during the phone conversation. Obtain accurate directions, and verify the spelling of your interviewer's name. If you will be interviewed by more than one person, get all of their names.
- If given a chance, ask for an interview on Tuesday at 10:30 a.m. This is considered the most opportune time. Avoid the start of the day on Monday and the end of the day on Friday.[2]
- Before you hang up, reconfirm the date and time of your interview. You could say something like *I look forward to meeting with you Wednesday, May 15, at 2 p.m.*

16-2c Learning About the Target Company

One of the best ways to become a stand-out candidate during the hiring process is to investigate thoroughly the target organization. Once you have scheduled an in-person or video interview, you need to start preparing for it. Never enter an interview cold. Recruiters are impressed by candidates who have done their homework. The good news is that it's never been easier to gather information about a prospective employer.

Scouring the Internet for Important Company Data. Search the potential employer's website, news sources, trade journals, and industry directories. Unearth information about the job, the company, and the industry. Learn all you can about the company's history, mission and goals, size, geographic locations, and number of employees. Check out its customers, competitors, culture, management structure, reputation in the community, financial condition, strengths and weaknesses, and future plans, as well as the names of its leaders. A good place to check is the About Us section on its website.

Analyzing the Company's Advertising. In addition to its online presence, examine the company's ads and promotional materials, including sales and marketing brochures. One candidate, a marketing major, spent a great deal of time poring over brochures from an aerospace contractor. During his initial interview, he shocked and

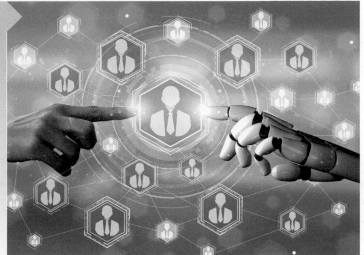

Blue Planet Studio/Shutterstock.com

impressed the recruiter with his knowledge of the company's guidance systems. The candidate had, in fact, relieved the interviewer of his least-favorite task—explaining the company's complicated technology.

Locating Inside Information.   To locate inside information, use social media sources such as LinkedIn and Twitter. On Facebook indicate that you "like" the company; comment shrewdly on its status updates and other posts. Check out employee review websites such as Glassdoor to get the inside scoop on what it's like to work there. Learn about the organization's culture and its values. Are opportunities for training and advancement important to you? How important is meaningful work? In one survey of American workers, nine out of ten reported that they were willing to earn less money to do more meaningful work.[4] Are you in this group?

To discover whether you know someone at the company or organization, use tools such as LinkedIn's JobsInsider toolbar. Your goal is to connect with someone who is currently employed by the company—but not working in the immediate area where you wish to be hired. Be sure to seek out someone who is discreet. Blogs are also excellent sources for insider information and company research. In addition, don't forget to google the interviewer.

As you learn about a company, you may uncover information that convinces you that this is not the company for you. It is always better to learn about negatives early in the process. More likely, though, the information you collect will help you tailor your interview responses to the organization's needs. You know how flattered you feel when an employer knows about you and your background. That feeling works both ways. Employers are pleased when job candidates take an interest in them.

16-2d Rehearsing Success Stories

To feel confident and be ready to sell your qualifications, prepare and practice success stories. These stories are specific examples of your educational and work-related experience that demonstrate your qualifications and achievements. Look over the job description and your résumé to determine what skills, training, personal characteristics, and experience you want to emphasize during the interview. Then prepare a success story for each one. Incorporate numbers, such as dollars saved or percentage of sales increased, whenever possible. Your success stories should be detailed but brief. Think of them as 30-second sound bites.

Practice telling your success stories until they fluently roll off your tongue and sound natural. Then in the interview, be certain to find places to insert them. Tell stories about (a) dealing with a crisis, (b) handling a tough interpersonal situation, (c) successfully juggling many priorities, (d) changing course to deal with changed circumstances, (e) learning from a mistake, (f) working on a team, and (g) going above and beyond expectations. Remember that you are being judged on your communication skills as well as your talents.

16-2e Cleaning Up Your Digital Presence

Potential employers definitely screen candidates' online presence using Google and social media sites such as Facebook, LinkedIn, and Twitter. One CareerBuilder survey revealed that 70 percent of hiring managers use social media to investigate prospective hires. Even more significant, 49 percent said they had found information that caused them not to hire a candidate.[5] What turned them off? The top reasons cited were (a) provocative or inappropriate photographs, videos, or information; (b) content about drinking or doing drugs; (c) discriminatory comments related to race, religion, and other protected categories; (d) criticism of previous employers or colleagues; and (e) poor communication skills.[6] Teasing photographs and provocative comments about drinking, drug use, and sexual exploits make job candidates look immature and unprofessional. Think about cleaning up your online presence by following these steps:

- **Remove questionable content**. Get rid of any incriminating, provocative, or distasteful photos, content, and links that could make you look unprofessional to potential employers.

- **Stay positive**. Don't complain about things in your professional or personal life online. Even negative reviews you have written on sites such as Amazon can turn employers off.

- **Be selective about who is on your list of friends**. You don't want to miss out on an opportunity because you seem to associate with negative, immature, or unprofessional people. Your best bet is to make your personal social networking pages private. Monitor your settings because they often change.

- **Don't discuss your job search if you are still employed**. Employees can find themselves in trouble with their current employers by writing status updates or sending tweets about their job searches.

16-2f Dressing for, Traveling to, and Arriving at Your Interview

The big day has arrived! Ideally, you are fully prepared for your interview. Now you need to make sure that everything goes smoothly. On the day of your interview, give yourself plenty of time to groom and dress.

Deciding What to Wear and When to Arrive.   What to wear may worry you because business attire today ranges from ultracasual to formal suits. The best plan is to ask your interviewer what is appropriate, advises career counselor Liz Ryan.[7] Ask this when the interview is arranged, and you will be greatly relieved. However, if that request doesn't bring results, think about the research you have done on the company. What is its level of formality? Take a look at photos of their social media sites and notice what people wear at the office. For job interviews it's always safe to dress conservatively.

Here's what you definitely should not wear for an interview, as reported at Monster.com: Flip flops, wedge sandals, ripped jeans or shorts, tank tops, halter tops, sandals, strapless tops and dresses, and athletic attire like yoga pants and sneakers. Also avoid anything that is too casual, too ill-fitting, too uncomfortable, too different from the company culture, too scented, and too revealing.[8]

As part of your interview preparations, make sure you can arrive at the employer's office without being rushed. If something unexpected happens that will cause you to be late, such as an accident or bridge closure, call the interviewer right away to explain what is happening. Most interviewers will be understanding, and your call will show that you are responsible. On the way to the interview, don't smoke, don't eat anything messy or smelly, and don't load up on perfume or cologne. Arrive at the interview five or ten minutes early, but not earlier. If you are very early, wait in the car or in a café nearby. If possible, check your appearance before going in.

Being Polite and Pleasant.   When you enter the office, be courteous and congenial to everyone. Remember that you are being judged not only by the interviewer but also by the receptionist and anyone else who sees you before and after the interview. They will notice how you sit, what you read, and how you look. Introduce yourself to the receptionist, and wait to be invited to sit. You may be asked to fill out a job application while you are waiting. You will find tips for doing this effectively later in this chapter.

Greeting the Interviewer and Making a Positive First Impression. When meeting the interviewer, make eye contact and smile warmly but don't extend your hand for a handshake. Although shaking hands was the standard greeting in the past, following the COVID-19 pandemic, we've seen a profound shift toward "touchless" greetings. Instead of offering your hand, you could tilt your head or give a friendly wave and say, *I'm pleased to meet you, Mr. Thomas. I'm Constance Ferraro.* If Mr. Thomas, the interviewer, extends his hand, you should accept it graciously as a sincere greeting. Don't recoil or launch into a lecture on cleanliness and the history of handshaking. Afterwards, if you wish, you could wash your hands promptly.

16-2g Fighting Fear

Expect to be nervous before and during the interview. It's natural! One survey revealed that job interviews are more stressful than going on a blind date, being pulled over by the police, or taking a final exam without studying.[9] One of the best ways to overcome fear is to know what happens in a typical interview. You can further reduce your fears by following these suggestions:

When German Chancellor Angela Merkel extended her hand to greet her cabinet minister, he rebuffed the gesture. During the COVID-19 pandemic, many people around the world gave up handshaking, kisses on the cheek, and hugging in greetings. How can one avoid the embarrassment of rejecting a proffered handshake?

- **Practice interviewing**. Try to get as much interviewing practice as you can—especially with real companies. The more times you experience the interview situation, the less nervous you will be. However, don't schedule interviews unless you are genuinely interested in the organization. If offered, campus mock interviews also provide excellent practice, and the interviewers will offer tips for improvement.

- **Prepare thoroughly**. Research the company. Know how you will answer the most frequently asked questions. Be ready with success stories. Rehearse your closing statement. Knowing that you have done all you can to be ready for the interview is a tremendous fear preventive.

- **Understand the process**. Find out ahead of time how the interview will be structured. Will you be meeting with an individual, or will you be interviewed by a panel? Is this the first of a series of interviews? Don't be afraid to ask about these details before the interview so that an unfamiliar situation won't catch you off guard.

- **Dress appropriately**. If you have checked with the interviewer in advance and know that you are dressed properly, you will feel more confident. When in doubt, tend toward more conservative, professional attire.

- **Breathe deeply**. Plan to take deep breaths, particularly if you feel anxious while waiting for the interviewer. Deep breathing makes you concentrate on something other than the interview and also provides much-needed oxygen.

- **Know that you are not alone**. Everyone feels some anxiety during a job interview. Interviewers expect some nervousness, and a skilled interviewer will try to put you at ease.

- **Remind yourself that an interview is a two-way street**. The interviewer isn't the only one who is gleaning information. You have come to learn about the job and the company. In fact, during some parts of the interview, you will be in charge. This should give you courage.

16-3 **During the Interview**

Throughout the interview you will be answering questions and asking your own questions. Your demeanor, body language, and other nonverbal cues will also be on display. The interviewer will be trying to learn more about you, and you should be learning more about the job and the organization. Although you may be asked some unique questions, many interviewers ask standard, time-proven questions, which means that you can prepare your answers ahead of time. You can also prepare by learning techniques to control those inevitable butterflies in the tummy.

16-3a **Sending Positive Nonverbal Messages and Acting Professionally**

You have already sent nonverbal messages to your interviewer by arriving on time, being courteous, dressing appropriately, and greeting the receptionist confidently. You will continue to send nonverbal messages throughout the interview. Remember that what comes out of your mouth and what is written on your résumé are not the only messages an interviewer receives from you. Nonverbal messages also create powerful impressions. You can send positive nonverbal messages during face-to-face and online interviews by following these tips:

- **Control your body movements**. Keep your hands, arms, and elbows to yourself. Don't lean on a desk. Keep your feet on the floor. Don't cross your arms in front of you. Keep your hands out of your pockets.
- **Exhibit good posture**. Sit erect, leaning forward slightly. Don't slouch in your chair; at the same time, don't look too stiff and uncomfortable. Good posture demonstrates confidence and interest.
- **Practice appropriate eye contact**. A direct eye gaze, at least in North America, suggests interest and trustworthiness. If you are being interviewed by a panel, try to maintain eye contact with all interviewers.
- **Use gestures effectively**. Nod to show agreement and interest. Gestures should be used as needed, but not overused.
- **Smile enough to convey a positive attitude**. Have a friend give you honest feedback on whether you generally smile too much or not enough.
- **Listen attentively**. Show the interviewer you are interested and attentive by listening carefully to questions. This will also help you answer questions appropriately.
- **Turn off your cell phone or other electronic devices**. Avoid the embarrassment of having your device ring, or even as much as buzz, during an interview. Turn off your electronic devices completely; don't just switch them to vibrate.
- **Don't chew gum**. Chewing gum during an interview is distracting and unprofessional.
- **Sound enthusiastic and interested—but sincere**. The tone of your voice has an enormous effect on the words you say. Avoid sounding bored, frustrated, or sarcastic during an interview. Employers want employees who are enthusiastic and interested.
- **Avoid empty words**. Filling your answers with verbal pauses such as *um*, *uh*, *like*, and *basically* communicates that you are not prepared. Also avoid annoying distractions such as clearing your throat repeatedly or sighing deeply.
- **Be confident, but not cocky**. Most recruiters want candidates who are self-assured but not too casual or even arrogant. Let your body language, posture, dress, and vocal tone prove your confidence. Speak at a normal volume and enunciate words clearly without mumbling.

Naturally, hiring managers make subjective decisions based on intuition, but they need to ferret out pleasant people who fit in. To that end, some recruiters apply the airport test to candidates by asking themselves the following: Would I want to be stuck in the airport for 12 hours with this person if my flight were delayed?[10]

When interviewing many candidates, recruiters may apply the airport test.

16-3b Preparing to Answer Interview Questions

One of the best ways you can compensate for lack of experience is careful preparation and well-rehearsed responses to typical interview questions. In addition, the way you answer questions can be almost as important as what you say. Use the interviewer's name and title from time to time when you answer. *Yes, Ms. Bradshaw, I would be pleased to tell you about . . . .* People like to hear their own names, but don't overuse this technique. Avoid answering questions with a simple *yes* or *no*; elaborate on your answers to better promote yourself and your assets.

Remember that your communication skills are being judged. Keep your answers positive; don't criticize anything or anyone. Strive to incorporate positive adjectives, appropriate inflection, and a confident voice tone.

During the interview it may be necessary to occasionally refocus and clarify vague questions. Some interviewers are inexperienced and ill at ease in the role. You may even have to ask your own question to understand what was asked: *By _____, do you mean _____?* Consider closing out some of your responses with *Does that answer your question?* or *Would you like me to elaborate on any particular experience?*

Always aim your answers at the key characteristics that interviewers seek: expertise, competence, motivation, interpersonal skills, decision-making skills, enthusiasm for the company, excitement about the job, and a pleasing personality. Remember to stay focused on your strengths. Don't reveal weaknesses, even if you think they make you look human. You won't be hired for your weaknesses, only for your strengths.

As you respond, be sure to use good English and enunciate clearly. Avoid slurred words such as *gonna* and *din't*, as well as slangy expressions such as *yeah, like,* and *ya know*. As you practice answering expected interview questions, it is always a good idea to make an audio or video recording. Is your speech filled with verbal static?

You can't expect to be perfect in an employment interview. No one is. But you can avert sure disaster by avoiding mistakes such as those described in Figure 16.3.

The following sections present questions that may be asked during employment interviews. To get you thinking about how to respond, we have provided an answer for, or a discussion of, one or more of the questions in each group. As you read the remaining questions in each group, think about how you could respond most effectively. For additional questions, contact your campus career center, or consult one of the career websites discussed in Chapter 15.

16-3c Warm-Up Questions

Recruiters usually start the interview with warm-up questions designed to get acquainted and put you at ease. They are also striving to gain an overview to see whether you will fit into the organization's culture. When answering these questions, keep the employer's needs in mind and try to incorporate your success stories.

1. Tell me about yourself.

   Experts agree that you must keep this answer short (one to two minutes tops) but on target. Use this chance to promote yourself. Stick to educational, professional, or business-related strengths; avoid personal or humorous references. Be ready with at least three success stories illustrating characteristics important to this job. Demonstrate responsibility you have been given; describe how you contributed as a team player. Try practicing this formula: *I have completed a _____ degree with a major in _____. Recently I worked for _____ as a _____. Before that I worked for _____ as a _____. My strengths are _____ (interpersonal) and _____ (technical).* Rehearse your response in 30-second segments devoted to your education, work experience, qualifications, and skills.

FIGURE 16.3   The Ten Biggest Interview Mistakes

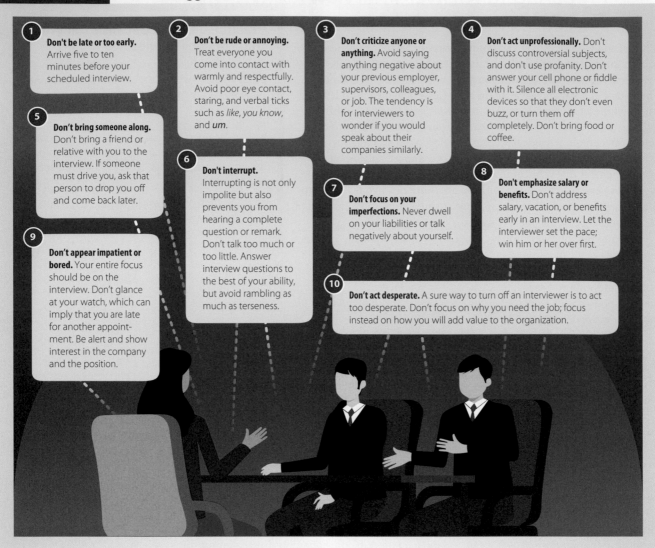

1 Don't be late or too early. Arrive five to ten minutes before your scheduled interview.

2 Don't be rude or annoying. Treat everyone you come into contact with warmly and respectfully. Avoid poor eye contact, staring, and verbal ticks such as *like, you know,* and *um*.

3 Don't criticize anyone or anything. Avoid saying anything negative about your previous employer, supervisors, colleagues, or job. The tendency is for interviewers to wonder if you would speak about their companies similarly.

4 Don't act unprofessionally. Don't discuss controversial subjects, and don't use profanity. Don't answer your cell phone or fiddle with it. Silence all electronic devices so that they don't even buzz, or turn them off completely. Don't bring food or coffee.

5 Don't bring someone along. Don't bring a friend or relative with you to the interview. If someone must drive you, ask that person to drop you off and come back later.

6 Don't interrupt. Interrupting is not only impolite but also prevents you from hearing a complete question or remark. Don't talk too much or too little. Answer interview questions to the best of your ability, but avoid rambling as much as terseness.

7 Don't focus on your imperfections. Never dwell on your liabilities or talk negatively about yourself.

8 Don't emphasize salary or benefits. Don't address salary, vacation, or benefits early in an interview. Let the interviewer set the pace; win him or her over first.

9 Don't appear impatient or bored. Your entire focus should be on the interview. Don't glance at your watch, which can imply that you are late for another appointment. Be alert and show interest in the company and the position.

10 Don't act desperate. A sure way to turn off an interviewer is to act too desperate. Don't focus on why you need the job; focus instead on how you will add value to the organization.

2. **Tell me what you know about us.**
   This is a killer question for those who have not done their homework. An outstanding candidate will be able to present considerable information about the company. Primarily, however, this question eliminates clueless candidates who have not bothered to do even minimal checking.

3. **What are your greatest strengths?**
   Reread your résumé and cover letter to review what you want to promote. Stress your strengths that are related to the position, such as *I am well organized, thorough, and attentive to detail.* Tell success stories and give examples that illustrate these qualities: *My supervisor says that my research is exceptionally thorough. For example, I recently worked on a research project in which I . . . .*

4. **Do you prefer to work by yourself or with others? Why?**
   This question can be tricky. Provide a middle-of-the-road answer that not only suggests your interpersonal qualities but also reflects an ability to make independent decisions and work without supervision.

5. **What was your major in college, and why did you choose it?**

6. **What are some things you do in your spare time?**

16-3d Questions to Gauge Your Interest

Interviewers want to understand your motivation for applying for a position. Although they will realize that you are probably interviewing for other positions, they still want to know why you are interested in this particular position with this organization. These types of questions help them determine your level of interest.

One of the best ways to fight fear before a job interview is preparing thoroughly. You can guess many of the questions that will be asked and prepare your responses in advance.

1. **Why do you want to work for [name of company]?** Questions like this illustrate why you must research an organization thoroughly before the interview. The answer to this question must prove that you understand the company and its culture. This is the perfect place to bring up the company research you did before the interview. Show what you know about the company, and discuss why you want to become a part of this organization. Describe your desire to work for this organization not only from your perspective but also from its point of view. What do you have to offer that will benefit the organization?

2. **What sets you apart from other people that might apply for this job?** Although the answer to this is on your résumé, this is a chance to really sell yourself. Most interviewers will usually sit back and see how well you can sell. This is when you review and expand on your summary of qualifications from your résumé.

3. Why are you interested in this position?

4. Why do you want to work in the _____ industry?

5. What interests you about our products (or services)?

16-3e Questions About Your Experience and Accomplishments

After questions about your background and education and questions that measure your interest, the interview generally becomes more specific with questions about your experience and accomplishments. Strive to show confidence when you answer these questions. If you are not confident in your abilities, why should an employer be?

1. **Why should we hire you when we have applicants with more experience or better credentials?** In answering this question, remember that employers often hire people who present themselves well instead of others with better credentials. Emphasize your personal strengths that could be an advantage with this employer. Are you a hard worker? How can you demonstrate it? Have you had recent training? Some people have had more years of experience but actually have less knowledge because they have done the same thing over and over. Stress your experience using the latest methods and equipment. Be sure to mention your computer training and Internet savvy. Emphasize that you are open to new ideas and learn quickly. Above all, show that you are confident in your abilities.

2. Describe the most rewarding experience of your career so far.

3. How have your education and professional experiences prepared you for this position?

4. What were your major accomplishments in each of your past jobs?

5. What was a typical workday like?

6. What job functions did you enjoy most? Least? Why?

Reality Check

The Candidate Who Never Made a Mistake

"Occasionally you bump into a talented and competent candidate . . . who's so lacking in the EQ components of humility and realness that you can't take a chance. This young man had a lot of the right stuff, but when he started telling us that he had never made a mistake in his life and didn't expect to, we knew we'd heard enough."[12]

—Jack and Suzy Welch, management consultants and authors

7. Tell me about your technical skills.

8. Who was the toughest boss you ever worked for and why?

9. What were your major achievements in college?

10. Why did you leave your last position? *OR:* Why are you leaving your current position?

16-3f Questions About the Future

Questions that look into the future tend to stump some candidates, especially those who have not prepared adequately. Employers ask these questions to see whether you are goal oriented and to determine whether your goals are realistic.

1. What are your long-term career goals?

   Formulate a realistic plan with respect to your present age and situation, but keep your response fairly general. If you are considering different career paths, keep your options open. Show an interest in the current job and in making a contribution to the organization. Talk about the levels of responsibility you would like to achieve. One employment counselor suggests showing ambition but not committing to a specific job title. Suggest that you hope to have learned enough to have progressed to a position in which you will continue to grow. Keep your answer focused on educational and professional goals, not personal goals.

2. If you got this position, what would you do to be sure you fit in?

3. This is a large (or small) organization. Do you think you would like that environment?

4. Do you plan to continue your education?

5. What do you predict for the future of the _____ industry?

6. How do you think you can contribute to this company?

7. What do you expect to accomplish in the first 30, 60, and 90 days on the job?

8. How do you keep current with what is happening in your profession?

16-3g Challenging Questions

The following questions may make you uncomfortable, but the important thing to remember is to answer truthfully without dwelling on your weaknesses. As quickly as possible, convert any negative response into a discussion of your strengths.

1. What is your greatest weakness?

   It is amazing how many candidates knock themselves out of the competition by answering this question poorly. Actually, you have many choices. You can present a strength as a weakness (*Some people complain that I'm a workaholic or that I'm too attentive to details*). However, hiring managers have heard that cliché too often. Instead, mention a corrected weakness (*Because I was terrified of making presentations, I took a college course and also joined a speakers' club*). You could cite an unrelated skill (*I really need to brush up on my Spanish*). You can cite a learning objective (*One of my long-term goals is to learn more about coding and programming*). Another possibility is to reaffirm your qualifications (*I have no weaknesses that would affect my ability to do this job*).

2. What type of people do you have no patience for?

   Avoid letting yourself fall into the trap of sounding overly critical. One possible response is, *I have always gotten along well with others. But I confess that I can be irritated by complainers who don't accept responsibility.*

3. If you could live your life over, what would you change and why?

4. How would your former (or current) supervisor describe you as an employee?

5. What do you want the most from your job?

6. What is your grade point average, and does it accurately reflect your abilities?

7. Have you ever used drugs?

8. Who in your life has influenced you the most and why?

9. What should I know about you that is not on your résumé?

10. How do you define success?

16-3h Situational Questions

A **situational question** is one in which interviewers describe a hypothetical situation and ask how you would handle it. These questions help employers test your thought processes and logical thinking. Situational questions are based on the type of position for which you are interviewing. Knowledge of the position and the company culture will help you respond favorably to these questions. Even if the situation sounds negative, keep your response positive. Here are a few examples with possible responses to the first two:

1. How would you respond if your fellow team members strongly resisted a proposal you made in a meeting?
   You might explain the rationale behind your proposal with specific examples of the benefits that the recommendation could bring to the team. If the team continues to oppose your proposal, you should let it go and move on.

2. What would you do if you knew that your boss gave your team data that was totally wrong? Let's say, for example, that in a team meeting your boss provided data that had not been updated, and you recognized the error immediately. Before responding, you should confirm that your figures are correct. Then you might tactfully share the correct data in a private conversation with your boss. You could suggest that the error was an oversight perhaps caused by figures that were released after an initial report, and say that you know that your boss would want to base the team project on accurate data. You would not correct your boss in front of the team, and you would try to understand why the mistake was made.

3. Your supervisor has just told you that she is dissatisfied with your work, but you think it is acceptable. How would you resolve the conflict?

4. Your supervisor has told you to do something a certain way, and you think you know a far better way to complete the task. What would you do?

5. Assume that you are hired for this position. You soon learn that one of the staff members is extremely resentful because she applied for your position and was turned down. As a result, she is being unhelpful and obstructive. How would you handle the situation?

6. A colleague has told you in confidence that she suspects another colleague of stealing. What would your actions be?

7. What would you do if an angry, disappointed customer confronted you? How would you resolve the customer's concern?

16-3i Behavioral Questions

Instead of traditional interview questions, you may be asked a **behavioral question** in which you are asked to tell a story. The interviewer may say, *Describe a time when . . .* or *Tell me about a time when . . . .* To respond effectively, learn to use the storytelling, or STAR, technique, as illustrated in Figure 16.4. Ask yourself what the **S**ituation or **T**ask was, what **A**ction you took, and what the **R**esults were.[15] Practice using this method to recall specific examples of your skills and accomplishments. To be fully prepared, develop a coherent and articulate STAR narrative for every bullet point on your résumé. When answering behavioral questions, describe only educational and work-related situations or tasks, and try to keep them as current as possible. Here are a few examples of behavioral questions:

1. Tell me about a time when you solved a difficult problem.
   Tell a concise story explaining the situation or task, what you did, and the result. For example, *When I was at CyberTech, we continually had a problem of excessive back orders. After analyzing the situation, I discovered that orders went through many unnecessary steps.*

S →	**T** →	**A** →	**R**
Situation	**Task**	**Action**	**Results**
Briefly explain the background and context of a situation. What happened? When? Where?	Describe the problem. What needed to be done? Why?	What did you do? How? What skills or tools did you use?	Explain the results (e.g., savings, greater efficiency). Try to quantify.

I suggested that we eliminate much of the paperwork. As a result, we reduced back orders by 30 percent. Go on to emphasize what you learned and how you can apply that learning to this job. Practice your success stories in advance so that you will be ready.

2. Describe a situation in which you were able to use persuasion to convince someone to see things your way.

   The recruiter is interested in your leadership and teamwork skills. You might respond as follows: *I have learned to appreciate the fact that the way you present an idea is just as important as the idea itself. When trying to influence people, I put myself in their shoes and find some way to frame my idea from their perspective. I remember when I . . . .*

3. Describe a time when you had to analyze information and make a recommendation.

4. Describe a time that you worked successfully as part of a team.

5. Tell me about a time that you dealt with confidential information.

6. Give me an example of a time when you were under stress to meet a deadline.

7. Tell me about a time when you had to go above and beyond the call of duty to get a job done.

8. Tell me about a time you were able to deal with another person successfully even though that individual did not like you personally (or vice versa).

9. Give me an example of when you showed initiative and took the lead.

10. Tell me about a time when you were asked to complete a task you had never performed before.

16-3j Salary Questions

Increasingly, state and local governments are adopting laws and regulations that prohibit employers from requesting salary history from job applicants. These laws are intended to help ensure that equal pay is offered for equal work rather than basing new salaries on past ones. Many have argued that a pay gap exists in part because of artificially lower starting salaries, especially for women, thus perpetuating wage inequity. Despite new laws in some states, naïve or rogue hiring managers may still pose such questions during interviews. What should you do if asked for past salary information? New grads may not have relevant past employment records, but for those who are changing careers, a salary question can be challenging. One way to respond is to deflect a question about past salaries by explaining that this position is not the same as your last job. How to respond to this and other potentially illegal questions requires tact and forethought, as explained in the following section titled Illegal and Inappropriate Questions.

Beyond being asked to reveal past salary, candidates may still be asked other salary-related questions. When the matter of salary is raised, it's wise to recognize that nearly all salaries are negotiable, depending on your qualifications. Knowing the typical salary range for the target position is very important in this negotiation. The recruiter can tell you the salary ranges—but you will probably have to ask. If you have had little experience, you may be offered a salary somewhere between the low point and the midpoint in the range. With more experience, you can negotiate for a higher figure. A word of caution, though. One personnel manager warns that candidates who emphasize money are suspect because they may leave if offered a few thousand dollars more elsewhere. See the accompanying Career Coach box for dos and don'ts in negotiating a starting salary. Here are typical salary-related questions:

Salary negotiation during an interview is critical. If asked what you want for salary, a strategic response might be, "I know what I'd *like* to make, but I'm excited about working with your organization. What is the budget for this position?"

1. What salary are you looking for?

   One way to handle salary questions is to ask politely to defer the discussion until you know that a job will be offered (*I'm sure when the time comes, we will be able to work out a fair compensation package. Right now, I'd rather focus on whether we have a match*). If salary comes up and you are not sure whether the job is being offered to you, it's time to be blunt. Ask, *Are you making me a job offer?* Another possible response to a salary question is to reply candidly that you can't know what to ask until you know more about the position and the company. If you continue to be pressed for a dollar figure, give a salary range with an annual dollar amount. Be sure to do research before the interview so that you know what similar jobs are paying in your geographic region. As an expert negotiator said, "In business as in life, you don't get what you deserve, you get what you negotiate."[17] See the accompanying Career Coach box for more tips on discussing salary.

2. How much do you think you are worth?

3. How much money do you expect to earn within the next ten years?

4. Are you willing to take a pay cut from your current (or previous) job?

5. What do you think is reasonable salary for this position?

16-3k Illegal and Inappropriate Questions

U.S. federal law states that "it is illegal to discriminate against someone (applicant or employee) because of that person's race, color, religion, sex (including gender identity, sexual orientation, and pregnancy), national origin, age (40 or older), disability or genetic information."[18]

Therefore, it is inappropriate for interviewers to ask any question related to these areas. Such questions become illegal, though, only when a court of law determines that the employer is asking them with the intent to discriminate.[19]

Many illegal interview questions are asked innocently by inexperienced interviewers. Shockingly, one survey revealed that a whopping 20 percent of interviewers admitted that they had unknowingly asked an illegal question.[20] Many interviewers do not know the law. Others are only trying to be friendly when they inquire about your personal life or family. Regardless of the intent, how should you react? If you find the question harmless and if you want the job, go ahead and answer it. If you think that answering it would damage your chance to be hired, try to deflect the question tactfully with a response such as *Could you tell me how my marital status relates to the responsibilities of this position?* or *I prefer to keep my personal and professional lives separate.*

If you are uncomfortable answering a question, try to determine the reason behind it; you might answer, *I don't let my personal life interfere with my ability to do my job*, or, *Are you*

Money Talk: Salary Negotiation Dos and Don'ts

Negotiating a salary offer may not be the first priority for new grads seeking entry-level positions. However, the following dos and don'ts offer guidance for traditional and nontraditional grads as well as tips for those who are progressing in their careers.

- **Do** make sure you have done your research on the salary you should expect for the position you are seeking. **Do** understand how geographic location affects salary ranges.

- **Don't** bring up salary before the employer does. **Do** delay salary negotiations until you know exactly what the position entails.

- **Do** be aware of your strengths and achievements. **Do** be sure to demonstrate the value you will bring to the employer.

- **Don't** tell the employer the salary you need to pay your bills or meet personal obligations.

- **Do** let the employer make the first salary offer. **Do**, if asked, say you expect a salary that is competitive with the market, or give a salary range that you find acceptable.

- **Don't** inflate your current earnings just to get a higher salary offer.

- **Don't** feel obligated to accept the first salary offer. **Do** negotiate salary if the offer made is inadequate.

- **Do** thank the employer for the offer when it is made. **Don't** try to negotiate right after the offer is made. **Do** take the time to consider all factors before making any job offer decisions.

- **Don't** be overly aggressive in negotiating the salary you want.

- **Don't** focus solely on salary. **Do** consider the entire compensation package.

- **Do** try to obtain other concessions (shorter review time, better title, better workspace) or benefits (bonuses, vacation time) if you aren't successful at negotiating a salary you want.

- **Don't** enter salary negotiations as part of an ego trip or game.

- **Don't** agree to the first acceptable salary offer you receive if you are not sure about the job or the company.

- **Do** get the offer in writing.

---

concerned with my availability to work overtime? Another option, of course, is to respond to any inappropriate or illegal question by confronting the interviewer and threatening a lawsuit or refusing to answer. However, you could not expect to be hired under these circumstances. In any case, you might wish to reconsider working for an organization that sanctions such procedures. Here are selected inappropriate and illegal questions that you may or may not want to answer:[21]

1. What is your marital status? Are you married? Do you live with anyone? Do you have a boyfriend (or girlfriend)? (However, employers can ask your marital status after hiring for tax and insurance forms.)

2. Do you have any disabilities? Have you had any recent illnesses? (But it is legal to ask if the person can perform specific job duties, such as *Can you carry a 50-pound sack up a 10-foot ladder five times daily?*)

3. I notice you have an accent. Where are you from? What is the origin of your last name? What is your native language? (However, it is legal to ask what languages you speak fluently if language ability is related to the job.)

4. Have you ever filed a workers' compensation claim or been injured on the job?

5. Have you ever had a drinking problem or been addicted to drugs? (But it is legal to ask if a person uses illegal drugs.)

6. Have you ever been arrested? (But it is legal to ask, *Have you ever been convicted of _____?* when the crime is related to the job.)

7. How old are you? What is your date of birth? (But it is legal to ask, *Are you 16 years [or 18 years or 21 years] old or older?* depending on the age requirements for the position.)

8. Of what country are you a citizen? Are you a U.S. citizen? Where were you born? (But it is legal to ask, *Are you authorized to work in the United States?*)

9. What is your maiden name? (But it is legal to ask, *What is your full name?* or, *Have you worked under another name?*)

Ethics ✓ Check

During a job interview, Cheryl was startled to be asked to provide her password and login credentials for her social media accounts. Is this an illegal or unethical request?

10. Do you have any religious beliefs that would prevent you from working weekends or holidays? (An employer can, however, ask you if you are available to work weekends and holidays or otherwise within the company's required schedule.)

11. Do you have children? Do you plan to have children? Do you have adequate child-care arrangements? (However, employers can ask for dependent information for tax and insurance purposes after you are hired. Also, they can ask if you would be able to travel or work overtime on occasion.)

12. How much do you weigh? How tall are you? (However, employers can ask you about your height and weight if minimum standards are necessary to safely perform a job.)

13. Are you in debt?

14. Do you drink socially or smoke?

15. Are you transgender or do you plan to transition in the future?

16-3l Asking Your Own Questions

At some point in the interview, usually near the end, you will be asked whether you have any questions. The worst thing you can do is say *No*, which suggests that you are not interested in the position. Almost as bad is using this time to continue to pitch yourself for the position. Instead, ask questions that will help you gain information and will impress the interviewer with your thoughtfulness and interest in the position. Don't forget that this interview is a two-way street. You must be happy with the prospect of working for this organization. You want a position that matches your skills and personality. Use this opportunity to learn whether this job is right for you. Be aware that you don't have to wait for the interviewer to ask you for questions. You can ask your own questions throughout the interview to learn more about the company and position. Here are some questions you might ask:

1. What will my duties be (if not already discussed)?

2. Tell me what it is like working here in terms of the people, management practices, work-loads, expected performance, and rewards.

3. What training programs are available from this organization? What specific training will be given for this position?

4. Who would be my immediate supervisor?

5. What is the organizational structure, and where does this position fit in?

6. Is travel required in this position?

7. How and by whom will my job performance be evaluated?

8. Assuming my work is excellent, where do you see me in five years?

9. How long do employees generally stay with this organization?

10. What are the major challenges for a person in this position?

11. May I have a tour of the facilities?

12. This job seems to be exactly what I'd really like to do. Do we have a fit here?

13. What is the next step in the hiring process?

14. What is the salary budget for this position?

15. When do you expect to make a decision?

16-3m Ending Positively

After you have asked your questions, the interviewer will signal the end of the interview, usually by standing up or by expressing appreciation that you came. If not addressed earlier, you should at this time find out what action will follow. Career coach Don Georgevich recommends asking the interviewer when a decision will be made and whether you may follow up. "Interviewers always say yes," he reports, "and now you have permission to call them. In fact, they will expect your call."[22] This is not the time to be shy. Too many candidates leave the interview without knowing their status or when they will hear from the recruiter.

Before you leave, summarize your strongest qualifications, show your enthusiasm for obtaining this position, and thank the interviewer for a constructive interview and for considering you for the position. Ask the interviewer for a business card, which will provide the information you need to write a thank-you message. Be sure to thank the receptionist. Departing gracefully and enthusiastically will leave a lasting impression on those responsible for making the final hiring decision.

LEARNING OUTCOME

4 Describe what to do *after* an interview.

16-4 After the Interview

After leaving the interview, immediately make notes of what was said in case you are called back for a second interview. Write down key points that were discussed, the names of people you spoke with, and other details of the interview. Ask yourself what went really well and what you could improve. Note your strengths and weaknesses during the interview so that you can work to improve in future interviews.

16-4a Do I Really Need to Send a Thank-You Message?

Reality Check

Wowing the Interviewer With a Thank-You From the Parking Lot

"Thank-you notes matter: They give you a terrific opportunity to follow up with the decision-maker right away. I encourage job seekers to get thank-you notes out (to each individual they've met in the interview process) immediately after the interview. Same day. From your laptop in the parking lot, if you really want to wow them."[23]

—Jenny Foss, *job search strategist, career coach*

Yes, you really should send a thank-you message after a job interview—if you want the job. One survey revealed that 80 percent of human relation specialists considered thank-you notes helpful following a job interview. Yet, only 24 percent actually received them.[24] When it's so easy to do, it's surprising that all serious candidates don't take advantage of this opportunity to show their good manners and enthusiasm for the job.

Generally, you have three options for sending a thank-you message: a handwritten note card, a word-processed letter on bond paper, or an e-mail. Texts would be inappropriate. Handwritten cards and letters are always impressive, but most managers today welcome e-mail. Your preparation and knowledge of the company culture will help you determine whether an e-mail message or a traditional thank-you letter is more appropriate. E-mail has the advantage of enabling you to include a link to your digital e-portfolio, LinkedIn account, or professional social networking profiles. If you choose to send an e-mail message, make sure that you use professional language, standard capitalization, and proper punctuation. Whatever format you choose, be sure to spell the name of the interviewer correctly!

Your message will be most effective if sent immediately after your interview. In your message, refer to the date of the interview, the exact title of the job for which you were interviewed, and specific topics discussed. Try to mention something you liked about the interview such as *Job interviews can be stressful, but you made me feel comfortable, and I am grateful for that.* Avoid worn-out phrases such as *Thank you for taking the time to interview me.* Be careful, too, about overusing *I,* especially to begin sentences. Most important, show that you really want the job and that you are qualified for it. Notice how the message in Model Document 16.1 conveys enthusiasm and confidence.

If you have been interviewed by more than one person, send a separate thank-you message to each interviewer.

16-4b Contacting Your References

Once you have thanked your interviewer, it is time to alert your references that they may be contacted by the employer. You might also have to request a letter of recommendation to be sent to the employer by a certain date. As discussed in Chapter 15, you should have already asked

Thomas M. Taylor

95 Grasslands Road, Valhalla, NY 10595
(914) 769-5002, thomastaylor@gmail.com

June 1, 2021

Ms. Victoria Sanchez
iDesign Marketing & Media
1055 Westchester Avenue
White Plains, NY 10604

Dear Ms. Sanchez:

Talking with you on Tuesday, May 27, about the graphic designer position in White Plains was both informative and interesting.

Thanks for describing the position in such detail and for introducing me to M. Mullins, the senior designer. His current project designing an annual report in four colors sounds fascinating as well as quite challenging.

Now that I've learned in greater detail the specific tasks of your graphic designers, I'm more than ever convinced that my computer and creative skills can make a genuine contribution to your graphic productions. My training in design and layout using PhotoShop and InDesign ensures that I could be immediately productive on your staff.

You will find me an enthusiastic and hardworking member of any team. As you requested, I'm enclosing additional samples of my work. I'm eager to join the graphics staff at your White Plains headquarters, and I look forward to hearing from you soon.

Sincerely,

Thomas M. Taylor

Thomas M. Taylor

Enclosures

Annotations (left margin):

Mentions the interview date and specific job title

Highlights specific skills for the job

Shows good manners, appreciation, and perseverance—traits that recruiters value

Annotations (right margin):

Uses customized letterhead but could have merely typed street and city address above dateline

Personalizes the message by referring to topics discussed in the interview

Reminds reader of interpersonal skills as well as enthusiasm and eagerness for this job

---

permission to use these individuals as references, and you should have supplied them with a copy of your résumé and information about the types of positions you are seeking.

To provide the best possible recommendation, your references need information. What position have you applied for with what company? What should they stress to the prospective employer? Let's say you are applying for a specific job that requires a letter of recommendation. Professor Sindaha has already agreed to be a reference for you. To get the best letter of recommendation from Professor Sindaha, help her out. Write an e-mail or letter telling her about the position, its requirements, and the recommendation deadline. Include copies of your résumé, college transcript, and, if applicable, the job posting or ad with detailed information about the opening. You might remind her of a positive experience with you that she could use in the recommendation. Remember that recommenders need evidence to support generalizations. Give them appropriate ammunition, as the student has done in the following request:

In a reference request letter, tell immediately why you are writing. Identify the target position and company.

Specify the job requirements so that the recommender knows what to stress.

Provide a stamped, addressed envelope.

Dear Professor Sindaha:

Recently I interviewed for the position of administrative assistant in the Human Resources Department of Host International. Because you kindly agreed to help me, I am now asking you to write a letter of recommendation to Host.

The position calls for good organizational, interpersonal, and writing skills, as well as computer experience. To help you review my skills and training, I enclose my résumé. As you may recall, I earned an A in your business communication class last fall; and you commended my long report for its clarity and organization.

Please send your letter to Mr. Camden Singer at Host International before July 1 in the enclosed stamped, addressed envelope. I'm grateful for your support and promise to let you know the results of my job search.

Sincerely,

16-4c Following Up

If you don't hear from the interviewer within five days, or at the specified time, consider following up. Of course, if you have remembered to ask the interviewer when a decision is expected and whether you may follow up, you are all set. Otherwise, the standard advice to job candidates is to contact the interviewer with a follow-up e-mail or phone call.

An e-mail to find out how the decision process is going may be your best bet because such a message is less intrusive than a phone call. An e-mail message also gives the interviewer time to look up your status information, leaves a paper trail, and eliminates annoying phone tag.[25] The following follow-up e-mail message would impress the interviewer:

Dear Ms. Sanchez:

I enjoyed my interview with you last Tuesday for the graphic designer position. You should know that I'm very interested in this opportunity with iDesign Marketing & Media. Because you mentioned that you might have an answer this week, I'm eager to know how your decision process is coming along. I look forward to hearing from you.

Sincerely,

If you follow up by phone, say something like, *I'm calling to find out the status of your search for the _____ position.* Or you could say, *I'm wondering what else I can do to convince you that I'm the right person for this job.* It's important to sound professional and courteous. Sounding desperate, angry, or frustrated that you have not been contacted can ruin your chances.

Depending on the response you get to your first follow-up request, you may have to follow up additional times. Keep in mind, though, that some employers won't tell you about their hiring decision unless you are the one hired. Don't harass the interviewer, and don't force a decision. If you don't hear back from an employer within several weeks after following up, it is best to assume that you didn't get the job, and you should continue your job search.

16-5 Preparing Additional Employment Documents

Although the résumé and cover letter are your major tasks, other important documents and messages are often required during the job-search process. You may need to complete an employment application form and write follow-up letters. You might also have to write a letter of resignation when leaving a job. Because each of these tasks reveals something about you and your communication skills, you will want to put your best foot forward. These documents often subtly influence company officials to offer a job.

16-5a Application Form

Some organizations require job candidates to fill out application forms instead of, or in addition to, submitting résumés. This practice permits them to gather and store standardized data about each applicant. Whether the application is on paper or digital, follow the directions carefully and provide accurate information. The following suggestions can help you be prepared:

- Carry a card summarizing vital statistics not included on your résumé. If you are asked to fill out an application form in an employer's office, you will need a handy reference to the following data: graduation dates; beginning and ending dates of all employment; salary history; full names, titles, and present work addresses of former supervisors; full addresses and phone numbers of current and previous employers; and full names, occupational titles, occupational addresses, and telephone numbers of people who have agreed to serve as references.

- Look over all the questions before starting.

- If filling out a paper form, write neatly using blue or black ink. Many career counselors recommend printing your responses; cursive handwriting can be difficult to read.

- Answer all questions honestly. Write *Not applicable* or *N/A* if appropriate. Don't leave any sections blank.

- Use accurate spelling, grammar, capitalization, and punctuation.

- If asked for the position desired, give a specific job title or type of position. Don't say, *Anything* or *Open*. These answers make you look unfocused; moreover, they make it difficult for employers to know what you are qualified for or interested in.

- Be prepared for a salary question. Unless you know what comparable employees are earning in the company, the best strategy is to suggest a salary range or to write *Negotiable* or *Open*.

- Be prepared to explain the reasons for leaving previous positions. Use positive or neutral phrases such as *Relocation, Seasonal, To accept a position with more responsibility, Temporary position, To continue education*, or *Career change*. Avoid words or phrases such as *Fired, Quit, Didn't get along with supervisor*, and *Pregnant*.

- Look over the application before submitting to make sure it is complete and that you have followed all instructions.

16-5b Application or Résumé Follow-Up Message

If your résumé or application generates no response within a reasonable time, you may decide to send a short follow-up e-mail or letter such as the following. Doing so (a) jogs the memory of the personnel officer, (b) demonstrates your serious interest, and (c) allows you to emphasize your qualifications or to add new information.

Dear Ms. Steinberg:

Please know I am still interested in becoming an administrative support specialist with Quad, Inc.

Open by reminding the reader of your interest.

Since submitting an application [or résumé] in May, I have completed my degree and have been employed as a summer replacement for office workers in several downtown offices. This experience has honed my word processing and communication skills. It has also introduced me to a wide range of office procedures.

Review your strengths or add new qualifications.

Please keep my application in your active file and let me know when my formal training, technical skills, and practical experience can go to work for you.

Close positively; avoid accusations that make the reader defensive.

Sincerely,

16-5c Rejection Follow-Up Message

If you didn't get the job and you think it was perfect for you, don't give up. Employment specialists encourage applicants to respond to a rejection. The candidate who was offered the position may decline, or other positions may open up. In a rejection follow-up e-mail or letter, it is OK to admit that you are disappointed. Be sure to add, however, that you are still interested and will contact the company again in a month in case a job opens up. Then follow through for a couple of months—but don't overdo it. You should be professional and persistent, not annoying. Here is an example of an effective rejection follow-up message:

Dear Mr. Mazahri:

Subordinate your disappointment to your appreciation at being notified promptly and courteously.

Although disappointed that someone else was selected for your accounting position, I appreciate your promptness and courtesy in notifying me.

Emphasize your continuing interest.

Because I am confident that you would benefit from my technical and interpersonal skills in your fast-paced environment, please consider keeping my résumé in your active file. My desire to become a productive member of your Transamerica staff remains strong.

Refer to specifics of your interview.

Our interview on _____ was very enjoyable, and I especially appreciate the time you and Ms. Issapour spent describing your company's expansion into international markets. To enhance my qualifications, I have enrolled in a course in international accounting at CSU.

Take the initiative; tell when you will call for an update.

Should you have an opening for which I am qualified, you may reach me at (818) 719-3901. In the meantime, I will call you in a month to discuss employment possibilities.

Sincerely,

16-5d Job Acceptance and Rejection Message

When all your hard work pays off, you will be offered the position you want. Although you will likely accept the position over the phone, it is a good idea to follow up with an acceptance e-mail or letter to confirm the details and to formalize the acceptance. Your acceptance message might look like this:

Dear Ms. Jackson:

Confirm your acceptance of the position with enthusiasm.

It was a pleasure talking with you earlier today. As I mentioned, I am delighted to accept the position of project manager with Innovative Creations, Inc., in your Seattle office. I look forward to becoming part of the IC team and starting work on a variety of exciting and innovative projects.

Review salary and benefits details.

As we agreed, my starting salary will be $54,000, with a full benefits package including health and life insurance, retirement plan, and two weeks of vacation per year.

Include the specific starting date.

I look forward to starting my position with Innovative Creations on September 15, 2021. Before that date I will send you the completed tax and insurance forms you need. Thanks again for this opportunity, Ms. Jackson.

Sincerely,

If you must turn down a job offer, show your professionalism by writing a sincere letter. This letter should thank the employer for the job offer and explain briefly that you are turning it down. Taking the time to extend this courtesy could help you in the future if this employer has a position you really want. Here's an example of a job rejection letter:

Dear Mr. Glazier:

Thank you very much for offering me the position of sales representative with Bendall Pharmaceuticals. It was a difficult decision to make, but I have accepted a position with another company.

I appreciate your taking the time to interview me, and I wish Bendall much success in the future.

Sincerely,

Thank the employer for the job offer and decline the offer without giving specifics.

Express gratitude and best wishes for the future.

16-5e Resignation Letter

After you have been in a position for a while, you may find it necessary to leave. Perhaps you have been offered a better position, or maybe you have decided to return to school full-time. Whatever the reason, you should leave your position gracefully and tactfully. Although you will likely discuss your resignation in person with your supervisor, it is a good idea to document your resignation by writing a formal letter. Some resignation letters are brief, whereas others contain great detail. Remember that many resignation letters are placed in personnel files; therefore, you should format and write yours using the professional business letter–writing techniques you learned earlier. Here is an example of a basic letter of resignation:

Dear Ms. Dowd-Garcia:

This letter serves as formal notice of my resignation from Allied Corporation, effective Friday, August 15. I have enjoyed serving as your project manager for the past two years, and I am grateful for everything I have learned during my employment with Allied.

Please let me know what I can do over the next two weeks to help you prepare for my departure. I would be happy to help with finding and training my replacement.

Thanks again for providing such a positive employment experience. I will long remember my time here.

Sincerely,

Confirm the exact date of resignation. Remind the employer of your contributions.

Offer assistance to prepare for your resignation.

End with thanks and a forward-looking statement.

Although the employee who wrote the preceding resignation letter gave the standard two-week notice, you may find that a longer notice is necessary. The higher your position and the greater your responsibility, the longer the notice you give your employer should be. You should, however, always give some notice as a courtesy.

Writing job acceptance, job rejection, and resignation letters requires effort. That effort, however, is worth it because you are building bridges that may carry you to even better jobs in the future.

Zooming In

Your Turn:
Applying Your Skills With Don Georgevich

Career coach Don Georgevich knows that you, his assistant, will soon graduate and be looking for full-time employment. To prepare you for potential interviews, he asks you to think carefully about the kind of work you want to do and the skills required for a position in that field. He talks with you about transferable skills because you, like many soon-to-graduate students, say that you have had little experience that relates directly to a job in your future careers.

Your Task

Identify three to five skills that employers seek among new hires in your career area. LinkedIn research revealed that the most important "soft" skills in demand today are creativity, persuasion, collaboration, adaptability, and time management.[26] A list from the National Association of Colleges and Employers named the following six top attributes desired by employers: written communication skills, problem-solving, ability to work in a team, initiative, analytical-quantitative skills, and strong work ethic.[27] In an e-mail memo addressed to Don Georgevich (but mailed to your instructor), describe a success story showing how you developed each skill or attribute that you name.

SUMMARY OF LEARNING OUTCOMES

1 Explain current trends as well as the purposes, sequence, and types of job interviews.

- Current trends in interviewing include (a) early-stage screening by technology; (b) longer, multiple interviews; (c) on-the-spot interviewing; (d) psychometric and skills tests; (e) behavioral and situational questions; and (f) group interviews.

- As a job candidate, you have the following purposes in an interview: (a) convince the employer of your potential, (b) learn more about the job and the company, and (c) expand on the information in your résumé.

- From the employer's perspective, the interview is an opportunity to (a) assess your abilities in relation to the requirements for the position; (b) discuss your training, experience, knowledge, and abilities in more detail; (c) see what drives and motivates you; and (d) decide whether you would fit into the organization.

- Screening interviews, conducted by telephone or video, seek to eliminate less qualified candidates.

- Hiring/placement interviews may be one-on-one, panel, group, sequential, or video.

2 Describe how to prepare *before* a job interview. Prepare for telephone screening interviews by ensuring professional answering techniques and screening incoming calls.

- Make the first conversation impressive by using professional, businesslike language, and having your résumé, a copy of the job description, a calendar, and a list of your references handy.

- Research the target company by scouring the Internet and the company's advertising to learn about its products, history, mission, goals, size, geographic locations, employees, customers, competitors, culture, management structure, reputation in the community, finances, strengths, weaknesses, and future plans.

- Strive to locate inside information through social media.

- Rehearse 30-second success stories that demonstrate your qualifications and achievements.

- Check your online presence and strive to clean up any digital dirt.
- Decide what to wear to the interview by asking the interviewer what is appropriate.
- To reduce fear before an interview, practice interviewing, prepare thoroughly, and remind yourself that interviewing is a two-way street.

3 Describe what to do during an interview.

- During your interview send positive nonverbal messages by controlling body movements, showing good posture, maintaining eye contact, using gestures effectively, and smiling enough to convey a positive, professional attitude.
- Listen attentively, turn off your cell phone or other electronic devices, don't chew gum, and sound enthusiastic and sincere.
- Be prepared to respond to traditional inquiries such as *Tell me about yourself*.
- Practice answering typical questions such as why you want to work for the organization, why you should be hired, how your education and experience have prepared you for the position, where you expect to be in five or ten years, what your greatest weaknesses are, and how much money you expect to earn.
- Be ready for situational questions that ask you to respond to hypothetical situations. Expect behavioral questions that begin with *Tell me about a time when you . . . .*
- Think about how you would respond to illegal or inappropriate questions, including salary questions. New laws in some states prohibit employers from requesting salary history from job applicants.
- Prepare your own questions inquiring about the job, the work load, training programs, your supervisor, and methods of evaluating job performance.

- End the interview positively by summarizing your strongest qualifications, showing enthusiasm for obtaining the position, thanking the interviewer, asking what the next step is, and requesting permission to follow up.

4 Describe what to do after an interview.

- After leaving the interview, immediately make notes of the key points discussed.
- Note your strengths and weaknesses during the interview so that you can work to improve in future interviews.
- Write a thank-you e-mail, letter, or card including the date of the interview, the exact job title for which you were interviewed, specific topics discussed, and gratitude for the interview.
- Alert your references that they may be contacted.
- If you don't hear from the interviewer when expected, call or send an e-mail to follow up. Sound professional, not desperate, angry, or frustrated.

5 Prepare additional employment documents.

- When filling out an application form, look over all the questions before starting.
- If asked for a salary figure, provide a salary range or write *Negotiable* or *Open*.
- If you don't get the job, consider writing a letter that expresses your disappointment but also your desire to be contacted in case a position opens up.
- If you are offered a job, write a letter that confirms the details and formalizes your acceptance.
- When refusing a position, write a sincere letter turning down the job offer.
- Upon resigning from a position, write a letter that confirms the date of resignation, offers assistance to prepare for your resignation, and expresses thanks.

Key Terms

screening interview *583*
hiring/placement interview *584*
one-on-one interview *584*
panel interview *584*

group interview *584*
sequential interview *584*
one-way video interview *584*

two-way video interview or (live video interview) *584*
situational question *595*
behavioral question *595*

Critical Thinking

1. Put yourself in the shoes of an employment recruiter. You're impressed by a job candidate's résumé and references. During her interview, she responded well and asked insightful questions about the company. She's the best fit of all the applicants you have interviewed thus far. But, oh, no! She failed to send a thank-you after she met with you. Should you cross her off the list? Jessica Liebman, a publishing executive who has been hiring for ten years, did just that. Ms. Liebman followed her own simple rule: If someone doesn't send a thank-you e-mail, don't hire that person.[28] No thank-you, no job! She claims that a thank-you note differentiates the "bad eggs" from the "good eggs." Do you agree with this reasoning? Why or why not? (L.O. 4)

2. In a LinkedIn survey of over 5,000 talent professionals, respondents reported that they value so-called "soft skills" equally or higher than hard skills.[29] Many recruiters, however, confess that they do not know how to measure emotional intelligence and other job-ready intangibles. How do you think a hiring manager determines whether an interviewee has strong emotional intelligence (L.O. 3)

3. Like criminal background checks and drug tests, social media background checks have become commonplace in today's recruiting. What are the pros and cons of conducting such checks as a primary or sole means of screening applicants?[30]

4. If you are asked an illegal interview question, why is it important to first assess the intentions of the interviewer?

5. **Ethical Issue:** A recruiter for an organization has an outstanding prospect for a position. As part of his screening process, the recruiter checks the online presence of the candidate and discovers from her social networks that she is 18 weeks pregnant—and happily so. He knows that the target position involves a big project that will go live just about the time she will be taking maternity leave. He decides not to continue the hiring process with this candidate. Is his action legal? Ethical? What lesson could be learned about posting private information online?

Activities

16.1 Document for Analysis: Lexie's Poor Interview Follow-Up Letter (L.O. 4)

Team

YOUR TASK Study the following poorly written interview follow-up letter. In teams or in a class discussion, list at least five weaknesses. It has problems with punctuation, wordiness, proofreading, capitalization, sentence structure, and other writing techniques you have studied.

415 South Cory Lane
Sunny Slopes, IN 47401
June 11, 2021

Mr. Jared M. Rogers
Watkins & Associates, CPAs
3205 East Covenanter Drive
Bloomington, IN 47402

Dear Mr. Rogers:

It was altogether extremely enjoyable to talk with you about the open position at Watkins & Associates, CPAs. The position as you presented it seems to be a excellent match for my training and skills. The creative approach to Account Management that you described, confirmed my desire to work in a imaginative firm such as Watkins & Associates.

I would bring to the position strong organizational skills, and I have the ability to encourage others to work cooperatively within the department. My training in analysis and application of accounting data and financial reporting; as well as my experience as a financial consultant in the mortgage industry would enable me to help with the backlog of client projects that you mentioned.

I certainly understand your departments need for strong support in the administrative area. I am definitely attentive to details and my organizational skills will help to free you to deal with more pressing issues in the management area. I neglected to emphasize during our very interesting interview that I also have a minor in finance despite the fact that it was on my résumé.

Thanks for taking the time to interview me, and explain the goals of your agency along with the dutys of this position. As I am sure you noticed during the interview I am very interested in working for Watkins & Associates because I need to get a job to start paying off my student loans; and look forward to hearing from you about this position. In the event that you might possibly need additional information from me or facts about me, all you need to do is shoot me an e-mail.

Sincerely,

Lexie Tsuneshi

16.2 Surviving Cattle-Call Interviews (L.O. 1)

`Social Media` `Web`

Group interviews are not for the fainthearted, and opinions on the practice are mixed. "Cattle-call" interviews can be stressful, shocking, even demeaning, some participants feel. One interviewee for an executive-level public relations position described being herded into a room with 200 other applicants where interviewers started bellowing questions at participants. Employers who like this tool say that cattle-call interviews are fair and efficient because they allow the quick ranking of candidates in categories such as teamwork, leadership, and stress management.

YOUR TASK To deepen your understanding of group interviews, search the Web for articles and blogs using the keywords *group job interviews* or *cattle-call interviews*. Job-search advice sites offer tips on coping with the anxiety of group interviewing. Collect the advice and report your insights in class or in a written document as determined by your instructor.

16.3 What Social Media Info Helps or Hurts Your Job Prospects? (L.O. 1, 2)

`E-Mail` `Social Media` `Team` `Web`

Hiring managers are increasingly searching social media sites to research job candidates. A significant Career-Builder survey revealed that most hiring managers aren't intentionally looking for digital dirt. Six in ten employers say they are merely looking for information about candidates "that supports their qualifications for the job."[31]

Surprisingly, it may not be what they find but what is missing that matters. More than four in ten hiring managers say "they are less likely to interview job candidates if they are unable to find information about that person online." Hiring managers who did find social media information online revealed that the following items turned them off:

Social Media Behavior Hurting Job Seekers

Provocative or inappropriate photographs, videos, or information	46 percent
Information about candidate drinking or using drugs	43 percent
Discriminatory comments related to race, religion, gender, etc.	33 percent
Complaints about previous company or fellow employees	31 percent
Poor communication skills	29 percent

Conversely, social media behavior that impresses recruiters includes the following: candidate's background information supported job qualifications (44 percent), candidate's site conveyed a professional image (44 percent), candidate's personality came across as a good fit with company culture (43 percent), candidate was well-rounded and showed a wide range of interests (40 percent), and candidate had great communication skills (36 percent).

YOUR TASK Conduct a social media audit in your course. Armed with the knowledge acquired in this chapter and the information in this activity, critically evaluate fellow students' social media sites such as Facebook, Instagram, Twitter, and LinkedIn. In pairs or larger groups, look for positive attributes as well as negative qualities that may repel hiring managers. Report your findings orally or compile them in an e-mail or memo. If you identify negative behavior, discuss remedies such as how to remove offensive material.

16.4 Using Glassdoor to Prepare for Interviews and Find Salary Data (L.O. 1, 2)

`E-Mail` `Social Media` `Web`

Many job seekers do not realize that the job and career site Glassdoor is a superb source of job-search information, postings, reviews, and salary data. Glassdoor provides anonymous posts by current and former employees revealing current information on company culture, salary comparisons, CEO approval ratings, interviews, and more. For authentic insider data about job interviews and other invaluable information, check out Glassdoor.

Let's say you wish to know what LinkedIn is like as an employer and how happy applicants are with LinkedIn's interview process. You would search on the company by name and could refine your search by targeting a specific job title and location. You would see that at 4.6, the career network has a high rating overall and that its CEO Jeff Weiner has achieved a stellar 98 percent approval rating.

YOUR TASK At the Glassdoor site, search for your dream employer. You can select from industries or search for companies by name. Examine the reviews and the interview modalities. How happy are interviewees and current workers with their employer? Share your results with the class and, if asked, report your findings in a document—a memo, e-mail, or informal report.

16.5 How Much Are You Worth? (L.O. 2, 3)

`Web`

Whether you are currently interviewing for a job or not yet in the market, it's good to know what you are worth.

Salary research can give you a better idea of what salary figure you should expect or shoot for. Remember, too, that negotiating a beginning salary can make a huge difference in your overall lifetime earnings. Many salary research websites provide excellent salary information, and most are free. *Salary.com*, the most popular salary-specific job site, not only provides salary data but also offers information on cost-of-living calculators, comparison tools, and negotiating tips. Other notable salary research websites include Glassdoor, PayScale, Indeed, and Salary List. Also consider checking salaries for occupations at O*Net Online, which provides figures compiled by the Bureau of Labor Statistics.

YOUR TASK For a job in which you are interested, consult three different salary research websites. Compare the salary information for a job if filled by a person with your qualifications, as well as your experience. Report your findings as your instructor directs.

16.5 Superwoman Conquers Stress Before Interview (L.O. 3)

Web

In the hours before a make-or-break job interview, Emma Valentiner was a bundle of nerves. She wanted to do well, but she was petrified that she would stumble. To relieve her anxiety, she prepared herself by donning what she called ridiculous underwear adorned with perky pugs and prickly cactuses. As she approached the interview room, she stopped by the restroom, disappeared into a stall, and struck a Superwoman pose. With hands on hips, shoulders thrown back, and feet firmly squared, she breathed deeply for a few moments and told herself she could conquer this interview. This confidence-building trick worked to relieve her stress and helped her enter the interview poised and feeling self-possessed.[32]

YOUR TASK Search news articles and Web blog posts for tactics or tips that new grads and others could employ to reduce anxiety before a job interview or a big test. Prepare a list of 10 ideas, including a few offbeat rituals such as Emma's. Write your list as a set of instructions and be ready to amplify if necessary. Report your advice in class or in a written document determined by your instructor.

16.6 Engaging Social Media to Investigate Jobs (L.O. 1, 2)

Social Media **Web**

Valuable insider information about a company's culture and day-to-day activities is available for those who are willing to search. Savvy job seekers increasingly access blogs, company Facebook profiles, LinkedIn pages, Indeed, Salary, Glassdoor, and Twitter feeds to investigate jobs and companies.

YOUR TASK Using the Web, locate a blog that is maintained by an employee of a company where you would like to work. Monitor the blog for at least a week. Also, access the company's Facebook and Instagram pages, check its LinkedIn presence, and monitor any Twitter feeds for at least a week. Prepare a short report summarizing what you learned about the company through reading the blog postings, status updates, and tweets. Include a statement of whether this information would be valuable during a job search.

16.7 Building Interview Skills With Worksheets (L.O. 3)

Successful interviews require diligent preparation and repeated practice. To be well prepared, you need to know what skills are required for your targeted position. In addition to computer and communication skills, employers generally want to know whether you work well with a team, accept responsibility, solve problems, are efficient, meet deadlines, show leadership, save time and money, and are a hard worker.

YOUR TASK Consider a position for which you are eligible now or one for which you will be eligible when you complete your education. Identify the skills and traits necessary for this position. If you prepared a résumé in Chapter 15, be sure that it addresses these targeted areas. Now prepare interview worksheets listing at least ten technical and other skills or traits you think a recruiter will want to discuss in an interview for your targeted position.

16.8 Telling Success Stories (L.O. 3)

You can best showcase your talents if you are ready with your own success stories that illustrate how you have developed the skills or traits required for your targeted position.

YOUR TASK Using the worksheets you prepared in **Activity 16.7**, prepare success stories that highlight the required skills or traits. Select three to five stories to develop into answers to potential interview questions. For example, here is a typical question: *How does your background relate to the position we have open?* A possible response: *As you know, I have just completed an intensive training program in _____. In addition, I have over three years of part-time work experience in a variety of business settings. In one position I was selected to manage a small business in the absence of the owner. I developed responsibility and customer service skills in filling orders efficiently, resolving shipping problems, and monitoring key accounts. I also inventoried and organized products worth over $200,000. When the owner returned from a vacation to Bermuda, I was commended for increasing sales and was given a bonus in recognition of my efforts.* People relate to and remember stories. Try to shape your answers into memorable stories.

16.9 Digging for Digital Dirt: Keeping a Low Profile Online (L.O. 2)

Social Media / **Web**

Before embarking on your job hunt, you should find out what employers might find if they searched your personal life in cyberspace, specifically on Facebook, Instagram, Twitter, and so forth. Running your name through Google and other search engines, particularly enclosed in quotation marks to lower the number of hits, is usually the first step. To learn even more, try some of the people-search sites such as 123people, Snitch.name, and PeekYou. They collect information from a number of search engines, websites, and social networks.

YOUR TASK Use Google, 123people, PeekYou, or another search tool to explore the Internet for your full name, enclosed in quotation marks. In Google, don't forget to run an *Images* search at **http://www.google.com/images**

to find any photos of questionable taste. If your instructor requests, share your insights with the class—not any salacious details, but general observations—or write a short memo summarizing the results.

16.10 Talent Assessments: Reviewing Test Scenarios (L.O. 1, 2)

Web

What do Foot Locker, Macy's, PetSmart, Nieman Marcus, Walmart, and Burger King have in common? They all have used pre-employment testing to identify applicants who will fit into the organization. Unlike classical aptitude tests that began in the military, today's online multiple-choice tests assess integrity, collegiality, and soft skills in general.

To give you a flavor of these talent assessments, here are three typical scenarios:

1. You have learned that eye contact is important in communication. How much eye contact should you hove when conversing with someone in a professional environment?

   A. At all times. You want to make sure the person knows you are paying attention.

   B. About 60–70 percent of the time

   C. Every now and then. You don't want to make the other person uncomfortable.

   D. About half the time

2. You are attending an important meeting with colleagues who are more senior than you are. How much should you speak at the meeting?

   A. You should look very interested but not speak at all unless they request it.

   B. You should speak only when the topic is in your area of expertise.

   C. You should try to talk as much as possible to show your knowledge.

   D. You should speak in the beginning of the meeting and every now and then.

3. You just found out that people at work are spreading a bad rumor about you that is untrue. How would you respond?

   A. Tell everybody that it is not true. You need to clear your name.

   B. Don't react to it at all. It'll blow over eventually.

   C. Find out who started it so you talk to them to make sure that they will never do it again.

   D. Talk to others about another coworker's rumor so people will forget about yours.

YOUR TASK Answer the questions; then compare your answers with those of your classmates. Discuss the scenarios. What specific skills or attributes might each question be designed to measure? Do you think such questions are effective? What might be the best way to respond to the scenarios? Your instructor may share the correct answers with you. If your instructor directs, search the Web for more talent assessment questions. Alternatively, your instructor might ask you to create your own workplace (or college) scenarios to help you assess an applicant's soft skills. As a class you could compare questions/scenarios and quiz each other.

16.11 Practicing Answers to Interview Questions (L.O. 3)

Team

Practice makes perfect in interviewing. The more often you rehearse responses to typical interview questions, the closer you are to getting the job.

YOUR TASK Select three questions from each of the following question categories discussed in this chapter: questions to get acquainted, questions to gauge your interest, questions about your experience and accomplishments, questions about the future, and challenging questions. Write your answers to each set of questions. Try to incorporate skills and traits required for the targeted position, and include success stories where appropriate. Polish these answers and your delivery technique by practicing in front of a mirror or by making an audio or video recording. Your instructor may choose this assignment as a group activity in class.

16.12 Anticipating Situational Interview Questions (L.O. 3)

`Team` `Web`

Situational interview questions can vary widely from position to position. You should know enough about a position to understand some of the typical situations you would encounter on a regular basis.

YOUR TASK Use your favorite search tool to locate typical descriptions of a position in which you are interested. Based on these descriptions, develop a list of six to eight typical situations someone in this position would face; then write situational interview questions for each of these scenarios. In pairs, role-play interviewer and interviewee, alternating with each question.

16.13 Examining Behavioral Interview Questions (L.O. 3)

`Team` `Web`

Behavioral interview questions are increasingly popular, and you will need a little practice before you can answer them easily.

YOUR TASK Use your favorite search tool to locate lists of behavioral questions on the Internet. Select five skill areas such as communication, teamwork, and decision making. For each skill area, find three behavioral questions that you think would be effective in an interview. In pairs, role-play interviewer and interviewee, alternating with each question. You goal is to answer effectively in one or two minutes. Remember to use the STAR method when answering.

16.14 Negotiating a Salary (L.O. 3)

`Team`

Negotiating a salary can be tricky. You want to get what you're worth, but you don't want to offend or scare off the recruiter—especially in a competitive job market. Worse yet, negotiating doesn't come naturally to Americans. "Most people in our country are not used to bargaining," says salary expert Matthew Deluca. "But if you don't bargain, you're not going to get all you should."[33]

YOUR TASK To build your negotiating skills, reread the Career Coach box on page 598. Then, role-play a situation in which a hiring manager offers a candidate a starting salary of $49,500. The candidate wants $55,000 to start. The candidate responds to preliminary questions and negotiates the salary offer.

16.15 Creating a Digital or Paper Interview Cheat Sheet (L.O. 3)

Even the best-rehearsed applicants sometimes forget to ask the questions they prepared, or they fail to stress their major accomplishments in job interviews. Sometimes applicants are so rattled they even forget the interviewer's name. To help you keep your wits during an interview, make a cheat sheet—either paper or digital—that summarizes key facts, answers, and questions. Review it before the interview and again as the interview is ending to be sure you have covered everything that is critical.

YOUR TASK Prepare a cheat sheet with the following information:

- Day and time of interview:
- Meeting with: [name(s) of interviewer(s), title, company, city, state, zip, telephone, cell, video, e-mail]
- Major accomplishments (four to six):
- Management or work style (four to six):
- Things you need to know about me (three or four items):
- Reason I left my last job:
- Answers to difficult questions (four or five answers):
- Questions to ask interviewer:
- Things I can do for you:

16.16 The End of the Handshake: A New Etiquette Emerges (L.O. 4)

`Web`

As a result of the COVID-19 pandemic, people around the world have changed their greeting style. To reduce the risk of contracting the virus, many switched from the Western custom of shaking hands to a wide range of alternatives. Assume you have been asked by the editor of your school blog to post an article reviewing the history of the handshake and how the greeting has changed as the COVID-19 pandemic appeared and spread. What alternatives have emerged not only in your country but around the world?

YOUR TASK Search the Web for current information about greetings that are considered polite, safe, and welcoming. What is the history of the custom of shaking hands? What alternatives have emerged to replace handshaking? Has the stigma of touching declined since the initial reaction to the pandemic outbreak? What advice would you give candidates who are being interviewed for jobs? Submit your findings in an e-mail or a format your instructor chooses. You may be asked to share your findings in a presentation illustrated with images.

16.17 Responding to Inappropriate and Illegal Interview Questions (L.O. 3)

Although some questions are considered inappropriate and potentially illegal by the government, many interviewers ask them anyway—whether intentionally or unknowingly. Being prepared is important.

YOUR TASK Assume you are being interviewed at one of the top companies on your list of potential employers. The interviewing committee consists of a human resources manager and the supervising manager of the department in which you would work. At various times during the interview, the supervising manager asks questions that make you feel uncomfortable. For example, he asks whether you are married. You know this question is inappropriate, but you see no harm in answering it. Then, however, he asks how old you are. Because you started college early and graduated in three and a half years, you are worried that you may not be considered mature enough for this position. However, you have most of the other qualifications required, and you are convinced you could succeed on the job. How should you answer this question?

16.18 Asking Your Own Questions (L.O. 3)

When it is your turn to ask questions during the interview process, be ready.

YOUR TASK Decide on three to five questions that you would like to ask during an interview. Write them down and practice asking them so that you sound confident and sincere.

16.19 Role-Playing Mock Interviews (L.O. 3)

Team

One of the best ways to understand interview dynamics and to develop confidence is to role-play the parts of interviewer and candidate in a mock interview.

YOUR TASK Choose a partner for this activity. Each partner makes a list of two interview questions for each of the eight interview question categories presented in this chapter. In team sessions you and your partner role-play an actual interview. One acts as interviewer; the other is the candidate. Prior to the interview, the candidate tells the interviewer the job he or she is applying for and the name of the company. For the interview, the interviewer and candidate should dress appropriately and sit in chairs facing each other. The interviewer greets the candidate and makes the candidate comfortable. The candidate gives the interviewer a copy of his or her résumé.

The interviewer asks three questions (or more, depending on your instructor's time schedule) from the candidate's list. The interviewer may also ask follow-up questions, if appropriate. When finished, the interviewer ends the meeting graciously. After one interview, partners reverse roles and repeat.

16.20 YouTube: Critiquing Interview Skills (L.O. 3)

Web

The adage *Practice makes perfect* is especially true for interviewing. The more you confront your fears in mock or real interviews, the calmer and more confident you will be when your dream job is on the line. Short of undergoing your own interview, you can also learn from observation. YouTube and other video sites offer countless video clips showing examples of excellent, and poor, interviewing techniques.

YOUR TASK Visit YouTube or search the Internet for interview videos. Select a clip that you find particularly entertaining or informative. Watch it multiple times and jot down your observations. Then summarize the scenario in a paragraph or two. Provide examples of interview strategies that worked and those that didn't, applying the information you learned in this chapter. If required, share your insights about the video with the class.

16.21 Interviewing Over Meals: Table Manners on Display (L.O. 3)

Web

Although they are less likely for entry-level candidates, interviews over business meals are a popular means to size up the social skills of a job seeker, especially in second and subsequent interviews. Candidates coveting jobs with a lot of face-to-face contact with the public may be subjected to the ultimate test: table manners. Interviews are nerve-racking and intimidating enough, but imagine having to juggle silverware, wrangle potentially messy food, and keep your clothing stain free—all this while listening carefully to what is being said around the table and giving thoughtful, confident answers.

YOUR TASK Researching tips can help you avoid the most common pitfalls associated with interviews over meals. Use your favorite search engine and try queries such as *interview dining tips*, *interviewing over meals*, and so forth. Consider the credibility of your sources. Are they authorities on the subject? Compile a list of tips and jot down your sources. Share the list with your peers. If you instructor directs, discuss the categories of advice provided. Then, as a class assemble a universal list of the most common interview tips.

16.22 Thanking the Interviewer (L.O. 4)

You have just completed an exciting employment interview, and you want the interviewer to remember you.

YOUR TASK Write a follow-up thank-you letter to Meredith Murillo, Human Resources Development, Cybersecure, Inc., 4400 Legacy Drive, Plano, TX 75024 (or a company of your choice). Make up any details needed.

16.23 Following Up After Submitting Your Résumé (L.O. 4)

`E-Mail` `Web`

A month has passed since you sent your résumé and cover letter in response to a job advertisement. You are still interested in the position and would like to find out whether you still have a chance.

YOUR TASK Write a follow-up e-mail or letter to an employer of your choice that does not offend the reader or damage your chances of employment.

16.24 Refusing to Take *No* for an Answer (L.O. 5)

After an excellent interview with Meredith Murillo of Cybersecure, Inc. (or a company of your choice), you are disappointed to learn that someone else was hired. However, you really want to work for CCS.

YOUR TASK Write a follow-up message to Meredith Murillo, Human Resources Development, Cybersecure, Inc., 4400 Legacy Drive, Plano, TX 75024 (or a company of your choice). Indicate that you are disappointed but still interested.

16.25 Saying *Yes* to a Stellar Job Offer (L.O. 5)

Your dream has come true: you have just been offered an excellent position. Although you accepted the position on the phone, you want to send a formal acceptance letter.

YOUR TASK Write a job acceptance letter to an employer of your choice. Include the job title, your starting date, and details about your compensation package. Make up any necessary details.

16.26 Demonstrating Your Growing Value to the Organization (L.O. 1, 4, 5)

Let's assume your boss has paid your tuition for this course. As you complete the course, he or she asks you for a letter about your experience in the course.

YOUR TASK Write a letter to a boss in a real or imaginary organization explaining how this course made you more valuable to the organization.

Test Your Workplace Etiquette IQ

New communication platforms and casual workplace environments have blurred the lines of appropriateness, leaving workers wondering how to navigate uncharted waters. Check your workplace etiquette IQ by deciding whether the following statements are true or false. Then see if you agree with the responses on p. Key-6.

1. As you enter the room for a job interview, the recruiter stands up to greet you but doesn't hold out his hand. You should smile, announce your name, and hold out your hand to shake in the conventional sign of collegial greeting.

   _____ True _____ False

2. At your job interview, the recruiter greets you with her hand extended to shake. Because you firmly believe that handshaking must be avoided, you should withhold your hand, smile, and give a cheery one-handed (or two-handed, if both are free) wave or nod so that the interviewer knows you are happy to be there but are observing healthy "touchless" greetings.

   _____ True _____ False

3. During a job interview, it's perfectly acceptable to jot down a few notes in a professional-looking binder or notepad—but not on an iPad or other electronic device.

   _____ True _____ False

Chat About It

In each chapter you will find five discussion questions related to the chapter material. Your instructor may assign these topics for you to discuss in class, in an online chat room, or on an online discussion board. Some of the discussion topics may require outside research. You may also be asked to read and respond to postings made by your classmates.

TOPIC 1: "Soft skills can make or break a hire—and they can also make or break a company," said Mark Lobosco, LinkedIn vice president. "As automation and AI [artificial intelligence] continue to reshape entire industries, companies and jobs, strong soft skills—the one thing that machines can't replace—are becoming absolutely vital."[34] In your field, what special skills will be required that machines can't replace?

TOPIC 2: What is your greatest fear of what you might do or what might happen to you during an employment interview? How can you overcome your fears?

TOPIC 3: If you are interviewing for a company where most of the employees are dressed very casually, including ripped jeans, should you wear similar clothes to a job interview with that company? Why or why not?

TOPIC 4: You confide in a friend that you don't feel confident about going to job interviews. She tells you that you need more practice, and she suggests that you apply for jobs that you know you don't want and accept interviews with companies in which you are not genuinely interested just so you can develop your interviewing skills. She says that interviewers expect some *shopping*. Do you agree? Should you take her advice? Why or why not?

TOPIC 5: Should job candidates be required to give their social media passwords to recruiters when asked? Explain your view. What does your state allow in this regard?

Grammar and Mechanics Review 16

Total Review

Each of the following sentences has **three** errors in grammar, punctuation, capitalization, usage, or spelling. On a separate sheet, write a correct version. Avoid adding new phrases, starting new sentences, or rewriting in your own words. When finished, compare your responses with those in the key at the end of the book.

EXAMPLE: Suki wondered how many companys use social media to check candidates backgrounds?

REVISION: Suki wondered how many **companies** use social media to check **candidates' backgrounds**. [Use period, not question mark.]

1. Despite the heavy use of e-mail many employers' use the telephone to reach candidates and set up there initial interviews.

2. Most interviews usualy cover the same kinds of questions, therefore smart candidates prepare for them.

3. When you are asked to tell about yourself experts agree that you should answer in no more than 2 minutes, and keep the response targeted on the job.

4. In interviewing job candidates recruiters have the following three purposes, assessing their skills, discussing their experience and deciding whether they are a good fit for the organization.

5. If your job history has gaps in it be prepared to explain what you did during this time, and how you kept up to date in your field.

6. Interviewing is a two way street and candidates should be prepared with there own meaningful questions.

7. Yired was asked whether she had a bachelors degree, and whether she had three years experience.

8. If you are consentious and want to create a good impression be sure to write a thank you message after a job interview.

9. When Yireds interview was over she told friends that she had done good.

10. Yired was already to send a thank-you message, when she realized she could not spell the interviewers name.

APPENDIX A
Document Formats

Although business communication channels are rapidly changing, many business documents continue to be sent in standardized formats. Becoming familiar with these formats is important because these documents carry two significant kinds of messages. Verbal messages are conveyed by the words chosen to express the writer's ideas. Nonverbal messages are conveyed largely by the appearance of a document and its adherence to recognized formats. To ensure that your documents carry favorable nonverbal messages about you and your organization, you will want to give special attention to the appearance and formatting of your e-mails, letters, envelopes, memos, and résumés.

A-1 E-Mail Messages

Despite social media, texting, and instant messaging, e-mail remains an important channel for conveying workplace messages. This section describes formats and usage. The following suggestions, illustrated in Model Document

A.1, may guide you in setting up the parts of any e-mail. Always check, however, with your organization to ensure that you follow its practices.

To Line. Include the receiver's e-mail address after *To*. If the receiver's address is recorded in your address book, you just have to click it. Be sure to enter all addresses very carefully since one mistyped stroke prevents delivery.

From Line. Most mail programs automatically include your name and e-mail address after *From*.

Cc and Bcc. Insert the e-mail address of anyone who is to receive a copy of the message. *Cc* stands for carbon copy or courtesy copy. Don't be tempted, though, to send needless copies just because it's easy. *Bcc* stands for blind carbon copy. Some writers use *bcc* to send a copy of the message without the addressee's knowledge. Writers also use the *bcc* line for mailing lists. When a message is sent to a number of people and their e-mail addresses should not be revealed, the *bcc* line works well to conceal the names and addresses of all receivers.

MODEL DOCUMENT A.1 Typical E-Mail

To: Karen Chitwood <karen.chitwood@enterprise.com>

From: Emily Katz <emily.katz@enterprise.com>

Subject: Responding to Your Inquiry About Jury Duty — Includes descriptive subject line

Hello, Karen, — Provides salutation to reflect friendliness and to mark beginning of the message

Yes, all employees who are summoned for jury duty service are eligible for paid jury duty leave. However, they are paid only for the days that they serve as jurors. On-call jurors who are not required to report for jury duty service are not eligible for paid jury duty leave. Depending on the employee's category, an hourly employee or an employee who works less than full time is eligible for time off with pay for jury duty for only those hours scheduled to work. — Uses single spacing within paragraphs and double spacing between

To initiate jury leave, you should indicate the time served on Attendance Form 540 in Section 7F of the Employee Handbook. Attach the jury notice and any monies you received to Form 540 and forward to your attendance reporting clerk. Please call Human Resources if you have questions or if you do not have a copy of the Employee Handbook.

Emily Katz
Coordinator, Human Resources
E-mail: emily.katz@enterprise.com — Closes with name and full contact information to ensure identification
Office: (513) 329-8861
Cell: (513) 893-3390

Subject. Identify the subject of the e-mail with a brief but descriptive summary of the topic. Be sure to include enough information to be clear and compelling. Capitalize the initial letters of main words. Main words are all words except (a) the articles *a*, *an*, and *the*; (b) prepositions containing two or three letters (such as *at*, *to*, *on*, *by*, *for*); (c) the word *to* in an infinitive (*to work*, *to write*); and (d) the word *as*—unless any of these words are the first or last word in the subject line.

Salutation. Include a brief greeting, if you like. Some writers use a salutation such as *Dear Karen*, followed by a comma or a colon. Others are more informal with *Hi, Karen; Hello, Karen; Good morning;* or *Greetings.*

Message. Ideally, cover just one topic in your message, and try to keep your total message under three screens in length. Single-space and be sure to use both upper- and lowercase letters. Double-space between paragraphs.

Closing. If you choose to conclude an e-mail with a closing, you might use *Cheers, Best wishes,* or *Warm regards,* followed by your name and complete contact information. Some writers omit an e-mail address because they think it is provided automatically. However, programs do not always transmit the address, and it may be lost in long e-mail threads. Therefore, always include it along with other identifying information in the closing.

Attachment. Use the attachment window or button to select the name of any file you wish to send with your e-mail. You can also attach a Web page to your message.

A-2 **Business Letters**

Business communicators write business letters primarily to correspond with people outside the organization. The use of business letters has declined significantly in recent years. E-mail is faster, more efficient, and less costly. However, business letters are necessary when the situation demands a permanent record, confidentiality, formality, or a persuasive presentation. The following information will help you format your letters following conventional guidelines.

Conventional Letter Placement, Margins, and Line Spacing. The following are conventional guidelines for setting up business documents:

- For a clean look, choose a sans serif font such as Arial, Calibri, Tahoma, or Verdana. For a more traditional look, choose a serif font such as Times New Roman. Use a 10-point, 11-point, or 12-point size.
- Use a 2-inch top margin for the first page of a letter printed on letterhead stationery. This will place the date on line 13. Use a 1-inch top margin for second and succeeding pages.
- Justify only the left margin. Set the line spacing to single.
- Choose side margins according to the length of your letter. Set 1.5-inch margins for short letters (under 200 words) and 1-inch margins for longer letters (200 or more words).
- Leave from 2 to 10 blank lines following the date to balance the message on the page. You can make this adjustment after keying your message.

Spacing and Punctuation. At one time typists left 2 spaces after end punctuation (periods, question marks, and so forth). This practice was necessary, it was thought, because typewriters did not have proportional spacing and sentences were easier to read when 2 spaces separated them. Professional typesetters, however, did not follow this practice because they used proportional spacing, and readability was not a problem. Influenced by the look of typeset publications, many writers now leave only 1 space after end punctuation. As a practical matter, however, it is not wrong to use 2 spaces, if done consistently.

A-2a **Business Letter Parts**

Professional-looking business letters are arranged in a conventional sequence with standard parts. Following is a discussion of how to use these letter parts properly. Figure A.1 illustrates the parts of a block style letter.

Letterhead. Most business organizations use 8½ × 11-inch paper printed with a letterhead displaying their official name, street address, Internet address, e-mail address, and telephone and fax numbers. The letterhead may also include a logo and an advertising message.

Dateline. On letterhead paper you should place the date 1 blank line below the last line of the letterhead or 2 inches from the top edge of the paper (line 13). On plain paper place the date immediately below your return address. Because the date goes on line 13, start the return address an appropriate number of lines above it. The most common dateline format is as follows: *June 9, 2022.* Don't use *th* (or *rd, nd,* or *st*) when the date is written this way. For European or military correspondence, use the following dateline format: *9 June 2022.* Notice that no commas are used.

Addressee and Delivery Notations. Delivery notations such as *VIA U.S. MAIL, E-MAIL, FAX TRANSMISSION, FEDEX, MESSENGER DELIVERY, CONFIDENTIAL,* and *CERTIFIED MAIL* are typed in all capital letters between the dateline and the inside address.

Inside Address. Type the inside address—that is, the address of the organization or person receiving the letter—single-spaced, starting at the left margin. The number of lines between the dateline and the inside address depends on the size of the letter body, the type size (point or pitch size), and the length of the typing lines. Generally, 1 to 9 blank lines are appropriate.

Be careful to duplicate the exact wording and spelling of the recipient's name and address on your documents. Usually, you can copy this information from the letterhead of the correspondence you are answering. If, for example, you are responding to *Jackson & Perkins Company*, do not address your letter to *Jackson and Perkins Corp.*

Always be sure to include a courtesy title such as *Mr., Ms., Mrs., Dr.,* or *Professor* before a person's name in the inside address—for both the letter and the envelope. Although many women in business today favor *Ms.,* you should use whatever title the addressee prefers.

Generally spell out *Avenue, Street,* and *Company* unless they appear as abbreviations in the printed letterhead of the document being answered.

Attention Line. An attention line allows you to send your message officially to an organization but to direct it to a specific individual, officer, or department. However, if you know an individual's complete name, it is always better to use it as the first line of the inside address and avoid an attention line. Placing an attention line first in the address block enables you to paste it directly onto the envelope:

Attention Marketing Director
The MultiMedia Company
931 Calkins Avenue
Rochester, NY 14301

Salutation. For most letter styles, place the letter greeting, or salutation, 1 blank line below the last line of the inside address or the attention line (if used). If the letter is addressed to an individual, use that person's courtesy title and last name (*Dear Ms. Davis*). Even if you are on a first-name basis (*Dear Dana*), be sure to add a colon (not a comma or a semicolon) after the salutation. Do not use an individual's full name in the salutation (not *Dear Ms. Dana Davis*) unless you are unsure of gender (*Dear Dana Davis*).

It's always best to address messages to people. However, if a message is addressed to an organization, consider these salutations: an organization of men (*Gentlemen*), an organization of women (*Ladies*), an organization of men and women (*Ladies and Gentlemen*). If a message is addressed to an undetermined individual, consider these salutations: a woman (*Dear Madam*), a man (*Dear Sir*), a title (*Dear Customer Service Representative*).

Subject and Reference Lines. Although experts suggest placing the subject line 1 blank line below the salutation, many businesses actually place it above the salutation. Use whatever style your organization prefers. Reference lines often show policy or file numbers; they generally appear 1 blank line above the salutation. Use initial capital letters for the main words or all capital letters.

Body. Most business letters and memorandums are single-spaced with double-spacing between paragraphs. Very short messages may be double-spaced with indented paragraphs.

Complimentary Close. Typed 1 blank line below the last line of the letter, the complimentary close may be formal (*Very truly yours*) or informal (*Sincerely* or *Cordially*).

Signature Block. In most letter styles, the writer's typed name and optional identification appear 3 or 4 blank lines below the complimentary close. The combination of name, title, and organization information should be arranged to achieve a balanced look. The name and title may appear on the same line or on separate lines, depending on the length of each. Use commas to separate categories within the same line but not to conclude a line.

Sincerely yours,   Cordially yours,

Jeremy. M. Wood   *Casandra Baker-Murillo*

Jeremy M. Wood, Manager   Casandra Baker-Murillo
Technical Sales and Services   Executive Vice President

Some organizations include their names in the signature block. In such cases the organization name appears in all caps blank line below the complimentary close, as shown here:

Cordially,
LIPTON COMPUTER SERVICES

Shelina A. Simpson

Shelina A. Simpson
Executive Assistant

Reference Initials. If used, the initials of the typist and writer are typed 1 blank line below the writer's name and title. Generally, the writer's initials are capitalized and the typist's are lowercased, but this format varies.

Enclosure Notation. When an enclosure or attachment accompanies a document, a notation to that effect appears 1 blank line below the reference initials. This notation reminds the typist to insert the enclosure in the envelope, and it reminds the recipient to look for the enclosure or attachment. The notation may be spelled out (*Enclosure, Attachment*), or it may be abbreviated (*Enc., Att.*). It may indicate the number of enclosures or attachments, and it may also identify a specific enclosure (*Enclosure: Form 1099*).

Copy Notation. If you make copies of correspondence for other individuals, you may use *cc* to indicate courtesy copy, *pc* to indicate photocopy, or merely *c* for any kind of copy. A colon following the initial(s) is optional.

FIGURE A.1 Block and Modified Block Letter Styles

Letterhead

Island Graphics
893 Dillingham Boulevard
Honolulu, HI 96817-8817

(808) 493-2310
http://www.islandgraphics.com

↓ Dateline is 2 inches from the top or 1 blank line below letterhead

Dateline — September 13, 2022

↓ 1 to 9 blank lines

Inside address — Mr. T. M. Wilson, President
Visual Concept Enterprises
1901 Kaumualii Highway
Lihue, HI 96766

↓ 1 blank line

Salutation — Dear Mr. Wilson:

↓ 1 blank line

Subject line — Subject: Block Letter Style

↓ 1 blank line

This letter illustrates block letter style, about which you asked. All typed lines begin at the left margin. The date is usually placed 2 inches from the top edge of the paper or 1 blank line below the last line of the letter head, whichever position is lower.

Body — This letter also shows mixed punctuation. A colon follows the salutation, and a comma follows the complimentary close. Open punctuation requires no colon after the salutation and no comma following the close; however, open punctuation is seldom seen today.

If a subject line is included, it appears 1 blank line below the salutation. The word Subject is optional. Most readers will recognize a statement in this position as the subject without an identifying label. The complimentary close appears 1 blank line below the end of the last paragraph.

↓ 1 blank line

Complimentary close — Sincerely,

↓ 3 blank lines

Mark H. Wong

Signature block — Mark H. Wong
Graphic Designer

↓ 1 blank line

Reference initials — MHW:pil

Modified block style, mixed punctuation

In the modified block style letter shown at the left, the date is centered or aligned with the complimentary close and signature block, which start at the center. Mixed punctuation includes a colon after the salutation and a comma after the complimentary close, as shown above and at the left.

Second-Page Heading. When a letter extends beyond one page, use plain paper of the same quality and color as the first page. Identify the second and succeeding pages with a heading consisting of the name of the addressee, the page number, and the date. Use the following format or the one shown in Figure A.2:

Ms. Sara Hendricks   2   May 3, 2022

Both headings appear 6 blank lines (1 inch) from the top edge of the paper followed by 2 blank lines to separate them from the continuing text. Avoid using a second page if you have only 1 line or the complimentary close and signature block to fill that page.

Plain-Paper Return Address. If you prepare a personal or business letter on plain paper, place your address immediately above the date. Do not include your name; you will type (and sign) your name at the end of your letter. If your return address contains 2 lines, begin typing so that the date appears 2 inches from the top. Avoid abbreviations except for a two-letter state abbreviation.

580 East Leffels Street
Springfield, OH 45501
December 14, 2022

Ms. Ellen Siemens
Escrow Department
TransOhio First Federal
1220 Wooster Boulevard
Columbus, OH 43218-2900

Dear Ms. Siemens:

For letters in the block style, type the return address at the left margin. For modified block style letters, start the return address at the center to align with the complimentary close.

A-2b Letter and Punctuation Styles

Most business letters today are prepared in either block or modified block style, and they generally use mixed punctuation.

Block Style. In the block style, shown in Figure A.1, all lines begin at the left margin. This style is a favorite because it is easy to format.

Modified Block Style. The modified block style differs from the block style in that the date and closing lines appear in the center, as shown at the bottom of Figure A.1. The date may be (a) centered, (b) begun at the center of the page (to align with the closing lines), or (c) backspaced from the right margin. The signature block—including the complimentary close, writer's name and title, or organization identification—begins at the center. The first line of each paragraph may begin at the left margin or may be indented 5 or 10 spaces. All other lines begin at the left margin.

Mixed Punctuation Style. Most businesses today use mixed punctuation, shown in Figure A.1. It requires a colon after the salutation and a comma after the complimentary close. Even when the salutation is a first name, a colon is appropriate.

FIGURE A.2   Second-Page Heading

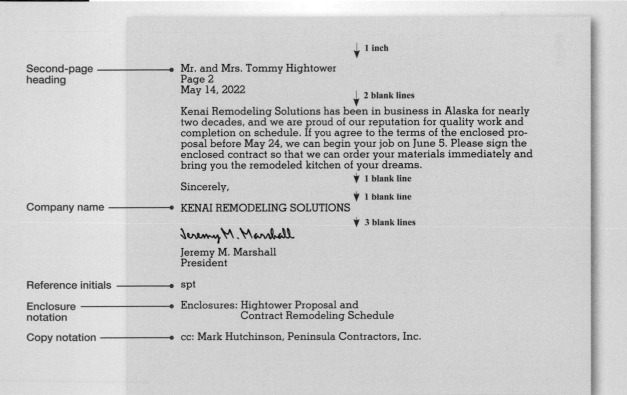

A-2c Envelopes

An envelope should be of the same quality and color of stationery as the letter it carries. Because the envelope introduces your message and makes the first impression, you need to be especially careful in addressing it. Moreover, how you fold the letter is important.

Return Address. The return address is usually printed in the upper left corner of an envelope, as shown in Figure A.3. In large companies some form of identification (the writer's initials, name, or location) may be typed above the company name and address. This identification helps return the letter to the sender in case of nondelivery.

On an envelope without a printed return address, single-space the return address in the upper left corner. Beginning on line 3 on the fourth space (½ inch) from the left edge, type the writer's name, title, company, and mailing address. On a word processor, select the appropriate envelope size and make adjustments to approximate this return address location.

Mailing Address. On legal-sized No. 10 envelopes (4⅛ × 9½ inches), begin the address on line 13 about 4¼ inches from the left edge, as shown in Figure A.3. For small envelopes (3⅝ × 6½ inches), begin typing on line 12 about 2½ inches from the left edge. On a word processor, select the correct envelope size and check to be sure your address falls in the desired location.

The U.S. Postal Service recommends that addresses be typed in all caps without any punctuation. This Postal Service style, shown in the small envelope in Figure A.3, was originally developed to facilitate scanning by optical character readers. Today's OCRs, however, are so sophisticated that they scan upper- and lowercase letters easily. Many companies today do not follow the Postal Service format because they prefer to use the same format for the envelope as for the inside address. If the same format is used, writers can take advantage of word processing programs to copy the inside address to the envelope, thus saving keystrokes and reducing errors. Having the same format on both the inside address and the envelope also looks more professional and consistent. For those reasons you may choose to use the familiar upper- and lowercase combination format. But you will want to check with your organization to learn its preference.

In addressing your envelopes for delivery in this country or in Canada, use the two-letter state and province abbreviations shown in Figure A.4. Notice that these abbreviations are in capital letters without periods.

Folding. The way a letter is folded and inserted into an envelope sends additional nonverbal messages about a writer's professionalism and carefulness. Most businesspeople follow the procedures shown here, which produce the least number of creases to distract readers.

FIGURE A.3	Envelope Formats

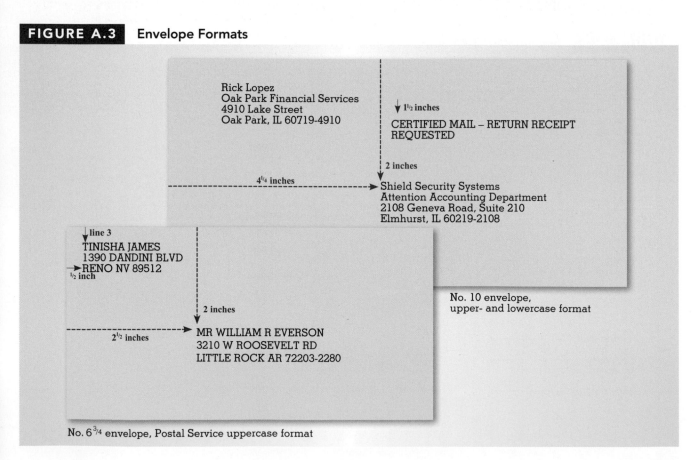

Rick Lopez
Oak Park Financial Services
4910 Lake Street
Oak Park, IL 60719-4910

↓ 1½ inches

CERTIFIED MAIL – RETURN RECEIPT
REQUESTED

2 inches

4¼ inches

Shield Security Systems
Attention Accounting Department
2108 Geneva Road, Suite 210
Elmhurst, IL 60219-2108

↓ line 3
TINISHA JAMES
1390 DANDINI BLVD
→ RENO NV 89512
½ inch

2 inches

2½ inches

MR WILLIAM R EVERSON
3210 W ROOSEVELT RD
LITTLE ROCK AR 72203-2280

No. 10 envelope,
upper- and lowercase format

No. 6³⁄₄ envelope, Postal Service uppercase format

FIGURE A.4 Abbreviations of States, Territories, and Provinces

State or Territory	Two-Letter Abbreviation	State or Territory	Two-Letter Abbreviation
Alabama	AL	North Carolina	NC
Alaska	AK	North Dakota	ND
Arizona	AZ	Ohio	OH
Arkansas	AR	Oklahoma	OK
California	CA	Oregon	OR
Canal Zone	CZ	Pennsylvania	PA
Colorado	CO	Puerto Rico	PR
Connecticut	CT	Rhode Island	RI
Delaware	DE	South Carolina	SC
District of Columbia	DC	South Dakota	SD
Florida	FL	Tennessee	TN
Georgia	GA	Texas	TX
Guam	GU	Utah	UT
Hawaii	HI	Vermont	VT
Idaho	ID	Virgin Islands	VI
Illinois	IL	Virginia	VA
Indiana	IN	Washington	WA
Iowa	IA	West Virginia	WV
Kansas	KS	Wisconsin	WI
Kentucky	KY	Wyoming	WY
Louisiana	LA	**Canadian Province**	
Maine	ME	Alberta	AB
Maryland	MD	British Columbia	BC
Massachusetts	MA	Labrador	LB
Michigan	MI	Manitoba	MB
Minnesota	MN	New Brunswick	NB
Mississippi	MS	Newfoundland	NF
Missouri	MO	Northwest Territories	NT
Montana	MT	Nova Scotia	NS
Nebraska	NE	Ontario	ON
Nevada	NV	Prince Edward Island	PE
New Hampshire	NH	Quebec	PQ
New Jersey	NJ	Saskatchewan	SK
New Mexico	NM	Yukon Territory	YT
New York	NY		

For large No. 10 envelopes, begin with the letter face up. Fold slightly less than one third of the sheet toward the top, as shown in the following diagram. Then fold down the top third to within ⅓ inch of the bottom fold. Insert the letter into the envelope with the last fold toward the bottom of the envelope.

For small No. 6¾ envelopes, begin by folding the bottom up to within ⅓ inch of the top edge. Then fold the right third over to the left. Fold the left third to within ⅓ inch of the last fold. Insert the last fold into the envelope first.

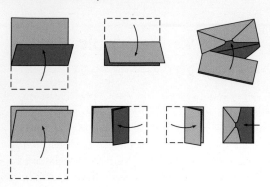

APPENDIX B
Citation Formats

Careful business writers properly cite the source of any data borrowed from others. Citing sources strengthens a writer's argument, as you learned in Chapter 11, while also shielding the writer from charges of plagiarism. Moreover, good references help readers pursue further research. As a business writer, you can expect to routinely borrow ideas and words to show that your ideas are in sync with the rest of the business world, to gain support from business leaders, or simply to save time in developing your ideas. To be ethical, however, you must show clearly what you borrowed and from whom.

Source notes tell where you found your information. For quotations, paraphrases, graphs, drawings, or online images you have borrowed, you need to cite the original authors' names, full titles, and the dates and facts of publication. The purpose of source notes, which appear at the end of a report, is to direct your readers to the complete references. Many systems of referencing are used by businesses, but they all have one goal: to provide clear, consistent references

Rarely, business writers use content notes, which are identified with a raised number at the end of the quotation. Usually at the bottom of the page, the number is repeated with a remark, clarification, or background information.

During your business career, you may use a variety of citation or documentation systems. The two most common systems in the academic world are those of the American Psychological Association (APA) and the Modern Language Association (MLA). Each organization has its own style for text references and bibliographic lists. The endnotes in this textbook represent a modified APA style. However, business organizations may use their own citation styles.

Before starting any research project, whether for a class or in a business, inquire about the preferred referencing style. For school assignments ask about specifics. For example, should you include URLs and dates of retrieval for Internet sources? For workplace assignments ask to see a previous report either in hard copy or as an e-mail attachment.

In your business and class writing, you will usually provide a brief citation in parentheses that refers readers to the complete reference that appears in a references or works-cited section at the end of your document. Following is a summary of APA and MLA formats with examples.

B-1 American Psychological Association Format

First used primarily in the social and physical sciences, the APA documentation format uses the author-date method of citation. This method, with its emphasis on current information, is especially appropriate for business. Within the text, the date of publication of the referenced work appears immediately after the author's name (Rivera, 2020), as illustrated in the brief APA example in Figure B.1. At the end of the report, all references appear alphabetically on a page labeled References. The APA format does not require a date of retrieval for online sources, but you should check with your instructor or supervisor about the preferred format for your class or organization. For more information about the APA format, see the *Publication Manual of the American Psychological Association*, Seventh Edition (Washington, DC: American Psychological Association, 2020).

B-1a APA In-Text Format

Within your text, document each text, figure, or personal source with a short description in parentheses. Following are selected guidelines summarizing the important elements of APA style.

- For a direct quotation, include the last name of the author(s), the year of publication, and the page number if available; for example, *(Meadows, 2020, p. 32)*. If no author is shown in the text or on a website, use a shortened title or a heading that can be easily located on the References page; for example, *(History, n.d.)*.

- If you mention the author in the text, do not use the name again in the parenthetical reference. Just cite the date; for example, *According to Meadows (2020)*.

- Search for website dates on the home page or at the bottom of Internet pages. If no date is available for a source, use *n.d.*

B-1b APA References Format

At the end of your report, in a section called References, list all references alphabetically by author, or by title if no author is available. To better understand the anatomy of an APA scholarly journal article reference, see Figure B.2.

FIGURE B.1 Portions of APA Text Page and References

Peanut butter was first delivered to the world by a St. Louis physician in 1890 (Rivera, 2020). As discussed at the Peanut Advisory Board's website, peanut butter was originally promoted as a protein substitute for elderly patients (History, n.d.). However, the 1905 Universal Exposition in St. Louis truly launched peanut butter. Since then, annual peanut butter consumption has zoomed to 3.3 pounds a person in the United States (Barrons, 2019).

Uses first word of Website title (History); has no author, no date

America's farmers produce 4.1 million tons of peanuts annually, about half of which is used for oil, nuts, and candy. Lisa Gibbons, executive secretary of the Peanut Advisory Board, says that "peanuts in some form are in the top four candies: Snickers, Reese's Peanut Butter Cups, Peanut M&Ms, and Butterfingers" (Meadows, 2020, p. 32).

Requires author's name (Meadows), date, and page number for direct quote

References

Print journal with volume, issue, date, and page numbers

Barrons, E. R. (2019, November). A comparison of domestic and international consumption of legumes. *Journal of Economic Agriculture, 23*(3), 45-49. doi: 10-1058-0885-7974.30.6.678

Blog article without date or page numbers

History of peanut butter. (n.d.). Peanut Advisory Board. Alabama Peanut Producers Blog. www.alpeanuts.com/consumer_interest/article.phtml?articleID=102

Magazine article

Meadows, M. A. (2020, May). Peanut crop is anything but peanuts at home and overseas. *Business Monthly*, 35(4), 31-34.

Book

Rivera, C. A. (2020). *The world's premier protein sources.* HarperCollins.

FIGURE B.2 Anatomy of an APA Journal Article Reference

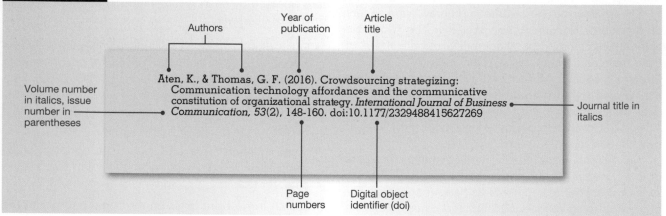

Authors · Year of publication · Article title

Volume number in italics, issue number in parentheses

Aten, K., & Thomas, G. F. (2016). Crowdsourcing strategizing: Communication technology affordances and the communicative constitution of organizational strategy. *International Journal of Business Communication, 53*(2), 148-160. doi:10.1177/2329488415627269

Journal title in italics

Page numbers · Digital object identifier (doi)

As with all documentation methods, APA has specific capitalization, punctuation, and sequencing rules, some of which are summarized here:

- Include the last name of the author(s) followed by initials. APA is gender neutral, so first and middle names are not spelled out; for example, (Aten, K., & Thomas G.F.).

- Show the date of publication in parentheses immediately after the author's name. A magazine citation will also include the month and day in the parentheses.

- Use sentence-style capitalization for all titles except journal titles. Do not use quotation marks.

- Italicize titles of magazines, newspapers, books, and journals.

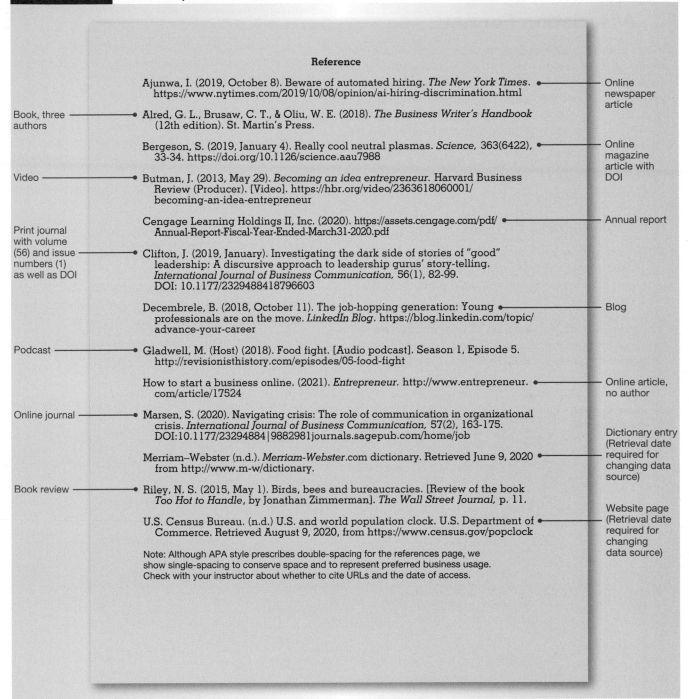

Reference

Ajunwa, I. (2019, October 8). Beware of automated hiring. *The New York Times*.
https://www.nytimes.com/2019/10/08/opinion/ai-hiring-discrimination.html — Online newspaper article

Book, three authors — Alred, G. L., Brusaw, C. T., & Oliu, W. E. (2018). *The Business Writer's Handbook* (12th edition). St. Martin's Press.

Bergeson, S. (2019, January 4). Really cool neutral plasmas. *Science, 363*(6422), 33-34. https://doi.org/10.1126/science.aau7988 — Online magazine article with DOI

Video — Butman, J. (2013, May 29). *Becoming an idea entrepreneur.* Harvard Business Review (Producer). [Video]. https://hbr.org/video/2363618060001/becoming-an-idea-entrepreneur

Cengage Learning Holdings II, Inc. (2020). https://assets.cengage.com/pdf/Annual-Report-Fiscal-Year-Ended-March31-2020.pdf — Annual report

Print journal with volume (56) and issue numbers (1) as well as DOI — Clifton, J. (2019, January). Investigating the dark side of stories of "good" leadership: A discursive approach to leadership gurus' story-telling. *International Journal of Business Communication, 56*(1), 82-99. DOI: 10.1177/2329488418796603

Decembrele, B. (2018, October 11). The job-hopping generation: Young professionals are on the move. *LinkedIn Blog*. https://blog.linkedin.com/topic/advance-your-career — Blog

Podcast — Gladwell, M. (Host) (2018). Food fight. [Audio podcast]. Season 1, Episode 5. http://revisionisthistory.com/episodes/05-food-fight

How to start a business online. (2021). *Entrepreneur.* http://www.entrepreneur.com/article/17524 — Online article, no author

Online journal — Marsen, S. (2020). Navigating crisis: The role of communication in organizational crisis. *International Journal of Business Communication, 57*(2), 163-175. DOI:10.1177/23294884|9882981journals.sagepub.com/home/job

Merriam–Webster (n.d.). *Merriam-Webster*.com dictionary. Retrieved June 9, 2020 from http://www.m-w/dictionary. — Dictionary entry (Retrieval date required for changing data source)

Book review — Riley, N. S. (2015, May 1). Birds, bees and bureaucracies. [Review of the book *Too Hot to Handle*, by Jonathan Zimmerman]. *The Wall Street Journal*, p. 11.

U.S. Census Bureau. (n.d.) U.S. and world population clock. U.S. Department of Commerce. Retrieved August 9, 2020, from https://www.census.gov/popclock — Website page (Retrieval date required for changing data source)

Note: Although APA style prescribes double-spacing for the references page, we show single-spacing to conserve space and to represent preferred business usage. Check with your instructor about whether to cite URLs and the date of access.

- Include the digital object identifier (DOI) when available for books and online periodicals.

- For references with URLs, do not include the words "Retrieved from" or "Accessed from" unless the data is designed to change over time as in dictionaries and encyclopedias.

- Include references to personal communications in the text but not in the reference list. Personal communications include e-mails, text messages, online chats, direct messages, personal interviews, telephone conversations, live speeches, memos, letters, messages, and other nonarchived sources.

- Break a URL or DOI only after a mark of punctuation such as a slash or period.

For an expanded list of contemporary APA documentation format examples, see Figure B.3.

B-2 Modern Language Association Format

Writers in the humanities and the liberal arts frequently use the MLA documentation format, illustrated briefly in Figure B.4. In parentheses close to the textual reference, include the author's name and page cited (*Rivera 25*). At the end of your writing on a page titled "Works Cited," list all the sources alphabetically. Some writers include all of the sources consulted. Include the URLs for Web references. For more information, consult the *MLA Handbook*, Eighth Edition (New York: The Modern Language Association of America, 2016).

B-2a MLA In-Text Format

Following any borrowed material in your text, provide a short parenthetical description. Here are selected guidelines summarizing important elements of MLA style:

- For a direct quotation, enclose in parentheses the last name of the author(s), if available, and the page number without a comma; for example, *(Rivera 25)*. If a website has no author, use a shortened title of the page or a heading that is easily found on the works-cited page; for example, *(History)*.

- If you mention the author in the text, do not use the name again in parentheses; for example, *According to Rivera (27)*.

B-2b MLA Works-Cited Format

In a section called "Works Cited," list all references alphabetically by author or, if no author is available, by title. As with all documentation methods, MLA has specific capitalization and sequencing rules. Some of the most significant are summarized here:

- Include the author's last name first, followed by the first name and initial, as (*Rivera, Charles A.*).

- Enclose in quotation marks the titles of articles, essays, stories, chapters of books, pages in websites, articles in blogs, individual episodes of television and radio broadcasts, and short musical compositions.

- Italicize the titles of books, journals, websites, magazines, and newspapers.

FIGURE B.4   Portions of MLA Text Page and Works Cited

Cites book author (Rivera) and page number

Cites journal author (Barrons) and page number

Peanut butter was first delivered to the world by a St. Louis physician in 1890 (Rivera 25). As discussed at the Peanut Advisory Board's website, peanut butter was originally promoted as a protein substitute for elderly patients (*History*). However, the 1905 Universal Exposition in St. Louis truly launched peanut butter. Since then, annual peanut butter consumption has zoomed to 3.3 pounds a person in the United States (Barrons 47).

America's farmers produce 4.1 million tons of peanuts annually, about half of which is used for oil, nuts, and candy. Lisa Gibbons, executive secretary of the Peanut Advisory Board, says that "peanuts in some form are in the top four candies: Snickers, Reese's Peanut Butter Cups, Peanut M&Ms, and Butterfingers" (Meadows 32).

Lists first word of blog reference (*History*) when no author is available.

Places period outside of author, page reference

Works Cited

Print journal with volume, issue, date, and page numbers

Blog article without author; includes publication date, URL, and access date

Magazine article

Book

Barrons, Elizabeth R. "A Comparison of Domestic and International Consumption of Legumes." *Journal of Economic Agriculture*, vol. 23, no. 3, 2019, pp. 45–49.

"History of Peanut Butter." *Alabama Peanut Producers Blog*, Jan. 2021, www.alabamapeanutproducers.com. Accessed 2 Feb. 2021.

Meadows, Mark A. "Peanut Crop Is Anything but Peanuts at Home and Overseas." *Business Monthly*, Apr. 2020, pp. 31–34.

Rivera, Carlos A. *The World's Premier Protein Sources*. HarperCollins, 2020, pp. 25–26.

- Include the URL for online references, unless your instructor or organization prefers to omit URLs.

- Do not identify the medium (such as *Web, Print, Video*) as required in *MLA Handbook*, 7e.

To better understand the anatomy of the format of an MLA scholarly journal article reference, see Figure B.5. For an expanded list of contemporary MLA documentation format examples, see Figure B.6.

FIGURE B.5 Anatomy of an MLA Journal Article Reference

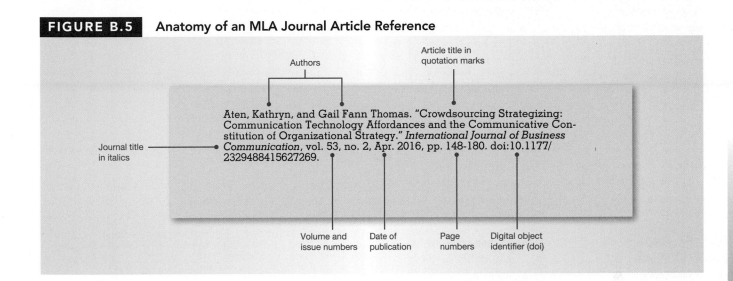

Works Cited

Book, more than one author, with *et al.*

Online video

Print journal with volume and issue numbers as well as DOI. Note: Citing a DOI is preferable to citing a URL.

Podcast

Online magazine article, no author

Print book review

Online newspaper article with access date

Online magazine article with DOI. Note: MLA style omits *http://* in URLs

Annual report

Blog article

Dictionary entry

Online journal with volume and issue numbers as well as DOI

Government publication

Ajunwa, Ifeoma. "Beware of Automated Hiring." *The New York Times,* 8 Oct. 2019, https://www.nytimes.com/2019/10/08/opinion/ai-hiring-discrimination. html. Accessed 17 July 2020.

Alred, Gerald J., *et al. The Business Writer's Handbook.* 12th ed. St. Martin's Press, New York 2018.

Bergeson, Scott. "Really Cool Neutral Plasmas," *Science,* Jan. 4, 2019, 363(6422), 33-34. https://doi.org/10.1126/science.aau7988. Accessed 14 Feb. 2020.

Butman, John. "Becoming an Idea Entrepreneur." *Harvard Business Review* 29 May 2013. hbr.org/video/23636180600001/becoming-an-idea-entrepreneur. Accessed 4 Jan. 2021.

Cengage Learning Holdings II, Inc. 2020 Annual Report. assets.cengage. com/pdf/Annual-Report-Fiscal-Year-Ended-March31-2020.pdf. Accessed 16 Feb. 2021.

Clifton, Jonathon. "Investigating the Dark Side of Stories of 'Good' Leadership: A Discursive Approach to Leadership Gurus' Story-telling." *International Journal of Business Communication*, vol. 56, no. 1, 2019: pp. 82-99. doi:10.1177/2329488418796603. Accessed 14 Sept. 2021.

Decembrele, Blair. "The Job-Hopping Generation: Young Professionals Are on the Move." *LinkedIn Blog.* Oct. 11, 2018. www://blog.linkedin.com/2018/october/11/the-job-hopping-generation-young-professionals-are-on-the-move. Accessed 21 Apr. 2020.

Gladwell, Malcom. "Food Fight," *Revisionist History*, season 1, episode 5, 2018. revisionisthistory.com/episodes/05-food-fight. Accessed 21 Nov. 2021.

Heuristic. Defined in *Merriam–Webster's Online Dictionary*, 11th ed. www.m-w/dictionary/heuristic. Accessed 13 Nov. 2021.

"How to Start a Business Online." *Entrepreneur.* 2021, www.entrepreneur.com/article/17524. Accessed 23 Dec. 2021.

Marsen, Sky. "Navigating Crisis: The Role of Communication in Organ izational Crisis." *International Journal of Business Communication*, vol. 57, no. 2, 2020. pp.163-175. doi:10.1177/23294884|9882981 journals. sagepub.com/home/job. Accessed 6 Nov. 2021.

Riley, Naomi Schaefer. "Birds, Bees and Bureaucracies." *The Wall Street Journal*. Review of *Too Hot to Handle*, by Jonathan Zimmerman. 1 May 2015, p. 11.

U.S. Department of Commerce, Census Bureau. U.S. population clock, 2020. www.census.gov/popclock. Accessed 9 Nov. 2020.

Note: Check with your instructor about whether to cite URLs and the date of access. Although MLA suggests using URLs only if necessary, many schools require students to include all URLs in their research papers.

APPENDIX C
Correction Symbols and Proofreading Marks

In marking your papers, your instructor may use the following symbols or abbreviations to indicate writing weaknesses. Studying these symbols and suggestions will help you understand your instructor's remarks. Knowing this information can also help you evaluate and improve your own e-mails, memos, letters, reports, and other writing. These symbols are keyed to your Grammar and Mechanics Guide and to the text.

Adj	Hyphenate two or more adjectives that are joined to create a compound modifier before a noun. See G/M Guide 20.
Adv	Use adverbs, not adjectives, to describe or limit the action. See G/M Guide 19.
Apos	Use apostrophes to show possession. See G/M Guides 31–33.
Assgn	Follow the assignment instructions.
Awk	Recast to avoid awkward expression.
Bias	Use inclusive, bias-free language. See Chapter 4.
Cap	Use capitalization appropriately. See G/M Guides 39–46.
CmConj	Use a comma before the coordinating conjunction in a compound sentence. See G/M Guide 23.
CmDate	Use commas appropriately in dates, addresses, geographical names, degrees, and long numbers. See G/M Guide 24.
CmIn	Use commas to set off internal sentence interrupters. See G/M Guide 25.
CmIntr	Use commas to separate introductory clauses and certain phrases from independent clauses. See G/M Guide 22.
CmSer	Use commas to separate three or more items (words, phrases, or short clauses) in a series. See G/M Guide 21.
Coh	Improve coherence between ideas. Repeat key ideas, use pronouns, or use transitional expressions. See Chapter 5.
Cl	Improve the clarity of ideas or expression so that the point is better understood. See Chapter 6.
CS	Avoid comma-splice sentences. Do not use a comma to splice (join) two independent clauses. See G/M Guide 3 and Chapter 5.
CmUn	Avoid unnecessary commas. See G/M Guide 26.
:	Use a colon after a complete thought that introduces a list of items. Use a colon in business letter salutations and to introduce long quotations. See G/M Guides 29 and 30.
Direct	Use the direct strategy by emphasizing the main idea. See Chapter 5.
Dash	Use a dash to set off parenthetical elements, to emphasize sentence interruptions, or to separate an introductory list from a summarizing statement. See G/M Guide 36.
DD	Use document design (white space, margins, typefaces, bullets, lists, indentions, or headings) to enhance readability. See Chapter 6.
DM	Avoid dangling modifiers by placing modifiers close to the words they describe or limit. See Chapter 5.
Filler	Avoid fillers such as *there are* or long lead-ins such as *this is to inform you that*. See Chapter 6.
Format	Choose an appropriate format for this document. See Appendix A.
Frag	Avoid fragments by expressing ideas in complete sentences. A fragment is a broken-off part of a sentence. See Chapter 5 and G/M Guide 1.

MM	Avoid misplaced modifiers by placing modifiers close to the words they describe or limit. See Chapter 5.
Num	Use number or word form appropriately. See G/M Guides 47–50.
Ob	Avoid stating the obvious.
Org	Improve organization by grouping similar ideas.
Par	Express ideas in parallel form. See Chapter 5.
Paren	Use parentheses to set off nonessential sentence elements such as explanations, directions, questions, or references. See G/M Guide 37.
Period	Use one period to end a statement, command, indirect question, or polite request. See G/M Guide 34.
Pos	Express an idea positively rather than negatively. See Chapter 4.
PosPro	Use possessive-case pronouns to show ownership. See G/M Guide 33.
Pro	Use nominative-case pronouns as subjects of verbs and as subject complements. Use objective-case pronouns as objects of prepositions and verbs. See G/M Guides 11–13.
ProAgr	Make pronouns agree in number and gender with the words to which they refer (their antecedents). See G/M Guide 17.
ProVag	Be sure that pronouns such as *it, which, this*, and *that* refer to clear antecedents. See G/M Guide 18.
?	Use a question mark after a direct question and after statements with questions appended. See G/M Guide 35.
Quo	Use quotation marks to enclose the exact words of a speaker or writer; to distinguish words used in a special sense; or to enclose titles of articles, chapters, or other short works. Words used in a special sense may also be shown with italics. See G/M Guide 38.
Redun	Avoid expressions that repeat meaning or include unnecessary words. See Chapter 6.
RunOn	Avoid run-on (fused) sentences. A sentence with two independent clauses must be joined by a coordinating conjunctions (*and, or, nor, but*) or by a semicolon (;). See Chapter 5 and G/M Guide 2.
Self	Use *self*-ending pronouns only when they refer to previously mentioned nouns or pronouns. See G/M Guide 15.
;	Use a semicolon to join closely related independent clauses or to separate items in a series when one or more of the items contains internal commas. See G/M Guides 27 and 28.
Shift	Avoid a confusing shift in verb tense, mood, or voice. See G/M Guides 4 and 5.
Sp	Check misspelled words.
Trans	Use an appropriate transition. See Chapter 5 and Chapter 12.
Tone	Use a conversational, positive, and courteous tone that promotes goodwill. See Chapter 4.
You	Focus on developing the "you" view. See Chapter 4.
VbAgr	Make verbs agree with subjects. See G/M Guides 6–10.
VbMood	Use the subjunctive mood to express hypothetical (untrue) ideas. See G/M Guide 5.
VbTnse	Use present-tense, past-tense, and part-participle forms correctly. See G/M Guide 4.
VbVce	Use active- and passive-voice verbs appropriately. See Chapter 5.
WC	Focus on precise word choice. See Chapter 4.
Wordy	Exclude wordy expressions, long lead-ins, unnecessary *there is/are* fillers, redundancies, and trite business phrases. See Chapter 6.

Proofreading Marks

Proofreading Mark	Draft Copy	Final Copy
⹀ Align horizontally	TO: Rick Munoz	TO: Rick Munoz
‖ Align vertically	166.32 132.45	166.32 132.45
☰ Capitalize	Coca-cola sending a pdf file	Coca-Cola sending a PDF file
⌒ Close up space	meeting at 3 p. m.	meeting at 3 p.m.
⯈⯇ Center	Recommendations	Recommendations
⟿ Delete	in my final judgement	in my judgment
⌄ Insert apostrophe	our companys product	our company's product
⋏ Insert comma	you will of course	you will, of course,
⁼ Insert hyphen	tax free income	tax-free income
⊙ Insert period	Ms Holly Hines	Ms. Holly Hines
⹂ Insert quotation mark	shareholders receive a bonus.	shareholders receive a "bonus."
# Insert space	wordprocessing program	word processing program
/ Lowercase (remove capitals)	the Vice President	the vice president
	HUMAN RESOURCES	Human Resources
⊏ Move to left	I. Labor costs	I. Labor costs
⊐ Move to right	A. Findings of study	A. Findings of study
○ Spell out	aimed at 2 depts	aimed at two departments
¶ Start new paragraph	Keep the screen height of your computer at eye level.	Keep the screen height of your computer at eye level.
⋯ Stet (don't delete)	officials talked openly	officials talked openly
∿ Transpose	accounts recievable	accounts receivable
bf Use boldface	Conclusions	**Conclusions**
ital Use italics	The Perfect Résumé	*The Perfect Résumé*

APPENDIX D
Grammar and Mechanics

In the business world, people are often judged by the way they speak and write. Using the language competently can mean the difference between success and failure. Speakers may sound accomplished, but when they put ideas in print, errors in language usage can destroy their credibility. One student observed, "When I talk, I get by on my personality, but when I write, the flaws in my communication show through. That's why I'm in this class."

D-1 How This Grammar and Mechanics Guide Can Help You

This grammar and mechanics guide contains 50 guidelines covering sentence structure, grammar, usage, punctuation, capitalization, and number style. These guidelines focus on the most frequently used—and abused—language elements. Frequent checkpoint exercises enable you to try your skills immediately. In addition to the 50 language guides in this appendix, you will find a list of 160 frequently misspelled words plus a quick review of selected confusing words.

The concentrated materials in this guide help novice business communicators focus on the major areas of language use. This guide focuses on principal language guidelines and troublesome words. Your objective should be mastery of these language principles and words, which represent a majority of the problems encountered by business writers.

The guidelines presented are founded on those appearing in *The Gregg Reference Manual, 11e*, by William Sabin; *HOW: A Handbook for Office Professionals, 14e*, by Lyn Clark and James L. Clark; and *Business English, 13e*, by Mary Ellen Guffey and Carolyn M. Seefer.

D-2 Grammar and Mechanics Guidelines

D-2b Sentence Structure

GUIDE 1: Avoid sentence fragments. A fragment is an incomplete sentence. You can recognize a complete sentence because it (a) includes a subject (a noun or pronoun that interacts with a verb), (b) includes a verb (a word expressing action or describing a condition), and (c) makes sense (comes to a closure). A complete sentence is an independent clause. One of the most serious errors a writer can make is punctuating a fragment as if it were a complete sentence.

Fragment	Improved
Because 90 percent of all business transactions involve written messages. Good writing skills are critical.	Because 90 percent of all business transactions involve written messages, good writing skills are critical.
The recruiter requested a writing sample. Even though the candidate seemed to communicate well.	The recruiter requested a writing sample, even though the candidate seemed to communicate well.

Tip: Fragments often can be identified by the words that introduce them—words such as *although, as, because, even, except, for example, if, instead of, since, so, such as, that, which,* and *when.* These words introduce dependent clauses. Make sure such clauses are always connected to independent clauses.

DEPENDENT CLAUSE   INDEPENDENT CLAUSE

Since she became a supervisor, she had to write more memos and reports.

GUIDE 2: Avoid run-on (fused) sentences. A sentence with two independent clauses must be joined by a coordinating conjunction (*and, or, nor, but*) or by a semicolon (;). Without a conjunction or a semicolon, a run-on sentence results.

Run-On

Rachel considered an internship she also thought about graduate school.

Improved

Rachel considered an internship, and she also thought about graduate school.

Rachel considered an internship; she also thought about graduate school.

GUIDE 3: Avoid comma-splice sentences. A comma splice results when a writer joins (splices together) two independent clauses—without using a coordinating conjunction (*and, or, nor, but*).

Comma Splice

Disney World operates in Orlando, EuroDisney serves Paris.

Improved

Disney World operates in Orlando; EuroDisney serves Paris.

Disney World operates in Orlando, and EuroDisney serves Paris.

Visitors wanted a resort vacation, however they were disappointed.

Visitors wanted a resort vacation; however, they were disappointed.

Tip: In joining independent clauses, beware of using a comma and words such as *consequently, furthermore, however, therefore, then,* and *thus.* These conjunctive adverbs require semicolons.

Note: Sentence structure is also covered in Chapter 5.

✓ Checkpoint

Revise the following to rectify sentence fragments, comma splices, and run-ons.

1. Although it began as a side business for Disney. Destination weddings now represent a major income source.

2. About 2,000 weddings are held yearly. Which is twice the number just ten years ago.

3. Weddings may take place in less than one hour, however the minimum charge is $25,000.

4. Limousines line up outside Disney's wedding pavilion, they are scheduled in two-hour intervals.

5. Most couples prefer a traditional wedding, others request a fantasy experience.

For all the Checkpoint sentences, compare your responses with the answers at the end of Appendix D.

D-2b Verb Tense

GUIDE 4: Use present-tense, past-tense, and past-participle verb forms correctly.

Present Tense	Past Tense	Past Participle
(Today I_____)	(Yesterday I_____)	(I have_____)
am	was	been
begin	began	begun
break	broke	broken
bring	brought	brought
choose	chose	chosen
come	came	come
do	did	done
give	gave	given
go	went	gone
know	knew	known
pay	paid	paid
see	saw	seen
steal	stole	stolen
take	took	taken
write	wrote	written

The package *came* yesterday, and Kevin *knew* what it contained.

If I *had seen* the shipper's bill, I *would have paid* it immediately.

I *know* the answer now; I wish I *had known* it yesterday.

Tip: Probably the most frequent mistake in tenses results from substituting the past-participle form for the past tense. Notice that the past-participle tense requires auxiliary verbs such as *has, had, have, would have,* and *could have.*

Faulty

When he *come* over last night, he *brung* pizza.

If he *had came* earlier, we *could have saw* the video.

Correct

When he *came* over last night, he *brought* pizza.

If he *had come* earlier, we *could have seen* the video.

D-2c Verb Mood

GUIDE 5: Use the subjunctive mood to express hypothetical (untrue) ideas. The most frequent misuse of the subjunctive mood involves using *was* instead of *were* in clauses introduced by *if* and *as though* or containing *wish.*

If I *were* (not *was*) you, I would take a business writing course.

Sometimes I wish I *were* (not *was*) the manager of this department.

He acts as though he *were* (not *was*) in charge of this department.

Tip: If the statement could possibly be true, use *was*. If I *was* to blame, I accept the consequences.

✓ Checkpoint

Correct faults in verb tense and mood.

6. If I was you, I would have went to the ten o'clock meeting.

7. Kevin could have wrote a better report if he had began earlier.

8. When the project manager seen the report, he immediately come to my office.

9. I wish the project manager was in my shoes for just one day.

10. If the manager had knew all that we do, I'm sure he would have gave us better reviews.

D-2d Verb Voice

For a discussion of active- and passive-voice verbs, see Chapter 5.

D-2e Verb Agreement

GUIDE 6: Make subjects agree with verbs despite intervening phrases and clauses. Become a detective in locating true subjects. Don't be deceived by prepositional phrases and parenthetic words that often disguise the true subject.

Our study of annual budgets, five-year plans, and sales proposals *is* (not *are*) progressing on schedule. (The true subject is *study*.)

The budgeted item, despite additions proposed yesterday, *remains* (not *remain*) as submitted. (The true subject is *item*.)

A vendor's evaluation of the prospects for a sale, together with plans for follow-up action, *is* (not *are*) what we need. (The true subject is *evaluation*.)

Tip: Subjects are nouns or pronouns that control verbs. To find subjects, cross out prepositional phrases beginning with words such as *about, at, by, for, from, of,* and *to*. Subjects of verbs are not found in prepositional phrases. Also, don't be tricked by expressions introduced by *together with, in addition to,* and *along with*.

GUIDE 7: With subjects joined by *and*, use plural verbs. Watch for true subjects joined by the conjunction *and*. They require plural verbs.

The CEO and one of his assistants *have* (not *has*) ordered a limo.

Considerable time and money *were* (not *was*) spent on remodeling.

Working out in the gym and jogging every day *are* (not *is*) how he keeps fit.

Tip: Subjects joined by *or* or *nor* may require singular or plural verbs. The verb should agree with the closer subject.

Either the software or the printer *is* (not *are*) causing the glitch. (The verb is controlled by the closer subject, *printer*.)

Neither St. Louis nor Chicago *has* (not *have*) a chance of winning. (The verb is controlled by *Chicago*.)

Tip: In joining singular and plural subjects with *or* or *nor*, place the plural subject closer to the verb. Then, the plural verb sounds natural. For example, *Either the manufacturer or the distributors are responsible*.

GUIDE 8: Use singular verbs for most indefinite pronouns. The following pronouns all take singular verbs: *anyone, anybody, anything, each, either, every, everyone, everybody, everything, neither, nobody, nothing, someone, somebody,* and *something*.

Everyone in both offices *was* (not *were*) given a bonus.

Each of the employees *is* (not *are*) being interviewed.

GUIDE 9: Use singular or plural verbs for collective nouns, depending on whether the members of the group are operating as a unit or individually. Words such as *faculty, administration, class, crowd,* and *committee* are considered *collective* nouns. If the members of the collective are acting as a unit, treat them as singular subjects. If they are acting individually, it is usually better to add the word *members* and use a plural verb.

Correct

The Finance Committee *is* working harmoniously. (*Committee* is singular because its action is unified.)

The Planning Committee *are* having difficulty agreeing. (*Committee* is plural because its members are acting individually.)

Improved

The Planning Committee members *are* having difficulty agreeing. (Add the word *members* if a plural meaning is intended.)

Tip: In the United States, collective nouns are generally considered singular. In Britain collective nouns are generally considered plural.

✓ Checkpoint

Correct the errors in subject–verb agreement.

11. The time and talent of Instagram was spent developing a blockbuster ad campaign.

12. Your e-mail message, along with both of its attachments, were not delivered to my computer.

13. Each of the Fortune 500 companies are being sent a survey regarding women in management.

14. A full list of names and addresses are necessary before we can begin.

15. Either the judge or the attorney have asked for a recess.

D-2f Plural Nouns

GUIDE 10: For nouns ending in *s*, *x*, *z*, *ch*, or *sh*, form the plural by adding *es*.

All *businesses* must pay their *taxes*.

The *Lopezes* purchased two *watches* as graduation gifts.

Nouns ending in *y* form the plural in two ways. When the letter before *y* is a vowel (*a*, *e*, *i*, *o*, *u*), form the plural by adding *s* only. When the letter before *y* is a consonant (all letters other than vowels), form the plural by changing the *y* to *ie* and adding *s*.

Several *attorneys* worked on the privacy cases.

Both *cities* provided extensive *libraries* for citizens.

D-2g Pronoun Case

GUIDE 11: Learn the three cases of pronouns and how each is used. Pronouns are substitutes for nouns. Every business writer must know the following pronoun cases.

Subjective (Nominative) Case	Objective Case	Possessive Case
Used for subjects of verbs and subject complements	Used for objects of prepositions and objects of verbs	Used to show possession
we		
I	me	my, mine
us	our, ours	
you	you	you, yours
he	him	his
she	her	her, hers

Subjective (Nominative) Case	Objective Case	Possessive Case
Used for subjects of verbs and subject complements	Used for objects of prepositions and objects of verbs	Used to show possession
it	it	its
they	them	their, theirs
who, whoever	whom, whomever	whose

GUIDE 12: Use subjective-case pronouns as subjects of verbs and as complements. Complements are words that follow linking verbs (such as *am, is, are, was, were, be, being,* and *been*) and rename the words to which they refer.

She and *I* (not *her* and *me*) will be collaborating. (Use a subjective-case pronoun as the subject of the verb phrase *will be collaborating.*)

We hope that Marci and *he* (not *him*) will join our team. (Use a subjective-case pronoun as the subject of the verb phrase *will join.*)

It must have been *she* (not *her*) who called last night. (Use a subjective-case pronoun as a subject complement.)

Tip: If you feel awkward using subjective pronouns after linking verbs, rephrase the sentence to avoid the dilemma. Instead of *It is she who is the boss*, say, *She is the boss.*

GUIDE 13: Use objective-case pronouns as objects of prepositions and verbs.

Send the e-mail to *her* and *me* (not *she* and *I*). (The pronouns *her* and *me* are objects of the preposition *to.*)

The CEO appointed Rick and *him* (not *he*) to the committee. (The pronoun *him* is the object of the verb *appointed.*)

Tip: When a pronoun appears in combination with a noun or another pronoun, ignore the extra noun or pronoun and its conjunction. Then, the case of the pronoun becomes more obvious.

Jason asked Jennifer and *me* (not *I*) to lunch. (Ignore *Jennifer and.*)

The waiter brought hamburgers to Jason and *me* (not *I*). (Ignore *Jason and.*)

Tip: Be especially alert to the following prepositions: *except, between, but,* and *like.* Be sure to use objective pronouns as their objects.

Just between you and *me* (not *I*), that mineral water comes from the tap.

Everyone except Robert and *him* (not *he*) responded to the invitation.

GUIDE 14: Use possessive pronouns to show ownership. Possessive pronouns (such as *hers, yours, whose, ours, theirs,* and *its*) require no apostrophes.

All reports except *yours* (not *your's*) have to be rewritten.

The apartment and *its* (not *it's*) contents are *hers* (not *her's*) until June.

Tip: Don't confuse possessive pronouns and contractions. Contractions are shortened forms of subject–verb phrases (such as *it's* for *it is, there's* for *there is, who's* for *who is,* and *they're* for *they are*).

✓ Checkpoint
Correct errors in pronoun case.

16. My partner and me have looked at many apartments, but your's has the best location.

17. We thought the car was her's, but it's license plate does not match.

18. Just between you and I, do you think the companies will merge?

19. Neither the boss nor me knows whether its broken, but its condition should have been reported to him or I earlier.

20. We received several applications, but your's and her's were missing

GUIDE 15: Use pronouns ending in *self* only when they refer to previously mentioned nouns or pronouns.

The president *himself* ate all the M&Ms.

Send the chocolates to Mike or *me* (not *myself*).

Tip: Trying to sound less egocentric, some radio and TV announcers incorrectly substitute *myself* when they should use *I* (*Jimmy and I* [not *myself*] *are cohosting the tournament*).

GUIDE 16: Use *who* or *whoever* for subjective-case constructions and *whom* or *whomever* for objective-case constructions. In determining the correct choice, it is helpful to substitute *he* for *who* or *whoever* and *him* for *whom* or *whomever*.

For *whom* was this software ordered? (The software was ordered for *him*.)

Who did you say called? (You did say *he* called)

Give the supplies to *whoever* asked for them. (In this sentence the clause *whoever asked for them* functions as the object of the preposition *to*. Within the clause *whoever* is the subject of the verb *asked*. Again, try substituting *he: he asked for them*.)

✓ Checkpoint
Correct any errors in the use of *self*-ending pronouns and *who/whom*.

21. The manager herself is willing to call whoever we decide to honor.

22. Who have you hired to investigate the data breach?

23. I have a pizza for whomever placed the online order.

24. The meeting is set for Wednesday; however, Matt and myself cannot attend.

25. Incident reports must be submitted by whomever experiences a personnel problem.

D-2h **Pronoun Reference**

GUIDE 17: Make pronouns agree in number and gender with the words to which they refer (their antecedents). When the gender of the antecedent is known, make the pronoun agree with it.

One of the men failed to fill in *his* name on the application. (The singular pronoun *his* refers to the singular *One*.)

Each of the female nurses was escorted to *her car*. (The singular pronoun *her* and singular noun *car* are necessary because they refer to the singular subject *Each*.)

Somebody on the girls' team left *her* headlights on.

When the gender of the antecedent is unknown, pronoun choice should be carefully considered. Some writers in the past substituted the wordy and awkward *he or she* (Each worker had his or her own work space). Recently experts have accepted the use of *they* (*their, them*) as a singular pronoun when the gender of the antecedent is unknown. In conversation the singular *they* was often heard, but careful writers avoided what was considered ungrammatical usage. Although the singular *they* is now accepted, some speakers and writers strive to find other ways to express an idea calling for a singular third-person pronoun.

When an employee does well, *they* (not *he or she*) should be praised. (*They* as a singular pronoun.)

When *employees* do well, *they* should be praised. (Alternative: Make the antecedent plural.)

When an employee does well, *that person* should be praised (Alternative: Avoid the pronoun.)

Every employee should receive *their* paycheck Friday. (*They* as a singular pronoun.)

Every employee should receive *a* paycheck Friday. (Alternative: Use an adjective instead of a pronoun.)

In particular, when referring to gender nonbinary, nonconforming, and fluid individuals, always use the person's self-identifying pronouns if you know the pronouns of the person being described. For example, they may ask that the gender nonspecific, singular pronouns *they/their* or *ze/hir*—not *he/his* or *she/her*—be used to refer to them. If you do not know an individual's self-identified pronouns, refer to the above examples and consider how to rephrase a sentence to avoid the use of pronouns.

GUIDE 18: Be sure that pronouns such as *it*, *which*, *this*, and *that* refer to clear antecedents. Vague pronouns confuse the reader because they have no clear single antecedent. The most troublesome are *it*, *which*, *this*, and *that*. Replace vague pronouns with concrete nouns, or provide these pronouns with clear antecedents.

Faulty	Improved
Our office recycles as much paper as possible because *it* helps the environment. (Does *it* refer to *paper*, *recycling*, or *office*?)	Our office recycles as much paper as possible because *such an effort* helps the environment. (*Effort* supplies a concrete noun for the vague pronoun *it*.)
The disadvantages of some mobile apps can offset their advantages. *That* merits further evaluation. (What merits evaluation: advantages, disadvantages, or the offsetting of one by the other?)	The disadvantages of some mobile apps can offset their advantages. That fact merits further evaluation. (*Fact* supplies a concrete noun for the vague pronoun *that*.)
Negotiators announced an expanded wellness program, reductions in dental coverage, and a proposal to move child-care facilities off site. *This* ignited employee protests. (What exactly ignited employee protests?)	Negotiators announced an expanded wellness program, reductions in dental coverage, and a proposal to move child-care facilities off site *This change in child-care facilities* ignited employee protests. (The pronoun *This* now has a clear reference.)

Tip: Whenever you use the words *this*, *that*, *these*, and *those* by themselves, a red flag should pop up. These words are dangerous when they stand alone. Inexperienced writers often use them to refer to an entire previous idea, rather than to a specific antecedent, as shown in the preceding examples. You can usually solve the problem by adding another idea to the pronoun (such as *this change*).

✓ Checkpoint
Correct the faulty and vague pronoun references in the following sentences. Numerous remedies exist.

26. Every employee must wear his or her picture identification badge.

27. Flexible working hours may mean slower career advancement, but it appeals to many workers.

28. Any renter must pay his rent by the first of the month.

29. Someone in this office reported that his computer had a virus.

30. Obtaining agreement on job standards, listening to coworkers, and encouraging employee suggestions all helped to open lines of communication. This is particularly important in team projects.

D-2i Adjectives and Adverbs

GUIDE 19: Use adverbs, not adjectives, to describe or limit the action of verbs. Use adjectives after linking verbs.

Andrew said he did *well* (not *good*) on the exam. (The adverb *well* describes how he did.)

After its tune-up, the engine is running *smoothly* (not *smooth*). (The adverb *smoothly* describes the verb phrase *is running*.)

Don't take the manager's criticism *personally* (not *personal*). (The adverb *personally* tells how to take the criticism.)

She finished her homework *more quickly* (not *quicker*) than expected. (The adverb *more quickly*) explains how she finished her homework.)

Liam felt *bad* (not *badly*) after he heard the news. (The adjective *bad* follows the linking verb *felt*.)

GUIDE 20: Hyphenate two or more adjectives that are joined to create a compound modifier before a noun.

You need an *easy-to-remember* e-mail address and a *one-page* resume.

Person-to-person networking continues to be the best way to find a job.

Tip: Don't confuse adverbs ending in *-ly* with compound adjectives: *newly enacted* law and *highly regarded* CEO would not be hyphenated.

✓ Checkpoint
Correct any problems in the use of pronouns, adjectives, and adverbs.

31. My manager and me could not resist the once in a lifetime opportunity.

32. Because John and him finished their task so quick, they made a fast trip to the recently opened snack bar.

33. If I do good on the exam, I qualify for many part time jobs and a few full time positions.

34. The vice president told him and I not to take the announcement personal.

35. In the not too distant future, we may enjoy more practical uses of robots and drones.

D-2j Commas

GUIDE 21: Use commas to separate three or more items (words, phrases, or short clauses) in a series. (Comma Series: CmSer)

Downward communication delivers job instructions, procedures, and appraisals.

In preparing your résumé, try to keep it brief, make it easy to read, and include only job-related information.

The new ice cream flavors include cookie dough, chocolate raspberry truffle, cappuccino, and almond amaretto.

Tip: Some professional writers omit the comma before *and*. However, most business writers prefer to retain that comma because it prevents misreading the last two items as one item. Notice in the previous example how the final two ice cream flavors could have been misread if the comma had been omitted.

GUIDE 22: Use commas to separate introductory clauses and certain phrases from independent clauses. (Comma Introductory: CmIntro) This guideline describes the comma most often omitted by business writers. Sentences that open with dependent clauses (frequently introduced by words such as *since, when, if, as, although*, and *because*) require commas to separate them from the main idea. The comma helps readers recognize where the introduction ends and the big idea begins. Introductory phrases of four or more words, and phrases containing verbal elements, also require commas.

If you recognize introductory clauses, you will have no trouble placing the comma. (A comma separates the introductory dependent clause from the main clause.)

When you have mastered this rule, half the battle with commas will be won.

As expected, additional explanations are necessary. (Use a comma even if the introductory clause omits the understood subject: *As we expected.*)

In the spring of last year, we opened our franchise. (Use a comma after a phrase containing four or more words.)

Having considered several alternatives, we decided to invest. (Use a comma after an introductory verbal phrase.)

To invest, we needed $100,000. (Use a comma after an introductory verbal phrase, regardless of its length.)

Tip: Short introductory prepositional phrases (three or fewer words) require no commas. Don't clutter your writing with unnecessary commas after introductory phrases such as *by 2020, in the fall*, or *at this time*.

GUIDE 23: Use a comma before the coordinating conjunction in a compound sentence. (Comma Conjunction: CmConj) The most common coordinating conjunctions are *and, or, nor*, and *but*. Occasionally, *for, yet*, and *so* may also function as coordinating conjunctions. When coordinating conjunctions join two independent clauses, commas are needed.

The investment sounded too good to be true, *and* many investors were dubious about it. (Use a comma before the coordinating conjunction *and* in a compound sentence.)

Southern California is the financial fraud capital of the world, *but* some investors refuse to heed warning signs.

Tip: Before inserting a comma, test the two independent clauses. Can each of them stand alone as a complete sentence? If either is incomplete, skip the comma.

Promoters said the investment offer was for a limited time and could not be extended even one day. (Omit a comma before *and* because the second part of the sentence is not a complete independent clause.)

Lease payments are based largely on your down payment and on the value of the car at the end of the lease. (Omit a comma before *and* because the second half of the sentence is not a complete independent clause.)

✓ Checkpoint
Add appropriate commas.

36. Before she enrolled in this class Erin used to sprinkle her writing with commas semicolons and dashes.

37. After studying punctuation she learned to use commas more carefully and to reduce her reliance on dashes.

38. At this time Erin is engaged in a serious yoga program but she also finds time to enlighten her mind.

39. Next fall Erin may enroll in communication and merchandising courses or she may work for a semester to earn money.

40. When she completes her junior year she plans to apply for an internship in Los Angeles Burbank or Long Beach.

GUIDE 24: Use commas appropriately in dates, addresses, geographical names, degrees, and long numbers. (Comma Date: CmDate)

September 30, 1993, is his birthday. (For dates use commas before and after the year.)

Send the application to James Kirby, 20045 45th Avenue, Lynnwood, WA 98036, as soon as possible. (For addresses use commas to separate all units except the two-letter state abbreviation and the zip code.)

Lisa expects to move from Cupertino, California, to Sonoma, Arizona, next fall. (For geographical areas use commas to enclose the second element.)

Karen Munson, CPA, and Richard B. Larsen, PhD, were the speakers. (Use commas to enclose professional designations and academic degrees following names.)

The latest census figures show the city's population to be 342,000. (In figures use commas to separate every three digits, counting from the right.)

GUIDE 25: Use commas to set off internal sentence interrupters. (Comma Internal: CmIn) Sentence interrupters may be verbal phrases, dependent clauses, contrasting elements, or parenthetical expressions (also called transitional phrases). These interrupters often provide information that is not grammatically essential.

Harvard researchers, working steadily for 18 months, developed a new cancer therapy. (Use commas to set off an internal interrupting verbal phrase.)

The new therapy, which applies a genetically engineered virus, raises hopes among cancer specialists. (Use commas to set off nonessential dependent clauses.)

Dr. James C. Morrison, who is one of the researchers, made the announcement. (Use commas to set off nonessential dependent clauses.)

It was Dr. Morrison, not Dr. Arturo, who led the team effort. (Use commas to set off a contrasting element.)

This new therapy, by the way, was developed from a herpes virus. (Use commas to set off a parenthetical expression.)

Tip: Parenthetical (transitional) expressions are helpful words that guide the reader from one thought to the next. Here are typical parenthetical expressions that require commas:

as a matter of fact	in addition	of course
as a result	in the meantime	on the other hand
consequently	nevertheless	therefore
for example		

Tip: Always use *two* commas to set off an interrupter, unless it begins or ends a sentence.

✓ Checkpoint
Insert necessary commas.

41. James listed 1805 Martin Luther King Street San Antonio Texas 78220 as his forwarding address.

42. This report is not however one that must be classified.

43. Employment of paralegals which is expected to decrease 12 percent next year is contracting because of the slow economy and automation.

44. The contract was signed May 15 2012 and remains in effect until May 15 2022.

45. As a matter of fact the average American drinks enough coffee to require 12 pounds of coffee beans annually.

GUIDE 26: Avoid unnecessary commas (Comma Unnecessary: CmNo). Do not use commas between sentence elements that belong together. Do not automatically insert commas before every *and* or at points where your voice might drop if you were saying the sentence out loud.

Faulty

Growth will be spurred by the increasing complexity of business operations, and by large employment gains in trade and services. (A comma unnecessarily precedes *and*.)

All students with high grades, are eligible for the honor society. (A comma unnecessarily separates the subject and verb.)

One of the reasons for the success of the business honor society is, that it is very active. (A comma unnecessarily separates the verb and its complement.)

Our honor society has, at this time, over 50 members. (Commas unnecessarily separate a prepositional phrase from the sentence.)

✓ Checkpoint
Remove unnecessary commas. Add necessary ones.

46. Car companies promote leasing because it brings customers back into their showrooms sooner, and gives dealers a steady supply of late-model used cars.

47. When shopping for a car you may be offered a fantastic leasing deal.

48. The trouble with many leases is, that the value of the car at the end of the lease may be less than expected.

49. We think on the other hand, that you should compare the costs of leasing and buying, and that you should talk to a tax advisor.

50. American and Japanese automakers are, at this time, offering intriguing lease deals.

D-2k Semicolons, Colons

GUIDE 27: Use a semicolon to join closely related independent clauses. Experienced writers use semicolons to show readers that two thoughts are closely associated. If the ideas are not related, they should be expressed in separate sentences. Often, but not always, the second independent clause contains a conjunctive adverb (such as *however, consequently, therefore,* or *furthermore*) to show the relation between the two clauses. Use a semicolon before a conjunctive adverb of two or more syllables (such as *however, consequently, therefore,* or *furthermore*) and a comma after it.

Learning history is easy; learning its lessons is almost impossible. (A semicolon joins two independent clauses.)

He was determined to complete his degree; consequently, he studied diligently. (A semicolon precedes the conjunctive adverb, and a comma follows it.)

Serena wanted a luxury apartment located near campus; however, she couldn't afford the rent. (A semicolon precedes the conjunctive adverb, and a comma follows it.)

Tip: Don't use a semicolon unless each clause is truly independent. Try the sentence test. Omit the semicolon if each clause could not stand alone as a complete sentence.

Faulty	Improved
There is no point in speaking; unless you can improve on silence. (The second half of the sentence is a dependent clause. It could not stand alone as a sentence.)	There is no point in speaking unless you can improve on silence.
Although I cannot change the direction of the wind; I can adjust my sails to reach my destination. (The first clause could not stand alone.)	Although I cannot change the direction of the wind, I can adjust my sails to reach my destination.

GUIDE 28: Use a semicolon to separate items in a series when one or more of the items contains internal commas.

Representatives from as far away as Blue Bell, Pennsylvania; Bowling Green, Ohio; and Phoenix, Arizona, attended the conference.

Stories circulated about Henry Ford, founder, Ford Motor Company; Lee Iacocca, former CEO, Chrysler Motor Company; and Shoichiro Toyoda, founder, Toyota Motor Company.

GUIDE 29: Use a colon after a complete thought that introduces a list of items. Words such as *these, the following,* and *as follows* may introduce the list or they may be implied.

The following cities are on the tour: Louisville, Memphis, and New Orleans.

An alternate tour includes several West Coast cities: Seattle, San Francisco, and San Diego.

Tip: Be sure that the statement before a colon is grammatically complete. An introductory statement that ends with a preposition (such as *by, for, at,* and *to*) or a verb (such as *is, are,* or *were*) is incomplete. The list following a preposition or a verb actually functions as an object or as a complement to finish the sentence.

Faulty	Improved
Three Big Macs were ordered by: Pam, Jim, and Lee. (Do not use a colon after an incomplete statement.)	Three Big Macs were ordered by Pam, Jim, and Lee.
Other items that they ordered were: fries, Cokes, and salads. (Do not use a colon after an incomplete statement.)	Other items that they ordered were fries, Cokes, and salads.

GUIDE 30: Use a colon after business letter salutations and to introduce long quotations.

Dear Mr. Duran: Dear Lisa:

In discussing social media conversations, the consultant said: "Finding the right balance will take time, if it is ever achieved. Unlike face-to-face conversations, there's really no good way yet for people to let one another know when they are revealing too much."

Tip: Use a comma to introduce short quotations. Use a colon to introduce long one-sentence quotations and quotations of two or more sentences.

✓ Checkpoint
Add appropriate semicolons and colons.

51. Marco's short-term goal is an entry-level job his long-term goal however is a management position.

52. Speakers included the following professors Cameron Piercy University of Kansas Lora Lindsey Ohio University and Michael Malone Central Florida College.

53. The recruiter was looking for three qualities loyalty initiative and enthusiasm.

54. Microsoft seeks experienced individuals however it will hire recent graduates who are skilled.

55. South Florida is an expanding region therefore many business opportunities are available.

D-2l Apostrophe

GUIDE 31: If an ownership word does NOT end in an s sound, add an apostrophe and s, whether the word is singular or plural.

We hope to show a profit in one year's time. (Add 's because the ownership word *year* is singular and does not end in s.)

The children's teacher assigned computer problems. (Add 's because the ownership word *children*, although it is plural, does not end in s.)

GUIDE 32: If an ownership word does end in an *s* sound and is singular, add an apostrophe and *s*.

> The witness's testimony was critical. (Add 's because the ownership word *witness* is singular and ends in an *s*.)

> The boss's cell phone rang during the meeting. (Add 's because the ownership word *boss* is singular and ends in an *s*.)

If the ownership word ends in an *s* sound and is plural, add only an apostrophe.

> Both investors' portfolios showed diversification. (Add only an apostrophe because the ownership word *investors* is plural and ends in an *s*.)

> Some workers' benefits will cost more. (Add only an apostrophe because the ownership word *workers* is plural and ends in an *s*.)

Tip: To determine whether an ownership word ends in an *s*, use it in an *of* phrase. For example, *one month's salary* becomes *the salary of one month*. By isolating the ownership word without its apostrophe, you can decide whether it ends in an *s*.

GUIDE 33: Use a possessive pronoun or add an apostrophe and *s* to make a noun possessive when it precedes a gerund (a verb form used as a noun).

> We all protested *Laura's* (not *Laura*) smoking. (Add an apostrophe and *s* to the noun preceding the gerund.)

> *His* (not *Him*) talking on his cell phone angered moviegoers. (Use a possessive pronoun before the gerund.)

> I appreciate *your* (not *you*) filling in for me while I was gone. (Use a possessive pronoun before the gerund.)

✓ **Checkpoint**

Correct any problems with possessives.

56. Both companies executives received bonuses, even when employees salaries were falling.

57. In just one weeks time, we promise to verify all members names and addresses.

58. The manager and I certainly appreciate you bringing this matter to our CPAs attention.

59. All beneficiaries names must be revealed when insurance companies write policies.

60. Is your sister-in-laws job downtown?

D-2m Other Punctuation

GUIDE 34: Use one period to end a statement, command, indirect question, or polite request. Never use two periods.

> Matt worked at BioTech, Inc. (Statement. Use only one period.)

> Deliver it before 5 p.m. (Command. Use only one period.)

> Stacy asked whether she could use the car next weekend. (Indirect question)

> Will you please send me an employment application. (Polite request)

Tip: Polite requests often sound like questions. To determine the punctuation, apply the action test. If the request prompts an action, use a period. If it prompts a verbal response, use a question mark.

Faulty	Improved
Could you please correct the balance on my next statement? (This polite request prompts an action rather than a verbal response.)	Could you please correct the balance on my next statement.

Tip: To avoid the punctuation dilemma with polite requests, do not phrase the request as a question. Phrase it as a command: *Please correct the balance on my next statement.* It still sounds polite, and the punctuation problem disappears.

GUIDE 35: Use a question mark after a direct question and after statements with questions appended.

> Are they hiring at BioTech, Inc.?

> Most of their training is in-house, isn't it?

GUIDE 36: Use a dash to (a) set off parenthetical elements containing internal commas, (b) emphasize a sentence interruption, or (c) separate an introductory list from a summarizing statement. The dash has legitimate uses. However, some writers use it whenever they know that punctuation is necessary, but they are not sure exactly what. The dash can be very effective, if not misused.

> Three top students—Gene Engle, Donna Hersh, and Mika Sato—won awards. (Use dashes to set off elements with internal commas.)

> Executives at Apple—despite rampant rumors in the stock market—remained quiet regarding dividend earnings. (Use dashes to emphasize a sentence interruption.)

> Japan, Taiwan, and Turkey—these were areas hard hit by recent earthquakes. (Use a dash to separate an introductory list from a summarizing statement)

GUIDE 37: Use parentheses to set off nonessential sentence elements, such as explanations, directions, questions, and references.

> Researchers find that the office grapevine (see Chapter 1 for more discussion) carries surprisingly accurate information.

Only two dates (February 15 and March 1) are suitable for the meeting.

Tip: Careful writers use parentheses to de-emphasize and the dash to emphasize parenthetical information. One expert said, "Dashes shout the news; parentheses whisper it."

GUIDE 38: Use quotation marks to (a) enclose the exact words of a speaker; (b) enclose the titles of articles, chapters, or other short works; and (c) enclose specific definitions of words or expressions.

"If you make your job important," said the consultant, "it's quite likely to return the favor." (Quotation marks enclose the exact words of a speaker.)

The recruiter said that she was looking for candidates with good communication skills. (Omit quotation marks because the exact words of the speaker are not quoted.)

In *The Wall Street Journal*, I saw an article titled "Communication for Global Markets." (Quotation marks enclose the title of an article. Italics identify the names of newspapers, magazines, and books.)

The term *videosize* means "to turn your message into a video for ease of access." (Quotation marks enclose the definition of a word.)

For jargon, slang, words used in a special sense such as humor or irony, and words following *stamped* or *marked*, some writers use italics. Other writers use quotation marks.

Computer criminals are often called *hackers* (or "hackers"). (Jargon)

My teenager said that the film *The Hunger Games* is *sick* (or "sick"). (Slang)

Justin claimed that he was *too ill* (or "too ill") to come to work yesterday. (Irony)

The package was stamped *Fragile* (or "Fragile"). (Words following *stamped*)

Tip: Never use quotation marks arbitrarily, as in *Our "spring" sale starts April 1.*

✓ Checkpoint
Add appropriate punctuation.

61. Will you please unsubscribe me from this mailing list as soon as possible

62. (Direct quotation) Our Super Bowl promotion said the owner will cost nearly $500,000

63. (De-emphasize) Two kinds of batteries see page 16 of the instruction booklet may be used in this camera

64. Tim wondered whether sentences could end with two periods

65. Stephanie plans to do a lot of chillaxing during her vacation

D-2n Capitalization

GUIDE 39: Capitalize proper nouns and proper adjectives. Capitalize the *specific* names of persons, places, institutions, buildings, religions, holidays, months, organizations, laws, races, languages, and so forth. Do not capitalize seasons, and do not capitalize common nouns that make *general* references.

Proper Nouns	Common Nouns
Michelle Deluca	the manufacturer's rep
Everglades National Park	the wilderness park
College of the Redwoods	the community college
Empire State Building	the downtown building
Environmental Protection Agency	the federal agency
Persian, Armenian, Hindi	modern foreign languages
Annual Spring Festival	in the spring

Proper Adjectives	
Hispanic markets	Italian dressing
Xerox copy	Japanese executives
Swiss chocolates	Reagan economics

GUIDE 40: Capitalize only specific academic courses and degrees.

Professor Donna Hernandez, PhD, will teach Accounting 121 next spring.

James Barker, who holds bachelor's and master's degrees, teaches marketing.

Jessica enrolled in classes in management, English, and business law.

GUIDE 41: Capitalize courtesy, professional, religious, government, family, and business titles when they precede names.

Mr. Jameson, Mrs. Alvarez, and Ms. Robinson (Courtesy titles)

Professor Andrews, Dr. Lee (Professional titles)

Rabbi Cohen, Pastor Williams, Pope Francis (Religious titles)

Senator Tom Harrison, Mayor Jackson (Government titles)

Uncle Edward, Mother Teresa, Cousin Vinney (Family titles)

Vice President Morris, Budget Director Lopez (Business titles)

Do not capitalize a title when it is followed by an appositive (that is, when the title is followed by a noun that renames or explains it).

> Only one professor, Jonathan Marcus, favored a tuition hike.

> Local candidates counted on their governor, Lee Jones, to help raise funds.

Do not capitalize titles following names unless they are part of an address:

> Mark Yoder, president of Yoder Enterprises, hired all employees.

> Paula Beech, director of Human Resources, interviewed all candidates.

> Send the package to Amanda Lopez, Advertising Manager, Cambridge Publishers, 20 Park Plaza, Boston, MA 02116. (Title in an address)

Generally, do not capitalize a title that replaces a person's name.

> Only the president, his chief of staff, and one senator made the trip.

> The director of marketing and the sales manager will meet at 1 p.m.

Do not capitalize family titles used with possessive pronouns.

> my mother, his father, your cousin

GUIDE 42: Capitalize all words of four or more letters in titles, subject lines, or headings—unless any of those words are the first or last words.

> I enjoyed the book *A Customer Is More Than a Name*. (Book title)

> Team Meeting to Discuss Deadlines Rescheduled for Friday (Subject line)

> We liked the article titled "Advice From a Pro: How to Say It With Pictures." (Article)

> Check the Advice and Resources link at the Career-Builder website.

(Note that the titles of books are italicized, but the titles of articles are enclosed in quotation marks.)

GUIDE 43: Capitalize names of geographic locations. Capitalize *north*, *south*, *east*, *west*, and their derivatives only when they represent specific geographic regions.

from the Pacific Northwest	heading northwest on the highway
living in the West	west of the city
Midwesterners, Southerners	western Oregon, southern Ohio
peace in the Middle East	a location east of the middle of the city

GUIDE 44: Capitalize the main words in the specific names of departments, divisions, or committees within business organizations. Do not capitalize general references.

> All forms are available from our Department of Human Resources.

> The Consumer Electronics Division launched an upbeat marketing campaign.

> We volunteered for the Employee Social Responsibility Committee.

> You might send an application to their personnel department.

GUIDE 45: Capitalize product names only when they refer to trademarked items. Do not capitalize the common names following manufacturers' names.

Dell laptop computer	Skippy peanut butter	NordicTrack treadmill
Eveready Energizer	Norelco razor	Plexiglas window
Coca-Cola	Uber ridesharing	Big Mac sandwich

GUIDE 46: Capitalize most nouns followed by numbers or letters (except in page, paragraph, line, and verse references).

Room 14	Exhibit A	Flight 12, Gate 43
Figure 2.1	Plan No. 1	Model Z2010

✓ **Checkpoint**

Capitalize all appropriate words.

66. vice president moore bought a new droid smartphone before leaving for the east coast.

67. when you come on tuesday, travel west on highway 5 and exit at mt. mckinley street.

68. The director of our human resources department called a meeting of the company's building security committee.

69. our manager and president are flying on american airlines flight 34 leaving from gate 69 at the dallas/fort worth international airport.

70. my father read a businessweek article titled can you build loyalty with bricks and mortar?

D-20 Number Usage

GUIDE 47: Use word form to express (a) numbers *ten* and under and (b) numbers beginning sentences. General references to numbers *ten* and under should be expressed in word form. Also use word form for numbers that begin sentences. If the resulting number involves more than two words, however, recast the sentence so that the number does not fall at the beginning.

> We received *six* text messages from *four* sales reps.

> *Fifteen* customers responded to our *three* cell phone ads today.

> A total of 155 smartphones were awarded as prizes. (Avoid beginning the sentence with a long number such as *one hundred fifty-five*.)

GUIDE 48: Use figures to express most references to numbers 11 and over.

> Over *150* people from *53* companies attended the two-day workshop.

> A four-ounce serving of Haagen-Dazs toffee crunch ice cream contains *300* calories and *19* grams of fat.

GUIDE 49: Use figures to express money, dates, clock time, decimals, and percentages.

> One item costs only *$1.95*; most, however, were priced between *$10* and *$35*. (Omit the decimals and zeros in even sums of money.)

> We scheduled a meeting for May 12. (Notice that we do NOT write May 12th.)

> We expect deliveries at 10:15 a.m. and again at 4 p.m. (Use lowercase *a.m.* and *p.m.*)

> All packages must be ready by 4 o'clock. (Do NOT write 4:00 o'clock.)

> When U.S. sales dropped *4.7* percent, net income fell *9.8* percent. (In contextual material use the word *percent* instead of the symbol %.)

GUIDE 50: Use a combination of words and figures to express sums of 1 million and over. Use words for small fractions.

> Orion lost *$62.9 million* in the latest fiscal year on revenues of *$584 million*. (Use a combination of words and figures for sums of 1 million and over.)

> Only one half of the registered voters turned out. (Use words for small fractions.)

Tip: To ease your memory load, concentrate on the numbers normally expressed in words: numbers *ten* and under, numbers at the beginning of a sentence, and small fractions. Nearly everything else in business is generally written with figures.

✓ Checkpoint

Correct any inappropriate expression of numbers or abbreviations.

71. Although he budgeted fifty dollars, Jake spent 94 dollars and 34 cents for supplies.

72. Is the meeting on November 7th or November 14th?

73. UPS deliveries arrive at nine AM and again at four fifteen PM.

74. The company applied for a fifty thousand dollar loan at six%.

75. The U.S. population is over 300,000,000, and the world population is estimated to be about 7,600,000,000.

Key to Grammar and Mechanics Checkpoint Exercises in Appendix D

This key shows all corrections. If you marked anything else, double-check the appropriate guideline.

1. Disney, destination

2. yearly, which

3. hour; however,

4. pavilion;

5. wedding;

6. If I *were* you, I would have *gone*

7. could have *written* . . . had *begun* earlier.

8. project manager *saw* . . . immediately *came*

9. project manager *were*

10. manager had *known* . . . would have *given*

11. time and talent *were* spent (Note that two subjects require a plural verb.)

12. attachments, *was* (Note that the subject is *message*.)

13. Each of . . . companies *is* (Note that the subject is *Each*.)

14. list of names and addresses *is* (Note that the subject is *list*.)

15. attorney *has*

16. My partner and *I* . . . but *yours*

17. was *hers*, but *its*

18. you and *me*

19. Neither the boss nor *I* knows whether *it's* broken, but its condition should have been reported to him or *me* earlier.

20. but *yours* and *hers*

21. *whomever*

22. *Whom* have you hired

23. for *whoever*

24. Matt and *I*

25. by *whoever*

26. Every employee must wear *their* picture identification badge. *OR: All employees* must wear *picture identification badges OR Every employee must wear a picture identification badge.*

27. slower career advancement, but *flexible scheduling* appeals to many workers. (Revise to avoid the vague pronoun *it*.)

28. Any renter must pay *their* rent . . . *OR: All renters* must pay *their* rent . . . .

29. reported that *their* computer . . . *OR reported that a computer* . . . .

30. communication. *These techniques are* particularly important . . . (Revise to avoid the vague pronoun *This*.)

31. My manager and *I* could not resist the *once-in-a-lifetime* opportunity.

32. John and *he* finished their task so *quickly* (Do not hyphenate *recently opened*.)

33. do *well* . . . *part-time* jobs and a few *full-time*

34. told him and *me* . . . *personally*.

35. *not-too-distant* future

36. class, Erin . . . with commas, semicolons,

37. studying punctuation,

38. program,

39. merchandising courses,

40. junior year, . . . in Los Angeles, Burbank,

41. Street, San Antonio, Texas 78220,

42. not, however,

43. paralegals, . . . next year,

44. May 15, 2012, . . . May 15, 2022.

45. fact,

46. sooner [delete comma]

47. car,

48. is [delete comma]

49. think, on the other hand, . . . buying [delete comma]

50. automakers are [delete comma] at this time [delete comma]

51. entry-level job; his long-term goal, however,

52. professors: Cameron Piercy, University of Kansas; Lora Lindsey, Ohio University; and Michael Malone, Central Florida College.

53. qualities: loyalty, initiative,

54. individuals; however,

55. region; therefore,

56. companies' . . . employees'

57. one week's time, . . . members'

58. appreciate *your* . . . CPA's

59. beneficiaries'

60. sister-in-law's

61. possible.

62. "Our Super Bowl promotion," said the owner, "will cost nearly $500,000."

63. Two kinds of batteries (see page 16 of the instruction booklet)

64. two periods.

65. *chillaxing* or "chillaxing"

66. Vice President Moore . . . Droid . . . East Coast

67. When . . .Tuesday, . . . Highway 5 . . . Mt. McKinley Street.

68. Human Resources Department . . . Building Security Committee

69. Our . . . American Airlines Flight 34 . . . Gate 69 at the Dallas/Fort Worth International Airport

70. My . . . *BusinessWeek* article titled "Can You Build Loyalty With Bricks and Mortar?"

71. $50 . . . $94.34

72. November 7 or November 14 [delete *th*]

73. 9 a.m. . . . 4:15 p.m. (Note only one period at the end of the sentence.)

74. $50,000 loan at 6 percent.

75. 300 million . . . 7.6 billion

Confusing Words

accede:	to agree or consent
exceed:	over a limit
accept:	to receive
except:	to exclude; (prep) but
adverse:	opposing; antagonistic
averse:	unwilling; reluctant
advice:	suggestion, opinion
advise:	to counsel or recommend
affect:	to influence
effect:	(n) outcome, result; (v) to bring about, to create
all ready:	prepared
already:	by this time
all right:	satisfactory
alright:	unacceptable variant spelling
altar:	structure for worship
alter:	to change
appraise:	to estimate
apprise:	to inform
ascent:	(n) rising or going up
assent:	(v) to agree or consent
assure:	to promise
ensure:	to make certain
insure:	to protect from loss
capital:	(n) city that is seat of government; wealth of an individual; (adj) chief
capitol:	building that houses state or national lawmakers
cereal:	breakfast food
serial:	arranged in sequence
cite:	to quote; to summon
site:	location
sight:	a view; to see
coarse:	rough texture
course:	route; part of a meal; unit of learning
complement:	that which completes
compliment:	(n) praise or flattery; (v) to praise or flatter
conscience:	regard for fairness
conscious:	aware
council:	governing body
counsel:	(n) advice, attorney, consultant; (v) to give advice

credible:	believable
creditable:	good enough for praise or esteem; reliable
desert:	(n) arid land; (v) to abandon
dessert:	sweet food
device:	invention or mechanism
devise:	to design or arrange
disburse:	to pay out
disperse:	to scatter widely
elicit:	to draw out
illicit:	unlawful
envelop:	(v) to wrap, surround, or conceal
envelope:	(n) a container for a written message
every day:	each single day
everyday:	ordinary
farther:	a greater distance
further:	additional
formally:	in a formal manner
formerly:	in the past
grate:	(v) to reduce to small particles; to cause irritation; (n) a frame of crossed bars blocking a passage
great:	(adj) large in size; numerous; eminent or distinguished
hole:	an opening
whole:	complete
imply:	to suggest indirectly
infer:	to reach a conclusion
lean:	(v) to rest against; (adj) not fat
lien:	(n) legal right or claim to property
liable:	legally responsible
libel:	damaging written statement
loose:	not fastened
lose:	to misplace
miner:	person working in a mine
minor:	(adj) lesser; (n) person under age
patience:	calm perseverance
patients:	people receiving medical treatment
personal:	private, individual
personnel:	employees
plaintiff:	(n) one who initiates a lawsuit
plaintive:	(adj) expressive of suffering or woe
populace:	(n) the masses; population of a place

populous:	(adj) densely populated	*then:*	adverb meaning "at that time"
precede:	to go before	*their:*	possessive form of *they*
proceed:	to continue	*there:*	at that place or point
precedence:	priority	*they're:*	contraction of *they are*
precedents:	events used as an example	*to:*	preposition; sign of the infinitive
principal:	(n) capital sum; school official; (adj) chief	*too:*	adverb meaning "also" or "to an excessive extent"
principle:	rule of action	*two:*	a number
stationary:	immovable	*waiver:*	abandonment of a claim
stationery:	writing material	*waver:*	to shake or fluctuate
than:	conjunction showing comparison		

160 Frequently Misspelled Words

absence	convenient	familiar	maintenance
accommodate	correspondence	fascinate	manageable
achieve	courteous	feasible	manufacturer
acknowledgment	criticize	February	mileage
across	decision	fiscal	miscellaneous
adequate	deductible	foreign	mortgage
advisable	defendant	forty	necessary
analyze	definitely	fourth	nevertheless
annually	dependent	friend	ninety
appointment	describe	genuine	ninth
argument	desirable	government	noticeable
automatically	destroy	grammar	occasionally
bankruptcy	development	grateful	occurred
becoming	disappoint	guarantee	offered
beneficial	dissatisfied	harass	omission
budget	division	height	omitted
business	efficient	hoping	opportunity
calendar	embarrass	immediate	opposite
canceled	emphasis	incidentally	ordinarily
catalog	emphasize	incredible	paid
changeable	employee	independent	pamphlet
column	envelope	indispensable	permanent
committee	equipped	interrupt	permitted
congratulate	especially	irrelevant	pleasant
conscience	evidently	itinerary	practical
conscious	exaggerate	judgment	prevalent
consecutive	excellent	knowledge	privilege
consensus	exempt	legitimate	probably
consistent	existence	library	procedure
control	extraordinary	license	profited

prominent	remittance	sufficient	unnecessarily
quality	representative	supervisor	usable
quantity	restaurant	surprise	usage
questionnaire	schedule	tenant	using
receipt	secretary	therefore	usually
receive	separate	thorough	valuable
recognize	similar	though	volume
recommendation	sincerely	through	weekday
referred	software	truly	writing
regarding	succeed	undoubtedly	yield

Key to Grammar and Mechanics

Chapter 1

1. The current graduating class will enter the most challenging job market in **years. Many** graduates do not know where to apply. [d, Guide 3, Comma splice. Use a semicolon or start a new sentence with *Many*.]
2. Researchers predict that a booming U.S. economy may not return **quickly. The** job market may take years to regain stability. [c, Guide 2, Run-on. Use a semicolon or start a new sentence with The *job*.]
3. Because recent graduates are entering a fast-paced, competitive, and highly connected digital **environment, communication** and technology skills are critical to career success. [b, Guide 1, Fragment]
4. Many applicants will apply for openings**; however,** those with exceptional communication skills will immediately stand out. [d, Guide 3, Comma splice. Use a semicolon or start new sentence with *however*.]
5. Surprisingly, many employers say that the ability to think critically, communicate clearly, and solve complex problems is more important than a candidate's undergraduate major. [a, Correctly punctuated]
6. The 9-to-5 job may soon be a relic of the **past if** millennials have their way. [b, Guide 1, Fragment]
7. Knowledge workers must be able to explain their **decisions; they** must be critical thinkers. [c, Run-on, Guide 2. Use a semicolon or start a new sentence with *They*.]
8. Informal communication travels through the **grapevine, which** is generally word-of-mouth communication. [b, Fragment, Guide 1]
9. Ethical companies experience less **litigation; they** also are the target of less government regulation. [d, Comma splice. Use a semicolon or start a new sentence with *They*.]
10. Even when an action is **legal, it** may violate generally accepted principles of right and wrong. [b, Fragment, Guide 1]

Chapter 2

1. Conflict and disagreement **are** normal and should be expected in team interactions. [Guide 7. Choose a plural verb to agree with the plural subjects *conflict* and *disagreement*.]
2. Have you **written** to other members of the virtual team? [Guide 4. Use the past participle verb *written*.]
3. One of the most frequently requested professional skills during job interviews **is** writing proficiency. [Guide 6. Choose a singular verb *is* to agree with singular subject *One*.]
4. I wish the CEO **were** more supportive of our current team project. [Guide 5. Use the subjunctive verb *were*.]
5. Better decisions and faster response time **explain** why organizations are using teams. [Guide 7. Choose the plural verb *explain* to agree with the plural subjects *decisions* and *time*.]
6. Neither the speaker nor members of the team **were** bothered by the technical mishap. [Guide 7. Make the verb agree with the closer subject *members*.]
7. Every piece of information including e-mails and texts **was** made public during the trial. [Guide 6. Choose the singular verb *was* to agree with the singular subject *piece*.]
8. A committee of students and faculty **is** examining strategies to improve campus conservation efforts. [Guide 9. Choose the singular verb *is* to agree with the collective noun *committee*.]

Chapter 3

9. Each of the newly hired employees must **choose** a team to join. [Guide 4. Use the present-tense verb *choose*.]
10. When two candidates have equal qualifications, the one who appears to be more polished and professional is more likely to be hired and promoted. [C]

1. Just between you and **me**, do you know how to curb ethnocentrism? [Guide 13. Use the objective case *me* as the object of the preposition *between*.]
2. During the bribery hearing, both **attorneys** questioned all witnesses thoroughly. [Guide 10. The noun *attorneys* does not change form when pluralized.]
3. Please send texts to my manager and **me** so that she and I both understand the situation. [Guide 13. Use the objective case *me* as the object of the preposition *to*.]
4. **It's** natural for most of us to gravitate toward those who are similar to us. [Guide 14. Use the contraction for *it is*.]
5. Starbucks has established itself successfully in China and India by adjusting **its** brand to local markets. [Guide 14. Choose the possessive pronoun *its*, which is written without an apostrophe.]
6. Please send your report to the administrative assistant or **me** when it's finished. [Guide 13. Choose the objective case pronoun *me* as the object of the preposition *to*.]
7. **All sales reps** must improve their writing skills to handle chat sessions. [Guide 17. Sensitive writers prefer a plural construction.]
8. The contract will be awarded to **whoever** submits the lowest bid. [Guide 16. Use the subjective case pronoun *whoever* as it functions as the subject of the verb *submits*.]
9. Most applications were made in time, but **yours** and **hers** missed the deadline. [Guide 14. Use the possessive pronouns *yours* and *hers*, which are written without apostrophes.]
10. It must have been she who sent the e-mail to Mason and **me**. [Guides 12 and 15. Choose the subjective pronoun *she* as it functions as the complement. Use the objective case *me* following the preposition *to*.]

Chapter 4

1. Writing concise, purposeful, and audience-centered messages is a skill that does not come **naturally** to most people. [Guide 19. Use the adverb *naturally* to describe the action of the verb *come*.]
2. **Well-written** business messages sound conversational but professional. [Guide 20. Hyphenate two or more adjectives that are combined to describe a noun.]
3. Many organizations use wikis to post **up-to-the minute** information about projects. [Guide 20. Hyphenate words combined to describe a noun.]
4. Most of our **newly written** team documents were posted **quickly** to the wiki. [Guides 20 and 19. Don't hyphenate *ly*-ending adverbs. Do add *ly* to the adjective *quick* to form an adverb.]
5. We all felt **bad** when one member lost her laptop and had no backup. [Guide 19. Use the adjective *bad* following the linking verb *felt*.]
6. The 3-x-3 writing process provides **step-by-step** instructions for preparing messages. [Guide 20. Hyphenate compound adjectives.]
7. The written report and its bibliography were a **three-week** project for our team. [Guide 20. Hyphenate compound adjectives.]

8. Our project ran more **smoothly** after Nazarnin reorganized the team. [Guide 19. Use the adverb *smoothly* to describe the verb *ran*.]
9. **Locally installed** online collaboration tools are **easy to use** and work well. [Guide 20. Do not hyphenate *ly*-ending adverbs nor hyphenate words that are familiar but are not joined to describe an adjective.]
10. Samantha thought she had done **well** when she wrote her part of the team report. [Guide 19. Use the adverb *well*, not the adjective *good*, to describe how she did.]

Chapter 5

1. More than 10,000 hungry professionals named yogurt, protein **bars, jerky,** and string cheese as the healthiest office snacks. [Guide 21. Use commas to separate three or more items or words.]
2. By learning to distinguish between dependent and independent **clauses,** you can avoid serious sentence faults. [Guide 22. Use a comma to separate an introductory phrase or clause.]
3. We hired Dalia **Aljaja,** who was the applicant with the best **qualifications,** as our new social media manager. [Guide 25. Use commas to set off internal sentence interrupters.]
4. When you use company **e-mail,** you must realize that your messages are monitored. [Guide 22. Use a comma to separate an introductory clause.]
5. Active-voice verbs are best in most business **messages,** but passive-voice verbs are useful when sensitivity is required. [Guide 23. Use a comma before a coordinating conjunction in a compound sentence.]
6. Although the company was founded on **April 15, 2015,** it did not show a profit until **June 30, 2020.** [Guide 24. Use a comma to separate an introductory clause.]
7. The new social media start-up, **by the way,** is flourishing and is expected to show a profit soon. [Guide 25. Use commas to set off internal sentence interrupters.]
8. After he **graduates,** Luke plans to move to Austin and find work there. [Guide 22. Use a comma to separate an introductory clause.]
9. Last fall our company introduced policies regulating the use of cell **phones, texting,** and e-mail on the job. [Guide 21. Use commas to separate three or more words or items in a series.]
10. The problem with many company telecommunication policies is that the policies are **self-policed** [delete comma] and never enforced. [Guide 23. No comma is necessary because the sentence is not compound.]

Chapter 6

1. New product names must be **interesting; however,** many of the best names are already taken. [Guide 27. Use a semicolon before the conjunctive adverb *however* to join closely related independent clauses.]
2. Although developers dreamed up a snazzy new **app,** it lacked an exciting name. [Guide 27. Don't use a semicolon unless both clauses are truly independent.]
3. Tech specialists find it difficult to name new **products; consequently,** they prefer hiring specialists. [Guide 27. Use a semicolon before the conjunctive adverb *consequently* to join clauses.]
4. A distinctive name helps establish the tone for a product; it acts as the primary handle for a brand. [C. Use a semicolon to join closely related independent clauses.]
5. Branding a product is a creative **endeavor;** the name becomes a product's shorthand. [Guide 27. Use a semicolon to join closely related independent clauses.]
6. Global names must be appealing in such faraway places as **Beijing, China; Yokohama, Japan;** and Dubai **City, United** Arab Emirates. [Guide 28. Use semicolons to separate items in a series when the items contain internal commas.]
7. One naming expert warned companies with the following **comment:** "Be aware of global consequences. For example, Bimbo is the name of a Mexican baking conglomerate. However, the word in English

has an unsavory meaning." [Guide 30. Use a colon to introduce long quotations.]
8. Company and product names are developed by combining the following three linguistic **elements:** morphemes, phonemes, and syntax. [Guide 29. Use a colon after a complete thought introduces a list of items.]
9. Some English sounds (such as L, V, F, and W) are considered **feminine;** others (such as X, M, and Z) are viewed as masculine. [Guide 27. Use a semicolon to join closely related independent clauses.]
10. Among the company officers judging new names were Daniele Waters, vice **president;** Rachel Lohr, **CFO;** and Lucia Rosales, manager. [Guide 28. Use semicolons to separate items in a series when the items contain internal commas.]

Chapter 7

1. In just one **year's** time, Chynna increased her blog followers by 50 percent. [Guide 31. Add an apostrophe and *s* when an ownership word does not end in an *s*.]
2. Max wondered whether all sales **managers'** databases needed to be updated. [Guide 32. If an ownership word ends in an *s* and is plural (*managers*), add an apostrophe.]
3. Even her friends resented **Olivia's** smoking in the hallways. [Guide 33. Add an apostrophe and *s* to make a noun possessive when it precedes a gerund.]
4. Many followers of **James's** blog commented on the overuse of the Reply All button. [Guide 32. If an ownership word ends in an *s* or an *s* sound, add an apostrophe and *s*.]
5. Our three top sales **reps**—Ryan, Ashley, and **Leah**—received substantial bonuses. [Guide 36. Use dashes to set off parenthetical elements containing internal commas.]
6. You must replace the ink cartridge (**see** page 8 in the **manual**) before printing. [Guide 37. Use parentheses to set off nonessential sentence elements.]
7. Success often depends on an **individual's** ability to adapt to change. [Guide 31. Add an apostrophe and *s* to show ownership.]
8. (Direct quotation) "The death of e-**mail,**" said Mike Song, "**has** been greatly **exaggerated.**" [Guide 38. Use quotation marks to enclose the exact words of a quotation.]
9. The most helpful article was titled "**Ten** Tools for Building Your Own Mobile **App.**" [Guide 38. Use quotation marks to enclose the title of an article.]
10. Our staffing meeting starts at 10 a.m. sharp, doesn't **it?** [Guide 35. Use a question mark after a direct question.]

Chapter 8

1. Our **district manager** and **director of operations** recommended the purchase a new **Nordictrack** treadmill for the health center. [See Guides 41 and 45 for explanations.]
2. The secretary of state of the **United States** urged members of the **European Union** to continue to seek peace in the **Middle East.** [See Guides 41, 39, and 43 for explanations.]
3. Passengers of **United Airlines** must exit the plane at **Gate** 2B in **Terminal** 4 when they reach **Seattle-Tacoma International Airport.** [Guides 39, 46]
4. My **aunt,** who lives in the **South,** has a **Big Mac** and a **Diet Coke** for **lunch** nearly every day. [Guides 41, 43, 45]
5. Our corporate **vice president** and **president** met with several **directors** on the **West Coast** to discuss how to develop **apps** for **Facebook.** [Guides 41, 43, 39]
6. Three countries with high tax rates are **Belgium, Germany,** and **Denmark,** reported **Professor Du-Babcock,** who teaches at the **City University of Hong Kong.** [Guides 39, 41]
7. Alyson Davis, who heads our **Consumer Services Division,** has a **master's degree** in **marketing** from **California State University,** Long Beach. [Guides 44, 40, 39]

8. Please consult **Figure** 2.3 in **Chapter** 2 to obtain **US Census Bureau** population figures for the **Northeast**. [Guides 46, 39, 43]
9. Last **summer** did you see the article titled "The Global Consequences of **Using Crops** for **Fuel**"? [Guides 39, 42]
10. Deidre plans to take courses in **management, economics,** and **history** in the **spring**. [Guides 40, 39]

Chapter 9

1. Amazon employees are said to spend **two** days every **two** years working in customer service. [Guide 47]
2. **Sixty-four percent** of consumers have made a purchase decision based on social media content. [Guides 47, 49]
3. Faced with a **$522 million** [delete *dollar*] deficit, the mayor sent pink slips to **15,000** city employees. [Guides 49, 48]
4. UPS deliveries are expected before **10 a.m.** and again at **4:30 p.m.** [Guide 49]
5. Although tweets can now be **280** characters, about **9 percent** are exactly **140** characters. [Guides 48, 49]
6. On **April 15** our attorney notified all **four** managers of the lawsuit. [Guides 49, 47]
7. You can burn **150** calories by walking as little as **30** minutes. [Guide 48]
8. A **five**-year loan for a **$25,000** new car with **20 percent** down would have monthly payments of **$356**. [Guides 47, 49]
9. Although he expected to spend **$50** or less, Jake actually spent **$65** for the gift. [Guide 49]
10. In the last election, only **one half** of the eligible voters turned out. [Guide 50]

Chapter 10

1. Colman complained that his **capital** investments had been **adversely affected.**
2. The **principal** part of the manager's persuasive message contained a **compliment** and valuable **advice.**
3. Before writing the sales message, did you **already analyze** the product's major and **minor** appeals?
4. In responding to the irate customer, Marilyn made a **conscious** effort to show **patience** and present credible facts.
5. Even in **everyday** business affairs, we strive to reach **further** and go beyond what is expected.
6. Before you **proceed** with the report, please check those **surprising** statistics.
7. It's **usually** better to de-emphasize bad news **than** to spotlight it.
8. **Incidentally**, passive-voice verbs can help you make a statement less **personal** when **necessary.**
9. Customers are more **accepting** of **disappointing** news if they are **assured** that **their** requests were heard and treated fairly.
10. The customer's complaint **elicited** an immediate response that carefully presented the facts and was not **too** long.

Chapter 11

1. Many jobs in **today's** digital workplace are never **advertised; they're** part of the hidden job market.
2. Some job seekers paid **$600** each to attend **12** sessions that promised expert job-searching **advice.**
3. One **credible** study revealed that **30** percent of jobs go to **companies'** inside candidates.
4. To excel at **networking**, a candidate must have **an easy-to-remember** e-mail address.
5. My friend wondered if I had **already** prepared a **30-second** elevator **speech**.
6. When Kaitlyn and **I** were collecting data for the **report**, we realized that **Twitter** and Facebook could be significant.
7. **Today's** workers must brush up their marketable **skills; otherwise**, they may not find another job after being laid off.

8. Being active on LinkedIn and building an impressive Internet presence **are** important, but the looseness of these connections **means** you shouldn't expect **too** much from them.
9. Just between you and **me**, one of the best **strategies** in networking **is** distributing business cards with your personal tagline.
10. On January **1** our company **president** revealed that we would be hiring **30** new employees, which was excellent news for everyone.

Chapter 12

1. Among the oddly named towns in the United States **are** [delete colon] What Cheer, **Iowa**; Peculiar, **Missouri**; and Cheesequake, New Jersey.
2. After our supervisor and **she** returned from their meeting at **2 p.m.**, we were able to sort the **customers'** names more quickly.
3. **Six** of the 18 workers in my department were **fired; as a result**, we had to work harder to achieve our goals.
4. **Jeffrey's** presentation to a nonprofit group netted him only **$300**, which is a tenth of his usual **honorarium**, but he believes in pro bono work.
5. Of all the discoveries and inventions in human **history**, the **four** greatest are said to be **these:** speech, fire, agriculture, and the wheel.
6. Our latest press release written by our **Corporate Communication Department** announces the opening of three Asian offices.
7. In his justification report dated September **1**, Justin argued that expansion to **12** branch offices could boost annual revenue to **$22 million**.
8. The practicality and advisability of opening **12** branch offices **is** what will be discussed in the **consultant's feasibility** report.
9. **Three** categories of **apps** (social media, productivity, and **entertainment**) are most popular for installing on smartphones.
10. Because some organizations prefer **single-spaced reports**, be sure to check with your organization to learn **its** preference.

Chapter 13

1. If you face **writer's block**, you should review your **three** main reasons for writing.
2. Our Manager and CEO both worked on the **30-page proposal, which** was due immediately.
3. Supervisors in **two departments** complained that **their** departments should have been consulted.
4. The RFP and **its** attachments arrived **too** late for my manager and **me** to complete the necessary research.
5. Although we worked **every day** on the proposal, we felt **bad** that we could not meet the **May 15** deadline.
6. Daryl had **three interviews**, and in each one he was asked to demonstrate his critical **thinking** [delete comma] and communication skills.
7. Although **short**, a successful mission statement should capture your business's goals and **values in** a few succinct sentences.
8. A proposal budget cannot be changed if costs **rise later; consequently**, it must be written **carefully**.
9. Entrepreneur Stephanie **Rivera**, publisher of **an** urban event **calendar**, relies on social media to broadcast her message.
10. Stephanie asked Jake and **me** to help her write a business **plan that** would guide her new company and garner **permanent** funding.

Chapter 14

1. A poll of **2,500** employees revealed that **four-fifths** of them said they feared giving a presentation more **than** anything else they could think of.
2. The **CEO's** assistant scheduled my colleague and **me** for a **15-minute** presentation to explain the new workplace sustainability initiative.
3. PowerPoint presentations, claims one **expert**, should be no longer **than** 20 minutes and have no more than ten slides.

4. The introduction to a presentation should accomplish **three goals:** (a) capture attention, (b) establish **credibility**, and (c) preview main points.
5. My accountant and **I** are **grateful** to be asked to make a short **presentation**; however, we may not be able to cover the entire budget.
6. A list with **40** tips for inexperienced speakers **is** found in the article titled "Quick Tips **for** Speakers."
7. In the **spring** our **company's** stock value is expected to **rise** at least 10 percent.
8. The **director** of operations made a **20-minute** presentation giving **step-by-step** instructions on achieving our sustainability goals.
9. The appearance and mannerisms of a speaker **definitely affect** a **listener's** evaluation of the message.
10. Because the **boss's** daughter was a dynamic speaker who had founded a successful **company**, she earned at least **$20,000** for each presentation.

Chapter 15

1. When searching for **jobs**, candidates discovered that the résumé is more likely to be used to screen **candidates than** for making hiring decisions.
2. If you have **ten** or fewer **years** of experience, **it's** customary to prepare a one-page résumé.
3. To conduct a safe online job search, you **should** [delete colon] (a) **use** only reputable job boards, **(b)** keep careful records, and (c) limit the number of sites on which you post your résumé.
4. **Today's** employers use **sites** such as Facebook to learn about potential employees, **which** means that a job seeker must maintain a professional online presence.
5. Although action verbs make a résumé appeal to a recruiter, applicant tracking systems often **look** for nouns in three **categories:** (a) job titles, (b) technical **skills,** and (c) certification.
6. Luca wondered whether it was **all right** to ask his professor for employment **advice.** [Replace question mark]

7. At last **month's** staff **meeting**, team members examined several **candidates'** résumés.
8. Rather **than** schedule **face-to-face interviews**, the team investigated videoconferencing.
9. **Eleven** applicants will be interviewed on **April 10**; consequently, we may need to work late to accommodate them.
10. Although as many as **25** percent of jobs are found on the **Internet**, the **principal** source of jobs still involves networking.

Chapter 16

1. Despite the heavy use of **e-mail**, many **employers** use the telephone to reach candidates and set up **their** initial interviews.
2. Most interviews **usually** cover the same kinds of **questions; therefore**, smart candidates prepare for them.
3. When you are asked to tell about **yourself**, experts agree that you should answer in no more than **two minutes** [delete comma] and keep the response targeted on the job.
4. In interviewing job **candidates**, recruiters have the following three **purposes:** assessing their skills, discussing their **experience**, and deciding whether they are a good fit for the organization.
5. If your job history has gaps in **it**, be prepared to explain what you did during this **time** [delete comma] and how you kept **up-to-date** in your field.
6. Interviewing is a **two-way street**, and candidates should be prepared with **their** own meaningful questions.
7. Yired was asked whether she had a **bachelor's degree** [delete comma] and whether she had three **years'** experience.
8. If you are **conscientious** and want to create a good **impression**, be sure to write a **thank-you** message after a job interview.
9. When **Yired's** interview was **over**, she told friends that she had done **well**.
10. Yired was **all ready** to send a thank-you **message** [delete comma] when she realized she could not spell the **interviewer's** name.

Test Your Etiquette IQ Responses

Chapter 1

1. **False.** Never sign anyone's name to a document without permission. No matter how innocuous it seems, you never know how perilous it could be for you.
2. **True.** Much depends on the relationship with your manager, but generally you can observe a common e-mail rule: Respond to e-mails within 24 hours. It's reasonable to set boundaries on your free time. By the way, if you are a manager or boss, don't send demanding e-mails or texts to employees on weekends or after hours.
3. **False.** Should you phone your vacationing coworker with a work question? Certainly not! Everyone deserves a vacation. Get your information elsewhere. It's also considerate to avoid sending texts or e-mail requests that demand immediate responses after working hours. If at all possible, wait until regular work time to conduct your business unless you know your receiver works 24/7.

Chapter 2

1. **False.** At a networking function, you should plan to spend about five to seven minutes with each person and then move on.
2. **False.** Never perform personal grooming tasks (such as combing your hair or clipping your fingernails) during a business meeting.
3. **True.** Always respect the personal space and privacy of individuals. Never open the closed door of a coworker or superior. Decide whether your business is important enough to interrupt the person by knocking.

Chapter 3

1. **False.** Americans tend to assume that others around the world do things as they do. Shaking hands and maintaining eye contact are accepted behaviors in the United States, but in other parts of the world, people may not want to shake hands, and eye contact may be offensive.
2. **False.** When abroad, it's wise to remember that Americans are often accused of being too loud, informal, and overly expressive with body language. Show restraint.
3. **True.** Show respect in more formal environments by opening doors and allowing older businesspeople to enter and be seated first.

Chapter 4

1. **False.** It's not wise to take even short personal calls at work. Before doing so, learn what your organization's policy is. Tell your friends and family your work hours, cautioning them not to call. Remember that how you act at work sends a message about your professionalism.
2. **False.** Among the most offensive people in open offices are *speaker freakers*, those who take their calls with speaker on. This practice is especially disruptive in open offices or those with cubicles. If you must have your hands free, get a headset.
3. **False.** First, don't shout to anyone over the top of cubicles. Second, don't eavesdrop on conversations. Third, never give advice to a coworker about information you overheard on any call. It's difficult working in close surroundings, but try to observe others' privacy and personal space.

Chapter 5

1. **False.** Don't friend everyone. It's important to maintain boundaries between your work life and personal life. Do you really want to see your boss in a bathing suit? Remember that Facebook is for friends; Twitter is for everyone.
2. **False.** The person facing you should always take precedence over an incoming text.
3. **True.** Although it's wise to warn coworkers by texting that you will be late, it's even better to make sure you are on time with proper planning.

Chapter 6

1. **True.** Never divulge confidential information told to you by employees. As a general rule, whether you are a manager or an employee, it's better not to discuss your own personal affairs with colleagues.
2. **False.** It is good manners to simulate a knock by tapping lightly on the wall before entering a cubicle; even better is to call or e-mail in advance to ask about a good time for your visit.
3. **False.** Do not expect to be good buddies with your boss, regardless of any similarity in age or personality. Realize that your boss is in charge. Be friendly at business functions, but don't strive to socialize outside of business hours.

Chapter 7

1. **False.** Never forward e-mail messages without first seeking the permission of the sender. A message sent to you was meant for your eyes only. The writer may have used a totally different tone if the message were going to the secondary audience.
2. **False.** Contrary to what some believe, e-mails should be held to the same standards as other workplace documents. Ditch the slang, use proper punctuation, and be sure to proofread before you hit Send.
3. **False.** Don't make instant enemies by storing smelly food in a communal refrigerator. And certainly don't warm it up the next day in the office microwave. If you must store something smelly in the refrigerator, double-wrap it and remove it as soon as possible. On the topic of office food, if you didn't put food in the refrigerator, don't eat it.

Chapter 8

1. **False.** Although it's acceptable to grab a bag of chips or a cookie on your way out the door, don't abuse your company's generosity. The office goal is to make your workplace comfortable, not help you entertain.
2. **True.** Etiquette authorities say that even though personal gifts may be prohibited within an organization, it is acceptable to show appreciation by sending a gourmet food basket or a subscription to a trade magazine for the entire office.
3. **True.** Business cards should be treated as gifts. After accepting a card, you should admire it and perhaps say something about it. Don't stuff it in your pocket or immediately write something on it.

Chapter 9

1. **False.** You should say, "Mr. Lopez, I would like to introduce Lucy Larios, a new office employee." The senior-ranking person should be mentioned first. However, when introducing a guest, client, or business partner, that person should always be the first to be introduced to coworkers and superiors, regardless of the peers' or supervisors' rank or seniority.
2. **False.** You should smile and calmly say, "I remember meeting you, but I can't remember your name." Don't try to bluff your way through your encounter. Because many people can't remember names, you should help others remember yours by announcing it when you greet someone who may have forgotten your name. Don't expect people to remember your name.
3. **False.** It is no longer necessary for a man to wait for a woman to extend her hand. Men and women are workplace equals today.

Chapter 10

1. **False.** It's always wise to talk with your superior about any behavior that seems to violate office expectations. However, it is true that more and more companies realize that allowing personalization of work spaces helps normalize the idea of a working parent having non-work commitments.
2. **False.** Never take home any office supplies. No matter how entitled you feel, it is thievery.
3. **True.** It is your responsibility to support your boss's decisions, even if you disagree with them. You can strive to make changes but do so constructively and through the proper channels.

Chapter 11

1. **True.** It may be disruptive to carry on a conversation in today's open offices. In addition, you don't want everyone to hear your conversation.
2. **False.** You should wait to sit down and ask where you may sit.
3. **False.** It is generally not a good idea to give personal or expensive gifts to your boss.

Chapter 12

1. **False.** Many workers dislike voice-mail messages. If possible, wait until she returns to talk with her in person or on the phone. Sending an e-mail is also possible.
2. **False.** Don't do it! As an employee, you have a responsibility to contact your employer regarding absence and lateness. If you text, it could give the impression that you have something to hide. It's better to make a phone call.
3. **True.** Delivering bad news such as a reprimand is better done privately. If your goal is to change behavior, private talks are more effective than humiliating public dress-downs.

Chapter 13

1. **False.** In an office environment, if everyone contributes and if you occasionally use the coffee or pastries, you are obligated to contribute. Always contribute your fair share toward group gifts, treats, or housekeeping.

2. **False.** Even office casual has its boundaries (e.g., no bare midriffs, no sloppy jeans or sweatshirts, no flip-flops). If you are striving for a promotion, try to dress one or two notches above office casual.
3. **False.** The first person should hold the door for whomever follows, regardless of gender.

Chapter 14

1. **False.** Sex, politics, religions, and other sensitive topics are off limits no matter how well you think you know the others.
2. **False.** Expect the host, whether male or female, to pay for a meal. Don't offer to pay for your own meal.
3. **True.** You should not order liquor, appetizers, or desserts unless the host does, and your meal should not cost more than the host's. If unsure about the most appropriate selections, ask your host for recommendations.

Chapter 15

1. **False.** Sharing your decision to search for another job with coworkers may make you feel more comfortable but doing so forces you into a position of weakness. A coworker could easily slip up, and your boss might hear of your decision long before you are ready to leave.
2. **False.** Hiring managers, recruiters, and human resources professionals are busy people. Don't waste their time and risk angering them with multiple applications.
3. **True.** This seems extreme, but it is a recommendation that makes sense for anyone whose phone never leaves his or her side. Hiring managers may be reluctant to invest in those whose lives revolve around their phones.

Chapter 16

1. **False.** In the time of the COVID-19 pandemic, a new greeting etiquette is emerging: Most people are striving to avoid shaking hands. In this situation it would be better to smile, announce your name, and wave or nod your head keeping your hands tucked away or busy holding something. Don't look awkward and try to explain why you are going "touchless."
2. **True.** This is tricky because you don't want to offend the interviewer. However, times are changing. Although handshaking was a time-honored greeting before the COVID-19 pandemic, many now prefer other ways to acknowledge each other. If you feel obligated to shake hands, you could do so, while avoiding touching your face, and then wash your hands or apply an antibacterial wipe as soon as possible.
3. **True.** Taking a few notes during an interview conveys a sincere interest in what your interviewers have to say and gives you a chance to jot down a question to ask at the appropriate time. However, some hiring managers think negatively of an applicant who shows up and starts taking electronic notes. Doing so forces the interviewee to lose eye contact with the interviewer.

References

Chapter 1

[1] Nordstrom expands in New York City with opening of flagship store. (2019, October 24). Press Release. *The Wall Street Journal.* Retrieved from http://wsj.com

[2] Andrews, T. M. (2017, September 12). Nordstrom's new concept: A clothing store with no clothes for sale. *The Washington Post.* Retrieved from https://www.washingtonpost.com

[3] Nordstrom is No. 16 in the Internet Retailer 2018 Top 1000. Retrieved from https://www.digitalcommerce360.com; Hatch, D. (2012, May 15). Nordstrom in fashion with social media, mobile tech. *U. S. News.* Retrieved from http://money.usnews.com

[4] Mau, D. (2018, July 20). Are influencer brands the key to bringing millennials to department stores? *Fashionista.* Retrieved from https://fashionista.com

[5] Elliott, L. (2016, January 24). Fourth industrial revolution brings promise and peril for humanity. *The Guardian.* Retrieved from https://www.theguardian.com; Manyika, J., Lund, S., Chui, M., Bughin, J., Woetzel, J., Batra, P., Ko, R., & Sanghvi, S. (2017, November). Jobs lost, jobs gained: What the future of work will mean for jobs, skills, and wages. McKinsey Global Institute. Retrieved from https://www.mckinsey.com

[6] Manyika, J. (2017, May). Technology, jobs, and the future of work. McKinsey Global Institute. Retrieved from https://www.mckinsey.com

[7] Hart Research Associates. (2018, July). Fulfilling the American dream: Liberal education and the future of work. Selected findings from online surveys of business executives and hiring managers conducted on behalf of the Association of American Colleges & Universities, pp. 14–15. Retrieved from https://www.aacu.org; Satell, G. (2015, February 6). Why communication is today's most important skill. *Forbes.* Retrieved from http://www.forbes.com

[8] National Association of Colleges and Employers. (2017, November). Job outlook 2018: How employers view candidates, p. 28. Retrieved from http://careerservices.wayne.edu; Hart Research Associates. (2018, July). Fulfilling the American dream: Liberal education and the future of work. Selected findings from online surveys of business executives and hiring managers conducted on behalf of the Association of American Colleges & Universities, pp. 14–15. Retrieved from https://www.aacu.org

[9] Duxbury, L., & Lanctot, A. (2017, April 20). Carleton University. Retrieved from https://newsroom.carleton.ca

[10] Solomon, G. (2018, August 9). Why mastering writing skills can help future-proof your career. *Forbes.* Retrieved from https://www.forbes.com

[11] College Board: The National Commission on Writing. (2004, September). Writing: A ticket to work . . . Or a ticket out: A survey of business leaders, p. 3. Retrieved from http://www.collegeboard.com; O'Rourke, IV, J. S. (2013). *Management communication: A case-analysis approach* (5th ed.). Boston: Prentice Hall, p. 9; Canavor, N. (2012). *Business writing in the digital age.* Los Angeles: Sage, p. 3.

[12] College Board: The National Commission on Writing. (2004, September). Writing: A ticket to work . . . Or a ticket out: A survey of business leaders. Retrieved from http://www.collegeboard.com

[13] Fottrell, Q. (2018, August 4). People spend most of their waking hours staring at screens. *MarketWatch.* Retrieved from https://www.marketwatch.com

[14] Bezerra, J., Bock, W., Candelon, F., Chai, S., Choi, E., Corwin, J., DiGrande, S., Gulshan, R., Michael, D. C., & Varas, A. (2015, January 15). The mobile revolution: How mobile technologies drive a trillion-dollar impact. The Boston Consulting Group. Retrieved from https://www.bcgperspectives.com

[15] Leveling up: How to win in the skills economy. (2016). PayScale. Retrieved from https://www.payscale.com

[16] Schawbel, D. (2016, May 17). How to win in the skills economy study. WorkplaceTrends. Retrieved from https://workplacetrends.com

[17] Marr, B. (2018, August 6). Seven job skills of the future (that AIs and robots can't do better than humans). *Forbes.* Retrieved from https://www.forbes.com

[18] Drucker, P. (1989, May). New realities, new ways of managing. *Business Month,* pp. 50–51.

[19] Surawski, B. (2019). Who is a "knowledge worker"—Clarifying the meaning of the term through comparison with synonymous and associated terms. *Management, 23*(1), 105–133. doi:10.2478/manment-2019-0007; Rasmus, D. W. (2012, June 24). What is an information worker? Serious Insights. Retrieved from https://www.seriousinsights.net; Baumol, W. J., Blackman, S. A., & Wolff, E. N. (1989). *Productivity and American leadership: The long view.* Cambridge, CT: MIT Press.

[20] Kelly, K. (2012, February 17). Q&A: Hacker historian George Dyson sits down with *Wired's* Kevin Kelly. *Wired Magazine* (March 2012). Retrieved from http://www.wired.com

[21] United States Department of Labor. Bureau of Labor Statistics. (2018, April 13). Occupational outlook handbook. Retrieved from https://www.bls.gov

[22] Bezerra, J., Bock, W., Candelon, F., Chai, S., Choi, E., Corwin, J., DiGrande, S., Gulshan, R., Michael, D. C., & Varas, A. (2015, January 15). The mobile revolution: How mobile technologies drive a trillion-dollar impact. The Boston Consulting Group. Retrieved from https://www.bcgperspectives.com

[23] Lohr, S. (2017, November 1). Where the STEM jobs are (and where they aren't). *The New York Times.* Retrieved from https://www.usnews.com.

[24] Rogers, K. (2018, September 7). Manufacturing is firing on all cylinders, but a lack of skilled workers is squeezing the sector. CNBC. Retrieved from https://www.cnbc.com

[25] Weber, L., & Cutter, C. (2019, May 10). A wake-up call for grads: Entry-level jobs aren't so entry level any more. *The Wall Street Journal.* Retrieved from https://www.wsj.com

[26] Belkin, D. (2017, June 5). Exclusive test data: Many colleges fail to improve critical-thinking skills. *The Wall Street Journal.* https://www.wsj.com

[27] Allcott, H., & Gentzkow, M. (2017). Social media and fake news in the 2016 election. *Journal of Economic Perspectives, 31*(2), 211–236. doi:10.1257/jep.31.2.211

[28] Rainie, L., & Anderson, J. (2017, May 3). The future of jobs and jobs training. Pew Research Center. Retrieved from https://www.pewinternet.org

29 Buckland, K., & Sano, N. (2018, February). Toyota's way changed the world's factories. Now the retool. *Bloomberg*. Retrieved from https://www.bloomberg.com

30 Forbes Human Resources Council. (2019, February 12). Lattice or ladder? 10 best ways for professionals to advance their careers. *Forbes*. Retrieved from https://www.forbes.com; Benko, C., Anderson, M., & Vickberg, S. (2011, January 1). The corporate lattice: A strategic response to the changing world of work. Deloitte. Retrieved from https://www2.deloitte.com; Benko, C., & Anderson, M. (2010). *The corporate lattice: Achieving high performance in the changing world of work.* Deloitte Development, pp. 3–4.

31 Rainie, L., & Anderson, J. (2017, May 3). The future of jobs and jobs training. Pew Research Center. Retrieved from https://www.pewinternet.org

32 Gee, K. (2017, October 17). These companies will pay you to learn your job. *The Wall Street Journal*. Retrieved from https://www.wsj.com

33 Househ, A. A. (2018, August 29). IBM taps other industries to create its new collar workforce. Workforce. Retrieved from https://www.workforce.com

34 Cited in Everson, K. (2015, June 29). Be a Boy Scout: Prepare for digital badging. Chief Learning Officer. Retrieved from http://www.clomedia.com

35 Morgan, H. (2014, September 3). How to be a better communicator in the workplace. *US News & World Report*. Retrieved from http://money.usnews.com

36 Madell, R. (2020, May 26). Job outlook for recent graduates. Retrieved from https://usnews.com

37 National Association of Colleges and Employers. (2017, November). Job outlook 2018: How employers view candidates, p. 28. Retrieved from http://careerservices.wayne.edu

38 Ibid., p. 30.

39 Hart Research Associates. (2018, July). Fulfilling the American dream: Liberal education and the future of work. Selected findings from online surveys of business executives and hiring managers conducted on behalf of the Association of American Colleges & Universities, pp. 14–15. Retrieved from https://www.aacu.org

40 Jones, J. M. (2018, October 9). Confidence in higher education down since 2015. Gallup blog. Retrieved from https://news.gallup.com

41 Association of Public & Land-Grant Universities. (2016). How does a college degree improve graduates' employment and earnings potential? Retrieved from http://www.aplu.org; Rampell, C. (2013, February 19). College premium: Better pay, better prospects. Economix Blogs, *New York Times*. Retrieved from https://economix.blogs.nytimes.com

42 Beach, G. (2018, June 26). Hard-pressed by soft skills, CIOs face talent challenge. *The Wall Street Journal, CIO Journal*. Retrieved from http://www.aplu.org

43 National Association of Colleges and Employers. (2017, November). Job outlook 2018: Career readiness, p. 32. Retrieved from http://careerservices.wayne.edu; National Association of Colleges and Employers. (2012, October 24). The skills and qualities employers want in their class of 2013 recruits. Retrieved from http://www.naceweb.org

44 Househ, A. A. (2018, August 29). IBM taps other industries to create its new collar workforce. Workforce. Retrieved from https://www.workforce.com

45 Statista. (2018). Number of monthly active Twitter users worldwide from 1st quarter 2010 to 2nd quarter 2018. Retrieved from https://www.statista.com; Internet Live Stats. (2018, October 15). Retrieved from http://www.internetlivestats.com

46 Shemkus, S. (2018, April 21). Think before you boycott: There are consequences. *The Boston Globe*. Retrieved from https://www.bostonglobe.com

47 Kitchen, M. (2018, October 5). How to disconnect from "always on" work culture. *The Wall Street Journal*. Retrieved from https://www.wsj.com

48 Kitchen, M. (2018, October 5). How to disconnect from "always on" work culture. *The Wall Street Journal*. Retrieved from https://www.wsj.com

49 Fujikawa, M. (2018, June 29). Japan's idea of a work-life balance: 99 hours of overtime a month. *The Wall Street Journal*. Retrieved from https://www.wsj.com

50 Kitchen, M. (2018, October 5). How to disconnect from "always on" work culture. *The Wall Street Journal*. Retrieved from https://www.wsj.com

51 Burjek, A. (2018, August 27). Don't ignore the negative effects of technology at work. *Workforce*. Retrieved from https://www.workforce.com

52 Gottschalk, S. (2018). *The terminal self: Everyday life in hypermodern times.* New York: Routledge, p. 14.

53 Wladawsky-Berger, I. (2017, October 6). The true state of globalization: Not dead, not completely OK. *The Wall Street Journal*. Retrieved from https://blogs.wsj.com

54 Irwin, N. (2018, March 23). Globalization's backlash is here, at just the wrong time. *The New York Times*. Retrieved from https://www.nytimes.com

55 Ip, G. (2018, June 27). That noise you hear is the sound of globalization going into reverse. *The Wall Street Journal*. Retrieved from https://www.wsj.com

56 Lam, B. (2016, January 15). Why are so many Zappos employees leaving? *The Atlantic*. https://www.theatlantic.com

57 Feintzeig, R. (2015, August 18). Radical idea at the office: Middle managers. *The Wall Street Journal*. Retrieved from https://www.wsj.com

58 Ibid.

59 Lam, B. (2016, January 15). Why are so many Zappos employees leaving? *The Atlantic*. https://www.theatlantic.com

60 Walker, S. (2018, May 18). There's a war on middle management and Tesla just joined it. *The Wall Street Journal*. Retrieved from https://www.wsj.com

61 Walker, S. (2018, May 18). There's a war on middle management and Tesla just joined it. *The Wall Street Journal*. Retrieved from https://www.wsj.com

62 Edmondson, A. C. (2012, April). Teamwork on the fly. *Harvard Business Review*. Retrieved from http://hbr.org

63 Tita, B. (2016, September 20). A new approach to new products. *The Wall Street Journal*. Retrieved from https://www.wsj.com

64 Edmondson, A. C. (2012, April). Teamwork on the fly. *Harvard Business Review*. Retrieved from https://hbr.org

65 Maurer, R. (2018, June 8). Experts puzzled by new BLS contingent workforce data. Society for Human Resource Management. Retrieved from https://www.shrm.org; Manyika, J., Lund, S., Bughin, J., Robinson, K., Mischke, J., & Mahajan, D. (2016, October). Independent work: Choice, necessity, and the gig economy. McKinsey Global Institute. Retrieved from https://www.mckinsey.com

66 Manyika, J., Lund, S., Bughin, J., Robinson, K., Mischke, J., & Mahajan, D. (2016, October). Independent work: Choice, necessity, and the gig economy. McKinsey Global Institute. Retrieved from https://www.mckinsey.com

67 Statista. (2020, January 28). Percentage distribution of population in the United States in 2016 and 2060, by race and Hispanic origin. Retrieved from https://www.statista.com; U.S. Census Bureau, Population Division. (2014, December). Percent of the projected population by Hispanic origin and race for the United States: 2015 to 2060 (NP2014-T11). Retrieved from http://www.census.gov

68 National Center for Education Statistics. (2018, February). Digest of education statistics. Retrieved from https://nces.ed.gov; Perry, M. J. (2018, June 18). Table of the day: Bachelor's degrees for the class of 2016 by field and gender. American Enterprise Institute, AEIdeas. Retrieved from https://www.aei.org

69 National Science Foundation. (2017, January). Women, minorities, and persons with disabilities in science and engineering. Retrieved from https://www.nsf.gov

70 Fry, R., & Stepler, R. (2017, January 31). Women may never make up half of the U.S. workforce. Pew Research Center. Retrieved from https://www.pewresearch.org

71 Toossi, M., & Torpey, E. (2017, May). *Older workers: Labor force trends and career options.* Career Outlook. U.S. Bureau of Labor Statistics. Retrieved from www.bls.gov

72 Donovan, A. (2017, October 31). Why older workers are a major value added to the workforce. *Forbes*. Retrieved from https://www.forbes.com; Miller, M. (2018, June 21). Companies need older workers: Here is why. *Reuters*. Retrieved from https://www.reuters.com

73 Davidson, P. (2018, March 5). Willing and able: Disabled workers prove their value in tight labor market. *USA Today*. https://www.usatoday.com

74 Eng, D. (2018, June 24). Where autistic workers thrive. *Fortune*. Retrieved from http://fortune.com

75 Based on Bacon, J. (2017, September 6). Optimizing mobile workers in an ever-connected world. *Forbes*. Retrieved from https://www.forbes.com

76 Gallup. (2017). State of the American workplace, p. 150. Retrieved from https://www.gallup.com

77 Shin, L. (2018, January 17). Work from home 2018: The top 100 companies for remote jobs. *Forbes*. Retrieved from https://www.forbes.com

78 Lohr, S. (2017, October 6). Don't get too comfortable at that desk. *The New York Times*. https://www.nytimes.com

79 Clark, P. (2016, February 19). Co-working spaces are going corporate. *BloombergBusiness*. Retrieved from http://www.bloombcrg.com

80 Sanders, S. (2019, April 23). The affluent homeless: A sleeping pod, a hired desk and a handful of clothes. *NPR*. Retrieved from https://www.npr.org; Chayka, K. (2018, February 8). When you're a "digital nomad," the world is your office. *The New York Times*. Retrieved from https://www.nytimes.com

81 Statcounter GlobalStats. (2020, January). Desktop vs mobile vs table market share worldwide. Retrieved from https://gs.statcounter.com; Clement, J. (2019, September 11). Mobile Internet usage worldwide—Statistics & facts. Statista. Retrieved from https://www.statista.com

82 Global mobile OS market share in sales to end users from 1st quarter 2009 to 2nd quarter 2018. (2018). Statista. Retrieved from https://www.statista.com

83 Daft, R. L., & Lengel, R. H. (1983, May). Information richness: A new approach to managerial behavior and organization design. [Technical report], p. 13. Retrieved from http://www.dtic.mil; Daft, R. L., & Lengel, R. H. (1986). Organizational information requirements, media richness and structural design. *Management Science 32*(5), 560. Retrieved from http://search.ebscohost.com

84 Short, J., Williams, E., & Christie, B. (1976). *The social psychology of telecommunications*. London: John Wiley.

85 Discussion based in part on Kaplan, A., & Haenlein, M. (2010). Users of the world unite! The challenges and opportunities of social media. *Business Horizons, 53*, 59–69. Retrieved from http://michaelhaenlein.com

86 Rozell, E. (2014, June 15). The office grapevine: Hurtful or helpful? *Springfield News-Leader*. Retrieved from http://www.news-leader.com; Steelcase Inc. (2007, August 9). Steelcase Workplace Index Survey examines "water cooler" conversations at work. Retrieved from http://www.prnewswire.com. See also Wademan Dowling, D. (2009, April 24). The truth about office rumors. *Harvard Business Review*. Retrieved from http://blogs.hbr.org; DiFonzo, N. (2009). *The water cooler effect: An indispensable guide to understanding and harnessing the power of rumors*. New York: Penguin, pp. 151, 174–175, 180.

87 Rozell, E. (2014, June 15). The office grapevine: Hurtful or helpful? *Springfield News-Leader*. Retrieved from http://www.news-leader.com

88 Langford, B. (2016, August 23). *The etiquette edge: Modern manners for business success*. AMACOM. Retrieved from https://proquest.com

89 Drexler, P. (2014, February 14). The value of annoying co-workers. *The Wall Street Journal*. Retrieved from http://www.wsj.com

90 Goman, C. K. (2006, June). I heard it through the grapevine. Paper presented at the International Association of Business Communicators, Vancouver, Canada.

91 Quast, L. (2013, October 14). New managers: 5 ways to stop negative office gossip. *Forbes*. Retrieved from http://www.forbes.com

92 Ibid.

93 Ott, M. (2018, October 12). Wells Fargo, haunted by scandal, reports higher third-quarter profit. *USA Today*. Retrieved from https://www.usatoday.com; Merle, R. (2016, September 13). Wells Fargo fired 5,300 workers for improper sales push. The executive in charge is retiring with $125 million. *The Washington Post*. Retrieved from https://www.washingtonpost.com; Wattles, J., Geier, B., Egan, M., & Wiener-Bronner, D. (2018, April 24). Wells Fargo's 20-month nightmare. CNN Business. https://money.cnn.com

94 Rauwald, C. (2018, June 13). VW agrees to $1.2 billion fine as diesel crisis grinds on. *Bloomberg*. https://www.bloomberg.com; Matussek, K. (2018, September 7). VW fights investors as diesel-scandal cost could top $35 billion. *Bloomberg*. Retrieved from https://www.bloomberg.com

95 Green, A. (2014, June 5). Managing: I caught my employee in a lie. Now what? *The Business Journals*. Retrieved from http://www.bizjournals.com; Campbell, R. (2014, March 11). The surprisingly large cost of telling small lies. *The New York Times*. Retrieved from http://boss.blogs.nytimes.com

96 Snyder, B. (2017, May 1). 7 insights from legendary investor Warren Buffett. CNBC. Retrieved from https://www.cnbc.com

97 Report to the nations: 2018 global study on occupational fraud and abuse. (2018). Association of Certified Fraud Examiners, p. 8. Retrieved from https://s3-us-west-2.amazonaws.com

98 Landrum, S. (2017, March 17). Millennials driving brands to practice socially responsible marketing. *Forbes*. Retrieved from https://www.forbes.com

99 Punishing CEOs for bad behavior: 2017 public perception survey. Stanford Graduate School of Business. Retrieved from https://www.gsb.stanford.edu

100 Green, J. (2016, May 9). CEO scandals dog company reputations years after they're fired. *Bloomberg*. Retrieved from https://www.bloomberg.com

101 Abrams, R. (2017, April 26). Rhonda Abrams: Women business owners will save America. *USA Today*. Retrieved from https://www.usatoday.com

102 Alvino, N. (2018, September 11). What working for Enron taught me about corporate ethics. *Entrepreneur*. Retrieved from https://www.entrepreneur.com

103 Spector, R., & Reeves, B. O. (2017). *The Nordstrom way to customer service excellence: Creating a values-driven service culture* (3rd ed.). Hoboken, NJ: John Wiley & Sons, p. 136.

104 Hatch, D. (2012, May 15). Nordstrom in fashion with social media, mobile tech. *U.S. News & World Report*. Retrieved from https://www.usnews.com

105 Spector, R., & Reeves, B. O. (2017). *The Nordstrom way to customer service excellence: Creating a values-driven service culture* (3rd ed.). Hoboken, NJ: John Wiley & Sons, p. 5.

106 Will Schwalbe quoted in Lam, B. (2015, May 15). Why emoji are suddenly acceptable at work. *The Atlantic*. Retrieved from http://www.theatlantic.com

107 Kerpen, D. (2016). *The art of people: 11 simple people skills that will get you everything you want*. New York: Crown Publishing, p. 96.

108 Caminiti, S. (2018, April 3). The dream job that's all the rage across America. CNBC.com. Retrieved from https://www.cnbc.com

109 Beach, G. (2018, June 26). Hard-pressed by soft skills, CIOs face talent challenge. *CIO Journal*. https://blogs.wsj.com

110 Pinsker, J. (2018, August 22). Phones are changing the texture of family life. *The Atlantic*. https://www.theatlantic.com

111 Otani, A. (2015, May 5). Five charts that show work-life balance is dead. *Bloomberg Business*. Retrieved from http://www.bloomberg.com

112 Taylor, C. (2012, January 6). Study: Social networkers have more ethics problems at work. Gigaom. Retrieved from https://gigaom.com

Chapter 2

[1] Sun, M. (2017, January 28). Lyft cuts staff: Does it have a new business strategy? *The Christian Science Monitor.* Retrieved from https://search.proquest.com; American Health Line. (2018, March 6). Lyft, Allscripts partner on health care ridesharing. The Advisory Board Company. Retrieved from https://search.proquest.com

[2] Burns, J. (2019, October 15). Lyft partners with ADT, Uber cuts 350 more in "final" layoffs as ride-hail criticism mounts. *Forbes.* Retrieved from https://www.forbes.com

[3] Lyft's big lift: Ride-hailing wars. (2017, June 10). *The Economist.* Retrieved from https://search.proquest.com

[4] Shields, N. (2018, October 1). Lyft more than doubled its revenue in H1 2018. *Business Insider.* Retrieved from https://www.businessinsider.com

[5] Oliver, M. (2017, July 18). Culture and hyper growth: Ron Storm on keeping Lyft's values alive. Constructive Culture. Retrieved from https://www.humansynergistics.com

[6] Buhr, S. (2015, September 15). TC Cribs: A look inside Lyft's quirky, hot pink HQ. [Video file]. Video posted to http://techcrunch.com

[7] Tjhayadi, H. (2015, June 5). What is it like to work for Lyft as a software engineer? Quora. Retrieved from https://www.quora.com

[8] "Excellent culture!" (2015, May 26). Glassdoor. Retrieved from http://www.glassdoor.com

[9] Moore, M. (2017, October 26). Capgemini and LinkedIn release new report on the digital talent gap: Employees are investing their own resources to remain competitive. Retrieved from https://www.capgemini.com

[10] Vozza, S. (2015, February 5). When companies stop excusing bad behavior. Fast Company. Retrieved from https://www.fastcompany.com

[11] Shellenbarger, S. (2018, July 23). You could be too much of a team player. *The Wall Street Journal.* Retrieved from https://www.wsj.com

[12] Gensler. (2016). U.S. workplace survey 2016. Retrieved from https://www.gensler.com

[13] Gallup. (2017). State of the American workplace, p. 131. Retrieved from https://www.gallup.com

[14] Newport, C. (2016). *Deep work: Rules for focused work success in a distracted world.* New York: Grand Central Publishing, p. 37.

[15] Coutu, D. (2009, May). Why teams don't work. *Harvard Business Review, 87*(5), 100. Retrieved from http://search.ebscohost.com

[16] Cain, S. (2012, January 13). The rise of the new groupthink. *The New York Times.* Retrieved from http://www.nytimes.com

[17] The collaboration curse. (2016, January 23). *The Economist.* Retrieved from https://www.economist.com

[18] Cross, R., & Taylor, S. (2018, January 30). How to manage collaborative overload. Babson Thought & Action. Retrieved from http://entrepreneurship.babson.edu

[19] *Virtual collaboration: Work from anywhere, overcommunicate, avoid isolation.* (2016). Boston: Harvard Business Review Press, pp. 2–3.

[20] Caminiti, S. (2018, April 3). The dream job that's all the rage across America. CNBC. Retrieved from https://www.cnbc.com

[21] Geiger, F. (2014, December 22). Germany's big firms pay price for small-town ties. *The Wall Street Journal.* Retrieved from http://www.wsj.com

[22] Lepsinger, R. (2015, April 27). 3 companies with high-performing virtual teams. LinkedIn. Retrieved from https://www.linkedin.com

[23] Discussion of Tuckman's model based on Robbins, H. A., & Finley, M. (2000). *The new why teams don't work* (2nd ed.). San Francisco: Berrett-Koehler, Chapter 29.

[24] Author Mike Staib quoted by Shellenbarger, S. (2017, November 28). Taking one for the team: Companies foster collaboration. *The Wall Street Journal.* Retrieved from https://www.wsj.com

[25] Haas, M., & Mortensen, M. (2016, June). The secrets of great teamwork. *Harvard Business Review.* Retrieved from https://hbr.org; Coleman, P. T., Deutsch, M., & Marcus, E. C. (2014). *The handbook of conflict resolution: Theory and practice* (3rd ed.). San Francisco: Jossey-Bass.; Janis, I. L. (1982). *Groupthink: Psychological studies of policy decisions and fiascoes.* Boston: Wadsworth, pp. 174–176.

[26] Emory University neuroscientist Gregory Berns quoted in Cain, S. (2012, January 13). The rise of the new groupthink. *The New York Times.* Retrieved from http://www.nytimes.com

[27] J. Richard Hackman quoted in Coutu, D. (2009, May). Why teams don't work. *Harvard Business Review, 87*(5), 105. Retrieved from http://search.ebscohost.com

[28] Coleman, P. T., Deutsch, M., & Marcus, E. C. (2014). *The handbook of conflict resolution: Theory and practice.* (3rd ed.). San Francisco: Jossey-Bass, p. 333. Janis, I. L. (1982). *Groupthink: Psychological studies on policy decisions and fiascoes.* Boston: Houghton Mifflin.

[29] Romero, L. E. (2016, January 20). What everyone should know about teamwork. *Forbes.* Retrieved from https://www.forbes.com; Scudamore, B. (2016, March 9). Why team building is the most important investment you'll make. *Forbes.* Retrieved from https://www.forbes.com

[30] Chinnery, K. (2010, May 13). At the end of the day. BRW. Retrieved from Factiva; Katzenbach, J. R., & Smith, D. K. (2015). *The wisdom of teams: Creating the high-performance organization.* Boston: HBR Press, p. 182. Ruffin, B. (2006, January).

T.E.A.M. work: Technologists, educators, and media specialists collaborating. *Library Media Connection, 24*(4), 49. Retrieved from http://search.ebscohost.com

[31] Anderson, K. (2015, September 13). Why and how to cultivate conviviality at work. *Forbes.* Retrieved from https://www.forbes.com; Ferrazzi, K. (2013, December 18). To make virtual teams succeed, pick the right players. HBR Blog Network. Retrieved from https://hbr.org; Holtzman, Y., & Anderberg, J. (2011). Diversify your teams and collaborate: Because great minds don't think alike. *The Journal of Management Development, 30*(1), 79. doi:10.1108/02621711111098389.

[32] Househ, A. A. (2018, September 14). Tradeswomen enter the male-dominated construction industry. *Workforce.* Retrieved from https://www.workforce.com

[33] Accountemps, Robert Half. (2018, July 30). Time spent (and wasted) in meetings. Retrieved from https://www.roberthalf.com; Austin, M. (2012, May 21). Wasted time in meetings costs businesses £26 billion. Techradar. Retrieved from http://www.techradar.com

[34] Fox, J. (2018, June 26). CEOs have to go to lots of meetings, too. *Bloomberg.* Retrieved from https://www.bloomberg.com

[35] Rogelberg, S. G., Shanock, L. R., & Scott, C. W. (2012). Wasted time and money in meetings: Increasing return on investment. *Small Group Research, 43*(2), 237. doi:10.1177/1046496411429170

[36] Owens, K. (2014, June 11). How to get employees to plug in to your meeting and not their devices. *Fast Company.* Retrieved from https://www.fastcompany.com

[37] Vozza, S. (2015, July 28). How 12 companies make meetings memorable, effective, and short. *Fast Company.* Retrieved from https://www.fastcompany.com

[38] Shellenbarger, S. (2012, May 16). Meet the meeting killers—In the office, they strangle ideas, poison progress; how to fight back. *The Wall Street Journal.* Retrieved from http://search.proquest.com

[39] Shellenbarger, S. (2017, November 7). Can you keep your meeting to five minutes? *The Wall Street Journal.* Retrieved from https://www.wsj.com

[40] Fisher-Yoshida, B. (2018, October 3). 3 tips to make the most out of your next meeting. *Inc.* https://www.inc.com

[41] Gallo, A. (2015, July 6). The condensed guide to running meetings. *Harvard Business Review.* Retrieved from https://hbr.org; Blenko, M. W., Rogers, P., & Mankins, M. C. (2010, September 27). *Decide and deliver: Five steps to breakthrough performance in your organization.* Boston, MA: HBR Press.

[42] Shellenbarger, S. (2016, December 20). A manifesto to end boring meetings. *The Wall Street Journal.* Retrieved from https://www.wsj.com

[43] One day, a community transformed—Servapalooza 2018. (2018). Retrieved from https://www.timberland.com

[44] Based on *HBR guide to making every meeting matter.* (2016). Boston: Harvard Business Review Press; Egan, M. (2006, March 13). Meetings can make or break your career. *Insurance Advocate, 117,* p. 24.

[45] Ferrazzi, K. (2015, March 27). How to run a great virtual meeting. *Harvard Business Review.* Retrieved from https://hbr.org

[46] Based on French, S. (2016, March 14). Ten etiquette rules for videoconferencing. *The Wall Street Journal,* p. R4. Retrieved from https://www.wsj.com

[47] *Running virtual meetings: Test your technology, keep their attention, connect across time zones.* (2016). Boston: Harvard Business Review Press; Schlegel, J. (2012). Running effective meetings: Types of meetings. Salary.com. Retrieved from http://www.salary.com; Cohen, M. A., Rogelberg, S. G., Allen, J. A., & Luong, A. (2011). Meeting design characteristics and attendee perceptions of staff/team meeting quality. *Group Dynamics: Theory, Research, and Practice, 15*(1), 100–101.

[48] Knowles, K. (2018, June 27). How to boss it like: Katharina Borchert, Chief Innovation Officer at Mozilla. *Forbes.* Retrieved from https://www.forbes.com

[49] Five reasons why your company needs to embrace video conferencing now. (2017). *Forbes.* Retrieved from https://www.forbes.com; Fox, J. (2014, October 8). Why virtual conferences will not replace face-to-face meetings. International Meetings Review. Retrieved from http://www.internationalmeetingsreview.com

[50] Zenger, J., & Folkman, J. (2020). *The new extraordinary leader: Turn good managers into great leaders* (3rd ed.), p. 168; Rowh, M. (2006, April/May). Listen up! Tune out distractions, and tune in to people. Here's how listening skills help lead to success. *Career World, 34*(6), 22. Retrieved from http://search.ebscohost.com; Robbins, H., & Finley, M. (1995). *Why teams don't work.* Princeton, NJ: Peterson's/Pacesetter Books, p. 123.

[51] Riordan, C. M. (2019). Three ways leaders can listen with more empathy. In: *Emotional intelligence: Mindful listening.* Boston: Harvard Business Review Press, pp. 29–37.

[52] Dean, S., & East, J. I. (2019). Soft skills needed for the 21st-century workforce. *International Journal of Applied Management and Technology, 18*(1), 17–32. doi:10.5590/IJAMT.2019.18.1.02. Retrieved from https://search-proquest.com; Boyle, D., Carpenter, B., & Mahoney, D. P. (2017, Fall). Developing the communication skills required for sustainable career success. *Management Accounting Quarterly, 19*(1), 1–9. Retrieved from https://search-proquest.com

[53] Coy, P. (2018, February). Maybe STEM isn't the future after all. Soft skills are coming on strong. *Bloomberg Businessweek.* Retrieved from https://www.bloomberg.com; Davidson, K. (2016, August 30). Employers find "soft skills" like critical thinking in short supply. *The Wall Street Journal.* Retrieved from https://www.wsj.com

[54] Bergh, C. (2018, July-August). The CEO of Levi Strauss on leading an iconic brand back to growth. *Harvard Business Review,* 34–35. Retrieved from http://ebscohost.com

[55] Daimler, M. (2016, May 25). Listening is an overlooked leadership tool. *Harvard Business Review.* Retrieved from https://hbr.org

[56] Crockett, R. O. (2011, March 14). Listening is critical in today's multicultural workplace. *Harvard Business Review.* Retrieved from https://hbr.org

[57] International Listening Association. (n.d.). Listening and speech rates. International Listening Association. Retrieved from https://listen.org

[58] Young, V. M. (2018, November 6). Fran Horowitz on listening and learning. *Women's Wear Daily.* Retrieved from http://ebscohost.com

[59] Stibitz, S. (2015, January 30). How to really listen to your employees. *Harvard Business Review.* Retrieved from https://hbr.org

[60] Devault, G. (2017, December 4). Learn when to use open-end or closed-end questions. The Balance Small Business. Retrieved from https://www.thebalancesmb.com; Open and closed-ended questions. (2015). PewResearchCenter. Retrieved from http://www.people-press.org

[61] Wellins, R., & Sinar, E. (2016, May). The hard science behind soft skills. *Chief Learning Officer, 15*(5), 51. Retrieved from http://ebscohost.com

[62] Colbert, A., Yee, N., & George, G. (2016, June). The digital workforce and the workplace of the future. *Academy of Management Journal, 55*(3), 733. doi:10.5465/amj.2016.4003

[63] Shellenbarger, S. (2018, October 9). The best bosses are humble bosses. *The Wall Street Journal.* Retrieved from https://www.wsj.com

[64] Doubek, J. (2016, April 17). Attention, students: Put your laptops away. NPR. Retrieved from https://www.npr.org

[65] Goudreau, J. (2012, March 22). Is your body language costing you a promotion? *Forbes.* Retrieved from http://www.forbes.com

[66] Birdwhistel, R. (1970). *Kinesics and context.* Philadelphia: University of Pennsylvania Press.

[67] Kinsey Goman, C. (2018, March 7). On National Women's Day, don't look less than you are. *Forbes.* Retrieved from https://www.forbes.com

[68] Zarrella, K. K. (2019, November 7). How much fashion is too much fashion at work? *The Wall Street Journal.* Retrieved from https://www.wsj.com; Glazer, E. (2016, June 3). J.P. Morgan says employees don't always have to wear suits. *The Wall Street Journal.* Retrieved from https://www.wsj.com

[69] Statista, (2019). Survey on the perception of people with tattoos in the U.S. 2015. Retrieved from https://www.statista.com; Singer, A. (2016, February 26). Tattoos in the workplace: The research Forbes was too lazy to do. *The Huffington Post.* Retrieved from http://www.huffingtonpost.com; Mishra, A., & Mishra, S. (2015, April). Attitude of professionals and students toward professional dress code, tattoos and body piercing in the corporate world. *International Journal of Innovative Research & Development, 4*(4), 324–331. Retrieved from http://www.ijird.com

[70] Hall, E. T. (1966). *The hidden dimension.* Garden City, NY: Doubleday, pp. 107–122.

[71] Valbrune, M. (2018, September 28). Gender-based dress codes: Human resources, diversity, and legal impact. *Forbes.* Retrieved from https://www.forbes.com

[72] Krischer Goodman, C. (2016, July 23). Does dressing casually affect productivity at the workplace? *StarTribune.* Retrieved from http://www.startribune.com; Cracking the dress code dilemma. (2015). Salary.com for Business. Retrieved from http://business.salary.com

[73] Pine, K. J. (2014, February 3). Sartorial decisions have repercussions. *The New York Times.* Retrieved from https://www.nytimes.com

[74] Shriver, M. (2014, May 28). Look like a leader: Secrets of executive presence. NBC News. Retrieved from https://www.nbcnews.com; Kennedy, M. M. (1997, September-October). Is business casual here to stay? *Executive Female,* 31.

[75] Krischer Goodman, C. (2016, July 23). Does dressing casually affect productivity at the workplace? *StarTribune.* Retrieved from http://www.startribune.com; Popick, J. (2012, September 21). 5 reasons to ditch your dress code. *Inc.* Retrieved from http://www.inc.com

[76] Gale, K. (2014, February 4). Free your style, free your thoughts. *The New York Times.* Retrieved from https://www.nytimes.com

[77] Rainie, L., & Anderson, J. (2017, May 3). The future of jobs and jobs training. Pew Research Center. Retrieved from http://www.pewinternet.org

[78] Manyika, J., Lund, S., Chui, M., Bughin, J., Woetzel, J., Batra, P., Ko, R., & Sanghvi, S. (2017, November). Jobs lost, jobs gained: What the future of work will mean for jobs, skills, and wages. McKinsey Global Institute, pp. 78, 80, 90. Retrieved from https://www.mckinsey.com

[79] Friedman, T. L. (2017, May 24). A road trip through rusting and rising America. *The New York Times.* Retrieved from https://www.nytimes.com

80 Mitchell, H. (2018, February 19). The big impact of a little rudeness at work. *The Wall Street Journal*. Retrieved from https://www.wsj.com

81 Taylor, S. G., Kluemper, D. H., Bowler, W. M., & Halbesleben, R. B. (2019, July 10). Why people get away with being rude at work. *Harvard Business Review*. Retrieved from https://hbr.org; Wallace, J. B. (2017, August 18). The cost of workplace rudeness. *The Wall Street Journal*. Retrieved from https://www.wsj.com

82 Porath, C. (2016, December). The hidden toll of workplace incivility. *McKinsey Quarterly*. https://www.mckinsey.com; Porath, C., MacInnis, D., & Folkes, V. S. (2011, April 17). It's unfair: Why customers who merely observe an uncivil employee abandon the company. *Journal of Service Research*. doi:10.1177/1094670511404393.

83 Newport, C. (2016). *Deep work: Rules for focused work success in a distracted world*. New York: Grand Central Publishing, p. 52.

84 Gulley, P. (2009, March). 'Til we meet again: Nothing like a good old-fashioned business meeting to turn a crisis from bad to worse. *Indianapolis Monthly, 32*(8). Retrieved from http://search.ebscohost.com

85 Shellenbarger, S. (2018, October 9). The best bosses are humble bosses. *The Wall Street Journal*. Retrieved from https://www.wsj.com

86 Ibid.

87 Hollon, J. (2007, November 13). Meeting malaise. *Workforce*. Retrieved from http://www.workforce.com

88 Zipkin, N. (2018, April 19). Why Elon Musk hates meetings. *Entrepreneur*. Retrieved from https://www.entrepreneur.com

89 Jackson, A. (2017, October 3). Elon Musk has reportedly used a brutal tactic to keep from wasting time in meetings. *Business Insider*. Retrieved from https://www.businessinsider.com

90 Scenario based on Shellenbarger, S. (2017, November 7). Can you keep your meeting to five minutes? *The Wall Street Journal*. Retrieved from https://www.wsj.com

91 Heitler, S. (2011, November). The art of listening: How open are your ears? *Psychology Today*. Retrieved from https://www.psychologytoday.com

92 Stibitz, S. (2015, January 30). How to really listen to your employees. *Harvard Business Review*. Retrieved from https://hbr.org

93 Heitler, S. (2011, November). The art of listening: How open are your ears? *Psychology Today*. Retrieved from https://www.psychologytoday.com

94 Statista. (2019). Compared to people without tattoos, which of the following characteristics do you think people with tattoos have? Retrieved from https://www.statista.com

95 Premack, R. (2018, October 5). Experts say there are 2 types of tattoos that are still a "no-go" at work—and they are likely to outright disqualify you from some jobs. *Business Insider*. Retrieved from https://www.businessinsider.com

96 Premack, R. (2018, October 4). Here's why experts say you still need to cover up your tattoos when you're interviewing. *Business Insider*. Retrieved from https://www.businessinsider.com

97 Premack, R. (2018, October 5). Experts say there are 2 types of tattoos that are still a "no-go" at work—and they are likely to outright disqualify you from some jobs. *Business Insider*. Retrieved from https://www.businessinsider.com

98 The Harris Poll. (2015). Tattoo takeover: Three in ten Americans have tattoos, and most don't stop at one. Retrieved from https://theharrispoll.com

99 McGinty, J. C. (2018, August 31). Tattoo industry wins over millennials. *The Wall Street Journal*. Retrieved from https://www.wsj.com

100 Carr, N. (2017, October 6). How smartphones hijack our minds. *The Wall Street Journal*. Retrieved from https://www.wsj.com

101 Dewey, C. (2015, August 26). When it is and isn't okay to be on your smartphone: The conclusive guide. *The Washington Post*. Retrieved from https://www.washingtonpost.com

102 O'Brien Coffey, J. (2011, September). How to manage smartphones at meetings. *Executive Travel Magazine*. Retrieved from http://www.executivetravelmagazine.com

103 Ibid.

104 O'Brien Coffey, J. (2011, September). How to manage smartphones at meetings. *Executive Travel Magazine*. Retrieved from http://www.executivetravelmagazine.com

Chapter 3

1 Yoder, S., Visich, J. K., & Rustambekov, E. (2016, March-April). Lessons learned from international expansion failures and successes. *Business Horizons, 59*(2), 233–243. doi:10.1016/j.bushor.2015.11.008. Retrieved from sciencedirect.com; Volk, A. (2014, November 9). Wal-Mart and workers' rights: A case study. *Harvard Political Review*. Retrieved from http://harvardpolitics.com

2 Pollock, L. (2014, October 30). Wal-Mart to close 30 underperforming stores in Japan. *The Wall Street Journal*. Retrieved from http://www.wsj.com

3 Boyle, M. (2018, June 4). Walmart's Brazilian blunder comes to an end with Advent deal. *Bloomberg*. Retrieved from https://www.bloomberg.com

4 Nassauer, S., Magalhães, L., & Purnell, N. (2018, April 29). Walmart looks to scale back in U.K. and Brazil, with an eye on India. *The Wall Street Journal*. Retrieved from https://www.wsj.com

5 Boyle, M. (2018, May 9). What Walmart will do next after buying in India, selling in U.K. *Bloomberg*. Retrieved from https://www.bloomberg.com

6 Cheng, E. (2019, September 30). China's giant middle class is still growing and companies from Walmart to start-ups are trying to cash in. CNBC. Retrieved from https://www.cnbc.com; Jacobs, H. (2018, May 1). Photos reveal what it's like to shop at Walmart in China—Which is shockingly different from the US and struggling to compete. *Business Insider*. Retrieved from https://www.businessinsider.com

7 Time to deliver: How Walmart approaches last-mile convenience around the world. (2019, August 22). *Business Wire*. Retrieved from https://www.businesswire.com

8 Michaels, D., & Nassauer, S. (2019, June 20). Walmart to pay $282 million to settle claims of corrupt payments abroad. *The Wall Street Journal*. Retrieved from https://www.wsj.com

9 Corkery, M. (2019, June 20). A "sorceress" in Brazil, a "wink" in India: Walmart pleads guilty after a decade of bribes. *The New York Times*. Retrieved from https://www.nytimes.com

10 Monllos, K. (2015, May 29). Is Walmart trying to brand itself as socially conscious? *Adweek*. Retrieved from http://www.adweek.com

11 TRA Research. (2019). TRA's brand trust report: India study 2019. Retrieved from http://www.trustadvisory.info

12 Neo, P. (2019, September 18). Brand new: PepsiCo, Coca-Cola and Nestle are some of the big names featured in our round-up. Food Navigator Asia. Retrieved from https://www.foodnavigator-asia.com

13 Morris, C. (2017, May 11). 10 iconic American companies own by Chinese investors. CNBC. Retrieved from https://www.cnbc.com

14 Moudoukoutas, P. (2018, August 4). What is China doing in Africa? *Forbes*. Retrieved from https://www.cnbc.com

15 Morris, C. (2017, May 11). 10 iconic American companies own by Chinese investors. CNBC. Retrieved from https://www.cnbc.com

16 Flitter, E. (2018, February 15). S.E.C. blocks Chinese takeover of Chicago Stock Exchange. *The New York Times*. Retrieved from https://nytimes.com

17 Perlberg, S. (2014, January 14). Some Americans are threatening to stop drinking Jim Beam now that it's owned by a Japanese company. *Business Insider*. Retrieved from http://www.businessinsider.com

18 Hanbury, M. (2018, August 2). 11 American companies that are no longer American. *Business Insider*. Retrieved from https://businessinsider.com

19 Lempert, P. (2018, August 9). Inside Aldi's $5 billion plan to become the third-largest grocer in the U.S. *Forbes*. Retrieved from https://forbes.com; Chaudhuri, S. (2015, June 11). Aldi details U.S. expansion plan.

The Wall Street Journal. Retrieved from http://www.wsj.com

20 Mourdoukoutas, P. (2019, January 21). Starbucks worst nightmare in China is coming true. *Forbes.* Retrieved from https://forbes.com; Fleming, A. (2013, September 3). The geography of taste: How our food preferences are formed. *The Guardian.* Retrieved from http://www.theguardian.com

21 Matousek, M. (2018, July 11). Here's what it's like to eat at McDonald's in 7 countries around the world. *Business Insider.* Retrieved from https://businessinsider.com; Kannan, S. (2014, November 19). How McDonald's conquered India. BBC News. Retrieved from http://www.bbc.com

22 Mourdoukoutas, P. (2019, January 21). Starbucks worst nightmare in China is coming true. *Forbes.* Retrieved from https://forbes.com

23 Ganesan, G., & Cavale, S. (2017, March 10). Mattel reworks China strategy amid elusive growth. *Reuters.* Retrieved from https://www.reuters.com; Carlson, B. (2013, September 26). Why big American businesses fail in China. CNBC. Retrieved from http://www.cnbc.com

24 Klement, P. (2018, March 8). International brand blunders: How NOT to enter a new market. GFluence. Retrieved from https://gfluence.com

25 Schooley, S. (2019, August 12). Lost in translation: 10 international marketing fails. *Business News Daily.* Retrieved from https://businessnewsdaily.com

26 Layne, R. (2019, December 10). Here's what's in the U.S.-Mexico-Canada Agreement, the new NAFTA. CBS News. Retrieved from https://www.cbsnews.com

27 U.S. Free Trade Agreements. (2019, July 8). Export.gov. Retrieved from https://export.gov/FTA

28 Schwab, K. (2017, March 17). Klaus Schwab: We need a new narrative for globalization. World Economic Forum. Retrieved from https://www.weforum.org

29 Kharas, H., & Hamel, K. (2018, September 27). A global tipping point: Half the world is now middle class or wealthier. Brookings. Retrieved from https://www.brookings.edu

30 Ibid.

31 Cheng, E. (2019, September 30). China's giant middle class is still growing and companies from Walmart to start-ups are trying to cash in. CNBC. Retrieved from https://www.cnbc.com

32 Gopinath, G., & Parker, C. (2019, April 11). An economist explains the pros and cons of globalization. Word Economic Forum. Retrieve from https://www.weforum.org

33 Visser, D. (2018, February 6). Snapshot: The world's ultra large container ship fleet. *Maritime Executive.* Retrieved from https://www.maritime-executive.com

34 Choe, T., Rosenberger, S. A., Garza, M., & Woolfolk, J. (2017). The future of freight: How new technology and new thinking can transform how goods are moved. Deloitte Insights. https://www2.deloitte.com

35 Smith, J. (2019, January 8). Warehouses test a new breed of AI robots. WSJ PRO Artificial Intelligence. Retrieved from https://www.wsj.com

36 Page, P. (2019, December 31). Today's logistics report: The top stories shaping supply chains heading into 2020. *The Wall Street Journal.* Retrieved from https://www.wsj.com

37 Press, G. (2019, November 22). Top artificial intelligence (AI) predictions for 2020 from IDC and Forrester. *Forbes.* Retrieved from https://www.forbes.com

38 Press, G. (2017, November 22). Top 10 hot artificial intelligence (AI) technologies. *Forbes.* Retrieved from https://www.forbes.com

39 Frey, W. H. (2018). *Diversity explosion: How new racial demographics are remaking America.* Washington, DC: The Brookings Institution, p. 2.

40 Radford, J. (2019, June 17). Key findings about U.S. immigrants. Pew Research Center, Fact Tank. Retrieved from https://www.pewresearch.org; Statista Research Department. (2019, April 29). United States' population growth projections for 2015-2060. Retrieved from https://www.statista.com

41 Based on Wil. (2015, February 24). Doing business in different cultures in English. EF English Live Blog. Retrieved from http://englishlive.ef.com; Sharma, R. R. (2019, September 9). Navigating cultural differences in a global business world. Retrieved from https://phys.org

42 Ganesan, G., & Cavale, S. (2017, March 10). Mattel reworks China strategy amid elusive growth. *Reuters.* Retrieved from https://www.reuters.com; Burkitt, L. (2013, November 7). Mattel gives Barbie a makeover for China. *The Wall Street Journal.* Retrieved from https://wsj.com; Wang, H. H. (2012, October 24). Why Barbie stumbled in China and how she could re-invent herself. *Forbes.* Retrieved from http://www.forbes.com

43 Attitudes on same-sex marriage. (2019, May 14). Pew Research Center. Retrieved from https://pewforum.org

44 Hall, E. T., & Hall, M. R. (2000). Key concepts: Underlying structures of culture. In Maryann H. Albrecht (Ed.), *International HRM: Managing diversity in the workplace.* Hoboken, NJ: Wiley-Blackwell, pp. 200–202; Hall, E. T., & Hall, M. R. (1990). *Understanding cultural differences.* Yarmouth, ME: Intercultural Press, pp. 183–184.

45 Figure based on Chaney, L. H., & Martin, J. S. (2011). *Intercultural business communication* (5th ed.). Upper Saddle River, NJ: Prentice Hall, Chapter 5; J. Chung's analysis appearing in Chen, G. M., & Starosta, W. J. *Foundations of intercultural communication.* Boston: Allyn and Bacon, 1998, p. 51; and O'Hara-Devereaux, M., & Johansen, R. (1994). *Globalwork: Bridging distance, culture, and time.* San Francisco: Jossey-Bass, p. 55.

46 Chaney, L. H., & Martin, J. S. (2011). *Intercultural business communication* (5th ed.). Upper Saddle River, NJ: Prentice Hall, p. 93.

47 Chen, M.-J., & Miller, D. (2010, November). West meets East: Toward an ambicultural approach to management. *Academy of Management Perspectives, 24*(4), 19ff. Retrieved from http://search.ebscohost.com; Sheer, V. C., & Chen, L. (2003, January). Successful Sino-Western business negotiation: Participants' accounts of national and professional cultures. *The Journal of Business Communication, 40*(1), 62; see also Luk, L., Patel, M., & White, K. (1990, December). Personal attributes of American and Chinese business associates. *The Bulletin of the Association for Business Communication*, 67.

48 Gallois, C., & Callan, V. (1997). *Communication and culture.* New York: Wiley, p. 24.

49 Copeland, J. (1990, December 15). Stare less, listen more. American Airlines. *American Way*, p. 32.

50 Gallois, C., & Callan, V. (1997). *Communication and culture.* New York: Wiley, p. 29.

51 Copeland, L., & Griggs, L. (1986). *Going international.* New York: Penguin, p. 94.

52 Ibid., p. 108.

53 Ibid., p. 12.

54 Mueller, J., & Stewart, M. G. (2018, March 23). Why are Americans still so afraid of Islamist terrorism? *The Washington Post.* Retrieved from https://www.washingtonpost.com

55 Stangor, C. (2000). *Stereotypes and Prejudice.* Levittown, PA: Taylor & Francis, p. 7; Chen, G. M., & Starosta, W. J. (1998). *Foundations of intercultural communication.* Boston: Allyn and Bacon, p. 40.

56 Varner, I., & Beamer, L. (2011). *Intercultural communication in the global workplace.* Boston: McGraw-Hill Irwin, p. 100.

57 Fish, J. M. (2014, February 25). Tolerance, acceptance, understanding. *Psychology Today.* Retrieved from https://www.psychologytoday.com

58 Tress, L. (2017, January 23). In the barren south, Israelis and Arabs work to green the Middle East. *The Times of Israel.* Retrieved from https://www.timesofisrael.com; Blumberg, A. (2015, April 21). In the Middle East, Muslims and Jews work in unison to care for the environment. *The Huffington Post.* Retrieved from http://www.huffingtonpost.com

59 Smith, M. (2019, August 30). Britons make the worst tourists, say Britons (and Spaniards

and Germans). YouGov. Retrieved from https://yougov.co.uk; Dale, R. (n.d.). British and French vie for "worst tourists" title. Center for Strategic & International Studies. Retrieved from http://csis.org

[60] O'Very, P. (2018, April 27). 20 countries that hate tourists from the United States. *Best Life*. Retrieved from https://bestlifeonline.com; Cahn, L. (n. d.). The worst tourists of 2019. *Reader's Digest*. Retrieved from https://www.rd.com

[61] Martin, J. S., & Chaney, L. H. (2006). *Global business etiquette*. Westport, CT: Praeger, p. 69.

[62] Hammer, M. R. quoted in Chen, H.-M., & Starosta, W. J. (1993). *Foundations of intercultural communication*. Boston: Allyn & Bacon, p. 247.

[63] Chaney, L. H., & Martin, J. S. (1995). *Intercultural business communication*. Englewood Cliffs, NJ: Prentice Hall Career and Technology, p. 67.

[64] Limbu, M., & Gurung, B. (2014). *Emerging pedagogies in the networked knowledge society: Practices integrating social media and globalization*. Hershey, PA: IGI Global, p. 72.

[65] Ali, S. (2018, October 5). Is social media making you lonely? *Psychology Today*. Retrieved from https://www.psychologytoday.com; Brody, J. E. (2018, June 25). To counter loneliness, find ways to connect. *The New York Times*. Retrieved from https://www.nytimes.com

[66] Walton, A. G. (2019, January 24). Loneliness linked to negative social media experiences, study finds. *Forbes*. Retrieved from https://www.forbes.com

[67] Vinnakota, R. (2017, January 24). How social media divides us. The Aspen Institute. Retrieved from https://www.aspeninstitute.org

[68] Shao, G. (2019, August 16). Social media has become a battleground in Hong Kong's protests. CNBC. Retrieved from https://www.cnbc.com

[69] Feng, E. (2019, August 20). How China uses Twitter and Facebook to share disinformation about Hong Kong. NPR. Retrieved from https://www.npr.org

[70] Girard, J. (2019, September 25). Visual color symbolism chart by culture. Lifewire. Retrieved from https://www.lifewire.com; Cousins, C. (2012, June 11). Color and cultural design considerations. Web Designer Depot. Retrieved from https://www.webdesignerdepot.com

[71] Kapur, A. (2019, November 1). The rising threat of digital nationalism. *The Wall Street Journal*. Retrieved from https://www.wsj.com

[72] Martinez, A. (2014, November 14). Why Mandarin won't be a lingua franca. Retrieved from http://time.com

[73] Haden, J. (2018, February 20). *Inc.* 11 sentences that guarantee the rest of your email won't get read. Retrieved from www.inc.com

[74] Levick, R. (2015, January 21). New data: Bribery is often an "unspoken rule" in China. *Forbes*. https://www.forbes.com

[75] Henning, P. J. (2019, August 19). A push to let the U. S. charge foreign officials with bribery. *The New York Times*. Retrieved from https://www.nytimes.com

[76] Kottasova, I. (2015, September 10). IKEA is making loads of money in Russia. Wait, what? CNNMoney London. Retrieved from http://money.cnn.com; Meyer, H. (2011, March 7). Corruption halts IKEA in Russia. *The Age*. Retrieved from http://www.theage.com.au; see also Bush, J. (2009, July 2). Why IKEA is fed up with Russia. *BusinessWeek*. Retrieved from http://www.businessweek.com

[77] Corruption Perceptions Index 2019. Transparency International. Retrieved from http://www.transparency.org

[78] Ibid.

[79] OECD. (2020). Intensifying anti-corruption and integrity efforts. Anti-corruption & integrity hub. Retrieved from https://anticorruption-integrity.oecd.org

[80] Watson, B. (2013, September 18). Siemens and the battle against bribery and corruption. *The Guardian*. Retrieved from https://www.theguardian.com

[81] Forsythe, B., & Hull, C. (2019, November 18). Former Alstom executive convicted of Foreign Corrupt Practices Act charges on agency theory. JD Supra. Retrieved from https://www.jdsupra.com; Viswanatha, A., & Barrett, D. (2015, October 19). Wal-Mart bribery probe finds few signs of major misconduct in Mexico. *The Wall Street Journal*. Retrieved from http://www.wsj.com

[82] McCann, M. (2017, December 22). Breaking down the guilty verdicts in FIFA corruption trial. *Sports Illustrated*. Retrieved from https://www.si.com; The FIFA investigation, explained. (2015, December 3). *The New York Times*. Retrieved from http://www.nytimes.com

[83] Koch, R. (2005, May 1). The Foreign Corrupt Practices Act: It's time to cut back the grease and add some guidance. *Boston College International and Comparative Law Review, 28*(2), 379–380.

[84] What's the cost of corruption? (2018, October 18). CNBC Video. Retrieved from https://www.cnbc.com

[85] The cost of corruption: Values, economic development under assault, trillions lost, says Guterres. (2018, December 9). UN News. Retrieved from https://news.un.org

[86] Manjoo, F. (2019, October 9). Dealing with China isn't worth the moral cost. *The New York Times*. Retrieved from https://www.nytimes.com

[87] Gentile, M. C. (2016, December 23). Talking about ethics across cultures. *Harvard Business Review*. Retrieved from https://hbr.org

[88] Mauro, P., Medas, P., & Fournier, J.-M. (2019, September). The cost of corruption: Graft results in lost tax revenue, but it also takes a social toll. *Finance & Development, 56*(3). Retrieved from https://www.imf.org

[89] Montero, D. (2018). *Kickback: Exposing the global corporate bribery network*. New York: Viking; Montero, D. (2018, November 16). How managers should respond when bribes are business as usual. *Harvard Business Review*. Retrieved from https://hbr.org; Hodgson, K. (1992, May). Adapting ethical decisions to a global marketplace. *Management Review, 81*(5), 54. Retrieved from http://www.dowjones.com

[90] Hunt, V., Yee, L., Prince, S., & Dixon-Fyle, S. (2018, January). Delivering through diversity. McKinsey Report. Retrieved from https://www.mckinsey.com

[91] Frey, W. H. (2018, March 14). The US will become "minority white" in 2045, Census projects. The Brookings Institution. Retrieved from https://www.brookings.edu

[92] Ibid.

[93] Older people projected to outnumber children for the first time in U.S. history. (2018, March 13). United States Census Bureau. Retrieved from https://www.census.gov

[94] Pew Research Center. (2018, April 11). Millennials are the largest generation in the U.S. labor force. FactTank. Retrieved from https://www.pewresearch.org

[95] GLAAD/Harris Poll. (2017, March 30). New GLAAD study reveals twenty percent of millennials identify as LGBTQ. Retrieved from https://www.glaad.org

[96] Flores, A. R., Herman, J. L., Gates, G. J., & Brown, N. T. (2016, June). *How many adults identify as transgender in the United States?* Los Angeles: The Williams Institute at UCLA. https://williamsinstitute.law.ucla.edu

[97] McGregor, J. (2019, July 7). How employers are preparing for a gender non-binary world. *The Washington Post*. Retrieved from https://www.washingtonpost.com

[98] Human Rights Campaign Foundation. (2019, June 19). Corporate equality index 2019, p. 17. Retrieved from https://www.hrc.org

[99] McGregor, J. (2019, July 7). How employers are preparing for a gender non-binary world. *The Washington Post*. Retrieved from https://www.washingtonpost.com

[100] James, S. E., Herman, J. L., Rankin, S., Keisling, M., Mottet, L., & Anafi, M. (2016). *The Report of the 2015 U.S. Transgender Survey*. Washington, DC: National Center for Transgender Equality. Retrieved from https://transequality.org

[101] Ibid.

[102] McGregor, J. (2019, July 7). How employers are preparing for a gender non-binary world. *The Washington Post*. Retrieved from https://www.washingtonpost.com

[103] Boykiv, Y. (2015, June 3). How to build and sustain a diverse team. Fast Company.

Retrieved from http://www.fastcompany.com

104 Phillips, K. W. (2014, October 1). How diversity makes us smarter. *Scientific American*. Retrieved from http://www.scientificamerican.com

105 Boykiv, Y. (2015, June 3). How to build and sustain a diverse team. Fast Company. Retrieved from http://www.fastcompany.com

106 Hunt, V., Yee, L., Prince, S., & Dixon-Fyle, S. (2018, January). Delivering through diversity. McKinsey Report. Retrieved from https://www.mckinsey.com

107 Bush, M., & Peters, K. (2016, December 5). How the best companies do diversity right. *Fortune*. Retrieved from https://fortune.com

108 Segal, J. A. (2015, October 1). How gender bias hurts men. Society for Human Resource Management. Retrieved from http://www.shrm.org

109 Brenan, M. (2017, November 16). Americans no longer prefer male boss to female boss. Gallup News. Retrieved from https://news.gallup.com; Smith, J. (2015, April 3). Study finds women are better bosses than men—Here's why. Business Insider. Retrieved from http://www.businessinsider.com

110 Separation of church and cubicle: Religion in the workplace. (2015, April 30). Wharton, University of Pennsylvania. Retrieved from http://knowledge.wharton.upenn.edu; U.S. Department of Justice. (2016, July). Combating religious discrimination today: Final report. Retrieved from https://www.justice.gov

111 Valet, V. (2019, January 15). America's best employers for diversity 2019. *Forbes*. Retrieved from https://www.forbes.com

112 Krawcheck, S. (2017). *Own it: The power of women at work*. New York: Crown Publishing, p. 37.

113 Meakin, L. (2019, June 14). BOE's Carney calls for diversity to stop groupthink in banking. *Bloomberg*. Retrieved from https://www.bloomberg.com

114 Capowski, G. (1996, June). Managing diversity. *Management Review*, 85(6), 16.

115 Gino, F. (2016, October-November). Rebel talent: If you want engaged employees, let them break rules and be themselves; we'll show you how. *Harvard Business Review*. Retrieved from https://hbr.org

116 Gay executives talk about the importance of being out at work. (2019, June 21). *Bloomberg*. Retrieved from https://www.bloomberg.com

117 Molinsky, A., & Jang, S. (2016, January 20). To connect across cultures, find out what you have in common. *Harvard Business Review*. Retrieved from https://hbr.org; Pfau, B. N., & Kay, I. T. (2002). *The human capital edge: 21 people management practices your company must implement (or avoid) to maximize shareholder value*. New York: McGraw-Hill, pp. 72–73, 75.

118 America's most hated companies. (2019, January 16). 24/7 Wall St. Retrieved from https://247wallst.com; Monllos, K. (2015, May 29). Is Walmart trying to brand itself as socially conscious? The value-focused chain seems to embrace corporate responsibility. *Adweek*. Retrieved from http://www.adweek.com; Hill, C. (2015, February 21). 4 reasons Walmart is the most-hated retailer in America. MarketWatch. Retrieved from http://www.marketwatch.com

119 Explore the Management Top 250. (2019, November 22). *The Wall Street Journal*. Retrieved from https://www.wsj.com

120 Horovitz, B. (2019, October 7). From the rooftops, big box stores are embracing solar. *The New York Times*. Retrieved from https://www.nytimes.com

121 McLaughlin, K., & Steer, A. (2019, November 6). Why Walmart and other companies are sticking with the Paris Climate Deal. *The New York Times*. Retrieved from https://www.nytimes.com

122 Schooley, S. (2019, August 12). Lost in translation: 19 international marketing fails. *Business News Daily*. Retrieved from https://www.businessnewsdaily.com

123 Transparency International. (2019, December 11). Wasta: How personal connections are denying citizens opportunities and basic services. Retrieved from https://www.transparency.org

124 Unless attributed otherwise, the scenarios are based on Richards, K. (2018, December 19). 5 major brand fails of 2018—And what every marketer can learn from them. *Adweek*. Retrieved from https://www.adweek.com

125 Schneider, E. (2020, January 10). 4 lessons from WW's unfortunate promoted tweet that ran while WWIII was trending: How to be nimble when the unexpected happens. *Adweek*. Retrieved from https://www.adweek.com

126 Marketing muck-ups: The biggest follies of 2011. (2011, December 12). *Advertising Age*. Retrieved from http://adage.com

127 Rai, S. (2018, November 20). Twitter CEO gets trolled after wading into India's caste debate. *Bloomberg*. Retrieved from https://www.bloomberg.com

128 British minister in cultural gaffe after giving Taipei mayor "taboo" watch. (2015, January 26). *The Guardian*. Retrieved from http://www.theguardian.com

129 Špaček, L. (2008). *Nová velká kniha etikety*. Prague: Mladá Fronta, p. 260.

130 Conlin, M. (2007, April 23). Go-go-going to pieces in China. *BusinessWeek*, p. 88.

131 Fifty-six percent of hotels in Japan bar visitors with tattoos from bathing facilities. (2015, October 22). *Japan Today*. Retrieved from https://japantoday.com

132 Shearer, E., & Matsa, K. E. (2018, September 10). News use across social media platforms 2018. Pew Research Center. Retrieved from https://www.journalism.org

133 Based on: Sewell, C. (2017, June 20). Russia's "gay propaganda" laws are illegal, European court rules. *The New York Times*. Retrieved from https://www.nytimes.com; Feder, J. L. (2013, November 20). Ikea pulls lesbian couple from Russian edition of its magazine. *BuzzFeed*. Retrieved from https://www.buzzfeednews.com; Sieczkowski, C. (2013, November 21). Ikea pulls lesbian couple feature from Russian magazine. *Huffpost*. Retrieved from https://www.huffpost.com; Strzelecki, M. (2019, July 1). Ikea risks boycott in Poland after firing anti-LGBT employee. *Bloomberg Quint*. Retrieved from https://www.bloombergquint.com; Noack, R. (2019, July 20). Polish cities and provinces declare "LGBT-free zones" as government ramps up "hate speech." *The Independent*. Retrieved from https://www.independent.co.uk

134 Statistics in this activity are based on the following sources: Facebook by the numbers: Stats, demographics & fun facts. Omnicore. Retrieved from https://www.omnicoreagency.com; Number of monthly active Facebook users in the United States and Canada as of 3rd quarter 2019. (2020) Statista. Retrieved from https://www.statista.com; Facebook Q2 2019 results. (2019). Retrieved from https://investor.fb.com; Internet World Stats. (2019). Miniwatts Marketing Group. Retrieved from https://internetworldstats.com; Internet penetration in Africa. (2019, June 30). Internet World Stats. Retrieved from https://internetworldstats.com

135 FCPA: A resource guide to the U.S. Foreign Corrupt Practices Act. (2012, November 14). U.S. Department of Justice and the U.S. Securities and Exchange Commission. Retrieved from https://www.justice.gov; FCPA & bribery: Travel expenses neither "reasonable" nor "bona fide." Whistleblower Justice Network. Retrieved from https://whistleblowerjustice.net; Martin, K., & Walsh, S. M. (1996, October). Beware the Foreign Corrupt Practices Act. *International Commercial Litigation*, 25–27; Lay-person's guide to Foreign Corrupt Practices Act (FCPA). (n.d.). United States Department of Justice. Retrieved from http://www.usdoj.gov

136 Berger, M. (2020, January 17). South Koreans find a focus for their ire: A U.S. ambassador's mustache. *The Washington Post*. Retrieved from https://www.washingtonpost.com

137 Fired Vancouver waiter: I'm not rude, just French. (2018, March 26). *BBC News*. Retrieved from https://www.bbc.com; Bachega, H. (2018, March 28). Fired Vancouver waiter case: Are the French really rude? *BBC News*. Retrieved from https://www.bbc.com

138 Alliance for Board Diversity. (2018, August 15). Missing pieces report: The 2018 board diversity census of women and minorities on *Fortune* 500 boards.

139 Catalyst. (2018, August 1). *Quick take: Why diversity and inclusion matter.* Retrieved from https://www.catalyst.org

140 Hunt, V., Yee, L., Prince, S., & Dixon-Fyle, S. (2018, January). Delivering through diversity. McKinsey Report. Retrieved from https://www.mckinsey.com; McKinsey & Company. (2015, January). Why diversity matters. Retrieved from http://www.mckinsey.com/insights/organization/why_diversity_matters

141 Hamblin, A. (2018, October 1). Should public companies be required to have women on their boards? California thinks so. *The San Diego Union-Tribune.* Retrieved from https://www.sandiegouniontribune.com; Egan, M. (2015, March 24). Still missing: Female business leaders. CNN Money. Retrieved from http://money.cnn.com; Ferrary, M. (2009, March 2). Why women managers shine in a downturn. *Financial Times.* Retrieved from http://www.ft.com

142 Solal, I., & Snellman, K. (2019, November 25). Why investors react negatively to companies that put women on their boards. *Harvard Business Review.* Retrieved from https://hbr.org

143 Greenfield, R. (2019, December 16). The problem with female CEOs isn't that they are female, it's that they are CEOs. *Bloomberg*, p. 12.

Chapter 4

1 VisibleThread. (2020). The Visible/Thread asset clarity index: Asset management 2019. Retrieved from www.visiblethread.com

2 Carrick, R. (2018, July 9). Why it's not your fault it's so hard to understand investing. *The Globe and Mail.* Retrieved from www.theglobeandmail.com

3 Casten, S. (2019, October 19-20). Quoted in Zweig, J. Time for advisors to speak in plain English. *The Wall Street Journal*, 32.

4 Maltby, E. (2010, January 19). Expanding abroad? Avoid cultural gaffes. *The Wall Street Journal*, B5.

5 Foderaro, L. (2009, May 18). Psst! Need the answer to no. 7? Just click here. *The New York Times*, p. A17.

6 Li, L. (n.d.). 10 stupid business ideas that made millions. Retrieved from www.entrepreneursforachange.com

7 Lewellen, E. (2014, November 13). Communication—Bypassing. *Transformative Thinking.* http://trans-think.com See also Sullivan, J., Karmeda, N., & Nobu, T. (1992, January/February). Bypassing in managerial communication. *Business Horizons*, 34(1), 72.

8 Brewer, E., & Holmes, T. (2009, October). Obfuscating the obvious: Miscommunication issues in the interpretation of common terms. *Journal of Business Communication, 46*(4), 480–496.

9 Halvorson, H. G. (2011, September 29). Too much communication at work? A simple fix. *Forbes.* Retrieved from ww.forbes.com

10 Udemy. (2018). 2018 Workplace Distraction Report. *Udemy for Business.* Retrieved from https://research.udemy.com

11 Littlefield, A. (2019, January 1). No, you don't have the attention span of a goldfish. Retrieved from https://www.ceros.com; Maybin, S. (2017, March 10). Busting the attention span myth. Retrieved from https://www.bbc.com/news/health-38896790

12 Drucker, P. (1990). *Managing the non-profit organization: Practices and principles.* New York: HarperCollins, p. 46.

13 Silverman, D. (2009, February 10). Why is business writing so bad? *Harvard Business Review.* Retrieved from https://hbr.org

14 Quoted in O'Hara, C. (2014, November 20). How to improve your business writing. *Harvard Business Review.* Retrieved from https://hbr.org

15 Visentin, L. (2015, May 28). Macquarie University revokes degrees for students caught buying essays in MyMaster cheating racket. Retrieved from www.smh.com.au

16 Arnold, V. (1986, August). Benjamin Franklin on writing well. *Personnel Journal*, p. 17.

17 Bacon, M. (1988, April). Quoted in Business writing: One-on-one speaks best to the masses. *Training*, p. 95.

18 Clark, B. (n.d.). The two most important words in blogging. Retrieved from www.copyblogger.com

19 Riesterer, T. (2019). You vs. we: Which is the best way to phrase a campaign? Retrieved from adweek.com

20 Adams, K. (2018, October 30). This baby gets $11,000 because her parents named her after Col. Sanders. *Louisville Courier Journal.* Retrieved from www.courier-journal.com

21 Google. (2012, January 30). E-mail message to Mary Ellen Guffey.

22 Lahey, S. Emojis at work: The good, the bad, and the legally binding. Retrieved from https://relate.zendesk.com; see also Mims, C. (2019, July 20). Yes, you actually should be using emojis at work. Retrieved from https://www.wsj.com

23 Geraghty, L. (2017). Positive tone: It's how you say it. Retrieved from http://wavelength.training

24 Canavor, N. (2012). *Business writing in the digital age.* Thousand Oaks, CA: Sage, p. 52.

25 Link, S. (2012, May 2). Use 'person first' language. [Letter to editor]. *USA Today*, p. 6A.

26 Agrawal, A. (2014, December 2). Why Office 365 is the best choice for collaboration. Retrieved from www.microsoft.com

27 Chang, J. (2019, October 30). Best mind mapping software of 2020. Retrieved from https://reviews.financesonline.com/p/wisemapping; Hurst, J. (2018, January 3). 15 best brainstorming and mind-mapping tech tools for every creative mind. Retrieved from www.lifehack.org

28 May, T. (2017, June 28). We're undervaluing collaboration. Retrieved from www.computerworld.com

29 Tomac, E. (2019, September 20). The 27 most annoying business buzzwords of 2019. Retrieved from https://www.trustradius.com/buyer-blog/27-most-annoying-business-buzzwords-of-2019-explained

30 E-write Online. Plain writing is a civil right. (2009). Retrieved from www.ewriteonline.com

31 Halvorson, H. G. (2011, September 29). Too much communication at work? A simple fix. Retrieved from www.forbes.com

Chapter 5

1 Hirscheimer, R. (2015, July 21). Interview with Mary Ellen Guffey.

2 2019 Run for Equal Justice. Retrieved from https://runforequaljustice.com/page.php?groupingID=miscellaneous1

3 Myevent.com. (2018). What our clients say. Retrieved from https://myevent.com/athons

4 Greenfield, R. (2014, July 29). *Fast Company.* Brainstorming doesn't work; try this technique instead. Fast Company. Retrieved from www.fastcompany.com

5 PC Magazine. (2017, August 21). The best mind mapping software of 2018. Retrieved from www.pcmag.com

6 Stormboard. (2018). Shared sticky notes and whiteboards. Retrieved from www.stormboard.com

7 Speier, K. (2016, January 7). Four examples of clever crowdsourcing campaigns. Retrieved from https://www.mainstreethost.com

8 CocaCola Journey Staff. (2018, February 23). Coca-Cola turns to consumers for sweetener innovations through crowdsourcing contest. Retrieved from https://www.coca-colacompany.com

9 Fawdrey, G. (2019, September 2). Challenging plastic waste. Retrieved from https://www.nesta.org.uk/blog

10 Rexrode, C. (2017, September 18). The soul of Citigroup. *Retrieved from The Wall Street Journal*, B1.

11 Rindegard, J. (1999, November 22). Use clear writing to show you mean business. *InfoWorld*, 78.

12 Kassel, M. (August 7, 2017). CEOs' simple trick on earnings calls: Saying "I," "we" and "us." *The Wall Street Journal*, R1.

13 Johnston, L. G. (2011, January 12). Avoid this simple comma splice error. Retrieved from www.businesswritingblog.com

14 Goddard, R. W. (1989, April). Communication: Use language effectively. *Personnel Journal*, 32.

15 O'Connor, P. (1996). *Woe is I.* New York: Putnam, p. 161.

16 PayScale. (2016, May 17). Leveling up: How to win in the skills economy. [Press release]. Retrieved from www.payscale.com

17 Bernoff, J. (2016, September 6). Bad writing is destroying your company's productivity. *Harvard Business Review*. Retrieved from https://hbr.org

18 Booher, D. (2007). *The voice of authority*. New York: McGraw-Hill, p. 93.

Chapter 6

1 Lefler, S. (2018, September 13). Taco Bell was voted the best Mexican restaurant in the country, and the Internet can't believe it. Retrieved from https://www.usmagazine.com

2 Horovitz, B. (2012, February 20). Taco Bell + Doritos = success? *USA Today*, p. B1.

3 Northrup, L. (2015, September 15). Taco Bell abruptly closes its upscale 'American-inspired' Taco Restaurant. Retrieved from http://consumerist.com

4 Taco Bell. (2019). How to eat vegetarian and meatless at Taco Bell. Retrieved from www.tacobell.com

5 Elbow, P. (1998). *Writing with power: Techniques for mastering the writing process*. Oxford, UK: Oxford University Press, p. 30.

6 Shankman, P. (2011, May 20). I will never hire a "social media expert," and neither should you. Retrieved from http://shankman.com

7 Adams, S. (2011, April 9-10). How to get a real education. *The Wall Street Journal*, C1–C2.

8 Fogarty, M. (2015, April 27). Quoted in Coster, H. Ten tips for better business writing. Retrieved from www.forbes.com

9 Bernoff, J. (2016, September 6). Bad writing is destroying your company's productivity. Retrieved from https://hbr.org

10 Sword, H. (2012, July 25). *Zombie nouns*. Retrieved from http://www.3quarksdaily.com

11 Beck, J. (2018, June 27). Read this article!!! Retrieved from www.theatlantic.com

12 Levitt, A. (2011, April 2). A word to Wall Street: "Plain English," please. *The Wall Street Journal*. Retrieved from http://online.wsj.com

13 Duffy, S. P. (2007, April 23). Attorney hit with $6.6 million malpractice verdict. Retrieved from http://www.corpcounsel.com

14 Wells, G. (2015, October 8). How grammar snobs no u ain't mr rite. *The Wall Street Journal*, A1.

15 The trouble with email. (2015, September 13). Retrieved from http://businesstodaync.com

16 Waller, N. (2018, October 23). I'm not mad. I'm just not using exclamation points. *The Wall Street Journal*, R7. See also Beck, J. (2018, June 27). Read this article!!! Retrieved from www.theatlantic.com

17 Van Grove, J. (2009, January 21). 40 of the best twitter brands and the people behind them. Retrieved from http://mashable.com

18 Bank of America Twitter Help. (2012, June 3). @AmyJo 63Owen. Twitter. Retrieved from https://twitter.com

19 JetBlue Twitter Help. (2012, June 4). VictoriaKlim @vikiybubbles. Twitter. Retrieved from https://twitter.com/#!/JetBlue

20 Southwest Airlines Twitter. (2012, May 15). Chris Cichon@cichonship. Twitter. Retrieved from https://twitter.com/#!/SouthwestAir

21 H&R Block. (2012, June 4). Carlos Noriega@calinelbarbaro. Twitter. Retrieved from https://twitter.com/#!/hrblock

22 Zinsser, W. (1976). *On writing well*. New York: HarperCollins.

23 O'Tool, G. (2012, April 28). If I had more time, I would have written a shorter letter. Retrieved from https://quoteinvestigator

Chapter 7

1 Brewster, T. (2020, February 10). Chinese government hackers charged with massive Equifax hack. *Forbes*. Retrieved from https://www.forbes.com

2 Unless otherwise noted, the scenario is based on conversations with members of the Averon team in 2019/2020 and on information on the company's website, Averon.com.

3 Averon closes new funding round bringing raise to $13.3 million. (2018, March 21). PR Newswire. Retrieved from https://www.prnewswire.com

4 Heath, N. (2018, September 24). Will Microsoft finally kill the password with its Authenticator upgrade? TechRepublic. Retrieved from https://www.techrepublic.com

5 Mobile fact sheet: Mobile phone ownership over time. (2019, June 12). Pew Research Center. Retrieved from https://www.pewresearch.org

6 Dean, J. (2016, October 25). Slack CEO Stewart Butterfield on the future of communication. *The Wall Street Journal*. Retrieved from https://www.wsj.com

7 The Radicati Group. (2019, April). Email market, 2019-2023. Retrieved from https://www.radicati.com; Clement, J. (2019, August 9). Number of e-mail users worldwide 2017-2023. Statista. Retrieved from https://www.statista.com

8 The Radicati Group. (2018, March). Email statistics report, 2018-2022. Retrieved from https://www.radicati.com

9 Tschabitscher, H. (2019, June 27). 19 fascinating email facts. Lifewire. Retrieved from https://www.lifewire.com; Lynkova, D. (2019, April 22). The surprising reality of how many emails are sent per day. Techjury. Retrieved from https://techjury.net

10 Duffy, J., & Moore, B. (2019, December 12). The best business messaging apps for 2020. *PC Magazine*. Retrieved from https://www.pcmag.com

11 Madrigal, A. C. (2014, August 14). Email is still the best thing on the Internet. *The Atlantic*. Retrieved from https://www.theatlantic.com

12 Elgan, M. (2018, March 31). Why email is the best social network. *Computerworld*. Retrieved from https://www.computerworld.com

13 Clement, J. (2019, August 9). E-mail usage in the United States—Statistics & facts. Statista. Retrieved from https://www.statista.com

14 Connley, C. (2018, June 5). Suzy Welch: 4 email mistakes that make people hate you. CNBC. Retrieved from https://www.cnbc.com

15 Gillett, R. (2017, February 21). 21 unprofessional email habits that make everyone hate you. *Business Insider*. Retrieved from https://www.businessinsider.com

16 La Roche, J. (2019, March 16). Goldman Sachs CEO reveals the valuable job skill he's finding "less and less." Yahoo Finance. Retrieved from https://finance.yahoo.com

17 Abramovich, G. (2019, September). CMO by Adobe. Retrieved from https://cmo.adobe.com

18 Koren, M. (2018, June 11). The most honest out-of-office message. *The Atlantic*. Retrieved from https://www.theatlantic.com

19 LaFrance, A. (2016, January 6). The triumph of email. *The Atlantic*. Retrieved from https://www.theatlantic.com

20 O'Connor, K. (2016, July 25). Email is forever. *The Houston Chronicle*. Retrieved from https://www.chron.com

21 Vaughan, A. (2018, January 16). BP's Deepwater Horizon bill tops $65bn. *The Guardian*. Retrieved from https://www.theguardian.com; Vance, A. (2014, December 4). The eight most expensive e-mail snafus in corporate history. *Bloomberg Business*. Retrieved from http://www.bloomberg.com

22 Ma, A. (2019, April 19). Nine years later, the BP oil spill's environmental mess isn't gone. *Mother Jones*. Retrieved from https://www.motherjones.com

23 Nagele-Piazza, L. (2018, June 15). Tips for managing workers' after-hour use of mobile devices. SHRM. Retrieved from https://www.shrm.org; Brandeisky, K. (2015, March 3). 5 things you didn't know about using personal email at work. *Money*. Retrieved from http://time.com

24 Bell, J. D. (2018, August 24). Firing for online behavior. SHRM. Retrieved from https://www.shrm.org; American Management Association. (2014, November 17). The latest on workplace monitoring and surveillance. American Management Association. Retrieved from http://www.amanet.org

25 Lamb, S. E. (2015). *Writing well for business success*. New York: St. Martin's Griffin, p. 139.

26 Bohns, V. K. (2017, April 11). A face-to-face request is 34 times more successful than an

email. *Harvard Business Review.* Retrieved from https://hbr.org

[27] Turk, V. (2020). *Kill reply all: A modern guide to online etiquette.* New York: Plume, Penguin Random House, pp. 9–10.

[28] Mobile fact sheet: Mobile phone ownership over time. (2019, June 12). Pew Research Center. Retrieved from https://www.pewresearch.org

[29] Strasburg, J. (2017, January 13). Deutsche Bank bans widely used text-messaging programs for business use. *The Wall Street Journal.* Retrieved from https://www.wsj.com; Bit, K. (2014, June 9). Cohen's Point72 bans instant messaging for some managers. *Bloomberg Business.* Retrieved from http://www.bloomberg.com; Rushton, K. (2013, December 15). JP Morgan to ban staff from instant messaging services. *The Telegraph.* Retrieved from https://www.telegraph.co.uk

[30] Campbell, D. (2019, March 27). Wall Street is losing its battle against encrypted apps like WhatsApp and WeChat as it tries to police employee communications—And even regulators are stumped. *Business Insider.* Retrieved from https://www.businessinsider.com; Keller, L. J. (2017, March 30). Wall Street's new favorite way to swap secrets is against the rules. *Bloomberg.* Retrieved from https://www.bloomberg.com

[31] Anderson, D. (2014). Best practices for employees to protect the company from hackers. *Entrepreneur.* Retrieved from https://www.entrepreneur.com

[32] Motor vehicle safety at work: Distracted driving at work. (2019, September 30). Centers for Disease Control and Protection. National Institute for Occupational Safety and Health. Retrieved from https://www.cdc.gov

[33] Jack in the Box SMS redemption rates 3-5x greater than email marketing. (2015, March 24). Tatango. Retrieved from https://www.tatango.com

[34] Based on Advice: Texting manners. (n. d.). The Emily Post Institute. Retrieved from https://emilypost.com

[35] Fischer, M. (2017, May 1). What happens when work becomes a nonstop chat room. *New York Magazine,* Intelligencer. Retrieved from https://nymag.com

[36] Warren, T. (2019, July 11). Microsoft Teams overtakes Slack with 13 million daily users. *The Verge.* Retrieved from https://www.theverge.com

[37] Peer review for Slack. (2019). Gartner Peer Insights. Retrieved from https://www.gartner.com

[38] Scott, C. L. (2020, March 5). So, you got Slack for your employees. Make sure you're ready for it. *The Wall Street Journal.* Retrieved from https://www.wsj.com

[39] Moses, E. R. (2019, October 11). Viewpoint: The legal risks of digital workplace apps. SHRM. Retrieved from https://www.shrm.org

[40] Scott, C. L. (2020, March 5). So, you got Slack for your employees. Make sure you're ready for it. *The Wall Street Journal.* Retrieved from https://www.wsj.com

[41] Based on Akhtar, A. (2019, September 4). Your guide to workplace slack etiquette. *Inc.* Retrieved from https://www.inc.com

[42] Locker, M. (2016, October 28). How to make a great podcast—A beginner's guide. *The Guardian.* Retrieved from https://www.theguardian.com

[43] Richter, F. (2019, March 7). The steady rise of podcasts. Statista. Retrieved from https://www.statista.com; Smith, A. (2015, April 1). U.S. smartphone use in 2015. Pew Research Center. Retrieved from https://www.pewinternet.org

[44] Winn, R. (2020, February 7). 2020 podcast stats & facts (new research from Jan 2020). Podcast Insights. Retrieved from https://www.podcastinsights.com

[45] Brogan, C. (2019, August 30). Is there any value in blogging and podcasting and all that media? Chris Brogan Media: Storyleader. Retrieved from https://chrisbrogan.com

[46] Comedy, news, society and culture podcasts most listened-to genres in podcasting. (2019, December 16). Edison Research. Retrieved from https://www.edisonresearch.com

[47] Yonchev, O. (2019, December 31). 7 social media trends to watch out for before 2020 hits. PR Daily. Retrieved from https://www.prdaily.com

[48] Beyond the Iron: The Caterpillar podcast. Retrieved from https://www.caterpillar.com

[49] Walmart Radio. (n.d.). Apple Podcast Preview. Retrieved from https://podcasts.apple.com

[50] Orman, S. (n.d.). Women & Money. Retrieved from https://www.suzeorman.com

[51] Day, M. (2018, March 27). The fraud and the four-hour workweek. *Jacobin.* Retrieved from https://jacobinmag.com; Schein, M. (2019, January 17). Tim Ferriss is everything that's wrong with the modern world (and why you should follow his lead). *Forbes.* Retrieved from https://www.forbes.com

[52] Podcast Directory. (2020, February). TED Radio Hour. Retrieved from https://www.npr.org

[53] P&G, GEICO love advertising on podcasts. (2019, June 6). Radio Ink. Retrieved from https://radioink.com

[54] Rose, J. (2020, February 26). 14 reasons to not listen to Suze Orman. Good Financial Cents. Retrieved from https://www.goodfinancialcents.com

[55] Dale, B. (2016, January 27). Five revenue strategies from a million dollar podcast. Observer Media. Retrieved from https://observer.com

[56] Sullivan, T. (2019, July 17). How to create your own successful podcast. *PCMag.* Retrieved from https://www.pcmag.com

[57] Shafrir, D. (2017, May 23). Seven elements you need to create a successful podcast. *Forbes.* Retrieved from https://www.forbes.com

[58] Houlahan, A. (2015, September 28). The importance of blogging for your brand. Retrieved from https://www.adamhoulahan.com

[59] Barnes, N. G., Mazzola, A., & Killeen, M. (2020, January 9). Oversaturation & disengagement: The 2019 Fortune 500 social media dance. University of Massachusetts Dartmouth. Retrieved from https://www.umassd.edu

[60] Ibid.

[61] To shave, or not to shave, in November. (2019, November 19). Transportation Security Agency. Retrieved from https://www.tsa.gov

[62] Arruda, W. (2018, February 15). Why storytelling is the key to success, and how to tell your story. *Forbes.* Retrieved from https://www.forbes.com

[63] Marriott, Jr., J. W. "Bill." (2012, January 1). About my blog. Marriott on the Move. Retrieved from http://www.blogs.marriott.com

[64] Beyond the box. (2020). Zappos.com. Retrieved from https://www.zappos.com

[65] Melody. (2017, May 31). Starbucks nixes the MyStarbucksIdea community: You can still submit ideas. StarbucksMelody: Unofficial Starbucks News & Culture. Retrieved from http://www.starbucksmelody.com

[66] Schultz, E. J. (2016, January 4). See the "Crash the Super Bowl" finalists' ads. *Advertising Age.* Retrieved from http://adage.com

[67] Pulse: Our teams, our stories, our careers. Target. Retrieved from https://pulse.target.com

[68] Harter, J. (2018, August 26). Employee engagement on the rise in the U.S. Gallup. Retrieved from https://news.gallup.com

[69] Scheiber, N. (2018, March 11). Lotto tickets are nice, boss, but can I have my bonus? *The New York Times.* Retrieved from https://www.nytimes.com

[70] Apostolopoulos, A. (2019, August 19). The 2019 gamification at work survey. TalentLMS. Retrieved from https://www.talentlms.com

[71] Gamification market 2012-2022. P&S Intelligence. Retrieved from https://www.psmarketresearch.com

[72] Smith, R. A. (2020, January 2). Work clothes, reimagined for an age of wearable tech. *The Wall Street Journal.* Retrieved from https://www.wsj.com; Gage, D. (2018, September 16). Wearable health monitors: Do they work? *The Wall Street Journal.* Retrieved from https://www.wsj.com; Schatsky, D. (2018, September 11). Wearables: The new workforce superpower. CIO Journal, Deloitte. *The Wall Street Journal.* Retrieved from https://deloitte.wsj.com

[73] Rayson, S. (2017, June 26). We analyzed 100 million headlines. Here's what we learned (new research). BuzzSumo. Retrieved from https://buzzsumo.com

[74] Plourde, D. (2020, January 30). Do you have what it takes? Top 20 most rugged jobs in America. Direct2Dell. Retrieved from https://blog.dell.com

[75] Chartrand, J. (n.d.). Do you have useless website content? Men With Pens. Retrieved from https://menwithpens.ca

[76] Spencer, J. (2019, November 25). How to start a blog: A really simple beginners guide on how you can create your own blog in just 20 minutes. MakeAWebsiteHub. Retrieved from https://makeawebsitehub.com

[77] Abramovich, G. (2019, September). CMO by Adobe. Retrieved from https://cmo.adobe.com

[78] Barnes, N. G., Mazzola, A., & Killeen, M. (2020, January 9). Oversaturation & Disengagement: The 2019 Fortune 500 social media dance. Center for Marketing Research, University of Massachusetts Dartmouth. Retrieved from https://www.umassd.edu

[79] More than half of employers have found content on social media that caused them NOT to hire a candidate, according to a recent CareerBuilder Survey. (2018, August 9). CareerBuilder. Retrieved from https://www.prnewswire.com

[80] Social media fact sheet. (2019, June 12). Pew Research Center. Retrieved from https://www.pewresearch.org

[81] Vogels, E. A. (2019, September 9). Millennials stand out for their technology use, but older generations also embrace digital life. Retrieved from https://www.pewresearch.org

[82] Desilver, D. (2019, August 29). 10 facts about American workers. FactTank. Retrieved from https://www.pewresearch.org

[83] Perrin, A., & Anderson, M. (2019, April 10). Share of U.S. adult using social media, including Facebook, is mostly unchanged since 2018. Pew Research Center: FactTank. Retrieved from https://www.pewresearch.org

[84] Barnes, N. G., Mazzola, A., & Killeen, M. (2020, January 9). Oversaturation & Disengagement: The 2019 Fortune 500 social media dance. Center for Marketing Research, University of Massachusetts Dartmouth. Retrieved from https://www.umassd.edu; Perrin, A., & Anderson, M. (2019, April 10). Pew Research Center: FactTank. Retrieved from https://www.pewresearch.org

[85] Quesenberry, K. A. (2018, January 2). The basic social media mistakes companies still make. *Harvard Business Review*. Retrieved from https://hbr.org

[86] Frier, S., & Wagner, K. (2020, February 27). TikTok marketers chase billions of views in uncharted terrain. *Bloomberg*. Retrieved from https://www.bloomberg.com

[87] Zhan, L. (2019, November 12). Will TikTok become the next Huawei? *Business Insider*. Retrieved from https://www.businessinsider.sg

[88] Cardon, P. (2015). Enterprise social networks (Internal social media platforms). *NBEA 2015 Yearbook: Recent and Projected Technology Trends Affecting Business Education*, p. 37.

[89] Better serving members using one social spot. (n. d.). Yammer Success Story: Featured Customers. Retrieved from https://cdn.featuredcustomers.com

[90] Wall, M. T. (2015, June 8). After employee disagrees on internal social network, IBM changes travel policy. LinkedIn. Retrieved from https://www.linkedin.com

[91] Neubert, S. (2016, February 11). Goodyear brings spirit of innovation to every facet of product development and delivery. Microsoft 365. Retrieved from https://www.microsoft.com

[92] Networking to save the planet. (n.d.). Yammer Success Story: Featured Customers. Retrieved from https://cdn.featuredcustomers.com

[93] Carley, S. (n.d.). Empowering employees for improved customer service and a better bottom line. Yammer Success Story: Featured Customers. Retrieved from https://cdn.featuredcustomers.com

[94] Brin, D. (2017, July 18). Agility, willingness to pivot are key for transforming companies: IBM's Gherson.

[95] Westwood, R. (2018, January 16). Are your employees wasting time on social media? Here are three benefits. *Forbes*. Retrieved from https://www.forbes.com

[96] The compliance risks of social media. (n.d.). Thomson Reuters. Retrieved from https://legal.thomsonreuters.com

[97] Samuel, A., & Marquez, S. (2018, May 29). Should companies let employees use social media at work? *The Wall Street Journal*. Retrieved from https://www.wsj.com

[98] IBM social computing guidelines: Blogs, wikis, social networks, virtual worlds and social media. (n.d.). IBM. Retrieved from https://www.ibm.com

[99] Bizzi, L. (2018, May 17). Employees who use social media for work are more engaged—But also more likely to leave their jobs. *Harvard Business Review*. Retrieved from https://hbr.org

[100] Chang, E. (2017, November 30). Why halting social media use in the workplace fails. *The Street*. Retrieved from https://www.thestreet.com

[101] Ramirez, C. (2018, September 24). Detroit officer fired over social media post. *The Detroit News*. Retrieved from https://www.detroitnews.com

[102] Bell, J. D. (2018, August 24). Firing for online behavior. SHRM. Retrieved from https://www.shrm.org

[103] Anderson, J., & Rainie, L. (2017, October 19). *The future of truth and misinformation online*. Pew Research Center: Internet & Technology. Retrieved from https://www.pewresearch.org

[104] Thompson, S. A., & Warzel, C. (2019, December 19). Twelve million phones, one dataset, zero privacy. *The New York Times*. Retrieved from https://www.nytimes.com

[105] Altschuler, G., & Tarrow, S. (2019, October 20). Combatting fake news on social media will take a village. *The Hill*. Retrieved from https://thehill.com; Shearer, E., & Matsa, K. E. (2018, September 10). *News use across social media platforms 2018*. Pew Research Center: Journalism & Media. Retrieved from https://www.journalism.org

[106] Schmidt, A. L., Zollo, F., Del Vicario, M., Bessi, A., Scala, A., Caldarelli, G., Stanley, H. E., & Quattrociocchi, W. (2017, January 31). Anatomy of news consumption on Facebook. *Proceedings of the National Academy of Sciences, 114*(12), 3035–3039. Retrieved from https://www.pnas.org

[107] Anderson, J., & Rainie, L. (2017, October 19). *The future of truth and misinformation online*. Pew Research Center: Internet & Technology. Retrieved from https://www.pewresearch.org

[108] Silverman, C., & Singer-Vine, J. (2016, December 6). Most Americans who see fake news believe it, new survey says. *BuzzFeed News*. Retrieved from https://www.buzzfeednews.com

[109] Flood, A. (2016, November 15). "Post-truth" named word of the year by Oxford Dictionaries. *The Guardian*. Retrieved from https://www.theguardian.com

[110] O'Sullivan, D. (2016). When seeing is no longer believing. CNN Business. Retrieved from https://www.cnn.com

[111] Bell, C. (2018, February 1). The people who think 9/11 may have been an "inside job." BBC News. Retrieved from https://www.bbc.com

[112] Harris, S. (2019, February 5). Making sense with Sam Harris—Jack Dorsey. Podcast episode #148. Retrieved from https://www.stitcher.com

[113] Stephens, B. (2019, May 3). Facebook's unintended consequence. *The New York Times*. Retrieved from https://www.nytimes.com

[114] Social media firms "failing" to tackle cyber-bullying. (2018, February 26). BBC News. Retrieved from https://www.bbc.com

[115] 2020 Businesses @work: Most popular factors. (2020). Okta.com. Retrieved from https://www.okta.com

[116] Vogels, E. A., & Anderson, M. (2019, October 9). *Americans and digital knowledge*. Pew Research Center: Internet & Technology. Retrieved from https://www.pewresearch.org

[117] 2020 Businesses @work: Most popular factors. (2020). Okta.com. Retrieved from https://www.okta.com

[118] Jurkowitz, M., & Mitchell, A. (2020, January 29). *An oasis of bipartisanship: Republicans and Democrats distrust social media*

[119] *sites for political and election news.* Pew Research Center: Journalism & Media. Retrieved from https://journalism.org

[119] Brooks, S. (2018, April 20). Business leader interview with Wendell Brown—CEO at Averon. *Enterprise Times.* Retrieved from https://www.enterprisetimes.co.uk

[120] De Querol, R. (2016, January 25). Zygmunt Bauman: "Social media are a trap." *El País.* Retrieved from http://elpais.com/elpais/2016/01/19/inenglish/1453208692_424660.html

[121] LaFrance, A. (2016, January 6). The triumph of email. *The Atlantic.* Retrieved from https://www.theatlantic.com

[122] Confessore, N., Dance, G. J. X., Harris, R., & Hansen, M. The follower factory. *The New York Times.* Retrieved from https://www.nytimes.com

[123] Based on Samuel, A. (2020, March 6). The tech habits of co-workers that drive us crazy. *The Wall Street Journal*, pp. R1–R3.

[124] Martin, G. (2019, April 18). Is a podcast right for every business? CO. U.S. Chamber of Commerce. Retrieved from https://www.uschamber.com

[125] Clark, D. (2014, October 28). How to launch a successful podcast – Fast. *Forbes.* Retrieved from http://www.forbes.com

[126] Montoya, M. (2012, October 16.) 5 ways Twitter can get you fired. Examiner.com. Retrieved from http://www.examiner.com

[127] Shanbhag, A. (2016, March 2). What happens when you quit social media? I found out. *Makeuseof.* Retrieved from http://www.makeuseof.com; Gaddis, B. (2016, February 9). Here's what happened when I quit social media. *The Huffington Post.* Retrieved from http://www.huffingtonpost.com; Hempel, J. (2015, August 2). I'm quitting social media to learn what I actually like. *Wired.* Retrieved from https://www.wired.com; Sparkes, M. (2013, April 11). Twitter and Facebook "addicts" suffer withdrawal symptoms. *The Telegraph.* Retrieved from http://www.telegraph.co.uk

[128] Rufus, A. (2017, July 14). The dangers of digital detoxing. *Daily Beast.* Retrieved from https://www.thedailybeast.com

[129] Connected leadership. (2019). Brunswick Group. Retrieved from https://www.brunswickgroup.com

[130] Gravier, E. (2019, June 26). The top 10 most "connected" CEOs on social media—And where you can follow them. CNBC.com. Retrieved from https://www.cnbc.com

Chapter 8

[1] The 2019 Pizza Power report. (2018, December). *PMQ Magazine.* Retrieved from www.pmq.com

[2] Kelso, A. (2019, January 22). How Domino's plans to continue dominating the pizza market. *Forbes.* Retrieved from www.forbes.com

[3] Wong, K. (2018, January 26). How Domino's transformed into an e-commerce powerhouse whose product is pizza. *Forbes.* Retrieved from www.forbes.com

[4] Ibid.

[5] Internet usage statistics: World Internet users and 2020 population stats. (2019, December 31). Miniwatts Marketing Group. Retrieved from https://internetworldstats.com

[6] Pulcinella, S. (2017, August 30). Why direct mail marketing is far from dead. *Forbes.* Retrieved from https://www.forbes.com

[7] Advice: Effective business letters. (n.d.). The Emily Post Institute. Retrieved from https://emilypost.com

[8] Why revisions and editing are worth your time: They're where the real writing happens. (2018, January 30). Hurley Write, Inc. Retrieved from https://www.hurleywrite.com

[9] Girard, J. (2018, February 1). Your name and your word. Joe Girard Blog. Retrieved from https://www.joegirard.com

[10] Reid, B. (2018, February 16). An unsigned email may create a contract. *Huff Post.* Retrieved from https://www.huffpost.com

[11] Can emails and messages constitute a legally binding agreement? (2016, September 12). DBL Law. Retrieved from https://www.dbllaw.com

[12] Based on Kostov, N., & Schechner, S. (2019, June 17). GDPR has been a boon for Google and Facebook. *The Wall Street Journal.* Retrieved from https://www.wsj.com; Satariano, A. (2018, May 6). What the G.D.P.R., Europe's tough new data law, means for you. *The New York Times.* Retrieved from https://www.nytimes.com; Wakabayashi, D., & Stariano, A. (2018, April 23). How Facebook and Google could benefit from the G.D.P.R., Europe's new privacy law. *The New York Times.* Retrieved from https://www.nytimes.com; Singer, N. (2018, April 8). A tough task for Facebook: European-type privacy for all. *The New York Times.* Retrieved from https://www.nytimes.com

[13] Wolford, B. (2020). Everything you need to know about the "Right to be forgotten." GDPR.EU. Retrieved from https://gdpr.eu

[14] Klemp, N. (2017, March 31). 10 rules of engagement: How to respond to social media complaints. Salesforce Blog. Retrieved from https://www.salesforce.com

[15] Ford, A. (2011, June 28). Develop a comment monitoring policy . . . Or use this one. Tymado Multimedia Solutions. Retrieved from http://tymado.com

[16] Harrison, K. (2019, May 7). 10 companies that totally rock customer services on social media. Business News Daily. Retrieved from https://www.businessnewsdaily.com; Banjo, S. (2012, July 29). Firms take online reviews to heart. *The Wall Street Journal.* Retrieved from http://online.wsj.com

[17] Gibbons, S. (2018, September 20). Why businesses need to see customer feedback as make-or-break. *Forbes.* Retrieved from https://www.forbes.com

[18] Stum, L. (2017, November 1). Seven reasons people don't read instructions. Learning Stream. Retrieved from https://www.learningstream.com

[19] Carrera, M. (2019, September 5). Diesel mocks "wardrobing" phenomenon with fall ad campaign. WWD. Retrieved from https://wwd.com

[20] Bernstein, E. (2015, August 10). Don't hit send: Angry emails just make you angrier. *The Wall Street Journal.* Retrieved from http://www.wsj.com

[21] Cox, K. (2016, March 14). The 8.5 steps to making an effective complaint that gets a solution. *Consumerist.* Retrieved from https://consumerist.com; Torabi, F. (2011, July 28). Bad customer service? 3 smarter ways to complain. CBS News. Retrieved from http://www.cbsnews.com

[22] Tran, T. (2020, March 3). What is social listening, why it matters, and 10 tools to make it easier. Hootsuite. Retrieved from https://blog.hootsuite.com; Morrison, K. (2016, March 18). 5 tips for using social listening to understand customers. *Adweek.* Retrieved from https://www.adweek.com

[23] Hoopfer, E. (2019, March 3). Social media LUV: How Southwest Airlines connects with customers online. *Dallas Business Journal.* Retrieved from https://www.bizjournals.com

[24] Doyle, A. (2020, January 29). You can get fired for what you post online. The Balance Careers. Retrieved from https://www.thebalancecareers.com

[25] Warren, K. (2018, April 11). 18 unbelievable things people did at work that got them fired immediately. *Insider.* Retrieved from https://www.insider.com

[26] Huddleston, T. (2019, October 10). Can you get sued over a negative Yelp review? Here's what you need to know. CNBC. Retrieved from https://www.cnbc.com; Posting a negative review online can get you sued. CBS News. Retrieved from https://www.cbsnews.com

[27] Local consumer review survey. (2019, December 11). BrightLocal. Retrieved from https://www.brightlocal.com

[28] Gino, F. (2016, October/November). Rebel talent: If you want engaged employees, let them break rules and be themselves. *Harvard Business Review*, p. 7. Retrieved from https://hbr.org

[29] Gurchiek, K. (2018, February 23). Saying "thank you," "I'm sorry" is simple but meaningful. SHRM. Retrieved from https://www.shrm.org

[30] Mau, E. (2019, December 18). Study examines the effectiveness of apology laws on reducing medical malpractice liability. Borden Ladner Gervais LLP. Retrieved from https://www.blg.com; State apology laws may not reduce risk of liability. (2017, February 15). ECRI. Retrieved from https://www.ecri.org

31 Molinsky, A. (2016, November 25). The 4 types of ineffective apologies. *Harvard Business Review*. Retrieved from https://hbr.org; Hollis, L. (2014, February 27). Sorry seems to be the hardest word. *Management Today*. Retrieved from http://www.managementtoday.co.uk

32 Sanchez, C. (2019, July 16). Nine ways to turn a customer complaint into a valuable lesson; 4. Stay focused on solutions and forego scripts. *Forbes*. Retrieved from https://www.forbes.com; Baer, J. (2015, June 24). How asking for help can turn haters into brand advocates. *Inc*. Retrieved from http://www.inc.com

33 Advice: Sympathy notes and letters. (n.d.). Emily Post Institute. Retrieved from http://emilypost.com

34 Ibid.

35 A case for the dwindling art of letter writing in the 21st century. (2014, June 5). Radio Boston WBUR. Retrieved from http://radioboston.wbur.org

36 Turkle, S. (2015, September 26). Stop Googling. Let's talk. *The New York Times*. Retrieved from http://www.nytimes.com

37 Based on Bailey, L. (2016, April 1). The 25 funniest fails that have ever happened on Twitter. *BuzzFeed*. Retrieved from https://www.buzzfeed.com; Henry, Z. (2017, November 30). These are the biggest social media fails of 2017. *Inc*. Retrieved from https://www.inc.com

38 Based on Klemp, N. (2017, February 9). 10 rules for responding to customers on social media. Appirio. Retrieved from https://hub.appirio.com

39 Based on Buddy Media. (2011). How do I respond to that? The definitive guide to Facebook publishing & moderation. Retrieved from https://www.hashdoc.com

40 Smith, C. (2020, February 21). 80 interesting Yelp statistics and facts (2020); by the numbers. DMR Business Statistics. Retrieved from https://expandedramblings.com

41 Barnes, C. M. (2018, August 27). You know you need more sleep. Here's how to get it. *Harvard Business Review*. Retrieved from https://hbr.org

42 Ibid.

43 Scenario based on Glazer, E. (2016, June 3). J.P. Morgan says employees don't always have to wear suits. *The Wall Street Journal*. Retrieved from https://www.wsj.com; Eisen, B., & Glazer, E. (2016, June 3). *The Wall Street Journal*. Retrieved from https://www.wsj.com

44 J.P. Morgan dress code leaves women guessing. (2016, June 7). Finews.com. Retrieved from https://www.finews.com

45 Binkley, C. (2016, June 3). Business casual can be complex, especially for women. *The Wall Street Journal*. Retrieved from https://www.wsj.com

46 Weinberger, M. (2018, December 1). Read the sweet letter that Microsoft sends to the newborn children of its employees. *Business Insider*. Retrieved from https://www.businessinsider.com

Chapter 9

1 Rechtin, M. (2016, March 29). FTC charges Volkswagen with false advertising. *Consumer Reports*. Retrieved from https://www.consumerreports.org

2 MacDuffie, J. P., & Zaring, D. (2019, March 21). Exhausted by scandal: "Dieselgate" continues to haunt Volkswagen. Knowledge@Wharton. Retrieved from https://knowledge.wharton.upenn.edu

3 Ibid.

4 Smith, A. (2018, May 4). Volkswagen ex-CEO charged with fraud in diesel emissions scandal. CNN Business. Retrieved from https://money.cnn.com; Bender, R. (2018, June 19). Fünf mal Haft, 70 Beschuldigte – Diese Manager sitzen wegen Dieselgate. *Handelsblatt*. Retrieved from https://www.handelsblatt.com

5 MacDuffie, J. P., & Zaring, D. (2019, March 21). Exhausted by scandal: "Dieselgate" continues to haunt Volkswagen. Knowledge@Wharton. Retrieved from https://knowledge.wharton.upenn.edu

6 "Er wusste nichts": So viel Geld zahlt Volkswagen jetzt an Winterkorn. (2015, September 30). *Focus*. Retrieved from https://www.focus.de; Porter, J. (2019, April 16). Ex-VW CEO charged over Dieselgate, faces millions in fines and 10 years in prison. *The Verge*. Retrieved from https://www.theverge.com

7 Grossman, D. (2015, September 23). What the VW scandal means for diesel cars. BBC Newsnight. Retrieved from https://www.youtube.com

8 Furchgott, R. (2019, August 22). Piled up in huge lots, Volkswagen's reworked diesels trickle to buyers. *The New York Times*. Retrieved from https://www.nytimes.com

9 McCartney, S. (2018, April 24). At Southwest Airlines, the minutes after disaster struck. *The Wall Street Journal*. Retrieved from https://www.wsj.com

10 Aspan, M. (2017, September 8). Why Equifax's response makes its data breach the worst ever. *Inc*. Retrieved from https://www.inc.com; Newman, L. H. (2017, September 24). *Wired*. Retrieved from https://www.wired.com

11 O'Brien, S. (2017, September 8). Equifax response to data breach leaves many consumers confused. CNBC. Retrieved from https://www.cnbc.com; Bracy, J. (2017, September 8). The Equifax breach, response, and fallout. IAPP. Retrieved from https://iapp.org

12 Chow, E. K. (2014, April 1). Why Courtney Love's "Twibel" lawsuit is good for the Internet. *The Huffington Post*. Retrieved from http://www.huffingtonpost.com

13 Gardner, E. (2015, August 27). Courtney Love ends defamation row with $350K settlement. *The Hollywood Reporter*. Retrieved from http://www.hollywoodreporter.com

14 Hals, T. (2019, December 6). Musk's defamation win may reset legal landscape for social media. *Reuters*. Retrieved from https://www.reuters.com

15 Safe communication: Guidelines for creating corporate documents that minimize litigation risks. (2016, August 17). FindLaw. Retrieved from https://corporate.findlaw.com

16 Lizotte, J. (2019, January 24). True stories: Hiring mistakes that can turn into costly discrimination claims. Score. Retrieved from https://www.score.org

17 Creelman, V. (2012). The case for "living" models. *Business Communication Quarterly, 75*(2), 181.

18 Veltsos, J. (2012). An analysis of data breach notifications as negative news. *Business Communication Quarterly, 75*(2), 198. doi:10.1177/1080569912443081

19 Canavor, N. (2012). *Business writing in the digital age*. Thousand Oaks, CA: Sage, p. 62.

20 Joyce, C. (2012, November). The impact of direct and indirect communication. International Ombudsman Association. Retrieved from https://www.ombudsassociation.org

21 Krzanich, B. (2016, April 19). E-mail to employees. Retrieved from https://newsroom.intel.com

22 Young Entrepreneur Council. (2014, October 1). 9 (polite) ways to reject a customer. *Inc*. Retrieved from https://www.inc.com

23 Kashtan, M. (2013, May 20). Saying "no" without saying "no": How to say "no" to someone so they know they still matter to us. *Psychology Today*. Retrieved from https://www.psychologytoday.com

24 5 ad trends to be wary of in 2020. (2020, January 7). Truth in Advertising. Retrieved from https://www.truthinadvertising.org

25 When responding to customer complaints online, answer with deliberate speed. (2017, July 31). *Forbes*. Retrieved from https://www.forbes.com

26 Schweitzer, M. (2006, December). Wise negotiators know when to say "I'm sorry." *Negotiation*, 4. Retrieved from Business Source Complete database.

27 Bentley, J. (2018). What counts as an apology? Exploring stakeholder perceptions in a hypothetical organizational crisis. *Management Communication Quarterly, 32*(2), 207. doi:10.1177/0893318917722635

28 Racine, M., Wilson, C., & Wynes, M. (2018, October). The value of apology: How do corporate apologies moderate the stock market reaction to non-financial corporate crises? *Journal of Business Ethics*, 1–21. doi:10.1007/s10551-018-4037-5. Retrieved from http://search.proquest.

com; Chance, D., Cicon, J., & Ferris, S. P. (2016, January). Poor performance and the value of corporate honesty. *Journal of Corporate Finance, 33.* doi:10.1016/j.jcorpfin.2015.04.008. Retrieved from http://search.proquest.com

29 ten Brinke, L., & Adams, G. S. (2015). Saving face? When emotion displays during public apologies mitigate damage to organizational performance. *Organizational Behavior and Human Decision Processes, 133.* doi:10.1016/j.obhdp.2015.05.003. Retrieved from http://search.proquest.com

30 Kador, J. (2009). *Mending fences, building bridges, and restoring trust.* San Francisco: Berrett-Koehler, p. 8.

31 Barwick, R. (2019, October 29). Boeing takes out full-page ads before CEO testifies. *Adweek.* Retrieved from https://www.adweek.com

32 Parmar, B. (2016, December 1). The most empathetic companies, 2016. *Harvard Business Review.* Retrieved from https://hbr.org

33 Our definition of empathy. (n.d.). The Empathy Business. Retrieved from http://theempathybusiness.co.uk

34 Parmar, B. (2016, December 1). The most empathetic companies, 2016. *Harvard Business Review.* Retrieved from https://hbr.org

35 Zaki, J. (2019, May 30). Making empathy central to your company culture. *Harvard Business Review.* Retrieved from https://hbr.org; 2019 state of workplace empathy. (2019). Businessolver. Retrieved from https://www.businessolver.com

36 Ross, M. (2018, November 22). 4 reasons why empathy is good for business. *Entrepreneur.* Retrieved from https://www.entrepreneur.com

37 Zhang, H. (2020, February 4). The New York Times increases digital subscription price for the first time. CNN Business. Retrieved from https://www.cnn.com

38 When responding to customer complaints online, answer with deliberate speed. (2017, July 31). *Forbes.* Retrieved from https://www.forbes.com

39 The Zendesk customer experience trends report 2019. (2019). Zendesk. Retrieved from https://www.zendesk.com

40 Wolfe, J. (2018, November 20). Want faster airline customer service? Try tweeting. *The New York Times.* Retrieved from https://www.nytimes.com; Guliani, B. K. (2016, February 15). Twitter's greater revenue is due to its faster responses. Digital Vidya Blog. Retrieved from http://www.digitalvidya.com

41 Armano, D. (2017). Digital transformation journey: Brands' secret weapon to combat marketing disruption. Edelman Digital. Retrieved from https://edelmandigital.com

42 MacDonald, S. (2020, April 8). 5 ways to reduce customer service response times.

SuperOffice. Retrieved from https://www.superoffice.com

43 Toister, J. (April 7, 2020). How quickly should your respond to email? Toister Performance Solutions. Retrieved from https://www.toistersolutions.com; MacDonald, S. (2020, April 2). New study: 62% of companies ignore customer service emails. SuperOffice. Retrieved from https://www.superoffice.com; Baer, J. (n.d.). 70% of companies ignore customer complaints on Twitter. Convince&Convert. Retrieved from https://www.convinceandconvert.com

44 Ahmed, M. (2017, January 13). Social media customer service statistics and trends. SocialMediaToday. Retrieved from https://www.socialmediatoday.com

45 Gibbons, S. (2018, September 20). Why businesses need to see customer feedback as a make-or-break. *Forbes.* Retrieved from https://www.forbes.com

46 Wolfe, J. (2018, November 20). Want faster airline customer service? Try tweeting. *The New York Times.* Retrieved from https://www.nytimes.com

47 Josephs, L. (2018, January 9). Between five minutes and five hours: How long airlines take to respond to your complaint on Twitter. CNBC. Retrieved from https://www.cnbc.com

48 Wagner, S. (2012, September 11). CEO addresses Sept. 10 service outage. Retrieved from http://www.pcworld.com

49 Ngak, C. (2012, September 10). GoDaddy goes down, Anonymous claims responsibility. CBSNews.com Retrieved from http://www.cbsnews.com

50 Forbes, M. (1999). How to write a business letter. In K. Harty (Ed.), *Strategies for business and technical writing.* Boston: Allyn & Bacon, p. 108.

51 Heathfield, S. M. (2019, June 25). How to fire an employee with compassion and class. The Balance Careers. Retrieved from https://www.thebalancecareers.com; Browning, M. (2003, November 24). Work dilemma: Delivering bad news a good way. *Government Computer News,* p. 41; Mowatt, J. (2002, February). Breaking bad news to customers. *Agency Sales,* p. 30.

52 Prossack, A. (2018, October 28). How to have difficult conversations at work. *Forbes.* Retrieved at https://www.forbes.com; Gallo, A. (2015, March 30). How to deliver bad news to your employees. *Harvard Business Review.* Retrieved from https://hbr.org; Ensall, S. (2007, January 30). Delivering bad news. *Personnel Today,* p. 31. Retrieved from Business Source Premier database.

53 Ziglar, Z. (2011, January 18). Dad, you do choose your daughter's husband. Retrieved from http://www.ziglar.com

54 Forbes Coaches Council. (2017, July 17). 14 ways to approach conflict and difficult conversations at work. *Forbes.* Retrieved from https://www.forbes.com

55 Lynch, L. J., Bird, E., & Cutro, C. (2016, October 17). VW emissions and the 3 factors that drive ethical breakdown. UVA Darden, Ideas to Action. Retrieved from https://ideas.darden.virginia.edu

56 Kiley, D. (2018, May 16). Volkswagen diesel scandal coming to a TV screen and movie theater near you. *Forbes.* Retrieved from https://www.forbes.com

57 Lynch, L. J., Bird, E., & Cutro, C. (2016, October 17). VW emissions and the 3 factors that drive ethical breakdown. UVA Darden, Ideas to Action. Retrieved from https://ideas.darden.virginia.edu

58 Ewing, J. (2019, July 26). "A few dirty tricks": Documents show Audi's role in Volkswagen emissions scandal. *The New York Times.* Retrieved from https://www.nytimes.com

59 Lorio, J. (2015, September 23). Volkswagen Group CEO Martin Winterkorn resigns in wake of diesel emissions scandal. *Car and Driver.* Retrieved from https://www.caranddriver.com

60 Glinton, S. (2016, January 11). "We didn't lie," Volkswagen CEO says of emissions scandal. NPR.org. Retrieved from https://www.npr.org

61 Vlasic, B. (2017, December 6). Volkswagen official gets 7-year term in diesel-emissions cheating. *The New York Times.* Retrieved from https://www.nytimes.com

62 Vozza, S. (2015, February 2). When companies stop excusing bad behavior. *Fast Company.* Retrieved from https://www.fastcompany.com

63 Bergh, C. (2018, July-August). The CEO of Levi Strauss on leading an iconic brand back to growth. *Harvard Business Review.* Retrieved from https://hbr.org

64 Green, A. (2017, January 3). Is it OK to fire an employee by phone or email? *Inc.* Retrieved from https://www.inc.com

65 Rand, B. (2019, January 23). University mistakenly emails 430 acceptance letters, blames "human error." ABC News. Retrieved from https://abcnews.go.com

66 Reeves, M. (2019, January 22). Never mind: "Big mistake" cited as USF St. Pete takes back 430 admission letters. *Tampa Bay Times.* Retrieved from https://www.tampabay.com

67 Rand, B. (2019, January 23). University mistakenly emails 430 acceptance letters, blames "human error." ABC News. Retrieved from https://abcnews.go.com

Chapter 10

1 Launching a new product to a competitive category. (2018, August 28). Cult Collective. Retrieved from https://web.archive.org/web/20180828003303/http:/cultideas.com/case-study/juul

2 Harrison, S. (2019, October 17). Juul, under heavy fire, pulls fruit-flavored pods from US. *Wired.* Retrieved from https://www

.wired.com; Maloney, J., & Mattioli, D. (2019, March 23). Why Marlboro maker bet on Juul, the vaping upstart aiming to kill cigarettes. *The Wall Street Journal*. Retrieved from https://www.wsj.com

[3] Nedelman, M., Selig, R., & Azad, A. (2018, December 19). #JUUL: How social media hyped nicotine for a new generation. CNN Health. Retrieved from https://www.cnn.com

[4] Tiku, N. (2018, July 23). Users sue Juul for addicting them to nicotine. *Wired*. Retrieved from https://www.wired.com

[5] Belluz, J. (2018, December 20). Juul, the vape device teens are getting hooked on, explained. *Vox*. Retrieved from https://www.vox.com

[6] Nedelman, M., Selig, R., & Azad, A. (2018, December 19). #JUUL: How social media hyped nicotine for a new generation. CNN Health. Retrieved from https://www.cnn.com

[7] Juul and the vape debate. (2018, December 17). CNN. [video]. Retrieved from https://www.cnn.com

[8] Harrison, S. (2019, October 17). Juul, under heavy fire, pulls fruit-flavored pods from US. *Wired*. Retrieved from https://www.wired.com

[9] Juul and the vape debate. (2018, December 17). CNN. [video]. Retrieved from https://www.cnn.com

[10] Nedelman, M., Selig, R., & Azad, A. (2018, December 19). #JUUL: How social media hyped nicotine for a new generation. CNN Health. Retrieved from https://www.cnn.com

[11] Belluz, J. (2018, December 20). Juul, the vape device teens are getting hooked on, explained. *Vox*. Retrieved from https://www.vox.com

[12] White, E. (2008, May 19). The art of persuasion becomes key. *The Wall Street Journal*. Retrieved from http://online.wsj.com; McIntosh, P., & Luecke, R. A. (2011). *Increase your influence at work*. New York: American Management Association, p. 4.

[13] Morgan, H. R. (2018, March 28). 3 reasons being aggressive in sales is an outdated and harmful tactic. *Forbes*. Retrieved from https://www.forbes.com

[14] Perloff, R. M. (2020). *The dynamics of persuasion: Communication and attitudes in the 21st century* (7th ed.). New York: Routledge, Kindle edition, Chapter 1.

[15] Cialdini, R. B. (2009). *Influence: The psychology of persuasion*. New York: HarperCollins, p. xiv.

[16] Ibid., p. x.

[17] Discussion based on Perloff, R. M. (2020). *The dynamics of persuasion: Communication and attitudes in the 21st century* (7th ed.). New York: Routledge, Kindle edition.

[18] Holmes, R. (2019, February 19). We now see 5,000 ads a day . . . And it's getting worse. LinkedIn. Retrieved from https://www.linkedin.com; Simpson, J. (2017, August

25). Finding brand success in the digital world. *Forbes*. Retrieved from https://www.forbes.com; Marshall, R. (2015, September 10). How many ads do you see in one day? Red Crow Marketing. Retrieved from https://www.redcrowmarketing.com

[19] Perloff, R. M. (2020). *The dynamics of persuasion: Communication and attitudes in the 21st century* (7th ed.). New York: Routledge, Kindle edition.

[20] Carter Hartley, L. (2019). *Persuasion: Convincing others when facts don't seem to matter*. New York, NY: TarcherPerigee, p. 37.

[21] Patel, S. (2016, January 4). 5 easy ways to build more business relationships as an entrepreneur. *Entrepreneur*. Retrieved from https://www.entrepreneur.com

[22] Kruse, K. (2016, December 19). 5 subtle ways to persuade and influence others. *Forbes*. Retrieved from https://www.forbes.com

[23] DeMers, J. (2015, January 20). 7 tech-based strategies for overcoming resistant sales leads. *Inc*. Retrieved from https://www.inc.com

[24] Kelly, J. (2020, February 24). Wells Fargo forced to pay $3 billion for the bank's fake account scandal. *Forbes*. Retrieved from https://www.forbes.com; Lorin, J. (2019, November 1). Hard-selling Fisher Investments won't take no for an answer, prospects say. *Bloomberg*. Retrieved from https://www.bloomberg.com; Young Entrepreneur Council. (2014, November 24). 8 pushy sales tactics that could harm your business. *Inc*. Retrieved from http://www.inc.com

[25] Carroll, R. (2018, December 21). Aspen retailers face legal retaliation over sales tactics. *The Aspen Times*. Retrieved from https://www.aspentimes.com

[26] Glazer, R. (2019, August 12). "Command and control" leadership is dead. Here's what's taking its place. *Inc*. Retrieved from https://www.inc.com

[27] Kumar, A. (2018, June 5). As Howard Schultz retires, will his impact on labor be one of his core legacies? *Forbes*. Retrieved from https://www.forbes.com

[28] Groth, A. (2020, January 29). Zappos has quietly backed away from holacracy. *Quartz at Work*. Retrieved from https://qz.com; Feloni, R. (2016, January 14). Zappos CEO Tony Hsieh explains why 18% of employees quit during the company's radical management experiment. *Business Insider*. Retrieved from http://www.businessinsider.com; Silverman, R. E. (2015, May 20). At Zappos, banishing the bosses brings confusion. *The Wall Street Journal*. Retrieved from http://www.wsj.com

[29] Grainger, B. (2017, December 5). Surviving the open office (really, it's not so bad). Evernote Blog. Retrieved from https://evernote.com

[30] Lucas, S. (2019, September 16). Employee buy-in to promote workplace engagement.

The Balance Careers. Retrieved from https://www.thebalancecareers.com; Gleeson, B. (2017, October 15). 5 powerful steps to improve employee engagement. *Forbes*. Retrieved from https://www.forbes.com

[31] Brandon, J. (2014, December 12). 20 leadership experts share their best leadership tip. *Inc*. Retrieved from http://www.inc.com

[32] Reh, F. J. (2019, June 25). How to run a cost-benefit analysis. The Balance Careers. Retrieved from https://www.thebalancecareers.com

[33] Baldor, L. C. (2018, February 3). Marines seek young, tough recruits in Super Bowl ad. *AP News*. Retrieved from https://apnews.com

[34] Fulmer, N. (2019, April 24). Is direct mail dead? Mail Shark. Retrieved from https://www.themailshark.com

[35] Haskel, D. (2019, January 16). The latest direct mail response data from DMA will leave you speechless. IWCO Direct. Retrieved from https://www.iwco.com

[36] Pulcinella, S. (2017, August 30). Why direct mail marketing is far from dead. *Forbes*. Retrieved from https://www.forbes.com

[37] Pulcinella, S. (2018, September 14). Direct marketing is thriving in millennial mailboxes: Here's how to make the most of it. *Forbes*. Retrieved from https://www.forbes.com

[38] Pulcinella, S. (2017, August 30). Why direct mail marketing is far from dead. *Forbes*. Retrieved from https://www.forbes.com

[39] Office of Inspector General. (2015, June 15). Enhancing the value of mail: The human response. United States Postal Service. Retrieved from https://www.uspsoig.gov; Lee, K. (2015, May 22). Seven reasons to make direct mail part of your digital marketing. ClickZ. Retrieved from https://www.clickz.com

[40] Pulcinella, S. (2017, August 30). Why direct mail marketing is far from dead. *Forbes*. Retrieved from https://www.forbes.com

[41] Paikin, L. (2020, April 23). Direct mail retargeting: Evolution and overcoming obstacles. *Forbes*. Retrieved from https://www.forbes.com

[42] Tweh, B., & Patel, S. (2020, January 14). Google Chrome to phase out third-party cookies in effort to boost privacy. *The Wall Street Journal*. Retrieved from https://www.wsj.com

[43] Jones, R. (2020, March/April). Facing the consequences: A look at some lesser-known costs of distracted driving. *Westways*, p. 16.

[44] Ziglar, Z. (2006). *Secrets of closing the sale*. Grand Rapids, MI: Revell/Baker Publishing, p. 57.

[45] McGinley, L. (2019, February 11). FDA launches tougher oversight of supplements. *The Washington Post*. Retrieved from https://www.washingtonpost.com

[46] Tchekmedyian, A. (2018, September 4). Gwyneth Paltrow's Goop to offer refunds

over "unsubstantiated" claims about health benefits. *Los Angeles Times*. Retrieved from https://www.latimes.com

47 Upadhyaya, K. K. (2019, January 23). "Iron Chef" Cat Cora awarded $565k in lawsuit against shuttered Meatpacking restaurant. *New York Eater*. Retrieved from https://ny.eater.com

48 Saad, N. (2019, September 3). Ariana Grande sues Forever 21 over failed deal and lookalike model. *Los Angeles Times*. Retrieved from https://www.latimes.com

49 Fair, L. (2016, July 15). It's no longer business as usual at Herbalife: An inside look at the $200 million FTC settlement. Federal Trade Commission. Retrieved from https://www.ftc.gov

50 Trying to lose weight? Watch out for false promises. Federal Trade Commission. Retrieved from https://www.consumer.ftc.gov

51 Electronic muscle stimulators. (2017, December 17). U.S. Food & Drug Administration. Retrieved from https://www.fda.gov

52 Hiltzik, M. (2016, January 6). If you weren't smart enough to know Lumosity was making bogus claims, the FTC has your back. *Los Angeles Times*. Retrieved from https://www.latimes.com

53 Wischhover, C. (2019, October 22). Skin care brand Sunday Riley got in trouble for writing fake reviews. It just settled with the FTC. *Vox*. Retrieved from https://www.vox.com

54 Musil, S. (2019, February 26). FTC settles its first case over fake paid reviews on Amazon. CNET. Retrieved from https://www.cnet.com

55 Haskel, D. (2015, April 14). 2015 DMA response rate report: Direct mail outperforms all digital channels combined by nearly 600%. IWCO Direct. Retrieved from http://www.iwco.com

56 Verblow, B. (2019, January 2). You've still got mail. Forrester. Retrieved from https://go.forrester.com

57 Nedelman, M., Selig, R., & Azad, A. (2018, December 19). #JUUL: How social media hyped nicotine for a new generation. CNN Health. Retrieved from https://www.cnn.com

58 Ibid.

59 Ibid.

60 Harrison, S. (2019, October 17). Juul, under heavy fire, pulls fruit-flavored pods from US. *Wired*. Retrieved from https://www.wired.com

61 Berger, L. L., & Stanchi, K. M. (2018). *Legal persuasion: A rhetorical approach to the science*. New York: Routledge, p. 5.

62 Larson, C. U. (2013). *Persuasion: Reception and responsibility* (13th ed.). Boston: Wadsworth, Cengage Learning, p. 17.

63 Kokalitcheva, K. (2016, March 21). These 8 employers will pay you to volunteer. *Fortune*. Retrieved from https://fortune.com

64 Based on Yu, R. (2009, 13 March). Hotels take action to pare down food, restaurant expenses. *USA Today*, p. 3D.

65 Kokemuller, N. (2018, November 6). Do restaurants have the right to automatically charge tips to your credit card? PocketSense. Retrieved from https://pocketsense.com

66 Scenario based on Federal Trade Commission. (n.d.). FTC fact sheet: It looks good . . . but is it true? Retrieved from https://www.consumer.ftc.gov/sites/default/files/games/off-site/youarehere/pages/pdf/FTC-Ad-Marketing_Looks-Good.pdf

67 Stillman, J. (2017, August 25). Here's how to spot fake online reviews with 90 percent accuracy, according to science. *Inc.* Retrieved from https://www.inc.com

68 Broida, R. (2019, March 4). How to spot fake reviews on Amazon, Best Buy, Walmart and other sites. *CNET*. Retrieved from https://www.cnet.com; Cohen, J. (2019, June 26). How to spot a fake review on Amazon. *PCMag*. Retrieved from https://www.pcmag.com

69 Stillman, J. (2017, August 25). Here's how to spot fake online reviews with 90 percent accuracy, according to science. *Inc.* Retrieved from https://www.inc.com

70 Cohen, J. (2019, June 26). How to spot a fake review on Amazon. *PCMag*. Retrieved from https://www.pcmag.com

71 Loveday, S. (2020, February 28). The cheapest electric cars for 2020. *U.S. News & World Report*. Retrieved from https://cars.usnews.com; Demuro, D. (2015, January 20). 8 least expensive electric vehicles. *Autotrader*. Retrieved from https://www.autotrader.com

Chapter 11

1 Seventh Generation. (2018, September 18). Seventh generation commits to aggressive science-based greenhouse gas targets, zero waste and 100 percent sustainable sourcing. Retrieved from https://www.globenewswire.com

2 Chhabra, E. (2018, December 22). Unilever is betting on this company to deliver sustainability at scale. Retrieved from https://www.forbes.com

3 Elliott, M. (2010-2013). Writing. Retrieved from http://marianne-elliott.com/writing

4 Hutchinson, O. (2018, May 7). 4 key questions on primary vs secondary research. *Euromonitor*. Retrieved from https://blog.euromonitor.com

5 Kennedy, C. (2019, February 7). Phone vs. online surveys: Why do respondents' answers sometimes differ by mode? Retrieved from https://www.pewresearch.org

6 Jaschik, S. (2019, January 7). Temple will pay $5.5M to settle suits over false rankings data. www.insidehighered.com

7 Peltz, J. F. (2019, July 28). How Starbucks has picked up steam again. *The Los Angeles Times*. Retrieved from https://www.latimes.com

8 Weeks, L. (n. d.). 50 thought-provoking quotes about libraries and librarians. *Ebook Friendly*. Retrieved from http://ebookfriendly.com

9 Attributed to Gaiman, N. (n.d.). 10 ways academic libraries are leading change. The Wiley network. Retrieved from https://www.wiley.com

10 Nutt, A. E. (2016, April 1). This scientist nearly went to jail for making up data. *The Washington Post*. Retrieved from https://www.washingtonpost.com

11 Hawkins, A. J. (2019, April 12). Electric scooters may not be around for long. Retrieved from https://www.theverge.com/2019/4/12/18307591/electric-scooter-sharing-bird-lime-uber-economics-big-picture; see also Korus, S. (2019, February 19). Electric Scooters: The unit economics may spell trouble. Retrieved from https://ark-invest.com

12 Stuart, E. (2016, January 19). ASU professor resigns amid plagiarism accusations. *Phoenix New Times*. Retrieved from http://www.phoenixnewtimes.com; Iyengar, R. (2015, November 25). 200 South Korean professors charged in massive plagiarism scam. *Time*. Retrieved from http://time.com; McCabe, F. (2014, December 2). UNLV fires professor accused of "serial plagiarism." *Review Journal*. Retrieved from http://www.reviewjournal.com

13 Kuratko, D. F. (2016). *Entrepreneurship: Theory, Process, and Practice* (10th ed.). Cengage Learning, pp. 45–46.

14 Writing Tutorial Services, Indiana University. Plagiarism: What it is and how to recognize and avoid it. Retrieved from http://www.indiana.edu

15 U.S. Census Bureau. (2019, May 23). Fastest growing cities primarily in South and West. Census Bureau press release. Retrieved from https://www.census.gov

16 Evans, C. L. (2018). *Broad band: The untold story of the women who made the Internet*. Portfolio/Penguin, p. 204.

17 Ibid.

18 Tufte, E. R. (1983). *The visual display of quantitative information*. Graphics Press, p. 107.

19 Frozen Fire. (2019). 5 tips for creating effective infographics. Retrieved from https://frozenfire.com

20 Reasons students hate writing essays or term papers. (n.d.). Retrieved from http://custompapers.com

21 Loten, A. (2019, February 25). Fast on its feet. *The Wall Street Journal*, p. R8.

22 Pennington, D. (2019, March 21). Facebook is rapidly losing millennials, US user base down 15 million since 2017. Retrieved from https://www.techspot.com

23 U.S. Food and Drug Administration. (2018, May 18). Final determination regarding partially hydrogenated oils (Removing

trans fat). Retrieved from https://www.fda.gov

24 Zhang, C. (2018, December 10). Food delivery apps serve as rising competitor for university dining halls. Retrieved from https://northwesternbusinessreview.org

25 Piper, K. (2019, January 9). The American public is already worried about AI catastrophe. Retrieved from https://www.vox.com

26 Tufte, E. (1990). *Envisioning information.* Graphics Press, p. 34.

27 Fung, E. (2019, October 26). Save the American mall? *The Wall Street Journal*, B5.

28 Park, A. (2011, January 6). Study linking vaccines to autism is "fraudulent." *Time*. Retrieved from http://healthland.time.com; see also Quick, J., & Larson, H. (2018, February 28). The vaccine-autism myth started 20 years ago. Retrieved from https://time.com

29 Harnish, A. (2019, October 25). Fighting vaccine hesitancy, one parent at a time. *The New York Times*. Retrieved from https://parenting.nytimes.com; Benn, S. (2019, September 20). Declaring vaccine hesitancy one of the ten biggest health threats in 2019 is unhelpful. Retrieved from https://medicalxpress.com

30 Perry, S. (2015, April 7). "Plagiarism, fraud, and predatory publishing" are polluting science, says bioethicist Arthur Caplan. *Minnpost*. Retrieved from https://www.minnpost.com

31 Iyengar, R. (2015, November 25). 200 South Korean professors charged in massive plagiarism scam. *Time*. Retrieved from http://time.com

32 Williams, T. (2017, July 12). Only a third of students enter college with research skills. Retrieved from https://www.goodcall.com

Chapter 12

1 Kafka, P. (2019, November 7). Now that Netflix has more streaming competitors, it suddenly cares about ratings. *Vox*. Retrieved from https://www.vox.com

2 Watson, A. (2020, January 22). Number of Netflix paid streaming subscribers worldwide 2011-2019. Retrieved from https://www.statista.com; Dunn, J. (2017, January 19). Here's how huge Netflix has gotten in the past decade. Business Insider. Retrieved from https://www.businessinsider.com

3 Porter, R. (2020, January 23). Netflix's new ratings math sacrifices clarity for flashy number. *The Hollywood Reporter*. Retrieved from https://hollywoodreporter.com

4 Reid, A. (2019, July 2.) Why messaging is the future of market research. *Entrepreneur*. Retrieved from http://entrepreneur.com

5 Based on Goldin, R. (2015, August 19.) Causation vs correlation. Sense About Science USA. Retrieved from http://www.senseaboutscienceusa.org; Rohrer, J. M. (2018). Thinking clearly about correlations and causation: Graphical causal models for observational data. *Advances in Methods and Practices in Psychological Science, 1*(1), 27–42. doi:10.1177/2515245917745629

6 Martin, A. (2020, September 1.) Fairphone 3 review: The only way is ethics? MSN.com. Retrieved from https://www.msn.com; Gibbs, S. (2019, September 18). Fairphone 3 review: The most ethical and repairable phone you can buy. *The Guardian*. Retrieved from https://www.theguardian.com; England, R. (2019, August 27). The Fairphone 3 packs in features while keeping its green credentials. *Endgadget*. Retrieved from https://www.engadget.com

7 Huff, A. (2020, 7 January). "Amazon Effect" may explain rising driver turnover in truckload. *Commercial Carrier Journal*. Retrieved from https://www.ccjdigital.com

8 The Bridgespan Group. (n.d.) How to talk about finances so non-financial folks will listen. Retrieved from https://bridgespan.org

9 Spotify reports second quarter 2019 earnings. (2019, July 31). Retrieved from https://newsroom.spotify.com

10 Ashton, R. (n.d.) Top ten writing tips for scientists. *Sciencebase*. Retrieved from http://www.sciencebase.com

11 Baron, J. (2018, 27 December). Tech ethics issues we should all be thinking about in 2019. *Forbes*. Retrieved from https://www.forbes.com

12 47 must-know live video streaming statistics. (n.d.). *Livestream blog*. Retrieved from http://livestream.com

13 Elliot, M. (2019, December 25). You won't believe how many original movies and shows Netflix released in 2019. *Showbiz CheatSheet*. Retrieved from from https://www.cheatsheet.com

14 Pupic, T. (2019, December 30). Bringing ethics back to business: Alethia. *Entrepreneur Middle East*. Retrieved from https://www.entrepreneur.com

15 McPherson, F. (2018). *Effective notetaking (study skills)* (3rd ed.). Wellington, NZ: Wayz Press, pp. 15–18.

16 Carey, B. (2014). *How we learn: The surprising truth about when, where, and why it happens.* New York, NY: Random House, pp. 81–83.

17 Giacomini, S. (2020, January 15). BMW Motorrad set yet another sales record in 2019. *Ride Apart*. Retrieved from https://www.rideapart.com; BMW Motorrad global sales increased in last 8 years. The 200k target is not a dream. MotorCycles Data. Retrieved from https://www.motorcyclesdata.com

18 Barrett, R. (2020, April 9). Harley-Davidson sales slow as coronavirus closes dealerships and threatens motorcycle events. *Milwaukee Journal Sentinel*. Retrieved from https://www.jsonline.com

19 Hoium, T. (2019, April 18). Why Harley-Davidson shares crashed 19.3% in December. The Motley Fool. Retrieved from https://www.fool.com

20 Head, A. J., & Eisenberg, M. B. (2009, February 4). Finding context: What today's college students say about conducting research in the digital age. Project Information Literacy Progress Report. The Information School, University of Washington. Retrieved from http://projectinfolit.org; Wilser, J. (2019, February 12). The neurological reasons you're up against deadlines, and how to make a change. *Comstock's Magazine*. Retrieved from http://comstocksmag.com

Chapter 13

1 Davenport, C. (2020, May 21). No one thought SpaceX would beat Boeing: Elon Musk proved them wrong. *The Washington Post*. Retrieved from https://www.washingtonpost.com

2 Carter, J. (2019, April 23). SpaceX: Everything you need to know. *Techradar*. Retrieved from https://www.techradar.com

3 Sheetz, M. (2019, October 19). SpaceX has spent "hundreds of millions" extra in building astronaut capsule for NASA, Elon Musk says. CNBC. Retrieved from https://www.cnbc.com

4 City of Hermosa Beach. (2020, April 15). Bids and proposals (RFPs & RFQs). Retrieved from https://www.hermosabeach.gov

5 Center for the Advancement of Science in Space. (n.d.). Unsolicited proposals. Retrieved from http://www.iss-casis.org

6 Moses, S. (2018, June 27). How to create impossibly good project proposals. Retrieved from https://www.workamajig.com

7 Piecewicz, Mary. Former proposal manager, Hewlett-Packard (personal communication with Mary Ellen Guffey).

8 Sant, T. (2012). *Persuasive business proposals* (3rd ed.). New York: AMACOM, p. 114.

9 McLaughlin, M.W. (n.d.). 12 tips for writing a winning proposal. Retrieved from http://c-nsc.org

10 Ouellet, D. (2020, January 7). What to do when an RFP asks for resumes. Retrieved from https://www.echelonone.ca

11 Ronald McDonald House Charities. (n.d.). Grants. Retrieved from https://www.rmhc.org

12 Greene, F. J., & Hopp, C. (2018, May 18). When should entrepreneurs write their business plans? *Harvard Business Review*. Retrieved from https://hbr.org

13 A business plan: Everything you need to know. (2017, February 3). SCORE Youngstown. Retrieved from https://youngstown.score.org

14 How much do business plan writing services cost? Go Business Plans. Retrieved from https://www.gobusinessplans.com

[15] Business.org. (2020). The 5 best business plan software and tools in 2020 for your small business. Retrieved from https://www.business.org

[16] 2020 new venture competition FINALS. (2020, May 21). UC Santa Barbara Technology Management. Retrieved from https://tmp.ucsb.edu; Acebu, E. (2015, December 16). Everything but the elevator. UCSB. Retrieved from http://www.tmp.ucsb.edu

[17] Starr, K. (2012, September 18). The eight-word mission statement. *Stanford Social Innovation Review*. Retrieved from http://www.ssireview.org

[18] Berry, T. (2014, June 25). True story: Why you don't want a business plan writer. U.S. Small Business Administration. Retrieved from https://www.sba.gov

[19] Smith, T. (2019, April 10). Buying college essays is now easier than ever. But buyer beware. NPR. Retrieved from https://www.npr.org

[20] Office of Civic Engagement & Service. (n.d.). Definition of service learning. Fayetteville State University. Retrieved from http://www.uncfsu.edu

[21] Inspired by McKeown, G. (2012, October 4). If I read one more platitude-filled mission statement, I'll scream. HBR Blog Network. Retrieved from http://blogs.hbr.org; also partially based on Ideas and inspirations for defining your own mission statement. (n.d.). Retrieved from http://www.missionstatements.com

Chapter 14

[1] Doumont, J. (2016, April 15). Lecture on presentation skills for UCSB Writing Program.

[2] Doumont, J. (2009). Effective oral presentations. Retrieved from http://www.treesmapsandtheorems.com and adapted from Doumont, J. (2009). *Trees, maps, and theorems*. Kraainem, Belgium: Principiae.

[3] Doumont, J. (2009). Effective oral presentations. Retrieved from http://www.treesmapsandtheorems.com

[4] Bughin, J., Hazan, E., Lund, S., Dahlström, P., Wiesinger, A., & Subramaniam, A. (2018, May). Skill shift: Automation and the future of the workforce. McKinsey Global Institute. Retrieved from https://www.mckinsey.com; 2020 Workplace learning trends report: The skills of the future. Udemy for Business. Retrieved from https://info.udemy.com

[5] Leveling up: How to win in the skills economy. (2016). PayScale. Retrieved from http://www.payscale.com

[6] Key attributes employers want to see on students' resumes. (2020, January 13). National Association of Colleges and Employers. Retrieved from https://www.naceweb.org; Job outlook 2020 survey. (2020, January). National Association of Colleges and Employers. Retrieved from http://www.naceweb.org

[7] Nakano, C. (2016, June 15). Presentation habits presenters don't like to admit. Prezi Blog. https://blog.prezi.com; Gallo, C. (2014, September 25). New survey: 70 percent say presentation skills are critical for career success. *Forbes*. Retrieved from http://www.forbes.com

[8] Average salary for jobs with public speaking skills. (n.d.) Retrieved from https://www.salary.com

[9] Gallo, C. (2014, September 25). New survey: 70 percent say presentation skills are critical for career success. *Forbes*. Retrieved from http://www.forbes.com

[10] Booher, D. (n.d.). 5 tips for executives who become public speakers. Booher Research Institute. Retrieved from https://booherresearch.com

[11] Dhu, P. (2016, August 16). 9 tips for quickly building rapport with your audience. LinkedIn. Retrieved from https://www.linkedin.com

[12] Medina, J. (2008). *Brain rules: 12 principles for surviving and thriving at work, home, and school*. Seattle, WA: Pear Press, p. 292.

[13] Gallo, C. (2020, January 6). What it takes to give a great presentation. *Harvard Business Review*. Retrieved from https://hbr.org

[14] Tufte, E. (2003). *The cognitive style of Powerpoint* (2nd ed.). Graphics Press; Duarte, N. (2008). *Slide:ology: The art and science of creating great presentations*. Sebastopol, CA: O'Reilly Media; Atkinson, C. (2018). *Beyond bullet points: Using PowerPoint to tell a compelling story that gets results* (4th ed.). Pearson Education.

[15] Reynolds, G. (2020). *Presentation zen: Simple ideas on presentation design and delivery* (3rd ed.). New Riders/Pearson, p. 308.

[16] Booher, D. (2003). *Speak with confidence: Powerful presentations that inform, inspire, and persuade*. New York: McGraw-Hill Professional, p. 126; Morr, K. (2016, July 5). How to choose the best colors for your presentations. Prezi Blog. Retrieved from https://blog.prezi.com; Ciotti, G. (2016, April 13). The psychology of color in marketing and branding. *Entrepreneur*. Retrieved from https://www.entrepreneur.com

[17] Hearn, H. J. (2017, December 11). 6 PowerPoint presentation tips. American Express. Retrieved from https://www.americanexpress.com; Bates, S. (2005). *Speak like a CEO: Secrets for commanding attention and getting results*. New York: McGraw-Hill Professional, p. 113.

[18] Gallo, C. (2020, January 6). What it takes to give a great presentation. *Harvard Business Review*. Retrieved from https://hbr.org

[19] Sommerville, J. (n.d.). The seven deadly sins of PowerPoint presentations. About.com. Retrieved from http://entrepreneurs.about.com; Avoid visual clichés when presenting. (2013, April 19). HBR. Retrieved from http://business.time.com

[20] Gallo, C. (2020, January 6). What it takes to give a great presentation. *Harvard Business Review*. Retrieved from https://hbr.org

[21] Hedges, K. (2014, November 14). Six ways to avoid death by PowerPoint. *Forbes*. Retrieved from http://www.forbes.com

[22] Miller, T. (n.d.). She's 22, from rural Zimbabwe, and a mogul in the making. Kiva. Retrieved from https://www.kiva.org

[23] Quoted in Reynolds, G. (2014, January 20). Coping with presentation anxiety & "stage fright." Presentation Zen. Retrieved from http://www.presentationzen.com

[24] Dray, K. (2017, March 27). Adele emotionally explains why she may never tour again. *Stylist*. Retrieved from https://www.stylist.co.uk

[25] Fleming, R. (2004). *The inner voice: The making of a singer*. New York: Viking, p. 109.

[26] Enright, P. (2007). Even stars get stage fright. NBC NEWS. Retrieved from http://www.nbcnews.com

[27] Eaton, K. (2016, June 8). Getting over stage fright with the help of your smartphone. *The New York Times*. Retrieved from https://www.nytimes.com

[28] Grant, A. (2015, September 2). 5 tips for speaking to multicultural audiences. *Fast Company*. Retrieved from https://www.fastcompany.com

[29] Aslani, S., Brett, J. M., Ramirez-Marin, J. Y., Tinsley, C. H., & Weingart, L. R. (2013, September 2). Doing business in the Middle East. Kellogg Insight. Retrieved from http://insight.kellogg.northwestern.edu. See also Wunderle, W. (n.d.). Through the lens of cultural awareness. Combat Studies Institute Press. Retrieved from http://usacac.army.mil; see also Marks, S. J. (2001, September). Nurturing global workplace connections. *Workforce*, p. 76.

[30] Brandel, M. (2006, February 20). Sidebar: Don't be the ugly American. *Computerworld*. Retrieved from http://www.computerworld.com

[31] Davidson, R., & Rosen, M. Cited in Brandel, M. (2006, February 20). Sidebar: Don't be the ugly American. *Computerworld*. Retrieved from http://www.computerworld.com

[32] Letting go of efficiency can accelerate your company—Here's how. (2015). First Round Review. Retrieved from http://firstround.com; The secret of Zara's success: A culture of customer co-creation. (2019, December). Martin Roll: Business & Brand Leadership. Retrieved from https://martinroll.com

[33] Grayson Riegel, D. (2017, July 5). 20 things that great presenting teams ask before they open their mouth. *Inc*. Retrieved from https://www.inc.com

[34] Gallo, C. (2015, March 26). How Steve Jobs made presentations look effortless. *Forbes*. Retrieved from https://www.forbes.com

[35] Popescu, A. (2018, January 25). Keep your head up: How smartphone addiction kills manners and moods. *The New York Times*. Retrieved from https://www.nytimes.com

36 Anderson, M. (2019, June 13). Mobile technology and home broadband 2019. Pew Research Center. Retrieved from https://www.pewresearch.org; Mobile fact sheet. (2019, June 12). Pew Research Center. Retrieved from https://www.pewresearch.org

37 Kamenetz, A. (2019, October 13). It's a smartphone life: More than half of U.S. children now have one. NPR. Retrieved from https://www.npr.org

38 Popescu, A. (2018, January 25). Keep your head up: How smartphone addiction kills manners and moods. *The New York Times*. Retrieved from https://www.nytimes.com

39 The Nielsen total audience report: Q3 2018. (2019, March 19). Retrieved from https://www.nielsen.com

40 Rainie, L., & Zickuhr, K. (2015, August 26). Americans' views on mobile etiquette. Pew Research Center. Retrieved from http://www.pewinternet.org

41 Hutchinson, A. (2018, September 11). Smartphone etiquette 2018 [Infographic]. SocialMediaToday. Retrieved from https://www.socialmediatoday.com

42 Booher, D. (2011). Speak with confidence. AudioInk.

43 Whitmore, J. (2017, January 10). 5 tips to reduce presentation anxiety. *Entrepreneur*. Retrieved from https://www.entrepreneur.com

44 Search YouTube or the top 100 speeches at American Rhetoric: http://www.americanrhetoric.com

45 Nisen, M., & Guey, L. (2013, May 15). 23 of the best pieces of advice ever given to graduates. *Business Insider*. Retrieved from http://www.businessinsider.com

46 Duarte, N. (2008). *Slide:ology: The art and science of creating great presentations*. Sebastopol, CA: O'Reilly Media, p. 64.

47 Reynolds, G. (2020). *Presentation Zen: Simple ideas on presentation design and delivery* (3rd ed.). Berkeley, CA: New Riders/Pearson Education, p. 68.

Chapter 15

1 Cengage Student Opportunity Index. (2019, May 15). College graduates optimistic about the future despite mounting loan debt and housing costs, new analysis finds. Retrieved from https://news.cengage.com

2 Bureau of Labor Statistics. (August 22, 2019). Number of jobs, labor market experience, and earnings growth: Results from a national longitudinal survey summary. Retrieved from https://www.bls.gov

3 National Association of Colleges and Employers. (2015). 2015 internship and co-op survey. NACE. Retrieved from https://www.naceweb.org

4 Mitler, L. (2019, May 7). Quoted in Shellenbarger, S. Job advice for grads: A tricky proposition. *The Wall Street Journal*, A11.

5 Doyle, A. (2020, January 30). What is the hidden job market? Retrieved from https://www.thebalancecareers.com; Laumeister, G. (2015, June 2). How to navigate the hidden job market. Retrieved from https://www.dailyworth.com; Collamer, N. (2013, August 12). 6 ways to crack the 'hidden' job market. Retrieved from http://www.forbes.com

6 Stewart, R. (2015, November 25). 4 reasons why job boards are still a useful tool for employers. TalentCulture. Retrieved from http://www.talentculture.com

7 Doyle, A. (2019, August 2). Top 6 best free job search apps. Retrieved from https://www.thebalancecareers.com; McCullum, K. (2019, April 21). 12 best job search apps to find your career. Retrieved from https://www.learninghowtobecome.org

8 Richardson, V. (2011, March 16). Five ways inside the 'hidden job market.' Daily Finance. Retrieved from http://www.dailyfinance.com

9 Barnes, N. G., Mazzola, A., & Killeen, M. (2020, January 9). Oversaturation & Disengagement: The 2019 Fortune 500 social media dance. Center for Marketing Research, University of Massachusetts Dartmouth. Retrieved from https://www.umassd.edu

10 Morgan, H. (2018, November 13). How companies recruit in 2018. Retrieved from https://money.usnews.com

11 Garriott, O. (2015, February 6). 10 LinkedIn tips for students and new grads. Retrieved from https://www.linkedin.com

12 Richardson, K. (2018, July 25). Why more millennials and young people should be using LinkedIn. Retrieved from https://www.thesociiproject.com

13 Better Team Facebook. (2019, October 2). How to post a job on Facebook. Retrieved from https://www.betterteam.com; Mauer, R. (2018, July 31). How to get started with recruiting on Facebook. Retrieved from https://www.shrm.org

14 Isaacs, K. (n.d.). How long should my résumé be? Monster. Retrieved from http://career-advice.monster.com

15 Isaacs, K. (n.d.). Career advice: Résumé help and job interview tips. Monster. Retrieved from http://career-advice.monster.com

16 Indeed Career Guide. (2020, January 27). How to write a summary of qualifications. Retrieved from https://www.indeed.com

17 Malacoff, J. (2019, August 27). 10 résumé tips you haven't heard before. Retrieved from https://www.glassdoor.com

18 Linkedin for Volunteers. (n.d.). Use your skills to make a positive impact. Retrieved from https://volunteer.linkedin.com

19 Hehman, E., Flake, J. K., & Freeman, J. B. (2015). Static and dynamic facial cues differentially affect the consistency of social evaluations. *Personality and Social Psychology Bulletin*, 1–12. doi:10.1177/0146167215591495

20 Fisher, C. (2015, January 21). Brand YOU year: How to brand yourself without sounding like everyone else. LinkedIn Official Blog. Retrieved from http://blog.linkedin.com

21 Adams, S. (2015, April 23). Seven ways to make LinkedIn help you find a job. *Forbes*. Retrieved from http://www.forbes.com

22 Kreps, L. (2015, June 25). The legal risks of lying on your résumé. Retrieved from http://www.shakelaw.com

23 CareerBuilder. (2015, December 31). Employers reveal biggest résumé blunders in annual CareerBuilder survey. Retrieved from http://www.careerbuilder.com

24 Ibid.

25 Qu, L. (2019, November 7). 99% of Fortune 500 companies use applicant tracking systems (ATS). Retrieved from https://www.jobscan.co/blog

26 Skillings, P. (2015, March 1). How to get the applicant tracking system to pick your résumé. Big Interview. Retrieved from http://biginterview.com/blog

27 Quint Careers. (n.d.). Applicant tracking systems 101 for job-seekers: Understanding the ATS technology that dominates online job search. Retrieved from http://www.quintcareers.com

28 U.S. Equal Employment Opportunity Commission. (2010, September 21). ADA, GINA, Title VVVII & ADEA: Video Résumés. Retrieved from https://www.eeoc.gov

29 Vaas, L. (n.d.). Résumé, meet technology: Making your résumé format machine-friendly. The Ladders. Retrieved from http://www.theladders.com

30 JobVite. (2017, May). 2017 Job Seeker Nation Study. Retrieved from https://www.jobvite.com

31 Scivicque, C. (2017). Are cover letters still relevant? Retrieved from https://www.ivyexec.com

32 Lareau, J. Quoted in Luckwaldt, J. (2015, September 28). Cover letters probably don't matter, but you still need one. Retrieved from http://www.payscale.com

33 Tanzi, T., & Dmitrieva, K. (2020, February 20). The job market is hot. So why are half of U.S. grads missing out? Retrieved from https://www.latimes.com

34 Gig In or Get Out. (2019, September 18). Retrieved from https://www.businesswire.com

35 Guina, R. (2019, January 22). The hidden job market—How to find a job that isn't advertised. Retrieved from https://cashmoneylife.com

36 Is LinkedIn a waste of time? (2020, January 18-19). *The Wall Street Journal*, p. D10.

37 Kolakowski, M. (2018, October 12). Phantom job postings. Retrieved from https://www.thebalancecareers.com/phantom-job-postings-1287159; Weber, L., & Kwoh, L. (2013, January 9). Beware the phantom job listing. *The Wall Street Journal*, pp. B1 and B6.

[38] Direct look at the largest generation in the US labor force. (2019, June 5). Retrieved from https://letsgo.akumina.com

Chapter 16

[1] Georgevich, D. (2020, March 24). Career coach. Personal communication with Mary Ellen Guffey.

[2] Zhang, L. (n.d.) The best (and worst) times to schedule an interview. Retrieved from https://www.themuse.com

[3] Green, A. (2011, February 7). How to prepare for a job interview. *U.S. News & World Report*. Retrieved from http://money.usnews.com

[4] Schor, S. (2018, November 6). 9 out of 10 people are willing to earn less money to do more meaningful work. Retrieved from https://hbr.org

[5] Career Builder. (2018, August 9). More than half of employers have found content on social media that caused them not to hire a candidate. Retrieved from https://www.prnewswire.com

[6] CareerBuilder. (2016, April 28). Number of employers using social media to screen candidates has increased 500 percent over the last decade. Retrieved from http://www.careerbuilder.com

[7] Ryan, L. (2015, March 21). What to wear to a job interview. Retrieved from http://www.forbes.com

[8] Ashford, K. (2020). 7 interview looks that say "Don't hire me." Retrieved from https://www.monster.com

[9] Active listening for interview success: How your ears can help you land the job. (2007, September 25). Retrieved from http://www.hcareers.com

[10] Hodas, S. L. Quoted in Korkki, P. (2009, September 13). Subtle cues can tell an interviewer "pick me." Retrieved from http://www.nytimes.com

[11] Chan, A. (2013, June 14). Top 10 interview tips for new college graduates. *The Huffington Post*. Retrieved from http://www.huffingtonpost.com

[12] Welch, S., & Welch, J. (2008, July 7). Hiring is hard work. *BusinessWeek*, p. 80.

[13] Martin, C. (n.d.). List of strengths and weaknesses: What to say in your interview. Retrieved from http://www.monster.com

[14] Mazur, T. Quoted in Dezube, D. (n.d.). How to interview to uncover a candidate's ethical standards. Retrieved from http://hiring.monster.com

[15] Tyrell-Smith, T. (2011, January 25). Tell a story that will get you hired. *U.S. News & World Report*. Retrieved from http://money.usnews.com

[16] Karsh, B. Quoted in Vogt, P. (2020). Entry-level salary (probably) isn't as negotiable as you think. Retrieved from https://www.monster.com

[17] Karrass, C. L. (n.d.). *In business as in life, you don't get what you deserve, you get what you negotiate.* Stanford St. Press.

[18] U.S. Equal Employment Opportunity Commission. (2016). Prohibited employment policies/practices. Retrieved from https://www.eeoc.gov

[19] Doyle, A. (n.d.). Illegal interview questions. About.com. Retrieved from http://jobsearchtech.about.com

[20] Career Builder. (2015, April 15). 1 in 5 employers has unknowingly asked an illegal interview question. Retrieved from http://www.careerbuilder.com

[21] Glassdoor. (2020, February 23). 8 inappropriate interview questions and how to tackle them like a pro. Retrieved from https://www.glassdoor.com; common interview questions: What you can ask and when it is legal. (n.d.). Retrieved from http://hiring.monster.com; Gerencer, T. (2019, February 12). Illegal interview questions an employer cannot ask [So don't answer!]. Retrieved from https://zety.com

[22] Georgevich, D. (2020, March 24). Career coach. Personal communication with Mary Ellen Guffey.

[23] Foss, J. (2012, May 12). 4 non-annoying ways to follow up after an interview. Retrieved from http://www.forbes.com

[24] Accountemps. (2017, November 17). A little thanks goes a long way. Retrieved from https://www.roberthalf.com

[25] Owens, Y. (n.d.). 3 rules for following up with a recruiter. The Muse. Retrieved from https://www.themuse.com

[26] Bersin, J. (2019, January 30). LinkedIn 2019 Talent trends: Soft skills, transparency and trust. Retrieved from https://ww.likdin.com

[27] National Association of Colleges and Employers. (2018, December 12). Employers want to see these attributes on students' resumes. Retrieved from https://www.naceweb.org

[28] Wilkie, D. (2019, April 10). No thank-you note? No job. Retrieved from https://www.shrm.org

[29] LinkedIn. (2019). Global talent trends 2019. Retrieved from https://business.linkedin.com

[30] Klazema, M. (2016, February 10). The pros and cons to strictly doing a background check on social media. Retrieved from http://www.socialmediatoday.com

[31] Career Builder. (2016, April 28). Number of employers using social media to screen candidates has increased 500 percent over the last decade. Retrieved from http://www.careerbuilder.com

[32] Shellenbarger, S. (2019, October 22). Find your job interview Zen. *The Wall Street Journal*, A12.

[33] Deluca, M. Quoted in DeZube, D. (n.d.). Ten questions to ask when negotiating a salary. Retrieved from http://career-advice.monster.com

[34] Lobosco, M. Quoted in Maurer, R. (2019, February 20). 3 trends that will shape recruiting in 2019. Retrieved from https://www.shrm.org

Index

Italicized page numbers indicate illustrative information in figures.

B

BaaAgent, 373
backchannel communication, 21
background, informal proposals, 459
bad-news messages, 244
 checklist for managing, 311–312
 cushioning in, 294–295, *296*
 to employees and public, 309, *310*
 in-person delivery, 307
 intra-organizational bad news, 306–312, *308*
 to job applicants, 309–311
 sandwich model for, 307
Balter, Dave, 373
bar charts, 395, *396*
Barry, James, 329
Barry, Margaret, 329
Bartolome-Williams, Leslie, 260–261
Bcc (blind carbon carbon), 205
behavioral questions, 595–596
benefits
 in negative messaging, 293–294
 of sales messages, 346
Bergstein, Joey, 369
Bernoff, Josh, 184
Bernstein, Elizabeth, 257
Berry, Tim, 463
Best Buy Influencer Network, 221–222
best news buffer, 291
Big Five personality types, 540
blockchain technology, 85
blogging
 market growth and, 220
 storytelling through, 220–225
 tips for effective blogging, 224–225, *225*
blogs, *13*
body
 of business presentation, 498–499, *499*
 formal business reports, 468, *471–480*
Boeing 737 Max 8 jet disaster, 292
Bonitasoft, 16
Boocher, Dianna, 495
bookmarking, in research, 381–382
books, secondary research, 379
Boolean search strategies, 381
Borchert, Katharina, 55
bossless organizational structure, 16
Bousis, George, 290
Boykiv, Yuriy, 105
brainstorming, 151
brainwriting, 151
brand, credibility and, 8
brand ambassadors, 222

branding
 blogging and, 221
 dress and, 63, 66
 job searching, 546–547, *547*
brick-and-mortar commerce, 7–8
bring-your-own-device (BYOD) policies, 213
Broussard, Alexis, 436–437
browsers, 380–381
budget, informal proposals, 459
buffers, in negative messages, 291, *296*
bullet points, in business presentations, 505
buried verbs, 184
Burns, Kevin, 353
business documents
 block style, *246*
 compliance requirements and security, 213
 customer relations and, 299–301
 documentation requirements, 390–391
 drafting phase, 245, *246*
 editing, proofreading and evaluation, 247
 eye appeal, 64
 formal business reports, 465–470, *471–480*
 headings in, 187–188
 informal business reports, 411–440
 letters, A–2 to A–8
 prewriting phase, business letters, 244–245
 reports, 383–390
business ethics, 25–29
 antibribery laws, 102–103
 culture and, 100–103
 global survey, *26*
business etiquette
 development of, 67–69
 slack messaging, 215–216
 text messaging and, 214, *214*
business organizations, diversity and, 105
business plans, 462–465
 components, 462–463
 internet examples of, 465
business presentations
 audience connection and engagement, 496–505, *499*, *501*, *503–505*
 body of, 498–499, *499*
 checklist, 516–517
 conclusion of, 500
 construction of, 508–511, *510–511*
 delivery, rehearsal and performance, 512–517

 effectiveness in, 493–495, *496*
 followup procedures, 516
 intercultural and team presentations, 517–521
 multimedia presentations, 506–511, *507, 509–511*
 preparation and anticipation, 510–511, 513–514
 purpose of, 495
 smartphone best practices, 521–524
 stage fright, 513–514
 types of, *494*, 495
Business Source Premiers (EBSCO), *380*
Butterfield, Stewart, 204
buzzwords, avoidance of, 184
bypassing
 as communication barrier, 122
 false advertising and, 121

C

calls to action, in blogging, 224–225, *225*
Cambridge Analytica, 251
CAN-SPAM Act, 212
Canva presentations, 505, *505*
CareerBuilder job site, 542, 588
career e-portfolio, 562, *562*
career fairs, 542
career objectives, in résumés, 549–550
career opportunities, preparation for, 540–541
careless language, 286
Carter, Lee Hartley, 328
Casteen, Sean, 120
causation vs. correlation, 414–415
celebrity endorsements, ethics concerning, 347
Cenek, Cyril, 288
Cengage and Wakefield Research, 538
Chan, Andy, 591
chronological résumés, 548, *556–557, 559*
churn, 338
citation formats, 394, B–1 to B–6
 in formal business reports, 469, *471–480*
Citigroup, 153
Claborn, Brandie, 299
claims
 checklist for writing, 263
 denial of, 296–297, 303–305
 persuasive claims, 336–337
 support for, 255
 writing process for, 254–259, *255*
clarity in writing, 182–185, *183*
 in negative messaging, 293–294